LAVDĀT EV IN CORDIS ET ORGANO

Larousse Encyclopedia of Music

based on 'La Musique: les hommes; les instruments; les oeuvres', edited by Norbert Dufourcq

Introduction by Antony Hopkins

Editor: Geoffrey Hindley
with special contributions by
Benny Green, Dr Everett Helm,
Donald Paine, Roger Smalley
and Stephen Walsh

HAMLYN
London · New York · Sydney · Toronto

The Larousse Encyclopedia of Music, with original
contributions to the English language edition, is based on
La Musique: les hommes; les instruments; les oeuvres first
published in France by Augé, Gillon, Hollier-Larousse,
Moreau et Cie, Librairie Larousse, Paris, under the editorial
direction of M. Norbert Dufourcq

First published in 1971 by The Hamlyn Publishing
Group Limited
London · New York · Sydney · Toronto
Astronaut House, Feltham, Middlesex, England

Sixth impression 1983

ISBN 0 600 02396 6

Phototypeset by Filmtype Services Limited, Scarborough,
North Yorkshire.

Printed in Yugoslavia

Contents

List of colour plates	9
Introduction	11
Preface	13

Section I
Music of the Oral Traditions 15

Introduction to non-European traditions 17
Music in ritual
Social functions of music
The instruments of music
The status of musicians and modes of performance
African music 21
The instruments
The drum
Vocal polyphonies
Music in society
The music of the Far East 25
Some general aspects
The music of China: history and theory
The music and the instruments
The music of Japan
Theatre music
Koto music
The music of Indonesia 30
History and theory
The gamelan
Music in India 33
The historical development
Musical instruments
The theory
The rāg
The tāl
The performance
The music of the Arab world 37
General characteristics
The pre-Islamic period
The Islamic period
Musical theory
Musical instruments

Section II
Monody and Rhythm 41

European folk music 43
Introductory remarks
The Mediterranean lands
Central and Eastern Europe
Northern and Oceanic Europe
Popular traditions and art music
Europe in the middle ages: historical background 49
The emergence of Europe
The power of the Church
The ascendancy of France
The culture of Provence

Italy
The background to the music 52
The Roman Catholic mass
Polyphony from organum to ars nova
Secular music
The ecclesiastical modes
The instruments of music 54
Some general remarks on the study of musical instruments
Musical instruments up to the 14th century
Instruments and their use during the 14th century
Origins: the music of the Church 58
Introduction
Jewish music
Byzantine music
Early Christian music
The slow progress towards a uniform rite in the
*   Western Church*
The Gregorian ritual at its height
The origins of notation
The sequence: a new type of melody
The history of plainsong to the 20th century
The first centuries of polyphony 65
The beginnings: diaphony and early organum
The school of Paris: the first great polyphonists
The motet
The evolution of the motet as a secular form
The conductus
Ars Nova in France 70
Introduction
The birth of a 'new art'
The isorhythmic motet
Guillaume de Machaut
Religious music in a secular age
Origins: the music of lay society 73
The world of secular music
The forms
The musicians
The elements of the art
The flowering of lyric song
The Meistersinger
Music for the dance
The musical drama in the middle ages 79
Origins of the medieval theatre
The spoken drama in French
The miracle and mystery plays

Section III
The Age of Polyphony 83

Europe of the Renaissance and Reformation:
    historical background 85
The Low Countries
Italy
Spain
The Reformation
England and France

The background to the music 88
The cantus firmus mass
The emergence of 'national' schools
The secular forms and instrumental music
Monody and the basso continuo
The instruments of music 90
The 15th century
The 16th century
Combinations of instruments and the great Renaissance
  collections
The repertoire
The growth of the ensembles
The beginnings of the instrumental forms
The art of the makers
The growing market for instrumental music
The Franco-Flemish school 97
English and Italian influences
Dufay
Johannes Ockeghem
Josquin des Prez
The masses and motets
Josquin's style
Jacob Obrecht
Lesser contemporaries of Josquin
The 16th century
Sweelinck
Music in France during the 16th century 108
The golden age of the French chanson
Janequin
Other composers of the chanson
'Measured music in the antique style' – Claude Le Jeune
Music and the Reformation
Instrumental music
Music in the lands of the empire 113
The beginnings of German polyphony
The first generation of German organists
Heinrich Isaac
Musicians of the Reformation
Ludwig Senfl
De Monte
Roland de Lassus
The compositions
Lesser composers and instrumental music
Music in Bohemia
Music in Italy 122
Italian music up to the end of the 14th century
The Laude
Italian secular music of the ars nova
Florence and the music of Landini
Secular music in the 15th century
The madrigal
Founders and pioneers
Cypriano de Rore and other madrigalists
The later masters of the madrigal
The school of Rome and the music of the Oratory
Palestrina
Music at Venice

Adriano Willaert and the founding of a tradition
Instrumental music at Venice
Giovanni Gabrieli
Music in the theatre: the beginnings of opera
The music of Spain 134
The Hispanic liturgy
The early sources of Spanish music
The court of Naples and Tinctoris
Spanish music in the 15th century
The 16th century in Spain
The school of Andalusia
The school of Castile and Victoria
Aragon
Instrumental and keyboard music
Portugal
England during the middle ages and the Renaissance 140
From the Norman Conquest to the Hundred Years War
The 15th century
Leonel and Dunstable
The court of Henry VIII
Taverner
The age of Tye and Tallis
The Golden Age
The English madrigal
Morley, Weelkes and Wilbye, the masters of the English
  madrigal
The lesser madrigalists and composers of the ayre
William Byrd
Orlando Gibbons and the viol fantasy
Lute and keyboard music

Section IV
The Age of Harmony 151

From Baroque to classicism: historical background 153
The Thirty Years War
England
France
The German lands
The background to the music 156
The Italian opera
New forms in religious music
Instrumental music
Instrumentation
The concerto and the symphony
The development of a harmonic language
The instruments of music 159
Violins and viols at the beginning of the 17th century
Instruments in early 17th-century Italian opera
Instruments in church music
Instruments in France and the orchestra of Lully
Viol music in the 17th century
Plucked stringed instruments
The woodwind
The brass
Italy: the language of music 167

The world of Italian opera
Roman opera
Venetian opera
The 'spectacular' in full spate
Monteverdi
Monteverdi and the 'New Music'
The operas
The religious music of Monteverdi
Music in the church
Carissimi and the oratorio
Instrumental music
The birth of the new instrumental forms
German music of the 17th century   178
Theory and practice: Michael Praetorius
The cantata and the Passion
Schütz
The development of German organ music
The northern and southern schools
Central German organ music and the continuators
   of the northern tradition
Secular music
French music before the age of Lully   185
The court air and related forms
The French court ballet of the 17th century
Religious music in France
Instrumental music: composers for the keyboard and lute
Ensemble music
English music in the century of Purcell   192
The reign of Charles I
Music under the Commonwealth
The birth of English opera
Music of the Restoration
Purcell
John Blow
The world of Bach   197
The life of the composer
The style
The works
The Italian Age   202
Instrumental music
Musical forms and styles
The schools of Venice and Bologna in the late 17th century
Corelli
Lesser Italian masters of the 18th century
Vivaldi and the school of Venice in the 18th century
Naples
The age of Italian opera
The school of Naples
Opera buffa
Religious music
The evolution of style and forms in sacred music
Italian composers abroad
Handel and music in England   214
Handel
The works of Handel
The ballad opera
English composers

Foreign musicians in England
Music in France from Lully to the death of Rameau 220
Musical institutions
Lully
Charpentier
Music under the Regency and the young Louis XV
Couperin the Great
Musical life under Louis XV
Taste and styles
Rameau
France and foreign music
Music in the German lands in the 18th century   227
The beginnings of classicism
Vienna in the first half of the 18th century
The court of the elector palatine at Mannheim
Music in Mannheim and Munich
Berlin
Carl Philipp Emmanuel Bach and the later Berlin school
Hamburg
Music at the court of Saxony-Poland
Gluck and the reform of Italian opera
The Singspiel and the German opera
The great age of classicism   236
Vienna and Salzburg
The development of the classical forms
The sonata and chamber music
Haydn
Instrumental music
Church music
Mozart
The music
The operas

Section V
The Romantics   245

The 19th century: historical background   247
France and Europe
The German lands
The Americas
The birth of new cultural traditions
The background to the music   250
The great age of symphonic music
Orchestras and concerts
The conductor
Scholars and critics
The instruments of music   253
The wind instruments in the 19th and 20th centuries
The flute
The clarinet
The oboe
The bassoon
Secondary types of wind instruments
The brass
The invention of the valve
The pianoforte

The harp
The age of Beethoven 263
Beethoven's life
The symphonies and concertos
The chamber music
The choral works
Secular vocal music and works for the stage
Beethoven's lesser contemporaries
Weber
The Lied before Schubert
The first generation of Romantics 273
Schubert's piano compositions and chamber music
The Lieder
The symphonies
Mendelssohn
Symphonic music
Chamber music and piano works
Schumann
The piano music
Lieder
Chamber music and symphonies
French music from the death of Rameau to
   the rise of Berlioz 281
The opéra-comique
From the Revolution to 1830
The fêtes and songs of the French Revolution
The romance
The théâtre lyrique
Berlioz the prophet 288
The works
The dramatic symphonies
The musician and writer
After Berlioz
Foreign composers in Paris
Meyerbeer and his contemporaries
Offenbach
The renaissance of French music
Gounod and Lalo
Saint-Saëns
Bizet
Chabrier
Franck and his followers
Franck's first pupils
Vincent d'Indy
Fauré
Polish music from earliest times to the end of
   the 19th century 303
The 13th and 14th centuries
Polish music during the Baroque period
Romanticism in Poland
Chopin
The music
The contemporaries of Chopin
Moniuszko
Secondary musicians
The end of the 19th and beginning of the 20th centuries
Hungarian music to the age of Liszt 313

Erkel and Mosonyi
Liszt
The symphonic poems
The importance of Liszt
Liszt and the musical life of his time
The symphony and opera in Germany 322
The music of Wagner
Man of the theatre and musician
Brahms
Piano works and chamber music
Symphonic music
Lieder and choral works
Bruckner
Music in Bohemia 330
Smetana
Dvořák
Lesser figures and the first period of Leoš Janáček
Russian music from the earliest times 334
Russian folk songs
'Sacred verses' and epic songs
The beginnings of art music
The Italians in Russia
Advent of a Russian school
Russia in the 19th century
Glinka
Glinka's contemporaries
Two rival camps
'The Five'
Mussorgsky
Borodin
Rimsky-Korsakov
Russian opera
Tchaikovsky: his life
The man and musician
Music in Italy 351
Rossini
Rossini's lesser contemporaries
Verdi
The music
Verdi's successors
The aftermath of Romanticism 359
Hugo Wolf
Mahler
The symphonies
Richard Strauss
The symphonic poems
The operas
Reger

Section VI
Music in the Modern World 365

The 20th century: historical background 367
The United States
Europe between the wars
Germany

The modern age
Background to musical developments in
    the 20th century   370
Crisis
New departures
The return to classicism
Serialism
The laws of chance . . .
. . . and electronics
Conclusion
The instruments of music in the 20th century   375
Music and electronics
Electronic instruments
Into the future
The school of Vienna   380
Schoenberg
The twelve-note system and the serial method
The aesthetic and style of Schoenberg's works
Berg
Aesthetic and style
Webern
Aesthetic and style
Stravinsky   387
Biography
The stage music
Stravinsky's musical language
Instrumental and choral works
Stravinsky's serial music
French music   393
Debussy
Piano works and chamber music
Orchestral and vocal works
Ravel
Piano works and chamber music
Orchestral and vocal works
Roussel
Dukas, Satie and lesser figures
Revolution and tradition
Honegger, Milhaud, Poulenc and the 'Six'
The school of Arcueil and Young France
The middle generation
The independents
Messiaen
Music in Germany and Austria   406
Hindemith
The development of his music
Hindemith's contemporaries
The younger generation
Hungary in the age of Bartók   413
Hungary after Liszt
Bartók
The musician
A new musical language
Kodály and his contemporaries
Italian music   418
Busoni
Futurism and other trends

The generation of Casella
From Neo-classicism to dodecaphony
Avant-garde serial composers in Italy
Music in Russia   425
Some minor figures
Prokofiev
His music
Nationalist composers in the Soviet Union
The central tradition
State directives and the arts
Shostakovich
American music   433
The beginnings
The first American composer
The 19th century
Shape-note music and folk hymnody
The beginning of a tradition
Charles Ives
The 20th century
Breakthrough
The second generation
Musical theatre
The contemporary scene
Music in England from 1800   445
The world of music
The Tudor and folk music revival
Renaissance
Elgar
Delius
Vaughan Williams and Holst
The next generation
Britten
Music in Scandinavia   455
Sweden
The 20th century
Norway
Grieg
Denmark
Finland
Sibelius
After Sibelius
Central European music   461
Poland
Szymanowski
Post-war Poland
Czechoslovakia
Martinů
Spanish music in the 19th and 20th centuries   467
The guitar
Music for the stage
Regional schools
Albéniz and Granados
De Falla and Turina
After de Falla
The younger generation
Portugal
The music of South America   475

The centuries of European influence: Mexico
The northern republics
The southern states of Spanish America
The music of the 20th century: Brazil
Villa-Lobos
The 20th century in Chile and Argentina
Mexico
Music in Switzerland   483
Bloch
German Switzerland
Frank Martin
Music in Belgium and the Netherlands   488
The birth of the Flemish school
The Walloons
Holland
Pijper
Badings and his contemporaries
Music in the Balkan countries   494
Yugoslavia
Rumania
Greece
Skalkottas
Yannis Xenakis
Music in Australia   501
Music of the Australian Aborigines
Traditional music
The colonial period
Percy Grainger and the 20th century

The contemporary world
Music in Canada   506
The school of Toronto
The school of Montreal
The World of Jazz   510
New Orleans
Chicago
The pianists and the Blues
Big band
Ellington
The first generation of virtuosi
The birth of 'modernism'
New frontiers
The 1960s and beyond
The last five years – new directions   524
Boulez
Barraqué and Carter
Xenakis, Ligeti and Penderecki
Stockhausen (I)
Live electronics
Stockhausen (II)
Peter Maxwell Davies
John Cage
Glossary of Technical Terms   534
Glossary of Musical Instruments   548
Supplementary reading list   556
Index   558
Acknowledgements   575

Colour Plates

1 A stringed instrument in the manner of a *viola d'amore.*
2 A panel from the Ghent altarpiece by Van Eyck.

3 The orchestra of the Japanese Imperial Court.
4 A 17th-century Indian miniature painting of the Spring *rāg.*
5 Brazilian Kamaiuras Indians playing large flutes.
6 A Vietnamese peasant musician playing a type of *sheng* mouth organ.
7 A Bolivian Indian blowing a conch shell.

8 *Angel Musicians,* a fresco by Benedetto Bembo in the ducal chapel at Milan.
9 *Christ Glorified* by Fra Angelico.
10 The tombstone of the 14th-century Italian composer, Francesco Landini.

11 A detail from the Memlinc altarpiece at Bruges.
12 *A dance at the court of Henry IV of France* by Louis de Caulery.
13 A late 16th-century positive organ.

14 *Lady at the Virginals* by Vermeer.
15 *The Concert,* a painting attributed to Costa.

16 A detail from Pieter Breughel the Elder's *The Peasant Wedding.*
17 A ceiling painting in the Rosenburg Castle, Copenhagen, showing musicians of the court of Christian IV of Denmark.

18 The organ of Salamanca Cathedral.
19 A portrait of Claudio Monteverdi by an unknown artist.

20 The Compenius organ at Fredericksborg castle, Denmark.
21 Costume and setting for a Turin ballet, 1647.
22 A performance in the Teatro Ducale, Turin, in 1681.

23 A decorated French single-manual harpsichord of the 1670s.
24 A 17th-century painting by Van Bronchorst showing a player of a theorboed lute.
25 A portrait of Henry Purcell by Clostermann.

26 A pastel portrait of Rameau by Carmontelle.
27 *The Scale of Love* by Watteau.
28 The first known portrait of Handel in England, by Philip Mercier.

29 *An Allegory of Music* by La Hire Laurent.
30 A painting by Pannini depicting a performance of an 18th-century opera.
31 A portrait of Haydn by Rössler.

32 A portrait of Mozart by Krafft.
33 A painting by Nicolas Lancret of the ballet dancer Camargo.
34 *The 14th Baron Willoughby and Family* by Johann Zoffany.
35 Four 19th-century metronomes.
36 A portrait of the 19th-century *primadonna,* Malibran.

37 A miniature of the young Beethoven.
38 Set from a 19th-century production of Beethoven's opera *Fidelio.*
39 A painting by Kupelweiser entitled *Landpartie der Schubertiana.*
40 Woodwind instruments of the 18th century.

41 A portrait of Chopin by Delacroix.
42 A portrait of Wagner by Lenbach.

43   A portrait of Verdi by Boldini.
44   The opera of La Scala, Milan.

45   A portrait of Mussorgsky by Repin.
46   Set designed by Leon Bakst for Rimsky-Korsakov's ballet *Scheherezade*.
47   A portrait of Richard Strauss by Max Liebermann.

48   *Le Foyer de danse à l'Opéra* by Degas.
49   The new ceiling of the Paris Opera by Chagall.
50   Backdrop design by Picasso for Satie's ballet *Parade*.

51   A scene from the Covent Garden production of Schoenberg's opera *Moses and Aaron*.
52   Dancers of the Red Army state ensemble.
53   A scene from the musical *Porgy and Bess*.
54   Negro slaves dancing.

55   Ben Webster playing the baritone saxophone.
56   Modern jazz organist.
57   Modern jazz drummer.

58   Scene from a performance of the ballet *La Création du Monde*.
59   The organ of the Royal Festival Hall, London.
60   A recording of an opera at a recording studio.

Introduction

To begin the introduction to an encyclopedia with the statement that facts are overrated and often irrelevant may seem perverse and paradoxical; yet the response to music is so much a matter of emotion and intuition that it is true to say that for the average listener, at any rate, his enjoyment is little affected by considerations of fact. If, as the result of a misprint in a programme, an entire audience in a concert hall was misled about the date of a composition, its key or its opus number, would it really affect individual reactions to the music? The performance would either succeed or fail in generating enthusiasm; emotions would be stirred or left dormant; the musical scholar might enjoy a moment of self-congratulation in detecting the error but otherwise it would pass unnoticed. These may seem strange words to come from someone who spends the greater part of his professional life exhorting music-lovers to use their minds more actively as they listen; but to be aware of a composer's creative processes, to follow the line of a musical argument, to recognise thematic relationships and transformations – these are not the same as to know facts garnered from a book of reference. Even if one's first realisation of these greater musical truths has been found in an analytical essay, it is still something that must be experienced in terms of sound and emotion to have its full impact. Music is music, and though we may speak or write a million words about it, nothing will change the fact that in the long run it must stand or fall by its ability to move us, to stimulate us, to entertain, to bore, to perplex, to illumine, to delight, to arouse hostility or to enlarge our capacity for spiritual experience.

The purpose of this book then is not to change music by simplifying in some mysterious way; it is to change us, the listeners, so that we may be better equipped to rise to music's challenge. I use the word challenge on purpose, for it is only too easy to be seduced by the sound of music without making any attempt to grasp its sense. A great composer is a master of a highly specialised language, and it is foolish of us to imagine that we are likely to comprehend that language unless we are prepared to make some effort commensurate with the intensity with which it states its message. We live in an age when the entire currency of music is in danger of being devalued since so much of our listening is done through machines, and machines do not complain if we treat them rudely. The gramophone or the radio are sufficiently impersonal for us to be able to talk while they are playing without feelings of guilt. We adjust their volume to our convenience, taming Beethoven's titanic voice when he prevents us hearing marital commands from the kitchen, or cutting off Mozart in mid-flight when the telephone rings. If there were no other argument in favour of preserving the live artist, I would still feel that at least he justifies his existence by ensuring that we do not forget our manners while he plays. Even though we may dislike the music, we respect the presence of the performer.

Yet though I may be wary of the machines, they have also helped to propagate music to an extraordinary degree unimaginable half a century ago. The long-playing record in particular has brought into being a new audience for the music of over five centuries and many cultures. We can now experience in our own homes performances of instrumental music of the Renaissance or the electronic sound of our own time, of madrigals or the Berlioz Requiem, of Scarlatti on the harpsichord or the complete piano sonatas of Beethoven. If our tastes are even more exotic and embrace the music of India or the Far East, that too is available, something to be remembered if your interest is stimulated by the admirable chapters about Eastern music in this book. Never before has the civilised world been so sound-conscious, as the makers of television commercials have discovered in their constant attempts to titillate the ear. However, being aware of sound is not necessarily to understand it, and there is always a danger that the aural palate may become insensitive if the diet is too rich and the listener too voracious in his appetite for new sensations.

If then, as I believe, the music itself is more important than the historical facts appertaining to it or the artist who performs it, what is the function of knowledge as represented by a book on this scale? To answer this question, I should like to suggest some of the qualities that I believe make up the ideal listener. Let us suppose that we are at a concert; our two immediate neighbours must serve as representatives of typical listeners. One experiences music almost entirely through his emotions. He is thrilled by sound itself; the weight of a Tchaikovsky climax overwhelms him; the sensuous beauty of a Brahms slow movement affects him like a good claret; he finds Mozart charming, if a little lightweight, loves the songs of Schubert but finds his instrumental music a trifle over-long, admires and respects Beethoven sometimes to the point of idolatry but considers the late quartets to be a bit above him. His enjoyment of music is genuine, enthusiastic, committed and personal, and not in any way to be despised.

Beyond him sits our paragon, the perfect listener. He shares all of our immediate neighbour's enthusiasms, but his reactions are constantly enhanced by the awareness of subtleties in the music and in its performance. Let us look into his mind for a moment to see the equipment he brings with him to increase his rapport with the music. The programme tells us that we are hearing a Beethoven quartet, the first of the Op. 59 set, and gives us a good deal of information about Count Rasumovsky, to whom the work was dedicated. It gives the date of composition, 1806, and the story of the quartet's publication. In its analysis of the four movements it draws particular attention to the Russian folk-tune in the finale, incorporated into the score by Beethoven in order to delight his Russian patron.

(Incidentally, and with deference to the musicologists, would our enjoyment of this piece be affected in *any* way if the opus number was to be changed to 52, if the Count had been a Slovakian ambassador named Silicowsky, if the final tune had been a Moravian folksong and so on? Of course not.)

What then do I expect my ideal listener's reaction to the music to be? In general terms, to appreciate every moment in the composition that has some special significance, not in the analyst's sense, like a dead moth pinned on a board, but as part of the whole interwoven tapestry of music. These strands are so complex and multifarious that the very first bars of this quartet might be said to reach back to early Haydn and forward as far as Sibelius. The accompanying figure is pure Haydn, but the cello theme starting so unexpectedly on the fifth note of the scale has a curiously modal flavour that shows us intimations of the opening of Sibelius' 3rd symphony.

This sense of period, this awareness of the very feel of time, will extend beyond the realm of music, so that one identifies with the intellectual climate of the age. Music is a sort of time machine, enabling us to experience vicariously the emotions and thoughts of men long dead; but it should also help us to be more in tune with the paintings, architecture, literature and poetry of the age from which it comes. Listening to Beethoven we become sensitive not just to the music but to the whole flavour of his era.

As the work progresses our ideal listener will respond to every sudden twist of harmony, to the subtleties of Beethoven's scoring, to the delicate balance of phrase against phrase. He will know precisely when the composer is stretching the vocabulary of his time, and appreciate those fleeting moments when he can detect the first signs of ultimate maturity. He will delight in the impish humour of the scherzo because he genuinely shares in the sense of fun that prompted Beethoven to write it, and not just because he has been told in a programme note that it is a humorous movement. The joys of the performance itself will be incidental rather than paramount, a shared love made manifest through the hands of the performers.

When I was asked to write the introduction to this encyclopedia I was greatly flatttered but also somewhat appalled. With my innate scepticism about the value of facts, how could I become involved in such a product? A survey of the material reassured me. Although it is invaluable as a book of reference, it is not arranged alphabetically, apart from the helpful glossary of musical terms. You cannot cheat by just looking up *Spontini* under *S*, or *Athens, Ruins of – see under Beethoven, list of works*. You must read, and in the process of reading you will learn just that background of culture that I was presupposing in my ideal listener. What pleases me particularly is the refusal to segregate music from the other arts. Inevitably, music reflects its environment. The creative energies of Bach or Haydn were directed into particular channels precisely because of the nature of their employment; they can no more be disassociated from their background than Debussy or Stravinsky can be from theirs. Many people would maintain that the first duty of an encyclopedia is to provide information; my own view is that it is still more important to *relate* information and, in doing so, to encourage the reader's mind to travel further from his original quest. If this seems to demand an initiative that presupposes more knowledge than you already possess, there are preliminary chapters to each section which give a broad background picture of the utmost value. The interlinking of music and cultural history is done in fascinating terms, enabling one to fill in all those fearful pockets of ignorance which conventional education seems to leave. Too often we learn subjects at school in compartments, isolating history from geography, literature from social conditions. This book is a valuable corrective to the narrow approach of the pedant. I am as sceptical of Instant Knowledge as I am of the academic's jargon; they are different aspects of the same misapprehension – stick a label on something and all will be well.

Here then is to be found not music but a preparation for music, not a dictionary but a distillation of knowledge. Most books of reference are used after an event has started a train of speculation. A question floats into the mind for some reason or another; let's look up the answer. Although it is possible with a little diligence to use this book in that way, I would suggest that the process be angled somewhat differently. Books about music are useless if they don't make you want to listen to the music itself. Try therefore to use the book as a stimulant to new experience rather than merely as an antidote to ignorance. Time and again I found myself thinking as I read the text, 'I must look out for that – it sounds interesting'. Being human, I shall probably forget to do so, but the challenge is there, and it is well worth while. All the more important then to try to act quickly, to follow up by hearing a record, a performance or a broadcast of the music. Instead of looking up answers, see if it is not more productive to use this book to provoke questions, questions that can only be adequately met by enlarging your own musical experience. There is much knowledge here, and wisdom too; but I am sure that I speak on behalf of all the musical scholars who have contributed their special skills to this comprehensive study when I say that it is all subservient to that art that goes beyond mere words, the art that enables us to reach across the gulf of time and share most vividly the intimate thoughts and emotions of Mozart, Beethoven or their fellows – the art of music.

ANTONY HOPKINS

Preface

A history of music published at the turn of the 20th century presents a special challenge to the compilers and offers the reader a far wider range of interest than would have been expected even twenty years ago. Artists in all fields and the public at large have been increasingly eager to explore the alien and the unfamiliar and this general tendency has been nowhere more marked than in music. Since the early years of the century our musical awareness has been gradually extended back into Europe's own past so that the music of J. S. Bach and Vivaldi are no longer the rarefied interests of the few, while audiences are growing ever more enthusiastic and informed about the great achievements of the Renaissance and medieval composers. Moreover, the process works in the reverse direction as jazz musicians and to some extent pop groups investigate and make use of the more advanced techniques pioneered by the vanguard of composers working in the field of 'serious' music. In the world at large the example of European composers is having its effect as far afield as Japan. In their turn the Westerners are studying the musical traditions of the Orient and of Africa and finding in them new sources of inspiration.

The reader will find a number of chapters which aim to introduce him to the basic principles of Indian, Arabic, Oriental and African music both as subjects of great interest in their own right and as interesting comparative studies, helping to illuminate his understanding of his own tradition. Then the early centuries of that tradition itself are given extended treatment. What the reader will not find here are learned speculations on the nature of ancient Greek or Assyrian music – as far as possible this history is concerned with living traditions.

When all has been said it is obvious that the great ages of classical and Romantic music, from Bach to Richard Strauss, as well as the masters of the present age, are still of most immediate and general interest and a large part of this work is accordingly devoted to them. It is equally clear that the art of jazz can no longer be regarded as a separate field from the history of music and a specially commissioned chapter on this subject provides, in the editor's opinion, a summing up which, despite its necessary conciseness, is both lucid and thought-provoking.

In so far as the present work is ultimately based on *La Musique: les hommes; les instruments; les oeuvres* originally published in Paris by Larousse and edited by the well-known French scholar, M. Norbert Dufourcq, it is heavily indebted to the work of the large team of experts that he enlisted. Nevertheless a number of considerations, such as the need for up-dating and the desire to redistribute the balance of treatment to make it conform more nearly with the interest of the English-speaking world, have led to a number of editorial decisions which, while we hope they may also be said to have improved the work, do certainly give it quite a different aspect from its French original. The English like the French edition is divided into six main sections, of which the first deals with the non-European musical cultures mentioned above and the remaining five are devoted to the development of the European tradition, but in an attempt to enable the reader to grasp the overall direction both of the musical events in these long periods and of the social and political developments in Europe, each main section is preceded by two short introductions. There are also two extensive glossaries which, with the comprehensive index, will, it is believed, make the book a valuable and easily used source of reference. To increase its usefulness in this respect, the English edition has, to the fullest possible extent, assembled the information relating to each main composer in one place. Thus by referring to the index the reader can quickly inform himself on Beethoven's life and works or on the music of Tchaikovsky or Mozart, without being obliged to follow up several references.

To increase the comprehensiveness of the work the editor has supplied new material in a number of chapters as well as writing the historical background pieces and all but one of the musical backgrounds. But it has also been thought desirable to call on contributions from a group of English and American scholars, whose help is here most gratefully acknowledged. Benny Green has written the new and extended chapter on the history of jazz; Dr Everett Helm has provided a new chapter on American music; Donald Paine, Precentor of Radley College, has written a new chapter for this edition on English music in the 19th and 20th centuries; Roger Smalley, of Kings College, Cambridge and himself a composer, has contributed a most valuable commentary on recent developments in the music of the last five years; and Stephen Walsh, journalist and broadcaster, has written a lucid and informative background chapter that precedes the section on the 20th century.

As Antony Hopkins has said in his foreword to the book, it is the art of music which is the focus of all our work, and it is the hope of the editor and the contributors that their efforts will serve to reinforce and buttress the reader's enjoyment of that art.

Section I

Music of the Oral Traditions

Introduction to non-European traditions

This section is concerned with a review of the vast musical domain which lies beyond the frontiers of the Western tradition of academic or 'art' music. During this century European awareness of these alien traditions has grown considerably from the dilettante interest of the 18th century in Turkish military music and the superficial study of their national folk traditions by the 19th-century Romantic composers. The revived interest of the 19th century in the origins of plainsong may also be regarded as part of the gathering impetus towards the eclectic inspiration which has been such an important feature of 20th-century music, as of the other arts. From the folk traditions of Europe itself to the *gamelan* orchestras of Indonesia, the drum rhythms of Africa as transmitted and transmuted by jazz and the principles behind the Indian *rāg*, European composers have availed themselves of the increasingly serious study which is going on in all fields of non-European music. The results of these researches are to be found not only indirectly in the influence they have on the compositions of some composers but also in the growing audiences for concert performances of Indian music and the increasing availability of all kinds of music in authentic recorded versions. Through these means we are able at the moment to assemble a wide survey of the stages in the development of man's various modes of self expression in sound. Just as in the West, so in the great civilisations of Asia, there is a distinction between the art music of the court and that of the priests, while in the music of Africa, once dubbed 'primitive', there is found a division in some areas between the professional and non-professional musicians. In this section we shall touch on music ranging from the most primitive to the most sophisticated, yet throughout we shall find certain general characteristics.

The oral tradition is, as a matter of fact, the strongest link binding together all the types of music which may be considered as belonging to the historical beginnings of music, and it is the most important single feature which the traditions studied here have in common. The very existence of this unwritten music depends entirely on oral acquisitions and preservations which are not the fruit of bookish intellectual speculations. The music of the advanced cultures that we shall examine, and which has some form of original schematic notation, does not invalidate this proposition, since these notations consist of summary forms of inscription which merely serve as a guiding line and as an *aide mémoire* for initiates.

A further characteristic shared by the primitive music of the oral tradition is that it is essentially a utilitarian music, with magical, symbolic or social functions. Such music is more than an entertainment, and even when it survives after the attitudes and customs that inspired it have vanished, its significance goes beyond that of mere aesthetics. Indeed, this music is considered by the players themselves to be the property of a specific human group and one of its important spiritual manifestations.

Music holds a revered place in the traditions of both the higher civilisations and the so-called primitive peoples. As we shall see music occupied a central place in the mythology and religious system of ancient China, it was the subject of a semi-mystical philosophy in the school of the Pythagorean philosophers of Greece, and it plays a dominant role in the myths of the most primitive of the Australian Aborigines, in the ceremonial and mythology of many African tribes and in the ancient Vedic rites of India. These myths acknowledge the immense power of music and the musician, but according to many of them sound itself was one of the primeval forces of creation; the voice of the priest, or the sound of an instrument, may be regarded as providing a vehicle for the voice of the creator. This belief may be held in a most literal sense; in the myths of the Tamil peoples the world is believed to have derived from the tambourine of the god.

Music in ritual

In most regions, both voice and musical instruments have a ritual and symbolic value. As an officiating member in a rite, the musician will be obliged to make his voice conform to a precise timbre and use it with a special technique determined by the circumstances. Sometimes he will give greater importance to voice production than to the words themselves and, similarly, he may prefer one type of musical instrument to another and choose a privileged direction for his playing. Thus, the long trumpet players in Islam take possession of space by turning in succession towards the four cardinal points of the compass, and the *shaman* informs his hearers of the arrival of the spirit by a pronounced change in rhythm in his drum playing. Similarly, bark horns with slow, low-pitched tones may incarnate evil spirits (in the Amazon region), whereas the lively, shrill piping of flutes represents the good spirits; in Gabon, the light notes of an arched harp indicate that a spirit is beginning to take possession of the instrument. During long centuries of evolution in the search for improved and new means of musical and semi-musical communication, both voices and instruments have often been distorted from their simple timbres. The voice may be deliberately developed to give a harsh grating sound, sometimes the registers of the voice are rapidly opposed in a manner reminiscent of the yodelling of the Swiss Alps and the Tyrol, the singer may direct his voice into various types of resonator and both voice and instrument may imitate the cries of animals. In Africa and Formosa music and song play an active part in hunting rites. The same applies to healing rites which are, perhaps, the most spectacular illustration of the magical power of music. The healing magician makes use of a large range of sound techniques, from song, instrumental rhythms and melodies (especially on the flute) to a series of incantatory proceedings such as cries, murmurings, disguised voices, the shaking of rattles and whistled sounds. The links with the language of such incantations and such magico-religious chants are very strong, and certain characteristics, such as the long-drawn-out fall of chromatic phrases, are frequent in this type of music. The use of strange timbres and cacophonies to repel or to personify evil spirits is varied and numerous; typical instruments are hand-rattles, clappers and friction drums. At least one example of this kind of music-making is to be found in parts of Europe in the Noise of Darkness made during the Holy Week rituals in the Catholic Church.

Social functions of music

Examples such as these reveal the functional and ritual importance of primitive music, but it also has an important place in the social life of the community. Birth, manhood initiation, marriage and death are all accompanied by music, and of these functions funeral ceremonies are probably the highest. In most beliefs, different notions of the transition of the soul from one life to another require the mediation of music. The central Asian *shaman* recalls the soul of the deceased by the sound of his drum; the weepers of Mediterranean countries grieve by psalmodising, crying out, shouting regrets, invectives or praises, and in West Africa the tinkling of bells indicates the exact moment when the deceased enters into another world.

There are many other ceremonies of all kinds which require music to be accomplished successfully. Examples are the *charivaris* or mock serenades for ill-matched or ill-reputed bridal pairs in French folk traditions and all the musical or noisy elements associated in almost all

traditions with seasonal festivities and ceremonies connected with such natural phenomena as rain making and fertility rites. The musical instruments used for such occasions are charged with symbols, in their timbre as much as in their shape or decoration. Examples are the ancient bronze drums of North Vietnam, the feathered rattles carved in the shape of birds used by the Indians of the North Pacific coast, and the little Sudanese drums made out of baobab fruits.

From earliest times, all these activities connected with man's subsistence have been associated with music. According to ancient beliefs, it was an essential element in enlisting the supernatural protection which ensured success. Important magical elements are present in the songs for the tilling of the soil, found in countries of Mediterranean culture, both European and Arab, such as the song to the oxen in southern France. These songs take the form of ornate recitative chants with free rhythms, which may be punctuated by exhortations shouted to the animals, and can be adapted to avert the effects of unexpected occurrences or accidents. The chants, delivered at full voice into space, frequently end in rising scales or ascending cries. Other songs and rhythms are linked with the techniques of collective work: weaving songs, songs for the transplanting of rice or the pounding of maize. The rhythmic structure of the song itself is modelled after the rhythm of the work and the songs often take the form of responses, or alternate passages between solo and chorus.

The magico-religious and social functions of primitive music are therefore of great importance. Apart from the rituals, magical practices, and the activities already described, music is all-powerful in other profane and religious situations. Songs of praise, love songs, epic and narrative songs, satiric songs, programme music (for pastoral flute, for example), calls, messages sent by whistling, horn or tambourine as well as performances of traditional dances and plays are all, in primitive or early societies, examples of music being used for more than merely entertainment.

Indonesian flute player in a state of ecstasy.

The instruments of music

From the beginning man made music both with his voice and with the gestures of his body, such as the clapping of the hands, the stamping of the feet in dance or the slapping of various parts of the body. To these sonorous effects provided by his physical nature he added the resources of the world about him, at first using raw untreated materials such as resonant stones, as in the lithophones of Togo or ancient Chinese music, or the empty carapace of a turtle used as a percussion instrument in Guyana, or the conch shell, still used in parts of South America. With only the slightest modification, other natural objects such as the gourd proved adaptable to the purposes of music and, with characteristic inventiveness, man even turned to the tools which he had himself devised for other purposes. It is probable that the gong originated from the simple cooking pot, while the earliest harp may have been a modified hunting bow.

The richness and variety of techniques of voice production or of types of musical instruments are very great and significant. To take one example, a style of voice production may be identified with a regional style; singers in countries bordering the Mediterranean sing with a head voice, while those in the Far East sing in nasal tones. Thanks to modern research and to recording *in situ* we are beginning to realise that in music of oral traditions, the timbre of voices or instruments is often as important a characteristic as the structure of the music itself.

In many religions, the musical instrument is an object used in worship, and is loaded with symbols; the *rudra-vina* in India, attributed to a divine or legendary figure, the *sheng* (mouth organ) or *ch'in* zither in China are examples. Shaped in the image of the divinity, the musical instruments may also be the emblem of the musician-gods (such are the panpipes, Apollo's *kithara* and Triton's conch) and in many cultures these instruments have become the allegorical symbol of music itself. In the European tradition the harp and lyre have often assumed this role. The instruments' forms may reproduce those of the human body (the arched harps of Equatorial Africa, Congolese horns and the whistling statues of Yucatan) or those of animals – the Japanese fish-shaped wooden drum and the phoenix-shaped mouth organ in Chinese tradition. Some groups of instruments coincide with human or social structures, as may be seen from the male and female gongs of South East Asia, the male and female drums of Africa and the polycalamous flutes known as 'children' and 'parents' in the Sunda Isles.

The status of musicians and modes of performance

Apart from itinerant or professional musicians, such as bards or African *griots*, the playing of musical instruments or the making of music is often reserved to a particular caste or clan. The Levites' responsibility for the music of the Temple of Jerusalem is but one example of this. The status of such groups is sometimes humble, and they are regarded as a group apart from the others in

above
Trumpet players at the feast of the New Year in Trichinopoli, India.

far left
Ceremonial drummers in Borneo.

left
A drummer accompanying a traditional sports festival, in the region of Teheran, Iran.

right
A young peasant performer on the dulcimer, from the Ukraine.

below
Greek street musicians playing a barrel organ and a tambourine.

bottom
Carnival musicians of Cuba.

cerned) be exclusively played by women while others may only be played by men, by young boys, by the representatives of a particular trade, or by initiates.

In the world of primitive music, both the methods of playing or singing and the circumstances of performance are closely linked to the development of genres and forms. It is consequently impossible to speak of a certain stage of polyphony without mentioning the structure, the resources of the musical instruments and the effects of a long tradition. It would be impossible to determine a rhythm without observing the gestures (whether of work or of dance) which the music accompanies, or without examining the relationships between the rhythm and the language of the song – this is especially true of music with a tonal language. Again, the whole vast field of improvisation can only be understood by taking into account the fact that an essential quality of the musician is the innate faculty of being able to make variations within the context of a set scheme of conventions and of being able to recreate formulas and motifs that are themselves marked by both routine and improvisation.

In all these different types of music we may find homophonic and monodic procedures: monody or homophony with responses or accompaniment, vocal or instrumental polyphony ranging from a melody on a drone bass to development by parallel intervals and to descant and even canon. Polyphonies by parallel intervals, usually vocal, may be in thirds, in fourths and sometimes in seconds. It should be noted that musicologists and ethnomusicologists do not always agree on the application of the terms 'polyphony' to music of oral tradition. Some, despite its strictly neutral sense of 'many sounds', find it misleading and only use it within the narrow limits of Western written music, preferring the term 'heterophony' for other instances. But advances in research and a wider knowledge of primitive music now tend to justify the use of the term 'polyphony' for these types as well.

The drone which is so characteristic of certain types of music and which is present in a great number of polyphonic or diaphonic pieces may be either vocal or instrumental. The voices execute intermittent hummings or repetitive 'rocking' motifs in fifths or octaves according to traditional conventions. Certain instruments, such as the hurdy-gurdy, zither, *sitar*, the bagpipes or the double shawm or hornpipe, may have a drone element incorporated, while in ensemble playing one or two separate instruments may hold the drone note.

Cantillation, as in readings of the Koran and Bible, recitative, psalmodic and melodic forms all play an extremely important role; they may be found side by side and often interpenetrate. For a long time it was believed that there was no formal structure in the most primitive forms of music but in fact there are rigid systems, both melodic and rhythmic, behind such music. Not only has the existence of archaic systems been found but the mechanism of structures ranging from the bitonic to the pentatonic has been determined. The same applies for larger, organised forms which can be either open or closed or cyclical; the Moroccan *nouba* for example is virtually a suite. Certain formulas for 'composition' would seem to be preferred and to characterise the musical content, such as repetitions of short motifs, straight or ornate repetitions of certain passages, acceleration particularly towards the end of the music, opposed registers and timbres, solo introductions and preludes, ascending, descending and linear cadences. In conclusion it should be emphasised that however great or slight the degree of systematisation in music of the oral traditions, improvisation according to conventional rules, which may be strict or comparatively free, is an essential feature. These rules and the cognate art of ornamentation form the basic equipment of the musician in these traditions.

respected society. Often however it is high; indeed, a special instrument such as the tambourine, or the category of music, such as that for a religious sanctuary, may determine both the place occupied by the musicians in the social structure and the hereditary privileges they enjoy. Such rules are very strict and involve tenacious prejudices. Moreover, certain musical instruments are subject to taboos and must or should (according to the degree of development reached by the country con-

African music

Africa may be roughly divided by a line parallel to the Equator and running south of the Sahara desert. Such an artificial boundary is obviously flanked on both sides by a blurred transitional zone, but the two large areas thus defined in northern and equatorial Africa are more or less homogeneous within themselves and differ notably from one another. Each includes enclaves owing allegiance to the other, and such a delimitation goes far beyond traditional linguistic, political, geographical and even anthropological frontiers. This chapter will be concerned with the musical culture to the south of this imaginary line, with what might be called 'pure' Negro music.

In this vast region there are of course a multitude of different musical traditions, varying from area to area, from district to district, and from tribe to tribe. Despite increasingly intensive research during this century, the huge field is far from being completely surveyed; however, enough is now known for us to be able to make a number of generalisations with some confidence. First, despite many very ancient survivals in some parts of the continent and in some musical usages – notably those connected with religion and magic – African music as a whole definitely does not belong to the most primitive stages of known musical development; when compared with other traditions such as that of the Australian Aborigines, it appears indeed as a comparatively recent art. Furthermore, in its instrumental resources and also in some of its musical idiom it shows clear evidence of the fruitful influence of both Islam and South East Asia. Secondly, the music with which we shall be concerned here is based entirely on the procedures of an oral tradition, having neither any form of notation, nor any systematic musical theory comparable to that found in Asia or Europe. Other features shared by the musical traditions of Black Africa are a common concern with elaborate and complex rhythms; a fascination with timbres which leads to countless modifications to single instruments and a preference for large instrumental ensembles producing very subtle combinations; a tendency to low-pitched vocalisations; a preference for collective rather than individual song; a frequently polyphonic arrangement of choral music, and the predominance of the pentatonic scale. In what follows we shall discuss African music under the main headings of the instruments; drum music; vocal polyphonic music; and the function of music.

The instruments

After the drum, which is undoubtedly the most widespread, popular and important of the instruments of African music, string instruments have the greatest variety. One of the most ancient in the world is the

A type of bow harp with calabash resonator.

musical bow still played in Africa in a number of varieties. In its simplest form it is an archer's bow plucked by the fingers of one hand while the other flexes the stave of the bow to vary the tension in the string and thus the pitch of the notes. It would seem at first sight that this was adapted from the weapon, but it has been suggested that in fact the bow was originally used as a musical instrument or that the two were invented independently. The sound is often amplified with some form of resonator; in its earliest form this was the mouth of the performer – by varying the size of the mouth cavity different harmonics could be made to resonate; in other forms, the resonator was a gourd attached to the bow. The length of the vibrating string can also be modified by a sliding noose, and the string is vibrated either by plucking or with a percussive stroke of the hand or a stick. In one type, even, the string is vibrated by the breath of the player. Yet another variant of this instrument is the ground bow, found in Uganda. Here one end of the bow is anchored in the ground, the string being set in a covered hole in the ground which acts as the resonator. The 'pluriarch' seems to be an extension of the musical bow principle. In effect this is several bows fixed to a single resonator formed by a box or a gourd, producing an instrument with the characteristics of a lyre and a lute. There is also a wide variety of harps, some of which, with ivory pegs and carved necks, are highly refined in their manufacture. One type of harp is the zither-harp, which may be as much as two yards long, and there are many true zithers, as well as lutes and lyres, of types only to be found in Africa.

Wind instruments are represented by different kinds of flute. In many parts, for example the region around Lake Victoria, it is believed to have magical properties, being used to assist at the performance of certain important social and communal acts. In addition to the flutes,

This flute player from the Cameroons uses his cupped left hand to extend the length of the instrument as required.

above
Marimba-type xylophones from the Congo; each key has a calabash as a resonator.

right
These 'thigh sticks' are hollow and the pitch is altered by varying the angle of the opening against the thigh. The girl on the left has a string of beads round hers to give a buzzing rattle to the tone.

African music also employs trumpets, not only the familiar end-blown variety but also animal horns, of ivory or other substances, with the narrow end stopped and the embouchure carved in the side of the tube. Some trumpets indeed are equipped with a finger hole to extend their melodic range somewhat, and trumpet sets are also found, five or six performers each playing a trumpet with one or two notes.

Finally we must mention the percussion instruments other than the drums, of which the most numerous are the xylophones, thought to have come to Africa from Indonesia. They range from the ground xylophone of the Yoruba of Nigeria, mounted over a pit which serves as a resonator, to the marimba type where gourds act as individual resonators to each of the keys. Some of these xylophones reach vast dimensions, and consist of several great bars of wood or bamboo which rest on the ground and may be played by one or two men, while others have as many players as there are keys, each man resting one of the tuned blocks across his knees. In other cases the instrument can easily be carried by the player.

We may also include in the category of percussion instruments the uniquely African *sansa*. It has many names and many forms but essentially it consists of a number of tongues, usually of metal but sometimes also of bamboo, which are anchored at one end to a sounding box and project up over a bar or bridge so that they are free to vibrate when struck. The instrument is played by holding the body of the sounding box (usually about eight inches long and six wide) with the fingers of the two hands and plucking the tongues with two thumbs. The *sansa* not only has a uniquely plangent and liquid sound but also has a feature remarkable among percussion instruments of any type: the vibrating length of the tongues can easily be changed and rapid tuning is thus possible.

As we have said, African musicians and their audiences delight in complexity and variety of timbres, and all the instruments described above are liable to be varied and modified from one tribe to another by a variety of means such as the introduction of *mirlitons* (membranes which give the tone a buzzing quality) to the wind instruments or the use of fret devices on the string instruments. But this delight in change and variety not only affects timbres but also extends even to tunings. The same basic instruments will be found played with different tunings in closely neighbouring tribes, just as the style of the music itself will change from one community to another. It is perhaps hardly surprising that there should be these kinds of distinctions between groups which are often isolated from one another and in any case are spread over a vast geographical area. In view of these considerations it is perhaps remarkable that one instrument, the drum, enjoys an almost universal ascendancy throughout the area.

The drum

One may reasonably assume that one cause of the drum's extensive distribution is the role it plays in communications. The carrying power of these instruments is considerable, and as a link between communities often separated by tracts of forest or bushland their value is obvious. Indeed their value as a means of communication persists; the talking drums have been used during the Nigerian war to signal the arrival of relief supplies. Furthermore, it is worth emphasising that the African drum has considerable precision as a means of communication. It is not merely a rhythm language operating on some kind of Morse code principle. In many cases the drums are tuned, so that they faithfully represent the actual sounds of the languages which are in most cases tonal (that is to say that pitch is an essential part of verbal significance).

The talking drum is still a vital part of musical tradition and is used in communal music for weddings and other such occasions. Westernised dance bands in Nigeria use the instrument on commercial recordings, and it is possible for a listener, unfamiliar with the record, to identify 'what the drum is saying'. However the drum has other, loftier associations. In one kingdom the omnipotence of the ruler is held to be limited in only one respect, that he cannot silence the royal drums, and in all African communities the royal drums are accorded great respect. Their manufacture is attended by special rituals and they may even be offered sacrifices.

As may be expected the instrument displays many types. Perhaps one of the most interesting is the variable pitch 'hourglass' drum. This has two heads which are generally tensioned by thongs connecting them along the length of the drum. In West Africa the nature of this drum has produced a remarkable degree of technical virtuosity. The drum is held in the crook of one arm and by increasing the pressure of the arm on the thongs the drummer can alter the pitch of the drumhead at will and may command a range of over an octave. Another drum which can be 'made to talk' belongs to the numerous family of the slit-drums. These are made from a hollowed out tree trunk or branch, so worked as to leave two lips either side of a thin slit which may extend the whole length of the drum or only part of the length. In the talking variety of the slit-drum the two lips are carefully whittled down so as to give one thick and one thin surface and hence two different pitches. There are many types of double-headed drums, of drums with a single head with bodies made of wood or clay, and of kettledrums which, like those of Europe, derive from Arab patterns. Some are played with sticks, others with the hands, and even the percussive technique may be determined by the status of the instrument being played. Drums may be played singly or more often in pairs, or they may be grouped in large 'batteries'.

Batteries as large as twelve drums are known, tuned to different pitches, and in performance each of these drums may be playing a different rhythm. The resulting complex is built up from a number of comparatively simple rhythms, but to maintain his part in such a turbulent sea of movement demands the highest degree of musicianship and experience in the drummer. C. M. Jones, one of the leading authorities on African music, has analysed the essence of African rhythm as tension. This results from the performance of conflicting rhythms on the different drums so that the beats of each are staggered as measured against a simple basic rhythm. In addition, the drums may be playing in different metres. The long rhythmic figures of the master drummer in the ensemble may be answered by a middle drum whose rhythm in its turn crosses that of the basic rhythm. In this highly elaborated art the elements of improvisation and convention are nicely balanced. It has been said that all African music is transmitted by oral traditions and this is also true of the drums; nevertheless the most skilled drummers are those whose natural inspiration can most imaginatively embellish the conventional rhythms, even while adhering to them.

Vocal polyphonies

Polyphony (we use the word simply to denote the simultaneous execution of several parts) is an important feature of African Negro music and, particularly, forest music. Three main kinds of polyphony are to be found, that of

the Bushmen and Pygmies, that of the Bororos and that of the Baoule. The Baoule are an important people of the Ivory Coast, whose music shows a predilection for a kind of 'diaphony' in parallel thirds. This would seem to be peculiar to this region and is used in singing long melodies which are in phrases of unequal length and punctuated by sustained notes, each linked to the other like garlands. When the chorus intervenes it does so powerfully and massively, stopping at perfect consonances, and producing a kind of struck chord which resounds for a long time and contrasts with the mobility of the diaphony while at the same time balancing it. It has been suggested that the interval of the third is part of the musical heritage which coastal Africa is believed to have assimilated from the Indonesian seafaring peoples.

In equatorial Africa different procedures are used in vocal polyphony. A singer is entrusted with the melody, on which he is expected to improvise according to his talents. The chorus sings a repeating bass figure of two or three notes, its formula sometimes changing during

below
Master drummers of the Ivory Coast.

bottom
Three Nigerian performers on the famous 'talking' drums; the simple frame drum on the right is purely percussive.

the development of the main song. Sometimes a second voice mingles with the first, either to give it a response or to add an entirely independent part. Both the Pygmies and the Bushmen differ from the rest of the Africans in their habit of yodelling and their way of combining voices polyphonically, each voice producing a kind of 'melodico-rhythmic loop' and overlapping the others in large ensembles which perpetually renew themselves. On the basis of recordings it has been possible to distinguish and write down the score for as many as seven distinct parts in a Bushman polyphony. Such songs are nearly always connected with dancing, with hunting rituals among the Pygmies and with healing rites among the Bushmen. Bushman and Pygmy melodies are usually pentatonic. The polyphony of the Bororos consists mostly of vocalisations but can achieve the most remarkable effects; certain Bororo choruses have been compared to 'the playing of an organ, since they are so sonorous, low-pitched and solemn'.

Music in society

Musical instruments are used in the most varied formations for ritual and social reasons quite as much as for musical effects. Whereas some instruments have become completely profane in their use, certain others have powerful religious or magical powers and women or non-initiates who see them may be punished by death. The outstanding example is the 'bull-roarer' a carved bob of wood attached to a cord which, when whirled through the air, produces a terrifying roar. Nearly all instruments have very strictly defined functions – a certain drum may only 'speak' in the presence of the king, a certain type of calabash is only used for funerals.

People whose lives are devoted to music because of their social function are to be found in nearly all parts of Africa, as in the case of certain royal choristers. In the regions influenced by Islam we find the *griots*, who enjoy a very special social status. As chroniclers of societies without a written language, their role, on every important occasion, is to recreate the history of the country, its great chieftains and families, by means of long, declamatory recitations which are either intoned or sung full-throatedly. But some *griots* are itinerant musicians and may even sometimes be acrobats, so that their roles of

epic singer, musician and entertainer show a remarkable affinity to those of the medieval European *jongleur*.

There are countless varieties of *griots*, including even the prostitute or procuress, among the Songhais people of the Niger. Her song may be said to be the *pièce de resistance* of her professional repertory of allurements, and her over-shrill, over-strained voice attains a degree of stridency that, together with her strict use of pentatonic scales, is very reminiscent of the Chinese theatre. When she is not a professional singer, the Sudanese woman, to take another instance, relies on melodic forms that are much simpler than those of the *griottes* and develop within a much narrower range. She may sometimes make use of a very shrill head voice but only to sing very quietly. When passing between the huts, one may sometimes hear a very light and murmuring yet shrill and small voice which is that of a woman humming to herself in her courtyard or her house. Such intimate songs have an incomparable charm.

For men also, vocal technique, melodic form, scale and instrumental accompaniment are all quite different according to whether the music is that of the *griots* or the peasants. Of course a *griot* repertory of a single tribe may include several different styles. The Hausa *griots* of the Nigero-Chad sultanates have a violent, emphatic style which has hardly anything in common with that of the rustic *griots*; this uses a relatively natural vocal emission and a more melodic and melodious song line. Generally speaking, a large part of the *griot* songs from Senegal through Nigeria to Chad conform more or less strictly to the following pattern: the singer begins abruptly by a sung word or a word shouted as loudly as possible at the top of his voice; this is followed by a chanted period in the middle register, and the song is ended in a low pitch by a descending inflexion. Even the strongest voice cannot stand this strain for long and the *griot*'s voice, which is nearly always recognisable on account of its husky timbre, is sometimes so broken that it would hardly seem capable of emitting any more sounds.

Despite the important Negro populations in Abyssinia and Egypt, to describe the music of these two countries would be to go beyond the limits of this short survey. In West Africa the music of Mauretania constitutes a bridge between the Islamic music of North Africa and Negro music. To the east of Africa, Madagascar provides the example of an equally composite musical world, but this time the mingling is between the music of Africa and South East Asia.

Ceremonial trumpeters from Uganda. The instruments are side blown; the mouthpiece can be seen in the one being carried on the left.

The music of the Far East

The art music of all the main countries of this vast area, China, Japan, Korea, Vietnam and Mongolia, is heavily indebted to a common theoretical base evolved by the theorists and musicians of the Chinese empire. These various traditions use the same types of instruments and a musical language based ultimately on similar principles. In this review we shall concern ourselves only with the music of China itself and the neighbouring but distinct tradition of Japan. We must leave aside not only the music of Korea, Vietnam and Mongolia but also that of the various ethnic minorities, which in their turn vary immensely. Before embarking on a more detailed analysis of the two main traditions of our study it may be as well to survey the general musical assumptions common to the area as a whole.

Some general aspects

In the Far East as in other parts of the world a distinction is made between popular music, called *sou youe* in China and *zo kugaku* in Japan (literally, 'vulgar' or 'ordinary' music) and erudite music, called *ya yue* in China and *Gagaku* (literally, 'elegant music') in Japan. It is not, however, always easy to define the precise boundary between them.

Secular popular music consists mostly of work songs and music for the festivals of the agricultural year, the epic singing of travelling bards and music for the popular theatre. In the case of the work songs, which are often unaccompanied, the texts are largely improvised, as is sometimes the music; the rhythm of the songs depends, of course, on the kind of work for which they are intended. On the other hand the music of the rural and seasonal festivals and their processions always requires instruments, of which the most favoured are the flute, the two-string fiddle, the three-string lute and drums and gongs. The last type of popular music to be mentioned includes the songs of itinerant physicians, the incantations of *shamans* and the Buddhist cantillations and psalmodies. The last mentioned, and indeed all kinds of ritual songs, often involve frequent changes of scale systems, of modes and of rhythms, and with this type of music we are already approaching the area of erudite or art music.

A fundamental difference between the popular and art music of the Far East is found in the matter of pitch. Whereas in the ritual music of the court the notes of the scale were related to an absolute fundamental tone which as we shall see was imbued with almost mystical qualities, in popular music the instrument would be tuned by ear to suit the range of the singer or in accordance with a tuning note given by one of the instruments themselves – probably the flute. Both types of music however employ scales which are basically pentatonic. But although the five-note scale is an essential feature of the musical idiom of the area, it displays various characteristic aspects. One of the most important is an essentially pentatonic structure to which two auxiliary notes have been added to produce some of the features of a seven-note scale. There is a variety of pentatonic scales built up on different intervals and used in various modes, but there are also continuous scales, and two-note, three-note and four-note scales. The general characteristics of the mode in Far Eastern music (more fully described in the treatment of Chinese music) are: an individual modal scale; a fundamental note which in art music is one of the twelve standard notes prescribed by theory; a characteristic melodic mood often expressed in specific ornamentations peculiar to the mode, and special rhythmic characteristics.

In general the art music traditions employ binary rather than ternary rhythms. In Korea the treatises mention rhythms in three and five beats but these are exceptional and in other Far Eastern countries ternary rhythms are found only in popular music, that of the court using binary rhythms of two, four, eight or sixteen beats. However it should be noticed that syncopated rhythm is relatively frequent; in Vietnam for example it was regarded as a sign of the player's virtuosity and constituted a form of ornament. In all traditions, free rhythm or the execution of fixed rhythm in rubato are frequent.

The rhythmic formulas, founded on one or more cell units, of which there are some two hundred in the music of the Japanese *Noh* theatre alone, appear extremely complex to the uninitiated. Yet they are in fact relatively simple basic formulas often made unrecognisable by the elaborate percussion ornaments and variations with which they are executed. The percussion instruments on which the rhythms are performed are played with the fingers, the palm of the hand or wooden sticks, and the resulting timbres are important elements in the music in their own right.

To conclude this survey of the musical idiom of the Far Eastern traditions, a word must be said about such elements of polyphony as are found in this music. Essentially it is melodic, and the polyphonic features which it

Musicians from Vietnam. The instruments, from left to right, are a form of the p'i-p'a, *a* koto *and a type of transverse flute.*

does display are primitive and largely fortuitous. In instrumental music all the parts sound in unison both at the beginning and at the end of the pieces, and on the strong accents of each bar they are either in unison or sound one of the perfect consonances such as the fourth or the fifth. For the weak accents all intervals are permitted and ornamental passing notes are added to the main melody. But although for much of the music the voices and instruments are out of unison, struck chords are never used harmonically, and if there is any sense in which this music may be said to have elements of counterpoint, it is the counterpoint of timbres.

The music of China: history and theory

From the earliest times, music enjoyed a lofty position in the Chinese social and cultural scheme of things. There were three chief fields in which it was employed: the festivals of the agricultural year, going back to a remote antiquity; the ceremonial of the imperial court; and the rituals of religion. According to theory, the function of music was to imitate and sustain the harmony between heaven and earth, resulting from the encounter between the male principle, *Yan* and the female principle, *Yin*. The musical system was based on twelve notes or *lü*, from which were selected the basic notes of a series of five-note scales. Chinese music is fundamentally pentatonic in character and although, for the purposes of theory, the twelve *lü* were arranged in a series superficially similar to the Western chromatic scale, this purely theoretical scheme was never employed as a scale in practical music.

The twelve *lü* were generated by calculations based on the interval of the fourth and the fifth, starting from a foundation note called the *huang chung* (literally, 'yellow bell'). Acoustic theory shows that the vibration frequencies of the *lü* are all powers of two and three, which in Chinese philosophy are the numerals of earth and heaven respectively. The foundation note itself was held to have an almost mystical character and was considered to be not only a musical note, but also one of the eternal principles of the universe and the basis of the well-being of the state. Consequently considerable care was taken to arrive at the correct fundamental note for each dynasty. Several methods were used to find the absolute pitch of the *huang chung*; according to one, the height of the pipe which gave the note had to be equal to 90 grains of millet of average size, laid end to end. The dictates of this highly involved theory decreed that the music of the twelve months of the year should use modes based on each of the twelve *lü* in turn. It was to facilitate the correct ordering of this sequence that the twelve-note 'scale' described above was used. From the earliest times, then, the notion of absolute pitch was central to Chinese music, and already by the first century BC an imperial office of music had been established to standardise pitch as well as to supervise the musical life of the empire generally. As we have seen, the twelve *lü* were never used as a chromatic scale. A choice was made from among them to provide the constituent notes of the various pentatonic scales which were used for composition. These five notes were held to correspond both to the five elements, earth, metal, wood, fire and water, and also to functions in society such as prince, minister and people. In addition to this five-note scale a seven-note scale using five principle and two auxiliary notes was also used.

An ancient Chinese statue of a deity playing the ch'in.

The music and the instruments

The two main elements of Chinese music are melody and timbre. Harmony, for so long the dominant means of expressive colouring in the West, is absent and is replaced, in the music of the large Chinese orchestras, by the rich multiplicity of instrumental timbres and the cloud of upper harmonics which these generate. The great orchestras comprised representatives of the three main instrumental groups, wind, percussion and strings, and were large by any standards, that of the Temple of the Ancestors at Peking consisting of as many as 150 performers. But apart from such large ensembles other important categories were that of solo song and solo instrumental music, notably that of the seven-stringed zither, the *ch'in*.

This instrument enjoys special prestige in the classical tradition of Chinese music and is believed to date back to the period of Confucius. For a long time it was the instrument of philosophers, accumulating around itself a whole body of scientific and philosophical lore, and requiring the discharge of a prescribed ritual before it could be played. The notation for it, which may date back to as early as the 2nd century BC, is one of the earliest systems of notation developed by Chinese musical theorists, who used ideograms to denote the notes of the scale and also employed tablatures and fingering charts for instruments such as the *ch'in*.

Solo song, with instrumental accompaniment, is also common in the popular music alluded to in the early section of this chapter. There is a close parallel between the melody and the poetry, a natural result of the tonal nature of the Chinese language, which was emphasised by the fact that certain verse forms came to be associated with specific modes. The resulting musico-poetic amalgam may be compared to the close interrelationship of music and verse found in the Indian *rāg*. As we have said, the *ch'in* was pre-eminent as a solo instrument, but its position came to be rivalled from the 7th century AD by the popularity of the short necked lute or *p'i-p'a*, which was much used to accompany songs. Some of the finest of these songs come from the period of the T'ang dynasty and the composers of this period developed the *p'i-p'a* as a solo instrument. It seems to have originated beyond the borders of the empire in central Asia but it was completely absorbed in the musical tradition of China, and its technique may have been modelled on that of the *ch'in*. Composers of this instrumental music often favoured a programmatic style, writing works designed to portray, for example, the sounds of warfare. In the late decades of the Sung dynasty and during the succeeding Mongol dynasty of the Yüan (1283-1368), the beginnings of a new musical art can be observed. This was the highly elaborate genre of the Chinese opera which in the 14th century evolved in two main directions, represented by the northern and southern styles respectively. This reached its highest classical achievement during the period of the Ming (1368-1644). The most distinctive feature to the Western ear is the high and forced falsetto singing of the male singers, but the opera, like other types of Chinese music, finds an important place for the art of the dance. There were two chief styles of vocal writing, roughly equivalent to recitative and lyric, and these would be carefully alternated to give variety to the performance which, consisting of many acts, might also last many hours.

In the foregoing brief survey of the general nature of music in the Chinese court and theatre we have mentioned two very important instruments. It is now time to give some account of the many other instruments employed, and here again we find ourselves confronted with an elaborate semi-philosophical theory unlike anything in Western music. The musical tone produced by a sounding body was considered to be an important attribute of the material of which it was made, and consequently the Chinese classified musical instruments according to their materials and distinguished eight categories as follows: the family of metal instruments included the bells and the gongs, which might be used separately or grouped together in carillons or chimes; next come the stone instruments of which the stone chime (*pien ch'ing*), consisting of a series of L-shaped plates, was one of the most important instruments in Chinese music; the silk category, including the all important *ch'in* and numerous other silk-stringed zithers and instruments including the *p'i-p'a* and the two-stringed fiddle; the bamboo instruments including the transverse flute (*ti*) and the panpipe; the wood and the skin instruments which were almost exclusively percussive. One of the major instruments of the Chinese orchestra was the *sheng* mouth organ. This consisted of fourteen or more pipes set in a gourd wind chest which was supplied with air by the player blowing through a side mouth-pipe. The *sheng* belonged to the gourd category of instruments, even though its characteristic tone derived from the vibrations of the free metal reeds at the base of the pipes. The free reed instruments of the West, such as the accordion and the harmonica, are probably direct derivatives of this Chinese instrument. The last category of instruments comprises those made of clay, whose chief representative is the globular flute, similar to the ocarina.

Such then were a few of the rich variety of Chinese instruments. These were used in the music both of the court and of the temple, and one large establishment is recorded as having 120 *ch'in* zithers, 120 zithers of other types, 200 *sheng*, 20 shawms and a full complement of percussion instruments, bells and stone chimes. A large orchestra, probably employing most of these instruments, would be used in conjunction with a choir of voices. As the choir sang the chant, each syllable being held on a long-drawn-out note, it would be doubled by the wind instruments and bell chimes while the zithers divided the long notes in strictly calculated ornamentations. The performance of the verses was punctuated by interludes performed on other instruments.

Musicians of the Peking opera; centre right is a player of the sheng.

The music of Japan

Probably the most ancient music to be found in Japan is the polyphonic folk music of the Ainu, the dominant race before the coming of the Mongoloid peoples in the second millennium BC, but now a very small ethnic minority confined to the northern part of the country. The earliest music of the Japanese themselves was the early chants of the Shinto religion but the real impetus to music here, as elsewhere in the Far East, was given by the Chinese influence. In the case of Japan this was active as early as the 3rd century AD when Chinese culture spread across the Sea of Japan following the conquest of the kingdom of Korea. In music as in the other arts, Korea came to be the essential intermediary between China and Japan, and in the 6th century Chinese court music followed the same routes as did the music of Buddhism, originating in India but heavily modified by its transmission through and sojourn in China. In the 8th century the Japanese court, no doubt following the example of China, founded an official academy or office of music, and this borrowing from the great power across the sea extended to musical theory and even to the adoption of many musical instruments.

Among the main instruments of Japanese music are: the *koto*, a zither which exists in two main forms, one of which is regarded as truly Japanese, the other being derived from the Chinese *ch'in*; the *biwa*, a short-necked lute derived from the Chinese *p'i-p'a*; the *sho* mouth organ, developed from the *sheng*; the *hichiriki*, a small, high-pitched double-reed instrument; and the *samisen*, a string instrument of guitar type, but without frets. The latter, originating in China, is played in its adapted Japanese version with a large plectrum like an axe-head, which is used to pluck the strings with a very heavy, almost percussive stroke.

But the highly eclectic art which was early Japanese music, although chiefly indebted to China, also drew heavily on the traditions of Korea, Manchuria and India. This involved not only the importation and adaptation of theory, instruments and styles but also the faithful continuation of traditions such as the court music of China and certain musical dramas from India. As a result it is still possible today to hear music performed by the imperial court orchestra of Japan, which is the direct descendant of music performed at the courts of 6th-century Chinese and Indian rulers. This *Gagaku* or 'elegant music' embraced a number of specific forms of which the severe *Bugaku*, which probably still retains many traits in common with the ancient Chinese model, is still performed. But fascinating as this semi-fossilisation of ancient Oriental music is, it may seem to a Western observer to be a somewhat artificial archaism, and there is much more to Japanese music.

Theatre music

In addition to the music of the Shinto temples, whose most characteristic forms are the *kagura* dance and *Saibara* songs which originated with the folk before being adopted by the imperial court, there is the repertory of the various forms of Japanese theatre. The parent form of the Japanese drama is the *Noh* theatre which arose in the 14th century as a secular version of the 'monkey dance' of Shintoism. The art of *Noh* is highly formalised, as is the music which accompanies it. This is performed by a unison chorus, a transverse flute, three *samisen* and three types of drum. The drums maintain a regular beat throughout the action, and the words of the drama must conform to this underlying rhythm; the vocal music is of two kinds, recitative-like declamation and song. In the late 15th and early 16th centuries a popular form of the highly stylised drama of the court was introduced, and, despite a chequered history at the start, firmly established itself. This *Kabuki* theatre was much less bound by artistic conventions than its more exalted parent and the mood of the dramatic performance was symbolised by the introduction of the *samisen* into the musical ensemble. It may be that the effectiveness of this instrument in the *Kabuki* led to its adoption in the *Noh* theatre itself; certainly it did not become common in *Noh* orchestras until the advent of *Kabuki*.

Another popular type of theatre was that using puppets and this, in its *Bunraku* form, also used the *samisen*, either one or more instruments accompanying the voice of the narrator. His function, like that of the manipulators of the puppets in the Javanese *Wayang kulit*, is three-fold – to narrate the action in a form of recitative, which amounts almost to a stylised form of speech, to speak the parts of the various characters and to provide such sound effects as are necessary.

Japanese musicians playing kotos *(foreground), drum, and flutes.*

Japanese theatre musicians; the two singers are accompanied by a samisen.

Koto music

Just as the Chinese *ch'in* zither had been one of the major musical instruments of its tradition, so the Japanese derivative *koto*, winning a sudden popularity in the 17th century, remained one of the most cultivated of all the instruments of art music. Over six feet long, it consists of a sound board over which are stretched thirteen waxed silk strings, anchored at either end and passing over movable bridges. These bridges can be adjusted by the player with one hand, while the other, equipped with ivory plectra attached to finger stalls on the thumb and first two fingers, plucks the strings. The esoteric art of the *koto* had been cultivated long before the instrument's 17th-century vogue. The tuning produces a pentatonic scale spread over two and a half octaves, and one of the most striking features of the music is its wide ranging leaps. In its most advanced forms the music of the *koto*, at first performed mainly with voice accompaniment, consists basically of a set of variations embellished with various types of ornaments which are codified in manuscripts whose secrets are known only to a few.

The music of Indonesia

History and theory

Between Malaya and New Guinea there lies a string of islands whose only link is navigation and the Malayan language, which forms the *lingua franca* of exchange and trade. The coastal populations of the countries now corresponding politically to Indonesia, the Malayan Federation and the Philippines, have been the object of successive waves of cultural influence from China, India, the lands of Islam and Europe. From the 2nd to the 12th centuries AD the cultural influence of Hinduism was paramount and the legends of the Hindu religion came to provide the basis of the poetry and theatre of Indonesia. These two arts are inextricably bound up with music, which was thus indirectly affected by the gradual ascendancy of Islam so that today only the island of Bali retains Hinduism as its religion. But despite the foreign origin of the two main religions of the region, the music of Indonesia, after it had recovered from the undoubted effect of Indian music, regained much of its native inspiration so that the influence of Islam in music was slight. Indeed the most important contribution was in the field of instruments; the spike fiddle found in some Indonesian orchestras is the direct descendant of the Arab *rabab*.

Thus despite successive periods of foreign influence the music of Indonesia is highly individual, indeed in important respects it contributes a unique experience in the world of music. The two major factors are the scales employed and the instruments. These will be examined in greater detail when we come to discuss the *gamelan* orchestras and their music; here we need only notice that apart from the *rabab* mentioned above and the occasional use of various types of flute, the instrumental resources of Indonesian music are predominantly of the fixed-note percussion type of which the family of xylophones are among the most important.

The two basic scales are the *pelog* and the *slendro*. Of these the most ancient is the *pelog*; it divides the octave into seven notes which are separated by unequal intervals and which are used as the focuses of a series of five-note scales for the actual composition of the music of the repertory. Thus the music of the *pelog* uses a five-note scale though these five are drawn from a seven-note sequence. Whereas the *pelog* is traditionally considered to be feminine and melancholic in mood and is used to accompany the narratives of the great legendary cycles, as well as for the music of the *gamelan*, the *slendro* is felt to have a masculine, grave and exalted character and, in addition to its use in the *gamelan*, is associated with the movements of the figures of the *Wayang kulit* shadow puppet theatre. The *slendro*, traditionally held to have been invented by a minor deity at the behest of Siva, the head of the Hindu pantheon, probably did not become widespread until the 8th century AD. Not only is it used as a five-note scale, as is the *pelog*, but it divides the octave into only five notes which are separated by approximately equal intervals.

Although the identifiably Indian elements in the music of Indonesia have now become submerged, we should not forget the important formative role which Hindu religion and culture played in earlier centuries. Among the most notable examples of this was the widespread adaptation and performance of Sanskrit drama which naturally demanded new music for its accompaniment and which took its place alongside the characteristic Indonesian art of the *Wayang*. Today the art song of the Javanese theatre takes the form of the cantillation of the poems of the drama and is consequently governed by the rhythm of the poetry and the succession of the rhymes. The same applies to the songs performed by the operator of the figures of the shadow theatre; it is his job not only to animate the puppets, but also to narrate the action, speak the parts of the characters with suitably distinctive voices and even to provide the sound effects where needed. In a brief survey such as this, it is unfortunately impossible to do more than allude to the function of music in the traditional drama of Indonesia, and we now must turn to a consideration of the most important single musical phenomenon of this region of South East Asia – the *gamelan* of Java and Bali.

The gamelan

The name applies both to the music and to the orchestras which perform it. At the outset, we should note that there are a wide number of distinctive types and that the art is widespread and rooted in the community life of the islands. Under the impact of Western music the *gamelan* is inevitably and regrettably losing some ground, but there are still thousands of these local orchestras and the art is by no means dead.

As has been said the instruments used are almost exclusively fixed-note varieties. The preference for this type of sound is emphasised by many facets of life in South East Asia and Indonesia. Even the rocking bamboo troughs of the irrigation systems in the paddy-fields are so designed that the ringing of bamboo on stone as they periodically pivot backwards and forwards produces a kind of mechanical music in the open fields. In certain tribal ceremonies and fertility rites the ground and trees are struck or pounded with carefully chosen percussion sticks, and even the repetitive business of pounding rice seems to yield music. These simple everyday sounds are echoed in the sophisticated music of the orchestra where metal and bamboo combine to produce a magical and unique effect. The major instruments are the bronze-keyed *saron*, the *bonang*, a chime of different sized gongs, various types of individual gongs, the two-headed drum, the metal drum and the many types of xylophone. In addition to these we should notice the small numbers of string instruments of foreign origin, chief among them the *rabab* and zither types, and the

A girl from Borneo playing a large gong; note the central boss.

flutes, of which the most important is the Javanese ribbon flute or *suling*. This last named instrument is not used in the orchestras of Bali and there are other differences between the two types just as there are differences between their various regions and according to the role which the music is playing. Not only the music but also the combination of instruments changes according to whether the *gamelan* is accompanying the *Wayang* theatre performance or a dance or a temple ceremony. But the great divide between the various types of ensemble is that between the *slendro* and the *pelog gamelans*.

Since the instruments of the orchestra have fixed notes and therefore cannot be tuned, a single ensemble cannot play music which is composed in both scales. Formerly it was common for the princes and other wealthy patrons to have two *gamelan* orchestras, one for music in each scale, while the poorer village communities would be able to support only one in either *pelog* or *slendro* scale according to tradition. The grandest musical establishments boast a third *gamelan* which can perform the 'royal arrangement', this being music using the two scales alternately.

A *gamelan* composition consists of three main elements each of which is consigned to a group of instruments. At the very centre of the composition is what we may call a nucleic theme which provides the basic material for the music of the three main elements. This theme, given in long-drawn-out notes by the *saron*, forms the foundation of the piece in a manner analogous to the *cantus firmus* of European music of the middle ages and the Renaissance. The *saron* group comprises also a number of single gongs, which punctuate the divisions of the foundation theme, and the *kendang* drum, which marks time for the ensemble as a whole while also indicating nuances and variations in the rhythm. Next above the theme comes the music of a group of higher pitched chime instruments, such as the *bonang* and the *gender*, the latter a xylophone with bamboo resonators. This group embroiders the main theme according to strict though not rigid conventions, but never departs far from its basic shape. The third tier in this structure of sound is provided by another group of instruments which perform an embroidery of rapid figurations of notes, related to the main theme but somewhat freer than the second group. As we have seen, the Javanese *gamelan* employs the stringed *rabab* and also the *suling* flute, and these instruments, of which the *rabab* is particularly important, perform what amounts to a counter theme with subtle variations.

A full *gamelan*, whether from Java, Bali, Thailand or Cambodia, produces an effect unique in music. The complete sonorous range may be as great as six or seven octaves and the resultant effect is a cloud of sound, shimmering and vibrant, a homogeneous texture whose constituent parts are constantly changing. It was this sound which so impressed Debussy when he heard the *gamelan* orchestra sent to the Paris international exhibition in 1889, while 20th-century composers in both Europe and America have studied and used its effects. It may be said that the immediate appeal of any alien musical tradition lies in the timbres of its instruments and it is in this area above all that the *gamelan* is especially rich.

above
Young Javanese musicians.

right
A gamelan *orchestra from Bali.*

Music in India

Music (*sangita*) in India is intimately linked with philosophy and religion. Sound is said to be of two kinds, the vibration of ether and the vibration of air. The former, 'unstruck sound', corresponds to Pythagoras' 'music of the spheres'. Inaudible to men, it is that in which the gods delight. The latter, 'struck sound', is the stuff of man-made music. It is believed however to reflect the laws of the universe and results from the union of physical breath with the fire of intellect. According to tradition the god Brahma taught song to the legendary sage Nārada who in turn transmitted it to humans.

The historical development

The earliest texts known are hymns to divinities, sacrificial formulas and incantations, grouped in the four collections known as *Vedas*. Sung recitation, often given the name of 'Vedic psalmody' and codified particularly in the *Samaveda*, was an essential element in the worship that the Aryans progressively established in the whole of India after their arrival from the plains of the upper Indus 1,500 years before the Christian era. It was generally delivered on three notes: a central note, a lower note and an upper note. Indians believe that their classical music originated in a development of the melodies of the *Samaveda*.

Legendary narratives, religious and epic texts were succeeded by a long series of theoretical treatises in Sanskrit. To mention them all would be impossible and superfluous, especially as they have been abundantly glossed over many centuries.

The most ancient treatise to have come down to us is probably the *Nātya–Shāstra*, dated variously within the period 200 BC to AD 400. It is a vast encyclopedia in verse and prose whose principal subject is drama and the dance (regarded in India as a subdivision of music). But its author, Bharata, whose historical existence has been contested, deals also with rhythm, measure, the different ways of developing a song, and even describes a method for the playing of drums.

The *Sangita Makarandah* attributed to the original Nārada is the work of a much later author (another Nārada?) belonging to the 8th or 9th century AD. The most important treatise of the medieval period is still the *Sangita–Ratnākara* of Shārangadeva (1210–47) which contains models for musical compositions.

The extent to which the style of north Indian music changed after coming into contact with Arab and Persian musicians is disputed, but the theoreticians had difficulty in reconciling the musical usage of their age with past theories. The *Rāga–Vibodha* (about the year 1610) of Somanātha illustrates this process and constitutes a veritable treasure house of musical knowledge.

In the south, Venkata Makhin wrote his *Chaturdandi*

Prakāshika in 1620, and by his attempt at a systematic classification he made the definitive separation of Indian music into two great categories: the music of the north, known as 'Hindustani' and that of the south, named 'Carnatic'.

In the present century, the thorough systematising work of V. N. Bhatkande, *Hindusthani Sangita Paddhati* has had extensive influence in the northern school.

Musical instruments

Indian writers stress that primacy in music belongs to the voice. It is through the voice that the union of audible sound and intellect is most immediately and subtly achieved, and the development of instrumental music has essentially been in imitation of the classical vocal tradition. However, a variety of instruments has appeared, and as early as the *Nātya–Shāstra* we find the grouping of musical instruments into four categories – stringed, wind, membranous percussion and metal percussion – a division that has been maintained until the present.

Of the stringed instruments used by the classical musicians, the most representative is the *vinā*, the traditional attribute of Saraswati, goddess of learning and the arts. While originally the term denoted a harp, in its classical form the *vinā* finds its closest Western equivalent in the lute. Having seven strings and twenty-four adjustable frets, the *vinā* is equipped with two resonators of gourd or wood, one at each end. When played it is placed either horizontally across the player's knees or slanting against the shoulder, the left hand stopping the frets and the right hand plucking with the plectrum or the finger nails.

In the north the *vinā* has been supplanted by the *sitār*. While similar in style to the *vinā*, the *sitār* is somewhat smaller and simpler. Originally developed with only three strings by Amir Khusru at the court of Sultan Ala-u-din in the 14th century, it now normally has seven strings, but fewer frets than the *vinā*. In the best instruments up to thirteen sympathetic strings are tuned to emphasise the notes of the chosen *rāg* (see below). While popular with the amateur, it can extend the virtuoso's skill to the limit.

The *sārod* has a heavy wooden belly hollowed and covered with parchment, a metal finger board, but no frets; its range is lower and its tone heavier and richer than that of the *sitār*. Less versatile than the latter, the *sārod* has become prominent in the hands of recent virtuosi.

The *tānpurā* (*tamburā*), limited to four strings and resonator, is used only to provide the drone for a singer or instrumentalist, while the *sārangi* and *esrāj* are akin to the violin, but of very gentle tone. They are played with a bow, and used chiefly to accompany singers.

The wind instruments include not only conches and horns, but also straight and transverse flutes. Iconography has popularised the image of the god Krishna as a cowherd playing the transverse flute (*vansha* or *bānsuri*) to charm the milkmaids in the forest of Brindāvan. In modern times the subtlety and brilliance achieved by virtuoso players on the instrument, which retains its simple unkeyed form, is very remarkable. The most common reed instruments are the *shahnāi* in the north and the *nāgasvaram* in the south. Akin to the oboe or shawm, these instruments are virtually without keys. As in the case of the flute, the player produces the whole range of intermediate tones (including extensive 'slides') by partially closing the holes and adjusting the breath. The *shahnāi* is particularly associated with outdoor wedding celebrations, but in recent times has been skilfully exploited to perform the whole range of the classical *rāgs*.

Membranous percussion instruments play a dominant part in traditional music. In the north, the *tablā bāyan* (normally abbreviated to *tablā*) is a pair of small kettle-drums, one for each hand. In the south, the more ancient *mridangam* is a single large two-headed drum. In both cases the drum-heads are treated to provide different surfaces in concentric areas, and thus different tones, which are further diversified by the style of striking with varying combinations of fingers and palm. Lastly, metal percussion instruments include bells, pairs of cymbals and small bells which dancers and dancing girls tie in clusters around their ankles. Here again intricate rhythmic sound patterns are evolved by the precisely articulated movements of the feet and ankles.

Indian classical music as described in the treatises and as it is practised today is based on a modal conception analogous to that of ancient Greece and the Arab world. It is governed by rules which became increasingly precise and complicated in the course of the centuries, but which were already present in their essentials in Bharata's treatise. We omit here the extremely complex history of the evolution of scales and the varied use of technical terms, and focus attention on the salient features of classical music as it is performed today. While what follows largely reflects the usage of the northern school, the essential features are shared by the Carnatic tradition.

The theory

Theoreticians claim that the interval of the octave (*saptak*) may be divided into 66 *shrutis*. In practice 22 of these are employed. The Western listener, however, is greatly helped by the discovery that the *shrutis* are commonly thought of as modifications of the seven basic notes (*svar*) and that the seven *svars* form a sequence (the Indian *rāg bilāval*) which is identical with the European diatonic major scale. The Indian solfeggio is *shadj* (SA) *rishabh* (RE) *gāndhār* (GA) *madhyam* (MA) *pancham* (PA) *dhaivat* (DHA) *nishād* (NI).

There is however no sense of key and consequently no harmony in Indian music and it is misleading to refer to SA as 'tonic'. Each note (*svar*) is felt to have its individual quality, heard in relation to SA. Thus SA and MA represent tranquillity, RE, sharp or harsh feelings, GA and DHA, solemn and serious moods, PA, joy and gaiety, and NI sorrow. The *svars* are also likened to the cries of animals: RE to the mooing of a cow, NI to the trumpeting of an elephant and so on. There is however a good deal of diversity in these comparisons.

The classic combination of North Indian music; from left to right: tablā, tamburā *and* sitar, *the latter played by Ravi Shankar.*

The 22 *shrutis* are thought of as modifications of the *svars* in various degrees, 'natural', 'flat', 'extremely flat', 'sharp' and 'extremely sharp'. The application of these modifications to the seven *svars* produces the twenty-two divisions of the octave. The foundation of classical music is the organisation of the *svar–shruti* system into hundreds of note complexes known as *rāgs*. (The forms *rāg*, *tāl*, etc. have been used rather than *rāga*, *tāla*, etc. in conformity with north Indian usage, where the final 'a', though etymologically justified, is not pronounced.)

The rāg

A *rāg* is a particular set of the seven *svars*, or a selection of them, (in their 'natural', 'flat' or 'sharp' forms), whose interrelationship and sequence are governed by strict rules. The musician's art lies in exhibiting, with innumerable nuances and ornamentations, the full range of note relationships which are admissible within the structure of the chosen *rāg*.

The *rāgs* are nowadays classified into ten *thāts*. According to the varying combinations of the natural, flat and sharp forms of the notes, each *thāt* or class comprises a large number of *rāgs*, and each has a *rāg* chosen as characteristic of its *thāt*. Other *rāgs* will omit certain notes either in ascent (*ārohan*) or descent (*avarohan*) or both. For example one in the *bhairavi thāt* omits RE and PA in both ascent and descent to produce a scale virtually identical with the pentatonic scale of Western folk music; while another omits RE and DHA in ascent, but uses all the *svars* in descent.

The *rāg* is further defined by the selection of one note for special prominence (*vādi*) and a second note (usually a fifth or a fourth distant from the *vādi*) as a supplementary point of emphasis (*samvādi*). The prominence given to the *vādi* together with a few sequences of two or three notes characteristic of a particular *rāg* may in themselves distinguish it from another *rāg* which employs the same set of notes. Added piquancy may be achieved by the occasional introduction of a note which does not belong to the *rāg* at all (*vivādi svar*), though obviously this must be done with great sensitivity, so as to heighten and not destroy the characteristic mood of the *rāg*.

As all these subtleties can be understood only in their relationship to SA, the latter is sounded more or less throughout the music as a drone, either through lightly touching the strings of the instrument which are tuned to SA, or through a separate drone instrument such as the *tānpurā* (which always accompanies a singer). However, this 'SA pedal' never assumes the 'harmonic' feel of a keynote. Indeed in some *rāgs* SA hardly occurs in the actual exposition, and this fact coupled with an insistence on the *vādi* and the *samvādi* can produce an effect on the Western listener at once baffling and poignant.

Each *rāg* has its own emotional character, and is associated with a particular time of day. Thus *bilāval*, a late morning *rāg*, is said to be inquisitive, signifying a mixture of joy and affection, while *bhairavi* suggests sadness mixed with passion and pleasure. The *rāg megh* (literally, 'cloud') is associated with the joy of the rainy season, whereas an all-night session of music-making will be brought to a close with the early morning *rāg bhairav* which embodies a dreamy invocation of the dawn. There is a famous anecdote which tells how Tan Sen, court musician of the 16th-century emperor, Akbar, sang a night *rāg* at midday with such power that darkness fell on the place where he stood. On another occasion, his enemies forced him to sing the *rāgdipak* ('lamp light') to such effect that he was nearly consumed by flames, and was only delivered by a timely execution of the *rāg megh*, which brought rain to quench the fire.

above
A bardic singer from north India accompanying himself on a two-stringed lute.

left
Musicians at the festival of Holi.

A Hindu god playing the flute.

There has also been a traditional division between the male *rāgs* (mostly in the bolder pentatonic style) and their consorts or *rāginis* (mostly the more subtle septatonic variety), and these emotional and imaginative associations have provided material for some of the most celebrated miniature paintings of India, where the various *rāgs* and *rāginis* are depicted as human figures against suitably evocative backgrounds.

The tāl

The second basic element of Indian music is rhythm or *tāl*. The *tāl* is a rhythmic cycle, comprising a fixed number of time units (*mātrā*) of equal value. These may be 6, 7, 8, 10, 12, 14 or 16 in number – to name only the most common. They are grouped by bars and like the *rāgs* each has its individual name. Thus *tintāl* has 16 *mātrās* in four bars (4-4-4-4); *jhaptāl* has 10 *mātrās* in four bars (2-3-2-3) while *sultāl* has 10 *mātrās* in five bars (2-2-2-2-2); *vishnutāl* has 17 *mātrās* in five bars (2-3-4-4-4). However, by far the commonest is *tintāl*. In performance, great importance attaches to the first beat of the cycle – *sam* ('together', having a common Indo-European root with the English word 'assemble'). While during the cycle the drummer and singer or instrumentalist may explore largely independent rhythms, with syncopation and displacement of accent (provided they maintain a mathematically exact division of the *tāl*), they must come together precisely on the *sam*. This moment can have an electrifying effect when it is demonstrated that despite their rhythmic deviations, both players have maintained intact the basic structure and time value of the *tāl*. Not infrequently an element of competition enters when the instrumentalist introduces a novel and complex rhythmic pattern which the drummer must then imitate, and vice versa, each outdoing the other in elaborating rhythms which still keep within the rules of the *tāl*.

Although the 13th-century treatise *Sangita Ratnākara* describes 120 *tāls*, contemporary virtuosi claim only twenty individual *tāls* in common use, though each may be performed slowly (*vilambit*), at moderate speed (*madhya*) or rapidly (*drut*). To assist him in controlling the vast number of rhythmic variants on the *tāls*, the drummer makes use of mnemonics or *bols* which relate to the numerous ways of striking the drum-head. Some relate to the left hand, some to the right, and some to 'riffs' for both hands.

The performance

In the classical style of performance, the first section (*ālāp*) will be a slow and meditative exposition of the *rāg*, and will delineate its mood. Its practical purpose is to fix the various notes of the *rāg* upon the mind and show their relationships in ascent and descent. Beginning with one or two notes the *rāg* is gradually extended (with much use of portamento – *mir*) until all the notes of the *rāg* have been sounded in all three octaves. The *ālāp* however is far more than an introductory device: in the hands of a master it becomes an eloquent soliloquy, improvised in free time with infinite subtlety and delicacy of feeling, enfolding performer and listener in a common devotion to the spirit of the *rāg*. The *ālāp* (which itself may last up to thirty minutes) may be followed by *jor* – again an improvisation within the strict rules of the *rāg*, but introducing rhythm. At this stage the percussion instrument may join in, and gradually the tempo increases until

(in instrumental music) the performance is brought to a brilliant climax in *jhālā*, a prestissimo section in which the plectrum on the higher drone strings (*chikari*) deftly weaves dazzling rhythmic patterns around the *rāg* theme. While the main part of any classical performance is largely improvised, set compositions are also played. These are known as *gat*, and essentially comprise a series of variations or short rhythmic elaborations (*tān*) of the *rāg* about a relatively fixed recurrent motif (*sthāyi*), rather after the manner of a European rondo.

Besides the strictly classical tradition so far discussed, throughout the length and breadth of India there is a great variety of folk music – mentioned already in the writings of the medieval theoreticians as 'regional' music – which escapes the rules.

Very popular among the tribal peoples of India, as amongst the village Hindus, are the drums of many kinds used to accompany village dancing – frame drums, single-skin vertical drums, small and large two-skinned drums, the timbals of the Santal dancers, the pottery timbals of the young Murias, the giant wooden drums of the Nagas of Assam. The bamboo transverse flute plays a privileged role, and there is also a motley collection of simple stringed and bowed instruments.

Above all, however, popular music has found expression in simple lilting or rhythmic song, often designed to accompany the different operations of farming and fishing, such as the famous boat song of Kerala. Frequently religious themes are prominent: songs of devotion to one or another god of the Hindu pantheon, known in the north as *bhajan*, songs related to the spring-time festival of Holi, sung dramas, or the extended outpourings of Vaisnaivite devotion in the group lyrics known as *kirtān* in Bengal and based on the legend of Krishna or the deeds of Rāma.

In modern times one outstanding composer, Rabindranath Tagore (1861-1941), has married his own Bengali words to composed lyrical tunes after the fashion of the romantic ballad. In Bengal his music (known as *Rabindra Sangit*) is immensely popular and has an immediate emotional appeal. Rabindranath based his melodies on the classical *rāgs*, but added elements of Western harmonisation. He was deliberately seeking a new style in which Indian tradition would be fertilised by a Western infusion and formalised classicism would be complemented by romantic lyricism. His music however, while highly regarded, is hardly accepted as classical, and he has had no outstanding followers.

The music of the Arab world

From Asia Minor to the Atlantic we may still find various types of music which, for all their variety, belong to the common tradition of Islam and which were spread to the cultural centres of the Near and Middle East, the Maghreb and Spain by the triumphant career of conquest in the 7th and 8th centuries. In this music, which grew out of pre-Islamic Arab music and the important contributions made by the Islamicised peoples–notably the Persians and Turks–the Arab element acted as a catalyst. But such a successful fusion could never have taken place if there had not been affinities between Arab music and regional popular music. Although the latter has been neglected in favour of the more sophisticated exercise of art music, it has still survived, especially as music for the celebration of family events, for the festivals of the agricultural year and among the humbler classes of society. Of such celebrations, that of marriage is the occasion for the most important performances, with songs and dances predominating. The further we move away from the centre of Islam's development, the more we will find regional peculiarities predominating in popular music. It is thus that the music of the Berber tribes has kept its own personality up to the present day. Moreover, although Islamic art music spread to an extraordinary extent, it did not take deep root everywhere. Java and to a lesser degree Mauretania and the Sudanese region are examples of Islamicised countries only slightly affected by it. Art music, however, is the common denominator of the whole musical region we are examining, and there is, moreover, a deep interpenetration between religious, popular and serious music.

General characteristics

The music of the Islamic world rests on oral tradition. Some medieval Arab theoreticians adopted a system of alphabetic notation for purely theoretical requirements and systems of notation were elaborated in 17th-century Turkey, but even these were never applied to the very complicated art of serious music for fear of fossilising it. There were well defined conventions certainly, but within these the skilled performer was expected to extemporise and enrich his material in a way fitting to his audience and the occasion. Just as the story-teller or a popular epic singer would never relate the same story twice in the same way, so the serious musician varied his performance of traditional themes.

The music is essentially monodic and executed within the linear framework of the melody, which either takes on the form of an austere, unadorned line or that of a highly embroidered arabesque punctuated by vocalisations and improvisations. The melody is developed through intervals comprising a variety of the tone and semitone, as well as an interval intermediate between

them and one somewhat greater than the tone.

Such music is characterised by a very great number of vocal timbres, and these give it refined nuances and great expressive power. Indeed everything is done to exploit the capacities of the human voice to the utmost. This predilection for the voice and vocal music caused instrumental music to take second place almost everywhere except in Persia, which had a strong tradition of instrumental music before the coming of Islam. But according to trustworthy theoreticians, even this music was similar in spirit to vocal music.

The music of Islam is essentially modal. This characteristic is common to many other types of music, especially that of India, and dates back to very ancient times. Since the 12th century, the generic term *maqam* has been used to designate the notion of the mode. The term may be related to the *maqama*, a literary genre which generally took the form of a series of tableaux linked together by a character who finds himself in picturesque situations which provide him with a pretext for improvising poems of great virtuosity. The modes are very numerous and bear names which may refer to a place, to a famous man, or to emotions, objects, qualities and so on.

In theory the *maqam* is a characteristic scale in which certain notes are stressed; these notes, or degrees of the mode, are often repeated and serve as supports for the melody, sometimes playing a role comparable to that of the keynote in European music. To modify the nature of the mode it is in practice only necessary to stress other notes in the same scale and change the main melodic or rhythmic formula. As a consequence, apart from the succession of intervals and the choice of stressed notes, it is the pre-existing melodic and rhythmic formulas and the conventions which determine their treatment in a given composition that form the essential part of the modal universe. Thus when a musician is asked to play or sing a mode, he executes not a scale but only a motif or theme stressing the characteristics of the requested mode. These formulas are consecrated by tradition and echo ancient songs or particularly successful motifs taken from the compositions of great past musicians. They provide the musician with the raw material for new compositions.

The pre-Islamic period

The music of the tribal encampments in the Arabian peninsula and in the Yemen, and in the towns and courts of the independent Arab kingdoms, was essentially vocal. The most widespread type of song among the Bedouin tribes was the *huda* song of the camel-drivers which had a rhythm said to mimic the movements of the camel's feet; it may originally have been a kind of charm against

right
The large tambourine shown here is common in Algeria; there are three cords stretched across the inside of the head that produce a rattling effect when the instrument is struck.

below
A dancer from Tunisia accompanying himself on the pipes.

the spirits of the desert and may have been very similar to the *buka* (funeral lament). Another type of song was the incantatory song, intoned at the moment of battle. Such songs were stark and simple in character and were given a rudimentary accompaniment by the *mizaf* (lyre), *qussaba* (flute) and *duff* (frame drum) and must have resembled the present popular songs of the Bedouin tribes and the peasants of the Middle East. More highly developed songs were to be found in the towns, as well as a greater variety of instruments including the *wann* and the *jank* (harps), the *tunbur* (long-necked lute) and the *surnay* (shawm). It is interesting to note that from the earliest times women had a prominent role as instrumentalists.

The Islamic period

Although the Moslem invaders were in a minority and culturally inferior to the civilisations they had conquered, they succeeded in imposing an impressive degree of unity on the heterogeneous elements that made up their conquests.

It would seem that pre-Islamic poetry, which was of a very high quality, was largely sung. It is probably in these songs, in which the music is subordinate to the words, that we must look for the origins of the Koranic cantillation.

Mohammed was basically hostile to the unregulated performance of art music, only permitting its use for the solemn reading of the Koran, the call to prayer and family celebrations. In other words he proscribed the performance of serious music for secular purposes. As some writers and theoreticians have pointed out, from the strictly musical point of view there was no fundamental difference between the cantillation of the *muezzin* and the vocalisations of a professional lay singer, or between the laws governing Koranic recitation and those determining secular art song. Mohammed may have attempted to prevent gratuituous musical performance because he foresaw that music in its secular applications might develop in such a way as to harm religious feeling. And in fact, as Arab music came into contact with the music of the conquered countries and especially that of Persia, it did gradually lose its solemn, serene character and increasingly became a source of diversion, both refined and exuberant. The growing virtuosity of performers and the multiplicity of stylistic experiments contributed to the rise of a host of famous musicians, who enjoyed fabulous salaries and soon rivalled in fame the very rulers and ministers who employed them.

The new developments were opposed by philosophers and theoreticians, who believed that they would lead the art into decline. They took a stand against the introduction of pleasure and luxury into music and demanded the reinstatement of the moral element; even some practising musicians fought bitterly against the moderns and sought for a balance between the extremes.

Islamic music achieved its first classical period under the Umayyad caliphate (661-750). During this period the musical form par excellence was the solo lute song and it was in the late 17th century, under Persian influence, that the lute gained its classic shape. Indeed the pressures of foreign styles were great and the first major Islamic musician, Ibn Misjah (d. 715), who travelled widely, rejected all such influences which did not conform to the spirit of Arab music.

A real quarrel between the ancient and modern schools of thought broke out in the 9th century under the first Abbasid caliphs, its most eminent proponents being Ishaq al-Mausili (d. 850) and the prince Ibrahim ibn al-Mahdi (d. 839), a famous singer in the 'romantic' style of Persia. Ishaq, the most powerful artistic personality of his age, and one of Islam's greatest musicians, rigorously defended the spirit of the old music, and particularly protested against the idea of virtuosity in music and excessive use of grace-notes which, he claimed, gave music an effeminate character. He seems to have had some success in slowing down the pace of experimentation.

His most brilliant pupil was Ziryab, who eventually had to leave Baghdad on account of his master's jealousy. He took refuge in Andalusia, where he introduced new teaching methods. From this period Spain was one of the greatest centres of Islamic music reaching its peak in the 10th century when the great theorist, Al-Farabi, was working. The achievements of Moorish Spain never again reached these heights but its music had important repercussions in the rest of Europe. This is demonstrated not only by the adoption of instruments such as the lute and the *rabab*, European name 'rebec', but also by the new impetus for theoretical researches which European scholars, such as Roger Bacon, derived from the work of their Arab predecessors. After the fall of Granada in 1492, the musical tradition of Moorish Spain was perpetuated in the countries of the Maghreb.

Even after the golden age of the Moslem empire music continued to flourish in the various regional centres, and while the old music received new infusions during the long period of Turkish domination, under the Ottoman empire, on the whole, it still remained true to itself. Even today, wherever it has escaped the influence of Europe, the serious music of the Arab world, in the East and in the Maghreb, has remained basically unchanged since the days of Abbasid Baghdad or Moslem Andalusia.

Musical theory

Given the absence of musical notation, the numerous writings on the art of music are our only source of information on Arab music in the past. These writings fall into two categories: literary and theoretical. In the first category, of which the most important work is the *Book of Songs* by Abu al-Faradj al-Isfahani, we find details of musical execution and the ethical and aesthetic ideas of the period in a more or less anecdotal form. The second category comprises specifically theoretical codifications. Arab musical theory, which developed so greatly from the 9th century onwards, received particular impetus from the Greek treatises which were translated in the same period. But it advanced beyond that of the Greeks in theoretical and acoustic experiments and registered monumental achievements which have left their mark on contemporary Arab music.

The most famous theoreticians were Al-Kindi (d. c.873), Al-Farabi (d. 950), Avicenna (d. 1037) and Safi al-Din (13th century). Their treatises begin with some general remarks which illustrate the personal ideas of the author; Al-Kindi lays emphasis on the almost mystical concept of universal harmony; the others tend towards a more rationalist concept of music. After a general definition of music, the theoretical study embraces four main branches: acoustics, rhythm, composition and instruments.

Some of the greatest achievements of the Arab theorists were in the study of notes and intervals, calculations of concordant and discordant intervals and the organisation of sounds into systems. The question of modes was first given complete treatment by Safi al-Din. All demonstrations and theoretical experiments were based on the favourite instrument of the period, the 'ud (four- or five-string lute) of which some of the frets were fixed, the others being movable. This gave rise to a wealth of nuances in performance which theory attempted to describe or to systematise.

Rhythm was considered extemely important. It was explained in terms of prosody, whose structure and terminology it borrowed, although music did not employ the sixteen metres of classical Arab poetry. The analysis of rhythm involved a study of time and percussion, which led to combinations of times and percussions in conjoined rhythms (with symmetrical elements) and disjointed rhythms (with asymmetrical elements) and lastly, the question of the fundamental percussions and embellishments which form a given rhythm. The second part of rhythmic analysis was an exposé of the seven rhythmic modes and their derivatives. By embellishing the obligatory rests between the main beats of the mode with light percussive beats, it was possible to obtain a great variety of rhythms starting from the basic modes.

The exposition of composition was also based on

Moroccan ladies playing three-stringed, long-necked lutes.

prosody but was also related to the *tagwid* (the 'ornamentation' of the reading of the Koran). In fact, melody completely assumed the form of classical Arab verse. In Arab poetry, each line is complete in itself, i.e. it contains an idea in its entirety. The result is that each line has its corresponding complete melodic phrase. This type of song was generally preceded by a recitative, a cry, a vocal or instrumental improvisation, or an instrumental prelude. The role of the musical instruments was usually to support the song, to double it and to provide interludes during which the singer might rest.

The alteration of all these elements and the search for contrasts led to the development of the more highly evolved forms of 'suites' which were given the name of *naubas* in Andalusia and *tafsil* in Turkey. This form of suite is still used in the Orient and North Africa.

Musical instruments

In the past as today, the favourite instrument was the *'ud* already alluded to. In the 8th century it had four strings, the two outer strings having Persian names, and the two inner strings Arabic names. A fifth string was later added so that two octaves might be obtained. Unlike the former *'ud*, and the European instrument, the modern version is without frets and has either ten or twelve strings, grouped in twos. The *luwitra* is derived from the *'ud* and has eight strings grouped in twos. Like the *'ud* it is played with a plectrum.

The *tunbur* is a long-necked instrument with strings plucked by hand. There were once two varieties of *tunbur*: that of Baghdad – of Arab origin – and that of Horasan. Both had two strings and were provided with frets. The present Turkish *tunbur* has the same form but eight strings, grouped by twos, each two tuned in unison. The *tar* and *setar* now played in Iran are practically the same. The *gunbri*, a popular instrument of the lute type, is widely found in several countries, notably in Morocco, the Sudan and Egypt. It generally has two strings to be plucked by hand and its sound-box may be made of the most varied materials such as tortoise or coconut shell.

The *qanun*, a trapezoidal zither, has seventy-two strings grouped in threes and is played with a plectrum. A similarly shaped instrument is the *santur*; this has thirty-six strings which are grouped by twos and played by being struck with two wands. Of the bowed instruments, the most important were those of a family consisting of varieties of the *rabab* differing in shape and having one or two strings played with a bow.

The wind instruments include a great variety of flutes of varying length; double-reed instruments of the shawm type; the *zurna* (in Turkey) which accompanies dances, the *gafta* which is very common in North Africa and is used among the Berbers to accompany dances, processions, pilgrimages and outdoor ceremonies, and lastly the double 'clarinet' type.

The percussion instruments include a great variety of frame drums known by the generic name of *duff*, some of which are furnished with small cymbals; the *zil* or the *znoudj*, small copper cymbals fastened to the thumb and index finger of each hand, and the *nuqayrat*, of the kettle-drum type, adopted in medieval Europe where the name was modified to *nakir* or *nakers*.

In conclusion, two points of particular interest in the history of the instruments of Arabic music should be emphasised. First, the number of important European instruments, such as the lute, the rebec and the kettle-drums, which have Arabic antecedents. Secondly it is interesting to note how in Arabic music as in other essentially melodic traditions, one instrument occupied a place of special esteem in the eyes of both performers and theoreticians. The status of the Arabic *'ud* is comparable to that of the *ch'in* zither in Chinese music or the *vinā* in classical Indian music; all three instruments held a privileged position in their cultures and were the focus not only of musical theory but also of semi-philosophical speculations.

A musician playing the Arab lute; note that the instrument is played with a plectrum and has no frets.

Plate 3 left
The orchestra of the Japanese imperial court; notice in particular the two koto players in the foreground.

Plate 4 below
A miniature painting expressing the mood of the Spring rāg. The artist was a member of the Bundi school of the 1660s.

Plate 5 right
Three Kamaiuras Indians of Brazil playing large flutes with the same principle of sound production as the European recorder.

Plate 6 below
A Vietnamese peasant musician playing a type of sheng *mouth organ.*

Plate 7 below right
A Bolivian Indian blowing a conch shell.

Monody
and
Rhythm

European folk music

Introductory remarks

In the foregoing section we have sketched in broad outline the main features of some of the great traditions in music of the world outside Europe. In so doing we have touched on some of the essentials of the language of music itself – melody, rhythm, timbre and the organisation of sounds in the 'horizontal' dimension. One great difference between these traditions of music and that of the West is their reliance on oral tradition as the prime means of transmission, the other obvious distinction, to be studied at length in all that follows, is the typically European concept of harmony and the rules which were evolved to govern the organisation of sounds in the 'vertical' as well as the 'horizontal' dimension.

In this second section we take up the central theme of this book – the European tradition itself. Almost exclusively our attention will be focussed on the development of art music, that is the music of the church and of the court, what the Japanese called 'elegant' music. And yet in Europe, as elsewhere, there was a continual interaction between the 'high' art and the music of the folk, and whereas the latter often derived motifs and even musical procedures from above, the composers in their turn derived much from the techniques and material of the folk musicians. Above all the practice of improvisation and ornamentation according to conventional procedures, which survived even in European art music longer than is sometimes realised, has remained basic in the folk music of Europe up to the present day. Hence the first chapter in this section on the roots of European music is about the true tradition of folk music as it survives today. From this, we turn to the roots of European art music in the plainsong of the Church and trace the development through until the end of the 14th century and the threshold of a great new development, the age of polyphony and the beginnings of those harmonic procedures which were to dominate the work of composers into the middle of the 19th century.

For the ethnomusicologist, Europe presents a unique diversity of musical traditions. These are expressions of the exceptionally wide range of cultural levels which have resulted from the successive waves of invaders – Slavs from the east, Vikings from the north, Arabs and Turks from the south – and from the rapidity with which new cultural developments have followed each other over the last 500 years. The pace of change has become so fast that the new is already being displaced before the old has entirely receded. As a result, and despite all the pressures they have had to bear, primitive social groupings have survived remarkably vigorously. They represent not only vestiges of earlier peasant cultures but may also reveal fossilisations of technique and musical vocabulary from the court music of earlier generations. It is in the more remote rural societies that these ancient musical traditions have survived and it is important to remember that the vast majority of the population of Continental Europe lived in such societies well into the 19th century. The social impact of the industrial revolu-

Part of the ceremonial attending a Yugoslav wedding.

tion was not felt to its full extent until the present century in many parts of the Continent. Even today we can see economic, social and cultural organisations with centuries-old traditions co-existing with highly industrialised societies. Furthermore we are justified in assuming that such groups have preserved an ancestral musical heritage of extreme antiquity which can help us to trace music back to a very remote past.

Folk music is now established as a legitimate object of serious academic research, but this was not always so. Not only did the nationalist romantic composers of the last century, who took an interest in the folk traditions of their countries for largely chauvinistic reasons, treat the resources of the folk largely as a quarry for colourful material for their orchestral compositions, thus distorting its nature, but even the academics who founded the science of comparative musicology tended to regard European folk music as little better than a degenerate offshoot of the tradition of art music. Such views are now almost entirely discredited and the two streams of academic and folk music are seen as flowing in parallel though separate channels, which are linked by tributaries carrying influences from one to the other. Research is particularly advanced in Central and Eastern Europe, which was where the first major work was undertaken; it has been conducted increasingly systematically in Italy and France and other parts of the continent.

Considering the large areas still to be explored in Europe, the actual state of our knowledge only gives us a fragmentary view which may at any time be rendered obsolete by new discoveries.

The traditional music of the European peoples may at first strike us by its diversity; a diversity of forms, styles, idioms, means of expression, functions and ages. From prehistoric times to the present day each successive stage

opposite
A 17th-century engraving of Reims Cathedral. Such triumphs of medieval architecture were paralleled by the development of magnificent music for the Church.

43

The procession of St Efisio in the streets of Cagliari, Sardinia.

in a long and complex past has left its traces in music as it has in the signs of material culture. Underlying all these developments lies an archaic musical language common to all the ethnic groups of Europe. This ancient musical heritage, which dates back to prehistoric times, has left its traces in the most remote peasant communities of the present day and allows us to get some inkling of the music of the nomadic shepherds and farmers who peopled Europe.

Its main characteristic features are: a somewhat crude melodic idiom proceeding by conjunct intervals and founded on elementary scale systems; an essentially monodic character, although we can also detect the use of antiphony and rudimentary polyphony; the most primitive types of instruments, such as horns of wood, bark or shells, whistles and drums etc.; and finally an essentially utilitarian function.

Such music is designed to make it easier for men to communicate between themselves or to conduct their work for religious rituals. At the next stage in the development of European rural societies we find regional characteristics in music; characteristics which distinguish

region from region, district from district and even village from village. These highly differentiated traditions, although derived ultimately from a remote common ancestor, now differ both in their content and, above all, in their techniques and instruments. In the survey which follows Europe has been divided into large geographic regions.

This procedure is not without its disadvantages since interpenetrating influences between neighbouring regions are so frequent that they make precise delimitation difficult; furthermore, as such interpenetrations are likely to lead to certain divisions in political unities, the same country may eventually be considered successively in several areas, as in the case of France which is touched by all the regions of survey. Nevertheless, the populations of these regions frequently display far greater community of culture among themselves than with their national compatriots.

The Mediterranean lands

This region is particularly rich in music to accompany the work of the farmer and the shepherd, the fisherman and the muleteer. Perhaps still more important, however, is the vast repertoire devoted to the rituals of the seasonal festivals and the great social events: music to celebrate the 'burial' of winter or the 'resurrection' of spring, music for cradle songs, for the lamentations of the dead, and the innumerable songs and dances which surround the festivities of marriage. Finally there is the category, not quite so large but almost as important, of 'table' songs, the music of the epic singer, without any precise function, which recounts the narrative of heroic events and actions of the past.

There are of course many diverse musical languages in this huge Mediterranean region. Traces may still be found of the ancient prehistoric structures dependent on scales of three, four and five notes, and there are abundant examples of melodies using seven-note scales and procedures reminiscent of the music of ancient Greece – a reminder that many of the coastal districts were once

Greek musicians playing an Aegean fiddle (left) and a deep-bodied lute; note that the lutenist is using a plectrum.

Greek settlements. Again there are traces of the much later Turkish influence in the occasional chromaticisms, but by and large the music of the Mediterranean peoples is fundamentally diatonic and its rhythmic patterns simple. We should notice, however, that Turkish influence is still strong in some Balkan countries and in Albania, Greece and eastern Yugoslavia instances can be found of asymmetric rhythms obviously imitative of the *aksak* rhythms of Turkish music. The best examples of these rhythms are in the vigorous acrobatic dances for men, danced to the *zurna* or *zurla* (a double-reed instrument) and the large double-headed drum (*tapan* or *tupan*). In distinction from these, the round dances which are found throughout the area, from the Balkans to Spain, are almost exclusively in one of the two simple rhythms. The same broadly applies to vocal music, except in the case of the epic narratives, where the rhythm of the music tends to be strictly governed by that of the words.

Vocal music falls into the three main types of recitative, syllabic (where each note of melody corresponds to a single syllable of text), and melismatic (where a syllable of text may be spread over several melody notes). In the very broadest terms we may say that the first two types are represented by the work songs and the music of the ceremonial, while the epics normally employ a melismatic technique. But any kind of classification like this is apt to be dangerous and in any case can take no account of the very important fact that the syllabic style may frequently be highly ornamented and may also alternate in a single piece with the melismatic style. Indeed it is just the amalgam of these elements which provides Mediterranean music with one of its most characteristic modes of expression. The *saetas* of Andalusia are a fine example of the style and it is most probable that they are heavily indebted to the Arab influence which penetrates the area at its western and eastern extremities.

Polyphonic folk music is not found exclusively in the Mediterranean region but does seem to exist in its greatest variety of forms there. Its most primitive manifestations are in the octave and fifth drone basses particularly common in Greece. But the drone itself has many variants, the number of drone instruments may vary and the drone note may be changed to give a rocking bass effect. Other rudimentary polyphonic effects are found in the accompaniment of the melody voice by another singing in parallel intervals whether in thirds, fourths, fifths, octaves or even parallel seconds. Finally, all these various elements may be combined to produce new and more significant polyphonic structures. Certain characteristics common to these polyphonic songs may be observed: they are strophic, each verse is opened by a solo voice, and at the end of the verse the voices reunite on the unison. Finally, the music of the choral voices is often embellished by the high-pitched ornamentations of a male falsettist, which in the final notes of the verse rise above the other parts in a succession of arabesques to end on the octave above the main unison of the choral voices.

Another important musical style of the Mediterranean peoples is that of accompanied monody. The voice may be supported by a simple rhythm instrument or by the scarcely melodic droning of a Jew's harp, while other instruments such as the various flutes, clarinets, fiddles or lutes perform ornamentations on the melody. The epic songs are usually performed in this manner, being accompanied by the singer himself, playing some kind of stringed instrument, such as the lyre or *bouzouki* in Greece, or the violin in Corsica. All these forms, however, are based on the fundamental practice of improvisation. Both singer and instrumentalists are performing within the context of a familiar structure, and the success of their performance depends on their skill in the art of elaborating it within the conventions of ornamentation which tradition allows.

Among the instruments of the regions, many betray an Arab origin; these include numerous types of drum, from the Portuguese *adufe* to the Yugoslav *def*, and of course the various instruments derived from the lute. There are also many indigenous instruments: the numerous types of flute, the various single-reed instruments of clarinet type, which may be played singly or as double or triple instruments, and the bagpipes – essentially single-reed pipes connected to an air reservoir. Finally we should mention the shawms, double-reed instruments which probably also derived from the influence of the Arab world.

Festival of the Liberation at Kruja, Albania. The shawm and drum combination are found in many Balkan countries.

above
Musicians on the way to a wedding in Rumania.

right
A fujara *player from Slovakia.*

Central and Eastern Europe

Highly differentiated ethnic groups are to be found side by side throughout this area and comparisons in the field of music are difficult. Some groups have lived in a state of relative isolation down to the present day, while others have long been penetrated and influenced by the mainstream of civilisation; socio-cultural, economic, geographic or religious factors have all helped to accentuate these existing regional peculiarities. Whereas, for example, certain Slav peoples have kept some of their ancestral musical customs intact, the equivalent was wiped out in the Germanic countries in the 16th century by the Lutheran Reformation, which imposed the choral singing, harmony and rhythms of art music. Even so, a few archaic melodic types have still survived even here, notably in southern Germany.

As we move away from the influence of the Mediterranean and the Orient, still strong among the Bulgars and the southern Slavs, we shall find that vocal tones tend to become softer, the resonance of instruments becomes gentler, strings are more commonly used than wind instruments, and songs become more strictly syllabic. But although melodic melismas are less frequent, the desire for ornamentation is no less strong. It makes use of other procedures, all more or less connected with the production of the voice itself, such as long-drawn-out notes opening, punctuating or closing Bulgarian songs; trill-quavers which Carpathian shepherds obtain by striking their throats with the palm of the hand; the clucking of Rumanian female singers, and the various whistles and call-and-signal cries of the mountain-dwellers of the Alps. Another speciality of the Alpine shepherds is the yodel, a technique which requires special gifts and training since it consists of the uninterrupted transition of a low or medium vocal system to a shrill register, or of a chest- or throat-voice to a falsetto. Although the original purpose of the yodel was long-distance communication between shepherds in the mountains, it gradually infiltrated into village music-making.

Throughout this region, as elsewhere in Europe, the preponderant musical idiom is diatonic. Certain chromatic elements are present in the Balkans thanks to Arab and Turkish influences, and here too pentatonic and sub-pentatonic scales and asymmetrical rhythms are more in evidence than elsewhere in the region. Indeed it was in Bulgaria that Bartók, in his capacity of folk musicologist, first encountered the European equivalent of the Turkish *aksak* rhythms, and consequently these are still sometimes called 'Bulgarian' rhythms.

The melodies for the most part have a syllabic and strophic structure, or proceed by the more or less strict imitation of an initial motif. Here also, as in the Mediterranean area, there is a large body of songs of the narrative epic type. It is perhaps worth stressing that in the Balkan countries, Bulgaria and Rumania in particular, this traditional narrative art style of bardic verse singing is still very much alive. Indeed, studies of the practice of this part-traditional, part-improvisatory art have been made in order not only to learn about the workings of the contemporary tradition but also indirectly to arrive at some understanding of how this art would have been practised in the ancient world, for it was to this tradition of epic singers that the first singers of the Homeric epics must have belonged.

Vocal polyphony in this region ranges from the rich complexities of the art of Georgia to the simplest style of drone accompaniment, or the use of parallel intervals (seconds in Bulgaria, thirds and sixths in Slovakia and

Silesia). The instruments are supplemented by bodily gestures such as the hand clap, more common here than in other regions, and percussion instruments of the rattle type are often found, while drums are not so varied as in the Mediterranean zone. However there are an immense number of string types, above all the many varieties of hurdy-gurdy played with a bow or wheel, while the lute family is represented by many types, of which the most famous is the balalaika from Russia. Finally we must mention the very prolific family of the zithers, both plucked, such as the Russian *guzla* and the Rumanian *cobza*, and played percussively, such as the *cymbalon* of the Hungarian gypsies, an instrument which has occasionally found its way into the symphony orchestra. The family of wind instruments is represented by various types of bagpipe and flute, notably the *kaval* or end-blown flute of Rumania.

Northern and Oceanic Europe

This vast area, which stretches from Brittany to the eastern frontiers of Finland, may be regarded in ethnic terms as comprising a central population of Germanic peoples, flanked to the west by a great arc of Celts. One of the most characteristic forms of this region is the song used to accompany the round dance, formerly found in every rural community but now chiefly confined to Brittany and the Faroe Islands. The melodies have a simple structure but within this display a remarkable diversity of form. One of the most interesting features of the region as a whole is the extensive and extremely skilled use of the pentatonic scale, which in the Celtic lands reaches a mastery found nowhere else in Europe. In the folk music of Scotland, Ireland, Wales and Brittany the melodic potential of the five-note scale is exploited to the full, and melodies sometimes embrace a range of two octaves. Among the non-Celtic populations, on the other hand, a form of diatonic scale is used, and the melody is often confined within a narrow range, perhaps the interval of a major third or a fifth or sixth. Antiphonal and accompanied singing is found in the *kan ha diskan* of central Brittany for example, and above all in the *penillion* of the Welsh bards. This latter form has retained much of its character as a high art form and was once one of the major accomplishments in the repertory of a court bard.

Ceremonial music may certainly be dying out but Christmas and New Year are still accompanied by songs to the accompaniment of the *rommelpot* (friction drum) in Flanders or by *pastorals* in Brittany.

Carnival time, the coming of spring or midsummer day are still occasions for important musical activities; wedding rites are still accompanied by a great deal of music, as in the west of France for example. Work songs of various kinds are still alive, such as the so-called 'grazing' songs or the animal calls made by Scandinavian herdsmen and breeders, the milking songs of the Hebrides, and the Scottish songs for fulling the tweed. In addition we have a vast body of vocal or instrumental music without any specific purpose, which is played on the slightest pretext whenever a family or village gathering takes place.

The distinctive musical instruments of this region are the triangular Celtic harp of Ireland and Wales, numerous varieties of violin such as the Norwegian *hardangerfele* with sympathetic strings tuned differently from the melody strings, the *kantele* zither of Finland, and many types of bagpipe from the strident Scottish pipes and the Breton *biniou bras* (unusual in having as many as three drones) to the soft-toned Irish union pipes whose wind pressure is supplied by bellows. The pipes indeed would

left
A peasant bagpiper from Hungary; the chanter has a horn bell and its joint with the bag is in the form of a ram's head.

below
A Finnish peasant playing the kantele *zither, the instrument of the ancient bards.*

seem to be the Celtic instrument par excellence and enjoy an honoured place in the military music of Irish, Breton and Scottish military regiments.

Popular traditions and art music

The interpenetration of popular and serious music, both secular and religious, is no recent phenomenon. In the 13th century the *Jeu de Robin et Marion* of Adam de la Halle exploited folk songs; the cries of itinerant sellers were illustrated in the 16th century by Janequin in *Les Cris de Paris*, while English composers such as Orlando Gibbons used the cries of London street-sellers as the basis of whole compositions. In the 15th century composers frequently used popular songs as the *cantus firmus* for a mass, and the practice continued into the 16th century when the song 'Io son abandonata' was used by Palestrina in the *Missa sine nomine*.

The Christmas serenade of the *pifferari*, the shepherd-mendicants of the Abruzzi, is drawn on by Handel in his *Messiah* (1741), and Haydn, Beethoven and many other composers drew on popular material.

As a result of the influence of the Romantic movement and the current of ideas stemming from it, composers made their own return to the sources by paying greater attention to the peasant music of Europe. In a period when the awareness of national characteristics was particularly strong, musicians found a way of exalting the musical characteristics of their own countries in peasant music, as did Chopin in his *Polonaises* and Liszt in his *Hungarian Rhapsodies*.

Since the end of the 19th century, traditional music has found its way into art music in various ways. Some composers have been content to dress it up with varying degrees of success, as in countless songs harmonised for voice and piano or for an *a cappella* chorus, thus bringing popular music to the concert hall in a form far removed from reality.

Other composers have simply 'lifted' a melody and incorporated it in an orchestral work, like d'Indy in his *Symphonie sur un thème montagnard*. Finally, composers translated the traditional music of various European regions into serious music and succeeded in restoring the particular features and climate of the music without imitating it. This is what Vaughan Williams and Benjamin Britten did, for example, for English music; Falla and Ravel, for Spanish music; Mussorgsky and Rimsky-Korsakov, for Russian; Bartók, for Hungarian; and Milhaud, for Provençal music.

A shawm player from western Brittany.

Europe in the middle ages: historical background

The emergence of Europe

The dim origins of Western art music may be located in the 4th century, the age of St Ambrose of Milan. The universal empire of Rome was in the last stages of decay, but to contemporaries this was by no means obvious. The Emperor Constantine had officially accepted the faith. But the rulers of the Church had no wish to see the end of the great temporal authority, hoping to use it to govern the world for Christ. The hierarchy of the Church had already modelled itself on the civil administration and the very plan of the first great Christian churches was derived from the Roman basilican halls of justice. The head of the Church in the west was the bishop of Rome, and he sought to establish his claim to the same kind of universal authority in spiritual affairs as his pagan predecessors had exercised in temporal. Nor should we forget that paganism itself remained powerful for centuries to come. Indeed during the reign of the Emperor Julian called the Apostate (361-63) it must have seemed that the Church faced a new period of humiliation. The episode proved short, but the Church now found itself threatened from within by the great heresy of Arianism. This, which denied the absolute divine nature of Christ, won huge numbers of converts and was not even overcome when the Emperor Theodosius I (d. 395) issued an edict enforcing belief in the doctrine of the Trinity. Arianism remained strong among the Vandals of North Africa and the Visigoths of Spain for a long time to come. The Church nevertheless could reckon two great victories from the reign of this emperor. First her success in winning the authority of an imperial edict for the enforcement of an article of faith; second, the incredible triumph of St Ambrose over the emperor himself. The bishop of Milan not only excommunicated the emperor for the sack of Salonika, a routine act of disciplinary savagery, but also refused to lift the ban until the emperor had sought absolution.

In imperial politics also the reign of Theodosius marked a watershed. The division of the empire between two or more rulers broadly responsible for the affairs of the east and west respectively was not new, but after Theodosius, who instituted his sons as co-emperors at Rome and Constantinople, the empire was never to be reunited. During the 5th century the two halves developed in very different ways. The eastern emperors were able to consolidate and strengthen their position and for the next thousand years the name of the Roman empire was upheld by an unbroken line of rulers who for much of that long period maintained that empire as the greatest power bloc in the Middle East. Such was the authority of the Byzantine emperors that the patriarch of Constantinople remained subservient to the emperor himself even in Church affairs.

In the west things were very different. Already at the beginning of the 5th century the pattern of future events had been hinted at as one barbarian commander after another sought to rule the empire through a succession of puppet emperors. From this time the territories of the western empire were divided up between the warring tribes of Franks, Ostrogoths, Visigoths, Lombards, Burgundians and many others, while across the channel the island of Britain was colonised by Germanic invaders. Yet if for Britain the 5th century ended with a return to paganism, in Ireland to the west the Celtic Church survived, though in isolation, while in Gaul the victorious Franks under their king Clovis accepted Christianity from Rome. Throughout the 6th century the successors of Clovis continued to extend their power eastwards and westwards, eliminating the power of the Burgundians and confining the Visigoths behind the Pyrenees. Despite its growing internal divisions, this Catholic kingdom was to be of particular importance to the popes, who found themselves beset by enemies.

In the middle years of the 6th century the Arian kingdom of Theodoric the Ostrogoth was replaced by the restored power of the Byzantine emperor Justinian, and this in turn was replaced as the dominant power in the greater part of Italy by the kingdom of the Lombards, who confined the Byzantines. The popes succeeded in holding their position in Rome and their hereditary territories in its neighbourhood, and the troubled 6th century closed with the glorious pontificate of Pope Gregory I. He is traditionally regarded as the formulator of the liturgical chant of the Church and the tradition has a symbolic significance. For St Gregory was unremitting in his struggle to maintain the unitary nature of the Christian faith, to resist all heretical tendencies which tended to weaken that faith, and hence the potential influence of the papacy, and to extend that influence wherever possible; his initiation of the conversion of England is the outstanding case.

The power of the Church

In furtherance of these aims a uniform Roman liturgy was to become a valuable weapon. During the 7th century the Church in England had had to combat the claims of the ancient Celtic rite, in Spain the very faith itself was almost extinguished by the victorious advance of the armies of Islam, and the proud traditions of the Visigothic kingdoms and the Visigothic rites were maintained by tiny states isolated from the rest of Europe. In the empire of the Franks also an independent tradition flourished and evolved; so when in the 750s the popes sent to the Franks to help against a new threat from the Lombards, it was with considerable surprise that the representatives of the two sides observed the difference between their respective liturgies.

The kingdom of the Franks, now under the rule of Pepin, one of the great Carolingian mayors of the palace, was the greatest power in Europe. The price of his help against the Lombards was papal recognition; accordingly the last of the descendants of Clovis was confined to a monastery and Pepin the Short, father of Charlemagne, was recognised by the pope as king of the Franks. The shadowy theoretical claim of the true Roman emperor at Constantinople to be the sole arbiter in secular affairs was ignored and the popes dramatically consolidated this new advance in their power when on Christmas day 800, Pope Leo III crowned Charlemagne emperor of the west. Increasingly the legitimacy of European monarchs came to be guaranteed by the unction of the holy oil of a church coronation. Thus in the 11th century, when the corrupt and weakened papacy was to be restored by the intervention of the Emperor Henry III, the theoretical supremacy of the spiritual power was too strong to be resisted, and during the great struggles of the later 11th and 12th centuries, the popes emerged the effective victors. But to win the contest they had deployed the full panoply of their spiritual power, which was debased by the political ends to which it was put, and when in 1307 Pope Clement VII decided to flee Rome for Avignon and the protection of the French king, the papacy had taken one step nearer to a new humiliation. This came seventy years later when, within a few months, the cardinals elected two popes and began the great Schism in the papacy which was to last forty years.

But imperial authority was under attack not only from the Church. The glorious reign of Charlemagne, which had seen the Christian religion extended by force of arms deep into the lands of the Saxons and a renaissance of learning and culture under the auspices of the Anglo-Irish monks such as Alcuin, was followed by wars and divisions which ended in the establishment of the kingdom of France to the west and the German empire in the east.

The empire, apparently the greatest power in Europe in the 11th century, gradually lost ground not only to the aggressive power of the papacy but also as a result of its own over-ambitious attempts to assert itself, not only throughout Germany, but in Italy as well. Many other causes contributed to its decline, and from the middle years of the 12th century the pride of political place in Europe was contested between the kingdoms of England and France.

After the conquest of England by the powerful duke of Normandy, the French king found that if he had lost one of his most unruly vassals he had also gained a dangerously powerful northern neighbour. During the first two centuries of its history the French monarchy, founded by the upstart Hugh Capet in the late 10th century, had struggled to maintain itself against a numerous and powerful feudal aristocracy whose greatest members, like the dukes of Normandy, the duke of Aquitaine or the counts of Anjou, were virtually independent princes in their own lands. However, unlike the empire, the French monarchy was hereditary and an important factor in its growing power was the dynasty's remarkable achievement in producing male heirs for 350 years.

The ascendancy of France

Most of the kings were competent rulers, and if to this we add the fact that France was the most populous and fertile region of the Continent it is not remarkable that, despite the frequent conflicts between the king and his great vassals, notably of course the king of England, France was without doubt the cultural leader of medieval Europe from the birth of the Gothic style in the Ile de France in the middle of the 12th century until the last years of the 14th century.

The French nobility had already won immense prestige for the leading part it played in the first crusade which triumphantly entered Jerusalem in 1099. This was of indirect benefit to the kings of France in that it drew off a large reservoir of discontented manpower and landless leaders. The crusades were the product of many forces: political ambition, genuine spiritual faith and the pressure of the overall rise in the European population in the 11th and 12th centuries all played their part. The consequences of the crusades were also numerous. They represented in fact the first great investigation by Europeans of the world beyond Europe, not the less significant because it was military, and led to extensive cultural borrowings from the Arab world. Perhaps the greatest single treasure which the Arabs had to offer was the writings of the Greek philosophers, but as we shall see the great Islamic civilisation influenced the music of Europe as well as its philosophy.

But contacts were made with Islam through the Mediterranean lands of Europe herself. The Norman kingdom of Sicily and its successor the brilliant court of the Emperor Frederick II provided a crucible where the civilisations of Byzantium, Islam and the adolescent culture of northern Europe were fused into a unique amalgam. To the west the gradual Christian reconquest of the Iberian peninsula brought Christian, Arab and Jewish philosophers into fruitful contact. By the end of the 14th century the kingdoms of Castile, Aragon and Portugal had reduced their ancient infidel enemies to the tiny foothold of Granada in the south and had not yet grown sufficiently arrogant to despise the immense cultural heritage of the conquered lands.

The culture of Provence

A new, specifically European courtly culture was being born, and it was in the relaxed atmosphere of southern France – in Provence and the lands of the dukes of Aquitaine – that it reached its first great expression. In the 11th and 12th centuries the Provençal lyric and the civilising and gentle code of courtly love, that exquisite convention of the troubadours, provided a new and softer elegance to counterbalance the more martial civilisation of the *chansons de geste* of northern France. Through the brilliant, beautiful and immensely rich and powerful heiress to the lands of Aquitaine, the duchess Eleanor, it extended northward to the lands of the young king of England, Henry of Anjou, whose sensational marriage to Eleanor, two years before he succeeded to the kingdom of England as Henry II, was to have such immense cultural and political repercussions over the next three centuries. From France, the ideals and poetic forms of Provence flowered eastwards into the German lands, contributing to the school of courtly poetry of the *Minnesänger*, and finally westwards to the Iberian peninsula. But perhaps their most important effect was on the rapidly maturing cultural environment of the towns of northern Italy.

Italy

Since the coronation of Charlemagne as king of Lombardy in the 8th century, the supreme feudal overlord in the heartlands of the ancient Roman empire had been the German emperor. The cultural influence of the remaining Byzantine colonies in the south was considerable and was reinforced by the treasures brought back to Italy from the sack of Constantinople after the notorious 'crusade' of 1204, manipulated by the powerful commercial republic of Venice. The political history of Italy during the middle ages was the successful rejection of imperial authority by the ever expanding city states of northern Italy, whose immense wealth derived from their position as the great entrepôts of the trade between the populous states of northern Europe and the luxuries of the East. The main cultural impetus in the 12th century had come from France but in the 13th century the converging streams of Sicilian and Provençal literature had met in the plains of Tuscany and produced at the beginning of the 14th century the poetry of Dante. This and the work of his great successors Petrarch and Boccaccio laid the foundations of the Italian leadership in European civilisation which the new force of humanism, already arising at the end of the 14th century, was to convert into outright domination in that vast adventure of the human spirit now called the Renaissance.

Three main points emerge from this bird's-eye view of Europe in the middle ages: the central position of the Church in cultural affairs, above all perhaps in music, which was such an important part of the daily service of cathedral or parish church; the preponderating influence of France from the 12th century to the end of our period; and finally the growing importance of secular culture. Originally served by the travelling bards and *jongleurs*, it reached its first mature expression in the courts of Provence and thereafter in the courts of the great nobles and in the wealthy cities of Italy, where it evolved an independent tradition which first rivalled, and in later periods was to overshadow, the Church-based civilisation of earlier centuries.

This equestrian figure represents Cangrande della Scala, ruler of Verona and an enthusiastic patron of the arts, who died in 1329.

The background to the music

In the first part of this general history of music an account has been given of the traditions of music outside the European. Despite their wide diversity these traditions were seen to have a number of features in common. They all relied primarily on an oral tradition, even though various types of notation were evolved for limited purposes. In none of the traditions do we find anything approaching the Western harmonic system and sense of tonality, but they are all essentially melodic. We have seen how the melodic and oral tradition survived in Europe in its folk music, and in what follows we shall study the crucial events which led to the evolution of polyphony in Western art music. By 1400, composers were writing freely in three or four parts, and the stage was set for the developments of the next two centuries during which the mature art of polyphony evolved.

The plainsong of the Church had its antecedents in the chants of Jewish synagogue music and in the practice of the Eastern Church, but from the 4th century the music of the Roman and Byzantine Churches began to diverge. However, the Roman liturgy and its music found itself challenged by the practice of the Celtic, Spanish and Gallican Churches. It was to be many centuries before any real uniformity was established, and when it came the shape of the liturgy owed much to the powerful Gallican tradition. From an early period the popes had attempted to achieve uniformity, and the great Pope St Gregory I has given his name to the chant still used in the Roman Catholic Church. But although Gregory was probably closely concerned with the music of the liturgy as well as its textual content, the 'Gregorian' chants date in their present form from no earlier than the 8th or 9th centuries.

A basic handicap to the dissemination and transmission of a uniform musical setting for the service was the absence of an efficient system of musical notation. Before the 9th century such notation as there was was little more than a memory aid; it could only indicate the general shape of the melody and was not able to record the pitch of its component notes, still less the rhythm. However by the 11th century an important advance had been made by the introduction of horizontal lines to represent the pitch of at first one, then two, three and finally four notes. With this development and the gradual evolution of differently shaped 'notes' to indicate different time durations, the foundations had been laid of a precise system of notation.

The Roman Catholic mass

It is important before embarking on the study of medieval music to describe the broad outlines of the office of the Roman Catholic mass, which was to provide the cradle of Western art music.

The mass is in several sections and these are of two main types. There are first those sections whose texts change according to the seasons of the ecclesiastical year or according to the feast days of the various saints. These sections, which are assembled in the *Graduale*, are collectively known as the Proper, since they have texts which are proper to the day on which they are sung. Distinct from them are the sections which go to make up the Ordinary, so called because their text remains the same throughout the year. In a sense the Ordinary forms the scaffolding of the whole structure of worship. It consists of five main sections, which are: the Kyrie, the Gloria, the Credo, the Sanctus (which embraces the Benedictus and the Osanna) and the Agnus Dei. The Lord's Prayer or Pater Noster and the Dismissal or Ite Missa Est, from which the whole service seems to have derived its name, are also parts of the Ordinary but are of little importance from a musical point of view.

It was in their attempts to lend variety to the music of the mass that musicians first began to formulate the principles of composition; it was from this origin that independent musical forms broke away; and finally it was the unchanging text of the Ordinary that led composers to produce the first major Western musical form. During the early and high middle ages however, the Ordinary had not achieved its dominating position, and some of the more interesting experiments arose in treatments of sections of the Proper. Two examples are the evolution of a primitive form of musical drama from the reading of the Gospel story and the rise of the sequence, a new melodic form, from the practice of extending the Alleluia with new material.

Polyphony from organum to ars nova

At some point, probably in the 9th century, music made a radical new departure; this was the performance of the music of the liturgy with two voice parts. The new style was termed *organum* and at its most primitive consisted simply of one voice singing the plainsong melody, being accompanied step by step at the interval of a fourth below by another voice. The origins of European polyphonic practice are obscure and the subject of numerous theories. One theory holds that polyphony originated in the East; another contests that part singing was an ancient art in north European folk music and that it gradually asserted itself in the monodic chant of the Church of Rome. Whatever its origins two-voice *organum*, sometimes called diaphony, opened a new field which was to produce its first fruits in the monasteries of central France in the 11th century. This was developed still further by the composers of the school of Paris so that the *organa* of the 12th and 13th centuries, known as the period of *ars antiqua*, were considerable achievements of composition. They comprised three types of music: monody, diaphony with the two parts moving step-wise together, the top one providing occasional embellishments, and a new manner in which a slow-moving lower part was accompanied by an upper part moving much more quickly.

Gradually the plainsong melody was relegated to the lower voice and composers came to treat this part, which 'held' the melody of the liturgical setting, as a basis for elaborate and florid upper parts. Since the plainsong melody was more or less fixed, it became known as the *cantus firmus* (fixed song) or the tenor (from the Latin *tenere*, 'to hold'). Musicians also actually changed the shape of the plainsong melodies and even the words of the text by inserting new passages. In a case for example where the first words of the mass, *Kyrie Eleison*, were set with each of the syllables stretching over many notes, new words might be added so that the invocation now read not simply *Lord have mercy on us* but *Almighty Lord of heaven and earth have mercy on us*. The process might also be applied to the music and a new piece of melody inserted. In both cases the new material was called a trope, and the troping of the music of the liturgy became very common, giving rise to new forms. The sequence which followed the Alleluia was a trope of single line plainsong; when the process was applied to two-part *organum* the result was the birth of the polyphonic motet. In such ingenious ways the musician found a way of expressing his individual creative urge within the context of the plainsong, which at first sight seems complete and invariable. To this tradition of increasingly complex composition the composers of the 14th century added their own revolutionary rhythmic procedures which introduced still further complexity into music and produced the art which they proudly termed the *ars nova*.

Secular music

The art of formal composition was born in the great churches of Europe, but an immense amount of music was performed outside their precincts. It is true that lay musicians were very willing to incorporate into their own work the advances made by their ecclesiastical colleagues, but as the middle ages progressed the temper of European society became increasingly secular. In the 14th century religious music suffered a temporary eclipse and the motet moved out of the Church into the world of courtly culture. Lay music had been represented by the epic song of the travelling *jongleurs*, the Latin songs of the travelling scholars or goliards, and the refined vernacular songs of the courtly troubadours of Provence and their successors throughout Europe. Above all the use of instruments, while found in religious music, was most extensively cultivated in the music of the court and of the folk. Here the most important advances during the later middle ages were to be made in the field of dance music. Thus, when the 14th century came to its close,

instruments and voices were becoming increasingly equal partners. Furthermore, composers had gained confidence in their handling of the most complex rhythmic combinations of many individual melodic parts. The development of a euphonious style and the beginnings of harmony lay in the future.

The ecclesiastical modes

In common with other essentially melodic musical traditions, plainsong recognised a system of modes which were, in fact, basic patterns for the ordering of the notes of the diatonic scale. These seven notes, represented by the white notes of the piano, provided the basic material of music well into the middle ages, and at some time, possibly in the 8th century, the plainsong melodies were classified as belonging to one of eight basic modes. This theoretical system was to be used by composers up to the 16th century when it was further defined by theorists and when it was already yielding ground to the emerging formulation of the practices of harmonic composition.

For the modes, strictly interpreted, could only apply to single melodies. The three fundamental characteristics were: the range of an octave; a 'final', the note on which music in that mode had to end; and a 'dominant', the note which provided a centre of gravity for the melody and the note on which any passage of text which had to be recited would be intoned. The eight modes were divided into four which were called the 'authentic modes' and four which were called 'plagal'. The first of the authentic modes had its final on the note D with a range of an octave above and its dominant note at A an interval a fifth above the final. Thus a melody in this mode would begin and end on D, would confine itself to the notes of that octave, going neither above or below it, and would tend to hover about the note A which would act as the backbone, so to speak, of the melody. For the second authentic mode the final was E and the dominant the C above; for the third the final was F and the dominant A and for the fourth the final was G and the dominant D. Each of the authentic modes was accompanied by a plagal mode which had the same final note but used a different octave and a different dominant note. To take one example, the plagal mode associated with the first authentic mode, while it had the final note of D, ran from the A below this note to the A above, in other words it was a fourth lower than the authentic mode; its dominant was F. Thus a melody in the first plagal mode would begin and end on D, would use the notes of the octave A to A and only those, and would tend to centre upon the note F. We should also notice that in each mode the two semitone intervals found in the diatonic scale occurred in different places. All the features described combined to give a characteristic flavour and mood to the melodies of the different modes and the distinction between 'major' and 'minor' familiar in classical harmony is a fossilised remnant of this.

Detail from the 11th-century Bayeux tapestry. King Harold is crowned, his people see a comet approaching and news is brought to him of it, which he interprets as a bad omen.

The instruments of music

Some general remarks on the study of musical instruments

In 1946 the French musicologist André Schaeffner made a comprehensive study of musical instruments. He described instruments from the ancient civilisations of Sumer, Egypt, Greece, and Rome, and those of the middle ages, Renaissance, and the classical and Romantic periods. The study drew comparisons between instruments that are still used in different parts of the world and others which had been popular in Asia several thousands of years ago, or in Europe four or five centuries ago. The study aimed to reveal the principles underlying the construction of musical instruments in general and, by the comparative method employed, focussed attention upon the similarities and relationships between the instruments of often widely differing musical traditions.

This was a splendid example of organology, the science of musical instruments, whose purpose is, as Schaeffner declared, 'the enumeration, description, classification and history of all instruments used in all civilisations and periods of mankind in order to produce sounds or noises for a purely aesthetic purpose, or for religious, magical or practical reasons'. Thanks to the work of Schaeffner and other organologists, notably Curt Sachs, the main

outlines of this vast picture have been drawn. Our concern in the sections on instruments in this book is much more limited. In the first place, our study will be confined to some six or seven centuries in the history of Western Europe. Secondly, rather than give detailed descriptions of the construction of the instruments themselves (found in the glossary), we shall try to give a general idea of the use of instruments in the various periods to be covered. In the earliest periods this means examining the various elements making up an ensemble and, given the lack of rules governing the sonorous balance of these groupings, at least revealing the habits imposed by a long tradition.

The medieval period presents many difficulties, for not only do the origins of the instruments now appear more complex than they were formerly thought to be, but even the raw materials of our study, the instruments themselves, are often lacking. Before the 15th century, all we have at our disposal are a few recently discovered and still little known specimens.

To study instrumental music during the middle ages, and its place in the life of the period, we must first rely on works of art such as paintings and sculptures, stained glass windows and tapestries. But we should treat such evidence, derived from works produced for reasons quite unconnected with the study of musical instruments, with reserve and compare it with that of literary texts. Yet we shall find that 'analogy in details is often a guarantee of verisimilitude' and it will be possible for the reader himself to see that the artistic representations tally fairly precisely with the contemporary accounts of chroniclers or poets.

Musical instruments up to the 14th century

We have few visual records of musical instruments between the 5th and 9th centuries. Paintings and sculptures influenced either by barbarian art, with its tendency towards abstraction, or by classical art, only show a few instruments, often directly inspired by Greco-Roman models.

The lyre and the zither, the two main plucked instruments of antiquity, and the *pandoura* (a kind of small two- or three-stringed lute) are to be found represented on ivories and Christian sarcophagi. But an 11th-century psalter, still influenced by the classical style, shows a carefully drawn lyre being played with a bow instead of being plucked. Apart from these, the *rote* is the 'barbarian' instrument par excellence. A plucked string instrument, it was considered to be specifically 'Britannic' by Venantius Fortunatus, the 6th-century bishop and historian. The harp is also mentioned in this same period, as is the organ.

In the 11th century, literary and artistic references to musical instruments become more numerous. Plainsong

On the left is a frame drum; the nakers on the right were small kettledrums of Arab origin.

played the main role in church music. It was generally sung unaccompanied, as can be seen from numerous miniatures; but on certain occasions it was supported by the organ, and at great festivals other instruments would be used. The presence of *jongleurs* in such ceremonies in the 10th century, before they were later banished from the sanctuary, shows that the Church could be faced with irritating moral problems especially in the matter of instrumental music. If such music was to be allowed to add to the splendour of religious ceremonies, by whom should it be performed? Could the Church tolerate that this music should be played by those same *historions* whose virtuosity gave profane music such dangerous charms? According to the different answers given to these questions, some themes were abundantly illustrated in musical iconography while others were glossed over. Whereas music as a liberal art, on the same level as rhetoric or arithmetic, is given a place of honour on the royal portal of Chartres cathedral, and the concerts of the elders of the Apocalypse are given an important place in miniatures, the music of *jongleurs* and mountebanks is generally relegated to the margins and borders of the same manuscripts.

If the images in which we see King David surrounded by his musician companions correspond to the way in which music was really played in church, we may see from a miniature in a 12th-century manuscript now in the Bibliothèque Nationale, Paris, that the harp is surrounded by such secular instruments as the *fretel*, a rustic type of pan-pipes, the cornett and the fiddel – all profane instruments – as well as by a bell chime, or carillon. Such an ensemble of instruments as those represented would certainly have added brilliance to the increasingly complex polyphonic compositions designed to accompany the liturgy and the majestic *organa* of the 12th and 13th centuries.

Quite apart from its place in the liturgy of the Church, music played a vital part in all aspects of lay society. Contemporaries used the terms 'high' and 'low' to distinguish the two main types of this secular music. The terms did not refer to the pitch of the music but rather to its volume and are perhaps more clearly understood as 'loud' and 'soft'. Such activities as hunting, warfare, and dancing out of doors were accompanied by strong sounding instruments. Miniatures frequently show a hunter blowing the traditional calls on a little horn made from animal horn; in warfare, troops had to be manoeuvred and the enemy frightened by the sound of great trumpets, like those often shown being played by the angels on the Day of Judgment. The doughty hero Roland, Charlemagne's captain, was said in an 11th-century poem to have sounded his 'horns and his *buisines*', the latter being long, straight, copper or silver trumpets with a flaring bell, while the most famous musical instrument associated with the name of Roland is the oliphant which he sounded at the fateful battle of Roncesvalles, this being a horn made from an elephant's tusk or other animal horn. As for percussion instruments, the 13th-century Frankish warriors brought back to Europe the small Arab kettledrums (nakers, Arabic, *naqqara*) which had struck fear into them in the battles of the crusades. The tabor, a two-headed drum, had already been in use for some time, as several 11th-century *chansons de geste* testify.

There was a passion for dancing at every level of society. A frequent instrumental combination was the pipe and tabor and also the shawm or other reed instrument, and tabor. The pipe and tabor were used by peasant musicians, by *jongleurs*, and to accompany the dances of the upper classes, and have survived as an ensemble to the present day. During this period too another instrument, later confined to folk musicians, was quite common at the festivities of the nobility. This was the bagpipes, which is found under many names, such as the *cornemuse* or the *estive*, and was revived as a fashion-

left
Early bowed instruments were often played in a vertical position with the bowing hand palm upwards.

below left
Double reed instruments such as this shawm (left), became more common in the 14th century. In the middle ages bagpipes were used in art music.

able toy by the sophisticated societies of the 17th and 18th centuries as the *musette*. Yet, as we have said, in the middle ages it was a respectable enough instrument for peasants and aristocrats alike. The same is true, to a perhaps even greater extent, of the hurdy-gurdy, known in the middle ages as the *organistrum, symphonie* or *chifonie*. At first it ranked as one of the more noble instruments and was one of the few capable of playing a number of sounds at once. By the 12th century it had become so large that it needed two players, as we may see from several paintings and sculptures of this period, especially the Glory portal of the cathedral of Santiago de Compostela. Both the bagpipes and the hurdy-gurdy were drone instruments and it is not surprising to find them in high favour at a period when the rudimentary harmonic element of Western music was not much advanced beyond the chords formed by the melody notes on a drone bass. But as harmonic awareness developed in courtly music, so the bagpipes and hurdy-gurdy gradually declined in the social hierarchy of music.

But throughout the middle ages the instruments played in the castle were not noticeably different from those to be heard on the village green. The great festivities and weddings that 12th-century romances describe with unprecedented wealth of detail show that dances of all kinds were accompanied by the same groups of wind and percussion instruments. An example is found in the 12th-century courtly epic, *Erec et Enide*: 'sound the tabor and the tambourine, play the bagpipes and the panpipes, the trumpets and shawms'. Such a group of 'high' instruments would be a fitting accompaniment to a high festivity but for the music of diversion during and after dinner in the great hall, the soft-toned 'low' instruments would be used. After the feast the *jongleurs* would appear, with harp and fiddel, to sing a lay of war or love. The accompaniment to a poem, which might be half recited, half sung, was performed by the singer himself. During the course of the song he would use the instruments to give backing to the words, but before the recitation began it was usual to play a prelude on the instrument in order to prepare the audience for what it was to hear next and perhaps to verify the tuning of the strings. The instrument would also provide interludes between the episodes of the narrative and a postlude after it had ended. The most complete instrument for this purpose was the fiddel. This bowed string instrument could play a sustained melodic line, embellished with decorations improvised by the performer according to well-known conventions, and together with a rhythm instrument

(possibly tuned) it constituted a small but sufficient ensemble for the accompaniment of highly elaborate poetry.

Up to the 15th century most musical instruments shared a common range of about two octaves and were consequently distinguished not by pitch so much as by timbre. A common grouping consists of harps, fiddels, rebecs, psalteries and hurdy-gurdies playing together. The melodic part might be played by the rebec and the accompaniment by the psaltery. A flute might replace the fiddel while the rote, and in the 13th century, the lute, came to take over the role of the harp.

These few examples reveal a conception of instrumental music that was far from being rudimentary and that was able to combine timbres agreeably, to balance an ensemble and probably bring out the intertwinings of movements of the polyphonic parts with lightness and clarity.

Instruments and their use during the 14th century

All the instruments so far described were still being played in the 14th century. The 'high' instruments that accompanied the processions of princes and their entries into their 'good towns' were described by contemporaries as 'gay and joyous' and were so loud that 'one could not hear God thundering'. The 'low instruments', that could be played 'without discordant notes', were used for playing dances, preludes, interludes and postludes during festivities in the castles.

Dances and the *baleries* of the courts were accompanied by fiddels, lutes and psalteries, as were lays of love and *balades*. In about 1340, Lefèvre de Resson, procurator to the *parlement* of Paris and a poet, who liked to spend his winter evenings listening to 'musicians playing sweet melodies', added motets, *virelais, comédies* and *rondeaux* to these sung poems and dances, and the *chalemie* (a reed instrument), the bagpipes, small organs and the double-reed dulzian to the list of instruments. He specifies that the psaltery has ten strings and the rebec, three. He also mentions different types of bagpipes from Slavonia and Germany, and among the percussion instruments lists the cymbals and the *choron*, the ancestor of the Gascony or Bearn tambourine still used today. In about 1376 he describes the bass reed instruments, the *grosses bombardes*, as new arrivals.

right
A fiddel being played under the chin with bowing hand palm downwards; also note the convex bow.

far right
Secular musicians performing a castanet dance with psaltery accompaniment.

In the same period Guillaume de Machaut, a distinguished poet as well as a composer, introduces lists of instruments into his poems. It is particularly valuable to have the comments of a professional musician on the instruments of his day. He distinguishes transverse flutes from those 'which you play upright when you flute' (like the recorder), and insists on the extreme diversity of '*flaios*' or flageolets, which can be either single or double. He also mentions the two-fingered flute (presumably the pipe played with the tabor) and attributes an Arab origin to the lute; lastly, he lists the *eschaquier* (*echiquier*, *exaquier*) *d'Angleterre*.

This strange instrument is first mentioned in 1360 when one was offered by Edward III of England to his prisoner, the king of France, John the Good. In 1388, John II of Aragon wrote from Saragossa to his brother-in-law, Duke Philip the Bold of Burgundy, to ask him for one; he describes the instrument as resembling an organ, in that it has a keyboard, but fitted with strings ('*ab cordes*'). The action by which these strings were sounded was not described and many theories have been advanced as to the exact nature of this mysterious instrument. It has been suggested that it was an early clavichord, a forerunner of the harpsichord or even a primitive predecessor of the piano. However, it is known that in the 16th century people danced to the accompaniment of the *echiquier*, and from this it would seem impossible that it could have been a clavichord, an instrument which at this time was remarkable for the finesse of its timbre and its weak volume. It seems equally unlikely that it was a harpsichord (or spinet) since early 16th-century descriptions exist of a combined instrument which could be played as both an *echiquier* and a spinet. It may in fact have been a type of the 'clavicembalum' described by Arnaut de Zwolle in about 1460. The action described for this instrument suggests certain similarities to the piano, since the strings were struck by a leaded weight which was projected towards the string when the key was depressed. But whatever it may have been, the new instrument seems to have enjoyed some success, judging by the number of contemporary references.

In addition to the professional musicians attached to the courts of rulers or great lords, who had gradually taken the place of the travelling *jongleurs*, there seem to have been a number of amateur musicians who, by the end of the 14th century and the beginning of the 15th, were playing instruments for their own pleasure. Boccaccio describes gatherings in which young lords and ladies made music together. Dioneo plays the lute and accompanies the singing of Emilia or, with Fiammetta on the viol, plays a dance '*soavamente*' (smoothly); while in view of what has been said above about the declining status of the bagpipes it is interesting to note in passing that it is the servant Tindaro who accompanies dances with the sound of his bagpipes. It seems, however, that the 'high' instruments such as the shawm, the bombard and the sackbut – our present trombone – were, in general, left to the professionals, whereas the amateurs preferred 'low' instruments, such as flutes and the strings. No doubt this is partly explained by a contemporary comment that the technique of playing the 'high' instruments with distended cheeks 'makes the face ugly'.

We get many other glimpses at music making in the middle ages from contemporary records. In a castle in Lombardy, the evenings preceding Christmas were spent not only in telling or listening to tales, but in playing the organ, the flute, the psaltery and the viol; there were songs to the harp and the company took great pleasure in listening to a consort of three rebecs of different sizes. In Germany people also liked to combine the viol with the lute, the voice with the harp, the lute and the '*clavechimbolon*' (the harpsichord). In England, the *Canterbury Tales*, to mention only one text, contain many allusions to the playing of instruments and to songs sung to the

psaltery or a small rebec, or 'in harmony with a cittern'. By the early 14th century the portative organ was often used by singers for their accompaniment. The *Roman de la Rose* is one of the contemporary texts in which it is mentioned.

During the reign of Charles VI of France, Parisians enjoyed music by superb harpists ('*souverains harpeurs*'), performers on the flute and virtuosos on the hurdy-gurdy. A rich bourgeois like Maistre Jacques Duchie had in his mansion in the rue de Prouvelles, 'a room filled with all manner of instruments, harps, organs, fiddels, citterns, psalteries and others' and was able to 'play on them all'. The poet Jean Regnier, who was sent to prison on political charges, said goodbye to his instruments which he 'kept for his pleasure and his *montjoye*'. Nor did monarchs and great lords neglect instrumental music. Charles V liked to hear low-pitched instruments at the end of his feasts, the duke of Guyenne took 'very great pleasure in the sounds of organs', Charles VI bought a 'well wrought' harp bearing his arms. We know that Charles of Orleans and his mother Valentine Visconti played the harp, which, at least since the time of Machaut, had had as many as twenty-five strings. In Italy, the lute was played by Aeneas Sylvius Piccolomini, the future Pope Pius II, cardinal Riario and Ippolita Sforza, the duchess of Calabria.

As the middle ages progressed the role of the instruments we have been discussing became increasingly important in all types of music. The organ had accompanied the plainsong of the service since the 9th century and as music became polyphonically more complex fully instrumental accompaniments were used. By the 15th century large organs with pedalboards and numerous stops were known. Instruments were assured of their place in dance music, a central part of medieval music making, and as the 'masques and interludes of the court' became ever more extensive, so instrumental ensembles gained increasing status. We shall see how these courtly entertainments blossomed into the elaborate occasional music for the great festivities held by the dukes of Burgundy and the courts of Renaissance Italy. In the 15th century, too, we find the first sizeable body of exclusively instrumental composition and thereafter music for instruments gradually develops as an independent branch of music.

A 14th-century hurdy-gurdy. The handle and wheel are very distinct but the instrument is shown without drone strings.

Origins: the music of the Church

Introduction

It is impossible to give a full account of the origins and earliest developments of the plainsong of the Church, the first great manifestation of European music. For the first six centuries of its existence it was maintained by an almost exlusively oral tradition and the literary sources which have survived are by no means exhaustive. Nevertheless it is clear that although medieval theoreticians accepted some of the theoretical bases of ancient Greek musical theory, the practice of music was far more heavily indebted to the traditions of Jewish music as developed in the Palestine-Syria region and as transmitted to the West through the music of the Eastern Church. Consequently our study of the birth of plainsong will begin with brief accounts of what is known of the music of the Temple at Jerusalem and the music of the Byzantine Church.

In its earliest form, then, Christian chant owed much to the music of the Temple and the synagogue. Of course, the precise melodic form of the classic plainsong repertory as it later developed was not the direct descendant of synagogal music, nonetheless the latter embodied many of the characteristics to be found in the music of the Church of the early middle ages. The solemnity of the holy text is raised to an exalted level by being intoned to a musical line; the rhythm of this music is free, being governed more by the rhythms of speech than by imposed patterns; antiphony, the singing of alternate sections of the chant by different singers or groups of singers, is employed; and finally, in addition to the chanting of the sacred texts, musical elements are used elsewhere in the liturgy. At this point it should also be stressed that not only in the music, but also in the very shape of the service and the planning of the divine office of the hours of prayer, Jewish modes of worship exercised a considerable influence on the practice of the first Christians who were, after all, themselves originally members of the Jewish faith.

The influence of Christianity's Jewish antecedents was most marked in the style of intoning the words of holy scripture, known as cantillation. As time went by, of course, these pre-Christian traits became increasingly attenuated as the new faith spread through Europe and the Middle East and as the basic traditions, derived from the Palestinian and Syrian communities, developed in the diverse environments of Alexandria, Rome, Gaul, the Iberian peninsula, Celtic Ireland and of course Constantinople herself. In the 6th century the practice of the Church of Antioch was still an important influence on the music of the Church of Rome and even today certain elements in the music of the synagogue survive in the Roman Catholic liturgy.

Jewish music

Our knowledge of the Biblical period is confined to literary references – the Bible itself and post-Biblical sources. According to a venerable tradition, the music of religious ritual was given its first formalisation by King David who, although probably not the author of many of the psalms attributed to him by the piety of later generations, was nevertheless probably both a composer and performer of considerable gifts. Moreover it is possible that it was he who confirmed the men of the tribe of Levi as the custodians of the music of the divine service. Up to the time of the founding of the kingdom by David and the building of the First Temple by his son Solomon we have only scattered evidence of the songs of the Hebrew folk; the Well-song, so important in the life of a desert people, the war songs, the Song of Miriam and the Song of Deborah. Descriptions are more detailed and abundant when we come to the beginning of the scholarly tradition of the music of the Temple, and the most important single source is the Book of Psalms. Despite many enigmas, this gives us a highly revealing musical terminology and the names of a great number of instruments. Certain headings to the psalms and other indications would seem to suggest that the use of modes, one of the most marked characteristics of all Middle Eastern music, was well known to the Levites. As to instruments, the most important would seem to have been the *hazozra*, a shrill trumpet, and the *shofar*, a ram's horn or he-goat's horn, both of which were later used as signals to mark certain phases in the service. The latter, which is still sounded today on certain high feasts, was especially associated with the sacrifice. In the secular field the main

Ushering in a Jewish festival with the sound of the shofar.

instrument was the *kinnor*, a form of lyre, the *'ugab*, a type of flute, the harp, the double shawm, analogous to the Greek *aulos*, the *tof*, a type of frame drum, and the cymbals.

The musical tradition of the Temple was rudely broken by the destruction of the First Temple and the exile of the Jews in Babylon during the 6th century BC. Most of the psalms seem to have been written in the years following the return to Jerusalem, and at this time too the practice of antiphonal singing between the cantor and the congregation seems to have become common. As we have seen, antiphony was one of the debts owed by Christian music to its Jewish predecessor. At its peak around the beginning of the Christian era, the elaborate music of the Temple was performed by a large choir of highly trained men singers, with boys sometimes added, and at this period many instruments also were employed. The Temple orchestra – for its size alone warrants the use of the word – consisted of lyres, harps, cymbals, the *hazozra* and *shofar* and, on special feast days, the double shawm referred to above.

The full glories of this art, whose secrets were jealously guarded by the Levites, the Temple musicians who retained the historic tribal name of their ancestors, was lost by the end of the 1st century. In AD 70 the Second Temple was destroyed by the troops of the Emperor Titus and in the years that followed the Levites themselves, like the great majority of the Jews, fled from Palestine. Nevertheless much of the tradition of Jewish music, which derived in part from the practice of the Temple, continued in the music of the synagogues, local centres of worship whose importance had increased after the return from Babylon. The synagogue music of the Dispersion lost the joyful character of that of the Temple and the large instrumental forces mentioned above were dispensed with. This was partly, no doubt, due to the fact that they had never formed part of the ceremonies of the synagogue; but it may also have been an outward mark of the mourning of exile and was enjoined by religious leaders to counteract the dangerous pagan associations of the instruments. Only the *shofar* was retained and is still used in services on New Year's day and at the feast of the Atonement. Despite the decline of the great Temple tradition, the Biblical cantillation of the modern synagogue no doubt echoes something of the old music.

This cantillation was in fact the recitation of the sacred text to a chant composed of a series of melodic formulas, whose basic form was to be respected, but which were subject to the improvisation of the local cantor. Cantillation was an important part of the service and a desire to retain the traditional formulas led to the elaboration of a system of notation using signs known as 'accents' (*ta amin*). From the 4th to 9th centuries three main forms of this notation developed, of which the final was the Tiberian Massorite, whose perfection is attributed to Ben Asher. It was in this form that the notational system was adopted throughout the Jewish communities. The accent signs used indicate both the grammatical and the musical nature of the phrase and both the musical formulas and the notational symbols change according to whether the music is for the text of the Pentateuch, the Prophets or the Psalms. The musical performance of the basic formulas represented by the *ta amin* may be either plain or ornate, the eastern Jewish communities tending by and large to favour the ornate style. The basic scales of this style of cantillation were in many cases tetrachords, as were the basic modes of Greek music, while the later cantillation of certain of the major prayers was based on eight modes. This was to be developed in Byzantine musical practice and the church modes of Western Europe.

In addition to the music of the liturgy and the Biblical text described, a rich fund of religious poetry began to develop in Palestine during the 6th and 7th centuries known as *piyyutim*. These *piyyutim* texts were interpolated within the basic prayers and gave considerable impetus to liturgic and paraliturgic chant. The tradition of this religious poetry was particularly enriched by the Jewish communities of Spain who gained much from their contact with Islamic culture and music. Indeed the melodies of the *piyyutim* are mostly of foreign origin and introduced a new musical form based on metric structure. After the expulsion from Spain in 1492, religious song flourished once again in Palestine in the shadow of the cabalistic Safed movement. In the later middle ages and thereafter, the diffusion of the *piyyutim* and the augmentation of the sung part of the service led to the establishment of the professional singer, the *hazzan* or cantor. His function and its interpretation afforded another instance of the difference between the eastern and western communities. Both showed the same preferences for high, soft, nasal voices and the same taste for improvisation and rich ornamentation, but whereas in the west the role of the *hazzan* became increasingly professional and subject to codified rules which related to a scholarly and stylised art, in the east this art always remained open to the talents of any layman with a good voice and was in consequence more spontaneous.

In the above we have attempted to present the basic essentials of Jewish music from the ancient period to the middle ages, with particular relation to their influence on the music of the early Christian Church. From an early period this consisted of two main and gradually divergent traditions, that of the east and that of the west, but it must be remembered that for a long time these traditions were closely interrelated and that several of the bishops of Rome, even as late as the 8th century, were Greeks. We cannot therefore discount the contribution of Byzantine tradition to the development of Western plainsong; indeed the corpus of Byzantine music is a magnificent achievement in its own right, as the researches of the 20th century, led by the work of Egon Wellesz, have shown.

Byzantine music

As in the West, Byzantine church music was derived from the practice prevailing in the area of modern Palestine and Syria; indeed the Eastern Church was an important vehicle for the transmission of this Jewish-based music to the West. It is worth noting that not even in the eastern Roman empire, so heavily indebted to Greek culture in both literature and language, was the practice of church music significantly affected by Greek models. But whereas in the West, the formulation of the liturgical chant became increasingly uniform, in the East the chant was made up of a number of melodic formulas which were embellished and connected according to the skill of the singer. From the 8th century however, a rudimentary notation began to develop which served as an *aide mémoire* as to the general shape of the melodic units handed down by oral tradition. This notation developed to give indications not only of melodic shape, but also of rhythm and, in the 13th century, of the values of intervals. By the 14th century the system was further refined so that the style of performance of certain groups of notes could be recorded.

In all its music the Byzantine Church adopted the mode, which as we have seen was common throughout the Middle East. The idea of the mode (the ancient Greeks used the word *tropos*), whether in Greek music or Byzantine music, may be said to comprise two main elements: that of a scale of notes arranged in sequence and separated by certain specific intervals; and that of the melodic possibilities and mood deriving from the use of these notes and these intervals. The eight Byzantine modes were, then, 'melody formulas' – sequences of notes each allowing specific melodic possibilities.

The glory of Byzantine music was its great corpus of hymns. Of these the *troparion* developed from a short verse originally interpolated in the singing of the psalms. The greatest of these hymns was the Akathistos, first sung to celebrate victory and subsequently assured a permanent place in the liturgy of the feast of the Annunciation.

Early Christian music

Such were the main streams from which the current of Western music flowed, but from an early period Christian music, although greatly indebted in its practice to the Jewish tradition, was familiar with the Greek notions of a theoretical *musica*. Song was not considered as part of the true music, which was a science on the level of the highest studies. Hence there was a gulf between song and 'music'. On one side there were the traditional singers who learned and transmitted important texts by memory but who were ignorant of musical theory in this rarified abstract sense. On the other side, there were the scholars for whom the study of *musica* comprised the analysis of verbal rhythm and the acoustic analysis of sounds.

The first Christian treatise on music was the late-4th-century *De Musica* of St Augustine. The first six volumes deal primarily with rhythm and the subsequent ones were to have treated melody. Thereafter other writers such as Boethius, Isidore of Seville and Bede wrote on the theory of music and, more important, *musica* was gradually brought in touch with the art of song. The two main streams find their first confluence in a written treatise in the *De Musica* (*c.* 850) of Aurelian of Rome, who was remarkable in that he was both an erudite musical theorist and knew the practical aspects of the art – indeed he may have been a singer in the imperial court chapel at Aachen. His treatise is in two parts, the first summing up the work of the theoreticians, the second describing the practice of 9th-century plainsong.

Many types of chant were practised in the early Church. The reading of texts made cantillation obligatory and the central place of the Psalter made the chanting of psalms very important. We are not sure of their precise melodic form but we do know that the verses were sung to the same melody, either by alternation between two groups of the choir, or without alternation, or with the response being given by the congregation. This responsorial chant is mentioned in the 3rd century, when there is a description of psalm singing in which the deacon sang the verse while the faithful responded with an *Alleluia*! This practice of antiphony was greatly extended in 4th-century Antioch and seems to have been established in Europe by the practice of Milan as formulated by St Ambrose.

Lastly we must mention the canticles and hymns of the early Church. Canticles are certain passages from the Bible which are designed to be sung and have a form similar to the psalms–they include the Magnificat and the Nunc Dimittis. The definition of the hymn has presented difficulties since the earliest times. For St Augustine it was 'the praise of God by singing'. If one of the three elements implied in this definition – namely praise, devotion to God, or song – is lacking, then there is, according to Augustine, no hymn. But this definition also covers psalms and canticles and we can further define the hymn if we add a fourth necessary element – that it should be sung by the congregation. As we have seen hymns are one of the great glories of the Byzantine liturgy, but they have also played an important part in

the worship of the Western Church. Traditionally the founder of strophic hymnody as we know it today is held to be St Ambrose, the 4th-century bishop of Milan, and the early hymns of the Church included the 6th-century *Pange Lingua* and *Vexilla regis* of Venantius Fortunatus and the 4th- to 5th-century Te Deum of uncertain and probably multiple authorship (the Dacian bishop Nicetas is thought to be the most likely author).

At this point we should consider the singers of this music. The officiating priest must certainly have chanted his orisons, as he now sings the Preface to the mass. Next we find the lector, whose duty was the public, cantillated reading of epistles, gospels and psalms. His function made him a teacher and we find frequent allusions to the psalms he taught to the congregation. The cantor, canonically designated by the hierarchy, only appeared later, for the first time, in the canons of the Council of Laodicea (348–81). It would seem that the cantor was not always part of the clergy. He is not to be found named in the lists of the different orders leading to the priesthood and, if he is named, it is only to indicate that the lectors and cantors do not form part of the clergy. The cantor was in fact the interpreter for the congregation, who probably responded to his chants, as to the invocations of the priest, with short cries of the *Kyrie eleison* type.

The slow progress towards a uniform rite in the Western Church

Because of the clandestine nature of the Church until the 4th century, the uniformity of liturgical principles and details which are now so familiar to us can be found neither in the liturgy of that time nor in what we know of the chants. Since the heads of the communities were free to improvise, in many cases there were differences between local churches. From this period the divergency of practice between the Western and Eastern Churches grew, the West tending towards a progressive unification while in the East local customs continued to be cultivated. In Europe the Gregorian rite slowly won universal acceptance whereas in the lands of the Orthodox Church

right
The Te Deum, in the version attributed to St Ambrose

below
St Ambrose of Milan, from a 5th century mosaic.

many different rites developed. There were frequent exchanges and reciprocal borrowings, but it was not only in music that the two Churches differed and in the 11th century came the schism between the two.

Yet in the West, too, diversity of practice between the regional churches was deep-rooted. Their existence as rival systems was hardly noticed in the 4th century, but thereafter the Ambrosian rite of Milan, the Visigothic rite in Spain, the Celtic rite in Britain and Ireland and the Gallican rite in France resisted the trend towards uniformity. Indeed, up to the 8th century and beyond, they held their own. Even after the advent of Roman Christianity in Britain in the 6th century, under the auspices of Gregory himself, the Celtic Church was

slow to give up its rite and Milan was equally tenacious. As to the Gallican rite, there are indications that it contributed almost as much as Rome to the gradual unification of the traditions. In Spain the Visigothic tradition persisted down to the 11th century.

The other great area of liturgical divergence was in the monasteries. The monastic liturgy took shape in the very heart of the Roman ritual and even today it is still very similar to the pattern laid down by St Benedict a century before Gregory. Differences remained which were only resolved by the Council of Trent in the 16th century, which promulgated the adoption of the Roman rite. Nevertheless, monastic rites were unaffected by this decree and towns that could prove that their customs were more than 200 years old could apply to keep them. For practical reasons the clergy opted for the printed books which were guaranteed by Rome, and only Toledo, Milan, Braga and Lyons asked to keep their earlier rites.

Some degree of uniformity had started to be apparent from the 4th century. With liturgy becoming abundant and addressing itself to a numerous congregation, its content had to be watched. The popes drafted an 'annual liturgy', the *cantilena circuli anni*, although there was no notation to specify exactly the nature of the pieces to be sung. Some of these versions, however, became famous, with the Leonine sacramentary, the work of St Leo (440–61) and the Gelasian sacramentary, the work of St Gelasius (492–96), constituting the main stages in the process. But none were as popular as the Gregorian. This was the work of Gregory I (590–604) who brought back the earlier texts and added to them; but it was not edited in the form in which it has come down to us and the Gregorian rite of later ages owed little to the 6th-century pope and saint.

The Gregorian ritual at its height

It is difficult to follow the parallel history of text and music in the period between the years 600 and 750. The Gelasian sacramentary had been widely circulated and the Gregorian ritual must have been superimposed upon it. Moreover, it seems that during this period Rome retained another custom, the old Roman, which is said to have been the ancestor of the Gregorian. Possibly the reformed Gregorian rite was used by the papal *curia* and

far left
Pope St Gregory the Great

left
Illumination showing musicians playing a chime of bells, a rebec and a wind instrument, either an oliphant or a cornett.

below
Heavenly musicians from the carved portal of the 12th-century cathedral of Santiago de Compostela.

right
Musicians portrayed on the cathedral of Santiago de Compostela; note that in both this and the previous picture only stringed instruments are shown.

below
Illuminated initial from a 16th-century antiphonary.

the other by the churches of the city, but nothing is certain. In any case, the old Roman ritual, which appears to have been less subtle and more prolix than the Gregorian, is now only represented by a few books and fragments in the liturgy.

The Gregorian rite is considered to have reached its apogee in the course of the 8th century. We should note the possibility of Eastern influence since several popes of the 7th and 8th centuries were Byzantine. The Gregorian rite first came to Gaul in 735 when Pope Stephen II was brought to Pepin by Chrodegand of Metz to seek protection against the Lombards. Chrodegand's astonishment at the sight of the Roman ceremonies has been described, but it seems more probable that it was the shock to the pope in seeing a ritual different from his own that was the impetus for the movement to extend Roman practice. Cantors were sent from Gaul to study in Rome while Rome sent books to the Gallican Church to hasten the modification of its ritual. But difficulties arose for a century: the music was not always written and the tradition was being lost; to train a cantor took about ten years and no sooner had the repertory been transmitted than it was altered. Moreover, everything would indicate that Rome was not always sending identical books. Nevertheless, the whole of Western Europe gradually adopted this Roman chant, soon after called Gregorian. The service books gradually became more or less uniform despite the difficulties just mentioned and the repertory was completed by the addition of new pieces with music modelled on the former repertory, as in the case of the service for the Dead or the Trinity mass, both of the 9th century. Indeed the new pieces were so numerous that it became necessary to note them down, where previously they had been handed down by oral tradition.

The origins of notation

As we have seen, a system of notation, primarily to aid the memory, had begun to develop in Byzantine music. A similar intention lay behind the earliest system of notation in the West. Signs resembling the accents in language came to be used to represent the main lines of the chant over the words of the manuscripts. Examples of this primitive notation, which was first applied to the new, mainly syllabic pieces, are to be found in some 9th-century manuscripts. Fairly quickly this system, suitable to music in which by and large individual syllables occupied separate notes of the melody, was adopted for the notation of the main liturgical repertory, which was rich in vocalised groups of notes sung to one syllable and called neumes. The early isolated signs were ill suited to indicate such sequences of notes or melismas; accordingly they were, like the sounds, joined together. The name for the sung element was transferred to the written element and hence the earliest form of Western notation is called neumes. But towards the end of the 10th century, attempts to give more exact indications of pitch gave rise to modifications which led to their being represented separately again.

A revolutionary step in the definition of pitch by notation was taken in the 11th century. This was the use of horizontal lines to indicate the relative pitches of certain notes. It seems reasonable to attribute the perfection of the stave to the Italian monk Guido d'Arezzo, who died in 1050, and within fifty years of his death it is found throughout Italy and in northern France. Yet, as with so many of the advances of Western music, something was lost by this refinement. A precise indication of the pitch of individual notes was now possible, but only of those notes with an exactly defined pitch in the system of tones and semitones then developing. Guido's stave could not take account of the passing notes of intermediate and indeterminate pitch described by the theoretical treatises, and indeed sung, which the imprecise system of grouped neumes had been able to indicate without attempting to specify.

The sequence: a new type of melody

New types of melodies, notably the trope and the sequence, made their appearance at the same time as the written music. They must already have been customary, since the liturgical scholar Amalaire recorded the existence of the trope in the early 9th century without making any comment. The trope, somewhat like the *troparion* of Byzantine music, was an interpolated passage of text or music in the body of an established liturgical chant. The trope could be long or short; it could be simply an additional musical phrase, sung to the vocalisation of a syllable of the existing text, or it could be new text added to an existing vocalisation. The sequences were tropes added to the vocalisation of the Alleluia, but their great number and their more highly developed form made them a genre apart. The only trope to be retained by the liturgy was repeated in the *Benedicamus Domino*: it was the Easter hymn *O filii* which had become independent. The repertory of sequences was somewhat richer but only five are now used; they include the *Veni Sancte Spiritus*, the *Dies Irae* and the *Stabat Mater*.

The history of plainsong to the 20th century

During the first centuries of its history, plainsong was the sole music of the Church. Combining the two musical elements of melody and rhythm, it reached its apogee in the 8th century; yet already the most primitive examples of two-part singing were probably beginning to develop and during the 9th century the performance of *organum* became common and its principles began to be formulated. From this time the monodic chant of the early Church lost ground to the demands of the increasingly complicated forms which polyphony assumed. We study the beginnings of polyphony in the next chapter but before doing so let us trace the subsequent history of plainsong.

Not only did the pure melodic line of the plainsong lose prominence by becoming simply one of a number of parts, even if the dominant one, but its basic character was distorted in other ways. The organisation of two or three parts was obviously more complex than that of a single line of melody. The endeavour to discipline the singers of the various parts led to the regularising of the metrical beat, and the rhythmic resilience and subtlety of the monodic chant, one of its chief glories, was lost. As polyphony advanced still further, the plainsong melody, originally the chief element of the music, to which everything else was subservient, was first moved from the upper part to the lower and then was degraded still further when fragments of plainsong were taken to form the basis of new polyphonic compositions. The next chapter describes the development of this new art, but we should notice here that very soon after its advent, the solemn celebrations of the mass were primarily polyphonic.

Yet even in the richest polyphonic mass, the cantillation of the preface, the epistle and the gospel were opportune reminders of the great art of the past; while in the worship of the poorer churches, which could not afford the luxury of a 'chapel' of singers and musicians trained in the art of part singing, the services were necessarily conducted in the old chant. As a result of its decline in status, the art of plainsong not unnaturally declined in quality also. The Council of Trent in the 16th century commissioned the great Palestrina to reorganise the ancient chant of the Church; but the spirit of the age was not in tune with the inspiration of the earlier centuries, and neither this work, nor the reforms of the 17th century, restored plainsong to its former glories. Indeed the so-called Medicean edition of the *Graduale* (1614-15) suffered from many defects, which included the suppression of the free rhythms and many of the ancient melodies. The numerous attempts at reform in the 17th and 18th centuries, chiefly in France, produced a condition of anarchy in the liturgy of the Church, and it was not until the work of E. A. Choron in the 19th century that the slow work of recovering the ancient music of the church began on a sound basis.

Perhaps the single most important event was the foundation of the Benedictine monastery at Solesmes in 1835; later in the century Charles Bordes (1863-1909) founded the Singers of St Gervais for the sole purpose of singing Gregorian chant and Renaissance polyphony and later, with Vincent d'Indy and A. Guilmant, the Schola cantorum. During the 19th century, indeed, a new interest in plainsong developed outside the ranks of

An early representation of the lute in Europe; note the use of a plectrum.

church musicians, and composers such as Berlioz showed interest in this long forgotten art. But it was the continuous work at Solesmes, where Gregorian chant was part of the daily liturgy that, despite some false starts and ill-conceived publications on the part of a few enthusiastic but hasty publishers, really laid the foundations of the modern restoration of plainsong.

In 1859 Solesmes had received a distinguished recruit, Dom Joseph Pothier who, with the aid of Dom Jausions, prepared an edition of the *Graduale* (published in 1883) and then of the *Antiphonary* (published in 1891). Meanwhile two monks, Dom Jausions and Dom Mocquereau, both collaborators of Dom Pothier, began to delve into the libraries again. It was during this period that Dom

Mocquereau conceived the idea of the *Paléographie musicale*, which began to appear in 1889, with the aim of providing all researchers with facsimiles of the main Gregorian manuscripts. This invaluable collection was the basis for most of the studies made of liturgical chant and still appears regularly. Moreover, as the technique of photography was perfected, the scriptorium and library of Solesmes grew richer, thus facilitating more precise studies and providing a great number of manuscripts.

Other research centres were gradually built up in the same way with the result that, far from being isolated, the abbey of Solesmes became the centre of a constantly spreading scholastic enterprise.

An illuminated initial from a late medieval manuscript.

The first centuries of polyphony

From the 9th century onwards, the history of music becomes gradually more concrete thanks to the survival of written sources and the development of musical notation. It is in this period that the great story of polyphony begins. This great advance in music coincides with the cultural revival initiated in the reign of Charlemagne and persisting in the following decades. The first evidence of polyphony and the first manuscripts with neumes date from this period.

The beginnings: diaphony and early organum

So far as we can now tell, the music of the classical world and of the synagogue was exclusively monodic. The music of the early medieval Church, the most important single formative force in the history of Western music, followed this tradition. In so doing it produced a liturgical chant of immense richness and variety which was one of the most beautiful artistic achievements of the middle ages known to us.

With the emergence of what has been called 'polymelody' in the 9th century, music took a new path.

Polymelody was simply the singing of different parts simultaneously and this new art was not to produce anything to compare with the splendours of the monodic chants for another three hundred years. The beginnings of polyphony were thus neither sudden nor spectacular and greatly resembled the rudiments of polyphony of the primitive cultures which are now being studied by ethnomusicologists. Nevertheless, in it lay the seeds of that wild and luxuriant growth, the music of the European tradition.

Although they may have aroused the admiration of contemporaries, the musical experiments of the 9th and 10th centuries were hardly advanced works of art. Quite simply the *organum*, as it was called, consisted of the liturgic chant accompanied step by step by a second voice at an interval of a fourth below it. Even here however there was scope for development since the two voices started in unison, which necessitated timid attempts at oblique and contrary movement. In practical terms this meant that, although throughout the rest of the piece the two voices moved together note for note and the contour of each melodic line was identical, at the beginning the two singers were on the same note and had to move away from each other for a brief moment in order to establish the interval between them. The reality was indeed

The praise of God and his saints was the first function of music in the earlier middle ages. Among the instruments the strings were particularly respected; note here the zither, centre right.

The great church of Notre Dame, Paris, the home of the first major school of polyphonic composition.

humble. All we have from this period is a short invocation, *Rex coeli, Domine* which is described in a theoretical treatise, the *Musica Enchiriadis*, written by a certain Otger though long attributed to Hucbald de Saint-Amand, a composer of sequences and probably also *organa*. But although it stands alone, this unique example is testimony to the birth of a practice which bore within it the seeds of the whole of medieval musical art. The plainsong of the liturgy was the absolute master in this note by note 'diaphony' and the second voice, the *vox organalis*, was in a state of absolute submission; nevertheless the fundamental procedure of polyphony had been created.

The next great step came in the 11th century. It will be seen that of the two parts in the primitive *organum* so far described, it was the humble *vox organalis* which nevertheless offered the greatest scope for development. It was after all to some extent an invented part, whereas the principal voice, with the plain chant of the liturgy, could not be melodically changed precisely because it was already an established, finished melody. In the 11th century, however, not only did the movement of the *vox organalis* become freer but, more important still, it went over to the *superius* or upper part, the *cantus*, or plainsong, being relegated to the lower voice. Furthermore the *vox organalis* almost constantly evolved by contrary motion; as the line of the *cantus* descended, that of the upper voice ascended and vice versa. This new style has been termed discant. But, although the parts now moved more independently, there was still a strict note to note relationship between them. The next two important changes were the liberation of the *vox organalis* from the strict demand that each note of the melody should correspond to a syllable of the text, and the developing practice of embellishing the notes of the *cantus* with a brief passage of shorter notes. The art of *organum* had now advanced to a stage where it could offer a vehicle for the expression of major creative talent.

The first evidence of the activity of such musical genius is found in France at the abbey of St Martial of Limoges, which exercised a seminal influence in the 12th century. The Limousin *versus* seems to have served as a model for the school of Notre Dame of Paris, which was to become the focal point of musical development in Western Europe. Thanks to the foregoing developments, the composer now had three musical elements to give variety and shape to long compositions. These were: the ancient monodic chant of the choir in unison, the discant *organum* in which two parts moved, usually by contrary motion, in a note to note equivalence, and the most advanced style of *organum* in which the top part embellished the slow moving plainsong melody with passages of short notes.

The school of Paris: the first great polyphonists

From the second half of the 12th century the region of the Ile de France was the nucleus of the ecclesiastical culture of Christendom for more than a hundred years. It was here that the Gothic style in architecture first reached maturity and here, too, that the first monuments of polyphony were created.

The magnificent *organa* composed by the two greatest masters of the School of Notre Dame of Paris, Léonin and his successor Pérotin, achieved a beauty and fluency which raise them far above the primitive polyphony of early *organum*. They were large scale compositions fully capable of expressing the deepest religious mysticism. They were composed to heighten the splendour of the ceremonies on important feast days, and were based not on the ordinary of the mass, but rather on the texts of the special prayers of the service of the day (called the Proper) and almost exclusively on graduals and Alleluias, whose plan they strictly respected. They constituted in fact a new and brilliant addition to the great Gregorian tradition.

For both the two-part *organum* of Léonin and the more complex three- or four-part *organum* of Pérotin, the basic procedure was the same. The principal voice or 'tenor', so called because it 'held' the line of the liturgic *cantus* in the lower part, extended its notes to support the vocalisations of the upper parts. The lengthening of the notes of the plainsong was so extreme that the ear easily loses the sense of a melody, hearing rather a series of long-drawn-out pedal notes. The solid substructure of the Gregorian chant is obscured and the attention of the listener is drawn away to the elaborated interlacings of the upper parts or *voces organales*. The effect is almost that of extemporisation on a slow moving theme. Nor is this impression wholly misleading, for contemporary treatises indicate that in a two-part *organum*, the shape of the *vox organalis* was sometimes left to the musicianship of the performer. Discanting to the book, as it was called, was of course governed by conventions and rules known to any competent musician. Little by little however, as the possibilities available became more and more numerous and the art consequently more demanding, the part of the *vox organalis* was written out and this practice became even more necessary when Léonin's double *organum* gave way to the triple and quadruple *organum* of Pérotin and his followers.

The typical pattern of one of these later works might be as follows. In the opening passage, the notes of the tenor are so long drawn out that when the note changes, the effect, to modern ears at any rate, is almost that of a modulation. The colouring of the music is completely changed as it moves from one basic pedal note to another and, although it is not entirely inapposite to introduce the term modulation, perhaps a happier analogy is with the changing appearance of a rose window in a Gothic cathedral as the sun moves round the sky. However after the first fifty bars (to use later terminology), the character of the music changes. The tenor moves more quickly, its melodic shape becomes more noticeable, and in some passages its rhythm follows that of the upper voices. The work concludes with a passage in which the tenor part reverts to the ponderous pace of the opening section and after this there might come a coda in which the upper voices vocalise above a held note in the bass. These florid decorative vocalisations at the end of a verse of the *organum*, or at the end of the whole composition, seem to have provided the soil from which grew the motet, the most important and influential musical form to flourish during the 13th and 14th centuries.

left
Lutes, psaltery and fiddel make
music to the glory of the Virgin.

below
A 17th-century engraving of Pope
John XXII (d.1334), who attempted
to limit the newly-found freedom of
composers and musicians by forbid-
ding certain intervals and melodic
procedures.

IOANNES XXI· DICTVS XXII· PONT· CXCVIII·
ANNO DOMINI MCCCXVI.

The motet

This form, which developed out of the polyphony of the *organum* and was first of all employed in the worship of the Church, very soon grew away from its origins and became the most important single form of musical expression, whether ecclesiastical or secular. Indeed, although the academic composers of the period were 'clerks' in the medieval sense of the word and therefore in the last resort 'church composers', the term was valid only in the most general sense. During the 14th century especially, the finest products of academic music were, with one or two outstanding exceptions, in the secular field. Nevertheless, the distinctions between 'religious' and 'secular', were far less clear than they were to become in later ages – in his famous bull of 1326, Pope John XXII fulminated against the introduction of profane words into the church *motetus*. Furthermore, the composers of the period were inevitably the heirs of the ecclesiastical polyphonic tradition and not of the tradition of the troubadours, the true ancestors of Western secular art music.

One of the earliest procedures for varying the music of the liturgy was the trope discussed earlier. New passages of music or text were interpolated into the existing musical structure, and from this early practice a new form, the sequence, had developed. When this same principle of interpolation was applied not to the monody of the plainsong but to the polyphonic structure of *organum*, the result was the polyphonic motet, which emerges, in France, in the second half of the 13th century. The plainsong tenor of the earlier *organum* with vocalisation was divided into a number of distinct musical units which corresponded to words or phrases of the text. Such melodic units or cells were set to phrases such as '*In veritate*', '*Mane prima*', or even short clauses. The divisions set up by the tenor were observed by the *voces organales* with each of the words constituting a section, called a *clausula*. These *clausulae*, which were in effect musical fragments, formed the vital element in the birth of the motet. It became increasingly common for musicians to vary the *organa* in their cathedral repertory by interpolating *clausulae* from one *organum* in another. When this was done, the original text of the *clausula*, which would of course be out of place in its new

setting, was dispensed with, and, instead, the interpolated section of music would be performed as a vocalisation. In this way the *organum* could be musically varied without, however, losing its original character. The next stage of the development towards the motet was the addition of words to the upper part of the *clausula*, and this part soon became known as the *motetus* (from *mot*, 'word'). As often as not this new text would be a commentary in the vernacular French on the sense of the Latin tenor and the basic elements of a new form were now present, a form which soon achieved an independent existence. The final stage in the evolution of the full motet of the 14th century was the addition of a third part, *triplum*, to the tenor and *motetus*. The result was a three-part work consisting of a slow-moving lower part, the original tenor sung to its original short Latin phrase; a faster moving middle part with a French or Latin text and above that a still more florid part which, in its turn, was often set to another text which might also be in French or Latin. Although the two lines of text might be not only different words but even a different language, the result was diversity rather than disorder since the two texts were related to one another in sense.

The evolution of the motet
as a secular form

After first being an integral part of the *organum*, the polyphonic *clausulae* came to be performed in isolation during the service, although we do not know in what circumstances. In fact the new form of the motet had difficulty in finding its place in liturgy, for hardly had it been created than it left the Church and won an unprecedented popularity, its success contributing to the decline of the *organum* itself. Composers more and more abandoned the great religious fresco to apply themselves to this finely worked miniature. Using a relatively limited number of *cantus*, they wrote new *voces organales* with new words. Soon the practice grew up of giving the upper voices French texts related less and less obviously to the Latin tag of the tenor; thus a tenor taken from a passage in praise of the Virgin would have superimposed above it a French love song. From being religious, the motet became merely edifying and by the end of the 13th century had become an exclusively profane form with only the tenor – which might well now be wordless, being performed on an instrument – witnessing to its liturgic origin.

The composite form of the medieval motet presents special problems to the modern listener. Not only do the words seem at first sight prejudicial to the unity of the music and the relationship between the parts obscure, but our inevitable tendency to think in terms of vertical harmony rather than to follow the individual lines is a further handicap. As we have said already, these parts are by no means strangers to each other. The sense of

each one is related to the idea expressed by the tenor, and until the very end of the 13th century this relationship, no matter how slight, was to survive. It is now often difficult to discover this relationship, especially when the composition depends on refined symbolic or allegorical relationships of meaning between the tenor and the other voices. The 13th-century motet, however, was ideally suited to beguile away the leisure hours of a refined society which delighted in musical and literary games, and may well have been performed by amateurs for their own entertainment rather than in a concert. It has also been suggested that in concert performance each of the voices may have been sung in turn while the others were replaced by instruments, all these texts being sung simultaneously only as a finale to the performance. In conclusion it may be observed that the simultaneous rendering of different, yet related, texts in this way is in any case met with often enough in 18th- and 19th-century opera.

We have now traced the work of the musicians of the medieval Church from the majestic monody of Gregorian chant through ever great elaborations to a fully fledged form of secular polyphony. But this too had its foundations in the chant of the liturgy. By the latter part of the 13th century however the plainsong tenor, once the dominant element in the music, was becoming nothing more than a device of composition. Already, in a great many motets in the Montpellier and Bamberg manuscripts, the syllables of the text of this tenor are no longer placed under the notes. The scribe contents himself merely with mentioning the opening word, apparently as a reference. From this it was natural to dispense with the words altogether and give the tenor to an instrument. Further developments robbed the plainsong tenor not only of its words but also of its formal

A fiddel player; note the grip high up the bow-stick.

integrity. In the isorhythmic motet, to be examined below, it became fragmented into sections of identical rhythm. In yet other forms the tenor was reduced to the briefest of phrases, now barely identifiable, which were repeated several times over during the composition.

The conductus

The success of the motet in the 13th century was striking, but it was not exclusive. Another form was being practised concurrently: the polyphonic *conductus*, both more unitary in the modern sense of the term and more immediately comprehensible. The fundamental difference between the motet and the *conductus* was that, unlike the former which was built on a pre-existing plainsong tenor, the *conductus* used a composed *cantus firmus*; it was thus an entirely original work although the actual process of its composition was not new. The procedure was still one of a successive accumulation of counterpoints above a foundation voice. This, as we have said, was written for the occasion and although comparable to the tenor of a motet, it had a livelier popular rhythm and was greater in length so that it did not have to be repeated, as in the motet. Being therefore less abstract than the tenor of the motet, this voice was less alien to polyphony,

which was to model its proceedings after it. Whereas in the motet the time values of the notes diminished as they ascended from the *duplum* to the *triplum* and *quadruplum*, the *conductus* had the same rhythm in all the voices and also the same text. Originally the *conductus* was a monodic processional song intended to accompany the actions of the priest or the faithful during the service – hence its name. But by the end of the 12th century it had been affected by the advent of polyphony. Although he wrote *conductus* for one voice, as in the *Beata viscera*, Pérotin also produced examples for two voices and for three voices, the latter in the very beautiful *Salvatoris hodie* intended for the feast of the Circumcision. Like the motet, the *conductus* failed to find a place in the liturgy. After having provided a whole collection of pious but extraliturgic pieces, it became increasingly profane while retaining the use of the Latin language. A good example of this secularisation is the anonymous *conductus*, *Veris ad imperia* which, with its refrain *Eia* and its spontaneous character of a popular dance, is a wonderful evocation of the awakening of nature at Spring's behest. All in all, the *conductus* was the Latin equivalent of the works of troubadours and *trouvères* and it may be this that explains its decline into total disuse in the first quarter of the 13th century. While the 'church' composers preferred the elaborations of the motet form, the troubadours and their successors evolved the polyphonic *rondeau* which we shall study in another chapter.

Angel musicians playing a chime of bells, a psaltery and a fascinatingly early representation of a clavichord.

Ars nova in France

Introduction

The later middle ages in Western Europe witnessed an increasing secularisation of social attitudes. This became marked in the 14th century, which opened with the humiliation of Pope Boniface VIII by the French king and the ever growing involvement of the Avignon papacy with worldly political considerations. The declining spiritual prestige of the Church which resulted was matched by a rising self-confidence and assertiveness in lay society growing from the development of the merchant classes and the increasing sophistication of courtly life. Yet there was no sudden break with the previous century. The profound mystical piety which had inspired the great works of Pérotin and his contemporaries had weakened in the second half of the 13th century and there was a progressive and irreversible tide in favour of an increasingly profane type of music, epitomised and encouraged by the development of the motet. This form evolved still further in the hands of the *ars nova* composers, as we shall see. First, however, let us examine one of the most representative works of the profane culture which was growing up in the early 14th century.

This was the *Roman de Fauvel*, written between 1310 and 1316, which both in its subject matter and its satirical posture summed up much of the spirit of the new age. The Church in France had been heavily compromised by the king's unscrupulous campaign against the papacy and the whole structure of medieval ecclesiastical Europe was critically weakened when the French king, despite the open opposition of the pope, was able to break the French order of the wealthy Knights of the Temple. *Fauvel*, a curious collection of music and verse whose text was written by Gervais de Bus, is directed against the abuses in the Church and is full of allusions to the royal campaign against the Templars. The hero of the work is the donkey 'Fauvel', who personifies all the vices of mankind. The name is an acrostic of the initial letters of these vices: Flattery, Avarice, Villainy, Vanity, Envy and Lâcheté (cowardice). The work contains 132 musical pieces, many by Chaillou de Pestain and Jehannot de Lescurel, both monodic and polyphonic. They include motets, *rondeaux*, lays, responses and sequences.

The birth of a 'new art'

The involved, and one may feel frequently arid manifestations of French *ars nova* were facilitated by important works in the field of theory. The 13th century had been dominated by absolute ternary rhythm varied by the use of the six rhythmic modes. These were derived from the metres of verse such as the anapaest or dactyl, and can in each case be used in three *ordines* or 'manners'. A single piece or voice would employ one rhythmic mode but the *ordines* of that mode could be varied at will. Binary rhythm was latent in 12th-century music but could only be obtained by means of subtle calculations on the basis of ternary values. In the 14th century, however, the invention of a new notation and other theoretical advances opened up vast new horizons to composers, who eagerly explored them. In about 1320, Philippe de Vitry, the future bishop of Meaux, codified the recent achievements of theory in several famous treatises, and gave one of them the proud name of *ars nova*, the term generally adopted for the musical art of the 14th century. In these years composers found themselves in possession of a notation which could satisfy all requirements and which comes close enough to our modern ideas. It has been said that 'The main initiative, dating from about 1320, must certainly be credited to Philippe de Vitry, who invented the bar signs'. Henceforth, the clef was closely to be followed by an indication of the time that had been chosen. The composers were freed from the rhythmic modes, and indulged themselves by using increasingly small note values which often gave the melody a rather unnatural, angular and tortuous character.

A 14th-century illustration of an episode in the career of the beast Fauvel, *the embodiment of the vices.*

The isorhythmic motet

Notation was not alone in contributing to this abstract striving after complexity. Thanks to the two greatest composers of the time, Philippe de Vitry, who was more than a mere theoretician, and Guillaume de Machaut, the motet ceased to be the miniature work it had been in the 13th century. It extended considerably in length and its structure became more complex.

Even in the 13th century the liturgic tenor, which had served as a foundation, was frequently divided into short fragments with identical rhythm. This isorhythmy (Greek, 'identical rhythm') was at first applied only to very short tenors of which each fragment consisted of three or four notes. In the 14th century, however, the tenor was generally much longer and the sections, themselves longer, were often punctuated by rests. Although it was still constant, the rhythm was less immediately noticeable and its subtle arrangement was primarily intellectual. The consequence was that its role changed. The relationship of meaning that we have observed in the 13th century between the *voces organales* and the tenor altered as a result of the latter's fragmentation; the tenor lost its identity and often seemed alien to the motet for which it provided the pretext. Furthermore, the instrumental character of the tenor, mentioned above, was emphasised when a new part came to be added under it. This new voice, called the countertenor, was also subjected to an isorhythmic pattern and was to contribute to a change in the aesthetic of the motet and its sound balance. On the one hand there were one or two parts which were written in short values and were manifestly vocal; on the other, two more slow-moving parts which were gradually to engender the idea of a bass that was already confusedly harmonic.

The upper parts, characterised by complete liberty in the 13th century, were also constrained to follow a determined rhythmic programme, each having one of its own. It was a considerable tour de force to construct such a complex ensemble in which diverse rhythms were superimposed lineally, having different lengths and being repeated a different number of times so as to conclude together. The champions of this 'arithmetico-melodico-rhythmic procedure' were held in great esteem, and Philippe de Vitry's skill was unanimously applauded. Petrarch wrote him several highly deferential letters and poets and musicians were not sparing in his praise. But it is difficult to have a clear idea of the composer since scarcely fifteen works, mostly isorhythmic motets, can now be attributed to him with any certainty. Even so, his works seemed to have been inspired more by a perfect mastery than by a true sensibility and this was characteristic of the *ars nova* as a whole.

Guillaume de Machaut

It may be regarded as not far short of miraculous that any form of lyricism emerged from this mesh of calculations. That there was such a miracle was due to Guillaume de Machaut, without whom the music of the 14th century might well have been stifled by the overpreponderance of technique. He showed as much sensitivity in his most strictly constructed motets as in his freer works. An admirable example is a motet in which he deplores the fickleness of Fortune, in lines of the very highest quality. Above a very well chosen tenor, *Et non est qui adjuvet* ('there is no one to come in aid'), there

above
A book of music notation of the 13th century.

left
A small lute and a double pipe of recorder type.

were developed two supremely assured parts, despite the rhythmic yoke they have to bear. While the *duplum* used symbolic language to describe the unenviable fate of the man who, trusting to Fortune, takes to sea in a flimsy coracle at the mercy of the winds, the *triplum* states that he is mad indeed who 'confides his trust in Fortune's promises'. Next follows a tirade against Fortune 'which shines outwardly and is filth within'. The melodic flow of each voice is astonishingly supple and natural without any trace of the laborious work behind it.

But the isorhythmic motet was not the sole form of erudite music. New forms were evolved and old forms elaborated while the ancient mode of monodic expression was never totally abandoned. Indeed, Machaut himself used it for his lays and complaints, thus carrying on the tradition of the *trouvères* of the preceding century. But in most cases he used polyphony. Although it was close to the lay in its form and its quasi-syllabism, the *virelay* was often given a second part without words, like

This Italian painting shows a lady playing the fiddel and, outside the charmed garden, young ladies dancing to the sound of the bagpipes.

Plate 8
A fresco by Benedetto Bembo in the ducal chapel, Milan, showing God the Father and God the Son surrounded by angel musicians.

the delightful *Se je souspir parfondement*, without losing anything in the way of the freedom and grace of a *trouvère* song. The *rondeau*, already made illustrious by Adam de la Halle, was extended by Machaut. The scheme was the same but each of the two or three elements making up the single motif of the *rondeau* acquired a new dimension of breadth. An exquisite example is *Rose liz printens verdure*, in which the lyrical element is expressed by the most beautiful melismas, completely Gothic in their form with their successions of sharp intersecting punctuations.

But it was the *ballade* that Machaut treated with the greatest refinement. Written in two, three or four parts and free from all constraint since there was no longer any question of *cantus firmus* or rhythmic formulas, it gave free rein to the composer's creativity. *Je puis trop bien ma dame comparer*, a *ballade* for voice and two instruments, is a typical example of Machaut's courtly, elegant but rather conventional lyricism. The intellectual character of the inspiration is even more accentuated in the double or triple *ballade*, of which Machaut appears to have been the inventor. By transposing the technique of the motet into this form, he had the idea of having the two or three verses of a *ballade* sung by two or three different voices, the disparity being resolved by the last line of each verse being the same. This was the case in the double *ballade Quant Theseus – Ne quier veoir*. To the first voice, which says something like 'I am not conerned with seeking after honour as did Theseus, Hercules and Jason', the second voice replies: 'little do the beauty of Absalom or the strength of Samson mean to me' and the two voices conclude in unison: 'I see enough, since I see my lady'.

Religious music in a secular age

We have seen how the central trunk of European church music sent out branches which spread into the secular world. The religious music of the 14th century was eclipsed by such secular music. Whereas religious music had constituted the greater part of the artistic production

of academic composers in the 13th century, it now seemed to be no more than a survival. However, an important new style of composition for the church service was beginning to emerge. It is to be found in a series of 'masses', which consisted of groups of pieces of unequal quality but all grouped together within the context of the mass. Although these ensembles of pieces, written in different styles by different composers, and known as the 'Besançon', 'Toulouse' and 'Tournai' masses, were artificial, nevertheless they established certain habits which were to be continued and developed by Machaut. Here we see the beginning of the mass as a musical form.

Perhaps the greatest achievement of the religious music of the 14th century was Machaut's *Notre-Dame* mass for four voices. This is now thought to have been written as a votive mass and not for the coronation of King Charles V as was long believed. Machaut worked before the introduction of the cyclic tenor by the English school in the 15th century, but achieved a unity far in advance of the masses mentioned above by other means. All the sections are linked together by a descending 'head' motif of four double quavers which is characteristic enough and appears frequently enough for us to regard it as the result of an organising intention; in addition there are the syncopated rhythms often repeated in identical forms; and lastly the striking analogies in the 'harmonic' colouring of the sections.

The mass is in six parts: the Kyrie, in four sections, the Gloria, the Credo, the Sanctus, the Agnus Dei and the Ite missa est. As in the Tournai mass, the Gloria and the Credo are without the liturgic *cantus firmus* and are written in the style of the polyphonic *conductus*. The similarity of the procedure in the four voices engenders successions of aggregates of notes which to the modern ear suggest series of chords. The *'Qui propter nos'* in the Credo, one of the most moving moments, is a striking example of this because of the way the notes to the words *'ex Maria Virgine'* are drawn out.

All the other sections of the mass use the technique of the motet except that all the parts use the same text. The tenor, though fragmented, seems to have regained its melodic role, lost as a result of the isorhythmic division; Machaut evidently hesitated to disfigure it and thus showed it a respect that had long ago become unfashionable. Even in the Kyrie, in which it was cut up into fragments separated by rests, it still remains recognisable. In the other parts it is almost uncut.

In this mass as in most of his other works, Machaut made use of the hocket, a device which was already known in the late 13th century. This was a mode of writing which fragmented the various melodic lines to the extreme and produced swarms of short notes which responded to each other from one voice to another. The technique is at first somewhat disconcerting to the modern ear but the enjoyment felt by the composer as he superimposed rhythmic elements one on the other is obvious, and the device undoubtedly has the effect of aerating the heavily stratified polyphony. The melodic lines do not exist any the less, and to execute these brief notes, the singer does not consider them in themselves but as a part of a melody of which only the parts are apparent. Machaut often employed the hocket to bring a section to a close with a sparkling display of contrasts.

Machaut so dominates his time as to eclipse his contemporaries, and seems to enshrine in himself a whole century of musical production. He stands between the extremes of conservatism and innovation, between those who devoted all their efforts to keep the traditions of the previous century as championed by Pope John XXII and those who fought for the new ideas, following the example of Philippe de Vitry. Avoiding the rigidity of doctrines, Machaut brought to his music a lyricism and a spontaneity which made him a precursor of the musical art of the next century.

Plate 9
Christ Glorified *by Fra Angelico.*
Of the many instruments note
particularly the straight trumpets,
portative organs and pipe and tabor
in the foreground.

Origins:
the music of lay society

The world of secular music

Up to this point we have been almost exclusively concerned with the music of the Church and the composers who wrote for it. In this chapter we turn to the parallel tradition of secular music and the mainly lay composers and performers who produced it. This music drew inspiration both from the traditions of the folk and the more self-conscious art of the liturgy. For example, we find *trouvère* compositions which are based on plainsong themes, and in the 14th century the two streams flow together and merge so completely that much of the finest work being produced by church composers, such as Machaut, are in the field of secular music. Not only did the motet, originally religious, rapidly become a favoured vehicle for secular compositions, but Machaut and his contemporaries wrote superb examples of exclusively secular forms, such as the *ballade* and the *rondeau*. It is quite likely of course that serious church musicians had occasionally produced songs and dance music before this, but it is only in the 14th century that the clear boundary between the two fields begins to blur, and after that period composers, while specialising in one field or the other, came to write quite naturally in either.

The division, moreover, was not merely one of subject matter, but also one of the style of composition. It was in the music for the worship of the Church that the elaborate art of polyphony first evolved and it was not really until the arrival of the motet in the 13th century that polyphony became at all common in secular music. Among the earliest manifestations of courtly music,

apart from the huge field of the dance, was the narrative song and epic. This had the most venerable ancestry, being essentially similar in type to the Homeric epics of ancient Greece, and it has survived down to the present day in the folk music of south-eastern Europe. As far as we can tell, throughout this long epoch of some three thousand years the basic nature of the performance has changed very little. The theme of the long poetic text is some past heroic action of the members of the community or of the ancestors of the aristocratic listeners; the verse will contain many repetitive formulas partly to give formal coherence but more importantly to aid memorisation. For we must not forget that these epics formed both the entertainment and the history of a civilisation based on oral tradition. The singer recites the epic to a highly repetitive melodic line which may consist of only one or two basic phrases, and accompanies himself on some stringed instrument such as the lyre or the harp. Finally, although the main line of the story and much of the verse will be faithfully rendered from one performance to the next, the bard is expected to demonstrate his own skill and further entertain the listeners by ornamenting the music and improvising, even on the words themselves, according to the conventions of his art. Such epic singing, found in one form or another in almost all musical cultures, was the stock in trade of the medieval *jongleur* or travelling minstrel. The great *chansons de geste* such as the *Song of Roland* and the *sagas* of the Norsemen would have provided the most important

far left
Minstrels and jongleurs *(from which comes the modern word 'juggler') provided early medieval society with its entertainment both serious and light. Here the man is playing a double shawm, the boy castanets.*

left
A dancer accompanying herself with hand bells.

An illuminated letter 'S' of jugglers in the modern sense and musicians playing a cornett and a rebec.

musical events at the courts of the aristocracy throughout Europe up to about the 11th century. But at that point a new style of song, whose theme was love and the cult of woman surrounded by the trappings of the new code of courtly love, rapidly rose to prominence in the south of France. It was soon the dominant poetic and musical form of Provençal culture, and from there spread to the rest of Europe.

Undoubtedly the music of the troubadours, or *trouvères* as they came to be known in northern France, dominated secular music, but there was also a large body of songs which had Latin texts, whereas those of the troubadours were written in the vernacular. Of these Latin songs perhaps the best known are the songs of the goliards, the name for the travelling scholars who thronged the roads of the middle ages. Although by virtue of their profession as students they had necessarily taken minor orders in the Church, their songs are dedicated to the joys of life, to love, spring and drinking. The earliest medieval Latin songs date back to the 9th century, but the flowering of the art came in the 12th.

The forms

As often as not, the names given by contemporaries to the lyric songs of the middle ages refer more to their subject matter than to their form. Nevertheless we can distinguish three types which were especially popular. These were the *ballade*, the *virelay* and the *rondeau*. The basic structural unit of these secular songs, both with vernacular and Latin texts, was the 'strophe', a unit of one or more lines linked by a common rhythmic pattern and a more or less elaborate rhyming scheme. Most of these songs repeated the music of the first strophe for each of the succeeding ones, but within the strophe there were various types of melodic procedure: the music might develop from line to line or it in turn might be made up of repeated and ornamented sections. From a very early date, the element which was to be the most important means of formal articulation made its appearance. This was the refrain. By and large we may say that in the *ballade* the refrain followed each verse, and that in

the *virelay* it preceded and followed each verse, as it did in the *rondeau*, the most complex form of the three. All these basic forms were, in their origins, songs to accompany the dance; indeed the derivation of the French *ballade* and the Italian *ballata* is the same as the modern English word 'ball'.

In addition to these strophic forms there were also asymmetrical forms such as the *lai* (German, *Leich*) which consisted of a number of verses of unequal length, each with its own music except for the last, which usually repeated the music of the first. There were also numerous variants on the strophic forms themselves such as the *alba* to the dawn (German *Tagelied*), 'Bacchic' or drinking songs, songs of the crusade and the *planctus* or complaint. In Germany, above all, the resources of the strophic song were exploited to the full in the various '*Weise*' or manners which came to be associated with specific performers.

The musicians

The troubadours wrote in the *langue d'oc* (Provençal and its dialects) and were localised to the south of the Loire, in the Limousin, Périgord and Toulouse regions and Provence, with important branches in Catalonia and, in the 13th century, at the court of Alfonso the Wise of Castile. Another branch developed in northern Italy from the end of the 12th to the beginning of the 14th century. These Italian troubadours composed in Provençal. The *trouvères*, who only began to appear in the second half of the 12th century, used the *langue d'oïl* (ancestor of modern French) and were numerous in northern France, where Arras was an important centre.

The *Minnesänger*, whose art was related to that of the troubadours, were mainly active in the Rhineland and Bavaria. They began to flourish in the late 12th century but were still active in the 14th; sometimes they used Latin but more usually old German.

Apart from the *planctus* and the political songs of the 9th and 10th centuries, which have largely been preserved in a mid-12th century codex of the Bibliothèque Nationale in Paris, we find the figures of Walafrid Strabo or Micon de Saint-Requier, joined by that of the parodising and 'irreverent' Sedulius Scottus (*c.* 820), called the '*Golias carolinus*'. He is followed by a few others, leading us to the 11th-century *Cambridge song-book* which is rich in *planctus*, political events (deeds of kings), idyllic or springtime couplets, erotic songs etc. At least two of these pieces reappear in other manuscripts with notations which enable us to read the melodic contour though not the rhythm. One, 'To the Nightingale', often attributed to Fulbert of Chartres (d. 1028), is filled with musical terms.

The poet most qualified to be considered as intermediary between this Cambridge collection and the poets of the 12th century is certainly the brilliant philosopher Peter Abelard (1079-1142). His love songs have been lost but six lyric pieces notated in neumes (*c.* 1132) have surived under the title of *Planctus*. The songs by Abelard may be regarded as a prelude to the goliard flourishing of the 12th century of which the most famous illustration is the collection *Carmina burana*. This comprises religious, political, moral, erotic, Bacchic and satirical songs which, with few exceptions, belong to the 12th century and can, in certain cases, be attributed to known authors and especially to Gautier de Châtillon (or Lille) (d. after 1181), now known to be a prolific *trouvère* with some famous works to his credit. He was preceded by Hugh of Orléans (b. 1095), known as 'Primat' and followed, in France, by Mathieu of Vendôme, by Pierre of Blois, some of whose profane songs have survived, and lastly by Philippe 'Chancellor of Paris', some of whose pieces were said to have been set to music by Pérotin.

Almost a contemporary of the Latin poets Primat and Abelard, William IX, duke of Aquitaine (1071-1127), is considered to be the first singer-poet in the vernacular; of his work eleven songs in the *oc* dialect and a small musical fragment have survived. He was the first of many. From Marcabru (active about 1130) to the end of the 13th century, we have the names of 460 troubadours who left behind some 2,600 songs although unfortunately only 263 are notated. Some of these songs have been preserved in collections but many are dispersed in isolated *codices*. Of the notated songs twenty-six are anonymous, the remainder being the work of forty-four authors, the last of whom died in 1282; the largest number attributable to a single composer are the forty-eight left by Guiraut Riquier but in many cases the composers are represented by only one or two pieces.

Sometimes these singer-poets were great lords like William of Aquitaine, or members of the lesser nobility like Bernard de Ventadour, the famous courtier of Eleanor of Aquitaine. Others were soldiers or clerics 'of poor family', but in this field, talent could raise the commoner-poet to the level of the aristocracy, while noble ladies tried their hand at the art. About 220 of the *trouvères* are known to us as authors of 2,200 songs, and of these the majority, unlike the troubadour and goliard songs, have been notated. They are in some twenty main manuscripts (the best being at Paris) or dispersed at random in a great number of French or foreign collections. Some 600 are anonymous – the others being attributed unequally to such princely *trouvères* as Thibaut of Champagne, king of Navarre (d.1253), the author of seventy-six songs, or such needy minstrels as Colin Muset, a fiddle-player and a good poet (*c.* 1200). In Germany, the first *Minnesänger* appeared towards the end of the 12th century; like the troubadours, they belonged both to the noble and humble classes of society.

Bernard de Ventadour, one of the most famous of the Provençal troubadours.

The elements of the art

If these works are to be studied and criticised, a decipherable musical notation is the first necessity. The first great problem confronting the musicologist in his study of the goliard, troubadour and *trouvère* songs of the 12th century is that we do not know the original notation of these works. The earliest notations for them are those in 13th-century manuscripts. The goliard songs have come down to us with 11th-century neumes or with late 13th-century neumes (*Carmina*). Fortunately some of these songs are found in 13th-century manuscripts with line notation in which at least the melodic outlines are legible; thus they may be translated into approximate if not exact musical versions.

Most of the troubadour songs preserved in collections of the early 13th century have notations, but often these, while they are written on three, four, five or six line staves and give the pitch of the notes, fail to indicate their duration. But perhaps the most vexed question in reviving the music of these medieval songs is that of rhythm. Even when the notation permits us to assign pitch and duration to the notes with reasonable accuracy, the rhythm is never clearly indicated. Despite the numerous theories of musicologists this remains a major stumbling block to the restoration of an art whose conventions are lost.

To the modern mind a particularly fascinating feature of this secular lyric music is its use of the C major scale. Undoubtedly, both goliards and troubadours learnt much from the music of the Church. We have seen how

some of these songs employed plainsong themes, and the ecclesiastical influence is even more apparent in the use of the modes by these lay musicians. Yet this C major scale, so commonplace in later music, is not represented in the classic ecclesiastical modes; it belonged rather to the '*musica naturalis*' of the *jongleurs* and histrions or epic singers who used the tonality of C. Thus, although they were forced to yield pride of place to the masters of the new lyric art, we see that in this respect they influenced their successors.

Although the medieval song is interesting in itself, it is even more so when considered in the light of its link with the past, its influence on other works of the time and on later periods.

Apart from musical theory, various elements of liturgic origin served as the starting point for the lyric composers of the period. Nevertheless, as early as the 16th century an Italian writer, G. M. Barbieri, was considering the possibility that the origins of medieval Western song could be found in Arab poetry and its Arabo-Andalusian and even Judaeo-Spanish ramifications. Barbieri's views were not in fact published until the 1790s but since that time the question has been discussed in an extensive literature. If in fact this Arabist theory were correct it would mean that the lyric song of medieval Europe had roots as far away as Iran. The ultimate sources of this music will probably always remain a matter for speculation but we know a good deal about the connections and borrowings between the various European forms. The *lai* with its multiple melodies often borrowed from songs

lore. If folk singers ever did in fact borrow from this material, they so profoundly changed the melodies of the *trouvères* that it is now impossible to find any link between an artistic version and a folklore version. Possibly liturgic melody, heard by everybody throughout the year, had somewhat more influence on popular song.

Borrowings between goliard and *trouvère* songs must also have been frequent; for example Gautier de Châtillon's piece *Veri(s) pacis* was sung to a melody by Blondel de Nesle, as was the anonymous Latin song *Procurans odium*. Both songs are to be found for two voices in several manuscripts and the question of who created the melody is still undecided.

The flowering of lyric song

In Germany, the *Minnesänger* borrowed freely from the output of the troubadours and *trouvères*. Of the *Minnesänger* songs of the late 12th century by Friedrich von Hausen, Bernger von Horheim, Heinrich von Morungen and others, many were derived from songs by Bernard de Ventadour, Chrétien de Troyes, Gace Brulé etc. In Spain nearly all the 13th-century *cantigas* of Sta Maria are written in *virelay* form and frequent melodic borrowings have been traced from Spanish folklore or from French songs and *lais*. Indeed the literary repertory of lyric song influenced everything around it. The *Sponsus*, the oldest known liturgical drama (*c.* 1100?), contains veritable songs, either in the Limousin dialect, or in Latin with a refrain in the vernacular, or in Latin without refrain. In later liturgic or semi-liturgic drama such borrowings from secular forms were common.

The lyric forms spread to the epic romance, such as the romance of *Tristan* (*c.* 1170) and the motet, while the structure of the *rondeau* was to be found again in the 'Latin *rondeaux*' which provided the rhythms for the dances of the clergy, held in the churches on certain feast days. More than forty *rondeaux* are preserved in a 13th-century manuscript in Notre-Dame de Paris, mingled with refrain songs.

The luxuriant spread of lyric music was limited neither in time nor in space. We may add to it the Italian *laudi* of the 13th and 14th centuries, and through the accompanied melodies of the late 14th and 15th centuries in France and elsewhere elements of it were revived in the court airs and lute songs of the 16th and 17th centuries. Although, unlike the *Minnesänger* melodies, of which some survived into the 19th century, the French *trouvère* melodies died out, they had still succeeded in defining a genre and a style whose fundamental elements were to determine the permanent characteristics of the French *chanson*.

The Meistersinger

The *Minnesänger*, who belonged to the aristocracy, were followed in Germany in the early 14th century by the *Meistersinger* or 'mastersingers' of the great cities, who represented the bourgeois class of craftsmen and merchants. Organised in guilds, they cultivated poetry and music according to strict formulas which singularly limited the free expansion of song forms. The apprentice mastersinger had to learn the rules mechanically and the apprenticeship was consequently long and complicated. Mainz, where Frauenlob, one of the last *Minnesänger*, had died in 1318, is believed to have been their birthplace, but schools soon sprang up throughout Germany. There were *Singschulen* at Augsburg in 1450,

above

The famous Minnesänger *Heinrich von Meissen, called* Frauenlob *('Praiser of ladies'), playing the fiddel with which he accompanied his lays. He is surrounded by musicians – bagpipes and psaltery to the right and a shawmist behind him.*

which in their turn were sometimes derived from *lais*. Moreover mutual borrowing between liturgic and profane music, between Latin and French song and vice-versa, appears to have been frequent; fragments of songs were used for the tenors of church polyphonies and the texts of refrains or entire couplets were used in motets. An essentially aristocratic and even academic form, these medieval lyrics seem to have left no traces in folk-

at Strasbourg where, in 1490, the mastersingers assembled to draw up statutes, at Fribourg in 1513, and later at Colmar, Ulm, Memmingen, Worms, Frankfurt, Prague, Dresden, Breslau, and Danzig. These unpaid artists included Hans Foltz, Fritz Ketner and Michel Beheim, author of 399 *Lieder*, who died in 1474 at the court of the Prince-Elector of the Palatinate; Jörg Wichram, who was active about 1560; and the weaver Nunnenbeck, who was the master of Hans Sachs (1494-1576).

Nunnenbeck, who set himself the task of instructing the people, wrote no fewer than 4,270 *Meisterlieder*. His example was followed by his disciples, the shoemaker Georg Hagen, who revised the Nuremberg tablature, and the tailor Adam Puschmann of Görlitz, who died in Dresden in 1600, and whose *Singebuch* of 1584 contains a list of 334 *Töne*. It has been described as 'a fossilised residue of the living tradition of the middle ages'. Mention must also be made of Benedict von Watt, born in 1568; he was laureate of the Nuremberg school where he won the *Schulkleinod* in 1592. The practice of *Meistergesang* continued until the end of the 17th century when, in 1693, Johann Christoph Wagenseil published a *Buch von der Meistersinger holdseligen Kunst* which enumerated all the arbitrary rules that Wagner ridiculed in his opera *The Mastersingers of Nuremberg*.

Music for the dance

One of the most important factors in the development of secular music away from the Church was the growing elaboration of dance music and the increasingly important place which this came to occupy in the courtly life of Europe from the 12th century onwards. From earliest times the dance was found everywhere throughout Europe but such was its vast popularity that the Church, while condemning in repeated papal bulls the excesses to which dancing could lead, was obliged to allow even the clergy certain indulgence to act as a safety valve. Indeed, a whole chapter could be written on the popular dances performed in the churches. There were ecclesiastical dances reserved for the clergy, such as the *rondeaux* of the Notre Dame manuscript and even certain dances performed by bishops and other dignitaries on special feast days – these included a *bergerette* recorded at Besancon. Until 1466 the clergy of Strasbourg were authorised to go in disguise to public dances, while at Venice in 1518 two cardinals performed a 'hat' dance. But these were exceptions to the general condemnation of the dance by the Church. Even in lay society there were degrees of abandon considered proper for the different strata of society and we shall see how, on their journey from the village green to the castle hall, many peasant dances were toned down to suit their more pretentious surroundings. Up to the 12th century little but the names of the dances have survived and we can have no clear idea of either the steps or the music to which they were performed; however we do know that the music for the dance was often provided by voices. As we have seen, such lyric forms as the *ballade, rondeau* and *virelay* were originally intended to accompany dances and, in the case of the *virelay* at least, this practice seems to have been known as late as the 14th century.

One of the most ancient forms of the dance was the group round dance. This was certainly known to classical writers, who held it to be an imitation of the circular movement of the stars around the Earth. Not only was it to be found in the cyclic chorus of the Greek tragedy, but also in the medieval *carole*, undoubtedly of pagan origin. Basically it consisted of a closed ring of male and female dancers turning around a tree, a fountain, or a

central personage who was eventually known as the 'devil'. In about 1190 it was given a transitional name, the *rondet de carole*, the word *rondet* designating any kind of versified song that provided rhythmic accompaniment for a dance.

Some troubadour and *trouvère* songs have been credited with a choreographic function and a famous song of the period, *A l'entrada del tems clar*, a *ballata* or *ballade*, appears to have been danced in chorus. It is possible that *pastourelles* were also performed with dialogue and mimed by *jongleurs*, and it is probably from this that the 13th-century pastorale, *Robin and Marion* by Adam de la Halle, developed. In the musical interludes of this piece, the actors moved and danced to *rondeau* refrains. While we may be sure that instruments were used to accompany the dances of their early period, we cannot be certain which instruments were used nor how they were combined.

The oldest notated dances now known to us – the *spagnola*, the *estampies* and royal dances – are of the 13th century and have no text; they were therefore instrumental but we do not know what instruments they were played on. Without specifying their uses, the authors mention the bow fiddel, the hurdy-gurdy, the hautboy, the bagpipes, the flageolet, the cornett and the tambourine. An 11th-century manuscript shows an acrobatic dancer practising to a double hautboy; in another a harpist is shown accompanying three dancers. The *Roman de Guillaume de Dole*, which is so rich in allusions to dances, only mentions the fiddler once or twice; most of the *rondeaux* and other dances were sung. 15th-century paintings frequently show bands of trumpets, bombards and cornetts playing dance music at balls; but it is the late 16th-century *Orchesographie* which gives us the most precise information on the orchestration of the *basse danse* – drum, cornett and voice – and this is confirmed by the instrumental indications for other dances such as pavans, galliards and *volte*.

Among the other dances of the period were the *ductia*, perhaps the lay equivalent of the ecclesiastical *conductus*, the *nota*, the *branle* and above all the *basse danse*. The *ductia* and the *estampies* were composed by the combination of various musical phrases called 'points' or *puncta*; the *ductia* consisting of three or four such 'points', the

opposite page top
The ceremonial investiture of a new knight required music; here we see a bowed fiddel and a lute being played with a plectrum.

A dance in a walled garden; shawms were commonly used for outdoor entertainment.

both the *carole* and the *tresque*. These dances differed from each other by the number and order of their paces and the reverences. The *branle* was danced 'sideways' (like the *carole*, towards the left first); it was a dance for 'several' which could be transformed into a round dance. The *branles* bore the names of their region of origin or their nature: *branle de Poitou*, *branle de Bourgogne*, the 'gay' *branle*, the torch *branle*. In 1588, Thoinot Arbeau published an analysis of nineteen *branles* and their corresponding music; he noticed that although the *branle de Poitou* had formerly been danced in 3:4 time, at Langres it was then commonly danced to a binary rhythm with the 'gay' *branle* being danced in 6:8 time.

Separate dances existed apart from these suites or *danceries*: the galliard (skipped), the *corrente* (the binary French *courante*), the *volta* (a more *risquée* dance); the noble pavan and above all, the *moresque* or 'morris', which was relatively ancient since the tragic *bal des Ardents* (1392) at the Court of Charles VI had included 'choreas sarracenicas'. In 1459 the *moresque* was danced in the presence of King Charles VII; in 1465, a sung *moresque* was performed by twelve dancers at Siena. It was disguised and often sung to burlesque words, and consisted of a ballet of soloists with small round bells who beat the time on the ground with their heels. In Italy, it had first been a sword dance.

Apart from the *moresque*, certain dance numbers were executed in the course of princely receptions during the dessert and were followed by aristocratic dances performed by the noble guests, who would sometimes be disguised and led by instruments.

A dance in quite another spirit was the *danse macabre*. Its text became widespread from the end of the 14th century and as a spectacle it anticipated the frescoes representing it. It required actors and was performed before an audience who took no part in the action.

Such dance spectacles, in which the knights and their ladies might perform, provided the origins of the ballet. Spectacular as it was, the *Ballet comique de la reine* (danced in Paris in 1581) was not only performed by professionals but also by a whole contingent of amateurs who had been well trained by *salon* dancing. It had been preceded by the Florentine pastorals (1539) with orchestra, song and dances; in 1542, Pan and the shepherds danced a sung *moresque* with instruments. In 1581 Lassus had published a *Libro de villanelle*, *moresche* for two or three voices.

Many dances, as we have mentioned, had a popular origin. Two Spanish dances, the frenzied chaconne of the muleteers and the sarabande, forbidden because of its licentious nature, rapidly rose to the rank of court dances, becoming modified and disciplined if only because of the weight of the robes and fancy dress and the encumbrance of the sword. In this way most of the former village dances attained the level of aristocratic society and then somehow became dissociated from the dance floor to evolve into the 17th-century instrumental suite.

top
A dance accompanied by a slide trumpet and pipe and tabor.

above
In place of the one-man combination of pipe and tabor, here separate players perform on tabor and transverse flute.

estampie of six or seven and the *nota* of four.

The *basse danse*, so called probably because unlike the *danses en haut* it was performed without leaps, was well known in the 14th century and was fully described in 1416. It was then a 'suite of dances', a series of some six figures with different rhythms and tempos: introduction (*capo*), *basse danse* proper, *quadernaria*, *saltarello* (*pas de Breban*, executed with a skip), *piva* (a popular dance to bagpipes), and return of the *basse danse*. In principle, the musical motif of the initial *basse danse* was used by the other figures, the rhythm being modified according to a previously established graduation, each figure being faster than the one before it. The *basse danse* was a dance by couples and was the dominant dance in aristocratic circles, but was not intended to be performed on the stage. It was sometimes performed to the accompaniment of songs and instruments.

Branles were first mentioned in about 1400 and constitute another series of dances which were derived from

The musical drama in the middle ages

Like all artistic activities in the middle ages, the theatre came within the province of the Church, at least in its beginnings. It was in the church, by the Church and for the Church that the elements of staging, dialogue and action were developed, which were gradually to engender a new art. This new theatre owed nothing to the accomplished technique of the Greeks and Romans. At the most all we can say is that, like the Greek theatre, it had originated in a form of worship. The works of some Latin playwrights were known to a few ecclesiastics, but from its origins as an aid to expounding the Bible to the illiterate laity, the development of medieval drama was continuous and had little or nothing to do with any classical precedents. From the 12th century, the purely musical element in the theatre became less and less important, and from this time on, from the point of view of the music historian, the medieval lyric theatre may be said to have started its decline.

Origins of the medieval theatre

The birth of the theatre was the consequence of two needs: to paraphrase the texts of the service by explaining them with the aid of increasingly lengthy dialogue elements, called tropes and, secondly, to illustrate the liturgical services which had thus been given dialogue in a lively and picturesque manner. By the device of the trope, parts of the service gradually became transformed into a spectacle. It was no longer really a service and it was not yet theatre, but the embryo had been created and it was from this that the serious medieval theatre developed.

The initial material was provided by Easter, the peak of the liturgical year. This is not surprising since the order of the ceremonies on holy days and the abundance

of prescribed rites were already a kind of theatrical spectacle in themselves. An introductory trope to the Easter introit, *Resurrexit*, had long been in existence. It was also to be found, although without any scenic indications, on one of the most ancient troparies of Saint-Martial of Limoges. It has been dated from about AD 930 and contains all the questions and responses that are found in the piece now regarded as the first true drama. It is the abbey of Fleury (St Benoit-sur-Loire) that seems to deserve the credit for having made a scenic use of the trope. The detailed narrative of a wonderstruck English monk, St Ethelwold, gives us much precise information. A monk, with a palm in his hand, represented the angel whose duty it was to announce to three other monks, playing the roles of the holy women, that Christ had risen. The short dialogue runs as follows:
 – Whom do you seek?
 – Jesus of Nazareth,
 – He is not here: but has risen as he foretold.
   Go and tell it abroad that he has risen from the dead.
 – Alleluia, the Lord is risen.
 – Come and see the place.
 – The Lord is risen from the tomb.
It was followed by the chant of the Te Deum.

As St Ethelwold mentioned, and as the final hymn clearly indicates, this short drama was performed at Matins, between the third lesson, which tells the story of the arrival of the three Marys at the tomb of Christ, and the Te Deum which ends the service. It was due to this position held in the service that the liturgical drama and then, later, the miracle and mystery play, traditionally ended with the chant of the Te Deum even after the spectacle had gone outside the church.

left
The play of the Three Marys.

far left
Woodcut from a late medieval edition of the plays of Terence; the plays of such pagan writers had been familiar to monastic copyists since the earliest period but the tradition of the live European theatre was born in the Church.

The variety thus introduced into the service was so greatly appreciated that the same dialogue, with a few slight changes, was carried over into the services of the other main feast-days, in the first instance that of Christmas, and later the feast of the Ascension.

From this point on the text of the dialogue was extended by the simple expedient of borrowings from the words and music of the liturgy; from the antiphons, which provided the introduction and commentaries, or from other parts of the service, like the tropes and sequences. There was still no thought of a truly new creation. The music and words of certain parts of the service were merely placed in a new context, the music remaining an essential part. The sequences, which were then composed of short pieces which responded to each other in pairs, were arranged so as to be incorporated in this dialogue. An 11th-century example, *Victimae Paschali laudes*, constituted a natural and logical development of the *Quem quaeritis*, since the question contained in the added trope was supposed to be pronounced by the apostles, who, running to the sepulchre, met the three Marys.

Another scene, if we may call it such, was provided by the Gospel itself, and relates how two angels appear to the weeping Mary Magdalene, followed by Christ, whom she at first takes to be the gardener. From the musical point of view this was a short drama in several episodes with dialogue; most of the questions and responses were elements of tropes or sequences interspersed with phrases that were usually borrowed from the antiphons of the service. A certain fantasy predominated in the use made of the materials but there was nothing among them that was not liturgical.

There must have been a considerable temptation to amplify such works even if it meant taking liberties with the sacred texts. The slightest allusions in the Gospels were exploited and also became scenes. Thus the *Quem quaeritis* was nearly always preceded by a dialogue between the Holy Women and a seller of aromatic spices used for embalming the dead. This was a purely imaginative dialogue which even included highly profane remarks on the price of perfume. Pilate also provided the pretext for further scenes, as did the Roman soldiers ordered to keep watch over the tomb.

Once scrupulous respect for the liturgic text had gone, the door was open to innovations. Admittedly, the subject was still closely linked with the divine service, yet even when it was still of an edifying nature it was no longer an integral part of the liturgy. The earliest 'dramas' belonged either to the rites for Easter, such as the Resurrection and the Supper at Emmaus, or to the rite for Christmas, such as the Prophets, the Adoration of the Magi, the Massacre of the Innocents, and the Lamentation of Rachel. From these dramatic dialogues, which were not an integral part of the liturgy, it was a short step to the composition of works which had nothing to do with the service; examples were the Conversion of St Paul, the Resurrection of Lazarus, and others inspired by more or less legendary tales borrowed from the Lives of the Saints. It was this new-style drama that was given the name of miracle play, and as early as the 11th century the miracle play competed with the liturgical drama and contributed to its decline. Since there was a movement away from liturgy towards pure dramatic invention there could no longer be any question of borrowing. It was necessary to create. The tendency was to repeat formulas so that the drama became gradually transformed, as did the sung miracle play, into an assemblage of strophic hymns, which therefore diminished its interest.

In one of these semi-liturgical dramas, the late 11th-century *Sponsus*, Latin was for the first time joined by the vernacular French. Most of the spectators would have been incapable of understanding Latin, and if we make a precise analysis of the work we shall see that each of the elements contained in the Gospel parable of the Wise and the Foolish Virgins is doubled by an element in French which is in effect a translation. One scene in French is, however, added to the Gospel account; in it the Foolish Virgins go to beseech the merchant to give them oil for their lamps. The abandonment of the liturgical language for invented episodes was to become commonplace, and these additions, which were so much appreciated and so ceaselessly developed, gradually ousted Latin from the theatre.

The *Sponsus* marks a stage in the history of the theatre both in the use of the two languages and in dramatic and musical terms. Dramatic, in the first place, since its construction reveals a noticeable progression from earlier dramas – an action leading progressively towards a denouement. It is interesting musically since it no longer contains the slightest element borrowed from liturgy: everything was written in measured verse and the free rhythm of Gregorian chant is no longer present.

Sketch for the Castel of Perseverance from the Townley cycle of plays.

The spoken drama in French

The *Jeu d'Adam* is generally considered by literary historians to be the first theatrical achievement worthy of the name. Certainly its considerable length, almost a thousand lines, far exceeds that of the *Sponsus*, which has only one hundred and seven. The sung responses scattered throughout the work are in reality the very framework of the play. The extensive dialogues that follow them are essentially intended to explain the ideas contained in the responses. The work is still musical in its conception but the importance of the dialogue gives the impression that music is no longer indispensable. Even when it was no longer played, its disappearance was hardly noticeable. The fact remains that even if it was not conceived in this spirit, the *Jeu d'Adam* was nothing other than spoken theatre with musical interludes. The considerable changes that had come about in this early drama between its creation and the 12th century corresponded with a notable weakening of religious feeling. It is almost certain that in this period the dramatic spectacle had gone out of the choir of the church to the parvis, where the preliminary pieces would have been less out of place.

The miracle and mystery plays

We may say that with the *Jeu d'Adam* the medieval lyric theatre entered its decline. One of the best of the later examples of sung drama is the Latin play of *The Three Maries* which was still performed in the 14th century by the nuns of Origny-Sainte-Benoîte. It is easy to recognise the schema of the primitive *Quem quaeritis*, but the extension of the various elements has gone to extremes. As in the *Sponsus*, the added scenes, such as a long dialogue between the merchant and the three Maries, are written only in the vernacular, but the traditional antiphons, responses and tropes are all present. But the play of *The Three Maries*, although true to the origins of the sung drama, was outdated and the theatre, which was now an independent form, was increasingly becoming a means of amusement. The cycle has thus come to an end and the sung drama tended to become once again an element of the liturgy. Indeed, 13th-century texts have survived which contain nothing that is not liturgical, that is not in Latin and that is not sung. At the same time the length of the works was reduced: a 14th-century *Annunciation* was no more than a simple trope sung between the antiphon *Ave Maria* and the Magnificat.

From the early 13th century onwards the miracle play increasingly took the place of the sung drama. It offered far greater possibilities for fantasy and variety. The saint would appear in stories which were sometimes starkly realistic if not even scabrous. The always latent desire to edify became less pressing than the desire to please and amuse. The pretext of the play remained religious but the theatre was already profane.

Although the manuscripts do not always indicate the fact, music was still important in these performances and, in some respects, the difference between the miracle plays and the drama of *Adam* was not great. But the spirit had changed profoundly. Whereas in *Adam* the sung responses had engendered dialogues, in the miracle plays song only intervened as stage music, according to the needs of the text. The choice of the piece to be played was a matter of so little importance that no precise references are to be found in the rubrics. The early 13th-century *Jeu de Saint Nicolas* by Jean Bodel d'Arras and the *Miracle de Théophile* by Rutebeuf only mention the

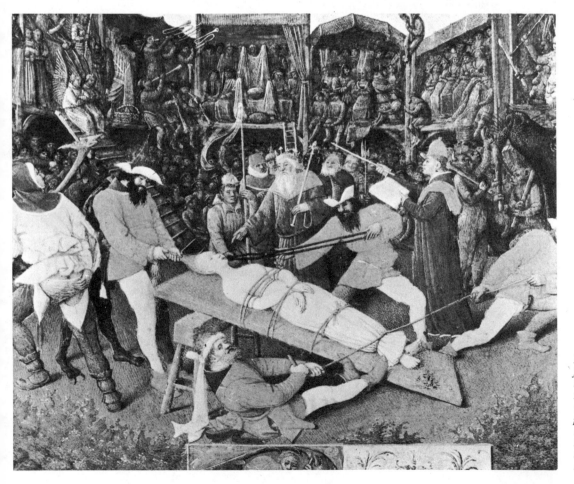

In this painting the artist has skilfully confused the world of the theatre – stage in the foreground, spectators in the rear – with the world of historical reality. The presentation of the martyrdom of St Apolline by the guild or 'mystery' of St Etienne seems almost to be the event itself rather than mere play acting.

Te Deum hymn which was to bring the performance to an end. Perhaps the best known 13th-century drama is the very appealing *pastourelle* of Adam de la Halle entitled *Jeu de Robin et Marion*. This aristocratic entertainment, composed in about 1283, was not properly speaking a work of music. Of its 780 lines, only 72 were sung, and even these musical interludes were borrowed from known airs. But what is remarkable is the perfect harmony of the alliance between music and speech.

The mystery play was born in the 14th century and supplanted the miracle play in the 15th. No more than its predecessor did it mention the use of music explicitly. But music still played a part, following the whims of the actors and the possibilities that arose. In the *Mystère de la Passion* by Arnoul Greban (15th century) certain pages were set to music, although the composers are unknown. The rubrics are vague and merely state, for example, that at the moment of the Resurrection the prophets 'must here sing some motet or joyful thing'. Music, from being an integral part of the drama, has now clearly become merely a decorative element. It retained quite an important role in the 16th century in the theatre of Shakespeare and played a dominant part in the elaborate interludes which became such a common feature of the entertainments of the 15th-century court of Burgundy, but it was not until the birth of opera in the 17th century that a true tradition of musical drama once again became part of European musical culture.

Manuscript page from the Jeu de Robin et Marion.

Section III

The Age of Polyphony

Renaissance and Reformation: historical background

By convention the modern era of European history is considered to have opened in the 16th century. In this brief survey we shall trace the radical developments on the political stage of Europe, and in the section which follows we shall see that equally important changes were taking place in the music. In the high middle ages the concept of Christendom was felt to be a real one, and its validity had been strengthened by the pressures from the alien faith of Islam on the West and East. In the 16th century this notion of Christendom, already weakened by the advance of the secular state in the 15th century, was torn apart by the events of the German Reformation, which divided the Continent in an unheard-of way – along lines of religious conviction. There had indeed been wars against heretics and schismatics in the middle ages but they were exceptions, and the notion that religious differences were the natural grounds for armed conflict between Christian rulers was revolutionary. Whatever the political or economic realities of the situation, many sophisticated Europeans of the 16th century saw the great issues of their time in a religious context. Certainly the political and religious division was an unavoidably real fact in the lives of composers. For those living in the more extremely Protestant states that centuries-old field of inspiration, the liturgy and music of the Catholic Church, was closed. Yet in their search after ever more elaboration in the music of the mass, the composers themselves had, it was claimed, obliterated the words and the sacred significance of the service, so that Luther singled out only Josquin des Prez for praise as a church composer.

The Low Countries

Josquin, like so very many of the major composers of the period, was born in the Netherlands. The cultural axis of Europe in the 15th century ran between the Low Countries and northern Italy, and this corresponded to political realities. The once mighty kingdom of France was humbled by the ravages of English armies, which, supporting their king's century-old claim to the French throne, occupied vast territories and were only expelled in the 1450s. Even then Calais was left to England and, in the following century, was to serve as the beachhead for the ventures of Henry VIII. In addition to foreign armies, France had also to suffer the feuds of the great magnates, which seemed likely to dismember the kingdom. The power of the dukes of Orleans, Anjou and Berry, and of the virtually independent duchy of Brittany, all reflected strong regional tendencies which were to be active again in the wars of religion within France in the 16th century. But most threatening of all was the state of the dukes of Burgundy. They controlled an almost continuous block of territory on the eastern frontiers of France; they had become to all intents and purposes independent rulers, and they aspired to the status of kings. The dream was not an idle one. Their possessions comprised the wealthy merchant and industrial regions of the Low Countries; their subjects numbered the greatest musicians and artists anywhere in Europe; their lands were governed by an increasingly effective and centralised administration, and their military capabilities were considerable. In wars between France and England they sided for much of the time with England, and the French kings had every reason to fear the might of their chief 'subjects'. In 1477 however, the chance of battle ended the career of the last duke, Charles, and, with the accession of his daughter Mary, the threat of a Burgundian state. But the wealth of the Netherlands, found in such towns as Antwerp, Amsterdam, Bruges and Ghent, ensured that the area – under Maximilian of Habsburg who married Mary, and his successors, soon to be kings of Spain – remained a powerhouse of artistic creativity and political independence for generations to come. At the end of the 16th century, this was expressed in the rebellion of the northern provinces from Spain, culminating in the independence of the Protestant United Provinces which were to form the base of the great Dutch maritime empire.

Italy

Throughout the 16th century, the Netherlands continued to produce a flood of composers, from Willaert to Lassus. Many of these great men emigrated, especially to the Renaissance courts which had sprung up in the urban civilisation of northern Italy. For centuries cities such as Florence, Venice, Mantua, Milan and Padua had grown strong on commerce, industry and banking, and when in the 15th century the many petty warring communes were succeeded by an uneasy balance of power between the great states of Venice, Milan, Rome, Florence and the kingdom of Naples, the conditions were ripe for the flowering of the great artistic movement which was launched by the writings of Dante, Petrarch and Boccaccio and which was driven on by the new enthusiasm for classical learning summed up in the term 'humanism'.

Yet if the dynamic behind the flowering of the north Italian cities was commerce and the fluid social structure which it encouraged, Naples and Rome, both important cultural centres, represented uncharacteristic polities for Italy. The kingdom of Naples was essentially a rural-based feudal monarchy of the type so common north of the Alps. Following the death of Frederick II in 1250, Naples had come under the rule of the French house of Anjou and had suffered the conflict between the

opposite
Detail from Holbein's The Ambassadors.

Angevins and the rival Spanish house of Aragon. Under Ferrante of Aragon, Naples enjoyed a brilliant period in the middle of the 15th century, and through Naples Spain first came into contact with the new ideas of the Renaissance. Finally it was the continuing conflict between France and Spain over Naples that made Italy the battlefield of Francis I of France and Charles V, emperor and king of Spain, in their struggle for European mastery in the opening decades of the 16th century. Against a backdrop of complex diplomacy involving all the major European states, and seemingly endless wars, one event stands out as sensational even in that age of turmoil. This was the sack of Rome by imperial troops in 1527.

Like Naples, Rome did not conform to the general pattern of Italian states. Not only its international prestige but also its wealth depended on the presence of the popes. The century leading up to the sack had been one of painful recovery and rehabilitation for the papacy. The 15th century had opened with the Church in disarray. The schism between two rival popes had begun in 1378; for forty years Europe lived with two and then three supreme pontiffs. Their rivalry for allegiance from the secular rulers could only strengthen the already strong tendencies towards secularisation in lay affairs and within the Church. Theorists, notably from the University of Paris, proclaimed not only the need for root and branch reform within the Church, but also the sovereignty of a universal council of the Church above the pope himself. In 1415, at the imperial town of Constance, such a council was convened under the auspices of the Emperor Sigismund. The crucial question was whether the Church should be reformed, or the new pope elected, first. The papalist party won this central point and the autocratic power of the popes was gradually reimposed; as the papacy recovered so did the fortunes of Rome as a city, and it grew into one of the most important centres of cultural patronage. In the 16th century the trend continued and Rome, together with the great maritime republic of Venice and the duchy of Florence, became one of the celebrated centres of Italian music.

Spain

The decline of Venice was linked with the shift in the focus of European trade away from the Mediterranean routes to the East, to the long sea routes round Africa, and above all to the westward sea lanes to the New World. Increasingly the ports of Spain and Portugal, the two great imperial powers, grew rich on this trade, and towards the end of the 16th century the English, French and Dutch began to make inroads into their preserves. The 16th century indeed was the century of Spain, and although it closed in the humiliating sequel of the defeat of the great Armada by England, nevertheless the apparent wealth of the Spanish crown and its client kingdom of Portugal was still the most dazzling in Europe. The golden age of Spain, as it was called, was so not only in political and economic terms, but also in the world of literature, painting and music.

In the year 1492, not only had Columbus discovered America, thus opening new fields of wealth and missionary endeavour, but the last foothold of Islam in Spain had been demolished with the conquest of Granada. In fact the Christian conquerors, valuing the industry and commercial acumen of their new subjects, had made extensive concessions to their customs and faith, but from the middle of the century new and more rigorous policies had been introduced. For Philip II, the new king of Spain, uniformity of religion among his subjects seems at times almost to have become an obsession; not only did he determine to exterminate all traces of Islam within Spain's frontiers, but he was also determined to crush the Protestant heresy of the Dutch. In this he merely intensified and extended his father's policy, for Charles V had sought by all available means to combat the spread of the new reformed faith from its birth within his German dominions. In 1558 Charles had abdicated, but his Catholic policies were continued in Spain and also in the empire by his younger brother Ferdinand I, the new emperor.

The Reformation

Evidence of popular disillusionment with the Church was to be found in many parts of Europe during the 15th century. In England the Lollards, followers of John Wyclif, although an underground and socially depressed minority, continued an underground existence throughout the century. In Bohemia the Hussites, inspired by the example of their martyred leader Jan Hus, asserted not only their doctrinal independence of Rome but also their political independence of the empire. In the Low Countries the Brethren of the Common Life and their great mystic, Thomas à Kempis, rejected the still growing corruption of the hierarchy. Throughout Europe people were turning away from the Church. But it was in Germany that this feeling took concrete shape and led to the great movement which came to be known as the Reformation. The monk, Martin Luther, who became the first great leader of the movement, relied heavily on the support of the secular power. It is perhaps no coincidence that this religious movement enjoyed ever increasing support from the German princes at a time when the new emperor, Charles V, was exerting himself to restore the ancient powers of the medieval empire. For the princes of that empire, who had long since thrown off all but the most nominal allegiance to that power, the ambitions of Charles must have appeared as a considerable threat, and the religious cause which Luther provided would for many have been an ideal pretext. For others the desire for reform was genuine and honorable however, and at long last the Church itself took to heart the century-long clamour for reform. At the council of Trent, convened, it must be said, only after it was obvious that the Church had lost something like a third of its flock, the main lines of this reform were drawn up. The members of the council endeavoured to deal with all aspects of church life and music was not neglected.

England and France

But in Protestant Europe these reforms had come too late, and the new churches which had sprung up had devised liturgies of their own which to a greater or lesser extent reflected the old usages. These new services demanded a new kind of music, often a much reduced musical content, and in a country like England some of the finest composers remained true to the old faith and continued to compose music for the mass. But for the majority of Englishmen, the close of the 16th century was a period of glorious national self-assertion against the defeated might of Spain and the Church of Rome which that power represented. The brilliant school of late Elizabethan and Jacobean composers echoed in their music a mood of national elation and self-confidence which in the political world, after the disastrous interlude of the reign of Charles I, led to the establishment of Great Britain as the pre-eminent naval power in a new Europe, increasingly attuned to global considerations.

But whereas England was spared the worst horrors of religious war, in France the conflict was long, bloody and recurrent. For the first sixty years of the 16th century the energies of France were absorbed by her conflict with the empire. But the teachings of the Reformation won a large following in France and in 1560 the first of the Wars of Religion broke out between the Catholic establishment and the Protestant Huguenots. For the next thirty years France was torn by civil war in which the Catholic family of Guise effectively controlled affairs, until the accession of the Protestant claimant, Henry of Navarre, as Henry IV in 1594. Henry brought a period of good government and religious peace; himself accepting Catholicism as the price of his throne, he passed the important Edict of Nantes which ensured toleration to the Protestants, at least until Henry's assassination in 1610.

During the 16th century France and the empire were both torn apart by the divisive forces of religious intolerance, and the conflict was to continue into the following century. Yet it is interesting that in both these states, as to a certain extent in England also, many composers wrote music both for the Catholic and for the Reformed Churches. We shall see in the musical introduction which follows the kind of musical changes which took place in the wake of the Reformation; it is important to remember that however intense the religious passions which lay behind these changes, the first generations of composers were prepared to draw their inspiration from both sources.

A contemporary engraving of the first colonists landing in Virginia.

The background to the music

In the two hundred years or so from the death of Machaut to that of Lassus in 1594, the history of music in Europe is one of consolidation and of important new departures. Thus by the beginning of the 17th century most of the major elements in the musical language of the Baroque and classical periods can be discerned. In this survey of the age of polyphony, we shall necessarily be concerned with generalisations, and the more detailed treatment of the history of the period in the chapters which follow will indicate qualifications to the simplified outline to be given here. Nevertheless we can consider this history under six main headings. These are: the introduction of euphony into polyphonic writing; the rise of the *cantus firmus* mass as Europe's first major musical form; the emergence of 'national' schools of composition; the birth of new secular forms; the beginnings of truly instrumental music; and the interrelated developments, at the end of the period, of monody and the *basso continuo*.

In the most general sense the word 'polyphony', which simply means 'many sounds', can be used of any music in more than one part. But it has special application to describe the writing of music in which the parts are all considered of equal importance and when combined produce not only independent horizontal movement but also euphonious combinations of chords. The composers of the *ars nova* had solved the most abstruse problems of rhythmic organisation in three or four parts; it is also true that the greatest master of the style, Guillaume de Machaut, had been able to compose music of great lyric beauty as well as rhythmic complexity. But the nature of the music was essentially horizontal, that is to say the melodic movement of each individual part was of greater importance than the total sonorous effect of the whole. One of the characteristics of *ars nova* compositions was the frequent and often violent dissonances produced by the conflicting parts. The harshness of this music was to yield in the 15th century to a new euphonious manner. This was first proclaimed in the works of the English composers who, led by John Dunstable and Leonel Power, had a decisive influence on the music of Europe. Their example was reinforced by the practice of less renowned composers in Italy. With the military campaigns of the later Hundred Years War many Englishmen came to the Continent, and as the century progressed more and more northern composers visited Italy at the invitation of the early Renaissance courts. Thus north and south combined to introduce new methods of composition. These were taken up by the great school of Flemish and Franco-Flemish composers which was to dominate the history of music during the Renaissance.

The key to the 'sprightly concordance' of the English, as a contemporary named it, was the use of the intervals of the third and the sixth. According to accepted theory, heavily influenced by the principles of acoustics of Pythagoras, these were classed as discords. It is probable that the English composers derived their revolutionary technique from the folk and popular music of their native land. Whatever the source of their inspiration and whatever the strictures of theory, the practical effects of the use of these despised intervals was immediately recognised by the Continental composers who gratefully hailed the new art and followed its example. The greatest master of the new smooth style was to be the Franco-Flemish composer Guillaume Dufay, who died in 1470; with his contemporaries and successors he developed a new language of polyphony which was fully exploited in the next century by men such as Palestrina and Lassus.

The cantus firmus mass

For a brief period in the first half of the 15th century the English school held the lead in European music, even if before its end it had retired into an insularity which was to persist with only one exception until the 20th century. Not only did Dunstable and his colleagues introduce the basis of a new musical vocabulary, but they seem also to have been the pioneers of an important formal device which made possible the organisation of the five major sections of the Ordinary of the mass as a single great unity. Towards the end of the 14th century there had been various attempts to introduce an element of unity, but it was only with the 'cyclic tenor', first employed it appears by the English, that the answer was found. The technique, once discovered, seems simple enough. It consisted in using the same basic *cantus firmus* for all the parts of the mass so that, sharing a common theme, they made up a single cycle of related pieces. Again it was to be Dufay who took and moulded this new form into a vehicle for some of the finest compositions in the whole repertory of European music.

The emergence of 'national' schools

It is somewhat anachronistic to speak of national schools in the 15th century, if by this is meant schools of composers consciously striving after a style with strongly nationalist traits. But it is nevertheless true that while the lead had been taken by French musicians from the school of Paris in the 12th century up to the end of the French *ars nova*, with the 15th century other regions of Europe produced the pioneers and the great masters. We have already mentioned the English, and they were soon to be eclipsed by the achievements of the Burgundians, a loose but convenient term for the 15th-century composers from the districts of Flanders and north-eastern France. This region, heavily influenced by

French culture but for the most part outside the political control of France, was to provide Europe with a brilliant and continuous stream of master musicians.

The characteristic talent of these Franco-Flemish composers was for involved yet flowing polyphony. Their example was followed with great enthusiasm in Italy but already, from the early 16th century, the Italians were beginning to make their own distinctive contributions. The Italian sense of the dramatic was to be strongly evinced both in the developing art of instrumentation and in a growing feeling for harmonic colouring.

During the Renaissance the strong musical tradition of the Spanish countries began to make itself felt on the stage of Europe both in religious music and in work for the keyboard. Indeed in this latter field the Spaniards were to be among the pioneers. In Germany too, the achievements of Flemings such as Isaak and Lassus began to be matched by the works of native composers, while the religious impetus of the Reformation found a characteristic expression in the popular religious hymn form of the chorale. Although the English school must be regarded as insular and out of touch with the European *avant-garde*, yet, throughout the 16th century, its composers produced music both distinctive in character and outstanding in quality. Finally the French, once the acknowledged masters, were now one school among many, even though the French *chanson*, a strongly idiomatic form, was one of the major musical types of the period.

The secular forms
and instrumental music

But the *chanson* was only one of many forms of secular vocal music and was overshadowed, as the century progressed, by the immense popularity of the Italian madrigal. In both these forms composers of Flemish extraction, such as Josquin des Prez, Arcadelt and Willaert, continued to set the pace. Besides the madrigal, which was to provide the vehicle for some of the finest of 16th-century music, the Italians also contributed more lightweight forms, such as the *frottola* and the *villanesca*. In addition to these French and Italian part songs, we should mention the German *Lied*.

Still more interesting than these developments in vocal music are the indications of the beginnings of specifically instrumental forms. The Italians took an important step when they took up the French *chanson* and adapted it for instrumental music under the name of *canzona da sonar*. In England, composers gave much of their attention to music for viols, and well into the 17th century the viol fantasy was to be one of the most fertile fields of English composition. But it was in compositions for the keyboard that a specifically instrumental style first evolved. The Italian *canzona da sonar* typified instrumental music of the period in so far as it was derived from a vocal form; it was to be a long time before music for instruments shook itself free entirely from the procedures of composition for voices. The rise of the violin at the end of the 16th century and the beginning of the next, and the growing number of virtuosi who cultivated it, was to be important, but significant steps had already been taken by Spanish and English composers for the keyboard. By the end of the 16th century in England, composers had worked out a technique of keyboard variations which, although often based on themes from popular songs, owed no debt to vocal techniques and was to contribute importantly to the development of a keyboard style on the Continent.

In the realm of music for instrumental ensemble, the perennially popular music for the dance was becoming increasingly important in purely aesthetic and formal terms during our period. From the earliest times, of course, the dance had been accompanied by instruments as well as singing. By the beginning of the 15th century the earlier types of vocal dance music such as the *carole* and the *rondeau* were yielding pride of place to purely instrumental music. During the 14th century the *basse danse* had become one of the commonest types of all and its popularity lasted well into the early Renaissance. It was in fact a suite of contrasting dances rather than a single one, and the combinations of such dance movements was to provide the earliest model for instrumental compositions. In fact the development did not reach full maturity until the middle years of the 17th century, but already in the 16th conventions are beginning to emerge, such as the coupling of the slow-moving and serious pavan with the sprightly galliard.

Monody and the basso continuo

In the 1580s and 1590s a small group of musicians and poets met in Florence to pursue some of the most exciting researches and experiments in Europe. They adopted the name of *camerata* and the object of their study was to revive the drama of Greek theatre in which, they believed, music and poetry had been ideally combined. The outcome of their work was a radical break with the prevailing orthodoxy in the world of art music, since they dispensed with polyphonic procedures in favour of a single melodic line accompanied by an instrumental bass and some plucked or keyboard instrument. This was the new art of monody from which was to grow the essentially operatic medium of recitative. From this small beginning there followed a series of developments which led to the production of the first true operas in Western music and, indirectly, to the style of composition known as *basso continuo*.

The *camerata* were certainly not the inventors of accompanied solo singing. There were models enough for them in the folk music of Tuscany, but by bringing it into the field of art music they provided a powerful impetus to the movement away from the old polyphony to the new style of the Baroque age in which expressiveness and contrast were everything. The new style abandoned the equality of the parts and in its place the bass and treble provided the main structure of the music, which the intervening parts clothed and embellished.

European composers did not discard the magnificent language of polyphony; indeed the old and the new styles continued to be used, often by the same composers, as alternative means of expression. But as the 16th century drew to its close so did the 'Age of Polyphony'. The old style had become an integral part of the musical language of Europe but from now on composers were to produce their greatest achievements in the exploration and development of the new concept of vertical structure and chordal harmony.

The instruments of music

The 15th century

If we exclude the organ, which was to have its own literature as early as the 14th century, it is not until the early 15th century that we find texts with precise instrumental designations. Among them is a brilliant and stirring 'tuba gallicalis', a fanfare on a broken chord of c major for three sackbuts, and a French song mentioning a 'contratenor trompette' (probably a slide trumpet). If the 'high' instruments 'made the company joyous' they also added to the solemnity of certain religious services. The use of wind instruments, particularly the brass, was permitted in church. In the manuscripts of this period we find a motet accompanied by two sackbuts and numerous fragments of 'trompetta' masses, the works of Franchois, Grossin, and Locqueville; sometimes the strings were combined with the 'wind' as during the consecration of Sta Maria dei Fiori at Florence in 1436 when 'the whole basilica resounded with such harmonious symphonies, accompanied by the sound of diverse instruments, that you would have said that it was the music of Paradise itself'.

The sumptuous feasts given by the dukes of Burgundy, which have so often been described, were the occasion for many musical interludes. In the course of the Feast of the Pheasant at Lille in 1454, held by Duke Philip the Good for a solemn dedication of the Burgundian nobility and the princes of Europe to a crusade for the recapture of Constantinople from the Turks, the music included 'une musette moult nouvellement', ('bagpipes in a new manner'), a German cornett, four 'clarons', as well as a lute, a 'dulzian with a concordant instrument', which must have been a harp if we go by tradition, two fiddels with a lute, and lastly four flutes. During the wedding of Charles the Bold and Margaret of York at Bruges in 1468, the 'haults menestriers' made their appearance disguised as goats and rams, and played a motet, the three goats playing on shawms, the ram on a 'sackbut trumpet'; lastly, a song was played by 'four wolves holding flutes in their paws'.

If we have insisted at some length on these groupings,

it has been to show that instrumental music had acquired two very different aspects by the second half of the 15th century: that of an ensemble of varied instruments which was to become the 'broken consort', and that of an ensemble of instruments of the same family, such as recorders, shawms and – at the end of the century – viols of different sizes with a range corresponding to that of a vocal trio or quartet.

The combinations of the 'broken consort' were not arbitrary and they respected certain traditional habits of balancing instruments. Pairs such as those of the 12th and 13th centuries, which consisted of a monodic plucked string instrument or wind instrument with percussion, still remained popular but ensembles were becoming larger. A *viola da braccio*, rebec or flute played the treble, a harp or lute, the middle and bass parts, and often all these instruments were combined. Sometimes they were joined by other strings such as the cittern, the psaltery or dulcimer and also, more rarely, by a spinet, while a small organ enveloped the 'consort' with its rounded, sustained sonority. This basic grouping continued into the 17th century when pieces are found for the violin, the lute, the spinet and the organ. The ensembles depicted by the Italian painters were generally simply redoublings of this 'consort'.

We should also remember that such percussion instruments as cymbals, triangles with jingle rings and various types of bells played an important part in 14th- and 15th-century music and musicians did not even hesitate to combine bells with a clavichord and a psaltery (Naples, the church of San Giovanni a Carbonara, fresco by Leonardo da Besozzo). Many other combinations are represented in paintings and miniatures. We may even see a Jew's harp combined either with a group of shawms, or with a *viola da braccio* and a little *tromba marina*. But in the second half of the 15th century we come to the earliest of the great treatises on musical instruments, which from now on amplify what we are able to learn from the visual arts. The treatise of Arnaut de Zwolle, dating from shortly before 1466, was quickly followed by the *De inventione et usa musicae* (*c.* 1487) of the famous theoretician and composer, Johannes Tinctoris. Both works contain much precious information, the first on the manufacture of instruments, the second on their provenance and their use.

Manuscripts of organ tablatures, which were rare at the beginning of the century, soon multiplied. That of the Charterhouse of Buxheim shows a wide religious and secular repertory and, in about 1470, reveals an ornate style composed of 'fioritura' and 'breaks' well adapted to the keyboard. A single piece, a French song, bears the indication: *in cytharis vel etiam in organis* ('for the organ or cythara') which shows that it could equally well be played on an instrument with plucked strings. Even so we still have to wait another thirty years before we find the first tablatures written for the lute. The technique of the lute had been undergoing a transformation which

15th-century court ladies playing a portative organ, two types of dulcimer, a bass shawn (centre above) a trumpet and a pipe and tabor.

was to help to make it the solo instrument par excellence for a century. Formerly it had been played with a plectrum or a quill, but during the last third of the 15th century players begin to pluck it with the fingers, which not only allowed more delicate playing and a more rounded, softer sonority, but also made possible the rapid execution of passages with two or more parts. Tinctoris indeed expressed his admiration for this new generation of lute players who, he said, 'can not only play one or two parts, but three or four at the same time, which is very difficult'.

The instrumental repertory was, however, still a tributary of vocal music, most works being transcriptions of motets or polyphonic songs. Only certain dances, fanfares, preludes or postludes may be considered as being strictly designed for instruments. It was in the course of the 16th century that the notion was gradually formed of two distinct musical domains, the vocal and the instrumental, with the latter affirming its independence more strongly as time went on. The way in which instruments were made played an important part in this 'liberation', whose stages we shall now attempt to trace.

The 16th century

Reaching this period, the organologist is on firmer ground and may feel that at last he has something concrete to work with. Naturally he must still examine the evidence of works of art, inventories, chronicles and poems, but now it is also possible for him to examine, at first hand, a sizeable number of instruments which have survived more or less intact as they left their makers' hands, to analyse their special characteristics and to discover the essential principles governing their construction. He can now read pieces written for the lute, the guitar, the cittern, the keyboard and even the flute while holding the instruments themselves. Not only does he have theoretical treatises, but he also has the opportunity of testing for himself the best method of playing the various instruments and the 'instructions' concerning each of them. Finally, he can gather even more valuable information concerning the tuning of instruments, bowing techniques, the fingerings used and the subtleties of execution such as legato playing, conventions of ornamentation and the art of 'divisions'.

It is worth insisting on the debt owed by instrumental music to the discovery of printing, for the importance of the invention in the preservation and diffusion of works was immense. Before the spread of printing, the music that accompanied the great events in the life of a city such as the entries of sovereigns, festivals held in commemoration of a victory, great weddings, impressive religious ceremonies or street processions, was often ephemeral. But from the first years of the 16th century this and many other types of music were recorded and dispersed to other centres.

First in Italy, then in Germany and later in France, publishers also brought out collections of works of the greatest virtuosos, often preceded by precise instructions to guide beginners. The first sections of Virdung's method, *Musica getutscht* (1511), Martin Agricola's work, *Musica instrumentalis deudsch* (1528) and Luscinius' *Musurgia* (1536) all contain precious information on nearly all the instruments then known, while the second part of Virdung's work, translated eighteen years later into French, brought the technique of the lute, the clavichord and the recorder within the reach of many amateurs. The skill of the musician became less and less the mystery of a profession or the privilege of the wealthy and was opened up to anyone with the will to learn.

But apart from these social considerations, instru-

From left to right the angels are playing a tromba marina, *a Jew's harp and a fiddel.*

mental music was of great importance in the history of music itself. It was not alone responsible for the abandonment of the modes, but it did contribute to the establishment of modern ideas of tonality. The player of any of the fretted instruments, like the guitar or the lute, necessarily adopted the division of the tone into two equal parts. Such a division represents a compromise in terms of pure acoustic theory; it was no doubt an imperfect system, but one that was gradually to be adopted by vocal music and was to end by dominating it.

The increase in sonorous range from three octaves in the middle ages to five in the course of the 16th century was also due to the manufacture of new instruments. The families of stringed or wind instruments which had formerly counted three and then four different sizes saw the addition of three or four new models towards the end of the century, the result being an unprecedented enrichment of the range of low-pitched tones.

The lute, organ and harpsichord, which have their own extensive literature, are dealt with in the chapters on the various schools, but in passing we should take note here of some of the earlier publications of works specifically for these instruments. They include works by Spinacino or De Dalza for flute, those of Franciscus Bossinensis for voice and lute, published by Petrucci between 1507 and 1511, the works for keyboard published by Anticho in 1517, and the rich series of collections of lute pieces published at Venice between 1536 and 1550. The 'tablatures' of German and French origin, the English repertory (almost entirely in manuscript until the last decade of the century) and pieces for the Spanish *vihuela* will be treated in special paragraphs in the chapters dealing with the music of these different

A music school. The quartet of bass viol players seem to be in earnest but the seats are being used by gamblers and spectators.

piece flutes, 30 shawms, 28 organs, 25 crumhorns, cornetts and bagpipes, 32 virginals, 26 lutes, 25 viols, 21 guitars, 2 clavichords, 3 combinations of organ and virginal (*épinette organisée* or *claviorganum*,), totalling 272 wind instruments and 109 string instruments.

Rich bourgeois patrons also had 'music chambers'. That of the Fugger family of Augsburg contained more than 140 lutes, all masterpieces by Laux Maler, Magnus Tieffenbrugger or Laux Bosch, instruments made of ivory or exotic woods, harpsichords by Francesco Ungaro and English masters, numerous violins made in workshops in Brescia and Padua, as well as more than a hundred different flutes. France does not seem to have had such important collections although one of Francis' councillors, a by no means wealthy bourgeois, did manage to gather not only a musical library but spinets, clavichords in various sizes, two large spinets, one being a double-spinet, viols, harps and rebecs.

Among the many people who took an interest in musical instruments in Italy was Isabella d'Este, the marchioness of Mantua, who excelled as a singer but who also played the clavichord. She was no mere dilettante. When she ordered Lorenzo Gusnasco, in charge of her antique collection, to buy a clavichord, she warned him that the action of the one that he had delivered to her sister, duchess of Milan, was far too stiff. She also asked Gusnasco to find a viol in ebony and ivory for her collection. As Sabba di Castiglione was to say later, an instrument must 'charm the ear as much as it must animate the spirit and ravish the eye'. Isabella's nephew Alfonso II, fourth duke of Ferrara, had 'two large musicians' halls reserved to players in his service, where they might gather when they wanted to play cornetts, trombones, dulzians, viols, rebecs, lutes, citterns, harps and harpsichords . . .' From this sort of contemporary comment we may gain useful information on the kinds of instruments to be found at Renaissance courts, while the famous series of engravings by Hans Burgkmair, *The Triumphs of Maximilian* (*c.* 1510), provides a vivid record of the part which the 'high' instruments played in the ceremony and pageantry of a great public occasion. The duke of Ferrara, whose large collection of instruments also included the set of six crumhorns now in Brussels, also took an interest in *avant-garde* experiments and owned the famous enharmonic harpsichord built by Nicolas Vicentino. The last of these great Renaissance collections we have space for in this brief survey is that consisting of some 200 wind and 50 string instruments, nearly all of a rare beauty, assembled by the archduke Ferdinand of Tyrol in his castle of Ambras near Innsbruck. This now forms the nucleus of the admirable collection in the museum of Vienna.

countries. But it is worth noting that more than 150 collections of works for the lute, the *vihuela*, the guitar and the cittern have survived until the present day and that works for the lute constitute almost nine tenths of the total, with Italy alone providing half this number.

In the course of the sections which follow, we shall consult these collections to learn the possibilities of the instrument and to determine the part that a lute could play in an ensemble, and we shall do the same for the spinet, the harpsichord, the clavichord and the organ. Lastly, we shall look at reproductions of these ensembles in Italian and Flemish paintings and German and French prints and see how they were made up. We shall also try to understand why some works succeed better than others when they are played on certain instruments and why what is good for one is not so good or so suitable for another.

Combinations of instruments and the great Renaissance collections

As we have seen, in the preceding century 'consorts' were of two kinds. There was the broken consort, made up of instruments of different families. This was widespread in the middle ages and was still much used in the 17th century. There was also the consort of instruments of differing sizes of the same family; this became increasingly frequent in the 16th century with the spread of the practice of constructing families of instruments over the whole sonorous range. There was no longer any question of 'high' or 'low' instruments but of open air ensembles and chamber ensembles, the first combining cornetts, shawms and sackbuts, with violins sometimes added. Such ensembles were those of the town musicians whose duty it was to play during public festivities and great rejoicings. The second type of ensemble consisted of soft instruments – transverse flutes and viols. These were the 'intimate' instruments that Francis I of France was to group in the 'music of the chamber', the brass and woodwind forming the music of the royal stables, the '*Grande Ecurie*'. (From a very early period the music of the hunt, centred on the royal stables, was an important part of court music. As time progressed it came to embrace the general field of open-air ceremonial music.) Francis' great rival, King Henry VIII of England, was a distinguished amateur musician and a competent composer. In 1547 he had a collection of some 380 instruments: 78 transverse flutes, 77 mouth-

The repertoire

We must now turn to the repertoires of works written for these instruments. In fact few works were written for a specific instrument and there are many prefaces to early publications which reveal the freedom accorded to the player and describe the pieces as 'suitable for voices or instruments'. In practice, every polyphonic work (song, '*frottola*', madrigal, motet, fantasy or dance) could feature in this repertory on condition that each of the parts was ornamented according to the nature of the instrument executing it, the ornamentation which might be improvised usually being left to the skill of the interpreter. Thus methods for instruments published at this time not only gave instructions in basic technique, but also in the equally important matter of ornamentation. The tutors included that of Hans Gerle, for lutes and viols, *Musica Teutsch* (1532) and *Musica und Tablatur*

(1546); the *Fontegara* (1535) for recorders and the *Regola Rubertina* for viols (1542-43) of 'the very illustrious' Silvestro Ganassi del Fontego; and lastly, the *Tratado de glosas sobre clausulas* (1555) of the Spaniard, Diego Ortiz. In the treatises devoted to the viols the technical section gives valuable indications for fingering, interestingly compared with that of the lute, and on how to hold the bow; for flutes, we find advice on tonguing, on the different methods of sound production and variation, on 'attack' and also, of course, on the different fingerings in use. These last, applicable both to the transverse flute and to the recorders known as 'nine-hole' flutes, might also serve for the playing of other instruments with fingerholes such as cornetts, shawms, and crumhorns. In 1533 the French publisher Pierre Attaingnant brought out two books of songs in which some were indicated as being suitable for one kind of flute or the other, while others were suitable for both. In their presentation, neither of these two collections, which were published in separate parts, differed in the slightest from those destined for the voice. Ornamentation was not written down but any competent player was expected to know the correct method of playing 'divisions' for his particular instrument.

According to Philibert Jambe de Fer, the viol was appreciated by 'gentlemen, merchants and other people of virtue' and, grouped in fours, sixes or eights, the instruments were praised for their extreme softness. Ganassi, in his method for the instrument, also dealt with the polyphonic technique of performance on the solo viol. Known as 'lyra viol' playing, this was extremely popular in England in the 17th century, and even gave rise to a new member of the viol family, somewhat smaller than the bass viol, which was often played across the knees and plucked in the manner of a guitar or lute. The *viola da braccio*, known from the mid-16th century as the violin, was still treated with a certain disdain until the later years of the century, being considered as suitable for 'dance or mummery', and its 'harsh' sound was condemned by some writers.

The growth of ensembles

During the 16th century instrumental ensembles tended to grow larger and the 'broken' consorts more diverse than previously, but, as might be expected, the principle that the melody line be carried by a sustaining instrument was maintained. This function might be performed by a recorder, flute or cornett, the intermediary parts being given to instruments with interrupted sonorities such as lutes, harps, or spinets, which were often supported by chamber organs with one or two stops – bourdon and flute. Ensembles of this kind, which might be formed by amateurs or professionals, were common throughout Europe. The painter called the Master of the Half-Lengths painted a charming scene representing three young women, one singing, the others playing the transverse flute and the lute, performing a setting by Claudin de Sermisy of Clement Marot's words '*Jouissance vous donneray*'.

A broken consort of this period might consist of spinet, recorder, lute and bass viol to which a cornett and sackbut might sometimes be added. Often enough the vocal parts of a madrigal were doubled by instruments, or these played additional parts. Anton Francesco Doni, a contemporary writer, describes an ensemble of two male voices, tenor and bass, two cornetts, flute, two viols, lute and organ.

Of all the instruments of this period, the cornett was the most highly prized. Made of wood and with finger-holes like a recorder but played with a mouthpiece

above
An allegory of love – the seated figure is not King Death, despite appearances, but Cupid. Note the bagpipes used for a court dance.

left
Noblemen and ladies dancing to the music of the pipe and tabor, later to be limited to folk music.

right
When first introduced to Europe the lute was played with a plectrum, as here; finger plucking became general by the late 15th century.

below
A lyra da braccio made by Giovanni d'Andrea; note the drone strings off the fingerboard.

similar to a trumpet's, in the hands of a skilful player it has a uniquely sweet yet carrying tone. Lacking all the refinements of the modern wind instruments, the cornett demands a complete mastery of technique and there are only one or two modern performers who can meet these demands. But in the Renaissance period, the 'masters of the cornett' were renowned for their virtuosity and were the highest paid players of the orchestra. Indeed princes competed for their services, and Monteverdi, one of the greatest composers of that or any other age, complained bitterly that his stipend as court composer at Mantua was lower than that enjoyed by the cornettists in his orchestra. The cornett was often used to carry the treble line in consort with an ensemble of sackbuts, but the latter instruments might, in conjunction with the bass viol, assume a role similar to that of the continuo instruments in the 17th century. In this capacity they gave weight to the harpsichord, the continuo instrument par excellence, amplifying both its restricted range and its fleeting sonorities, and enriching the balance of the ensemble as a whole. In passing it should be noted that, since its invention in the 15th century as an improvement on the old medieval slide trumpet, the trombone has remained unaltered in its basic structure. Nevertheless, it is useful to retain the old name of sackbut for the early instrument, which had a narrower bore, a less markedly flaring bell and consequently a somewhat thinner tone than the modern orchestral trombone.

As time went on and particularly after 1560, instrumental ensembles became more important. From the early practice of allotting each part to one instrument with the general harmonic element being provided by the lute, organ or other keyboard instrument, things became more complex. A good example of this is the music which Lassus organised for the wedding of William of Bavaria to Renée de Lorraine at Munich in 1585, in which instruments were used on a large scale. A motet of eight parts was performed by three 'concerts' or groups of instruments: one of eight large flutes, one of eight viols and one of eight sackbuts; in addition there was a harpsichord and a theorbo. In another motet, this time of seven parts by Lassus himself, five cornetts, two sackbuts and an organ were used in conjunction with a chorus of twelve singers. This combination is very reminiscent of the Venetian practice which was to reach its high point in the *Sacrae Cantiones* of Giovanni Gabrieli.

The 'interludes and concerts' given in 1589 at Florence for the wedding of the grand duke Ferdinand de' Medici and Christine de Lorraine is another highly instructive instance of Renaissance instrumentation. For the first time this is indicated precisely, for each successive scene. Ornamented airs by Peri and Caccini were to be sung to the lute and chitarrone, others by Malvezzi, to the lute, the chitarrone and the bass *lyra da braccio* ('*arciviolata lyra*').

Nevertheless the principles of instrumentation had not greatly changed since the previous century. The treble was held by an instrument of flowing sonority such as the flute or violin. The intermediate parts were given to plucked strings and in many of the pieces three large lutes and three small lutes, with a single or double harp as occasion demanded, are scored for; in others, this ensemble is joined by a cittern, mandora, psaltery or chitarrone. This somewhat lightweight centre was reinforced in some pieces by tenor viols, while a sonorous background was assured by three chamber organs with eight- and four-foot bourdons (wood stops), two cornetts and four sackbuts. In some other pieces, a *viola bastarda* is added; this was a type of bass viol. The cornetts and sackbuts figured in purely instrumental '*sinfonie*' which served as overtures, and also in the ensembles accompanying certain of the choruses. There are clear-cut examples of calculated effects of 'instrumental colour-

ing'. Three female voices are accompanied by two *lyra da braccio*, a harp and sometimes, in certain sung episodes and popular types of dance (Cavalieri's final ballet), by two guitars, one 'Spanish', the other 'Neapolitan', and a tambourine with 'silver bells'.

Instrumental ensembles like those of the interludes, both varied and well balanced, were the true descendants of a long tradition, and that adopted by Monteverdi for *Orfeo* belonged to the same lineage.

The French fêtes of the second half of the 16th century, mostly organised under the auspices of Catherine de' Medici, also belonged to the same tradition. The most famous is the *ballet comique de la reine* given in 1581. The arrangement was made by an Italian, Balthazar de Beaujoyeux, but the words and music were those of members of the French palace academy. The instrumentation closely resembled that of the Florentine interludes but was far less precisely indicated. In both cases some forty instrumentalists were required. In the French ballets there were also soft-toned organs concealed in grottoes to 'intervene at the right place'. The violin family was also fully represented but it was excluded from the ensemble of the 'gilded vault' to which the major polyphonic works were devoted and was confined to the accompaniment of the ballets on the stage. Indeed this family of instruments was not to be secured in its place at the top of the musical hierarchy until very much later.

The beginnings of the instrumental forms

Such were some of the developments in Italian, French and German religious and secular music, and such were some of the ensembles of instruments and voices which were used as the 16th century advanced. At the end of the century, the passages for instruments alone were beginning to take on a degree of independence. Terms such as *ricercare*, *canzona da sonar*, *toccata* and *fantasia* came into regular use as designations of instrumental pieces; as yet they had no exclusive application and certainly must not be regarded as distinct 'forms', but they were indications that instrumental music was acquiring a new status, and during the 17th century instrumental forms were to emerge.

In the case of the fantasia, this process was most actively developed in England. The four-, five- and six-part viol fantasies of Dowland, Byrd and Gibbons, together with their late successors by Purcell are among the very finest works in the European tradition of instrumental music.

In England also the art of the broken consort found an able exponent in Thomas Morley. His remarkable *Consort Lessons* (1599) consist of a number of pieces written for an ensemble of six instruments, namely treble and bass viols, bass recorder, cittern, lute and pandora. The parts for the three melodic instruments describe harmoniously overlapping curves, and the cittern and pandora give a simple but effective harmonic support for the extremely ornate polyphony.

In Italy the instrumental *canzona* (*canzona da sonar*) was also flowering to perfection. Andrea Gabrieli had usually written for eight instruments, but his nephew Giovanni commonly employed as many as twenty or more. His *Sacrae Symphoniae* of 1597 include a *canzon in echo* for eight cornetts and two sackbuts, and the *sonata pian e forte* for violin, cornett and six sackbuts. The brilliance of the instrumental colouring, and the splendour of these wind instruments as they resounded below the vaults of San Marco fired the imagination of Heinrich Schutz, and the influence of Gabrieli is apparent in much of the work of this German master.

Together with these new developments, dances continued to be an important part of the instrumental repertory. They were of two main kinds: airs for dancing that were played on the violin, the pipe and tabor, or a flageolet also accompanied by a drum, as we learn from the writings of Thoinot Arbeau (1588); secondly, *danceries*, which Arbeau describes as dancing airs that had been 'set to music', that is, arranged with a number of polyphonic parts. These *danceries* were played on 'violins, spinets, transverse and nine-hole flutes, shawms and all sorts of instruments'. The airs for dancing came within the province of the minstrels. The *danceries*, however, suitable for a quartet of shawms or an ensemble of cornetts and sackbuts, were taking on the aspect of works of art, to be heard rather than danced, and the dance 'suites' which became widespread throughout Europe in the 17th century were directly derived from them.

The art of the makers

In the 16th century the art of the instrument maker reached considerable heights. The stage of experiment was rapidly overcome with each new type, and to realise this we need only look at the wonderful *lyra da braccio* made by Giovanni Andrea da Verona, dated 1511, in the museum of Vienna, or the beautiful harpsichord by Jerome of Bologna (1521) in the Victoria and Albert Museum, London. It was Italy that led the field as it had done in the printing of music, closely followed by Germany. Among the greatest Italian makers of clavichords, spinets and harpsichords were Domenico de Pesaro, Francesco Hungaro (a Hungarian who worked at Padua and Venice), Giovanni Antonio Baffo, Bertolotti of Venice and Vitus de Transuntinis, who built an instrument closely resembling the enharmonic harpsichord of Nicolas Vicentino mentioned above. We should also remember the name of Giovanni Cellini (*c.* 1460-*c.* 1527), the father of Benvenuto, who, according to his son, built some remarkable wooden-piped organs and some of the most beautiful harpsichords ever created, as well as viols, lutes and harps.

In the late 16th century one of the greatest families of European instrument makers began work in the Netherlands. About 1580 Hans Ruckers began to produce keyboard instruments, modelled on the work of Italian workshops, which with those of his sons Johannes and Andries made their workshops in Antwerp famous. The finest lutes, it would seem, were those made by the Germans Laux Maler, Laux Posch, Hans Frey, Georg Gerle and Magnus Tieffenbrucker in the mid-16th century. They were highly prized by contemporary musicians and collectors and still hold their reputation. After 1570, the Paduans, Venetians, Brescians and

above
A gentleman in an allegorical setting playing the bagpipes, an instrument that was to enjoy several fashionable revivals.

left
An early Renaissance instrument maker's shop; notice particularly the cymbals, straight trumpet and panpipes at the bottom right.

Romans created superb citterns, theorboes and chitarroni with ivory and ebony bodies and encrusted and engraved necks of exceptionally rich workmanship, while in Venice the workshops of Matteo and Giorgio Sella gained European fame for their keyboard instruments. In England John Rose of London created a new instrument, the wire stringed pandora, but the period of the greatest workmanship was in the 17th century. The end of the 16th century saw the manufacture of fine examples of the small organs with three or four stops known in Italy as *organetti*. They were used in ensembles rather than as solo instruments and combined a wooden bourdon with an eight-foot flute and a two-foot stop and sometimes, as in Italy, a reed, like that of the *pivette* (bagpipes) which was required for a sonata in the interludes of 1589.

Antonio Siciliano of Venice and Gaspar da Salo of Brescia have left us some of the most remarkable viols and violins of the period, and by this time the towns specialising in violin-making were already Cremona, the home of the great Amati family, and Brescia.

There does not appear to have been any one country specialising in the making of wind instruments in the 16th century. Soft and transverse flutes, recorders, shawms, cornetts, trumpets and sackbuts were made at many centres and were generally of uniformly high quality.

The growing market for instrumental music

The general popularity of instrumental music is perhaps indicated by the fact that, on average, French publishers issued tablatures for lutes and citterns and guitars in a first edition of 1,200 copies, whereas only about 500 were printed for vocal works. Such numbers indicate a large public, which would have consisted of professional musicians, 'maistres d'instruments de musique et luths', and enlightened amateurs. In common with other European centres, Paris had many workshops, each with its sign displayed in the street. On entering, the customer would find a wide selection of instruments displayed on little woollen rugs at prices within the reach even of those with only modest means. If we go back to the period preceding the financial crisis which afflicted Europe in about 1559, a pair of citterns, tenor and bass, cost little more than a sizeable oaken chest. For about half this sum, it was possible to buy a lute and its case. The firms of instrument makers varied greatly in importance. The largest represented a considerable capital investment and would employ numerous craftsmen. At his death, one maker left about 600 finished lutes and as many mandoras; another, 350 finished instruments and some forty in preparation, including 169 mandoras and 78 flutes. But as well as these giants there were many small family businesses, and somewhat larger enterprises with two or three apprentice assistants.

Whereas the professionals were the best buyers (it has been calculated that each used on average at least ten instruments), many instruments were also bought by private individuals for their own pleasure. The Parisians, for example, preferred rebecs made according to the 'manner' of Cambrai, lutes in the 'manner' of Flanders, Germany, Venice, Padua and even Lyons, as well as the great centres of Cremona and Brescia.

An apprentice would reckon to spend about four to six years with his master and would travel far to serve with a famous maker. Englishmen went to Paris and Parisian apprentices to the trade of flute maker often went to Lyons, at least up to about 1540. After that date, there was a flourishing trade in Paris in flutes, recorders and shawms, which came to be sold in sets.

The 16th century had been an extraordinarily fertile period in the history of instrument making. It was an age of experiment and research in every direction. New types were invented, experiments were constantly being made to obtain greater perfection in intonation and tone quality and theoreticians collaborated with the makers. This activity continued into the early 1600s but, as was to be expected, this intensive period of exploration was followed by one of consolidation. During the 17th century, apart from the important improvements made in the design of certain of the woodwind instruments, the trend was towards selection and standardisation.

above
The beautifully decorated back of a bass viol.

right
A double-manual harpsichord and a spinet built into the same case.

The Franco-Flemish school

The area now covered by the north-eastern corner of France, Belgium and Luxembourg may be regarded as the powerhouse of European music during the 15th and 16th centuries. The cultural environment of the region was largely French, and the major political unit, the state of the dukes of Burgundy, was ruled by a line of French dukes, but, as we have seen, in political terms Burgundy was drawing away from France. Although in musical terms it is perhaps a little artificial to speak of a distinct 'Burgundian' school, nevertheless these great Franco-Flemish composers evolved an increasingly international musical style in which the *ars nova* of France played a subsidiary role to the inspiration of Italian and English music. Of these two traditions the latter exerted considerable influence on the Continent during the first half of the century, while the second became increasingly important as the Rome of the renewed papacy established itself as one of the major musical centres of Europe.

We should remember that there had been commercial exchanges between Flanders and Italy since the 12th century and that intellectual and artistic activity was already flourishing at that time. Although these musicians have customarily been called 'Franco-Flemish' or 'Netherlandish' they rarely remained in their own country. They were truly international artists, constantly voyaging on the roads of France, Italy, Spain or Germany. They were very conscious of the exchanges of ideas and influences that transcended all national frontiers, and they trained pupils in far-off countries, thus creating the traditions of the golden age of vocal and instrumental counterpoint.

We have said how little the 14th century had esteemed liturgic, or at any rate religious, inspiration, and how superbly isolated Guillaume de Machaut's *Notre-Dame* mass was despite the appeal of earlier works like the 'Tournai' mass. But even if the superiority of profane music was overwhelming, sacred music was by no means exhausted; at the end of the century, when sacred music again featured largely in manuscripts, it gave proof of a noticeable development.

After its profane career during the 13th and 14th centuries, the motet showed a decided tendency to return to the Church. Latin motets became increasingly numerous and although inspiration was still not completely religious, it turned towards the celebration of important events, which were often now unconnected with the life of the Church; while the mass, although it had not yet produced the great unitary ensembles that were to be so common during Dufay's generation, gradually fixed the procedures for the composition of each of its constituent sections.

English and Italian influences

The Franco-Flemish composers certainly felt the influence of the Italian *ars nova* which, unlike the French style, did not neglect religious inspiration. Its intuitive character rejected the abstract constructions that were so sought after by the French musicians. The art of the Italian composers of the 14th century, led by Landini, was characterised by its smoothness, its naturalism and its 'abandonment to music'. After Landini's death in 1397 there was a brief reversion to French influences, despite their decadent aspects. But thanks to Jean Cigogne, a native of Liège who had emigrated to Italy and Italianised his name to Ciconia, Italian music regained its former simplicity, later to be such a revelation to the young Dufay.

The early 15th century also saw the development in England of a school of predominantly religious music. The Old Hall manuscript, which dates from about 1420, illustrates the priority held by religious music, in contrast to the music of the Continent. The two great names in this school were those of Leonel Power and John Dunstable. Their works were distinguished by the decorative quality, fine workmanship and abundant embellishments of their ample melodies, and also by their rich, mellow harmony, which carefully avoided any unprepared discords and had a sweet euphony which contrasted strongly with the harshness of French *ars nova*. But the main interest of their work lay in the use, for the first time, of one and the same *cantus firmus* to

Duke Philip the Good of Burgundy, one of the most magnificent of 15th century patrons of the arts, painted by the great Rogier van der Weyden.

bind together all the parts of the mass. Thus developed a form known as the cyclic mass, which was to be of immense importance in the history of polyphonic music.

Possibilities for encounters between English and French musicians were multiplied by the Hundred Years War. The English presence on French soil was not limited to military occupation. Artists and musicians came flocking to France. Dunstable himself was chaplain to Henry V's brother, the duke of Bedford, who after the king's death became English regent in France. The court of Burgundy especially was the melting-pot in which all the various musical styles intermingled. The Englishmen who worked there were numerous and their talent must have been greatly appreciated since one of them, Robert Morton, taught counterpoint to the future duke, Charles the Rash. It is highly likely that it was here that Dufay first became acquainted with the English style.

Dufay

With the death of Machaut in 1377 French music lost its leader and the next great master of international stature in Continental Europe was to be Guillaume Dufay, born about the year 1400, probably in the region of the town of Cambrai. The young musician, like many after him, began his career in the famous choir school of Cambrai, but before he was twenty he had already journeyed to Italy. Here he was in the service of the Malatesta family of Rimini and Pesaro and the earliest known

of his 200 odd surviving works is the vocal and instrumental composition, *Vasilissa* (Greek 'queen'), *ergo gaude*, written to celebrate the departure of Cleofe Malatesta for Constantinople to marry a Byzantine prince in 1420. Dufay seems to have remained in Italy for another thirteen years, during which time he served for a while in the papal chapel of Eugenius IV. He is next found at the court of Savoy, but his connection with the city of the popes continued although he received his income from a prebend at his '*alma mater*', Cambrai cathedral. Like so many of his contemporaries, Dufay led a cosmopolitan life, serving both the dukes of Savoy and the dukes of Burgundy, travelling much in Central Europe and enjoying a huge international reputation. He earned the respect not only of fellow composers like the Italian Antonio Squarcialupi, but also of princes, amongst whom one of the most illustrious was Lorenzo de' Medici. He died in November 1474 at Cambrai where he had spent much of the later period of his life.

In the 15th century religious music regained much of the prestige it had enjoyed prior to the *ars nova* style of the 14th. The reasons for this are by no means fully understood but several factors contributed. The declining prestige of the Church, hastened by forty years of papal schism, together perhaps with the terrible awareness of human mortality which was etched into the European mentality by the Black Death in the 1340s, bred a new movement of popular piety. One of the most significant manifestations of this was the Brethren of the Common Life, which originated in the Low Countries with the mysticism of Jan Van Ruysbroeck in the 1380s and came to be known as Devotia Moderna. Even more widespread was the fervour for the Marian cult. In Italy,

as we shall see, this popular piety, stimulated by the preaching of such men as S. Bernardino of Siena, gave rise to a type of religious song known as *laude*, while composers themselves were much affected by it. Dufay's little masterpiece *Vergine bella* is a good example. Other possible causes for the revival of religious music as such are to be found in the renewed importance of the papal chapel itself as a musical centre and, perhaps most important of all, the fact that for professional musicians the most challenging formal development of the age was the exclusively ecclesiastical form of the cyclic mass.

No matter what the reasons were, religious music held a pre-eminent place in Dufay's work. It is worth noting that, as his career progressed, Dufay gradually turned from song to devote himself to liturgic music. But as early as his first stay in Italy, he was experimenting in this domain with the mass *Sine nomine* in three parts, which dates from about 1420. This early work by Dufay is somewhat old fashioned; it does not have a *cantus firmus* and shows other points of relationship with the 14th-century works composed for the chapel of Avignon. For example, Dufay had not yet freed himself from the angular style of *ars nova*. But from the start we can detect his determination to achieve unity between the various sections of the mass, founded, in this early instance, on a close melodic and rhythmic kinship. The *Sancti Jacobi* mass illustrated Dufay's desire to make experiments in the elaboration of the fixed framework of the mass. To the parts of the Ordinary, Dufay added elements of the Proper, but he still chose different *cantus firmi* for different parts.

It was only in his later masses that Dufay fully exploited the immense artistic possibilities of uniting the various parts of the mass with a single *cantus firmus*. Although such an innovation might appear to us to be merely logical, we must not forget how revolutionary it was at the time and the consequences springing from it. Earlier attempts at unification had not succeeded in breaking the autonomous nature of the various parts. The creation of the unitary mass, in so far as it marked the arrival of the first major unitary musical form of major dimensions, had immense significance for the history of music.

Like Machaut's *Notre-Dame* mass and early English examples, Dufay's great ensembles used four voices. However, whereas the English composers placed the *cantus firmus* in the bottom part, Dufay gave it to the third voice. The vocal quartet was fairly clearly subdivided into groups of two voices of very differing character and exchanges between them were nonexistent. The two lower voices, written in long values, rarely departed from a hieratic strictness, while the upper voices, written in much shorter values, had a pronounced melodic form; imitations, which were still infrequent, were only between the upper voices.

The *Caput* mass is certainly Dufay's first unitary cyclical work. The English origin of the *cantus firmus* (from the Sarum rite), and the absence of the Kyrie in the oldest version, in conformity with the English practice, are eloquent testimony to Dufay's indebtedness to English composers for the formal technique of the cyclic tenor. As for the mass *Se la face ay pale*, it may perhaps be the first mass to have been composed with a profane theme. But it is in his last three masses, *Ecce ancilla Domini*, *L'Homme armé* and *Ave Regina coelorum*, all three works of his old age, that Dufay shows the greatest mastery and perfection.

To give still greater unity to his work, Dufay used the 'head motif'. The device, which was not new, consisted of the use of a short two- or three-bar figure which was repeated at intervals at the beginning of important phrases in the upper voices. Dufay seems to have attached great importance to it since, in his last masses, this head motif became ampler and was used with great subtlety.

However, in his music there is a pretty strict division of function between the *superius*, or upper part, and the tenor, or third part. The *cantus firmus* was only very rarely given to any other voice than the tenor, and the head motif was almost exclusively confined to the *superius*. Dufay's immediate successors, chief among them Johannes Ockeghem, were to integrate the four parts by giving both head motif and *cantus firmus* to all the voices with increasing freedom. Nevertheless we can only admire the mastery with which Dufay constructed works of such unprecedented breadth and melodic suppleness. This was one of his essential contributions to the music of succeeding generations.

His contribution to liturgical music was not limited to masses, but before we go on to his motets we must first mention his immensely popular hymns and three-part sequences, as well as his several Magnificats. In these works he used the new compositional device of *fauxbourdon*, which he may indeed have invented. Here again we can trace the influence of the English school since *fauxbourdon* was almost certainly an attempt to harness the euphonious harmonies of English discant, in which three voices improvised in a succession of six-three chords, for the purpose of formal composition. One of the most important distinctions between Dufay's *fauxbourdon* and English discant was that Dufay placed

A statuette of a Morris dancer, a popular form of entertainment in northern Europe.

right
A society lady playing a small
portative organ.

below
The Cloth Hall and Belfry, Bruges.
The splendours of Flemish late
Gothic surrounded the composers of
this school on every hand.

the melody in the top voice rather than the bottom voice.

The path taken by Dufay may perhaps be followed most easily in his motets. From the motet with isorhythmic tenor to the freer compositions that opened the way for the 16th-century motet, the degree of evolution was remarkable. In his work *Vasilissa, ergo gaude*, Dufay was inspired by the *ars nova* aesthetic, using a liturgic tenor in an angular style. But even more remarkable were his religious, if not liturgic, motets. He seems to have abandoned the form of the isorhythmic motet from about 1450 and henceforth, free from the old constraints, he gradually elaborated the aesthetic of the new style of motet. The combination of French and Latin texts became increasingly rare and the language became unified in favour of Latin. As the unity of the text became gradually established so the religious character of the work became more important. Finally, even though the *cantus firmus* was still present, it no longer played the part of the fundamental voice; later it tended to be omitted altogether. *Vergine bella*, Dufay's moving prayer to the Virgin set to the words of Petrarch, is an example and does not employ *cantus firmus*. It was in these motets that had been freed from imposed themes, even more perhaps than in his songs, in which a form was obligatory, that Dufay displayed a hitherto unprecedented lyric vein and the treasures of his extremely rich and vibrant sensibility.

Although the music of the transitional period between the death of Machaut and about 1420 apparently remained faithful to the style and the genres made famous by Machaut, signs of an evolution which were profoundly to change musical aesthetics had already begun to appear. Machaut had been interested in the *ballade* form. His successors also devoted themselves to it but they so increased its complexity that taste gradually moved towards the simpler *rondeau*.

In Italy Dufay was able to meet other French musicians who had emigrated there, like Ciconia and Hugo de Lantins, many of whose songs, like the delicate *Pour resjouir la compaignie*, so obviously displayed Dufay's influence in the careful way it made use of imitation between the two trebles.

In the field of song as in that of church music Dufay reveals himself a master. He practised all the genres in use in his time, as well as composing *ballades*, a form whose popularity was gradually declining. But his great triumph was in the *rondeau*: a more spacious *rondeau* than that of the 14th century, and one that usually had sixteen lines. They varied greatly in their inspiration: from the merry spirit of *He! Compaignons* to the sentimental richness of *Adieu m'amour*, which already suggested Ockeghem's manner, by way of the gracious spirit of such courtly pieces as *Pourray-je avoir vostre mercy*. But Dufay did not feel in the least obliged to submit to tradition; he composed without restraint, and with a verve, gaiety and warmth of human feeling far removed from the erudite ratiocinations of *ars nova*.

The names and works of many of Dufay's French and Burgundian predecessors and contemporaries are known to us, notably that of Hugo de Lantins, born in the bishopric of Liège and practising early in the 15th century at Venice. But the only Continental master who could rival the great Dufay, and then only in the field of secular music, was his exact contemporary and friend, Gilles de Binche, known as Binchois. This exquisitely talented musician was born at Mons in the county of Hainaut about the year 1400. Through the elaborate dynastic marriage policy of the dukes of Burgundy, Binchois' homeland became part of their growing state in the 1420s, and from about 1430 probably till his death in 1460 he made a successful career in the service of the great dukes. Despite his immense reputation during his lifetime and in the following century little is known about him, but it appears that as a young man he was for a time a soldier before taking clerical orders; we know that he was also in the service of the earl of Suffolk at Paris during the year 1424 and possibly longer.

Binchois' fame rested on his secular compositions, but settings of sections of the mass by him survive, as do a number of hymns, Magnificats and a Te Deum. It would seem that he never attempted the major compositional exercise represented by the cyclic masses of his great contemporary, nor in the surviving mass sections by him do we even find the use of the *cantus firmus* device; where he does use plainsong themes they are freely paraphrased and usually given to the upper voice. As we might expect of a composer renowned for his *chansons*, his greatest success in religious compositions is in the shorter mass-sections, such as the Kyrie, Sanctus and Agnus Dei, and in the hymns where he uses the *fauxbourdon* technique described above and also employs the intervals of the third and the sixth, first made 'respectable' by the English school. It is worth noting that Binchois' religious style was often similar to that of his *chansons*, indeed the almost seductive character of one Agnus Dei by him has melodic inflexions and cadences that would not have been out of place in a profane composition. Some of his motets such as his *Ave Regina coelorum* are extremely beautiful, and in his admirable Pentecostal hymn he wrote highly successful responses between high and low voices.

In his secular compositions Binchois drew on the poems of such writers as Charles, Duke of Orleans, Christine de Pisan, Alain Chartier and other lyricists in favour at the Burgundian court. The immense popularity of his *chansons*, *ballades* and *rondeaux* rested on the grace and suppleness of their melodies, for they were for the most part technically unpretentious. At their best, however, as for example in the four-part *Filles à marier*, an exquisite and lively admonition to young girls, they are without equal in their field. Other outstanding examples are *De plus en plus se renouvelle*, with a magnificent and spacious melodic line and *Triste plaisir et douloureuse joye*, which touchingly expresses the melancholy latent in Chartier's text.

Binchois displayed a delicate mastery in his chosen field, but his inspiration was less varied than that of Dufay. He never travelled and thus never renewed his essentially courtly style. The movement of the parts in his work was more rigid than Dufay's, and the admittedly gracious and supple melodies are often supported by somewhat unvocal lower parts which may well have been performed by instruments. But we should note that in Dufay's as in Binchois' work the musical phrase carefully respected the division of the lines and was modelled upon it. Each line carried its melody, and submission to the poetic context was still so great that repetitions of words or groups of words were very rare.

Johannes Ockeghem

The following generation, led by its most distinguished representative, Ockeghem, was to take up and develop the heritage of the age of Dufay. Whereas Dufay's church music, and particularly his masses, sometimes suffer from a certain lack of human warmth, Ockeghem's works are marked by their expressive and emotive intensity.

He was born in Hainaut about 1420 and in his mid-twenties was for a brief period a member of the choir of Antwerp Cathedral. But soon after this he left the territories of the duke of Burgundy, going first to work in the chapel of the duke of Bourbon and then, from 1454, serving the kings of France until his death, about 1495,

at Tours. He enjoyed the esteem of his royal masters, becoming master of the royal chapel and even treasurer of the great abbey of St Martin at Tours, and the respect and affection of his fellow musicians, as the various laments and epitaphs written for him testify. His known compositions comprise some twenty *chansons*, fourteen masses, of which eleven are complete, a requiem mass and about ten motets, and his complete output seems to have been remarkably small for a composer with such a vast reputation. However, as will be seen, the quality of that music fully justified the admiration which his contemporaries had for him and gives the lie to the belief, common until recent years, that Ockeghem was notable chiefly for the number of his pupils and the arid academicism of his work.

Everything that we know about him indicates that Ockeghem's most important work was done in the field of religious music and it is above all in his masses that his genius stands fully revealed. In general the overall polyphonic texture of his work is quite different in character from that of Dufay. In Dufay's four-part works there is a fairly strict distinction between the upper two parts and the more slow-moving lower parts. In the work of Ockeghem the parts become increasingly similar in character and function. The *cantus firmus*,

Johannes Ockeghem surrounded by a group of singers.

from being the foundation on which the composer built his music, might now be heard in all the voices as the work proceeded. We are at the beginning of a revolution in musical thinking, and are moving from the concept of a safe and sure basic melody, a *cantus firmus* in its old strict sense, towards the much later idea of a generating theme which provides the germ of life for the musical development of all the parts of the piece. In other important respects Ockeghem evolved a musical texture which was much more homogeneous than that of his great predecessor. Both tenor and contra-tenor parts were given greater melodic and rhythmic freedom and his music, with that of Busnois to be studied next, offers the first examples in the work of a major composer of imitation in all parts. Together with the principle of the unifying theme, such as the *cantus firmus*, imitation was one of the most important devices developed by composers for giving coherence and unity to their increasingly elaborate structures. In the music of Dufay and his contemporaries the upper two parts had occasionally imitated phrases after one another, but the device was at a rudimentary stage and never extended to the other parts of the polyphony. But as the 15th century progressed two related developments made the extension of the practice possible and indeed necessary. These were the increasing equality of the melodic interest in all the parts and the widening of the sonorous range. In the music both of Busnois and of Ockeghem the bass voice is written lower relative to the other parts than had

The castle of the counts at Ghent, the scene of many splendid festivals.

previously been the practice, and with the resultant clarification of the lines of the four voices, as they pulled away from one another in pitch, imitation became more possible. In general we may say that whereas in the music of the earlier period the parts, while occupying roughly the same vocal register, had been distinguished by strongly marked differences of melodic treatment, now they enjoyed melodic equality but were differentiated by increasingly wide distinctions of pitch.

In the first decades of the 16th century the principle of imitation was more systematically developed by composers. In the work of Ockeghem its full possibilities are already apparent, and here is displayed the immense skill, versatility and audacity of his counterpoint. Yet Ockeghem's work was distinguished not so much by musical acrobatics as by the sovereign grace, naturalism and duration of melodies of an unprecedented breadth as well as by the fluidity of a polyphony which never betrayed either the effort behind it or the procedure underlying it.

None of the religious compositions of his mature period has less than four parts. They may be based on a liturgic *cantus firmus*, like the mass *Ecce ancilla Domini* and the rather archaic *Caput* mass or, as is more frequently the case, on a profane *cantus firmus*, like the mass on the perennially popular tune *L'Homme armé*. Alternatively the base theme may be an original one, as in the masses *Cuiusvis toni* and *Prolationum*, in which the author gave himself up to the most difficult technical speculations. In all these works we can only admire the quality of the lyricism and the power of conception which enabled Ockeghem to produce great masterpieces while constantly extending the language of polyphony. The *Missa Prolationum* contains, for example, the first canon cycle, a device to be used later by both Palestrina and Bach. In his *cantus firmus* masses he exercised characteristic imagination on the now established technique in new and adventurous ways; a fine example is the *Missa Forseulement*, in which the *cantus firmus* is provided by both the upper part and the tenor of one of his own *rondeaux*.

Of Ockeghem's nine motets, most were written to antiphons to the Virgin. In these, plainsong material is used but is paraphrased with characteristic originality, while the *Gaude Maria*, a late work, shows the ageing composer fully alive to the work of the younger generation, employing imitation between pairs of voices. We should also mention the curious *Ut heremita solus* in four parts: a vast and rather mysterious paraphrase with an unidentified tenor frequently repeated with long notes.

The mighty genius of Ockeghem found its fullest scope in the great religious works here briefly reviewed, but the few surviving *chansons* reveal his considerable talents in the field of secular composition and were much admired by his contemporaries and long after. They include a setting of John Dunstable's beautiful *O rosa bella* and the delightful *L'autre d'antan*, but he seems to have preferred to work in a more subdued vein and inclined towards lyrics which sang of grief and melancholy such as the *rondeau*, *Forseulement l'attente*, used in the mass referred to above. Just as his religious music is marked by the grandeur and power of its expression, so the most remarkable characteristic of these secular works is their emotional intensity.

But the finest composer of secular music of Ockeghem's generation was Antoine de Busnes, called Busnois. Little is known of his life, but it is recorded that he was in the service of Charles the Bold before the latter acceded to the dukedom of Burgundy in 1470; that although a court musician he was a priest and held many church appointments, and that he was on the staff of the church of St Sauveur of Bruges at the time of his death in 1492. Only a few of his religious compositions survive. They include a mass on the popular song *L'Homme armé*, which although it makes interesting use of canon shows nothing of the contrapuntal ingenuity of Ockeghem, confining the *cantus firmus* for the most part to the tenor. It is perhaps worth noting that in this piece both the part above the tenor and that below it are marked '*contra*'. Here we seem to have the first move towards the nomenclature of the second and fourth parts which has now become standard: the *contratenor altus*, the higher of the two, was soon to become shortened to 'alto'; the *contratenor bassus* to 'bass'. Of Busnois' other religious works we need only mention a motet (*c.* 1465) dedicated to Ockeghem, who was possibly his teacher, and a four-part *Regina coeli* in which he again makes use of canon.

His secular works included *chansons*, a *ballade* in Flemish and *rondeaux*. Their immense popularity is demonstrated by their wide diffusion in contemporary French, German and Italian manuscripts, while his famous and beautiful Italian song *Fortunata desperata* served as a *cantus firmus* for masses by Josquin des Prez and Obrecht. His preferred theme was love and, besides drawing on the work of contemporary poets, he also wrote his own texts, which often are devoted to the praise of his mistress Jacqueline. His melodies are graceful and spontaneous, and their spirit, while often joyful, could also be both melancholy and moving, as in the *chanson*, *Ha! que vile*. In these works the upper part holds the greatest musical interest; nevertheless the polyphony displays a homogeneity in keeping with contemporary developments in religious music, but unusual and interesting in secular works.

Josquin des Prez

With this great name we reach the culmination of medieval musical art, and indeed one of the high points in all music. His greatness was recognised in his lifetime and was confirmed by the esteem in which his works continued to be held after his death. An abundance of copies, transcriptions and new editions of his work continued to be published up to the 17th century. Indeed such was his legendary stature that long after his music had ceased to be performed he is mentioned with respect

by the late 18th-century English historian of music, Sir John Hawkins.

He was born probably in Hainaut about the year 1445, and began his career as a choir boy at St Quentin. But although he sprang from the fertile musical soil of the Franco-Flemish region, which is the subject of this chapter, he soon followed the example of many of his great predecessors from the region, and went as a youth to Italy, serving at the court of Milan. Then, from 1486 to about 1494, he served at the papal court. In the last years of the 15th century he worked at Ferrara, but from 1503 to 1515 he was composer to the court of Louis XII of France. After the king's death, he retired first to Brussels and then to Condé, where he lived until his death in 1521.

The masses and motets

Like his great predecessors, Dufay and Ockeghem, Josquin produced some of his finest music in his polyphonic masses. But he did not limit himself to the mass, and indeed the most exalted flights of his genius are found in his motets. He helped to establish the rules for this genre which, outside France at any rate, was to have a great future.

A few early masses by Josquin show their dependence on earlier techniques. As in Dufay's masses, the profane tenor is not integrated into the polyphony of his mass *Hercules, dux Ferrariae*. For the main part, the tenor remains alien to the melodic context. The rigidity of the

below left
Charles the Bold, the last of the magnificent dukes of Burgundy and himself a lover of music. The portrait is by Van der Weyden.

below
The figure on the right in this allegorical scene is thought to be Josquin des Prez, perhaps the greatest of the masters of the Franco-Flemish school.

above
A canon by Josquin.

right
Flemish tapestries were famed throughout Europe; in this detail from the Triumph of the Church *the artist has depicted a number of early Renaissance instruments.*

theme and the search for an absolute symmetry are largely responsible for the impression of archaism given by this mass.

But this sort of composition was exceptional in Josquin's work. Although he did not hesitate to adopt any of the procedures used by his predecessors and even accentuated them, he followed Ockeghem by directing all his efforts towards a total fusion of the *cantus firmus* into the musical texture. This endeavour, which is already apparent in one of his first masses, *Ave maris stella,* was to be continued without a break right up to the great achievements of his mature period, the masses *De Beata Virgine, Da pacem,* and *Mater Patris,* which provides an early example of the parody mass, and *Pange lingua,* in which a strict equality between the parts was at last achieved. Henceforth the *cantus firmus,* formerly a separate and identifiable line, is integrated into the body of the music. It may be found in any of the parts, between which imitation becomes increasingly free. In a word we may say that the spirit of the *cantus firmus* was respected rather than the letter.

In the mass *Pange lingua,* which is perhaps his most accomplished work, the theme is present everywhere, whether by its melodic curve or its characteristic intervals. Contemporary admiration for Josquin's masses is shown by the fact that the publisher, Petrucci, devoted no less than three books to them, reprinting the first two, whereas no other composer received more than a single printing of one volume.

Both mass and motet were inspired by the same spirit and started by borrowing styles that were very similar. It is Josquin who deserves the credit for having created the new motet, in which the old *cantus firmus* technique, while not brutally rejected, is supplanted by a 'pervading imitation' to produce an almost fugal texture. In Josquin's music the motet becomes a marvellously free form in which the entire range of religious sentiments can be expressed.

It is in the free motet that we may see the extent to which the tenor role had been modified. When necessary Josquin did not hesitate to use it, but it no longer appeared as the starting basis for the composition. It seemed rather to be inserted in the polyphonic texture like a quotation, and to have only suggested itself to the composer by virtue of its sense in relation to the subject being treated. It was thus that in the five-part *Stabat Mater* he made such conscious use of the profane song *Comme femme desconfortée* ('Like a grief stricken woman . . .') as the tenor.

Josquin's style

The intellectual enjoyment that Josquin derived from raising and solving the most complex problems of composition is obvious. But one of the most marked characteristics of his work is his constant desire to vary the choral effects. The full choir generally is reserved for short fragments while duets or trios ceaselessly alternate with the quartet. Josquin thus avoided a monotony that was not always absent from the works of the next generation who employed his techniques. The balance of the full choir and duo and trio sections is often arranged symmetrically but more interesting than this are the indications of a tonal sense which can be clearly detected in the chordal structure.

Finally we may notice Josquin's conscious exploitation of the 'programmatic' qualities of music, which to a later generation have become clichéd, but in his time were fresh and compelling. Thus an idea of descent, fall, humiliation or prostration was to be expressed by a descending inflexion or a fall in stages

Plate 11
Detail from the Memlinc altar-piece at Bruges.

Plate 12
A dance at the court of Henry IV
of France.

towards low notes, as in the five-part *Miserere*. Similarly, in his *De profundis*, Josquin wrote the psalmist's lament for the low voices alone. His resort to the trio in the fragments relating to the Trinity was also symbolic as was the unison for words like *unigenitus*. His evocation of *tribulatio* by means of sharpened notes and the way he described sentiments of joy or sadness by using major and minor chords was already in the spirit of the madrigal. The great and prolonged reputation enjoyed by Josquin's music has perhaps already been sufficiently stressed, but it is fitting to conclude this survey of his religious music with the view of an Italian of the late 1560s, who compared him to Michelangelo.

Yet Josquin has also justly been called the greatest *chanson* composer of his age. The claim is justified both by the variety of formal structure in his *chansons* and by the texture of their polyphony. With him the growing homogeneity of the polyphonic texture, already observed in Busnois, was finally achieved and the four-part setting became habitual. Like his many lesser contemporaries, Josquin wrote at first for three voices, as in most of the songs published by Petrucci in 1501 in the *Odhecaton*. But he very soon broke away from this manner and created a different type by making the song benefit from the technique that had been perfected in the motet. He made a definitive break away from the fixed forms of poetry, thus making possible the musical freedom implied by the repetition of words or groups of words and creating a greater freedom in the relations between the lines and the melody; secondly, he made four-part writing a standard practice and even introduced the quintet or sextet, unprecedented innovations; thirdly, he perfected uniformity of the polyphonic texture, which made possible the use of imitation throughout the parts.

Although he did not neglect such forms as the Italian *frottola* (e.g. *Il Grillo*, which was already completely harmonic), Josquin worked mainly in the field of the French *chanson*. His *chansons* were further characterised by their brevity, clarity and their use of more pronounced rhythms, which became typical of the genre. *Faulte d'argent* or *Basiés-moy* already suggested Josquin's style. But Josquin's *chansons*, like those of Ockeghem, were often imbued with a spirit of gravity which brought them close to the motet, as in the admirable *Déploration de Johannes Ockeghem*, which, with its sincere and heartrending accents, was one of the peaks of his secular achievements.

Jacob Obrecht

Obrecht was a Dutchman, his family stemming from the neighbourhood of Bergen-op-Zoom in Holland. He was born on St Cecilia's day in 1450 or 1451. Apart from brief periods of service at the court of Ferrara in Italy, he passed most of his career in the Low Countries and north-eastern France, working at Antwerp, Cambrai, Bruges, Bergen itself and also Utrecht, where as a young man in his mid-twenties he had the great humanist, Erasmus, as one of his choirboys. He returned to Italy at the end of his life and died of the plague at Ferrara in 1505.

In some respects Obrecht's music reveals a certain degree of conservatism in its techniques. This tendency is seen in some of his motets where the *cantus firmus* is given the long-drawn-out notes of an earlier age, and the composer makes comparatively little use of imitation. But Obrecht's genius is revealed most fully in his masses, and here, while the traditional technique of the *cantus firmus* is fundamental to the music, he shows fluency and mastery in the way in which he manipulates

and exploits the device. In the *Missa super Maria zart* on a German song to the Virgin, he divides the *cantus firmus* melody into twelve sections and only gives the whole of the melody at one point and that, the Agnus Dei, towards the end of the mass, so that it serves as a focus of climax. In other masses such as the *Ave Regina coelorum* he makes use of an ostinato effect, the lower voices at the end of the Credo repeating a carillon motif to the words *et resurrexit*; in others, among them the mass *Sub tuum praesidium*, he used several *cantus firmi*, so that the seven-part Agnus Dei employs three antiphons to the Virgin simultaneously. Some of Obrecht's most complex treatments are found in the masses on Hayne van Ghizeghem's *De tous biens plaine* and *Fortunata desperata* by Busnois. In these the *cantus firmus* is subject to the most elaborate deformations – for example the notes are given in reverse order, or in the order of their time values. Despite such highly intellectual games, which are comparable to, and may in some cases have inspired, the calculations of modern serial composers, Obrecht's religious works contain some of the finest examples of Renaissance polyphony both technically and aesthetically. He often reveals a somewhat conservative approach but, again in the *Missa Fortunata desperata*, which draws on all the parts of the original song for its material, an approach can be seen to the parody mass form which was to be so popular as the 16th century progressed. In addition to his twenty-five masses and thirty-one motets, Obrecht produced a number of songs, the majority of which are in Dutch. They give further examples of his great inventiveness and verve. They are often based on popular songs although some, without words, seem to have been especially written for instruments. One of the best-known of his secular works is the part song *La tortorella*, still popular with continental choral societies.

Lesser contemporaries of Josquin

One of the greatest of these was Heinrich Isaak (*c.* 1450–1517), by origin a Fleming, by inclination cosmopolitan and by employment in the later years of his life, a German. Indeed, although his career up to his mid-forties lay largely at the court of Lorenzo de' Medici in Florence, Isaak's contribution to German music during the last twenty years of his life as court composer to the Emperor Maximilian I was so considerable that he was once thought to be a German by origin. In consequence his music is treated in the chapter on German music.

Another leading composer, once thought to be German but probably of Flemish origin, was Alexander Agricola. He was a follower of Josquin, whom he had met in Italy, and he had worked at Milan in the service of the Duke Galeazzo Maria Sforza from 1471 to 1474. In 1500 he was 'chaplain and singer' of Philip the Handsome, the Habsburg duke of Burgundy, whom he accompanied to Luxembourg, Paris and Spain. There he died at the age of sixty, leaving a considerable number of profane and religious works which are to be admired for their richness of melody, their skilful scoring and their variety of inspiration.

Gaspar van Weerbecke was a native of Oudenarde and a cleric in Tournai, and was invited to Milan in 1472 to be a member of the chapel that the Sforza duke had just founded. He soon became its director and brought Josquin there. Gaspar was later a papal chorister and then served Philip the Handsome; he returned to Rome in 1499 and remained there until 1509. His known works include six masses, five of these being distinguished by publication in a one-volume edition by Petrucci, who also published a number of

Plate 13
A beautifully preserved positive organ from the late 16th century. Note the gravity bellows, the two stops to the right of the keyboard and the fact that the instrument was designed to be stood on a table. This unusual instrument, designed with the characteristic. square shoulders of the violin, was built with a number of sympathetic strings, in the manner of a viola d'amore.

his motets. The mass *Princesse d'amourettes* is distinguished by the breadth of the melody, and the constant renewal of inspiration in the motets reveals a churchman who was used to translating liturgical texts with a pious and intelligent degree of emotion.

Johannes Ghiselin, also called Verbonnet, pursued part of his career in Italy. He was at the court of Duke Hercule d'Este at Ferrara in 1491, and in 1503, after returning to his own country, he served the guild of Notre Dame at Bergen-op-Zoom. He wrote masses based on songs, and in his motets a harmonic style often appeared in opposition to passages written in counterpoint.

Marbriano de Orto was dean of Ste Gertrude at Nivelles, where he was buried in 1529. He was a

member of the pontifical chapel, a chorister of Philip the Handsome, and from 1515 he was the first chaplain to the Archduke Charles (the future emperor, Charles V). In 1505 Petrucci devoted a book to masses, and, in 1506, another book to his Lamentations. He skilfully cultivated the art of the *cantus firmus* mass, and his motets had variety, expressiveness and fervour, while his secular works include a moving four-part lament on the death of Dido, based on a passage in the Aeneid.

Pierre de La Rue (1450?–1518) was one of the greatest of Josquin's contemporaries. Born probably at Tournai, he spent much of his life in the service of Philip the Handsome, and, after his death, that of his wife Margaret, regent for the Habsburg power in the Low Countries. De La Rue left thirty-six masses,

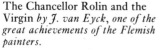

The Chancellor Rolin and the Virgin *by J. van Eyck, one of the great achievements of the Flemish painters.*

thirty-seven motets, a fine Requiem and a number of secular pieces. Most of his masses were of the traditional *cantus firmus* type with the tenor rendered in long notes while the other voices were written with greater animation. Like Obrecht, De La Rue often contrasted two duet voices, one in a high register, the other in a low register, to the ensemble of the voices. In his four-part mass *Ave Maria*, a fifth part was introduced in the Credo to render the antiphon on which the whole work was based in long notes. In general, the melodic curve had breadth, though it is often divided into incidental sections in canon.

The last of these Franco-Flemish contemporaries of Josquin to be mentioned here is Loyset Compère, a native of the St Quentin region, who died in that town in 1518. His style, in his masses, motets and in his secular works, shows many characteristics of an earlier generation, and in many ways he belongs more to the age of Busnois and Ockeghem than that of Josquin.

The 16th century

During this period the Franco-Flemish region of our present study continued to produce a stream of master musicians who worked far from their homelands. Many, like Willaert or Cypriano de Rore, fertilised the field of Italian music, while Philip de Monte and the mighty Lassus contributed their genius to the music of the empire – their work is dealt with, therefore, in the chapters on Italian and German music respectively. But there was also a host of other talented musicians. Jacobus Kerle (1532–91), born at Ypres, spent his working life between Italy, Prague and Augsburg; Jacob Vaet (1536–67), from Courtrai, was de Monte's predecessor at the imperial chapel; Pierre de Mandricourt, a native of Béthune, died in the service of Philip II of Spain; Giaches de Wert, from Antwerp, went to Italy while still a youth and stayed there, serving at the court of Mantua from 1564 until 1590. In addition to these there were also three major figures: Nicolas Gombert, Clemens non Papa and Thomas Crequillon.

Nicolas Gombert, born in southern Flanders towards the end of the 15th century, was held to be a disciple of Josquin, in whose memory he composed a lament. From 1525 to 1540 he was master of the children of the chapel of Charles V, whom he followed to Madrid. He next came to Tournai where he was made a canon. A prolific composer, he wrote ten masses, eight Magnificats, 160 motets and no less than one hundred finely wrought secular *chansons*. Among the motets we should mention the *Vita dulcedo*, an exquisite prayer to the Virgin. In the *Diversi diversa orant*, the voices sang the four antiphons of the liturgical years, and his *Pater noster* was long famous. In his music Gombert shows a preoccupation with, and mastery of, the procedures of counterpoint, demonstrating a special predilection for imitation at very close intervals.

Clemens non Papa, or to give him his real name, Jacques Clément, seems to have taken the nick-name 'non Papa' to distinguish himself from the poet Jacobus Papa, his contemporary. Jacques Clément was choir master at St-Donatien at Bruges and died in about 1558 at Dixmude. He was endowed with a rare facility for composition and left 158 motets of four to seven parts, parody masses and songs. Particularly outstanding among this enormous production were his profoundly felt lamentation, *Vox in Rama audita est*, the motet to the Virgin, *Maria vernans rosa* and another dedicated to Saint Barbara, *Ave Martyr gloriosa*; while particularly popular in his own day were the *Souterliede heus*, a collection of little songs from the Psalter based in many cases on Dutch folk songs and designed to be sung in the home. The best of Clément's work already heralded the music of Roland de Lassus, and even Palestrina; his music is distinguished by its enormous texture and its happy use of word painting.

Thomas Crequillon succeeded Gombert in the chapel of Charles V and aimed at the same ideal in his religious music. He was similarly prolific and left behind him sixteen four- to six-part masses, 116 motets, two cycles of Lamentations and numerous *chansons*. He was canon of Béthune when he died in about 1557.

Sweelinck

The last great composer from this region until the 20th century was the Dutchman Jan Pieterszoon Sweelinck. He was the son of an organist and was born at Deventer in 1562. He went to Amsterdam when his father was appointed to the great organ of the Oude Kerk. After the death of his father in 1573, Jan inherited his post and kept it for forty-eight years.

He spent his life uneventfully at Amsterdam. He was a zealous composer and also one of the greatest masters of the organ. He was also a highly renowned teacher and pupils came to him from every country. He trained the best German musicians and his son, Dirk, who had been born in Amsterdam in 1599, succeeded him in 1621 in the organ-loft of the Oude Kerk.

Jan Pieterszoon's works for organ and keyboard have survived entirely in manuscript. But between 1592 and 1619 his vocal compositions were published in Antwerp, Amsterdam, Haarlem, Leyden, Berlin and Hamburg. His imposing body of works includes 22 French *chansons*, 4 Italian madrigals, a collection of French and Italian rhymes, 7 canons to Latin words, 153 *Psalms of David* in the French version of Clément Marot and Theodore Bèze, 3 *Epithalamia* to Latin texts and 37 *Cantiones sacrae* or Latin motets which featured the intervention of a continuo bass. The complete works of Sweelinck were published between 1895 and 1902.

Sweelinck was a musician of cultivated mind and composed in every kind of vocal music that was in vogue at the time, writing to French, Dutch, German, Italian and Latin texts. In his motets he combined his mastery of counterpoint with deep religious inspiration and, in his secular pieces, with fantasy and sentiment.

In his instrumental work, which was largely composed of organ pieces, Sweelinck accomplished a magnificent synthesis between the variation technique of the English virginalists and the brilliant style of the Italian organists. He had known emigré English composers such as Peter Philips and John Bull and, on the other hand, he knew the works of Claudio Merulo and Giovanni Gabrieli, which were circulating everywhere throughout the Netherlands.

It was Sweelinck's achievement to have introduced a new cohesiveness of organisation into keyboard music and to have prepared the way for the sublime achievements of the German organists. Sweelinck composed his contrapuntal fantasies in three or five parts, treating his theme in long notes at first, and then in increasingly reduced diminutions. His *Fantasias in the manner of an Echo* are still popular because of the possibilities of varied registrations that they offer the organist. Finally, Sweelinck's variations on chorales are immensely important in the early history of the organ chorale.

M. Joannes Petri Swelingus Amstelo-batavus, Musicus et Organista toto orbe celeberrimus, vir singulari modestia ac pietate, cum in vita, tum in morte omnibus suspiciendus. Obijt M.DC.XXI.XVI. Octob. Æt. Lx.
Jan Muller sculp. 1624

Sweelinck, the last great Dutch composer for three hundred years.

Music in France during the 16th century

After the death of Machaut at the end of the 14th century, French music lost its inspiration and French musicians their leadership in Europe. The lead instead was taken by composers who originated beyond the frontiers of metropolitan France in the Franco-Flemish region to the north-east. This region continued to provide Europe with many of her most distinguished musicians throughout the 16th century, but in France at least the death of the great Josquin des Prez marked the end of Flemish predominance. Already with the career of Antoine Brumel (1460?–1520?), a somewhat younger contemporary of Josquin's, the resurgence of truly native French talent can be seen. He spent the first part of his working life in northern France, at the cathedrals of Chartres, Laon and Notre Dame de Paris. In about 1500 he moved south to Lyons and some five or six years later went to work at that great musical centre, the court of Ferrara. Brumel's output included some impressive motets; sixteen complete masses, in which he treats the plainsong *cantus firmus* with a freedom and a degree of imitation through the parts which is in tune with contemporary developments, and a number of *chansons* which show the move towards greater simplification which was to characterise the history of the genre during the 16th century.

One of Josquin's most talented contemporaries in France was Jean Mouton, whose birth place was near Boulogne but who, after an early career in the cathedrals of Amiens and Grenoble, entered the service of the French kings. He died in 1522. The distinctive features of Mouton's style, which was modelled faithfully on that of Josquin, were the smoothness of his melodic line and his remarkable inventiveness in developing the 'thematic' possibilities of the *cantus firmus* or other plainsong material which he used. His religious music – he wrote few secular works – reveals considerable gifts, but perhaps his greatest importance in the history of music lies in the fact that as the teacher of Adriano Willaert he formed an important link between the tradition of Josquin and the Venetian school.

The golden age of the French chanson

During the 16th century the two most popular forms of secular vocal music were the Italian madrigal and the French *chanson*. All the greatest composers of the first half of the century won much of their reputation from their compositions in these forms. But before going on to a study of the *chanson* and its composers, we should mention some of the music publishers who played such an important part in the dissemination of new music and the rapid building-up of European-wide reputations for the composers. The name of the Italian, Petrucci, has already been mentioned and we have seen how his

commercial calculations as to print runs for the various composers occasionally provide us with a measure of their relative popularity. The greatest name in French music publishing in the 16th century is that of Pierre Attaingnant, working at Paris from 1528 to 1549. His long list of publications of music of all kinds includes some seventy collections containing almost 2,000 *chansons*. Another famous firm was that established in the middle of the century by Robert Ballard and Adrien Le Roy – indeed this company was to remain one of the leading Parisian publishing houses up to the Revolution. There were many other important printers who introduced such innovations as the oval-shaped notes usual ever since, and the careful printing of the words under the notes to which they refer, but of them we have only space to mention one of the most important outside France – Tielman Susato, working at Antwerp from the 1530s to the 1560s.

It has been said that the madrigal and the *chanson* dominated the secular music of the 16th century, and as might be expected they interacted upon one another. The principal difference between the two types was that the music of the *chanson* was basically determined by the verse structure of the poetry, whereas the madrigal was essentially shaped by the emotional content of the words. It is therefore not surprising that one of the most important factors in the rise of the *chanson* was the new and freer style of French poetry initiated by Clément Marot (1496–1544). The language he used was more colloquial than the somewhat formal diction of his immediate predecessors, while his preference for short stanzas and his turning away from the fixed forms of the middle ages both favoured the move to simplicity found in the music of his contemporaries, who had in their turn been influenced by the *frottole* produced by the great Flemish composers.

The death of Josquin marked the beginning of what might be termed a national revival in the field of song. Whereas Josquin's manner was perpetuated in the north-eastern territories, France came once again into the mainstream of European music by creating a truly French style that was perfectly adapted to song, a genre which was to hold a predominant place in musical activity for a long time to come. The word *chanson* became a generic term which for a whole century was applied to almost all types of secular music with several parts and French words. We shall see that in the course of the century the meaning of the term was to be profoundly modified.

We may distinguish two main stages in the history of the *chanson*. The great period was approximately between 1525 and 1550 and roughly corresponded with both the reign of Francis I and the career of the composer Janequin. During this period religious music in France suffered a momentary eclipse. What was then known as the 'Parisian' *chanson* differed noticeably from Josquin's *chanson* although it was directly derived from it. All in all, it constituted a very successful synthesis between northern polyphony and the French spirit of musical clarity and simplicity. The form enjoyed an unprecedented popularity. By taking short texts–quatrains or ten-line stanzas with eight or ten syllables–as a basis, the *chanson* became more lively and therefore more popular. Counterpoint was pruned; there was a radical abolition of everything in the score that could not be immediately heard during the performance. The imitative entries of successive voices were retained, but this typically polyphonic procedure was considerably tightened up so that it was rare for a voice to utter more than four or five notes before being joined by others, and the complexities of extensive imitation were thus avoided.

A rapid declamation tended towards syllabism and frequently repeated notes; melismas were rare; the phrases, though shaped around the lines, were not unduly constrained by them since repetitions of words were frequent; moreover the phrases were often short and the cadences numerous and well-established; there was a very marked impression of a forthright rhythmic beat, though this did not always avoid weakness, being too often expressed by stereotyped melodic or rhythmic formulas. Although the subordination of the music to the text was evident, the early *chanson* was aimed more at conveying a general impression than at stressing the details of the words. There was little use of word painting, what there was being limited by and large to the musical transcription of words like 'fly', 'dance' and 'laugh'. To conclude, it should be noted that like the popular song the *chanson* sometimes resorted to a refrain which had only a remote relationship to the poem and which might even be merely a series of syllables without any meaning.

Janequin

What we have just said only holds good for certain *chansons* by Janequin, whose genius was varied. Although he took a genuine delight in making sacrifices to fashion–of which he was one of the main promoters–he displayed a consummate art of composition in many lyric pieces which are among the finest of his work, such as the *Pleust a Dieu que feusse arondelle*.

Clément Janequin was a major exponent of the French *chanson* and indeed the most representative French composer of the century. He was born in Poitou and as early as 1528 had achieved the distinction of a one-man edition published by Attaignant. About this time he seems to have been working in the Bordeaux region but, thanks to the patronage of the de Guise family and others, his career progressed and from about 1548 he was living in Paris; from the mid-1550s enjoyed a measure of royal patronage. Shortly before his death in 1560 he complained of old age and poverty, but could at least console himself by reflecting on his Europe-wide reputation. He left close on 300 *chansons* which show his mastery of the genre both in its earlier form, as the Parisian *chanson*, and in its later types, to be described below. Even when handling courtly verses which now seem to be cliché-ridden and unnatural celebrations of the theme of love, Janequin produced beautiful and moving music as in *Ce faux amour d'arc et de flèches s'arme*. But some of the finest flights of his genius are to be found in his programmatic pieces such as *La Guerre*, based on the battle of Marignano, or the charming evocation of the famous lark in *L'Alouette* and of bird song in *Le Chant des oiseaux*, all of which display an immense musical inventiveness which never becomes mere procedure.

above
Music-making outdoors in the 16th century.

left
Francis I by Jean Clouet, about 1528.

Other composers of the chanson

Although he was the greatest master of the *chanson*, Janequin was by no means the only one. We should mention Claudin de Sermisy (*c.* 1490-1562), who for much of his career was in the service of the kings of France, and was one of the musicians at the Field of the Cloth of Gold, the brilliant meeting between Francis I and Henry VIII of England in 1520; he also wrote church music. His numerous popular *chansons*, many of which were arranged for lute and keyboard versions, were both more lyrical and more sober than those of his great contemporary, some being adapted to sacred texts. Claudin's work is also notable for the Italian influence which is clearly apparent in it, as it is in that of Pierre Sandrin.

Activity in the domain of the so-called 'Parisian' *chanson* was far from being limited to the capital, although most of the collections were put out by the great Parisian publishers. Musicians throughout France kept the Parisian printing-presses well supplied with songs, and the commercial success of this popular new form was such that foreign publishers did not hesitate to follow the movement; Susato of Antwerp was one of those who thus helped to diffuse this essentially French art throughout Europe.

The transition to the second period of the *chanson* was far from abrupt and the Parisian *chanson* continued its successful career well after signs of evolution had appeared. New influences led to an even greater simplification of counterpoint, and harmonic treatment of the lower parts became an increasingly established feature of the *chanson* in the form of an air. Pierre Certon (d. 1572), seems to have been one of the first musicians to have made systematic use of this method of composition in his *Premier Livre de chansons* of 1552. He was followed by N. La Grotte, whose rather simple harmonisations became highly popular, and by Pierre Cléreau.

It was also in this period that the Italian madrigal began to make its influence felt; the *chanson* imperceptibly began to move towards the madrigal. The

above
Manuscript, in the shape of a heart, of a love song by Baude Cordier.

right
An anonymous 16th-century painting entitled Le Repas en musique.

fugato style fell into total disuse, being considered too intellectual, and expressivity became essential. Sonorities became richer; like the madrigal, the *chanson* increased the number of parts, which rose from five to six, and the Italian influence is most strongly seen in the enrichment of the harmony of the French song. But outright imitations of the Italian madrigal were rare in France, and the polyphonic *chanson* continued its career and remained a lively form. Guillaume Costeley (1531?-1606) was one of the last representatives of the old manner. His very personal style was one of extreme refinement and rare delicacy. Even Claude Le Jeune made occasional use of the declining genre. But it may have been Antoine de Bertrand who made the most original contribution. His slightly Italianate style was free from a harmonic bias and showed particular attention to the arrangement of the voices.

'Measured music in the antique style' – Claude Le Jeune

Shortly before 1570, at the very time when Italian influence in France reached its peak, an attempt was made to renew French musical language. The poets of the group called the Pléiade, led by Ronsard and Du Bellay, tried to adapt French verse to Greco-Latin rhythms and compose what Vauquelin de La Fresnaye called 'measured verse in the antique style'. Musicians who had been attracted by the classical texts that the humanists had brought to light made use of the Latin poets. In 1555 Goudimel had published the *Quinti Horatii Flacci odae*, now lost. It is not surprising then that the experiments of the Pléiade should have interested composers, while humanists saw it as an opportunity to attain the ancient ideal of an intimate union between poetry and music. The poet Baif and the musician Thibault de Courville worked jointly and the Académie de poésie et de musique was founded in 1570. The enterprise was encouraged by the kings Charles IX and Henry III, who even made it into an official institution, although it was dissolved in 1584.

The first effect on music was not surprisingly in the field of rhythm. The lines were based on a scheme by which syllables, designated as either long or short, were arranged according to certain rules; the result was a somewhat formless and pre-imposed musical rhythm. Such an artificial system could only produce fine music in the hands of a master such as Claude Le Jeune. The second consequence was that the bass voices were obliged to conform to a strict discipline and to model their rhythm upon that of the top voice. Only a few composers submitted to this discipline but their influence was real, despite the secrecy which surrounded the music played during the sessions of the Academy – it was forbidden to copy this music or make it known outside the circle.

The greatest exponent of the style advocated by the Academy was Claude Le Jeune (*c.* 1527-1600) whose influence increased progressively towards the end of the century. Outstanding examples of his music are *Printemps*, which appeared in 1603, his psalms in measured verse, and books of tunes. The *Printemps* is the most attractive collection to have survived: it consists of thirty-nine pieces, of which six employ the old style of stratified polyphony. According to the ode at the beginning of the collection Le Jeune composed the work in his old age. While paying tribute to the new style, he borrowed two famous songs from Janequin, *l'Alouette* and *le Rossignol*, giving them a fifth part. In the *Printemps* Le Jeune displays both the eclecticism of his genius and all the colours of his musical palette, and ends the masterly work with a gigantic dialogue in

seven parts with rhymed lines in the purest Italian tradition. There is no doubt that to his mind, perfection was only to be found in 'united tastes'.

The best known of his followers is Jacques Mauduit (1557-1627). Although he was a very skilful composer of *chansonnettes* and occasionally produced little masterpieces like *Voici le verd et beau may*, he never reached the level of his illustrious predecessor.

Music and the Reformation

With the Reformation, religious music in France began to regain its popularity. The revival of interest began with the progressive elaboration of the psalter, which was intended to give the new community a common fund of prayers. Between 1539 and 1562 both the poetic text, translated by Clément Marot and Theodore Bèze, and the musical text, whose authors or adaptors are mostly unknown, were gradually elaborated. The rules of notation were codified by Loys Bourgeois (d. after 1557) who was long believed to be the author of a good number of melodies. The constitution of the psalter was established by 1562. Henceforth these simple, and in many cases popular tunes, whose only aim was to sustain prayers, were to serve as a pretext for innumerable polyphonic compositions which were destined not for religious services – since the reformers were opposed to them – but to counteract the influence of 'licentious' secular compositions. Both Catholics and Protestants drew on this fund of melodies for polyphonic settings. They included Bourgeois, Janequin, Certon, Le Jeune and above all, Claude Goudimel.

The year of Goudimel's birth is not known but his first publication, a book of *chansons*, appeared in 1549, and his conversion to Protestantism can be dated to about 1560. He was murdered in the St Bartholomew massacre in 1572. His *chansons* are fine examples of their type, and before his conversion he produced motets and masses, but it is for his psalm settings that he is best remembered. Sometimes his harmonisations followed

Claude Le Jeune.

the syllabic divisions of the psalm, sometimes they used the song as a tenor and clothed it with polyphony.

The Reformation also produced the flowering of a 'spiritual' or 'new' song, usually with a moralising text which was sometimes inspired by the Bible. In works of this kind by Claude Le Jeune and others the most interesting and audacious innovations made their appearance: a striving after expression and symbolism which was reminiscent of the madrigal; a juxtaposition of homorhythmic sections with passages written in imitation, and above all, a frequent increase in the chorus accompanied by a sometimes considerable lengthening of the works, which became veritable vocal symphonies.

Instrumental music

Soon after the invention of printing, though in France later than elsewhere, collections of instrumental music began to appear. From 1529 to 1533 Attaingnant published some ten collections of music for lute, organ and flute. But these only rarely contained original works for instruments; for the most part they were either straightforward transcriptions of vocal music, or adaptations that differed only slightly from the vocal style. In 1529 the *Brief and Easy Introduction* for the lute appeared; the following year, a series of dances consisting of *bassedanses*, *recoupes*, *tourdions*, *branles*, pavans and galliards; in 1531, the *Tablature for the organ* and the *Thirteen motets* transcribed for the keyboard.

It was not until about 1550 that other instrumental collections appeared. The change of style that we have seen in vocal music was to be found again in instrumental music and there is no doubt that the two modes of musical expression influenced each other in many ways. The publishers Fezandat and, above all, Le Roy and Ballard, continued Attaingnant's work by publishing some thirty collections of music for lute, cittern, zither and mandora. Besides transcriptions, the famous lutenist Albert de Rippe published some thirty very well constructed fantasias which allowed room for virtuosity, while Guillaume Morlaye adapted dances and psalms for the lute and the guitar. But by and large the French 16th century failed to produce any outstanding body of instrumental music.

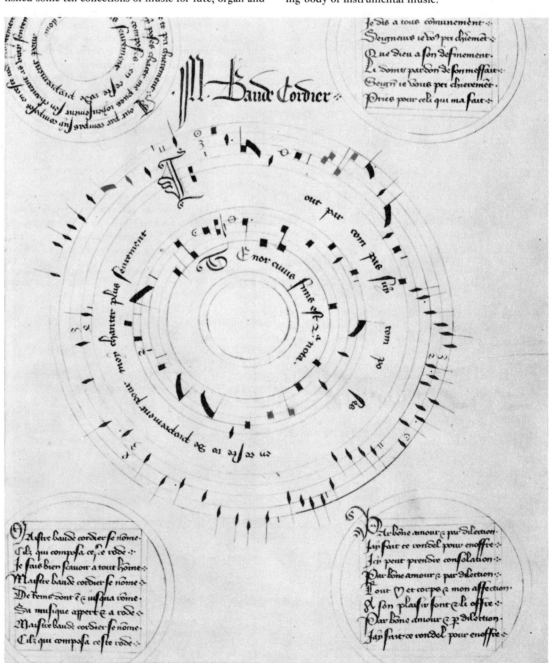

A rondeau by Baude Cordier.

Music in the lands of the empire

In view of its later commanding position it is interesting to note that German music was a comparatively late developer. Not until the 17th century were there any German composers who could be classed in the very first rank of European music. Already in the middle ages the term Germany (*Almania*, *Allemagne*) had been used to denote roughly the same geographical region as it was to cover in later ages. However, it also applied to the, lands of the empire in general, which included districts such as the county of Flanders, the chief jewel in the crown of the dukes of Burgundy and now part of the country of Belgium. By the 15th century the once powerful political unit of the empire had fallen apart into a number of independent duchies, counties and imperial towns and had taken on the patchwork appearance which it was to retain until well into the 19th century. Consequently in this chapter we shall be concerned with the music of a number of centres, chief among which were the imperial court centred upon Vienna and Prague, the court of Bavaria at Munich and the court of Saxony at Dresden.

The earliest evidence of a specifically German style was found in the monophonic *Lieder* of the *Minnesänger*. Just as their art had been deeply affected by the example of the Provençal troubadours, so that of their successors, the earliest representatives of German polyphony, was dominated by the music of the great Franco-Flemish school. Before, however, launching into a general consideration of the development of polyphony in Germany let us remember that from a very early period German musicians were beginning to show their mastery in the field of instrumental composition and above all that of music for the organ, in which they were later to excel. From the beginning of the 15th century organs and organists from beyond the Rhine were famous; in 1403 we find a certain Fredericus Schaubankes commissioned to build a new organ for Notre Dame in Paris, and in 1415 Heinrich of Saxony won the competition for the appointment of organist there.

The beginnings of German polyphony

In the earliest collections of German polyphonic music, of which the most important are the Lochamer, Schedelscher and Glogauer songbooks, works by the Flemings Dufay, Binchois, Ockeghem and Busnois and the

The town musicians of Nuremberg; shawms and sackbuts are in the foreground, a flute and large tabor behind.

Englishmen Dunstable, Walter Frye and Robert Morton, occupy an important place, and even a number of settings of the German song *Christ ist erstanden* ('Christ is risen') follow Franco-Flemish rather than German manner by placing the melody in the upper part. Nevertheless traces of a German style can be seen emerging, if only in the preference by the German composers represented for the melodies of their great predecessors the *Minnesänger*.

The two leading German-born composers of vocal polyphony in the later 15th century were Adam von Fulda, chiefly remembered for his treatise *De musica*, though some of his *Lieder* won considerable popularity, and Heinrich Finck. Born in about 1445, Finck was for some time in the service of the Polish court at Cracow; from about 1509 to 1513 he worked in the chapel of the duke of Württemberg at Stuttgart and died in 1527 as director of music at the Habsburg court of Ferdinand I at Vienna.

In his magnificent religious music, such as his six-part mass, he displays considerable contrapuntal skill and free use of imitation, while his German *Lieder* reveal a very personal sensibility and imagination. Finck's music shows signs of an unmistakably German idiom, for example his tendency to group two of the four parts together and a characteristic use of dissonances, but he did compose in the style of the French *chanson*, as for example in his *O schönes Weib*.

Finck's greatest contemporary, known rather for his instrumental than for his vocal compositions, was Paul Hofhaimer. Regarded as the greatest organist of his time, Hofhaimer was born near Salzburg in 1459. His career began as court organist to the archbishop of Innsbruck, but then from 1490 to 1519 he was in the service of the Emperor Maximilian I, who raised him to the nobility. He died in 1537, having been for the last eighteen years of his life chief organist at the cathedral of Salzburg. His many fine polyphonic *Lieder* display

affinities with the works of Finck; like them the melody is usually in the tenor, the overall style is one of rich lyricism, and a truly polyphonic sense is revealed in the almost complete equality enjoyed by the four parts. Nevertheless, in some ways, such as their somewhat stiff construction marked by frequently occurring block cadences in all the parts, these works reject the flowing manner of the contemporary Franco-Flemish school and revert to earlier types.

The first generation of German organists

As may be judged from his career, Hofhaimer enjoyed a contemporary reputation as an organist, being regarded as the greatest performer of his day. Unfortunately little of his music has survived although his example inspired a whole school of pupils.

Like Hofhaimer, the Italian Landini and so many other organists, Conrad Paumann, the first of the long line of German organists, was blind. Born in 1409 and owing his early musical training to the generosity of a rich patron in his home town of Nuremberg, he began his career as the organist of St Sebald's church there. From 1451 until his death in 1473 he was at the Bavarian court in Munich and, although he travelled to Italy, he refused many tempting offers from other patrons. His blindness seems to have bred a rather timorous nature, for on a visit to Italy he is said to have refused an invitation for fear that the envious Italian organists would poison him. Paumann is now chiefly remembered for his *Fundamentum organisandi*, a treatise on composition with special reference to the organ; he shows how to write counterpoint to a tenor and also gives instruction in the art of decoration by diminution.

Documents from the 14th century show the early popularity of the organ in Germany and from the first half of the 15th century we have three collections of works for the instrument which are perhaps the earliest examples to have survived anywhere of music written specifically for an instrument. Of these three the most interesting is that collated by Adam of Ileborgh in 1448. The music still clearly betrays its origins in adaptations from vocal works, but already at this early date we find a marking for a pedal part. This, together with the remarkably wide range of the keyboard written for, indicates that although the little portative organ was used in Germany—indeed Paumann was famed for his virtuosity on it—the German masters were already turning to an instrument with the essential characteristics of later models.

The most famous collection of early organ music is the Buxheim Organ Book, dating from about 1460. It contains some 250 compositions, all of which, save a dozen or so preambles, are arranged from earlier vocal works such as sections of the mass, motets and *chansons*, many of which are by Flemish or English composers. It should be noted in passing that all the organ music, like much other keyboard music both at this period and for some time to come, was recorded not in the notation used for vocal compositions, but in various types of tablature which differed between the national schools. As if to mark out their claim on a territory which was later to become their province alone, the German composers used a very elaborate system which combined features from the tablatures of Italy, France and Spain.

The last name to be noted in this early group of German organists is that of Arnolt Schlick (1455-1525), also blind and a native of Heidelberg. Many of his compositions, which stand second only to those of the great Hofhaimer, are contained in his *Tablatures of songs of praise and little songs for the organ and the lute*, pub-

One of the magnificent series of wood engravings known as the Triumphs of Maximilian *and dedicated to the Emperor Maximilian I.*

Heinrich Isaak

Three of the greatest figures in the German musical scene of the 16th century were of Flemish origin: Isaak, Lassus and de Monte. Born in Flanders, or possibly Brabant, about the year 1450, Isaak went to Florence in the early 1480s where he succeeded Squarcialupi as organist at the Baptistry and became music tutor to the children of Lorenzo the Magnificent. His music there included settings of some of Lorenzo's poems and a setting of Politian's lament on the prince's death. In the troubled years which followed the expulsion of Lorenzo's son Piero from the city in 1494, Isaak left to find employment elsewhere and became court musician to the Emperor Maximilian I. But after 1497, with his patron's permission, he divided his time between Vienna, Innsbruck, Constance and Florence, the home town of his wife. Indeed he was so happy by the banks of the Arno, after the restoration of the Medici in 1517, that he submitted his resignation to the emperor, whereupon Maximilian appointed him his diplomatic representative to the court of Tuscany. Isaak died in Florence that year, leaving a very considerable quantity of music. Before the work of Finck and Isaak, German vocal polyphony was remarkably retarded, but their masses introduced a new sophistication. In most of his masses Isaak followed common practice, usually drawing on plainsong for most of his material, although two are based on German *Lieder*.

The chapter of the cathedral of Constance commissioned him to compose a setting of the whole of the Proper of the mass, an enormous task which he undertook without hesitation. The *Choralis Constantinius*, the first polyphonic setting of the Proper, was completed by his favourite pupil, Ludwig Senfl, and published in Nuremberg at some time between 1550 and 1555. In the field of secular music Isaak showed himself to be a truly international composer. He could interpret Italian, Flemish, French and German with equal facility and was able immediately and intuitively to capture the spirit of foreign texts. An admirer and contemporary of Josquin des Prez, his *oeuvre* includes every type of music practised in his day.

Title page from a collection of organ works by Arnolt Schlick.

lished in 1512. In these the old manner of composing to a slow moving tenor drawn from a plainsong melody still lingers, but the style is unmistakably an instrumental one. Apart from his compositions, Schlick is an interesting figure because of his concern for the mechanics of organ building. Like the great Johann Sebastian Bach after him, he was recognised as an expert and his advice was sought by church authorities on the maintenance of their valuable instruments, as well as by the builders themselves.

It is not surprising to find that he was the author of the first work printed in German on the subject of organ construction. After him the tradition of organ composition is continued by the disciples of Paul Hofhaimer, the so-called 'Paulomines' who included in their number Othmar Luscinius, admired by the humanist Erasmus both for his wide knowledge and for his talents as a musician.

Later in the 16th century German music continued to develop in the hands of such men as Hans Cotter (*c.* 1485-1541) of Strasbourg, who died as a Protestant exile in Berne, and Leonhard Kleber (*c.* 1490-1556), organist at Pforzheim. In their liking for alternating chordal passages with rapid runs we can discern the dim origins of the typical toccata style of a later age. But immediately after them the desire for elaborate decoration reduced the keyboard style of German composers to a period of bombastic and meaningless virtuosity. Shortly after 1570 there appeared a group of organ tablatures by Nicholas Ammerbach (*c.* 1530-1597), organist of St Thomas, Leipzig; Bernhard Schmid (d. *c.* 1596), organist of Strasbourg cathedral; and Jacob Paix (d. *c.* 1617), organist at Lauingen. These contained transpositions of the authors' and their public's favourite motets, *Lieder* and *chansons*, together with German, Italian and French hymns, not to mention dances. These composers are known collectively as the 'colourists' since their compositions are often highly elaborate arrangements with a great deal of additional 'embroidery', which adds up merely to a superfluity of ornamentation. Nevertheless their technical expertise may be said to have prepared German composers for the new style of the 'variation' which, originating in the work of the English and the great Dutchman, Sweelinck, breathed new life into all organ music.

Musicians of the Reformation

As we have seen in the historical introduction to this section, the Protestant Reformation drew its inspiration from many roots deep in the history of Europe in the 15th century, but it was nevertheless the effective agency of one man, Martin Luther (1483-1546) which precipitated this great historical movement. Luther himself loved music and had considerable respect for its powers. As a youth he had learnt to play the lute and was sufficiently well versed as a musician to correct an ill-written score and even to compose melodies and simple part works. He admired much of the liturgy of the old church and the work of some Catholic composers, above all that of Josquin, but also that of De la Rue, Senfl and Finck. In consequence music held an important place in the Reformed religion and he took a hand both in the reform of the liturgy and the devising of the new congregational music. This performed an essential function in the extension of lay participation, which he believed should be an important part of religious worship.

Neither during the life of the great Reformer, nor for a

long time after, was there any degree of liturgical uniformity in the services of the 'Lutheran' family of Protestant Confessions. Luther himself introduced both a Latin mass, in the *Formula missae . . .* of 1523, which differed little from the Catholic form, and a German mass. They were devised with the help of Conrad Rupsch, *Kapellmeister* to Frederick the Wise of Saxony, and Johann Walther, but neither of these forms was adopted in its entirety, serving rather as the basis for the liturgies of the various communions of the Reformed Church. Indeed it was in the field of congregational song that German Protestantism made its greatest contribution both to religious music and to the musical tradition of Germany. Luther's sources for this were the chants and hymns of the Catholic Church, the religious songs of pre-Reformation Germany, of which a famous example is *Christ ist erstanden*, and old religious, secular or even popular songs whose melodies were retained but given new words; finally there were the songs written specially for the new religion, as often as not to words by Luther himself.

Every endeavour was made to familiarise the laity with the new music through both schools and adult singing groups. In 1524 the first collection of Protestant canticles was published, with a foreword by Luther himself, by Johann Walther (1496-1570). Called the *Geystliche Gesangk Buchleyn*, or the 'Little Book of Sacred Songs', it went into numerous editions. One of these the *Newe deudsche geistliche Gesenge* (1544) was published by Georg Rhaw (d. 1548), an important figure who in 1524 founded a printing firm in Wittenberg devoted to the service of the Reformation; it is especially interesting in having numerous contributions from such leading Catholic composers as Senfl himself and Arnolt von Bruck. Among the more important of the first generation of Protestant composers represented in the collection are Benedictus Ducis and Sixtus Dietrich, who was obliged to quit the service of the cathedral of Constance when he joined the Reformed Church.

During this century Protestant Germany had no native composer of the stature of Lassus, who had a profound influence on Catholic and Protestant musicians alike, yet in the figures of Johannes Eccard and Leo Hassler we can discern considerable musical talents. Another important influence was the restrained polyphony of the French school, which is seen in some of the finest works of Eccard based on German religious *Lieder*. Born in 1553, Eccard studied under Lassus at Munich before taking up a career in the distant German outpost of Königsberg (now Kaliningrad) in East Prussia, whence he moved, in 1608, to Berlin, where he died in 1611. He wrote both secular and religious works, using German and Latin texts in the latter, and the influence of his master Lassus is apparent; indeed the career of Eccard, emphasising as it does the universality of music in a world of divided faiths, was not untypical in Lutheran Germany.

This religious ambivalence is even more marked in the work and life of Eccard's greater contemporary Hans Leo Hassler (1564-1612). During his comparatively brief yet distinguished life, this man served both the Protestant Elector of Saxony and the great Catholic merchant prince Octavian Fugger II. He composed masses and Catholic motets, though it appears that he was by persuasion a Protestant. His style is distinguished by its elegant gracefulness, and the

Italianate manner of his teacher, Andrea Gabrieli, is everywhere apparent, especially in his liking for poly-choral writing. His works include *Canzonetti* for four voices, *Cantiones sacrae*, four-, five-, and eight-part madrigals and, as well as the masses mentioned above, Protestant motets and psalms for four parts.

Ludwig Senfl

Of the German-born composers of the 16th century the Catholic, Ludwig Senfl, was perhaps the most distinguished. Born about 1490, he entered the imperial chapel as a boy and received his musical training at the hands of the great Isaak, whose favourite pupil he soon became. He remained at the court of Maximilian until the emperor's death in 1519. In the early 1520s he took up an appointment in the Bavarian court establishment in Munich. The date of his death is unknown but it probably occurred about 1556. Although a Catholic, he seems to have been on friendly terms with Luther, at whose request he wrote a motet on the Reformer's favourite anthem, *In pace in id ipsum*. But Senfl's many-sided genius is revealed by his equal mastery in the mass and in his delightful German *Lieder*, which have been described as the high point of the first century of the polyphonic German *Lied*. Even here his debt to and mastery of the Franco-Flemish style of his master Isaak is apparent, but it is still more marked in his religious works, which include motets of noble yet lyrical contrapuntal character and both parody and *cantus firmus* masses. Among these last named it is interesting that Senfl, like so many of his great predecessors, employs the song *L'Homme armé* for one of his most interesting exercises; throughout the mass the *cantus firmus* from the *chanson* is sounded simultaneously with a second one based on a plainsong melody.

We have already seen that, like Senfl, Arnolt von Bruck (*c.* 1500-54) was one of the Catholic musicians who contributed to the Protestant collection *Neue Gesenge*. From 1510 he was in the service of the Habsburg ruler Ferdinand I, becoming his *Kapellmeister* in 1527. He wrote a large number of secular and religious *Lieder*, psalms, hymns and motets, in which he displays an admirable mastery of five-part polyphony. The fact that he was on occasion willing to draw his inspiration from Lutheran texts is perhaps the more remarkable in that he was an ordained Catholic priest.

left
Philip de Monte.

below left
Ludwig Senfl.

De Monte

With Philip de Monte we come to the first of the two giants in German music of the period. They represent the last of that multitude of outstanding musicians which the Franco-Flemish school bestowed on European music. In de Monte the tradition of Josquin and Dufay is carried forward, but of equal importance is his introduction of the main stream of Italian influence into German music. Born in Malines in 1521, he probably learnt the rudiments of Latin and music at the school of the church of St Rombaut, the principal parish there. He must have gone to Italy as a comparatively young man for in 1540 he is already practising as a music teacher at Naples. His first book of five-part madrigals was published in Rome in 1554 and had a resounding success, but soon after we hear of the young master in Antwerp. Here he was recruited as a member of the chapel of Philip II of Spain, with whom he visited England at the time of the king's marriage to Mary Tudor. Although in London for only a year, we know that de Monte met the young William Byrd and his father there, and it would seem that the two composers corresponded for many years thereafter.

Presumably he returned to Italy to resume his promising career, for in May 1568 he was living in Rome when he accepted the summons of the Emperor Maximilian II to take up the appointment of director of the imperial chapel. De Monte remained in the service of the imperial court for the next thirty years and unlike his famous predecessor Isaak seems to have discharged the duties of his onerous post conscientiously, travelling rarely except as the court moved between Vienna and Prague. The composer's immense industry and thorough attention to his responsibilities square well with what we know of his character, for he was described by a contemporary as a 'quiet unassuming man, as gentle as a girl'. Nevertheless, thanks to his immense talents and energy his reputation at his death had spread throughout Europe and was second only to those of Palestrina and the great Lassus himself, whose friend de Monte was.

The impact of the prolonged sojourn of this great master at the centre of German musical life was great.

Apart from a tour of the Netherlands in 1570 to recruit singers for the chapel, and attendance on the Emperor Rudolf II at the diet of Ratisbon in 1593, where he met Lassus, de Monte seems hardly to have moved from the court. Nor is this perhaps surprising when we reflect that, under Rudolf, the court was one of the most brilliant and cosmopolitan in all Europe. Yet despite this long career in Germany de Monte seems to have produced no examples of the German *Lied*, reserving the glories of his art for the Italian madrigal form, of which he was a master. So important indeed was his contribution in this field that it has been thought more fitting to deal with his madrigals in the chapter on Italian music and to confine our attention here to his religious music.

At the time of his death in 1603, de Monte had written, in addition to 1,200 madrigals and 45 French *chansons*, some 320 motets and 38 masses. In sheer bulk of output de Monte can stand comparison even with Lassus, and he has also been held to be the equal of his great contemporary in the quality of his work. This claim may be questioned and there is no doubt that in the variety of his inspiration and the versatility of technique he is outshone by the 'divine Orlando'. Yet if his style is sometimes less bold and dramatic, it is often inspired by greater warmth and sensitivity. His technical subtleties

in the handling of the parody mass almost always enable him to make more complete and exhaustive use of his model, for de Monte achieved a near perfect synthesis between the often secular piece on which the parody was based and the sacred purpose of the final mass; as a result the music is admirably adapted to the liturgy while its combination of subtle yet simple counterpoint and the richly varied resultant harmony makes it worthy to stand with the highest achievements of that great age of religious polyphony.

Roland de Lassus

Perhaps the greatest single international figure of 16th-century European music was Roland de Lassus, who was born in Mons about the year 1532 and who died some sixty years later at Munich after a life full of honour and achievement. Like many of his predecessors and contemporaries he travelled widely and his name is known in the Italian variant of Orlando di Lasso, the Latin, Orlandus Lassus and the French, Orlande. Since the major part of his career was spent at the court of Munich, it seems fitting to employ the Germanic version of his name.

Lassus had such a beautiful voice as a boy that it excited the cupidity of the recruiting agents in search of young singers for the courts of Europe, for whom the Franco-Flemish region was still the major hunting ground. Twice he was abducted from his church school; twice his parents fetched him back. On a third occasion, however, they did not dare refuse to let their son enter the service of Fernando Gonzaga, viceroy of Sicily for the Emperor Charles V. From Sicily he went to Milan in about 1550, where he was able to complete his musical education under the Fleming Hermann Werrecoren.

About 1550 Lassus left to enter the service of the Marquis de la Terza in Naples. Here he remained for about three years and no doubt exploited to the full the opportunities offered by one of Europe's major cultural centres. Next we find him in Florence, and in the spring of 1553 he was in Rome as choirmaster of St John Lateran, but only for a brief period, for his parents were seriously ill and he returned home to Mons. After travelling in England and France, he settled down in Antwerp, where he lived for about two years (1555-56). In 1555 Susato published his *Primo Libro*, a collection of works including seven Italian madrigals and some *villanesche*, French *chansons* and four-part songs, and in the same year Lassus had a book of five-part madrigals published in Venice.

In 1556 Lassus was summoned from Antwerp to Munich to become principal tenor in the choir of Albrecht V, Duke of Bavaria. He was still only twenty-four but with this appointment began a connection which was to last until his death. He learnt German and in 1560 married Regina Wächinger, daughter of a lady-in-waiting to the court. In 1564 Lassus was appointed ducal *Kapellmeister*, a post he occupied until his death. His conscientiousness and immense talents were fully appreciated by the duke and his son William V. The correspondence between Lassus and the young heir testifies to a close friendship; these letters are a delightful conglomeration of riddles, puns, jokes, nonsense and Rabelaisian stories, all mixed up in an exuberant combination of Milanese, French and German *patois*.

Like the head of any major musical establishment, Lassus was often obliged to journey in search of singers and instrumentalists; in this way he came to visit Nuremberg, Frankfurt, Venice (where he met Andrea Gabrieli) and Paris, where the publishers, Le Roy and Ballard, who were to publish much of his music, intro-

Roland de Lassus.

duced him to the master musicians of the court of Charles IX. In 1574 Lassus received a magnificent offer to work at the French court and in 1580 he rejected a similarly tempting invitation from the Saxon court at Dresden.

At the musical festival of Evreux in 1575 he won first prize with his motet *Domino Jesu Christe*; eight years later he gained a similar distinction with another motet, *Cantantibus Organis*. In 1585 he made a last journey in Italy, in the course of which, at Ferrara, he was received with princely honours by Duke Alfonso II. On his return to Munich he began to show signs of the hypochondriac melancholia which was with him until his death in 1594.

The compositions

Lassus, perhaps the most prolific composer of all time, left an enormous quantity of work. One might well ask oneself how the principal director of a ducal chapel could have found time to write more than 1,580 religious compositions and some 800 secular works. Nor was his music remarkable chiefly for its quantity. Like Josquin before him he dominated Europe and was known by contemporaries as 'the divine Orlando', the 'Belgian Orpheus', the 'prince of music', and the many honours with which he was overwhelmed included membership of the papal order of the Golden Spur.

By the time he was twenty-five he was already one of the greatest masters of his craft. From then onwards, an absolutely dedicated worker, he produced a seemingly unending flow of brilliant compositions, which always give the impression of absolute spontaneity. In his madrigals he combined an Italian finesse and vivacity with Flemish mastery of counterpoint, and produced sensitive musical equivalents to the poems of Boccaccio, Sannazaro, Fiamma and Ariosto. The wealth of invention displayed in his 140 French *chansons* still astonishes, and these works represent one of the high points of the form. Lassus gave a new turn to this genre, borrowing all the rhythmic and rich harmonic qualities of the madrigal to give his *chansons* much of their unique quality. Perhaps their most distinctive characteristic is an almost bewildering variety of moods; some have an infectious gaiety and are straightforward frolics, others are exer-

cises in technique or impressions of nature; others, again, are gentle and sad, the outpourings of a melancholy soul. He was inspired in turn by the poems of Alain Chartier and Villon, and by the sonnets of the Pléiade poets, du Bellay, Marot, Ronsard and Baïf. His secular and religious German *Lieder*, his *Mauresque Villancicos* and Italian *villote* show the facility with which he assimilated the idioms of every important form in contemporary music.

However, it is the religious works which constitute the most important part of his production. In these he shows himself to be as calm and austere in his devotion to the faith as he is whimsical, comic, capricious, sensual and wholly human in his secular music. The great majority of his surviving fifty-three settings of the Ordinary of the mass are parodies of secular polyphonic works, *chansons* and madrigals, of motets or of masses both his own and by other composers.

The celebrated mass, *Douce Mémoire*, a parody of a *chanson* by the French composer Pierre Sandrin, is a work of touching piety, perfectly adapted to the liturgy. The profoundly meditative Kyrie, the acclamations of the Gloria, the invincible rhythm of the Hosannah which follows the Sanctus, the dreamy meditation of the Benedictus, and the moving Agnus Dei, with rising progression to the Miserere Nobis, all give this mass an almost mystical fervour.

Of the one hundred settings Lassus wrote for the Magnificat, forty are parody treatments, making use of themes of Latin motets and secular songs; others are composed in the manner of liturgical psalmody. But it is in the motets that Lassus reveals his originality. The diversity of sacred texts allowed him continuously to invent new relations between words and music and to produce infinite harmonic variations and a variety of moods from the majestic to the idyllic. Sometimes he uses plainsong, as in his *Da pacem*, or in his anthems to the Virgin, but most often he draws on his own imaginative gifts; above all he seeks to give expression to the words. His occasional boldness is effectively counterbalanced by his developed sense of harmonic procedures; he contrasts polyphony with unison, binary with ternary rhythm, a graceful continuous melodic line with recitatives broken by silent passages. The *Penitential psalms*, written for the private use of Duke Albrecht, the *Sybilline prophecies*, the *Sufferings of Job* and *Lamentations of Jeremiah* are works of both lyricism and profundity.

Lassus at the keyboard with the musicians of the Bavarian court.

While the example of Lassus inspired composers throughout Europe, his influence was of course particularly evident in the work of his pupils, notably Eccard and Gregor Aichinger (1564-1628). Aichinger's religious work is very considerable and comprises motets, masses, vespers, several books of *sacrae cantiones* for four and two voices (1590-97) and numerous organ pieces (1606).

Lesser composers and instrumental music

Among the pupils of Lassus we should also mention the talented Leonhard Lechner (1553-1606) who, although the son of a Catholic family, was converted to Protestantism and served as *Kapellmeister* at the court of Stuttgart. His music is remarkable for its dramatic power and emotional intensity, qualities particularly evident in the fifteen *Spruche von Leben und Tod*, which reveal his sure command of techniques ranging from fluent polyphony to chordal writing. But perhaps Lechner's chief interest to a later generation lies in his St John Passion, which has been described as the finest of late 16th-century German Passions. Other examples of this genre, which was to occupy an increasingly important place in German music, include the Matthew Passion by Walther; written in the middle of the century, this foreshadowed the type of dramatic setting which the genre was to receive at the hands of the 17th-century German composers.

In the later 16th century a new and increasingly important influence came to be exerted in German music by the style of Rome, which enjoyed a growing prestige throughout Catholic Europe following the reforms instituted in the Council of Trent and exemplified in the works of the great Palestrina. Many of the German composers to be affected by the new manner were indebted to Jacobus Kerle (1532-91). A native of Ypres who spent much of his career in Italy, where as we shall see he played an important part in the revival of religious polyphony, he passed the later years of his life in the lands of the German empire and was a member of the court of Rudolf II at Prague, where he was instrumental

in spreading the knowledge of the new style. This found its first expression in the works of such German-born composers as Aichinger, while Blasius Amon (*c.* 1560-90), who may have been a pupil of Andrea Gabrieli, shows the spread of yet another Italian style to Germany; for Amon adopted the two choir technique which was such a hallmark of the music of the Venetian school, and was probably the first German to do so.

Instrumental music occupied a special place in German musical life. We have seen how some of the earliest purely instrumental compositions were German compositions for the organ. The organ had been an important participant in German performances of the mass since the 14th century but sackbuts and cornetts were also commonly used at the imperial court, indeed in the field of wind music in general the Germans had a European reputation. The strength of this tradition, like that of the organ tradition in Germany, must in part have rested on the many skilled makers, of whom Hans Neuschel (d. 1533) is probably the best known – a set of silver sackbuts which he constructed for the papal chapel earned a papal audience and a handsome reward. But another factor contributing to the high place of the wind instruments in Germany was undoubtedly the many towns who maintained their own musicians or *Stadtpfeifer*. The function of these instrumentalists was to provide music for ceremonial occasions, in which the trumpet fanfare had an important role, and to provide music for the entertainment of the citizens in the form of the so-called *Turmmusik* ('tower music'). This kind of municipal participation in music was not unique to Germany – the English town waites performed similar functions – but it was particularly strong there and was parallelled by the strong tradition of bourgeois vocal music represented by the lodges of the *Meistersinger*.

Music making in the home was immensely popular in 16th century Germany and here the lute held a special place. Like their compatriots who wrote for the organ, the German lutenists employed a tablature unique in Europe. The earliest examples were published by Schlick and by the lutenist Hans Judenkönig of Gmund, whose tablature was published in Vienna in 1523. In 1523 Hans Gerle of Nuremberg produced his *Musica Teutsch*; this was a manual teaching the viola da gamba, viola da

The town of Nuremberg, one of the important centres of the German Mastersingers.

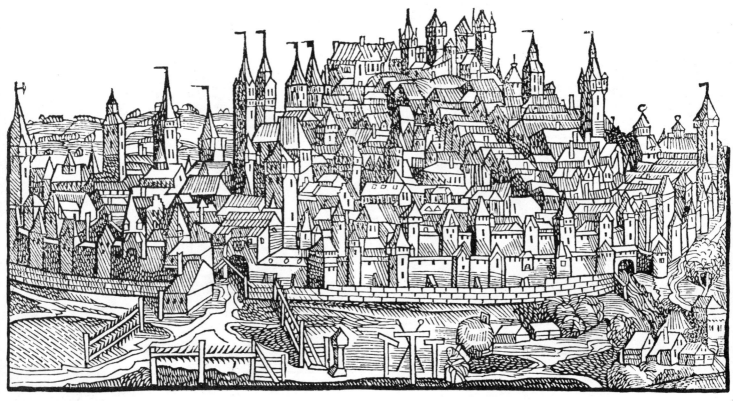

braccia and lute, and explaining how to transpose vocal parts. Besides this work he also published two books of lute tablature. The works of Melchior and Hans Neusiedler, natives of Hungary, but 'Burgesses of Nuremberg', contained transpositions for the lute of works by Hofhaimer, Isaak and Ludwig Senfl as well as French and Italian composers. Valentin Graew, lutenist to the King of Poland, published sets of fantasias in Lyons, Paris and Cracow between 1553 and 1565 which are very personal and excellent transpositions of French and Polish *chansons* as well as of polyphonic compositions and madrigals by Janequin, Gombert and Lassus.

Music in Bohemia

Throughout the middle ages the main impetus of European music had lain in the western lands and above all in France. In Germany sacred polyphony had been remarkably retarded and the situation was still worse further east. Indeed it was not until the 12th century that Bohemia became a Catholic country, having been first converted to Christianity by the Eastern Orthodox church missionaries, Cyril and Methodius. During the high middle ages Bohemian religious music was remarkable for the degree to which folk music influenced it. The golden age of the arts in Bohemia came during the reign of the ruler Charles IV, Bohemian king and emperor. He it was who laid the foundations of the magnificent imperial capital which was to be so important a centre of music under the Habsburgs in the 16th century. During his reign liturgical music developed in rich variety and the stage seemed set for the gradual, if belated, development of a national Czech school of music. This prospect was closed when Bohemia fell under the domination of the followers of the great reformer Jan Hus.

The Hussite movement provided a focus for lay anger at the growing corruption of the Church and for nationalist resentment against the increasing Germanisation of the country, which resulted from the subordinate position it had come to occupy in the empire after the death of the great emperor Charles. It opposed everything in religion which tended to detract from the primitive simplicity of early Christianity and as a result not only was the place of music challenged by the most

radical reformers, but the 'decadent' art of polyphony in all its forms was opposed. The melodies of the Hussite songs and of their 16th-century successors, the songs of the Czech Brethren, were often strong and beautiful, and provided themes for the national school of the 19th century, but it was not until the birth of Jacobus Gallus in 1550 that this eastern region of the empire produced a polyphonic composer of European standing.

In fact Gallus, often known under the Germanised version of his name, Handl, was a Slovene, but the greater part of his career was passed in Bohemia, and in 1581 he settled in the Bohemian and imperial capital of Prague, where he died in 1591. Gallus was a zealous Catholic and although most of his music was religious the influence of the Roman school is not pronounced and even the influence of Lassus, more easily discernible, is not strong. Indeed his style, which in its use of double chorus effects seems to borrow from the Venetians and in its skilful polyphony is clearly indebted to the Franco-Netherlandish school, cannot easily be classified. Nevertheless, despite contemporary criticisms, Handl's stature as a composer is not in question. It is indeed movingly demonstrated in the large collection of motets published in a number of volumes under the corporate title of *Opus musicum* between the years 1586 and 1591. In addition to these, which reveal the full range of his varied technique, he also composed a number of parody masses, madrigals and other works.

Music in Italy

While it is true of all European music that the fields of folk, popular and art music overlapped and provided each other with mutual inspiration, it is also true that in Italy music owed a special debt, in the development of a specifically Italian style, to the example and inspiration of popular and folk idioms.

Italian music up to the end of the 14th century

Italy made no significant contribution to the evolution of polyphony in the high middle ages, and we shall look in vain for any Italian equivalent to the great *ars antiqua* movement of the school of Notre Dame at Paris. It was only during the 14th century with the coming of *ars nova* that Italian composers began to approach the achievements of the masters north of the Alps, and then with the rise of the great Franco-Flemish school, the role of the peninsula remained secondary until well into the 16th century. Northern musicians made a point of visiting Italy during their apprentice years, many being lured by the rich offers made by the immensely wealthy rulers of the Italian states, whose courts were becoming the new centres of European culture. Many composers of northern origins passed the most significant parts of their careers in such service, and the importance of their example and teaching was as great in Italy as in other parts of Europe. But in their turn the northerners were increasingly affected by the native style of their adopted country, and by the 17th century this style had become one of the determining factors in European music as a whole.

The hallmark of the Franco-Flemish school was its mastery of a fluent, beautiful, but usually complex contrapuntal style, in which the free movement of the various parts was essential. The Italian composers of the 16th century on the other hand, while drawing heavily on the example of the many northerners in their midst such as Arcadelt or Willaert, and while showing themselves to be adept in the polyphonic manner, brought a new clarity of harmony and an interest in harmonic procedures and chordal writing which was to breathe a new spirit into European music. Although we have here run far ahead of our theme, this anticipation is not irrelevant since the essential clarity of the Italian style is found at the very beginnings of Italian music.

The Laude

In Italy, of course, as elsewhere in Europe, polyphonic music was used in the service of the Church during the 13th century. Evidence of its existence is provided by such things as rubrics, dating from 1215, prescribing the

A religious procession in an Italian town with musicians and singers in the foreground.

use of numerous polyphonic compositions at the cathedral of Siena, and by the testimony of Salimbeno de Adamo, a Franciscan from Parma, who records the use of two- and three-part *conductus* during the singing of the office. A few examples of Italian polyphony survive from the period but their interest is historical rather than artistic.

In the field of secular music the position is even worse, for although we know that music was an essential accompaniment to many forms of poetry, the poet often accompanying himself on a musical instrument, the art was in essence an improvisatory one. No compositions have survived except those of the northern school of troubadours of the 12th century, who had consciously sought to emulate the work of their Provençal colleagues and used the Provençal language.

The first truly Italian contribution to Western sacred music came in the field of religious song, of which the earliest recorded examples are the hymns of St Francis of Assisi. We are justified in assuming that these had considerable importance in the early history of the genre since St Francis, determined that all men should understand his message, used the vernacular for the text and probably relied heavily on popular song for the music. Thus from the beginning the growing musical form was free of any commitment to either the language or the traditional music of the Church. It is unfortunate that no trace remains of the music to which these hymns were originally sung, yet we know that the famous *Invocation to the Sun* was intended to be sung, since a stave has been drawn at the beginning of the oldest known manuscript. The hymns of St Francis may well have been the forerunners of the *laudi spirituali*, sacred songs in the vernacular, which were to be immensely popular from the 14th century onwards and were to gain a new lease of life in the 16th. They became closely associated with the Marian cult, popular in Italy as in the rest of Europe, and an evening service of song and prayer to the Virgin became such a prominent feature of lay musical life that most Italian towns of any size had their own confraternities, recruited mainly from the artisan and lower orders of society. The *laudi*, which had no place in the liturgy, were probably performed by their devotees in private houses, at open air meetings or in procession. Later indeed, in the 16th century, they were to hold their meetings in the church itself, but after the regular service was over. All in all these essentially monophonic songs were, in their origins, a spontaneous expression of popular lay piety. As such they are a remarkable testimony to the melodic sense of the Italian layman, though the later polyphonic settings are perhaps

of greater interest to the musical historian.

Nevertheless it should be noticed that although the words were the essential element, the music was no mere adjunct, and indeed in many cases it is the music that brings these simple texts to life. It has been said that in this respect the *laude* is the first example of that intense concern for an integration of music and text which has so often characterised the music of Italian composers.

Italian secular music of the ars nova

The three secular forms most frequently employed by the 14th-century composers in Italy were the madrigal, the *caccia* and towards the end of the century the *ballata*. Of these perhaps the most favoured was the madrigal. The origins both of the form and of its name are obscure. It has been suggested that the word may be a corruption of the Latin *materialis*, possibly used to distinguish *cantus materialis* (secular song) from *cantus spiritualis* (religious song). More important than the interesting matter of origins is the fact that the early madrigal of the *ars nova* period has little or nothing in common with the form of the same name which was to dominate the secular music of Italy in the middle of the 16th century.

In its early form the madrigal was a short poem composed of two- or three-line verses, ending with a *ritornello* of one or two verses. The music, more often than not for two parts, remains the same for each verse but changes in the final *ritornello*. The madrigal is essentially a high art form, and retains a serious and expressive mood

above left
Trumpets and shawms providing the music at a feast.

left
A woodcut illustration of three gallants serenading a lady.

Dancing to the sound of the bagpipes.

throughout, accented by long ornamental vocal passages which protract each verse. Opposed to it was the more light-hearted *caccia* (literally 'hunt'). Usually written for three voices, it was characterised by a canon in the upper two voices, though this did not necessarily run the whole length of the piece. The *caccia* was a freer form than the madrigal, which rarely had more than three lines to the verse and usually had eleven syllables to the line; moreover the *caccia* was essentially programmatic. It was set to a picturesque poem, punctuated with numerous onomatopoeic words, which evoke, if not always a hunt, at least open air scenes such as fishing, market places, battles and so on. The composer tries to capture the atmosphere in the writing of the canon, interweaving the two voice parts as much as possible, and adding exclamatory interpolations rendered in an almost impressionistic fashion. The *caccia*, which is certainly one of the most original forms of *ars nova*, nevertheless seems only too often merely a *tour de force* written to show off the composer's brilliance as a contrapuntalist.

These two forms were superseded in popularity in the latter half of the 14th century by the *ballata*, originally a monophonic form, similar in structure to the French *virelay*. The *ballata* can be traced back as far as the 13th century, but with the accession of interest in the form it became the subject of polyphonic treatment and both two- and three-part *ballate* were produced by such composers as Francesco Landini.

We have seen in our study of music in northern Europe in the early and high middle ages that the dominant inspiration in the age of *ars antiqua*, which witnessed the evolution of polyphony, was a religious one. We have also seen that with the 14th century a new secular spirit was abroad and the *ars nova* style of Phillippe de Vitry and his successors found its most natural expression in non-religious music. It is perhaps therefore not surprising that Italy, the region of Europe where a modern historian has identified the rise of the first truly secular states of Europe, should have produced its first composers of any importance during the century of the *ars nova*. Its flowering may be partly explained by a new attitude to patronage among the princely families and a new interest on their part in music. In view of the leading place of French music at the time, it is interesting that an Italian contemporary, Marchettus of Padua, credits the

new impetus to music patronage to a ruler of French descent. In a dedication written in 1324, Marchettus praises Robert of Anjou (king of Naples in succession to his great ancestor Charles) as the first Maecenas of music in the peninsula, for the consort of singers which he gathered around him at his Neapolitan court. But Naples, although perhaps the first, was soon followed by many other musical centres such as the court of the Visconti at Milan and that of the della Scala family of Verona and, from 1328, Padua.

Indeed the first performance of polyphonic madrigals recorded in Italy is noted as having taken place in Padua in 1332. Like the music of the French *ars nova* it often displays an untoward complexity of expression which contrasts particularly strongly with the touching simplicity of the *laude*. The names of only a few 14th-century Italian composers have come down to us and of these one of the earliest is Giovanni da Cascia, originally a native of the district of Florence and also called Johannes de Florentia. After a period as organist at the cathedral of Florence he was in the service of the della Scala at Verona in the 1340s and 1350s, and appears also to have spent some time at the court of the Visconti. Thirty of his compositions are known; the majority are madrigals but they also include three *caccie* and a setting of the Credo of the mass. Da Cascia produced some of the most accomplished madrigals of his time – a graceful and supple melody is enriched by beautiful melismas in the upper voice and supported by solid harmonic writing. Variety is given to the whole by a skilful alternation between syllabic declamation and embellished melody.

One of da Cascia's distinguished contemporaries is known to us only by his first name of Piero. In fact nothing is known of his life though it appears, from his choice of texts, that he worked for the courts of Milan and Verona. Piero's chief claim on our attention lies in his masterly and pioneering work in the *caccia*; indeed in this he reveals himself as one of the first Italian composers to grasp the full expressive possibilities of canon. All told we have only eight of Piero's works but their quality is outstanding and his *caccia*, *Con dolce brama*, which describes the entry of a boat into harbour and picturesquely reproduces the cries of the pilot and the seamen, may be considered a perfect model of the genre.

Of a younger generation was Jacopo da Bologna. He

embodied to the full the somewhat arrogant professionalism of the composers of the *ars nova*, complaining that the world had too many little men who, simply because they had produced a few compositions, thought themselves the equals of the great Italian ancestor of *ars nova*, Marchettus of Padua, or of de Vitry himself. Jacopo was at Verona from about 1340 to 1345, and must have known da Cascia there, but he later went to Milan where he was to produce some of his most important compositions. Some thirty madrigals, a *caccia* and a motet of his survive, and he also composed a piece in the popular genre of the *laude*, while his motet *Lux purpurata* is dedicated to Luchino Visconti, who died in 1349. Jacopo was one of the composers who contributed most considerably to the development of profane polyphony in Italy; his work is remarkable as much for the surety of his melodic sense as for the fecundity of his imagination, the variety of his rhythms and the independent movement of the voices.

Florence and the music of Landini

The music of 14th-century Italy culminates with two important figures, one Italian, the other – an augury of what was to be the trend in later centuries – a native of Liège. Towards the end of the century Florence became the most important musical centre of the peninsula, and even here the burgeoning influence of French types can be seen. With composers like Donato, Gherardello, whose *caccia*, *Tosto che L'alba*, was justly famous, and above all Francesco Landini, Florence could justly claim a special eminence.

Landini (*c.* 1325-97), one of the first of that long line of blind organists which presents such an interesting feature of musical history, was also a considerable composer. The son of a painter, it was perhaps not surprising that the artistically gifted child should have turned to music after a tragedy which robbed him of his sight. He enjoyed immense fame as an executant on the portative organ and a contemporary has movingly described the profound emotional effect his performances had on his hearers. Compared with other Italian composers of the 14th century, Landini left a considerable opus which indeed accounts for no less than a third of all the surviving compositions by Italians during the period. His fifty-four works include no fewer than 140 *ballate* in two and three parts, an eloquent testimony to the vogue which this form, freer and more emotionally expressive than its predecessors, the madrigal and the *caccia*, enjoyed, and Landini's compositions in the genre convincingly demonstrate the emotional power of which Italian music of this period was capable. Already, however, even in his work we may trace the beginnings of Franco-Flemish influence, and with the music of Johannes Ciconia (*c.* 1335-1411) the great incursion had already begun. A native of Liège, he was one of the first northerners to live and work in Italy. His works include many motets (some of which are isorhythmic, a type of composition apparently not much favoured by Italian composers), two- and three-part madrigals, *caccias* and *ballate*.

Secular music in the 15th century

Between the brilliant era of *ars nova* of the 14th century and the extraordinary efflorescence of the madrigal in the 16th, native Italian music may be said to have gone into recession. The musical vein of the Italians was over-shadowed, though not of course completely stifled, by the superior gifts of the Franco-Flemish composers. In addition to the cosmopolitan church circles and the princely courts, which were particularly susceptible to foreign influences, there were also the middle classes and more modest courts; these had always shown a marked predilection for popularly inspired performances, from which the most typical forms of Italian music were later to emerge. In this way, parallel to the Franco-Flemish current, we can follow throughout the 15th century another and purely Italian stream which, although perhaps less splendid, leads in an uninterrupted flow to the madrigal.

Unfortunately the first records of this new art have not come down to us, since more often than not it consisted of an improvised art of a recitative style with extempore accompaniment to a performance of poetry. Also lost to us for the same reason are the improvised Florentine *rispetti* and *cantipanchi*, songs of epic deeds and love which were sung at Carnival time from trestle stages in the Piazza San Martino, and some of which, like those of Antonio Guido, were celebrated throughout Italy. Lost too are the *ballate* of the Venetian, Leonardo Giustiniani (*c.* 1398-1446), whose gifts as a composer and executant were much vaunted by his contemporaries.

An interesting feature of Italian city life, particularly that of Florence, is the degree to which the pursuits and entertainments of the various classes of citizens overlapped. By reviving popular poetry and the splendours of the 'vulgar' tongue, which had been in decline since the times of Petrarch, Lorenzo de' Medici himself, together with other poets at his court, contributed greatly to the survival of secular song, which in Italy, perhaps more than anywhere else, derives from the language of the people. Lorenzo's Italian poetry included songs for the carnival celebrations before Lent and during the month of May, which under him took on a new luxury and splendour. An important part of the display was the

An allegorical painting of the great Lorenzo de' Medici receiving embassies and gifts from other princes.

Isabella d'Este.

processions of guild and court floats representing the city trades and mythical scenes reflecting on the glory of the Medici. Lorenzo wrote the words for songs of both aristocracy and commons; they were set for several voices and sung in the open air, probably from the processional floats themselves. They are simple little pieces, with none of the complex counterpoint or melodic refinements of *ars nova*, but are full of life. This minor art form has the merit of providing the first written record of some of the basic characteristics of Italian musical genius, that is to say a clear harmonic structure with the emphasis on the melody in the upper part, supported by chords in the other voices and occasionally displaying a precocious sense of tonality.

The most popular secular song form in Italy at the turn of the 15th and 16th centuries was the *frottola*. It was evolved in the north, at the court of Mantua, where Isabella d'Este was the enlightened patron of a brilliant group of poets and musicians at her court. Formally it consisted of a number of six-line verses with a four-line refrain. Like the carnival songs it relied heavily, particularly for its words, on the popular tradition; musically it was distinguished by syllabic treatment of the words and the punctuation of the lines with chordal passages. The role of the marchioness of Mantua in the revival of a national school of music in Italy has frequently been stressed, and it was indeed immense. The poets of the quiet little court of Mantua, far removed from political disturbances, found their inspiration in their native tongue and composed unpretentious poems, simple *poesia per musica*, made to stir the imagination of musicians. One of the most celebrated poets at the court of Mantua at that time was Serafino dall'Aquila (1466-1500). He enjoyed a high reputation for the exquisite way in which he combined words and music in his improvised lute accompaniments to his poems. For the Mantuan court, as for most Italians, poetry of any kind could only be fully enjoyed when accompanied by music.

The *frottola* had an extraordinary success in Italy, and even Franco-Flemish composers like Josquin des Prez, Isaak, Agricola and Compère were attracted by the form. But the majority of *frottolists* were Italian; forty names have come down to us, among which the most outstanding are Bartolomeo Trombonchino (d.*c.* 1535) and Marchetto Cara (d. *c.* 1530). Their work contributed greatly to the development of the *frottola* due to their imaginative use of long phrases, their innate sense of melody, their very sure sense of the rhythm of language and their interest in the meanings of words.

Two other forms popular at the beginning of the 16th century were the *strambotto*, a single eight-line stanza usually melancholy in mood, and the *canzona*, which was at first very similar to the *frottola* but showed an advance on the latter in the choice of texts (for example the poems of Petrarch, Michelangelo and Sanazzaro) and in the quality of the music itself. A fine example is Cara's *canzona*, *Da tuo bel volto*, which already has the delicacy characteristic of the madrigal.

The madrigal

This type of composition in its 16th-century form first appears in a book entitled *Madrigali de diversi autori*, printed in Rome in 1530 by Valerio Dorico, which includes works by two composers: Costanzo Festa, an Italian, and Philippe Verdelot, a Frenchman. Both shared in the birth of this new art form. That these two composers should be included side by side indicates that Italian and northern musicians, despite opposing tendencies, were beginning to evolve a common art form. The madrigal may be called the point where Italian and Flemish art meet; the techniques of the Franco-Flemish motet and the Italian *frottola* combined to produce one of Europe's greatest musical achievements. From beginnings which show its early similarities to its predecessors the Italian *canzone* and the French *chanson*, the madrigal reached a characteristic form. This was fully polyphonic, although the chordal effects of the *frottola* were retained for moments of punctuation, and the text enjoyed equal importance in all the voices. Other distinguishing features were that the madrigalist usually chose a text of literary quality and aimed to express the content of that text in his music.

Hence a madrigal was not simply words set to music but an attempt to produce a fusion of the two, and consequently the music for each verse was often different. The many other factors contributing to the madrigal's rise included the return to Petrarch's verse, encouraged by the humanist Pietro Bembo; the growing status of secular music as a medium of serious expression and no longer simply a form of amusement; the very concept of expressiveness itself in music; and finally the fact that from the first the madrigal received the concentrated attention of major composers. By 1540 the appearance of works by two other composers from beyond the Alps, Jacques Arcadelt and Adriano Willaert, proclaimed the maturity and potentialities of the new form.

Founders and pioneers

Of the two founding fathers of the form, Verdelot and Festa, the first, said by Vasari to be a Frenchman, seems to have died about 1540 and to have spent much of his working life in Florence and Venice. His first madrigals appeared in the early 1530s, and they reveal a variety of techniques, natural in the work of a pioneer, from purely chordal to heavily imitative. He wrote fine examples of the form in three, four and five parts. Although best known for his secular works, Verdelot also wrote religious music, though he seems to have approved the reforming policies of Savanarola at Florence in the mid 1490s.

Like Verdelot the Italian Costanzo Festa is first remembered for his madrigals, and like him he wrote religious music. This includes four masses, some forty motets and thirty hymns; the influence of the Franco-Flemish school is very apparent in his work, though not predominant. It is hardly surprising that this should have been so when we realise that when he joined the papal choir in the early years of the century it was mostly staffed by French and Flemish musicians. He remained at the papal court until his death in 1547, but like Verdelot he was publishing madrigals from the 1530s. He excelled at writing in three parts.

But if Festa and Verdelot may legitimately claim to have been the pioneers of the 16th-century madrigal, the two composers considered below were undoubtedly its first great masters. Jacques Arcadelt (*c.* 1504-67), a Netherlander by birth, was active in Florence, the third great centre of the early madrigal, in the 1530s. Later he went to work in Rome, where among other things he was commissioned to provide settings to poems by Michelangelo. Apart from religious music and madrigals Arcadelt also wrote a number of French *chansons* and the style is reflected in his madrigal writing. But it was above all his madrigals that won his great contemporary fame in Italy, and their sweet melodies, pure vocal style and excellent four-part harmony justify the immense number of reprints of his works which were brought out.

Adriano Willaert is the most important single figure in the history of Italian music in the first half of the 16th century and, as such, receives fuller treatment for his important church music in a later section. His first published madrigals appeared in 1536 and they betray the natural influence of the composer's Flemish home, though this is combined with Italian elements. The Flemish traits persisted and in the publication *Musica Nova* (1559), devoted to Willaert's madrigals, the fluency and brilliance of his contrapuntal writing is outstanding. Indeed the effect of Willaert's music on some of his contemporaries was such that one of them records that he felt he did not know what music was until he heard the compositions of Willaert.

left
Adriano Willaert, the Flemish composer who, as director of music at St Mark's Venice, was one of the most important figures in 16th-century Italian music.

below left
Cypriano de Rore, another great Flemish composer who made his mark on Italian music.

Cypriano de Rore and other madrigalists

Two pupils of Willaert, Nicolo Vicentino and the Fleming Cypriano de Rore, were to make further important contributions in different ways to the chromatic development of the madrigal, which had been tentatively initiated by their master. In the chromaticisms of his music Vicentino (1511-72) made an important contribution towards the freeing of music from the old modal system, although the theories which he propounded in his *Antica Musica ridotta alla moderna prattica* embodied ideas which he believed represented the practice of ancient Greek music. Cypriano de Rore (1516-65) was yet another of those Flemings who spent much of his career in Italy. He worked in Venice (where he studied under Willaert), Ferrara and Parma, and in the last year he worked for a time as the music director at St Mark's. His work displays a progressive wealth of harmonic colouring, and contributed to a greater freedom and a more daring use of chromatics. His interpretation of Giovanni Della Casa's beautiful poem *O sonno*, where text and music are inseparable, is characteristic of his delicate symbolism. Barely twenty years after the beginning of the genre he had raised the madrigal to such artistic heights that few of his contemporaries were able to follow him. However, Giovanni Nasco, Vincenzo Ruffo and Domenico Ferrabosco retained a certain originality in their delightful madrigals, which are far removed in style from the austerity of their contemporaries. The two great masters of religious music, Palestrina and Lassus, also devoted some of their creative

talent to the writing of madrigals, but with differing results. While the Italian master always remained essentially conservative and, in spite of his keen sense of harmonic colouring, far removed from the true lyric style of the madrigal, Lassus deliberately involved himself in chromatic experiments and succeeded more than any other composer before him in making the madrigal a real musical poem. His compatriots Philip de Monte and Jacques de Wert represent the last point at which northern musicians shared in the history of the madrigal.

The Fleming Philip de Monte, who made his greatest contribution to the music of Europe as *Kapellmeister* to the imperial court, also produced over a thousand madrigals, which represent the flowering of the classic style of the 16th-century madrigal. His work was not pioneering in terms of technique, but displays his immense talents as a musician and a remarkable fluency in his handling of contrapuntal techniques. His compatriot Jacques de Wert (1535-96), who spent most of his working life at the courts of Mantua and Ferrara, was greatly admired by his contemporaries for his madrigals. In these de Wert was clearly influenced by the style of his adopted country though the characteristic Flemish love of polyphony is still there; his penchant for word painting was shared by other madrigalists of the period, but his harmonic procedures may be said to anticipate some of the aspects of later tonality.

The later masters of the madrigal

The end of the century saw the appearance of a number of talented Italian composers and three outstanding ones: Marenzio, Gesualdo and Monteverdi. Luca Marenzio (1553-99) combined in his works all the musical characteristics which, up to then, had only been roughly defined, and imprinted his own original personality on them. With him, chromatic harmonies are not gratuitous experiments, but are used to express anguish, sorrow or passion; all the images with which the texts of madrigals abound are admirably translated into music. His writing displays a wealth of styles – vertical harmony, clearly articulated recitations, long lyrical melodies, simple arrangements for four voices and more complex compositions for two choirs. He often displays a Virgilian sweetness, which earned him the name of 'the gentle swan of Italy', and his elegance and delicate melancholy are well adapted to the langours of the Petrarchian poetry which he so loved.

Carlo Gesualdo (*c.* 1560-1613), a Neapolitan gentleman, was a man of quite different character, passionate both in his life and in his work. He is notorious for having murdered his wife, her lover, and a child whom Gesualdo was convinced was not his own. The music fully reflects the violent temperament of the man. Although at the end of his days he wrote some remarkable motets, it is by his madrigals he is best known. In these he displays most openly his ardent southern temperament; he pushes to extreme lengths the most daring contrapuntal and chromatic harmonies; he prefers, as it were, a certain harmonic imbalance and his embellish-

ments often verge on the extravagant, but it is impossible to deny his emotional power.

Claudio Monteverdi, one of the greatest Italian composers of his time, is famed for much else besides his madrigals but these constitute a significant part of his work. The first four of his books are devoted to perfect examples of the form, but with the fifth (1605) he completely broke with the past to follow a new line. He brought new life to the genre by using recitative style and choral writing, which introduced a dramatic tension into these works directly supported by the sense of the words. The boldness of his harmonies and modulations, criticised as 'modern' by the purists of the time, is never gratuitous but always subordinate to the demands of the text. Furthermore the provision of true continuo parts for all the madrigals of book five was an important technical innovation which anticipates the manner which was to dominate European music in the Baroque age. Some of Monteverdi's finest madrigal compositions are to be found in the sixth book, published in 1614.

During the latter half of the 16th century the art of the madrigal, once the preserve of the Franco-Flemish composers, had passed firmly into the hands of the Italians. As the century progressed the madrigal underwent some modification, one of the most important and interesting developments being the increasing frequency of dramatic elements and, related to this, the appearance of solo voice madrigals with instrumental accompaniment. This was fully in tune with the growing interest in the art of monody, which we shall return to at the end of this chapter. Some of the finest solo madrigals were those published in 1601 by Luzzasco Luzzaschi (*c.* 1545-1607). He was a pupil of de Rore at Ferrara and was himself for many years director of music at the court there, being a teacher of Frescobaldi. The 1601 collection, which also contains accompanied madrigals for two and three voices, is particularly interesting. It is the first to contain a keyboard accompaniment in which the vocal parts are written out in full, moreover the solo voice part is printed with the elaborate ornamentations so common in performance at the time. Other Italian madrigalists who should be mentioned here are Marc Antonio Ingegneri (d. 1592), a pupil of Ruffo and one of Monteverdi's teachers, and Andrea Gabrieli (*c.* 1520-86). Gabrieli and his nephew Giovanni were the outstanding masters of late Venetian music. Andrea's first madrigals date from the 1540s and as his style develops he applies the typically Venetian device of the double choir to the madrigal, producing works of great rhythmic drive and massed sonorities.

In the last decades of the 16th century there developed the new hybrid style of madrigal, usually known as the 'dramatic' or 'dialogue' madrigal. The 'dramatic' madrigal was influenced by the new forms of secular drama and has a marked affinity with the developing *Commedia dell'Arte*, in which action was much less important than the players' characterisation of practical jokers and buffoons. It was for such players as these that Michele Verrotto of Novara wrote what he called a 'dialogue' for ten voices, a bizarre sequence of scenes in which questions and answers are exchanged in a medley of languages. The 'dialogue' madrigal was often in a number of scenes and always dealt with everyday events, very different from the elegance of the madrigal proper. Thus a good early example by the aristocratic Mantuan composer, Alessandro Striggio (1535-87), is entitled *The chatter of laundry women*; it contains no action, but consists entirely of a lively dialogue between gossips concerning minor happenings in their village life. Striggio, who visited England, also composed music for *intermedi* and was a fine performer on the lute and on the viol.

We are indebted to Giovanni Croce, the director of music at St Mark's, Venice, for a piece entitled *Amusing masquerades and buffooneries for carnival*, published in

Portrait believed to be of Monteverdi as a young man.

Plate 14
Lady at the Virginals *by Vermeer.*
*The instrument was sometimes
played in a standing posture.*

Plate 15
The Concert, *attributed to Costa*.

1590, a series of scenes in which beggars, fishermen and peasants from Frioul engage in cheerful badinage; he also wrote *The musical panacea*, a series of tableaux, which according to the author would cure all ills.

The finest of these so-called 'choral dramatists' was Orazio Vecchi (1550-1605), a man of culture, archdeacon of Correggio and musical director of Modena cathedral, writer, poet and talented musician. In 1597 his masterpiece, *Amfiparnasso*, which he called a *commedia harmonica* (or musical comedy), was published in Venice. It was expressly not intended to be acted but it does not lack dramatic effect, for despite the web of polyphony Vecchi was well able to portray his different characters, drawn from the world of *Commedia dell' Arte*. The music has considerable rhythmic and harmonic richness.

Side by side with the madrigal there developed the more modest *villanescha*, which enjoyed a considerable vogue at the end of the century in the slightly modified form of the *villanelle*. It carried on the pleasing and spontaneous tradition of the *frottola*, but without the latter's popular appeal, for it was composed for the same sophisticated public as the madrigal. The earliest published examples appeared in Naples in 1537 under the title of *Canzone villanesche alla napolitana*. It was in this city too that it first reached its maturity and its best practitioners were to be found. But the year 1545, when Willaert published his *Canzone villanesche* in Venice, marks the beginning of a period when the *villanelle's* popularity was to spread further afield. Ten years later the *villanelle* had crossed the Alps with Lassus, who published fifteen of these compositions in Antwerp. Finally, in the second half of the century, all the finest musicians were practising the art – Marenzio, Jacques de Wert, Vecchi and Caccini. The *villanelle* even survived the madrigal, which had already long disappeared when the last collection of *villanelles*, under the title of *Prima Scelta di villanelle a due voci*, was published in Rome in 1652.

The school of Rome and the music of the Oratory

Although in terms of musical history the prime Italian achievement of the 16th century was in secular music, it also produced some of the finest religious music of all time. Palestrina, the greatest composer of the school of Rome, was also the greatest single Italian figure of the period. While Gabrieli has been described as the Titian of music, Palestrina was the Raphael, and just as their styles differed, so did the fields of their achievements. For apart from a book of fine madrigals, of which he later professed himself ashamed, Palestrina devoted himself almost exclusively to the music of the Church and set an example to all Europe as to how that music should be written following the reforms of the Council of Trent.

The most important of his predecessors were Costanzo Festa (d. 1545), whose madrigals have already been described, but who also wrote a great body of fine religious music including forty motets, and Jacobus Kerle (1532-91) a Fleming who passed most of his life in the region of Rome until, in the last ten years of his life, he settled in the empire. His notably devotional *Preces* of 1562 may have had some influence on the deliberations of the Council, but it must also be remembered that Rome was the centre of an important revival in popular devotional music.

The *laude spirituali*, whose early form we have already dealt with, enjoyed a remarkable flowering in polyphonic settings in the second half of the century as a result of the activity of St Philip Neri. From the meetings of a small number of pious men under the guidance of

BASSO PRIMO
MADRIGALI
GVERRIERI, ET AMOROSI
Con alcuni opufcoli in genere rapprefentatiuo, che faranno per breui Epifodij frà i canti fenza geíto.
LIBRO OTTAVO
DI CLAVDIO MONTEVERDE
Maeítro di Capella della Sereniífima Republ ca di Venetia.
DEDICATI
Alla Sacra Cefarea Maeftà
DELL' IMPERATOR
FERDINANDO III.
CON PRIVILEGIO.

IN VENETIA,   D
Appreffo Aleffandro Vincenti.   MDCXXXVIII.

left
Title page of the eighth book of madrigals by Monteverdi.

below
The Oratory of St Philip Neri, Rome.

Neri, there evolved the Congregation of the Oratory, which met regularly for worship. The only music permitted at these meetings were the *laudi*, which were sung before and after the sermon, which had now become more or less part of the liturgy.

Giovanni Animuccia, whose masses and motets are composed in accordance with the spirit of the Council of Trent, published two books of *laudi* on behalf of the Oratory. The year before his death in 1571 he became musical director at the Oratory, and he explains that although his compositions are written for as many as eight polyphonic parts, he has done his best to avoid 'fugues and other rash inventions in order that the sense of the text should not be obscured'.

Influenced by the sermons, which were invariably based on scriptural texts, and which had tended to become more and more like dramatic narratives, dramatic features were introduced into the texts of the *laudi* themselves. These were often in the form of 'dialogues'. Thus, the *Dialogo della Nativita del Nostro Signor* by Animuccia, written in 1570, where question and answer are distributed between twin choirs presenting two groups of the Faithful, or the very realistic episode from *The Prodigal Son*, seem like rough drafts for the oratorios of the next century, where characters are clearly differentiated and true dialogue is established.

Giovanni Pierluigi Palestrina.

Palestrina

Giovanni Pierluigi, who adopted the name of his native town of Palestrina, was born about the year 1524. It is possible that Arcadelt was one of his teachers in the art of music. In the art of self-advancement he would seem to have needed no instructor – soon after his appointment as master of the Julian Chapel in Rome, he dedicated to the pope, Julius III, a book of masses (1554), in the first of which he arranged for the printer to mark the entry of each new voice with the pope's coat of arms.

After a few years of service with the papal choir Palestrina was dismissed when Pope Paul IV enjoined celibacy on all members of the choir. Palestrina, who had been married since 1547, already had a family and was to marry again when his first wife died. By this second marriage to a wealthy widow the composer found himself with a flourishing furrier's business on his hands. Despite his duties as director of the Julian Chapel, to which he was reappointed in 1571, he seems to have made a success of commerce and was comfortably off at his death in 1594.

In a number of sessions which were spread over a period of some twenty years, the Council of Trent undertook the reform of many aspects of the Roman Catholic Church. An important part of the Council's work was concerned with the music of the service. Reform had been dear to the heart of Pope Marcellus II, who had reigned briefly during the year 1555, but it was a canon of the Council of Trent issued in 1562 that became the authoritative pronouncement in matters of church music. By this it was ordained that the music of the service must be purged of all secular, 'lascivious or impure' matter and must be devoted not only to the delight of the ears but, above all, to the worship of God and the encouragement of faith. To this end the music was to be clear and lucid and nothing was to interfere with the easy intelligibility of the text. The musical inspiration of Palestrina was fully in sympathy with the new requirements and his music is generally regarded as the perfect model of the style demanded by the Council.

Yet the compositions of Palestrina are much more than mere exemplars of a certain type of religious music. His secular work is confined to eight instrumental *ricercari* attributed to him and four books of madrigals for four and five voices published between 1555 and 1594. As might be expected these collections contain much magnificent music, even if they can hardly be regarded as advanced examples of the madrigal. The characteristics which mark his religious style – a sparing use of chromaticism and careful preparation of all dissonances – are found here; because of them his work lacks the dramatic intensity of the work of some of his contemporaries. But it was for his religious compositions that he earned the title of 'Prince of Music' and the epithet 'The ocean into which all streams have flowed'. His work, which avoids any dramatic or violent accents, presents a uniquely sensitive blend of the harmonic, or 'vertical' aspects of music with the polyphonic, or 'horizontal'. Despite many of the conservative elements in his music, Palestrina shows a sensitive awareness of the principles of tonality and chordal progression as they were emerging in the work of some of his contemporaries, though he avoids the use of major and minor chords as expressive elements, never straying far outside the limits set by the mode in which his music is written. The peak of his achievement is usually considered to be in the 105 masses, of which the celebrated *Missa Papae Marcelli* (dedicated to Pope Marcellus II) is an outstanding example. The masses employ the current parody and paraphrase techniques but some of them use the ancient methods of the straightforward *cantus firmus* mass. In addition to the masses, Palestrina composed much else and some of his most superb music is to be found in his motets, among which the four-part *Sicut cervus* is outstanding. But in everything he wrote this great Renaissance master rarely fell below the highest level, and, in its balanced and supple counterpoint and its lucidity of construction, his music represents one of the classic achievements of sacred polyphony.

Music at Venice

Of the Franco-Flemish musicians in Italy during the 16th century, Adriaan or Adriano Willaert was of special importance. In his thirty-five years as *maestro di capella* at St Mark's, Venice, he was the founder of a tradition of music which not only made Venice the greatest single Italian music centre, but which was also to have great importance in the music of other European countries as its influence spread in the following century.

At this time Venice was probably the richest and certainly the most stable of the Italian states. The days of its expansion were over but the wealth and glory of the Serene Republic was still legendary in Italy, and was expressed not only in the richly coloured and dramatic work of her painters, but also in the music of the great school of composers which, as we shall see, displayed similar qualities. At the centre of this musical activity was a single great institution, the church of St Mark, whose style and music made its influence felt throughout the surrounding towns within the sphere of the republic. St Mark's was a large musical establishment; at the head came the *maestro di capella* or musical director, and below him a number of other musicians, chief of which were the first and second organists. These two instrumentalists did not simply represent a chief organist and his deputy, but were each in charge of a separate instrument, for St Mark's had two choir lofts facing each other; this was to play an important part in the development of the Venetian style.

Adriano Willaert and the founding of a tradition

At the time of his appointment Willaert had already been in Italy a number of years. An amusing story is told by Zarlino, one of his successors, about his early years. Apparently the papal choir, to the delight of the young composer, had performed one of his works, but we can imagine his disillusionment on hearing that the choir had only performed the piece because they thought it was by the great Josquin – when they discovered who the composer really was they dropped it from the repertory. Presumably it was restored when the 'unknown' was appointed to the most coveted musical appointment in Italy. Willaert's talents and renown as a madrigalist have already been described, but he was equally outstanding in the field of religious music, particularly in the motet, and as a teacher the influence of his Flemish style was to be felt throughout the century, being detectable even in the work of Palestrina.

The typically Venetian style of antiphonal composition was to reach its apogee in the works of the two Gabrielis, but it was Willaert who pioneered the style in Italy. He must have been affected by the fact that this manner of performing the psalms and choral music was common in the north; the principle was not unknown in Italy but in Willaert's hands, and in the environment of St Mark's, it reached a new degree of formalisation, and its dramatic and colouristic qualities were seized on and extended by his successors. The style was to be particularly fertile in the field of instrumental music. Here, however, Willaert was not so active, being represented only by a three-part piece in the contrapuntal manner of the *ricercare* and lute adaptations of madrigals for solo voice by Verdelot. It is as a composer of vocal music that he is remembered, and his last great contribution in this field was to the evolution of vocal declamations, probably influenced by the humanistic ideals current in Italy, which laid great stress on the clear presentation of the words of the text.

Willaert died in 1562 and was succeeded in 1563 by Cypriano de Rore. De Rore, an ageing man, found the duties too arduous and returned to the service of his former patron the duke of Parma (1564); dying the next year. Although for most of his career de Rore was working outside Venice, he was a pupil of Willaert and the style of his master is apparent in his works, particularly his religious music. His madrigals have already been mentioned but he also wrote a number of masses, motets and a St John Passion. These works reveal a sensitive handling of the text only to be expected from a master of

below
The Sistine Chapel with its frescoes by Michelangelo is one of the great monuments of the Italian Renaissance.

bottom
An allegorical depiction of Musica playing a small positive organ.

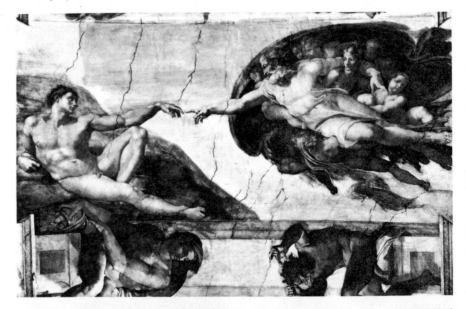

the madrigal, but they show none of the pioneering inspiration which was behind his secular vocal music.

In 1565 the post of *maestro di capella* passed to yet another of Willaert's pupils. Gioseffo Zarlino, who died in 1590, has left only a few compositions. These are highly competent, but it is as a theorist that he is most celebrated. His *Institutioni Harmoniche*, published in 1558, was soon translated into French, Dutch and German. The book devotes much of its time to an exposition of the theory of musical practice in the first half of the century. But it also contains a highly significant section in which Zarlino not only recognises the importance of the major and minor harmonies, increasingly obtrusive interlopers into the world of the modes, but puts far greater emphasis on their place in music than any former theoretician. The breakdown in the system of the modes was almost inevitable after the birth of polyphony, but the process had been a gradual one, and it was in the course of the 16th century that the pattern of the harmonic system of later generations began to emerge. The work of Zarlino is a major theoretical landmark in the recognition of the new system. As might be expected, he suffered attacks for his boldness but we may reflect that it was not unfitting that this theorist of the new elements of 'colour' in music should have held the chief post in the musical establishment of Venice.

Instrumental music at Venice

The organists at St Mark's included in their number many outstanding composers, of whom the most important were Merulo, Andrea Gabrieli and his nephew Giovanni. All of these wrote fine instrumental music but all of them also produced many excellent vocal compositions.

Claudio Merulo (1533-1604) held the post of first organist for some twenty years, resigning in 1584 and spending the last twenty years of his life at Parma. Two years after his arrival at Venice he went into partnership as a music publisher, his first publication being a collection of Verdelot's madrigals. Merulo himself wrote a number of fine if unadventurous madrigals and also

Joseph Asioli Cor Sculps

Claudius Merulus Corrigensis

Claudio Merulo.

masses and motets; in the last he occasionally employed the antiphonal choirs. But his most important work was in the field of keyboard music and here he contributed significantly to the brilliant genre of the toccata, introducing advanced contrapuntal sections and showing considerable imagination in his handling of harmony.

Merulo was succeeded as first organist by his older contemporary Andrea Gabrieli (*c.* 1520-86). Gabrieli produced masses, a number of distinguished motets and a setting of the psalms. In editions of both the motets and the psalms, he indicates that the works may be performed by either voices or instruments and provides alternative methods of performance – it would be surprising if in some performances the two were not combined. But Andrea also made notable contributions to keyboard music, his *ricercari* and *canzone* representing one of the peaks of this type of composition in the 16th century; these works, in which elaborate 'fireworks' passages, admirably suited to the keyboard, alternate with serious polyphonic writing, have a markedly individual character. He also wrote for instrumental ensemble but here both he and most of his contemporaries were to be outstripped by his nephew Giovanni Gabrieli.

Giovanni Gabrieli

This composer, who lived between 1557 and 1612, has been called 'the musical Titian of Venice' and his music is rich in harmonic and textural colour. For four years as a young man he had been at Munich with Lassus, but in 1585, when his uncle and teacher became first organist at St Mark's, Giovanni was appointed to the second instrument and remained in this position until his death. He was among the first Venetian composers to use the *basso continuo*, the compositional device which came to characterise the music of the Baroque age. Some of his music shows the features of the earlier tradition but even in his superb madrigals the characteristic colour of his style is apparent, and in his motets the polychoral tradition of Venice reaches its magnificent climax. In these works, Gabrieli wrote in four-, five- and six-part polyphony, the music being performed by two, three or four separate choirs of voices or instruments and voices. The effect of such elaborate ensembles distributed in the body of a church, so that the listener is assailed by music on all sides and can hardly expect to hear the same sonorities in successive performances of any given work, is both exhilarating and moving. Gabrieli's compositions for instruments alone are still regarded as among his greatest work and in this field, through his German pupils such as the German, Heinrich Schütz, he was to influence the music of all Europe.

In 1593 Giovanni, in collaboration with his uncle, published a number of *Intonazioni d'organo*, short keyboard preludes, semi-improvisational in manner, which were used at various points in the service to give the reciting note to the priest, or the pitch to the choir. Giovanni's *ricercari* based on a principal theme are among the more important anticipations of the art of the fugue. With the publication of the fourteen *canzone* and two *sonate* in the collection *Sacrae Symphoniae* (1597), he established one of the outstanding landmarks in the Venetian school of instrumental music. The most famous piece is the *Sonata pian.e forte* which is the first known work for an instrumental ensemble to have markings in the score to indicate changes in volume dynamics, and is also one of the first to specify the instruments to be employed for the various parts. But the collection contains other, perhaps more important, innovations, particularly in the *canzona da sonar*.

From the middle of the 16th century this type, derived ultimately from the French *chanson*, had been a favourite with Italian composers for instruments. It consisted of a large number of short contrasting sections one after the other in chain fashion. His predecessors had shown great ingenuity in giving a sense of unity and continuity to the sequence; Giovanni Gabrieli extends the process in one of his *canzone* by repeating the first section, almost as a refrain, after each new 'variation'. He also expanded the instrumental resources, writing examples for as many as twenty-two instruments. In addition to the *Sacrae Symphoniae* he also published a collection of *canzone e sonate* in 1615. With Gabrieli the instrumental *canzona* developed as an independent musical form and was impregnated with an entirely new spirit. The consummate art with which he balances the instrumental choirs, the way in which he controls responses and dialogue, his perfect mastery of thematic elaboration, his feeling for harmony, his powerful dynamism and the subtle colouring of his music leave all former attempts by his predecessors far behind.

Music in the theatre: the beginnings of opera

At the end of the 15th century the court theatre, which had developed on the model of religious plays (of which there were so many in Florence), was beginning to have more and more importance for music. One of the first non-religious plays, the *Orfeo* of Politian, presented in Mantua in 1471, had had musical interludes, or *intermedi*, written for it. Little by little these *intermedi* developed into an art form in their own right. They found particularly favourable conditions in Florence, where princely masquerades, which had succeeded the popular carnival displays, followed each other in succession at the court of the Medici. In 1539, Francesco Carteccia wrote *intermedi* for the wedding of Cosimo I and, in collaboration with Alessandro Striggio, for the marriage of Francesco in 1565.

In 1576 the humanist, Giovanni de' Bardi, founded the *camerata fiorentina*, where Greek aesthetics were discussed, where the *stile madrigalesco* was bitterly attacked and 'classical' monody – one voice with instrumental accompaniment – extolled. The academy did not invent monody, which had long been commonly enough used by Italian popular and folk musicians, nor were they the first to introduce the accompanied voice into art music; what they did was to lay a greater stress than ever before on this style of monody and to develop from it the important art of recitative. At first the *camerata* were more concerned in their discussions with literary and dramatic questions, but although music thus took second place, the beginnings of a new idea appear in a madrigal composed in 1579 by Pietro Strozzi for the wedding of Francesco de' Medici and Bianca Cappello, and sung by a character representing 'Night'. In 1589, at the festivities held in connection with the marriage of Ferdinand I, a performance was staged of *Pellegrina*, a comedy divided into six long acts. Several composers collaborated, including not only Cristofano Malvezzi and Luca Marenzio, but also Giovanni de' Bardi himself, together with three 'advanced' young composers, Emilio de' Cavalieri, Giulio Caccini and Jacopo Peri. Some of the melodies were ornamented with long vocal passages improvised by Caccini, which mark the first step by this composer towards the style of ornamented recitative which he was to develop later. The end of the century saw the rise to prominence of the figure of Cavalieri, whose theatrical experiments culminated with the production of his *Rappresentazione dell'anima e di corpo* in 1600. At the same time, urged on by Jacopo Corsi and Ottavio Rinuccini, the Florentine *camerata* was turning its attention to music in drama. In 1595 it encouraged Peri to compose his *Dafne* and, in 1600, *Euridice*, in which he brought the style of *recitativo* to perfection. With these works, the way was open to the operas of Monteverdi.

above left
Giovanni Maria Artusi, who had a considerable reputaion as a musical theorist.

left
An early bass stringed instrument. Notice the flat peg disc, the 'C' holes and the deep gouts in the waist.

The music of Spain

The Iberian peninsula, although more or less isolated from the rest of Europe by the Pyrenees, is by no means a simple ethnic or cultural unity within itself. In the west of the Pyrenees are the Basques, whose seven provinces constitute a single ethnic unit across the Franco-Spanish border. South-east from here lies Catalonia, which throughout the middle ages was much more closely related to Languedoc, with which it has affinities of language, than to Castile. We shall see the consequences of this influence on the liturgy and hence on the music of this region.

The Romanisation of the Iberian peninsula, a colony which bred emperors and poets, had been so complete that the barbarian Visigothic invaders fell under the cultural influence of Roman Spain. Thus Seville in the time of St Isidore (c. 570-636) was already one of the greatest centres of learning in Europe. In 711 the Arab invasion brought a violent end to Romanised Spain and established a new culture at Cordoba (founded in 756 as an independent emirate) and other centres where Greek science and philosophy were closely studied long before they passed to Western Europe. Confronting the Arabs were the Christian kingdoms of Oviedo, founded by the almost legendary Pelayo about 719, Navarre, created a kingdom in 750, and Castile, which gained its independence about 950. These became centres of a revived Christian culture. From 840 Santiago de Compostela on the north-west coast was one of the greatest pilgrim shrines in Europe, and the road leading there became the main thoroughfare for the exchange of ideas with the rest of Europe; it was hence the combined influences of Europe and Islam which inspired the artists and musicians of Spain.

The Hispanic liturgy

Between the 6th and 8th centuries Spain evolved its own liturgy, sometimes called 'Visigothic' or 'Mozarabic'. Since it contained elements of pre-Visigothic ritual, and since it was never exclusive to the Mozarabs (Christians living in Arab-dominated territories), 'Hispanic' is a more appropriate term. The Hispanic liturgy has in fact many features in common with the Syriac rite. These can be explained partly by the Eastern Empire's influence on its Iberian colonies, partly by the ties between the Peninsula and the Levant forged by travellers, and partly by certain heresies common to both regions. The Hispanic liturgy also owed much to the Milanese rite, especially the Ambrosian hymns, but most of all to the Roman. Its connection with the Gallican rite is more complex and it may in fact have influenced it. It is known to us by some twenty ancient manuscripts, the most important being a 10th-century collection of antiphons in the cathedral of Leon.

On Palm Sunday, 1077, prompted by various reasons such as his preference for Rome, dynastic relations with France and the Cluniac movement, Alfonso VI of Castile promulgated the abolition of the Hispanic rite, an act which was ratified by the Council of Burgos in 1080. However, the rite did not suddenly disappear, nor was it ever completely abandoned. For example, under the Arab domination Toledo, the old Visigothic capital, had retained the Hispanic form and although it accepted the Roman rite after the Christian reconquest in 1085, the liturgical tradition was not only not entirely abandoned, but survives to this day. In the west, Braga and Coimbra also retained the Hispanic ritual until the end of the 11th century.

An exception must also be made of Catalonia, which was under Frankish influence; Barcelona was captured in 801 by Charlemagne and not retaken by the Moors until 864. As late as the 12th century the memory of Catalonia as a 'march' or 'countship' of the Carolingian Empire remained very much alive in the minds of Christian and Arabic historians alike; in a number of texts, in the *Poema del Mio Cid* (c. 1140) for example, we still find reference to the Catalans as *Los Francos*, the French. Thus it was through Catalonia and the neighbouring states that the early medieval tropes were introduced into Spain.

The Hispanic liturgy, although often classed with Eastern rites because of Syriac influences, is undoubtedly of Western origin. Its order is largely that of the Latin mass and possesses certain unique forms which, although their equivalents are sometimes found in other non-Roman rites, have musical and liturgical features entirely their own.

At the beginning of the 16th century the service books of the Hispanic liturgy were edited under the care of Cardinal Ximenés de Cisneros, who established a special chapter to celebrate the Hispanic mass in the cathedral of Toledo. In the middle of the 18th century a further edition was printed and, since the last century, work has been going forward on a definitive edition based on the most authentic manuscripts of this rite.

Some manuscripts indicate that the substitution of the Roman ritual for the Hispanic took place at a much earlier date in some parts of the country than is usually supposed, while others show that non-Roman manuscripts were still being copied until a comparatively late date. In the 13th century Gonzolado Berceo, the first known Castilian poet, was using the vocabulary of the Hispanic ritual in his poems.

In this context the position of Catalonia was indeed quite exceptional. Not only was the Hispanic ritual not cultivated in Catalonia, but under the impetus of French liturgical centres it developed a very important para-liturgical school of its own, which was like none other in Spain.

Liturgical drama was practised at a very early date and still remains a living art throughout eastern Spain,

A vihuela.

either in the form of a *consueta*, a more or less elaborate liturgical work based on a Biblical story, or a performance of the *Song of the sibyl*, which was an addition to the Christmas liturgy; or in the form of *fiestas* or mystery plays. The most famous of these was the *Fiesta de Elche*, the music of which, according to legend, is of miraculous origin although parts of it can be ascribed to early Renaissance Spain. In Catalonia also we find early examples of ecclesiastical dance music. A manuscript entitled *Llivre Vermell* (the Red Book), from the Abbey of Montserrat, contains songs and dances consecrated to pilgrims, with 14th-century musical notation.

The early sources of Spanish music

The Arab influence on Spanish music has been much exaggerated; one theorist has tried to trace all musical art in Europe from Arab chants. However, links there obviously were, as was shown in 1948 with the discovery of a collection of Hispano-Hebraic poems based on an Arabic model. These poems, with refrains in Spanish (in Mozarabic dialect), extend from some time prior to 1042 until the 13th century. Some fifty of these Spanish refrains, or what are in fact little poems in their own right, have been brought to light by further researches.

The number of purely musical documents of the period is not very large, but what exists is very interesting. Of the whole copious output of Gallego-Portuguese troubadour music only the 13th-century *chansons* of Martin Códax have survived. On the other hand the music of 420 *chansons*, from Alfonso X the Wise of Castile's collection of *Cantigas* (1252-84), dedicated to the Virgin and describing the story of her miracles, have come down to us in three manuscript volumes. These *Cantigas de Santa Maria* are one of the most interesting of medieval musical manuscripts and contain a vast collection of poems in the Gallician dialect as well as many miniatures depicting musical instruments. It is now generally accepted that the king himself was closely involved in the composition.

Polyphony was practised in Spain from quite an early date. A 12th-century manuscript from Santiago de Compostela, contains as many as twenty compositions for three or more parts, which justifies Compostela's claim to have been one of the earliest seats of European polyphony. Moreover a certain Lucas, *magnus organista* of Tarragona, who died in 1164, seems to have been the precursor of Pérotin himself in the development of the higher forms of polyphony. However, in the following century the schools of Toledo, Ripoll and Tortosa derived their inspiration from that of Notre-Dame de Paris. The existence of an Arab school at Cordoba, where polyphony was said to have been taught in the 11th century, has never been established. An important memorial to Spanish polyphony in the early 1300s is provided by the manuscript collection of the Cistercian convent of Las Huelgas, which also bears witness to the wealth and variety of religious services at the convent. Court records of Aragon, Castile and Navarre seem to show that in Spain the courts, too, contributed to the development of polyphonic music.

In the 15th century Spain's connections with France were numerous and fruitful. Aragon and its court in particular maintained constant relations with the papal court of Avignon and that of Burgundy, whose musical traditions they followed. Spain also had many close contacts with the papal court of Rome; we need only remember Spain's part in Italian politics and the Spanish popes, Calixtus III (1455-58) and Alexander IV (1492-1503).

above
An illustration from the 14th-century Llivre Vermell, *depicting monarchs kneeling before the Pope.*

above left
Portrait of Cardinal Ximenés de Cisneros in Toledo Cathedral.

below
A page from the Cantigas *of Alfonso X the Wise.*

The court of Naples and Tinctoris

But the most direct contact between Spain and the main European traditions was through the court of the Aragonese kings of Naples, who extended the traditions of their Angevin predecessors. The brilliance of the reign of Alfonso V the Magnanimous (1443-58) was continued under his successor Ferrante, and Naples was one of the leading cultural centres of 15th-century Europe, boasting among its members the poet Sannazzaro, one of the most popular poets of the madrigalists of the next century. In music the court of Ferrante showed even more impressive achievements than that of his father, its leading figure being the Fleming Johannes Tinctoris (*c.* 1435-1511).

Although a competent composer (he enjoyed some reputation during his lifetime), Tinctoris is chiefly remembered as a theorist. He wrote twelve treatises which together constitute a major source for the music of the early Renaissance and, although he wrote a standard history of music, Tinctoris makes it plain that in his opinion the only music worthy of the name is that in the style which, in succession to 14th-century *ars nova*, originated in the 1420s. Like the French writer, Martin le Franc, he credits the English school, led by Dunstable, with founding the style, while listing Dufay, Binchois and Ockeghem as its great continuators. In his treatment of the modes he shows that he was aware that with the coming of polyphony the whole modal structure was destined to decay as harmonic considerations came more and more to the fore, while his treatment of intervals is a natural extension of this awareness. Like other theorists of his day Tinctoris pays much attention to the practice of improvisation, confirming yet again its influence on composition, and he also gives evidence that instruments were commonly used in the church music of his time. Although most of his career was spent in the service of a Spanish court, Tinctoris has little respect for the guitar, saying that its 'thin' tone meant it was of little use except as an instrument for women and for the performance of love songs.

Among the other musicians at the court of Naples was the Spanish born Johannes Cornago, whose works include a mass of particular interest, coming as it does at the dawn of the European 'Age of Discovery'–this is the *Missa mappa mundi*. He also wrote a number of works with Spanish words including examples of the *villancico*, the Spanish equivalent of the *virelay*.

Spanish music in the 15th century

Cornago represents the native Spanish school at the court of Naples. In its home land this tradition was already strong; one of its most interesting features was a group of musical treatises in the vernacular, including one by Fernando Esteban of Seville written about 1410. Although these works are for the most part limited in scope they reveal a knowledge of developments outside Spain – one mentions Dunstable, Dufay and Ockeghem – and in the *De musica practica* (1482) of Ramos de Pareja, gave birth to a work of great importance. Pareja published his book in Italy where he was apparently living from the 1470s. His treatise is one of the very earliest on music to be printed but its real interest lies in its highly controversial treatment of musical intervals and the scale; he even dared challenge Guido d'Arezzo's venerable hexachord system. His

Coplas de zambardo:

Title page of Coplas de Zambardo *by Juan del Encina.*

theories were fully in tune with the practical developments in music at his time, yet they set off a major academic storm.

There are four particularly important sources of Spanish 15th-century music. The first is the *Cancionero de Palacio*, which contains the compositions used in the ducal chapel of the house of Alba; according to the index, it originally comprised 551 pieces, but only about 460 have survived. Several of these, although written on a single stave, can be sung in canon, and one of them can even be reversed. The *Cancionero de la Colombina* (i.e. from the library of Ferdinand Colombus, the son of Christopher, which is housed in Seville) contains one hundred pieces, of which twenty are repeated in the Palacio Collection. The *Cancionero del Real Alcázar de Segovia* has thirty-eight Spanish *chansons* which are included with French and Italian *chansons*, and a number of religious works, some of which are by Netherlandish composers. The fourth source is the library of the Cathedral of Tarragona, which houses what is undoubtedly the richest collection of Spanish ecclesiastical music of this period.

The most common forms of composition at this period were the strophic *villancico*, the Spanish equivalent of the *virelay*, which had largely been abandoned by French composers in this period. The refrain (*estrivillo*) of the *villancico* is often of popular origin – or at least popular in style. The *romance*, a sort of epic lyric ballad which proceeds by long declamatory passages (*laisses*), consisted of a number of verses whose music is almost invariably repeated every fourth stanza.

Among the most important composers of this school were Cornago, who after his services at the court of Alfonso the Magnanimous joined the choir of Ferdinand the Catholic; Juan de Anchieta (1460-1523), of the chapel of Queen Isabella and later of Prince Don Juan and one of the finest church composers of his period; and the renowned Francesco de Penalosa (*c.* 1470-1528), who served in the chapel of Ferdinand but on the king's death in 1417 went to Rome. His contrapuntal skill is shown in an *ensalada* (*quodlibet*) in which four *villancicos* are combined. In the reign of Alfonso V of Portugal (1438-81) Tristan da Silva, the first important Portuguese composer, devoted himself to making a collection of the king's favourite music; unfortunately this anthology, like most of da Silva's own work, has not survived.

The 16th century in Spain

The most interesting composer at the turn of the century was Juan del Encina; he was born at Salamanca about 1469 and died some time after 1530. At one time he served the second duke of Alba, and also received favours from Pope Leo X in Rome, at whose court he stayed for five years; he also undertook a journey to the Holy Land. As well as being a composer, Encina was also a poet of great delicacy, and translated the *Bucolics* of Virgil. He was a pioneer in the Spanish secular theatre and several of his compositions, which are presented in the *Cancionero de Palacio*, are based on Virgil's *Eclogues*, and were written for stage presentation.

During the long reigns of Charles V (1517-56) and Philip II (1556-96) Spanish music, especially church music, reached its highest level of perfection and there was no lack of expert musicians of international calibre. Instrumental music, especially for organ and *vihuela*, attained an excellence equal to anything being produced in Europe while Spanish religious polyphony, which had distinctive individual qualities, was in the very first rank not only in its spiritual intensity but also in its musical achievement.

The school of Andalusia

Three great schools contributed to the astonishing wealth of Spanish religious music in this period: Castile, Catalonia-Aragon, and Andalusia. Among the many composers of the Andalusian school were Pedro Fernandez de Castilleja (d. 1547), nearly all of whose works have been lost though his status may be guessed from the fact that Guerrero named him 'Master of Masters'; Juan Navarro (*c.* 1530) who died in Mexico about 1610 and was author of the first work devoted entirely to music to be printed in the New World. The most important of all the Andalusian school were Guerrero and his great teacher, Morales.

Francisco Guerrero, born at Seville about 1528, was also a pupil of his brother Pedro – himself a competent composer. He was director of music at Jaen and Malaga, but in the 1550s he returned to Seville where he was to become musical director of the cathedral and where he was to stay, apart from a period in Rome and a visit to Palestine, until his death in 1599. His works enjoyed widespread popularity and were published in France, Italy and Flanders – a remarkable achievement for a Spanish composer of that period. He composed many masses and motets, a Matthew and a John Passion as well as many versions of the Magnificat and other Maryan works. His secular music is represented by the *Canciones y villanescas* of 1589, some of which are apparently parodies of religious pieces. Guerrero's main characteristics are the serenity and gentle lyricism of his music, and, if not the greatest, he is one of the most 'Spanish' composers of the 16th century.

The outstanding figure of the Andalusian school and one of Spain's greatest composers is Cristobal de Morales, the 'Divine Morales' as a modern writer has called him. He was born at Seville in 1500 and may have been a pupil of his father, whom we know to have been musician to the Duke of Medinaceli, and certainly studied under Fernandez de Castilleja. In 1535 he went to Rome, where he was admitted into the papal choir. His abilities were quickly recognised there, to judge by the important commissions he received – a cantata written for the reconciliation of Charles V and Francis I of France, commissioned by Pope Paul III in 1538, and a motet in honour of Ippolito d'Este's elevation to the cardinalate in 1539. He returned to Spain in 1545 with ten months leave of absence; as events turned out this was to be indefinitely extended until his death. We find him successively at the cathedral of Toledo, at Malaga, and also, perhaps, at Seville. Apart from two Italian madrigals and two compositions set to Spanish words, the whole of Morales' output (now in course of publication) was religious in character. His style is extremely austere, devoid of contrapuntal complexities, but at the same time it has a profoundly emotional quality obtained by his use of extremely bold harmonic progressions.

In the field of secular polyphony the most gifted Andalusian master was Juan Vasquez. Born at Badajoz in about 1500, he studied at Seville and worked at Burgos, in the north, before returning to Seville, where he died in about 1560. He left a very fine Office for the Dead, but his songs are sheer masterpieces, some of them being set to words by unknown poets such as Garcilaso and Boscan, while others are set to anonymous traditional poetry. Such is the beauty of these songs that nearly all vihuelists published their own transcriptions of them.

Cristobal de Morales.

The school of Castile and Victoria

Among musicians of the Castilian school we find the names of Juan Escribano, who died at Rome in 1558; Bartolomé de Escobedo (d. Segovia, 1564), cantor at Salamanca and later at Rome, where some of his compositions are preserved; Francisco Soto de Langa (1534-1609), who died in Rome and worked at the Oratory with St Philip Neri and Animuccia, and Diego Ortiz, distinguished for his instrumental compositions. But the most important of all the Castilian school was Luiz de Victoria, who is the only Spaniard who can be put on the same plane as Lassus and Palestrina.

Victoria was born in Avila somewhere between 1548 and 1550, and died in Madrid in 1611. In Spain he was a pupil of Escobedo; but he went to Rome in the 1560s and Palestrina seems to have been his master; at all events, there was, incontestably, a reciprocal exchange of influence between the Italian master and his Spanish disciple. After a successful twenty years in Rome he returned to Spain for good and settled in Madrid in the service of the widowed Empress Marie, daughter of Charles V. Victoria seems never to have written a single secular work and, unlike Morales who occasionally borrowed secular motifs as themes for his masses, was never inspired by other than religious melodies. He was a brilliant but unostentatious composer who never made a gratuitous display of his marvellous technical ability as a contrapuntalist. He never hesitated to make full dramatic use of religious texts, sometimes obtaining the most striking results by the use of ex-

Portrait of Luiz de Victoria, the most important musician of the Castilian school.

tremely bold dissonances. He composed some twenty masses for four to twelve voices, about forty-five motets, eighteen versions of the Magnificat, an Office for the Dead, and another for the Sunday before Easter, which is among one of his masterpieces, and a number of hymns, litanies, psalms, anthems and other works for the Church.

Aragon

The masters of the Catalan-Aragonese school are also numerous. In Aragon we find Melchor Robledo, who died in Saragossa in 1577, and Sebastian Aguilera de Heredia, organist and composer, who went to Flanders in the suite of Isabella, daughter of Philip II.

Mateo Flecha the Elder, born at Prades about 1483, belonged to the Catalan school; he died at the monastery of Poblet in 1553. He directed the music at the cathedral of Lerida before entering the service of the Infantas Maria and Joanna. Flecha occupies a particular place in Spanish music for his *ensaladas*, which were published in Prague in 1581 by his nephew, Mateo Flecha the Younger, and some of which were adapted by the vihuelists. Flecha the Younger (1520-1604) was also a composer and produced a number of madrigals.

Joan Brudieu, by birth a Frenchman, was music director at Urgell for forty years and died there. In 1585 he published a collection of sixteen madrigals, five of which are to Catalan texts, and in addition has left a very fine Requiem.

Among the many collections of secular polyphony, including works by composers of all the three main schools, is that published in Venice in 1533 under the title of *Villancicos de diversos autores*, better known as the *Cancionero of Upsala*, because the only known extant copy was found in the library of that city. Among collections preserved in other libraries, the National Library of Madrid and those of several Italian towns, the most important is the one that forms part of the collection of the dukes of Medinaceli.

Instrumental and keyboard music

In this field the Spanish composers made an early and distinguished contribution. Although virtually no music has survived from the 15th century, there is plenty of evidence to indicate the widespread cultivation of instruments which we must postulate to explain the glories of the 16th. The Spaniards were above all distinguished in music for the string *vihuela* and the organ.

The vihuelists represent a tradition unique to Spain, composing as they did for an instrument hardly cultivated elsewhere. There is now no doubt that the plucked *vihuela* so frequently referred to in Spanish musical records is in fact a guitar with six courses of strings. It was used for courtly music while the four-stringed version was the popular instrument. Of the extensive body of music composed for it during the 16th and 17th centuries, some of the best occurs in the first printed collection. This was the *Libro del musica de vihuela de mano intitulado El Maestro*, published by the aristocratic composer, Luis Milán, at Valencia in 1536. Milán (1500-c. 61) describes the pieces, which include a number of *villancicos* and fantasias, as for beginners, but their polish and elegance assure their composer a high place in the history of instrumental music. In all some ten volumes of 16th-century *vihuela* music by Spanish composers have been · preserved. Besides

Milán they include Enriquez de Valderrábano (1547), Diego Pisador (1531), Alonso Mudarra (1546), Miguel de Fuenllano – another blind musician – and Esteban Duza (1576). Publications by Venegas de Henestrosa, Santa Maria and Cabezón also contain compositions for *vihuela*.

The repertory consists of works for accompanied solo voice – Spanish and Portuguese *romances* and *villancicos*, together with Italian sonnets and *chansons*; there are also several settings of classical Latin texts, which are among the first indications of Renaissance accompanied monody. The purely instrumental pieces are either transcriptions of polyphonic works – Spanish or Franco-Flemish – or else of dances, *tientos* (preludes), *fantasias* and *diferencios* (variations). The *diferencios* are particularly interesting inasmuch as they constitute the first examples of the theme-and-variations genre which became so important in later instrumental music. Towards the end of the 16th century the *vihuela* was largely replaced by the guitar, which with the addition of a fifth string had acquired new artistic possibilities. The modification is traditionally attributed to Vicente Espinel, poet and musician (1551-1624), whose first treatise, *Guittara Espanola* (1583) was republished many times right up to the end of the 18th century.

Although little has survived, its quality is such as to put the Spanish school of organists in the forefront of European composition. The *Libro de Cifra nueva* by Venegas de Henestrosa, published in 1557, contains works by leading Spanish and Italian composers, and the *Declaración* by the theorist Juan Bermudo contained organ music by Spanish masters. The greatest of Spanish organists was Antonio de Cabezón, court musician to Charles V and Philip II; his works were published posthumously by his son Hernando, who succeeded him to the Chapel Royal. Cabezón was born in 1510 at Castrojeriz and died in Madrid in 1566. Blind from birth, he started his career at the age of eighteen as musician to the empress; he travelled Europe as a member of her household and this gave him the opportunity to meet all the best musicians of his day. His style, which was better adapted to the organ than that of most of his contemporaries, makes use of all the technical possibilities of counterpoint, while remaining essentially instrumental in character. Its grandeur and inventiveness have led to its comparison with the work of J. S. Bach himself.

To a later age one of the most valuable contributions by a Spaniard to instrumental music must be the *Tratado, de glosas . . . en la musica de violones*, published in Rome in 1553 by Diego Ortiz (*c.* 1510- after 1570). In his book, which is rich in musical examples, Ortiz gives detailed treatment of the highly important art of ornamentation and improvisation as applied to the music of bowed stringed instruments.

Portugal

In comparison with Spain, research on old Portuguese music is still relatively slight. In the collection of *chansons* in the Biblioteca Publia Hortensia, Portugal possesses a pendant to the Spanish collection of 15th- and 16th-century music. Gil Vicente (1465?-1536?), who was active as a writer for the theatre from 1502, is credited with being the creator of the Portuguese theatre and the originator of music for the stage. Unfortunately his musical production has been lost and we only have his notes for stage directions and a few popular songs, preserved from other sources, which he introduced into his plays. Apart from the chronicler Damião de Goes (1501-53), whose three motets have

been preserved, the greatest Portuguese polyphonists belong to the school of Manoel Mendes, musical director in his native town of Evora, where he died in 1605.

His pupils Duardo Lobo (*c.* 1565-1643), Filipe de Magalhaes, Diego Dias Melgaço and Soares Rebello were to become well known in the following century. Grigorio Silvestre de Mesa (1522-70), a distinguished composer, was organist at Granada Cathedral. He also led a flourishing school of vihuelists (the Milan volume contains three Spanish *villancicos* and three in Portuguese dedicated to Prince Don João), but little is known of their work.

England during the middle ages and the Renaissance

In the high middle ages the insularity of England, which has become such a cliché, was in fact not very marked. The short sea passage across the Channel was a great deal less arduous than the passage across the Alps or the Pyrenees or the forests which lay between France and the empire. The fruitful contacts between the island and the Continent were made still more numerous by the fact that for hundreds of years the kings of England held large territories in the realm of France. Compared with today, however, all European centres were comparatively isolated and tended to breed independent traditions. England was no exception and indeed she produced a strikingly original musical language. In the centuries immediately following the missionary endeavours of St Augustine from Rome in the early 7th century, however, England was comparatively cut off, and the first indications we possess of the originality of English music are found in its plainsong. Indeed a liturgical rite, independent of Rome and based at Salisbury Cathedral, very quickly made its appearance. At the time of the Reformation this Sarum rite (from the Latin name for Salisbury) served as the basis for the Anglican liturgy. Like the Ambrosian rite, it was more luxuriant and more colourful than the Gregorian, and tended to vigour of expression rather than to the purity of line of the Roman liturgy. The importance of the Sarum rite in the history of English music has never been sufficiently stressed. It was this which provided the *cantus firmus* for many English church polyphonists, and inspired much of the music of composers of the Reformation. Although we have no knowledge of any other music prior to the Conquest, there is every evidence of the existence of an old established musical tradition. In the important field of polyphony, it seems very possible that Britain, thanks to its own original folk music, was already versed in the art of part-singing long before the Continent. The famous philosopher and theologian, Johannes Scotus Erigena (810-77), describes in detail two-part polyphonic music, to which he already applied the term *organa*.

From the Norman Conquest to the Hundred Years War

Throughout these centuries French was the language of the court, nobility and clergy. However, the exceptional musical contribution made by Anglo-Saxon England is quite a different matter. There existed here an authentic polyphony quite unique in Europe. This was not scholastic but genuine folk music; at the end of the 12th century Geraldus Cambrensis describes a part song for several voices which had long been sung in the Celtic parts of the island – in Scotland, Wales and Ireland. The extraordinary originality of this polyphony resides in the systematic use of thirds and sixths. These inter-vals, according to theory based on Pythagorean ideas, were still regarded on the Continent as dissonant, as opposed to the consonant intervals of the fourth and fifth, which now seem much cruder to our ears. In northern England, two-part songs were common and we even have a late 12th-century example from the Orkneys; this English form of diaphony was called gymel (from the Latin *gemellus*, a twin). This 'twin' song is distinguished not only by its use of thirds, but also by the way in which the parts are frequently crossed. In these part songs it seems that even a primitive sort of canon was employed.

This art of secular polyphony was paralleled in English church music, as is proved by the late 11th-century tropiary of the cathedral of Winchester. This contains 150 *organa* for two voices, but unfortunately the form of notation employed has made it impossible to decipher the exact form of these early *organa*, which would seem to pre-date the work of the French composer Léonin by a full century. Another example of early English church polyphony is some early 12th-century two-voice responses which show similarities to the works of the school of Limoges. As elsewhere in Europe, there were few important theoreticians in England during this period. Mention must be made of the *De musica mensurabili* of John Garland, who went to study and teach in Paris in about 1210. But much the most interesting work is by one of his anonymous contemporaries, a monk of Bury St Edmunds, who also studied in Paris. By a stroke of remarkable luck the notes which he took in the lectures there have survived and have proved an invaluable source for the study of the style and theories of the great school of Notre Dame.

The principal examples of music of the *ars nova* period in England are to be found in manuscripts in Worcester Cathedral and the abbey of Bury St Edmunds. The more original works are found in the Worcester manuscript and here we find the intervals of the third and the sixth adopted by church musicians. A good example of the style is the *conductus, Redit aetas aurea* written for the coronation of Richard the Lionheart, himself a composer. Although in England composers continued to write *organa* during the 13th century at a period when they had died out in France, this did not retard development in other fields and the bilingual motet was also cultivated, French and Latin or English and Latin being used. Even here we notice an original English feature in the practice of having the voices exchange parts. In view of the predominance of French it is not surprising that the first motet with English text, *Worldes blisce*, appears comparatively late – about the year 1270. It was to be followed by others among which *Fowles in the Frith, Edibo thu, Jesu Christes milde moder*, are examples using gymel. But the most remarkable musical composition of the English 13th century, indeed one might almost say of Europe, is the isolated but splendid *Sumer is icumen in*. A justly famous piece, this is far and away the earliest example of six-part poly-

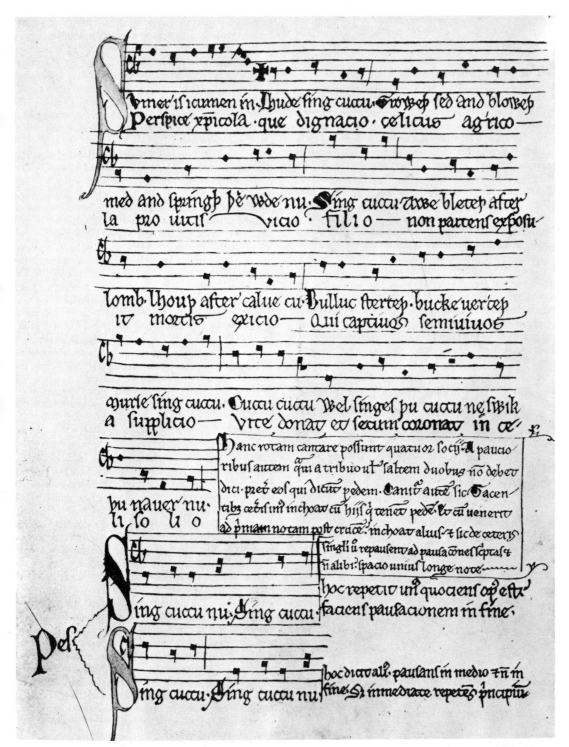

Perhaps the most famous of all medieval compositions, the round Sumer is icumen in, *composed, probably at Reading Abbey, in the late 13th century.*

phonic writing since it seems unlikely that it was composed later than the year 1280. This lyrical invocation to summer is in the form of a four-part round supported by the two lower voices performing a simple, four-bar repeating figure in the bass, also in canon. This device, called a *pes* (Latin, 'foot') was frequent in English music of the period and is mentioned by the theorist Walter Odington, a monk of Evesham active in the early 14th century. Our knowledge of 14th-century music in England remains scant through the paucity of the remaining sources. Of these the most important is the Old Hall manuscript, found at the place of that name in Hertfordshire, but the schools of Worcester and Bury St Edmunds still remained active. The characteristic thirds and sixths of the style known as 'English descant' are found. In this the melody is usually in the lower voice and is accompanied by two upper voices at the interval of a third and a sixth above it. Originally a method of

vocal improvisation, it was already being adopted by composers and, after its arrival on the Continent with the English school of the 15th century, was to be adopted by the Fleming, Dufay, and others, and modified to produce the style known as *fauxbourdon*.

These original sources of English music were supplemented in the 13th century when English musicians familiarised themselves with the masterpieces of the school of Notre Dame. When grafted on to the rich native tradition the style was enriched and modified, so that in England *ars antiqua* took on an extremely original aspect. From this time onwards written works become more and more abundant; these are mainly religious and most of them are in the form of a trope or *conductus*. All these works are anonymous, as are those of the 14th century, a period when England assimilated the glories of *ars nova* without herself contributing anything outstandingly new.

The 15th century

Although the composers of Tudor and Jacobean England were to write music the equal of anything to be found elsewhere, and the genius of Purcell was to outshine the work of his European contemporaries, yet it is nevertheless true that only once in the whole course of musical history did England actually determine the direction of the main stream. After the brief but glorious generation which ended with the death of John Dunstable in 1453 the English school, which had led the field, became increasingly isolated from Continental developments. We know that the Continentals themselves recognised the importance of the English contribution and it is a tragedy that even before the end of the century the Flemish theoretician, Tinctoris, after recording the great contribution of Dunstable and his school, lamented the 'wretched poverty of invention' of the English in his own age.

The effective cause of English influence may be traced in the revival of the Hundred Years War in the 1410s. This meant a military presence in France for the next forty years and with it a flood of English musicians crossed the Channel to serve the chapels of the regent and his great nobles. The two elements of the artistic contribution were the introduction of a new 'harmonic' sense which followed the revelation of the euphonious effect of the English use of thirds and sixths; and secondly the immensely important formal device of the cyclic mass. In this a single plainsong tenor was employed in all the sections of the mass, and a tight new unity of form was achieved.

Much of the surviving English music of the 15th century is contained in two manuscripts, both of the greatest importance: the Old Hall manuscript (*c.* 1420) and the splendid Eton Choir Book (*c.* 1500). The Old Hall manuscript consists of a very large number of mainly liturgical works of the late 14th and early 15th centuries, which teach us something of the music immediately preceding Dunstable. It contains the names of numerous composers, many of whom must have worked in the Chapel Royal of Henry IV and Henry V. Indeed it is possible that two of the mass sections are attributable to Henry IV himself. The Eton Choir Book provides an inestimable source of knowledge concerning everything relative to music at the beginning of the Tudor period. Although the 15th century has not yet yielded any instrumental compositions, mention should be made of the installation at this time of organs in many of the English churches.

In this page from the Bedford Hours *John Dunstable's patron, the duke of Bedford, is shown kneeling before St George.*

Leonel and Dunstable

One of the interesting features of the Old Hall manuscript is that it is almost exclusively devoted to works for the church service. It is possible that this English penchant for religious music may have been one of the contributory causes to its revival throughout Europe. The most important composer represented is Leonel Power, usually known by his Christian name, who may well have spent some of his career on the Continent in view of the number of his works to be found in Italian manuscripts. However he seems to have spent most of his working life at Canterbury Cathedral and died about 1445. He wrote a practical handbook to music in English, the *Tretis of the Gam*, but it is his fifty-odd compositions that are important. They include mass sections and motets, many of which were on Marian themes. Some make use of the isorhythmic technique, and the works of his early period exhibit certain archaisms. However, those of his later period approximate to the style of Dunstable so that attribution is not always certain. But the mass *Alma Redemptoris Mater*, which is probably the first to use the cyclic technique, is almost certainly by Leonel, who thus enjoys an honoured place in the history of the development of musical form.

But it was John Dunstable who dominated the European stage in the 1420s and 1430s and continued a revered master until his death in 1453. He went to France as a young man in the service of the duke of Bedford and seems to have passed the rest of his life on the Continent, many of his sixty surviving compositions being found in Italian manuscripts. He was described by both Tinctoris and the French writer Martin le Franc as the founder of a new style in music. The line of polyphonic development runs direct from him through the Franco-Flemish school to Lassus and Palestrina and it is not exaggerating to see Dunstable as the father of the first generation of modern music.

The 'Burgundian' composers were said by contemporaries to have followed the English in a number of points but the most significant is what le Franc described as 'sprightly consonance', which was to lead to a new harmonic awareness and thus in due course to the ultimate collapse of the modal system. But Dunstable's music was also much admired by Binchois and Dufay for the fluid and supple melodic line in the top voice, where the English master, departing from usual practice, often placed the chant. Only three of Dunstable's surviving works are secular but they include his most celebrated composition, the exquisite *O rosa bella*. In addition to his innovations he also wrote isorhythmic motets producing, with Dufay, the finest late examples of the form, of which we must mention the motet *Veni sancte spiritus*. This, it has been suggested, was composed for the coronation of Henry VI as king of France at Paris in 1429.

It was Dunstable who elevated the national musical language of his native England to the level of a universal style. The euphony of his music, so much admired by his contemporaries, consisted not only of a masterly use of the typically 'English' consonances of the third and the sixth, but also of the careful 'preparation' of dissonances if they were employed. It was this 'perpetual euphony', perfectly expressed in the motet *Quam pulchra es*, which may be said to mark the dividing line between the music of the middle ages and the music of the Renaissance. Dunstable's influence can be seen in the music of Dufay but is even more marked in that of Binchois, and it is interesting to note that a body of the surviving Dunstable manuscripts were preserved at the French town of Dijon where Binchois worked.

All in all, we may say of Dunstable's music that the richness of its sonorous effects, the grace and expressive elegance of the melodic curve and the perfection of the counterpoint, all proclaim him one of the great masters of music. In the half century after his death many English composers won important posts and earned respect abroad, men such as Robert Morton and Walter Frye at the court of Burgundy or the theorist John Hothby in Italy, but they never approached the front rank.

While it is true that English music turned in on itself and became conservative in style, there were developments of interest and some fine works were composed, as we can see from the Eton Choir Book. A somewhat earlier manuscript dating from the middle of the century contains the two earliest known polyphonic settings of the Passion according to St Matthew and St Luke. These are followed by later settings, notably that by Richard Davy (*c.* 1467-1516) which gives effective treatment to the crowd scenes and the *dramatis personae* of the story, while one of Davy's contemporaries, John Browne, produced a fine Magnificat, also preserved in the Eton manuscript. These compositions in general are marked by something of the same over-elaborate splendour of King's College chapel in Cambridge or Henry VII's chapel in Westminster Abbey, and it is to the carol, an ancestor of the English part song, that we must look for a more spontaneous musical inspiration.

Like its close relation the ballad, the carol derived ultimately from a dance form but by the middle of the 15th century it had lost this connection, had become a composed as opposed to a purely popular form and on occasion had even found a place in the liturgy. It could be on any subject and was distinguished as a form by the self-contained refrain or 'burden' which followed each verse. One of the finest of medieval carols was the magnificent Agincourt song written to celebrate that famous victory: 'Our king went forth to Normandy, with grace and might of Chivalry. There God for him wrought marvellously, wherefore England may call and cry: *Deo gracias*.' Like the Italian *lauda*, the carol was used by the Franciscans as a mode of popular religious music and although the polyphonic carol was an 'art' form it did have a strong popular appeal. Gradually carols of the nativity came to displace all

other types and today the word has only this meaning of a Christmas song.

The court of Henry VIII

It is fitting that this king's name be associated with a period of English music. He was no mean composer himself and gathered at his court a number of musicians who, if not in the forefront of European developments, produced some superb music. The greatest name of this period is that of Robert Fayrfax (*c.* 1460-1521). For thirty years he served the first Tudor king, Henry VII, and remained in service at the court of his son. The ageing composer was one of those who accompanied the brilliant and flamboyant young monarch to France for that great festival of chivalry and diplomacy, the Field of the Cloth of Gold, in 1520. Despite his commitments at court Fayrfax retained the post of director of the choir at the abbey of St Albans from 1498 until his death. Six of his masses, one of which may be the earliest English parody mass, a number of motets, two Magnificats and some secular works survive. In his religious music, Fayrfax shows immense technical

A Salve Regina from the Eton Choir Book.

Two parts of a motet by an English composer of the mid-16th century.

competence and a mastery of complex rhythms, and in his interest in imitation at least, he is in tune with developments in contemporary Europe.

But it was in the field of instrumental music and secular song that the freshest and most interesting work was being done in the first decade of the young monarch's reign. Already with the keyboard works of Hugh Aston and also John Redford, the English composers, possibly aware of the music of the Spaniard, Cabezón, were beginning to lay the foundation of a keyboard style which had thrown off its earlier debt to vocal music. In its maturity at the end of the century in the hands of men like John Bull, it was to contribute to the European developments in this field. We also find compositions for instrumental consort, which indeed is hardly surprising at the court of a monarch who had one of the finest collections of instruments in Europe.

From the beginning the rhythms of the dance were important, again hardly surprising as Henry himself was a fine dancer and wrote at least one piece of dance music. But some of the most beautiful music at the court was the part songs, above all the exquisite and moving compositions of William Cornyshe (1465-1523). A friend of the king, Cornyshe was not only a courtier but also a musician, poet and actor and wrote entertainments for the court after Henry had introduced the fashion for 'maskes' from Italy. Together with foreign fashions Henry also introduced foreign instrumentalists. But in addition to a wealth of secular music England also produced magnificent composers for the church service, and of these none was greater than John Taverner.

Taverner

Born about 1495 in Lincolnshire, Taverner became master of the choristers at Lincoln Cathedral when he was thirty, but within the year had taken up the post of organist at Cardinal Wolsey's college (now Christ Church) at Oxford. After the disgrace of his patron he returned to his home county, where he lived for most of the rest of his life. His chiefly religious output includes eight masses, all without the Kyrie as in the English manner, and over twenty motets. Although he followed convention in basing many of his works on Gregorian

chant melodies or secular songs – a famous example of this is his *Westerne Wynde* mass – Taverner writes music inspired by a more than conventional fervour. His long melodic melismas, which at times seem to forget the verbal substructure which supports them, are borne aloft on a current of pure meditative lyricism.

Taverner occupies a special place in the history of English instrumental music, though almost, we might say, inadvertently. One of the types of instrumental composition most cultivated by English composers was the so-called *In nomine*. Since these pieces have in common only a *cantus firmus* derived from a plainsong antiphon, *Gloria tibi trinitas*, and since the words *in nomine* do not appear in the text of the antiphon, the terminology presented something of a problem to later generations. In fact the theme which formed the *cantus firmus* was found almost in its entirety in Taverner's mass on the antiphon at his setting of the words *In nomine domine* at the opening of the Benedictus section of the mass. The first instrumental *In nomines* were in fact derived by Taverner himself from this section of his mass.

Almost exactly contemporary with Taverner was the first Scottish composer of any stature whose works have survived. This was Robert Carver, whose works include a nineteen-part motet *O bone Jesu* (*c.* 1546) and the only known mass on the tune *L'Homme armé* by a British composer. Another fine Scottish composer of the period was Robert Johnson (d. 1554) who according to tradition was chaplain to Anne Boleyn. His compositions include twelve motets and works for keyboard and for viol consort.

The age of Tye and Tallis

The sensational break with the authority of Rome in 1534 had less effect on the liturgy and worship of the Church in England than might be imagined. In the first instance King Henry's argument with Rome was an administrative one – who governed the existing ecclesiastical hierarchy, not what the faithful should believe or how they should worship. True, the use of an English Bible was ordained within two years but English did not become the official language of the service until much later, and until Henry's death few crucial changes were made in the liturgy. In the short reign of his son Edward VI there were signs of a vigorous reforming tendency but it was followed by the Catholic reaction under Mary and then the compromising policy of Elizabeth which, although it forbade the use of the mass as such, permitted the occasional use of Latin motets and in any case left music with a considerable place in the service. The consequence of this long-drawn-out period of change was that in the long term English musicians found themselves deprived of the inspiration of the mass, once a major musical form. But for composers living under Henry VIII even this did not apply, while Elizabeth's policy of semi-toleration meant that it was quite possible for the greatest English composer of them all, William Byrd, to remain a Catholic all his days and yet write not only masses and motets but also music for the Reformed Church. Even the long-term effects were not so dramatic as has been sometimes suggested, since even in Italy itself the music of the Church was being strongly challenged by secular forms such as the madrigal and, from the early 17th century, music for the stage and the opera. After the generation of Palestrina it would never again be possible for a composer to build up a great reputation on the strength of his masses and motets alone.

The working lives of Tye and Tallis span the whole

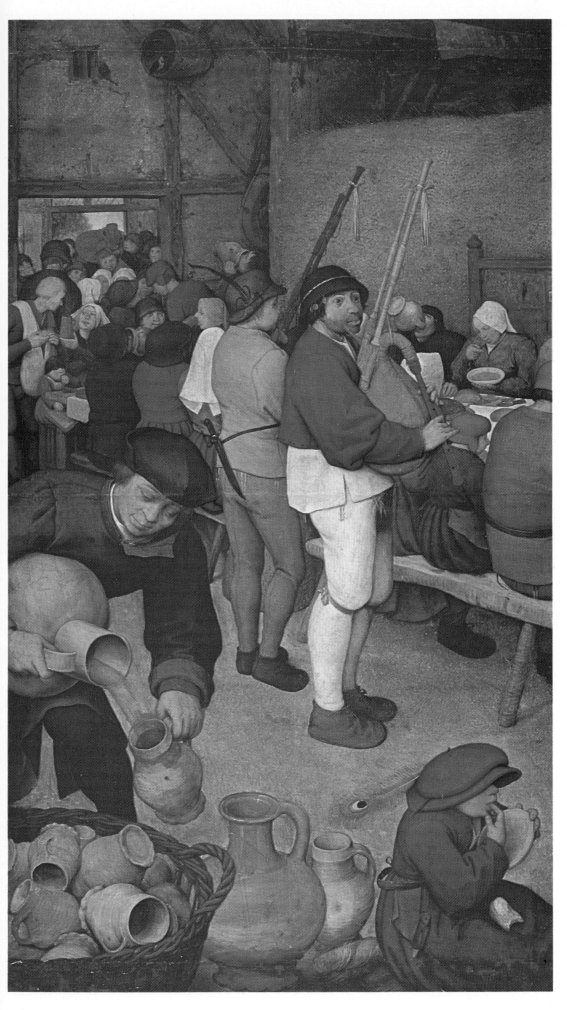

Plate 17

A ceiling painting in the Rosenburg castle, Copenhagen, showing musicians of the court of Christian IV. Notice the bass sackbut at the bottom and the cornettists to the right.

of the historical developments just outlined. Christopher Tye was born in the Isle of Ely in 1498 and after training as a chorister at King's College, Cambridge, he returned to Ely Cathedral and remained there until his retirement to become rector of a neighbouring parish in 1561. His music includes motets and masses, one of them on the song *Westerne Wynde*, three English anthems, which are in effect simply motets with English words, and works for viol fantasy including sixteen *In nomines*. The style is that of a supreme technician but despite the breadth of his music it lacks the intensity of deep inspiration. One of his more important works for the Reformed Church was a four-voice setting of a metric version of the *Acts of the Apostles* (1553). A greater man than Tye was his son-in-law Robert White, whose tragically early death at the age of thirty-four in 1574 robbed English music of a composer of genius. Of his sacred music, both Latin and English, perhaps the outstanding work is the mighty and moving setting of the *Lamentations*. In his works he shows a sure handling of imitation, and in the *Lamentations* his harmonic skill is revealed characteristically in his imaginative handling of the cadences.

Other composers of this central period of the 16th century include Richard Farrant (d. 1580), who produced some fine anthems for the English service and a number of keyboard pieces; John Shepherd (d. 1557), whose works include an outstanding mass, on *Westerne Wynde*, and William Mundy (1529-91). John Merbecke, of little note as a composer, earns a special place in the history of the music of the Reformed English Church for his *Booke of Common Praier noted* (1550) which, although outdated by the publication of the second Book of Common Prayer in 1552, showed great sensitivity in its adaptation of music to the English language. But the giant of English church music in the middle decades of the century was undoubtedly Tallis and to him we now turn.

Thomas Tallis (*c*. 1505-85) began his career in the pre-Reformation musical establishment and was the organist at Waltham Abbey at the time of the dissolution of the monasteries in 1540. Tallis, thanks to his considerable talents, had no difficulty in gaining a position in the royal chapel and served there under four successive sovereigns until his death. In 1575 he was granted, with William Byrd, the monopoly of music publishing for twenty years, and like his partner contributed seventeen motets to the thirty-four which they published in that year under the title of *Cantiones sacrae*. It goes without saying that his technical accomplishments were of the highest but he was also an inspired composer. His forty-part motet *Spem in alium* is not simply a *tour de force* of technical mastery but is also one of the inspired moments of vocal music. In it Tallis uses his large resources for massive effects and passages of dialogue between choirs of various sizes which echo within the mighty structure of the whole; the disciplined and poignantly effective use of apparently excessive forces is reminiscent of Berlioz's handling of his vast orchestras and choirs. Tallis' masses, motets, responses and hymns for the Latin service are all distinguished but perhaps his greatest Latin work is the superb five-part *Lamentations of Jeremiah*. The music is rich with telling dissonances and false relations, the special characteristics of English music up to the time of Purcell, which result from the simultaneous use of the ascending and descending forms of the minor scale. His music for the English service, which includes anthems, services and hymns, shows no falling off from the generally high level of his Latin works and is still to be heard in the cathedrals of England. Finally, Tallis, of whose considerable output only part has survived, made important contributions to keyboard music and must be classed as one of the originators of the brilliant toccata style.

An Italian engraving of the English composer Thomas Tallis.

The Golden Age

The period from the defeat of the Spanish Armada to the death of James I represents one of Europe's most brilliant 'golden ages'. In less than forty years England gave the world Marlowe, Webster and Bacon, the prose of Sir Walter Raleigh and of the Authorised Version of the Bible, the scientific researches of Gilbert and Harvey and the music of Byrd, Gibbons, Morley, Weelkes, Wilbye, Bull and Dowland, all geniuses of the first rank, and a host of richly talented followers.

Elizabethan civilisation was the fruit of an exceptionally favourable political and social marriage. The year 1588, which saw the defeat of the 'Invincible Armada', ushered in an age inspired by a new sense of self confidence, optimism and, to be frank, unpleasantly aggressive chauvinism. It was really from this moment that music and theatre began to spread their wings. In the theatre for which Shakespeare wrote, music held an important place, and composers actively collaborated in plays, which they enriched with numerous ayres accompanied on the lute or viols. Unfortunately, thanks to the essentially ephemeral nature of the occasion, much of this music is now lost.

But perhaps one of the most remarkable features of the Elizabethan age was the popularity of music making. In a period when public concerts were still unknown, the abundance of musical publications is explained by the great demand for music by amateurs. Everyone sang madrigals, most sizeable households possessed a chest of viols, and the virginal, for which the keyboard composers poured out such floods of fine music, was still more popular – the queen, herself a devoted virginalist, setting the example. As for the lute, such was its popularity that it was even to be found in barbers' shops, so that customers might pluck a few chords while awaiting their turn. Any young man unable to take his proper place in a vocal or instrumental consort became the laughing-stock of society. If the people had opportunities to shave to the joys of music, popular music also greatly inspired composers, and the intimate

right
Portrait, presumably of the
English music publisher John Day,
from the title page of one of his own
publications.

below
The Chapel Royal at St James's
Palace.

right
Portrait, presumably of the English music publisher John Day, from the title page of one of his own publications.

below
The Chapel Royal at St James's Palace.

fusion of art music with popular and folk elements remains one of the imperishable charms of the music of this golden age. Excepting large choral and orchestral works Elizabethan music embraces every style and genre. But although it cannot offer us anything comparable to the large-scale splendour of the Venetians, the beauties of the keyboard and chamber music may be regarded as ample compensation.

Religious music plays a definitely lesser role compared with the preceding period, even though it is represented by the masterpieces of Byrd and Gibbons, not to mention those of Morley, Weelkes, Tomkins and Peter Philips. Apart from Philips, Byrd was the only composer in England to write music for Latin texts. Philips, a practising Catholic, preferred to live on the Continent, where he enjoyed a considerable reputation. It is a piece by Philips that lies on the music stand in Jan van Breughel the Younger's painting *Sound* in a series on the Five Senses. But the greatest single body of this music in late 16th-century England was that represented by the late but brilliant flowering of the English school of madrigalists.

The English madrigal

It is an interesting fact that despite the aggressive chauvinism of Elizabethan England in political matters, her musicians and writers were willing, indeed eager, to adopt foreign and particularly Italian achievements. The all-conquering vogue of the madrigal during the last twenty years of Elizabeth's reign and the early years of the next had precedents – the native tradition of part-song writing and the occasional traces of Italian influence from the 1550s had prepared the ground for the English passion for the madrigal – but it suddenly gathered momentum after 1588, following Nicholas Yonge's *Musica Transalpina*, published in that year. In his preface Yonge indicates that he had been led to edit and publish the collection because the group of amateur singers to which he belonged were regular and enthusiastic performers of Italian madrigals. There is plenty of evidence that Italian madrigals had been circulating in England in increasing numbers for at least the last fifteen years. Almost immediately the English composers began to produce their own madrigals. But these were by no means slavish imitations of their models. The English madrigal was generally lighter and gayer in mood than the Italian; despite the magnificent riches of contemporary English poetry the composers either preferred to use Italian madrigal texts or turned to minor English writers, whereas one of the distinguishing features of the Italian school had been its preference for texts of great literary merit. Unlike the Italians however, the English composers were writing for an almost entirely amateur public, for whom the generally undemanding sentiments and comparatively simple technical demands were ideally suited. As Gustave Reese has said in his monumental *Music in the Renaissance*: 'In every way the English madrigal was a less esoteric and more popular movement' (than the Italian). Of more than thirty talented composers the great names are Morley, Weelkes, Wilbye, Tomkins and Gibbons, while Byrd also produced notable if few examples.

Morley, Weelkes and Wilbye, the masters of the English madrigal

Thomas Morley (1557-1603) was a pupil of Byrd and was organist at St Paul's for a time before entering the Chapel Royal in 1592; in 1598, the monopoly of music printing passed to him. Although his music does not touch the more serious vein to be found in the work of his madrigalist successors, yet as the composer of the light madrigal he had few equals. More than 100 madrigals and part songs by him survive and they were published in numerous collections, of which the first was *Canzonets . . . for three voices* (1593), which included serious madrigals as well as such light delights as 'Arise, Get up, My dear!' It was followed by *Madrigalls to Foure Voices*, the first English publication to use the actual word 'madrigal' of English compositions; then came the *First Booke of Balletts* in 1595, with such famous songs as 'Now is the month of Maying', in which he successfully adapts and indeed improves upon the *balletti* of the Italian, Gastoldi. His strong and fresh harmonic sense is to be found in all his work while *Canzonets for two voices* contains some of his most attractive music. But Morley also composed a number of fine two-, three- and four-part fantasies for viols, and in his didactic *The First Book of Consort Lessons* (1599) compiled a valuable collection of magnificent music by him-

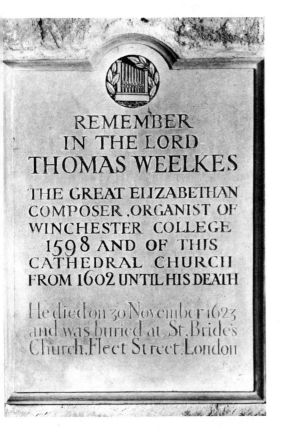

REMEMBER
IN THE LORD
THOMAS WEELKES
THE GREAT ELIZABETHAN
COMPOSER, ORGANIST OF
WINCHESTER COLLEGE
1598 AND OF THIS
CATHEDRAL CHURCH
FROM 1602 UNTIL HIS DEATH

He died on 30 November 1623
and was buried at St. Bride's
Church, Fleet Street, London

The lesser madrigalists and composers of the ayre

Even before the publication of Wilbye's *Second Set* of madrigals in 1609 the brief, late flowering of the English madrigal was in decline. Even in the ambitious collection of the works of twenty-four composers edited by Morley under the title *Madrigals, the Triumphes of Oriana* in 1601, few of the contributions reach the highest flights. The collection does however show the strong influence of Italian models, an influence even more apparent in the work of John Ward, whose set of *English Madrigals to three, four, five and six parts* (1613) show the composer's admiration for the rich style of Monteverdi. Francis Pilkington (c. 1562-1638) published madrigals in 1613 and 1624, but his finest work was in his ayres.

The ayre had a venerable ancestry in English popular song of the 16th century, but the first collections did not appear until 1597 when John Dowland's *First Booke* and arrangements for voice and lute of some of Morley's canzonets were published. Dowland, one of England's greatest song writers, was also a renowned lutenist and he is treated more fully in the section of this chapter on instrumental music. From the first, composers of ayres usually provided settings for three or more voices, and arrangements of the same piece for solo voice, the lower parts being adapted for lute accompaniment with a bass viol strengthening the bass. The most famous Elizabethan ayre is Thomas Morley's 'It was a lover and his lass' published in 1600, and the form remained popular well into the reign of James I. The ayre might be serious and emotional or light and gay; the poet composer Thomas Campion (1567-1620), who wrote his own verses, excels at the second type, but the ayres, 'There is a garden in her face' and the deeply felt religious 'Author of Light', also reveal a considerable musical talent. Campion wrote a poetical treatise and, more important, a work on the 'making of four parts in counterpoint'; it shows a comparatively advanced sense of harmony and was reprinted many times in the course of the 17th century.

left
The memorial to Thomas Weelkes in Chichester Cathedral.

below left
Monument to the brilliant young organist and director of music at both Canterbury and Exeter cathedrals, Matthew Godwin, who died at the age of seventeen in 1586.

self and others for a broken consort. This, which may have been published with professional groups such as the London waits in mind, is also an interesting document in the history of Renaissance instrumentation; Morley's consort was made up of lute, pandora, cittern, bass recorder, and treble and bass viol.

Thomas Weelkes (c. 1575-1623) who, after taking his degree in music at Oxford, took up the position of organist at Chichester, was clearly influenced by the work of Marenzio. He was the most daring of the English composers and the audacities of his chromatic harmonies as well as his deeply emotional style sometimes evoke the music of Gesualdo. His first book of madrigals, in three and six voices, was published in 1597 when the composer was in his early twenties and reveals remarkable maturity of style. Only three years later in his *Madrigals of 5 and 6 parts, apt for viols and voices,* he brought the whole art of the English madrigal to the apogee of its achievement; the five-part 'O care wilt thou despatch me' and the breath-taking six-part 'Thule the period of Cosmographie' are fine examples of his work. Following his appointment at Chichester Weelkes seems to have abandoned not only secular composition but also all interest in *avant-garde* experimentation. His church music displays skill and emotional intensity but it avoids the daring adventures of some of his madrigals.

John Wilbye (1574-1638) who, despite the comparatively small number of his compositions is considered perhaps the finest of the English madrigalists, was a Norfolk man and as a youth entered the service of the Kytson family as a musician. Following a grant of land in 1613 he became a landed gentleman in his own right and thereafter was apparently too busy attending to his lands to attend to his music. Undoubtedly he enjoyed greater prestige in his own time as a respected member of the gentry than he could have hoped for as one of England's leading composers. Of all the madrigalists he displayed the most sensitive understanding of the Italian composers, but he is equally remarkable for his intuitive and imaginative settings of English prose, and his finest works tend to music which is purely abstract and bears no relation to the madrigal.

Twenty-one light but perfect songs by Philip Rosseter (1568-1623) appear in a volume in which he collaborated with Campion; Robert Jones, John Danyel and Thomas Ford all produced one or two masterpieces in the genre, notably Ford's 'Since first I saw your face'. Indicative of the increasing lay public for music at this time is the popularity of the catch. This was a type of round often set to punning and ribald words, which continued a feature of English life right up to the 19th century. The earliest examples are those published by Thomas Ravenscroft in his collections *Pammelia* (1609), *Deuteromelia* (1609) and *Melismata* (1611).

William Byrd

The life of William Byrd, 'never without reverence to be named of the musicians', embraces the golden age of English music. He was born in 1543, probably at Lincoln, where for a time as a young man he was organist. From there he went to become a member of the Chapel Royal, where he was joint organist with Tallis. In 1575, as we have seen, the two men were granted the monopoly of printing music and published in that year a joint collection of motets under the title of *Cantiones Sacrae*. When Tallis died ten years later Byrd assigned his share in the lease to Thomas Easte. Under Easte's direction were published Byrd's *Psalms and Sonnets* (1588), *Songs of Sundrie Natures* (1589), two further

volumes of *Cantiones Sacrae*, two books of *Graduals* (1605 and 1607) and another volume of *Psalms, Sonnets and Songs* (1611). Byrd died in London in 1623. It is perhaps worth remarking that although a Catholic, Byrd not only received royal letters patent conferring on him a monopoly, but throughout his life composed music for both the Latin and the Anglican services.

In the field of church music Byrd stands with Lassus, Palestrina and Victoria, but he also wrote for all the genres current in contemporary England, both sacred and secular, excepting only compositions for the solo lute. His finest work is in the religious field and as a whole his style tended to be elevated and serious. Capable of sublime melody and moments of deep emotion, as a contrapuntalist excelling even his master, Thomas Tallis, and like all English composers a master of audacious harmonic strokes, Byrd was also a deeply religious man, as is apparent from the music of his three masses in three, four and five parts. These powerful and concise masterpieces are much shorter than their English forerunners and dispense with the *cantus firmus* technique altogether, though making fluent use of imitation. The sixty-nine motets in the three collections of *Cantiones Sacrae* include many masterpieces, among them the *Diliges dominum*, in which Byrd exhibits his polyphonic virtuosity with an eight-part crab canon, and the brilliant *Haec dies*; of the masterly motets which remain in manuscript, mention should be made of the *Lamentations* and a *Vidi, Domine quoniam tribulor*, which exhibits his chromatic audacity. Byrd's music maintains a consistently high level – thus the well-known *Ave verum* from his first book of *Gradualia*, despite its beauties, should be regarded as a representative rather than outstanding example of his art.

Byrd's music for the Anglican service includes masterpieces such as the *Great Service*; basically in five parts, this work is one of great polyphonic complexity. Finally we must mention Byrd's anthems; these are both full and 'verse', that is with alternating solo and choral passages, a form which Byrd did much to shape.

Byrd also composed a sizeable body of secular music of great quality. Above all he proved himself a master of the solo song with polyphonic accompaniment. Unlike many of his contemporaries and successors who used the lute as the accompanying instrument, he preferred the consort of viols and the result is some of the finest songs

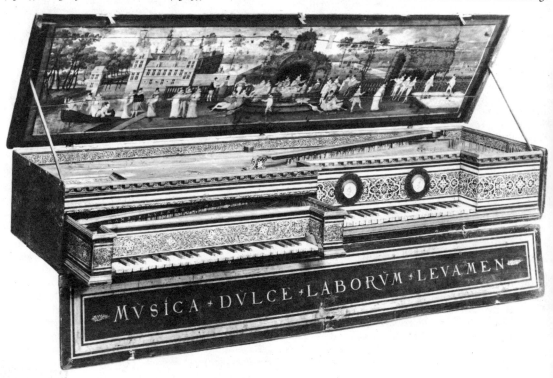

for chamber performance in the whole repertory. Apart from a few published examples such as the magnificent *O Woful Orpheus*, some of the most beautiful of Byrd's songs, such as the exquisite 'Lullaby My sweet little darling', have survived in manuscript. In these Byrd is a true follower of the English tradition of song writing, but when asked to provide an Italianate madrigal for *Italian Madrigals Englished* (1590), he stepped right into the first rank of the young school of madrigalists with his magnificent six-part 'This Sweet and Merry Month of May'.

Byrd wrote at least 150 pieces for the keyboard, including forty pavan and galliard pairs and the splendidly programmatic *The Bells*, while some of the fantasies, notably one surviving in manuscript form in the beautifully written *My Lady Nevell's Booke*, have been compared to the works of Bach. But as an instrumental composer Byrd excels in his compositions for viol consort and is one of the first great masters of this very English form. His works include a six-part fantasy, in which the popular tunes *Walsingham* and *Greensleeves* are used; another, also in six parts; one in five parts, which is in fact a set of variations on the song *Browning*; and a number of *In nomines*.

Orlando Gibbons and the viol fantasy

In this field Byrd was outshone by his young contemporary Orlando Gibbons (1583-1625). His father was one of the Oxford waits, and both his brothers and his sons were musicians and composers – Orlando himself seems to have been named after the famous Orlando di Lasso. His rise was rapid; in 1605 he was organist at the Chapel Royal, in 1619 virginalist to King James I and in 1623 he was appointed organist to Westminster Abbey.

Gibbons, who has been called 'the last of the Elizabethans', wrote some of his best music for the Anglican service and his full anthems, such as the six-part *Hosanna to the son of David* and the eight-part *O clap your hands*, have been called the last high point of the old polyphonic style in England. Although his verse anthems are of uneven quality, they too comprise masterpieces such as *Almighty God who by thy son*, and were important in shaping the development of the new form. Gibbons also wrote fine secular music for voices: madrigals, such as the rich and beautiful *The Silver Swan*, and what is in effect a vocal *In nomine* on the street cries of London. Similar fantasies were written by other composers such as Richard Deering.

From the beginning of the century, the popularity of dancing at the Tudor court had given rise to a sizeable body of music, and with the famous *In nomine* setting of Thomas Tallis, a new genre had entered the repertory of music for viol consort which was to be immensely popular with composers. But together with this the fantasy was the most cultivated form and, until its last glorious flowering in the music of Purcell, was to provide the vehicle for some of the finest flights of inspiration in English instrumental music. Besides his *Cries of London* Gibbons also wrote twenty-four viol fantasies. Some of the longer ones are broken up into small sections and in this respect show the formal influence of Italian models, but in their melodic and rhythmic variations and the way in which they use imitation they are entirely English. Most of the composers of the period wrote fantasies for the viol consort. But the noblest composition of the period for this ensemble was not a fantasy, but the great set of *Seaven passionate Pavans* with which the lutenist John Dowland opened his *Lachrimae* collection, published in 1605.

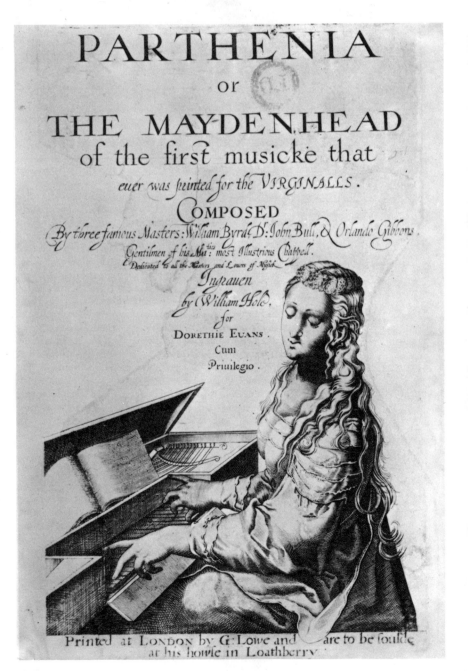

left
The bust of Orlando Gibbons in Canterbury Cathedral.

below
'Parthenia or the Maydenhead of the first musicke that ever was printed for the Virginalls' (*that is the first in England, c. 1611*); '*by three famous masters: William Byrd, Dr. John Bull & Orlando Gibbons.*' *The puns presumably appealed to contemporaries.*

above
Oberon's Palace, from a set for Ben Jonson's Masque The Faery Prince.

above right
Portrait presumed to be of John Bull, the English composer.

Lute and keyboard music

The late 16th and early 17th centuries witnessed a remarkable blossoming of English compositions for the lute. Men such as Francis Cutting, Alfonso II Ferrabosco (1575-1628), Robert Johnson and Michael Cavendish all produced fine music, while such publications as William Barley's *A new Booke of Tabliture* (1596) and Thomas Robinson's *Schoole of Musicke* (1603) catered for the growing body of amateur performers.

John Dowland, the greatest English lutenist, spent much of his career out of England. In the early 1580s he was in the service of the English ambassador in Paris, then after a stay in England when he took his degree in music at Oxford, he went to Italy where he met Marenzio. From 1598 to 1609 Dowland was employed as court lutenist to Christian IV of Denmark; after his return to England he finally obtained a court appointment, but his fame in his own country never equalled that which he had enjoyed abroad. His talents as a song composer were rich and deep and in all his works his gift for poignant and wide ranging melodies is apparent. His published works, mostly of ayres, appeared in four volumes between 1597 and 1613, the last one being entitled *A Pilgrim's Solace*. He excelled both in gay and in serious music but his finest compositions were elegiac in mood and the motto *Semper Dowland, semper dolens* he applied to himself. Such songs as 'Come away sweet love', 'Shall I sue', 'Weep you no more sad fountains' and of course the eloquent 'Flow my tears' on his famous tune *Lachrymae*, reveal his power as a song composer, but his lute compositions, which comprise numerous fantasies and dances, are no less magnificent. Perhaps the greatest of all of them is the complex yet moving fantasy *Forlorne hope*.

The English contribution to the formation of a truly keyboard style reached its culmination in the works of William Byrd, John Bull and their contemporaries. There are three important sources of the music. The earliest is the *Mulliner Book*, which was assembled by Thomas Mulliner from the 1540s to the 1580s; it includes work by numerous composers including Redford and Tallis. The *Fitzwilliam Virginal Book*, the most comprehensive of the collections, contains compositions dating from the 1560s to about 1612, while the beautiful *My Lady Nevell's Booke* is devoted exclusively to Byrd.

Although composers such as Tallis wrote for the organ, most of the music would have been played on the various instruments of harpsichord type, which the English termed collectively 'virginals'. At first English keyboard composers tended to base their compositions on plainsong melodies, but as these gave way to shorter themes such as popular tunes, metrical hymns and dances, permitting frequent repetition, the characteristic art of the English keyboard variation came to maturity. Furthermore, the preponderance of the bass and treble parts made for increasing harmonic variation, and a florid style of ornamentation was developed.

Among the most important composers, other than Byrd, whose work has already been noted, were Peter Philips, John Bull and Giles Farnaby (d. 1620). Besides his florid and harmonically advanced keyboard music, of which fifty pieces survive, Farnaby wrote twenty fine four-voice canzonets.

Philips, a Catholic from birth, is known to have been in Antwerp from 1590, and then for a time served as organist in Brussels Cathedral. Thereafter he held various posts and enjoyed a wide reputation until his death in 1633. He wrote much fine sacred music and also madrigals, but his works for keyboard may well have influenced his Dutch contemporary Jan Sweelinck, who was also a friend of John Bull. Born in 1563, Bull soon gained an appointment at the Chapel Royal, where his teacher was the composer and organist William Blitheman. In 1596 he was appointed as the first music professor at Gresham college on Queen Elizabeth's personal recommendation. His fame abroad equalled his reputation at home and, in 1613, he left England for the employ of the Habsburg governor of the Netherlands and became organist at Antwerp Cathedral in 1617. His compositions for keyboard reveal a fiery and passionate temperament and although their brilliance occasionally prohibits profound expression he remains one of the most important composers of early keyboard music.

Section IV

The Age of Harmony

From Baroque to classicism: historical background

During the period which is the subject of the following chapters, the age of the Baroque was succeeded by the age of the Enlightenment; a century of violent devastating war by an age which endeavoured to rationalise war as an instrument of policy; an age in which the arts were all inspired by the spirit of dramatic contrast was followed by a century which vaunted the spirit of detached rationalism even in the arts themselves.

The Thirty Years War

The first half of the 17th century was dominated by the Thirty Years War, which ravaged the lands of Germany and central Europe between 1618 and 1648. The struggle was confused and alliances were formed and broken across both religious and political boundaries, but the outcome was a severe weakening in the power of the Habsburg empire, and a Europe in which France was soon to emerge as the greatest power. The conflict opened with the rejection of the claims of the Catholic house of Habsburg by the Protestant peoples of Bohemia, who elected as their king a prince of the empire, Frederick the Elector Palatine. The imperial armies overcame the insurgents, and by 1623 it must have seemed that a civil struggle in the empire, in which religion was only one element, had been terminated. But the Danish king, Christian IV, fearing an extension of imperial power in northern Germany, now entered the war ostensibly in the Protestant cause. Denmark was utterly defeated by the great imperial general Wallenstein, and by 1629 the Habsburg emperor Ferdinand II found himself again unchallenged. But now he pressed his advantage too far, and introduced measures which threatened to invalidate the claims of many Protestant princes to the ecclesiastical lands which they had taken over at the time of the Reformation.

Nevertheless, it was another of the Scandinavian monarchs, the great Gustavus Adolphus of Sweden, who next took up the Protestant cause. His aims, too, were political as well as religious, and he was supported by Catholic France, and joined by the Protestant prince, John George of Saxony, who only now deserted his allegiance to the emperor. In 1632 the great Wallenstein was defeated at Lützen, although Gustavus of Sweden was killed in the battle. The continuing devastation of German land by foreign troops gave rise to a growing resentment in Protestant as well as Catholic Germany. In 1635, after further imperialist reverses, a war-weary Germany came to the conference table. Saxony offered very favourable terms to the emperor, having changed sides once again. However, the failure to reach agreement with the Swedes led to the reopening of hostilities, and France, for whom the discomfiture of the Habsburgs was of more importance to French policy than purely religious considerations, openly entered the war on the side of Sweden. The war became general.

By the terms of the Peace of Westphalia in 1648, Sweden and France won considerable territorial concessions, and the Habsburg power in Europe was severely weakened. In Germany, Saxony, which had suffered severely in the later stages of the war, and Brandenburg emerged as the dominant states, but more significant was the fact that the provisions of the peace made notable steps towards the concept of religious toleration. Never again was religion to be advanced as a serious pretext for war.

The religious motives proclaimed by the participants at the beginning of the Thirty Years War were fully in tune with an age still dominated by the consequences of the religious struggles of the previous century. These preoccupations were kept alive by the determined counterattack of the Catholic Church, known as the Counter Reformation. But it was not only with arms that the champions of the old Church fought back. The Society of Jesus, founded by St Ignatius Loyola in 1540, besides playing a major part in the spreading of Christianity outside Europe, also formed a spearhead of the counterattack against heresy in Europe. It exploited all possible types of appeal in its endeavour to win back people to the Church. It developed a form of religious drama, encouraged the essentially dramatic tendencies of Baroque art, and was an important formative influence in the dramatisation of the liturgy.

England

Alone among the major states of Europe, Britain had survived the 16th century without the turmoil of religious wars. But latent religious conflict there was between the Church of England and the Puritans and other nonconformist sects. These religious divisions, strengthened by the strong support given to the Church by James I, and still more by his son Charles, were an important element in the explosive situation which produced the English Civil War. Social and economic factors certainly played a large part, but contemporaries saw the struggle in terms of king versus parliament, bishop or no bishop. After the execution of Charles I in 1649 and the ten year protectorate of Oliver Cromwell, and then his son, no English king could ever hope to emulate the oppressive absolutism so effectively set up in France by Louis XIV. Charles II brought a taste for many French fashions on his return, not least important a passion for French music and French musicians, but he had more wisdom than to try to import the French system of government. After 1688, the year of the Glorious Revolution, which brought the Dutchman William III and his Stuart wife Mary to the throne in place of the Catholic James II,

153

the principle that the sovereign power in Britain was the king in parliament was assured.

The natural talent and enthusiasm of the English for music, which flowered so brilliantly in the Elizabethan and Jacobean ages, were not seriously inhibited by the protectorate, which merely banned music from church. Indeed this period saw the performance of the first opera in England, and with Henry Purcell it seemed as though a new golden age was about to dawn. But the taste for foreign music, fashionable during the Restoration period, was still strong, as was shown by the ardour with which the court and society flocked to patronise the Italianate operas of Handel in the next century. It would seem as though this second wave of foreign fashion coming so hard on the heels of that of the Restoration would finally mute the voice of native English music. Nor indeed did 18th-century England produce many men of the first rank in the arts. The energies of the nation were fully engaged elsewhere; in the corrupt and delighted exploitation of an assured political constitutionalism; in the pursuit of an empire in India; in the extension of trade, and in the continuous and absorbing occupation of fighting the French.

France

During the 16th century, France had been torn by civil wars which, in fact, reflected deep religious, social and geographical divisions in the country. It seemed as though unity and peace were to be restored by Henry IV, the Protestant claimant who turned Catholic. But he was assassinated in 1610, to be succeeded by his nine-year-old son Louis XIII. Louis was content to leave the direction of affairs in the hands of his two great ministers, cardinals Richelieu and Mazarin. They initiated a policy of centralisation in politics and orthodoxy in religion, which was to be continued and perfected in the reign of Louis XIV. Furthermore, by quelling the rising of the second Fronde, Mazarin put an end to aristocratic opposition and the possibility of further armed faction. Mazarin continued to direct French affairs until his death in 1661, but then Louis XIV, who had come to the throne in 1643 at the age of five, took control.

Louis's long reign, from 1661 to 1715, may be said to describe an arc with its highest point in the middle 1680s. Thereafter the commanding position of France in European affairs began to decline under the financial strain of an aggressive and acquisitive foreign policy, and the increasingly effective coalitions of other European powers.

Parallel with this cycle of military and political prestige, the reign of the 'Sun King' displays a natural progression from the brilliance and flamboyance of youth to the staid and oppressive piety and correctness of the court of the king's old age. Yet throughout there run the twin motifs of the wealth of France and the king's punctilious and unrelenting devotion to the business of governing. In affairs of state, the old nobility 'of the sword' was replaced by the new nobility 'of the robe', chosen from all ranks of society. Versailles, whose architecture and court etiquette provided the model for countless imitations, became the jewelled setting for an astonishing new concept in European monarchy, and the glittering cage for an aristocracy robbed of all power but invited to expend its immense resources in an orgy of conspicuous consumption.

The artistic establishment which served the court was also run on authoritarian lines. Music, art and literature were all subject to the most stringent control. While Lully enjoyed an outright monopoly of stage productions and directed the musical life of the court, the painter Charles Le Brun controlled the work of painters, sculptors and engravers, and the craftsmen at the royal furnishing factory at Gobelins.

Despite the drain on government finance by the wars of Louis XIV, and, still more serious, the weakening of the country's economic potential by the renewed persecution of the industrious and skilled classes of Protestant Huguenots, the wealth of France was such that she recovered within a few years of the death of Louis. The years of the regency saw the birth of a new lighter manner in art which came to be known as Rococo. But new wars coupled with the still more crippling effects of an archaic system of taxation produced a crisis situation. Deprived of their full power in the central government, the nobility jealously clung to their privileges, which resulted in injustice and oppression in other ranks of society. In 1789, a desperate attempt to involve the nation in the reforms so vitally needed led, in fact, to revolution.

The German lands

Austria remained the greatest power in south-east Europe, but the power of the Habsburgs invited continued incursions from their enemies. Almost unaided Austria had to resist the last great campaign of Islam against Europe. In 1683, the Turks were before the gates of the city of Vienna with their Hungarian allies and the siege was only raised in the nick of time by a Polish army. Thereafter the eastern and southern frontiers of the empire were assured. Vienna became one of the most beautiful European capitals; new palaces and parks were built to adorn the city, which became the metropolis for a vast area of diverse traditions and peoples owing a common allegiance to the name of Habsburg.

In north Germany, however, a new power was rising which was to rob the Austrian emperors of much of their territory, and in the next century supplanted their German hegemony. This was the kingdom of Prussia. The true founder of the Prussian state was Frederick William I. He welded his poor territories into a politically cohesive unity and laid the foundations of a powerful military machine. It was this tool which his son Frederick II (the Great) used to extend the possessions of his house in a succession of daring and ambitious wars. Thanks to the exertions of Frederick II, Prussia was able to exploit her position as a leading military power to profit from the partitions of Poland at the end of the 18th century. But Frederick had other pretensions than those of military conquest. Influenced by the philosophy of the French Enlightenment, and ambitious to emulate the glories of Versailles, he set up at Potsdam outside Berlin a brilliant court, where of all the arts the most favoured was music.

The medieval and Renaissance greatness of Poland was reduced during the 17th and 18th centuries thanks largely to a powerful and anarchic nobility. Austria and Russia, and later Prussia, played an increasingly important part in her affairs. With Russian support, Augustus II of Saxony was elected king of Poland in 1697 and the title remained with Saxony for the next sixty years. For Saxony itself the period was a mixed one. The ambitions of Frederick II of Prussia drove him to attack his north German neighbour as well as the lands of Austria. But although the political prestige of Saxony declined steadily during the 18th century, her electors Augustus II and Augustus III proved lavish patrons of the arts. Dresden, their capital, became one of the most beautiful cities of Europe, and other cities in their dominions, notably Leipzig, where J. S. Bach spent the last twenty-seven years of his life, were important cultural centres.

There were many other German states, ranging from Hanover, whose electors were also kings of England, to the small but wealthy Hanseatic town of Hamburg. Music was promoted by the considerations of prestige which led these countless states to lavish their patronage on the maintenance of opera houses, of which that at Hamburg was an outstanding example. As we shall see, one of the most famous and important musical establishments during the 18th century was at another German court: this was the orchestra of Mannheim, the capital of the Elector Palatine, Charles Theodore. This multiplicity of the sources of patronage in Germany was immensely important since it increased the possibilities of talent being taken up and cultivated. Beethoven began his career at Bonn, one of the lesser courts, while Haydn served the Esterhazy, one of the great princely families of the empire.

But in Germany, as in other parts of Europe, the character of patronage itself was gradually changing. The trend was first seen in Italy where in the 1630s the first public opera house opened its doors. From then on, as the spectacle became ever more expensive, opera came to depend more and more on the resources of public theatres. Italy herself was already well past the greatest days of her commercial prosperity. The trade lines of Europe had shifted to the north, and the Italian

towns and duchies, financially weakened by the consequent retraction of their commerce, were still further exhausted by the extortions of the imperial powers of Spain and Austria, which by the middle of the 18th century had divided the peninsula between them. Only Venice and a small number of lesser republics and the papal states retained their independence. Yet Italy continued to be one of the mainsprings of the European musical genius, and the fashion for Italian music and musicians spread throughout Europe, even as far afield as the court at St Petersburg, where, after the reign of Peter the Great, the rulers of Russia pressed ahead with a policy of Westernisation.

In the field of thought, the greatest impulse in the civilisation of Europe was the new and aggressive spirit of rationalism of the French thinkers known as the *philosophes*. Inspired by the discoveries of the 17th-century scientists such as Galileo and above all Sir Isaac Newton, they introduced the new principles into the realm of philosophy, and summed up their attitude in the Great Encyclopaedia. The frankly materialist principles of the work and its denial of the still accepted religious orthodoxies shocked contemporaries. The 17th century had seen the exclusion of religion from politics; the following century saw the assault pressed into the realm of thought.

An 18th-century view of the interior of the Farnese Theatre at Parma.

The background to the music

The 17th and 18th centuries witnessed the formation and climax of a new language of musical expression and also of new musical forms. The opera, a true child of the Baroque love of drama, and the symphony, perfected during the classical era, were major contributions to the world of musical form, while the language of tonality which finally supplanted the use of the modes worked a revolution in the very nature of composition.

The Italian opera

The birth of opera can be dated with some precision to the last decade of the 16th century. In the first instance it was the result of what we might call a research programme. From the 1570s, a group of musicians and poets had been working in Florence with the express intention of rediscovering and recreating the lost art of the ancient Greek theatre. There, they believed, music had played an integral role, quite different from its largely decorative function in the emerging secular drama of the Renaissance. The heart of the problem was to devise a system of declamation which would enable the actors to give all the text of the play in music. The first fruit of this experimentation was an essentially non-melodic musical line. This early monody, as it was called, was an intellectual and aristocratic art appealing to the cognoscenti rather than the masses. The great step which assured the vitality of opera as a popular form was taken not in Florence but in Rome. Here, a more dramatic style of the monody was evolved, known as recitative, and here also the scenic scope of the spectacle was greatly enlarged. These trends were confirmed and strengthened in Venice, whose musical tradition had long been essentially dramatic in inspiration; the first public opera house was opened there in the 1630s. From this point on Italian opera was taken up throughout Europe; only in France was the trend resisted, although attempts were also made in Germany to produce a national style. As the popularity of opera spread, so did its appeal to sensationalism; by the middle of the 18th century, the target of parodies and lampoons, Italians opera had become an art drained of true expressive possibilities. Consequently when Gluck produced his *Orfeo ed Euridice* at Vienna in 1762, with the declared intention of reasserting the primacy of plot and structure, the 'reform opera' found many sympathetic listeners.

New forms in religious music

In the age of the Baroque, the passion for drama infected even the music of the Church. Making use of the new style of monody and recitative, Italian composers began to produce a new type of vocal composition with instruments, based either on sacred or secular texts, known as the cantata. The distinction between the Italian religious and secular cantata was one of subject matter, but as developed by German composers the church cantata evolved as a recognisably different form. The Italians themselves introduced choruses at a relatively early date, but in Germany it came to include an instrumental introduction, separate passages of aria and recitative, choral sections and, most distinctive of all, passages in which chorale melodies were set, often for performance by choir and congregation together. This was the cantata which reached its perfection in the hands of J. S. Bach.

The spirit of the secular stage was still more apparent in the oratorio. Its antecedents lay in the order of worship used in the Oratory of St Philip Neri which, in its turn, grew out of the strong movement of lay piety in 16th-century Italy. The services of the Oratory, specifically designed to appeal to the lay mind, were open to the influences of lay society and were affected by the tendencies towards the dramatic in secular music. Some of the earliest operas had themselves had religious themes and the religious opera as such became well established at Rome in the opening decades of the 17th century. The oratorio which developed alongside the early opera was, in truth, distinct from it only in dispensing with the stage setting. The oratorios of the great Giacomo Carissimi were essentially operas for concert performance. Some of the finest examples of the form were to be produced by German composers, and in the 18th century it enjoyed a new lease of life in England where the oratorios of Handel were received with immense enthusiasm by the newly emerging bourgeois concert-going public.

But although these Italian forms spread rapidly, French, German and English composers were also pursuing other developments peculiar to their own traditions. In France the Latin motet, an essentially choral form, continued to be written, while in England it had given birth to the anthem as far back as the 16th century. The full anthem, choral throughout, and the verse anthem with passages for solo voice, were cultivated by English composers from Byrd to Purcell. As elsewhere, instruments came to play an increasingly important part in church music; in the work of Purcell as in that of his continental contemporaries, the distinction between church anthem and music for the theatre was largely a matter of the text. In Germany, however, religious music produced a major and truly spiritual form in the Passion. With antecedents stretching back into the 15th century, the setting of the story of the suffering and death of Christ had evolved until it achieved the status of a separate form. Like most other major types of vocal music, it could not avoid being affected by the prevailing interest in drama, but in the hands of the 17th-century German composers such as Schütz, some of the most deeply moving religious music of all time was written.

Instrumental music

Not only were instruments major partners with the voices in the new types of compositions described above, but fully independent forms of instrumental music were emerging. The most fertile field for this development was that of the dance. An integral feature of European court and peasant society, the dance had a musical repertory of its own with a venerable ancestry. The interchange between folk and courtly music was considerable and many dances moved up in the social scale, so to speak, from the rumbustious and hot-blooded world of the village wedding or social celebration, to the more elegant, though scarcely less passionate, world of the court. Very many of the Renaissance dances of polite society were formalised versions of peasant originals. As the 17th century advanced, their progress continued so that a new manner of music arose which was no longer intended for dancing, although it retained the names and rhythms of its prototypes. It was in this increasingly formalised dance suite that specifically instrumental concert music began to emerge.

Another important area of instrumental music was in the interludes and *sinfonie* of the operas and in the sonatas and *canzoni* for instruments. The last named, which were derived from vocal forms, took on a life of their own in the 17th century. By its end, the trio sonata, for two melody instruments, a bass and a harmonic accompaniment, and the solo sonata, for one solo instrument and accompaniment, were well established.

But by this time composers had a number of instrumental forms available. The literature of the keyboard, whose history can be traced back to the 15th and 16th centuries, was already extensive. In Germany composers for the organ developed the chorale prelude, a type of variation on the chorale melody, and used the combination of the free prelude followed by an elaborate fugue. Italian composers, chief among them Domenico Scarlatti, were writing 'sonatas' of three or four contrasting movements and everywhere the format of the multi-movement dance suite was being adapted to the requirements of the keyboard. By the end of the 18th century, three main forms of concerted music for instruments were coming to dominate all music outside the theatre. These were the concerto, the symphony, and the chamber music ensemble for strings.

Instrumentation

All these forms expressed in different ways the capabilities of a combination of instruments unheard of at the beginning of the 17th century but commonplace by its end. This was an orchestra based on the members of the violin family. The violin, which emerges almost fully formed in the middle of the 16th century, was at first regarded as unfit for refined music and suitable only for dances and 'mummeries', but its power and brilliance could not be denied. From being used for dramatic coloristic effects, it rapidly gained equality with the viol and then, thanks in large measure to its prestige in the court music of France, displaced its rival completely. When the 17th century opened, the language of instruments was that of contrast. Giovanni Gabrieli and the school of Venice set a fashion for contrasting groups of instruments using different tone colours and different dynamics of volume. Far from aiming to blend the instruments into a homogeneous sound, such composers luxuriated in the rich and piquant conflict of many timbres. This may have been in part because the very structure of the instruments themselves, particularly those of the wind families, made any kind of blending impossible. The strident tones of the shawms could not 'blend' with the soft sound of the viols, nor the nasal qualities of the crumhorns offer anything but contrast to the clear, hollow sounds of the Renaissance recorder.

But as the 17th century progressed, a natural shift of taste towards a more uniform instrumental combination was assisted by two factors. These were the adoption of the sharp-toned violin as the basic string instrument, and the important improvements in the design of the wind instruments. For the first time, indeed, these approached a homogeneity of tone within their own range. The loss of piquancy in the orchestral sound which resulted from these developments was happily surrendered in exchange for the new-found euphony. Moreover composers were acquiring ever growing confidence in the use of the language of tonality, which in itself opened up new territories of musical colour. Thus the delights of contrasting instrumental timbres began to give place to those of contrasting and changing harmonies.

The concerto and the symphony

Timbre of course remained, but it was no longer central. However the Baroque delight in contrast was perpetuated in the concerto grosso, which was evolved at the end of the 17th century by the Italian composers Torelli and Corelli. These were extended works in three or four movements, and were written for a string orchestra in which a group of solo instruments was contrasted with the full orchestra. The form reached its fullest expression in the concerti grossi of Vivaldi and Handel, and the Brandenburg concertos of J. S. Bach, who introduced other instruments besides strings. From the middle of the 18th century the concerto grosso yielded in popularity to the three-movement solo concerto in which a single instrument was set against the whole orchestra.

As it was first used, the word *sinfonia*, if it had any special significance at all other than indicating a piece of music for instruments, tended to refer to the introductory passage or overture before the scenes of an opera. One of the greatest of late Baroque opera composers, Alessandro Scarlatti, made a significant advance when he standardised his *sinfonie* into a three-movement form – a slow movement flanked by two faster ones. Moreover these works were outstanding in their own right and were sufficiently complete and independent of their opera to be performed as separate concert pieces. With the introduction of a minuet after the slow movement in the second half of the 18th century, the symphony gained its classic four-movement form, which was perfected by Haydn and which formed the basis of the string quartet.

Common to both of them was the use of what is generally called first movement sonata form. Evolving during the first half of the 18th century, this was to be the most important single structural element in music during the classical period. It consists of two main sections, the exposition and the development, and concludes with a recapitulation of the first of these. The essential ingredients were the contrast of themes, and a harmonic movement from the tonic key at the beginning of the piece into the dominant, and then back to the tonic for the conclusion. This simple basic structure was to prove immensely fertile and was the characteristic form of the classical period.

The development
of a harmonic language

The increasing complexities of polyphony led inexorably to the breakdown of the modal system in which pitch, range and interval had all been linked in an essentially melodic sense of pattern. A new sense of the organisation of sound was bearing in upon composers as they became more and more concerned with the 'vertical' effect of many notes sounding together, rather than the 'horizontal' lines of numerous melodies. The importance of the chord of the triad grew, as did the coloristic effect of the major and minor third. These elements, fully appreciated by practising musicians in the 16th century, were confirmed in both practice and theory by the rapid adoption of the harmonic bass known as the *basso continuo* in the early 1600s. This, another innovation of the Italians, reveals that composers thought in terms of two lines of music, of the

melody and the bass. The inner parts might be written out in full or they might be left to the interpretation of the keyboard player. A typical 'continuo' part would simply give the bass line with figures above the notes to indicate which of the chords available on those notes were to be used.

The harmonic language was already familiar, and as the 17th century progressed it was to become ever more sophisticated and well defined. The essential notion of tonality was introduced, with its idea of a 'home' key which provided the focus of a piece or a section of music; in relation to this home key, the 'tonic', other keys were considered to be either near or remote. Laws were evolved for the movement, or 'modulation', between the keys of this tonal hierarchy, and, with the incorporation of the major and minor 'modes', the essentials of a new musical vocabulary was present. The old art of polyphony continued a vigorous and glorious existence in the contrapuntal music of J. S. Bach, but it too used the maturing harmonic language. The age of polyphony which had grown from the art of church monody was supplanted by the classical age.

The great organ of the Baroque church at Passau, Austria.

The instruments of music

We have seen how, in the 16th century, instrumental music was gradually becoming emancipated from being no more than an imitation of vocal music; but, nonetheless, this long remained the model for instrumental composition. The history of instrumental music in the 17th and 18th centuries is largely the story of the establishment of a truly independent instrumental idiom.

But before embarking on this necessarily brief survey of the many trends and developments of the period with an account of the music of the early 17th century, it is important to make some mention of the tremendous literature which the century produced on the subject of instruments, their manufacture and origins. Perhaps the most important authors are the German Michael Praetorius, whose *De organographia*, the second volume of the *Syntagma musicum* (1619), includes the vast 'Treatise on Instruments', while the *Harmonicum instrumentorum libri IV*, the Latin edition of the preceding work, contains some notable differences from the French text published in the same year; the Frenchman, Pierre Trichet, whose *Traité des instruments de musique*, written in about 1640, while perhaps less scholarly than the works of Praetorius, is full of very pertinent observations; and Marin Mersenne, author of the very important *Traité des Instruments* (1636-37). The *Masurgia universalis* (1650) by Athanase Kircher is a considerably smaller work than the others we have mentioned, but on certain points is more comprehensive.

Violins and viols at the beginning of the 17th century

The introduction of violins into serious music is a dominant feature of this period. We have already encountered the various bowed instruments known in the 16th century, such as the viols, the *lyras da braccio*, *violas bastarda* and the violins. In his *Orfeo* Monteverdi writes principal parts for doubled '*viole da brazzo*' in five parts, that is to say ten instruments of the violin family. A similar ensemble was used in the *Ballet comique de la Reyne*; here, as we have seen, the violins were confined to accompanying the stage ballet, while the music for the action in the golden vault, which included the *sinfonia*, was entrusted to lyres and viols.

The introduction of violins into serious music did not however result in the immediate disappearance of the viol. In scores like Monteverdi's *Orfeo* the violin had, so to speak, made the grade, but well into the century the viol enjoyed the favour of many musicians, particularly in northern Europe. In 1640 Pierre Trichet wrote: 'Viols are very proper for concerts of music inasmuch as they mix with voices and join in with other types of instruments, and by reason of the clearness of their tone and the facility of execution to which they lend themselves, while the sweet harmony which they produce causes

them to be used more than other instruments'. Marin Mersenne, however, showed a marked predilection for the violin, in particular for *Les Vingt-quatre violons du Roy*, the twenty-four violinists of the French court. Of them even Trichet wrote: 'Those who have heard them avow that they have never heard music more ravishing or more powerful'. And here we come to the hub of the matter. For nobody denied the power of the instrument; it was precisely the quality which had caused it for so long to be compared unfavourably with the 'sweet harmonies' of the viol.

Instruments in early 17th-century Italian opera

Continuing our study of the instrumentation of Monteverdi's *Orfeo* we next look at the use of the plucked string instruments. In this pastorale the instrumental passages are given names such as *toccata* (the overture), *ritournelle* or *sinfonia*, all of which have the same instrumental texture (as was true later of the operas of Cesti). However, one should not attach to these terms the meaning given to them today to describe a precise musical form. For the *toccata* overture which precedes the prologue five violins are joined by three bass viols, two violone or contrabass viols, two harpsichords and two chamber organs, trumpets and sackbuts (a brilliant combination), and later by a five-part chorus. The voices are accompanied by violins, three chitarroni and, from time to

An illustration from the important work on instruments, contained in his De organographia (1619), by the German Michael Praetorius, showing members of the viol family grouped round an early type of violin.

time, a harpsichord and a recorder to provide fresh colour. Another *ritornello* is given to the harpsichord, two chitarroni and two small *violons à la française*, by which Monteverdi probably meant the *pochette* used by dancing masters, pitched an octave higher than the violin and small enough to be carried in the pocket.

For the scenes set in the underworld Monteverdi has recourse to more sombre instrumentation – a regal (a small organ), cornetts and sackbuts. For a delicate *ritornello* marked *pian piano* he employs a chamber organ, a bass viol and a violone. In act three, in Orpheus's aria *Passente spirito*, the violins break in with a bold sweeping passage, and finally in act four he introduces (no doubt to drown the noise of the scene shifters) bass citterns, whose brilliant sonorous tone is used to reinforce the chitarroni, violins, contrabasses, organs and harpsichords. The *basso continuo* accompaniment, the first suggestion of which is found in the intermezzi of *La Pellegrina* and in the *Ballet comique de la Reyne*, is here definitely established for the first time and is used from start to finish of the opera as an accompaniment to all recitatives, arias and choruses, and, according to the mood of the scene, is played either on harpsichords or chitarroni, or on a combination of chitarroni and organ, or on regals and sackbuts.

From this account we can clearly see the wealth of instrumental resources in the early 17th century and the care with which Monteverdi deployed them. In his *Pomo d'Oro* (1667) Mercantonio Cesti shows an equal attention to the business of instrumentation. His 'infernal scenes' are scored for regal, cornetts and two sackbuts, and in Proserpine's aria in the first act he adds a bassoon. For Aurindo's lament he uses four viols and an organ, a combination which enhances the emotional quality of this impressive, dissonant music. In another work by the same composer, *La Serenata*, written in 1662 for the birthday of the grand-duke Cosimo III of Tuscany, there are annotations in the manuscript score, clarifying certain details of the instrumentation and showing in particular what is meant by the 'French manner'. 'The symphonies [we read] should be played in the French manner, by doubling the parts: six violins, four altos, four basses, and one contrabass, and one spinette *aigue* (i.e. in an octave higher than standard pitch), a harpsichord, one theorbo and one chitarrone; the soloists to be accompanied by a *spinettone a doi registri*, a theorbo and contrabass and a chorus of eight, accompanied by the same instruments, to which should be added a bass viol and a *spinette aigue*, the sonatas should be played by the whole orchestra.'

Instruments in church music

By the beginning of the 17th century not only had the value of contrasting strings with wind been understood, but also the value of combining the two together. But in church music, which for some time to come continued to consist for the most part of music for two contrasting choirs, the first method was the one most commonly used. This style of opposing choirs of instruments and voices, which originated in Venice, was taken up in Germany by Schütz, and elsewhere in Europe. For example, for the funeral of Charles III of Lorraine at Nancy in 1608 – of which we have a pictorial record in the engraving by Claude de la Ruelle – two rostrums were erected; one for the 'great Choir', consisting of some twenty singers, four cornetts, one shawm, two sackbuts and two bassoons; the other for the 'little Choir' of twelve singers and four instrumentalists – one lute, one theorbo, one *lyra da gamba* and one bass viol.

In Spain the practice of using several different 'choirs' is found in the compositions of J. B. Comes, among them a *Dixit Domine* for four choirs, the first of which is accompanied on the harp, the second on the organ; the third is scored for solo voice (alto or countertenor), two cornetts, one sackbut and one bassoon; the fourth has an accompaniment of *vihuelas* and a second organ.

In Lübeck, Buxtehude used a similar system of contrasting tonal values. In his *Benedicam Dominum* (among other compositions) he employs two vocal choirs which alternate with 'choirs' of instruments – one composed of cornetts, trumpets, sackbuts and bassoons, the other of violins (the continuo being provided by the organ, bass viol and violone), all uniting in the end in one great splendid fanfare.

In France in the first half of the century, however, there seems to have been no standard practice. Despite the funeral music mentioned above it seems that instruments were not often used in churches at all. The vocal motets for two choirs by G. Bouzignac and N. Formé seem to have been unaccompanied, though it is probably not wrong to assume that the organ was sometimes used, while instruments seem to have been largely excluded from Parisian churches up to the 1650s. It would seem that matters were arranged differently, however, for the coronations of the kings in Reims. At the coronation of Louis XIII in 1610, 'on the approach of the king, when

above
An elegantly decorated 17th-century hurdy-gurdy.

right
This type of small Italian clavichord of the late 16th century was to be displaced by larger keyboard instruments as the age of the Baroque advanced.

Plate 18
The baroque organ was one of the summits of the instrument maker's art and perfectly matched the mighty compositions for it by Bach and his contemporaries. This superb case is that of the organ of Salamanca.

Plate 19
Claudio Monteverdi.

he was at some one hundred paces distant, [they] began to play several pieces of music and fancies made expressly in honour of His Majesty. These they performed on the cornett, which was chosen for this purpose as above all instruments, the trumpet excepted, it is the most brilliant . . .'

The music provided for the coronation of Louis XIV is still better known, thanks to the engravings of Lepautre. These show a rostrum of singers, six theorboes and a bass viol; a group of trumpets, drums and shawms, and finally, in the nave of the cathedral, a band of 'twelve large oboes'. Two fantasies 'for the oboes' by Louis Couperin bear the date 1654 and it is interesting to speculate as to whether they were in fact written for this occasion.

This type of disposition of instruments by 'choirs' or 'concerts' was not reserved exclusively for religious music. One example among many of its use for secular occasions is afforded by a banquet given at Nuremberg in 1649. Here four groups of singers and instrumentalists were situated in the four corners of the hall. The first consisted of eleven singers, a cornett, flute and violin, a violone and a chamber organ; the second, of four singers, eight 'violas' (it is not specified whether they are viols or violins) and a theorbo; the third, again four singers, alto, tenor and bass sackbuts, a regal and two harps; and the fourth choir consisted of two voices, three bassoons of different pitches and another regal. This combination of instruments recalls ensembles used by Lassus eighty years previously at the court of Bavaria, but in addition the Nuremberg music has a fifth group consisting of two sopranos accompanied by a theorbo, and purely instrumental music for strings.

Instruments in France and the orchestra of Lully

During the reign of Louis XIII, the violin family assumed a position of consequence in the orchestra, and henceforth was to become more and more important. The *Vingt-quatre violons du Roy* were always called on for the royal ballets and court fêtes, although lutes and viols were still often used to accompany singers. Thus in the *Grand Ballet de Nemours* of 1604, some *airs* are played on the lute and some on violins, and in a scene of a ballet given in 1617 'The music being composed for sixty-four voices, twenty-eight viols, and fourteen lutes, was conducted by the Sieur Mauduit, and was so concerted that the whole orchestra seemed but a single voice'.

Lutes still continued to be used for some years for ballet. In 1615, Robert Ballard conducted a 'music for lutes' for the *Ballet de Madame*, and Chancy (one of the 'Masters of the King's Music') also conducted a 'consort of lutes' in a ballet of the *Triumphs* in 1635. But it would seem that this was one of the last occasions when a consort of lutes was mentioned, although theorboes were called upon to provide the *basso continuo* together with a harpsichord. From time to time, other instruments made their appearance in ballets, but only for some picturesque intermezzo. Thus watercolour drawings of 1626 show a group of guitarists assembled on the stage, and, to give a representation of 'American' music, a group playing gongs and bagpipes.

The court ballets were the great occasions for employment of the *Vingt-quatre violons du Roy* but of course they did other work. For the most part, this consisted of dances, which included voltes, galliards, *passamezze* and *branles* grouped in suites, in alternate binary and ternary forms; gavottes, sarabands, pavans and the Breton *passepied*. There are also numerous *courantes* (always in simple triple time), and ballets grouped in *entrées*, sarabands, *courantes* and galliards, which give some

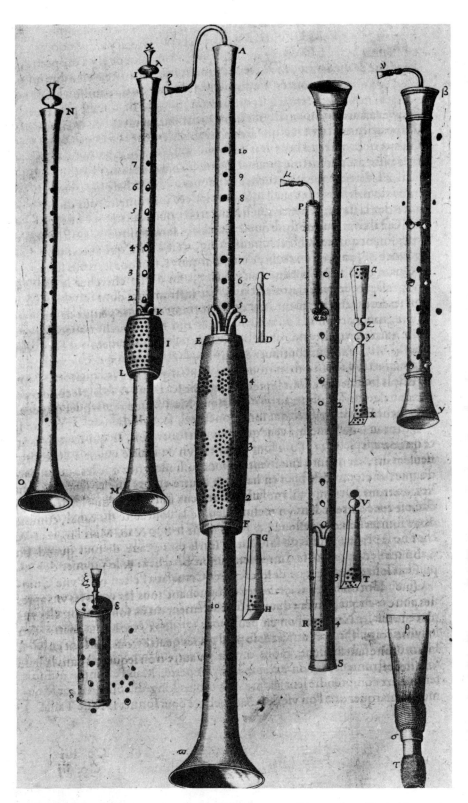

indication of the purely instrumental side of the dances given at the court of Henry IV. All these pieces formed, then, part of the repertoire of the first generation of the *Vingt-quatre*, which were organised definitively as a 'band' in about 1610-20. The work of the second generation of the *Vingt-quatre* has been preserved thanks to the Kassel Manuscript, a collection we owe to certain German amateurs who were interested in the French king's music. The twenty pieces which were copied between 1650 and 1670 are all works by Parisian instrumentalists. They are often much akin in style to the three dances which usually constituted a suite in the classic period of the form: an *allemande*, a *courante*, and a saraband.

The basis of Lully's orchestra was five violin sections, often doubled, tripled, and sometimes even quadrupled,

This page from Marin Mersenne's treatise on instruments shows a bass shawm (centre) with, to the right, a curtal and (bottom left) a rackett. Other types of shawm and a reed are also illustrated.

which played the *ritournelles*, supported the choruses, and supplied obbligatos for solos. He used transverse flutes but also, and more generally, recorders. All the flutes play either in unison with the strings, or sometimes short concerted pieces on their own. Sometimes oboes are joined with crumhorns. Trumpets are provided with brilliant parts, and are occasionally used with kettle-drums in fanfares using traditional rhythms and motifs governed by one of the most jealously guarded conventions in music at that time – the rules and usages of the trumpeters' and drummers' guilds. In the *Princesse d'Elide*, Lully introduces bagpipes, guitars and hunting horns, while the theorbo was still used extensively.

Yet only rarely did Lully use all the instruments at once. He preferred to deploy them in groups following the practice indicated by the Venetians, alternating them with each other and/or with the voice parts. Yet the skill with which Lully organised his players was admired beyond the borders of France and served as a model for composers both there and abroad.

Viol music in the 17th century

Jacobean England saw the golden age of the viol. The dances and above all the fantasies for as many as six instruments of English composers were works which for pure invention, subtlety of texture and counterpoint, gaiety and emotional appeal, yield nothing in quality to any instrumental works being produced anywhere in Europe. And if it is true to say that the viol fantasy enjoyed a late flowering in England, it is also true that its last manifestations, the fantasies which Purcell produced in 1680, are among the most expressive achievements in instrumental music of any age. The violin also makes its appearance in works by John Cooper, called Coperario (d. 1626) and others, while English composers, like others in Europe, wrote for the broken consort, and also left many compositions for the lyra viol, an instrument uniquely popular in England.

The surviving French repertory is less rich than that on the other side of the Channel. The fantasias of N. Metru (1642) for two parts never achieve real grandeur, but there is a group for four viols by Etienne Moulinié showing fine contrapuntal writing, rhythmic variety (alternating double and triple time), and lively codas, into one of which he discreetly introduces some very expressive chromatic passages. The last French compositions for consorts of viols known to us are those by Louis Couperin, although the two of his fantasias in the Bauyn manuscript are not polyphonic pieces in which each part introduces a theme of equal importance. Only treble and bass are written out in full, in conformity to demands of the *basso continuo* style of composition.

The contribution made by Germany and Italy to the repertoire of consorts of viols in the 17th century is negligible. After 1680, the viol as an ensemble instrument began to disappear in Europe. As a solo instrument, however, the bass viol enjoyed a new lease of life into the second half of the 18th century, and its popularity was nowhere greater than in England where, as late as the 1760s and 1770s, the German virtuoso C. F. Abel enjoyed a considerable vogue. But despite this protracted popularity, reflected also in France by the careers of Marin Marais and his son Roland, the bass viol could not withstand the triumphant progress of the cello in the hands of such masters as the great Italian virtuoso, Franciscello. The viol's fine and delicate tone could never equal the expressive power of its rival, and the pamphlet published by Hubert Le Blanc in 1740 under the title of *A Defence of the bass viol against the pretensions of the violin and the violoncello* was no more than a duel

above
This still life detail from a 17th-century painting shows a pandora, a shawm and, on the floor, a sopranino violin.

right
Some early cellos have rope holes in the bottom of the neck so that they could be carried in procession.

f honour. Yet in its rise to fame, the cello had first to displace the unwieldy five-stringed bass violin which, like many other instruments produced in the prolific experimentation of the 16th century, was discarded in the 17th.

The battle between the bass viol and the cello was nevertheless real. The *violoncello piccolo* and the *viola pomposa*, with their smaller proportions and strings tuned to fourths and fifths, bear witness to the attempt to achieve a compromise between the two families. Bach himself wrote accompaniments and solos for them in his Passions and cantatas, yet by the end of the 17th century their future was already doomed. The virtuosity and wonderful tone of the great school of French cellists (the brothers Janson and Duport) had confirmed the cello as a solo instrument.

Plucked stringed instruments

Among these the most important were the lute and its late 16th-century derivations; at the beginning of the 17th century these new instruments received the fullest attention in Italy. H. Kapsberger, a German who spent all his life in Venice and Rome, wrote two collections for chitarrone, while his Italian contemporaries left *capricci*, *canzoni*, church sonatas for theorbo and organ, and chamber sonatas for theorbo and harpsichord. And throughout the century in Italy it was instruments of this family which were most used for accompanying voices and providing the *basso continuo*, frequently a demanding part. It is worth emphasising the point, since modern performances of continuo parts are often confined to harpsichord or bass viol and are sometimes pedestrian and unimaginative. We have already remarked on the variety of Monteverdi's continuos in his *Orfeo*, but in his church sonatas for two violins and organs he also sometimes substitutes chitarrone for viol so as to provide a more biting attack. This arrangement was adopted by Arcangelo Corelli among others, for his *Sonate a tre*.

In France and the Low Countries, much music was written for lute ensembles. J. B. Besard (d.*c.* 1625) provides us with several examples of music for the lute in his *Norvus partas* (1617) in which we find *branles*, *courantes*, *voltes* and *passamezzi*, together with transpositions of songs and psalms and a *sinfonia* for three lutes. In Nicolas de Vallet's *Secret of the Muses* (1615) there are also transpositions of dances and songs of the own for four lutes, one treble, two tenor, and one bass.

Lutes also served as a basis for broken consorts, like that used by the Italian Pietro Paoli Melii for a *Balletto detto ardito gracioso* in 1616. This was scored for two tenor lutes, a bass lute, a double harp, a theorbo-cittern (or archcittern), while a violin and flute played the treble, and a harpsichord and bass viol the bass. Sometimes a mandora was added to the lutes to bring the upper parts into relief but, as Mersenne said, 'their sharp tone is so penetrating that the lutes have difficulty in making themselves heard'. The guitar was not introduced into Italian broken consorts until the end of the 17th century. In France we find some duos for guitars, and a prelude, *allemande*, saraband, gigue, fanfare with counterpart', were published in the *Guitare royal* and dedicated to Louis XIV. In the 18th century, the guitar remained popular as an accompaniment to songs; it never featured in orchestras except when arrangements including it were made of fashionable *airs*.

The harp, on the other hand, seems to have enjoyed a more important role than is at first apparent. Although few scores exist in which it is specifically mentioned, there are a great many pictures in which it is shown in

company with other instruments, including a cornett and bass viol, and we may perhaps assume that the harpist doubled one of the harmony instruments according to some generally recognised convention. In Spain, indeed, a harpist was appointed to the Chapel Royal and Cabezón composed music suitable 'for the keyboard, harp or *vihuela*.

Vivaldi composed a great deal of music for plucked stringed instruments. This included a concerto for mandolin, two violins, lute and bass, and three concertos for lute, violin and bass. The lutes specified for the second group are *liuti soprani*, an octave higher in pitch than the standard instrument. In these concertos the lute's role was varied; often it was accorded richly decorated parts, while the violin confined itself to the basic framework. Sometimes the violin and lute were played strictly in unison. In some slow movements the tune is given solely to the lute, while the violin and bass provided a discreet accompaniment with long-drawn-out phrases.

The popularity of the lute lasted longer in Germany than elsewhere. The last of the great lute virtuosi was German. Leopold Weiss, who died in 1750 and had been court lutenist at Kassel since the 1710s, left many fine works for his instrument. The last lute performance in Paris seems to have been given by Kohaut, a Czech, in a *concert spirituel* in 1796. Works by him for lute and cello, played by him and Duport, were very coldly received and the experiment was not repeated.

This strange instrument, invented in 1629, emerged from an attempt to adapt the keyboard principle to that of the hurdy-gurdy.

above
*Musicians in an arcadian setting;
the group on the left are playing a
cornett, a rackett and a bass
recorder.*

above right
*A huntsman playing on the tightly
wound helical horn from which the
modern orchestral horn was
probably ultimately derived.*

The woodwind

In France the wind instruments formed part of the
establishment of the Grand Ecurie (i.e. the royal stables).
Taking the brass as well as the woodwind, they comprised shawms (later the oboes), curtals (later bassoons), crumhorns, bagpipes and fifes and drums, horns,
trumpets and sackbuts. We have seen how some of these
instruments were used at the coronation of Louis XIV,
and in the nave of a cathedral they would have made a
splendid sound. But they were also much used for open-
air festivities, 'because of the great noise they make'.
Some of their repertoire has been preserved for us thanks
to the copies made by André Danican Philidor, himself
a player of the crumhorn, hautboy, trumpet and kettledrum, besides being a composer. The crumhorn, which
has a characteristic nasal tone and of which there was a
complete family, was used, according to Mersenne, as a

consort instrument in groups of four, five and six
Between 1600 and 1650, the main wind instruments ir
Italian music were the cornett, trumpet, sackbut and
bassoon. Works which survive for various combinations
of these instruments include a duet for trumpets, sonata
for trumpet and organ, a sonata for violin and sackbut
a sonata for cornett, violin and sackbut, and a *sinfonia
tertia* for cornett, two violins and bass viol.

In England, many composers wrote for wind instruments – Antony Holborne (d. 1603), who wrote for the
King's Trumpeters, being one of the finest. Just as composers often insisted that their music was equally suitable for instruments or voices, so when writing for wind
they often indicated various combinations of instrument
which could be employed. The Englishman John Adson
for example, suggests that a five-part piece be played
either on viols, cornetts or three sackbuts, and in Italy
the players were often left free to choose between cornett
and violin, sackbut, or bass viol. A carved German ivory
dating from the beginning of the century shows two
groups of instrumentalists; at the base, the side-blown
flute and hautboy are depicted playing together, while
the crumhorn remains silent; in the foreground are a
cornett, a bass recorder, a rackett, a treble recorder and
a sackbut and a silent panpipe. These instruments may
well have formed a broken consort in which the recorder
and the cornett played the treble parts, while the bass
recorder and trombone played the middle parts, the bass
being consigned to the rackett.

During the first half of the 17th century, the woodwind, 'high' instrument of the Renaissance, steadily lost
favour with composers and musicians. Lully, master of
the French musical scene, shared this attitude, yet it was
nevertheless Paris that launched the great revolution in
the design of woodwind instruments. It started with a
group of musicians from the Grand Ecurie, chief among
them Jean Hotteterre and André Philidor. All the
members were outstanding virtuosi, but in addition
many were composers and some had reputations as
manufacturers of shawms and bagpipes. From this little

rcle, four completely redesigned instruments were orn: the recorder as we know it today; the transverse ute with conical bore; the oboe and the new bassoon, hich was a very different instrument from the old urtal or courtant.

The first thing that strikes one about these instruments that they are made in several sections instead of from ne piece of wood, as had been the case hitherto. In this ay it was possible to make the finger holes more ccurately, and more accessible. Another characteristic – lthough this does not apply to the recorders – is the hick rings of ivory at each joint to reinforce the wood, which gives these instruments an elegant appearance. The alterations to the holes and reduction of the bores made the recorders more precise, and altogether easier o play, though the instrument paid the price in a much nfeebled tonal range.

The improvement to the transverse flute was the bandonment of a cylindrical for a conical bore, and with he provision of a B flat key shortly after, the flute, for which Mozart wrote and on which Böhm must first have layed, was complete. But it was with the shawm that he most progress was made. The aim of the innovators vas to give the instrument a sharper register, wider ange, and greater subtlety of tone. The bore was slightly educed throughout, becoming slightly wider at the ase. The higher notes were obtained by reducing the inger holes in diameter, the pirouette was abandoned, nd the distance between finger holes was reduced. Keys vere soon added to give both an A flat and an E flat which were well in tune, and the oboe of Bach and Handel had been born. It seems to have been played for he first time by Jean Hotteterre and André Philidor in a ballet by Molière and Lully in 1657. It proved a success: this new instrument was able to express every shade of feeling; it has the sweetness of a recorder, with greater power and variety'.

We first come across the word bassoon at the beginning of the 17th century, used to describe the instrument which was formerly known as the curtal. This too was modified by one of the Hotteterre group who, by dividing the body into four segments and altering the holes, made the classic bassoon of the 18th century, known in England as the French bassoon. Lully employed it in 1674, but it is probable that it was used ten years earlier.

In addition to their ingenuity in the redesign of the woodwind, the Hotteterre family made a considerable contribution to the literature of the instruments. Particularly important was the *Principles of the Side-blown or German flute; Recorder, or sweet flute; and hautboy*, published in 1720, by Jacques Hotteterre. Despite its other name, the side-blown flute was adopted more quickly in France than in Germany, and it was for this instrument that composers like Marin Marais and J. M. Leclair wrote.

In Germany the famous flautist Johann Joachim Quantz (1697-1773) wrote an important book on his instrument which, incidentally, contains a very interesting treatise on ornamentation. Nevertheless, in Germany, the recorder enjoyed the favour of many major composers. Bach, for example, made frequent use of it in his cantatas, and in fact *flauto* in a Bach score means the recorder; if he requires the transverse flute, he often marks the score explicitly *traverseria*. Bach was not alone in the use of the recorder, which was not completely excluded from the orchestra until the 1750s.

A literature soon began to develop for the bassoon, but it must be remembered that its predecessor, the curtal, had already intrigued composers long before the improvements we have mentioned had taken place. In one of his *Symphoniae sacrae* (1639) Schütz had used three bassoons and an organ in support of treble and alto voices (*In lectulo noctes*), and in his *In te, Domine, speravi* combines a solo alto voice with one violin and a bassoon

and organ continuo. There are also instances of its use in the work of other composers.

We have no space here to discuss the many works for woodwind of this period. They included the concerti of Vivaldi and J. S. Bach; a number of the latter's cantatas and the *Sinfonie* of Alessandro Scarlatti – these are in fact concerti grossi, in which two wind instruments (two flutes or flute and oboe, etc.) answer one another, or are combined with a group of strings. Bach also had a particular liking for the oboe d'amore, with its plangent tone and a range half way between an oboe and a cor anglais.

A decorated French cello case of the early 18th century which probably belonged to a musician of the Chapel Royal.

right
This magnificent double manual harpsichord is from the shop of a French maker and is dated 1679.

below
A mid-17th-century bass sackbut; note the wide bell.

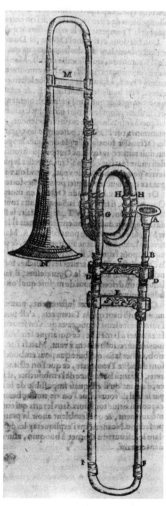

The brass

In the 17th century, trumpets and horns, formerly used only for war, ceremonial music or the hunt, were introduced into serious music. At first they were simply used as 'effects'; for example horns are used in *Le Nozze di Teti e di Pelso* by Cavalli, performed in Venice in 1639, and in Lully's *La Princesse d'Elide* given at Versailles in 1664, simply to give colour to the hunting scenes. These early horns, taken almost direct from the hunting field, were pitched at least a third higher than the modern orchestral horn. They were constructed of a tube of a fairly wide conical bore, some five and a half feet in length, wound in a tight helix of four or five loops and with a slightly flaring bell. In the mid-17th century improvements were made to this instrument, very probably in France, and, we may guess, among the musicians of the Grand Ecurie. These resulted in a horn of a narrow bore and a more flaring bell, wound at first in two loops and then, towards the end of the century, in one elegant loop. The instrument was soon known in England, where it was given the name of the French horn. It gradually gained acceptance for a limited role in the orchestra. The first scores known to specify them were for an opera at Hamburg in 1705 and a concerto for trumpets, hunting horns, oboes and kettledrums in 1728.

Like the trumpet, the horn, being simply a natural single open pipe, sounded only the notes of the harmonic series available to it. The first step in making the instrument somewhat more flexible was taken in the 1710s, when it became common to alter the pitch of the instrument, and hence the harmonic series available, by the insertion of extra lengths of tube (called crooks) to give the desired key. But the major advance towards making the horn a solo instrument was the discovery of hand stopping by the German hornist, Anton Joseph Hampel. This added a few notes in some of the gaps of the natural series, and it was basically for this instrument that Mozart wrote his horn concertos. It is impossible to discuss the use of the horn in 18th-century music without some allusion to technicalities, but for a more detailed account of these and also of the development of the trumpet, the reader is referred to the glossary of instruments at the back of the book.

Italy: the language of music

In the introductions to this section we have already described some of the elements which went to make up the explosive compound which was Baroque art, and have seen that they were also present in music. By the end of the 16th century the Franco-Flemish impetus, which had been felt throughout European musical life, was losing its force. Though its characteristic delight in polyphony was to be extended in Germany for a long time to come, it was yielding pride of place to the lyric-harmonic spirit of Italy. This was expressed in the arts of monody and recitative which originated in Florence and the highly coloured instrumental *concertato* style of Venice. Before proceeding any further, however, it is important to re-emphasise that for most of the 17th century, and particularly during the first fifty years, many terms which later were to have well defined meanings were used freely in different contexts. Words such as *sinfonia*, *sonata*, *toccata*, *concerto* etc. referred without much real discrimination to instrumental compositions which exhibited few definable formal characteristics. As the century progressed they were to be more closely defined – such terms as *sonata da camera* and *sonata da chiesa* or *trio sonata* were used with increasing frequency and significance. But since it is really in the first decades of the century that composers began to search for new and independent forms for instrumental music, we need not be surprised if at first these forms lacked definition.

But problems of terminology must not blind us to the fact that, in the 17th century, music took a radically new departure in ways which can be readily recognised if not always precisely defined. The old style, although no longer dominant, continued to be used by composers as an alternative mode of expression, and was still active in Germany; the new style may by gross over-simplification be summed up in the one word – contrast. In the polychoral style of Venice, large forces of instruments and voices were deployed in contrasting and sometimes opposing choirs. Instruments themselves came to play an increasingly independent part in the musical texture. Dynamics of volume, the contrast between loud and soft passages within the same piece of music; the contrasts between fast and slow *tempi*; between harmonic or contrapuntal textures ('old' against 'new', we might almost say); between the contrasting tone colours of the instruments; and finally the contrasts between the melody in the top part and the bass – all these were exploited to the full expressive effect. None were new to music, but the consistent and fully conscious use of them as major factors in composition produced a new kind of music, to which expressiveness, the power to affect the emotions of the hearers, was vital.

In technical terms the most important innovations were recitative, to be described more fully later in this chapter, and the manner of composition known as *basso continuo*. This more than anything else signified the displacement of the polyphonic style, in which all voices had been of roughly equal importance. In the new manner only the outer parts, the treble and the bass, were written out in full by the composer, the inner parts being left to the discretion and virtuosity of the player of the continuo instrument, usually keyboard. It had been increasingly common practice in the 16th century for the voice parts to be doubled by plucked instruments, such as members of the lute family, citterns or pandoras. In *basso continuo* composition the keyboard did not double lines of existing music but provided the harmonic filler material between bass and treble line or lines.

The *basso continuo*, once thought to have been invented by the Italian Lodovico Viadana, and found in *Concerti* published by him in 1602, evolved in the last years of the 16th century, to be formalised in the early years of the 17th. By 1607 Agostina Agazzari had already published a treatise giving instruction in the execution of the new art. His preference in instrumentation was that strings rather than wind should provide the bass line and it was soon general for the bass to be held by the bass viol or a violone and the intermediate parts of the harmony to be filled out from the keyboard. Often enough, especially in the earlier examples, the composer ensured that the harmonies supplied were the ones he wanted by writing figures above the bass line to indicate the chords required. As the century progressed and conventions became accepted, this practice was discarded in Italy and a competent keyboard player was expected to provide the continuo part without the aid of a 'figured bass'.

In its beginnings the *basso continuo* performed an important function in binding together the growing forces of the Baroque orchestra. It became possible only when harmonic practice and theory had advanced to a certain stage, and later, when a violin sonata might consist of only two written lines yet be performed with bass, melody and full harmony, it provided the vehicle for a highly sophisticated mode of composition in which composer and performer were unmistakably partners. Like all important innovations it degenerated in the course of time into conventionalism but it had, for a while, been the characteristic vehicle of some of Europe's finest music. All the elements of contrast here described, supported by the *basso continuo*, went to make up the musical texture of the new and typical Baroque art of the 17th-century opera.

The world of Italian opera

This new art developed into what may be called, without any exaggeration, the musical spectacular. With origins in the courtly diversions of earlier generations and the speculations of Florentine intellectuals, opera

right
*View of the interior of the Teatro
Olimpico at Vicenza.*

right
*View of the interior of the Teatro
Olimpico at Vicenza.*

below
*Reigning supreme when this chapter
opened, the lute was rapidly
declining in favour when it closed.*

was born about the year 1600 but, within a generation, it had emerged from the halls of privilege and the inner sanctum of scholarship to become public property. It was indeed largely instrumental in the establishment of the Italian public theatre, open to all on payment of an entrance fee. This showed something of the democratic aspect of the English theatre; even if the classes were still segregated by boxes, the pit and the balcony, no social barriers existed at the gaming tables in the foyers or circles of the theatres.

It was not, of course, the first time that music had played a part in theatrical performances, whether at court or in the church. What was new was the idea of a spectacle conceived entirely in musical terms. This 'music drama' was largely made possible by the recitative, first formulated by the Florentine composers Cavalieri and Caccini. We have touched on the work of the circle to which they belonged, and have seen that its inspiration was the hope of reviving the principles of ancient Greek drama, which was believed to have used music as an integral part, as well as the art of vocal monody familiar in the popular and folk music of north Italy. Recitative was a musical but essentially unmelodic manner for the declamation of ordinary speech. When it had been perfected, the way was open to a drama which could dispense entirely with the spoken word. Music need no longer occupy a secondary, supporting role in which choruses, ballets, intermezzi, songs or madrigals were interpolated into the main action, but now assumed a position of equal importance with the text.

The experiments of the *camerata* of Florence had become increasingly concerned with the problem of a musical equivalent for the spoken word after Jacopo Corsi, himself a poet, had taken the lead in the group on the departure of Count Bardi and Caccini for Rome in the early 1590s. The first public performance of true recitative was almost certainly in Jacopo Peri's music (now lost) to Ottavio Rinuccini's opera *Dafne*; this was presented in its definitive form by Corsi in Florence in 1595 and 1597. It was followed by two settings of a further libretto by Rinuccini on the theme of *Euridice*, one setting being by Peri, the other by Caccini. In 1600, a religious music drama, *Rappresentazione dell'anima e di corpo*, was performed at Rome. It was by Emilio de' Cavalieri, who had been sent from Florence to Rome on diplomatic business, and may be regarded as the true harbinger of opera in the papal city.

The early art of the Florentine recitative was very much for the cognoscenti, being generally dry and academic, but it was to be transformed for future opera by the work of Monteverdi. By approximating more closely to the free style of *arioso* and by carefully adapting the recitative to the dramatic demands of the text, he was to create an instrument of vigorous lyric dramatic expression, first revealed to the world in his opera *Orfeo* performed at Mantua in 1607.

Roman opera

Monteverdi was able to arrange private performances of his operas at Cremona, Milan and Genoa. But these comparatively small north Italian courts were insufficient to support the luxuriant new growth, and the dimensions of the 17th-century opera were set by the lavish spectacles presented at Rome at the court of the Barberini pope, Urban VIII. This magnificent patron commissioned the famous Barberini theatre to designs by the great Baroque architect Bernini; it held some 3,000 people and was open to both the Roman and the visiting aristocracy. It was inaugurated in 1632 with a performance of the religious opera *Sant' Alessio* by Stefano Landi, a member of the papal chapel.

Rome was for a time the centre of operatic development. Not only did its composers and stage managers extend the dimensions of the spectacle but, in musical terms, their operas began to emphasise the distinction between the emotional mood of the aria and the narrative function of the recitative. Among the most important composers were Landi himself, Domenico Mazzochi, whose secular opera *Catena d'Adone* (1626) stands out from the predominantly religious subject matter of his colleagues, and his brother Virgilio, who collaborated in the composition of the first comic opera *Chi soffre, speri* (1639), and also wrote numerous cantatas and oratorios. Marco Marazzoli, who was Mazzochi's collaborator, also worked in Venice.

Marazzoli was not the only Roman composer to travel abroad. Most interesting perhaps are the Italians who went to Paris; among them was Luigi Rossi who was called to the French capital by the exiled Barberini, where his *Orfeo* was produced in 1647. It was not the first Italian opera seen in Paris; an Italian company had performed there two years previously at the invitation of Cardinal Mazarin, but it made a considerable impression, no doubt because it deliberately appealed to French taste, incorporating among other things a number of ballets. Another group of musicians left Rome to seek their fortunes in north Italy. They were Benedetto Ferrari, Francesco Manelli and his wife, Madalena. It was their company, which included the singer Felice Sances, that opened the new San Cassiano theatre at Venice with a performance of Ferrari and Manelli's opera *Andromeda* in 1637. In the same year Sances left to take up a post at the imperial court at Vienna, and later was to be one of the pioneers of Italian opera in Prague.

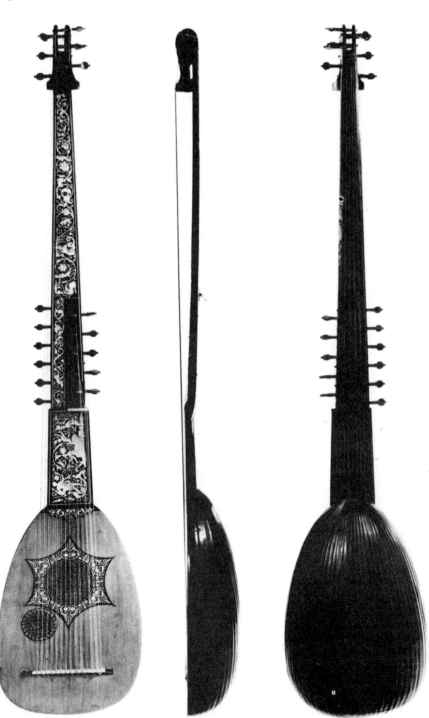

below left
Pope Urban VIII, an important patron of the developing art of opera.

below
This beautifully decorated chitarrone is a perfect example of the massive and elaborate modifications of the simple lute which were used for continuo parts. Front, side and back views of the one instrument are shown.

right
*St Mark's Venice, one of the great
musical establishments of Italy.*

below right
*Numerous models of harpsichords
with divided keys and specially
tuned strings were invented to
obviate some of the problems of
using untempered pitch on keyboard
instruments.*

Venetian opera

The opening of the San Cassiano theatre in Venice
marked a major departure in the history of opera in
Italy. The refined and rarefied art of the Florentines had
been quickly transformed into a great public spectacle,
a change which as we have seen owed much to the Roman
composers and also to Monteverdi, from 1613 *maestro
di capella* at St Mark's in Venice. It was in this city,
with the opening of the San Cassiano theatre, that the
era of the public commercial opera house was born and
a revolution initiated in Italian national life. The theatre
became the common meeting place of people of all
classes who gathered to see the show and to congregate
round the gaming tables. Here they mixed to a degree
which would have seemed intolerable in the previous
century and which was certainly indicative of changes
to come. The 19th-century Italian theatre crowds, for
whom the cry *Viva Verdi*, interpreted as *Viva Vittore
Emanuele re d'Italia* (king of Italy), was a nationalist
slogan, were the heirs to a tradition in which the
theatre had long been a central feature of national life.

And whatever the different contributions, such as
those of Rome, Florence or Venice in the early years of
opera, the musical style quickly became an Italian one.
The movement of composers and musicians between
the cities was a central factor in this evolution. This
communication between musical centres was increased
still further by the formation of touring companies such
as the famous *Febi Armonici*. After touring in north and
central Italy, they went to Naples where they later
established themselves. After this somewhat late introduction to opera, the Neapolitans were to develop an
individual style which in turn was to feed back into the
mainstream of Italian opera in the early years of the next
century.

As opera put down new roots in Naples and the touring companies were active in northern Italy, opera in
the great Venetian tradition (begun by Monteverdi
whose work is dealt with extensively below), was
developed by many gifted composers, chief among
whom were Pietro Francesco Cavalli (1602-76) and
Mercantonio Cesti (1623-69). In their hands opera in
the Venetian style continued to extend the spectacular
nature of its staging; the music became increasingly
absorbed with the aria and *arioso* passages which were

to give full scope to the rising body of virtuosi singers,
headed by the *castrati*.

Cavalli, who entered the musical establishment of St
Mark's in 1617 and for the last ten years of his life was
maestro di capella there, shows the influence of Monteverdi both in his fine church music and in his operas.
But in the latter field he made advances, favouring a
more rhythmic manner in his recitatives and giving
the chorus an ever less important role in the musical
structure. He was one of the Italians who produced
opera at Paris, his *Ercole Amante* being produced for
the wedding of Louis XIV in 1662. But opera in the
Italian style never gained great popularity at the French
capital, where music came to be dominated by Lully
who, although Italian-born, assiduously cultivated the
French manner. Cavalli is known to have written more
than thirty operas, most of which were produced at
Venice; among the finest were *Didone* (1641) and *Il
Giasone*. Among the composers working at Venice in
the tradition of Monteverdi and Cavalli was Carlo
Pallavicino (1630-88), who also spent some time at
Dresden, but many others were influenced by the
Venetian school, among them Stradella, Agostino
Steffani (1654-1728), most of whose career was spent in
Germany, and above all Marc Antonio Cesti.

Cesti, who reputedly wrote more than a hundred
operas, was a true cosmopolitan, working at Rome,
Vienna, Innsbruck, at Venice for a brief period, and
dying at Florence. His style, softer and perhaps more
graceful than that of Cavalli, is nevertheless indebted to
the Venetian master. More than his older contemporary,
he catered to the ever-growing demand for spectacle
and sensation, sacrificing the dramatic unity of his
works to the exigencies of the singers' virtuosity, and
separating to a greater extent than had his predecessors
the elements of recitative and aria, the latter becoming
frankly a vehicle for vocal brilliance. The role of the
chorus was reduced still further and the splendours of
the decor became still more overwhelming. In Cesti's
most famous work, *Il Pomo d'Oro*, presented at Vienna
for the marriage of the Emperor Leopold I to Margaret
of Spain, there were no fewer than twenty-four scene
changes in the four acts. Whole vistas dissolved before

the spectators to reveal yet further glories; gods and goddesses appeared floating among the clouds, and the whole, lit it should be remembered by naked candles, was manoeuvred with precision by elaborate machinery which was the pride of Baroque theatre.

The 'spectacular' in full spate

Such a spectacle was exceptional no doubt, but it was only a remarkable example of the kind of display common throughout the courts of Europe as the 17th century progressed. These theatrical performances became a matter of the most intense rivalry between rulers and princes. A production might be recorded in richly decorated 'programmes' portraying the splendour of the sets and carrying the libretto of the opera in many languages so that the whole, which in effect constituted a propaganda hand-out, could be distributed to the admiring, and it was hoped envious, eyes of foreigners. Even to the imperial exchequer the expense of mounting such a spectacle was considerable, and in the case of *Il Pomo d'Oro* the organisers attempted to recoup some of their outlay with a public performance, still something of a rarity outside Italy.

The works themselves were as astonishing as their settings. Mythology was confounded with sacred drama (it is worth remembering that even in the 'sacred representations' of the 14th century and later, elaborate machinery was already employed). Pagan deities joined in dances with companies of angels; demons shared the stage with monsters, magicians and fairies; the scene passed in quick succession from sea-borne regattas to *fêtes champêtres* and cavalry battles. Nor did the composer hesitate to match this dramatic phantasmagoria with musical anomalies. Songs alternated with popular dances; tragic airs with comic or burlesque scenes which had little or no dramatic function. Plaintive laments and lullabies were followed in quick succession by warlike songs accompanied by trumpets and hunting horns. Finally we must devote some attention to the singers, for whom the whole vast structure was a setting. They exploited their situation to the full, pouring forth the most ingenious vocal acrobatics that the innumerable singing schools could devise. They exerted themselves to outdo the solo instruments of the orchestra (the great Farinelli of the next century was to challenge and defeat in both floridity and breath control a virtuoso on the trumpet). To extract the last possible ounce of sensationalism, they even resorted to physical acrobatics.

It was in this situation that one of the most astonishing vogues in musical history arose. This was for the voices of the eunuch singers known as *castrati*. Many a gifted boy soprano was operated on before the age of puberty in an attempt to preserve his voice. For many of the victims of this sophisticated barbarism the result was a career in provincial obscurity, or outright failure. But in a few cases the operation succeeded in making possible a voice of stupefying unreality of tone and technical perfection. The high pure treble register of the boy, coupled with the power of an adult man's body, was further reinforced by the fact that training and development were not interrupted by the year or two of rest enforced by the breaking of the normal male voice. The audiences, even of the smallest theatres, expected to thrill to the demonstrations of vocal expertise of which the *castrati* were capable and the demand grew throughout Europe, reaching its peak in the middle of the next century. The singers developed a successful personal repertoire which could be taken from one theatre to another without much alteration, and its items inserted as the need arose into the most diverse works. Of the

two most famous 'sopranists' of their time, Loreto Vitori remained in Italy, while Baldassare Ferri, who served at the courts of Warsaw, Stockholm and Vienna, was the rage of all Europe. He was created a knight of St Mark by the Venetians and left an estate of 600,000 crowns to charity on his death, in Perugia, in 1680. We shall find his success paralleled by many later singers.

top
A performance of Cesti's opera Il Pomo d'Oro *given at Vienna in 1677.*

above
Set design for Il Pomo d'Oro *by Lodovico Burnacini*

Monteverdi

The place of Claudio Monteverdi in the history both of opera and of music is so important that it demands separate treatment. Undoubtedly the greatest Italian composer of the 17th century and one of the major European composers of all time, he excelled in all the main branches of his art except that of purely instrumental music. His madrigals have been described in an earlier chapter; here we shall be concerned chiefly with his dramatic and religious music.

Born at Cremona in 1567, he began his career as a choir boy in the cathedral there, where Marc Antonio Ingegneri was his teacher. At the age of twenty-three he entered the service of the Gonzagas of Mantua as musician and composer, meeting there de Wert,

Gastoldi and Viadana. He travelled in the entourage of the duke on an expedition against the Turks in Hungary, and then in 1599, to Brussels, where he no doubt gained valuable first-hand experience of the music of the late Franco-Flemish school. Its continuing influence in Italy is witnessed by the polyphonic style of Monteverdi's earliest church music, but he was soon to become a conscious revolutionary against the old manner, which he himself termed the *prima prattica*, and one of the leaders of the *avant-garde*, or the *seconda prattica*. On the death of the Mantuan *maestro di capella*, Benedetto Pallavicino, in 1601, Monteverdi was successful in his application for the post, and took Mantuan citizenship.

right
A 16th-century plan of Cremona.

below
Fresco in the ducal palace of Mantua, the town where Monteverdi held his first major post.

Some years previously he had married Claudia Cattaneo, one of the singers at the court, and her death in the early years of the new century hit him hard. His time at Mantua was indeed an unhappy one, for, despite his great talents and reputation, the duke was reluctant to meet the composer's demands for a raise in salary. In 1612 Monteverdi finally resigned his post. In the following year he was unanimously elected to the most coveted post in Italian musical life, the directorship of St Mark's, Venice. Here he remained for the rest of his life, for although his official duties involved him only in the composition of religious music, not only was the money excellent (the authorities doubled the former salary for the post to keep him), but so also were the conditions of work. While discharging his official obligations, Monteverdi was able to compose dramatic works and other secular music for performance in the great houses of Venice and even at the courts of other cities. After the opening of public opera houses at Venice, Monteverdi was able to see his last masterpieces performed before the largest audiences of contemporary Europe.

Monteverdi and the 'New Music'

One of the first shots in the battle between the old and new styles had been fired by the Florentine Caccini in his collection *Le Nuove musiche* (1601). This was a collection of a number of monodies and some madrigals, but was of particular interest on account of its preface in which Caccini outlined the principles of the new music. The aim of music should be to heighten the emotional content of the text and not merely to provide a backdrop for word painting. He criticised the structures of the polyphonists, praised the expressive powers of monody, and gave practical comments on the new manner of natural singing which was needed to give the maximum emotional expression to the line. Central in the new school, with which Monteverdi identified himself and of whose style indeed he was the chief architect, was the demand that all the resources of music should be called up to express a text as naturally as possible.

The conflict of attitudes was neatly summed up by contemporaries in the two Latin maxims; for the old school: *Harmonia Orationis Domina est*, 'Music is the mistress of the word'; for the new school: *Oratio Harmoniae Domina absolutissima*, 'The word is the absolute mistress of the music'. The conflict between the generations is no new phenomenon in art, and it should be stressed that the most characteristic features of Monteverdi's style had well established antecedents. His expressive use of chromaticism, and the abruptness of some of his modulations, had been anticipated in the works of Marenzio and Gesualdo. The arts of monody and recitative were certainly not 'invented' by Monteverdi, and his colourful instrumentation was, essentially, a masterly extension of the principles of Gabrieli. But Monteverdi's stature derives not from the invention of any new forms of musical expression but the creative powers which he brought to existing styles, transcending, transmuting and integrating them into music which ranks with the greatest of all time.

For the excellence with which he handled the new style and the profound modifications which he wrought in it, he may indeed be classed as one of its pioneers. Certainly he was a self-confessed devotee. In a reply to a patron who asked of him his objections to handling a conventional pastoral theme he made the significant remark: 'The story in no way inspires me and to be honest I even had some difficulty in understanding it . . . *Arianna* moved me as a true cry from the heart; *Orfeo* as a heartfelt entreaty to the gods, but I just do not see the point of this tale. This being the case, your highness, what purpose, exactly, do you expect the music to serve?' His devotion to the new music had been apparent in the fourth and fifth books of madrigals. In a preface to the fifth book Monteverdi had answered the embittered criticisms made by the arch-traditionalist Giovanni Artusi in his treatise *Of the Imperfections of Modern Music*, saying that music should rest on the fundamental truths of nature and that it should express the full range of human passions, from tranquillity to anger, from joy to despair.

The operas

Monteverdi's *Orfeo*, with a libretto by Alessandro Striggio and performed in Mantua in 1607, was the first great masterpiece in the history of opera. It is important in that monody, although playing a large role, is not so predominant as in the earlier operas of the Florentines. In *Orfeo* there is a large variety of forms: choruses and dances are interspersed between the arias and passages of recitative, while these already reveal the contours which they are to fill as opera develops. It has already been said that the recitatives embody a major contribution to the development of opera, yet despite his sympathy with the modern manner, Monteverdi is too fine a musician to allow the music to suffer by a slavish subordination to the words. The facility with which the musical line of the recitatives, both accompanied and unaccompanied, follows the every inflexion of the dramatic sense, verges on the miraculous.

Monteverdi's dramatic sense and feeling for structure is one of the distinguishing features of the work. Instruments are used to portray moods and emotions: a choir of sackbuts (the ancestor of the trombone) is associated with the regions of Hell. In general the instrumentation shows great sensitivity, while the score is one of the first in which the exact instrumentation is marked throughout. The orchestra itself is worthy of note as an example of the resources available to the composer to a large Italian court. It consisted of: strings – ten 'little violins' *à la française*, three bass viols and two violone; wind – two recorders, two cornetts, four sackbuts and three trumpets; and continuo instruments – two clavichords, two positive organs, a regal and a double harp.

It was the year after the performance of *Orfeo* that Monteverdi's wife died and the composer, weighed down with grief, wrote the opera *Arianna* to a libretto by Rinuccini. The work is lost save only for the deeply moving and famous *Lament* which reduced the audience to tears on its first performance. Another work surviving from about this period is the delightful *Ballo delle Ingrate* to another text by Rinuccini. It tells the sad story of the fate, after death, of ladies who in this life refused the pleas of their lovers; allowed a brief return to earth, they advise the female members of their audience not to commit the crime of which they were guilty. Yet even in this light-hearted piece, the voice of the composer of the *Arianna* is heard in the aria in which the last of the *Ingrate* makes her final farewell to the world of light.

above
Modern production of Monteverdi's opera L'incoronazione di Poppea *at La Scala, Milan, in 1953.*

left
Rest on the flight into Egypt *by Caravaggio.*

An allegorical picture showing St Cecilia, the patron saint of music, playing the lute. Notice however the violin at her feet and the double bass violin with its six strings and high shoulders.

Many of Monteverdi's dramatic works have been lost, but among those to have survived is the *Combattimento di Tancredi e Clorinda* performed at Venice in 1624. The work, a secular cantata rather than a true opera, is performed by viols and keyboard and three singers, one of whom has the role of narrator. The instruments are used in a masterly fashion to contribute to the action, and it is interesting that Monteverdi here made use of tremolo and pizzicato in the string parts for programmatic effects, such as the portrayal of the battle scenes.

Not the least remarkable feature of Monteverdi's outstanding career is the fact that his greatest masterpiece, and one of the summits of operatic achievement of all time, was completed in his seventy-fourth year. Whereas his first public opera for the Venetian stage, *Il ritorno d'Ulisse in patria* (1641), had, in accordance with convention, dealt with a mythological subject, the mighty *L'incoronazione di Poppea* (1642) chose an historical one from imperial Rome under Nero. Yet the fact that this is the first historical opera is a point of secondary interest, in comparison with the phenomenal power which the composer showed in portraying all aspects of human emotion and personality in the widest possible range of situations. In Monteverdi's last great triumph, music becomes the full and sufficient vehicle of the drama.

The religious music of Monteverdi

We have already referred to the collection of three-part motets in the polyphonic manner which, under the title *Sacrae cantiunculae*, Monteverdi had published when still only fifteen. His next collection of religious music was that of 1610, containing the famous *Vespers*, a six-part mass on a theme by the Franco-Flemish composer Gombert, and other works. The mass shows Monteverdi's confident mastery of the *prima prattica*, a mastery which was to be demonstrated in his subsequent publications of religious music, *Selva morale e spirituale* (1641), which, containing a four-part *a cappella* mass, is a veritable polyphonic tour de force, and the posthumous publication *Messa . . . e Salmi* (1650). This includes the magnificent *Laetatus sum* – a masterpiece of the *concertato* style for six voices, two violins, two sackbuts, two curtals (early bassoons) and *basso continuo*.

Although published while he was still in the service of the Mantuan court, the 1610 collection is dedicated to the pope and may, as has been suggested, have been intended for performance at Rome. This may well be true of the mass, but the mighty *Vespers* of 1610, 'Vespers in the concerto style composed on *canti firmi*', were presumably written for the ducal chapel of Mantua. They employ large vocal and instrumental forces, and demonstrate the immense expressive potentialities of the modern style, the *seconda prattica*.

As published, the settings of the psalms for the *Vespers* were interspersed with cantata treatments of other psalms not connected with the service, and the volume also contains the *Sonata sopra Sancta Maria*. Modern performances of the *Vespers* often include these works as well.

Music in the church

We have seen that operas, especially those of the Roman school, often had religious themes and that the handling of the subject matter, whether religious or secular, was the same. Furthermore the developments in music intended for performance in churches were parallel to those in theatrical music. The main difference, for example, between a religious opera and a church oratorio was that the latter would be given in concert performance without settings or costumes. Even this drawback was greatly compensated for by the introduction of 'spectacular' elements into the music. The austere polyphony of Palestrina was expanded by a new Baroque sonority, and a musical language created which was fully in tune with the architectural fantasies of a Bernini or a Borromini. The lead was taken by composers working at Rome, but we must be careful here, as in the realm of secular music, of making hard and fast regional distinctions. The polychoral style, which was to find a natural setting in the great Roman basilicas, had nevertheless been developed, if not to the same grandiose extent, in Venice. Similar music was soon heard in Assisi and Loretto, and all the great Italian churches. Although no longer holding pride of place, the old style of polyphony continued to be followed by some composers, but the weight of church patronage was behind music in the new styles of *concertato* compositions for voices and instruments, and the lyric monody written for solo voices and instrumental accompaniment.

The fertile field of monody in fact gave birth to one of the most characteristic types of church composition in the cantata. The first recorded use of the word seems to be in a volume published by Alessandro Grandi in 1620, and by this time the type was more or less established. Its origins, however, are to be sought in the development of the monody by Caccini and others, and in the increasingly dramatic treatment of the madrigal as exemplified in the later collections of Monteverdi.

In the early history of the cantata, as elsewhere, we can observe the blurring of the distinctions between church and secular music. Based on either sacred or secular texts, the cantata was at first a series of arias and recitatives for solo voice with instrumental accompaniment. But additional voices were soon introduced and, as the cantata developed, choruses were also used until, with the music of German composers later in the century, the dimensions of the form changed completely. In Italy, the early cantata quickly gained in popularity and for a time enjoyed a position comparable to that of the madrigal in the 16th century. The fashion became general, cantatas with sacred texts were performed in churches, monasteries and convents, while secular cantatas were to be heard at festivals and in the academies. But though the texts differed, the form was identical.

The main centres of cantata composition were Florence, Rome, Venice and later Bologna. In the first half of the century, the structure was firm and on a comparatively small scale, while later it became larger and the compositions more individual. The distinction between recitative and aria became ever more marked, and a melodramatic trend became more and more obvious. The principal composers were the prolific Luigi Rossi (1598–1653), whose *Lament of the Queen of Sweden* on the death of Gustavus Adolphus in battle was his most renowned work in the genre; Alessandro Stradella; Giovanni Legrenzi (1626–90), who published a volume of solo cantatas in the 1670s; and above all the great Carissimi. But although one of the most popular and prolific composers of cantatas, he enjoys a still greater importance as the greatest single creative force in the shaping of the second major form of Italian church music – the oratorio.

Carissimi and the oratorio

What was to become the major dramatic form of 17th-century Italian composers of church music had its roots in the *Laudi spirituali* and the Exercises of the Oratory of St Philip Neri. With the explicit aim of attracting lay members to his new congregation, Neri had enlivened its meetings by introducing music before the sermon and concluding with songs of praise inspired by the liturgy of the day. As the 16th century drew to a close, these *laudi* and the music of the Oratory inevitably became affected by the increasing introduction of dramatic elements into other musical forms, such as the madrigal, and also reflected the interest in monody which was sweeping the Italian musical world. The musical exercise of the Oratory developed in two distinct ways under these influences. On the one hand emerged the art of the fully fledged religious opera, which made use of staging and costumes and other aspects of visual spectacle. On the other the oratorio, though hardly less dramatic musically, dispensed with the trappings of the theatre, being always given in concert performances.

Emilio Cavalieri's *Rappresentazione dell'anima e di corpo*, the first musical drama of any kind to be seen in Rome, was performed in the Oratory of Sta Maria in Vallicella in 1600, and was the ancestor of the many religious operas to be produced by Roman composers as the century progressed. No distinction was made in the treatment of sacred or secular texts, but it was no doubt thought more fitting that the papal opera house, the Barberini theatre, should be inaugurated with a performance of Landi's religious opera, *Sant' Alessio*. In any case, the terms secular and sacred applied only to the general theme, for the action might well contain comic or burlesque scenes obviously secular in inspiration. Indeed the distinction between the sacred and the secular was of so little real significance that during Lent,

Giacomo Carissimi.

when all theatres as such were closed, the performances of the non-scenic oratorios of the churches were thronged by the theatre-going public. Carissimi, the father of the oratorio, has been called the great seculariser of church music and in the hands of him and his successors, the oratorio won a popularity in Italy which for a time rivalled that of the opera itself.

Giacomo Carissimi was born near Rome in 1605 and in his thirtieth year took up the appointment at San Apollinare, the chapel of the German college of Jesuits at Rome, which he was to hold until his death. A tall, gaunt man of melancholy aspect, he remained frugal and austere in his wants despite his sizeable income. His reputation as a composer quickly spread throughout Europe and his pupils included the Germans, Christoph, von Kerll and Krieger, and the Frenchman M.-A. Charpentier. It was thanks to copies by these and others that many of Carissimi's works have survived, since he published little, and at the suppression of the Jesuit Order in 1773, the great collection of his works at San Apollinare was destroyed or dispersed.

Carissimi drew on all the resources of the contemporary instrumental and theatrical music in the composition of his cantatas and oratorios. In his hands the oratorio, often based on episodes in the Old Testament, achieved the level of epic drama while depending not on action but on the words sung. The succession of choruses, *arioso* passages and recitative, linked by the narrator, are welded into a dramatic unity of great power in which the music provides both the setting and the interpretation. His oratorios include many masterpieces, among them the superb *Jephte* as well as *Baltazar*, *Jonas* and *Judicium Salomonis*, together with the sacred histories including *Abramo e Isacco* and *Job*. In addition to his religious works, Carissimi also produced a large number of secular cantatas which, although lacking the warmth of those of the Neapolitan composer Luigi Rossi, are nevertheless considerable works. In general, Carissimi's music is marked by a strongly developed harmonic sense. Indeed the confident, often bold, modulations reveal a true mastery of what amounts to a new awareness of the harmonic idiom. To this he adds the talent essential for a 17th-century dramatic composer, an absolute mastery of declamatory recitative.

Among the continuators of the oratorio were Alessandro Scarlatti (whose important operatic output is dealt with in a later chapter), Bernardo Pasquini and Alessandro Stradella (1644–82). A passionate man whose career formed the subject of a 19th-century romantic opera, Stradella found himself involved in love affairs and elopements which drove irate rivals to a number of attempts at assassination, the third of which, at Genoa in 1682 was successful. Yet despite an active and, it seems, largely fugitive life (which may in some degree account for Purcell's reputed admiration of his work), Stradella produced much fine music – not only in the field of the oratorio. He made important contributions to the development of the accompanied aria, and, by adopting a division of the orchestra into contrasting groups, *concertino* and *grosso*, was, in his development of the *sinfonia da chiesa*, a pioneer of the concerto grosso as later developed by Corelli.

Girolamo Frescobaldi.

Instrumental music

The two great formative influences on the evolution of keyboard music during the 17th century were the Dutchman J. P. Sweelinck and the Italian Girolamo Frescobaldi. Frescobaldi, the younger of the two by twenty years, was born at Ferrara in 1583. There he was a pupil of the organist Luzzasco Luzzaschi, through whom he no doubt became acquainted with the work of the madrigalist, Gesualdo, Luzzachi's friend. He worked and studied for a time at Rome before travelling with Guido Bentivoglio of Ferrara to Brussels (1607-8), where he gained first-hand acquaintance with the music of Sweelinck himself. He passed the rest of his career, apart from a six year period at Florence, in Rome. Frescobaldi's fame as an executant spread all over Europe and pupils flocked to study under him. Among them was the German J. J. Froberger, while some fifty years later Johann Sebastian Bach studied the works in the *Fiori Musicali*.

The hallmarks of Frescobaldi's style were clarity of harmonic structure, the fullest exploitation of thematic material in a wealth of masterly sets of variations, the incorporation of the art of the virtuoso into compositions of the highest musical worth, and the cultivation of a pure and cantabile line. In addition to his keyboard music he wrote madrigals and music for instrumental ensembles. His *canzoni*, like those of some of his con-

temporaries, exhibit an important trend away from the multi-sectional form towards the three or four 'movements' of the later sonata. Yet despite his great fame, Frescobaldi's example was followed far more eagerly abroad than at home. Apart from his pupil Michelangelo Rossi, it was not until the work of Bernardo Pasquini that an important Italian composer followed him.

Pasquini (1637-1710), who worked in Rome, was not only a fine composer but was also a distinguished teacher. Despite clear affinities with Frescobaldi, his music contained important new elements, amongst which the clear differentiation between the instrumental characteristics of the organ and the harpsichord was prime. The joy which he took in the technical possibilities of the latter instrument is obvious, and even his vocal and theatrical compositions are impregnated with the spirit of the harpsichord. Both his own compositions and those of his many pupils, among them Durante and the German Georg Muffat, opened the way to the development of a style specifically attuned to the harpsichord. Apart from the purely technical features of Pasquini's music, he may also be classed among those musicians who contributed to the development of the chamber music style of the 18th century. Pasquini was chamber musician to Prince Borghese and later to Queen Christina of Sweden, who lived in Rome from 1654 and was a major patron of the arts, and he played an important part in introducing the harpsichord as an indispensable feature of elegant society concerts.

The birth of
the new instrumental forms

As the 17th century progresses two trends can be observed. The first was the gradual emergence of the instrumental consort – strings of the violin family and harpsichord – as the basic group in music for both large and small instrumental ensembles. The rich and piquant instrumentation of the Venetians, in which strings, wind and continuo instruments are combined while still retaining their marked individuality and relatively equal standing, gradually gives place to an orchestra in which, although many of the same instruments are present, a hierarchy is established dominated by the violin family, doubled and supported by the woodwind, with the brass performing increasingly specialised functions. This development, which parallels the structural hierarchy of the music introduced by the technique of the *basso continuo*, is closely associated with the rise of the violin and especially with the prominence which it was to enjoy at the French court.

The second important trend is the gradual establishment of the instrumental forms. The general interchangeability, already noted, of such terms as sonata and concerto gives way to specific forms such as the trio sonata, the solo sonata and the concerto grosso in the last decades of the century. The important part played by the dance suite in the development of instrumental forms has already been mentioned and we shall have occasion to return to it. It consisted of a number of contrasting movements based ultimately on popular and courtly dances but more and more intended for concert performance and with increasingly little to do with dances. The dance suite already contained the embryo of a more formalised grouping in the contrasting pairs, such as pavan and galliard, and the *passamezzo* and *saltarello*, long accepted by convention. The *canzona da sonar*, derived by Italian composers from the vocal form of the French *chanson* in the 16th century, continued as a reminder of the original dependence of instrumental music on vocal forms into the first decades of the 17th.

Music for instruments only achieved an equal status

Plate 20
*The magnificent and important
Compenius organ at Fredericksborg
castle, Denmark. It dates from the
1610s.*

ith vocal music during the 17th century, and it is not herefore surprising that the evolution of instrumental orms was somewhat late. Yet by the end of the century he sonata for solo instrument with continuo was a ecognisable and increasingly popular form, though for most of this period the trio sonata for two solo instruments, bass viol and harpsichord was more common. Its origins may be seen in the *Libro delle sinfonie e gagliarde* published at Venice by the Jewish composer Salomon Rossi (1570–*c.* 1630). Rossi, who signed himself 'Hebreo', was held in high regard at the court of Mantua where he served, being spared the humiliation imposed on his co-religionists of wearing a distinctive yellow badge. The collection contains one four-part piece entitled 'sonata' and a number of three-, four- and five-part *sinfonie*; of particular interest, in view of later developments, is the preponderance of three-part works. Rossi subsequently published some twenty years later a further instrumental collection of *sonate*, *sinfonie*, *gagliarde* and *corrente* for two violins and chitarrone, and also three- to eight-voice settings of psalms for the synagogue. Another important early composer of chamber music was the violin virtuoso Biagio Marini (1597–1665) who was born at Brescia, one of the chief centres of violin-making, and who travelled widely in Italy and Germany before his death at Venice in 1665. His *Affeti musicali* (1617) contains 'sinfonie, canzone and sonate balleti' in one, two and three parts which are suitable for performance by violins or cornetts, bass violin or sackbut and continuo. Towards the end of his life he also published *Sonate da chiesa e da camera* for two to four parts with continuo and guitar.

The distinction of form implied by the terms church sonata (*da chiesa*) and chamber sonata (*da camera*) did not exist, the main difference between the two being primarily that the former had a somewhat graver mood. Far more important was the emergence of the trio sonata and the sonata for solo violin. The solo sonata was promoted by the rise of the violin virtuosi, among the first of whom was Giovanni Battista Fontana, called 'da Violoni'; his reputation in the first years of the century matched that of the great cornettist, Ludovico Cornale. Some of the first instrumental solo com-

positions, whether with or without accompaniment, were written for these two executants and are technically much bolder than those which were written at the end of the century. It is as though composers for the violin wished to exploit every possibility of the new instrument before systematising its *tessitura* and adopting the standard compass established by Corelli. The capabilities of these early violinists are shown by the works of Marini and others, notably Carlo Farini, himself a virtuoso. His *Capriccio stravagante* published in 1627 is for four stringed instruments, but the first violin part stands out by reason of its florid nature and its use of unusual techniques such as double stopping, tremolo and even the use of the wood of the bow; these and others are called for by the composer in the numerous imitations of the cries of various animals, the beggar's hurdy-gurdy, the soldier's drums and trumpets etc. Sensational as such tricks were, they heralded the beginning of a fashion which was more than a passing vogue, for the violin was gradually to assume the topmost place among musical instruments. Its position was assured by the prestige accorded to the virtuosi of the *Vingt-quatre violons du Roy* at the courts of the French kings.

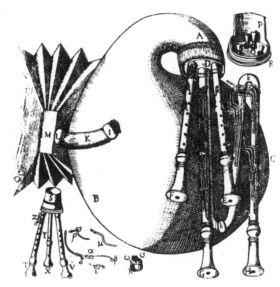

above left
In Italy as in France peasant instruments enjoyed a fashionable vogue; an example is the bellows-blown bagpipe or musette.

left
Colonnade by Bernini in the Piazza San Pietro at Rome.

German music
of the 17th century

The Baroque age witnessed the formulation of a characteristic German style and the characteristic German musical forms. The sacred and the secular cantata and Passion music all underwent new and exclusively German modifications, while in the field of instrumental music the German organists developed the great structures of the chorale prelude and the prelude and fugue which were to be so magnificently perfected in the hands of Bach. The history of the music of the period is complicated by both politics and religion, but as a broad generalisation we may say that as the century progressed the lead passed from the Catholic lands of the south to the Protestant states of the north.

After the conclusion of the Thirty Years War at the Peace of Westphalia in 1648, calm was restored and the numerous German states confirmed within boundaries which were to remain basically unchanged for the rest of the century. The most important courts were the following: Vienna, capital of the Habsburg Empire, provided employment for many musicians and was one of the centres of Italian influence; to the west lay Salzburg, where the powerful archbishops held court, and Munich, capital of the electors of Bavaria; to the west again was the duchy of Württemberg and its capital, Stuttgart. In the north the electoral court of Saxony at Dresden was, thanks to the great Heinrich Schütz, one of the main musical centres, while in the Saxon university town of Leipzig, his contemporary Schein was musical director at the church of St Thomas. Immediately north of Saxony lay the lands of the electors of Brandenburg, with their capital at Berlin, and to the northwest the great Hanseatic city of Hamburg provided a long line of distinguished musicians and composers. The last of the numerous musical centres of the German 17th century to be mentioned here is the town of Kassel, in the duchy of Hesse.

Theory and practice:
Michael Praetorius

Peculiar to Germany was the preponderant position enjoyed by one particular form of religious music; this was the chorale, the harmonised congregational hymn of the Lutheran Church. Its melodies came from various sources including, very often, folk or popular music. Three main chorale anthologies had been published during the 16th century by Georg Rhaw (1544), Lukas Osiander (1586) and Sethus Calvisius (1597). Its growing significance in the 17th century is heralded by the collection *Musae Sionae* of Praetorius, who distinguishes three types of treatment. As the century progressed the chorale became a regular feature of the church cantata and the basis, as we shall see, of a number of distinct keyboard forms.

Despite the considerable amount of music which he

composed, some of it very fine, Michael Praetorius (1571-1621) is still chiefly remembered for his theoretical works. Besides the religious music in the nine volumes of the *Musae Sionae* (1605-10), which also contains works by other composers, and many other collections of church music, Praetorius also wrote secular music. His most interesting single publication in this field is the *Terpsichore* (1612) which comprises over 340 six-part settings of dance melodies by Parisian masters. He also wrote a number of organ pieces including some on chorale melodies. But it is with the monumental *Syntagma musicum* that Praetorius made his great contribution to the history of music. In its three large volumes, it provides an invaluable survey of the musical practice of his day. The first volume describes the compositions both secular and religious of contemporaries. The second, the famous *De organographia*, contains an exhaustive description of the instruments of music (and, in later editions, valuable illustrations) including an account of German organs and their registration. The third section of this important work describes the vocal and instrumental forms as they were developing at the time, with extensive indications as to modes of performance.

Cui chorus assurgit Musarum & Musica tota,
Hac Michaël Prætor Musicus est facie.

Michael Praetorius, important as both theoretician and composer.

178

The cantata and the Passion

The cantata developed in two distinct forms, the secular cantata being most cultivated in the south. It handled a usually dramatic theme in a series of arias and recitatives and was used by such composers as Georg Aichinger and Christoph Erbach at Augsburg, the Italian Valentini at Vienna and later von Kerll at Munich. Such composers were receptive to new ideas from Italy, and it was above all the cantatas of Carissimi that produced a definite change in style from the earlier essentially monodic cantatas to a richer form using both soloists and choir and a larger orchestra.

During the middle years of the century, the Protestant composers of the north evolved a major new musical form to grace the music of the Reformed Church. Taking as their starting points the motet in its *concertato* manner and the native German chorale and combining these with the dramatic expression of the church cantata, they produced an elaborate form which usually called for soloists, chorus and orchestra. This German church cantata was a work of several sections, which usually opened with a chorus and closed with a chorale in which the congregation might join. The text, though explicitly religious, often drew on various sources such as the words of the chorale and original passages of a lyric of contemplative nature, as well as Biblical texts. The form approached the oratorio and, with the introduction of full arias and recitatives, even that of secular opera. This development was summed up and promoted by the libretti published in the first years of the next century by the poet and preacher Erdman Neumeister (1671-1756), who was explicitly influenced by the form of Italian opera and finally freed the cantata from its ancient associations with the motet. Quite apart from his contribution to the formal development of the cantata, Neumeister provided separate cantata texts for each Sunday and all the feast days in the Church year. Bach was one of the many composers who made use of his texts.

The first published examples of the new church cantata appeared at Leipzig in 1662 in a collection to which the great Schütz himself wrote a preface of warm approbation. Some twenty years later Carl Briegel, *Kapellmeister* to the court of Hesse-Darmstadt, produced a *Musikalischer Lebens-Brunn* with texts for Sundays and feast days throughout the year. Johann Christoph Bach, the uncle of Sebastian, left a grandiose and colourful cantata depicting the struggle between the Archangel Michael and Satan. But the greatest exponent of the form before Bach himself was Buxtehude, who established the musical conventions of the form, using organ and orchestra, regularly providing a symphonic overture and writing recitative as well as chorus and solo passages.

The Passion as a religious form had a long history. Examples are known from the 15th century, but by their masterly development of it the German composers of the 17th century raised it to a new height. In its earliest form, the Passion consisted of the reading of the Gospel account of Christ's sufferings and death in the liturgy for Holy Week. The narration by a solo voice was punctuated by a chorus representing the crowd. Three soloists, besides narrating the story, also took the parts of the main actors in the story; in some settings the words of Christ himself are sung by all three in unison. During the 17th century the greatest German Passions are those by Schütz, but the fine *St Matthew Passion* by Johann Sebastiani (1622-83), who was *Kapellmeister* at Königsberg for the electors of

Brandenburg, is especially interesting because it introduces chorale sections like those to be found in later Passion music. In its fullest form this consisted of a solo voice giving the narration, other soloists taking the parts of the *dramatis personae*, choruses which not only play the crowd scenes but also comment on the story and amplify it with reflective meditations, reflective arias for solo voice, and chorale settings suitable for audience participation.

Musicians at the court of Christian IV of Denmark, one of the main centres of music in northern Europe and heavily influenced by German styles.

right
Heinrich Schütz, one of Germany's greatest composers.

below
A fine 17th-century German trumpet.

talent for dramatic interpretation in musical terms of the characters and situations of his religious texts, and his masterly exploitation of his resources, whether on the large scale of his earlier works, or the austere and restricted plane of the late Passions. Like all great masters Schütz evolved an unmistakable and individual style, but his debt to the Italians was both acknowledged and considerable. His music is remarkable for the success with which he accomplished his aim of faithful expression of the words of his text, whether it was German or Latin. To this end he welded the elements of the Italian *concertato* style, the use of contrasting choruses and contrasting solo and chorus passages, and the compositional technique of the *basso continuo* recitative, into a powerfully expressive musical language.

Schütz's talent for dramatic interpretation is found in many of his works, but above all in his oratorios. This Italian form seems to have been introduced to German composers by way of Vienna where Antonio Bertali, as director of the imperial chapel from 1649, gave the first performance of an Italian oratorio in Germany. Schütz was one of the earliest as he was among the greatest German composers of the form. The early *Story of the Resurrection* given at Dresden in 1623, in which the narrative is related by a tenor solo and the commentary provided by choruses, was followed towards the end of his life by the profoundly moving and mighty composition *The Seven Words of Jesus on the Cross* and the *History of the Joyful Nativity of Jesus Christ*, which in instrumental resources and the masterly handling of recitative and chorus reveal their Italian models. His first masterpiece in the 'grand Italian manner' had been the settings of the *Psalms of David as motets and concertos for eight and more voices . . .* published at Dresden in 1619, and the exquisite *Symphoniae sacrae* (twenty-seven three- to five-part 'German Concertos') of 1629 show their debt to Monteverdi in the richness of their instrumental colour. Already the early *Cantiones Sacrae* of 1625 had used four voices in *a cappella* style, and the restricted resources of the *Kleine Geistliche Konzerte*, dictated by the exigencies of the war period, had shown Schütz fully able to compose great music for small ensembles. In the three Passions from the later period of his life, he chose limited instrumental and vocal forces for some of the greatest of all music. The three authenticated Passions are those according to St Matthew, St John and St Luke; a fourth, according to St Mark, though not unworthy of the master's hand, is probably not his. In his old age, Schütz complained that his young contemporaries were losing the art of counterpoint, and had indeed commissioned a motet from his former pupil, Bernhard, in the 'pristine contrapuntal style'.

Schütz

Heinrich Schütz was born in the middle German town of Kostritz in Thuringia, in October 1585. His father, after a successful life as a lawyer which culminated in his election as mayor of Weissenfels, ended his days in retirement as landlord of an inn whose name he changed from The Golden Bagpipe to Chez Schütz; it was still standing in the 1960s. Like many famous composers both before and since, Schütz owed the start in his career to a fine treble voice, and as a boy of thirteen was recruited to the choir of the court of Landgrave Maurice the Learned of Hesse-Kassel. Under the landgrave's patronage, he not only received his first musical training, but in due course entered the University of Marburg. In 1609 his patron sent him to study music under the great Giovanni Gabrieli, an event important for the whole history of German music since, on his return to Germany in 1613, Schütz was a major agent of the transmission of the principles of the Venetian style to German composers. Schütz readily acknowledged his debt to his Italian master, and his affection and respect seem to have been reciprocated, as Gabrieli bequeathed him his signet ring on his death.

After four years as court organist at Kassel, Schütz was released by the landgrave to take up the important appointment of *Kapellmeister* at the Saxon court of Dresden. Here he married and became the friend of Schein, the cantor of St Thomas's, Leipzig, for whose death Schütz composed a six-part motet. From 1629 he was again in Italy, buying instruments for the Dresden orchestra and studying the instrumental and stage music of Monteverdi. Saxony was sorely hurt by the depredations of the Thirty Years War so that the musical establishment had to be seriously curtailed, and Schütz himself was obliged to take employment elsewhere, working for a time at Hamburg, and from the mid-1630s at the royal court of Copenhagen. As the war drew to a close, he returned to his post at Dresden and in 1651 retired to the family property, the old inn Chez Schütz, where his sister kept house for him. He died in 1672.

Schütz's predominantly religious output is inspired by his own profound piety, and his stature as a composer derives from the emotional power of his work, his

The development of German organ music

The chorale prelude, as its name implies, was a keyboard piece based on the melody of a chorale, the typically Lutheran congregational hymn. Its period of development may be defined as running from the works of Samuel Scheidt (d. 1654) to those of J. S. Bach. It may have had its origins in the organist's practice of playing over the chorale melody as an introduction to the congregational singing of the hymn. No doubt the embellishments added by the organists to the 'old favourites' must have irritated many of the faithful, though not always imaginative, worshippers, and we know that Bach, who continued to perfect the form long after its decline in popularity, was criticised by his church authorities for the liberties which he took with the old tunes. From its simple beginnings three main ypes developed. In one, the chorale was used as a *cantus firmus* which appeared section by section at intervals throughout the work; in the second type it might be used for a series of variations which formed a musical commentary on the verses of the text; in the third type a section of the melody only was taken as a theme for elaboration.

In everything that they wrote the north German organists displayed the utmost contrapuntal elaboration, and nowhere was their mastery of this better displayed than in the classic combination of the prelude and fugue. In this, a piece in the free manner of a fantasia or toccata was followed by a fugue, whose opening subject might on occasion catch up the opening phrase of the toccata. Here, as in the cantata, the difference between the northern and southern styles was apparent. As we shall see, the northern school learnt much from the south in terms of keyboard technique, but it went far beyond it in developing the fugue. In the art of the south Germans, led by Froberger, this may be described as a series of fugal variations on single subjects in three sections and with few, if any, episodes. In the north the fugue became increasingly complex, using double and triple counterpoint in the development of one or more main subjects and their accompanying countersubjects.

The northern and southern schools

As the century progressed two major schools of organ composition flourished in Germany and eventually flowed together in the works of J. S. Bach. They represented the religious and geographical division of the country between north and south.

Together with Schütz and Schein, Samuel Scheidt (1587-1654) makes up that group of composers sometimes called the three great 'S's' of German music. From 1609 to 1630, he was in the service of the margrave of Brandenburg at Halle, but was dismissed following a dispute over his responsibilities to the choir school of one of the city churches. His last years were spent in tragic circumstances; four of his children died in the plague, and he himself was buried in a pauper's grave.

Decisive in the development of Scheidt's organ style was the year he spent at Amsterdam as a pupil of Sweelinck. From him he learnt the basis of the keyboard variation technique which the Dutch master had developed from the example of the English virginalists, and Scheidt's own style was modelled on the contrapuntal idiom of the Flemish-German polyphonic motet. Towards the end of his life, Scheidt wrote to a colleague: 'I have remained true to the old style of composition and the strict rules of counterpoint'. But he had contributed essentially to the development of his art in the chorale variations for organ, while his toccatas and fantasias for the harpsichord are of equal importance. Among his most important publications were the three-volume *Tablatura nova* (1624) and the *Tablaturbuch* (1650), but he wrote much else including *Cantiones sacrae* (1620) and *Concerti sacrae* (1621) for voices and instruments.

His younger contemporary Johann Jacob Froberger (1616-67) grafted the style of the Italian masters on to the tradition of German keyboard composition. Attached to the imperial court, Froberger travelled widely

below left
Samuel Scheidt.

below
Georges de la Tour's painting of an old man playing the hurdy-gurdy.

in Europe visiting Holland, England, Brussels and Paris, where he met Chambonnières and Louis Couperin among others.

An avowed disciple of the Italian master Frescobaldi, Froberger nevertheless greatly extended his master's achievements, particularly in the field of fugal writing, exploring and stabilising the conventions for the treatment of a subject and its countersubject. In this, and his successful integration of the French style into German compositional technique, he must be regarded as one of the most important architects of the German organ keyboard style, in both his organ and his harpsichord music. Other members of south German schools were Johann Kaspar von Kerll (1627-93) and Wolfgang Ebner who was, like Froberger, attached to the imperial court. Kerll, although a Saxon by birth, spent his career in the south between Vienna and the Bavarian

court at Munich. Kerll had studied in Rome under Carissimi and although his compositions for keyboard represent his most important work, culminating in the *Modulatio organica* (1686) for organ, he wrote a number of religious works as well as many operas of which only the libretti now survive.

Central German organ music and the continuators of the northern tradition

To the northern and southern schools of organ composition we must add a third, which was to be that of the central German school. Strictly speaking, Bach may be said to have belonged to this tradition, but such a classification has little meaning since in his universal

A mounted drummer, a member of one of the most exclusive groups of professional musicians.

genius the achievements of the three schools were amalgamated and transcended. However, it is important to recognise the work of one of Bach's predecessors, Johann Pachelbel (1653-1706). Born in Nuremberg, he was for a time, at the start of his career, assistant organist at St Stephen's in Vienna and so came into contact with the south German school. One of the finest performers of his day, Pachelbel, who from 1677 occupied posts in central Germany, becoming a friend of Bach's family at Eisenach, did much to unite the south and middle German schools. His music was distinguished by the cantabile nature of his part writing, the essential simplicity and clarity of his harmonies, and his skill in rhythmic variation.

The north German tradition, initiated by Scheidt, was continued by many great names of which we should mention Matthias Weckmann, Adam Reinken and Buxtehude. Weckmann (c. 1619-74) was a pupil of Schütz (his 'fatherly friend') at Dresden and then for a time, at Schütz's advice, of Jacob Praetorius of Hamburg, who had studied under Sweelinck. Weckmann's own music reveals the influence of both Schütz and Sweelinck, but also shows that he had studied the works of his friend Froberger. Their friendship, surprisingly, started when Weckmann defeated Froberger in a keyboard competition at Dresden where Weckmann was joint *Kapellmeister*. In 1655 Weckmann was called to Hamburg, an increasingly important centre of music, where the Sweelinck tradition was most notably upheld by Heinrich Scheidemann (1596-1663) and his pupil Reinken. Weckmann himself contributed significantly to the life of the city by the weekly series of concerts which he inaugurated under the name of *Collegium musicum*. Patronised by the rich merchant oligarchs of the city, these concerts were the means of introducing the most important contemporary music from the great centres of the south, such as Dresden, Munich, Vienna and the Italian courts.

Though a lesser figure than Weckmann, Jan Adam Reinken (1623-1722), of Dutch descent, is assured of his place in the history of the German organ school if only because of the admiration for him shown by the young Bach, an admiration warmly reciprocated. A true continuator of the Sweelinck tradition in organ composition and a pupil of Scheidemann's, Reinken also took part in the music of the Hamburg opera, being one of its co-founders in 1678, and co-director for some years thereafter. In addition to compositions of all kinds for keyboard, he published in 1687 a collection of works for strings (suites, *courantes*, *allemandes*) entitled *Hortus musicus*, which Bach drew on in some of his organ works.

With Dietrich Buxtehude (c. 1637-1707), we come to one of the leading figures of the north German school of the latter part of the 17th century. As an organist his compositions rank with the best of those of his contemporaries, but his outstanding work was done in the field of sacred choral music. He was born a Danish subject in Holstein, probably at Oldesloe, and after studying under his father, held posts successively at Hälsingborg and Elsinore. In the late 1660s, he became organist at the important church of St Mary of Lübeck where he revived the *Abendmusik* concerts, which had been begun by his predecessor Franz Tunder as weekday entertainments for businessmen attending the Lübeck exchange. Buxtehude greatly extended the scope of these concerts and wrote some of his finest music in the cantatas which he composed for them. Nearly 120 of his cantatas have been preserved in manuscript, drawing their texts from the Latin and German Bibles, from the chorales of the Lutheran Church, from religious and even secular poetry. It is in this music that Buxtehude displays the qualities of inventiveness and lyricism which justify his reputation as one of the finest of all Bach's north German predecessors. But his forty or so surviving organ com-

positions, including chorale variations, preludes and fugues, *canzone*, chaconnes and toccatas, are eloquent testimony to his mastery at the keyboard, and fully explain why the young Bach should have made the long journey from Arnstadt to Lübeck on foot to hear the master play.

Secular music

Apart from the keyboard music already mentioned, the secular output of German 17th-century composers comprised dance suites, *Lieder*, polyphonic music for the violin (a peculiarly German genre), opera and secular cantatas.

The history of German opera in this period exhibits two parallel developments. On the one hand, there was the direct imitation of Italian and French models, and on the other, the search for a German style for the alien form. The three main centres for the diffusion of Italian influence were Munich, Vienna and Dresden, where Italian composers such as G. A. Bontempi, and Germans like J. K. von Kerll, worked. As early as 1627, Schütz had composed music to a *Dafne* of which only the libretto by Opitz has survived, but it seems probable that the work was more in the nature of a secular cantata than of a true opera. The search for a German operatic idiom was pursued to a greater or lesser extent at Weissenfels and Hamburg, where the new theatre opened with a series of operas on religious themes and themes specifically related to Hamburg. But the conventions of classicism soon asserted themselves and the music increasingly displayed the influence of Italian as well as French models. But performances in German were continued well into the 18th century, and while it was served by such distinguished composers as Handel and Telemann, the opera at Hamburg continued to enjoy success.

German composers were very prolific in the field of music for chamber music ensembles, songs and especially the very characteristic German genre of unaccompanied contrapuntal music for violin. Like so many styles of the 17th century, this was to reach its

The birthplace of Dietrich Buxtehude.

perfection with J.S.Bach, but in the hands of such masters as J.J.Walther, Heinrich Biber and Johann Schop of Hamburg, it had been shown to be a medium capable of a fuller range of expression than mere virtuosity. Yet of course, the new virtuosity of violinists in the 17th century was important and a matter of admiration, and led to some remarkable feats, such as that of the performer Nicolas Bruhns, who improvised two-part fugues on the violin while providing himself with a bass part on the pedal board of the organ.

But instrumental music of all kinds was produced in quantity by such composers as Schein and Rosenmuller. Johann Rosenmuller (1620-84) was one of the finest composers of his generation. He worked in Leipzig, Venice, and for the last years of his life at Wolfenbüttel, and in his numerous compositions displays an easy familiarity with, and complete assimilation of, the Italian and French styles. His works, much admired by contemporaries, include dance suites for violins and viols and other instruments, and fragments of religious compositions have also survived.

Johann Hermann Schein (1586-1630), who held posts at Weissenfels and Weimar before becoming cantor at St Thomas's, Leipzig, was, with Scheidt and Schütz, one of the central figures of German 17th-century music. He wrote much fine music for the Lutheran service, which can be found in the two collections *Cymbalum Sionium* (1615) containing Latin and German motets for

from five to twelve voices, and the *Opella nova* (two volumes, 1618 and 1626). This last contains some sixty cantatas with *basso continuo*, more than half of which are for three voices, and like the previous collection shows the composer's familiarity with the new Italian style. His collection *Fontana d'Israel* of 1623 is subtitled 'in the pleasing Italian madrigal style'. His secular compositions are perhaps even more interesting than his religious ones. The *Musica bosareccia*, 'in the Italian *villanesca* manner', comprise three collections of German *Lieder* many of which use the *basso continuo*, while the *Banchetto Musicale* of 1617 contains no fewer than twenty dance suites for four and five voices, in which Italian dances feature prominently.

Finally, in this brief survey of secular music, we should mention the sizeable output of secular as well as religious songs during the period. The poet and musician, Heinrich Albert, cousin of Schütz, used the *basso continuo* in the German *Lied* in his religious and secular songs, published in eight volumes between 1638 and 1650 and important as early German examples of Italian monody. They inevitably show the strong influence of Italian composers such as Caccini and Monteverdi. Other important collections of songs were the *Arien* published by Schütz's pupil, Adam Krieger, in 1657, and the *Weltliche Arien* by Johann Theile (1646-1724), whose *Adam und Eva*, a *Singspiel*, had been commissioned for the opening of the Hamburg opera.

Title page of the commemorative Abendmusik *given for Buxtehude in 1707.*

French music
before the age of Lully

In France as in Italy the most interesting developments in music during the 17th century took place in the theatre. France, resisting the enthusiasm for Italian opera which swept through Europe, not only developed an operatic style of her own, but also evolved a characteristic stage spectacle – the dance – which was the ancestor of modern ballet.

The court air and related forms

During the second half of the 16th century, France had been torn by the wars of religion which were only resolved, and that temporarily, by the accession of Henry IV. During his reign, the important Edict of Nantes of 1598 ushered in a period of religious toleration and a generation of peace. Thus at the end of the 16th century a war-weary country turned with enthusiasm to the delights of music, and the following period was marked by a profusion of aristocratic and bourgeois patronage and a rapid spread of amateur participation. Composers, while working in the same spirit as the Italians, devoted their talents to essentially French forms, chief among them the airs of the court, which were to become constituent elements in the *ballets dramatiques*.

As in Italy, so in France, monody had a long and popular tradition. At the beginning of the 16th century, this had been re-expressed in the strophic songs of the towns (*voix de villes* and hence *vaudeville*), so that with the decline of the polyphonic *chanson* at the end of the century, it is not surprising to find this essentially less complex type of music being revived in a new guise in the *air de cour*. The term is first found in the title of a collection by the music publisher Adrien le Roy, *Livre d'Airs de Cour miz sur le luth*, published in 1571. Le Roy explains in his introduction that these new *chansons* are lighter than earlier examples, and explicitly refers to the fact that they are in the style once described as *vaudeville*. In fact, many of the songs are in effect solo voice settings of polyphonic *chansons*, with the other parts arranged for the lute accompaniment. Like the English lute song, these new *airs* won immense popularity with the nobility and the wealthy citizenry. The lute was the king of instruments; Henry IV commissioned airs from Malherbe and Guédron to charm his latest conquests, and of an evening his successor, Louis XIII, sang the airs of Boesset in the company of courtiers and musicians.

Like most musical forms at the beginning of the 17th century the *air de cour* was a term with a wide definition. It often signified a serious and affected refined style of song, but it might loosely be applied to the *chanson* of classic type, to *airs* for the ballet or even to recitative. However, it was associated with a recognisable and distinct type of strophic song usually concerned with expressions of love or with a romantic theme. In this sense the melody of the *air de cour* could be sung either with or without accompaniment.

Its most distinctive feature is its flexible rhythm, not unlike that of the *musique mesurée* of the later *chanson* composers. In many cases the *air de cour* assumed an affected charm and langorous mood, though Pierre

Musicians to a French court ballet of the early 17th century.

185

Diagram of a clavichord from the
important French work on musical
instruments by Marin Mersenne,
published in 1636.

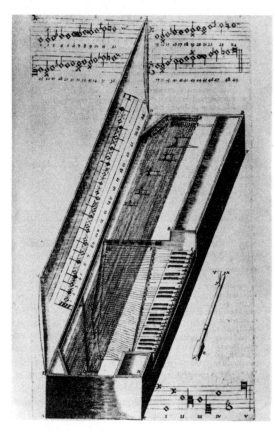

Guédron (d.c. 1620) gave it clearer and more compact
form. His *airs* have none of the bold harmonies common
to Italian monody; they are unpretentious and easy on
the ear, with a free accompaniment which alternates
between the major and minor. His successors, Antoine
Boesset (c. 1587–1643) and Etienne Moulinié (d.c. 1660)
moved in a different direction. Boesset's music has an
elegiac quality, and is valued for the beauty of its melodic
lines, the subtle emphasis of the word setting and for its
charm and delicacy. Influenced by Pierre de Nyert
(1597–1682), who had travelled in Italy and hoped 'to
adjust the Italian method to the French', Boesset modified his style. His phrases became longer, he used repetitions, and employed wide melodic intervals – everything
with which the French had up to now reproached the
Italians. Etienne Moulinié was another lyricist whose
airs have great expressive beauty. His later *airs*, in
common with all those composed after the death of
Boesset, dispense with the lute, its place being taken by
a continuo part.

From about the 1630s the new *air en rondeau*, in
which the opening words and tune are twice used as a
refrain, and the *air* which continued the tradition of the
air de cour, were written in increasingly lively rhythms
and their forms became ever clearer and more and more
compact. The elegant and simple *airs* of Michel Lambert
(d. 1696) were mostly written for two voices and *basso
continuo*. Sébastien Camus (d. 1677) often wrote an
introductory instrumental prelude before each piece, an
unusual feature for the *air*.

In its many forms the *air* was to be an important
element in the dramatic forms of the ballet and the
French opera, and it is to the ballet that we now turn.

The French court ballet
of the 17th century

Dancing had long been a feature of the great entertainments at the court, just as it was immensely popular with
all classes of society. It had played a part in the medieval
dramatic presentations of the mystery plays, and at court
had not only a recognised place in the ceremonies and
celebrations but had, during the 15th and 16th centuries,
achieved a certain stability of form. During the 17th
this was to contribute essentially to the development of
the French opera and the *ballet mélodramatique*, its
precursor.

In the time of the Valois, Italian choreographers,
attracted to the court of Catherine de' Medici, performed
figured dances with entirely novel steps whenever
masques, jousts, and tilts were held. In the 1570s, the
humanist ideal of combining poetry, music and dance in
the style of ancient classical drama had a great influence
on these *divertissements*. The *Paradis d'Amour* (1572),
for example, was a mythological allegory with music, in
which Mercury sings a recitative, and which also
featured dancing and mechanical stage props.

The *Ballet comique de la Reyne*, given before an invited
audience at a wedding at the court of Henry III in 1581,
anticipated the 17th-century court ballet. This spectacle, a combination of comedy, music, songs and dances,
was conceived and directed by a Piedmontese, Baldassarino di Belgiojoso, who adopted a French style for his
name – Beaujoyeux. By borrowing the sylvan gods of the
Italian pastorales he provided a mythological setting for
the play. The sumptuous sets, rich costumes, mobile
scenery and stage properties all helped to create the
atmosphere of enchantment and illusion. In the 17th
century, ballet comprised choruses and dancing and
spoken and sung recitatives (called *airs*), with poets such
as Malherbe and Tristan l'Hermite contributing to the
words. The ballet started with the chorus; this was
followed by thirty '*entrées*' consisting of dances or panto-
mimes, and the presentation ended with a '*grand ballet*'
in which the king himself and his courtiers joined.
Recitatives and *airs* with lute accompaniment preceded
the *entrées*; passages of dialogue for duet occurred only
rarely. Violins, viols, lutes, cornetts, oboes, flutes and
bagpipes played during the interludes and accompanied
the dances while the musicians themselves, wearing
suitable costume, took part in the *entrées*. These ballets,
whose antecedents lay in the entertainments at the
court of 15th-century Burgundy, were immensely
popular and were performed on every possible occasion
in public halls, at the court, and in private residences.

During the reign of Henry IV, a new type of ballet,
the *ballet mascarade*, enjoyed a considerable vogue. This
was presented without scenery and had no continuous
plot. It consisted of a series of burlesque scenes which
might contain a mixture of songs, spoken or sung recitatives, dances and even, occasionally, acrobatics. Concurrently with this, changes were taking place. The unity
of chorus, declamation, *air* and dance, evident in Beaujoyeux's early example of the *ballet comique*, was restored
and in 1607 the *ballet mélodramatique* was born. The
most important figure in this development was Pierre
Guédron, whose *Déliverance de Renaud* (1617), written
in collaboration with Boesset, was the prototype for later
French opera. Guédron, who was inspired by the
Italians, provided the first examples of the recitative
adapted to the soft French manner. His recitatives are
often set for voice and lute and are remarkable for their
pathos and restraint.

After Guédron and under Boesset, his successor as
director of music at the court, a new convention with a

marked artificiality of form came into vogue. This was the *ballet à entrées*. The *Ballet de la reyne représentant le Soleil* (1621), with four acts representing the four seasons, prefigures in some aspects the opera of Rameau. Lyric rather than dramatic qualities distinguish Boesset's works. Towards the end of his life, he collaborated in the composition of a *Ballet de la Félicité* in honour of the birth of the future king Louis XIV.

Under Mazarin, who introduced Italian opera, the ballet suffered a brief eclipse and Franco-Italian musical polemics remained a subject of debate for a long time after this period. The styles were undoubtedly different; the contemporary musical theorist Marin Mersenne notes the distinction between the calm, voluptuous music of the *airs de cour* and the passionate accents of the Italian recitative. Frenchmen like P. de Nyert, who had visited Rome, had not concealed their admiration for Italian art. Yet presentations of *La Finta Pazza* (1645) by Sacrati, with sumptuous settings and effects by Torelli, *Egisto* (1646) by Cavalli and *Orfeo* (1647) by Luigi Rossi, made little impact. Nonetheless they created a favourable atmosphere for the development of the French pastorale and musical 'comedies'. The *Opéra d'Issy* by Cambert (*c.* 1628–77), subtitled 'the first comedy in music to be presented in France' (1659), is a mixture of pastorale and comedy. The *Ballet de la nuit*, in which the young Lully took part in 1653, was also inspired by the pastorale, as the *ballet mélodramatique* had been previously. In the prologue the composer makes use of a simple, free and expressive recitative reminiscent of the style of Guédron. Thanks to this return to a long neglected style, a new step had been taken in the direction of the music drama.

After the wars of the Fronde, Mazarin staged further Italian operas but, to gain popularity, had court ballets included in them. Ballets were also interspersed between the scenes of Cavalli's *Ercole amante* given on the occasion of Louis XIV's marriage in 1662; apart from these French elements, Cavalli's works met with little success. Yet Italian opera had shown both French audiences and composers that drama could be delivered in entirely musical terms. Ten years later, an opera by French composers and in the French manner was to win such acclaim that French opera swept the musical world of Paris.

But until the success of *Pomone* in 1670, the theatre-going public continued to prefer the ballets of Isaac de Benserade and Lully to the operas of the Italians. The court ballet satisfied French taste. The sumptuousness of the costumes was in every way as great as that of the decor, and the nobility spent fortunes in order to take part in the ballet at the side of the king. They liked shimmering materials, they wore masks, they were not afraid of appearing either grotesque or extravagant. The ballet for them was a living lyric, ill-defined as an art, and a distraction cultivated by an ever more powerful and burdensome royal absolutism.

Religious music in France

During the 16th century the style of religious music remained faithful to polyphony. However, during the reign of Henry IV, under the influence of Italian innovations, French composers began to experiment with accompanied monody. This style, and the technique of the *basso continuo*, gave musical expression to the individualistic nature of Renaissance thought and society. In France as elsewhere the old and the new manners of composition continued side by side; composers were torn between two conflicting influences, sometimes moving forward, sometimes sharply back. The aria and recitative were more quickly adopted in circles which were wide open to foreign influences, particularly court circles where the musicians of the chapel were in close touch with those of the royal chamber, as well as in some of the Parisian conventual establishments which attracted an elite group of men of the world.

The music of Eustache Du Caurroy still conforms to the laws of polyphony, but he uses a double choir with great sensitivity and has left rare examples of psalms sung by alternate choirs in the 'antique style' with Latin words (*Vox Domini super aqua*). Nearly all the works of his contemporary, Jacques Mauduit, a Catholic musician from De Baïf's Academy, have been lost, but Mersenne has preserved for us some fragments of his *Requiem* mass, written in 1586 in memory of Ronsard, which according to Claude Binet 'was enlivened by all manner of instruments', as well as eleven French and Latin motets with solemn metrical verses by Baïf.

A woman musician entertaining a nobleman at the harpsichord.

Under Louis XIII and the regency of Anne of Austria, composers sometimes hesitated to employ new musical forms. Jean de Bournonville (*c.*1585-1640) is chief among those of the conservative school, while Nicolas Formé, pupil and successor to Du Caurroy at the Chapel Royal, was not insensible to the influence of the secular music which was enjoying such tremendous success at court. He often let his imagination run loose here and borrowed freely from the technique of court ballet, using successive harmonic chords, metrical rhythm and repeated notes.

Another musician, Guillaume Bouzignac, a native of Languedoc, who before 1634 was in the service of

Guillaume Charlonye, governor of Angoulême, also composed motets and *dialogues* between soloists and choir with non-liturgical texts. In fact the small 'choir' sometimes consists of only one soloist. Bouzignac has a taste for effects, contrasting harmonies and embellishments, and in sacred pieces which anticipate the oratorio he shows a real sense of drama. He does not make use of operatic recitative, but borrows certain elements from the madrigal to stress the significance of words. His solo passages suggest that they were accompanied by a figured bass.

In 1652, the first of the French motets with a figured bass were published. These were the *Cantica Sacra* (for one, two and three voices) by Henry Du Mont, who became master of the royal chapel in 1663. These were followed by motets once attributed to Antoine Boesset, though in fact probably by his son, Jean-Baptiste. Boesset employs imitation, but also uses an instrumental bass in polyphonic passages which blends in with the vocal bass parts; when the voice is silent, its place is taken by an instrumental bass to complete the harmony.

Boesset also composed a Magnificat written throughout in *concertato* style. Soloists and chorus constantly alternate and the development of a harmonic sense is marked. In 1658 Etienne Moulinié published his *Meslanges de sujets Chrétiens*... for three, four and five parts. Although he wrote a *Missa pro defunctis* (1636) in the old style, he was nonetheless perfectly acquainted with 'modern' art. His *Meslanges* are permeated with Italian influence and employ a *basso continuo* (found also in his third *Book of Aires*, 1635) and double choir. The motet, with organ accompaniment, had become a concert piece.

Jean Veillot (d. 1661), of the Chapel Royal, who was the author of the Te Deum for the marriage of Louis XIV with Maria Theresa, also wrote, besides short vocal pieces with *basso continuo*, an anthem for double choir in *concertato* style, as well as two motets for double choirs with symphonies. Here the orchestra doubled the voices of the full choir, while the soloists were supported by a *basso continuo*. These last works anticipate the *grand motet*, to which Henry Du Mont was soon to give definite form.

Thus we find the style of religious music completely transformed. The non-liturgical *grand motet*, though still using Latin, contained recitatives for solo voice, more or less dramatic *dialogues*, choruses, instrumental accompaniment and symphonic interludes. As well as the motet, psalms translated or paraphrased into French were used in the fight against the attractions of Protestantism. These psalms appealed to a large music-loving public and to men of the world. At the beginning of the 17th century Philippe Desportes's translation had an unprecedented vogue, though it was superseded by that of Antoine Godeau, bishop of Grasse and Vence as well as master of ceremonies at the Hotel de Rambouillet. His *Paraphrase des Psaumes de David en vers françois* (1648) inspired not only Louis XIII himself (who set four of them to music), but also Thomas Gobert, director of the Chapel Royal, whose settings of the psalms could be sung either as a vocal duet, or as a solo with *basso continuo*. At the same time, the Jesuits and Capuchins initiated the publication of edifying songs and hymns for unaccompanied solo voice in different centres of France and in Rome.

Instrumental music: composers for the keyboard and lute

In France, as in the other major European traditions, the evolution of instrumental music really gathered momentum during the 16th and 17th centuries; indeed in this field French composers were somewhat behind their colleagues in Italy, England and Spain. It was not until the work of Jehan Titelouze that the French produced a major composer for the keyboard. His immediate predecessors, Guillaume Costeley the Norman (d. 1606) and the famous *chanson* composer Claude Le Jeune (d. 1600), had written fine instrumental music, but it was not exclusively keyboard in style and was equally suitable for performance on viols or spinets. Even Du Caurroy gives no precise instructions as to how his *fantaisies* are to be performed. He paraphrases themes borrowed from liturgical chants or secular *chansons* and develops them either in fugal style, or in the form of variations. These fugato passages by Du Caurroy, and the *Twenty-four fantasias on the twelve modes* by C. Guillet (1610), which are written primarily for organ, show the continuing tendency of organ music to discard the restricting elements in vocal music, while still retaining a basically polyphonic style.

A highly gifted artist, Titelouze had a passion for musical theory which he discussed in the correspondence he maintained with Mersenne. His *Hymnes* (1623) and Magnificat (1626) for four voices are in *ricercare* form. The long sustained plainsong subject for full organ (first verse) is later given to the alto or tenor, or sometimes to both in a fugal chorale. These *ricercari* are characterised by their meditative, flowing melodic line, and by their straightforward lively themes. Without underrating the importance of vertical harmony, even Titelouze remained faithful to the past. Nevertheless, his austere, monumental art is so rich in new possibilities that he must be considered as the founder of French organ music.

Among his successors is Etienne Richard (*c.* 1621-69). A follower of the modern style, he adapted a suite of dances for lute to the organ, using the language of harmony and tonality suitable to the keyboard instruments. The harmonic or 'vertical' manner was also to be used by Louis Couperin in his chaconnes for keyboard, which show the influence of the Italian, Frescobaldi, though in his settings of liturgical verses and in his fantasias, his style is more idiomatically polyphonic.

François Roberday (1624-72), like Titelouze, still cherished the old polyphonic traditions, but later he too discovered Italian music and the daring melodic rhythm and harmonic riches of Frescobaldi. The *Fugues et Caprices* (1660) in four parts, 'principally for the organ',

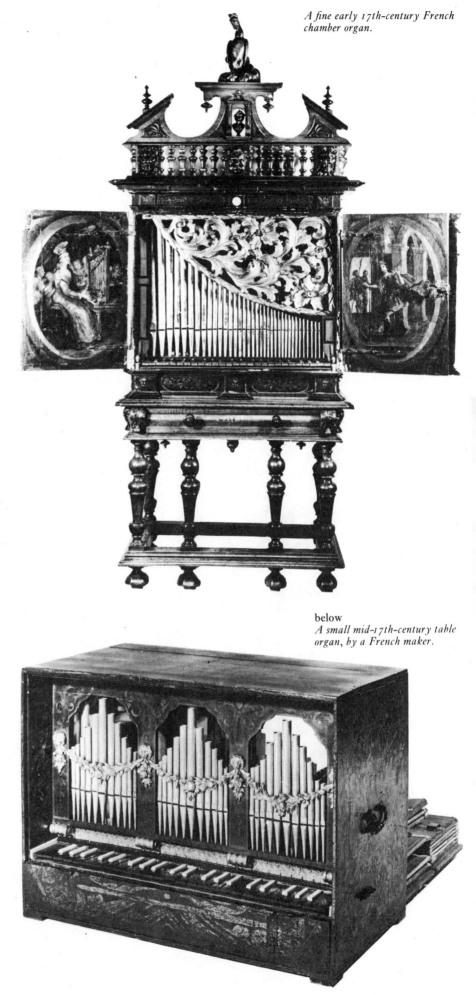

A fine early 17th-century French chamber organ.

below
A small mid-17th-century table organ, by a French maker.

resemble the style of Titelouze, but, in their boldness of treatment and diversity of rhythm, they look to the future. Roberday's fugues are more constructed than those of Titelouze, his melodic line is more expressive and above all his harmonies are more fully thought out.

At the beginning of the 17th century, the harpsichordists adopted the style of the *air*, but borrowed from the lutenists their free contrapuntal style (imposed by the technical limitations of the instrument) and their rapid diatonic scales. Jacques Champion de Chambonnières succeeded his father Jacques Champion as royal lutenist in 1638, before assuming, a little later, the post of harpsichord player to the king which he retained until 1662. He composed dance suites with a tonic-dominant-tonic modulation. He retained the traditional counterpoint forms, with bold melodic expositions. In his gigues he almost achieves a fugal form, but his chief merit is his extreme simplicity.

Chambonnières's pupil, Louis Couperin, organist of St Gervais, was a more distinguished musician than his master, and a much more original composer. His suites are more vigorous and have a great variety of expression; his *allemandes* are sometimes solemn, sometimes gay,

his sarabands, sometimes tranquil in mood, sometimes tempestuous. In the *Preludes*, he uses bold modulation, and combines arpeggios with ornamental phrases, alternating with passages in canon. In his *fantaisies* and duos, he uses a fugal form throughout. On one occasion he attempted to represent in musical terms the death of a lutenist killed falling downstairs (*Le Tombeau de Blancrocher*). His work is typical of the indecision with which so many composers of his age were afflicted. Louis Couperin swings from the modern – when he sometimes reaches the height of pure emotion – to the archaic style of composition, when he reverts to a mood of severe solemnity.

As we have already seen, no instrument of the period enjoyed such popularity in France as the lute, although it had already been abandoned in Italy by virtuosi. To learn the lute was part of the education of all gentlefolk. Gaultier gave lessons to Anne of Austria and Richelieu. Among those ladies 'whom one would have assumed to be goddesses descended from Parnassus', the Marquise de Termes, Mme de Joyeuse, and Mlle de la Barra were renowned for their skill, as were Ninon de Lenclos, pupil of Denys Gaultier, and Marion de Lorme, in the

A singer in an ale house accompanied by guitar and small violin note the violinist's already old-fashioned way of holding the instrument.

fashionable world of gallantry.

During the last third of the 16th century lutenists, in preference to polyphonic *chansons*, transcribed popular *airs* and dances. Antoine Francisque (*c.* 1570-1605) in his *Trésors d'Orphée* (1600) included preludes, fantasies and dances. Jean-Baptiste Besard (*c.* 1567-1625), a native of Besançon, also included transcriptions of court *airs* in his *Thesaurus harmonicus*. In the *Livres de Lutte* (1611-14) of Robert Ballard, lute teacher to Louis XIII, the transcriptions of dances are written in the form of variations, and arranged in suites of two or four movements. The French suite, which was derived from lute music, was never bound by any hard and fast rules. A single fragile link connects the different pieces – all are written in the same key.

Under Louis XIII and during the ministry of Mazarin, there were a number of brilliant lutenists. Ennemond Gaultier (*c.* 1575-1651), gentleman-in-waiting to Marie de' Medici, excelled in preludes, fantasies, suites, chaconnes and *tombeaux* (instrumental elegies). His *coranto*, *Les Larmes* ('Tears'), with its syncopated rhythm, approaches the pathos of the famous piece, *Lachrymae*, by Dowland, and expressed the most tender, delicate and almost Romantic feelings. His cousin Denys Gaultier, the teacher of Ninon de Lenclos, published the *Rhétorique des Dieux* in 1640, a collection of dance *airs* whose titles conform to the affected 'classical' style of the age: *Phaeton struck by lightning, Diana in the Forest*, etc. Their beauties lie in the flowering melodic line, the trills and ornaments, and the varied tonal colours and simple harmony appropriate to the lute. In his *Pièces de Lutte* (1669), the dance *airs* are grouped in four suites, each in a different key. Besides the lute, other instruments of the same family were employed. In 1629, F. de Chancy published a *Tablature for the Mandora*. The guitar, which had been esteemed in France for more than half a century, also had its place in the court ballet.

Ensemble music

In France as in England, much ensemble music was produced for the viol. In the reign of Louis XIII and under Mazarin's ministry the number of consorts of viols increased, both at court and in Parisian and provincial circles.

But it was the violinists formerly attached to the Ecurie who formulated the first real rules for musical ensembles. 'The great band of twenty-four violins' (*La grande bande des vingt-quatre violons*), founded in 1592, became in about 1620 the first real permanent orchestra, with six treble violins, six basses, four altos, four tenors, and four 'quints' (five-stringed basses). Like the lutenists, this band introduced popular dance music to the court, and helped to pave the way for the dance suite. The repertory of the first generation of the *Vingt-quatre*, of which Praetorius published some three hundred examples in his *Terpsichore Musarum* (1612), included numerous *branles, correnti*, gavottes and Breton *passepieds*. Twenty suites by the succeeding generation have much more variety and scope than those of their predecessors, and some anticipate the future French overture. Just as with the music of the lutenists and harpsichordists, here free polyphony alternates with free harmonies; there are many repeats and calculated false relations and the occasional dissonance, equivocally and constantly changing from major to minor. The stylised dance form brought about a split in the ranks of instrumentalists. A distinction was now made between serious and popular music. Serious dance music, much of which had in fact nothing specifically choreographic about it, was performed at concerts. It may be regarded as the beginning of pure 'symphonic' music and in the first place was confined to the violin family, whose expressive power had now come to be appreciated.

French violinists rapidly became established beyond the borders of their own country and the courts of Europe danced to French music. In England, Charles II brought back a taste for French music on his return from the continent at the Restoration, while in Italy the fashion for *correnti* and *balletti à la française* spread during the second quarter of the century.

Dance music had a determining influence on the evolution of the *concertato* style or symphony. While the 'tune' or the sung recitative is independent of strict musical form, popular dances introduced into serious music a basic melodic framework and rhythm, a dynamic regular beat and tonality. Dance 'tunes' definitely established a relation between treble and bass and modified the whole concept of composition, even before the introduction of *basso continuo*. Dances also suggested the possibility of novel harmonies which led to tonality. Harmonic instruments were also early in the field and contributed to this tonal evolution by adopting methods of temperament (an adjustment in tuning to get rid of gross inaccuracies in the intervals between certain notes) and the equivalent of a modern modulatory key system by which the octave is divided into twelve semitones.

Another illustration from Marin Mersenne's book on musical instruments; it shows a trumpet hung with the royal banner and illustrates the harmonic series of the instrument. Note also the mute.

English music in the century of Purcell

The end of the golden age in English music coincided with the end of the reign of James I. Byrd and Weelkes died in 1623, Orlando Gibbons in 1625 and John Bull, living abroad, in 1628. It is true that Wilbye lived on into the late 1630s, but he had already abandoned music.

The reign of Charles I

Only Thomas Tomkins continued to maintain the great traditions. Born in 1572, and thus the senior of Weelkes, Wilbye and Orlando Gibbons (all of whom predeceased him), he composed some of the greatest masterpieces in the tradition of English polyphonic church music, and also many fine examples of the verse anthem. He was organist at Worcester Cathedral for some fifty years until, in 1646, Puritan legislation against church music forced him to retire as a practising musician. He continued to compose, but mostly keyboard and instrumental pieces. His great stature as a composer is revealed in his church anthems and services, published by his son in the collection *Musica deo sacra* in 1668. These, which are in from four to ten parts, show Tomkins to have been a master of great originality and power, capable of massive choral effects and tense chromatic climaxes. His justly famous and moving madrigal, 'When David heard that Absalom was slain', is one of the most poignant laments in all vocal music.

If Tomkins was the only major composer active in England during the reigns of James I and Charles I, there was at least a number of talented men who made some contribution to the musical life of the country during these years.

Henry Lawes (1596-1662) wrote the music to Milton's masque *Comus* (1634), and also composed many fine songs. His brother William (1602-45) devoted himself largely to instrumental music, which included a number of bold examples of the traditional English art of the viol fantasy. Compositions for voices and instruments combined, in the manner of the late madrigals of Monteverdi, became increasingly popular thanks to composers such as Martin Peerson (d. 1650) and Walter Porter (d. 1659), who may even have studied under this Italian master. John Jenkins (1592-1678), court composer to both Charles I and Charles II, also wrote viol fantasies, although his *Twelve sonatas for two viols and a base* (1660) follow Italian models. William Child (d. 1697) who also served both these kings, wrote much church music as well as catches and ayres and a number of compositions for instruments.

However, the main event in the history of music of this period was the growth of a body of music for the theatre which prepared the ground for the brief appearance of English opera. The first half of the 17th century was the great period for the masque, in which courtiers and their ladies, and even the king and queen themselves, took part; it was almost the exact equivalent of the French court ballet. Combining poetry, drama, scenic architecture, decor, music and dancing, its sumptuous spectacles enjoyed great success from the close of the 16th century. The architect Inigo Jones, creator of mobile scenic

A MASKE

PRESENTED

At Ludlow Castle,

1634:

On *Michaelmasse* night, before the
RIGHT HONORABLE,

IOHN *Earle* of Bridgewater, *Vicount* BRACKLY,
Lord *Prasident* of WALES, And one of
His MAIESTIES most honorable
Privie Counsell.

Eheu quid volui misero mihi! floribus austrum
Perditus ————

LONDON,
Printed for HVMPHREY ROBINSON,
at the signe of the *Three Pidgeons* in
Pauls Church-yard. 1637.

Plate 23 above
This beautifully decorated and embellished single-manual harpsichord comes from a French workshop of the 1670s.

Plate 24 left
This 17th-century painting gives an admirably detailed presentation of a theorboed lute. Notice the three peg boxes to carry the many strings.

Plate 25
Henry Purcell.

effects, was the master of decor; Ben Jonson was the chief poet. Music played a subsidiary role and often one or two ayres for the lute are all that remain to us. Often the music was provided by several composers, the most important being Nicholas Lanier (1588-1666), also a fine painter, and the two Lawes brothers. *Lovers made men* (1617) by Inigo Jones, Ben Jonson and Lanier, had a particularly great success. The music is now lost, but it appears that in this work Lanier consciously adopted the style of the Italian recitative.

Music under the Commonwealth

In 1641, a House of Commons now dominated by men of Puritan persuasion legislated for the closing of the public theatres. For some ten years the king had governed the country without recourse to Parliament, and within two years a complex of social, economic and religious factors, added to a tense political situation, were to plunge the country into a civil war which ended in 1649 with the execution of the king and the establishment of the Commonwealth. Puritanism, which in some ways reflected the beliefs of European Calvinism, had been a strong force in all classes of English society since the later years of Elizabeth's reign. The closing of the theatres was a quite simple though dramatic Parliamentary gesture against the fashions of the court. It also squared with a moral reaction felt by many people against the growing licentiousness of the theatre; a licentiousness which returned in the works of the Restoration dramatists, whose immensely witty plays can still provoke a puritan reaction in our own day. During the troubled years of the 1640s, music, in common with all the arts, went through difficult times. Its problems were to be compounded when religious principles led Parliament to prohibit the use of music in churches, while some fanatics in the army destroyed both organs and music books in various cathedrals. Yet to see this in perspective we should remember that Calvinist courts on the continent had similar prohibitions against church music; one need only quote the example of Anhalt-Cöthen where J. S. Bach, some seventy years later, was obliged to confine himself largely to secular compositions. We should also remember that the often quoted passion which Oliver Cromwell had for music was shared by many of his co-religionists. Indeed, the Protector himself seems to have had little objection even to church music, one of his favourite relaxations being to listen to the motets of Richard Deering, an English Catholic composer of the previous generation.

The musical life of England during the Commonwealth, if not of the high quality of the past, was certainly active, and the 1650s witnessed a flood of publications. In 1651, the publisher John Playford put out his *English Dancing Master*, which was to go through twelve editions by 1703. It may well have served as the home tutor for some of the guests at the wedding of Cromwell's daughter in the Banqueting Hall in Whitehall, when the dancing went on to the small hours of the morning. In the following year Playford published *Music's Recreation on the Lyra viol*, and three years later a *Brief Introduction to the Skill of Music*. In 1653 Henry Lawes published his *Ayres and Dialogues* for voice and lute or bass viol, which came out in its third edition in 1658, while in the year after that appeared one of the most famous English practical music tutors, Thomas Simpson's *Division violist*. The English passion for music in the home continued to flourish as it had during the golden age, though the madrigal was gradually being replaced by the less complex form of the catch, represented by Hilton's *Catch that Catch Can* (1652, 1658, 1673). Furthermore,

John Playford, whose numerous publications played a major part in the musical life of the Commonwealth period.

although the art of spoken drama was denied its public, the masque continued to flourish in the homes of the gentry. Finally, it was under the Commonwealth that the first English opera was produced.

The birth of English opera

The masque *Cupid and Death*, performed in 1653, is a little masterpiece of musical drama. The book by John Shirley was set to the music of Christopher Gibbons (1615-76) and Matthew Locke (1630-77). Gibbons, who was the son of Orlando, had served in the royalist army during the war and was to be organist of the Chapel Royal under Charles II. He wrote a number of pieces for viols and voices that are sometimes mistakenly attributed to his famous father. Locke, who became court composer to Charles II, wrote a number of other pieces of stage music including *Psyche* (1673), an 'opera' with spoken words by Thomas Shadwell, and music for performances of Shakespeare's *Tempest* and *Macbeth*. His other work includes a treatise on composition with *basso continuo*.

The short history of early English opera begins with the performance of *The Siege of Rhodes* in 1656. The music was contributed by five composers, among them Henry Lawes and the young Matthew Locke, and the words by Sir William Davenant. Davenant, who had been court poet to Charles I and was in effect poet laureate under the Commonwealth, was reputedly Shakespeare's bastard son and, as an actor manager, had been one of the first to use women actors. He had visited Paris and, possibly under the influence of the court ballets he had seen there, decided on a similar venture in England. In May 1656, probably to test the attitude of the censorship, he had a trial run – *The First Dayes Entertainment at Rutland House by declamation and Musicke after the Manner of the Ancients*. Meeting with no opposition, he followed this with *The Siege of Rhodes*, set to music throughout, in the autumn of that year. Possibly opera was smiled on by the authorities because of its serious and 'improving' nature; *The Cruelty of the Spaniards in Peru* and the *History of Sir Francis Drake* were both performed in the Cockpit in Drury Lane before 1660. Be that as it may, English opera was off to a fair start, and its failure to establish itself during the Restoration must be attributed to the predominance of French taste at court, or to a national distaste for the art.

Music of the Restoration

In music, as in so much else, the house of Stuart was a disaster for England. After a century of rule by the Tudors, monarchs who cultivated the art and had pretensions to be musicians themselves, England found herself with a dynasty which either showed little or no interest in music (Charles I's enthusiasm for music extended only to the founding of the office of Master of the King's Musick), or admired only the foreign product.

Indeed the return of Charles II in 1660 marks a decisive turning point in the history of English music. Under the influence of the monarch's personal tastes, formed during his long stay in France, we find a cosmopolitan artistic invasion which was to sweep away the last vestiges of the golden age. To be sure, the examples of Lully and the Italians were to enrich with new elements the work of several English composers of the first rank of this period. However, the Restoration brought with it no resurgence of native talent despite the presence of an English composer of world rank. Henry Purcell, worthily seconded by his older contemporary John Blow, was not followed by a renewed flourishing of the national school and, deprived of nourishment from a healthy tradition and ill-supported by those in power (who only regarded it as conferring prestige on them and

A scene from a modern production of Purcell's opera Dido and Aeneas.

as an opportunity for lavish entertainment), music fell into decline.

Religious music had been directly suppressed under the Commonwealth and it was necessary to re-establish a continuity of tradition. This was the task of Henry Cooke (1615-72), known as 'Captain Cooke' from his rank in the royalist army, who was appointed as Master of the Children in the Chapel Royal. A competent composer, actor and singer, Cooke wrote some thirty anthems as well as part of the score of *The Siege of Rhodes*. But his chief merit lies in the fact that he trained a new generation of musicians among whom were Blow, Purcell and Pelham Humfrey; the latter (1647-74) received a royal grant to study in Italy and France and followed Cooke at the Chapel Royal.

There was no question of reviving the old polyphonic style since too many continental influences and the personal taste of the king were opposed to it. Also, with the introduction of the verse anthem, orchestras were now introduced into churches, with violins to the fore, supplanting the old viols as they had already done in chamber music. The new concerted harmonies with continuo displaced the polyphonic fantasy. The *Consort of Four Parts* (1660) by Locke, which combines the fantasy with elements of the dance suite, was the last of this genre to be published while its glorious crown, the *Fantasies* of the young Purcell, was to remain in manuscript. The Italian trio sonata admired by Purcell was having a growing success, but above all it was dances in the manner of Lully that won the royal favour.

Charles II, in fact, formed a band of twenty-four violins on the same pattern as the *Vingt-quatre violons* of the French king. This was under the musical directorship first of a German, and later of a Frenchman, Louis Grabu, a somewhat feeble imitator of Lully who for ten years enjoyed every mark of royal favour. Charles II had even hoped to attract Lully in person to his court, but instead was obliged to be content with Cambert, who was in fact an excellent musician and had, with his partner Perrin, won a royal monopoly in France for operatic performances. No doubt delighted to obtain such a brilliant position after being cheated of his monopoly by Lully, Cambert enjoyed a brief success in London before his unsatisfactory career ended in 1677 with his murder by his valet.

In the meanwhile, thanks to the efforts of Locke, Blow and Purcell, English opera was mounting the steps of its brief career. It must, however, be emphasised that the number of operas in the strict meaning of the word, that is works entirely sung, were extremely few. Moreover the works were short, like the two masterpieces, *Venus and Adonis* by John Blow and *Dido and Aeneas* by Purcell. Most popular was a hybrid entertainment in which the core of the action was entirely spoken, the music being confined to ayres, dances, instrumental preludes, interludes and 'masques'. A masque at this period signifies an *entrée* of ballet mixed with songs. Purcell's scores for these semi-operas with masques were much more developed and elaborately orchestrated than those for the small-scale operas. Unfortunately the texts were usually of a quite deplorable quality – Shakespeare and the great Elizabethans were shamelessly adapted to suit the taste of the day.

A most important element in the musical life of England was the creation of public concerts, a field of activity in which the country was half a century in advance of France. John Banister, the violinist (1630-79), ex-director of Charles II's twenty-four violinists organised the first paying concerts between 1672 and 1679. The programmes which were of excellent quality were chosen by the public themselves. Later, Thomas Britton (1657-1714), coal merchant and enthusiastic music lover, organised a series of weekly instrumental concerts from 1678 until his death, in which the most illustrious musicians participated including Handel himself. In 1689, Robert King, himself a composer, also started public concerts, which had great success. But such concerts fostered the invasion of foreign virtuosi, who accentuated the cosmopolitan flavour of musical life. The fine traditions of vocal and instrumental polyphonic pieces performed in the home were now no more than memories. The lutenist Thomas Mace, in his treatise *Musick's Monument* (1676), summons up with legitimate nostalgia the remembrance of things past.

Purcell

Henry Purcell, England's greatest composer, was born in the year 1659. Despite the most recent and intensive research, little is known of his life. He was for a time in the choir of the Chapel Royal, where his teachers were Henry Cooke and Pelham Humfrey, by whom he was no doubt introduced to French music. He also received lessons from John Blow, who in 1680 surrendered his position of organist at Westminister Abbey to his brilliant young pupil. Although little is known of this 'British Orpheus', perhaps no English composer before or since enjoyed such acclaim and admiration from his contemporaries. At the age of eighteen he had been engaged as a composer at the court of Charles II, and five years later he became organist in the Chapel Royal and keeper of the king's instruments. Throughout his life Purcell devoted his immense talents to commissions which would now be regarded as beneath the notice of a serious composer: mediocre theatrical productions, royal birthdays, and official celebrations of all kinds. Yet it is obvious that he himself found nothing untoward in such work, and although we may regret that the society he served gave no scope for the full genius of a composer obviously capable of the finest flights of operatic composition, we have no cause to be discontented with the superb body of music that he left us. It is typical of the man that *Dido and Aeneas*, which despite its brevity is the first major English opera, was written to the commission of a friend for performance by his pupils at a school for girls in Chelsea. The grace, gaiety and humour of much of the score is well suited to its occasion, but the great dramatic moments are not avoided or rendered with a conventional pathos. The lament of Dido, written to that most typically Purcellian device – composition on a ground – is one of the most deeply felt and moving moments in opera. Purcell's immense power of invention within the seemingly constricting formula of the ground bass is more brilliantly, if perhaps not more profoundly, in evidence in his mighty chaconne in G minor which, in the realm of instrumental music, ranks with the chaconne from the D minor solo violin sonata by J. S. Bach. His instrumental compositions also include the magnificent fantasies for viols and the sonatas for three and four parts for violins, bass viol and continuo, with which Purcell proclaimed his intention of introducing the Italian style to the English. All these works reveal a unique and poignant sense of harmony which, if it derives in part from the English tradition of the golden age and perhaps also from the Italian madrigalists at the beginning of the 17th century, is nevertheless unmistakably his own. His chamber compositions for instruments include, besides, a number of fine keyboard pieces.

In addition to his one true opera *Dido and Aeneas* (1689), Purcell wrote five semi-operas which, like the earlier masque, employ spoken as well as sung passages. All these works contain much fine music. They are: *Dioclesian*, with a text by the actor Thomas Betterton after Beaumont and Fletcher; *King Arthur*, by John

THO.⁹ BRITTON,
The Musical Small Coal-man.

above
John Blow, the most important of Purcell's contemporaries.

left
Thomas Britton, a prosperous coal merchant who was one of the first to organise public concerts.

The manuscript of the opening bars of Purcell's famous Golden Sonata.

Dryden; *The Tempest*, adapted from Shakespeare; *The Fairy Queen*, a reworking of his *Midsummer Night's Dream*; and the *Indian Queen*, to which Dryden also contributed. Yet, as Handel was to find in his turn, the English had no great love of opera in any form, and Purcell's largest output for the stage was in the form of incidental music for straight plays. In fact he provided the music for more than forty plays, among them a number by Dryden, but perhaps the best known of this music is that he wrote for Congreve's comedy *The Double Dealer* and for S. Behn's *Abdelazar*.

With such an obvious penchant for the theatre, it is interesting to find that Purcell wrote his most extended and ambitious works for the ceremonial occasions of the birthday of Queen Mary II, and for the annual celebrations of St Cecilia's day, the patron saint of music; of these latter probably that for the year 1692 is the most famous.

Purcell has frequently been compared with Mozart and there are abundant similarities. Both had tragically short lives (both died at thirty-six), both were overflowing with creative genius (Purcell wrote over five hundred works), both were gifted with a prodigious variety of inspiration, unrivalled psychological insight, a power of expression equally striking in sorrow as in joy, and a common genius for the theatre. In all these respects Purcell was probably the most complete musician of the second half of the 17th century. Purcell excels in every sphere – operas, music for plays, cantatas, church and chamber music, and keyboard music. His vocal works far exceed his instrumental compositions in number, although the quality of his instrumental music is equally high. His premature death, as much as the ungrateful period in which he lived, have prevented him from being recognised at his true worth as one of the greatest composers of all time. Purcell, like many a great artist, was not a creator of musical form and had to content himself with the scanty resources which England at the close of the 17th century offered him, from the hybrid semi-opera to the trio sonata in its early stages.

His receptive genius enabled him to fuse the most diverse and contradictory influences in the crucible of his feverish personality. His fantasies for strings, his full anthems, and a thousand details in the writing of his other compositions, reveal his attachment to the great English masters of the past. But at the same time, he was open to the new trends from the continent. From the French he learned the art of the overture *à la française*, the chaconne, the colour of his orchestration and his conception of theatrical ensembles; from the Italians his use of *concertato* style, the trio sonata, his expressive use of chromatics (he had studied Monteverdi) and his dramatic recitatives and *da capo* arias. Yet all unite in a style full of grace, power and poetry, in which unpredictable gaiety, akin to traditional folk music, rubs shoulders with poignant melancholy. An interpreter of every human passion, Purcell could write with great power while at other times his music is imbued with a profound sadness.

John Blow

Purcell was to be the last great English composer for two centuries and he reigned supreme during his life. But there was nothing to indicate the dark eclipse of native English music which was to follow him. His contemporaries were indeed lesser men, but such a composer as John Blow (1649-1708) was a worthy, if secondary, figure. At the early age of nineteen he had been appointed as the organist of Westminster Abbey and though, as we have seen, he surrendered the post to his brilliant young pupil, he resumed it on the death of the latter. His admiration for the younger man was unfeigned and one of his greatest compositions is the *Ode on the Death of Mr Henry Purcell*. His imagination was not equal to his ambition but on occasion, as in this ode, and in the *St Cecilia Ode* of 1684 he rose close to the level of his greater countryman. With the death of Blow, English music was in true decline and few if any figures of the 18th century achieved a similar stature.

The world of Bach

The life of the composer

Johann Sebastian Bach (1685-1750) was the youngest son of Johann Ambrosius Bach, one of the town musicians of Eisenach. The Bach family had been musicians for at least a century and, in addition to a grammar school education, the young Sebastian received a musical training, at first from his father and then from his father's cousin, the organist Johann Christoph Bach (1642-1703). By the time he was ten both of the young Bach's parents had died, and he was taken into the family of his brother, another Johann Christoph who worked as organist at Ohrdurf, having been a pupil of Pachelbel. When he was fifteen Bach was sent to the *Gymnasium*, or high school, of St Michael's, Lüneburg. Two of the major figures in the central German tradition were organists in Lüneburg when Bach took up his studies there: the elderly J. J. Löwe (1629–1703) who had been a pupil of Schütz, and Georg Böhm (1661-1733), who from 1698 had been attached to the church of St John's at Lüneburg, and who, as a composer, strongly influenced Bach's organ compositions. Furthermore, Bach came into contact with the French style. The French dancing master and violinist at the French chapel of the nearby court of Celle gave lessons to the musicians of Lüneburg. In addition, Bach made many journeys to the important musical centre of Hamburg, where he became the friend and admirer of the ageing Jan Adam Reinken, the organist at St Catherine's church and heir to the tradition of Sweelinck.

In 1703, when he was eighteen, Bach was offered an appointment as violinist at the court of Weimar and then, a few months later, the post of organist at St Boniface's church in Arnstadt, which he accepted. But, although now a full-time professional himself, Bach certainly did not regard his apprenticeship as at an end, and, obviously deeply attracted by the north German tradition, made the long journey to Lübeck on foot to hear the great Buxtehude. It is possible that Bach also considered applying for the succession to Buxtehude's post, but like others, Handel among them, he was probably deterred by the fact that the appointment carried with it the obligatory marriage to Buxtehude's thirty-year-old daughter. Whatever the intentions behind Bach's Lübeck visit, his employers at Arnstadt were not surprisingly displeased that, without any notification to them, Bach had extended a four-week leave of absence to four months. Although he received a salary notably better than any of his predecessors or of his successor, the fiery organist was involved in increasingly acrimonious disputes with his superiors and, in 1708, took up a post at the city of Mühlhausen. After a year Bach moved again to become court composer to the duke of Saxe-Weimar. For the first years his life was happy and honourable, but Bach seems to have been constitutionally unable to avoid controversy and became involved in court politics. In 1717 he was again seeking a new appointment and accepted the directorship of music at the little court of Anhalt-Cöthen. He obtained his release from Weimar only after the most persistent demands and a period of imprisonment for insubordination to the ducal wishes.

Up till this time Bach had written mostly religious music, and at Weimar had composed some of his finest works for organ as well as many of the great cantatas. But religious music had little place at the Calvinist court of Cöthen. The duke however, himself a musician, maintained a sizeable musical establishment and he and his court conductor became close friends. For a time Bach, whose reputation as an executant had spread far and wide, seemed to have found the ideal conditions for his work. His home life was an important factor, for we should remember that he had been an orphan from the age of ten, and a true home of his own must have seemed very desirable. At Weimar, as soon as he had achieved a degree of financial security, he had married his second cousin Barbara Bach, who was to bear him many children, among them the talented Wilhelm Friedemann (1710-84) and the great Carl Philipp Emanuel (1714-88). In 1720 Barbara died and although he married again some eighteen months later, the blow was a heavy one. His second wife, Anna Magdalena Wilcken, daughter of the court trumpeter at Cöthen, was herself a professional musician but, like her predecessor, she took on the running of an ever-growing household. Towards the end of his period at Cöthen, Bach's output probably fell off as the emphasis on music at the court weakened under the influence of the duke's wife. Once again Bach considered the possibilities of a new job.

In 1722, Johann Kuhnau, cantor of St Thomas's

The console used by Bach himself at the organ of St Boniface, Arnstadt.

church, Leipzig, died. The post was one of the most responsible and important appointments for a church musician in Protestant Germany, involving as it did the direction of the music in the main churches of the city, and in the university. The town council, having been disappointed in negotiations with the great Telemann of Hamburg and the lesser, but then renowned, Johann Christoph Graupner (1683-1760) of the court of Hesse-Darmstadt, decided to 'content' themselves with the director of the less prestigious court of Cöthen. For his part Bach regarded the move from directorship to that of cantor as a loss in prestige, but the new post offered the possibility of a higher gross income and he was anxious that the sons of his growing family should have the chance of a university education. Bach inaugurated his reign at Leipzig on the Good Friday of 1723 with a performance of the *St John Passion*, and his years there were to be marked by the production of some of the greatest religious compositions of all time. Yet throughout this last great creative period of his life the composer, who had a headstrong will and a quick contempt for the stupidity of the official mind, found himself time and again in conflict both with the town authorities and the director of the grammar school. Bach's official duties included the teaching of Latin to the boys at the school or the provision of an adequate deputy.

After a brief interlude in the early 1730s when the school was under the directorship of a rector who fully respected the genius of the cantor, Bach was confronted by an ambitious young rector named Ernesti, who was determined to make the school a great academic centre and had no time for musical distractions. All out war ensued and by the early 1740s Bach seems to have withdrawn from his teaching responsibilities by mutual consent. He may have won some help in his struggle from the title of 'Composer to the Court of Poland and the Elector of Saxony' conferred on him in 1736. He received a further royal accolade when, in 1747, he visited the court of Frederick II of Prussia at Berlin, where his son Emanuel was serving. The story is well known of how 'old Bach', as the king called him, was invited to test the numerous Silbermann pianos and harpsichords in the palace, astonishing the court with the fluency and profundity of his improvisations. It was on this occasion that he made a fuller acquaintance with the comparatively recent piano, and had a low opinion of what he found. No doubt with the courtier's sense of interest in a royal reward, Bach is reputed to have asked Frederick for a theme for contrapuntal variation. The result, based on a truly royal theme, he called the *Musical Offering* and dedicated it to Frederick. Unfortunately for Bach the 'gift' was accepted in the sense in which it seemed to have been offered and he received nothing for this masterpiece. At Leipzig too, Bach's talents as a musician, while sometimes grudgingly admitted, were never duly recognised. Within weeks of his death in July 1750, after an unsuccessful operation to restore his failing sight, the relieved town council, remarking that the school needed a cantor rather than a conductor, appointed a pliant nonentity in Bach's place and found a pretext for reducing the customary pension to the dead musician's widow.

The style

Despite the very large number of works by Bach which survive, it is possible that we have today only about half of the composer's total output. Of the five Passions which he wrote, only two are now known, and it seems probable that in addition to the two hundred cantatas which have come down to us another hundred are lost. Yet we can be fairly sure that no works which may yet come to light will alter in any significant way our appreciation of Bach's mighty musical personality. Bach himself said that anyone who had worked as hard as he had done could have achieved as much. This apparently modest comment can probably be discounted as the reply to some innocent but slow-witted enquirer into 'how he did it'. Yet there is no doubt that he did work. The ingredients of genius cannot be analysed, but the constituent elements which went to make up Bach's superbly integrated style can be traced. The young musician was indefatigable, not only in his pilgrimages to hear the music of his German contemporaries, but also in his study of the music of Italian and French composers both past and present. He built up a large library of his own manuscript copies of the works of

below right
The case of the organ in the town church of Arnstadt.

below
Leipzig in the 18th century.

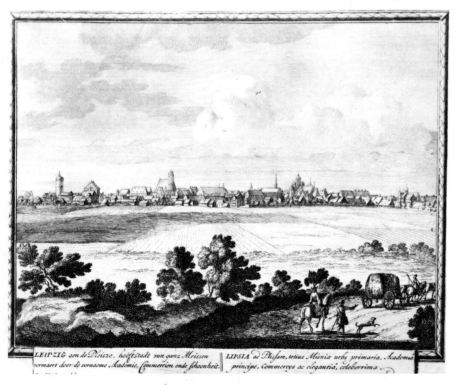

LEIPZIG aen de Pleisze, hooftstadt van ganz Meissen || LIPSIA ad Plisam, totius Misniæ urbs primaria, Academia vermaert door de vornaeme Academie, Commercien ende schoonheit || principe, Commerces ac elegantiâ, celeberrima.

such men as Vivaldi, Corelli and Frescobaldi, and did not hesitate to make use of their material in his own compositions. The practice was commonplace at the time, but whether he drew on the work of others or on earlier compositions of his own, Bach transmuted such borrowings into his own brilliant new coinage.

Nevertheless, although fully in touch with new developments, Bach's style rests firmly on the foundation of 17th-century German polyphonic writing, and in consequence was considered outdated by some of his contemporaries. If, for us, the music of Bach is synonymous with order, it is easy to understand how to the 18th-century ear, already acclimatised to a more 'pleasing' lightweight style, it was felt to be unsympathetic and erudite. But although the contrapuntal idiom is central to Bach's musical language, he achieved a profound and unequalled synthesis of the contrapuntal with the harmonic element. His musical structures, rich with melodic lines in all the parts and with beautiful and daring resultant harmonies, the profusion of which astonished and delighted Mozart, are built up into great units which possess an internal balance and overall sense of structure that may be described as architectural. In addition to his astounding gift for melody, the harmonic assurance and audacity of his music and the mighty sense of structural and formal perfection which inspires all his mature works, Bach had a powerful and awe-inspiring control of climax. In his instrumental music in particular, he frequently takes a single melodic or harmonic configuration and develops it exhaustively to build a climax which depends not on rhythm, nor on contrasting dynamics of volume, nor on crescendo, but on the accumulation of a number of musical statements derived from the original motif. A classic example of this cumulative effect is in the great toccata for organ in F major, while in the harpsichord cadenza of the Brandenburg Concerto No. 5, the series of lesser climaxes is brilliantly contrived to give the fullest possible effect to the sense of liberation and achievement reached in the final one.

No account of J. S. Bach's artistic personality would be complete that did not stress his deep religious inspiration. Despite the many dramatic elements in his cantatas, the natural legacy of the century of the Baroque, these works, which include some of his most mature masterpieces, reveal their composer's deep religious faith. This reaches its apogee in the choruses of the *St Matthew Passion* and the tremendous Sanctus of the Mass in B minor, while more than two hundred works for organ were all composed for performance in the church service and to the greater glory of God. In this respect the period at Leipzig, despite its many tribulations, must be regarded as the culmination of Bach's career. It is perhaps interesting to reflect that the veneration of this supremely religious composer has never stood higher than in our own day, when the spirit which inspired him would seem to be at its lowest ebb. For both the modern composer and the modern audience the works of Bach are profoundly satisfying; there can be few lovers of music insensitive to the works of a man who, perhaps more completely than any other before or since, united the intellectual and emotional drives of the human spirit.

The works

These may be divided into five periods of which the first, corresponding to the early years of his career at Arnstadt and Mühlhausen, show the young composer exploring and experimenting. A number of organ works, preludes and fugues, toccatas, and canzonas date from this period, during which he also composed his first cantatas and the light-hearted *Capriccio on the departure of his brother*.

During the years at Weimar, Bach's cantata composition shows him influenced by the work of the Lutheran ecclesiastic and poet, Erdmann Neumeister, who wrote cantata libretti which he regarded as nothing more or less than sections of an opera composed of

A page from Bach's manuscript of one of his chorale preludes.

alternating recitative and arias. At Weimar, too, Bach composed some of his most renowned works for organ, among them the great Passacaglia and double Fugue in C minor and the still more famous Toccata and Fugue in D minor. At Weimar he wrote a number of masterly compositions which, like so many other works by him, were destined to be used as exercises by his pupils. Forty-six chorale variations, which Bach entitled *Orgelbüchlein* or 'Little Organ Book', reveal Bach's attachment to the German tradition of the 17th century, and indeed the intention of the book was to teach the young organist how to develop a chorale in various ways, an art which was beginning to be outmoded even at the

time of writing. The dedication ends with words which sum up Bach's approach to music: 'To the glory of all highest God and to the instruction of my fellow men'.

The years in the congenial atmosphere of the court at Cöthen were devoted chiefly to instrumental music. Only seventeen cantatas survive and very few organ works, though these latter do include the splendid Fantasia and Fugue in G minor. But among the compositions for the court orchestra were the Brandenburg Concertos, the orchestral overtures in C major and B minor; the six partitas and sonatas for solo violin, of which the second partita in D minor has the mighty chaconne as its final movement, and the solo sonatas for

Johann Sebastian Bach by Haussman.

cello. At this time also Bach wrote a large number of keyboard concertos, many of which were transcriptions of the work of other composers, the two violin concertos, in E major and A minor, and the concerto for two violins in D minor. Among the many keyboard works were the dramatic *Italian Concerto*, the *Chromatic Fantasia and Fugue*, written in about 1720 though given its final form in 1730, the English and French suites and, above all, the twenty-four preludes and fugues in all the major and minor keys, known as Book I of the *Well Tempered Clavier*. With a companion completed in 1744, they are familiarly referred to as the 'Forty-eight', and comprise a treasure house of contrapuntal expertise and sheer musical beauty which were to make them the bible of professional musicians from the time of Bach himself to the present day. The German word *Klavier* is neutral in its application, meaning simply keyboard. It is obvious from the nature of the pieces, particularly in Book II, that they were written for different instruments – the majority no doubt for the clavichord but many for the harpsichord and a few for the organ. The idea of writing a cycle of pieces through the twenty-four keys was not new with Bach (at least one other German composer, J. F. C. Fischer, had produced a similar series), but with his set Bach put the seal of approval on the system of equal tempered tuning. (For the whole subject of temperament and the context in which Bach produced these compositions, the reader is referred to the glossary of technical terms.)

For the first fifteen years of his time at Leipzig his output was to be primarily religious. The *St John Passion* composed at Cöthen for his inauguration in his new post, with its perfection and balance of form and the drama and power of expression of the music itself, contrasted strongly with the uninspired music of his predecessor, but it was only a foretaste of what was to come. The poignancy and grandeur of the great *St Matthew Passion* of 1730 were hardly to be surpassed by Bach himself. From the majestic and disturbing opening chorus the hearer is aware that he is involved in a work of sublime tragedy and, in the ordering of the various arias, choruses and chorales which together make up this mighty composition, Bach reveals himself not only as a great musician but also as a great dramatic poet. As a unified work of art, the St Matthew Passion is excelled not even by the awe-inspiring Mass in B minor. The Kyrie and Gloria of this work had been written in

1733 to mourn the passing of the Saxon elector and to greet the accession of his successor; the dimensions of the work preclude its use in the liturgy whether of the Reformed or the Catholic Church. The music abounds in moments of sublimity and remote grandeur, and the composer's mature and confident mastery of counterpoint is apparent throughout. Of the many other religious compositions of the Leipzig period, the finest are the six cantatas now known collectively as the *Christmas Oratorio*, together with the Magnificat, the six Latin motets and the superb series of cantatas.

Bach continued to compose a certain amount for the harpsichord and indeed produced, during this time, the set of *Thirty Variations on an Original Aria*, the so-called *Goldberg Variations* (1742), which form one of the peaks of this type of composition. Commissioned by Count Keyserling, the emissary of the Saxon court at Leipzig, to be performed by his household musician J. G. Goldberg to while away the count's sleepless hours, they earned Bach one hundred pieces – the highest fee he ever received.

In the last ten years of his life, Bach seems to have retired more and more into his music from the turbulent world of local politics and school-mastering. The other great cycles of his last years are the *Musical Offering*; the canonic variations for organ on the chorale melody *Vom Himmel hoch da komm ich her* (1747), which constitute the summit of the art of counterpoint and which have inspired Stravinsky to compose a parody imitation; and finally *The Art of Fugue*, so-called by his son Emanuel who published it. In this, the master takes a theme and demonstrates the fugal and canonic variations which are possible on it. The work is not scored for any specific instrument, and the final fugue is incomplete, as if to challenge the student who has progressed that far to put his knowledge into practice and finish the work. There have indeed been such attempts, of which the most satisfying is that of the English scholar and musician Donald Tovey. But the mystery which hangs over this work and Bach's intentions when writing it will probably never be solved. The manuscript ends just as the theme on the name of the composer B-A-C-H has been introduced as the third subject. On the manuscript score his son Carl Philipp Emanuel wrote 'At this point, where the theme B-A-C-H is introduced as counter-subject, the composer died'.

GEOFFREY HINDLEY

The last page of Bach's manuscript of The Art of Fugue.

The Italian Age

In the last twenty years of the 17th century and during much of the 18th century, Italy maintained her musical supremacy while France, inspired by Italy's technical and formal discoveries, also contributed to the formation of that European style which was eventually to find its full development in the music of the composers of the German countries. Italian supremacy was affirmed, above all in the fields of instrumental music and opera. But decline always follows an apogee. There was to come a point when it seemed that the perfection of form, vocabulary, language and technique could be taken no farther: the talent of Italian composers, rich as it was, was exhausting itself on such stilted forms. The lead passed into other hands and such giants as Haydn and Mozart prepared for a new style, dispensing with tradition and creating a new form which finally opened the way to the composers of the 19th century. In opera, another great German composer, Christoph Willibald Gluck, was to protest against the sterility of the Italian convention. But in their heyday, both Italian opera and instrumental music had led Europe, and in this account of music in the 'Italian age' we shall begin with a study of instrumental music.

The muse Terpsichore playing a chitarrone. The instrument became obsolete during the 18th century but was sometimes shown in allegorical paintings.

Instrumental music

In the second half of the 17th century the instrumental style of the Italian school developed rapidly. In keyboard composition, the styles of organ and harpsichord works separated finally and unmistakably while, at the same time, a specific instrumental style of writing for the violin was also beginning to emerge. The first important form which is fully recognisable by the mid-17th century was the trio sonata, which was to prepare the way for later types of chamber music and even played a part in the origins of the symphony.

The Italian composers of the later 17th century were quick to improve on the no doubt rudimentary, but already established musical forms to which they were the heirs, and their works often anticipate those of the 18th-century masters of central Europe, who were happy to seek inspiration from them. It is well known, for example, that the great J. S. Bach studied the works of Vivaldi, many of which he transcribed for harpsichord. In the middle decades of the 18th century, both the technique and the prodigious inventive faculties of Giuseppe Tartini opened the way to a great age of virtuosity whose most brilliant representative was another Italian, G. B. Viotti.

Musical forms and styles

The end of the 17th century and the whole of the 18th century saw an ever-increasing search for unity on thematic and formal levels.

The sonata for two violins with *basso continuo* was the form preferred by the majority of composers, but, by a somewhat artificial convention, it was subdivided between the *sonata da chiesa* and the *sonata da camera*. The church sonata generally consisted of five or six movements, with indications of tempi. It was usually in three parts, was imitative in style, and was intended for a small instrumental ensemble. The chamber sonata preserved the form of the old dance suite, with its dance titles and, by and large, afforded greater freedom of composition. In all these forms composers tended to reduce the number of themes and in some cases produced monothematic structures which, paradoxically, preceded the bithematic sonata. Giovanni Legrenzi and G. B. Vitali in the late 17th century sketched in the first outlines of this evolution, Corelli gave it precision, and Vivaldi developed it.

The other important tendency was towards the stabilisation of the number of movements at three.

Corelli, however, did not adhere to the composition in three movements derived from the Italian overture or *sinfonia*, but generally adopted five movements separated by two intervals: *grave* and *allegro*, *vivace*, *largo* and *allegro*. Vivaldi, on the other hand, frequently returned to a ternary construction, but omitted repeat sections in fast movements to give them greater unity.

At the beginning of the 18th century the more advanced composers were beginning to dispense with the continuo bass. This often entailed instrumental rescoring which gave enhanced colour and timbre, and stressed the individuality of instruments; an individuality which led inevitably from the early concerto grosso to the orchestral symphony on the one hand, and to the sonata and concerto for soloist on the other. While the early concerto grosso contrasted a group of soloists with an orchestral ensemble, Vivaldi substituted a violin solo for a trio holding dialogue with the orchestra; from then on we have an ensemble consisting of a part for soloist, four parts for *concertino* and eight parts for concerto grosso. Here, quite plainly, is one of the original forms of the orchestral symphony and of the concerto for solo instrument and orchestra.

The development of instrumental technique also contributed to the rise in importance of the soloist, in turn opening the way to a new generation of great virtuosi. The most marked development was in string instruments, particularly in the violin and cello, with Corelli and, later, Boccherini. But the invention of the pianoforte by Christofori in about 1709 was, at the end of the century, to have a profound influence on keyboard music. The new instrument was not at once adopted. Nevertheless the style of works for the harpsichord gradually evolved with Scarlatti and Clementi towards the future style of the piano. In this evolution, Domenico Scarlatti represents an important landmark, particularly from the point of view of form.

He often anticipates the bithematic sonata and, while he preserved the pattern of the binary movements of the suite, certain of his works have an embryonic central development and a partial re-exposition which foreshadow the classic ternary form of the sonata.

When in due course this development achieved its full flowering with Beethoven, the Italian, Clementi, also revealed considerable genius in the handling of form and there are curious interreactions between the works of the two masters, who shared a mutual respect. As examples one may instance the sonatas which Clementi wrote between 1788 and 1790, in which he uses elaborate themes and harmonies in a manner which Beethoven was not to apply till twenty years later. In the Suites of 1815 and 1820, however, it was Clementi who followed Beethoven, orientating his style in a direction which foreshadowed the lyricism of Chopin and even at times the symphonies of the great German Romantics.

Thus this period is one of transition between the pre-classic and classic forms, but also, towards the end, one stirred by the new forms of the dawning Romantic era.

The schools of Venice and Bologna in the late 17th century

At the end of the 17th century the Venetian school, which had already anticipated the dialogue and contrast of the concerto in compositions for double choirs, now produced one of the greatest pioneers in Italian instrumental music in the person of Giovanni Legrenzi (1626–90). He was born in Bergamo where, from his earliest youth, he played the organ. In 1665 he went to Venice where he was made director of the Conservatorio di Mendicanti (1672), and in 1685, his powers of in-

vention and brilliant talents for orchestration won him the appointment as director of the music of St Mark's. He expanded the orchestra of the cathedral to thirty-four players: eight violins, eleven violas, two tenor violas, three bass viols, four theorboes, two cornetts, one bassoon and three trombones. Theatrical music allowed him full scope for his talents as an orchestrator, but it was in the realm of purely instrumental music that he proved himself a truly significant composer. He was one of the first to write for the combination of two violins and cello, and thus did much to establish the trio sonata which was to reach its full flowering with Corelli. In the 1660s he was writing solo violin sonatas in three separate movements, and thus lent his authority to another important formal development, while his sonatas for four instruments, published as *La Cetra* in 1673, show a remarkable balance between the different parts. The quality of his thematic material was equally fine and both Bach and Handel borrowed from him – the first employing one of his themes for an organ fugue, the second for his oratorio *Samson*.

Antonio Veracini, born in the middle of the 17th century, made his contribution to violin technique and the sonata form with thirty sonatas for two violins and continuo. These, published by the composer between 1692 and 1696, testify to the stylistic maturity of the trio sonata by the end of the 17th century, and seem to have influenced the works of his nephew Francesco Maria Veracini (1690–*c.* 1750). F. M. Veracini, however, was renowned throughout Europe as a virtuoso violinist rather than as a composer, and his many works include twenty-four violin sonatas with continuo. Another composer whose work, like that of Antonio Veracini, is of interest in the history of the trio sonata

The Concert *by Pietro Longhi. The violin dominated the 18th-century orchestra; its technique was developed in Italy.*

Giuseppe Torelli, the leading composer of the late 17th-century Bolognese school.

was Giovanni Battista Mazzaferrata (d. 1691), whose twelve sonatas for two violins, bass viol and continuo were published in 1674.

It is clear that the composers of the school of Bologna played a decisive role in the formative period of the classical instrumental style, and the prestige of the school and the city's Accademia Filarmonica persisted throughout the 18th century. Morizio Cazzati (1620-77), generally considered the founder of the school of Bologna, made notable advances towards giving true formal unity to the trio sonata, while his sonatas for five and four instruments have been described as masterpieces. Nevertheless, despite the merits of his own work, his position as the teacher of G. B. Vitali is perhaps even more important.

Giovanni Battista Vitali (*c.* 1644-92), whose musical career was divided between Bologna and Modena, exercised a very strong influence on the development of instrumental composition. The quality of his melodic inspiration, his mature sense of tonality which is revealed in a meticulous ordering of the tonic in relation to its neighbouring keys, coupled with a delight in rich sequences of modulation, would be sufficient in themselves to place him in the ranks of the masters. But in addition to these contributions to the very vocabulary of the language of classical music, he did much to bring thematic unity to the different movements of the sonata. An Italian musicologist has pointed out that the four movements, *grave, prestissimo, allegro* and *largo*, of the second sonata of Vitali's *Artifici musicale a diversi stromenti* are all based on the same motif. This device of a single linking theme obviously has affinities with the *cantus firmus* mass, while in instrumental music the use of a single thematic nucleus for an extended work was the basis of the cyclic sonata of the 19th century. Vitali's son, Tommaso Antonio, who was to become a member of the duke of Modena's orchestra and the Accademia Filarmonica of Bologna, followed in his father's footsteps, although his trio sonatas (1693) and 'concerti di sonate' for violin, cello and continuo (1701) seem designed to meet the contemporary delight in virtuosity for its own sake.

Among other composers of the Bolognese school at this time, there was also Pietro degli Antoni (d. *c.* 1720), president and one of the founder members of the Accademia Filarmonica, and composer of many violin sonatas with continuo, as well as organ sonatas.

Giovanni Battista, his brother, published between 1687 and 1697 seven books of organ music, as well as works for violin, cello and harpsichord. It seems beyond doubt that their compositions were known to both J. S. Bach and Handel.

Giovanni Battista Bassani, who worked at Bologna, Ferrara and Bergamo, left twelve unusually elegant church sonatas for two violins and continuo (1683), which reveal his preoccupation with devising a harmonic scheme as a means of conferring a greater degree of unity on the sonata form. His original and personal sense of rhythm occasionally anticipates the future *scherzo*, and his style shows affinities with that of Corelli.

It was also at Bologna, in 1685 and 1691, that Giovanni Battista Bononcini, whose European career was to include the famous feud with Handel in London, published his *Trattenimenti, concerti e sinfonie* for three instruments, which remain faithful to the traditions of the genre. Another Bolognese musician, the cellist Giuseppe Maria Jacchini, was probably the first composer of a concerto for cello and orchestra (1701).

Giuseppe Torelli (1658-1709), however, remains without any doubt the major composer at Bologna during the period. His talent and genius far and away dominate the productions of his compatriots. Moreover, he had an excellent knowledge of the technical resources of instruments, and he himself played the violetta (an early cello) and tenor viol in the cathedral orchestra. Almost all his working life as a composer and instrumentalist was passed at Bologna. A contemporary of Corelli, Torelli produced many fine examples of the emerging concerto grosso form, although he does not appear (despite the dates of publication) to have preceded the latter in the genre. If one is to believe the German musician Georg Muffat, similar works by Corelli (although not actually published before 1714) had already been performed in Rome in 1682. Of the eight collections of compositions for strings by Torelli which were engraved for publication, only seven have survived, but the opus numbers in their order of publication tell us much of the workings of his creative mind. His compositions range from trio sonatas (1686) to the *Concerti grossi with a pastorale for the festival of the Nativity* (1709), by way of the twelve *Sinfonie* (1687) and the *Sinfonie e concerti* (1692). Many of Torelli's works survive in manuscript and these include what are perhaps the earliest examples of the solo violin concerto. For his concerti grossi he adopted the plan of the Italian overture in three movements and, in much of his music, enriched his orchestration with many additional instruments: trumpets, trombones, oboes and kettledrums. But his feeling for orchestral colour belongs to the developing tradition of the 18th century, rather than to the past. His music appeals with its ease, grace and freshness, but it lacks deep emotional appeal; it is for this reason perhaps, that posterity has preferred the richer and more finished works of Corelli.

Corelli

Arcangelo Corelli (1653-1713) was born in Bologna, where he had his early training. But from 1675 he lived in Rome, and it was here that he published his principal works and thereby raised the prestige of a city which, at that time, could boast no instrumental composers of stature. Of Corelli's Roman predecessors, Michelangelo Rossi (1600-74) had written works for the organ and harpsichord which are full of original rhythmic discoveries; Bernardo Pasquini (1637-1710), a remarkable teacher to whom such men as Krieger,

Muffat, Durante and Domenico Scarlatti came for advice, also wrote many works for harpsichord and seems to have attempted to perpetuate the style of Frescobaldi. But the tradition of that great Roman master had few Italian admirers, and it seemed to have died out at the beginning of the 18th century with Domenico Antonio Giordani, organist of the church of the Twelve Apostles and author of *Rules for the realisation of a basso continuo* (1724).

In many respects the work of Corelli forms the link between the 17th and 18th centuries. No doubt others before him showed greater originality, but no one of his time displays a nobler concern for measure and balance, or for formal perfection and grandeur. Despite his Bolognese training he incarnates the classical age of Italian music, and owed much to the Roman tradition. Corelli's works were the fruit of slow and considerable deliberation. He was already twenty-eight before he published his first collection of church sonatas (1681). Four years later he produced his first chamber sonatas for two violins, violone and harpsichord. His mastery was fully confirmed with his fifth collection, which appeared at the very dawn of the 18th century – the dedication to Sophie-Charlotte of Brandenburg is dated 1st January 1700. The first part of the collection comprises six church sonatas for violin and bass, the second, six chamber sonatas. The collection ends with a final sonata, twenty-three variations on the popular theme *La Follia di Spagna*, which brings us to the threshold of the homophonic style of virtuoso playing. However, although himself a skilled violinist, Corelli still used traditional compositional methods. The sonatas of the fifth collection contain many fugal passages and even 'true' fugues, and his undramatic cantabile style was to have a profound influence on subsequent compositions for the violin.

His greatest work is to be found in the twelve concerti grossi. Although these were published posthumously at Amsterdam in 1714, Corelli himself seems to have prepared them for publication and had signed the dedication at Rome in December 1712. It would seem that the composition of these concerti grossi had occupied him over a period of thirty years. The first eight are in the solemn manner of the church sonata; in the last four he reverts to the mood of the *sonata da camera*, heading the movements with dance titles. The number and the arrangements of the movements vary with each work, but the instrumental balance remains unchanged throughout. Corelli contrasts the two violins and cello of the *concertino* group with the two violin parts, viola and bass (sometimes doubled) of the *ripieno*; each group is supplied with an independent harpsichord or organ figured bass part. The fairly schematic notation of certain slow movements of the fifth collection seems to call for improvised ornamentation, but the composition of the concertos is much more complete.

Corelli was not merely an inspired composer, but, as one of the greatest of the early violinists, he considerably enriched the technical resources of his instrument. His teaching gave birth to a tradition which in the work of his pupils, Geminiani and Locatelli, provided the basis of all future developments in violin technique.

If he himself did not actually invent the musical forms which he employed, Corelli gave them a nobility and perfection which make him one of the greatest 'classicists'. Dr Charles Burney, the English music historian, commented towards the end of the 18th century of Corelli's concerti grossi that their 'ensemble effects are so majestic, so solemn and so sublime, that they disarm all criticism and make us forget everything else composed in this style'.

At Naples at the end of the 17th century the concerto grosso form seems to have been anticipated in the work of Alessandro Stradella (d. 1682). His orchestral con-

Arcangelo Corelli, one of Italy's finest composers and an important figure in the history of the violin.

certos, symphonies and trio sonatas reveal a splendid mastery of composition and an unusual concern for formal harmonies, and he introduces music in the style of the concerto grosso into the overtures and *intermezzi* of his works for the theatre, frequently dividing the orchestra into two distinct groups corresponding to the *concertino* and *grosso*.

It was in the 18th century that the supremacy of Italy was definitely established in the realm of instrumental music. The great masters were Vivaldi at Venice, Tartini at Padua, and the Scarlattis of Naples, but there were many other fine composers who contributed to Italy's European hegemony.

Lesser Italian masters of the 18th century

The great master of the 18th-century Bolognese school, Fr Giovanni Battista Martini (1706-84), had an encyclopedic knowledge of music which is shown not only in his vocal compositions (to be discussed later), but also in his works for organ and harpsichord (1741-47), in which the principles of traditional counterpoint and the seductive, delicate and playful character of the fashionable *style galant* are mixed.

In Piedmont Giovanni Battista and Lorenzo Somis (1686-1763 and 1688-1775), pupils of Corelli and Vivaldi, both wrote violin sonatas and concertos while Gaetano Pugnani (1731-98), a pupil of G. B. Somis and Tartini, earned a European reputation as both a composer and executant. The Lombard organist and composer Giovanni Battista Sammartini (1698-1775), known as San Martini of Milan, wrote some 2,800 compositions of all sorts including symphonies, quartets, trios, violin and harpsichord sonatas, and flute duos. His first symphony with four movements, written in 1734, marks an important landmark in the history of symphonic form and he was among the first composers to turn away from the *basso continuo* method of composition, making important contributions to the developing first movement sonata form.

Vivaldi and the school of Venice
in the 18th century

The son of a violinist of repute and probably a pupil of
Legrenzi, Antonio Vivaldi (1678-1741) taught between
1703 and 1740 at the Music Seminary of the Ospizio
della Pietà, one of the four original institutions of Venice
which were both hospice and convent. These foundations cared for the sick and for the upbringing of children, whose education included a solid musical background.

The girls of the Pietà sang and also played one or
more instruments – violin, harpsichord, organ, flute,
oboe, bassoon and even trumpet. Vivaldi thus had at his
disposal a permanent orchestra with an exceptional
range of timbres, which explains the abundance of his
orchestral compositions. He also wrote some forty
operas and oratorios, but their quality is not notably
higher than that of other contemporary works, and it is
as a composer of instrumental music that he is chiefly
remembered. In this field well over 500 works which can
be definitely attributed to him survive; among them are
75 sonatas for two and three instruments, 23 symphonies and 454 concertos, 96 of which were grouped together and published in collections during his lifetime.
He holds a major position in the history of musical form
as one of the most important figures in the development
of the solo concerto, and he was no less an innovator in
symphonic writing; its pre-classic form reached the
height of precision in his operatic overtures as well as in
the orchestral passages of his concertos. His music,
characterised by dramatic contrasts of dynamics and
harmony and with a passion and lyricism then rare in
instrumental music, was criticised in his own time as
eccentric, and after his death was almost entirely forgotten until its revival in the 1930s. Yet his themes,
rhythm and coloratura passages possess an originality
which fascinated professionals, and we know that Bach
transcribed ten of his concertos.

Many of Vivaldi's contemporaries added lustre to
the Venetian school, among them Tommaso Albinoni
(1671-1750), a close friend of Vivaldi and also esteemed
by Bach, who used one of his themes as a subject for a
fugue. It has been claimed that Albinoni was the first to
introduce the minuet into the symphony, and that he
thus antedates the Mannheim composers. However
this may be, the suppleness of his thematic material
places him among the precursors of the symphonic
style and even Romanticism in music. Mention should
also be made of Antonio Lotti (1667-1740) whose works
include a trio of great charm for flute, oboe and continuo, and Alessandro Marcello (1684-1750), composer
of twelve solos for violin and several concertos. His
brother, Benedetto (1686-1739), wrote fine examples of
all the main genres (both vocal and instrumental),
among them as numerous concertos, one of which for
oboe Bach transcribed as a harpsichord concerto. Baldassare Galuppi (1706-85), a pupil of Lotti, was most successful in his works for the theatre, but also composed a
number of instrumental works, among them harpsichord
sonatas in from one to four movements, seven concertos
for strings and a trio sonata. The last of these lesser contemporaries of Vivaldi to be mentioned here is Domenico
Alberti (1710-40). In his short career he wrote both
operas and motets but is chiefly remembered for his
forty harpsichord sonatas. His consistent use of the
broken chord bass, now known as the Alberti bass,
marked an important milestone in the development of
the homophonic style of composition which was
gradually displacing the continuo.

Towards the middle of the 18th century, the school
of Venice found its fame challenged by that of the
neighbouring town of Padua. This was due solely to the
talents of one man, Giuseppe Tartini (1692-1770), one
of the most important figures in the history of the violin.
He was the son of a wealthy nobleman and was educated
in turn for the Church, the law and the army, becoming
meanwhile a champion fencer and skilful violinist.
After an adventurous youth which led him into a secret
marriage before the age of twenty, he settled in Padua

as first violinist in the orchestra of San Antonio. Here, despite the poor money, he stayed for the rest of his career. But Tartini's supreme mastery as a violinist, the beauty of his tone and, above all, the expressive intensity of his playing, soon brought him an international reputation. In 1728 he established a school for the violin at Padua, and the pupils of the 'master of the nations', as his contemporaries dubbed him, were to include Nardini and Pugnani among many others. As a teacher, Tartini paid special attention to the right rendering of ornamentation and wrote, about 1750, the first 18th-century treatise on this important subject (Leopold Mozart was to draw heavily on it for his own work on the subject). Tartini's standing as a composer is also very high. Throughout a long and active career he produced hundreds of violin sonatas, and many concertos which, in their formal excellence and melodic and harmonic inventiveness, stand second only to the works of Corelli and Vivaldi. Tartini was also responsible for improvements to the violin itself, in lengthening the bow and thickening the strings, which gave the instrument a mellower tone.

Pietro Nardini (1722–93) introduced his master's style and technique to Germany, where Leopold Mozart and Schubert praised the evenness of tone, beauty, sweetness and emotive quality of his playing. He left Germany in 1769 to become concert master at the court of Florence. His sonatas, duos and quartets, though not the equal of Tartini's, reflect the advances in form which were made as the 18th century progressed.

Naples

Although Neapolitan musicians were mainly concerned with music for the theatre, a number of them can be counted among the pioneers of the modern style of orchestral symphonic works and chamber music. Indeed, in the work of Alessandro Scarlatti, some of the most significant pioneer work in the new instrumental style grew out of the opera. For it is in the instrumental *sinfonie* to his operas, with their typical three movement form of fast-slow-fast tempi, that historians of music trace the beginnings of the classical symphony. The first example of this 'Italian' type of *sinfonia* is to be found in an opera Scarlatti wrote when he was about

left
Niccolò Jommelli, Neapolitan opera composer of both serious and comic operas.

below left
Domenico Scarlatti, the great Neapolitan keyboard composer who spent much of his time at the court of Spain.

twenty-five. But he also wrote many independent instrumental works and the French writer Romain Rolland has said that, by the complete freedom of his chamber music, 'Scarlatti was able to perfect the orchestra'. The works written during the last ten years of his life were of extraordinary diversity. They included sonatas in four parts for strings and a dozen *Sinfonie di concerto grosso* where the strings are sometimes joined by two flutes, sometimes by a flute and oboe, or sometimes by flute and trumpet. Scarlatti also wrote serenades of which one of the most interesting is the *Serenade for the Prince of Stigliano*, employing solo voices and chorus, two flutes, two oboes, two horns, two bassoons, supported by a string band.

Domenico Scarlatti (1685–1757) followed in his father's footsteps. In the seventeen symphonies he has left us, the grouping of the wind instruments varies from work to work. However, it was in particular his compositions for harpsichord which brought him European fame.

Scarlatti introduced fantasy and grace and lively rhythmic invention into the apparently unchanged form of the binary sonata. His own very personal harpsichord technique has great melodic charm, as well as bold harmonies of astonishing modernity, and is characterised by his lavish use of ornamentation. Sometimes a nostalgic note creeps in, only to disappear like a fleeting sad memory driven out by a joyous mood. To some extent his work reflects the atmosphere of Spain, where he lived for nearly a quarter of a century, and greatly influenced Spanish composers like Fr Antonio Solér (1728–83). Thematically he anticipates the bithematic sonata, whose form he had in effect already outlined.

In addition to the Scarlattis, other Neapolitan musicians produced interesting instrumental music. The three- or four-part *sinfonie* of Giovanni Battista Pergolesi had a direct influence on modern orchestral style and form. The same can be said of his violin concertos and of the concertos and sonatas for organ and harpsichord written when he was at the Naples Conservatory.

Leonardo Leo (1694–1744), a master of Neapolitan opera, also composed toccatas for harpsichord as well as cello concertos of remarkable formal beauty, and a *sinfonia* which enchanted Mozart. Niccolò Jommelli, another opera composer (1714–74), visited central Europe, and while he was in Stuttgart the orchestra there played his concerto for harpsichord and orchestra,

as well as his symphonies and operatic overtures. Indeed, the majority of the masters of Neapolitan opera, when they lived abroad, particularly those in London, cultivated chamber music. Eloquent testimony of this type of work can be found in the compositions of Antonio Sacchini (1730-86) and the opera composers Giovanni Paisiello and Nicola Porpora. Domenico Zipoli (1688-1726) is of particular interest since he went to the Argentine and was one of the first to introduce the new European style, which he had inherited from his masters Scarlatti and Pasquini, to South America.

FARINELLI.

The age of Italian opera

It has been possible to mention only a few of the leading Italian composers active in the main musical centres north of the Alps during the 18th century. It is possible to gauge the extent of their ascendancy if we remember that during the lifetime of Bach, from about 1685 to about 1750, at least eighty Italians worked in London at one time or another; over one hundred in Vienna, twenty-five at St Petersburg, forty at Dresden and, perhaps most surprising of all, as many as fifty visited Paris. Their contribution to the developing language of European music was immense. Some idea has been given of the Italian achievement in the field of instrumental music, but for contemporaries the impact of Italian music was still more noticeable in the theatre.

For the first half of the 18th century Italian opera continued to enjoy the supremacy which it had won in the 17th. With the vogue for Italian composers and their music went that for Italian singers. Castrati such as Farinelli (1705-82) and Cafarelli (1703-83) enjoyed a success which has been aptly compared to that of the great film stars in the heyday of Hollywood.

The classic style of the high art of Italian opera was known as *opera seria*. The plot, usually on some historical or mythological theme, was of little importance. The *opera seria* was essentially a series of florid arias linked in the most tenuous manner by passages of recitative, intended to recount the development of the story but in fact generally regarded by the audience as periods of relaxation. Towards the end of the century, a French visitor to Rome observed that the game of draughts was the ideal diversion to while away the tedium of the recitative, which in its turn served to correct a most ungentlemanly devotion to draughts. Such orchestral interludes as there were served, like the

Plate 26 left
Pastel portrait of the great French composer Rameau.

Plate 27 below
The Scale of Love *by Watteau; the guitar in one of its fashionable roles in the 18th century.*

Plate 28
The first known portrait of Handel in England, by Philip Mercier.

recitatives, primarily as intervals between the arias while the chorus was almost entirely dispensed with. The aria acquired a three-part form in which the opening section was followed by a contrasting one and was then repeated. Known as the *da capo* aria, this was the dominant formal element in *opera seria*.

From the first quarter of the 18th century the artificial and often bombastic convention of *opera seria* was the target of lampoon and pastiche in the northern countries – and even in Italy itself. But despite this, and despite the rise of a new, lighter form, the *opera buffa*, the serious convention held its own both in Italy and abroad. As early as 1764 Gluck had proclaimed the reform of the *opera seria*, introducing tighter dramatic construction and reducing the preponderance of vocal virtuosity, but the taste for the art did not die a sudden death and Mozart was to write two fine examples.

The school of Naples

The emphasis on the aria was already apparent in the operas of the later 17th-century Venetian composers, but the strict demarcation between aria and recitative and the full development of *opera seria* as just described were the work of the Neapolitan school.

Opera came to Naples comparatively late, but from the 1650s Venetian and Roman operas were regularly performed there and Neapolitan composers began to evolve their own characteristic style. Two composers, while working within the new convention and doing much to shape it, produced outstanding work and avoided the worst superficialities of their successors. These were Francesco Provenzale and Alessandro Scarlatti.

Provenzale (1627–1704) is often regarded as the founder of Neapolitan opera. The thematic unity of his arias, the beauty of his melodic line, the daring of his harmonies and the genuine emotion of much of his music reveal a true musical talent. He also wrote oratorios and sacred dramas, and the annual performances of these by his pupils at the Conservatorio di Loretto encouraged the growing taste for opera at Naples. But it was undoubtedly Alessandro Scarlatti (1660–1725) who brought Italian opera to the peak of its possibilities.

Born at Palermo in Sicily, Scarlatti spent the first years of his career at Rome, serving for a time in the musical establishment of the exiled Queen Christina of Sweden. From 1684 to 1702 however, he was musical director to the court of Naples where, apart from various periods of renewed employment at Rome and also at Florence, he passed the greater part of his life. From *La Rosaura* in 1690 to *Mitridate Eupatore* in 1707, there is a steady development in the vocal music of the operas. Particularly noticeable is the progressive perfection attained by the *da capo* aria. In the operas from the 1710s to *La Griselda* in 1721, Scarlatti accorded an increasing importance to the orchestra, giving it an ever more dramatic role and in some aspects anticipating the works of Gluck. Indeed, in his latest works, Scarlatti attained a dramatic power and mastery which at times was to startle his contemporaries. Furthermore, he was disinclined to make concessions to the Italian public's obsession with the solo voice, and his later compositions enjoyed greater popularity in Germany than in Italy. Nevertheless, the works of Alessandro Scarlatti can with justice claim to be the highest achievements of 18th-century Italian lyric drama.

After Scarlatti, Italian composers paid ever less attention to the dramatic demands of the plot. The singers, given every opportunity and encouragement to display their talents, took extraordinary liberties with the texts, adding variations and improvising freely. It is all too easy to forget the extent to which such extemporisation continued in European music, and this is to be borne in mind when listening to modern literal performances of the scores.

The size of orchestras continued to grow, but the chorus intervened less and less frequently in the action. That it did not disappear altogether was due mainly to the poet Pietro Metastasio (1698–1782). In his many opera texts – for Vinci, Caldara and the German Hasse, among others – he proved himself the most talented librettist of the 18th century. He had a sure dramatic instinct and took a keen interest in the production of his works. By his insistence on giving strict directives to his composers, Metastasio helped to develop the psychological aspect of scenarios which Gluck was to make full use of.

Among Alessandro Scarlatti's successors who made distinguished contributions to *opera seria* were his son and pupil Domenico, whose operas were performed in Rome and London between 1711 and 1720; Leonardo Vinci (1690–1730), one of the first to interrupt recitatives with orchestral passages in the attempt to stress the psychological significance of the action; Antonio Caldara (1670–1736), author of more than 80 operas and serenades and 30 oratorios, distinguished for their fluent melody and highly esteemed in Vienna and Germany; and Leonardo Leo (1694–1744) a pupil of Provenzale and renowned for his church compositions and comic operas. His pupil Niccolò Jommelli (1714–74) made moves to reinstate the chorus, and other reforms. He also introduced to Italian music the subtle and expressive style of orchestral writing of the school of Mannheim, a style he had become familiar with during his fifteen-year period at Stuttgart. Tommaso Traetta (1727–79), a pupil of Durante whose dramatic instinct was outstanding, developed a style which was among the most important contributions by an Italian to the reform of the *opera seria*.

Finally in this brief summary of the Italian composers of *opera seria*, two names are of special interest. These are Nicola Porpora and Niccolò Piccini. Porpora (1686–1768) spent much of his working life in Naples, but also held numerous appointments abroad. These included three years in London (1736–39), and a period in Vienna where the young Haydn was for a time his pupil. It is indeed as a teacher that Porpora is now best remembered. His pupils included the renowned singers Cafarelli and Farinelli, the German composer Hasse

An artist's impression of the great teacher Porpora (centre) among a group of pupils.

and many others. In their virtuoso arias, Porpora's operas betray the inclinations of an outstanding singing teacher, and they did not outlast their vogue. With Piccini (1728-1800) however, we come to a great musical talent. Born in southern Italy, he, like so many of his contemporaries, passed much of his career in northern Europe and during his long stay in Paris (1776-89) became the unwilling centre of a faction opposed to Gluck's opera reforms. But his first success had been at Rome in 1760, with the production of his comic opera *La Buona figliuola*, based on Richardson's novel *Pamela*. Both the charm and the elegance of his music, as well as the subtlety of his orchestration, justified the composer's fame, and his personal admiration for Gluck was to be reflected in his later work.

Opera buffa

In the first two decades of the 18th century, the serious and artificial form of *opera seria* gave birth to a new, gayer and more light-hearted entertainment. At an early date a custom arose of introducing two comic interludes between the three traditional acts of the opera. Almost as soon as the idea of these interval pieces took shape, attempts were made to give the two new isolated acts a common continuous plot.

As opposed to the historical or mythological characters portrayed in serious opera, *opera buffa* portrays the man in the street – labourers, artisans, business men and so on. Instead of sumptuous palaces and temples, we are shown the humble dwellings of the poor; in place of grave and solemn declamation, the dialogue is vivid and high-spirited. As for the actual production, nothing could be more modest. While serious opera demanded a whole troupe of performers, *opera buffa* was content sometimes with no more than a bass, a female singer and perhaps an occasional mime.

Leo, Vinci, Piccini and Jommelli all wrote spirited *opere buffe* full of verve, while Niccolò Logroscino (1698-1767) was known in his time as 'The god of the Opera Buffa'. The great masters of the 18th century, however, were Giovanni Battista Pergolesi (1710-36),

Baldassare Galuppi, Giovanni Paisiello and Domenico Cimarosa.

In 1732 Pergolesi displayed his gift for comedy and had a triumphant success with *Lo Frato'n amorato*, the Neapolitan dialect libretto of which gave him the opportunity to depict popular manners and characters with grace and humour. Three years later he returned to dialect comedy with *Il Flaminio*. But among his many delightful masterpieces, pride of place must be given to *La Serva Padrona* (1733), which was to have such a strong influence on the origins and development of French *opéra-comique* after its first production in Paris in August 1752. He is also remembered for his setting of the Stabat Mater for female voices.

Baldassare Galuppi (1706-85) composed seventy-two serious operas and forty *opere buffe*, for which most of the libretti were supplied by the great playwright Goldoni. Galuppi, however, was most at home with comedy, although on occasion he showed a strong feeling for the theatre and could handle large choruses; the writing of some of his operatic finales is indeed often remarkably ingenious and grandiose in its effect. Paisiello (1740-1816) composed more than a hundred works for the theatre. The richness of his invention is legendary, for he wrote as many as four *opere buffe* a year. His works are pervaded with a delicate humour and his ensembles reveal a supple and detailed technique. The wit of his *Barbiere di Siviglia* (1782) so enchanted Rossini that he more or less took over the libretto in 1816 to compose his own version of the opera. Contemporaries were disgusted by the presumption of the young newcomer in attempting to rival the great Paisiello, and Rossini's *Barber* established itself only after some disastrous early performances.

Among the eighty or so works of Paisiello's rivals, one must single out *Il Matrimonio Segreto* composed by Cimarosa (1749-1801) during his brief stay in Vienna and based on *The Clandestine Marriage* by Colman and Garrick. Following the one hundred consecutive performances (when the opera was performed in Naples in 1793), it has continued to enjoy success up to our own day. Stendhal boasted of having heard 'this masterpiece of wit, elegance and refinement' more than a hundred times, and described it as 'a work which can be compared with Mozart'.

right
The orchestra was usually conducted by the composer from the harpsichord at this time. In this later artist's impression the famous comic opera composer Paisiello is depicted.

below
The brilliant young Giovanni Battista Pergolesi.

In the first years of the 19th century the era of the old *opera buffa* came to a close. But as the genre had spread across Europe, it contributed to the evolution of new musical forms, particularly that of the French *opéra-comique*, and it also had a discernible influence on certain forms of the German *Singspiel*.

Religious music

During the 18th century, opera after the style of Naples dominated the Italian musical scene. Of course at Naples itself, composers wrote much else besides opera. Leo wrote many masses, oratorios and motets, while another pupil of the great Alessandro Scarlatti, Francesco Durante (1684-1755), wrote religious music of considerable polyphonic complexity. Outside Naples, the main musical centres continued to maintain a separate identity, especially in the field of religious music.

Rome remained an important centre of music worthy of its great past. In their concern to maintain the fame of the Roman school, even while making innovations, her composers remained faithful to the principles of the Palestrinian tradition. Giuseppe Pitoni (1675-1743), Pasquale Pisari (1725-78), and Giuseppe Jannaconi (1741-1816) at St Peter's, and Giovanni Battista Casali (1715-92) at St John Lateran continued to use a scholarly counterpoint which affirmed the polyphonic structures of their grandiose vocal compositions.

At Bologna the fame and authority of Fr Giambattista Martini (1706-84), whose foreign pupils included Johann Christian Bach and Mozart, assured the city's continuing status as an international centre of the Italian style. The majority of central European musicians made pilgrimages to this ecclesiastical master, whose enthusiasm, science and erudition had considerable influence. The fame of Martini at Bologna was rivalled at Padua by that of Fr Francesco Antonio Vallotti (1697-1780), reckoned one of the greatest composers of church music of his day. He applied in his compositions the theory of intervals and dissonances that he propounded in his *On the theory and practice of modern music* (1779), and also taught these principles to his pupils, notably to the future Abbé Vogler and Luigi Antonio Sabbatini (1739-1809), whose didactic works long held a place of authority.

The proud traditions of the Venetian school were upheld by Agostini Steffani (1654-1728) who, thanks to his many musical and diplomatic appointments, greatly contributed to the spread of Italian music in Germany. He divided his activities between the theatre, instrumental music, and religious compositions; his symbolic interpretation of texts, his power of expression and melodic quality assure him of an honoured place among composers. The same may be said of Antonio Caldara (1670-1736), a member of the chapel of St Mark's, where he was singer and cellist. His thirty-one oratorios, masses and motets remain to this day in the repertoire of the churches of Austria, Bavaria and Switzerland.

However, the greatest Venetian composer of church music of the first half of the 18th century was probably Antonio Lotti (1667-1740), who was *maestro di cappella* at St Mark's for the last four years of his life. He practised all branches of composition and his works reveal a complete mastery of the arts of counterpoint and an inspired melodic gift. His immense talents put him in the first rank of contemporary composers, above all of religious music, and the many singers and composers whom he trained are a proof both of his value as a teacher and of the vitality of the Venetian school. The most important of his pupils are Benedetto Marcello and

Baldassare Galuppi, whose theatrical works have already been referred to. Styled the 'Prince of Music' by his contemporaries, Benedetto Marcello taught many talented pupils. He was known, above all, for his setting of an Italian paraphrase of the first fifty psalms *Estro poetico-armonico* (1724-27) and for his satirical work the *Teatro alla moda* (1721). This, under the pretence of offering advice to would-be opera composers, attacked with superb irony the symptoms of decadence already apparent. As for Galuppi, his modern leanings did not go so far as to permit him to abandon the Palestrinian style in his religious compositions, but his cosmopolitan training enriched his language and his notions of form. With justice he is often classed as one of the immediate precursors of the classical sonata for harpsichord, and the dramatic unity that he brought to his opera finales was in tune with the newest ideas in this field.

All these composers wrote religious music, some even concentrated on it, yet it may be said that, in almost every case, their sense of the theatre was greater than their depth of feeling, and their dramatic works are much superior to their religious compositions.

above
Pergolesi's manuscript of a page of the Salve Regina, *one of his last compositions.*

left
Padre Martini, the respected composer and teacher; Mozart was among those who took lessons from him.

right
Muzio Clementi, who spent much of his career in London.

below right
Luigi Cherubini, a distinguished composer and theoretician who worked mainly in Paris. He was admired by Beethoven.

The evolution of style and forms in sacred music

The mass, the motet and the psalm on the one hand, the cantata and the oratorio on the other, evolved quite rapidly during this period. The spirit of the vast polyphonic structures of the past still lived on in certain works, notably in the use of different vocal groups, the variable number of which often exceeded the traditional double choir of the Venetian school. It was thus that Pitoni wrote masses and psalms for twelve or sixteen parts, divided into three or four choirs, and he also composed motets for twenty-four or thirty-six parts, scored for six or nine choruses. But, alongside these exceptional works, compositions for three, four or five parts remained in vogue; however, one may observe that the work of some composers who sought variations in the number of parts exhibits an over-preoccupation with form.

The continuo, with or without supplementary instruments, generally took the place of an accompaniment, but the development of works with recitatives, arias and choruses quite soon necessitated a fuller use of the orchestra. Nevertheless, until the end of the 18th century, the Palestrinian *a cappella* style retained its high reputation and there was hardly a composer who did not write at least one or more works faithful to the old

traditional style. The oratorio, the Passion and the sacred history continued the trend set in the 17th century, using the declamatory style of the theatre and assuming an operatic form. Instrumental music played an increasingly greater role and the importance of the overture and introductions to the arias, as well as the symphonic density of the accompaniment, became more and more characteristic. Italian church music was, at the end of the 18th century, on the brink of complete decadence. Devoid of all spiritual substance it now appeared, in relation to the text which it clothed, like a sumptuous vestment beneath which one could seek in vain for sincerity or feeling.

Italian composers abroad

During the 17th and 18th centuries, Italy made handsome repayment for the immense debt which it had incurred from northern Europe during the Renaissance. In the 17th century, the styles of Italian music were spread throughout Europe by northern composers who went to study in Italy itself. In the 18th century, there was what amounted to a mass migration of the Italians themselves. Some of these composers passed the greater part of their creative careers abroad and for this reason a number of them deserve special treatment.

In 1737, Giuseppe Sammartini (1693–*c.* 1770), who had by that time been in London about ten years, published there his *Dueti per flauti* and his *Sonate a tre*; in these he partially dispensed with the use of the continuo. Sammartini, who crowned a successful career in England as director of music to the Prince of Wales, was also a talented oboist and greatly esteemed as a concert player. Felice di Giardini (1716–96) was praised as a virtuoso violinist on his triumphal tours through Europe before settling first in London, and then in Russia. His enormous instrumental output happily combines the expressive dynamism of the Mannheim school with the charm of the *style galant*.

Francesco Geminiani (*c.* 1685–1762) settled in London in 1714, where he contributed immensely to the development of English violin technique. Of his seven treatises on theory, the most important is undoubtedly *The Art of Playing on the Violin*, first published in about 1740. His concerti grossi based on Corelli's violin works show a fine feeling for orchestration and instrumental colour, while his twelve violin sonatas, published in 1705, were of particular interest as early examples of compositions which dispensed with the continuo.

Pietro Antonio Locatelli (1695–1764) enjoyed an equal reputation in his day. He settled in Amsterdam in 1720 and was one of the boldest innovators in violin technique. The virtuosity of his *Caprices* was classed by his contemporaries, not slow to criticise his audacity, as extravagant. His concertos and sonatas, grandiose in inspiration and noble in construction, are rich in poetry, melody and dramatic feeling.

Giovanni Giuseppe Cambini (1746–1825), pupil of Fr Martini, settled in Paris in 1770, where he achieved success with his works for the theatre. However, it is as the composer of 140 quartets and sixty symphonies that Italian scholars have recently accorded him a place of importance, since they claim to see in these the last manifestations of the early Italian tradition in instrumental music.

Muzio Clementi (1752–1832), one of the most talented of these Italian exiles, came to London in 1773. A man of unusual musical culture for his time, he knew intimately the works of Bach, Handel and Domenico Scarlatti. He conquered the audiences of Europe in tours legendary for his virtuosity on the piano, in which he employed an entirely modern style of playing. In Vienna in 1781 he was declared victor in a piano competition with Mozart himself. In London, Clementi was active not only as a composer and teacher, numbering among his pupils J. B. Cramer and John Field, but also in the world of music publishing and piano building. As a publisher, he produced the English editions of many of Beethoven's works following his meeting with the German composer in Vienna in 1807. As a piano builder he introduced many important improvements. But Clementi's many-sided activities have sometimes obscured his gifts as a composer. His works include 106 piano sonatas, which Beethoven greatly admired, as well as manuals of instruction (famous among them the *Gradus ad Parnassum*), while his orchestral music included a number of large-scale symphonies. Only six of these have survived, yet, contemporary with Beethoven's ninth symphony they mark a high point in the history of Italian instrumental music.

With Luigi Cherubini (1760–1842) we enter the 19th century, and his career will be dealt with more fully in another chapter. But it was in 1788 that he settled in Paris, and his instrumental works – a symphony, six string quartets, a quintet, six sonatas for piano – belong to the great evolutionary tradition we have traced here, while holding the promise, in language, expression, and compositional refinement, of the approaching Romanticism of the 19th century.

We have described the outstanding contribution made to piano music by the London Italian, Clementi, but in the field of ensemble music he was far outstripped by Luigi Boccherini, who died in Madrid in 1805. Born in Lucca in 1743 into a family of musicians, Boccherini studied the cello under his father. At thirteen he was sent to Rome, while a journey to Milan to visit Sammartini, and three stays in Vienna, all before the age of twenty-one, put the seal on his reputation as a virtuoso and saw his debut as a composer – six quartets with obbligato parts were published in 1760. After a fruitless

attempt to establish himself in his native town, he led the wandering life of a virtuoso until he settled in Spain in 1769. Here he worked for various patrons, but, in the unsettled conditions of that country during the Napoleonic wars, he failed to gain lasting or secure employment and died in Madrid in 1805 in great hardship.

Apart from his celebrated minuet, the name of Boccherini fell into oblivion until comparatively recently, but now the riches of his chamber music are becoming known to an ever growing public. To his contemporaries, Boccherini, in 1760, was first and foremost a virtuoso cellist who had assimilated the technical innovations of the violin school of Corelli and Tartini and had developed and applied them to the cello. In 1765, he formed a quartet in Milan, together with Nardini, Manfordi and Cambini. Boccherini's influence was two-fold; on virtuosi like the Duport brothers, Romberg and Viotti, and on the composition of chamber music by writing obbligato parts for each instrument. He himself wrote an enormous amount of chamber music: twenty-seven sonatas for cello and six for piano and violin; forty-two trios; ninety-seven quartets; 176 quintets (113 for two cellos), and seven nocturnes for wind ensembles.

Already possessing the Italian birthright of elegance and brio, the youthful Boccherini discovered the music of Germany and Austria; in Mannheim he learnt the reforms of Stamitz, in Vienna he found the first indications of *Sturm und Drang*. His work acquired a truly Romantic lyricism and passion which earned it the epithet of bizarre, while its composer was described by a contemporary as 'a writer infatuated with strange and complicated modulations'. His further discovery of Spanish music with its 'Andalusian' peculiarities of key ornamentation, borrowed from guitar technique, and dance rhythms such as fandangos and sequidillas, brought other new elements, not always completely assimilated, to Boccherini's compositions. The result is a highly personal idiom which won the admiration of Gluck, and to some extent influenced Mozart and Haydn.

An open-air concert. Violins predominate but note the bass shawms to the right and the horns (being held as in the hunting field) to the left.

Vendesi da Giovanni Chiari Libraio nella Condotta in Firenze

Handel and music in England

The exhaustion of the native English talent for music during the 18th century is one of the great mysteries of musical history. Undoubtedly there was a falling off in the number of good composers after the death of John Blow, and in the two and a half centuries of glorious achievement from Dunstable to Purcell there had been momentary lapses of inspiration. But what was it that made the decades after 1700 so catastrophic?

It is possible to point to many causes. Like the rest of Europe, England was inundated by the incursion of Italian musicians and their music, and by the passion for opera. But England was particularly badly prepared for such an invasion. The years of the Restoration monarchy had set a fashion for things foreign which was crushingly reinforced, especially in music, by the accession of the German house of Hanover. Furthermore, while in Germany the numerous courts and self-governing cities offered many centres of patronage, each with strong native traditions, and while the French had a strong, if sometimes oppressive, machinery of royal patronage, England had only one centre of any importance – namely London – and virtually no system of patronage whatsoever. Again we may point to the lack of any great teaching institutions like the ones from which the Italians were able to launch their assault on Europe. Perhaps most telling of all, the English never came to terms with the opera. In an age when religious music was everywhere an offshoot of the predominant secular style, the wealth of good music produced for English cathedrals in the 17th century appears almost as an irrelevance in terms of general musical history. Finally, of course, no sooner had the vogue for Italian opera lost something of its force than the English composers had to contend with the overpowering tradition of the Handel oratorio.

However, although her composers produced few great works, the musical life of England was an active one throughout the century. The number of public concerts increased and in 1710 the Academy of Ancient Music was founded, which performed the masterpieces of composers of the 16th century, both English and foreign. In 1741 the Madrigal Society was founded, originally for the performance by working men of the works of the English madrigal school. From 1724 the reconstituted Three Choirs Festival of the cathedrals of Worcester, Gloucester and Hereford began a tradition of concerts which stretches down to the present day, and which inspired imitators, most important of which was the Birmingham triennial festival, founded in 1764.

It seems as if, exhausted by two centuries of intense creative effort, England now turned more and more towards its glorious past, and admirable editions (in particular the vast anthology of *Cathedral Music* compiled by Boyce) made the masterpieces of the golden age accessible once again. It was also this period that saw the birth of English musicology, so active to this day, with the publication of two monumental works: *The General History of Music* in five volumes (1776), by Sir John Hawkins (1719-89) and the great *History of Music* (1776-89) by Dr Charles Burney (1726-1814), whose judgment perhaps should be accepted with reserve when he pronounces an opinion on composers of the past, but who is a mine of information concerning his contemporaries.

Finally, this picture of musical life in 18th-century England would be incomplete without mentioning the innumerable clubs where gentlemen of the time gathered to sing catches and glees. The earliest of these clubs was the Hibernian Catch Club founded in Dublin in 1680, while the Gentleman's Catch Club of London, which was to number the Prince Regent among its members, was founded in 1761.

In the first decades of the 18th century Italian opera ruled supreme, and Giovanni Battista Bononcini, a rival with Handel for public favour, made the Neapolitan style familiar to Londoners. Stifled by this foreign invasion English composers also attempted, with mediocre success, to adopt the Italian style both for the stage and for the concert hall, where foreign domination was just as strong. One of the most illustrious disciples of Corelli, the great violinist-composer Francesco Geminiani, arrived in England four years after Handel and made a brilliant career for himself. Nevertheless it was Handel who dominated the musical life of England in the first half of the century.

Handel

The family of Handel was of Silesian origin. Georg, the father of the composer, was a distinguished physician in Halle and at the court of Saxe Weissenfels, where he numbered many of the court musicians among his acquaintances. When already over sixty he married for the second time and his second son by this marriage, Georg Friedrich, was born in 1685.

At a very early age the child showed extraordinary musical gifts which his father categorically refused to encourage, intending his son for the legal profession. However, on one occasion, on a visit to the court at Weissenfels when Georg Friedrich was only seven, he dared to try out the organ in the presence of the duke and his *Kapellmeister* Johann Philipp Krieger, both of whom urged the father to give his son a musical training. On returning to Halle, Georg Handel placed his young prodigy in the municipal school in order to pursue regular studies, but also arranged for him to have harpsichord lessons. The young Handel was fortunate in his teacher, F. W. Zachow, whom the contemporary musical historian Mattheson described as 'as benevolent as he was talented'. Recognising the outstanding gifts of his young pupil, he gave him an excellent grounding in the technique of keyboard instruments, the arts of counterpoint, of composition and instrumentation. He led him through a comparative analysis of German and Italian cantatas and sonatas, and a manuscript notebook dated 1698, which Handel kept all his life, contains the copies he made of the works of such masters as Kerll, Froberger and Alberti.

Although his father died in February 1697, Handel continued his legal studies and entered the university in February 1702. In March he was appointed temporary organist of the cathedral, where he had the use of an excellent instrument of twenty-six registers. Increasingly aware of his musical powers, Handel involved himself in the musical life of Halle.

Yet despite his wide circle of friends, among them Telemann, and his success as a composer and a virtuoso of the organ and oboe, Handel still cherished the ambition to go to Hamburg. Finally abandoning his legal studies, he left Halle for Hamburg in March 1703. Passing through Hanover he made the acquaintance of the Italian Agostino Steffani, who was later to be instrumental in his returning to work there.

In Hamburg he got work as a violinist in the opera orchestra. In 1705, Handel produced two German operas with Italian interludes, with great success. But things were going badly at the theatre and the young composer went to seek his fortune in Italy in 1706, producing his opera *Rodrigo* at Florence. He travelled to the main centres, visiting Rome, Naples and Venice, where he met Lotti and Marcello; he frequented courts and academies, looking and listening to all he could, composing much instrumental work, Latin psalms, cantatas, and making himself a considerable reputation as a keyboard virtuoso.

After the immense success which his opera *Agrippina* enjoyed in Venice in 1709, Handel seems to have considered a visit to Paris, the great musical centre of northern Europe. But he finally accepted the post of *Kapellmeister* at the court of Hanover. However, as soon as possible, he obtained leave to go to London to put on an opera. Arriving in England in December 1710, Handel wrote, in fifteen days, *Rinaldo*, an Italian opera which was warmly received. Its success continued and Handel was granted a second leave of absence from Hanover. As soon as he arrived, Handel put on his *Pastor Fido* and, by order of Queen Anne, composed his magnificent Te Deum to celebrate the Treaty of Utrecht. He gave no more thought to the court of Hanover and led the tranquil life of an artist *grand seigneur* in the household of Lord Burlington until the queen died suddenly in August 1714. George, Elector of Hanover, was proclaimed king of England with the title of George I and arrived in London for his coronation. At first Handel was out of favour but was soon restored with the success of *Amadigi*, and later when, in July 1716, the king paid a visit to Hanover, Handel was invited to accompany him. It was about this time that the Saxon composer took out papers of naturalisation as an English subject, and adopted the anglicised version of his name, George Frederick Handel. Then, for three years from 1717, he directed the private chapel of the duke of Chandos. It was now that he reached his most mature style, testing himself in all branches of composition.

From these happy years date the Chandos Anthems, three Te Deums, *Acis and Galatea*, the first version of the oratorio *Esther*, and the eight suites for harpsichord. In 1720 a society of wealthy amateurs founded a Royal Academy of Music for the performance of Italian opera at the Haymarket Theatre. The intrigues and the rivalries between actors and actresses ended in the dispersal of the troupe after the season of 1728. In the midst of worries and fatigue, Handel found time to write the four anthems for the coronation of George II in 1727; they include *Zadok the Priest*, performed at every English coronation since.

After the collapse of the Academy, Handel joined

left
Portrait of the young Handel by a contemporary German miniaturist.

below
Oratorio was to dominate the English musical scene as the 18th century progressed; here we have Hogarth's view both of it and of the state of cathedral music.

year, harassed by cabals, dogged by bankruptcy and three times struck down by illness. For twenty years he struggled as impresario and composer to impose Italian opera on a largely hostile public which had been only too diverted by the irreverent spoof represented by the *Beggar's Opera*. During these years Handel had produced two oratorios, *Esther* and *Deborah*, and in 1741 he returned decisively to this new form. Having completed the *Messiah*, he journeyed to Dublin, where the first hearing of the masterpiece was given in April 1742. Returning to London, he found himself the victim of hostility for four years, but the solemn *Occasional Oratorio* (1746), written 'to encourage the English resistance' to the Stuarts, and *Judas Maccabaeus*, composed in 1747 to celebrate the Battle of Culloden, assured the triumph of the Saxon master in Great Britain.

The following year he found himself threatened by blindness. Painfully he finished the last act of *Jephtha* and then submitted to three operations for cataract. Becoming blind, he did little composing and passed the last seven years of his life in solitude and contemplation. Occasionally he attended performances of his oratorios and during the intervals would play one of his organ concertos.

On 6th April 1759, he played the harpsichord at a performance of the *Messiah*. It was his last effort. Returning home, he took to his bed; in his final illness he said, 'I wish I may die on Good Friday, in the hope of meeting my dear Lord and Saviour on the day of His Resurrection'. He died on Saturday 14th April, and was buried in Westminster Abbey, in Poets Corner.

The works of Handel

Handel began his career, like so many of his contemporaries, as a composer of Italian opera. In this he not only achieved great success but also produced much fine music. Although he did not react against the conventions of the art, he sought to introduce greater variety by his use of choruses and instrumental interludes. But apart from their purely musical qualities, his operas have real dramatic attributes and reveal his psychological perception; beneath the marvellous and grandiose names of mythology, Handel reveals convincingly human heroes. The revival of Handelian operas, which began in Germany in the 1920s, has continued up to the 1960s and has made headway in England; among the best known are *Rinaldo* (1711), *Admeto* (1727), *Berenice* (1737) and *Serse* (1738). His strictly religious music includes a number of choral anthems whose style reveals French influence and that of Purcell; the great Te Deums such as that for the Treaty of Utrecht and also the one for the victory of Dettingen in 1743, in which Handel makes brilliant use of contrasting colours; the Chandos Anthems and the coronation anthems.

But it is of course for his oratorios that Handel is so very famous in England. In these we find the same variety of inspiration as in the operas. Half of the oratorios are on secular themes, but it is the religious ones, inspired by the deep faith of their composer and conceived on the grand scale, that revolutionised English musical life. Originally performed during Lent when the theatres were closed by law, the oratorios soon grew to be something more than substitute opera, becoming a major feature of the English musical scene and launching a tradition of choral singing that inspired Haydn and impressed Berlioz. In their structure the oratorios closely follow the pattern of Italian opera, using recitatives, arias and dramatic scenes in much the same way. But in the oratorios Handel gave a much greater importance to the chorus, and it is in these mighty choral ensembles that

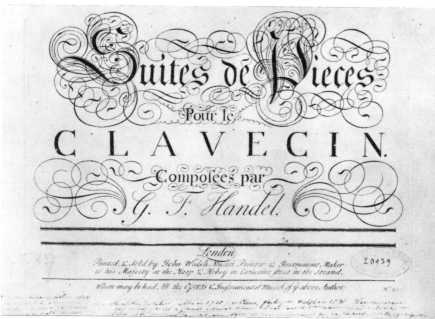

top
Performance of an oratorio; possibly it is Handel conducting. Note that the cello is rested on a small table to increase its resonance and the double bass is being played pizzicato.

above
Title page of a set of Handel's suites for harpsichord.

forces with the manager, Heidegger, in order to make use of the theatre, and left for Italy to recruit the finest singers he could find. He was in Venice when he learned that his mother, already blind, had been struck with paralysis. He hurried to Halle. There he received a visit from Wilhelm Bach who, on behalf of his father, invited him to spend a few days in Leipzig, but Handel declined the invitation; after a year's absence it was time to return to London and take up once more the fight for public acceptance of Italian opera.

He plunged into the battle against the rival 'Opera of the Nobility' sponsored by the Prince of Wales and directed by Bononcini, writing two or three operas a

Plate 30
The spectacular splendours of Italian opera in its heyday are fully displayed in this 18th-century painting.

Plate 31
Joseph Haydn.

he produced his greatest music. Of the many religious oratorios, among the greatest are *Saul* (1739), *Israel in Egypt* (1739), *Judas Maccabaeus* (1747) and *Jephtha* (1752). The *Messiah*, which stands alone, is remarkable in many respects, and not least for the fact that it was written in three weeks. At its first performance in Dublin in 1742 it was received with instant acclaim, but its success in London was much slower. Beethoven said of Handel that he of all composers knew best how to achieve grand effects with simple means, while Haydn quite simply called him 'the master of us all'. The *Messiah*, which inspired these comments, also in part explains them. The secret of Handel's magic may be the unique blend which he achieved between the grace of French music, the harmonic intensity of Italian, and the polyphony of north Germany. Among Handel's secular choral works we should mention the *St Cecilia Ode*, *Alexander's Feast*, and *L'Allegro, il Penseroso ed il Moderato*. This third work was based on a text derived from Milton and adapted by Handel's respected friend and librettist Charles Jennens. He had been largely responsible for the book of the *Messiah*, and Handel recognised a deep debt to him and consulted him on both musical and textual matters. As an instrumental composer Handel wrote the overtures and interludes to his stage works and much else besides, notably concertos for organ, suites, fugues and sonatas for harpsichord, violin sonatas and the orchestral suites *The Water Music* (1715) and *Music for the Royal Fireworks* (1749). Some of his noblest compositions for instruments are the twelve stately concerti grossi, published in 1739.

left
The classic portrait of Handel in his prime by the English painter Thomas Hudson.

below
The irreverence of The Beggar's Opera *made it the rage, but this caricaturist was appalled by its 'vulgarity'. The debasement of public taste is illustrated by the elegantly dressed musicians playing the instruments of the mountebank, such as the stick and bladder; under the stage the lute and lyre pine away while Harmony flies to the refuge of the 'legit' theatre. The noise of the singers is like the braying of animals.*

The ballad opera

The most original work in English music during the 18th century was the famous *Beggar's Opera*, with a biting libretto by John Gay (1685-1732), which was a tremendous success at Covent Garden. This violent social satire transposed the insipid Italian pastorale to the criminal underworld of London, and drew the harsh but permanently valid moral that the rich have all the vices of the poor, but that the poor alone are punished for them. Brought up to date by Bertold Brecht and Kurt Weill two centuries later in their *Die Dreigroschenoper* ('The Threepenny Opera'), and more than once made into a film, the scenario of the *Beggar's Opera*, depicting immortal types like Macheath and Polly Peachum, has lost none of its punch. The music contributed greatly to it success, and in reaction to grand opera, Gay chose sixty-nine songs. For the most part they were popular English, Scottish, Irish and Welsh airs, but they included derisive parodies of arias from popular operas, or airs by the divine Purcell and – sacrilege! – by the great Handel himself. Gay engaged a composer of German origin, John Pepusch, to 'mix the sauce', orchestrate the songs, and write the overture. The success of the *Beggar's Opera* led immediately to a flood of ballad operas based on popular songs and ballads (more than a hundred and twenty were produced in the following decade). But although faithful to national traditions, this form of musical entertainment was limited as much by its very nature as by the mediocre talents of the composers.

Such men as Charles Dibdin (1745-1814) and William Shield (1748-1829) were only slight talents who were soon to be forgotten. Dibdin, who based his musical career on the training (such as it was) received as a chorister, won great popularity with songs and 'table entertainments'. He composed well over a hundred ballad operas, for many of which he also wrote the words, and he also wrote a history of music. Stephen Storace (1763-96), half Italian by birth, was of a higher calibre

and, after studying in Italy, won a certain success with the production of operas in Vienna. Here he met Mozart, with whom he and his sister became friends – Nancy Storace was a fine coloratura soprano and was the original Susanna in *The Marriage of Figaro*. Storace wrote many stage works after his return to London, among them *No song, No supper* (1790) and *The Cherokee* (1794). They indicated potentialities which might have developed into real achievement had it not been for his early death.

English composers

Under the oppressive shadow of Handel the not inconsiderable talent of men such as Croft, Greene and Roseingrave put out only tender shoots.

William Croft (1678-1727), successor to Blow at the organ of Westminster Abbey, master of the children of the Chapel Royal, and composer, wrote, apart from a number of violin sonatas, predominantly religious music. The bulk of his more important work is in two collections, *Cathedral Music* containing thirty anthems and a funeral service still used, and *Musica Sacra* (1724) containing anthems for from two to eight voices. Among his best work is 'Hear my prayer O Lord' for six solo voices and a choir in five parts. In the English tradition, Croft makes poignant use of dissonance to express the sufferings of the sinner.

Croft's successor at the Chapel Royal was Maurice Greene (1695-1755), who from 1735 was also Master of the King's Musick. A prominent figure in English musical life, Greene was a founder member of the Royal Society of Musicians in 1738. He was also a close friend and admirer of Handel's, although the two were to fall out over Greene's friendship with Handel's rival, Bononcini. His compositions include *Forty Select Anthems* – among which are the beautiful 'Lord, let me know mine end' – three oratorios, and a *St Cecilia Ode* (1730). It was he

Dr William Boyce, perhaps the major native English composer of the 18th century.

who began the collection of English church music which was to provide the foundation for William Boyce's *Cathedral Music*. Greene also wrote a certain amount of secular music including *A Collection of Lessons for the Harpsichord* (1750), as well as catches and glees.

One of the most interesting figures in early 18th-century English music is Thomas Roseingrave (1690-1766). In Italy from 1710, he became a friend of Domenico Scarlatti, whose music made a deep impression on him. After his return to England he published a collection of Scarlatti's sonatas which aroused much interest; Arne, Boyce, Pepusch, Stanley and Greene were among the original subscribers, while another English composer published an arrangement of twelve of the sonatas as concerti grossi. The English vogue for Scarlatti seems to have been considerable and led Burney to refer to the 'Scarlatti sect'. Roseingrave's own keyboard compositions, *Fifteen Voluntaries and Fugues* (1730) and *Six Double Fugues* (1750), reveal a highly individual talent in which his experience in Italy is combined with a characteristically English delight in chromaticism and dissonance.

The second generation of English 18th-century composers was made up of somewhat stronger personalities who withstood foreign influence better than their older contemporaries. Thomas Augustine Arne (1710-78) enjoyed considerable fame during his lifetime for his operas, of which he wrote thirty, and for his incidental music to Shakespeare, of which songs such as 'Where the bee sucks' are well known. Arne's talent was for fresh, delightful melody, but his music is not distinguished by its originality. He is of course best remembered today for one song, 'Rule Britannia!' which in its original version appeared in Arne's masque, *Alfred*, performed at Cliveden in 1740.

In a century which produced little in the way of original English musical talent, the instrumental music of William Boyce (1710-79) deserves special mention. He was successively composer and then organist to the Chapel Royal. At the early age of twenty-seven he undertook the musical direction of the Three Choirs Festival and from 1755 he was Master of the King's Musick. Boyce's three-volume *Cathedral Music* (1760-72) was a treasury of the greatness of England's past, and he himself composed a number of anthems and oratorios in addition to much stage music. But it is the twelve trio sonatas, second in popularity only to those of Corelli during their day, and above all the eight symphonies, that contain Boyce's finest music. The influence of Handel is apparent, but the strong and vigorous music contains a number of purely English traits.

In form the symphonies belong to the pre-classical period of the Mannheim school and some seem to have originally been stage overtures. In some cases Boyce opens with a French overture, in others he adopts the tripartite form, fast-slow-fast, of the Scarlatti *sinfonia*.

The organist John Stanley (1713-86), blind from the age of three, was a pupil of Greene and late in life became Master of the King's Musick, as well as organist to the Chapel Royal. His work, which was commended by Handel, included oratorios and stage music, but his best work is for instruments, notably the six concertos in seven parts for string orchestra.

Foreign musicians in England

In 1762, three years after the death of Handel, the youngest son of J. S. Bach, Johann Christian (1735-82), came to England. 'Bach of Milan' was now the 'London Bach', and henceforth it was he who dominated the English scene just as Handel had done before him. Unlike Handel, however, who had fought for mastery, 'Mr John Bach' found England completely receptive and willing to be conquered afresh after a generation of foreign domination. In addition to the craze for singers, there was now a similar craze for pianists, and Johann Christian himself increased the vogue for the instrument at a memorable concert in 1767 when he played one of his own concertos. Known as a composer of symphonies and chamber music, Johann Christian Bach had equal success with his Italian operas. Furthermore, in 1765, he founded with his compatriot Karl Friedrich Abel (1723-87), a virtuoso player of the bass viol and also a talented composer of symphonies, a series of subscription concerts which flourished for twenty-five years. In the cosmopolitan atmosphere of 18th-century Europe, London, in addition to such residents as Handel, Geminiani, Bach and Clementi (whose career is described in the chapter on 18th-century Italian music) had, like other great cities, a number of distinguished visitors.

In 1764 the eight-year old Mozart was on tour, while the great Haydn, in the full flood of his powers, made two visits in 1791 and 1794, when the performances of each of his twelve great London symphonies were greeted, and rightly, as major events. Thus during the 18th century England presents the aspect of a minor colony of European music. Cultivating the glories of her past and devoted to the art of spoken drama, she was content to accept the domination of foreigners in the field of music and was not to recover from this self-imposed cultural helotry for another century.

From a title page of a music tutor for 'gentlemen and ladies'.

Music in France: Lully to the death of Rameau

On the death of Mazarin in 1661, Louis XIV took the reins of power into his own hands, and there began the most remarkable episode in the history of European absolutism. Louis was to develop an ever-tightening grip on not only the political but also the cultural life of France, and his intentions were clear from the outset, even in the very specialised field of music. In 1661 he appointed Lully as Superintendent of Music and founded the Royal Academy of Dancing. Two years later he reorganised the music of the Chapel Royal and appointed four assistant musical directors. Within the next six years he gave the first great musical fête at Versailles and established the Royal Academy of Music. For almost a century, musical life in France was to be virtually state-controlled. The royal musicians were appointed, according to their particular competence, to the establishments of either the Chamber, the Chapel or the Ecurie.

The tradition of what has come to be known as the 'Music of Versailles' was maintained throughout the whole of the long reign of Louis XIV, the Regency, and during the first twenty years of Louis XV. But although the standard of music at Versailles tended to decline even before the deaths of Leclair and Rameau in 1764, in Paris, where musicians were closely associated with the philosophers and theoreticians and in touch with a new musical public through private and public concerts, it was able to develop freely.

Louis XIV himself was by no means an ordinary amateur musician. He had taken part in ballets since the age of five, he danced to the violin of Lully, and studied the guitar and the harpsichord. It was he who appointed composers like Lully, Louis Delalande and Couperin the Great. It was he who supervised and criticised the opera when necessary. He lived in a world of music. It was as much part of the ceremonial of his palace as it was of his private life. He paid the salary of the *Petits violons* out of his own privy purse, and gave orders for his victories to be celebrated with sumptuous Te Deums. Nor was he neglectful of the musical education of his children, both his legitimate and natural offspring, to whom he appointed Charpentier, Delalande and Couperin as teachers.

This profusion of royal patronage overwhelmed the taste of a society eager to display its submission to the autocrat. Even the most ephemeral successes of Ver-

Louis XIV as patron of music. Despite the importance of the Twenty-four violins in the music of the court, the artist has given the viols greater prominence; note also the fashionable musette *bagpipes.*

sailles were repeated in Paris by the Royal Academy. Music lovers, bourgeois and aristocrat alike, were quick to learn that such and such a piece had met with the king's approval on its first hearing at Versailles, and flocked to see it.

Musical institutions

The origins of the Chapel Royal date back to the very beginnings of the monarchy itself, but the Ecurie and the Chamber were not founded until the 16th century. The Academy, Louis XIV's own creation, in so far as it divided its activities between Versailles and Paris, was, nevertheless, less subject to royal authority than the other three. Under Louis XIII the Chapel Royal was restricted to only a few choristers and instrumentalists. However, Mazarin considerably increased its numbers while Louis XIV expanded the establishment still further. The musical directors received four new assistants and the choir might consist of as many as sixty to eighty choristers even including, from the late 17th century, some women and, if required, thirty instrumentalists. A certain number of players were accredited to the Chapel and these were reinforced, when necessary, by the violins of the Chamber and several instrumentalists from the Ecurie.

The musicians of the Chamber, as their name implies, were called upon to perform for the private delectation of the king, and to provide music for the ballet. The most important group of musicians of the Chamber were the famous *Vingt-quatre violons* (Twenty-four violins) under their musical director. The formation of this band of musicians dates back to the Valois, when the finest violinists of the capital were recruited to play at court balls. It seems that the original recruitment was by lot, and that the post was handed down from father to son over several generations. During the first years of Louis XIV's reign the *Vingt-quatre* were doubled by a band of much younger violinists known as the *Petits violons*, whose primary function was, it seems, to entertain the young king. Some of these were the sons of the *Vingt-quatre* and were later promoted to the official band.

Besides bowed instruments, which also comprised the whole of the viol family, the Chamber also included the plucked stringed instruments such as lutes, theorboes and guitars, the wind (oboes, flutes and recorders), a harpsichord and singers.

The third band, known as the Ecurie (which dated from the time of Francis I) performed either mounted on horseback or on foot. The musicians of the Ecurie comprised all the instruments of the violin family, oboes and bassoons, the bagpipe family, trumpet, kettledrums and even conches. All these instruments performed in processions and open-air parades, either in part or altogether. The Chamber and the Ecurie were employed in two capacities. They were engaged to play either in concerts (to which the audience was required to listen in silence before applauding) or on ceremonial occasions, when they would play individually or in groups of the same family of instruments to announce, say, the entrance of the king, the serving of each course at a royal banquet, or the arrival of ambassadors.

The last institution, the Royal Academy of Music, was founded on the lines of the Italian academies. It comprised not only some of the best soloists of the age, but also some of the best dancers (the very best were enrolled in the Royal Academy of Dancing), as well as some of the instrumentalists and singers from the other establishments. There were also a number of musicians independent of the royal institutions, and after the death of Louis XIV the Academy grew to such an extent that it

was able to recruit its own personnel and enjoyed a much greater degree of freedom from royal control.

It seems that the state organisation of the musical institutions was not buttressed by such a carefully thought out system of training. As soon as his voice began to break, the young musician seems to have had two ways open to him. If his father was an instrumentalist, he might decide to follow in his footsteps. Otherwise he might aim to ascend by degrees to the tribune of the grand organ of the local church or cathedral, where he would be under the supervision of the organist in matters of keyboard technique and composition. In the former case, the father would apprentice his son for two to five years to a violinist of repute. The young man might lodge with his master and would learn from him the essentials of musical theory. A keyboard player would first try to find a modest position in some conventional establishment, or would act as understudy to his master at the grand organ. Later he too would earn a livelihood by giving lessons, and gather around him in his turn a group of pupils. Musical education, therefore, was largely a question of example or maxims transmitted by word of mouth.

Such a career would not be especially lucrative, but it did have certain compensations. Provided he had any talent, any young man lucky enough to join either of the royal bands of violins was bound to succeed, for the highest ambition of most musicians was to work at court. But the circle was difficult to break into, for appointments to the Chamber, Ecurie and Chapel were often bought and handed down from father to son.

The coronation of Louis XIV in the cathedral of Reims in 1654. In the foreground are the musicians: trumpeters and drummers on the left, trombones, cornetts and shawms on the right.

right
*The Florentine-born Jean Baptiste
Lully, Louis XIV's director of
music.*

far right
Michel Delalande.

Lully

Undoubtedly the greatest name in French music of the
17th century was that of the Florentine, Jean Baptiste
Lully (1632-87). He came to France as a boy and seems
to have learnt the elements of music in his country of
adoption. After the disgrace of his patroness, Mlle de
Montpensier, the niece of Louis XIII, Lully succeeded
in winning a position as one of the violinists at the court
of the young king Louis XIV. His talent for court
politics had much to do with his rise to the heights of the
French musical world, and from the outset he won the
friendship of the fourteen-year-old Louis, dancing at his
side in many ballets and enjoying an important place in
the royal household. In 1661 he was appointed superintendent of the music of the Chamber and was firmly
launched on his brilliant career. In the 1660s Lully
collaborated with Molière, providing the incidental
music to a number of his plays, among them the
Bourgeois Gentilhomme. But in 1669, after many years
of coolness, the French musical world suddenly took to
its heart opera in the Italian style. The successful entrepreneurs, the poet Perrin and his composer Cambert,
obtained the royal licence for such theatrical entertainments and seemed to have the world at their feet. Lully
was determined to control the new vogue and succeeded
not only in getting the monopoly for himself but in having
the legal proceedings instituted by his rivals quashed.
In collaboration with the pliant if not outstanding librettist Philippe Quinault, he was to produce a new lyric
drama annually until the year of his death. All these
works, which adapted the opera to the French taste, had
mythological or semi-historical themes. They opened
with an overture in the French manner, a *grave* passage
followed by a fugato section. This was followed by a
prelude in honour of Louis XIV himself and five acts in
which declamatory recitatives, choruses and arias were
interspersed with dances. Yet despite his address as a
courtier and lack of scruple as a businessman, Lully's
immense success was ultimately due to his talents as a
musician. His secret is to be found in the mastery he
showed in all the matters related to his art, as a violinist,
composer, actor, singer and dancer. Furthermore,
despite his Italian origins he had a deep feeling for
French prosody.

His music developed in a number of well-defined
stages. First comes a group of *grands ballets* rich in
dramatic scenes, such as *The Muses* of 1666; then a
number of 'musical comedies', also written in collaboration with Molière, which show affinities with the ballet.
Lully then returned to the manner of the early 17th-
century French *pastorale* with works such as *Les Amants
Magnifiques*, which was produced in 1670, the year after
the success of the opera of Perrin and Cambert. Thereafter he wrote primarily *tragédies-ballets* or lyric dramas
of which *Psyche* was the first, produced in 1671.

Lully, in the words of a contemporary, 'softened the
manner of the Italian recitative to the French taste', and
wrote arias and dialogues which transmitted the meaning
of the text with the aid of music. The composer deepened
and enriched his understanding for French prosody by
visits to the theatre, where he heard the works of Racine
declaimed by the great tragedienne Marie Champmesle.
But besides evolving a musical equivalent for the declamation of French dramatic verse in a recitative which
used musical intervals for expressive and symbolic purposes, he enhanced the stature of his scores with dramatic
choruses, vocal dialogues and trios, and employed the
orchestra dominated by the violins to full descriptive
effect.

Lully also wrote a certain amount of religious music,
but he was essentially a composer for the stage. He was
faithful to the French aesthetic which he did so much
to form and in which the dance and noble, expressive
recitative were sovereign.

Charpentier

Lully's supremacy as a theatrical composer was not to
be challenged, but in the field of religious music he was
outshone by far by his brilliant young contemporary,
Marc Antoine Charpentier (*c.* 1636-1704). He served a
number of distinguished patrons, among them the future
regent of France, and in his early sixties was appointed
to the staff of the Ste Chapelle. His output included
divertissements, overtures and interludes for the Comédie
Française, an opera *Medea* (1693) and two theoretical
treatises. But his finest achievement is his religious music,
which both by its quantity and quality assures him a
place in the forefront of French composers of his age.
He wrote more than a hundred motets, fifty-eight set-

tings of the Tenebrae for Holy Week, twelve masses, twenty-four sacred dramas and many other compositions for the church. In all his work he displays an original melodic talent, a piquant sense of harmony, a mastery of counterpoint, a refined sense of orchestration, and above all an ability to fuse the conflicting elements of drama and devotion into a whole unique in his generation. His work was of a double significance in French religious music. He took the *grand motet* which appeared settled in the form of a cantata for solo voice and orchestra, and by introducing two, three or even four soloists and contrasting choruses, gave it greater flexibility. Secondly it was Charpentier who gave to the oratorio a truly French character.

The last of the French composers to be described here who contributed to the splendours of music in the age of Louis XIV (although the last period of his career spanned the ten years of the regency) is Michel Richard Delalande (1657-1726). A Parisian by birth, he belongs to the great tradition of the French keyboard composers, and was one of the musicians who gave lessons to the children of Louis XIV. Delalande entered the Chapel Royal in 1683, and over the next forty years was both assistant director to the Chapel and superintendent of the music of the Chamber. Despite his talents as a harpsichordist and organist and the fact that his music betrays his debt to the tradition of Lully, he excelled as a composer of religious rather than secular music. Nevertheless he wrote a number of ballets and *divertissements*, as well as his *Symphonies pour les soupers du roi*, which enjoyed great popularity.

His achievement as a church composer rested not only on his immense skill as a musician, but also on a profound knowledge of the Latin language and its metrical quantities. By a dexterous variation of the rhythm of the music and the sensitive use of instrumentation, Delalande illuminated the meaning of the religious text with true insight. Accepting the cantata-motet with its sequence of separate 'numbers', he used dialogues between the vocal forces in a way similar to Charpentier. His style, which blended contrapuntal procedures reminiscent of the north German composers with the harmonic idiom of Lully, is overlaid with a delicate lyricism.

André Campra (1660-1744) was active during the last thirty years of the reign of Louis XIV and for a large part of that of Louis XV. His many appointments included service with the regent and he ended his career as director of the Chapel Royal, a post he held from 1723, and as conductor at the opera. The successor to the tradition of Lully, Charpentier and Delalande, but half Italian by birth, Campra well knew how to adapt their style to the possibly more frivolous taste of the age of Rococo and gave a greater place in his work to the light Italian *arietta*. Campra was an ordained priest and seems to have hesitated all his life between the music of the church and that of the theatre, but among his most important contributions to French music were those in the new genre of the opera ballet.

Music under the Regency and the young Louis XV

During the Regency musical life continued as vigorous as ever but music at Versailles was, temporarily, abandoned and musicians now brought new life to the salons of the royal residences in Paris. Something of the oppressive grandeur and nobility of the court of the Sun King was lost, and the lofty temple of official music was rudely shaken in 1715 when *opéras-comiques*, the parodies of grand opera, were first performed at the great annual Paris festivals. After his coronation at Reims, Louis XV once again established all the former officers of the royal musical household at Versailles, but for him music was merely an ornament, not an art to enrich the cultural life of France.

In 1725 were founded the first public concerts in France, the *Concerts spirituels*, which opened in the Tuileries with the king's consent. Indeed, whatever his shortcomings as a musical patron, Louis XV employed the great François Couperin as his court claveciniste and Rameau as composer-in-ordinary. However, although Louis XV, like his grandfather, commissioned Te Deums to be sung in all the churches of his kingdom, this was not so much from personal taste as from established custom. He seems to have shown hardly any real interest in music and then only to please his mistresses. Mme de Pompadour delighted in music and organised private concerts of her own – a fashion quickly taken up by the great town houses in Paris. But sponsored royal

This contemporary group portrait probably depicts the violinist Antoine Forqueray and the two Hotteterre brothers, flautists who redesigned the woodwind instruments.

Contemporary pencil portrait of Louis Couperin.

music was already on the decline, war necessitated economic restrictions and, towards the end of the reign of Louis XV, the four great musical institutions were forced to amalgamate.

Couperin the Great

One of the great musical dynasties of the Baroque age was that of the Couperins, and the greatest of them was François Couperin (1668-1733), who succeeded his uncle as organist at St Gervais in 1685, becoming organist at the Chapel Royal in 1693. He was one of the musicians who were charged with the musical education of the children of Louis XIV, and he was appointed claveciniste to the court of the young Louis XV. Couperin wrote a number of organ works including organ masses, distinguished by both their power and their lyricism, and vocal works, among which are three magnificent sets of Tenebrae of great poignancy. But it is nevertheless as a composer of instrumental music that Couperin achieved his finest flights. This included ten concertos entitled *The Reconciliation of the Styles* (i.e. the French and the Italian), seven trio sonatas, *The Nations*, written between 1692 and 1726, and two trios – *The Apotheosis of Corelli* (1724) and *The Apotheosis of Lully* (1725). Despite the picturesque titles of these works, the music marks a superb blend of abstract and programme music.

Himself a keyboard virtuoso, Couperin produced a treatise on harpsichord technique and four volumes of compositions for the instrument. Comprising 240 pieces in all, these are arranged in twenty-seven groups of pieces with a common tonality, which Couperin termed *ordres*. In most of these pieces the dance suite gives place to programmatic pieces – portraits of human characters, landscapes, animals and moods, though in some cases the titles, such as *Les tic toc choc*, make it somewhat difficult to identify the subject. The music derives its quality from its great melodic charm and delightfully capricious part writing. It avoids exact symmetry but in its conciseness of expression and the confident lines of its contrapuntal development it borders on perfection. The prevailing mood is of melancholy and irony heightened by a tense nervousness of rhythm.

Musical life under Louis XV

From the second half of the 17th century, when the first private concerts were beginning to be held in Paris and the provinces, professional musical life was tightly organised. Celebrated lutenists and organists invited their close associates, and soon some of the aristocracy, to visit their homes in order that they might hear a particularly beautiful voice or a virtuoso harpsichordist. These musical and social gatherings, originally organised by artists themselves, were little by little taken over by members of the nobility who, as frequenters of the court, were able to introduce the music which they had heard at Versailles to a wider public.

A little later, we find a Maecenas like the minister of state, La Pouplinière, following the same example. A passionate devotee of music, he was rich enough to maintain one of the best orchestras in Paris, which included foreign players who were the first to introduce the clarinet to France. Apart from French conductors from Paris and the provinces, such as Rameau, he also engaged the services of comparatively young foreign conductors such as Stamitz and Gossec. These private concerts may possibly have been stimulated by the young Louis XV's support for the public *Concerts spirituels*. Be that as it may, such distinguished private performances together with the *Concerts spirituels* provided a wide range of music (including motets, cantatas and oratorios), and were becoming more and more audacious in their choice of foreign works and in the increasing size of their orchestras.

The Church, too, was far from neglecting the powerful influence exercised by music. Music occupied a privileged place in both parish and collegiate churches. True, it was liturgical music, but nevertheless it was concert music as well, and there were many religious establishments that prided themselves on their modernity by engaging violinists and the finest singers of the Opera Academy to perform in their churches at a first presentation of some motet or music for Tenebrae.

Taste and styles

The music maintained by the king at Versailles and that performed at public and private concerts were developing different and distinctive styles. The three types of music in which the French were interested were the theatre, religious music and dancing; all three demanded the co-operation of singers and instrumentalists, either as soloists or in groups. Of all entertainments the *opéra-lyrique*, or music drama (an historical or mythological tragedy set to music, and including ballet) was the most popular. For audiences drawn from all ranks of society it was essential that the words of the play, although clothed in music, should be clearly understood. By developing his own style of accompanied recitative, Lully attempted to find a compromise between pure music and the declamatory speech of actors. The recitative served for narrative, dialogue or dramatic expression, while the subsequent grand aria provided a sort of meditative soliloquy which gave the audience present an opportunity to reflect on the dramatic episode just performed. The chorus (as in Greek tragedy) intervened to advise, exhort or dissuade the principal characters. At intervals in the action the spectator was entertained by the antics of buffoons or else by dances borrowed from the old court ballet. There was also a long prologue in which the king's military prowess and glory were extolled and the whole performance was preceded by an overture. This, the French overture, invariably consisted of a dignified, slow movement in 'dotted' rhythm twice repeated, which led directly into a short, quick fugato movement for strings. A trio of reed instruments and trumpets played an equally important part in the composition of the orchestra as the five string sections. Lyric dramas established on these lines persisted until after the death of Rameau.

Apart from writing lyric dramas some composers, inspired by the Baroque decor and stage machinery introduced into France from Italy by J. Torelli and the Vigarani (father and son), revived many aspects of Louis XIII's *ballet de cour* and borrowed the most spectacular features from the 'Lullyst' operas, in order to create *opéra-ballet*. Although each act was designed to give the fullest opportunities for a vocal display of arias, *ariettas* and recitatives, the most important feature was the dances, adroitly worked into the tissue of the dramatic scheme. The leading exponents of *opéra-ballet* were Campra and his successors Destouches, Montéclair and Desmarets, who were to provide Rameau with the means to instil new life into the performances given by the Royal Academy of Music.

It was during this time that fairground artists first began to parody the 'Lullyst' tragedies and his most pompous arias, and to introduce comic elements into pseudodramatic situations. After being banned for a short while, these performances were officially recognised and given the name of *opéra-comique*. Despite Rameau's attempt to revive the old traditional *comédie musicale* with his opera *Platée*, written in the early 'Lullyst' manner, *opéra-comique* continued to flourish. It was well served by Dauvergne and Duni, who, inspired by the Italian *opera buffa* which had earlier been presented in Paris, altogether abandoned stories of mythological gods in favour of sentimental bourgeois situations.

Throughout this period the recitative had become infinitely more supple and varied, while sacrificing some of its original force. The same thing happened to the aria, which now ranged from the grand aria to the *arioso*, the *da capo* aria and the short, fast *arietta*. The opera chorus was assigned either a more or less static role or, as in Rameau's *Platée*, that of a moving, colourful crowd which intervenes only momentarily in the action.

Recitatives, arias and choruses, however, were not confined only to theatrical performances; they were also the basis of a sacred style of opera or dramatic cantata, known by the French as the *grand motet*. These motets were a part of the repertoire not only of the Chapel Royal and the Chapel of the palace, but also of the cathedral of Notre Dame and the *Concerts spirituels*. They took the form of dialogues between large and small choirs, or, as in the case of Du Mont's compositions, a large choir and soloists. After Lully the form became more defined, especially in the works of Delalande, the greatest exponent of the *grand motet*. Campra's sacred arias are influenced by Italian music; Rameau's motets are outstanding for their incomparable polyphony. Apart from the *grand motet*, which continued to be performed throughout the whole of the 18th century, the Te Deum occupied a very important place in the repertoire of sacred music. It was essentially ceremonial music to be sung on special occasions. The *grands motets* were always accompanied by strings and solo wind instruments and the organ. In the time of Louis XIV these compositions had a certain spiritual quality, but later it is not unusual to find choruses written in dance rhythm.

The dance suites, so popular in France ever since the *ballets de cour* of Louis XIII, had gradually assumed a definite pattern, in which the dances were arranged alternately in contrasting or related binary form. These

Marin Marais (1656–1728), composer and violinist. He is here shown playing the bass viol 'lyra' fashion.

were suites for lute or harpsichord and even the organ, in the form of settings of semi-liturgical verses. At certain critical moments in the action, dance suites were introduced into the lyric dramas and they were of course the mainstay of the *opéra-ballet*. They were also included in the repertoire of the Chamber under the title of *Symphonies pour les soupers du roi* or *Concerts royaux*, and offered, with their lively flavour of *bourrées*, rigadoons and gigues, a sharp contrast with the slow stateliness of sarabands and minuets. French taste was for a long time completely satisfied by *allemandes* in counterpoint, gay gavottes, variations for chaconnes and *passacaglias* (to which sometimes a voice part was added), and it was not until the end of the 17th and beginning of the 18th century that composers began to adopt the form of the Italian trio sonata. The time was approaching when the science of music and technical virtuosity were of greater interest to composers than choreography – something quite new in 17th-century music.

Rameau

Born at Dijon in Burgundy in 1683, Jean Philippe Rameau was the son of an organist and began his own career on that instrument. On his father's advice he visited Italy to study but stayed there only a year, returning to France in 1702. From 1705 to 1708 he was in Paris but was not to settle there permanently for another fifteen years. During this period he worked in his home town of Dijon and then as organist at the cathedral of Clermont-Ferrand. It was here that he published his famous *Traité de l'harmonie* in 1722. Theoretical considerations of his art were to remain of primary importance to Rameau, but from the early 1730s he had another ambition – to make a name for himself in the theatre. His aim was to improve upon the forms cultivated by his predecessors, and between 1733 and 1764 he composed some thirty works which contain the choicest pieces of the French lyric theatre. They comprised all the current forms: lyric tragedies of which the first, *Hippolyte et Aricie* (1733), enjoyed an immediate success and roused the bitter opposition of the traditional followers of the style of Lully; heroic ballets such as the *Indes galantes* (1735) and comedy ballets such as *Platée* (1745). In these and other works, Rameau displayed an equal mastery of all the main types of vocal and instrumental music. His recitatives and arias are expressive and written in a rich diversity of styles. The choruses range from the picturesque to the dramatic, while the orchestra expresses fully the various aspects of this strong yet deeply felt music. In the subject matter

above
Jean-Marie Leclair (1697-1764), composer and ballet master at the French court and the court of the Netherlands.

right
Louis Nicholas Clérambault (1676-1749), one of France's outstanding organists and keyboard composers.

bottom right
André Danican Philidor (1726-95), the outstanding member of a long-lived family of French musicians; he was also a master chess player.

of his stage works he remained within the tradition of Lully, but his musical language employed a more expressive melodic line, richer harmonies and a more fully differentiated and colourful instrumentation which makes use, for example, of the clarinet and the horns, relative newcomers to the French orchestra.

As a theoretician, Rameau's aim was to find absolute natural principles on which to base the theories and practice of European harmony, believing that their secrets were to be discovered in the tones and overtones generated by the very simplest of resonating bodies. As a public controversialist Rameau had something of the acerbity and impatience of a Voltaire. He was constantly involved in argument: from the performance of *Hippolyte et Aricie*, when his own music was under attack from the Lullysts, to the acrimonious dispute of the 1750s over the relative merits of French and Italian music in which he no doubt also saw his own standing, along with that of other French composers, as being in question. But little is known of him as a man. A contemporary and friend who knew him in early life said of him, 'He is locked up, body and soul, in his harpsichord; once he has ceased to play and has closed it he seems to have withdrawn from the world.' What we do know of him suggests an essentially kindly man, while his music, not least important of which are the four books of keyboard pieces published before 1741, reveals an immense musical talent. He died in 1764.

France and foreign music

The development of French music was by no means entirely dependent on standards set by Versailles. A common European idiom was being evolved which was to combine characteristics peculiar to France, Italy and Germany.

Contacts with Germany were frequent. A number of French musicians visited Germany and we also find a very large number of Germans in Paris and at Versailles. Telemann stayed for some time in Paris, where he became familiar with French musical principles. Mention should also be made of the German musicians from Mannheim who introduced the beauties of the clarinet to France, and neither should we forget the first visit of the young Mozart to the court of Versailles in 1763.

Most fruitful of all were France's relations with Italy, though the results often caused violent fluctuations in French musical standards. Louis XIV, the grandson of Catherine de' Medici, had never disguised his admiration for Italian music. On the other hand, Lully, a Florentine, in order to please his royal master, gave his music a French flavour. Marc Antoine Charpentier, the pupil of Carissimi, introduced certain Roman features into his music. Italian violinists like Guignon were acclaimed in Paris in the first half of the 18th century and there is no doubt that Italian violin technique was assimilated by the *Vingt-quatre violons*. France accepted the oratorio, sonata and cantata and adopted them. Similarly, France welcomed the large number of Italians who visited Versailles and Paris. Among these were not only singers and instrumentalists, but machinists (i.e. designers of the mobile Baroque theatre props), librettists, virtuosi and composers – too many to name here – who came to France to entertain her kings and left a profound imprint on the music of Versailles and Paris.

The contrast between the Italian and French styles of music was bound to produce clashes. The French recitative was opposed by the Roman and Venetian *arioso*; the French overture described above, by the three-movement Scarlatti overture; French *fantaisie*, by Italian symmetry; and the restricted tonality of the one, by the chromatic harmonies of the other. Nevertheless, there were composers such as Couperin, Delalande and Rameau, who were capable of reconciling these differences.

The gods of the French national party were Lully and Rameau, whose imaginative yet intellectual music was considered infinitely superior to the lyric, lively and emotional style of Italian composers. In 1752, the controversy came to a head in the dispute known as the *Guerre des Bouffons*. A company of Italian comedians enjoyed great success in that year with Pergolesi's comic opera *La Serva Padrona* and the result was a still more acrimonious debate on the merits of French and Italian music. The musical and literary world of Paris was divided into two camps. Jean Jacques Rousseau went so far as to claim that there was no French music worthy of the name, to which Rameau made a disdainful and haughty reply, quoting all his works and his books on theory. This, however, did not prevent Italian singers and *opera buffa* composers from having many French supporters.

Music in the German lands in the 18th century

Although the death of Schütz in 1672 does not actually mark a break in the history of German music, it nevertheless coincides with a political and economic revival among the states of Germany. This revival was to have a profound influence in every field of German cultural activity. The Peace of Westphalia formally abrogated even the theoretical powers of the Habsburg emperor outside his hereditary lands and the rulers of the now virtually autonomous states were quick to exploit the recovery of the country from the worst consequences of the Thirty Years War. In the long run, cultural taste was determined by the religious partition of the country between the Catholic south and the Protestant north, and the music continued to reflect this division. Of the many German centres of music during the 18th century, the most important were the city of Hamburg and the court of the electors of Berlin in the north; the court of the electors Palatine at Mannheim; the Saxon-Polish court at Dresden; the court of the Bavarian dukes at Munich in the south; and the Habsburg capital of Vienna.

The beginnings of classicism

The great tradition of north German Protestant polyphony reached a grand climax in the works of J. S. Bach at Leipzig, but the formative work which was to lead to a new style took place elsewhere and Leipzig did not contribute to these developments. Paradoxically, the little town of Celle was more significant for the future history of music in Germany, since the French chapel of the dukes of Brunswick there provided an opportunity for German musicians, among them the great Bach himself, to become acquainted with the French style which was so important in shaping the new musical language.

It was the states of Prussia, Saxony and Austria which were to dominate the political history of Germany during the 18th century, and their capitals were to witness for the first time the fusion of a native musical heritage with the main European current.

As a result of the Catholic Counter Reformation, we already find differences at the beginning of the 17th century between traditional Catholic music and traditional Protestant music. This trend became even more apparent after the Thirty Years War, when the Protestant north produced the greatest composer of the whole German school, Johann Sebastian Bach, while in the Catholic south, more open to the influences of Catholic France and Italy, a new cosmopolitan language, the *Stil galant*, was developing and was to lay the foundations for the great Viennese classics.

Protestant composers, even those who visited Italy, were less susceptible to the southern art than their Catholic colleagues. They borrowed the form, but enriched it with a more or less traditional idiom of their own. Even at the beginning of the 18th century, German Protestant musicians were still taught by masters who transmitted what one may describe as 'ideological' musical theories, still partly inspired by the principles of the middle ages.

A musician working in this tradition had to comply with certain formalities, but it was counterpoint, above all, that provided the image, the reflection of the universal order in which he saw himself involved. The composer, while always a servant of God, was also always a craftsman. The rules of his craft, the rational element, supported him in his work and provided him with some degree of freedom from that creative ecstasy that was soon to take first place. This self-consciously German Protestant tradition, while actively prepared to learn from Catholic Italy, nevertheless regarded the latter with a certain reserve; south Germany, on the other hand, eagerly accepted the Italian influence. Ever since the Counter Reformation, the Church of Rome, imbued with a new fervour, had set an example of pomp and splendour unequalled anywhere else, and had instilled new life into all the arts. In southern Germany, particularly in Bavaria and Austria, most of the really important musical posts were held by Italians, who set the tone of musical activity. Counterpoint retained a place in the tradition of south Germany and Italy for a long time to come, although it was gradually dispensed with thanks to French influences. It was a tradition with which Mozart was perfectly familiar, even before he discovered its potential in the music of Bach. But it had in general come to be regarded more and more as an academic

The chapel of the north German court of Celle, an important centre of French influence in the early 18th century.

exercise, or as ideally suited to *a cappella* church music. In the 18th century the distinction between this type of sacred music and other styles of composition was common to Italy, France and south Germany.

The French influence on the music of south Germany is paralleled by the growth of the Rococo style of architecture there. Before the death of Louis XIV there had been an increasing tendency to soften the forms of Baroque architecture. Even if the exteriors of the buildings still retained their heavy, often classical outline, the interiors were becoming lighter and more graceful and were decorated in a style of whimsical ornamentation which the French called the *style galant*. This trend applied not only to architecture but also to poetry, painting and music, and was eventually to affect the arts throughout Germany. But it was eagerly seized on by south Germany, particularly in Bavaria and Austria, where a brilliant Rococo art, quite individual in style, came into being. The foundations of the musical counterpart of this movement had already been laid in Vienna, but it was Georg Muffat (1653-1704), a Savoyard, who had studied first with Lully, then in Rome, who was largely responsible for introducing the so-called *goût mixte* (mixed taste). As organist at Strasbourg and then Salzburg, he composed numerous keyboard works whose blend of the Italian and French styles was to be very influential in the south. The characteristic of the new style, which caused such a stir at the beginning of the

18th century and which owed so much to French influence, was precisely that of Rococo – the search for something almost intangible, an evanescent beauty, and the rejection of anything calculated or constructed – in short, of anything Baroque. This *style galant* was in fact a combination of Italian, south German and French styles, each of which made its own particular contribution. Italy provided the forms and a sensuous charm; south Germany, a certain melodic simplicity clearly related to the *Lied*; France, not so much a musical style as a particular French aesthetic – a perfection of detail and, as it were, polished manners – in fact, the essence of the *Stil galant*, as it was known in Germany.

J. S. Bach himself made use of Italian (and for that matter French) forms, and also of the French taste for detail, if only in a use of ornamentation which showed kinship to the art of Couperin. But otherwise Bach was far removed from this new style – not for him these superficial charms, these delightful 'badineries and smiling pretty melodies' so dear to the hearts of the public.

We have stressed the decisive importance of French influence, which was responsible for providing this new style with so much subtlety and animation, but it must be remembered that these particularly French qualities were only slowly assimilated into the music of the grand style – masses, oratorios and operas – which for a long time yet remained filled with pomp and circumstance. It was, in particular, in the field of chamber music designed for Rococo salons, that the new style was immediately evident. While composers still retained established musical forms, they imbued them with a new language and significance. The form of the suite for example, although still occupying a privileged place for some time to come, was to be gradually replaced by the sonata. This development was made all the easier because of the affinity of the sonata to the 17th-century *sonata da camera*, which had so often consisted of a series of movements in dance rhythm. These dance movements, however, were soon to become so stylised that even the original names of the dances were forgotten, and it was not long before the new sonata with its bithematic first movement form became the most important vehicle of instrumental music for both chamber and symphonic compositions.

In this evolution, the Italians, especially those active in Vienna, played a not inconsiderable role, especially after the reconstitution of the imperial Chapel Royal under Charles VI in 1712.

The church of the monastery of Ottobeuren, typical of the splendour of south German Rococo architecture.

Vienna in the first half of the 18th century

Austria, thanks to Leopold I (1658-1705), had once again become one of the great European powers, and all the magnificence and pomp of the monarchy were reflected in its imperial capital. The court and nobility, the Church and bourgeoisie, all rivalled each other in their enthusiasm for the arts, and made Vienna one of the most important cultural centres of Europe. In its uniquely cosmopolitan atmosphere were gathered the arts of France, Italy and Germany; the country under Joseph I (d. 1711), Charles VI (1711-40) and Maria Theresa (d. 1780) continued to enjoy all the benefits of a cultural golden age.

The most important of the Italians at Vienna were the brothers Bononcini – Giovanni Battista and Antonio, who were there from 1700 to 1711; Giuseppe Porsile (1680-1750), who was attached to the Viennese court from 1720 to 1740; and most important of all, Antonio Caldara (*c.* 1670-1736), who remained permanently in Vienna from 1716 until his death. It was Caldara's in uence that was the most apparent on Austrians of the ounger Viennese school, such as Georg Christoph Wagenseil (1715-77). The close collaboration between talian and German musicians is apparent in a work in he National Library of Vienna; this is the 'pastoral able' *Euridice*, written in 1750 by Wagenseil, Ignaz Holzbauer (1711-83), Hasse, Jommelli, Galuppi, Berasconi and others.

The Italian influence at Vienna is best exemplified in he works of the Viennese court *Kapellmeister* (from 715), Johann Joseph Fux (1660-1741). Fux is also the learest example of a composer adopting the two styles, old and new, for the distinct functions of ecclesiastical and secular music. His famous Latin treatise on the art of polyphonic writing, *Gradus ad Parnassum* (1725), remained a standard treatise on counterpoint for two centuries, and his own capacities in this manner of composition are dazzlingly revealed in the *Missa Canonica*. Inspired by the Palestrinian tradition in his many church compositions, Fux drew heavily on the Neapolitan style in his eighteen operas, which also incorporate elements of Austrian folk music, while his instrumental music, which includes thirty-eight trio sonatas, is clearly based on the work of Corelli.

The year 1740, in which the Emperor Charles VI died, marked a sensible decline in musical standards, more or less coinciding with the deaths of Caldara (1736) and Fux (1741). The Silesian Wars and the Seven Years War (1756-63) were a drain on the country's resources. Court music was restricted and the theatre, with its sumptuous productions, suffered equally. The dominant names in musical life were those of Wagenseil, Johann Georg Reutter (1708-72), who wrote mainly church music and opera, and Gottlieb Muffat (1690-1770), son of Georg Muffat, who wrote more particularly for the organ and harpsichord. All three were to die within seven years of each other. From 1746 to 1750 Holzbauer was attached to the court theatre; three years after leaving Vienna he was appointed *Kapellmeister* at Mannheim. For a time the impetuous flow of Viennese music seemed to be drying up, though instrumental composition remained at a fairly high level. But it was at this time that a new musical language emerged and the Baroque tradition came to be abandoned completely, and it was in Vienna, between 1740 and 1759, that Joseph Haydn, the first of the three great classical composers, received his musical training. The beginning of the decline of musical life at the court of Vienna coincided with a corresponding rise in the standards of the chapel and the school of Mannheim.

The court of the elector palatine at Mannheim

Just at the time when other states were putting their house in order after the Thirty Years War, the Palatinate, a modest political power, suffered the most appalling devastation at the hands of French troops. Cultural life suffered equally and the Residenz of the elector was transferred from Heidelberg to Mannheim in 1720. Recovery was slow but was to lead to the brilliant and renowned Mannheim school. That such a minor chapel should become one of the most famous orchestras in Europe was above all due to the elector Charles Theodore and to the musicians he recruited from the Habsburg lands, chief among them being the Bohemians Johann Stamitz (1717-57), Franz Xaver Richter (1709-89) and the Viennese Holzbauer. When they arrived in Mannheim their artistic personalities were already developed. Stamitz, who joined the court orchestra as a cellist in 1741, was already celebrated although he was only twenty-four, and was appointed *Kapellmeister* four

Franz Xaver Richter, one of the important Bohemian composers at the court of Mannheim. Notice his use of a roll of music as a conductor's baton.

years later; the violinist and composer Richter arrived when he was thirty-eight; Holzbauer (whose works are unknown to us), after five years in Vienna, was forty-two when he settled at the palatine court. After 1740, the school of Mannheim dominated that of Vienna, but her musicians had no need to formulate a new musical language. They built on foundations laid elsewhere. The Viennese school to which these men at first belonged, abandoning the Baroque, had already developed a musical language to the taste of the 18th century, and therein lay its importance.

There were also a number of Italians at Mannheim while Christian Cannabich (1731-98), a native Mannheimer and pupil of Stamitz, maintained the tradition of his master when he became director of instrumental music in 1774. Quite apart from their achievements as composers, the musicians of Mannheim were renowned for their orchestra. Its discipline, of a degree hitherto unknown, and its precise articulate bowing, produced extreme subtleties of tone and variations in dynamic, and its example was to initiate a revolution in European orchestral technique. Besides performing at concerts of instrumental music the orchestra would have had numerous other duties, notably at the court theatre, where opera and ballet were very popular.

Although the school of Mannheim achieved an instrumental melodic style of its own, its leading exponents were interested in other things besides, particularly in the sonata form and the questions of instrumentation and scoring which would resolve the uneasy distinction between chamber music and symphonic music. In Vienna, although there was already a relatively clear distinction between sonatas written for several instruments, *sinfonie* and *divertimenti*, the distinction between chamber music and orchestral or symphonic music proper still remained vague. In Mannheim, the distinction was much more precise and consistent. Stamitz and Richter wrote many fine four-movement symphonies, while Cannabich carried on their work, reaching new heights in the field of thematic development and instrumentation. These works had direct influence on their successors, notably the young Mozart, but it would be a mistake to draw too sharp a contrast between the two schools of Vienna and Mannheim. Both flowed from the same source and both were to contribute to the formation of the classical Viennese style; in 1778 the elector who had succeeded to the throne of Bavaria moved his capital to Munich, taking much of his orchestra with him.

Music in Mannheim and Munich

The brilliance of the Mannheim school was dimmed after the move of the electoral court to Munich, but the recently founded national theatre remained an active centre of the town's musical life. For the next twenty years a large number of *Singspiele*, melodramas and operas were performed there, amongst them most of the works of Mozart. More important in ensuring a continuing influence for the music of Mannheim and Munich in Germany and abroad was the career of the Abbé Vogler (1749-1814).

The son of an instrument maker of Würzburg, he came to Mannheim in 1771 and was soon granted a scholarship to study in Italy. He worked in Bologna with Martini and at Padua with Vallotti, also meeting Hasse in Venice. Ordained priest in Rome, he returned to Mannheim in 1775. Here he founded a conservatory, the first establishment of higher musical education in Germany.

Vogler followed the court to Munich where, with other Mannheimers such as Ignaz Holzbauer and Cannabich, he continued the traditions of Stamitz. But from 1784, although recently appointed *Kapellmeister*, he abandoned his functions at court in order to tour. His talents as an organist were enthusiastically appreciated, notably in London and Paris, and he assisted in the founding of conservatories in Stockholm, Prague and Darmstadt. The most fascinating period in the career of this active and enquiring musician was the tour he made of Morocco, Algiers and Turkish-occupied Greece in the 1790s. His declared aim was to study the conditions in which choral music (i.e. polyphony) had its origins, because he believed that it arose at a time when the oral tradition of music was more important than notation. In 1807 he settled at Darmstadt, where his pupils included Weber and Meyerbeer.

After the 16th-century glories of the reign of Albrecht VI and his director of music, Lassus, the tradition of music was continued at Munich under the auspices of Johann Kaspar von Kerll (1627-93), who also served for a period at Vienna. He wrote operas and keyboard music which did much to integrate the style of Frescobaldi into south German music. Kerll had been a pupil of Carissimi and this Italian influence at Munich was to be reinforced, both by the taste for Italian opera at court and by the influx of numerous Italian musicians. Thus despite close political ties with France, which in their turn produced a number of artistic contacts, Italian music remained predominant at Munich, being represented by Agostino Steffani and Evaristo Felice dall'Abaco (1675-1742), an important figure in the

development of the Italian style in chamber music.

Under the elector Max-Joseph III (1745-77), who was not only a patron of music but himself a composer (among other works, he wrote a Stabat Mater), Italian opera found a new home in the Residenz theatre, built by F. Cuvilliés and opened in 1753. On the death of the elector, the Bavarian crown was assumed by the elector palatine, and as we have seen the musical establishment of Mannheim was transferred to Munich.

Berlin

The composers of Berlin, in comparison with those of Vienna and Mannheim, tended to become increasingly academic. It was, of course, a Protestant court and although it may be said to have belonged to the pre-classical movement, there are still certain backward-looking tendencies in its music. The restricted finances of the state only allowed for a very modest cultural life, reflected in the fact that in 1683 the court chapel consisted of only thirteen musicians.

Frederick II of Brandenburg (1688-1713), crowned king of Prussia in 1701 as Frederick I, encouraged a degree of development at his court consistent with his new royal dignity. But the promise of growth was arrested in its development during the drab and joyless reign of Frederick William I (1713-40), known as 'the soldier king'.

Bitterly at odds with a father who opposed every indication of his son's obvious talents in the arts and literature, the young heir apparent, the future Frederick II, set up his household outside Berlin, at Rheinsberg. Here he gathered around him a musical establishment which included the great C. P. E. Bach, and which was to form the basis of the royal musical establishment at Berlin when he finally ascended the throne in 1740. Frederick himself was both a gifted flautist and a composer of above average ability. His instructor on the flute and later court composer was Johann Joachim Quantz (1697-1773), who had left a post as oboist at Dresden for the young prince's service. Quantz, who wrote some 300 flute concertos and also the important

An artist's impression of Frederick II of Prussia playing a flute concerto at his palace of Sans Souci.

treatise on the technique of the instrument, *Anweisung die Flöte traversiere zu Spielen* (1752), composed numerous other instrumental works.

Frederick's *Kapellmeister* was Carl Heinrich Graun (1704-59) who, besides organising the music of the court, was also in charge of the Berlin opera, which was opened by a performance of his *Caesar and Cleopatra* in 1742. He wrote a number of other operas, but his best work is religious and chief among it is a Passion cantata, *The Death of Jesus*, performed at Berlin almost annually until 1884. Another composer who served for a time at Berlin was the Bohemian, Georg Benda (1722-95), who was chamber musician from 1742 to 1750. However, his most important work was done after he had left the Prussian capital, and he is of particular interest for his melodramas. The melodrama is a musical dramatic form in which the actors speak their words against a musical background. It had already been anticipated by *Pygmalion* in 1770, with words by J. J. Rousseau, but Benda's *Ariadne auf Naxos*, first performed in 1775 and admired by Mozart, is generally regarded as the first example of the genre.

Carl Philipp Emanuel Bach and the later Berlin school

Of the composers who lent lustre to the court of Frederick the Great and formed what may be regarded as a Berlin school, the greatest by far was C. P. E. Bach (1714-88), who as court keyboard player was responsible for his father's visit to Berlin in 1747. Perhaps the most gifted of the many talented sons of the great Sebastian, Carl Philipp Emanuel was known to his contemporaries as 'the Bach'. He studied law at the universities of Leipzig and Frankfurt-an-der-Oder, receiving his musical education at the hands of his father. When he was still only twenty-four he entered the service of the young crown prince of Prussia. Bach remained at Berlin for some thirty years, before succeeding Telemann at the Johanneum in Hamburg in 1767. There he continued the tradition of public concerts initiated by his predecessor, while his house became the centre of a literary circle which included the poet Klopstock and the critic and dramatist Lessing.

Bach's immense reputation rested both on his skill

as a performer and on his compositions, while he also wrote an important treatise on keyboard technique, *Ein Versuch über die wahre Art das Clavier zu Spielen* (1753, 1762). Bach's music, which includes, as well as 200 keyboard pieces and fifty keyboard concertos, many other works for instruments and much church music, represents an important landmark in the development of the *style galant* towards the new classicism. His talent for thematic development, combined with great powers of passionate and sensitive expression, make his piano sonatas among the first great works for the newly popular instrument. They were to have a significant influence and affected the work not only of Haydn but also of the young Beethoven.

Apart from the influence exercised by Italian music at Berlin, the pronounced taste for counterpoint displayed by Quantz, the brothers Graun, and Benda, is much more closely related to the works of Telemann than to those of the Viennese or Mannheim schools. Instead of the *Stil galant* we find a 'sentimental style' with the accent placed on slow movements. Although a member of the Berlin Chapel Royal, Bach was too much of an individualist to fit comfortably into this school and broke away to pursue his own path. To his influence on the later Viennese classical composers should be added that of two other isolated figures – his brother Johann Christian (a Catholic convert, active in Milan and London) and Johann Schobert (*c.* 1720-67), a native of the former Austrian province of Silesia, who lived in Paris from 1762, where he was a member of the Prince de Conti's orchestra.

In 1775, J. F. Reichardt succeeded J. F. Agricola as

left
Johann Joachim Quantz, Frederick II's master of music and himself a talented flautist.

below
Carl Philipp Emanuel Bach, one of Germany's greatest 18th-century composers.

Johann Christian Bach, youngest son of the great Johann Sebastian, by Sir Joshua Reynolds. Bach spent much of his career in London.

director of the royal chapel in Berlin. A talented composer who was to meet Beethoven in Vienna in 1808, he was interested in the world of literature and philosophy, notably the works of Goethe, setting a number of his *Lieder* and four comic operas. Reichardt also published reviews and musical journals in which he speculated on the evolution and future of music. As a writer and critic he made important contributions to the history of the *Singspiel*, while the *Concerts spirituels* which he founded on the model of those of Paris ran from 1783 to 1797 and were a major contribution to the music of Berlin.

Under the successors of Frederick II the musical reputation of Berlin remained high. In 1791 Carl Friedrich Fasch founded the *Singakademie*, which after his death in 1880 was continued by his pupil Carl Friedrich Zelter (1758-1832). Under his direction it became notable for its performances of the works of the long-neglected J. S. Bach, giving, in 1829, the first revival of the *St Matthew Passion* under Zelter's pupil Felix Mendelssohn. In the first years of the 19th century Prussia underwent a major educational, as well as military, reorganisation and Zelter was responsible for supervising the new structures of musical education. During the first quarter of the new century Berlin experienced an intense musical life. The *Singspiele*, performed at the national theatre from 1786, contributed to the evolution of German opera, private concerts rivalled public performances, while Zelter's educational reforms provided favourable conditions for the expansion of music.

Musicians sought to augment their official incomes from other sources. From the Collegium Musicum concerts at Leipzig, Telemann received fees as conductor, and he was to repeat this pattern during his years at Hamburg. J. S. Bach himself had, as director of the Leipzig concerts, supplemented his cantor's salary while his son Emanuel also performed at concerts for the same reason. But it was the eldest of Bach's sons who was to be one of the first musicians to attempt to live solely as a freelance. Wilhelm Friedemann Bach (1710-84) was his father's favourite son and a musician of considerable promise, for whom Sebastian, with loving care, wrote the *Clavierbüchlein* or 'Little Book of Keyboard Music' in 1720. He inherited to the full his father's wayward temper but none of his application. Before he was forty he abandoned regular employment,

attempting to live by *ad hoc* commissions as composer and performer, being particularly admired for his improvisations. But neither the social environment nor Bach's own bohemian way of life, the subject of a 19th-century Romantic novel, augured well and he was at times reduced to selling manuscripts from his father's collection and even to forging compositions. As a composer however, Friedemann Bach left a quantity of fine keyboard music which frequently anticipates the tension and emotionalism of the Romantics.

Hamburg

The prosperous commercial capital of northern Germany had, throughout the 17th century, been one of the most influential centres of music, and the glories of the music of its churches and the renown of its organists had made it a Mecca for the musicians of northern Germany. Towards the end of the century the opera added a new focus for the musical life of the city. From 1699 its director was Johann Mattheson (1681-1764) who, some fifteen years later, also took over direction of the music at the city's cathedral. In 1728 he had to resign his official positions because of deafness and from then on devoted himself to composition and theoretical writings. The best known of these are the important *Vollkommene Kapellmeister* (1739), an invaluable guide to the practical musicianship of Mattheson's day, and the *Ehren Pforte*, a useful but not entirely dispassionate biographical dictionary of musicians.

But by far the greatest figure in the music of Hamburg during the 18th century was Georg Philip Telemann. Born in Magdeburg in 1681, Telemann, like his great contemporary and friend Handel, was destined for a career in the law. As a musician he was largely self-taught but, while a student at Leipzig University, he made such a name for himself in music, both as a composer and as the director of the concerts of the Collegium Musicum (an amateur student music group which he founded), that he decided to turn professional. His early appointments included that of *Kapellmeister* to a Polish prince, in whose service he studied the works of Lully and also made acquaintance with Polish folk music. From 1708 to 1712 he held appointments at Eisenach, where he met members of the Bach family, and at Frankfurt where he extended his musical experience as director of a series of concerts. During these years Telemann enjoyed an immense reputation in Germany, receiving offers of employment from various princes. In 1721 he was appointed to the important post of director of music at the Johanneum at Hamburg, with responsibility also for the music of five of the city's main churches. This post he held until his death in 1767, though in 1722 he was able to improve his conditions of employment by applying for the post of St Thomas cantor at Leipzig, eventually filled, to its governors' disappointment, by a second best – none other than J. S. Bach.

In a life's work probably unrivalled for quantity in the history of music, Telemann produced innumerable instrumental works, more than forty operas, forty-six oratorios and twelve complete cycles of cantatas for the church year, as well as secular cantatas and many occasional pieces. Some of these works are the run-of-the-mill products of any 18th-century professional composer, but many are of outstanding quality and go far towards justifying his great contemporary reputation. Although four years older than Bach, Telemann outlived him by seventeen years, and his style shows a development, not found in Bach's work, from the north German Protestant Baroque towards the lighter *style galant*.

Plate 32 left
Wolfgang Amadeus Mozart, detail of a portrait painted by Krafft after the composer's death.

Plate 33 below
A painting by Nicolas Lancret of the famous ballet dancer Camargo. Note the musicians and particularly the pipe and tabor on the left, very fitting to the artificiality of the scene.

Plate 34
*Al-fresco music-making in 18th-
century England*. The Sharp family
by the Thames at Fulham, *a
painting by Johann Zoffany*.

GEORGIVS PHILIPPVS TELEMANN
REIPVBLICAE HAMBVRGENSIS DIRECTOR
CHORI MVSICI.
Natus Magdeburgi MDCLXXXI. die 14 Martii.

GIO. ADOLFO HASSE DETTO IL SASSONE
Primo Maestro di Cappella di S.M.
il Re di Polo. Elet. di Saf...

left
J. A. Hasse, a major composer of Italian opera.

far left
Georg Philipp Telemann, director of music at Hamburg and a major figure in German musical life.

Music at the court of Saxony-Poland

Despite severe devastation during the Thirty Years War, Saxony emerged from the struggle as one of the major German powers. Its prestige was further enhanced when, in 1697, its elector succeeded with Russian help in his bid for the vacant throne of Poland. Only two years later the ruler of Brandenburg proclaimed himself as king of Prussia, determined, no doubt, not to be outdone by his rival. In fact by the end of the 18th century Berlin had overtaken Dresden in purely political terms though the latter was for a long time superior in cultural affairs.

Music had continued to flourish even after the death of Schütz, although the chronic state of rivalry between the numerous Italian musicians at court and the Germans had led eventually to the establishment of two separate chapels. With the accession of Frederick Augustus I (the Strong) in 1694, a brilliant age began in the culture of Saxony. To obtain a crown he had cynically surrendered his Protestant beliefs for Catholicism and, to maintain the splendour of this new royal status, expended immense sums on the beautification of his capital, Dresden, and on the acquisition of that mysterious and highly valued Oriental ware – porcelain. Indeed it was as the result of researches sponsored by him that its secret composition was discovered.

The music of the Protestant faith of the vast majority of his subjects, to which the queen also remained loyal, was upheld in all its grandeur in the Leipzig of J. S. Bach – at the capital it was overshadowed by the music of the court. This was reinforced by numerous Italians such as F. M. Veracini and Antonio Lotti, who visited Dresden for two years, as well as by the additional forces made available by the Polish Chapel Royal, and it reached its apogee in the next reign under the native Saxon director, Johann Adolf Hasse. But the splendour and brilliance of Dresden was dimmed when, during the course of the Seven Years War, the artillery of

Frederick II bombarded the city, destroying many of its buildings and innumerable treasures, including Hasse's valuable musical library.

For thirty years in the middle of the century, Hasse had been one of the most renowned opera composers of his day. After a debut at the Hamburg opera, he went to study under Porpora and Scarlatti in Naples in 1722. This was followed by a six year appointment in Venice, at the end of which he returned to Dresden in 1734 with his wife, the famous opera singer Faustina Bordoni. He wrote over fifty Neapolitan operas and travelled much in Europe and Italy, where he was hailed as the 'divine Saxon'. After the death of Frederick Augustus II he retired to Venice, where he spent the last ten years of his life.

The Slav lands to the east of Germany were comparatively late in developing a tradition of serious music. Bohemia, which was within the ambit of the German empire from the early 14th century and thus open to the influence of the music of Western Europe, produced in Gallus a composer of considerable stature during the Renaissance. During the 18th century, Bohemians played an important part in many centres, notably Mannheim. Poland too had developed an independent musical tradition during the middle ages and had had close contacts with Western Europe during the Renaissance. With accession of the Saxon kings, Polish involvement in Western developments became still closer.

Gluck and the reform of Italian opera

Christoph Willibald Gluck was born in 1714, the son of a head forester who served numerous princely houses. Little is known of the composer's early life except that his father unremittingly opposed his musical ambitions. Before he was eighteen the young Gluck had left home and, after studying in Milan under G. B. Sammartini, had made his debut in 1741 with an opera to a libretto by the great Metastasio. After ten years spent touring

Europe, directing his Italian operas and giving concerts, sometimes appearing as a virtuoso on the glass harmonica, he settled in Vienna in 1752. There, while continuing to produce *opera seria*, he also wrote a number of French *opéras-comiques*, commissioned by the director of the Viennese Burgtheater. In 1762 however, with the first performance of *Orfeo ed Euridice*, Gluck proclaimed himself the master of a radically new operatic style, and, although he continued to write Neapolitan opera, the new so-called 'reform' operas overshadowed his other works. In the 1770s he was invited to Paris, where the new style won an ardent following of amateurs and literati, who vehemently advocated the 'reform' against the claims of the traditional style represented by the works of Niccolò Piccini. But despite his prestigious visits to the French capital Gluck did not settle there. He died in Vienna in 1787.

At the heart of Gluck's new opera, in the development of which his librettist R. da Calzabigi played a vital role, was an insistence on the primacy of the dramatic plot. Music should advance and support this and interpret the emotions of the poetry. The tyranny of the soloist was to be overthrown and the musical over-elaboration of the arias discarded. The overture should be regarded as the dramatic introduction to the action and not merely as a brilliant curtain raiser; the sequence of arias and recitatives should follow no convention other than the dictates of the dramatic development, and the chorus was to be restored to the central place in the action that it had occupied in Greek drama. Even in Gluck's early operas there were hints of what was to come. *L'innocenza giustificata* (1755), based on a theme later to be used by Spontini in *La Vestale*, contains two innovations: for the first time a composer interrupted an aria before a cadence because the dramatic interest demanded it, and the chorus participated in the action. In *Orfeo*, *recitativo secco* frequently gave place to accompanied recitative; the arias, freed from all ornamentation, escaped from the tyranny of the repeat *da capo* section; and the orchestra and the chorus took part in the dramatic development. After a group of operas in the Italian manner the reform was resumed with *Alceste*, performed at Vienna in 1767 and published in 1769, with an historic preface in which Gluck stated his principles.

In the operas written and rewritten for Paris, Gluck was to go still further. *Iphigénie en Aulide* (1774) inaugurated the era of the symphonic overture which contains the dramatic action of the ensuing opera. *Orphée* (1774), an entirely remodelled version of the original Italian work, contained new arias and the role of Orphée, originally for *castrato*, was now set for tenor. The French version of *Alceste* (1776) is also very different from the original version. In *Armide* (1777), a setting of a poem by Quinault which Lully had already set to music, the orchestral writing attains a remarkable evocative power. *Iphigénie en Tauride* (1779) completely excluded the ballet and finally realised the ideal of the unified dramatic form towards which Gluck had worked throughout his life.

The Singspiel and the German opera

In the second half of the 18th century the composers of the Germanic countries freed themselves little by little from the influence of Italian opera. In this movement towards a national dramatic style, the form of the *Singspiel* played a determinant role. With antecedents in the Italian *opera buffa* and the French *opéra-comique*, the *Singspiel* had as its national forerunners the *Schulkomödie* (college comedy) and the *Stegreifkomödie* (impromptu comedy). The *Schulkomödie* flourished particularly in south Germany, and those that J. E. Eberlin composed for Salzburg delighted Mozart.

At Vienna the *Stegreifkomödie* easily mingled the aristocratic style and the popular style, including dances on occasion. In its beginnings it showed preference for Italian *opera buffa* in contrast to the northern *Singspiel* which generally adopted the French style. Its most famous representatives were Ignaz Umlauf (1746-96) and his son Michael (1781-1842), who also conducted the first performance of Beethoven's ninth symphony in 1824; Ditters von Dittersdorf (1739-99) now remembered principally for his symphonies, and the Mannheimer, Ignaz Holzbauer, whose German opera *Günther von Schwarzburg* (1776) impressed both Mozart and Gluck.

The *Singspiel* in north Germany, where it had first been introduced by troupes of wandering actors, traced its origins to fairground theatre and may stem ultimately from the jigs performed by English travelling companies in the late 16th century. But its history as a stage form really begins with the work of J. A. Hiller (1728-1804) and his librettist C. F. Weisse. Believing that French operas showed a better sense of the theatre than Italian, Hiller borrowed the subjects of the majority of his works from the French repertoire. His scores contain popular *Lieder* in couplets, little airs, duets and choruses of a fair quality. Folk songs are the basis of *Die Jagd* (1770), but when the peasants address the prince they express themselves in the *style galant alla polacca*; the nature of the subject even allowed a descriptive piece on the stage on the occasion of a storm.

Goethe, who had seen the French *opéras-comiques* of Jean-Jacques Rousseau and Favart at Frankfurt during the French occupation, was also interested in the *Singspiele* of Hiller. He himself wrote the libretto for an operetta, *Erwin et Elmire* (1775), based on an episode in the *Vicar of Wakefield*, with music by Johann André. Others followed and Goethe's letters to his composers contain very pertinent remarks on the expressive character of melody, the rhythm of the dialogue, and the nature of the orchestration. In one, he even suggests that a single musical motif could be introduced at various points to emphasise the similarities between certain recurring dramatic situations and thus reinforce the continuity of the work.

As the *Singspiel* developed, exotic, serious, historic and popular elements are all present, while the fantastic element which anticipates Mozart's *Magic Flute* is represented by the *Oberon* (1790) of P. Vranicky. We can also discern the trend towards German bourgeois drama of the 19th century in *Der Dorfbarbier* (1796) by Johann Schenk and *Die schweizer Familie* (1809) by Joseph Weigl. The theatrical works of Johann Christian Bach are also a part of the history of the *Singspiel*. His very personal style appears as a sensitive synthesis of the structural strength of the classical language (a poetic sensitivity close to that of the literary and pre-Romantic musical works of the 1770s), while the seduction of the melodious, Neapolitan opera led him towards the clarity and charm of the *style galant*.

The *Singspiel* contributed towards creating an opera of national character to combat the influence of Italian dramatic music, but it was Mozart, influenced by the *style galant* throughout his youth, who composed the first major examples of German opera.

Like Rococo architecture, its musical counterpart, the *style galant*, flourished best in a cosmopolitan atmosphere. It may be for this reason that in Germany it manifested itself earlier and more vigorously in the Catholic south, for the Roman Church is by nature cosmopolitan in a way that German Protestantism, conscious always of its national background, could never be.

Seen as a whole, it is clear that there remained a sharp division between the two traditions in Germany, despite many reciprocal relations, until the middle of the 18th century. But for all that German music has not suffered. At the same time as J. S. Bach was bringing the northern tradition to its glorious culmination with some of the mightiest works in the history of Western music, the Catholic south was preparing the way for a new art which, for the first time in history, was to earn German-speaking composers their place as the leaders of Europe.

The German poet and polymath Johann Wolfgang Goethe, who contributed to the development of the Singspiel.

The great age of classicism

In the foregoing chapter we traced the developments in German music which led to the evolution of a new musical language known, primarily for its formal perfection, as classical. Similar developments are to be seen in the visual arts, which from the 1770s witnessed the rise of the Neo-classical school. Neo-classicism was particularly strong in France and, with the advent of the Revolution in 1789, acquired political overtones. These had already been hinted at in the *Oath of the Horatii*, the painting by Jacques Louis David that seemed to be an admonishment to the frivolous and decadent world of the *ancien régime* to return to the virtues of Republican Rome. The movement had been inspired partly by the discoveries unearthed in the excavation of the ancient Roman towns of Pompeii and Herculaneum and by the books on ancient classical art published by the German scholar, J. J. Winckelmann. Although Gluck's determination to restore the opera chorus to the position of importance which the chorus had enjoyed in Greek tragedy to some extent parallels the overt return to ancient models proclaimed by the painters and sculptors, classicism in music was very much a continuous development from what had gone before. Its prime glories, the perfection of the symphonic form, the sonata and the string quartet, had easily identifiable roots in the early years of the 18th century.

But while art and music were proclaiming the beauties of classical form, poets and philosophers in England and Germany were already preparing the ground for a revolution in European culture which was to be known as Romanticism. Central to this was a new respect for the world of nature as a worthy subject of inspiration in itself, and an emphasis on the importance of the artist's personality and his right, indeed obligation, to express the emotions of his heart in his work. The musical language of Mozart sometimes gives hints of what was to come, while even Haydn was indirectly affected by the new current of thought, choosing a work by the important 'pre-Romantic' poet, James Thompson, as the basis of his oratorio *The Seasons*. But it was with the works of Beethoven that musical Romanticism first proclaimed itself. In what follows here we are concerned with the two great masters who preceded him and created the great school of Viennese classicism, in which Beethoven came of age as a composer and to which he himself also belongs.

Vienna and Salzburg

For more than a century Vienna had been one of Germany's main musical centres. With the careers of Haydn, Mozart and Beethoven it came to a pre-eminence in the musical life of Europe which it retained, with few interruptions, up to the early years of the 20th century.

G. C. Wagenseil (1715-77) wrote a number of symphonies, quartets and piano concertos, and was also a fine teacher, being in charge of the musical education of the daughters of the Empress Maria Theresa. J. G. Albrechtsberger (1736-1809), court organist from 1772, was a still more significant figure. Admired by Mozart as a composer, he counted Czerny and Hummel amongst his pupils, while Beethoven sought him out as a contrapuntal theorist and teacher in preference to Haydn. His *Composition Method*, written in 1790, exerted a certain influence after 1814 when it was translated. Joseph Starzer (1726-87), first violin at the imperial court, collaborated actively in the foundation of the *Tonkünstler Sozietät* (Society of Musicians); Leopold Hoffmann (1730-93), from 1772 choirmaster of St Stephen's cathedral, had the young Mozart as his assistant in 1791. K. Ditters von Dittersdorf (1739-99), author of some hundred symphonies, introduced into his fresh and elegant works the elements of popular music and of the *style galant*, as well as Italian mannerisms. Finally mention should be made of J. B. Vanhal (1739-1813). His music shows traces of Romantic inspiration and it contributed, by its light style in which folk influences break through, to the eclecticism which characterises Vienna at this period.

Artistic activity in Vienna was intense, as much in the domain of aesthetic theorising, composition, publication and the manufacture of instruments, as in that of official or private concerts. The rich bourgeoisie and the nobility eagerly cultivated chamber music; in 1778 the new National and Court Theatre, which was to

Karl Ditters von Dittersdorf, an important exponent of the early classical symphony.

become, in the words of the Emperor Joseph II, 'one of the means of constructing the nation', was founded. Ditters von Dittersdorf was among the composers who wrote for it, while the works of Mozart were performed at the theatre founded by Schikaneder. Thanks to the initiative of Baron Gottfried Van Swieten (Haydn's librettist and Beethoven's protector), Sunday morning concerts were given in the hall of the court library, while in 1812 the *Gesellschaft der Musikfreunde* (Association of the Friends of Music) was founded; later this was to lead to the foundation of the conservatory.

Gradually, thanks to the intensity of her musical life and the achievements of her composers, Vienna was to throw off the influence of Italian music in favour of a German style. In the 18th century also, Salzburg, residence of the prince-archbishops, home of Mozart, and a city with long musical traditions, achieved a certain prominence. The French style had been introduced at the end of the 17th century by Georg Muffat, a pupil of Lully, while Caldara had practised the Italian style there. But a group of German musicians, one of the chief being Mozart's father Leopold, began to supersede their foreign models.

Leopold Mozart, shown here with his children Wolfgang and Anna at the piano, was a composer and talented violinist. The portrait is of Wolfgang's dead mother.

The development of the classical forms

All the classical forms used the basic three-part or ternary form, known as first movement sonata form, which evolved throughout the 18th century. As perfected by Haydn, it consisted of three well-defined sections: an exposition in which two contrasting themes are stated, the first in the tonic of the piece, the second moving into the dominant; a central development section in which the musical ideas of the two themes are exploited; the movement is completed with a recapitulation of the material in the exposition. The essential, bithematic element of the form had been foreshadowed in the works of Domenico Scarlatti, and C. P. E. Bach is generally regarded as its creator. The classical composers not only refined and articulated the form of the first movement, but also gave shape to the overall four-movement pattern of the sonata. The first movement was characteristically an allegro in sonata form; this was followed by a slow movement – an adagio or andante in song form; a minuet, a dance form, with or without trio; and a finale often in sonata form, or a rondo or variations.

The symphony, which has been defined by the French scholar E. Borrel as merely a 'sonata for orchestra characterised by the multiplicity of the performers on each instrument and by the diversity of tone colours', conforms to this plan which Stamitz and the Mannheim school had anticipated. Haydn, the first great master of the classical symphony and in many ways its architect, sometimes preceded the first movement with a slow introduction and composed variations in the guise of a finale. Mozart largely followed this pattern, but with Beethoven the form of the sonata and that of the symphony were to acquire a new breadth.

The reciprocal influences of composers on each other were numerous at this period, but there is no more striking example than that of Haydn and Mozart. The allegros of the earlier symphonies of Haydn are still examples of pure virtuosity, but in his London symphonies he recalls the emotion-charged fast movements of Mozart. In his turn, the young Mozart rendered homage to his friend by declaring that Haydn's quartets had served as models for the six quartets which he dedicated to him.

Like the symphony, the concerto had its origins in the early 18th century, springing from the concerto grosso, and acquiring its formal structure from the *sinfonia* or Italian overture, with its sequence of fast, slow and fast movements. But whereas the symphony was augmented by the addition of the minuet or scherzo, the concerto remained a three-movement form. In the pre-classical period, the most favoured solo instrument was the violin, though the trumpet, oboe, cello, flute or viola were also written for. From the early classical period, for upwards of a century, the piano, followed at some distance by the violin, was the favourite instrument. But of course the classical composers also wrote for other instruments. Besides twenty concertos for keyboard, Haydn wrote nine for violin, six for cello, one for *clarino* (trumpet) and several others for different instruments; amongst the fifty odd concertos of Mozart, twelve are likewise for various instruments. The role of the solo instrument was strengthened in the classical first movement form because of its fundamental intervention in the thematic exposition and the central development; its virtuosity could be given free course in the cadenza, formerly improvised but henceforth written out. The concerto for several soloists did not contrast a small group with the *tutti*, as did the concerto grosso, but rather a series of soloists conducted a dialogue with the orchestra. This entailed a considerable amplification of the traditional three movements, as is seen in the concerto for flute and harp by Mozart and also the triple concerto of Beethoven.

The sonata and chamber music

Forerunners of the great classical composers such as Leopold Mozart and Wagenseil had written keyboard works employing first movement sonata form, while certain sonatas by Georg Benda were written in ternary form. In the sonatas of Johann Christian Bach we find the smiling and easy grace which characterises his symphonic writing. However, in the field of keyboard composition and chamber music, as in the symphony and concerto, classical perfection is reached in the works of Haydn and Mozart. Their favourite instrument remained the piano but Haydn also composed sonatas for the tenor string instrument, the baryton,

right
The opening of a violin sonata by Mozart, dedicated to 'my dear wife' in the first year of their marriage.

below right
Prince Nicolas Esterhazy (1765-1833) who brought the ageing Haydn back to his court as titular Kapell-meister.

and sonatas for violin and piano. Mozart wrote sonatas for two pianos, for piano for four hands, for violin and piano, and for bassoon and cello. The amplification of the second subject, the accentuation of the duality of the themes in the central development, and the daring modulations of Haydn, prepared the way to the language of Beethoven. In addition to sonatas, composers, chief among them Haydn, Mozart and Beethoven, also wrote sets of variations, a survival from an earlier generation.

Chamber music, more apt than the orchestra for the expression of the composer's inner life and emotions, developed rapidly. The trio, quartet and quintet became vehicles of the highest musical expression, the quartet being the most important. The origins of the string quartet go back to the middle of the 18th century, and the first essays in this form in Germany and Austria were those of Stamitz, Starzer and Leopold Hoffmann. Both Haydn and Mozart used the form of the sonata in their first movements.

Haydn

Franz Josef Haydn, one of the three greatest composers in Europe in the half century between 1760 and 1810, was born, the son of a wheelwright, at Rohrau in Lower Austria in 1732. His father, who was musically inclined, must have been delighted when the fine treble voice of his eight-year-old son gained him a place in the choir of St Stephen's cathedral, Vienna. Because of his family's poverty Haydn had to pick up his training in musical theory where he could. For a time he worked as accompanist in Porpora's singing academy, receiving the treatment usually accorded to servants, but also being given a certain amount of theoretical instruction as payment. He had been composing from his teens, and as his reputation grew he received his first appointment, soon after which he felt secure enough to marry. It was a disastrous marriage and for the next forty years the genial and good-natured composer had to suffer a domestic life dominated by an insensitive and unmusical termagant. In 1761 began Haydn's famous connection with the Esterhazy family and he became *Kapellmeister* in 1766. For some thirty years Haydn directed the musical establishment of this enlightened and wealthy family, and when the establishment was disbanded in 1790 the prince allowed Haydn to retain the title *Kapellmeister* and paid him a handsome pension. When the music of Esterhazy was restored, Haydn returned to his post, but during the ten intervening years he had made full use of his independence, travelling to London for two seasons (1791-92, 1794-95) where he achieved an immense success. The second

…eriod at Esterhazy was distinguished by a remarkable …te flowering of the composer's talent, during which he …omposed his greatest masses and the two oratorios, *The Creation* and *The Seasons*. Deeply in sympathy …ith the burgeoning sense of national solidarity in the …erman lands, Haydn's last days were darkened by the …under of French guns bombarding Vienna, and he …ed the day after Napoleon entered the city in 1809.

Instrumental music

…t should not be forgotten that Haydn was for a time the …eacher both of Mozart and Beethoven, both of whom …cknowledged his genius and from both of whom, with …he humility and vigour of genius, he was willing to …arn in his old age. The friendship of Mozart and …aydn, marked by deep respect on both sides, is one of …he most famous in the history of music and, because …f the mutual influence of each on the other, one of the …most fruitful. Haydn's compositions, which display a …erfect blend of lyricism, strength, formal elegance and …estraint, embody in a unique way the spirit of clas-…icism in music. Yet one of their most characteristic …spects is the composer's rich vein of wit, while it is …nteresting to notice the number of occasions on which …e resorts to a telling use of folk elements.

It is symbolic of the affection felt for Haydn that, …during his own lifetime and ever since, many of his …works have been given nicknames. But it is the bane of …Haydn the composer that this practice has sometimes …obbed his music of the admiration which is due to its …remendous stature. A favourite story of musical …history is that of how 'The Farewell' got its name. When …he musicians of the court of Esterhazy, growing dis-…contented with an overlong stay in the summer residence

left
Haydn, aged sixty, composing at the keyboard.

below left
Poster announcing the first performance of Haydn's Creation *in March 1799 in Vienna. Anxious to assure the artistic integrity of his work in performance, Haydn, with the utmost tact, requests that the audience do not call for encores of individual numbers.*

of the symphonic effects of Beethoven. Haydn, who ha[s] taken the four-movement symphony of the Mannhei[m] composers, had moulded it into a vehicle for the ex[?]pression of the most profound musical ideas. H[is] contribution to the world of chamber music is equal[ly] great and he is rightly known as the father of both th[e] string quartet and the symphony, not because he 'i[n]vented' them, but because in his hands they first reache[d] their full stature. One of his most important advance[s] which may be dated from the so-called Russian quarte[ts] of 1781, was the conscious exploitation of the bith[e]matic sonata form to give the development section [of] the three-part form its true significance and weigh[t]. In all Haydn wrote eighty-four string quartets, muc[h] other chamber music including over a hundred work[s] for the baryton (which was played by his patron), an[d] more than fifty piano sonatas. The importance of h[is] work in this last field is becoming increasingly recognise[d]

Church music

Haydn has left fourteen masses (of which six are wit[h] full orchestra), two Te Deums and other works. In thes[e] works the composer freely abandons himself to hi[s] inspiration and concerns himself little with liturgica[l] requirements. The Benedictus of the *Mariazell* mas[s] repeats note for note a secular air from an earlier opera, *Il Mondo della luna*. But perhaps nowhere is the fervou[r] of the composer's conviction more marked than in thi[s] mass where the pure *cantilena* of the Ex Maria Virgin[e] contrasts with the heart-rending chromaticism of th[e] Crucifixus which follows it. Haydn respects, according to the ancient canonical rules, the first words of the tex[t] of each part of the mass, but he does not hesitate t[o] isolate, to repeat or to superimpose certain phrases o[r] fragments of the text, alternating fugal choruses and richly ornamented airs with introductions and instrumental *ritornelli*. Earlier masters treated the mystery o[f] the incarnation in the Credo with gravity, which the[y] expressed in note values; Haydn was more willingly inspired by the traditions and style of 18th-century operatic singing. But he brings to his melodies a[?] nobility, a grandeur and an expressive sense which make the use of such means acceptable.

Haydn's masses have often been classed as 'sacred music of the concert hall' rather than as liturgical, suitable for use in a service. Haydn himself met with this kind of criticism and replied: 'I do not know how to

and wishing to return to their homes in Vienna, persuaded Haydn to act, the composer promptly wrote a symphony in which the music of the last movement is gradually reduced so that it ends with only one desk of violins on the platform. Even the great series of symphonies written for the London tours have received sobriquets: No. 94 in G is 'The Surprise', because of the sudden loud chord in the opening of the slow movement which, as Haydn himself observed, would make the ladies wake up; No. 100 in G makes use of the martial sounds of the bass drum and cymbals and is hence 'The Military'; while No. 103 in E flat is 'The Drum Roll'. Yet it is in these works that we find some of the greatest passages in terms of expressive power, imagination and lyrical intensity in the whole repertoire of symphonic music.

The last symphonies contain passages which recall the manner of Mozart and others which anticipate some

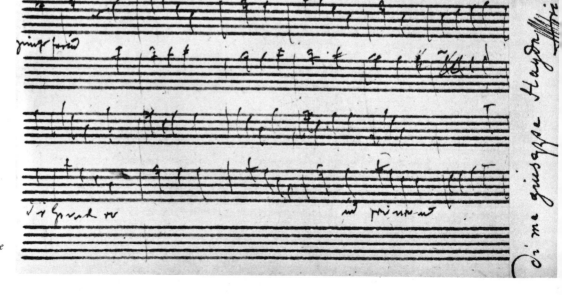

write otherwise. When I think of God, my heart is so full of joy that the notes flow like a fountain: and, since God has given me a joyous heart, He will pardon me for having served Him joyfully.' With such great works as the *Drum* mass in C (1796), the *Nelson* in D minor (1798), and the *Harmony* in B flat major (1802) to his account, one can only assume that Haydn's confidence was justified.

Apart from his masses, Haydn also gave a new impulse to the oratorio and the cantata. In his works the profundity of religious sentiment fuses, without incongruity, with the most simple descriptive elements of musical language, affirming Haydn's belief in the eternal presence of the Creator, which shows the picturesque in nature and creation. His cantatas and his first oratorio rarely escape from the operatic style. Quite different is *The Seven Last Words from the Cross*. Conceived in 1785 in the form of seven sonatas for strings preceded by an introduction, then transcribed for string quartet, it was much reworked in 1796. Haydn wrote a text for solo voices and choruses, slightly altered the instrumentation and added an epilogue on the shaking of the earth which accompanied the death of Christ. The unrelieved, elevated style of the resulting oratorio produces, despite the many beauties of the music, a certain monotony. It is otherwise with *The Creation* (1798) and *The Seasons* (1801). These were written under the influence of the strong impression which Haydn had received on hearing performances of Handel's oratorios in London, and both libretti drew on English sources; the first using passages of the Bible and Milton's *Paradise Lost*, the second James Thompson's poem *The Seasons*.

The Creation, beginning with an evocation of primeval chaos, passes on to describe the three periods of creation: the formation of the heavens, the appearance of life on earth, and the creation of the first man and woman. The score is rich in descriptions of nature yet, as the French scholar Félix Raugel has said, 'The theological and the actual, the epic and lyric, are intensely united in both libretto and score, and in the Allelujah! which closes the second part, and the grand fugal finale, the composer reveals himself as a powerful composer and an apostle of glory.'

Mozart

Wolfgang Amadeus Mozart, music's most precocious, as he was perhaps her most talented, genius, was born at Salzburg in 1756. His father, Leopold Mozart (1719-87), court composer at the archiepiscopal court, was a gifted composer and a talented violinist in his own right, being especially remembered for his violin tutor (1756). He was quick to recognise his young son's brilliance, and as his daughter, Maria Anna (1751-

Salzburg in the 18th century.

above
Mozart as a boy.

right
Mozart as a young man.

1829), was also precociously gifted as a singer and keyboard performer, the elder Mozart launched into a series of tours from 1762 which made the family, and above all the young Wolfgang, internationally famous.

This first period of his career may be said to have ended in 1773 with his second visit to Italy. It says much for the strength of Mozart's talent, as well as its careful supervision, that he was not spiritually destroyed by the hot-house conditions of these early years. As it was, his phenomenal devotion to work, which was to remain with him throughout his life, enabled him to benefit to the full from the rich experience of the musical life of Europe offered him by these visits to all the main Italian centres, to Paris, Vienna and even to London, where he profited by his meeting with J. C. Bach. However, although Mozart the musician survived, it is almost certain that the physical demands of the punishing schedules of engagements of these early years sapped his physique and weakened his frail constitution, and contributed to his early death.

He continued to tour Europe, visiting among other places Mannheim. During the 1770s Mozart held a post in the orchestra of the court of Salzburg, but he suffered the most ignominious treatment from the archbishop, and in 1781 provoked his own dismissal. From then on he lived freelance in Vienna, earning his living as a composer and performer – most of his piano concertos were written for his own concerts. Yet despite the acclaim enjoyed by his operas and his continuing reputation, lacking the protection of any form of copyright law and subject to the fickleness of fashion, Mozart died of uraemia, neglected by all save a few friends and his devoted wife Constance Weber, and was buried in a pauper's grave.

The music

Mozart's wide knowledge of contemporary European music, including personal acquaintance with many of the great Italians, and his familiarity with the great music of the past, notably the works of J. S. Bach which he heard and admired on a visit to Leipzig, were progressively blended by him into an unmistakable personal style in which his own unparalleled genius dominated. That style combines formal elegance with deep expressiveness. The delight of nuance, the sense of tonal colour and the flexibility of style save Mozart's strong vein of lyricism from all Romantic excess, and preserve for it the delicacy and supreme elegance of classicism. And on the occasions when it expresses tragedy in human terms, it is tempered with a serenity which relieves it of all pretentiousness. His music is pervaded by a grace and charm which can never conceal the strength, vigour and directness of his expression. In its once and for all perfection, Mozart's work rises from the profoundest depths of musical inspiration.

His astonishingly prolific output included some twenty operatic works, seventeen masses, twenty-one piano concertos, concertos for violin and also for wind instruments (notably the famous horn concertos), twenty-seven string quartets and six string quintets, as well as much other chamber music and forty-one symphonies. Of these the best known are No. 29 in A; No. 35 in D (the *Haffner*); No. 36 in C (the *Linz*); No. 38 in D (the *Prague*); and the last great three, all composed in the summer of 1788, No. 39 in E flat, No. 40 in G minor and the so-called 'Jupiter', No. 41 in C.

After Haydn, Mozart made the next major contribution to symphonic writing. It was he who was the first to make the symphony 'sing' by introducing into the initial allegro an elegiac element conceived in the spirit of the adagio; an admirable example is the initial phrase of the fortieth symphony. Mozart sought greater diversity, charm and sweetness of sonorities. He individualised the tone colours of the instruments and made far more effective use of the wind instruments than Haydn, who learnt from him in this respect, had done in his early works. Mozart particularly appreciated the fullness of timbre of the clarinet, often substituting it for the oboe in his symphonies and using it in many chamber music ensembles. He was also very fond of the sonority of the French horn, which in the symphonies is frequently given the function of strengthening the blending between the strings and the woodwind. The prevailing harmonic style predominated in his music, but he was also an absolute master of fugal writing, as is demonstrated by the final section of the 'Jupiter' symphony. The concern for expressiveness led him to expand the development and modulating bridge sections, and also the final rondo, in which he frequently introduced a second melodic idea which took on a considerable importance in his last works.

The form and the plan of the sonata also took on a new breadth with Mozart, and his melodic line is more obviously affected by Italian styles than that of Haydn. The purity of line and the grace of the contours set off his delicate and tender, sometimes nostalgic, lyricism, which foreshadows the *Sehnsucht* of the Romantics. His contemporary, Friedrich Wilhelm Rust (1739-96), brought these melodic elements (above all in the slow movements) to an emotional power which heralded very directly the great adagios of Beethoven.

The seventeen completed masses and one Requiem by Mozart comprise six solemn masses and eleven short masses intended for the ordinary Sunday service. All but three were composed at Salzburg. Mozart also wrote various other religious works. The forces employed range from the simple vocal quartet accompanied by the organ, to soloists and choirs with full orchestral accompaniment. The form, the syntax and the language are based on the symphonic writing of the time. A work such as the unfinished Grand Mass in C minor extends far beyond the usual liturgical framework. The different parts of the text are entrusted to various vocal groups and the soloists alternate with choirs of four, five or eight voices. The work ends in the second part of the Incarnatus of the Credo, which remains in suspense, a flute and a voice entwined together in Paradise. In his masses the Incarnatus and the Crucifixus, the mystery of the Incarnation and the redeeming death on the cross, rank among the most moving passages that he wrote.

The operas

Among the greatest of all Mozart's works are his compositions for the stage, and it is interesting to notice how many of these works have elements of the *Singspiel* as well as of the opera proper. It was certainly not by accident that Mozart turned towards a national form of art. In a famous letter written from Vienna to his father in February 1783, he says: 'I must now tell you my *idea*. I do not think that Italian opera can last much longer . . . and, for me . . . I am also in favour of German opera . . . even if it costs me more pains, I like it still better . . . Each *nation* has its opera . . . : why shouldn't we Germans have it? . . . I am writing at present a German *opera* "for myself" . . . But all this is still a secret until it is finished'.

Mozart's intentions are clear enough. He wanted not only to use German words, but also to seek a means of expression that was specifically German. The majority of his operas, even those based on Italian libretti, show a tendency towards a *Singspiel* style, found particularly in *The Abduction from the Seraglio* (1782), in which the subject and the characters and atmosphere also recall the contemporary vogue for Turkish things. In 1791, with *The Magic Flute*, he achieved the final and perfect synthesis of German language and music in an enlarged form of the *Singspiel*.

Mozart also wrote examples of Italian *opera seria* and

Scene from a performance of Mozart's opera The Magic Flute *at the Royal Opera House, Covent Garden.*

opera buffa. *Idomeneo* (1781) and *La Clemenza di Tito* (1791) belong to the former category and use the forms and traditional vocal style of Italian opera, but the intense, almost pathetic, lyricism of the former and the sobriety of style and the simplicity of means which characterise the latter show what mastery Mozart had attained in serious opera. Yet it is in the realm of *opera buffa* that Mozart has won the highest glory. In *The Marriage of Figaro* (1786), the adaptation of Beaumarchais' work to musical ends profoundly modified its character and structure. Mozart's music and the libretto of Lorenzo Da Ponte's work is lighter, merrier and perhaps more human than the French play, through which revolutionary winds were already blowing. Mozart certainly did not ignore the social status of his characters, but his artistry transfigures it, and the vivacity of the dialogue in the *recitativo secco* often alternates with arias of a delicate and serene sensibility such as those of the Countess, and that of Susanna in the last act. The dramatic element becomes more intense in the opening scene of *Don Giovanni* (1787) and in the final scenes with the statue of the Commendatore, but with *Così fan tutte* (1790), the dramatic element is relegated to second place. Here the plot is slight and the subject is nothing but an easy pretext for the most airy and most divine music. Perhaps nowhere did Mozart's poetic sense blossom more happily than in this work.

For his final work for the theatre, *The Magic Flute*

(1791), written on the eve of his death and rich in the symbolism of Freemasonry, Mozart returned to the style of the *Singspiel*. In this work the orchestra attains an exemplary fullness and a supreme mastery, as much in the overture as in the introductions to the arias and in the accompaniment, but the diversity of vocal effects is no less remarkable. Wagner loved the work and considered it the first German opera.

The above classification of Mozart's operas must not be taken too strictly. *Don Giovanni* for example, which Mozart entitled *dramma giocoso*, abolished the former division of styles. Drama and comedy mingle in it, with a fantasy and a freedom truly Shakespearean.

If the Italian influence makes itself felt principally in the arias, the recitative often reveals Mozart's admiration for the melodramas of Georg Benda, in which, as he said, 'one does not sing, one declaims', and in which, 'from time to time, one also speaks with musical accompaniment, which always makes a more magnificent impression'.

The psychological truth of the situations and the characters, the purity of form and the restrained architectural elegance, the transparency of the harmony, the freshness of the melodic inspiration, the limpidity of the orchestration and the delicacy of the tone colours, all these combine to give Mozart's operas their atmosphere of fantasy, their precise balance and their profundity of meaning.

'Le thé à l'anglaise' *at the house of the Princesse de Conti. Such society concerts were an important part of musical life and the young Mozart, shown here at the keyboard, quickly became a favourite.*

Section V

The Romantics

The 19th century: historical background

The 18th century had seen the consolidation of social and political systems throughout Europe which, whatever their potential for good in the hands of a benevolent despot, were founded in oppression and autocracy. In the vast Austrian empire a welter of different races – Italians, Czechs, Magyars, Slavs and many others – found themselves the subject of a German house and its mainly German ministers. In France the bulk of the population, even including the wealthy bourgeoisie and the increasingly critical intelligentsia, were without any effective say in the government of the state. For the northern Germans, to autocratic government and social injustice was added the scandal of national disunity and its consequent political weakness. Meanwhile, in Great Britain, a new and socially explosive system was coming to birth; a system based simply and explicitly on the money and profit motive; a system which was to bring decisive wealth to a new class of entrepreneurs who were to reinforce the ranks of the bourgeoisie clamouring for a say in the running of affairs. It was a system which ruptured and destroyed the old loyalties of a former age and laid bare for what it was the social structure which for centuries had, in the last resort, rested on oppression. The exploitation of man by man, which in earlier ages had been clothed, though with increasing difficulty, by religious beliefs and a theory of reciprocal social obligations, stalked the stage of industrial Europe in the 19th century, indecent in its nakedness. In theory, the aristocrat was to offer his subjects, in return for their toil, protection and justice; the notion was archaic and threadbare but in the society that was to follow such principles were not to be recognised even notionally. The theory of the free labour market, and the right of each man to make for himself the best bargain he could and to take the consequences, rationalised a situation in which those who controlled the means of production dictated the terms of the market place. Darwin's law of evolution – 'the survival of the fittest' – which propounded the survival of those individuals best fitted to their environment by a process of natural selection, appears now as an ugly pun on the social conditions actually existing in industrial Europe – those most 'fit' to survive the murderous conditions of employment and exploitation were also those who were tough, ruthless and above all already powerful. The new industrial society was to emerge only after a long period of piratical gangsterism.

France and Europe

Led by the forces of a powerful bourgeoisie thirsty for power, the French Revolution had brought forth an army of the discontented which later came to threaten the bourgeoisie themselves. Meanwhile a new spirit of French nationalistic self-assertion made the heirs to the Revolution the lords of all of continental Europe and themselves the new oppressors. In the wake of the Industrial and French Revolutions came a tidal wave of social and political upheaval which did not finally work itself out in Europe until the early 20th century. Two forces were at work. The bourgeoisie were determined to gain a voice in the control of affairs which, in countries subject to imperial rule, meant also national 'liberation' also led by the bourgeoisie; secondly, there was the pressure of the industrial proletariat on the bourgeoisie itself for the recognition of its human rights.

In Germany and Italy the aim, not exclusively anti-imperial but rather that of national unity, was effectively achieved in both instances in the 1860s. In central Europe and the Balkans the aim was liberation from the foreign domination of the Habsburgs and the Turks. Yet the general pattern which emerged all over Europe was the hardening of the idea of the nation state – a political system in which the great majority of the citizens were of one race, sharing a common language and living in a geographically unbroken territory. The idea that this was the natural and proper mode for the government of society was virtually the invention of the 19th century.

The spirit of national rebellion first arose in Greece, where the basic issue of the people against established authority was confused for some since the people were Christian and the heirs of the ancestors of European civilisation, while the authorities were infidel and the arch enemies of that civilisation. But in the Paris Revolution of 1830 the same issue was fought out between the thrusting bourgeoisie and the old-established régimes. The example of Paris was followed elsewhere and most notably in Poland, where the driving force was a nationalist resurgence following half a century of quiescence. The revolution in Warsaw, which inspired the self-exiled Chopin in Paris to write his famous *Revolutionary Study*, was effectively suppressed by the might of Russia.

The German lands

Whatever else it had done, the great French Revolution had crystallised for all Europe the idea of the sovereign nation state and had presented a working example of a government where qualifications other than noble birth or the will of an autocrat fitted a man for the highest public service. In Germany the impact of French ideas and the necessity of repelling Napoleon confirmed the already strong sense of national identity and gave birth to the dream of German unity. In the Austrian empire the idea of nationalism proved explosive; in Prussia, the largest non-Austrian German state, defeat at the hands of Napoleon caused a series of long needed reforms not only in the military establishment but also in education and even musical education. Prussia's essential contribution to the final European victory over Napoleon gave her the position of leader in the war of liberation against the French and from 1815 Prussia and Austria were to contest for the leadership of a united Germany. After the tumult of the Revolutionary and Napoleonic wars it was the aim of all European statesmen to ensure a period of international peace and internal social stability. In the former aim they were astonishingly successful – not until the Austrian defeat by Prussia at Sadowa in 1866 was the continent to see the movement of great armies. In the latter aim the failure of the statesmen, bent on the restoration of the old order under the leadership of the Austrian chancellor Metternich, shapes the history of the next generation.

Again the events of the French Revolution are instructive, for although France already approached the ideal of the nation state, her armies had undertaken a war of conquest in the name not of dynastic rights but of the rights of man. No matter how great the disillusionment after Napoleon's assumption of the imperial title, summed up by Beethoven's despairing cancellation of his dedication of the *Eroica* symphony to Napoleon, the ideal was not forgotten. The French might have reverted to the splendours and pretensions of an imperial age, perfectly summed up in the art and architecture of the time, which found its inspiration in the art of Egypt and Rome. Others still had the ideal – now their own liberation – to fight for.

The storm broke anew in 1848, the year of revolutions. Again the epicentre was Paris; the French, somewhat ahead of their colleagues elsewhere, were finding that political revolutions did not apparently change society. In the same year the Communist Manifesto was published marking the beginning of the first systematic theory of social revolution. Within four years of the collapse of the discredited régime of Louis Philippe, the French Republic had again foundered and there opened the epoch of the Second Empire under a descendant of Napoleon who chose the title of Napoleon III. The age of the Second Empire in France is generally and reasonably regarded as the apotheosis of the bourgeoisie, unbelievably well symbolised by the Paris opera house. The attitudes of the empire had long been in the making. Admired were not the sturdy gusts of iconoclastic realism of the painter Courbet but the smooth efficiency of an academic art, faultless in its technique but equally innocent of the fire of passion or the breath of inspiration. In music the age was well served by the immense but often pretentious operas of Meyerbeer and still better by the works of his less gifted imitators. Meanwhile the only composer of genius produced by France between the death of Couperin and the rise of Debussy was reduced to earning his livelihood as a journalist. While Auber produced operas Berlioz scribbled inspired criticism for the *Journal des Débats*.

The complacent society of the Second Empire, under constant attack from its artists and shocked to its core by the audacity of the Impressionists and the sacrilege to the classical past committed by Manet's *Déjeuner sur l'herbe*, dissolved in the humiliation of military defeat. It had only strength enough, in the heat of a national emergency, to ensure the corruption and death of the last effort of social protest by aborting the birth of the Paris Commune.

Yet for the triumphant forces of the German armies, surprised by the ease of their defeat and capture of Napoleon III and his capital, the events of 1870 set the seal on a struggle for German self-assertion; and the proclamation of William I of Prussia as emperor of Germany in Versailles brought to reality another dream – that of German unity. The passions of '48, which had led Wagner to join the ranks of the insurgents in Saxony, were for a time forgotten; the demands for social justice were drowned for a time in a sea of national enthusiasm. In the thirty years which brought the century to a close the Germans were interested in making good their position as one of Europe's leading powers by asserting their claims to a share in the overseas empires which France, England and even Belgium were carving out for themselves. Yet though the military and political triumph of Berlin was assured, the cultural lead still lay with Vienna – not only the home of the waltz king Johann Strauss but also the chosen home of the northerner Johannes Brahms. From Vienna it was the music of Mahler which was to carry on the tradition launched by Wagner, a Saxon by birth and the preferred protégé of the Bavarian king Ludwig.

But if the Germans seemed to have achieved some of their ambitions, elsewhere the struggle for national identity continued. In 1867 the Austrian empire, following its crushing defeat at Sadowa, had been compelled to concede a considerable degree of independence to its greatest single subject territory, and the Emperor Franz Josef went through a separate coronation ceremony as king of Hungary. The Austro-Hungarian empire had been born and the struggle of the Magyar petty nobility to be masters in what they regarded as their own house was near to being won. For the other subject peoples of the empire fortunes had varied. In 1861 Victor Emmanuel of Sardinia was crowned first king of a united Italy. It was the end of the first stage of an independence struggle which had been led by such great figures as Cavour, Garibaldi and Mazzini. But the states of Czechoslovakia and Poland were to wait another fifty years before their aspirations to nationhood were to be fulfilled.

The Americas

For the kingdoms of Spain and Portugal the century was one of mixed blessings. The threat to nationhood posed by the usurping régimes established by Napoleon was averted, but the breath of national liberty blew across the Atlantic to infect the populations of their South American colonies. By the end of the century the old world of Latin America had changed beyond recognition and where once the Iberian monarchy had reigned supreme a crowd of vigorous and newly independent states had arisen. Yet although the Latin American states had won this independence only in the wake of the Napoleonic turmoil in Europe, an example of successful rebellion had been set decades before by the revolt of the North American colonies from Britain and the foundation of the United States. For another century the Americas – both North and South – were to remain heavily indebted to Europe for the inspiration of their cultural life, but the new states had been established and in the 20th century they were to bear a rich cultural harvest.

The comparatively late development of independent cultural traditions in America is to be explained not only by their slow awareness of their separate political identity but also by the reluctant sloth with which the colonial classes, conscious and proud of their European descent, came to recognise the rich traditions of the conquered Indian populations as a source of inspiration. For if it is true to say that in Europe an appreciation of the folklore tradition was the source of national regeneration, it is also true that in South America, especially, the only available folklore was that of a conquered and despised population, while in he north the folklore heritage was that of a population which was not so much ignored as actively exterminated. But in Europe itself the search for national identity led scholars, artists and musicians to research the folk legends and memories of a distant past. It is hardly surprising that even in the most sophisticated of European societies, classical themes, once the mainstay of art and music, came a bad second to the legends of the medieval and more distant past of the northern European peoples themselves. The German philosopher Herder had, in the mid-18th century, proclaimed the tales and songs of the folk as the true source of a nationally identifiable culture, and the medievalising novels of Sir Walter Scott inspired the Romantics with a vision of history which fitted their own predilections.

The birth of new cultural traditions

After generations of domination by a foreign imperial power the artists of central Europe, many of whom spoke most easily the language of their conquerors, could hope to find their identity only in the traditions of the peasantry whom they themselves had so long despised. For Chopin and Liszt, the dimly perceived traditions of their native folklores provided a point of departure from which to frame a musical language which squared with their desire for a sense of national individuality. It matters little that a true understanding of that folk tradition was to come only much later; even the distorted elements which were available to them were sufficient to lend a nationalistic colour to their work while the more easily accessible literary tradition of the folk provided for Liszt and his Czech contemporary Smetana another strong source of inspiration.

Even in the great empire of Russia the century-long cultural hegemony of Italy, and above all France, had to be destroyed. Again the sources of inspiration lay with the legends and melodies of the peasantry – slaves in all but word and speaking a language which, for many of the cultural and artistic intelligensia so desperately seeking an identity, was less familiar than French. In Russia the political upheaval preparing throughout the 19th century was to be explicitly social, and when it eventually came, had few nationalist overtones. But before that great event the cultural life of the nation was divided between the Westerners and the Easterners – between those who believed that the future of Russian cultural life lay in the exploitation of the riches which centuries of association with Western culture had bequeathed, and those who saw salvation only in the conscious and unremitting revival of the indigenous art of the people.

Such were the terms of the struggle as seen from the

capitals of Eastern and Central Europe. For the Italians, involved also in the fight for freedom but with an age-long tradition of immense cultural achievement behind them, the natural route to national self-assertion was the continuing statement of the arts and styles that had guaranteed their ancient ascendancy. Thus we find in the 19th century that Italian music, for so long of seminal importance in the life of Europe, seems to be arrested in the repetition of the once novel, still delightful but by now stultified mannerisms of an earlier age.

It is perhaps a little ironical that the Germans, viewed by so many as the self-assured imperial power, found the same need for the discovery of national self-identity. From the operas of Weber at the beginning of the century and the vitally important work of the brothers Grimm, German writers and musicians exhibited an interest in establishing a true national identity common with that of many other European peoples but coming strangely from the nation which had produced a pantheon of musical genius which could name Bach, Beethoven, Haydn and Mozart. Yet in the 19th century political and social considerations assumed a new importance, and in these terms Germany was a nation without a tradition. Hence the anxious search for legitimate progenitors which led Wagner to cast his magnificent musical conceptions in a philosophical and mythological form which, however well rooted in a largely Germanic past, can only cause a later generation to pause in astonishment.

Aloof from all these struggles for identity and national confidence stood Great Britain. Choosing to disregard the tragedy of Ireland and its helpless, decimated population, she felt able to look out with condescending pity on the European struggles which affected but did not touch her. For although it was here that Karl Marx saw the natural birthplace of his revolution and fortunately found refuge in the library of the British Museum to expound his thesis, yet the ruling class of England felt, with, as it turned out, reason, that it knew better. Across the sea the Irish starved and emigrated, to the great detriment of their country and the eternal shame of England; at home the innocents of Peterloo were massacred and the idealists of the Chartist movement laughed to scorn. Yet in a century during which every other major European country was rent by bloody revolution the English, who spawned the industrial proletariat and hence, according to Marx, the revolutionary force that would destroy their body politic, came through with a death toll directly attributable to civil disobedience of fewer than fifty.

In the world of music the English produced nobody. But in Byron and Scott, Britain gave Europe two writers whose works, with the plays of Shakespeare so at odds with the cold classicism of the French, were to inspire many works of music during the century of Romanticism.

The Galerie des Machines *built for the Paris International Exhibition of 1889. It spanned 375 ft and was 1400 ft long.*

The background to the music

During the 19th century the European musical scene was enriched by the emergence of a number of new national schools of composition. Composers from Hungary, Bohemia, Poland and Russia all developed a mature national style of symphonic and operatic music during this period, while in Scandinavia the scene was being set for a similar if somewhat later flowering. In all these cases the emergence of a distinctive and highly self-conscious idiom was of course the result of a number of causes, though some were common to all of them, namely the new sense of national self-awareness in Central Europe during the period, an eager and increasingly informed interest in the native traditions of folk music on the part of some of the composers, and the premium set upon the expression of subjective convictions and longings by the Romantic aesthetic.

The possibilities of music as the vehicle of a personal emotion and for the expression of universal longings had been shown by Beethoven. With the career of Beethoven, the lead in Europe's musical life had passed irrevocably to Germany and it was events in the German countries that were to determine the future course of its development during our own century. The origin of this German mastery lay in large part in the fact that, thanks to their great musical traditions and their growing sense of national identity, the Germans were the first to evolve a national style to challenge the orthodoxies of the international Viennese style.

In an age such as our own, which is so contemptuous of the literary allusion or inspiration in art, it is perhaps difficult to appreciate to the full the extent to which the Romantic composers drew their inspiration from the works of their literary contemporaries, among the chief of whom were Byron, Scott and Hugo, or from the works of Shakespeare. Yet the productions of Romantic music are commonly titled either with the name of the book or character on which they are based, or with some description, of which Berlioz's *Fantastic Symphony, an episode in the life of the Artist* may be taken as representative. There had of course been examples of descriptive music in earlier periods, though in the past such music had usually been content with the onomatopoeic mimicry of the noise of the battlefield or the calls of birds. But the 19th century can legitimately claim to have invented programme music in the sense of music intended to express literary and even philosophical concepts, or to portray emotional states.

The great age of symphonic music

It is hardly surprising, with the mighty example of the Beethoven symphony and the continuing improvements to the orchestra, that instrumental music, in Germany at least, was the most important of the various types of composition. Even the operas of Wagner to some extent support this contention, for it was his aim to make the opera as far as possible the dramatic equivalent of the symphony, regarding both voices and instruments as parts of a 'total work of art', and using in his operas principles of thematic development with much in common with those of the symphony. In Paris, however, the passion for opera was uncomplicated and complete. The public demanded luxurious and pretentious spectacle and since, apart from Berlioz who refused to pander to the common taste, there was no French composer of any great attainment, the field was led by Meyerbeer, a composer of German extraction but with a remarkable sense of the demands of his French public. In Italy too opera was the centre of interest but, until it was saved by the music of Verdi, it seemed too content to remain superficial and delightful but without profundity.

To give scope to the new urge of composers for self-expression the balanced and closed forms of the classical period began to be extended and loosened. After a long period of gestation from the late 17th century to the 1760s, these forms had achieved a stable and final or classical shape only comparatively recently. But the moment of classical balance is rarely long lived in any cultural environment. From the first symphonies of Beethoven and indeed even the later works of Haydn and Mozart, it is obvious that the elegant and versatile framework of the symphony was soon to be called upon to express extremes of emotion that would eventually burst it asunder. Beethoven himself began a number of processes that his successors were to take to their logical, and ultimately destructive, conclusion. He developed conventions of thematic development in the first movement sonata form; for the stately minuet he tended to substitute the more vigorous *scherzo*; he enlarged the size of the orchestra, introducing the trombones for the first time to symphonic writing, and in his last symphony, even used a choir of voices. These indications of the future were to be the seeds of a veritable revolution in symphonic music.

During the course of the century both the orchestra and the symphonic idiom were to be changed beyond recognition at the hands of Schubert, Berlioz, Liszt and Mahler. By the latter part of the century Beethoven himself, who had done so much to point the way to the latterday innovators, came to be regarded as one of the architects of classicism so that Brahms, who held aloof from the startling developments of the new music, remained loyal to Beethoven's example. Despite the huge operatic achievements of Wagner and Verdi it is nevertheless perfectly true to say that the 19th-century form par excellence was that of symphonic music. The symphony itself changed its dimensions so radically as to become all but unrecognisable and in Liszt's symphonic poem, or tone poem, it spawned a new form. This, which was in one movement, used the principles of the thematic development already familiar from the symphony but was frankly descriptive in intention. The symphonic poem was meant to convey some mood, landscape or even to portray in musical terms the career of some legendary or historical hero.

Orchestras and concerts

To express the wide range of ideas and visual sensation that were to become of ever-increasing importance as the century progressed, composers could draw on the resources of an orchestra both larger and more flexible than anything known to their predecessors. As we shall see in the section on instruments, a number of revolutionary technical improvements gave the whole of the wind section a new aspect; the piano was modified almost beyond recognition and throughout the century makers and inventors devised new instruments or added refinements to the old ones. All these things led composers to give increasing attention to the complex subject of orchestration, and in 1843 appeared Berlioz's treatise on the subject, which was the earliest and is still one of the best.

During the 19th century the whole musical life of Europe underwent an important change. This may be most simply summed up by saying that during this period instrumental music went public. There had been various types of public concerts in England, Germany and France since the late 17th century but the dominant form of public entertainment outside England had been the opera, and it was only in the 19th century that, in Germany at least, the public symphony concert came to rival the opera house. Yet the composer and his works were liable to the most testing ordeals in the world of the 19th-century concert hall. The sheer size of the concerts, or so it seems to the modern observer, must have prevented the audience from fully appreciating the masterpieces performed. A famous instance is the concert put on by Beethoven in December 1808. The programme comprised two symphonies, the fifth and the sixth, the *Choral Fantasy*, a dramatic scene, three piano improvisations by Beethoven himself and two movements from his Mass in C, not to mention a piano concerto. This concert programme was not an isolated instance and later it became the practice not only to present an immense number of works but also to perform only one or two movements of a symphony or to intersperse the full performance with operatic arias or lightweight showpieces by some popular virtuoso instrumentalist.

In England the vast popularity of choral music since the time of the founding of the Three Choirs Festival in the 1710s had ensured a wide audience for the Handelian oratorios and the sacred concerts which soon sprang up beside them. The result was that the tradition of public concert music was perhaps stronger in England than elsewhere, while the opera was of course correspondingly weaker. Another result of the oratorio was the strong tradition of choral singing which has continued unbroken from the time of Handel to our own day. In the 19th century it undoubtedly played a part in the rapid rise of choral societies in Germany, and these provided yet another outlet for the vast and growing popular interest in music.

But it was of course the piano that provided the most significant vehicle for this popular culture, while such instruments as the guitar, the harp, and the flute were also widely cultivated by amateurs. The widespread popularity of the masterpieces of the concert hall as also of the 'hit' operatic arias led to the production of many adaptations of orchestral pieces for the piano or chamber music ensembles, and arrangements of operatic airs.

The conductor

The 19th-century symphony orchestra was something completely new in European music and it produced a new figure in the world of music – the conductor. He was preceded by a new and dynamic generation of leading violinists who, in the first decades of the century, did much to discipline the growing orchestral forces. The size and complexity of the scores were making it increasingly difficult for a performance to be directed by the composer himself from the keyboard of the harpsichord, on which he had once also been expected to provide the continuo bass of the music. Rehearsal and discipline, largely in the hands of the resident first violin of the orchestra, were to become more and more important and violinists such as F. A. Habeneck did much to prepare the way for the orchestras of the later part of the century. It was during this period too that the conductor's baton, which had been known in some form or another in the performance of choral music since the 15th century at least, became accepted as the normal mode of directing the orchestra.

Composer-conductors such as Spontini at Berlin, Weber at Dresden, Ludwig Spohr and of course Mendelssohn at the Gewandhaus Concerts of Leipzig, developed a tradition of discipline and rehearsal in the orchestra which made possible both the widening of the orchestra's repertory and the performance of such technically complex works as Beethoven's ninth symphony. The tradition was reinforced in the second half of the century by the example and work of Liszt and Berlioz both in Paris and elsewhere. Weimar, the centre of a new type of music, was, also under Liszt, the home of the new style of dynamic conducting of which Wagner was to be one of the greatest exponents.

The conductor took unto himself more and more the direction of the performance and the trend was to reach its height in the work of Hans von Bülow, who was to rehearse not only the different sections of the orchestra – woodwind, brass and strings – but even the individual 'desks' or pairs of players of which the string sections were made up. By the end of the century the conductor was firmly established as the new '*primadonna*' of the world of music. Just as Handel had voiced the feelings of many of his 18th-century colleagues when he inveighed against the liberties that singers took with their arias, and in the early 19th century composers had got into the habit of writing out the cadenzas of their concertos so as to protect themselves against the extravagances of virtuosi performers, so Verdi, towards the end of that century, complained that the conductor had now replaced the singer as the composer's worst enemy.

And he apparently had good reason. Even the great conductors were prepared to alter the work of their predecessors – Wagner was one of the many who 'improved' Beethoven's *Eroica* symphony, while others arranged his piano sonatas for orchestral performance. Besides these heroic feats of vandalism the reduction of a vast symphonic score to a keyboard arrangement could at least plead the justification that it was bringing the work to a wider audience. It was thus, during the century when the composer's instructions were becoming ever more explicit, and the liberty of the solo performer ever more restricted, that the interpretative position of the conductor became the chief danger to the composer's original intention. And if the work of Beethoven himself was not regarded as sacrosanct we can well imagine how the works of earlier composers fared; practical or performing editions were published of many early works, such as the sonatas of Domenico Scarlatti or

Purcell's opera *Dido and Aeneas*, and in the light of these strange and inventive 'editions' it is perhaps not surprising that the 19th century should also have been the age of the birth of musicology.

Scholars and critics

The 19th century was a time of new disciplines and scientific studies. The work of the brothers Grimm in Germany, of Sir William Jones, the great Sanskrit scholar in England, and of many others, gave rise to the scientific study of languages; in Germany scientific rigour came to be applied to the study of history. Germany too was one of the great centres of a revived study of medieval music, well in tune with the temper of the neo-Gothic age in the arts as a whole, that was to blossom into the now well-established discipline of musicology.

The 18th century had been a time of considerable activity in the field of musical history; in the 19th it gained a new dimension as scholars began to research not only the biographies of the great musicians of the past, but also their music, with a new respect and interest. In the hands of such distinguished scholars as the Belgian Fétis and the German Ambros the study of the history of music was made both more exhaustive and more erudite, and the music of the middle ages and the Renaissance, once regarded as quaint and interesting only as the prelude to the more 'mature' art of a later generation, became objects of study and interest in their own right.

The major work done on the earliest Gregorian chants of the Church has been referred to in an earlier chapter, and here we need only observe that the work of the scholars of the monastery of Solesmes was extended and supported by scholars in many other countries. The 19th century even began to probe the world of music outside the European tradition though, it must be confessed, much in the spirit in which its predecessors had studied Europe's more remote music. However, it is important to emphasise the underlying significance of all these studies. Such antiquarianism was a new thing in European musical life, which had formerly tended to confine itself primarily to the music of the present and the recent past. The researches of the 19th century prepared the way for the characteristic 20th-century concert repertoire which is continually extending its range back in time. Bach, who at the time of Mendelssohn was considered a somewhat esoteric taste, is now one of the classics of the concert hall, while the music of the Elizabethans and of Monteverdi, of Schütz and

Gabrieli, is now regularly performed. In our own day this real interest in the music of the past has brought the work of still earlier composers to the notice of an ever-growing body of music lovers.

Finally in this brief review of the main trends of music during the 19th century we must describe the important place that formal criticism came to assume. For the first thirty years of the century the field was led by the *Allegemeine Musikalische Zeitung* published by Breitkopf and Härtel and edited by J. F. Rochlitz, a man of considerable acumen and sensitivity who may claim to be the first European professional music critic. His most famous follower was to be the Viennese Eduard Hanslick, whose bitter hatred of, and vicious attacks on, the later music of Wagner have since become almost legendary. Second only to literature in the artistic scene of the 19th century, music had become the focus of heated debate and the interest of a large and increasingly well-informed public and it was for this reason that the many music journals that appeared both in Europe and the United States were published.

Nor did the composers themselves remain silent. Wagner wrote with a vitriolic pen on many subjects, with music high on the list, but a still more vital contribution was made by Schumann in his *Neue Zeitschrift für Musik* (published from 1834), and by Berlioz in his mordant and polemical contributions to the *Journal des Débats* between 1835 and 1863. These two men added to their stature as composers by the superb and incisive quality of their criticism and, especially in the case of Berlioz, proved themselves excellent prose stylists. The battle of words between the champions of the new music, Liszt, Wagner and Berlioz, and those of classicism, Schumann and later Brahms, with Hanslick as their powerful advocate, rumbled throughout the century and reached an almost pathological intensity in the pro-Wagnerian outpourings of Hugo Wolf.

Such conflicts between the old and the new had been seen before at fairly regular intervals since the Renaissance, but during the 19th century, with the widening of the audience for music of all kinds and because of the central position that it held among the arts during the Romantic movement, they became more intense, more decisive, and in consequence displayed a far wider spectrum of opinion. In common with his colleagues in the other arts the musician had thrown off his allegiance and sense of 'responsibility' to the old world of private patronage on which he had previously depended. The critical battle was now joined, not only with the professional opponents, but also with the bourgeois public itself, now the new patrons and involved willy-nilly in the aesthetic disputes which, in one form or another, have continued to our own day.

A caricature of Berlioz by Grandville.

The instruments of music

The revolution in orchestral textures which was one of the most characteristic achievements of the Romantic composers was only possible because of the intense period of mechanical invention in the early decades of the century, which led to radical changes in the wind section of the orchestra. Another remarkable aspect of 19th-century music making was the flood of pianos that invaded the drawing rooms of Europe; here again the makers were in the forefront of a revolution which affected not only music but society itself. In view, therefore, of the importance that mechanical inventions assumed during this period this chapter on musical instruments will be largely concerned with the work of the makers.

The wind instruments in the 19th and 20th centuries

Despite the experiments and improvements in the 17th century the wind instruments continued to present a number of problems until, in the 19th century, a series of revolutions in their design produced the instruments with which we are familiar today. In the case of the woodwind the problems were of three main types. First there was the fact that the tone quality was not homogeneous throughout the register, certain notes tending to require great care on the part of the performer if they were to be both in tune and of the same acoustic characteristics as the rest. As composers became increasingly interested in homogeneity throughout the whole orchestral range the inequalities of the woodwind were more and more obtrusive. Secondly, there was the difficulty of ensuring accurate intonation throughout the range. This derived from the need to pierce the holes accurately for acoustic purposes but also to ensure that they lay easily under the fingers. To iron out some of the worst faults of intonation performers had to devise a series of 'cross-fingerings' which involved often difficult placings of the fingers to achieve the best possible intonation. This produced the third problem of the woodwind, namely that of agility and the sure execution of rapid passages in any key that the composer, deploying a more and more elaborate harmonic language, might demand. The classical instruments of the 18th century also had certain limitations of range, but more important than this was still the fact that music written in keys remote from the natural key of the instrument involved the performer in the maze of the tricky cross-fingerings described above. Though virtuosi could be expected to handle such difficult parts there are well-known instances of critics complaining of faulty intonation and inadequate execution on the part of orchestral players.

In the case of the brass instruments, the problem was essentially different. The natural horn or trumpet was merely a simple open tube confining an air column, the vibrations of which yielded the notes of the natural harmonic series. In accordance with fundamental acoustic laws there are wide gaps in the lower range of the harmonic series, and thus the natural horn or trumpet had a consecutive scale only at the very top of its compass. Furthermore certain of these notes were not accurately in tune from the point of view of the diatonic scale. Early in the 18th century horn players had discovered that they could improve the intonation of the bad notes, and even 'fake' some notes not in the series at all, by stopping the bell of their instrument with the left hand. During the early 19th century ingenious inventors even tried to apply this principle to the trumpet and produced an instrument in which the bell, instead of projecting directly away from the player, was curved round to his hand. Known as the *demi-lune* (French, 'half-moon') it was only a pale copy of the hand horn and completely lost the natural brilliancy of the trumpet proper. The answer to this problem of the 'missing notes' both for trumpet and horn was eventually to be a mechanical one.

It will be apparent from what has been said thus far that many of the passages in the youthful works of composers such as Berlioz and Wagner could not have been performed on the wind instruments as they existed in 1810. Yet a player possessing the latest models of the 1850s would have been equipped to play the full orchestral repertory of the next century. From this time on, the wind players were saved from the hazards of notes liable to be out of tune or of veiled tonal qualities; of notes missing altogether from their range; and of difficulties or impossibilities in this or that musical passage which did not pose problems for other instruments.

Before the end of the 18th century the attitude of performers towards all new mechanisms had passed from their former conservative hostility to a positive interest. The seven-keyed flute, on which one could even play in the hitherto difficult key of D flat, and the Viennese keyed trumpet, on which rapid diatonic or chromatic passages over two octaves were possible for the first time in the history of the trumpet and for which Haydn wrote his trumpet concerto, came into use during this period. The first years of the 19th century brought important improvements in the very mechanism itself. The axle-mounted key, pivoted between metal pillars, was a major advance and the high point, hastened by the immense success of virtuosi on wind instruments during this period, was attained in 1832 with Böhm's flute. This was to open the way to a complete modernisation of woodwind mechanism. Meanwhile the valve mechanism for brass instruments, patented by Stölzel and Bluhmel in Berlin in 1818, revolutionised the compass of instruments already existing and prepared the way for the invention of new brass instruments. After the middle of the century, progress was in general less

above
Detail of a clarinet mechanism, showing clearly the ring keys over the open holes.

above right
The orchestra of the Paris Opera in the later 19th century, from a painting by Edgar Degas.

radical. However, divergences in tone quality created certain rather lively national contrasts in the conception and the use of woodwind and brass, in particular in the Germanic countries on the one hand, and in France and those countries dominated by French industry on the other hand.

The flute

The 'eight-keyed flute' of the first third of the century, associated with celebrated soloists such as Drouet, Tulou and Nicholson, retained the classical bore with a cylindrical head and a conical body and, as originally, six holes for the fingers. All the keys except the two lowest were 'closed' keys, i.e. keys which were opened by the action of the player, as opposed to 'open' keys, keys which remained open until closed by the player. The works and the tutors of the period testify to the prodigious virtuosity of the performers, though much of the vast 'repertoire for eight keys' designed primarily for amateurs now appears banal in the extreme.

Theobald Böhm's innovation in 1832 was to furnish the instrument with an 'open hole', i.e. a hole which normally is never closed, for each semitone of the scale. To operate the closed keys of the old flute the player had to move three or four fingers from their positions over the unkeyed finger holes. Böhm adopted an ingenious solution to this problem. In his mechanism the keys for holes other than the finger holes were mounted on axles which also carried rings which encircled the finger holes; thus, by simply using his finger to close the finger hole, the player depressed a ring which activated a key on another part of the instrument. The 1832 mechanism was retained without any important modifications and remains today by far the best of all woodwind instruments and the only one which can be considered as approaching perfection. But Böhm was also not satisfied with the acoustics of his 1832 flute and finally, in 1847, he introduced the cylindrical bore with parabolic head joint still in use. Böhm had also made metal instruments and in this too he was eventually followed, so that the best instruments today are no longer made of wood. The advantages of the 'cylindrical Böhm flute' were mainly appreciated outside Germany and especially in France; it not only inspired solo music of an unprecedented quality but also contributed to giving the flute a new place as an orchestral instrument, of which Debussy and Ravel took advantage.

The clarinet

The great German soloist Baermann first performed Weber's works for solo clarinet on an instrument with eight keys. This exploit must however have been accompanied by slight inequalities in the sound and intonation in rapid passages in the lower register. These defects partially disappeared with the Russian Ivan Müller's clarinet (Paris, about 1811) which carried the number of keys to thirteen. The 1820s saw the improvement of Müller's system; about 1840, the models by C. Sax and E. Albert of Brussels acquired great renown; and certain models subsequently devised based on Müller's system, still made today, are often called 'Albert system'. The system attained its maximum complexity in German clarinets of the late 19th century and of our own day. But in 1843 H. Klose, professor at the Paris Conservatoire, and the maker Auguste Buffet, jointly patented the model universally known today under the name of the 'Böhm clarinet'. This adapted ring keys to the clarinet and also provided for two alternative keys for the little fingers, to avoid sliding the finger from one key to another, which rendered legato surer. The Klose-Buffet model was rapidly adopted in France but only towards the end of the century, or later, elsewhere.

But besides the questions of mechanism and convenience under the performer's fingers, there are the important ones of the body, the mouthpiece and the reed, all of which influence the tone. The bore had been enlarged a little about 1840 in order to give more power, but the Germans have retained the old form of the bore, cylindrical as far as the top of the bell. They have also retained the short and pointed form of mouthpiece, which is used with a straight but hard reed. The Belgian and French makers, on the other hand, began the widening out of the bore higher up and sometimes even created an enlargement near the mouthpiece. The mouthpiece was also enlarged and used with a larger but relatively soft reed. The German clarinet can however claim to be capable of reproducing with some fidelity the tone quality which captivated Mozart and Weber, whilst the Franco-Belgian makers have created the more brilliant quality of the modern clarinet.

The oboe

At the beginning of the 19th century the two-keyed oboe could boast of having been for a century the principal woodwind instrument. At this period, it was felt to have few defects and supplementary keys were only slowly adopted. German performers led this movement and Sellner's thirteen-keyed oboe of the 1820s long exercised its influence on the German conception of the instrument. The rest of its construction hardly changed: large bore in the upper part of the body, sudden enlargements called 'steps' in the bore at the joints and the traditional rim at the internal extremity of the bell. The present-day Viennese oboe of Zuleger is the last representative of the 'classical' oboe.

The modern oboe is the work of Parisian makers and more especially of the Triébert family who rationalised the bore, introducing an entirely conical form, and created the 'simple system' oboe – still made for

beginners. The new layout and the keys for the little fingers remain in subsequent models. The Klose-Buffet 'Böhm system' oboe never won wide popularity with musicians. The Triéberts' 'system 5' (1849), which allowed the production of the C and B flat by means of a thumb plate, is still in favour in England, but is supplanted elsewhere by the 'system 6', known as the Conservatoire model, which appeared in 1876. In this model the C and B flat are obtained by means of a ring moved by the right hand. From the beginning of this century the Paris Conservatoire system began to be adopted by German performers.

The bassoon

The classical bassoon, which had from five to eight keys, presented certain irregularities in the tone quality and intonation and demanded exceptional dexterity from the performer. One could, up to a certain point, say the same of the other instruments of the period, but with the bassoon even the fundamental scale was affected.

The addition of keys during the course of the first quarter of the 19th century allowed the production of the chromatic scale in the lowest fifth and facilitated the execution of certain trills. Nevertheless, bassoon makers in France and Belgium and their Italian and English imitators remained faithful to the classical instrument, improving the bore and the sonority but not carrying out radical reforms, which would have facilitated the production of the notes at the expense of the traditional quality of the sound.

This conservative conception of the bassoon was challenged by the German performer, Karl Almen-raeder, who, with the help of the physicist G. Weber, produced a new model in 1825. The present-day Heckel bassoon is the latest development of it. The conical form of the bore became more regular and the positioning of the holes was considerably altered. The obligatory use of keys suppressed certain of the most difficult fingerings of the classical bassoon. However these alterations affected the tone, although the Heckel family brought a great improvement to the instrument. This tone, very different from that of the French bassoon, has no less of an evocative eloquence in the hands of the best performers.

Secondary types of wind instruments

In the alto and bass categories, Böhm revived the bass flutes with the alto flute in G and the bass flute in C, whose utilisation proved difficult; the practical bass flute, with inverted head for bringing the finger plates nearer to the performer's body, was introduced at the end of the century. Amongst the deeper oboes, Mahillon in 1875 and Lorée in 1889 revived the oboe d'amore for performing Bach. The cor anglais retained in general a curved form in France and an angular form in Germany until after the middle of the century. The straight form did not gain importance until later. An octave below the oboe, Triébert's *hautbois baryton* of 1823 with a straight bell had little success amongst composers and the straight forms of Lorée (1889) and Heckel (Heckelphone, 1904) were hardly more successful.

Among the clarinets, the basset horn in angular form was fairly well known in Germany up till about 1830 and was later rescued from oblivion, by Mahillon and others, for playing Mozart's works. The alto clarinet which is, in short, a truncated basset horn with a wider bore, was rarely made before Adolphe Sax constructed a model for military bands which is still used fairly often. The bass clarinet, after inconclusive attempts at the end of the 18th century, was developed in the early 19th century. The shapes varied enormously in attempts to reduce the dimensions of the instrument and make it more manageable, but its modern form is basically attributable to Sax. The most important attempt at a contrabass clarinet was perhaps the Besson pedal clarinet of 1889, which has won only limited recognition in our own time and is then used for large ensembles or for film music. It is the recent model by Leblanc of Paris which is the best known. A satisfactory form for the contrabassoon was not arrived at until that of the German maker Heckel in the 1860s–the model now universally used.

The saxophones, with a conical brass tube and a mouthpiece related to that of the clarinet, were patented by Adolphe Sax in 1846. They achieved their first success in the military bands for which they were first designed. Despite the initiative of composers such as Bizet and Massenet and later Vaughan Williams, the saxophones have never become integrated into the symphony orchestra, despite their immense popularity in jazz. As for the brass sarrusophones with a double reed, they only achieved an intermittent success, even in bands, although the contrabass had at one time been used in place of the contrabassoon in French orchestras.

Finally we should mention the serpent which, although played with cup mouthpiece like the trumpet, was made of wood. It remained in use in military bands during the 19th century and, in England, after 1850. It was generally furnished with at least three brass keys. The first half of the century was also the great period of the straight serpent, constructed in various forms, such as that of the *basson serpent*, or Russian bassoon, copied from that of the bassoon; the English bass-horn whose parallel tubes in copper or wood were, at their lower ends, fixed in a box; and the *serpent Forveille* (about 1820), a hybrid of the preceding two and very popular in France. Despite its, to us, unscientific conception the serpent, too, had its virtuosi who won considerable reputations for themselves.

The brass

In their modern forms these instruments obtain a complete scale by means of a slide, only possible of course on instruments with a tube of uniform diameter, keys or valves.

A trumpet with a short slide, drawn backwards, was used in English orchestras throughout the 19th century for the performance of the classical works. A French model by Courtois (about 1850), equipped with a slide closer to that of the trombone, offered more musical possibilities than the English model. Yet, despite its accuracy of intonation, superior to that of the valve trumpet, this instrument was hardly noticed.

The trombone changed but little in the course of the century, with the exception of the German preference for an enlarged bore and for starting the enlargement of the bell higher up. The primary object of this modification was to amplify the sound of the bass trombone. Later it was also applied to the tenor, at first in Germany and then, but only well after 1900, in other countries.

Before the perfection of valve mechanisms, keys,

similar to the closed keys of woodwind instruments and serpents, were employed on brass instruments even up to the middle of the 19th century. Keyed trumpets were still being made in 1840. The keyed bugle, invented in Dublin in 1810 by Halliday, derived from the natural bugle and was still the principal brass instrument of European and American military and brass bands in 1850, but it was then largely displaced by the modern valved flugelhorn.

The ophicleide, invented by the Parisian maker Halary in 1817, is a bass version of the keyed bugle. This instrument, scored for by Mendelssohn in his *Midsummer Night's Dream* and remarkable for its tone and its technical qualities, was still made well after 1900.

Keys could not be successfully applied to the French horn, whose tone depended on the combination of a narrow bore and a very developed bell, and in France, despite the adoption of valves, the handhorn, heir to a great tradition, remained the basic teaching instrument till the end of the 19th century.

The invention of the valve

The revolutionary development in the brass was the introduction of the valve. The principle was to vary the length of instrument, and thus its pitch and range of harmonies, by diverting the air through a supplementary tube or by cutting off lengths of the existing tube.

Valves are mentioned in German documents between 1815 and 1817 as the invention of Heinrich Stölzel, who, with Friedrich Bluhmel, took out a patent in 1818 relating to improvements to the horn. Thereafter a number of improved systems were introduced with the chief object of attaining ever more accurate intonation; by the 1840s the main lines of development of the French and German horns were emerging.

From 1820, in Germany, the professionals' interest in valves increased. The horn with fixed mouthpipe was the precursor of the modern German double horn in which the horn in F is combined with a horn in B flat alto to form a single instrument furnished with a selection lever worked by the thumb. In France on the other hand the old valve horn was modified so that it could take the terminal crooks of the natural orchestral horn. Its adoption goes back to 1827, but was not general until after the middle of the century. The Parisian makers also borrowed a narrower bell section

from the traditional hunting horn, obtaining a more brilliant sound than in the wider bore instruments which were always preferred in Germany.

From the addition of valves to the horn was also born the cornet. Its origin was the little circular horn used in Germany as a small hunting horn and post horn, and, in France, solely for the latter use. The simple cornet only permitted rudimentary fanfares, calls and signals, but valves immediately turned it into an instrument with a melodic flexibility and ease of execution without precedent, thus assuring its success. It seems to have been made first in Germany about 1825. Several reputable soloists assured the vogue of the new instrument and in many European orchestras outside Germany it threatened to displace the trumpet.

The natural trumpet of the beginning of the 19th century pursued its military career as a model with a single fold in its tube. For orchestras and bands the

below
A modern French orchestral horn with piston mechanism.

bottom
A tenor trombone.

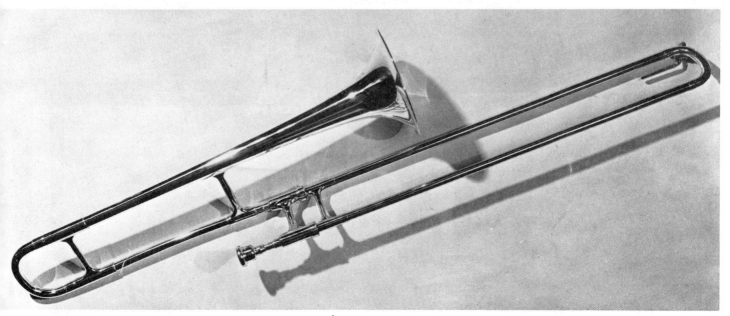

twice folded trumpet was fitted with a tuning slide on one of the folds. Valves were added to this model in Germany about 1820. The trumpet, usually pitched in F, was furnished with 'crooks' for the lower keys.

Valves were even fitted to the acoustically perfect trombone and it achieved such a success about 1870 that it appeared to challenge the existence of the slide trombone in the majority of countries. In the 20th century the older version of the instrument has largely reasserted itself in the symphony orchestra.

The revival of the trumpet and its great popularity nowadays are due to the adoption of the modern trumpet in B flat or C, whose production began at the end of the century. Its higher range makes it a more flexible instrument than the trumpet in F. However, although the trumpet in its new form beat off the challenge of the cornet, part of the tone of the classical trumpet had disappeared. The nearest one now gets to this is the trumpet calls and fanfares played on cavalry trumpets or heralds' trumpets in E flat. The small trumpets in D and F were introduced by Mahillon after 1890 for playing parts written for 'clarino' by Bach and other 18th-century composers.

The first modern tuba, which French makers could in fact have derived by adapting valves to the ophicleide, was produced in Berlin in 1835. The Germans also invented new valve instruments for playing the alto and tenor parts in band music. The old tenor horns etc. were followed in France by numerous models, among them Sax's saxhorns (1845). This family extended from the soprano to the contrabass, and Sax's latest models completed the basic equipment of altos, tenors, baritones, basses, etc. of the bands and brass bands of France, England and America from that day to this.

The rapid progress of the brass band, a popular institution during the second half of the century, was due to the solidity and simplicity of these instruments; all, including the cornet and flugelhorn – the trebles of the family – use the same fingering.

The pianoforte

It seems that the practical invention (c. 1709) of the 'gravicembalo col piano e forte' can be attributed to the Italian maker Bartolommeo Cristofori, who had the idea of combining in one the qualities of two keyboard instruments then in use: the clavichord and the harpsichord. Of the former, he borrowed the action (struck string), but replaced the metal blade which set the strings in vibration by wooden hammers whose heads were covered with leather. Of the second, the harpsichord, he retained a row of jacks which, fitted with cloth, formed the dampers. His new instrument, described in the *Giornale dei litterati d'Italia* (Venice 1711), permitted 'the production of a sound more or less powerful . . . according to the degree of force with which one depresses the key . . . Not only *piano* and *forte* are produced, but also various degrees of loudness.' Cristofori offered viable solutions for the three main problems of the new action: an effective mechanism for projecting the hammer at the string – called the throw of the hammer; secondly, the escapement, that is to say the ability of the hammer to fall back freely, without rebounding, after it has struck the string and even before the finger has been lifted from the key; and thirdly, the damping of the sound.

We possess two of his instruments from the 1720s, one in the Metropolitan Museum in New York, the other, dated 1726, in the Musikinstrumenten Museum of the Karl-Marx University of Leipzig. All the mechanical elements of the modern pianoforte are found in these early specimens, but, despite the composition of several pieces for the new instrument – among others, twelve sonatas by Ludovico Giustini (Florence, 1732) – it did not have much initial success

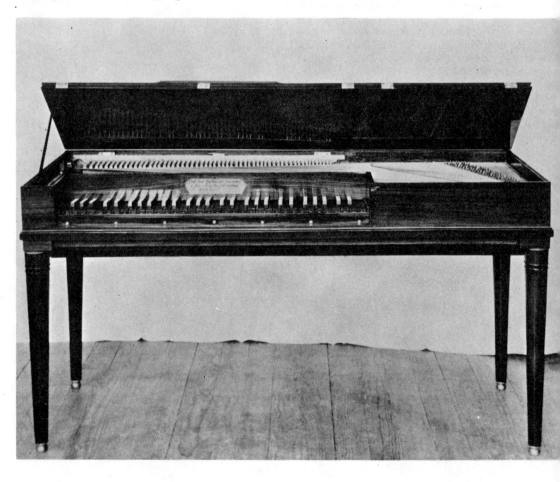

An early French square piano of 1771.

This may well have been because its wide dynamic range did not compensate for the dullness of its tone in comparison with that of the harpsichord. Furthermore much of Cristofori's work appears to have been forgotten. Early experiments by the Parisian maker Jean Marius towards a '*clavecin à maillets*' did not lead to a true piano. Marius failed to solve the problem of the throw of the hammer and none of his prototypes seem to have had an escapement.

Gottlieb Schroter, organist, theoretician and maker, had more success, and in about 1717 produced a hammer mechanism for which he is regarded as the inventor of the pianoforte in Germany. But it was not until the 1740s that the use of a hammer mechanism became widely accepted. At about this time Gottlieb Silbermann adopted a new system, called 'Prell mechanism', which solved the problem of rapid repetition of notes; the mechanism was further perfected by Andreas Stein in the 1770s, who added an escapement, and this became celebrated throughout Europe under the name of the 'German or Viennese action'.

From this time the pianoforte interested more and more composers. In a letter addressed to his father and dated October 1777, Mozart describes a visit to Stein's workshop and expresses an enthusiastic admiration for the instruments that he had just tried. 'I must give my preference to the pianos of Stein, because they damp the sound much better . . . . When I play loudly, I can leave my finger on the key or take it off, the sound ceases at the very instant that I make it. I can make my touch just as I wish: the sound is always the same. His instruments have above all the advantage over the others that they are made with an escapement. Now, out of a hundred piano makers, not one worries about this; and yet, without an escapement, it is absolutely impossible for a piano to continue vibrating after the note is struck. The hammers, when one presses the keys, fall back the moment they strike the strings . . . , whether one continues to press the key, or to let it go . . . .'

Nevertheless the influence of Cristofori did persist in Germany, where his action was improved thanks to the researches of Silbermann and of another of his pupils, Johannes Zumpe. This new action spread rapidly, and numerous pianofortes utilised it in France, Italy and England as well as in Germany; they have a greater sonority than Stein's instruments, but their touch is heavier. In England, although the discovery of the pianoforte goes back to the early 18th century, it did not become a practicable proposition until the middle of the century.

The Silbermann-Zumpe type was introduced in 1775. The English makers were soon to be stimulated further by the arrival of Johann Christian Bach in London and more importantly by the arrival of Zumpe himself. From then on the reputation of the English square piano became such that its action soon became known as the 'simple English action'. Used by Johann Christian Bach, Zumpe's instruments were considered the best until, in 1783, John Broadwood took out a patent for an 'English grand action', which in its turn soon gained considerable fame.

The earliest pianofortes generally retain the shape of the harpsichord, and the strings are stretched lengthwise. The most common instruments, the so-called square pianos, had the appearance of a rectangular table, with the keyboard in one of the long sides and the strings stretching along the length of the instrument; the strings of all these early pianos were usually single in the bass and double in the treble.

Compared with Germany and England, France was somewhat late in the commercialisation of the piano; it was only after the arrival in Paris in 1768 of the Erard brothers from Strasbourg that France became a significant centre of manufacture. Sébastien Erard produced his first piano in 1777 and won a considerable reputation; enjoying royal protection, he continued to increase his clientele, but with the Revolution he left France for a time, settling as a refugee in London in 1792. There he continued his researches, taking inspiration

above
A caricaturist's view of the craze for the piano in the drawing room.

below
The action of a modern grand piano.

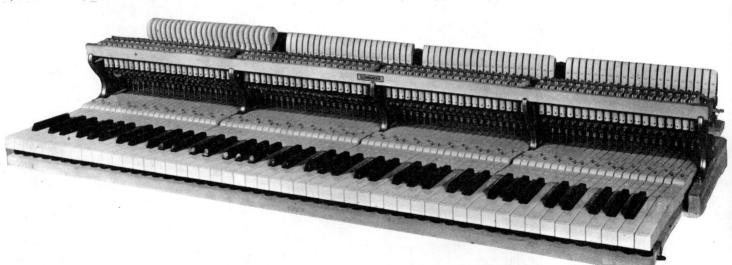

from the progress accomplished by the English makers. He completed another grand pianoforte in 1796, based essentially on the English action.

Erard's aim henceforth was to combine the qualities of the German action, in which the keyboard lent itself to rapid execution, with those of the English action, with its rich and powerful sonority. In 1818 he completed the construction of the 'double escapement' for which he is famous, but, now an old man, Sébastien left the practical realisation of the design to his nephew Pierre Erard, who obtained the patent in 1821. This action, in which the hammer remains constantly in touch with the key, even after its travel, allows the repetition of the note without waiting for the action to regain its position of rest. The largest firms adopted it under licence; Broadwood in England, Steinway in the U.S.A., Steinweg and Bechstein in Germany, and the firm of Pleyel, founded in Paris in 1809.

The piano had now attained a compass of at least six octaves, and the invention of the iron frame by the American Babcock about 1825 also increased its power. Thanks to this important improvement the frame could carry a much heavier stringing. In the highest registers the notes were now triple strung, while the single bass strings were made of wound steel. At this time also makers often fitted their instruments with a number of pedals which allowed, besides the *piano* and sustaining effects, such effects as bassoon, kettledrum, lute, bells and others.

By the first years of the 19th century the harpsichord had lost its position as a privileged instrument to the piano. By the 1770s C. P. E. Bach, Haydn and other major composers were writing for it; Mozart wrote almost the whole of his keyboard music for the piano and Beethoven rapidly adopted it. It is interesting that Beethoven's eight earliest sonatas were still conceived 'for harpsichord or pianoforte', but with the first concerto (1795) the option is no longer open. By the year 1802, the harpsichord no longer appears in the titles

above
View of a Pleyel grand piano with its lid removed; the tension of the strings on the iron frame is some twenty tons.

right
An upright piano with the case removed to show the action; note that the strings are crossed diagonally to reduce the height of the instrument.

of his works, and the style of the music is totally unsuitable for it, being clearly adapted to the '*Hammerklavier*', the German term for the piano, which Beethoven expressly uses. Once the instrument was established in the concert hall, a number of tutors were published for it, among the best known being Muzio Clementi's celebrated *Gradus ad Parnassum*, published in 1817; it is remarkable that this, the first full tutor for the piano, still remains in use. The piano soon became the instrument of the Romantic composers and performers, who had their individual preferences as to makers. If Chopin used instruments by Pleyel, English performers remained faithful to Broadwood, while Mendelssohn and Liszt preferred Erard pianos.

Liszt was fully appreciative of the work of the makers and was a close friend of Pierre Erard. In a letter of June 1839, after a concert given at La Scala in Milan he wrote 'My immense success is due, in part, to your magnificent instrument .... Now one can no longer say to me that the piano is not a convenient instrument for a large hall, that the sounds are lost there, that the nuances disappear .... It is recognised as a fact here that never has a piano produced a similar effect ....'

By the 1840s then, the concert grand, which had developed from much less powerful instruments over a period of some forty or fifty years, had reached the dimensions and capabilities that made it a fully mature solo concert instrument. It is important to remember that the piano used by Mozart and Beethoven was a much smaller and quieter one than that to which Liszt refers above, and was less powerful than the one on which their music is performed today. But while they conquered the concert hall the makers did not neglect the large and growing domestic market for the piano. The upright type of instrument had been experimented with during the 18th century despite the handicap it offered to the gravity controlled return of the hammers, while the arrangement of the lowest strings was equally difficult to resolve, taking into account the length that they must necessarily attain. From the end of the 18th century, however, the English makers Stodart and Southwell, soon followed by the Viennese Matthais Müller and Isaac Hawkins of Philadelphia, succeeded in producing such instruments. But it was not until the year 1811 that the English maker Wornum produced a small model, which was rapidly taken up by the drawing-room society of the emerging bourgeoisie. The range went down to the G below the bass staff and the action was an adaptation of the English double action. The French firm of Pleyel, recognising the commercial potentialities of such an instrument, began a large production programme in 1815 and soon these 'pianinos' were as common in France as in England.

It was then that the idea of arranging the strings diagonally was taken up again; it had already been utilised in the middle of the 18th century by Frederici for his pyramidal piano, but now it had a new interest. In 1827, the Parisian makers Blanchet et Rollet exhibited at the Louvre their first 'bridge piano', in which the strings are stretched diagonally from the upper left hand corner to the lower right hand corner. A hollow in the form of an arch, formed at the bottom of the case to make room for the feet of the performer, explains the curious name of the instrument.

The following year (1828) Henri Pape, associated with the firm of Pleyel, designed his 'piano in the form of a console', whose height did not exceed one metre, and in which the problem of the strings was resolved with great ingenuity. The lowest strings in it were, in effect, crossed above the highest, and this procedure was to revolutionise the traditional technique. It was soon applied to other types of piano, which acquired 'more tone' and stayed better in tune.

It was in this form that the 'upright' was to conquer the drawing rooms of Europe. Although its mechanism was basically established, it acquired a number of external forms, adapting itself to the taste of the day: oval, circular, hexagonal, the secretaire-piano, etc. Furthermore, to meet the demands of the essentially amateur public, mechanisms for automatic 'transposition' were adapted to the instrument so as to facilitate accompanying the voice or to simplify the execution of a piece. Some makers introduced a mobile keyboard, others a second keyboard fitted above the fixed keyboard. Other improvements included a patent for the addition of a pedalboard and it was for a piano of this type that Schumann wrote in 1845 his *Six canonic studies* and the *Six sketches*.

By the 1850s and 1860s the piano had, to all intents and purposes, reached its modern form. Of the different pedals used during the Romantic period, the makers retain no more than two, those for *piano* and *forte*; though about 1880 the firm of Steinway brought back the use of a third pedal (for the large instruments) which allows the notes of the three lowest octaves to be sustained while those of the treble are damped normally.

For a century and a half the piano has occupied a privileged place as the pre-eminent instrument of professionals and amateurs. During the 19th century it served, to some extent, the function of the gramophone and radio. A vast number of arrangements of orchestral organ works and operas were published for their use and through this medium a wide audience was able to gain acquaintance with a large repertoire of symphonic works, even when it was not possible to reach a concert

The harp's vogue as a society instrument, well established in the 18th century, continued into the 19th.

hall. Since the Second World War the piano has suffered a progressive disaffection. Amateurs have turned to the gramophone or instruments such as the guitar, while the interest in old music has robbed the piano of its unquestioned ascendancy even in the concert hall.

The harp

The first important move towards making the harp a more flexible instrument came in 1720 when the Bavarian instrument maker, Hochbrucker, a lutanist of Donauwerth (Bavaria), devised a mechanism which made a new range of keys available. Seven pedals, placed against the pedestal of the instrument, by means of a transmission system passing through the pillar, moved hooks, which, pulling against each string and shortening its length, raised the pitch by a semitone. Each pedal affected a given note of the scale in all its octaves so that operating the pedal in effect put the instrument into a new key.

The pedal harp was introduced into France in 1749 at a concert at the house of the wealthy patron, Le Riche de la Pouplinière, and then in the same year at a *Concert spirituel*. Ever since, the harp has taken its place in concerts, and large orchestras always include one and often two harpists. From then on the instrument became increasingly familiar to Paris audiences though there was little harp music as such, harpists contenting themselves with playing harpsichord pieces or realising continuo parts on the instrument. Some of the earliest pieces specifically for the pedal harp were in fact published by Hochbrucker's son Christian in 1760. The composer utilised a technique of writing designed to increase the sonority of the instrument: short arpeggios for the right hand, covering an octave or a tenth, supported by full basses. In 1770 Francesco Petrini advanced the technique of the harp by producing harmonics for the first time and by writing wide arpeggios, often covering four octaves.

In four of his symphonies this Italian composer combined a harp with a flute, two horns, two violins and a bass, but among the most important advances in harp technique were made by Krumpholz, harpist in Prince Esterhazy's orchestra, who from 1777 lived in Paris. In twelve preludes Krumpholz summed up the technique of the instrument, adding to the developments of his predecessors the discreet use of enharmonic notes, which allowed the instrument more flexibility in modulation, for Hochbrucker's harp could only be used in the keys most usual in the 18th century.

For a long time the instrument remained in this state. The improvements of the makers were principally concerned with the mechanism, since the hooks which raised the pitch of the strings also pulled them out of the plane of the other strings, thus causing twisting. In 1782 the French maker, Georges Cousineau, made an important improvement when he replaced the hooks by mobile vanes which pinched the strings in order to shorten it whilst leaving it in its normal plane. Despite the improvements brought to Hochbrucker's invention the instrument was still definitely incomplete, as certain keys were beyond its capabilities, and Krumpholz asked the piano maker Sébastien Erard to remedy this major defect in the harp. Erard's first advance was to replace Cousineau's pinching mechanism with a brass disc furnished with two projecting studs between which the string passed. On rotating the disc, the two studs gripped the string and shortened it without displacing it from its original position. The patent for this mechanism was belatedly taken out in London in 1794

although one can place its invention as early as 1786.

After this first success, Erard continued to concern himself with the harp and in 1811 created the double action which is still employed to this day. This full-sounding instrument was presented in 1815 to the Académie des Sciences of Paris. In this new harp a second disc, placed beneath the first, served to shorten the string so as to obtain a second semitone. Each pedal can be set in three notches placed one above the other (in the lowest position for the sharp, in the middle for the natural and at the top for the flat). The instrument possesses a compass of six and a half octaves.

Sébastien Erard's double action harp, despite having the advantage of being able to play in all the twenty-four keys, met with opposition in its country of origin, primarily from François-Josèphe Nadermann, who was not only a maker of single action harps, but was from 1825 professor of the harp at the Paris Conservatoire. It was not until his death in 1835 that Erard's improvement was introduced to the curriculum, despite the fact that it enjoyed the support of Fétis and had been in use in England for some years.

In the 19th and 20th centuries attempts at designing chromatic harps were inconclusive; reviving the principle published by Marin Mersenne in the 17th century, the harpist François-Josèphe Dizi invented a harp with two parallel rows of strings, an example of which is still preserved in the museum at Chantilly.

In 1843 the German maker Pape took out a patent for a harp with crossed strings which seems never to have been constructed. About 1895 Gustave Lyon, then Director of the firm of Pleyel, constructed a chromatic harp on the same principle of the crossed strings, which had only a limited success, despite a rich repertoire including Debussy's two *Danses*. Taught at the Brussels Conservatoire in 1900 and at the Paris Conservatoire in 1903, the chromatic harp was largely eclipsed in 1936 on the death of Gustave Lyon.

During this time the double action harp was established and the technique of writing for it had progressed, thanks to Nicolas-Charles Bochsa, François-Josèphe Dizi and especially Elias Parish-Alvars. The latter was a brilliant virtuoso and the creator of numerous sound effects, such as a guitar tone achieved by plucking near the soundboard, harmonics in chords of the third, the fifth and even the six, and new types of glissandi.

In their compositions, 20th-century harpists have sought to widen the palette of sound of an instrument whose possibilities are far from being fully exploited.

below
The harp of the Empress Josephine.

below right
A contemporary diagram of the mechanism of Erard's double action harp.

The age of Beethoven

The fifty-seven years of Beethoven's life, from 1770 to 1827, span the period which witnessed the emergence of Romanticism as the unchallenged and supreme principle of European culture. The career of Beethoven himself was of decisive importance both in music and in the world of the arts as a whole, and shows the development from the world of classicism to the threshold of high Romanticism. Carl Maria von Weber, who may be regarded as the first purely Romantic composer, was born in 1786 and came to his maturity when the age of classicism was already in decline, while Schubert, who only outlived Beethoven by a year, was almost thirty years his junior, and his mature music reveals only a few connections with the classical style.

Beethoven's life

Ludwig van Beethoven, whose figure overshadows the whole of 19th-century music, was born at Bonn in 1770, the son of one of the court musicians there. His grandfather, a native of Malines, had settled at Bonn some forty years previously, and the memory of Beethoven's origins is preserved in his use of the Dutch 'van' rather than the German 'von'. His father was neither a good musician nor a particularly good father, and while still in his teens Beethoven had to take over the responsibility of maintaining the family when his father lost his job. Yet the young composer was brought up in a musical environment and from an early age revealed gifts which earned the praise of both Mozart and Haydn. Beethoven's intention of taking lessons from Mozart in Vienna was frustrated when he was obliged to return to Bonn to attend his dying mother, whom he deeply loved.

His first teacher, C. G. Neefe (1748-98), himself of Flemish ancestry, was a composer of modest attainments, producing music mainly for the theatre at Bonn. As a teacher, however, he gave Beethoven an excellent grounding, introducing the youth to the *Well Tempered Clavier* of J. S. Bach and to the symphonists of Mannheim. Eventually, despite the interruption of his career by the necessity for him to shoulder his father's family responsibilities, Beethoven settled in Vienna in 1792 at the age of twenty-two. He took lessons from Haydn, yet despite his great respect for the latter as a composer, he found him too easygoing as a teacher and instead went to more exacting pedagogues – J. G. Albrechtsberger and A. Salieri. He rapidly made his name as a concert pianist among the fashionable salon society of the Austrian capital, and made the acquaintance of Prince Lichnowsky and the Brunswick family. During this period Beethoven also had a succession of love affairs, but despite a passionate nature and an expressed longing for marriage he never took a wife.

The birthplace of Beethoven at Bonn.

While he was still under thirty the tragedy which was to darken the rest of his life began to make itself apparent. From about the year 1796 signs of an incipient deafness became increasingly difficult to ignore. It is possible that the affliction was brought on by the dysentery from which Beethoven suffered. Whatever the cause his despair was terrible and pours itself out in the testament which he wrote to his brother during the summer months of 1802, spent at a country retreat in Heiligenstadt. For the last ten years of his life this deafness was to all intents and purposes complete, and he had to resort to the use of conversation books. In 1815 his brother died and Beethoven took legal action to justify his claim to the guardianship of his nephew. But the outcome was disastrous. Beethoven's possessive affection provoked withdrawal and hostility, and one can only imagine the crushing blow to Beethoven's spirit when, in the year before his own death, his charge attempted to commit suicide.

Beethoven seems to have been the first composer to attempt to live exclusively as a freelance from the very beginning of his career. We have seen that Mozart had chosen this way after the humiliations of his first employment and, like him, Beethoven often found himself in financial difficulties. In 1808 he was on the point of accepting the post of *Kapellmeister* at the court of Jerome Bonaparte at Kassel when a group of his wealthy and aristocratic friends banded together to guarantee him a sufficient income if he would stay in Vienna. He did so, though soon afterwards circumstances combined to rob him of the greater part of the pension; nevertheless at his death Beethoven, who on occasion proved himself fully capable of a degree of sharp practice in his business dealings, was by no means a poor man.

Beethoven wrote masterpieces in all the main musical genres practised during his time. In the consideration of his work we shall treat it under four broad headings: the symphonies; the chamber works, which will include both his piano sonatas and his quartets; secular vocal music and stage works; and religious choral works.

above
The young Beethoven.

right
A square piano, dated 1800 and built by Ignace Pleyel of Paris, owned by Beethoven.

The symphonies and concertos

From the outset it should be emphasised that for Beethoven music was a means of expressing his ideas on humanity and also a means of escaping from the constricting condition of life. Above all he projected into his art not his own sufferings or his own life but the ideals which he set against them in himself. From the age of twenty-two he had dreamed of setting to music Schiller's *Ode to Joy*; he only realised his project in 1823, in the great ninth symphony, where he introduces voices into symphonic form for the first time. Yet this work, which concludes in one of the most triumphant and joyful movements in all music, was written at a time when everything seemed to overpower him, when all joy seemed to fly from him. The seventh and eighth symphonies, which are imprinted with a sense of perfect well-being, date from 1812, a period (for Beethoven) of turbulent emotions and disappointments in love. Thus music was for Beethoven the language of an intense interior life, sometimes peaceful and sometimes in revolt, the language of the ideal which he carried within himself and which the world could not satisfy. This explains how the expressive problem dominated the formal problem with him; the physical means, instruments and voices were amplified, the themes acquired a personality more accentuated than previously, and the contrasts, between the ideas and between the different groups of instruments which expressed them, are more clearly marked. Four of his symphonies in particular have a strongly programmatic aspect as statements on the composer's outlook on life and the world. The third in E flat, the *Eroica* (1803), commemorates by turns the combats, the triumphs and the death of the ideal hero; the fifth, in C minor (1804-08), portrays the spirit of man overcoming the trials of fate; the sixth in F (1808), the *Pastoral*, evokes the various impressions which the artist felt at the spectacle of nature; and the ninth in D minor, the *Choral*, expresses human joy, heroism and redemption by love.

In Beethoven's hands the symphony was greatly modified. The themes became by their proportions veritable musical ideas; the modulating bridge which joins the two themes in the exposition was expanded, as was also the central development. The coda was extended and gave birth to a concluding development in which, in nearly every case, the themes of the central development are repeated, but in a more condensed manner. An introduction, sometimes very important, preceded the first movement, which was linked to it. The slow movement was sometimes in sonata form but most often appeared in the form of a song in three or five sections or in the form of a theme with variations; the minuet became faster, and was soon displaced by the more lively scherzo, which was frequently accompanied by a second trio section. In his finales, Beethoven sometimes used first-movement sonata form and sometimes rondo form, but he also employed the rondo-sonata form, of which he was the creator; sometimes, especially in his piano sonatas and chamber music, he

Title page of Beethoven's Eroica *symphony with the dedication to 'General Bonaparte' scratched out.*

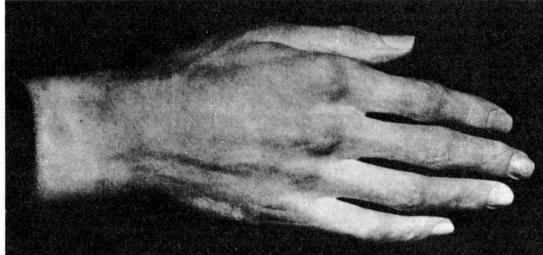

above right
Ludwig van Beethoven, who as man and composer dominated the world of music in the first half of the 19th century.

right
A cast of the hand of Beethoven, himself a great pianist.

esorted to the fugue or the variation. The sonata and the symphony of Beethoven are therefore extremely varied in their form, but the concern for unity which dominates these works often led the composer to establish thematic relationships which anticipated the appearance of the cyclic sonata.

The message made itself more obvious by moulding the framework according to its own form: hence the long development sections in the symphonies, the speeding up of the minuet which was transformed into the scherzo, the use of the amplifying variation, the presence of grand introductions designed to create the atmosphere, and the intrusion of words when pure music no longer suffices. In affirming the supremacy of the idea over the form, Beethoven not only profoundly modified the expressive content of the symphony, but he turned upside-down the laws which governed the genre and precipitated the rejection of the traditional forms, thus opening the way to Romanticism. Yet although his work leads into, and did much to shape the Romantic movement, for a long time it retained traits of the classical world. In the symphonies this is very apparent. Each has its own distinguishing character, yet in all both classical and Romantic elements are present. Besides the works already described, the others, in order of composition, were as follows: No. 1 in C major (1799), No. 2 in D major (1802), No. 4 in B flat (1806), No. 7 in A major (1812) and No. 8 in F major (1812).

Beethoven's stature as an orchestral composer is evidenced also by the seven concertos that he wrote. Of these probably the best known are the superb violin concerto in D major, written in 1806 and in the following year arranged by Beethoven himself for piano and orchestra, and the fifth piano concerto in E flat (1809), the *Emperor*. He wrote four other piano concertos: No. 1 in C major (1789), No. 2 in B flat (1795), No. 3 in C minor (1800), and No. 4 in G major (1806); and a triple concerto for piano, violin, cello and orchestra in C major (1804).

The chamber music

Yet despite the power and the sheer size of many of the symphonic works, Beethoven was to reveal the full depths of his inspiration through the medium of chamber music and above all the string quartet. The extension of the classical forms which we observed in the symphonies is to be found also in the piano sonatas. Furthermore, in certain examples, notably Opus 31, No. 2 and Opus 110, he introduces passages of instrumental recitative. These two works have declamatory passages which are reminiscent of the theme of the *Ode to Joy* and the instrumental recitative in the last movement of the ninth symphony before the entry of the voices. The procedure shows to what extent music might, for Beethoven, take on a dramatic aspect. Yet these theatrical and spectacular tendencies contrast strongly with the expression of a profoundly contemplative inner life to be found in his adagios, a contrast which epitomises the permanent conflict within him. Many of his piano compositions are marked by it, with their Romantic outbursts and their flights to the higher registers of the keyboard as if to free the melody from the hold of the bass. In this one is tempted to see an image of the man who strives to tear himself away from earthly attachments in order to attain the summits of the ideal. Yet as his creative Odyssey progressed Beethoven turned more and more towards an ascetic and contemplative mode of expression. The last of his piano sonatas dates from 1823, and a careful study of them

reveals a progressive shift towards the compositional techniques of the string quartet. From 1824 Beethoven composed almost exclusively for this latter medium and in it the visionary and ascetic nature of his work reaches its apogee. The last five quartets, together with the 'Great Fugue' for string quartet, composed between 1824 and 1827, are now generally regarded as the summit of Beethoven's achievement, though for many years after his death the advanced nature of their musical language made them incomprehensible to many critics. Above the opening bars of the last movement of the finale of the last quartet, Beethoven wrote the words '*Muss es sein – Es muss sein! Es muss sein!*' ('Must it be? It must be!'). On the threshold of eternal silence, a mind so long in conflict had found its resolution.

The choral works

The text of Beethoven's only oratorio, *Christ on the Mount of Olives*, is a paraphrase of the Gospel account. The agony of Jesus and his arrest are contained in two scenes. The music portrays the praises of a celestial choir, the threats of the soldiers, the supplications of the disciples, the resigned surrender of Christ and the intervention of a seraph, who invites men to reflect on the mystery of the Redemption. Towards the end of his life, Beethoven formed the project of writing a second oratorio, *The Victory of the Cross*.

He also composed seven secular cantatas. *The Glorious Moment*, written in 1814 on the occasion of the Congress of Vienna, takes universal love as its theme. More interesting are the two cantatas of 1790: *On the*

A contemporary impression of Beethoven in the streets of Vienna.

Death of the Emperor Joseph II and *On the Accession of the Emperor Leopold II*. Certain pages of these youthful works, such as the peroration of the funeral cantata, show a certainty of writing and a surprising expressive maturity which led Romain Rolland to declare that they 'constitute the imposing foundation of Beethoven's genius.'

Beethoven composed two masses: the Mass in C major (1807), and the Mass in D, the *Missa Solemnis* (1823). The Mass in C affirms the humility of the believer and his confident abandonment of himself to the mercy of an all-powerful God. The work is written for orchestra, choir and vocal quartet, and a concern for formal unity is evident in it from beginning to end. An example of this is the way in which Beethoven brings back the melody of the Kyrie for the concluding Dona Nobis Pacem.

The Mass in D, on the other hand, is an immense fresco of vast proportions, a human and religious drama rather than a liturgical work. It is written for full orchestra, including contrabassoon, three trombones, timpani and organ ad lib with choirs and a quartet of soloists. The three sections of the Kyrie follow the form of the andante of a sonata. The three principal divisions of the Credo use musical symbolism: rhythmic breadth and fugal entries for the affirmation of the faith, inflection of the melody by large descending intervals on the word *descendit*, use of a quartet of strings and a flute by themselves for supporting the vocal soloists in the mystery of the Incarnation, and the trombones in the Last Judgment. The whole is crowned by a masterly fugue, while the Crucifixus is one of the most humanly heart-rending pages that Beethoven wrote. From its beginning, the Sanctus abandons the solemn and glorious tone in order to adopt that of the intimate prayer, until the point where it breaks out into the vigorous accents of the Pleni sunt coeli and the Hosanna. The score of this great work is punctuated with comments which reveal Beethoven's deeply religious nature. Above the opening bars of the Kyrie he wrote: 'Come from the heart, it can return to the heart'; in the margin of the Credo: 'God above all other . . . God has never abandoned me', but for the Agnus Beethoven specifies: 'Prayer for internal and external peace', and, when the trumpets and kettledrums evoke fratricidal wars, he writes again: 'One must pray, pray, pray . . . '. Yet he seems to have had doubts about the religious value of his work, for, well after the completion of this mass, he declared, during the course of a conversation with a colleague, 'Pure church music should be performed only by voices . . . That is why I prefer Palestrina; but it is absurd to imitate him without possessing either his mind or his religious conception'.

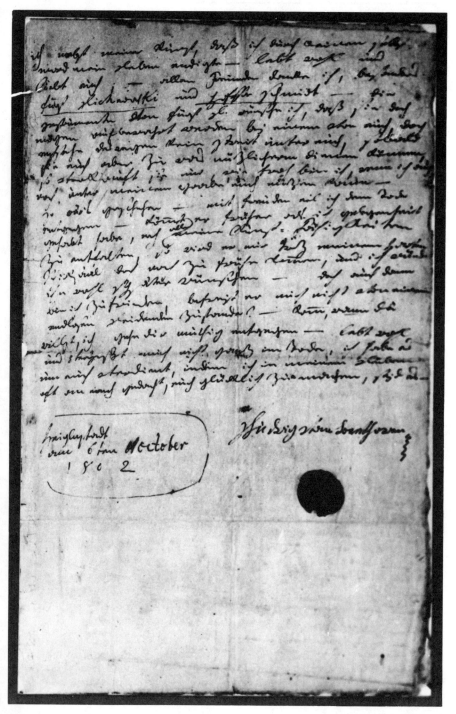

The Heiligenstadt Testament, *in which Beethoven poured out his miseries after he had become convinced of the irreversible nature of his deafness.*

Secular vocal music and works for the stage

In addition to 126 Scottish, Irish and Welsh folk songs which he harmonised for the English publisher Thomson, Beethoven composed nearly seventy-five *Lieder*. Many of them, such as the eight melodies of 1792, do not rise much above the level of similar contemporary pieces. But with *Adelaide*, in 1795, appeared a sense of dramatic declamation which developed through the six *Lieder* of Gellert (1803) to the severe style of *An die Geliebte* (1811), and continued to affirm itself up to *Elegische Gesang* for vocal quartet and string orchestra (1814).

Beethoven was one of the first to write *Lieder* in which musical expression and poetic expression were intimately united, such as *Wonne der Wehmut* ('The delights of melancholy'). The music is descriptive (*Cry of the Quail*), elegiac (*Mignon*) or picturesque (*Die Meeresstille*, 1814-15) for chorus and orchestra. By the symphonic spirit of the accompaniment, by their warm lyricism, by the choice of great human themes and the pantheistic spirit which animates them, Beethoven's *Lieder* are close to the Romantic spirit which was already blossoming in the works of Schubert at the same time.

Beethoven had composed two songs for a *Singspiel* called *The Beautiful Shoemaker* (1792), and two others within the limits of the stage music for Goethe's *Egmont*. His notebooks for 1823-26 tell us that he projected the writing of an opera on the poem *Melusine* by Grillparzer, in which each appearance of the fairy was to be underlined by a sort of *Leitmotiv*; yet the only complete proof that we have of his dramatic inspiration is his *Fidelio*.

The first rough sketches can be placed about December 1803. The libretto was taken from *Leonore or Conjugal Love*, which had been performed in Paris in 1798.

Dealing with historical events during the revolutionary terror thinly disguised as an episode in Spanish history, it gained its author a certain notoriety. Nevertheless its story of unjust political imprisonment and unshakeable conjugal devotion was perfectly suited to the expression of Beethoven's passionate belief in the ideals of liberty and the universal power of human love. His librettist, Sonnleithner, added several scenes to the original at the composer's request. Completed in November 1805, *Fidelio* had only three performances; but later revivals (1806-14) incorporated various reworkings to which we owe in particular, among the four successive overtures, that of *Leonora No. 3*.

Beethoven chose the form of drama blended with music, which was associated in certain aspects with the *Singspiel*. But in *Fidelio* the music took on an importance new to this style. With Beethoven, the music totally transcends the drama and itself becomes the centre of the action and the focus of the drama. The extraordinary amplitude of the overtures and of the symphonic developments in the introductions and codas emphasises the pre-eminence of the music. The new scenes were added for musical reasons and include the quartet in the first act, the trio, the march, Pizarro's aria, the duet with Rocco, the finale of the first act, Florestan's aria (much more developed than in the French version), the quartet and, above all, the imposing five-part finale.

Fidelio reveals a serious endeavour to combine the symphonic element with the dramatic element and in this respect to some extent foreshadows the work of Wagner. As for the comparatively trite theme of the French work, Beethoven transfigured it. In this work, as with the late sonatas and quartets, Beethoven reveals the very depths of his humanity in music which is almost ascetic. Love – whether it be conjugal love, pure love or the love of liberty – is the theme; it is a love which finds its highest expression in human fraternity and reconciliation.

Beethoven's total deafness in the last eight years of his life must in some measure account for the introspective and metaphysical aspects of the music of the last sonatas and the last quartets. The world of appearances was progressively rejected; deaf to the clamour of life, he seems to have had ears only for the mysterious harmonies which rose within him. To translate and express them he forged what was virtually a new musical language, a language which was to be fully understood only by later generations. Indeed, Beethoven's entire creative career bears witness to a conflict between the past and the future, between pure classicism and pure Romanticism, between the form and the idea, between life and the ideal. Quite apart from its immense stature in terms of sheer artistic achievement it has a great, if secondary, interest for us, precisely because on the one hand it sums up the legacy of earlier generations and on the other opens the way to the future.

Beethoven's lesser contemporaries

During his life Beethoven enjoyed a respect and European reputation which is paralleled only by that accorded to Michelangelo. After the death of Haydn there was no star in the musical firmament that was not dimmed by his brilliance and only his younger contemporaries, Weber and Schubert, can be compared with him. Nevertheless there were, of course, a number of talented composers working in Germany during the opening decades of the 19th century, amongst whom Dussek, Hummel and Ries may be cited here.

All three were renowned pianists, Johann Ladislaus Dussek (1760-1812) also enjoying a reputation as a virtuoso on the glass harmonica, which had such a vogue in the second half of the 18th century. Dussek was one of the many lesser Czech masters who enriched the history of German music during the 18th century. He travelled widely throughout Europe, spending eight years in London, where his venture in music publishing ended in bankruptcy. He occupies an important place in the history of piano technique, being the first to introduce the singing manner to piano playing. Although he wrote two operas and church music it is on his numerous keyboard works that his reputation is founded.

Johann Nepomuk Hummel (1778-1837) was for two years a pupil of Mozart and, from 1804 to 1811, *Kapellmeister* to the Prince Esterhazy – during the first five years acting as deputy for the aged Haydn. He was more important as a pianist than as a composer. Superficially his style is clearly influenced by that of Mozart, but virtuosity too far outweighs inspiration. However, both by the example of his own playing and by his important piano method, which contained the first rational treatment of the subject of fingering, Hummel contributed significantly to the virtuoso technique of the school of Chopin and Liszt. Last of this trio of pianists is Ferdinand Ries (1784-1838), who studied for four years under Beethoven himself. Between 1813 and 1824 he enjoyed considerable success as pianist and composer to the Philharmonic Society in London, and from 1826 until his death he was a leading figure in the musical life of Frankfurt.

Finally in this treatment of some of Beethoven's contemporaries we must mention the strange figure of the writer and musician Ernst Theodor Amadeus Hoffmann (1776-1822). His tales of the fantastic and the supernatural provided the material of Offenbach's opera *Tales of Hoffmann* and also inspired many other Romantic artists, notably Schumann. He was an important music critic, held musical directorships at Bamberg, Leipzig and Dresden and composed music of all kinds, his Romantic opera *Ondine* having a direct influence on the work of Weber.

Weber

Carl Maria von Weber (1786-1826) was destined for a musical career by his father, and at the age of ten took lessons from Michael Haydn (1737-1806), brother of Joseph. He published his first compositions at the age

Ear trumpets with which Beethoven strove to overcome his tragic deafness.

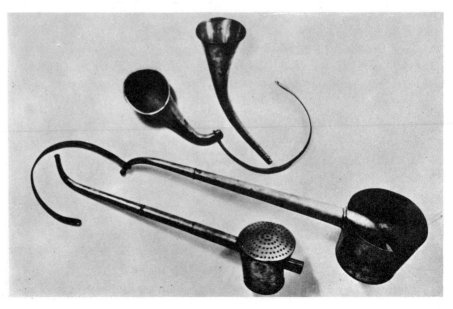

of thirteen, and after his first attempts at the *Singspiel* studied for a time under the Abbé Vogler. From 1816 he was a director of the opera at Dresden, but he died in London while there to conduct his opera *Oberon*. To his contemporaries Weber's music seemed to embody the spirit of the new Germanism which had grown up in response to the challenge of Napoleonic France, and during his life some of his best known music was his settings of the patriotic poems, *Lyre and Sword*, of the young Theodor Körner.

In his comparatively brief career Weber wrote over three hundred works, in which dramatic music is represented by a dozen *Singspiele*, several melodramas and a single true opera, *Euryanthe*. His success in the style of the *Singspiel* was precocious and rapid. The comic intrigue *Die Macht der Liebe und des Weins*, written in 1798 at the age of twelve, was followed two years later by *Das Waldmädchen*, whose success somewhat surprised the composer himself. In 1804 appeared *Rubezahl*, based on a popular legend, a work in two acts of phantasmagoric character with choruses of spirits, genies and nymphs. In 1810, with *Silvana*, the title of 'Romantic opera' appeared for the first time. Although the work itself could more accurately be described as an *opéra-comique*, the term accurately embodies Weber's place as the true pioneer of German Romantic opera, which was to be assured with the production of *Der Freischütz* some ten years later. It was preceded by *Abu-Hassan* (1811) a Turkish piece in one act, and *Preziosa* (1820), based on Cervantes and utilising themes taken from a recent collection of Spanish airs. *Der Freischütz* (1821), which showed affinities to Hoffmann's *Ondine* in its use of the fantastic, was a national work par excellence, and was hailed as such. Drawing on all the expressive powers of folk music it is

Carl Maria von Weber as a young man.

a fully German work. *Oberon*, staged in London in 1826, was inspired by one of C. M. Wieland's narrative poems. Once again it was a fantastic work but here the fantasy is benign and friendly.

Weber's only completely sung opera was *Euryanthe* (1823). The plot is taken from an old French legend of a virtuous woman wrongly accused. The intrigue which Weber introduced into the theme of the legend allows one to suppose that Euryanthe was unfaithful, and that she was so because she knew things which she ought not to know; this idea of the 'secret' was to be taken up by Wagner in *Lohengrin*.

All Weber's stage works share certain common characteristics. In all of them the orchestra is important in the dramatic development. In the tradition of Gluck's reform Weber's overture forms a prelude to the dramatic action. It is no longer, as in *Fidelio*, a symphonic overture in which the musical ideas are developed in the spirit of the drama, but an overture in which the music itself is cast in a dramatic mould, proceeding by contrasts and antitheses, its principal interest coming from the perfect balance between its dramatic and musical values. In the course of the action Weber depicts his characters with a remarkable precision, using purely musical means. Through the vividness of his orchestration he establishes his heroes as human types, but elevates them from the individual to the universal level. A judicious choice of tone colours and rhythms enables him to express the fantastic, the hallucinatory, the strange and the terrible.

In a real sense Weber may be regarded as the first essentially Romantic composer. Beethoven, like him, was profoundly inspired by nature but, with Beethoven, nature is a serene and pantheistic force, whereas for Weber it is causative, participating in and working upon the emotional life of humanity, and in his works the comic and the sublime are juxtaposed. He boldly utilises the whole gamut of the full orchestra's tone colours and shows particular originality in his handling of the brass, notably the horns. By the individualisation of tone colours and their mode of grouping, Weber created immense expressive possibilities, thanks to which musical drama was suddenly enriched with a new means of expression. Through the choice of certain harmonic progressions and their extremely varied deployment he contributed to the formation of a musical vocabulary of which Wagner was to make considerable use.

However, it was the field of melody, especially his use of popular melody, which proved the most fertile aspect of his talent. Wagner emphasised the point in his critical work *Opera and Drama*, which was dedicated to Weber. 'It is a characteristic trait of German popular melody that it manifests itself less in its short, lively and individual rhythms than in broad melodic passages joyful yet full of feeling. German *Lieder* performed without any harmony are absolutely inconceivable to us. Everywhere we hear them sung by two voices at the least; artistry urges the addition of the bass and the middle part to construct the whole edifice of this harmonic melody. This melody is the fundamental basis of Weber's popular opera which, freed from all particular local or national associations by the broad and general expression of the feeling, speaks to the heart of man because it appears unreservedly human and without the least disguise.'

This inextricable involvement with popular melody is the most striking characteristic of Weber's dramatic works, whether it be expressed in a single line (which is infrequent), or collectively in choruses of a rare beauty. These choruses seem to express one of the characteristic ideas of German Romanticism – that a people is to be considered no longer as a group of individuals but as a collective soul which has a reality of its own.

The Lied before Schubert

In this field, as in so many others, Beethoven, as we have observed, made an important contribution. During the second half of the 18th century a revival had begun which prepared the ground for the glorious flowering of the *Lied* in Schubert's music. We can distinguish two lines of development, first and less important being the growth of a tradition of nationalist German songs of which Weber's settings of Körner's *Lyre and Sword* was the natural continuation; the second was the more purely musical work of Haydn and Mozart, which was to provide a greater inspiration for Schubert. The philosopher Herder, whose emphasis on the fundamental importance of folk art and tradition as the roots of national identity and human experience was so influential, was probably the first to use the word *ein Volk*, 'a people', in the sense of a national ethnic community. And he regarded song as the most direct expression of this community. Furthermore by 'songs of the people' (*Volkslieder*), Herder meant not only peasant and nursery songs, but those of religious tradition. He believed that to renew the poetic and musical arts it was necessary to return to popular sources, to collect the old songs transmitted by oral tradition and revive them by reintroducing them to the people.

Inspired by these ideas Berlin composers actively attempted the resurrection of folk art. The *Rheinweinlied* (1776) of Johann André (1741-99), and the collections of songs in the folk idiom of Reichardt and Schulz that appeared from 1781, are examples. Their prefaces echo the principles of Herder: 'The melody must be very simple and must so exactly grasp the bearing of the text that words and music must henceforward be inseparable'.

However it was Goethe who was most eagerly set by German composers up to the Romantic period. Zelter set to music many a poem by his friend, and in 1809 Reichardt published his collection of *Lieder*, odes, ballads and romances of Goethe, which was probably the most important work of this genre in Germany before Schubert. Towards the end of this period, in 1818, there appeared the ballads for voice with piano accompaniment by Johann Carl Löwe (1796-1869); half-way between the *Lied* and the forms of dramatic music, these ballads, already Romantic in spirit, were ultimately based on folk idiom. Such a movement in the direction of popular song was hardly neccessary in southern Germany, where the old traditions had remained very much alive. C. F. D. Schubart (1739-91) and J. R. Zumsteeg (1760-1802) freely introduced the style of the folk song into their compositions, using literary texts by such poets as Schiller.

The intimate collaboration of composers and poets led music little by little towards the spirit and the form of the 19th-century *Lied*. As early as 1775 Gluck had written seven songs on poems by Klopstock – *Odes and Lieder by Klopstock for Singing to the Klavier*; in 1778 J. A. Steffan (1726-1800) published in Vienna the first volumes of a series of collections of German *Lieder*. The spirit of the *Singspiel* penetrated the *Lied* of the Viennese school. The rigidity of the north German style became supple, the melody became more lyrical and with less angular rhythm, and instrumental technique gave a greater importance to the accompaniment. The principal representatives of this school before the Romantic period were Haydn, Mozart and Beethoven himself.

Haydn is represented principally by two volumes of twelve *Lieder* (1781-84) and twelve English songs

Set for a 19th-century production of Weber's opera Der Freischütz.

(1796) several of the poems being by Shakespeare. Close to the popular style of the *Singspiel*, and with generally strophic, supple and ornate melismata, though occasionally borrowing the dramatic declamation of the aria, the *Lieder* of Haydn made an important advance in the treatment of the accompaniment. This, which had been used merely to double the voice in the right hand, was fired with a new 'symphonic' spirit; with its preludes, interludes and postludes it developed in the sense of a musical commentary on the text, sometimes descriptive, sometimes expressive.

Except for a setting of Goethe's *Das Veilchen* the texts of Mozart's songs are poor. Nevertheless in the variety of their form, in their diversity of expression, embracing humour and tenderness, and in the grace of a language whose airy purity did not exclude profundity, Mozart's thirty-four *Lieder* for voice and piano attained the summits of beauty. The earlier examples, composed

between 1768 and 1772, are still written on two staves, and recall the simple instrumental style of the collections of *chansons dansées* which were numerous at that time. *Das Veilchen*, however, which appeared in 1785, is a concise little drama whose delicate emotion revealed the exquisite sensibility of the composer as much as his dramatic instinct. Vehemence tempered by gracefulness animates the through-composed *Lied*, 'When Louise burnt her unfaithful lover's letters'.

In the last years of his life Mozart wrote songs of youthful freshness such as *Nostalgia of the Spring*; occasionally a more elegiac tone and a certain expressive nostalgia shine through, directly announcing the début of the Romantic *Lied*. To these varied merits is added a technique which provides a judicious balance between voice and keyboard, maintained without fettering a lyricism whose sense of nuance always forms and tempers the composer's most passionate outbursts.

Two impressions of Weber conducting.

Plate 37 left
A portrait of the young Beethoven.

Plate 38 below
*Set from a 19th-century production
of Beethoven's opera* Fidelio.

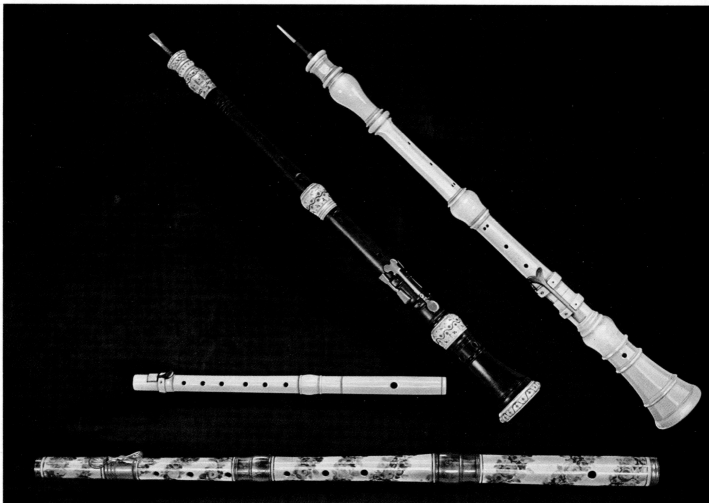

The first generation of Romantics

Franz Peter Schubert was born in Liechtenthal near Vienna, in January 1797. His father, a Moravian peasant schoolteacher, married a cook in Vienna, Elisabeth Vietz. Franz was their twelfth child. After acquiring the rudiments of music from his father he became a boarder at the municipal college, where choristers were trained for the imperial chapel and where the pupils formed their own orchestra. Here he completed his education in an atmosphere of work which was to cause him one of his first bouts of melancholia. He helped his father in his teaching until he was twenty-one, but he had composed from boyhood and by the age of seventeen was capable of such a masterpiece as *Gretchen am Spinnrade*. For the rest of his brief life Schubert devoted himself to composition and performances for a wide circle of friends on whose patronage he relied. During a working career of less than twenty years Schubert produced a torrent of work. This included various operas and *Singspiele*; music for the stage; seven masses, as well as a large number of individual sacred compositions; nine symphonies and several overtures; string quartets, quintets and one octet; sonatas for various instruments as well as some twenty piano sonatas together with some numerous fantasies, variations etc., for four hands; about fifty choral works and over six hundred *Lieder*.

Schubert's piano compositions and chamber music

The relative lack of musical form so evident in his piano sonatas probably derives from the fact that his sonata themes are hardly ever themes in the proper sense of the word, but seem rather like 'wandering songs'. Schubert's music is essentially melodic and song-like and he often seems to 'lose his sense of direction' in the formal context of the sonata and gets caught up in the mazes of his imagination before finally returning to a classical summing up. His sonatas are spread over the last thirteen years of his short life. They obviously owe much to Mozart both in form and style; at first glance, his scores seem to offer few harmonic differences from those of the preceding generation. However, there is in fact a complete difference in texture. Free modulations of key succeed each other in moods of reverie or liveliness and the characteristic Schubertian dichotomy between the major and minor is ever-present. Beethoven first introduced a similar 'free style' in his *Bagatelles*, but it was Schubert who brought the style to perfection with his *Impromptus* and *Moments musicaux*. These are generally conceived in the form of the scherzo, and reveal powers of imagination which shatter all previous traditional Viennese concepts. These compositions contain some of Schubert's very finest work on a small scale.

The freedom of his expression is perhaps even more obvious in the fantasies, *divertissements* and duets for piano. The piano duets are virtuoso concert pieces and have great depth of feeling. They show evidence of true improvisation and even of delirium. The most striking of the piano works are the fantasy in G minor, which is really a kind of sonata, the mighty *Wanderer* fantasy in C, the sonata in C major for piano duet and the extraordinary *Divertissement à la Hongroise*.

In his chamber music, Schubert, while clearly the heir to Mozart and Haydn in matters of formal structure, gives free rein to his inexhaustible inventive powers. He employs the simplest means to achieve the most miraculous tonal combinations, sometimes using complex counterpoint, interweaving parts or making one part answer to another in a manner until then hardly known. The sonatinas for violin and piano have a charm and original quality all of their own. The sonata in A major (1817) is a profound work, as is the famous sonata of 1824 for piano and the now obsolete stringed instrument, the arpeggione, whose part is today played on the cello. The two trios for piano and strings of 1816-17 are filled with Schubertian melancholy, particularly in the slow movements.

Schubert very soon found in the string quartet a medium which ideally suited his talent. The first was written in 1811; the last at the very end of his life. During these seventeen years his music assumes various colours, but the structure remains more or less constant and, throughout, there is always complete freedom of expression in his chromatic harmonies and the boldness of his modulations. Schubert's quartets almost invariably evoke the atmosphere of the *Lieder*. This is not only because he often uses the same themes for works in the two genres, but mainly because he establishes and develops in the quartets a lyrical dramatic mood similar to the songs; thus the passage marked *allegro ma non troppo* in the A minor quartet establishes an overwhelming feeling of sadness in the space of only two bars by the sudden introduction of a very simple but beautiful melody. In the D minor quartet the use of the *Death and the Maiden* theme has no symbolic significance, but the general tone of the work is very similar to the dramatic ballad style of the song of the same name. The G major quartet is an example of a very advanced style of harmonic writing which anticipates the mature Brahms and the young Richard Strauss.

Of the two quintets, the *Trout* piano quintet is probably the best known; it is in no way classical in form, and the introduction of a double bass with only one violin, viola and cello gives the piece a special interest. But the string quintet in C major with two violins, a viola and two cellos is Schubert at his purest and most sublime.

The great F major octet for two violins, viola, cello, double bass, clarinet, horn and bassoon is in fact a great divertimento in the Mozartian tradition. Written in 1824, and so full of irresistible charm, it also inevitably reminds one of the famous Beethoven septet.

The Lieder

Schubert's most important contribution was in the field of *Lieder*. Without exception the Schubertian *Lieder* have a concise framework, but within this he uses his prolific imagination to express every shade of poetic meaning – tenderness, drama, evocations of the countryside etc. But at the same time they are filled with great simplicity; his melodic line often has the artlessness of a folk tune and the piano accompaniment is often the simplest possible. Furthermore, Schubert displays an instinctive but profound understanding of the potentialities of the human voice. His subtle sense of rhythm enabled him to render the most delicate inflections and accents of the German language in terms of music; his rhythms change according to the mood of the poem, sometimes serene and calm, sometimes impassioned and febrile. Nature, love and death are his preferred themes. One can classify his immense production under two main headings: the lyric (love songs), and the heroic or dramatic (ballad style).

Although Schubert sometimes composed settings for mediocre poems like those by Müller, he nearly always chose fine texts, drawing on the works of such poets as Schiller, Goethe, Mattheson, Klopstock, Ossian, Aeschylus, Petrarch, Dante, Novalis, Uhland, Walter Scott, Shakespeare and Heine. His first major work in this field, when he was seventeen, was his setting of Goethe's *Gretchen am Spinnrade*. This was one of the first *Lieder* in which the piano accompaniment was of real significance (1814). The famous *Erlkönig* (1815) is one of the great masterpieces of dramatic folk ballads, and in it the piano accompaniment is almost symphonic; this technique was to be even further perfected in the *Doppelgänger*, where Schubert gives the piano a sort of chaconne-line bass accompaniment. Little by little he

above
Franz Schubert.

right
Schubert's house in Vienna.

was developing the ability to contrast light and shade by alternate major and minor keys and striking modulations; a fine example of this is the *Wanderer*, on which the C major piano fantasy is based.

In his ballads Schubert sometimes indulges in some curious experiments. The most typical example is the twenty-five-minute-long *Der Taucher*, on the epic ballad by Schiller, which is more like an operatic aria or even a one act opera than a ballad. In this work Schubert shows a sense of the theatre which, alas, he was never able to realise in his attempts at opera.

His genius and originality as a song composer is still further revealed in his three great song cycles: *Die schöne Müllerin* (1823), comprising twenty songs; the *Winterreise* (1827) with twenty-four, and the last, the *Schwanengesang* with fourteen, a symbolic title chosen by its publisher since it was written in 1828, the year of Schubert's death. In Schubertian usage the word 'cycle' does not carry the comparatively strict formal implications it was to bear later in the 19th century; Schubert did not aim at a thematic development through these large song collections, but wished rather to produce a poetic, dramatic and psychological unity.

The symphonies

Here, it must be said, we find ourselves on less original ground. Schubert appears to have learnt little from Beethoven. His thematic material is often rudimentary, but his harmonic resourcefulness and modulations of key, without having the inexhaustible richness of the quartets and *Lieder*, are still often characteristic of Schubert's inventiveness. 18th-century influences are evident in the first five symphonies (1813-16) and, reading between the lines, we can often see allusions to Italian music. Probably the most popular Schubert symphony is the two-movement 'Unfinished', No. 8 in B

minor (1822). Perhaps because of its very popularity this deeply inspired and moving work is liable to be underrated. Yet the greatest of the whole series is nevertheless the ninth – the 'Great' C major of 1828, not only by reason of its proportions and development, but by its glowing inspiration. Writing of it the critic Alfred Einstein has said: 'Its form is more drawn out and repeated than actually developed, which makes it difficult to interpret, particularly the finale which is difficult to "put across" after what has just preceded'. Schubert's particularly rich use of the woodwind and the brass is a notable feature in this work.

Schubert's seven masses are characterised by certain academic impersonal qualities rarely found in his other compositions and by excessively sentimental passages

below
A room in Schubert's house, now a museum.

bottom
Schubert was helped by the patronage of his friends: this painting by Moritz von Schwind gives an impression of a 'Schubert evening' when they gathered to hear the composer play.

(seldom carried to such extremes in religious works of this nature). An example is the Sanctus of the A flat mass (1822), a work which opened the way to the sentimental Romantic sacred music of the future.

In 1826 he wrote the so-called 'German' mass and in 1828 the mass in E flat, both of which, like the masses in B flat, are subjective in style. This fact may be explained by a little-known prayer written by Schubert, which ends: 'Almighty God, plunge me in the waters of Lethe, make me another man, more vigorous and courageous.'

Of all the masses the most original is the 'German' mass, based on German texts. Schubert used relatively few instruments so that the work might be easy to perform. It has a markedly Lutheran flavour; not only are the words in the vernacular, but the sections of the mass do not follow the traditional Catholic liturgy and have the character of hymns or canticles. The music is no less unorthodox than the liturgical structure; it is directly inspired by folk songs, chorales, and sometimes by *Ländler*. This was an Austrian waltz-type dance of which Schubert also wrote a number of piano examples.

above
A page of manuscript of one of Schubert's songs.

right
Heinrich Heine (1797–1856), whose poems were set by both Schubert and Schumann.

Mendelssohn

Felix Mendelssohn-Bartholdy was a classical musician whose style was formed by Palestrina, Bach and Handel, but his manner is often Romantic. The son of a well-to-do Jewish family, converted to Protestantism, and brought up in comfortable circumstances, he was by temperament agreeable, calm, collected and refined – in short, everything that was contrary to the tormented Romantic spirit. In the deepest recesses of his nature all was orderly. Yet its warmth and enthusiasm gives his music the personal emotional quality that fully entitles him to be called a Romantic, although in fact he is more often sentimental than volcanic. But his melodic and orchestral invention reveal him to be a true poet.

Mendelssohn was born in Hamburg in 1809 into a banking family (the name Bartholdy was assumed by his father when he gave up Judaism). Two years after the birth of Felix the Mendelssohn family moved to Berlin. Having given very early proof of an undoubted musical talent, Felix was sent by his parents to the celebrated Zelter for theory and Ludwig Berger, a pupil of Clementi, for piano.

He gave his first public performance at the age of nine. In the following year he entered the *Singakademie* and started to compose. In 1825 he visited Paris where Cherubini advised his father to allow him to devote his career entirely to music. At seventeen he wrote his masterpiece, the overture to *A Midsummer Night's Dream*. Two years later, he unearthed and edited Bach's *St Matthew Passion*, and conducted its performance at the *Singakademie* in Berlin in 1829. In the same year he started on his European tours, and his nine visits to Britain were of particular importance to the musical life of England. At the age of twenty-four he was appointed director of the Lower Rhine music festival in Düsseldorf (1833). Two years later he settled in Leipzig as conductor of the Gewandhaus Orchestra, where he was in part responsible for founding one of the most famous music conservatories in Europe; there he died in 1847, at the age of thirty-eight.

In his oratorios, *St Paul* and *Elijah*, written for the Birmingham Festival of 1846, despite the obvious influence of Bach and Handel, his music never achieves the fullest depths of feeling and fervour. But his brilliant fugal writing has real grandeur and his polyphonic scoring is superb. For both oratorios Mendelssohn relied entirely on the Biblical texts.

Symphonic music

The *Italian* (1833) and *Scottish* (1842) are undoubtedly the most popular of the symphonies and possess a freshness and poetry that well justify their success. One finds here the same charm, elegance, verve and sure touch that make the composer's travel letters and watercolours so enchanting. The *Reformation* symphony (1829-30), commissioned for the tercentenary of the Augsburg Confession, is essentially a religious work and is written in a deliberately austere and formal manner. This is particularly evident in the first movement, where Mendelssohn makes use of the three-fold Dresden Amen which Wagner also used for the Grail motif in *Parsifal*; this solemn mood is recaptured in the finale with the introduction of the chorale *Ein' feste Burg ist unser Gott*.

The overtures are evocative and to some extent can be considered as predecessors of the symphonic tone poem. From its very first miraculous opening bars the *Midsummer Night's Dream* transports us straight into the fairy world of Shakespeare.

The *Hebrides* overture, despite the composer's famous remark that 'the development smells more of counterpoint than of fish oil, seagulls and cod', is very evocative of the scenery of the Western Isles, and the music conjures up the image of waves, seagulls and rocky shores under scudding clouds.

In the two piano concertos it would seem that Mendelssohn was only trying to provide a vehicle for the virtuosity of the soloist, but it is quite a different matter when we come to his violin concerto, written for his friend Ferdinand David. Here the melodic line is very lovely and has a happy and peaceful intimacy.

Chamber music and piano works

Although Mendelssohn was attracted by small instrumental ensembles, it cannot be said that this was a medium in which he displayed his inventive gifts at their best. However, one must not underestimate the real dramatic power of the C minor trio or of the A minor and F minor quartets, the last of which was written in memory of his beloved sister. Nor should we overlook the string octet in E flat major, a masterly youthful work whose originality lies in the fact that it is a sort of 'chamber symphony'.

But undoubtedly Mendelssohn's most original works are those he wrote for the piano, in particular the forty-nine *Songs without Words*. These are one-movement pianoforte solos, throughout which a well-marked song-like melody progresses with accompaniment. The piano writing, though owing much to Bach, Mozart and Beethoven, is nevertheless markedly individual. The pieces owe their success primarily to their originality and simplicity and also to the mixture of genuine feeling and good taste they display, as well as to their conciseness and what one might call their 'romantic mood'. Moreover, the perfection of the contrapuntal writing, which was facilitated to some extent by the technical improvements made to the piano at this time, has an additional interest.

The *Variations sérieuses*, despite their title, are by no means austere. They are in fact the most sublime variations, of great technical interest, and they provide the executant with an opportunity to display his virtuosity to the full. The title was given by Mendelssohn to

above
Mendelssohn's autograph manuscript of the opening bars of his arrangement of the fifty-fifth psalm, 'Hear my prayer'.

FELIX MENDELSSOHN BARTHOLDY.

left
A caricature of Mendelssohn by the fin de siècle *artist Aubrey Beardsley.*

differentiate them from the variations and *pots-pourris* based on popular tunes which were so fashionable at the time. The whole work, based on a splendid, solemn theme, is fine and noble throughout, yet very moving.

Schumann

Robert Schumann, the middle class boy from the provinces who was to become one of the greatest Romantic composers and one of the most outstanding geniuses in the whole history of music, was never quite able to accomplish what he believed to be his mission. He was in fact a revolutionary, though he did not want to break with the past. There was something fundamentally conservative in Schumann's nature, and although he felt it his destiny to fuse modern and traditional art, he never succeeded. Whenever he reverted to traditional methods, he failed. He himself was aware of this and this was why he welcomed the young Brahms with such enthusiasm – 'this eaglet descended from Hamburg' – for here he felt was someone who would succeed in the mission in which he himself had failed.

Yet Schumann occupies one of the most important positions in German music. Everything he wrote displays his critical acumen and it was only after the most exacting deliberation 'that he allowed his art to take flight on the wings of his many-sided genius and give expression to the twin daemons by whom he was possessed – the heroic Florestan and gentle Eusebius.' However, in his very earliest works, when the eternal child in him was still free, he did realise himself completely. It was in the last period of his life that he was unable to follow his star.

Schumann was born in Zwickau, in Saxony, in 1810. His father was a bookseller – an important factor in the evolution of a musician who was to be the first Romantic with a real knowledge of literature and philosophy. In the backroom of his father's shop the young Schumann discovered the marvels of poetry, fiction and history.

A little later he combined his study of music with the classics. Sent to Leipzig to study law (1828), he continued his musical studies, especially the piano with Friedrich Wieck. With Wieck's help he would become a virtuoso pianist, or so he thought. But this hope was soon to be dispelled. Owing to an appliance which he had invented to hold the third finger motionless while practising, he permanently damaged the phalanges of his left hand and was obliged to abandon the piano altogether. It was only then that he decided to devote himself to composition. His first piano works date from this period, and also his first literary musical criticisms. His acuity and influence as a critic are marked by his introduction of the genius of Chopin to the German public.

During the Leipzig period he fell deeply in love with his teacher's daughter, Clara Wieck, herself an accomplished pianist. His feelings for her were soon reciprocated, but it was only after many years of struggle (indeed, after Schumann had brought a lawsuit) that Wieck finally gave his consent to their union (1840). It was a very happy marriage and for the next four years Schumann composed with greater facility and in greater quantity than ever, but signs of nervous disorder were already becoming apparent.

In 1843 Mendelssohn, who had recently founded the Leipzig conservatory, offered Schumann the position of professor of pianoforte and composition. But at the end of the year he resigned from the post and went to live in Dresden, where he began to show further signs of nervous collapse. Because of the Revolution of 1848 he was obliged to leave Dresden and accepted a post at Düsseldorf, where he made the acquaintance of the young Brahms. Health reasons obliged him to give up his official work, although he still continued to conduct until finally, in February, 1854, while in a fit of mental depression, he threw himself into the Rhine. He was rescued but thereafter was confined in an asylum near Bonn where he died two years later.

The piano music

From his very first piano score, the whole of Schumann – the hero of Romanticism – is revealed. The writing is individual and confident, but it often reflects his despair at not being able to marry the woman he loved. The young musician's moods of despondency and exasperation were nurtured by his readings of Jean-Paul, Heine and Hoffmann, and it is this that gives his work a quality which is as much pictorial and literary as musical. With his very first piano pieces he established a style (as did Beethoven) which, though very varied in mood, was never to change throughout his career as a composer. His piano compositions are nearly always based on short themes which he develops by harmonic progressions and which in turn affect the melodic line, a dialogue which is very revealing of Schumann's troubled state of mind. Schumann was very quick to break away from classical forms. All his compositions seem rather like pages from a personal diary – fragmented, concise, condensed and profuse in musical invention.

Opus 1 (1830), the *Abegg Variations*, were written as a compliment to an early love, Meta Abegg, on three themes formed by the notes contained in her surname. The literary side of Schumann is apparent in his opus 2, *Papillons*, 'Butterflies' (1832), which is written in the form of a suite of twelve waltzes inspired by the last pages of Jean-Paul's novel *Die Flegeljahre*, 'Years of Indiscretion'.

In his subsequent piano pieces, Schumann is particularly interested in finding new technical procedures, which he himself described as 'a labour of Hercules'. These are: *Studies on a theme of Paganini I*

Robert and Clara Schumann.

and *II* (1832-33); *Intermezzi* (1832); *Impromptus on an Air by Clara Wieck* (1833; revised 1850) and the *Davidsbündlertänze* (1837); the *Davidsbund* or League of David was an imaginary group opposed to all 'Philistines', often referred to in Schumann's journal and of which Eusebius and Florestan were the protagonists.

After *Papillons* we have an even more typically Schumannesque composition in *Carnaval* (1835). In this he vividly brings to life all the characters of his own secret world – Pierrot, Harlequin, Eusebius and Florestan, who all represent different aspects of his own character – as well as paying homage to Chopin and Paganini, and not least to his friends, by concluding the whole suite with the brilliant *Davidsbündler March against the Philistines*.

The opus numbers of his catalogued works are not in strict chronological order. After the sonata, Opus 11 (1835) and the *Fantasiestücke*, Opus 12 (1837), we find the sumptuous *Etudes symphoniques*, Opus 13, studies in the form of variations, almost orchestral in power, which were in fact written in 1834. This is followed by the *Concerto without orchestra* in F minor, Opus 14 (1836), later reworked as a sonata. Masterpiece after masterpiece followed each other – the ideally poetic *Kinderszenen* (1838), in which the eternal child in Schumann recaptures all his youth in some of the most delightful piano music he ever wrote; *Kreisleriana* (1838), 'music which is fantastic and mad', as Schumann himself wrote; and finally the 'bustling' Fantasy in C (1836), 'a long complaint', as the composer described it to his beloved Clara.

Lieder

Of the 250 *Lieder* written by Schumann, the first 130 were composed in the year 1840. Although Schumann's *Lieder* are directly descended from those of Schubert they differ from the latter's in more than one respect. It is true that they have similar themes (love, nature, death, legend) and both composers sometimes use texts by the same poets. But Schumann was to enrich the style, to make it more complex, more intense, more dramatic. Furthermore he was to depart further and further from folklore subjects for the world of German poetry. In addition, his piano accompaniments are really commentaries and enhance the atmosphere of the poem. We have already noted that in his piano works Schumann has a predilection for the musical cycle and he wrote four great song cycles: to texts by Heine, the *Liederkreis I* (1839); Eichendorff, *Liederkreis II* (1840); Chamisso, *Frauenliebe und Leben* (1840); and also by Heine, the *Dichterliebe* (1840). Apart from these poets his favourite authors were: Jean-Paul, Hoffmann, Goethe, Byron and Shakespeare, but he also sometimes turned to Schiller, Uhland, Hebbel, Mörike and others. But it was always to Heine that he returned and for whose poems he wrote his finest songs.

In a cycle such as the *Dichterliebe*, Heine blends his poetry with an irony that is apt to grow bitterest when his lyric mood is sweetest, and it is just this element that

The age of Mendelssohn and Schumann was also that of the Strauss family. This contemporary print of a galop indicates that 19th-century social life was not always inhibited. Notice that the orchestra in the gallery is led by a violinist.

Schumann saw reflected in himself. Although Schumann's melodic line is always lyrical and filled with simple tenderness, the piano accompaniment cuts sharp and deep and admirably interprets Heine's double meaning. The same applies to his settings of the eight poems by Chamisso, *Life and Love of a Woman* – the first meeting, betrothal, wedding, joys of marriage and the bitter separation by death are all reflected here in his music.

Chamber music and symphonies

In this field, Schumann is perhaps not quite so much at home as elsewhere. But in the three trios, for piano, violin and cello, the instrumental parts are clearly defined, sometimes treated broadly or with bravura, sometimes tenderly or with a sombre pathos. Every facet of Schumann's character is reflected in these works. Just as the trios reflect the tormented Schumann, so the three string quartets, written much earlier (1842), reveal the joyous side of his nature. Of all Schumann's chamber music, these are the most free and are the works in which he shows himself most at ease in a classical idiom.

Schumann towards the end of his life.

Two of the greatest chamber works, the piano quartet and quintet, also date from 1842. The quartet provides the piano with an almost concertante part. Despite its distinctive Schumannesque characteristics outside influences are very evident: Beethoven in the initial allegro movement; Mendelssohn in the scherzo; Bach in the finale. The quintet succeeds brilliantly. Here again the piano intervenes with great authority. The three themes in the first movement have the same impetuosity and force as the A minor piano concerto; the second movement with its awesome funeral march theme is pure Schumann, and if the scherzo is not quite so rich musically, it is nevertheless unequivocally a product of the fantasies of Eusebius and Florestan.

It is a commonplace to say that Schumann was an indifferent orchestrator; but although many great composers and eminent conductors have re-scored these four symphonies they have thereby sacrificed the light and shade of Schumann's genius. However interesting these arrangements may be as exercises, they only succeed in making the symphonies trite and standardised, and for a very good reason. However 'clumsy' Schumann may have been, he found just the right orchestra for his music.

The character of the first symphony is sufficiently explained by its date, 1841, the year after the composer's marriage. All four movements abound with exuberant happiness. The instrumentation is clear and open and full of colour. The second, in C major (1846), is very different. The anguish, the 'torment of the soul' of which Schumann was to speak later, is very apparent in the unusual harmonies, complex rhythms and often dense texture of all four movements. The third symphony, in E flat major (1850), usually known as the 'Rhenish', is again in contrast to the two preceding. It seems to be filled with the glad, soft light of the Rhineland; the grand, noble and tumultuous opening movement is evocative of the Rhine in its course, and the solemn fourth movement was inspired by services at Cologne cathedral.

The fourth symphony, in D minor (1851), is the freest of all. The first version was completed in 1841, but was later entirely redesigned and re-orchestrated. Originally it was to have been called *Fantaisie symphonique*. The work unfolds like an improvisation through a series of movements which are in turn mysterious, febrile, or filled with a melancholy charm or robust dynamic force. Of the five overtures Schumann has left us, *The Festival Overture* (1853) was written for a special occasion in honour of Rhine wine, but the heroic and splendidly aggressive *Julius Caesar* (1851) is perhaps the most remarkable.

Among works for soloists and orchestra, which include the cello concerto in A minor (1850), the A minor piano concerto, Opus 54 (1841-5), is far and away the most important. Its first movement was originally conceived as a fantasia, and the work was completed in 1845 by the addition of the intermezzo and finale. Nowhere is Schumann's double personality, Eusebius and Florestan, more clearly apparent than in this work. The concerto seems to have almost the freedom of an improvised work and achieves a rare balance between piano and orchestra. It is probably the first time that such an intimate relation between the two had ever been attained and that without any sacrifice to the virtuosity of the soloist.

French music from the death of Rameau to the rise of Berlioz

In France the advance of the bourgeoisie had begun in the arts before the Revolution, and it came to impose its fashions for seeing, feeling and even its mode of life. A new clientele prompted creative artists to abandon official, politico-mythological themes and turn towards the real, to evoke daily life in its most familiar aspects. In music, the *opéra-comique* succeeded the *tragédie-lyrique* and the *opéra-ballet* in popular esteem. New relationships were established between the creative artists and this vast new body of public patrons – in painting with exhibitions and in music with concerts. Newspapers appeared, providing a new means for the diffusion of thought and a forum for discussions in which connoisseurs and laymen, philosophers and encyclopedists took part. The lightening of the atmosphere at the court that followed the death of Louis XIV was felt in the arts as the age of the Rococo dawned. In music, the somewhat rigid notion of strictly separated dynamic levels of volume gave way more and more to an art of subtle gradation, crescendo and diminuendo, of sensitivity and nuance – an art summed up in orchestral terms by the compositions and manner of performance of the school of Mannheim. The harpsichord, which by the admission of even one of its most zealous servants, François Couperin, was incapable of crescendo or diminuendo, was increasingly less suitable to the composer's purpose. However, even in his harpsichord music, Couperin came close to the mood of the new sensibility, expressed in the novels of Richardson in England and the canvases of Watteau in France, which was to colour much artistic expression for the next century. In music, counterpoint and fugal writing gave way to a generally homophonic structure and accompanied melody; Cimarosa's *La Serva Padrona* (*The Maid become Mistress*), swept the tragedies of Rameau from their pre-eminent position, while new instruments came to the fore to serve this new-born aesthetic.

The first appearance of the pianoforte at a *Concert spirituel* was in 1777, but although the instrument enjoyed increasing popularity in France, French composers, apart from Méhul, produced little of merit.

During the reign of Louis XVI, the harp had a considerable vogue. Played by Marie-Antoinette herself, this instrument was introduced into the orchestra. Its vogue was heightened by a number of virtuosi and it came, with the guitar, to rival the pianoforte as an accompanying instrument for *romances*. The majority of the composers of *romances* with guitar were guitarists trained by the eminent Spanish composer and virtuoso, Fernando Sor (1778-1839), whose works and teaching instigated, in France as in Europe, a veritable renaissance of the instrument.

Rameau, the great master of the *tragédie lyrique* and the *opéra-ballet*, responded to the new mood. In *Zoroastre* (1749), the last of his great tragedies, he renounced mythological themes in favour of the Masonic Creed. He condensed the dramatic element by suppressing the prologue and by replacing the French overture by an Italian overture whose programme summarised the leading ideas of the drama.

New historical themes came to be used in operas, and Roman subjects took root in their turn with *Sabinus* (1774) by Gossec, but musical innovations, properly called, were limited. However, Gluck, whose reforms were imminent, exercised his influence in France even before his arrival in Paris.

The opéra-comique

The French *opéra-comique*, quite distinct from the Italian *opera buffa* became, by an amalgamation of previous minor vocal forms, the predominant lyrical expression. In the first decades of the century there was a fierce conflict between the powerful Opéra and the rival theatres. The smaller theatres were forbidden to give performances using music throughout, but in 1714, on payment of a heavy fee, they were at last permitted to make use of specially composed as well as folk and popular songs. Italian influence advanced so that a second performance of Cimarosa's *La Serva Padrona*, in 1752, launched the famous *Guerre des Bouffons*, a noisy and spectacular manifestation of the opposition between French and Italian music. The *opéra-comique*, now a recognised genre, became an institution and in 1762 joined with the Comédie-Italienne, but by the end of the 18th century the classical *opéra-comique* had passed its best. Its pursuit of realism even led it to introduce characters taken from everyday life on the stage (an example is *Annette et Lubin* by Gossec). Such audacious naturalism was not to be repeated in France until the operas of Bizet.

During the second half of the 18th century France produced no major composers, but Paris held a privileged place as a music publishing centre and as a focus of musical activity. Foreign symphonists came to France and often settled there to live, and French musicians went abroad.

François Martin, Blainville and Gossec were the true initiators of the symphony in France between 1745 and 1765. The characteristics of the concerto grosso and the trio sonata were abandoned under the Italian influence, and in the 1770s, thanks to the example of the school of Mannheim, the symphony triumphed. The Mannheimer, Franz Xaver Richter, held the musical directorship of Strasbourg for a time and attracted many disciples. Thus the French symphony arrived at maturity by a synthesis of Italian and German elements, but apart from compositions in the related form of the *symphonie concertante*, the French achieved nothing outstanding and, from the 1790s, the ascendancy of Viennese classicism was complete.

A concert in a nobleman's house. Note that the hornist is using his hand in the bell and that the cello, as yet without a tailpin, is supported by the player's legs.

In France, as in Italy and central Europe, the quartet developed parallel with the symphony. From the 1750s nearly 150 collections of quartets, both French and foreign, were published in Paris. Those of Boccherini enjoyed such a vogue that at the beginning of the 19th century Pleyel published, under Boccherini's name, quartets written in his style by another composer.

Religious music passed from the church to the concert hall; for nearly fifty years, the motet constituted the principal box office success for the *Concerts spirituels*. The new audience, 'listeners' rather than 'faithful', demanded entertainment rather than music for prayer or meditation. Larger forces were employed, and the resulting possibilities of contrasts between vocal and instrumental were exploited. Motet composers in fact tended to use orchestration in the manner of the instrumental concerto, which heavily influenced their work. Increasingly large-scale religious works, such as Gossec's *Messe des Morts*, formed the prelude to the elaborate musical occasions with which the religion of the Revolution was to be celebrated. The first French attempt at the oratorio goes back to 1727, but the mythological or sacred subjects and texts later gave place to new themes, always drawing nearer to present reality. A secular ode, *Carmen saeculare*, composed by Philidor on poems by Horace, was, by its exaltation of the Roman virtues and its undeniable sense of architecture, an important contribution to the civic repertoire. In 1785, La Dixmerie proposed, in his *Letter on the present state of our entertainments*, that concert programmes should include 'pieces in the heroic genre, pieces in which one would recall certain events glorious for the nation and dear to its memory'. Future politicians, like Siéyes, dreamt already of the new role that they were going to assign to the art of music.

From the Revolution to 1830

The French Revolution bred new political institutions, new social relationships appeared, and a new spirit breathed. Such a revolution had immense repercussions on the arts. In music, the Revolution signified at first a change of purpose, involving a modification of the material means of expression and of the relationship of the public with creative artists, and the founding of such establishments as the Conservatoire.

Yet the Revolution had only a brief period which could properly be called revolutionary. From a republic too republican for certain interests, it began to revert to a regime of personal power. The evolution of music was

The Belgian-born composer François-Joseph Gossec, who worked in Paris through the Revolution and the Restoration.

Marie-Antoinette at the keyboard.

dictated by these events. From an art truly popular by its inspiration, its destination and even its interpretation, it reverted to forms of expression and or organisation which existed before the Revolution, and musical teaching became increasingly restricted.

The authoritarian regime imposed Bonaparte's preferences for Italian music, 'which does not make a noise and does not prevent one from thinking of affairs of state'. It extolled this music which soothed in all circumstances and was not too academic. Artistic creation during the Consulate and the Empire seemed congealed and France produced no significant music during the first decades of the 19th century. For a time Paris ceased to be a musical capital. To a growing craze for the declining Italian opera, and for archaic vocal forms momentarily revived, was added a passion for foreign music in the new instrumental forms. Musical theory was more advanced than composition. Such was the case with Antonin Reicha (1770-1836), an important theoretician of Czech origin and teacher of Gounod, Berlioz and César Franck, whose works only tentatively indicate future developments. The bourgeoisie and the aristocrats of the Restoration showed the same taste as Napoleon; Rossini and Boïeldieu were soon preferred to Beethoven. In France, despite the superhuman achievements of Beethoven, music had once again become an art of decoration and amusement. But the new revolution of 1830 was to lift music out of its torpor and the awakening was announced by the best works of Hérold and, above all, the *Eight Scenes from Faust* of Berlioz (1828), which paralleled the poetry of Hugo and Lamartine and the canvases of Géricault and Delacroix.

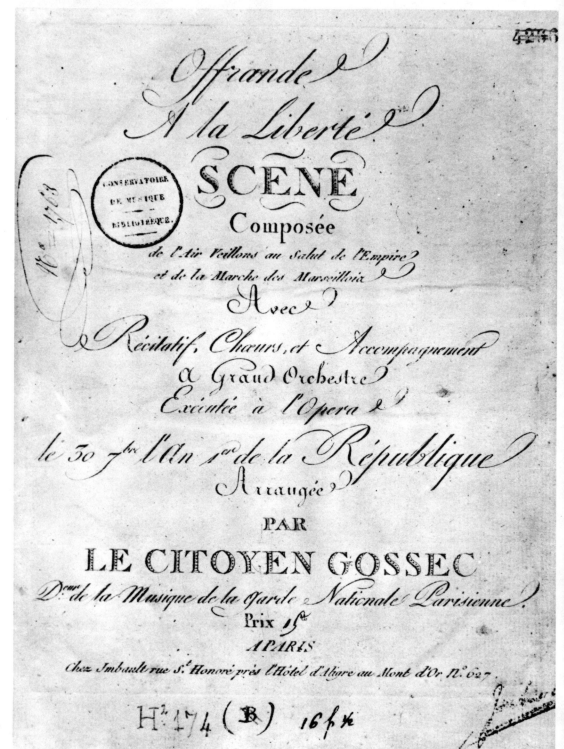

Title page of 'An offering to Liberty', given at the Paris Opera in the first year of the Republic. The music is by 'Citizen' Gossec, director of music of the Parisian National Guard.

The fêtes and songs of the French Revolution

During the first years of the Revolutionary regime, music faithfully followed the course of events, on which, from now on, its mission was to comment and glorify. As the forms of political life moved away from those of the *ancien régime*, so music moved away from its antecedents. In its less than ten years of life, the new *répertoire civique* blossomed out in conditions that favoured improvisation rather than tradition.

The new expressive music of the time corresponded to the political and social transformation. Its first repercussion was on existing forms of expression, which survived or not according to the extent to which they adapted themselves to the new circumstances. This was especially true of the *chanson*. The three years between the taking of the Bastille and the proclamation of the Republic produced *La Carmagnole* and the *Ça ira*, whose words were adapted from old songs by d'Alayrac. The early years of the Republic also produced the *Hymn to Liberty*, later, as the official Napoleonic song, to take the title of *Veillons au salut de l'empire*. The first national fêtes were organised in 1791. Music took pride of place. It was transferred from the church to the street, and from the concert to the public square.

In music, the new civic spirit which followed the collapse of the *ancien régime* accorded ill with the use of the traditional sacred texts. These were to be resolutely and definitively abandoned after the proclamation of the Republic. But already the *Marseillaise* had been born. It was imposed as the 'new Te Deum', to use Goethe's words. The suppression of Roman Catholicism was followed by the birth of a new civic liturgy, with its own 'proper' and 'ordinary'. The former was devoted to the glorification of new deities (the Supreme Being, Agriculture, Hymen, Old Age etc.); the second gave birth to hymns celebrating the joyous or solemn events of national life. These hymns, despite their occasional character, were often of high quality. It is worth noticing that foreign musicians participated in the national fêtes, and not only men such as Cherubini, who had long been settled in France. Luigi Cherubini (1760–1842) settled in Paris in 1788 on the advice of Viotti. He wrote many operas in a highly personal style that owed much to the Gluck reform and led Beethoven to regard Cherubini as the greatest of his contemporaries. He was an important figure in the music of the early Republic, but was out of favour with Napoleon. In 1821, however, he became director of the Conservatoire, holding this post until the year of his death.

As a general rule the large choral scores were written for three men's voices, the symphony orchestra being replaced by a band. Indeed, during this period the wind band took shape, finding its first original repertoire in military marches, overtures and one-movement symphonies. Certainly circumstances did not always lend themselves to a massive deployment of choirs and instrumentalists. The decadal fêtes were often celebrated with hymns for one voice with reduced accompaniment, the combination most used being the sextet.

Year II of the Republic constituted the culminating point of the Revolution. It marked similarly the apogee of civic music with the *Chant du départ* which followed the Feast of the Supreme Being, a perfect example of authentic popular art. The evening before, musician members of the Institut National were active in the various districts of Paris teaching the song to willing amateur choral singers. This active role was to become impossible after the revolution of Thermidor. 'After Thermidor, the flame which had illuminated the first

left
Nicolas D'Alayrac (1753–1809), who composed comic operas and contributed to the music of the Republic.

below
The court theatre at Versailles.

years of the Revolution was extinguished. Yet despite everything, France still remained a republic and the *fêtes civiles* continued to be celebrated, expressing in their own way the attitude of the national conscience, up till the day when the resumption of the religious festivals put an end to them.'

The romance

The *romance*, with fully written-out accompaniment in place of the old figured bass, was the successor to the *airs sérieux* of the previous generation.

The theme is generally unhappy love; to this was to be added the troubadour genre, presaging the 19th-century return to medievalism. A collection of *romances* by François Devienne for harp and flute bears witness, as do some works by Grétry and Méhul, to the introduction

of subjects of topical interest in the music of the Revolutionary period. But the *romance* was hardly suitable for development as a popular art and faded away momentarily to reappear under the Empire as a nostalgic reminiscence of 'the good old days' of the middle ages, whose vogue was established throughout Europe by the historical Romantic novels of Walter Scott. By and large French *romances* of this period use mediocre texts, and are a series of monotonous and complaisant formulae for voice and piano. Nevertheless, the output was not entirely negligible. Méhul and Boïeldieu composed many excellent *romances* while Mozart, Beethoven and Weber all wrote examples of the type.

Furthermore the *romance*, born on the fringe of public life and thus escaping the Italian ascendancy, constituted the most original, if not the most typical, form of musical expression of the Empire, and in the course of these fifteen years it attained its full blossoming. After 1815 it declined, prey to a veritable mass production of flat and vacuous curtain-raisers. But the decline of the *romance*

André Ernest Modeste Grétry (1741–1813), Belgian-born composer of opera, who enjoyed a long run of successes after settling in Paris in the 1830s.

was assured when Liszt and the tenor Nourrit revealed Schubert's *Lieder* to the French public. The latter's influence affected a number of his French contemporaries. Nevertheless, up to the 1920s, the *romance* itself maintained a twilight existence in fashionable salons.

The théâtre lyrique

The tradition of the lyric theatre was maintained and even renewed during the Revolution by the presentation of hymns and patriotic pieces beside old or new works on traditional themes. Mythological, historical and biblical subjects were to take over after 1800, but the end of the *fêtes nationales* obliged composers to turn towards the theatre. Napoleon here again made his preferences felt, imposing Paisiello and Spontini, his favourite Italian composers, on the French public.

The *opéra-comique* knew a new period of popularity, particularly during the reign of the restored Bourbon king, Charles X, until the moment when the prodigious success of Rossini's *Barber of Seville* consecrated the triumph of the new Italian opera and opened France to other masters of *opera buffa*. Up to 1830 the genre was cultivated by French composers, of whom Boïeldieu and Hérold were the most applauded.

On the whole, music in the theatre, as in the church, resurrected forms of expression which had achieved their complete evolution long before in the palmy days of the *ancien régime*. Spontini's operas constituted a skilful synthesis of Gluck and Mozart. But by their pomp and declamatory grandeur, his *La Vestale* and *Fernand Cortez* perfectly reflect the Empire period, a fact which naturally contributed to their success. They also display a new sense of instrumentation which did not escape the attention of Berlioz, and these experiments in orchestral writing remain the most positive aspect of the theatrical music of the Empire and the Restoration.

Boïeldieu's *opéras-comiques* completely satisfied those who, in music as in politics, had neither learned nor forgotten anything. The musical language recalled an earlier epoch and the libretti were calculated to titillate and please the bourgeois audiences of a restored monarchy; the dialogue amusingly censures the taste of the time and peasants are portrayed returning land to their *seigneurs*.

New stars – Meyerbeer, Halévy, Bellini, Donizetti – arose, and for nearly twenty years assured the survival of a mummified genre which was to stand in the way of Berlioz's innovations and obstruct the development of an authentic Romantic musical theatre.

The reopening of the choir schools and the chapels under Napoleon's aegis implied a renewal of their repertoire. The ceremonials and triumphs of the Empire were celebrated to the Te Deum rather than by the secular cantatas, which decreased in number and were, in general, morose, solemn and academic. Here, as in stage music, Napoleon imposed his preferences for Italian art. His official musician Paisiello composed the mass for the coronation. Other prominent religious compositions of the period included a mass by Méhul and the Te Deums of Gossec and Martini.

With the return of the Bourbons, music was reorganised on the model of the former Chapel Royal. Coronations and funeral services, amongst other solemnities, were new pretexts for grandiose compositions deploying numerous performers. Cherubini reigned during the fifteen years of the Restoration, producing the last specimens of classical religious music, while the old oratorio had a final flowering with Lesueur.

Only in 1828, with Habeneck's foundation of the *Société des concerts du Conservatoire*, did the concert

retrieve its erstwhile importance in musical life. Napoleon's official pianist was the Czech, Johann Ladislas Dussek. French instrumental compositions of this period are rare, and their worth lies principally in their researches into instrumental writing. This is the case with the four symphonies of Méhul and with the last symphony in seventeen parts by Gossec. It was with the symphony in D by the Italian Cherubini that the classical symphony in France reached its final point. The same remark also applies to the six quartets that Cherubini composed.

However, if the period we have been reviewing was poor in great creative talent there were many fine executant musicians. Among them was the violinist Rodolphe Kreutzer (1766–1831), who deigned to accept the dedication of Beethoven's great sonata, while the Duport brothers made European reputations as cellists.

Etienne Nicolas Méhul (1763–1813), French opera composer.

Berlioz the prophet

Hector Berlioz, a contemporary of Hugo and Delacroix, is the only great French Romantic composer. His sudden appearance, like some volcano in the middle of the sea, shook the debilitated world of French music. The man and his music can be compared to a brilliantly lighted stage set where it is at first difficult to pick out many of the essential features. This Romantic hero, always contradictory by nature, runs the risk of only being half understood, by reason both of his opinions and of his behaviour.

During his lifetime his music was denigrated in France, when it was not ignored, yet the establishment was so impressed by his Requiem Mass that he received the cross of the Légion d'Honneur. His music can be as gentle as it can be vehement; he was naturally inclined to the theatre, but the staging of his works can still present problems.

He was born in the Dauphiné in December 1803, the son of a country doctor. His father formed his taste in literature – Virgil, La Fontaine and Shakespeare were his favourite authors – but did nothing to encourage his musical gifts. At eighteen he had studied the principles of harmony and had learnt to play the flageolet (rather badly) and the guitar (tolerably well) and knew the shepherds' songs of his homeland. At twenty-five he was already a master of his craft and had composed *Eight Scenes from Faust*, his first masterpiece. He studied at the Paris Conservatoire under Antonin Reicha and J. F. Lesueur and at twenty-seven secured the Prix de Rome with his cantata *La Mort de Sardanapale*. He had fallen in love with an English actress, Harriet Smithson, and his passion for her led him to write the *Symphonie Fantastique*. Love died soon after their marriage in 1833, but despite a new attachment Berlioz waited until Harriet's death in 1852 before marrying again. Berlioz enjoyed a European reputation, touring widely and en-

Hector Berlioz.

Plate 41
Chopin, a portrait by Delacroix.

Plate 42
Wagner by Lenbach.

joying the friendship and admiration of Liszt and, for a time, Wagner. But in Paris his works were less successful than those of fashionable followers of the manner of Meyerbeer. Humiliation for Berlioz was completed by the fact that he often had to review their works.

The works

All the works of Berlioz have a certain theatrical quality, either explicit or implied, and he both remodelled existing forms and invented others. His overtures, for example, are in fact symphonic tone poems, free interpretations of the writings of Scott, Shakespeare and other literary heroes of the Romantic period. *Waverley* and *Les Francs-Juges* (1827-8) already display an assured technical mastery, and with *King Lear*, *Rob Roy* and *The Corsair*, Berlioz laid the foundations for the greatest of his overtures, *Roman Carnival*, written in 1844 and based on themes from his opera *Benvenuto Cellini* (1838).

The symphonies are, more accurately speaking, imaginary operas. But for all his innate Romanticism we should never lose sight of his debt to Beethoven, nor of his very personal form of composition, based on variations and contrasting themes. The 'programme' of the *Symphonie Fantastique*, which recounts the course of the composer's passion for Harriet Smithson, he regarded as crucially important. Now, however, the true interest lies in the orchestral colour of the five tableaux, beginning with the exaltation of the first movement and leading up to the hallucinatory mood of the last two; in between, parenthetically, we are introduced to the hero's passion in scenes set in a ball room and in the country-side. This splendid evocation of Romantic love is also a masterpiece of thematic development, more because of the different transformations it contains than because of the variations on the theme of the *idée fixe*. This device, literally a 'fixed idea', identified with a certain mood or occurrence, and having obvious affinities with the *Leitmotiv* of Wagner, was much used in *Harold in Italy* (1834). This extremely original work was commissioned by Paganini, though he never played it, objecting that the viola part was not sufficiently brilliant. Berlioz combines the concerto style, necessitated by the demands of the solo viola, with symphonic writing. In the *Symphonie Funèbre et Triomphale* (1840) – march, funeral oration and hymn with chorus – Berlioz makes admirable and dramatic use of the resources of military bands.

The dramatic symphonies

Romeo and Juliet (1839), whose influence Wagner confessed to, and *The Damnation of Faust* (1846) are among Berlioz's finest operatic works; in them he uses chorus, soloists and orchestra in a series of 'scenes'. This treatment of the great works of Shakespeare and Goethe, a method perhaps better suited to the cinema than the theatre, dispenses with the problem of continuous action. In the *Symphonie Fantastique* and *The Damnation of Faust* the interest is centred on a series of different tableaux and on their emotional content. Berlioz sometimes interprets his literary models very freely; he attached great importance to the episodic scenes of the Faust legend and even added material based on earlier versions of the legend such as that of Marlowe.

A group of musicians listening to Liszt at the piano; standing are Berlioz (left) and the German composer and theoretician Carl Czerny.

Berlioz's sacred music is equally characterised by its dramatic and pictorial content. The imagination is captured as much by the great burst of brass in the *Grande Messe des Morts* (1837) and in the *Te Deum* (1849) as by the deliberate avoidance of any grandiose effects which characterises the charming and gentle *Enfance du Christ* (1854). One must overlook the outward form to seek the essence of these works; the writing for the voice parts is often admirable, and, although old forms are often refurbished, there is nothing of pastiche about them.

Berlioz's operas contain marvellous music but ultimately fail to achieve their full effects on the stage because of a lack of internal cohesion. Berlioz was naturally attracted to opera as a series of juxtaposed tableaux but, in contrast to his symphonies, failed to impose his own personality completely on the medium. The best passages from *Benvenuto Cellini* (1838) and in particular from *The Trojans*, written in 1856, suffer from being inserted between conventional scenes in the manner of Spontini or the old *opera seria*, which had been revived during the time of the Revolution. *Beatrice and Benedict* (1862), much less ambitious than *The Trojans* and based on Shakespeare's *Much Ado about Nothing*, is perhaps the most accomplished of Berlioz's operas and reflects an unusual side of his nature in which tenderness and humour predominate. Shakespeare provided the perfect

libretto for Berlioz, but Berlioz ennobled the '*romances*', or arias by his orchestration and his remarkable gift for tonality. Such arias, however, do not lend themselves to dramatic outbursts and free declamation. This explains also the relative failure of Berlioz's songs, even though the cycle of *Les Nuits d'Eté* (1841) contains some delightful ideas which were later to inspire Gounod, Fauré and Duparc.

The musician and writer

Berlioz's *Traité d'instrumentation et d'orchestration modernes* (1844) was the first major essay on orchestration and remains a classic. He may legitimately be seen as the pioneer of a new art of the orchestra and his frequent demands for large numbers of instruments and voices came from his interest in the mastery of contrast. In the hands of Berlioz the orchestra becomes a rustling forest where singing birds call to one another, the roars of the lion are heard in the distance or suddenly overhead the thunderstorm breaks. The brilliance and contrast of his colours tempt us to compare him to Delacroix. Nevertheless there remains something disturbing about the art of Berlioz with its self-assertive mixture of nonconformity and naïvety, and his perfect knowledge of the rules of harmony; his bold innovations often display a violence which has brought wild fluctuations in the critical estimation of his music.

As a music critic writing mainly in the *Journal des Débats*, his innumerable articles are, with those of Schumann, some of the most brilliant of their kind. Among the numerous collections which reveal his considerable talents as a stylist, *Evenings in the Orchestra* is particularly witty and pungent; his autobiography is a literary achievement of great stature and, with his *Letters*, gives us a faithful portrait of the man, passionate, uncompromising and contradictory yet with a bubbling sense of fun.

After Berlioz

Berlioz is the perfect example of the genius born before his time. His temperament and gifts make him an ideal contemporary of the great 19th-century French musical renaissance which was to begin with Fauré, Debussy and Ravel. Despite the contradictory aspects of his character and music, his genius far and away outweighs any of his weaknesses and places him on a lonely pinnacle. Berlioz had no disciples, and, apart perhaps from Liszt and Schumann, none of his admirers fully understood him. Moreover, this isolated figure soon became forgotten in France and his message only reached French musicians towards the end of the century. It is always the originality of his genius that first attracts the curious, who ultimately come to love his compositions. Their panache has latterly guaranteed them considerable popularity; but their subtleties are admired by professional musicians.

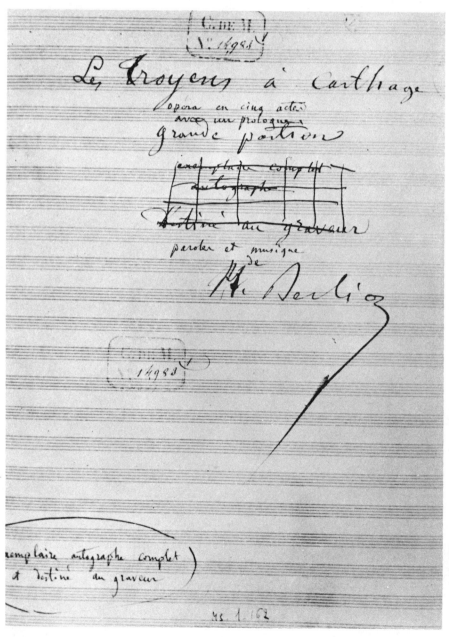

The title page of Berlioz's manuscript of The Trojans.

Foreign composers in Paris

In France the Romantic period was one in which opera and virtuoso performers flourished, but the majority of French musicians were far too influenced by foreigners. The contribution made to France by these foreign visitors, among them Rossini, Meyerbeer, Wagner, Verdi, Liszt and Chopin, was not entirely negative. Concerts in Paris were improving. The recitals of Liszt and Chopin were very different from purely virtuoso performances. Beethoven symphonies were performed at the concerts of the Conservatoire. Enthusiasm for German music became still more widespread when, from 1835, Liszt, accompanying Adolphe Nourrit, the greatest tenor of the age, in performances of Schubert's songs, spread the vogue for the *Lied* throughout France and thus hastened the decline of the popularity of the French *romance*.

The Opéra was the centre of Romantic Paris at that time, and Paris itself was the most important musical capital for the foreigner. Rossini had just brought to a close his series of masterpieces with *Le Comte Ory* (1827) and *William Tell* (1829), two French works; he then retired from the world of music for reasons which have always remained mysterious. But he continued to live in Paris until his death in 1868, during which time he composed a quantity of piano music and French and Italian songs, a beautiful *Stabat Mater* (1841) and the *Short Solemn Mass* (1864), music in which a combination of humorous parody, severe classical style and a surprising harmonic genius all contribute to present a hitherto unknown picture of the composer. Bellini wrote his *I Puritani* (1835) for the Théâtre-Italien while Donizetti produced two French works in 1840. Verdi often stayed in Paris, where he fulfilled two commissions for the Opéra – *The Sicilian Vespers* (1855) and *Don Carlos* (1867). The success of the first was not repeated, for Verdi's later style was already too obscure for the worshippers of Meyerbeer.

Meyerbeer and his contemporaries

Giacomo Meyerbeer (1791–1864), of German-Jewish origin and born Jakob Liebmann Beer, made his début as a pianist at the age of seven and studied under Zelter and the Abbé Vogler. From 1815 to the late 1820s he was studying and composing Italian opera, with much success in Italy, but he owed his European fame to his conquest of Paris in the 1830s, although from 1842 he lived and worked mostly in Germany. The success of *Robert le Diable* in Paris in 1831 assured him a position from which no one could oust him while he lived, a position which was further enhanced by *Les Huguenots* (1836) and *Le Prophète* (1849). The grandiose operas of Meyerbeer, inspired by Spontini and nourished on Weber, now appear over-sensational but they sometimes reveal considerable talents for melody and orchestration, most particularly in *L'Africaine*, performed posthumously in Paris in 1865. Even Wagner and Verdi were not altogether exempt from his influence. Last but by no means least of the foreign musicians to be mentioned here is Richard Wagner. His two main visits to Paris (1839–42 and 1859–61) are interesting as much for his ties with France as for his several French songs and the French version of *Tannhäuser*, which received such a humiliating rebuff at the Paris Opéra in 1861.

French opera, whether historic or *comique*, differed little from that of the Italian models. The overtures of Auber (1782–1871), from *La Muette de Portici* to *Fra*

Scene from the production of Berlioz's vast opera The Trojans *at the Royal Opera House, Covent Garden, 1957. Jon Vickers (centre) as Aeneas.*

above
*Giacomo Meyerbeer, the German
composer whose operas dominated
mid-century Paris.*

right
*J. L F. Halévy, a composer of
operas.*

Diavolo and *The Black Domino*, still pass for very charming light music. Ferdinand Hérold's (1791-1833) last two operas, *Zampa* (1837) and *Le Pré-aux-Clercs*, particularly the latter, outrivalled Rossini's *Comte Ory* in success. Hérold died at the age of forty-two, and with him any hopes for an early revival of French opera. Adolphe Adam (1803-56), whose ballet *Giselle* is performed today for reasons other than any purely musical merits, also wrote *Postillon de Longjumeau* (1836) and *Si j'étais roi* (1852), but neither he, nor J. L. F. Halévy (1799-1862), despite the latter's immense success with *La Juive* (1835), whose colours have now faded, were able to counteract the influence of Meyerbeer and reinstate French opera. This goal was to be achieved by Halévy's two pupils Gounod and Bizet.

Although he was not really a man of the theatre, mention must also be made of Félicien David (1810-76), commended as a melodist and orchestrator by Berlioz. His oratorio *The Desert*, written after a visit to the Middle East, of which in fact it shows very little trace, has always been considered a model of exotic Romanticism; it was sufficiently well thought of in its time for Offenbach to parody it. Ambroise Thomas (1811-96), whose official career led from the Prix de Rome to the directorship of the Conservatoire, wrote a number of operas in which he combined the surest Italian effects with the Romantic style of Meyerbeer; only *Mignon* (1866) is remembered today.

At the other extreme of Romantic music in the Paris of this time were the virtuosi of the piano. Several French executants both of this and of the preceding generation also composed music. Among them were not only Hérold, but also Adrien Boïeldieu (1775-1834) who had served at St Petersburg for eight years and enjoyed a certain operatic success with *La Dame Blanche*. Alexandre Boëly (1785-1858), in his compositions both for piano and for organ, shows a predilection for the older style of musical forms. But virtuosity reigned supreme in keyboard music. Other French composers included Charles Alkan (1813-88), whose piano music is enjoying a certain revival; the keyboard composers among the foreigners established in Paris included Stephen Heller (1813-88), Friedrich Kalkbrenner (1785-1849) and Sigismond Thalberg (1812-71). But of course Chopin, who lived in Paris from 1831 until his death, and Liszt (from 1823 to 1847) put all other pianists in the shade. France was a contributory factor in the development of their creative genius – Chopin was a friend of Delacroix, and Liszt of Berlioz. But they in their turn exercised a considerable influence on all future French music – Chopin on Fauré and Debussy; Liszt on Saint-Saëns and Ravel.

One of the most significant developments in music in France during the 19th century was the revival of interest in the church music of the polyphonic age. Alexandre Choron (1771-1834), founded the Royal Choral Society for the performance of sacred and classical music and published several works by composers of the old school. Napoléon Joseph Ney (1803-57), son of Napoleon's marshal, continued Choron's work and founded the Society for Concerts of Religious and Classical Vocal Music. From this was born the School of Louis Niedermeyer (1802-61), which encouraged the study of the music of the 16th to the 18th centuries, including Bach, and which still exists. Apart from church music Niedermeyer also composed a number of historical operas and the celebrated romantic aria *Le Lac*, from the poem by Lamartine. He assumed the direction of Choron's conservatory and it was his teaching that inspired many French composers, in particular Gabriel Fauré and Messager. The joint publications of Niedermeyer and Joseph d'Ortigue (1802-66), the friend of Berlioz, restored Gregorian plainsong to its proper place. The influence exercised on Parisian music by the Belgian

left
Scene from a 19th-century production of Meyerbeer's opera Robert le Diable.

below
Painting by Dufy of a 19th-century provincial production of Adrien Boïeldieu's opera La Dame Blanche.

composer and critic, François-Joseph Fétis (1784–1871), was also very considerable, not only by reason of his writings on composition, but because he reintroduced earlier styles of music. The teachings and compositions of the Czech scholar Antonin Reicha (1770–1836), professor at the Conservatoire, whose knowledge of counterpoint and folk music was unsurpassed, left a great impression on Liszt, Berlioz, Franck and Gounod.

Offenbach

One of the finest composers among the near contemporaries of Berlioz was the operetta composer Jacques Offenbach (1819–80). His operetta, which employs spoken dialogue as well as singing, is derived from the French *opéra-comique* and the German *Singspiel*; the plots are always simple and amusing, but his chief originality lies in his satire. He pokes fun at the world of classical myth and mythology, while using it as a vehicle for his satire of the society of the Second Empire, the very society that applauded him.

Born in Cologne in 1819, he was brought to Paris in 1833 by his father, who was a touring musician and also cantor of the Jewish congregation. Jacques became a pupil at the Conservatoire and later played the cello in the orchestra of the Opéra Comique. His first compositions were for the cello, and he also entertained fashion-

able salons by playing the buffoon with his instrument. In 1855 he became manager of a small theatre and in the same year acquired the Théâtre Comte, which he renamed *Bouffes Parisiennes*, where his success was immediate and lasting. In 1858 he discovered Meilhac and Ludovic Halévy, who became his librettists. With *Orpheus in the Underworld* he started a vogue which has long outlived him.

Of all his operettas, the most outstanding are *Orpheus* (1858) and *La Belle Hélène* (1864), both of which are mythological and political satires; *La Vie Parisienne* (1866) and *La Grande Duchesse de Gérolstein* (1867) are satires on social and military life. His satire lies not only in the libretti, but also in his music which, like the works which Rossini wrote after he had retired from public life, parodies operatic styles. But Offenbach was also inspired by popular dance tunes and songs and, although his music is unpretentious, it has grace and charm and is of sufficient calibre to carry the weight of the more serious *Tales of Hoffmann* (produced in 1881), which he considered his best work.

Offenbach's successors tried their best to imitate him, but were never able to recapture the mordant wit which was the basis of his unfailing success.

The renaissance of French music

It was only the work of César Franck and five of his lesser contemporaries that saved French music from complete vacuity between the time of Berlioz and Fauré. The songs of Gounod, the operas of Bizet, the chamber music of Lalo, the formalism of Saint-Saëns and the piano pieces by Chabrier all contributed to save French music from the complacency of bourgeois art. Franck, who has been called the French Wagner, and his disciples, dominated the scene, but it was the work of his five contemporaries which prepared the ground for a typically French musical language and opened the way to the achievements of Fauré and his successors.

Gounod and Lalo

Charles Gounod (1818–93), inspired by Mendelssohn's genius, found in it traits which would best serve the purposes of French music: a fresh sensibility, a sensual Romanticism and a mastery of musical dialogue which precluded exaggeration. French music, particularly opera, had been haunted by grandiloquence; indeed Gounod himself more than once succumbed, and an antidote was needed. Where the stormy Berlioz failed to wean the French public from its taste for the ostentation of historical grand opera and the seductions of mere virtuosity, Charles Gounod, far less talented but also less abrasive, was to carry on the work. Fauré, Duparc and even Ravel recognised and respected his basic aims. The score of *Faust* (1859), admittedly an uneven work, contains many subtleties. Today we can admire in the charming intimacy of the garden scene, the prelude and the choral recitatives, the emotional power of true inspiration; while the comic opera, *Le Médecin malgré lui*, based on Molière's play, is a faultless work, filled with charm and humour.

Two of his scores which deserve to be better known because of their freshness and delicacy are the first symphony in E flat, and the *Little Symphony for Wind Instruments* (1879). In these he adapts the manner of the Viennese school to delicate new harmonies in the best French tradition. Gounod's finest work, however, is in

A contemporary caricature of Offenbach.

his two hundred songs which, despite their Romantic origins, are quite devoid of any insipidity. The imperceptible irregularities in the symmetry of the melodic line, the adroit use of dissonance, the unexpected modulations and the happy balance between voice and piano often surpass in quality even the songs of Fauré which they inspired.

In the work of Gounod and also Lalo may be seen the first indications of the revival of French song writing before Fauré and Duparc. The fine, though perhaps not spectacular talents of Edouard Lalo (1823-92) are best known in his *Symphonie Espagnol* (1873), and his symphony in G minor is worthy to take its place beside those of his contemporaries, Franck, Saint-Saëns and d'Indy; his chamber music, like his songs, has an intimate and serious quality which contributed to the revival of French music. Lalo was influenced by Schumann and Mendelssohn, but he understood how to guide his music towards picturesque instrumental colour sharpened by a sense of rhythm which was, no doubt, due to his Spanish origins.

Despite its immediate success, his opera *Le Roi d'Ys* (1888) appears a bit old-fashioned today, partly because of the imbalance between its real musical qualities and the exigencies of a feeble plot. The overture with its great cello solo and the best passages in the opera deserve to be remembered. But Lalo was at his best when writing for orchestra, as is clear from his ballet *Namouna* and the G minor symphony. Both have charm, subtle rhythms and varied orchestration, with original tonal combinations, although neither are works of extreme brilliance.

above left
Edouard Lalo.

left
A drawing by Ingres of the youthful Gounod at the piano; the composer is playing a work by Mozart.

The strikingly brilliant scores for solo instrument, i.e. the *Symphonie Espagnole* for violin, the cello concerto and piano concerto, have nothing like the same qualities despite their great popularity. Two of his most interesting scores are the string quartet and the third trio.

Harmonically, the songs of Lalo complement those of Gounod, for, although they may not have the same charm, the richness of the instrumental accompaniment, their rhythmic invention and understanding of the best French Romantic poets bring Lalo close to the spirit of the German *Lied*.

Saint-Saëns

Despite a long life of immense productivity Camille Saint-Saëns (1835-1921), who started his career as an infant prodigy, never managed to acquire the reputation of a really great master. Although he was largely responsible for the restoration of French musical standards – indeed, Ravel had the greatest admiration for him – his brilliant but academic style was already outdated by the beginning of the 20th century. Moreover, his reputation as a composer suffered from the obstinacy of his opinions and his aggressive character; this 'French Mendelssohn' unforgiveably lacked the charm of his model and the ability to express a truly genuine melancholy with the same sensitivity. Nevertheless, Saint-Saëns was an erudite and purist composer who exercised a beneficial influence on French music, particularly after he had discarded his thralldom to Wagner.

One of his most important works, the opera *Samson and Delilah*, was first composed as an oratorio, and was rearranged three years later and produced in its present form by Liszt at Weimar in 1877. The importance of the choruses betrays its origins, and is best passages are reminiscent of Mendelssohn's oratorios, but the richness of the orchestral writing and the bewitching arias of Delilah are essentially operatic. It completely eclipses a long list of historical operas written to exorcise the spell of Wagner but unfortunately exhibiting an equally

above
A contemporary caricature of Camille Saint-Saëns.

right
A scene from Saint-Saëns' opera Samson and Delilah.

destructive dependence on the work of Meyerbeer.

Together with his tone poems, such as the *Danse Macabre* (1875), not so inspired as those of Liszt but very well orchestrated, his best orchestral work is the third symphony with organ accompaniment, dedicated to Liszt. It is written in two movements, each of which is divided respectively into an allegro and andante and a scherzo and finale. The first movement, with its lovely meditative middle passage for organ, is the more successful of the two. However, the less ambitious second symphony is more original and is perhaps preferable to the false brilliance of the finale of the third.

Saint-Saëns the purist was nevertheless the author of one of the best of all musical jokes, the *Carnaval des Animaux* (1886) written at the expense of rival composers but with a fine feeling for orchestral colour. But Saint-Saëns' most original work is to be found in his chamber music. The first trio was so much admired by Ravel that he took it as a model for his own; other fine works are the poignantly sad first violin and cello sonata, and the delightful, sparkling septet for trumpet, piano and strings.

To appreciate Saint-Saëns' piano writing we must look to the adroit way in which he manipulates the *Variations on a theme of Beethoven* and the music of the five concertos. Although here he introduces no innovations, the music is always delightful and perfectly adapted to the instrument.

Bizet

Were it not for the precious last four years of his life, the name of Georges Bizet (1838–75) would scarcely be known to us today. Only towards the end of his life was his admiration for Mozart, Rossini, Schumann and Mendelssohn, and to a minor extent for Wagner, to replace the taste which he had formerly shared with his contemporaries for the operas of Meyerbeer, for virtuosity and for the French *romance* form of song. Although the discipline of his last compositions owes much to the great masters just quoted, his true personality was even further developed under the influence of Spanish and Provençal music. Bizet himself was not seeking profundity or immortality; he was a man looking for a quick road to success, more sensual than intellectual, but dogged by misfortune and haunted by the fear of death.

The c major symphony is an agreeable work clearly influenced by Mozart and Rossini; the *Jeux d'enfants*, a suite of twelve piano duets which were later arranged for orchestra, is a marvel of life and gaiety. Originality may not be the dominant feature of these little pieces but they have a picturesque descriptive quality, bright harmonic colours and adroit combinations of timbre.

The orchestral suite from the incidental music for *L'Arlésienne* (1872) had an immediate success. The Provençal airs which Bizet borrowed provided his melody with a characteristic quality of their own, but only a brilliant and non-conformist orchestrator could have invented such bold harmonies.

Like all Bizet's other operas, *Carmen* (written between 1873 and 1874 and produced in 1875) received a cold reception. Some people were scandalised by the subject, the tragedy of a girl in a cigarette factory and her love for a bullfighter, others were irritated by what they considered the too 'symphonic' music. After fifty performances France proceeded to neglect completely, for ten years, a work which was a worldwide success. The violence of the story of *Carmen*, based on Prosper Merimée's novel, was still something remarkable in the time of Gounod and Saint-Saëns. But Bizet had at last found a means of expression which was ideally suited to

left
A pencil portrait of Georges Bizet in Rome in 1860.

below
Harry Belafonte and Dorothy Dandridge in a still from Carmen Jones, *a film version of Bizet's famous opera.*

his capabilities an opera divided into short scenes, which gave him an opportunity of using all his imaginative gifts and in which the realism of the theme exceeds the bounds of ordinary operatic convention. There can be few operas in which the style is so composite or the music of such unequal quality; in which masterly scoring alternates with sentimental musical platitudes. Nevertheless we can admire unreservedly the whole of Carmen's role (closely linked with dance rhythms), the quintet, the card trio and intermezzi and many of the other items. Very occasionally the music is heightened by Wagnerian influence, but what brings the opera to life is the Spanish source which, under Bizet's pen, miraculously becomes more genuinely 'Spanish' than the real thing. Once again a folk subject brings out all the composer's most audacious harmonies; his vocal ensembles are quite remarkable, and he uses the orchestra as a commentary to the action on the stage.

Chabrier

Emmanuel Chabrier (1841-94), admirer of the Impressionists, fervent Wagnerian, associate of the circle of César Franck, friend of Verlaine and Manet, is becoming increasingly appreciated. His works encourage a diversity of opinions – for some he is an entertainer, for others

Chabrier at the piano, a sketch by one of his friends.

a prophet. Chabrier tirelessly revised his scores and, uncertain of his vocation and rarely taken seriously as a composer, forced himself against everything in his nature to admire the works of Wagner and César Franck. His extreme sensitivity was better hidden behind a burst of laughter than behind ponderous Wagnerian harmonies, and it was he who handed on the tradition of musical wit from Rossini to Satie. But Chabrier also remained a real country man at heart, and was able to introduce a fresh element into French music, which was being stifled by the bourgeois salons of the Second Empire.

After some youthful essays in the operetta style in collaboration with Verlaine, Chabrier, in his mid-thirties, successfully produced a number of light stage works which contain some of his best music. His later work is influenced by his determination to admire Wagner at all costs, a resolve, encouraged by Franck and d'Indy, which stifled Chabrier's real genius in dusty mythological clouds of legend and was only to make his faults and shortcomings the more obvious. But Chabrier's songs have down-to-earth realism and humour and represent a type of song which was to take root in the French tradition. Of his orchestral works, *España* is a synthesis of all Chabrier's impressions of the Spanish *jota*. The healthy 'vulgarity' of Chabrier's tunes serves as an outline on which to build a brilliant orchestration whose fast rhythm gives greater cohesion to the movement.

La marche joyeuse, originally written for the piano (1890), is a fine example of Chabrier's droll wit. The piano was, indeed, the instrument best suited to Chabrier's talent as a composer. In his piano compositions his imagination never runs to excesses and his inclination to sentimentality is not so obvious as elsewhere. Two collections of piano pieces are of particular importance: *Les pièces pittoresques* (1881), together with the piano pieces of Franck and Fauré, give the first indications of a new trend in French piano music, and are already orientated towards the future school of Impressionism and musical picture making. In these two pieces, much of them disguised as humorous studies of the countryside, it is the quiet passages which are the most remarkable from the point of view of sheer instrumental invention. Passages in his compositions give us some idea of the brilliant technique of Chabrier's own piano playing. But he never regarded sheer virtuosity as an end in itself, though virtuosity is an indispensable pendant to this essentially vital music. In the three *Valses romantiques* for two pianos, Chabrier further enriches an already original style of piano composition by the increasingly liberal use of dissonance.

Franck and his followers

The contribution made by Franck and his followers has often been underestimated. The last representatives of the school of César Franck (1822-90) are contemporaries of Messiaen and Boulez, and their music now seems to us academic. But the school of Franck launched a trend which was responsible for raising French music to its apogee. The musical vocabulary of the school, however, was not equal to its aesthetic ideals, although it possesses a poetry of its own which compensates for the unambitious ideas of Gounod, Bizet, Saint-Saëns, Lalo and Chabrier. Yet it is invariably the rigidity of this school which is so criticised.

César Franck's character, both sensual and passionate but imbued with a simple mysticism, a mixture of solid bourgeois qualities and disinterested idealism, seems hardly that of a man destined to play an important part in the history of music. Franck's development both as a composer and as a major musical influence was very slow and tentative. We can divide his career into three phases. The first as a child prodigy, youthful virtuoso and teacher; then the second phase, his appointment to the organ loft of Ste Clothilde, Paris, a turning point in his life, which was marked by his first important composition, the six *Pièces pour orgue* – the revered teacher had now really entered the world of music as a composer. The third phase began with the quintet, composed at the end of his life.

Among Franck's works, those which are inspired by an imaginary visionary ideal are the exact opposite to those which were inspired by purely musical ideals. In the first category he never produced anything but secondary works, and even his most ambitious compositions in this field only emphasise his weakest points. In the second category we include his tentative youthful essays in the field of abstract music, on which he improved continuously all his life, for it is his musical architecture, his attention to and admiration for classical forms that are at the very root of the 'Franckist' ideal.

All his life César Franck turned to Biblical subjects for a number of ambitious oratorios which were, however, only half successful. Even more controversial than the oratorios are his two operas, which only too clearly show Franck's inability to conceive dramatic action or situations, except in very pedestrian terms; nor can it be said that the medium of song writing suited his genius. Following in the footsteps of Saint-Saëns, Franck also tried his hand at writing tone poems. His last is for piano and orchestra, though he does not make as much use of the possibilities of the solo instrument as he was to do a year later in the *Symphonic Variations. Psyche and Eros* (1887), a curious and long composite work with choral

introduction, is much less successful than the symphony written in the same year.

It was abstract music that had preoccupied the composer from his earliest youth. In the F minor string quintet of 1880 a truly orchestral chamber style blossomed out. The symphonic style of the piano writing encouraged an orchestral treatment of the strings. A single main theme runs through all three passionate movements and only bursts into a major key at the conclusion of this great work, in which Franck reveals his inner self more openly than ever before. With the violin and piano sonata he has achieved a thoroughly successful piece, not only because of the perfect balance between the two instruments, but also because the cyclical treatment here gives a degree of freedom to the exposition of the first three movements. It is only in the finale that Franck yields to the temptation to use a somewhat pedantic canon which deprives the work of genuine spontaneity. The string quartet, however, does not attain the same heights; Franck's powers of inspiration have been interrupted in full flight by an over-preoccupation with form. Indeed, the demands of the cyclic system give rise to so many unnecessary complexities that it is quite impossible to derive any pleasure from the form of this, the first quartet from the new school of French music.

In his organ music Franck shows a taste for serious composition at a time when French organ music in general was falling into a state of decadence, and in the three *Chorales* of 1890 his organ style reaches its peak. In these Franck introduces the cyclic 'system' used by his predecessors, Schumann and Liszt, which emphasises the importance of the theme of the chorale. His message as a composer, which is clearly expressed in

César Franck (seated centre) surrounded by a group of musicians; standing immediately to the composer's left is the Belgian violinist Eugène Ysaÿe.

A box at the opera in 19th-century Paris.

songs, which included settings of Baudelaire, and in which we find by turns the influences of German *Lieder*, French *romances* and the French *chanson*. Duparc, more perhaps than any other Frenchman, suffered from the influence of Wagner, but in his best songs he was able to avoid this, learning instead from the music of Gounod and Berlioz. In this way he achieved a brief but brilliant synthesis, something not altogether surprising in one who had once declared: 'I believe firmly in belonging to no school whatever!' After Duparc, many other composers were to acknowledge their debt to Franck, among them Charles Bordes, Ernest Chausson, J. G. Ropartz, and the Belgian, Guillaume Lekeu (1870-94), who despite his early death produced a most moving violin sonata.

Charles Bordes (1863-1909) is remembered much better for the impulse he gave to old music, which was little known in his day, than as a composer. He published and performed a number of Renaissance works and was also one of the first to make Bach's cantatas known in France. He was also a passionate devotee of folk song and is remembered for his large collection of Basque popular music. He was a co-founder of the Schola Cantorum which Vincent d'Indy was to make the centre of the Franck school.

Ernest Chausson (1855-99) was a pupil first of Franck and then of Debussy. Like many of Franck's disciples his musical ideals conflicted with his musical intuition; a work like his tone poem *Vivianne* is preferable to his lyric drama *King Arthur* and the symphony in B flat, both of which are directly inspired by Wagner. *Le poème*, for violin and orchestra, has an almost perfect elegiac quality. Chausson expresses the best of himself in works in which he admits his own limitations, in which he dreams in a sort of semi-twilight, and in which he makes no attempt to continue in the French tradition.

Joseph Guy Ropartz (1864-1955) left Massenet's teachings to follow in Franck's footsteps. But one can recognise the influence of his earlier master in his impressionist Debussy-like style, in the Breton folksong elements of his music (he came from Brittany) and in his lyric drama *Le pays*. He wrote tone poems, including *Dimanche breton*, symphonies, of which the first is based on a Breton chorale, a number of little pieces for strings and woodwind, songs, compositions for both piano and organ, and six string quartets which deserve to be better known. Ropartz is best known for his promotion of the school of young French music in his capacity as a conductor.

this music, serves to buttress his powerful sensual and religious emotions, and finds a means of expression which entirely balances them. Franck's importance lay in the manner in which he promoted the more serious aspects of music at a time when French musical taste was all too inclined towards a meretricious facility. He displayed a very personal harmonic language (despite his debt to Wagner), and a preoccupation with unity which is no less praiseworthy for being based on the somewhat artificial cyclical system. When he is content to make the cyclical form short and adaptable, as it is in the sonata for piano and violin and in the *Prelude, chorale and fugue*, it is very successful, but when it is used to clothe a long distinctive theme, as it is in the quartet, the system is more difficult to defend.

Franck's first pupils

Henri Duparc (1848-1933), Franck's first pupil, was forced by illness to retire from music at an early age and produced comparatively few works. He was a cultivated musician and pitiless critic, not only of other people's music (excepting that of Franck) but equally of his own. His admiration for Wagner and the German Romantics is apparent in his collection of fourteen

Vincent d'Indy

D'Indy's lofty, almost inhumanly intransigent character, his devotion to the Franck school, his corresponding aversion for the 'Six' and for Schoenberg, Stravinsky and Richard Strauss, and his lack of understanding of any music between Bach and Beethoven (or, for that matter, between Beethoven and Wagner) was complemented by his revivals of earlier music by Monteverdi, Destouches and Rameau. Unquestionably d'Indy (1851-1931) had a considerable effect on a section of the French musical elite; he was, among other things, one of the founders of the Schola Cantorum. However, his dogmatism in musical theory did not deafen him to the call of his homeland, the Cévennes, and it is in his *Symphonie sur un chant montagnard français* and in his *Spring day in the mountains*, rather than in his polemical and theoretical works, that one will find the real timeless music of d'Indy.

After several attempts at composing dramatic legends d'Indy showed his real gifts in *Fervaal*, *L'étranger* and

La Légende de St Christophe. Although influences of Wagnerian music are to be found in these works, the folk idiom from the Cévennes and elements of Gregorian plainsong permeate the scores and lighten them. D'Indy was undoubtedly more interested in the musical essence and dramatic construction of his scores than in the characters of his subjects. The best aspects of his orchestral writing are to be found in his symphonic works. The symphonic trilogy *Wallenstein* still remains somewhat impersonal, but the *Symphonie sur un chant montagnard français*, with its principal piano part, takes a worthy place among the new style of French piano concertos initiated by César Franck and Fauré. The composer here opens the door on to the landscape of the Cévennes and the music is pervaded by a fresh breeze and the scent of the countryside, which drive out any trace of strict formalism. His two other symphonies do not have quite the same precision. The *Fantasy on popular French themes, A Spring day in the mountains* and the *Mediterranean diptych* (1925-6), with their simple lyric themes, are preferable in every

way to the symphony, and his scores are never more appealing than when he forgets elaborate structure and allows himself to be inspired by nature. These two styles, that is to say the scholastic and the 'folk', also pervade his many chamber works.

Vincent d'Indy's literary works are imbued with an equally vigorous style and, although they have some importance, they read less like biographies of César Franck, Beethoven and Wagner, than like acts of worship. His *Course of Composition*, partly re-edited by his pupils, remains an excellent work provided one overlooks his exaggerated admiration for Franck, whom he compares with Beethoven.

The French musical consciousness, which for so long had been hypnotised by overwhelming foreign influences, now began to rouse itself following the military and political disasters of 1870. Fauré, Debussy, Ravel, Dukas, Roussel and Satie all thought of their art in French terms, and all referred back to a French musical tradition; they could assess the value of foreign influences without being deflected from their own course

below left
Charles Bordes, composer and musical scholar.

below
'Monsieur Jules', *a caricature of Jules Massenet (1842-1912), whose numerous successful operas show a sure melodic and dramatic sense.*

301

as Chabrier had been. French music was to find its natural bent by freeing itself of traditional tonality and adopting other close harmonic relations such as modality, polytonality and atonality.

Fauré

Gabriel Fauré's music has to be known extensively, and in context, for its harmonic refinement to be duly appreciated. His simple way of life and belated official recognition after years of financial insecurity concealed a great personality whose sensitivity increased with his spiritual development. As a man he was known as a charming and witty talker, who preferred to keep silent on the subject of the deafness which descended on him as an old man. During his long life (1845-1924) Fauré held many posts in Parisian churches; from 1877 to 1896 he was at the Madeleine, but it was not until he was approaching old age that he was appointed as director of the Conservatoire (1905). The charm of his music is such that it tends to hide the more serious aspects of his better compositions, and we must not fail to remember him as the more stringent composer of the second quintet, *Pénélope*, the twelfth nocturne, the

Gabriel Fauré.

string quartet, *Prometheus* and the *Preludes*. In the same way the quiet religious spirit of the Requiem has been so admired that the significance of Fauré's affinity with Greek art has been overlooked. He was content to make use of traditional musical forms, but bent musical rules to meet his own ends with such skill that, although we cannot apply revolutionary terms such as 'atonal' to his work, we can only admire the originality of his texture, melody and harmony. Yet the originality of his modulations and vigorous use of counterpoint are often marred by a too great musical symmetry and an excessive use of elegant instrumental figuration.

In his piano music Fauré was content to make use of the short style of composition which Romantic composers had made fashionable. Evocative shadowy titles like nocturne, barcarolle and prelude were sufficient to inspire him. Up to the time of the sixth nocturne, written in 1894, his impromptus, romances, barcarolles and nocturnes reveal many delightful passages which help to enhance a style of *musique de salon*, ideally suited for displays of virtuosity. The last five of his nocturnes and the collection of *Nine Preludes* (1910) contain the essence of a pianistic oeuvre which is as varied in texture as it is sometimes stripped to bare essentials. Every mood is represented in these pieces, from youthful impetuosity to a mood of hopeless despair; from the stark line to the grand powerful effect; from the search for harmonic and instrumental effects to utter simplicity. These masterpieces have none of the facile charms which have made his youthful but much less important works so popular; in the same way this also applies to the delightful *Ballade for piano and orchestra* (1881), which has eclipsed the far greater *Fantasy for piano and orchestra* (1919).

His chamber music, together with his piano compositions, constitutes the summit of Fauré's art, particularly the works of his maturity: the piano quintet (1921), the second sonata for piano and cello and the string quartet (1924) are among some of the finest examples of chamber music ever written.

Although Fauré is justly acclaimed as one of the great song writers, the beauty of his compositions is marred by their uneven poetical texts. Only the sober poems of Jean de la Ville de Mirmont allow Fauré's moving songs to attain, as they do in *L'Horizon chimérique*, a perfection comparable with his last instrumental works. Nevertheless Fauré has stamped French song with his own unique musical genius.

Prometheus and *Pénélope* (1900 and 1913) are two little-known examples of Fauré's dramatic art. The former is of astonishing power and grandeur; the latter presents the strange phenomenon of a drama in which music and nobility of sentiment replace scenic action. Both are difficult to produce on the stage. *Prometheus* consists of incidental stage music on a vast scale, with an abundance of spoken dialogue, and demands large orchestral and vocal resources for performances in the open air. *Pénélope* defies all stage production, and the extremely difficult score does not have the brilliance required to move the audience.

Religious music never inspired Fauré to his best, and the popularity of the rather 'smooth' music of the Requiem (1887-8) contributed to his reputation as a sentimental rather than as a profound composer. It would appear that Fauré's religious sentiments did not find their true outlet in church music, except perhaps in the modest but successful Low Mass.

As an orchestrator Fauré remains a mystery. He had little interest in orchestrating his work and entrusted this task to others in an almost light-hearted way. Yet the skill with which he orchestrated certain sections of, for example, *Prometheus*, which we know to be by his own hand, indicates that despite his lack of inclination he had considerable talent in this field.

Polish music from earliest times to the end of the 19th century

By the 10th century the Slavonic tribes of Poland were ruled by a sovereign prince. The process of unification, and an increase in a national consciousness, had been hastened by the struggle against the invading Teutonic knights, whose pretext for aggression had been the conversion of the pagan Slavs. In the 10th century Poland shrewdly adopted Catholicism and, though the knights continued their campaigns, the Poles at least derived the benefits of religion and plainsong. The oldest Polish plainsong manuscripts date from the 11th and 12th centuries and their neume notation is further evidence of the influence of Western European music. The first Polish anthem belongs to the 11th or the beginning of the 12th century. Gregorian plainsong was used in particular in the monasteries. But this foreign element was only slowly assimilated and, for a long time, the liturgy retained many forms which were typically 'folk'. Moreover, folk elements gradually permeated Gregorian chant and the result was local liturgical practices, like those of Cracow and Gniezno. The close relation between popular and ecclesiastical music is most obvious in the sequences in the liturgical mystery dramas and masked plays, popular in the 13th century and performed by strolling clerks, similar to the goliards of Western Europe. They sang in Latin, but clerks of humble origin and the musicians in the towns performed in Polish. About 80 musical settings of hymns and Latin sequences for single voice, one by the first Polish composer known to us by name, Wicenty of Kielce, a canon of Cracow, have survived from the early 14th century. Injunctions forbidding ecclesiastics to mix with *jongleurs* and minstrels reveal the extent to which popular elements were infiltrating into art music.

The unification and growing wealth of the country in the 14th century produced a very high level of cultural life. Even as early as 1025 the funeral of King Boleslas was celebrated with solemn music and his heir was greeted with songs in the style of the *sirventes*. The most famous Polish religious and patriotic hymn, *Bogurodzica* (Mother of God), bears a certain resemblance to a 13th-century French *trouvère* melody, while a prince of Silesia composed songs on the model of the German *Minnesänger*.

The 13th and 14th centuries

Recently discovered records of Polish polyphonic music date back to the turn of the 13th and the 14th centuries. The two manuscripts are written in a style reminiscent of the *organum* of the school of Paris, and we know that several Polish clerics studied in Paris in the early 13th

Polish town musicians of the 16th century.

The palace of the Polish kings at Warsaw.

century. Several motets for two and three voices and, later, several *chansons* with Latin or Polish texts, composed in the manner of an *organum* or of 14th-century ballads, testify to the development of polyphonic music in Poland, but the influence of *ars nova* on Polish music only becomes apparent at the beginning of the 15th century.

Comparatively few musical documents of the 14th century have survived; there are, however, several religious songs set to Polish-Latin or Polish words. In addition there is a certain amount of documentation on consorts of singers and instrumentalists at the royal court, including Russian performers on the *guzli* zither and dancers and permanent musicians of the Chapel Royal.

The first important Polish composer, Nicolas of Radom of the Chapel Royal, lived during this period. Both *ars nova* and Franco-Burgundian influences are apparent in his compositions. His vocal and instrumental pieces, both sacred and secular, show technical maturity and a forceful personality; his works include three three-part masses and a Magnificat written in *fauxbourdon*.

Manuscripts in Polish libraries contain Italian and Netherlandish pieces of the first half of the 15th century; the secular compositions in these collections, among them a hymn in honour of the city of Cracow and a panegyric on the royal family by Nicolas of Radom, mark the beginning of the emancipation of secular music from

liturgical influences. Monody continued to be used in sacred song and is often both rhythmically and melodically derived from folk songs. It was, however, the royal court that remained the centre of musical life in the 15th century. Contemporary accounts give the names of a number of court musicians, and in 1422 we find the first mention of a harpsichord player. The standard of this Polish court was high, and among the foreigners who studied at Cracow was the German, Heinrich Finck.

Municipal music also flourished although statutes for the formation of musical guilds were only accorded in the 16th century. Among the musicians employed by the city authorities were trumpeters, posted at the gates and on towers on the walls to summon the populace to hear proclamations, to announce the visits of kings or archbishops, or to assemble the citizens to defend their town against invaders.

The Renaissance in Poland was a golden age for both religious and secular music. Relations with European musicians increased; Polish music followed the same current, the same style and similar stylistic mannerisms as those of Italian, German and French music. But Polish composers also began to develop a national style – particularly in secular and instrumental music – which now began to spread beyond the borders of their own country.

Sigismund I founded a college of music which attracted almost as many celebrated foreign musicians as Poles. It was from here, the centre of polyphonic music in Poland, that Netherlandish and Italian influences spread throughout the country.

During the first half of the 16th century a great number of composers, both of vocal and keyboard music, appear on the scene. Keyboard tablatures have survived, notably those of John of Lublin and of the Monastery of the Holy Ghost at Cracow as well as the lute tablature of Cracow. In vocal music the Polish composers developed a grand style in cyclic masses for four to eight parts, taking *cantus firmi* from motets or, more rarely, from secular themes. They also composed graduals, laments and motets, and all their work shows the influence of the Netherlandish and Roman schools. The tablatures mentioned above contain pieces in madrigal style, Polish dances and popular songs in characteristic dance rhythm and town and court songs. The Polish dances are arranged in pairs in a manner analogous to the pavan-galliard combination but they have, already, a distinctive Polish style of their own and we now begin to find this style reflected in foreign, especially German, tablatures. One even finds mazurka rhythms in some Protestant canticles. There are also examples of music for the lute – dances, songs with lute accompaniment, or adaptations of vocal pieces for lute, while the tablature of John of Lublin contains the oldest surviving examples of Polish organ music, both introits and adaptations of vocal music.

During the second half of the 16th century the *chanson* became an increasingly popular form, while the Reformation produced both monodies and polyphonic compositions; the song books contain not only sacred songs but also wedding, mourning and even satirical songs. Mikołaj Gomólka is the author of a celebrated psalter (1580) based on Polish texts. Among the 150 psalms one find traces of foreign secular forms, such as the *villanelle* though their melodic and harmonic construction is strongly influenced by Polish folk songs, and their rhythm by folk dances. But there are also subtle polyphonic psalms, and the 16th century saw the flowering of polyphonic song inspired by both Latin and Polish texts.

By the end of the Renaissance something of the Venetian polychoral technique had already penetrated into Poland. The finest examples are by Mikołaj Zieleński (c. 1550-1615), whose *Offertoria* and *Communiones* were printed in Venice in 1601, but recently evidence of earlier and other composers using this technique has been discovered. Features of Zieleński's *Communiones* suggest that these vocal works were intended to have instrumental accompaniment – an indication of the Venetian influence. Thus we see that Polish music embraced every musical style that was being developed by the West – cycles of masses, motets, secular polyphonic *chansons*, religious canticles for several voice parts (mostly with Polish words), and music composed expressly for the lute, organ and harpsichord, as well as dances with a strong nationalist flavour based on folk music. The 16th century also witnessed the publication of a large number of Polish theoretical treatises, as well as commentaries and criticisms of similar foreign treatises.

Finally, in this account of Polish music up to the age of the Baroque, we should mention the books of plays annotated by theatrical producers, which show how considerable was the part played by music in theatrical productions. Although none of this theatre music has survived it prepared the way for opera in Poland, the first opera being produced in 1621.

Polish music during the Baroque period

There was a political and cultural decline in Poland during the 17th century. The political influence of the magnates was greatly enhanced by Poland's expansion to the east, when vast tracts of land fell into the hands of the feudal lords. They now constituted a Polish oligarchy, which exercised a powerful grip on the sovereign, and internal conditions in the country became more and more chaotic. When the Polish nobles, supported by Russia, elected Frederick Augustus I of Saxony as their king, with the title of Augustus II, the Elector Frederick of Brandenburg retorted by crowning himself King in Prussia and laid claim to that other part of Prussia which was subject to Poland (1701). On the death of Augustus II forty thousand Russian troops entered Poland and placed his son on the throne in place of a Polish claimant. The reigns of Augustus II and III were among the darkest periods in Polish history. The

A typical Polish folk dance.

country was ravaged by foreign armies of Saxons, Swedes and Russians, and from now onwards Russian influence became more and more preponderant. The century ended with the great partitions.

These events, and the *dirigiste* attitudes of the Counter Reformation, brought about a concomitant decline in the cultural life of the country. In this atmosphere of general decline, however, music continued to flourish. The Jesuits, well aware of its power, encouraged the study of music in their schools; sacred music was especially benefited, though the music of the court continued to develop.

The first performance of an Italian opera in Poland was given in 1621 at a princely house. The royal court first began to take an interest in opera after the future King Ladislas IV visited Florence in 1625, when Francesco Caccini had composed *La Liberazione di Ruggero*

Chopin as a young man, a drawing by Princess Eliza Radziwill.

dell' Isola di Alcina in his honour. After 1628 several operas were given at the court of Warsaw with Italian singers and, naturally, in Italian. We learn from the financial accounts that the royal opera, which accompanied the court and gave performances in Cracow and other Polish cities, maintained a staff of forty-nine musicians, including Italians and a few Germans, and twenty-six Polish composers and executants.

At the end of the 17th century, Augustus II transferred the Chapel Royal, and the whole of the royal opera company, from Warsaw to Dresden. After 1699 the Dresden company only visited Warsaw and Cracow occasionally, and by degrees German influence was to replace that of the Italians. In 1724 Warsaw acquired its own national opera house, but only after 1765 did the public at large have access to it.

Although the introduction of true opera was delayed, Polish composers were writing monodic songs in the early years of the 17th century. The majority of works of the Chapel Royal at Warsaw, the most prolific musical centre in Poland, was for massed choirs, fine examples being the *Offertoria* and *Communiones* by Zieleński. In the 17th century several Italians were replaced by Poles. Among these were Martin Mielczewski, who wrote a number of psalms and sacred concertos for combinations of voice and instruments, and Adam Jarzebski, who composed a ballad on Warsaw, twenty *canzoni* for two and four voices and several concertos for two, three and four instruments. Barttomeij Pekiel, composer of the first Polish oratorio, used both monodic and concertato techniques – his masses being the equal of anything produced in contemporary Europe. Jacek Różycki is the most representative composer of instrumental music in the second half of the 17th century.

The first Polish sonata for two violins and organ continuo of which we have any knowledge was composed about 1700 by Stanislas Sylvestre Szarzynski. Szarzynski's ten surviving works have an exceptionally pure melodic line and show extraordinary talent, while the *canzoni* by Andrej Rohaczewski and the later preludes by Jean Podbielski are very representative of early Baroque music. There are also a large number of compositions for harpsichord, popular with the nobility and bourgeoisie; but it was religious music that was far and away predominant. The most distinguished of the composers is Grzegorz Gerwazy Gorczicki, who in his *a cappella* compositions reverts to the tradition of the late Roman school but who, in his combined vocal and instrumental works, employs the Baroque *concertato* form.

To sum up, the development of music during the Baroque period is characterised by a number of things: a considerable increase in the number of musical ensembles, both vocal and instrumental; the enrichment of instrumental music by new forms – such as the *canzone* for organ, chamber orchestra and violins and the *sonata da chiesa*, as well as fantasies; the creation and performance of operas and oratorios; an increase in the production of musical instruments and finally the increased activities of Polish nationals, who replaced foreign musicians.

The music schools also contributed to an increased repertory of dance music and the evolution of a specialised style of music for dancing. Dance music was also developed in town and country, thanks to the municipal musicians' corporations. There are many references to these dances in Polish writings; some were imported from abroad, as we can see from the Polish variants of their foreign names. But it was in this period that definite form was given to such Polish national dances as the mazurka, krakovia and polonaise; this last was a stately dance in triple time which was to find its way into the music of several Western European composers, including Bach.

Romanticism in Poland

The Romantic movement in Poland is represented by a composer of exceptional importance – Frédéric Chopin. It is a mistake to assume that Chopin owed everything to his own original genius, for in fact he leaned for support on the music of preceding centuries. From the obliteration of Poland as an independent state, following the 18th century partition by the Prussians, Austrians and Russians, it was only through the medium of the arts that a real sense of unity and national consciousness survived. Poland was, in any case, economically and socially retarded and the peasants had long been exploited; under partition this exploitation was now in the hands of foreigners while education was Russified and Germanised. Only in the territories annexed by Russia was industry developed; the power of the bourgeoisie increased and a rudimentary capitalism began to take shape. The development of a strong and aware bourgeoisie led in Poland, as elsewhere, to the growth of patriotic sentiments and of struggles for freedom.

The Russian zone, in particular, was the scene of constant agitation; but the Prussian and Austrian territories were also affected. In consequence of these troubles, insurrection broke out in 1830-31; further revolts broke out between 1846 and 1848, but each time these were cruelly suppressed by the occupying powers. Later risings were no more successful in liberating the country. Each insurrection led to new repressive measures, and the number of emigrants increased in relation to the deepening of patriotic sentiments. Nevertheless, there were changes; the peasants became landed proprietors and what remained of feudalism disappeared, while capitalism in the towns brought with it, to a certain degree, the propagation of learning and a revival of cultural and scientific studies. Among the artists who most fully expressed the national yearning for independence were the great poet Adam Mickiewicz and the composer Frédéric Chopin. Although Chopin himself was not directly involved in the patriotic ideological movement, all the specific characteristics of Polish Romanticism are reflected in all his work. Not only the European classics but also authentic Polish folk music played a major part in the formation of his style and contributed to its dramatic power, despite the fact that he spent the second half of his life in Paris (1831-49).

Chopin

Frédéric Chopin was born near Warsaw in 1810 of a French father and a Polish mother. By the time he was eight he had emerged as a precociously talented pianist and was sent to study under Joseph Elsner of the Warsaw conservatory. His full professional career began when he was aged seventeen, although his Opus 1, a rondeau, had already been published in 1825. The intense musical life of Paris acted as a magnet to all the finest musicians of the day, much as London does today, and in 1830 the twenty-year old virtuoso travelled to the French capital, giving concerts at Vienna and Munich en route.

In Paris he became the admired friend of Liszt, Berlioz, Bellini and the novelist Balzac among others; he made a European reputation as virtuoso and composer, and was much sought after as a teacher. There had already been signs of the consumption which was to kill him and in 1838 he went to live in Majorca for a year's recuperation. At about this time he had met the novelist

below
Contemporary caricature of Georges Sand.

bottom
Chopin reads the newspaper while his friend Maurice Sand works.

Georges Sand and she went with him to the Mediterranean. This was one of the most creative episodes in Chopin's life and he wrote the *Twenty-Four Preludes*, which contain some of his finest music. The love affair with the strong-willed Georges Sand became increasingly strained and in the last years of his life she deserted him.

In the spring of 1848, the year of the revolution in Paris, Chopin travelled to London and toured Britain, giving many concerts on behalf of the Polish refugees from the unsuccessful revolutions. But the strain was too great for his weakened constitution, and he died in 1849 after his return to Paris.

The music

The bulk of Chopin's music is for solo piano; he also composed two concertos for the instrument. He arrived on the musical scene at a time when the instrument had reached the conclusion of its first long period of development, and Chopin's piano, both in subtlety and power of

Georges Sand, a portrait by Delacroix.

expression, approximated much more to the modern grand than it did to the piano of Mozart. It was to Chopin's apparently effortless mastery that the instrument owed much for its ascendancy as the dominant means of musical expression during the high Romantic period and beyond. His virtuosity, aided by an unconventional fingering technique, was a matter not simply of rapid figure work. Chopin deployed a unique range of touch and tone quality and a tightly expressive control of dynamics of volume, to which was added his legendary use of rubato rhythms. He was the founder of the 19th-century school of cantabile playing and Liszt, to some extent, modelled his style on that of Chopin.

The rudiments of certain aspects of Chopin's style as a composer are to be found in the work of his predecessors, the Irishman John Field and the Austrian J. N. Hummel. Chopin's nocturnes are clearly modelled on those of Field and Hummel's pianistic technique, which foreshadows that of the Polish composer, but of central importance in the formation of Chopin's style are the traditions of Polish folk and art music.

The period of Polish music immediately preceding the emergence of Chopin was poor in great talent. One finds the influence of the classics (Haydn and Mozart were much more influential on the work of Polish composers than was Beethoven) crossed with elements of *style galant* – the heritage of a former period – and with that of a *style brillant*. This latter was the result of the great flowering of music throughout Europe and the increasing virtuosity of musical interpretation. Poland was equally involved in the general musical trend which was felt throughout all Europe. The movement was particularly apparent in Lvov and Warsaw, where it was echoed in concerts, in music publishing, in the manufacture of musical instruments, in musical instruction and in the foundation of musical societies. Chopin grew up in this atmosphere. His music is a synthesis of all the trends which characterised Polish music of the end of the 18th and beginning of the 19th centuries. These he raised to the highest level of musical achievement, while he gave new life to European Romanticism by the introduction of his own individual style and Polish elements. Throughout Europe Romanticism was more closely identified with national characteristics than any earlier style. This was true not only of the emerging schools of Central Europe and Russia, and of the slow revival of music in Spain and England, but even of the great traditions of such major musical countries as France, Germany and Italy.

Chopin dug deep down into folk songs and peasant dances from Masovia, Kujavia and the districts of Lublin – such as the mazurka. Elements of the mazurka can be found in his waltzes and songs, in his concerto in F minor, and the *Fantaisie*, Opus 13. Cracovian elements appear in the *Cracovienne*, Opus 14 and the finale of the E minor concerto. Chopin returned to the stylised dances which we find in such abundance among his Polish predecessors, extracting from authentic folk music what was useful to him. It was the modality and complex tonal principles of Polish folk music that inspired Chopin to harmonic innovations, to innovatory rhythmic structures and to what were later to be termed agogic accents – that is accents of phrasing, rather than of strict metric qualities, as evoked in Chopin's famous rubato. The specific character of Polish songs imbues all the melodies of the composer, even when they have no direct connection with a folk tune model, and contributes much to the overall unity of his style.

Chopin not only sublimated popular traditions, but in his polonaises he harked back to the traditions of the courtly dances of the 17th century. Whereas the polonaises of Chopin's older contemporary Oginski acquired the sentimental character of *musique de salon* and also something of the nature of programme music, those of

Chopin have the grandiose effect of a great canvas into which the composer introduced all possible pianistic techniques. For his countrymen they seemed to be a perfect embodiment of a noble Polish past, though for Chopin himself they were perhaps rather an outlet for the pent-up nationalist feeling of an exile from an oppressed fatherland.

His music is not strictly programme music, but his letters point to historical connections. We can read battle scenes into his A major and A flat polonaises, and the famous *Revolutionary study* was directly inspired by the events of 1831. His polonaises are certainly not purely dance music, but dramatic and noble. He makes the same changes in his mazurkas; he forgets the original bourgeois, aristocratic or folk models to achieve short lyric concert pieces.

Not only musical and choreographic traditions infused the nationalist style of Chopin, but also literary traditions. Quarrels between the Romantic and classic poets turned Warsaw society topsy-turvy during Chopin's youth. The innovatory form of his piano ballades, which comprise elements of rhapsodies, was born during this period. It has been suggested that there is a direct link between Chopin's ballades and Mickiewicz, but the hypothesis is insufficiently supported. Nevertheless it is obvious that Chopin takes up the epic and fantastic genre of ballads and transforms them into purely instrumental music. Polish intellectuallism certainly fired the imagination of the youthful composer, imbuing it with patriotic tendencies and opinions on Poland's historic situation; its influence is to be traced in all his work right up to his last mazurka, written with the trembling hand of a dying man. The musical expression of his work is a distant and indirect reflection of the ideological situation of his country: the tension created by the preparations for the struggle for liberty of his country introduced a dramatic force into his sonatas, ballades and scherzos;

we even find it in the preludes, nocturnes and études.

Chopin's role as the representative of the spirit of Poland was soon accepted throughout the world; his contemporaries in the world of music recognised his importance as a composer and performer – in addition to Liszt's admiration he earned the highest praise from Schumann. Today we are particularly conscious of his dramatic expression and recognise his immense contribution to the piano music and musical Romanticism of the 19th century, but, nevertheless, he is also to be recognised as an outstanding genius who is the incarnation of the national Polish style.

The contemporaries of Chopin

No doubt because he lived abroad for the greater part of his creative life, and also partly because of the conservative attitude of the Polish, Chopin left no followers or imitators in Poland. The work of some Russian composers such as Scriabin, Lyadov and Balakirev was influenced by Chopin, but it was not until the 20th century that a Pole, Karol Szymanowski, returned to the traditions of Chopin on a new basis. Most of Chopin's contemporaries came from the Warsaw Conservatory, particularly from Elsner's class.

Josef Nowakowski was a composer of orchestral pieces and chamber and piano music; Tomasz Nidecki, conductor of the Viennese orchestra and later that of Warsaw, wrote several stage works and some religious music. Together with them, mention must be made of Ignacy Feliks Dobrzyński (1807-67), one of the most important composers in Poland in the 19th century, who received first prize for a symphony, written in the Polish spirit, at an international meeting of composers in Vienna. The

The Young Poland group.

309

Chopin in the costume of Dante, a drawing by Delacroix.

Sonnets of the Crimea and *Phantoms*, based on texts by Mickiewicz, are still performed. Moniuszko has also left us some religious works including a Requiem, masses, motets and litanies, as well as some instrumental works (the *Baijka* overture and two quartets). His style shows elements reminiscent of the music of Schubert, Mendelssohn, Bellini and Glinka.

Secondary musicians

There were a number of secondary musicians, dominated by the talent and personality of Moniuszko, who devoted their talent to light operetta and vocal lyrics – among them were Antoine Katski, a virtuoso pianist who studied under John Field in Moscow, and his brother Apollinaire (1827-79), who refounded the Warsaw Conservatory, of which he was director from the 1860s. Moniuszko's influence on these composers is very apparent, particularly in their melodic line, which is characteristically Slav. To the same generation belong Adam Minheimer, composer of operas very much like Meyerbeer's in style, Ludwik Grossman, and Franciszek Mirecki, who lived for a long time in Italy, where his numerous operas were performed.

Henryk Wieniawski (1835-80), a contemporary of these musicians, was one of the greatest violin virtuosi of the 19th century, attaining world fame and being sometimes compared with Paganini. Wieniawski started his musical career as an infant prodigy and, at the age of eight, joined the violin class at the Paris Conservatoire. He held posts in St Petersburg and Brussels, where he was a professor at the conservatory, while his numerous concert tours included one of the United States during the years 1874 to 1877 with the pianist Anton Rubinstein. Relations between these two musical 'prima-donnas' were often strained – it is recorded that on one occasion Wieniawski refused to play because he had not received equal billing with Rubinstein. His main compositions are two violin concertos, polonaises and mazurkas (*Légende* and *Souvenir de Moscou*), caprices, a series of variations and two collections of *études-caprices* for violin, and the *Modern school for solo violin*.

Five composers in the second half of the 19th century showed innovatory tendencies. They all died young, which prevented them from fully developing their talents and overcoming the conservatism which, at this period, was predominant in Polish music. Julius Zarebski, a remarkable pianist and composer and a pupil of Liszt, combines in his works (such as his piano concerto and polonaises) the styles of Liszt and Chopin, and displays certain glimmerings of Impressionism. Eugeniuz Pankiewicz uses particularly interesting harmonies in his songs and arrangements of folk music. Antoni Stolpe displays neo-Romantic and Wagnerian tendencies in his piano sonata and chamber music. Antoni Rutkowski displays similar stylistic tendencies. Henryk Jarecki, in his opera *Mindowe*, certainly inclines to Wagnerian drama. It was tragic for the state of Polish music in the early 20th century that this young talent was prevented from expanding.

The end of the 19th and beginning of the 20th centuries

In the second half of the 19th century German influence was reinforced in those territories annexed by Prussia, as it was in Galicia, which was under Austrian government. An intense diffusion of the literature and art of the occupying powers served as a means to Germanise the

progress of research into Polish folk music was much advanced by Oskar Kolberg (1815-90), who published a twenty-nine volume collection of folk songs classified by region; his works, which include a number of dances in the national style and an opera, are less important.

Moniuszko

Despite the European stature of Chopin, more important in the musical life of 19th-century Poland was the work of Stanislaw Moniuszko (1819-72), who has been called the father of Polish national opera but may, with justice, be considered the father of a national Polish style in music. He was active at the time of the revolutions and his work specifically reflects the feelings that predominated in Polish society at that period. The opera *Halka*, based on folklore and his most celebrated work, is an artist's reply to the revolutions during the years 1846-48, and conveys his sympathetic understanding of the problems of social injustice. From a musical point of view the work is specially interesting because it uses a technique similar to the Wagnerian *Leitmotiv* and shows the influence of Weber in the handling of the orchestra. Of his other operas, *The Haunted Castle* (1865) was the composer's reaction to the state of mind of Polish society after the January insurrection of 1848. Patriotic sentiments also imbue operas such as *The Countess* and *Verbum nobile*, while the theme of social injustice is portrayed in *Paria*.

Moniuszko's operas are full of tuneful arias whose origins can be found in traditional Polish folk music, although they are very considerably influenced by Italian opera. Moniuszko applauded the reforms made by Wagner although he did not adopt all his theories. Many of Moniuszko's ballets, operettas and melodramas created a great deal of interest in the society of his time, as did his cantatas, of which the most outstanding,

far left
Stanisław Moniuszko.

left
Henryk Wieniawski, the great 19th-century Polish violinist.

below
Paderewski giving a concert at St James's Hall, London, in 1892.

country, and in this respect music played a major part. But, as far as education and culture were concerned, it was quite a different matter in the territory occupied by Russia, where, after the emancipation of the serfs, industry, able to make use of cheap labour, progressed rapidly, leading to technical and scientific developments and advances in education.

The level of musical culture was the same in the three annexed territories. Musical teaching was just as widespread in Warsaw as it was in Lvov and Cracow (1860 was the year in which the Warsaw Conservatory was re-opened; it had been closed by the Russians after the January Insurrection). Singing, which was particularly encouraged by choral societies, helped to retain the character of Polish folk song in the Prussian zone. On the other hand, symphony concerts and operas introduced Western European influences.

The music schools, particularly the conservatories of Warsaw, Cracow and Lvov, produced musicians for the numerous symphony and opera orchestras; at the same time a number of great virtuoso musicians made their appearance. Some of them achieved world fame, such as pianists like Aleksander Michalowski, Natalia Janotha and Ignacy Paderewski; violinists like Henryk Wieniawski, Apollinaire Katski and Stanislaw Barcewicz; the cellist Aleksander Wierzbillowkz; and many singers who made a career for themselves outside Poland, such as Władysław Mierzwinski, Aleksander Brandowski, all the Reszko family and Marcelina Sembrich-Kochanska.

Władysław Zeleński and Zygmunt Noskowski were the most important composers after Moniuszko. Zeleński (1837-1921) rejected all innovations since Wagner and 'The Five' and is much more akin to Schumann, Mendelssohn and Chopin; for the last forty years of his life he was director of the Cracow Conservatory. He displays his talent best in vocal works, particularly in songs for solo voice. A very sweet and melodic line is characteristic of his operas and, although his dramatic works are somewhat thin, they have a markedly Polish character, as has his symphonic and chamber music.

Zygmunt Noskowski (1846–1908), a pupil of Moniuszko's, introduced the tone poem into Polish music for the first time with *The Steppes*. But he was responsible for introducing not only this type of programme music, but also a science of orchestration, very rich in texture. He also wrote a number of operas, symphonic and chamber music and a collection of songs for children which enjoyed a great success in Poland, although it must be admitted that stylistically they are no advance on Schumann.

A whole galaxy of technically excellent composers belongs to the same generation as Zeleński and Noskowski, and all of them remained faithful to Romanticism. But the most distinguished Polish musician of this period was, undoubtedly, Paderewski. Ignacy Jan Paderewski (1860–1941), perhaps the most famous pianist who has ever lived, began his studies at the Warsaw Conservatory when he was aged twelve, and was teacher of the piano there from 1878 to 1883. He continued to study at other European centres, notably Berlin and Vienna. After his first triumphant concert tour (1884–87) he was established as the leading pianist of his time; in 1909 he was appointed director of the Warsaw Conservatory, but four years later made another visit to the United States, where he had bought an estate. After the founding of an independent Polish state, following the Treaty of Versailles, Paderewski was first Polish ambassador in Washington and then, 1919–20, Polish president and foreign minister. Although he resigned from political office to devote himself to his concert career between the wars, he accepted nomination as president of the Polish regime in exile after the German invasion in 1940. Paderewski's just fame as an executant has obscured his achievements as a composer, but his works included the opera *Manru* (1901), a symphony, some remarkable songs, and many beautiful piano pieces. He also published an edition of Chopin's works and a study of Chopin's music as well as his own memoirs.

The tradition of Romanticism remained predominant in Poland after the 19th century, and her composers opposed the introduction of new Western European trends into Polish music.

above
Zygmunt Noskowski.

right
Autograph of part of Chopin's study in G flat major.

Hungarian music to the age of Liszt

With the conversion of the country under King Stephen I (d. 1038) Hungary joined the community of Western Christendom. In musical terms this Christianisation had two important results; not only did it mean the introduction of Gregorian plainsong as the music of the Church, but it also led to closer contact with the secular culture that was soon to develop in the West. Within Hungary itself the divisions between the aristocracy, descended from the invading Magyars, and the peasants, basically of Slav origin, was never wholly obliterated and with the Turkish conquests of the 16th century another element was to be added to the complex mesh of Hungarian music.

The descendants of St Stephen ruled in Hungary for three centuries and during this period the musical life of the nation consisted of three elements – folksong, the songs of the *jongleurs* and epic singers, and the plainsong of the Church. Contacts with the West include the presence of numerous Hungarian clerics at Paris university in the early 13th century and we know that the German *Minnesänger* Oswald von Wolkenstein and also the north French *trouvère*, Peire Vidal, visited Hungary. It was from the 12th century too that we have the first records of Gregorian plainsong used in the Hungarian church, but the music was purely monodic and was to remain essentially so for a long time to come. In addition to vocal music there is documentary evidence of the use of musical instruments in Hungary during the middle ages, especially wind instruments of all kinds; the bagpipes, as elsewhere in Europe, were to be found both in the village and at court.

The 14th century opened with a decade of anarchy which was terminated by the accession of the Angevin house, French in origin but, through the vagaries of dynastic marriages, having claims on the kingdom of Naples and now on that of Hungary. After a period of consolidation the Angevins, during the reign of Lewis the Great, inaugurated a period of brittle but dazzling imperial splendour for medieval Hungary. In cultural terms the close links with Italy, and even with Flanders in the north, which the reign of the Angevins brought, were of importance, but it was also during this period that the power of the nobility, so important in Hungarian social and later cultural life, was advanced in return for their quiescence in royal policies. During the 15th century Hungary was again in decline until the glorious reign of Matthias Corvinus (1458-90), a true Renaissance ruler who not only confirmed the political power of his kingdom but also was a great patron of the arts, founding at Buda one of Europe's great libraries.

Yet throughout the middle ages the musical life of Hungary was dominated by foreign styles, first of the Church and then, with increasing contacts with other European courts, of the growing art of secular music. The popular music of the folk, which from the few surviving pieces of evidence seems to have been vigorous and thriving, was despised by polite society and no native school of composers developed to integrate it into the stream of high cultural life. Whereas the medieval schools of France, Italy, England, Spain and, more significantly, Poland, all drew strength from their local traditions, the musicians of Hungary seem to have been content with the styles of their Western neighbours. The close link between folk and high art, which proved of such seminal importance elsewhere in Europe, was never truly established. The medieval lyric and epic poetry of Hungary, however, was a strong tradition, and the melodies which have survived reveal both their popular origins and an already identifiable Hungarian character. But it was not until the 16th century that this vigorous popular tradition was in any real way integrated into art music.

During the last years of the 15th century, a papal nuncio described the singing of the Hungarian Chapel Royal as the finest he had heard anywhere, and a Western musician of great stature, Adriano Willaert, visited the country for a time. But the impetus which music might have derived from his influence, and indeed the whole cultural life of Hungary, was disrupted by the victory of the Turks at the disastrous battle of Mohacs in 1526. Confusion grew when the Austrian house of Habsburg laid claim to the Hungarian throne and, after a disruptive period of warfare, the country found itself broken up into three regions: the central plains, dominated by the Islamic Turks; the principality of Transylvania in the east, governed by native Hungarian rulers in vassaldom to the Turks; and Habsburg Hungary in the west. To these political disasters was added the religiously divisive element of the Reformation, which

Matthias Corvinus, King of Hungary (1440-1490).

for a time seemed likely to convert Christian Hungary into a Protestant nation.

During the 14th and 15th centuries the music of the Church had received an added stimulus from the fact that many of Hungary's churches received organs during this period. The development of an ecclesiastical musical culture seemed to be advancing, and the trend could only have been reinforced by the visit of Willaert. Yet it is not until the 17th century, with the Franciscan monk Janos Kajoni, that we come to the first identifiable Hungarian composer of vocal polyphonies. He was also an organist and organ builder, and transcribed compositions by Schütz and Viadana for his instrument. The development of polyphonic church music in Hungary was retarded not only by the political events already mentioned but also, perhaps, by the fact that the leaders of the Calvinist Reformation in the country followed the practice of their co-religionists elsewhere in Europe by adopting the melodies of the folk to their religious texts. Moreover, the metrical psalms of the Huguenots, not-

ably those of Claude Goudimel, also enjoyed a considerable vogue. The value of popular songs as a medium of religious edification was recognised by the Roman Catholic Church in Hungary during the 17th century, and a council set in hand the preparation of an edition of popular melodies for church use. But the most important figure in the slow process of integrating the art of the folk into the music of high culture was the great chronicler of the Turkish wars, Sebestyen Tinódi (1505-56). Intent on inspiring a national Hungarian spirit in the face of the Turkish invasions, he visited the sites of the great Hungarian achievements of the past and wrote his verse *Chronicle*, which was published in 1554. Besides being a poet, Tinódi was also a lutenist and composer, and the twenty or so songs that his chronicle contains are the first important collection of Hungarian music. They draw not only on the melodies of the folk but also on church music, and even have elements from the music of the Turkish conquerors themselves. Their popularity was great; Sir Philip Sydney, who visited

A 16th-century engraving of Budapest.

Hungary towards the end of the century, reports the popularity of the national epics, and some of the melodies are still sung today. As a lutenist, Tinódi was outshone by others, most notable of whom was Valentin Bakfark (1507-76). During the 16th century a number of talented Hungarian musicians left their troubled homeland and gained great reputations for themselves in Western Europe. Among them some of the best known were the Neusiedler family who, although of Hungarian origin, spent most of their careers in Germany where their fame as lutenists was widespread. Bakfark, on the other hand, spent the first twenty years of his active life in the service of Hungarian nobles and then of the king himself, who ennobled him. However, he travelled widely in Europe, working at the Polish court and staying in France and Italy, where he died. He published two books of tablatures for the lute, which contain adaptations of works by Josquin, Gombert and Clemens non Papa, as well as some distinguished original polyphonic compositions.

During the 16th and especially the 17th centuries the aristocratic courts of Hungary cultivated music. Like many other courts of the time they maintained a body of trumpeters for state occasions, but keyboard music was also much appreciated and the works of the English virginalists seem to have enjoyed a certain vogue. The evidence of Hungarian activity in the field of keyboard music is contained in four large collections made during the 17th century. The work of Janos Kajoni has already been mentioned. The other collections were made by anonymous hands though it is possible that one of them was by Janos Wolmuth, the organist of the church of Sopron. This, the latest of the four, dates from 1689 and is written in modern notation. These collections are interesting not only because they show the extent to which Hungarian composers learnt from the techniques of the West, such as the English manner of variations, but also because they contain a number of dances and songs which clearly derive their inspiration from the Hungarian tradition, including the music of the Slavs.

A. Das Schlos
B. Die Ober Stat
C. Die Juden oder wasser Stat.
D. Die Hinder Vor Stat
E. Ein Pallast vnd Zollhaus in der Obern vor Stat
F. Die Vnder vor Stat.
G. Pest
H. Warme Bäder

I. Das Blockhaus welchs die Turcken angesteckt vn verlassen
K. Alt Gemeür von einer ver-wusten Stat in einer Insel
L. Turckische begrebnusen
M. Aufgeworffene Schantzen der auf die Stat beschossen worden
N. Die Thonau.
O. Die Schiffprucken.

ON DEN CHRISTE BELEGERT GEWEST. AÑO. 1598 Menf October

During the 17th century the courts of the Hungarian aristocracy remained important in the musical life of the nation, though their preference for foreign styles and performers remained. However, towards the end of the century, Pal Esterhazy (1635-1713), a member of that great family whose services to the arts were to be considerable, pointed the way to a new period of achievement among native Hungarian composers. He was an amateur of letters and music, a performer on the harpsichord and also a composer of some talent. In 1711 he published his *Harmonia Caelestis* at Vienna, a collection of compositions, many liturgically inspired, which show not only the expected influence of the school of Venice but also a close understanding, on the part of the princely composer, of the popular melodies of his native country. However, the development of an independent Hungarian national culture was effectively arrested when, in 1711, the Habsburg armies, which during the previous century had driven the Turks from their position in the country, routed the armed forces of Prince Rakoczy of Transylvania and brought Hungary finally under the control of Vienna. During the 18th century Hungarian culture came under the sway of the Austrian capital.

The maintenance of some semblance of an independent Hungarian tradition of art music now fell to the very numerous class of petty nobility and the almost guerilla forces who continued to oppose the rule of the Habsburgs. These freedom fighters, known as *kuruc*, assembled and developed a repertoire of songs and dances which represented one of the greatest flowerings of Hungarian popular music. These melodies show elements, not only of their strongly influential popular sources, but also of the Baroque and Rococo music of the courts; they have been preserved in collections known as *melodiaria* made between the 1770s and 1810s, many of them in the Calvinist colleges of Hungary. Not only was this *kuruc* music distinctive in its style but it also cultivated its own instruments, chief among them the violin, the zymbalom, a type of dulcimer peculiar to Hungary, and the *taragota*, a type of double-reed instrument similar to the Turkish *zurna*.

Towards the end of the 18th century there emerged a new genre of 'developed' folk music known as *verbunkos*. Some of these dances were used in the recruitment of the resistance forces and much of this music was performed by the gypsy musicians of Hungary who came to the country at the end of the 15th century. *Verbunkos* music drew on a variety of sources – Turkish music, Balkan

right
Pal Esterhazy.

below
A musical evening in the early years of the 19th century; notice how one of the members of this aristocratic gathering is playing the 'national' instrument, the peasant zimbalom.

folk music and popular Viennese and Italian styles. In the period of its first great flowering it was led by a number of virtuoso fiddlers of whom perhaps the most famous was Janos Bihari (1764-1827). It may have been he who composed the famous Rakoczy march. It rapidly became the song of the freedom movement against the Habsburgs, but its origins probably lie in the music of the *kuruc*; Berlioz's famous setting of it, later incorporated in the *Damnation of Faust*, was composed for a concert of his music in Pest which, not surprisingly, was a sensational success. A central figure in the development of the *verbunkos* style, Bihari formed a group of musicians and toured Europe, becoming famous for his Hungarian 'gypsy' music. This music was undoubtedly vigorous and stirring but it was not in fact genuine folk music, being too heavily coloured by the eclectic nature of its inspiration and the strong elements of Western art music which its practitioners introduced. After the great spontaneous flowering of the early 19th century the element of composed and contrived music became more marked. Dance suites were written with strong affinities to Western types and the most famous of all Hungarian dances, the *csárdás*, with its slow first section followed by a fast section, which is often regarded as a typical traditional Hungarian folk dance of some antiquity, dates from this period.

In Hungary, as elsewhere in central Europe, the 19th century was a period during which the growing sense of national identity and purpose exploded into revolutionary activities against the imperial Habsburg power. This political drive was everywhere accompanied by a strong nationalist movement in the arts. We have traced some of the roots of Hungarian music; it was in the 19th century that these were amalgamated into a style which could not only be classed as Hungarian, but which also, in the gigantic figure of Franz Liszt, was to have important repercussions in Europe. Even as early as the beginning of the 17th century some Italian composers had made use of their knowledge of the Hungarian idiom, then emerging, to give additional characteristic colour to some of their works. But it was only with Liszt that the country produced a master of independent stature whose music demanded respect without consideration of any ulterior nationalist appeal which it might have. Yet, although he dominated the scene, Liszt did not stand alone in Hungary, and before studying his music we will describe the work of his contemporaries.

Erkel and Mosonyi

Ferenc Erkel, who was the composer of the Hungarian national anthem, and has also been called the father of the Hungarian national opera, was born at Gyula in 1810. By the age of twenty-eight he was already director of the national opera house and later in life was to be principal of the national conservatory. He wrote eight operas, all set to Hungarian libretti, the most popular of which, such as *Hunyadi Laszlo* (1844), were patriotic in tone and based on the stories of Hungary's past heroes. During his long life (he died aged eighty-three) Erkel devoted his energies to the establishment of a purely Hungarian national style and his work was almost totally unaffected by the revolution in European musical sensibilities which was being worked by Wagner. Erkel, whose achievement was gratefully recognised by his countrymen, not only laid the groundwork of a Hungarian style of composition, but also inaugurated a national concert life with the launching of the Philharmonic Concerts in the 1850s.

He was supported by the work of others, notably Mihaly Mosonyi (1815-70). Largely self-taught as a composer, Mosonyi, who was also a professional double bassist, took pupils in composition and advanced the

A Hungarian folk dance.

right
Liszt as a young man, by Ingres.

below
The opera at Budapest.

cause of Hungarian music, not only by his own works, but also by articles in the first Hungarian musical journal. This was founded in 1860 by his pupil Kornel Abranyi, who had also studied under Chopin. Mosonyi's compositions included three operas, one of which was accepted by Liszt for performance at Weimar (though subsequently withdrawn by the composer), church music, including a gradual, two symphonies and examples of the other main musical forms of his day. Another of Mosonyi's pupils was Odön Mihalovich (1842-1929) who from 1887 to 1919 was director of the national conservatory, where his leanings towards Liszt and Wagner contributed to the introduction of wider currents into Hungarian musical life. During the 19th century Hungarian composers were in effect, divided between two schools, the 'westerners' and the 'populists', led by Erkel, whose style was self-consciously indebted to the *verbunkos*, a manner which was also gaining a certain currency outside Hungary.

This survey of Liszt's lesser contemporaries would not be complete without a mention of Joszef Joachim (1831-1907), the great Jewish violinist who, although born in Hungary, spent most of his life in Germany. After his concert début at the age of seven he studied at Vienna and Leipzig. He was there for six years and worked with Mendelssohn in the orchestra of the Gewandhaus, Leipzig. In the 1840s he visited London for the first time, where his popularity was such that he made an annual visit to the English capital for many years to come. For a time in the early 1850s Joachim apparently changed his loyalties in the great struggle which raged in Germany between the old school and the new. He left Leipzig and took the post of leader of the orchestra at Weimar, where Liszt, the warm admirer of Wagner, led the forces of the new music. But Joachim's inclinations were with the more traditional style and after his appointment to the court of Berlin in the 1860s he became an advocate of this manner, whose chief champion was now Brahms. Joachim's fame as a concert violinist was Europe-wide but he also proved himself capable of outstanding ensemble playing, and the quartet which he formed occupies a particularly important place in the history of music for its fine performances of the late quartets of Beethoven, reckoned for many years after the composer's death to be unplayable.

Liszt

Ferenc Liszt, most commonly known by the German version of his name, Franz, was born in 1811 at Raiding, not far from Eisenstadt, now in Austria. Like many of his compatriots Liszt learned German as a first language and never fully mastered Hungarian. His father, a member of the Hungarian petty nobility, employed in the service of Count Esterhazy as an accountant, was himself an excellent musician, playing the piano, violin, guitar and flute; he had known Haydn and Cherubini. Noticing the precocious interest taken by the little Ferenc in music, he transferred to him all the pent-up dreams of an unfulfilled virtuoso and gave him his first lessons. At nine years of age the young boy was applauded for the first time in public at the Esterhazy palace. He made such an impression on the aristocratic audience that they contributed to a bursary for him to continue his studies in Vienna, where he studied the piano with Czerny and composition with Salieri.

In 1823 he went to Paris, where he spent a great part of his life. There the Italian opera composer, Ferdinando Paer, who became his teacher, made him compose an opera (*Don Sanche*) at the age of twelve and a half; it met with little success, however. At fifteen Liszt wrote twelve

Etudes pour piano, which later, in 1838, were to become the twelve *Etudes d'exécution transcendante* and of which the fourth was adapted as the tone poem *Mazeppa*. At the same time he started on the innumerable European tours which made him world famous as a virtuoso pianist.

Admired and adulated everywhere, Liszt frequented the company of men in the public eye: Berlioz, Chopin and the leaders of the Romantic movement in literature, in particular Lamartine and Victor Hugo. Liszt himself had a highly developed literary taste; his favourite authors were Montaigne, Kant, Pascal, Châteaubriand, Lamenais, Constant and Senancourt. It may well have been his passion for literature that led him to attempt a full reconciliation of poetry with music in his symphonic poems. His interests also included philosophy, and as a youth he had entertained the idea of entering the priesthood. However, just when he was on the point of taking orders, the revolutions of 1830 directed his enthusiasm towards other ideals of humanity and social reform.

In 1834 Liszt came to know the Countess Marie d'Agoult (who was to become well known as a writer under the pseudonym of Daniel Stern), and their elopement caused an immense scandal in polite society. The liaison, which lasted for ten years, forced Liszt to live outside France – in Geneva, Rome and the Rhineland. In Germany Liszt developed a passion for the German poets – Heine, Goethe, Schiller and Uhland. In 1840 he paid a visit to his hometown of Raiding, where the gypsies feted him and may well have inspired his *Hungarian Rhapsodies* of 1852. Marie d'Agoult gave him three children, one of whom, Cosima, was herself later to cause a scandal by leaving her husband Hans von Bülow for Richard Wagner.

In February 1847 Liszt, who three years previously had broken off his liaison with the countess, became the lover of Princess Caroline Sayn-Wittgenstein who, unsuccessfully, tried to have her marriage annulled to marry the composer. Without any doubt, the Princess Sayn-Wittgenstein, who exercised a great influence on Liszt, helped to develop his creative genius. Installed in Schloss Altenburg at Weimar, Liszt transformed the city into the musical capital of Europe. He himself conducted Wagner's *Tannhäuser*, *Lohengrin* and *The Flying Dutchman*; Berlioz's *Benvenuto Cellini*; *Faust* and *Manfred* by Schumann, and many other works. Here he also composed some of his own best works, among them the *Dante Symphony* (1857), the piano sonata in B minor (1853), the greatest work for piano of the high Romantic period, *The Preludes*, the *Faust Symphony* and the *Gran*

left
The Countess Marie d'Agoult, who eloped with Liszt.

middle left
Princess Caroline Sayn-Wittgenstein, who became Liszt's mistress in the late 1840s.

bottom left
Liszt's silent practice keyboard, which he took with him when travelling.

mass, also referred to as the *Graner Fest Messe*.

But his situation in Weimar caused a great deal of envy; the new ruling prince was parsimonious in the funds allotted for music and Liszt's mode of life provoked increasing indignation in society. In the 1850s he became a tertiary of the Order of St Francis of Assisi and, after breaking with the princess, went to Rome, where he received minor orders and was presented to an honorary canonry by the pope; from this time Liszt carried the title of Abbé.

He quarrelled with Wagner and his own daughter Cosima at the beginning of their liaison in 1867; not on moral grounds primarily, but rather because Hans von Bülow, Cosima's husband, was Liszt's loyal disciple. Later, the ageing Liszt relented and Wagner's triumphs were the great consolation of his old age, in particular the inauguration of the theatre at Bayreuth (1876), when Wagner paid him public homage. Nevertheless, Liszt retired more and more from worldly affairs and his last work was the *Requiem*. Three years later he took part in numerous ceremonies organised on the occasion of his 75th birthday, when he conducted the *Gran* mass in London and the symphonic poem *St Elizabeth* in Paris. These were his last journeys; he died of pneumonia in July 1886 in Bayreuth.

The symphonic poems

Liszt, involved with literary circles and a man of considerable culture, was, with Wagner, the most literary of the Romantic composers. Liszt wrote scarcely any abstract music, and even his B minor sonata – his undoubted masterpiece – is really a poem translated into terms of music.

The symphonic poem was Liszt's greatest contribution to musical form. His inspiration as a composer came primarily from literature. There had been examples

A fashionable ballroom in 1860.

of programme music before him – Beethoven's *Pastoral* symphony, although not inspired by literature, was a more complete example of programme than anything before, and Berlioz's *Symphonie Fantastique* was a further step on the road. Weber's overtures were also well adapted to a programmatic scheme, while Goethe, in a letter, had suggested using a basic theme in an opera which could be freely treated with modifications of tempo, tonality, and so on, to suit the dramatic situation. All these preliminary ideas were ultimately resolved in the music of Liszt.

He wrote thirteen symphonic poems, among them *The Preludes, Orpheus, Prometheus, Mazeppa* (on a traditional Hungarian hero), *Hungaria, Hamlet, The Battle of the Huns* and *From the Cradle to the Grave*. Their magnificent quality does not rely on a given literary theme and the works are not 'programme music' in a pejorative sense, that is, merely descriptive and following a scenario step by step. The poem furnishes Liszt with the general atmosphere and colour of his theme – in *Mazeppa*, a wild horse-ride and a triumphal march; in *The Preludes*, various 'psychological moments', which echo the words of the poet Joseph Autran without, however, trying to translate them into musical language. Saint-Saëns praised Liszt, with good reason, for having created a style which was neither symphony nor overture, but an authentic marriage of poetry and music, the first borrowing from the second its pure poetic value and not just the words of the text. Liszt's music is a summary of and not a commentary on its poem.

This particular quality, which is so very much part of Liszt's genius, is perhaps even more forcibly stressed in the *Dante* and *Faust* symphonies, and even in the *Gran* mass, which in the ultimate analysis reveals itself as a highly inspired symphonic poem with chorus. No other composer has combined so perfectly the role of musician and poet as Liszt.

The importance of Liszt

'My sole ambition as a composer is to hurl my javelin into the infinite space of the future', Liszt once declared. And indeed his works have many prophetic aspects which foreshadow developments even of the 20th century. That he was able to achieve this was, first, because he had such a solid musical foundation. In his religiously inspired music we find the influence of Gregorian plainsong, Palestrina, and Roland de Lassus, while a profound knowledge of Bach heightens his organ music. Springing from a background of the purest tradition, Liszt nevertheless seems to be one of that rare breed of 'absolute' creative artists, a true innovator.

'I am a mixture of gipsy and Franciscan', is another of his observations. Here was a man who was both a thinker and passionate at the same time, a contemplative who was constantly and simultaneously aware of 'the two worlds'. Liszt himself was profoundly and sincerely conscious of the existence and interpretation of the spiritual and the physical, and his music links the one with the other. Examples are legion; one of the most typical is the *Fountains of the Villa d'Este*, which begins with a concrete visual picture but which fades into a vast meditation on the beauties of creation itself.

Liszt was a visionary for whom music represented a means for the total expression of nature and feelings; in his need to convey this he used entirely new musical forms and this made him one of the great forerunners of modern music. He believed that no chord could sound absolutely foreign to a given key, however far removed it might seem, and in his later works he dispensed with the classical rules of modulation. From

Plate 43
Verdi at the age of seventy-three.

Plate 44
*The famous opera house of La
Scala, Milan.*

here it is only a step to atonality. The whole of the Wagnerian musical style is already sketched in the great symphonic poems of Liszt, which indeed sometimes seem like drafts for Wagnerian operas.

In many of his works, particularly in the *Fountains of the Villa d'Este* and *Nuage gris*, Liszt appears as the precursor of Impressionism, and anticipates Debussy's shifting harmonic scheme and techniques used by Ravel. The *Years of Pilgrimage*, begun when Liszt was twenty-four, show remarkably early indications of this style; he resumed work on them twenty years later in the calm surroundings of Weimar and completed them between 1863 and 1882. Liszt achieves representations no less faithful than those of a great painter, but, in the words of the French musicologist Alfred Leroy, 'With the descriptive and narrative element there is closely linked an emotional and emotive psychological element, an intuition which links the real with the eternal.'

Liszt and the musical life of his time

The significance of Liszt's achievements as a composer has sometimes been underrated. However, his talents as a pianist and his importance in the history of piano technique have never been questioned. His own phenomenal talent made him the greatest pianist of his, possibly any, generation, but more important was the influence which his teaching and the practice of his pupils had on the development of the technique of the instrument. He enlarged the conventional range of the piano, and developed such techniques as the double trill, tremolos with crossing hands and glissandos. To this he added a cantabile style of playing, derived from the example of Chopin, and in short made the piano the equal of the orchestra. His own transcriptions of the largest of symphonic works, such as Beethoven's ninth symphony and the *Symphonie Fantastique* by Berlioz, demonstrated to the full the extent to which Liszt revealed and developed the resources of the piano. Without the pioneering achievement of the *Transcendental Studies*, the modern pianistic repertoire would be unthinkable. It was the achievement of Liszt to transform the piano from the instrument of bourgeois drawing-room entertainment into one of epic power and poetic expressiveness. In the musical life of Germany, Liszt was the champion of the 'new school' of music, which saw literary and programmatic elements as essential parts of music and made harmonic and orchestral explorations of ever increasing audacity.

The ageing Liszt playing for fashionable salon society.

The symphony and opera in Germany

Richard Wagner was born in Leipzig in 1813. His father died when he was still a child, and he was brought up by his mother and actor step-father, and later by his uncle. In 1814 the family moved to Dresden where Richard was to begin his formal education. In 1827 he returned to Leipzig where he studied philosophy, harmony and counterpoint, and where he made his first attempts at composition – two rather simple, but nevertheless Wagnerian piano concertos, a symphony, some studies for *Faust*, and his first work for the theatre, *Die Feen*. In 1833 he was appointed *répétiteur* at Würzburg, and, in the following year, director of the Magdeburg opera, where he wrote the words and music for *Das Liebesverbot* (Forbidden Love), based on Shakespeare's *Measure for Measure*. In the same year (1836) he married a pretty singer, Minna Planer, with whom he lived for twenty-five years but who brought him little happiness. We next find the composer in Leipzig, Königsberg and Riga and then in London and Paris, where he was reduced to such financial straits that he was compelled to support himself by arranging dance music and writing songs, novelettes and articles. He stayed in Paris until 1842 and in France composed *Rienzi* and *The Flying Dutchman*.

In 1842, *Rienzi* was performed at the Dresden opera house, where it was so well received that the following year Wagner was appointed director of the opera by the king of Saxony. *The Flying Dutchman*, however, which had been put on ten weeks after *Rienzi*, was received with much less enthusiasm. *Tannhäuser*, produced in 1845 (he had written the book in Paris), met with the same fate. However, undeterred, he set to work on *Lohengrin*.

The revolutionary was now aroused in the disappointed musician. In 1848, the year of revolutions throughout Europe, he became involved in the Saxon revolutionary movement and actually manned the barricades in an insurrection in Dresden. On the failure of the revolution, he was obliged to flee to Weimar, and thence, with the help of Liszt, to Zurich. It was here that he began writing his first theoretical treatises.

The success of *Lohengrin*, which had been produced at Weimar thanks to Liszt, brought some comfort to the exile, who at this time started work on the cycle of *The Ring*. It was in Zurich that he embarked on the passionate love affair with Mathilde Wesendonck, the wife of a rich industrialist, which inspired him to start writing *Tristan and Isolde*, but which also obliged him to leave Switzerland and take refuge in Venice, where he finally completed the score. He had a hard fight to have his work produced, especially in Paris, where, in 1861, *Tannhäuser* met with a notable lack of success.

The composer then travelled all over Europe conducting concerts of his music. In 1864, we find him in Vienna, miserable and in debt; then in Switzerland and Stuttgart, where he received a summons from King Ludwig II of Bavaria to come to Munich. The eccentric and passionate young monarch was devoted to Wagner and his music, and *The Flying Dutchman*, *Tannhäuser* and *Tristan* were all performed at Munich. But court intrigue obliged the composer, once again, to live in exile.

He had in the meanwhile separated from Minna, and the scandals attached to his name in Munich were partly due to the liaison which he had formed a little earlier with Cosima, daughter of Liszt, and wife of the pianist and composer Hans von Bülow. The scandal came to a head when Cosima presented the composer with his first daughter. Wagner then went to live at Triebschen, near Lucerne. Here he spent many happy and fruitful years writing *The Ring* and *The Mastersingers*. In 1870 Cosima obtained a divorce and married Wagner.

Good relations were now re-established with Ludwig II and the Bavarian court, and he and Wagner worked on the project for a national theatre where the composer's work could be produced under the best conditions. A suitable site was found at Bayreuth in 1872. The building of the theatre was completed in 1876 and it was officially opened in August of the same year. In 1882, Wagner achieved a crowning success with his production of *Parsifal*. The following winter, for reasons of health, he visited Venice, where he died of a heart attack. He lies buried at Bayreuth in the garden of his villa Wahnfried.

The music of Wagner

Despite all his contradictions, it was with Wagner that German musical Romanticism was to be most fully realised. Schumann still belonged to what one might call the bourgeois school of Romantics, to the sentimental school of Biedermeier poets. Wagner, although a late-comer to music, was immediately in advance of his time and discovered a new outlet for Romanticism. It was no vain boast on his part when he said he would be the musician of the future. He was prophetically correct – musically and technically. But he was also the supreme example of the German artist of the Bismarckian period and, in his grandiose Bayreuth productions, he reflected to perfection the image of the Germany of his day.

Wagner's youthful, liberal ideals were derived from the Young Germany movement and in particular from authors like Heine and Heinrich Laube. It was this background that inspired him to write his only historico-poetical opera, *Rienzi* (1838-40).

His philosophic development was rapid. His first important opera was *The Flying Dutchman*, a symbolic and legendary drama based on the concept of man's regeneration through love, a concept which he was to toy with for a long time to come. *The Flying Dutchman*

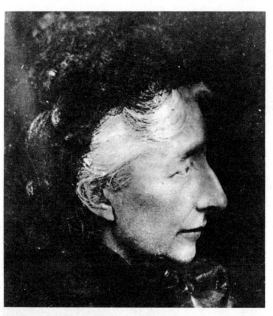

far left
Richard Wagner.

left
Cosima Wagner.

below left
A 19th-century production of
Lohengrin.

The Festival theatre at Bayreuth.

vegetarianism, anti-alcoholism, vivisection and the regeneration of man by some hazy synthesis of humanism, Christianity, Buddhism and theosophy. From this emerged *Parsifal* (1877-82), based on the legend of the Holy Grail, where once again we find the idea of renunciation combined with an element of mystical eroticism.

Man of the theatre and musician

Wagner was one of the great masters of opera. Up to and including *The Flying Dutchman*, Italian influences are very evident in his music, but in this opera, although there are still some echoes of the Romantic, historical grand opera, we are already aware of a trend towards the style of the drama ballad which he was to realise with *Lohengrin* and *Tannhäuser*. But Wagner was soon to abandon history entirely for mythology. His greatest contribution was undoubtedly *The Ring of the Nibelung*. This vast work, which draws on Germany mythology for its subject, is a cycle of four full-scale operas – *The Rhinegold* (*Das Rheingold*), *The Valkyrie*, *Siegfried*, and *The Twilight of the Gods* (*Götterdämmerung*). The gods, giants and dwarfs of myth are used by Wagner in a libretto which, despite its occasionally creaking machinery, achieves a powerful allegorical statement of the corrupting and destructive effect of the lust for power in hearts which have renounced the universal principle of love. To express the broad and ambitious sweep of his ideas, Wagner began to develop new operatic techniques. He discarded the rigid rules of recitative and aria and blended them into a new type of musical expression which was analogous to continuous spoken dialogue.

To assess Wagner's rightful place in music, it is essential to remember what he himself declared: 'Any critic who makes a distinction between my harmony and instrumentation is doing me as much injustice as someone who tries to isolate my music from my poetry, or my songs from their words.' It is this fusion of different elements, this successful application of the technique of 'total art', which makes any purely musical criticism misleading, if not altogether useless. Wagner's art possesses many more original ideas than original music. But the music is so complex and so ingeniously contrived, interwoven with so many motifs, that one is apt to forget the components in admiration of the whole that they form.

If Wagner's melodic line possesses any originality, it is not so much because his themes in themselves are original as because of the manner in which they are manipulated. But where he was really original was in the provision of a continuous melodic scheme which accorded with his principle of continuous declamation and action; this scheme gave an entirely new look to lyric declamation and broke away completely from the use of arias.

On the other hand, his use of the *Leitmotiv*, which was born of his need to represent symbols in musical terms, is masterly. The idea of using different musical themes to identify different characters or elements in programmatic music was not entirely new, but in Wagner's hands it becomes a means of advancing the dramatic development, and of psychological exposition.

In his first works he borrowed his harmonic procedures, particularly from his friend Liszt, but later, by extensive use of the chromatic scale, he advanced into new territory and not only presided over the decline of the classical system of diatonic harmony, but inaugurated a new era which was later to lead to Schoenberg and his school.

was immediately followed by *Tannhäuser*, based on the legend of the eponymous medieval minstrel torn between sacred and profane love. This fitted in perfectly with Wagner's own preoccupation with the conflict between spiritual and sensual love. *Lohengrin* (1846-48), based on the legends surrounding the quest for the Holy Grail, is concerned with good and evil in man. In the first version of *The Ring* we again find Wagner the socialist. Capitalism, represented by the Giants, opposes the oppressed workers (the Nibelungen). But in the second and final version, politics are replaced by 'Love' (Brunhilde), while Wotan represents the moral pessimism of Schopenhauer. But the composer had not abandoned politics. In his books *Art of the Future* (1850) and *Opera and Drama* (1851), Wagner the democrat postulates, in an elaborate exposition of his ideals, that only through popular art can a nation be completely integrated. Ideas continued to flow from him. *Tristan and Isolde*, which derives from a story in Arthurian legend and which has as its themes mystical eroticism and renunciation of the world, was written in 1857-59 and inspired by his love affair with Mathilde Wesendonck. *The Mastersingers* (1862-67) is based on the society of the singing guilds of medieval Germany and expresses Wagner's nationalistic and Christian ideals. Like *Tristan*, it has autobiographical overtones. Three years later, at the time of the Franco-Prussian war, we find him extolling the Prussian victories and dedicating poems to Bismarck.

He continued to pour out wordy and polemical writings on every subject under the sun – racism, hygiene,

In his book *Opera and Drama*, Wagner declared that music must be the servant of the drama. The vast orchestral forces he employed do not conflict with this intention. The Wagnerian orchestra in some respects takes the place of the ancient classical chorus in Greek drama, inasmuch as it explains and comments on the action of the drama. In his operas there are protracted passages where the characters remain not only motionless, but silent, while the orchestra interprets wordlessly what passes in the depths of their souls. With Wagner there are no fixed instrumental rules. One can only admire the skill with which he creates a unique and often magical atmosphere, and the way in which, by frequently doubling the parts, he creates an impression of depth.

It was a long time before Wagner was able to achieve what he had set out to do. It was not until he was thirty-three that, with *Lohengrin*, his musical language and technique really took shape and his dramatic qualities were fully realised. From then onwards, up to the time he wrote *Parsifal*, he continued ceaselessly to perfect his own dramatic formula and to produce music whose purpose was essentially functional and which was designed to intoxicate and overwhelm the listener. And this music, almost physical in its impact, which creates an atmosphere and plunges the listener into another world, still conveys a message.

Brahms

Johannes Brahms was above all a German from the north. It has been said that Hungarian and Viennese influences harmed his art, but such a point of view is completely incidental and superficial. Brahms's genius is essentially Nordic. He is both a classical and a Romantic composer, and his works constitute a major link in the evolution of German music. He established the balance between Beethoven, the classical composer

turned Romantic, and Schumann, the Romantic who tried in vain to be classical.

A conservative northerner and devout Lutheran, his inclination was for orderliness and strict form. But there was a contradictory side to his nature. Even as a boy, Brahms read not only Theodor Storm, but also the works of E. T. A. Hoffmann, Tieck, Jean-Paul and Eichendorff. The Scandinavian sagas and Nordic legends in Herder's collection of folk tales and ballads also helped to develop the dreamy, imaginative side of his character. Thus his work, while largely couched in classical forms, is Romantic in temper. There was nothing fortuitous about his art; he had an instinctive need to communicate, even when engaged on a commissioned work or on something written for some

below
The 1954 Bayreuth production of Tannhäuser *by Wieland Wagner.*

bottom
Wagner surrounded by friends and admirers.

solemn occasion. Brahms borrows classical forms, which he treats with due respect but which he is not afraid to mould to his own ends. His sonatas, symphonies and concertos all conform strictly to the traditional style established by Beethoven, but at the same time he enlarged their scope. Instead of the usual two themes, the allegro movements of his sonatas often consist of as many as three or four, while his variations have a breadth and freedom hitherto unthought of. The same can be said of his slow movements; sometimes his finales take the form of a chaconne or rondo.

Brahms was born in Hamburg, in May 1833, of humble parentage. He received his first instruction from his father, a double bass player in local theatres and dance halls. By the time he was fourteen the young Brahms was already a professional pianist, and played the piano in cafés and sailors' taverns. Later, he toured northern Germany with the Hungarian violinist E. Reményi, who introduced him to Joachim. Through the latter he came to meet Schumann and Liszt, to whom he played his first piano compositions. Liszt recognised his talent, but it was to Schumann's enthusiasm, expressed in a long article in the *Neue Zeitschrift für Musik* (1853), that the young man owed his initiation to the musical life of Germany.

In 1854 he was appointed court director of music to the prince of Detmold-Lippe. In 1862 he settled in Vienna where he accepted the post of conductor of the Singakademie. From now on his whole life was bound up in his music. The even tenor of his existence varied very little: in the spring, holidays in Italy and Sicily; in the summer, working vacations by the Swiss and Austrian lakes or in the Black Forest; in the winter, Vienna. Even when he achieved international fame bitter arguments raged over his work, even in Vienna, and he became, at first unwillingly, the champion of the anti-Wagnerian school in Germany.

Brahms died in Vienna in 1897 after a life without incident. There were no great emotional love affairs; every day was devoted to his art. He had several women friends, indeed very close friends, but no more. He had a horror of marriage (equal to his horror of opera, as he used to say jokingly). His alleged affair with Clara Schumann seems to have no foundation whatsoever, though his admiration for her was very great.

The birthplace of Brahms in Hamburg.

Piano works and chamber music

His piano works were not written in order to display technical virtuosity, but they have a marked orchestral quality. Indeed the *Handel Variations* (1861) have been arranged for orchestra with tremendous success by the English composer Edmund Rubbra. Several phrases are often repeated which give his piano music a peculiar flavour all its own – progressions in thirds, sixths and octaves, which, with the use of double suspension, provide almost symphonic effects. His use of wide melodic intervals should also be noted and finally, as in his other works (perhaps even more so than in the piano compositions), the superimposition of strong rhythms and abundant syncopation.

His piano works can be divided into three groups. The first group consists of youthful works: three sonatas (1853-54), four *Ballades* (Opus 10) and a scherzo. The second group comprises the so-called technical pieces, that is to say all the variations written in his maturity (1854-73). The third group includes all the contemplative lyric pieces, and practically everything written after the *Klaviersticke*, Opus 76, all works of his old age (1878-93).

The first group is inspired by Brahms's Nordic background and youthful reading. The three sonatas are all classical in form but developed in Beethoven's third manner. Although very carefully constructed, they are far from formal and can be compared to Nordic ballads, full of heroic and contemplative passages inspired by folklore and legend. The third sonata, Opus 5, is the most remarkable of the three, by reason of its breadth and cyclical form. This is no less true of the admirable *Ballades*, Opus 10, based on an old Scottish ballad and forming a satisfying artistic whole.

Variations always had a particular appeal for Brahms, and he used them in his symphonies and sonatas. He wrote six sets for piano: on a theme by Schumann (1854); on an original theme; on a Hungarian theme; a set for four hands on another theme by Schumann; on a theme by Handel (1861) and finally a set on a theme by Paganini (1863). Despite his obvious interest in the technical resources of the piano, which he stretches to the limit, it is first and foremost the imaginative, emotional appeal of his music that counts.

The *Lyrische Stücke* are mostly works of his old age, the so-called contemplative period. They can be classified by their mood; for example the *Intermezzi*, *Fantasien* and *Caprices* are dreamy and meditative; the *Ballades*, *Rhapsodies* and *Romances* are more literary in character, and strongly accented like ballads.

From this point of view, special attention should be paid to the last four of the great cycles, Opus 116, 117, 118 and 119, which constitute some of the most extraordinary pieces in all Brahms's piano music. In these pieces we find the same Nordic inspiration as infused his youthful work. They have the same intimate and exalted passages, and we find the same flashes of heroism, though perhaps less now that he was approaching the end of his days. On the other hand, a new mood of melancholy creeps in, perhaps due to old age and ill-health, which runs through the whole cycle and has something of the poetic feeling of Theodor Storm.

Of all the twenty-four chamber music compositions, not one is a bravura piece; all are meditative and introspective. They all adhere strictly to the formula employed by Beethoven, but although Brahms makes no new contribution in this respect, his invention is extremely rich and he is more prodigal with his themes in these works than in any other form of composition. There is always something intimate and pure about his chamber music. The source of his inspiration is sometimes evident for example in those works inspired by nature (usually tinged with melancholy) like the piano

above
Brahms with Johann Strauss, the 'Waltz king' (1825-99). Brahms had considerable respect for Strauss's talents as a musician and much admired the piquant rhythms, vigorous melody and fine sense of instrumentation that distinguished his waltzes.

left
Brahms as a young man.

327

and cello sonata, the two clarinet and piano sonatas, and the *Schwarzwald* trio for clarinet, piano and horn. To these must also be added the trio for piano, cello and clarinet, the great clarinet quintet (1891), and the two string sextets. Very rarely, with the exception of the third piano quartet, are there any tragic overtones in these works.

Symphonic music

Brahms was already in his forties before he wrote a symphony. He had, of course, already written orchestral music, such as the magnificent *Variations on the St Anthony Chorale* (1873). The four symphonies were written over the following years: No. 1 in C minor (1855-76); No. 2 in D major (1877); No. 3 in F major (1883) and No. 4 in E minor (1885). Brahms did not attempt to introduce any particular innovations and his symphonies are in the style of an expanded sonata, rich in themes and variations. The scoring is very individual, vigorous, clear and full of melodic invention.

His four concertos are closely related to the symphonies. The first for piano and orchestra (1858) is undoubtedly the most typical of Brahms. It is representative of his robust Nordic character and makes no

concessions to virtuosity. It has been criticised on the grounds that the piano is too much part of the orchestra, but this is just what makes it so original, and it is in fact probably the most powerful of all his concertos. The second piano concerto belongs to the traditional Romantic style and is to some extent more Viennese. It contains some superb piano writing but lacks the depth of the first. The magnificent violin concerto (1878) is similarly inspired. The violin and cello concerto (1887), like many of the works written in his old age, recalls the poetic mood of his youth. Here we find again the Nordic Brahms, the brusque passages, poetic melancholy and accented phrasing which characterise the epic ballad style.

Lieder and choral works

Of some three hundred compositions for voices, a very large proportion are in the style of the *Volkslied*. Although Brahms was to a great extent a literary composer, in the field of *Lieder* he was much more the successor of Schubert than of Schumann. His *Lieder* rarely have long piano preludes or postludes, the piano accompaniment being sometimes as simple as a folksong, though sometimes it is much more elaborate, resembl-

Brahms's autograph manuscript of one of his songs.

ing Schumann's piano accompaniments in this respect.

Of Brahms's two song cycles the first was the *Romanzen aus Magelone* (1862), a suite of fifteen *Lieder* for baritone and piano, each usually linked to the next by spoken words. The whole cycle is treated in the style of a ballad, with a rhythmic and melodic invention which makes this long work one of Brahms's grandest creations. The piano accompaniment is richer than usual and more symphonic. The texture is dense and often complex, and indicative of the quasi-symphonic cycle which was to follow. This second cycle, the *Four Serious Songs* (1896), written more than thirty years later, is altogether different in character. It is a religious work, composed when Brahms was approaching the end of his life. The cycle consists of four long songs for contralto or baritone with piano accompaniment, and is in the form of a four-part cantata based on texts from the scriptures. Despite their sacred and austere character they possess a certain warmth, and the general spirit is that of preparation for death. Occasionally one is reminded of the *German Requiem*. There is the same grandiose dramatic declamatory style, and the piano accompaniment is reminiscent of an organ or even an orchestra.

The *German Requiem* (1857-68), for soprano and baritone solo, chorus and orchestra, is not a liturgical composition. The seven long movements, based on German texts from the Old and New Testaments chosen by Brahms himself, have an essentially Lutheran quality. The style of the music is very free. The chorus has the principal role, the two solo voices only intervening in short passages from time to time.

A little-known but extremely beautiful vocal work is *Rinaldo*, a cantata for tenor solo, male chorus and orchestra, based on a text by Goethe which in turn was inspired by Torquato Tasso's *Gerusalemme liberata*, a poem abounding in dramatic incidents and which fascinated Brahms. In spite of his antipathy for opera, this work, with its recitatives and arias, curiously resembles lyric drama – something we would never expect of Brahms.

Bruckner

In an ultramodernist period Anton Bruckner's music appeared simple and unadventurous, yet his unsophisticated nature was to produce gigantic compositions. He was a devout Catholic but at the same time his spirit was troubled, and he was constantly haunted by terrifying fantasies. At the age of forty-three he suffered a nervous breakdown. His lifelong fears increased, as did his obsessions with the pleasures of the table, with marriage, with morbid stories and with music critics. To escape from these obsessions he sought refuge in music and God.

Bruckner was born in 1824 at Ansfelden in Lower Austria into a family of music teachers. He settled in Vienna in 1868, where he was appointed court organist and professor at the conservatory. Several European tours made his name well known to the public. From 1891, famous, but a sick man, he began to show signs of mental deterioration. He was unable to finish his ninth symphony and died in Vienna in 1896.

From his many compositions we can safely select nine symphonies, three masses, one Te Deum and a string quintet to be discussed here. These works were produced in two main creative periods. During the years 1871 to 1876 he wrote the second symphony, in C minor; the third in D minor; the fourth in E flat major; and the fifth in B flat major. Between 1879 and 1887 Bruckner wrote the string quintet; the Te Deum (1881-84); and the symphonies No. 6 in A major, No. 7

in E major (1883) and No. 8 in C minor (the *Apocalyptic*).

While Bruckner obtained little benefit from the example of Wagner in the harmonic evolution of his works, his symphonies constitute a sort of orchestral answer to Wagnerian drama. The resemblance is not simply one of proportion alone, for Bruckner's majestic and solemn themes have a certain affinity with those of Wagner. Moreover there is something Wagnerian in Bruckner's orchestration; he borrowed some of his contemporary's methods and was able to give a quite individual depth to his orchestral scores.

As far as form is concerned, his symphonies are merely greatly expanded versions of the Beethoven symphonies. However, Bruckner's amplifications are not the result of careful thought; there is a curious lack of structure, particularly in the amount of repetition and in the multiplicity of instruments he uses, this not always with justification.

The chorale plays an important part in his climaxes. Passion, which is generally lacking in Bruckner's symphonies, is replaced by solemnity, which is sometimes almost grandiloquent and has a certain descriptive naïveté, but which is imbued with sincere religious feeling. There are occasional flashes of true beauty, but real emotion is rarely found in the works of this master, who seems to have been overwhelmed by the grandeur of God and creation.

Anton Bruckner.

Music in Bohemia

From a very early period music held a central place in the culture of the ancient kingdom of Bohemia. As it came to be surrounded by the German lands of the empire it could not avoid interpenetration by cultural influences of the Western European tradition, but these external forces were counterbalanced by the vigour and quality of the musical life of the Bohemians themselves. The English music historian, Dr Burney, who visited the country towards the end of the 18th century, called Bohemia the 'conservatory of Europe' and described the immense musical activity in all sections of the community, especially remarkable in the outlying country districts.

The first major composer of Bohemian extraction, Jacob Handl, called Gallus, has been treated in the section on German music of the 16th century, and, because of the political subjection of Bohemia to the Habsburg empire after the battle of the White Mountain in 1620, the careers of all the important Czech musicians,

such as the outstanding violinist and composer Heinrich Biber (1644-1704), are inextricably involved in the musical life of the German lands. The contribution of musicians from Bohemia and Moravia to European music in general reached its height in the 18th-century German court of Mannheim. During this century, however, Czech musicians were to be found all over Europe. We have noticed the activities of the Benda family in Berlin and we should also mention the composer Leopold Anton Kozeluch (1754-1818), who, in the service of the Habsburg court for much of his career, won a European reputation, writing an immense amount of music, including thirty symphonies and thirteen piano trios. Yet Kozeluch was outshone by the work of his younger contemporary active in Paris, J. L. Dusik, better known as Dussek (1760-1812), while earlier in the century Josef Mysliweczek (1737-81) had earned from the Italians the sobriquet of the 'divine Bohemian' for his operas. Thus from the 16th century Bohemia had been directly in touch with the Central European tradition from which it had received much and to which it had also given much.

Christianity came to the lands of Bohemia, which then formed part of the empire of Greater Moravia, in the 9th century, but it was not fully established until the 10th, when St Wenceslas (d. 926) did much to ensure its success. The religion of Rome was inevitably attended by the advance of Gregorian plainsong in the music of the Church, and the native propensity for music was not slow to accept this new stimulus. In the mid-13th century we read of the installation of a new organ in the church of St Vitus in Prague, and music, as all the other arts, reached a high point during the reign of the Luxemburger king who, as Charles IV, was also Holy Roman Emperor (1346-78). Under him the influence of French musicians came to the fore and the art of the *ars nova* was introduced, Machaut himself visiting the court at Prague. The house of Luxemburg had succeeded to the throne after the native line of the Premyslids had died out in the person of Wenceslas III in 1306. During his reign the predominant influence in secular music had been German, and Wenceslas himself composed in the tradition of German *Minnesang*, while the great Heinrich von Meissen, called Frauenlob, had visited his court.

Quite apart from these foreign influences, there is evidence of a strong native tradition, represented by popular canticles such as the *Hymn of St Wenceslas*. In the 15th century this popular tradition was to come into its own when the religious rebellion of the reforming Hussites ousted the imperial house for a time and severed Bohemia from the empire at large. Anticipating the practice of the leaders of the European Reformation of the next century, the Hussites opposed the use of elaborate liturgical music in worship, encouraged the practice of congregational hymn singing and, most significant of all, not only used the vernacular language but also drew on the repertoire of popular song for the melodies of these hymns. The influence of these Hussite

Bedřich Smetana.

hymns was deep, long-lasting and extensive. In the first decade of the 16th century two collections were published containing some 90 hymns, and another collection appeared later in the century. Not only did the practice of the Hussites of encouraging the congregational singing of hymns in the vernacular and set to popular melodies influence the other European Reformers (and even at a distance John Wesley in England), but also their very tunes were to be found used in some of the Lutheran chorales of the German Reformed Church.

The last great period of Bohemia came during the reign of the Habsburg emperor Rudolf II, who made Prague one of the most brilliant capitals of Europe, frequented by artists and scientists of all nationalities, among them Jacob Handl. Rudolf reluctantly accepted the strength of the Reformist Church in Bohemia but, when his successors in the early 17th century attempted to revoke Rudolf's edict of religious toleration, the outcome was a rebellion which plunged Bohemia into a decade of chaos and set in train events which led to the great Central European conflict known as the Thirty Years' War. Yet, despite its fierce determination, the Reformed Church of Bohemia was scattered and the German grip on the national life, tightening throughout the 16th century, became complete. It remained so until the middle of the 19th century, when the leaders of the national revival spoke Czech rather than German and the composers, notably Smetana, composed to Czech libretti.

Smetana

The ground was already prepared for a national composer of wide gifts such as Bedřich Smetana (1824-84). The nationalist Czech musical movement could base itself on a long and solid classical tradition and, whereas the talents of Liszt and Chopin were able to flourish only in Western Europe, the mainstream of European music having been so poorly represented in their homelands, Smetana was able to develop his abilities in Bohemia itself at a very early age, thanks to his knowledge of the great classical masters. He became a first-class pianist and his early works consist almost entirely of dances and miniatures written for piano. In Prague he heard Liszt and later Berlioz and, at an early date, ranged himself on the side of the musical *avant-garde*. Henceforth he associated himself with progressive and nationalist ideas held by the Czech international elite of the time, which even the repression of the revolution of 1848 was unable to discourage.

In this year, indeed, Smetana founded a school of music in Prague, but eight years later conditions in Bohemia led him to go to Sweden, where he directed a concert society at Göteborg. On his return to Bohemia he found a more liberal atmosphere and he soon joined the vast effervescent nationalist movement, which was crowned by the inauguration in 1862 of a provisional Czech national theatre for the performance of opera, ballet and plays. Smetana, who had declared his allegiance to the school of Wagner, set himself the task of composing a repertory of Czech operas. His historic opera, *The Brandenburgers in Bohemia*, though written in 1863, was not performed until 1866 – the year in which Smetana became director of the national theatre. The immense success of the premiere of his first opera was not repeated with *The Bartered Bride* later in the same year. But the date marks the birth of a truly national Czech school of music. Since its first production, *The Bartered Bride* has been performed more than 2,500 times at the National Theatre, Prague, alone.

Yet despite the importance and popularity of this opera Smetana wrote others of greater stature. Almost a national figurehead, Smetana sang the glorious legendary past of Bohemia and in his grandiose lyric dramas, *Dalibor* and *Libussa*, produced examples of national opera at its finest. The latter work was not performed on the stage until 1881, on the occasion of the inauguration of a new building for the National Theatre, erected by public subscription. In the meanwhile, in 1874, Smetana

Scene from a 1956 production by Sadlers Wells of Smetana's The Bartered Bride.

presented a French-inspired *opéra-comique*, *The Two Widows*. In October of the same year Smetana became suddenly deaf. He reacted courageously to his infirmity and devoted himself unrelentingly to composition. It was during this period (1874-79) that he bequeathed to Czech music his great cycle of symphonic poems *My Country*, six masterpieces which successively sing of Bohemia's legendary past (1, *Vysehrad*, 3, *Sarka*); of the beauties of the countryside (2, *Vltava*, once known throughout the world under its German title, *Moldau*, and 4, *The Fields and Forests of Bohemia*); and finally, of the great periods in Bohemian history (5, *Tabor* and 6, *Blanik*). Then Smetana turned again to the lyric theatre with three *opéras-comiques*, *The Kiss* (1876), *The Secret* (1878) and *The Devil's Wall* (1882). But overwork and physical suffering finally led to a mental breakdown and, like Schumann, he ended his life in an asylum.

In some fields of music Smetana was successful in creating a valid national repertory. His aim was to evolve a Czech tradition of composition, monumental and lofty in expression, which would integrate the inner spirit of Czech folk music with the great achievements of the European pioneers of his day. His eight operas are all still performed in Czech theatres and some have passed into foreign repertories. The influence of Liszt, Berlioz and Wagner is apparent in his heroic operas, and his light-hearted ones have an almost Mozartian wit and vivacity. Like many 19th-century Romantics, Smetana often quoted or initiated folk melodies in his major works; the spirit of folk music coloured his thinking and was an important contributory factor in the shaping of his highly original musical language. The cycle *My Country* and the symphonic poems composed in Sweden, *Richard III*, *Wallenstein's Camp* and *Hakon Jarl*, are all stamped with the innovatory influences of the programme music of Berlioz and Liszt. Smetana was scarcely attracted at all to abstract music, and his three great chamber works, the piano trio and the two string quartets, of which the first is subtitled *From my life*, are essentially autobiographic. Finally, he composed a very large number of piano pieces of such dazzling virtuosity and refinement of language that his collection of *Czech polkas and dances* can well be compared with the best of Chopin.

Dvořák

Antonin Dvořák (1841-1904), Smetana's junior by seventeen years, was a composer of very different character. As the son of a butcher-cum-innkeeper in a village near Prague, he always remained a simple and sincere person, a man very much attracted to the soil. His lucid inspiration flows naturally, his fertile imagination and freshness evoke Schubert, while his peasant exuberance and attraction to abstract music place him as a distant descendant of the classical tradition of Haydn. Like Smetana, Dvořák aimed to establish the Czech national school as the equal of any in the world but, whereas his attempts at opera did not equal the achievements of his great compatriot, he staked out an incontestable Czech claim in the field of the symphony and chamber music. This, however, did not prevent Dvořák from trying his hand at every sort of music, but with very unequal results. The performance of his patriotic cantata *Hymnus: the Heirs of the White Mountain* (1872) made him known to the Prague public. A grant from the Austrian ministry of fine arts gave him a small but guaranteed income until Brahms was able to obtain a contract for him with the German publisher Simrock. From the publication of his *Moravian duets* and *Slavonic Dances* in 1878 his fame as a composer spread, particularly in England, a country which he visited no less than nine times between 1884 and 1896. He also visited the United States, where he held the post of artistic director of the New York conservatory from 1892 to 1895.

Dvořák composed nine symphonies. Undoubtedly the most famous is the one in E minor, which he subtitled *From the New World*, as it was composed in 1893 in New York. But the sixth in D major, the seventh in D minor and the eighth in G major all have a remarkable perfection of language. His earliest symphonic compositions (1865-75) also contain some remarkably fine passages. Dvořák also wrote three concertos – for piano in G minor, for violin in A minor and for cello in B minor (1894), of which the last is perhaps the most popular in the repertory of its instrument. Among his other symphonic works, the *Symphonic Variations* and the dazzling *Scherzo capriccioso* are outstanding. In his cycle of overtures, *Carnival*, *Nature* and *Othello*, he turned towards the symphonic poem, of which he wrote five examples in the year 1896-7, but among his most popular works are the two sets of *Slavonic Dances*, written in 1878 and 1886. Seven great string quartets (he composed fourteen in all) dominate his chamber music and the finest of them are quite equal to those of Schubert and Brahms; Dvořák also wrote four trios, two quartets and two quintets (all for strings and piano), a sextet and other works.

All his life Dvořák hoped to write an opera which would equal the success of Smetana's masterpieces. He

Antonin Dvořák.

Anton Dvořák.

made no fewer then eleven attempts and devoted the last years of his life to this end. Although *Dmitri*, the plot of which begins where the story of *Boris Godunov* ends, and *The Jacobin* in particular, contain much excellent music, Dvořák was only able to achieve his ambition with the colourful *The Devil and Kate* (1899), fairylike *Russalka* of 1900, and *Armida* (1904).

Dvořák was the true creator of Czech oratorio and his activity in the field of religious music culminated in four great works: the Stabat Mater, the Mass in D, the Requiem (1890) and the Te Deum (1892), which can be favourably compared with similar works by Liszt, Bruckner and Verdi.

Lesser figures and the first period of Leoš Janáček

The third great founder of the Czech national music was Zdeněk Fibich (1850-1900). After study with Moscheles in Leipzig and Richter in Paris, he returned to Prague in his early twenties. Fibich is essentially a Romantic composer, whose mentors were Wagner and Liszt; he had much less interest in folk music and its idioms than either of his two greater compatriots. Among his operas, which owe much to Wagner, those which are still performed as part of the national repertory include *Hedy*, *Sarka* and, best known of all, *The Fall of Arkun*. However, his most remarkable contribution to the lyric theatre consists of a series of melodramas, a genre which was specifically Czech in origin, having been virtually created by the 18th-century Bohemian composer, Jiri Benda. Fibich brought the form to its fullest expression with the trilogy of *Hippodamie* (1889-91). The declamation is sustained by an extremely intricate orchestration on the Wagnerian principle of the *Leitmotiv*. Several chamber works, three symphonies and innumerable piano pieces complete Fibich's considerable oeuvre.

Other members of this generation are Vilem Blodek (1834-74), composer of a one-act popular *opéra-comique*, *In the Well*; Karel Kovařovic (1862-1920), a pupil of Fibich, conductor and director of the National Theatre and author of several operas; and, lastly, Oskar Nedbal (1874-1930), whose operetta *Polish Blood* has delighted audiences all over the world.

Born in Hukvaldy, in the north of Moravia, Leoš Janáček (1854-1928) remained passionately attached to his native land. He spent his life in Brno, the capital of Moravia, and was for long regarded as a talented composer of merely local importance. By his life span Janáček appears to belong to the later 19th century but it must be admitted that he developed late and musically his essential works belong to the art of the 20th century, of which he was indeed one of the boldest pioneers. *Jenufa*, the third of his ten operas, met with no success at its first performance in Brno (1904), but the Prague performance in 1916 was a crown of glory for the sexagenarian composer. Stimulated by success, Janáček, still young in body and mind, gave proof of an extraordinary fertility of invention. Thus, eight years older than Debussy, he became a leading figure of the international *avant-garde*.

left
Dvořák (centre) with two fellow musicians in 1892.

below
Title page of the score of Dvořák's Stabat Mater, *autographed at Worcester in 1884 by Dvořák, who conducted, as well as by the soloists and members of the orchestra.*

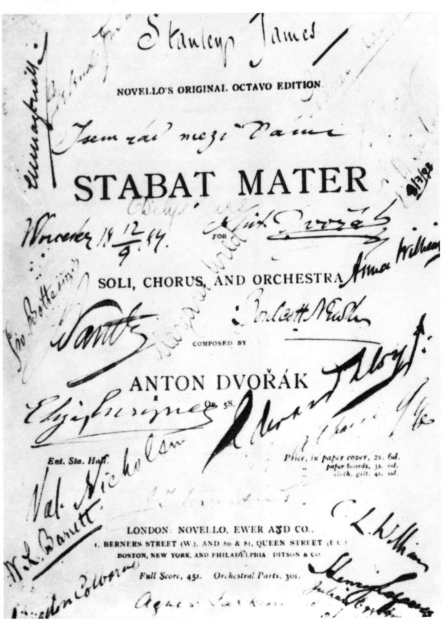

Russian music
from the earliest times

The foundations of the first Russian states were laid in the 9th century, when the original Slav populations of the great river systems of central Eurasia came under the sway of Scandinavian princes from Sweden and Denmark. The *raison d'être* of these nascent states was trade and the great towns such as Kiev and Novgorod were staging posts on the routes from northern Europe to the Black Sea and the Byzantine empire. In the last quarter of the 10th century, Vladimir of Kiev was finally converted to Orthodox Christianity, and may be regarded as the first Russian ruler in the historical sense of the word. Thus, from the beginning, Russian culture drew its inspiration from three sources – from the native Slav traditions, from the mythology of the Scandinavian world and from the dazzling brilliance of the civilisation of the Eastern Roman Empire. Of these, far and away the most important was that of Byzantium, and the music of the Russian Church still bears the traces of its origins in the chants and liturgy of Constantinople. But the influence of the Nordic world, especially on secular music and folk music, is not to be forgotten and it is in this world that the *buylini*, a Russian type of *chanson de geste* sung to the accompaniment of the *guzli*, finds its origins.

As elsewhere, the tradition of court music was to be fossilised in the music of the folk for centuries to come,

but Russian folk music, covering as it does such a vast area, is peculiarly rich and was much influenced by oriental sources. Even as far north as Novgorod we find evidence of Persian and Armenian merchants, and the music of these and other Eastern countries coloured Russian folk music and was an important source of inspiration to some of the 19th-century nationalist composers. Long and full melismatic melodies seemed to have exercised a peculiar appeal on the Slav spirit, and those of Armenia, which may extend over an octave and a half, were among the chants which infiltrated Russian folk and, later, art music. There are also marked similarities between some Russian folk melodies and those of Italy, while other songs betray the contact through their titles – *Ledenetz*, a corruption of Venezia, or *Gvidon*, a corruption of the man's name Guido. Finally we should take into account the important contacts with German and Hungarian traditions.

Nor were such contacts limited purely to folk and court music. The miracle and mystery plays performed in Russian churches seem to be indebted in some cases to Western models – among the most popular was that of the 'Tsar' Nebuchadnezzar and the three children of Israel whom he consigned to the flames of the fiery furnace. This Biblical story was also very popular in the West, but the Leningrad Museum still displays a

Russian peasant musicians; notice the method of bowing the cello and holding the violin.

magnificent piece of stage property for the furnace itself. There are even traces of classical legend in the mystery plays, probably the result of contacts with the Byzantine empire. For the seafaring merchant community of Novgorod the underworld of antiquity became a 'submarine kingdom', while in other parts of Russia Orpheus took the name of Sadko and his lyre was, naturally enough, transformed into the *guzli*.

The flourishing state of Russian music was severely inhibited in the late 12th century when Bishop Cyril Turovsky was instrumental in the promulgation of severe proscriptions of the arts. Above all he castigated music, which he regarded as an emanation of Hell itself. In many cases artists, formerly enjoying the patronage of the courts, had two alternatives: either to remain in the towns as popular entertainers, giving birth to the Russian equivalent of the *commedia dell' arte* – a tradition embodied in such 19th-century operas as *Sadko* and *Prince Igor*; or to retire to the more distant provinces where their work contributed to the 'living museum' of folk art.

The 'decentralisation' thus caused explains on the one hand the incredible richness of this folk source and on the other hand the fact that there are to be found in the extreme north of Russia, at Archangel, for example, songs reminiscent of Kiev, the south and the whole of the life of the warm climates.

left
Guzli *players.*

below
Title page of an Italianate opera on a Russian theme, produced at St Petersburg in 1791.

Russian folk songs

Russian folk song, like that of most traditions, was determined essentially by the rhythm and old pagan festivals of the agricultural year. The pantheon of the Slavs was founded on Sun and Earth worship. The Sun possessed several incarnations: Yarilo, the sun god; Dajdbog, sun father of the harvest; Svarog, the beating heat of the sun at midday; and Hors, the sun of light. Another deity of great importance was Peroun, the god of storms, thunder and lightning.

The pagan elements in folk traditions remained vigorous long after the introduction of Christianity. As late as 1849 the Russian musicologist and folklorist, Iakuchin, was able to observe clear evidence of such survivals. Indeed the pagan calendar of seasonal feasts was so strong that, after the conversion to Christianity, the religious authorities were obliged to take account of them and to endeavour to make the church feasts coincide with the pagan traditions. The 'cycle of songs' began the night following the winter equinox, which later became Christmas Eve. It was believed that on that night 'the sun veered towards the summer' and that it was prudent to obtain its benevolence. In the villages groups of young men and girls went from house to house, receiving presents and singing *koliada* of great beauty, and the custom is still maintained in the Ukraine.

The great feasts of the spring equinox with their carnival songs followed, then the incantations and the spring round dances, which Stravinsky has so well evoked in his *Rite of Spring*. These round dances of spring, which formed a very important rite for the community, were in fact usually slow and grave. The movable carnival feasts, which were later to become the church festivals of 'Shrovetide', commenced eight weeks before the first full moon of spring. They were devoted to driving away the forces of winter, symbolised in scarecrows which were set on fire with great ceremony amidst songs and dances. Seven weeks after the first full moon of spring was the feast of Russalia, which was intended to clear the woods of the *russalky*, or dryads, and of all the bad genies which attacked

Peter the Great.

innocent ramblers.

June 24, the time of the summer equinox and later the Christian feast of St John, was consecrated to Kupalo, the ancient god of the fire cult; it was the occasion of immense rejoicings and ritual songs preceding the important work of the harvest. Jointly with these 'seasonal songs' there existed those connected with family rites. The Slavs practised an ancestor cult; at the great feasts they drank to their health and sang for them. During the Russalia, in its Christianised form of Whitsun, the community met at the cemetery and held banquets on the tombs, performing joyful songs and dances to entertain the dead.

The wedding gave rise to some of the most complex of the musical rites: twenty-one pieces of vocal music preceded the nuptial blessing. There was much singing and dancing but the bride lamented, in deference, at the idea of being separated from her parents. The various songs and dances followed in a strictly regulated and quite immutable sequence, indeed each village had what one might call its own 'scenario', and judged a wedding by the standard of the performance of this scenario. The bride was helped in her part by a 'weeper' who doubled her in certain episodes; second in importance only to the bride were the two matchmakers, then came the bride's maid of honour and friends. The preparations for a wedding commenced with the plighting of troths. The female matchmaker came to arrange things with the parents, without consulting the interested party. Following this the suitor was solemnly received, a candle was lit in front of the icons, the couple 'consented' and the future wife sang her first plaintive ballad. The following day they met again on the occasion of the blessing of the betrothal, and the future wife lamented again twice over – the second lament lasted about forty minutes. This was followed, always in song, by the visits to the parents, to the future mother-in-law and to friends, the reception of the groom and the reunions with friends, at which rounds were sung and danced. Then came the eve of the great day itself, the most picturesque element of the 'scenario'. The young girl was led in great pomp to the bath. Before her departure she sang for her friends; then the bath attendant received her with a long and beautiful

cantilena, to which the bride replied with a short lyrical song. And, on the way back, she stopped in front of her parents to perform yet another lament. In all there were twenty-one items of prenuptial music.

'Sacred verses' and epic songs

The earliest sacred verses (Russian, *dukhovny stikh*) were by monks, inspired by the Old and New Testaments, the Apocryphal Gospels and the Byzantine religious legends. Like the sermons of the friars and the mystery plays of the West, the aim was to give their preaching greater impact; thus were born the hymns of *Adam and Eve*, *Alexis, man of God*, *The Virgin*, *St George*, *The Unfortunate Lazarus* and the *Book of the Dove*, in which King David himself teaches St Vladimir the origin of all things. The melodic line is simple, sober and austere, in the manner of plainsong, but is obviously modified by folk transmission and enriched by the ornamentation of peasant musicians. Christianity and pantheism are still found intermingled.

Jointly with this cycle of sacred music there developed an epic cycle, born in the princely courts. The bards, whilst accompanying themselves on the *guzli*, sang of the personal exploits of the prince and those of his host; as it descended to the people, the cycle would be extended, and to the personal exploits of the prince were added those of imaginary personages derived from local legends. With the epic songs one finds oneself in the presence of a professional art handed down from father to son, with each family of bards possessing its own repertoire and method of singing and narration. Mussorgsky and Rimsky-Korsakov had the opportunity of hearing the bard Riabinin, a late representative of the tradition of the 13th and 14th centuries. The essential characteristics of this tradition were the use of the ancient modes, a severe style, a free prosody and a singing recitative accompanied by arpeggios on the *guzli* and confined within the narrow limits of an interval of a fourth.

The beginnings of art music

From the 12th to the 16th centuries the Church dominated the arts and from this period date the most beautiful and the purest chants of the Russian Orthodox Church. During the reign of Tsar Feodor (1584-98), an English traveller observed theatrical '*entremets*' at the Russian Court, of the type to be seen in Western European countries, with the participation of jesters and poets; while under Boris Godunov (1598-1605), whose son and daughter learned to play the harpsichord, 'each regiment in the army had at its disposal twelve drums, twelve clarions and several shawms'. The first Romanov tsar, Michael (1613-45), favoured comedians and singers and encouraged the importation of organs, clavichords and harpsichords. Two years after his death, his son, yielding to the influence of the patriarch Joseph, authorised a decree demanding the destruction of all 'impious' musical instruments – fifty full chariots were collected and were burned in great pomp on the banks of the Moscva river. Later however, in 1672, Russia witnessed its first musical theatrical performance, this being *The Book of Esther, drawn from the Bible*, with music and songs by the German Johann Gottfried Gregory. Its success was such that the tsar charged Gregory to found a school of theatre and music, but the enterprise was short-lived.

Plate 45 left
Mussorgsky by Repin.

Plate 46 below
One of the sets designed by Léon Bakst for the first production (1910) of Rimsky-Korsakov's ballet Scheherezade.

Plate 47
*Richard Strauss at the age of
fifty-four; a portrait by the German
painter Max Liebermann.*

Under Peter the Great (1682-1725) Russian culture and civilisation were subject to a programme of Westernisation. He called in Western engineers and ship-builders and also architects, painters and musicians The emperor organised his celebrated assemblies, at which he himself sketched *caprioles*, the boyars danced clumsy minuets, blushing young ladies, embarrassed by the newly imported decolletage, cooed *pastourelles* and *bergerettes*, and sentimental romances, translated into Russian, were sung. The Austrian ambassador, Count Kinsky, invited polite society to serenades in which the horn virtuoso Leichtenberg performed. Ethnic Russian music was rigorously proscribed, except on the occasion of the great religious festivals and on the express condition that the songs were edifying.

In 1730, for the coronation of the Tsarina Anne, King Augustus III of Poland sent the artists of the Dresden Opera, among them a troupe of Italian singers, and they appeared in Russia for the first time. Their triumph was such that, the next year, the empress had a group of

musicians recruited in Italy. In 1734, an excellent French ballet-master, Jean-Baptiste Landé, arrived in St Petersburg. He was to be the true founder of choreography in Russia and, in 1738, the imperial theatre school was founded.

The Italians in Russia

Francesco Araja (1700-67), who had arrived in Russia with his Italian librettist Bonifaci, was the first important figure in the history of the Russian lyric theatre. In the reign of Elisabeth, daughter of Peter the Great, he produced on average one opera per year; after a time he was joined by two collaborators, Raupach and Manfredini. When Araja went back to his native Naples in 1759, Raupach succeeded him; but Manfredini came to grief with his opera *Charles the Great* and was forced

Sunday morning service in contemporary Russia.

337

right
*Alexander Pushkin, Russia's
greatest Romantic poet, whose work
inspired many composers.*

below right
Mikhail Glinka.

to leave Russia in some haste.

Locatelli came to try his luck in 1757, at a time when Russian musicians, very timidly, were attempting to gain a hearing. A certain Volkov, for example, ventured to compose 'an opera in the Russian style', *Taniucha or The Happy Encounter*, performed at the Free Theatre in 1756. The reign of Catherine the Great (1762-96) was to initiate a decisive turning-point in the history of Russian music by favouring the flowering of nationalism and preparing the gradual decline of Italian influence, but Italian music continued to be brilliantly represented. Manfredini was succeeded by the talented Galuppi, who was applauded for *The Shepherd King*, *Dido Abbandonata*, and then a very beautiful *Iphigenia in Tauris*, now unjustly forgotten. The most famous successor to Galuppi was the great Paisiello, whose setting of *Dido Abbandonata* was one of at least sixty contemporary versions, while his *Barber of Seville* was first performed in September 1782 at St Petersburg in the presence of Catherine the Great.

In 1784 the fiery and boisterous Sarti, a great specialist in counterpoint and Cherubini's teacher, reigned supreme at the theatre. The batteries of six cannons and the bells which he used in his Te Deum, and his operas such as *Castor and Pollux*, written 'in the most authentic Greek style' according to a contemporary, so charmed the ears of the Tsarina that she bestowed letters of nobility and a gold sword upon him. Secure in riches but physically and creatively exhausted, Sarti set out to return to his native Bologna in 1802 but died en route. Martini succeeded him jointly with Cimarosa. The works of Gluck, Mozart, Monsigny, Grétry, Philidor and Méhul were also performed, though with modest success; *The Marriage of Figaro* and *The Magic Flute*, indeed, passed unnoticed.

Advent of a Russian school

From the second half of the 18th century a reaction set in against foreign music. A zealous propagandist of Russian nationalism, despite her German origins, Catherine the Great tolerated this movement and even encouraged it. Indeed she personally compiled, with the collaboration of several ghost writers, the libretti of five operas and a 'grand historical spectacle' of national inspiration: *Févéé* (i.e. *Phoebus*), a satire against the powerful aristocrat Potemkin, set to music by Martini. At the same time numerous 'ballad operas' were being performed, setting villagers on the stage, contrasting them with the townspeople and their corruption and largely utilising the themes of the best known folksongs. Among these were *Aniuta* and above all the celebrated *Miller, Sorcerer, Liar and Matchmaker* by Sokolovsky, whose production in 1779 marked a major date in the history of Russian music. The work, which consisted of strictly national music, was performed up to the beginning of the 20th century. Prompted by the predilections of Catherine some of the Italian composers active at St Petersburg introduced Russian folk melodies into their scores. The same process to a more marked degree was to be observed in the work of native Russian composers, chief amongst them Dmitri Bortniansky (1751-1825).

After receiving lessons from Galuppi in St Petersburg he was granted a stipendium at the instance of Catherine to continue his studies in Italy. Here he produced a number of operas and also wrote a symphony, chamber music and piano sonatas. But he returned to Russia where, for the last thirty years of his life, he was director of the Chapel Royal. Bortniansky earned the sobriquet of the 'Russian Palestrina' and his church music owed much to the polyphonic style still cultivated in Italy for sacred music. But, in that he endeavoured to graft on to this alien stock the idiom of a native Russian art, he may be regarded as a true ancestor of the nationalist school of the 19th century. Maxim Berezovsky (1745-77) had preceded him but, despite his excellent work, he was largely ignored in Russia and it was Bortniansky, who devoted himself expressly to a study of medieval Russian chant in order to find the roots for a truly Russian idiom in church music, who is rightly remembered as the forerunner of much that was to come.

As the 18th century progressed there gradually developed what we might call the chrysalis of a national tradition. Protected from the wintry blasts of polite censure from a society sycophantically devoted to Western art in all its forms through its adoption of French and Italian fashions, and nourished inwardly by a growing attentiveness to the idiom of the folk, it needed only the hot summer of Napoleonic Europe, in which so many nationalist dreams hatched, to emerge as one of the most brilliantly coloured butterflies of the 19th century.

Russia in the 19th century

The rich resources of Russian folk culture and Russian church music held an immense reserve of musical inspiration and material for the formation of a national school; but, during the 18th century, Russian folk music was treated with a condescending interest like some sort of rather vulgar divertissement. Glinka, the first major Russian composer to take national music as his inspiration, was to be made aware of this. When his first opera *Ivan Sussanin* was produced in 1836 he was reproached with the accusation that 'the coach-

men in the streets sing this sort of stuff'. True, the Napoleonic wars induced a newly awakened patriotism in Russia as elsewhere in Europe, and Russians began to turn to their national heritage. Even leading foreign composers at the court began to use Russian folk themes in their compositions, though, in the words of a critic of the time, 'they hastened to drown these themes in Italian sauce'. No one as yet understood, as Glinka was to declare later, that 'we (composers) are adapters at the service of the people'. The struggle to establish a truly Russian music was to be an uphill one.

With justice, Glinka is considered the father of Russian music, but the part played by Verstovsky and Dargomizsky should not be minimised. To some extent the former was the precursor of Glinka, the latter his true continuator. Indeed Glinka, with *Ivan Sussanin* and *Russlan and Ludmilla*, never had any real followers except for a few young composers and Dargomizsky. The latter was determined to follow the nationalist road traced by Glinka, but also, without having expressly wished it, he became the inspiration and artistic guide to a group of bold self-taught composers comprising Balakirev, César Cui, Borodin, Mussorgsky and Rimsky-Korsakov – the celebrated 'Five' who were to constitute the second period of the Russian school. Together, Glinka and Dargomizsky dominated the first period and their contribution can be summed up in Glinka's words: 'I want to unite the songs of the Russian people with the good old occidental fugue, in legal marriage'.

Glinka

Mikhaïl Ivanovich Glinka was born in 1804 at Novo-spasskïe in the Government of Smolensk and was brought up on the estate of his father, a wealthy land-owner. As a child he loved to hear the songs sung by his

The Bolshoi Theatre of Moscow in the mid-19th century.

nurse and listen to the church choir and carillons. He studied music, as did all the young nobles of his time, learnt the violin and piano and took a few singing lessons. His debut as a composer came about by chance when he composed a set of variations to please a cousin. Encouraged by his first, if still clumsy, experiments, Glinka decided to study composition and, in 1830, with this end in view, he undertook a long tour through Germany, France and Italy, in the course of which he made the acquaintance of Berlioz, Donizetti, Bellini, Mendelssohn and of Dehn, a disciple of Beethoven who taught him composition in Berlin. A confirmed bon viveur, he died of a liver complaint at the age of fifty-three in 1857.

It was in Berlin that Glinka first conceived the idea of his opera *Ivan Sussanin*, inspired by nationalist and patriotic feelings, which was given its first performance, under the title of *A Life for the Tsar*, in St Petersburg in 1836. The use of folk elements in the music drew the kind of criticism which we have already noted, but inevitably Glinka's style in this, his first opera, was heavily influenced by his training in Italy and Germany. He took a further step in the direction of a specifically Russian style with his second opera, *Russlan and Ludmilla*, produced at St Petersburg in 1842. The story, which concerns two lovers who are eventually united despite the opposition of magical powers, is taken from Pushkin, and the opera brought the orientalising tradi-

tion firmly into Russian music.

Tchaikovsky was to say that everything in the subsequent school of Russian music was foreshadowed in the work of Glinka, and from the two operas we can trace two important themes which were to be developed by his successors. *Ivan Sussanin*, based on the story of the eponymous 17th century peasant hero, gave rise to a type of popular music drama of which Borodin's *Prince Igor* or Mussorgsky's *Boris Godunov* are the natural successors. The supernatural element found in *Russlan and Ludmilla* is taken up again in the fantasmagoric world of Rimsky-Korsakov's *Golden Cockerel*.

In addition to these two seminal works Glinka wrote a number of fine songs, some in the Italian manner, others reflecting the style of Schubert. He also composed the two great orchestral overtures, *Jota Aragonese* and *Summer night in Madrid*, as well as the fantasia *Kamarinskaya*.

Glinka's contemporaries

Alexander Dargomizsky (1813-69) was very much drawn to the principles of his predecessor Glinka, but differed from him in his tastes in foreign music. Glinka preferred the Germans and Italians; Beethoven and Bellini were his gods. Dargomizsky on the other hand turned first to France – to Auber, Halévy and even Adolphe Adam. After composing a 'grand opera' entitled *Esmeralda*, based on Hugo's *Notre Dame de Paris*, he wrote a grandiloquent *Triumph of Bacchus*; then suddenly he produced his lyric masterpiece *Russalka*, with a libretto based on Pushkin's *Water Sprite*. The remarkable *Stone Guest*, also based on Pushkin, was completed by Rimsky-Korsakov and produced posthumously; numerous passages already anticipate *Boris Godunov*.

Mussorgsky considered Dargomizsky as the true father of realism in music, and the earlier composer himself said, 'I want truth; I want sound to express words directly'. He applied this principle to his operas as well as to his 'realistic' songs like the *Earth Worm*, *The Old Corporal* and *The Titular Councillor*, which had an immense influence on Mussorgsky.

Glinka composed his music before the words, necessitating the distortion of the verbal rhythm of the libretto. Dargomizsky, on the other hand, in *Russalka* and the *Stone Guest*, is careful to follow Pushkin's texts. Thus, parallel with Glinka, he introduced a new principle into Russian music, that of melody motivated by the meaning of the words. This principle was to be used by Mussorgsky, most notably in *Boris Godunov*, by Rimsky-Korsakov in *Mozart and Salieri*, by Stravinsky in *Mavra*, by Prokofiev in all his operas, and by Shostakovich in *Katerina Ismailova*.

Alexander Serov (1820-71) occupies a place apart in Russian music. His three operas, *Judith*, *Rogneda* and *The Power of Evil*, have enriched the repertory of Russian opera houses without, however, leaving any school or creating any tradition. This may be because he was caught between two powerful influences and was not independent enough to free himself from them. His great idol was Wagner but his operas, apart from a few pages of *Rogneda* which are clearly affected by *Tannhäuser*, are much more reminiscent of Meyerbeer. However, *The Power of Evil*, which he was unable to complete, is inspired by nationalist sentiments and is based on a text by Ostrovsky, the great dramatist. Here we find a certain harshness, an almost 'plebeian' element, which cuts right across the idealism of Glinka and Rimsky-Korsakov. There are no trimmings, no *fioritura* passages, only deliberately 'stark' truculence, reminiscent of scenes in *Boris Godunov*, of Stravinsky's *Petrushka* and

Anton Rubinstein.

of much of Shostakovich.

Young Russians in 1860 found themselves caught between two fires in the conflict, which exists today, between 'Slavophils' and 'Occidentalists'. The former attached themselves to the 'Russian genius'. They despised all occidental importations, believing that their national heritage was sufficiently rich in all fields to meet their needs. Among the ranks of the 'Slavophils' were writers and poets like Dostoyevsky, Nekrassov, and, particularly, Turgenev and Tolstoy; they also numbered among them the intellectual Vladimir Stassov, who was the *eminence grise* of the nationalist composers of 'The Five', Mussorgsky and his friend the architect Victor Hartmann, who inspired *Pictures from an Exhibition*. The 'Occidentalists', for their part, demanded a universal civilisation in the tradition of Peter the Great and claimed that Russia was a part of Western Europe. This conflict of views was to become increasingly apparent in Russian music.

Another source of conflict was the moral, social and political malaise which was felt by all the young generation. First the French revolution and then the Decembrist revolt had borne fruit. A spirit of liberalism was blowing through the country with ever increasing force and contributed to the emancipation of the serfs in February 1861. Many small landowners were ruined overnight. A great gap now divided the 'absolutists' and the 'liberals', which helped to increase the disquiet existing among the youth of the country. Some thinkers, among them artists like Dostoyevsky and Mussorgsky, already foretold even greater upheavals to come.

In the 1860s thinking Russians were tormented by 'an accursed problem': the practical and social purpose of their very existence. No longer was there any question of living merely for pleasure; it was necessary to serve in order not to be classed in the category of Oblomov's 'supernumerary men'. 'Man is a social animal and he should remain so', declared Mussorgsky. Man therefore should try to live in society and to make society the sole and constant object of all his preoccupations. 'You cannot be a poet, you must be a citizen', said the poet Nekrassov.

During this period the musical situation was in no way a brilliant one, judging by the comments of Anton Rubinstein. 'Russian opera for a long time now has received a bad press. I wrote my operas in German and Italian precisely because the Russian theatre was stubbornly opposed to opera and the élite of society had no musical culture whatsoever. There are a quantity of dilettantes whose judgments on music are false and narrow-minded. They demand nothing from the arts, and music in particular, except to accommodate their taste for banality. The works now in fashion – by Puccini, Rossini, Bellini and many others – pass for models of incomparable beauty and depth. The public is incapable of understanding other beauties than barren and facile melodies; it is unwilling to recognise that music has a serious mission . . .'

There was no conservatory in Russia and, to acquire even the basics of theoretical musical knowledge, it was necessary to study abroad, as Glinka did. By force of circumstances, therefore, young Russians who were attracted to music were dedicated, often self-taught men like Dargomizsky.

Two rival camps

By a singular coincidence, in the year 1862, when 'The Five' were formed as a group, the first Russian conservatory was founded in St Petersburg under the direction of Rubinstein. From the beginning the teaching there raised a howl of protest from the Slavophils, nor were they entirely unjustified. True, it was difficult to use manuals of instruction other than those of Western Europe, but the actual teaching could well have taken the Russian school into account. Moreover, the instruction in composition was entrusted to Zaremba, a Russianised German who had in fact remained German to the core. Moreover, for Zaremba, the history of music ended with Mendelssohn, Schumann was non-existent and as for Glinka and the other Russians, they were 'savages and candle eaters'.

Rubinstein, having made himself the champion of this school, now founded a whole series of conservatories, beginning with one in Moscow to which he appointed his brother Nicolas as director. Tchaikovsky was one of the first products of the St Petersburg conservatory and later became a professor at that of Moscow. Opposed to these academic musicians was the dynamic group led by Balakirev and Vladimir Stassov, which the latter had dubbed 'The Mighty Handful'. The members of the conservatory, for their part, referred to this group as '*braillards*' or 'brawlers'.

'The Five'

This group was formally founded in 1862, but despite the name we must include, in addition to the five main figures – Balakirev, César Cui, Mussorgsky, Borodin and Rimsky-Korsakov – the names of Gussakovsky, Lodygensky, Scherbatchov and, later, Lyadov. Its leader and

Mily Balakirev, a drawing by Léon Bakst.

literary inspiration was Vladimir Stassov, both a socialist and a chauvinist imbued with the 'Slav genius', who imposed Russian nationalist ideas on the group. The 'musical and artistic director' was Mily Balakirev.

Born in 1836, Balakirev was attracted to music from his childhood. Unfortunately, due to lack of money, his musical education was restricted to ten piano lessons, although he later became a fine player. At the age of thirteen he was taken up by the wealthy historian and critic Ulibishev. He first gave Balakirev copying work to do, later commissioned him to carry out arrangements and finally entrusted him with the direction of the small orchestra he maintained, which was large and skilled enough to perform the symphonies of Haydn and Mozart and the first four by Beethoven.

Balakirev learnt to compose by dissecting the works of the great masters. Ulibishev introduced him to Glinka, who approved of his first attempts at composition. Greatly encouraged, the young man left for St Petersburg, determined to revolutionise music, if not completely to remake it. Here he recruited shock troops, amateurs, because with professionals he had a sense of inferiority. They were an officer of the corps of engineers, César Cui; a lieutenant of the guard, Mussorgsky; two chemists, Gussakovsky and Lodygensky; a military doctor, Borodin; a naval cadet officer, Rimsky-Korsakov, and a young diplomat, Scherbatchov. He taught them to compose by a very practical method: they played piano arrangements for four hands of the works of the masters, after which these were commented on and thoroughly analysed.

The group was comparatively short-lived. It was an artificial creation and united too many diverse personalities; moreover, those affiliated to it were impatient to escape Balakirev's often too despotic rule. The latter, deserted by his brood, sought consolation in mysticism and in the creation of a free musical school and free public concerts. The results were disastrous and, alas, completely extinguished the enthusiasm of this fanatical musician. After outliving all his companions in arms with the exception of Cui, Balakirev died in 1910.

His compositions are coloured by his devotion to three idols, Glinka, Berlioz and Schumann, and to a secret divinity, Liszt, who greatly influenced his piano music (the slow movement of *Islamey* is a 'love dream' translated into Russian with oriental *nuances*). He liked neither Bach, Haydn nor Mozart while the epithet 'Italian' from his lips became an insult. The spiritual heir of Glinka, Balakirev united the cult of German musical Romanticism with a taste for Russian folk music. He composed slowly, but the list of his works is relatively important. They include: two symphonies, very classical in style, *Thamar* and *Russia*; an overture; incidental music for *King Lear*; numerous scherzos, mazurkas and waltzes; a sonata; some forty songs, and the celebrated oriental piano fantasy *Islamey*, once the concert pianist's great virtuoso piece.

The works of the prolific César Cui (1835-1918) are seldom performed today. He was French by origin and a pupil of the Polish composer Moniuszko, being the only one of 'The Five' to have studied music, in the academic sense, at all deeply. His music reveals the talents of a miniaturist, though it is somewhat impersonal in outlook; but, unaware of his limitations, he wrote ten rather grandiloquent operas, which owe something to the idiom of classic 'grand opera', more than three hundred songs, and a very large number of piano pieces.

Alexander Borodin.

Mussorgsky

A member of a very old and aristocratic military family, Modest Petrovich Mussorgsky was born at Karevo in the Government of Pskov in 1839. Destined for an army career, he was educated at two military preparatory schools, but at the same time he took piano lessons and showed promise of becoming a great virtuoso. In 1856, after receiving his brevet as a lieutenant, he entered the Preoprajensky guards, an infantry regiment. Here he made the acquaintance of some music-loving officers, who introduced him to Dargomizsky, who in turn introduced him to Balakirev and César Cui. Under their influence he decided to leave the army and devote himself entirely to musical composition. Financially ruined overnight by the abolition of serfdom, he was obliged to find work in a junior capacity as a clerk in the ministry of forestry and waterways. His life as a minor official and his failure as a composer soured his character and he started drinking heavily. However, the legend of his alcoholism has been greatly exaggerated and many of the symptoms he displayed were in fact due to epilepsy. His friends left him and he died alone and in poverty in 1881 in a military hospital to which he had been admitted by charity.

Although a 'pupil' of Balakirev, Mussorgsky was of necessity mainly self-taught. Once again, however, legend has exaggerated; after leaving the army, he wrote nothing for two years, two years in which he probably devoted his time to improving his musical knowledge. Nevertheless, he enjoyed the characteristic advantage of the talented self-taught man in that he found no difficulty in forgetting the rules, which is the prerequisite of originality. He considered music not as an end in itself, as a manifestation of beauty, as something subjective and theoretical to be carefully planned, but as a means of communication with his fellow men. 'I want to speak to man in a language of truth', he declared. For Mussorgsky the impression, words and music form an indissoluble whole, the vocal line or melody being born of the language and motivated by its meaning. He carves out great configurations of sonorous splendour which are unfettered by any rules, each work creating its own individual form. In consequence Mussorgsky's harmony is quite free. It is not derived from any manual but is dictated solely by ear and frequently escapes from a given key (this fact greatly shocked Rimsky-Korsakov, who revised and 'corrected' his work), to achieve purely impressionist sound effects dictated solely by a desire to 'paint'. Examples abound but particularly worthy of note are: the three chords in fifths which conclude the *Trepak of Death*, which remain suspended in the air and seem to open perspectives on to the infinite; the two tenths in the final bar of *The Forgotten One*, which convey a feeling of anguish and utter desolation; or again, the end of the song, *The Harpist*, in which Mussorgsky shows such an audacious musical instinct that at the time it seemed quite mad. Finally we should instance the delicate and fluid harmonies of his cycle *Without Sunshine*, which so ravished Debussy. 'Life wherever it may be found, the truth however bitter it may be, a bold and sincere language – that is what I aspire to, that is what I want, and I am afraid of failing'.

With his passion for universal human truth, Mussorgsky hated flippancy, prettiness and 'pure beauty'. His contemporaries sometimes decried his music as mere naturalism. He provided his critics with some trenchant contradictions, beginning with *Pictures from an Exhibition* (1874), whose source of inspiration, some mediocre drawings and watercolours, was sublimated by an almost Impressionistic technique and attains the heights of Symbolism. Written originally for piano, this work has been the subject of five arrangements for orchestra, of which the best known is that by Ravel.

After the challenge afforded by *The Marriage*, in which he had attempted to set the most prosaic of Gogol's stories to music, Mussorgsky wrote two 'popular dramas', his great opera *Boris Godunov* (1874) and the unfinished operas *The Khovansky Affair* and the *Sorotchinsky Fair*. A little while before his death he had planned a third, based on the rebellion of Pugachov. It was the troubled periods of Russia's history that always attracted him the most, for, as he said, it was at such times that the soul of the people was the better revealed. 'Whatever I do', he wrote, 'it is the Russian people whom I see pass before my eyes – grand, vast, majestic and magnificent'. We have mentioned the way in which Mussorgsky's works were 'corrected and improved' by Rimsky-Korsakov but his masterpiece, *Boris Godunov*, was not only not exempt from this treatment but was not given it in its original form until fifty years after its first production. The libretto is based on a play by Pushkin on the life of the Tsar Boris, who died in 1605, and fully confirms the composer's sympathies with the Russian people. Rimsky-Korsakov also completed the unfinished *Khovansky Affair* and produced a rewritten version of Mussorgsky's remarkable orchestral work *St John's Night on the Bare Mountain*.

Mussorgsky's songs cannot be classified but are rather little worlds of their own, 'microcosms', similar to the *Préludes* of Debussy, for example. He wrote three song cycles – *Enfantines*, *Songs and dances of death* and *Without Sunshine*, and to these we could add *Scenes from town and village* and musical satires like *The Classic* and *Guignol*.

Borodin

The natural son of a Georgian prince, Alexander Borodin was descended from the kings of Imeretia, a little country in the Caucasus. He was born in St Petersburg in 1833; his father was sixty-two, his mother twenty-five. At a very early age he learnt to play the flute. At thirteen he composed a concerto for flute and piano, followed by a trio for two violins and cello on a theme from *Robert the Devil* by Meyerbeer. His mother was not at all pleased; she had determined that he should study at the faculty of medicine, and entered him there at the age of fifteen. He left the faculty six years later to work in a military hospital, but his naturally delicate constitution combined with a sensitive aversion to blood caused him to faint on the first occasion that he had to attend to the wounded. He gave up practising as a doctor, obtained the post of laboratory assistant and later was given the chair of chemistry at the St Petersburg military academy of medicine. He distinguished himself as a research chemist with brilliant results in the study of aldehydes and the discovery of aldol. He also founded a school of medicine for women. Although attracted to music, Borodin fully involved himself in the academic round

César Cui.

right
A scene from the Polovtsian dances in Borodin's opera Prince Igor.

below
Rimsky-Korsakov.

and did not take his own compositions seriously. He died suddenly in 1887 at a masked ball.

Nevertheless, of all 'The Five' he was the most fully qualified as a practising musician, being a competent performer on four instruments and a regular participant in chamber concerts. He was also an academic in his manner of composing, combining a scientific knowledge of occidental music with an oriental spontaneity, not to mention a certain typically Russian naïveté. His first love in music was Mendelssohn, but in 1850 he made the acquaintance of Mussorgsky and later of Balakirev, and henceforth joined their circle, transferring his artistic allegiance to Glinka and dedicating *Prince Igor* to his memory. The work is a direct descendant of *A Life for the Tsar* and *Russlan and Ludmilla*.

On his own admission, melodies came spontaneously to Borodin's mind, melodies which are broad and full, rich and heavy like oriental incense. Everything served him as a pretext for music: the ears of corn which covered the plains like a golden carpet, the melancholy call of a shepherd, groups of peasants meeting on a walk, the grey waters of a river under the rain, and even a reading of an account of Japanese tortures. Borodin's music is haunting because everything he wrote is highly melodic and has a certain naïve spontaneity and candour. His masterpiece is undoubtedly *Prince Igor*, which he began in 1869 but nevertheless left unfinished at his death eighteen years later. The opera was partly rearranged and finished by Rimsky-Korsakov, Glazunov and Blumenfeld. Here Borodin's true genius is firmly established; it is a great epic, which is borne along with vast vivid splashes of colour. Unfortunately, Borodin was unable to work on a theme or develop it and the result is almost a superabundance of 'tunes', irresistibly beautiful, but not well integrated into the texture of the work.

With unused material from *Prince Igor* Borodin composed his epic second symphony, known as the 'Russian Eroica', and his symphonic picture *In the Steppes of Central Asia*. These two works, so frequently performed, should not make us forget his other symphonies, his two quartets, the *Petite Suite* for piano, or his fourteen remarkable songs, with their delicate harmonies. No other Russian composer of the 19th century approached Borodin's mastery in the field of chamber music in the great European traditions.

Rimsky-Korsakov

Nikolai Andreyevich Rimsky-Korsakov was born in 1844 in the little town of Tikhvin in the Government of Novgorod. His personal life was uneventful. He fell in love with music at the age of four and resigned from the imperial navy when he was twenty-two to devote the rest of his life to his first love. In 1871 he was appointed professor of composition and instrumentation at the St Petersburg conservatory and conductor of the St Petersburg orchestra. This obliged him first to make a thorough study of musical theory under the supervision, by correspondence, of Tchaikovsky. He died near St Petersburg in 1908.

'God does not bless the tears of sorrow, God blesses the tears of celestial joy'. Thus sings Fevronia in Rimsky-Korsakov's opera *Kitezh*. It is a phrase which might well sum up all the composer's work. He was contemplative by nature, detached from practicalities and human passions, which he regarded with a good-natured indulgence tinged with a discreet scepticism. But he was also an active man in his own fashion and he created his own very individual world, which he presented through the magic lantern of his musical genius like the astrologer in *The Golden Cockerel*. (He once joked that the singer taking this part should take himself, Rimsky-Korsakov, as a model when he applied his make-up). The subjects which attracted Rimsky-Korsakov were not psychological or historic dramas or those dealing with conflicting passions, but fairy tales and folk legends whose simplicity lends itself to many variations. He also sought a truly Russian idiom. Mussorgsky had discovered it in the ever relevant truths of history–'the past in the present'. Borodin had found it in epics. Rimsky-Korsakov discovered that the profound wisdom of the Russian people could equally well be found and was perfectly expressed in their marvellous folk tales and legends. He was perhaps the greatest poet of fantasy in music who has ever lived. He had an innate taste for the fairy-like sounds of an orchestra and realised the possibilities of musical colouring to a singular degree. Like all 'The Five', he took Berlioz's *Treatise on Orchestration* as his basis, but he considerably expanded on it. Rimsky-Korsakov's orchestration has an almost physically intoxicating quality which foreshadows Ravel and Stravin-

The great Russian bass, Chaliapin, in the title role of Rimsky-Korsakov's opera Boris Godunov.

sky. The colouring of *Daphnis* and the great carnival scene from *Petrushka* are all directly derived from his research.

Of all Russian composers of his period, Rimsky-Korsakov was the most prolific. He wrote fifteen operas, four symphonies, three concertos, one trio, two quartets, one quintet, one sextet, five symphonic poems, two fantasies, four collections of piano pieces, some thirty songs, religious music, two works on musical theory and a very important collection of memoirs (*Chronicles of my life*)—a major work for a proper understanding of Russian music in the 19th century and at the dawn of the 20th. Although he turned his hand to all sorts of musical forms, his real bent was in the field of opera and symphonic poems. The latter are comparatively well-known, but excessive inportance is still attached to *The Great Russian Easter*, and *Scheherezade* is still often preferred to *Antar* which, though less spectacularly sumptuous, is the more intense work. We must also mention *Sadko*, the *Spanish Capriccio*, *Epitaph* and *Dubinushka*. His first opera, *Ivan the Terrible*, was followed nearly ten years later by his first masterpiece in the form, the irresistibly fresh and pastoral *The Snow Maiden* (1882). There followed the fairy-like *Sadko* (1898), *Tsar Saltan*, which can rightly be considered as the one and only genuine Russian *opera buffa*, the impressionist *Kastchey*, the staggering *Kitezh*, a kind of Russian *Parsifal*, and the mordant *Golden Cockerel* (1909) with its advanced chromaticism.

Russian opera

Because of its origins, Russian opera presents striking peculiarities. Until the time of Glinka, it was confined to servile imitations of Italian *opera seria* and *opera buffa*, and sometimes French *opéra-comique*. In composing *A Life for the Tsar*, Glinka had recourse to motifs related to folk themes and his harmony in many cases is based on folk modes. Thus, almost spontaneously, there came into being a fusion of opera with 'popular' songs.

In consequence there arose an operatic form unique to the Russian lyric theatre. In it the popular or folk songs neither lost their identity, no matter how much they were elaborated, nor gave the artificial impression of being special 'numbers' added for national 'colour'. In Western operas the intimate fusion of folk and art forms achieved by Russian opera is missing. The French *chanson* became the devitalised *romance*; what it gained in sophistication it lost in primitive flavour. Both Berlioz and Gounod use the folk song *King of Thule* and in both versions it loses its authentic folk flavour, becoming a conventional operatic aria. Whereas, to take only one example among many, Varlaam's song in *Boris Godunov* remains a true folk melody. Another essential and distinctive element of Russian opera is the frequency, richness and musical variety of the choruses. With Western opera, choruses were complementary to the soloists—a crowd of passive characters much more closely linked to the theatrical conventions of 'grand opera' than dependent on the actual music itself. 'Ah, these choruses!' exclaimed Glinka, 'They arrive from God knows where, sing God knows what and make off as they came in . . . ! Padding!'

For Russian composers the chorus represents a fundamental part of the music drama, an essential background and accompaniment. The chorus, never forgetting its 'popular' origin, became a collective *dramatis persona*, an essential to the action. It is not just a crowd of passive spectators, nor does it merely serve to comment on the drama in the manner of classical choruses; it is itself one of the participants, is constantly part of the action and plays just as important a role as any of the soloists. Mussorgsky noted on the first edition of *Boris Godunov* to come from the printers: 'I conceive the people as a collective character animated by a single idea. This is my objective in art, and one which I hope I have attained here'. In Russian operas, too, the ballet was never introduced gratuitously; it always forms part of the action, as for example the *Polovtsian dances* from *Prince Igor*, the underwater tableau in *Sadko*, and the polonaise in *Boris Godunov*.

A scene from Kastchey *by Rimsky-Korsakov.*

The attention to musical and theatrical aptness was so great among Russian composers that each of their operas possesses its own markedly individual style. This was even carried through to the style of recitative, which is different for each of the main characters. By this is meant something not only totally different from the classical *recitativo secco*, but also different from Wagner. With the latter we find that the hero of the *Ring* or of *Tristan*, as well as characters like Sachs, Walter or Parsifal, all have the same inflexions of voice and the same musical vocabulary. With the Russians, on the other hand, the style of recitative changes from one work to another. The characters in *Prince Igor*, for example, express themselves in their recitatives in a quite different manner from those in *Boris*, *Sadko* or *Kitezh*; never in fact, one might say, in all fifteen of Rimsky-Korsakov's operas, are there to be found identical formulas for lyric declamation.

The composer was above all anxious to translate the actor's words into music as accurately as possible. But he also wished to call to mind the style of the old Russian epics; like the old French *chansons de geste* these had been half sung, half declaimed and always in different modes and different styles. Instead of adopting the conventional recitative style of European opera Russian composers ever since Glinka had turned to these medieval epics or *buylini*, each of which had its own individual mode and style.

Russian opera is rarely entirely tragic throughout – *Boris Godunov* and *The Khovansky Affair* are exceptional. Usually Russian operas, like Shakespearean drama, have light-hearted aspects to them, while they tend to finish in a major key. Russian folk song is divided into two major categories: the first, dating from pagan times, is dedicated to Yarilo, the Sun-god, and is filled with light and warmth; the second, which originated at the time of the Tartar rule in Russia, is equally filled with lamentation and sadness. The pagan songs are particularly colourful and picturesque, and composers tended to opt for this type. *Prince Igor* for example, although the story of a defeat, is always radiant and optimistic, and modern Soviet composers, too, seem very drawn to this tradition.

Finally, Russian opera possesses a very important characteristic which, by the nature of things, is rarely recognised by non-Russians. In almost every case the libretti are of very high quality. This is due to the very high poetic understanding of Glinka and Dargomizsky and 'The Five' and the importance they all attached to the words of the opera. Unfortunately, however, these libretti, many of which, like the poetry of Wagner, are in themselves works of art, are practically untranslatable for stage performance because of their very stylised language and the syllabic accentuation proper to the Russian vocabulary.

The problem of the relation between words and music in opera was of particular importance to Russian composers. There were two trends diametrically opposed to each other: one adopted by Glinka, the other, by Dargomizsky. For Glinka it was the music that came first and foremost; Dargomizsky, on the other hand, claimed not to have changed a single comma of Pushkin's poetic text. The successors of Glinka and Dargomizsky veered between these two extremes, but if one is to judge by Mussorgsky, Rimsky-Korsakov and even Prokofiev, it was music that finally triumphed, a triumph assured by a form of melodic and personal recitative which Mussorgsky defined as 'a melody motivated by feeling' and which we find even in Prokofiev's *War and Peace* and Shostakovich's *Katerina Ismailova*.

Opposing 'The Five' were the composers brought up in the classical and Romantic tradition, men who had a solid technical background but who, Tchaikovsky apart,

A scene from Rimsky-Korsakov's opera The Golden Cockerel.

were singularly uninspired. At their head was Anton Rubinstein (1829-94), of whom César Cui said: 'He is not a Russian composer, but a Russian who composes'. This epigram was accepted everywhere, particularly abroad, and was applied indiscriminately to all the followers of the academic school – to Tchaikovsky and later to Rachmaninov, Scriabin and Glazunov. But in fact the academic composers were no less Russian than the others; indeed, sometimes they were closer to the true national idiom, cultivating a genuine folk music and not an imaginary one. Only their means of expression were different and were derived from Western sources. The first of them lacked any real drive, but it would be a great mistake to minimise the importance of Tchaikovsky, whose achievement is respected by musicians of such different stamp as Prokofiev, Stravinsky and Shostakovich.

Tchaikovsky: his life

Piotr Ilyitch Tchaikovsky was born in 1840 at Votkinsk, in the Government of Viatka. From childhood he was attracted to music, an attraction which in him amounted to a neurosis. After passing his examinations at Law School, where he associated with Apukhtine, a 'fatalist' and late Romantic poet whose work made a great impression on him, he became a civil servant. But he did not remain long as such, for no sooner was the St Petersburg conservatory founded (1862), than he enrolled as a student and obtained such brilliant diplomas that he was immediately engaged as professor at the Moscow con-

above right
A scene from a production of Swan Lake *by Tchaikovsky.*

right
Ballet was of central importance in Russia during the later 19th century and has remained so to the present day.

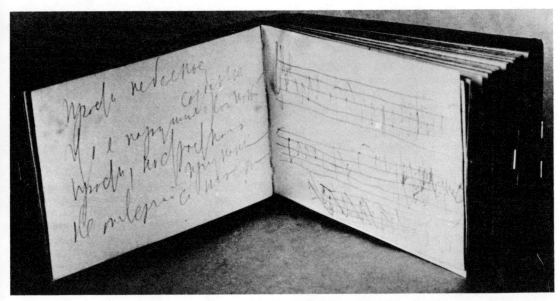

left
Tchaikovsky's notebook for the opera The Queen of Spades.

below
Tchaikovsky at Cambridge in 1893, where he received an honorary doctorate.

servatory. His first attempts at composition met with little success, and he lived, poor and miserable, from day to day, until 1876, when he met a wealthy patron, Nadezhda von Meck. A curious contract was drawn up between them; his benefactress undertook to look after the material needs of the composer on condition he never saw her and maintained contact by correspondence only. Despite his homosexual inclinations Tchaikovsky married but the outcome was disastrous and nearly drove him to suicide in 1878. Thereafter the composer led an uneventful life, travelling a great deal in Europe and even in the United States. He died of cholera in St Petersburg, eight days after conducting the first performance of his *Pathétique* symphony (1893).

The man and musician

Three key phrases, which may be said to sum up his work, stand out in Tchaikovsky's voluminous correspondence of more than 3,000 letters with Nadezhda von Meck. In one letter he wrote, 'I am a *Russian, Russian, Russian,* to the marrow of my bones'. In another, 'This evening I feel sad and am shedding tears because this morning while wandering in the woods I was unable to find a single violet. What an old sniveller I am . . . !' And the other quotation so revealing of his personality reads, 'Fate . . . hangs over our heads like the sword of Damocles and inexorably distils a slow and deadly venom. One must bend to it and abandon oneself to boundless despair . . .'

Tchaikovsky was perhaps the most truly Russian of all Russian composers, though, having received a Western education, he preferred classical forms. The 'Five' invented themes with a Russian character which they poured into a national mould, providing them with exotic colouring. Tchaikovsky, on the other hand, used authentic folk melodies, but submitted them to occidental treatment. Moreover, he is the only great Russian composer of his generation who owes nothing to the orientalising influence.

Tchaikovsky is also often reproached for his excessive post-Romantic sentimentality. He himself admitted that the charge was sometimes justified. Certainly, he reveals himself completely in his music and in this respect incarnates one aspect of the Russian character. But Tchaikovsky is quite capable of sounding the depths of profundity in his music; the trio in A minor in memory of Anton Rubinstein is an example. A Schumannesque idea of fate constitutes the major theme of Tchaikovsky's music, to such a degree that it ends by becoming a record of his own struggle against destiny. The general plan of his symphonies and concertos is a first and very 'pessimistic' movement, followed by the second, serene, gracious and sad, the third, an allegro, often in dance rhythm and the fourth, overflowing with vitality – though the *Pathétique*, in which, in the guise of a peroration, the composer writes his own Requiem, is an exception here. His themes are ample, decorative and striking, and he sometimes uses them as *Leitmotive* in long crescendos in successive waves, in a manner which owes much to Beethoven. The orchestration is rich but without any attempt at spectacular effects; Shostakovich has said that to listen to a work by Tchaikovsky is equivalent to a lesson in instrumentation.

Tchaikovsky's output exceeds even that of Rimsky-Korsakov. His instinct was for symphony and ballet but for practical reasons he wrote ten operas, though of uneven quality. Among them however, are the masterpieces *Eugene Onegin* (1879) and the *Queen of Spades* (1890), after Pushkin. For his own pleasure he wrote a great deal of chamber music, also uneven in quality. We can forget his piano pieces, but the A minor trio and the serenade for strings are music to remember. He also wrote sacred music.

But it is his symphonies that earn him a place of honour. Of these the *Manfred* symphony (1885) is a truly Romantic symphony in the style of Berlioz and Liszt. But perhaps the greatest is the sixth, called the *Pathétique* by the composer himself, in B minor. In addition he wrote the *Little Russian*, No. 2 in C minor (1873), which makes use of folk tunes; the first in G minor (1868); No. 3 in D major (1875); No. 4 in F minor (1878) and the fifth in E minor (1888).

Tchaikovsky also composed three piano concertos, of which the first is undoubtedly the most popular, one violin concerto and admirable symphonic poems like *Romeo and Juliet* and *Francesca da Rimini*. After his achievements as a symphonist the most important part of Tchaikovsky's output was in the field of ballet, with three great masterpieces to his credit: *Swan Lake* (1877; St Petersburg production 1895), *Sleeping Beauty* (1890) and *Nutcracker* (1891). But above all Russian music is indebted to Tchaikovsky for having brought the mainstream of Western music into the Russian tradition.

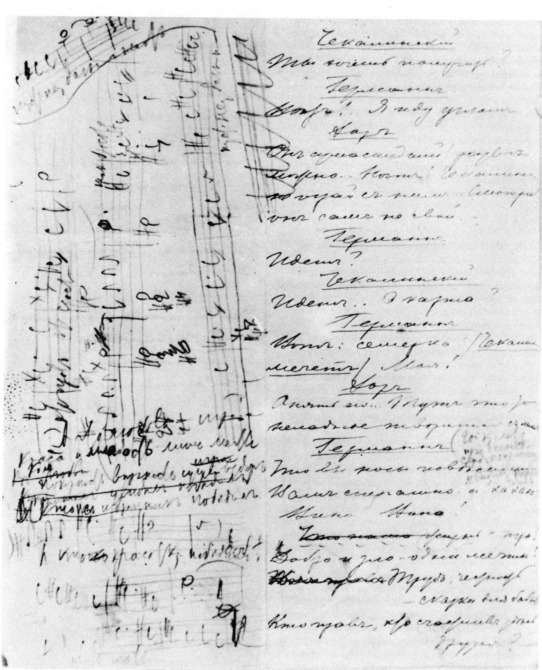

Page from Tchaikovsky's notebook for The Queen of Spades.

Music in Italy

The Italian devotion to opera, by far the most prominent feature of the musical life of the country from the middle of the 17th century, developed the proportions of an obsession during the 19th. As a result the history of music in Italy in this period is to all intents merely a chapter in the long story of Italian opera. In the field of instrumental music Italy continued to produce worthy successors to the tradition of Corelli, Vivaldi and Scarlatti, but the emigration from a theatre-dominated musical scene, which these same men had begun, snowballed, so that at the turn of the century some of the finest Italian composers were working abroad: Cherubini in Paris, Clementi in London, Boccherini in Madrid and Giovanni Battista Viotti (1755-1824), one of the most brilliant violinists of his day and a composer of some talent, in Paris and London.

Besides these important figures there were also lesser men who, nevertheless, achieved fine work abroad.

Giovanni Giuseppe Cambini (1746-1825) worked for fifty years in Paris where, inevitably, his numerous operas won great success, though the bulk of his work was taken up by a huge output of instrumental music. This included some ninety symphonies and *symphonies concertantes*, nearly 150 string quartets and quintets, seven concertos and some 400 other instrumental works. Among other Italians working abroad who made valuable contributions to the repertoire of chamber music were F. A. Radicati, who died in Vienna in 1823, and Ignazio Raimondi, who worked in London from 1790 until his death in 1813.

Yet it was for their operas that the Italians won European fame. At the age of sixty Giovanni Paisiello, whose *Barber of Seville* was only one in a long series of successes, was called to the court of Napoleon. Three years later, in 1805, the Empress Josephine appointed the Italian Gasparo Spontini (1774-1851) to be her

Gioacchino Rossini.

court composer. Spontini earned the respect of Berlioz for his *La Vestal* (1807) and was also important as a conductor, giving the first authentic performance of Mozart's *Don Giovanni* at Paris. He remained at the French capital under the Bourbon restoration, but then in 1820 went to Berlin where he remained for some twenty years. Such were some of the Italians who in the early 19th century continued the long tradition of Italian music in Europe north of the Alps.

At this time the political conditions in Italy itself were being shaped both by the campaigns and conquests of the Napoleonic regime in the north Italian plain, and by the awakening determination of the Italians themselves to achieve national unity and independence. With the defeat of France in 1815, the unified Napoleonic state in the north of Italy was broken down again into its constituent parts. Despite its incompleteness and short life, the Napoleonic settlement of Italy was an important lesson to the new radical and nationalist groups which came to dominate Italian politics in the struggle for national independence and, above all, unity.

In music, as we shall see, the Italians felt no strong attraction to Romanticism which, north of the Alps, was to provide such an important stimulus to nationalist aspirations. For centuries an authentic Italian style had, together with the French manner, coloured and to a large extent shaped much of European music. The Italians had no need to search for a national idiom and neither they nor the French, save of course for the monumental exceptions of Berlioz and Verdi, produced any important Romantic composer. For Romanticism was essentially a central European and, above all, a German phenomenon. The great classical school of Vienna, represented by the works of Haydn and Mozart and the young Beethoven, was firmly rooted in the international Franco-Italian tradition of 18th-century Europe. But in the fervid nationalist atmosphere of early 19th century Germany, seeking unity like the Italians, Romanticism provided the ethos for the first truly German art, which the rediscovery of Bach in the 1820s did much to reinforce.

It was natural therefore that Italian composers should follow the dictates of their audience, devoted to the beauties of the voice and a facile, brilliant style of vocal writing, and continue the exploitation of a national style which had reigned supreme in Europe for so long. But the decline in the standard of Italian opera had already been progressing for some time, and by the early 19th century it seemed, to outside observers, to be complete. The devotion to vocal display led to simple melodic lines, heavily ornamented, resting on a harmonic structure of the least imaginative type.

'As far as the Roman theatres are concerned, I would much sooner not speak of them, since nothing is more depressing than always having to repeat the same criticisms and to see the epithets pitiable, ridiculous, detestable, dashed off by one's pen'. Thus wrote Berlioz in 1832.

However, some new elements were introduced and the massive reforms achieved by Gluck in the 1760s found some faint echo in Italy, thanks largely to Giovanni Simone Mayr (1763-1845), a composer of German extraction. He came to Italy in his youth and soon settled in Venice. His first operatic success came in 1794 and for the next quarter of a century he devoted himself to the stage, being the leading composer in Italy until the debut of the brilliant young Rossini. Among his pupils was the young Donizetti and his school was distinguished by a concern, new in Italian opera, for brilliance of orchestration. Mayr, following the example of the Gluck reform opera, also gave a new prominence to the chorus, but his aim was also to adapt the techniques of the new opera to the tastes of his Italian audience. Nevertheless, a blow had been struck against the Italian infatuation with the voice, and Rossini was to owe part of his reputation to his own imaginative orchestration.

Rossini

Gioacchino Antonio Rossini – the 'Swan of Pesaro' for some, 'Signor Crescendo' for others because of his introduction of some of the techniques of the Mannheim orchestra – was born in Pesaro in 1792. His father was inspector of slaughter-houses and town trumpeter and horn player. His mother, a baker's daughter, studied singing and obtained engagements in the theatre when her husband was imprisoned for his republican opinions. Little Gioacchino's education was entrusted to a pork butcher and then to a blacksmith until, when he was only eight, he gave proof of quite exceptional musical gifts. At the age of fourteen, he composed an opera, *Demetrio e Polibia*.

At fifteen he entered the music school of Bologna, where he studied both the cello and the piano and received instruction in composition from Mattei. Under his supervision, Rossini made an intensive study of the work of Haydn and Mozart, notably their quartets, and earned the nickname of '*il Tedeschino*' (the little German) because of his enthusiasm for their music. He left the Liceo at Bologna when he was still only eighteen, and in addition to his opera had composed two symphonies and a set of variations for wind instruments, prompted by a taunt from his father that he did not understand the horn. In 1810 he made his theatrical debut in Venice with *La Cambiale di Matrimonio*. This was moderately successful, but Rossini received numerous commissions. Thenceforth he composed unceasingly, everywhere and anywhere: in his bed, on inn tables, in postchaises, so that in the space of thirteen years he had written more than thirty operas. These included *Tancredi* and *The Italian Girl in Algiers*, whose premiere in Venice in 1813 firmly established his name.

Over the next ten years he wrote on an average two operas a year. Among them was the highly successful *Elizabeth, Queen of England* (1815), important because, among other things, the voice parts are written out in full – a check on the singers, who until that time had been used to being allowed almost total freedom by composers in the decoration of their parts. The success of *Elizabeth* may have derived in part from its overture, which Rossini was to use in the following year for his

Scene from a production of Rossini's opera William Tell *at the Drury Lane Theatre, London, in 1844.*

Barber of Seville. It is for this comic masterpiece that Rossini is still best remembered. At its first performance it was met with blank hostility from the audience, who regarded Rossini's decision to set the selfsame libretto as the masterpiece of Paisiello as brazen presumption. However, *The Barber's* second performance, also in 1816, was a complete success and thereafter Rossini's rise was so meteoric that contemporaries, in an excess of hyperbole, compared him to Napoleon.

In 1824, two years after his marriage to the Spanish *primadonna* Isabella Colbran, Rossini was appointed director of the Théatre Italien in Paris. Here he was named to musical appointments at court and wrote *Il Viaggio a Reims*, an official work for the coronation of Charles X, which he revised as the remarkable *Count Ory*. His other two important compositions were the *Siege of Corinth* and, in 1829, *William Tell*, his major work for the stage.

The Barber of Seville had taken him only thirteen days, but Rossini worked for more than six months on *William Tell.* After its success he gave up writing for the theatre; he was only thirty-seven. In 1836 he went back to Italy, living in Bologna and then Florence, but in the 1850s he returned to Passy, near Paris, where he died in 1868. During the course of his long retirement he won a reputation as a bon viveur and gourmet – the dish tournedos Rossini was invented by him – but he composed practically nothing except a spectacular Stabat Mater, a mass, a few songs and some charming 'little nothings' ('the sins of my old age'), which he wrote for his Sunday visitors. Some of these were used by Respighi for his ballet *La Boutique Fantasque*, and their quality and charm in their own right are now being rediscovered.

An anxiety to please seemed almost inseparable from Rossini's character. As Wagner noted, 'if he heard that such and such a town particularly liked to hear the *roulades* of singers and that another, on the contrary, preferred languorous songs; then for the first, he provided nothing but *roulades*, for the second, languorous songs. Where he knew an audience liked percussion in

Joan Sutherland in the title role of Donizetti's opera Lucia di Lammermoor.

353

right
Gaetano Donizetti.

below right
Vicenzo Bellini.

the orchestra, he immediately started the overture of a pastoral opera with a roll on the drums'. But the desire to please was natural enough in a 19th-century opera composer, and even Berlioz was not above writing his great setting of the Rakoczy march specifically for a concert in the Hungarian capital.

Nevertheless, despite a keen awareness of the box office, Rossini did not escape criticism. In Italy he was suspected as an innovator because of his interest in German music; in northern Europe he was sometimes condemned as a conservative because of his refusal to follow the full precepts of Romanticism. There are hints in the nationalist and popular fervour of the choruses of *William Tell* (which delighted Berlioz) that, had he continued to compose, Rossini might have gone far to accept Romanticism. It is perhaps because he realised that his genius lay in an idiom which had been worked out and that if he attempted to adjust to the contemporary style he would fail, that he abandoned serious composition for the theatre. Maybe it was that after a career of astonishing productivity he looked forward to

a life of ease. Whatever his secret, Rossini wrote music for the comic stage that sparkles and bubbles over with life and laughter, and the hurly-burly of a well-produced *Barber* is irresistible.

Rossini's lesser contemporaries

The decade of Rossini's birth also witnessed the birth of a number of talented but lesser men. Giuseppe Mercadante (1795-1870), who from 1840 was director of the Conservatory of Naples, won considerable success with his operas, from which Verdi himself learnt. From the late 1830s, Mercadante's operas show some evidence of his admiration for the work of Meyerbeer, in that he attempted to give somewhat greater formal cohesion to his stage works than was usual among Italian composers. He also wrote a number of orchestral compositions and music for the church, some of which earned the approbation of Liszt. Giovanni Pacini (1796-1867), who enjoyed the perhaps unremarkable sobriquet of 'master of the *cabaletta*' (the final short section of a certain type of aria), was a renowned composer of opera in the years between Rossini's retirement and the rise of Verdi. He wrote more than ninety operas, a symphony, chamber music, and music for the church, and his work often displays great facility for orchestration. More important and talented than these were Gaetano Donizetti (1797-1848) and Vicenzo Bellini (1801-35). Even among a nation of composers where facility was almost *de rigueur* Donizetti's rapidity of composition was astonishing. Like Rossini and many other composers of the period he was, for a time, under contract to the impresario Domenico Barbaja, undertaking to write twelve operas in three years. Between 1816 and 1844 he wrote some seventy operas in addition to a number of string quartets, symphonies and music for the church. In an intensely active career Donizetti also worked as a director, conducting the first production of Rossini's Stabat Mater, and for five years was teacher of counterpoint at the Naples Conservatory. Despite his technical mastery and fine dramatic sense Donizetti was a composer of uneven inspiration. Among his best known operas are *Lucia di Lammermoor* (1835), based on a novel by Sir Walter Scott set in 17th-century Scotland; and the comic operas *The Daughter of the Regiment* (1840), *The Elixir of Love* (1832), and *Don Pasquale* (1843).

Bellini, whose tragically early death robbed Italian music of an outstanding talent, had the characteristic Italian facility for melody and wrote in the Italian tradition of *bel canto*. This vocal style, in which brightness of tone and virtuoso agility are at a premium, was in marked contrast to the somewhat lugubrious and fulsome style which was to pass for operatic singing once the tradition of Wagnerian musical drama was established. Although the music of Italian opera was less portentous than German, and in truth less capable of weighty expressiveness, yet, when the music of a master of the style like Bellini is sung by a voice able to meet its exacting demands, we can fully understand its immense vogue. Bellini's operas were *Norma* (1831), a tragedy about a Druid priestess and a Roman soldier, *La Sonnambula* (1831) and finally *I Puritani*, set in the English Civil War and first produced in Paris in 1835.

One of the most celebrated of all 19th-century Italian musicians was the great violinist Niccolò Paganini, whose astonishing virtuosity gave birth to the legend that he was in league with the devil. Born in Genoa in 1782, the son of a small shopkeeper, he received lessons on the mandolin from his father and retained an interest in plucked instruments all his life.

He was a virtuoso guitarist as well as violinist. His father soon sent him to study with qualified teachers and the young Paganini made his public debut when he was eleven. His self-willed independence drove him to leave home at an early age, travelling as a freelance virtuoso and winning notoriety both by his talent and his wild living. He was such an obsessive gambler that before the age of eighteen he had staked and lost his very violin. For three years he held an official appointment but gave it up in 1805, and thereafter travelled restlessly throughout Europe until his death in 1840. Paganini's life is wreathed in legend; he certainly had many love affairs, astonished audiences with his outstanding technique and amassed a huge fortune which he left to his illegitimate son, Achille. It is perhaps not surprising that Paganini was a poor ensemble player, yet despite his nervous brilliance as a performer, his own compositions include many which are more than mere displays of virtuosity.

Verdi

Unlike Wagner, that other great man of opera in the 19th century, Verdi was never a theoretician. He might more aptly be described as a 'natural force', a spontaneous musician, a man of simplicity, and unique. '*Io son un paesano*' (I am a peasant) he replied to King Victor Emmanuel when the latter wished to ennoble him. Proud of his origins, Verdi wanted to speak to the masses and not to an intellectual elite. 'The theatre yesterday evening was filled to bursting: that's the only gauge to success', he wrote.

Giuseppe Verdi was born at Roncole, a little hamlet in the commune of Busseto, not far from Parma, in 1813. His parents, who kept an inn which was also a wine shop and grocery store, entrusted his education to the village padre. The church organist took him under his wing and instructed him in the first rudiments of musical theory, and taught him to play the organ, so well indeed, that at the age of eleven, Giuseppe himself became organist at Roncole and Busseto. He played so beautifully that the commune awarded him a stipend to allow him to study at the Milan Conservatory; but he was not accepted, the examiners holding a less glowing opinion of his talents at the keyboard than his fellow villagers. But Verdi was determined on music and took private lessons to reinforce his own studies. He worked to the end of his life to perfect his technique, continuing to advance it. Thus his two greatest masterpieces are his last two operas, *Otello* (1887) and *Falstaff* (1893), composed in his seventies. He died in Milan in 1901.

Verdi made his debut in the theatre in 1839 with *Oberto*, which had an instant success at La Scala, Milan, and resulted in contracts both with La Scala and with the publisher, Ricordi. His next opera, *Un Giorno di Regno*, was a fiasco, but *Nabucco* (1842) was a triumph, both musically and politically. The principal 'character' of this opera is in fact the Jewish people in captivity in Babylon, but they sing of their lost country in terms which the Milanese had no difficulty in applying to their own situation under the Austrian yoke. The chorus, *Va, pensiero sull'ali dotate*, was soon sung all over Italy, and the name of Verdi, the militant repre-

Scene from a production of Bellini's opera Norma, *at the Royal Opera House, Covent Garden. Joan Sutherland as Norma.*

sentative of Italian independence ('a musician wearing a helmet', as Rossini put it), became a sort of symbol. His name was scratched on the walls of houses and public monuments, being the perfect and hardly veiled code word for 'Vittorio Emmanuele Re D'Italia'.

The success of *I Lombardi alla prima crociata* was even greater. In the following year *Ernani* was acclaimed in Venice. Then there followed in Milan, Venice and Rome, *Attila*, *I Due Foscari*, *Giovanna d'Arco*, *Alzira*, and *Macbeth*; in London, *I Masnadieri*; in Paris, *Jerusalem* (a new version of *I Lombardi*); at Trieste, *The Corsair*. After the production of *Luisa Miller* in 1849 at Naples, Verdi settled on his country estate and, like his idol Shakespeare, lived the life of a landed gentleman. He gave careful attention to the business of estate management and was a generous landlord and employer. He followed the hunt and represented his district in the newly united kingdom of Italy, but his inspiration as a composer strengthened as the years went by. *Rigoletto* (1851), *Il Trovatore* (1853) and *La Traviata* (1853), assured him of European fame, and henceforth success was assured. *The Sicilian Vespers* (1855) was produced in Paris; *Simon Boccanegra* (1857), *Aroldo* (1857) and *Ballo in Maschera* (1859) in Italy; *Forza del Destino* (1861) in St Petersburg; and *Don Carlos* (1867) in Paris.

Beginning with *bel canto* opera (even in *Traviata*, in Violetta's aria in the first act, there are repeats which early on give the soprano the possibility to introduce *fioriture* embellishments) Verdi never ceased to move forward and enlarge his technique. Although he in no way accepted Wagner's theories or aesthetic, Verdi

Scene from a production of Verdi's opera Aïda *at the Opéra, Paris.*

recognised the latter's contribution to orchestration and was more and more careful to enrich his own works. One is aware of this in *Aïda* (1871), and even more so in *Otello* (1887) and *Falstaff* (1893), which, apart from their volume of sound and the fact that Verdi abandoned the practice of dividing the operas between arias and recitatives, owe no further debt to Wagner.

After losing his friend, the great Romantic writer Manzoni, Verdi composed his mighty and beautiful Requiem (1874). He himself died in Milan in 1901. His very last compositions were the *Four sacred pieces* (1898) which show a definite tendency towards the music of Palestrina.

The music

Verdi drew his inspiration from what we may call the great source books of the Romantics: from Shakespeare – *Macbeth*, *Otello*, *Falstaff*, the libretto for the last two being provided by the poet and musician Arigo Boito; Schiller – *Joan of Arc*, *Luisa Miller*, *Don Carlos*; and Victor Hugo – *Ernani*, *Rigoletto* (based on *Le roi s'amuse*), and a work which remained no more than a project.

Verdi had an absolute understanding of the theatre, the great theatre open to masses of spectators. His music is always controlled by the demands of the drama and the plot, not in the manner of Wagner with his calculated network of *Leitmotive*, but in a seemingly irrational and spontaneous fashion which has a dramatic fitness, the feeling for a phrase rather than for the text word by word.

His methods are usually simple and direct and always make a true dramatic impact. He was a fighter, and his taste for combat, from which amorous passion was rarely absent, inspired some of his most noble music. His music is to the point and does not pretend to the symbolism which was important in the work of Wagner. Verdi is afraid neither of theatrical excesses nor of conventions, but at the same time succeeds in sublimating the convention of Italian opera and transforming it into great art.

It cannot be too strongly emphasised that although Verdi made the great Italian contribution to the music of the Romantic period, yet his art grew naturally out of the native tradition to which he was heir. There are obvious parallels between his career and that of Wagner and, like the German, he achieved a synthesis which provided a vehicle for the highest flights of dramatic art. Yet it was the style developed and perfected by Rossini, Bellini and Donizetti that Verdi took and shaped into a medium of great tragic expression. If his plots do not have the carefully ordered structure that Wagner achieved, they possess an organic vigour which not only expresses the native passion of the composer but also must owe much to his reading of Shakespeare. Nevertheless, as he matured in his art, Verdi, who was always learning and improving on his musical mastery, most notably in his understanding of the orchestra, also succeeded in exerting more effective control over the libretto and dramatic structure of his operas. But in the last analysis Verdi stands revealed as a grand master in the Italian tradition. When Wagner spoke of opera as never-ending melody he seems to be speaking of a different world from that inhabited by the mighty yet singing melodies of Verdi's masterpieces. In Verdi, Italian opera, so long despaired of by the musicians of Europe, emerged transfigured but recognisably the heir to its great past and the culmination of a great tradition.

Verdi's successors

After the triumph of Romanticism in the music of Verdi, Italian opera composers, towards the end of the 19th century, turned to an idiom which in some ways had affiliations to the various schools of realism and naturalism which had developed in European painting and literature in the last decades of the century. The movement, called *verismo* (the Italian word for realism) was distinguished as much by its subject-matter as by its musical style. Composers such as Puccini, the leading composer of the style, preferred plots based on contemporary life to the heroic and Romantic themes of Verdi. Nevertheless, in a sense Verdi's *La Traviata*, the tale of a courtesan in the high society of the period, tended towards *verismo*, while Bizet's *Carmen*, the tragedy of a girl worker in a cigarette factory, was obviously part of the same movement.

Giacomo Puccini was born at Lucca in 1858, the son of a family of musicians. His talents were soon recognised and he went to study at the Milan conservatory where his teachers included Amilcare Ponchielli (1834-86). Ponchielli's most famous opera, *La Gioconda*, tells the story of a young street singer and was set to a libretto by the poet and composer Arrigo Boito (1842-1918), taken from the work of Victor Hugo. Thanks to

Giuseppe Verdi, the greatest figure in Italian music of the 19th century.

right
Scene from a production of Puccini's Madame Butterfly, *at the Royal Opera House, Covent Garden.*

below
Giacomo Puccini.

the financial support of friends, who by now included Boito himself, Puccini was able to mount a production of his first opera which, although no astonishing success, led to a contract with the publishers Ricordi. This enabled him to devote himself to operatic composition at the early age of twenty-five. Nevertheless, his reputation was not established until the performance of his uneven but promising *Manon Lescaut*, based on the novel by the Abbé Prévost, in 1893.

Three years later followed his masterpiece *La Bohème* (1896). The success of the work was due in large part to the sensitive collaboration between the two librettists, G. Giacoso and L. Illica, and the composer. The story is taken from the mid-century novel by the Frenchman Henry Murger and the opera gives a touching if somewhat over-romanticised picture of student life. There followed *Madame Butterfly* (1904), taken from the American writer David Belasco's successful play on the subject of a tragic love story between an American naval lieutenant and a Japanese girl; *Tosca* (1900), a somewhat maudlin tale of feminine 'honour' and political corruption based on the novel by Victorien Sardou; *The Girl of the Golden West* (1910), again from a play by Belasco; and the unfinished *Turandot*, set in ancient imperial China. Puccini died in 1924.

Puccini, who made his typically Italian gift for delightful melody a medium for dramatic expression, enjoyed a phenomenal popularity with his public, although the critics' opinion of his work long remained adverse. The two other best known Italian *verismo* composers were Pietro Mascagni (1863-1945) and Ruggiero Leoncavallo (1858-1919). Their two famous works are Mascagni's one-act *Cavalleria Rusticana* (1890), a tale of rustic chivalry which has as its theme a Sicilian blood feud, and Leoncavallo's two-act *I Pagliacci* (1892), in which the real and stage lives of a group of village players are melodramatically juxtaposed.

Puccini, Mascagni and Leoncavallo may be regarded as the last representatives of the long tradition of Italian lyric theatre which had reached a new and glorious height of expression with the work of Verdi. Despite his heroic example, the music of these three successors is on a plane so much lower that it seemed to herald a new epoch which would repeat the history of the first decades of the 19th century. However, in the 20th century, led by such men as Malipiero and Casella, Italian music was to accommodate itself to the main stream of developments north of the Alps, while in Berlin the truly original figure of Busoni was to give a new direction to the age-long tradition of Italian composers abroad.

The aftermath of Romanticism

After the heroic period of Bismarck's Germany, in which the numerous German states had found political cohesion under the kings of Prussia, and the strong sense of German nationalism had been resoundingly reinforced by victory over France in 1871, there followed years of commercial and industrial expansion under the regime of the Emperor William II. Neither under Bismarck nor under the personal rule of William did Germany enjoy any great democratic freedom, but the wealthy industrial and commercial elite, inheriting a tradition of patronage from the age of the little German courts, deployed their riches in the peaceful generation before 1914 to finance an active cultural life. Artists and writers were in revolt against the principles of the Romanticism of the previous generation, but in music this movement enjoyed a somewhat longer life.

The late flowering of Naturalism in Germany was tinged with the Symbolism which had originated in France and Belgium. Among the chief champions of this new movement were the writers Gerhart Hauptmann and Stefan George (who was much more inclined to Symbolism). Naturalism and Symbolism were quickly superseded by Expressionism, a typically German phenomenon, whose first and terrifying representatives were the no longer young Frank Wedekind (1864-1928), and the tragic Georg Trakl. Among later Expressionist writers we might include the names of Rainer Maria Rilke, Franz Kafka and Franz Werfel. In the world of music, matters were not settled quite so quickly, and Romanticism remained a powerful force for some time to come.

Under Prussian hegemony, it seemed sometimes that the intellectual faculties of the German people had become atrophied. Music was restricted to a theatrical style, adapted to grandiloquent dreams. The exaltation of nationalism and pan-Germanism, from which Austria was not altogether exempt, produced an artistic trend which was not so much neo-Romantic as Baroque-Romantic. This is particularly apparent in the music of the period.

But out of all the torrents of music produced at this time, what remains? Perhaps the names of only nine or ten composers survive, and of these only three or four can be classed in the first rank, most of them Austrians. But it should be added that the reign of William II, closely linked with economic prosperity and expansion, was responsible for a major sociological revolution in the world of music, from the point of view both of the public and of the artist. Bereft of the social function that it had previously enjoyed, music, in Germany as elsewhere, entered the field of consumer goods. After his death, Wagner was acclaimed as the great Prophet of music and Bayreuth his Mecca. But it was not the intellectuals who supported his cult but the newly confident capitalist society. It was with their money that the Bayreuth festivals were financed, and it was they who gave names like Siegfried and Sieglinde to their sons and daughters.

Wagner, as we have already observed, set out to create music whose purpose, first and foremost, was to cast a magic spell. But to practise magic cults one must have sorcerers. These sorcerers were the orchestral conductors. At the end of the 19th and beginning of the 20th centuries, the conductor was to enjoy a social and artistic distinction such as he had never known before. Henceforth he was no longer just a simple local official musician, but very soon grew to be what he is today – a star who may well be a greater public attraction than the music he conducts.

Hugo Wolf

Of all the composers of the late Romantic period, the Austrians Hugo Wolf and Gustav Mahler made the most important contributions to the musical patrimony of Germany.

Wolf was born at Windischgrätz in 1860 and studied at the Vienna Conservatory, from which he was expelled for unruly behaviour. All his life, which was spent in comparative penury, he remained an undisciplined character, dividing his time between attempts at orchestral composition and the writing of a very considerable number of *Lieder*. At the same time he was a very active and virulent music critic. He was a highly sensitive, overexcitable man, and was eventually placed in the care of a psychiatric home in Vienna. It was here that he died, insane, in 1903.

His main works, some 200 *Lieder*, were composed at incredible speed between 1888 and 1891. His output can be divided into two groups. The first comprises a collection of piano pieces and chamber music, mostly unfinished, with the exception of the *Italian Serenade* for string quartet (1892); a symphonic poem, *Penthesilea* (1883); and an opera, *The Corregidor* (1896), which, though forgotten, is not lacking in verve and originality. The second group consists of the *Lieder*.

The bulk of Wolf's songs are found in great cycles: twenty-two poems by Eichendorff (1889); fifty-three by Mörike (1888); fifty-one by Goethe (1890); forty-four of the *Spanische Liederbuch* (1891); and finally, his three last settings of poems by Michelangelo (1898).

Wolf has been called 'the Wagner of *Lieder*', and there is some truth in this description. But although he was a great admirer of Wagner, he was never a mere imitator and he himself admitted to an intense respect for the *Lieder* of Schumann, refusing indeed to set any text used by Schumann. What he did was to adopt certain Wagnerian theoretical principles and use them in an individual way within the framework of his own poetic world. He was the first composer of *Lieder* to make use of the Wagnerian principle of continuous declamation. His melodic line and phrasing does not follow the metre of

right
Engelbert Humperdinck (1854-1921), whose opera Hansel and Gretel (*1893*), *which makes free and original use of Wagner's* Leitmotiv *principle, won him an immense reputation.*

below
Hugo Wolf.

the verses, but lays stress on the meaning of the words, rather in the manner of *recitativo arioso*.

Hugo Wolf was a man of letters; the written word for him was all-important. But, and this is a very important point, he never made any concessions where the piano parts were concerned. It was essential that the voice and instrument should form a complete unity and that the piano should not be just an adjunct. Wolf's approach to the place of the piano in his songs is clearly allied to Wagner's theory of the operas as a 'total artwork'. In fact, his vocal line is often like a Schoenberg *Sprechgesang*, and it is the piano part that provides the expression (in the same way as the orchestra does in a Wagner opera), and possesses an unbelievable subtlety in the translation of the poem into musical terms. Wolf's technical mastery, which was both highly original and personal, and his hypersensitivity, which led to hallucinations and eventual madness, lends his music subtlety and complexity and conveys the most illusory psychological nuances. He was able to interpret the intellectual lyricism of Goethe, the sparkling humour of Eichendorff, the delicacy of Mörike and the fleeting moods of the Spanish and Italian songs translated by Heyse and Geibel.

Mahler

Gustav Mahler was born in 1860 at Kalischt in Austrian Moravia. After a brilliant student career at the Vienna Conservatory, he embarked on the profession of conductor, which he practised all his life. After appointments in various European cities, he lived in Leipzig for a while where he worked with Artur Nikisch. In 1888 he was appointed director of the Budapest opera and in 1897 of the court opera in Vienna. This he completely reorganised, but animosity and intrigue obliged him to resign ten years later. In 1907 he was engaged as chief conductor at the Metropolitan Opera House, New York. At the height of his fame he fell ill and returned to Europe, stopping for a short while in Paris to receive medical treatment before proceeding to Vienna, where he died in 1911.

Despite his exhausting career as a conductor, Mahler was an extremely prolific composer. The catalogue of his works extends from 1880 to 1910. His principal works are the ten symphonies, some of which use choirs and are, in a sense, the symphonic apotheosis of the *Lied*. To these ten symphonies, the last of which remained unfinished, should be added *The Song of the Earth*, which is scored throughout for two soloists and large orchestra.

He also composed song cycles with orchestral accompaniment, among them four *Lieder eines fahrenden Gesellen* (*Songs of a Wayfarer*, 1884); twelve *Lieder aus Des Knaben Wunderhorn* (1899); and five *Kindertotenlieder* (*Songs on the Death of Children*, 1902).

Mahler was a hypersensitive artist, torn between his love for the marvels of nature – forests and bird songs – and the sufferings revealed by psychoanalysis in the innermost depths of man. His music is an expression of both his inner torments and his spiritual impulses (towards God, nature, beauty and purity). His work has been called 'the last farewell of modern man to the beautiful fading dream of Romanticism'.

Mahler's aesthetic did not spring from an instinctive spontaneous urge, but was rather the result of a conscious synthesis of his musical tastes and his spiritual aspirations: popular song, Beethoven, Bruckner, Wagner, deism and even a type of pantheism.

From a purely musical point of view, Mahler takes chromatic harmonies, first introduced with *Tristan* and *Parsifal*, to extreme lengths. In this respect he forms the link between Wagner and Schoenberg, who was soon to complete the destruction of the foundations of classical tonal harmony. As a composer, Mahler, undoubtedly one of the most original artists of his time, was an intellectual and a powerful ideologist. He broke away from traditional forms and created symphonies of gigantic proportions, with overwhelmingly rich orchestral texture, inspired by the spiritual and poetic demands of the work.

The symphonies

The first symphony, in D major (1888), known as the 'Titan', is entirely orchestral. It is a stream of melody, singing of nature and youth. The second, in C minor (1888-94), is called 'The Resurrection', and may have sprung from Mahler's conversion from Judaism to Catholicism. The final movement introduces a chorus and female solo voices, and is set to words by the 18th-century German poet Klopstock. The third symphony, in D minor (1896), an evocation of nature and creation, is scored for viola, chorus and orchestra. The fourth, in G major (1900), is much shorter and simpler than the third and is idyllic in mood.

The fifth, in C sharp minor (1902), which dates from the time of his marriage, is relatively happy, but the musical language looks to the future, using a sort of 'progressive tonality' and even atonality. The sixth symphony in A minor (1904), known as 'The Tragic', is one of the vastest of all Mahler's works and ranks among the greatest symphonies ever written. It uses purely orchestral means and is filled with a dramatic tension in which Mahler seems to lay bare the depths of his soul. The seventh symphony, in E minor (1905), known as 'The Song of the Night', is also entirely orchestral. The sub-

Gustav Mahler.

title is due to the second and fourth movements, which are respectively entitled 'Evening Music' and 'Dance of the Shadows'. Mahler's eighth symphony, in E flat (1907), is known as 'The Thousand', from the massive resources it employs. It is written for voices throughout and requires a large number of singers and instrumentalists: eight soloists, three choirs (one of children) and a huge orchestra with various additional instruments. It is inspired by man's passage through life to death. It might almost be described as an oratorio, the first movement of which is based on the hymn *Veni Creator*, and the second on the final scene of Goethe's *Faust*. The ninth symphony in D major (1909), purely orchestral, is mysterious, funereal and satanic – a work of despair. Mahler left it unfinished and it was completed by Bruno Walter.

The tenth symphony, also unfinished, was originally planned to have five movements, for all of which Mahler made sketches, but only the brief scherzando and the fine, broad adagio movement were completed. In the work Mahler makes use of advanced harmonies, similar in style to Schoenberg. A completed version of the symphony, by the English musicologist Deryck Cooke, was performed in 1964. *The Song of the Earth*, one of the most moving and disturbing of all Mahler's works, was written in 1908. It is, in effect, a symphony for tenor, contralto and orchestra, and the text is based on a collection of Chinese poems.

Richard Strauss

With Richard Strauss we are transported into a completely different world – a world both modern and classical, and yet unique inasmuch as Strauss avoided the post-Wagnerian mainstream which led Schoenberg to the development of twelve-note music. He, too, forms a bridge between two epochs, but he has none of the feverish and disturbing qualities of Mahler. He epitomises the German musical heritage. There is something

of the juggler about Strauss; no matter whether he is indulging in the most incredible feats of counterpoint or whether he is paying homage to Mozart, Liszt, Berlioz, Wagner or Brahms, his personal identity is immediately established within the space of two bars or in a simple succession of chords.

He was born in Munich in 1864. His father, Franz Strauss, was first horn player in the royal orchestra in Munich. There is no connection whatsoever, it should be noted, with the Viennese Strauss family of waltz composers. Richard Strauss studied music, in particular conducting, in his native city under Hans von Bülow, and he was to become one of the greatest conductors of his time. His artistic and intellectual education was developed under the influence of Alexander Ritter and Wagner, although some of his earlier works show an affinity with Brahms. His reputation as a conductor won him an early invitation to Bayreuth, and after appointments in Munich and Berlin he became director of the Vienna opera house (1919-24). He conducted the first performances of his own works in most of Europe's main music centres, and divided his time between the musical capitals of the world and his mountain retreat at Garmisch, in Bavaria. It was there that he died in 1949. His most important contribution to music was in the field of harmony. He did not, however, turn to the chromatic atonality of Mahler, but concentrated on emancipating traditional tonality. He first developed a type of chordal polyphony with only attenuated tonal support, but later his tonality became much stronger.

Strauss's other main innovation was in his orchestration. Never before had Germany known such an accomplished, powerful and bold colourist. Taking Berlioz as his model he developed orchestral possibilities with astonishing virtuosity. In the world of opera Strauss made a sort of synthesis between continuous declamation in the Wagnerian style and the Mozartian recitative, to produce a very personal style of musical conversation of extraordinary suppleness. Strauss is one of the modern masters of lyric declamation.

His career, roughly speaking, can be divided into two

Friedrich von Flotow (1812–83), author of numerous operas of which Martha *(1847) was the most successful.*

distinct periods, although they overlap slightly. In the first period he reveals himself as a master of symphonic form; he is an idealist, a true son of the great Romantics, but an idealist not devoid of scepticism, who could never suffer the metaphysical agonies of a Mahler. This first period, which covers all the symphonic poems, is followed by the period from about 1905 until 1941, during which his main concern was with dramatic works. In this latter period he reveals himself as a master of opera – a Baroque musician whose growing scepticism is allied to a considerable degree of sensuality.

The symphonic poems

After a charmingly descriptive tone poem, *Aus Italien*, a sort of musical documentary, he passed without any transition to his masterpiece *Don Juan* (1889), a bravura work which brilliantly illustrates the eternal hero's unrequited search for love and his final descent into Hell. Masterpieces continued to flow from his pen, most with an autobiographical background. *Death and Transfiguration* (1890) is an almost religious work which expresses the idea of redemption by death; *Till Eulenspiegel* (1895), based on the medieval legend of an irreverent travelling jester, is a tone poem concerned with thwarted idealism, scornful of bourgeois conventions, sarcastic and 'popular'. *Thus spake Zarathustra* (1896) is a Nietzschean poem in music – a contemptuous, heroic and superhuman work of an exasperated idealist; *Don Quixote* (1898) is a poem of pure idealism and illusions which the hero regrets on his deathbed, while *Ein Heldenleben* or 'The Life of a Hero' (1899) is a poem of proud idealism in which Strauss caricatures the 'enemy' (i.e. the critics) and displays a pessimism equivalent to that of the hero who becomes resigned to the futility of his work and the concept of freedom of choice. The *Sinfonia Domestica* (1904) is a semi-serious, semi-humorous poem of domestic bliss, while the *Alpensymphonie* (1915) is another musical documentary evoking the ascent of a mountain.

Strauss ended his career with the *Metamorphoses*, a masterpiece written for string orchestra in the style of Bach on a theme by Beethoven, but in which shades of Wagner are evident.

The operas

After two early works heavily influenced by Wagner, Strauss produced his first truly original opera with *Salome*, written in 1905. A tragedy in one act based on Oscar Wilde's verse play, it is a tragic yet perverse erotic drama filled with sudden violence, written in an original musical style which suddenly inclines to polytonality. *Elektra* (1909), another one-act tragedy, is a drama of madness and revenge. The libretto, by Hugo von Hofmannsthal, is based on the play by Sophocles. Throughout the opera the tension mounts, culminating with the singers almost shouting. This is reflected in the score, which becomes increasingly polytonal as the plot evolves. *Der Rosenkavalier* (1911), to an original libretto by Hofmannsthal, is a magnificent musical comedy in three acts – a story of gallantry set in 18th-century Vienna. After the former barbarous themes, we have here a sensitive, gracious and frivolous Baroque Austria, sensual almost to the point of eroticism, but nevertheless profoundly human. Here Strauss returns to a more traditionally solid tonal language despite the introduction of a profusion of extraneous chords, which serve no particular purpose other than pure decoration. *Der Rosen-*

kavalier is one of the highlights of Strauss's art.

Another masterpiece, more serious in mood, is *Ariadne on Naxos* (1912, revised version 1916), a one-act opera with prologue, with an original libretto by Hugo von Hofmannsthal. Nowhere else are all the different aspects of Strauss's art so manifest. In this work, despite its modernity, the composer comes closest to the music of the 18th century. But it is not just the music that belongs to this period; Strauss also adopts typical 18th-century forms like those of the *opera buffa* and *opera seria*, which are ingeniously mixed in two parallel plots, one within the other. It should also be noted that, despite his principles of continuous declamation, he returns here to the *recitativo secco* and the use of arias. Furthermore, the orchestra consists of only thirty solo instruments.

Die Frau ohne Schatten (*The Woman without a Shadow*, 1919), in three acts, with a libretto again by Hofmannsthal, is a fairy tale inspired by a Persian legend. For *Intermezzo* (1924), a two-act 'bourgeois comedy', an 'opera in shirt-sleeves', Strauss is his own librettist and brings to the stage an amusing episode of married life. Nevertheless, the handling of the musical conversation shows incomparable virtuosity.

Die Schweigsame Frau (*The Silent Woman*, 1935) is an *opéra-comique* in three acts, the libretto for which was an adaptation by Stefan Zweig of a farce by Ben Jonson. The co-authors attempt to recapture the style of the *commedia dell'arte* by using a fast *recitativo secco*, reminiscent of the classical *opera buffa*. Strauss's last operatic work, *Capriccio* (1942), is a 'theoretical comedy' in one long act and bears the sub-title, 'A musical conversation'.

Reger

Max Reger was a much less inventive and imaginative composer than Strauss, and was much more drawn to pure music. His principal merit lies in the fact that at this very uncertain and critical turning-point in the history of German music, he was able to resuscitate the inheritance of pre-classical polyphony.

Reger was born in 1873 in Brand in Bavaria, the son of a schoolmaster, who gave him his earliest instruction in music. He himself taught at the conservatory of Wiesbaden. Returning home, he suffered a long illness, but in 1901, barely recovered, he settled in Munich where he taught at the conservatory, and later in Leipzig. He died in Leipzig in 1916 from a heart attack.

Most of his works are instrumental: violin and cello sonatas which are models of this style of composition; one hundred organ pieces (fantasias, chorales and variations); four string quartets; and several orchestral works, in particular the splendid *Variations and Fugue on a Joyous Theme by Johann Adam Hiller* and *Variations and Fugue on a Theme from 'The Magic Flute'*.

Reger is an inspired artist, both in the austerity of his style and in the facility and perfect mastery of his technical resources. One might say that he continued and accentuated the classic side of Brahms's genius. There are few remaining traces of Romanticism. He was a magnificent craftsman who made a great contribution to musical language. In his canons, fugues, chorales, variations and sonatas, in appearance classically simple, he developed under the banner of J. S. Bach the chromatic harmonies of Wagner and created a sort of panchromaticism which anticipates the atonal school. In some ways Reger also anticipates serial music, but he remained apart from the great upheavals of his time, apart from all *avant-garde* movements.

Two of Reger's contemporaries who, although they long outlived him, continued to write in a basically post-

Romantic style well into the 20th century, were Pfitzner and Karg-Elert. Of these, Hans Pfitzner (1869-1949) was the more important figure, although he was not only a staunch continuator of the late Romantic idiom but was also a voluble opponent of modernism. Born in Moscow he came to live in Germany at an early age, where he worked not only as composer but also as conductor and writer on music. Nevertheless, despite his avowed allegiance to Romanticism, Pfitzner had a highly individual style and produced much fine music, not only in his masterpiece, the opera *Palestrina*, but also in his three symphonies, and in his choral works and chamber music.

Sigfrid Karg-Elert (1877-1933), although a composer of secondary importance, united two of the great historic streams of German music. In his youth he was encouraged by Grieg and wrote a symphony. Other works were to include vocal and choral works and above all music for the organ. His style is essentially post-Romantic but in his organ compositions, notably the *Chorale Improvisations* and the *Chorale Preludes and Postludes,* he took up, and applied afresh, the great tradition of Baroque German organ music, providing an interesting and often inspired commentary on the idiom of the great J. S. Bach. But the future of German music was to lie elsewhere, and although the mighty example of Bach was to some extent to inspire the new pioneers, they took a far more fundamental approach to his ideas than did this last master of a long defunct tradition.

A scene from Strauss's opera Der Rosenkavalier

Section VI

Music in the Modern World

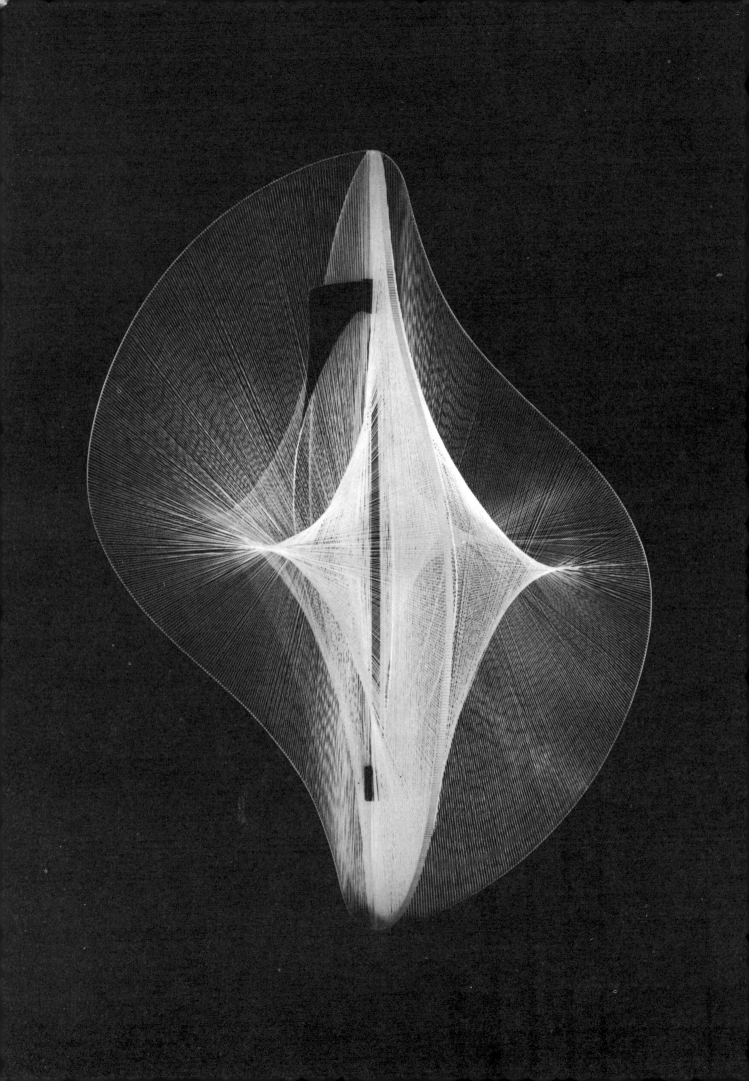

The 20th century: historical background

It was in the 19th century that the shadow of Europe began to lengthen in the world at large; the search for empires became a race, with the whole of the non-industrial world as the course. Not only the backward areas of tropical Africa, but even the great and venerable civilisation of China were considered fair game, so that when the 20th century opened there was hardly a part of the inhabited world without a European presence. The importance of this fact cannot be too much stressed since it was the prelude to the shaping of the contemporary world in which, in some form or another, European concepts such as the nation-state, the intrinsic value of curiosity and scepticism, the importance of physical well-being and the theoretical right of everyone to enjoy it in some form, are generally accepted.

But scarcely less dramatic than the impact of European ideology on the world at large was the rapid spread of its technology. To the new dynamic of the industrial 'take-off' was added the revolution in communications which shrank the distances that had previously insulated one civilisation from another. Thus the impact of a new culture exploding in the most energetic continent was inevitably felt with growing force throughout the world. These developments affected the arts. In many periods since the 12th century Europe had eagerly taken up the ideas of alien cultures, but in the 19th century the process was accelerated. The cult of Chinese blue-and-white procelain and the woodcut prints of Japan at the end of the 1860s heralded a new period during which European artists were to study non-European civilisations with open and receptive eyes. Then, in the first years of the 20th century, we find the interest shifting to the art of the primitive peoples of Africa and the South Seas and to the distant pre-Christian and indeed pre-civilised past of Europe itself.

In music the impact of these interests is found much later than in painting, though it is true that as early as the 1880s Debussy had been deeply impressed by the Indonesian gamelan music that he heard at the Paris exhibition. Nevertheless, from Stravinsky's *Rite of Spring*, influenced by the rhythms and rituals of a pagan past, composers throughout Europe found sources of inspiration in the most diverse places, including the equally sophisticated art of classical Indian music. The extension of European influence led also to the formation of an international language in the arts of architecture, painting, literature and music. Thus, important contributions are being made to the international musical idiom that has developed from the European past by composers from once remote Japan. The international community led by the industrially advanced nations is the direct result of the industrial revolution of the last century and the communications revolution of this.

Europe also involved much of the rest of the world in her ancient conflicts in the two great World Wars. Both of these extensive and bloody conflicts were followed by the break-up of exhausted empires. The first was terminated by the settlement of Versailles in 1919 which, among its other momentous decisions, presided over the final dismemberment of the Austrian empire. Poland, Czechoslovakia and Hungary gained full independence for the first time in centuries. After the Second World War it was the turn of the colonial empires outside Europe to disintegrate, as the metropolitan powers endeavoured to recover from the exhaustions of the war.

In the modern world, the once determining power of Europe in world affairs has been inherited by her two great descendants – Russia and the United States. For both, 1919 was a turning point, but in very different ways. Russia had in fact withdrawn from the war two years before the peace was signed, when, in 1917, her imperial regime was overthrown by the great Communist Revolution. It must have seemed to the many artists and writers who had looked forward to the Revolution in anticipation of a new social order, that all their hopes had been fulfilled. A new social order there certainly was, and in its first years the revolutionary state proved itself a sponsor not only of social reform but also of artistic adventure and discovery. But after this first period of 'the great experiment' as it has been called, artists and musicians were obliged to abandon the free-ranging experimentation which elsewhere was to be the hallmark of the arts during the 20th century. After the firm establishment of Stalin in 1927, Russia was devoted to the programme of building Socialism in one country; artists were to contribute whole-heartedly to the objective by producing works which would inspire the people in their great endeavour. Writers, painters and even musicians were to choose heroic or worthy themes and to avoid abstruse and difficult techniques. It is not surprising that despite the magnificent music of Prokofiev and Shostakovich, no composer resident in the Soviet Union is known as a leader of the *avant-garde*, even though one of the greatest figures in 20th-century music, Igor Stravinsky, was Russian. However, the intensity and thoroughness of Russian musical education, combined with the large reservoir of talent her academies have to draw on, has enabled her to produce many of the world's finest instrumentalists.

The United States

For America, 1919 proved a turning point of an unexpected kind. Her industrialists had already launched a new epoch in the industrial revolution with mass production methods that were to have their first and most dramatic impact with the car – perhaps the greatest single agent of social change during the first half of the century.

In the early 1900s America was still in the throes of recovering from the aftermath of a civil war which, in its violence and exploitation of mechanical weapons, has

opposite
Linear Construction No. 2,
by Naum Gabo, 1949

367

been classed as the first conflict in the era of modern warfare. To civil war were added the disruptive effects of the new industrial technology and the vast immigrant populations which had fled across the Atlantic from the troubles of 19th-century Europe. Social anarchy, an intense political life and industrial innovation, all contributed to keep America concerned with her own affairs and isolated from the European world although, in view of her immense wealth, such isolation was becoming absurd. When the United States eventually entered the First World War it was under President Wilson's watchword of a war to make the world safe for democracy. The decisive financial and material aid that America brought to the demoralised Western powers gave her a major part in the Versailles settlement and in the founding of the world's first, if ill-fated, international body – the League of Nations. But America was unwilling to involve herself any further and, in a momentous vote, Congress refused to ratify the commitments which President Wilson had made on behalf of his country. A new age of American isolation had set in and for another twenty years, during which the ancient power of Russia was withdrawn and the greatest industrial power in the world was in voluntary retreat, the statesmen of Western Europe were able to regard themselves as the arbiters of the world.

Europe between the wars

The artificiality of the period was at first increased by the fact that, after her defeat and the humiliating terms of the Treaty of Versailles, Germany was no longer a factor in the equation of European politics. For a brief period, the ambitions of Mussolini to revive the glories of Rome could be taken seriously and the indecision of the democratic powers of France and England could, for a time, pass unnoticed.

In the United States the cry was for a return to 'normal', yet the period opened with the majestically naïve attempt to prohibit alcohol, and the twenties were in fact distinguished by social and political corruption on a vast scale, the virtual collapse of the rule of law and, of course, the Charleston. Europe too had hoped to sail forward on a sea of euphoria; 'the war to end war' was over, the defeated had been punished with swingeing penalties and the victors were ready to enjoy themselves. But in Germany the crushing load of reparations contributed to terrible inflation, while in Britain discontent and disillusion grew rapidly as the working man came to realise that the homes for heroes which the country had promised its victorious army were never going to materialise. Yet despite the breaking of the General Strike in 1926, disaster was to hit the country from quarters quite beyond its control. In 1929 the Wall Street Stock Exchange crashed, and if Europe's statesmen had perchance forgotten the realities of world power they were brutally forced to recognise them as the terrible backwash of the American collapse was felt throughout the world. Unemployment was general and horrible and the politicians seemed powerless to do anything about it. Not surprisingly many people in Western Europe, both among the workers and the intelligentsia, turned to Communism from a capitalist system which seemed to have destroyed itself.

Anger and despair at the conditions prevailing in Europe, as felt by the artists of the period, is reflected, for example, in the Dadaist rejection of all so-called civilised pretensions and the poignant bitterness of Picasso's painting *Guernica*. In music, the breakdown of the old European order had been presaged by the virtual collapse of the tonal system in the early work of Webern and Schoenberg, while the contrast between the opulent self-confidence of pre-war Europe and the distracted and impoverished world of the twenties is reflected even in the orchestral resources used. The days of the mammoth orchestras of the late Romantics were over, and composers came to favour smaller, often almost chambersize, ensembles.

Germany

The inter-war years were a story of poverty and humiliation, briefly illuminated by the Weimar Republic's eventual mastery of its immense problems, and terminating in the dark night of Nazi hysteria and barbarism. The immediate post-war sense of national humiliation was exploited by Hitler in the 1920s with his great lie of the 'stab in the back'. This claimed that Germany had been defeated not in the field, but by the Republican politicians to whom the military government had consigned affairs in the last months of the war. Hitler's brilliance as a propagandist is further demonstrated by the name of his Nationalist Socialist party, which combined the two most powerful forces in German politics. Yet despite this and the considerable financial backing he received from industry, Hitler never achieved an outright majority in the Reichstag before he came to power. After the failure of his attempted *coup d'état* at Munich, he determined to win power within the constitution and was eventually appointed chancellor through shrewd manipulation of the political situation in Berlin. Now began a regime that mesmerised, yet impressed, all Europe. Under Hitler, Germany showed an apparent sureness of purpose and a real strength that exposed the hesitations of the democracies and pointed out the weaknesses of Fascist Italy. Externally Hitler was all the time testing the resolution of Britain and France and preparing the military might of Germany.

Intervention on the side of the Falangist forces in the bloody and terrible Spanish Civil War gave the German military an ideal opportunity to flex its muscles. That war was perhaps the last conflict in which Europeans could feel that ideals were involved. At home Hitler directed his energies to confirming his grip on every aspect of German life. Like the Communists whom he hated so much, he took art very seriously indeed, recognising in the free expression of ideas the most dangerous enemy common to all totalitarian regimes. Like Russia too, Germany saw purges of the governing party, the setting up of an insidious and vicious secret police, the abrogation of the last safeguard of personal constitutional liberty, and the persecution of 'undesirable' elements. Even before the filthiness and horror of the wartime extermination of Jews and Slavs and other oppressed minorities, Germany already had a record of official anti-Semitism at least as long as the rule of the Nazi party, and many distinguished Jews in scholarship and the arts fled abroad, particularly to America. But they were not the only emigrés, since Hitler was also determined to stamp out all examples of 'degenerate' art, a term which embraced all the more *avant-garde* work and which drove many artists abroad.

The modern age

The Second World War was a bloody demonstration of the menace constituted by the power and pride of the nation-state, and by a simplistic ideology put across with all the resources of a modern communications industry.

Since the war the presence of the communicators has become all pervading; education, entertainment, commerce and advertising all multiply the variety and number of stimuli that, every day, beat upon modern man. Artists of all kinds are the creators of this storm of information, of visual and emotional stimuli, and they in turn are affected by the bewildering diversity of ideas and objectives that have arisen in this century to shake the already uncertain assumptions of the past. The theories presented by psychologists on the roots and nature of the human personality, the work of anthropologists in researching the social structure and the artistic world of remote cultures, the discoveries of physicists and physiologists on the nature of the material world and its perception by man, have all provided inspiration to film makers, dramatists, painters and sculptors, while the study of modern society itself by sociologists has pointed to new directions for architects. In a century where the sciences have come to dominate the thought-world, as well as to shape the environment, of society, musicians have inevitably been deeply

affected. For many *avant-garde* composers a knowledge of higher mathematics is an essential part of their technical equipment, for others a full understanding of electronics.

Although every age is tempted to regard itself as unique, it does seem as though the artists of this technological society are developing techniques which will effect a revolution in the very nature of man's perception of himself and the world around him. One of the leading geneticists has said that, within the foreseeable future, our understanding of the innermost secrets of the mechanism of the human intellect will be such that men will no longer be able to comprehend the message and intentions and assumptions lying behind the great achievements of man as an artist. Such a claim must at the moment appear as doubtful to the layman, but, despite the apparently chaotic and kaleidoscopic state of the *avant-garde* in the arts of today, it is clear that the artists themselves are exploring the world in revolutionary ways, and their works seem to demand from us new eyes and new ears if we are to understand them.

Expectation *by Richard Oelze,* *1936.*

Background to musical developments in the 20th century

To the average listener the most striking difference between 20th- and pre-20th-century music is that, whereas the latter is perceptibly an unbroken thread of development from style to style, the former seems suddenly and unaccountably to break with tradition and to seek a whole new definition of that much abused word, 'music'. This is a misconception yet it is also a root cause of the difficulty many sensitive people experience in coming to terms with modern music. The trouble is that most of us were brought up to an essentially 19th-century conception of music. We feel that it is primarily an expression of emotion; is essentially melodic; is bounded by classical form; is to be played by one or more of a limited range of (largely orchestral) instruments.

Such an attitude is narrow and suffocating. Its implication that all significant advances in musical history have been tied up with the refinement of melody is untrue. Further, it ignores the truism that our own century is the most tradition-conscious era in history. Indeed, in its freedom from a constricting traditional*ism*, it is substantially dependent on its increased awareness of its own ancestry, and this is as true in music as in anything. In fact, whereas past centuries have often been unaware of the precise nature of their debt to the past, our own has studied it, analysed it, and used it consciously to expand the language of art.

The background to 20th-century music stretches beyond the 19th century to the middle ages and extends not only to Europe but also to Africa, Asia and even Polynesia. Wagner and Liszt represent only one of several major sources of modern music. Of at least comparable importance was Debussy's revolutionary view of harmony, timbre and rhythm, which not only encouraged his successors to treat these elements with less solemnity, but inspired them to look beyond their immediate environment for stimulus; or Brahms's neo-classicism, which showed how supremely the past could enrich the present; or Mussorgsky's sensitivity to his environment, particularly speech patterns. Wagner's importance is that, as a result of changes precipitated by his work, music reached a crisis which had to be resolved consciously.

Crisis

Wagner's revolution was at bottom harmonic, but through harmony it struck at every element of music – melody, rhythm, form and, less directly, timbre. Harmony is defined by key, or tonality, that peculiar homing device which ensures, to take a simple example, that 'God save the Queen' ends on the note with which it started. In music of the 18th and 19th centuries, harmony takes its character from its relationship to the tonic chord of the home key, and in its turn it is harmony which enables that key to be changed, by a logical process known as modulation. In Baroque music tonality is essentially stable. The early classical composers – up to Haydn – use modulation more freely, though main sections still tend to be in one key, with modulation taking place at certain critical moments. In later music modulation increased still further and development sections, for example, where tonality is at its most fluid, became more extensive.

Wagner's music marks the climax of this movement. In parts of *Tristan and Isolde* (1859) modulation is so continuous that sense of key ceases to exist; it is significant that Wagner achieved this in opera, where form is partly determined by non-musical considerations. Tonality is so fundamental to classical form that no symphonic composer would willingly have embraced Wagner's innovations at that time. Brahms and Bruckner, the greatest contemporary symphonists, did so only superficially, while Liszt – a close disciple of Wagner – used extra-musical 'programmes' in his symphonic poems to 'plug the gap' left by tonality.

Melody, which may shape or be shaped by harmony, grew correspondingly more chromatic. Rhythm, which in classical music is to a large extent subject to the cadential feeling of key and modulation, was in danger of losing its definition altogether. To Wagner's successors these were terrible facts. For a time, in the music of Strauss, Mahler and Scriabin, among others, an uncomfortable equipoise was held between inspiration and total collapse. And then, at about the turn of the century, matters arrived at a crisis, in the person and work of a perhaps less spontaneously inspired genius, Schoenberg.

New departures

Arnold Schoenberg (1874-1951) is generally cast as the 'villain' of modern music, though in fact his development was logical and evolutionary, his cast of mind classical. His early works are thoroughly in the Wagner tradition – sprawling single-movement compositions in which tonality, though present, is increasingly uncertain, followed by a series of much finer pieces – the second quartet, *Erwartung*, *Pierrot Lunaire* and some songs. In these, tonality is gradually relinquished, and a precarious continuity is achieved either by the composer's mastery of counterpoint and variation, or – in the case of *Pierrot* – by abandoning large form in favour of clusters of complementary short movements. For the traditionally-minded Schoenberg this situation came dangerously close to anarchy, and for some years he worked at a compositional method which, without in any way retreating from the extreme pre-war position, would provide it with a more practical and rational basis.

Schoenberg's pre-war music, along with that of his

pupils, Alban Berg (1885-1935) and Anton Webern (1883-1945), descends directly from Wagner. So greatly, however, did Wagner dominate the horizon that a reaction was inevitable. In some outlying quarters the reaction had actually been going on for some years, for instance in the nationalist movements of Russia, Czechoslovakia and Scandinavia, but these were for the most part purely local manifestations, and the most powerful movement away from Wagner began in Paris.

By 1900 this movement was well under way, led by two very different musicians, Claude Debussy (1862-1918) and Erik Satie (1866-1925). Satie was a confirmed anti-Wagnerite from early in his career, and he implemented his dislike of Germanic bombast in general by writing his own music in a dry, economical style whose satirical aim is heavily underlined by facetious titles which almost too emphatically depreciate their creator's seriousness. Nevertheless Satie's influence was enormous. Without him the post-war music of the French Group, the 'Six', would have been radically different, and he was the first of many French composers to incorporate jazz and popular idioms in his music in an attempt to revitalise rhythm and melody.

Debussy, on the other hand, began as an admirer of Wagner and never entirely shed the influence from his music. Nevertheless, it was in a completely new direction that his own importance lay, that of tone-colour and texture. Like the French Impressionist and Pointillist painters and Symbolist poets, with whom he is often bracketed, Debussy was acutely sensitive to his materials – that is to the texture and sonority of music for their own sake – and much of his music, both for keyboard and for orchestra, is thought out exclusively in these terms. Of special importance was his use of harmonic sequences for their colouristic rather than tonal implications, and also his fondness for the whole-tone scale, which similarly has the effect of negating tonality. In both respects he was influenced by non-European (particularly Javanese) music.

In spite of these novel features Debussy's music remains predominantly tonal, in feeling if not in structure, which is why he was able to make continued use of classical form supported by a Lisztian fondness for poetic imagery. His treatment of tone colour, however, was to have far-reaching importance for a much later French *avant-garde*, as well as influencing his own younger contemporaries, notably Bartók. And the strong rhythmic energy of his later orchestral and piano works leads naturally into the ballet scores of Stravinsky and Ravel.

Towards the end of the 19th and in the early 20th century two aspects of nationalism began to assume greater importance in the search for viable alternative styles: the use of speech patterns to determine melodic shape, and the influence of true folk music. The use of folk song in art music was of course no new development, though hitherto it had invariably appeared as local colour, never as a functional aspect of style. For Vaughan Williams in England, Bartók and Kodály in Hungary, however, folk song was a central influence, and all three composers gathered authentic material by research in the field. The discovery of irregularities of folk rhythm and melody (including certain melodic intervals) which did not occur in Western art music had a crucial effect on, in particular, the style of Béla Bartók (1881-1945), which became much tougher and acquired a new, almost Expressionist intensity under the tortured spell of the folk modes. In his mature work Bartók remained responsive to outside stimuli, and his music reflects many of the trends in European music up to the Second World War – Schoenbergian Expressionism, the harsh polytonality of the 1920s, and a mellower Neo-classicism in the 1930s. Yet his individuality is never in question, and he stands unquestionably as one of the major creative figures of the century.

The other main aspect of nationalism, speech patterns, could strictly apply only to vocal music, but the attitude which accompanied it was important. In Mussorgsky, for instance, speech patterns meant realism – a truth to life rather than Romantic fantasy – and it was this quality which attracted the Czech composer Leoš Janáček (1854-1928), and for a time Igor Stravinsky. Stravinsky's main pre-war scores are the ballets he wrote for Diaghilev's company in Paris, in which the dominant influence is still that of his teacher, Rimsky-Korsakov. But these scores also reveal a power of rhythm and an almost Debussian feeling for the colouristic values of (in this case largely dissonant) harmony quite alien to the exotic, 'picture-postcard' music of Rimsky-Korsakov. It is therefore no surprise that the influence of Mussorgsky and of peasant realism finally takes over in the ballet *Les Noces*, written during the war, a score which in its austere economy of means and brilliant, hard-edged instrumentation (for four pianos and percussion) must rank among the great revolutionary works of all time. For Stravinsky it pointed the way forward. His other wartime works all make a virtue of necessity in their chamber-music scoring, and the hard, clear outlines this produces lead directly into the Neo-classical period of the twenties.

The return to classicism

Before the 1914-18 war music was struggling to free itself from outdated conventions, but without any sure sense of what alternative direction to take. The war, itself a logical outcome of forces similar in type to those which affected the arts, altered European society radically. The violence of the upheaval made it unthinkable for a serious artist to go on writing as he had done in 1914, and it is therefore hardly surprising that the various idioms that emerged in the twenties had little of the spontaneity which had characterised musical style for upwards of 200 years.

Above all, the war placed in perspective the inflated gestures of late Romanticism, which now seemed indulgent and over-confident, and it was as a reaction against such music that Neo-classicism quickly gained a footing. Traditionally, the first Neo-classical score is Stravinsky's *Pulcinella*, a ballet based on music by the 18th-century Neapolitan composer, Pergolesi. However, a number of earlier examples can be traced – in the piano suites of Debussy and Ravel (especially the latter's *Le Tombeau de Couperin* of 1917), in Prokofiev's *Classical Symphony* (1916), and in the pastiches of the German Italian, Ferruccio Busoni (1866-1924), who was the first to propose a return to classical styles as an alternative to the grandiloquence of late Romanticism. At various times Stravinsky drew upon Bach, Gesualdo, even Tchaikovsky. His finest Neo-classical works, however, are those which suggest a more generalised approach, or even, like *Oedipus Rex* or the *Symphony in Three Movements*, profit from the lesson of Neo-classicism without harnessing any recognisably classical style.

Although Stravinsky stands alone in the extent and mastery of his Neo-classical output, a number of other composers were profoundly influenced by the movement. Bartók's later works, for instance, are mellower and fresher as a result of the classical wind which blows through them, while the leading French composers of the period, Ravel and Roussel, both profited from this new intellectual stimulus. Not even Schoenberg was unaffected, though the leading German exponent was Paul Hindemith (1895-1963). Hindemith's classicism was more doctrinaire than Stravinsky's and extended beyond musical style to the very practice of composition;

here his attitude was essentially that of a Bach or a Haydn, the attitude of the craftsman contrasting strongly with the self-conscious inspiration of the 19th century.

If Hindemith represents the serious side of the reaction, an altogether more flippant and outrageous approach was that of the Parisian group, the Six, and of certain other composers domiciled in Paris, including Prokofiev and occasionally even Stravinsky. Like Satie, the Six took their stand not only against Romantic gestures but against all pomposity and pretentiousness in art, and their music, though influenced by an academic kind of Neo-classicism, also makes studied use of jazz and popular idioms in its (frequently desperate) attempts to sound inconsequential. Their main weapon, however, was the discord, which they used not as a logical extension of harmony but as a deliberate shock-tactic, resulting in a brusque, unsympathetic style sometimes described as polytonality. Polytonal music is, of course, any music in which more than one key is in operation at a time (in Ravel's duo for violin and cello, for instance, the two parts are for a time written with different key signatures). With the Six, however, noise value is often more apparent than logic, and the result often sounds dated and unmotivated.

Their use of jazz and popular idioms was more significant. Jazz was the new experience of the twenties, and in the temper of that decade it is not surprising that many composers, from Stravinsky to Ravel, Milhaud to Hindemith, found themselves fascinated by its piquant rhythms and harmonies. Popular music, the music of Irving Berlin and George Gershwin, also came from America to tantalise composers like Weill and Krenek, who sought to convey the aimless decadence of Germany in the 1920s. The influence of Mahler and of Berg's *Wozzeck* is also apparent in the operas which Weill wrote in collaboration with Brecht. It is striking, all the same, that while the jazz idiom turns up repeatedly in the serious music of this period, its whole aesthetic point, that of improvisation, is ignored.

Two other short-lived movements of these years deserve mention before we pass on to a consideration of serial technique: microtonalism and the so-called *bruitismo* of the Futurists. The use of intervals smaller than a semitone had, of course, ample precedent in non-European (particularly oriental) music and in the folk music of Central Europe. Yet, curiously, its impact on Western European music was slight, despite the conscientious advocacy of the Mexican composer, Carrillo, and the Czech, Alois Hába, both of whom saw in it the extension of language sought at this time by all serious composers. The Futurists, less scholarly though more practical, had even before the war extended the boundaries of music to include noise, particularly the machine-age noise of automobiles, aeroplanes and armaments, though the musical value of their work seems to have been small. Of much greater importance was the Parisian Edgar Varèse (1885-1965), who emigrated to the United States in 1916 and found there an industrially developed but musically backward society which offered unique opportunities for the progressive composer. Varèse worked at first under the influence of Debussy, though impressed rather by his fellow-countryman's general attitude to sonority than by his sensibility, which was in every respect more refined than his own. Varèse's music is thoroughly in the spirit of a machine society, and directly evokes its sounds and atmosphere, while at the same time anticipating the abstract freedom of sonority which only electronic music could provide.

The furthest-reaching of the new idioms, however, was, significantly, Schoenberg's serial technique: significantly because it was the only one to have developed logically rather than as a reaction. For Schoenberg its logical connection with his pre-war works was of critical importance. In late Romantic music, whether by Strauss,

Berg, Reger or Schoenberg himself, themes built from the twelve notes of the chromatic octave occur quite frequently, not on any rational basis but simply because the blurring of tonality naturally tends to give the twelve notes equal importance. It was this which provided the foundation for serialism, though it took Schoenberg almost eight years to relate the two, during which time he preserved a rigid silence.

The discovery of the twelve-note method, and its appearance in Schoenberg's music in 1923, mark a turning-point in music, though it was many years before the method gained wide acceptance. Two circumstances account for the delay. On the one hand, there was the peculiarly intense, devotional atmosphere surrounding Schoenberg and his two main disciples, Berg and Webern, none of whom had the slightest idea of publicising their art, nor of compromising it to meet popular taste halfway. On the other, there was the striking fact that two at least of these three (Schoenberg and Berg) applied the technique in a consciously restricted way which made it harder for lay audiences to perceive that new listening habits were needed for its full appreciation. For Schoenberg serialism was associated solely with pitch, while the form and rhythm of his music remain essentially classical. Berg's music shows a still more marked compromise with 19th-century procedures – a 'tonal nostalgia' which led him to construct his note-rows in such a way as to permit the use of tonal harmony.

Webern's music, by contrast, is thorough in its exploitation of the new technique. Unlike those of his colleagues, his pre-serial works are marked by an extreme conciseness of form and a logic of thought which lead naturally into his first twelve-note scores. But in addition he shows an interest in colour and duration (i.e. rhythm) which in the main they do not show, and his output thus tends to develop consistently in all its parts, in contrast to Schoenberg's, which sometimes seems to forge ahead in spite of itself. Webern's music was to become of extreme interest to the post-Second World War generation. Its highly charged brevity of form and its use of instrumental colour as an organic part of the music both appealed to later composers. But perhaps still more influential was his individual approach to dodecaphony itself, in particular his fondness for logically constructed note-rows whose internal relationships are calculated down to the last detail. The work of the pioneer twelve-note composers is considered more fully in the chapter on the Viennese school and it need only be emphasised here how significant Webern's intuitively logical approach to his art was.

Serialism

The work which did more than any other single composition to advance the extension of serial technique, which owed so much to Webern, was Olivier Messiaen's *Quatre études de rhythmes* for solo piano. Yet Messiaen's music as a whole has nothing to do with serialism. Its sources are the harmonic-sound technique of Debussy, and a profound, almost mystical Roman Catholicism, expressed in a manner also characteristic of Indian (specifically Hindu) music and, latterly, in the intensive use of bird-song, which, for Messiaen, symbolises the transcendental religious quality. Since the war Messiaen's influence has been twofold. As a teacher in Paris he produced, almost single-handed, the leading *avant-garde* composers of the post-war years. As a composer his mastery of numerical rhythmic techniques (which for him possess a clear mystical symbolism), combined with the striking originality of his music, has had a profound effect on composers of many styles and nationalities, not all of them members of the *avant-garde*.

Nevertheless, the main outcome of his influence has been that most esoteric of all 20th-century techniques, total serialism. In the third étude, which is called *Modes de valeur et d'intensités*, serialisation takes place in rhythmic durations and dynamic intensities as well as the usual pitch elements, and although Messiaen uses these procedures in a highly personal and specialised way related to the 'modes of limited transposition' which occur elsewhere in his music, they were seized on by his pupils as a ready solution to the problems of language which followed the Second World War as they had the First. The combined influence of Webern and Messiaen was irresistible for these composers, dominated by the Frenchman Pierre Boulez (b. 1925) and the German Karlheinz Stockhausen (b. 1928).

For both these composers the writing of totally serial music was to prove only a phase in a larger development. In the uncertain European society left by the war a totally ordered art had obvious attractions. However it soon became apparent that since total serialism meant also total freedom of possibility it could no longer be felt that its organisation had much artistic meaning: in other words, the more thoroughly organised music became, the more chaotic and *un*ordered it tended to sound in performance. As a result both Boulez and Stockhausen retired from their extreme serialist position and both composers began to admit the element of chance into their music, while Stockhausen, whose serial works had led him naturally into the new electronic media, was able to combine electronics with chance, or aleatory, principles through the agency of live modulation of performed music.

The laws of chance . . .

Aleatory music was by no means new. Indeed, quite apart from the omnipresent factor of interpretation, chance had been playing a part in serious music since the American composer Charles Ives (1874-1954) had experimented with polyrhythm and polycounterpoint in the early years of the century, and in jazz for almost as long. Ives's philosophy, as expressed in his apparently chaotic but in reality precisely imagined works, derived from the Emersonian theory of Transcendentalism, the immanence of God in the human environment. Any musical material, from whatever source, was grist to Ives's mill and was frequently juxtaposed in quite unexpected ways to produce a thrilling sense of vitality and immediacy, coupled now and then with a haunting – almost Debussian – Impressionism.

Ives's methods had a profound effect on those of his successors who were able to hear performances of his music, and in particular they underlie the aleatory principles propounded in the forties by the Schoenberg pupil, John Cage. A student of Zen Buddhism, Cage gradually moved farther and farther from the principle of art as a function of the will, substituting chance as the vital element in musical experience. His works introduce such factors as the throw of a dice, or notes arranged according to the imperfections in a piece of manuscript paper, and even more than Ives does he admit extraneous sounds as component parts of his music. Audience participation or noise from quite irrelevant sources are accepted, and he has also used live electronic modulation – of both musical and non-musical sounds – as an integral part of an output which has become increasingly difficult to define in terms of 'composed' works.

In general, Cage's ideas have generally been more influential than his music, but in any event few European composers have been prepared to accept so extreme a

position in their own works. The aleatorism of Boulez, Stockhausen, Luciano Berio or Witold Lutosławski remains that of a mind unwilling completely to abdicate control of its material though interested in the structural fluidity and shifting textures which the element of chance introduces.

. . . and electronics

As originally developed, electronic and taped music represented a position diametrically opposed to that of Cage, its function being to enable a work, as heard, to be in all respects according to the precise wishes of its composer – even to the extent of removing conventional limitations of sonority imposed by traditional instruments. The first tape composition was made at the French Radio studios by Pierre Schaeffer in 1948, his technique being that of *musique concrète*: the manipulation, that is, of pre-recorded everyday sound (*objects sonores*) to create an original work of art. Some six years later the development of sine-wave generators at Cologne enabled the first concert to take place of music in which every sound was electronically synthesised.

In both techniques a problem soon appeared which may not previously have occurred to their exponents: how to keep an audience's undivided attention without any visible apparatus of performance. Despite the enormously expanded range of sounds, the problem was a real one. Two possible solutions have since emerged. First, the combination of taped sounds with music to be performed live (e.g. Stockhausen's *Contacts*). Second, and perhaps more fertile ground for the future, the use of electronic modulators to collect live performed sounds and transform them in conjunction with filters, generators, potentiometers, and so forth. In this field too Stockhausen has maintained his creative lead over all rivals, and has, virtually single-handed, brought about a rapprochement which would at one time have seemed unthinkable – the alignment of techniques associated with total serialism and those which by their nature involve chance or improvisation.

Conclusion

The extreme complexity of some modern music, coupled with the pretentious solemnity with which many of its lesser exponents continue to regard themselves, has done much harm to the image of art as an expression of contemporary thought. Confronted with an average present-day programme-note the ordinary listener might be forgiven for assuming that the music is too 'difficult'. Boulez's music is 'difficult', by any standards; that of Stockhausen, Berio and the present-day Polish composers for whom texture has become an autonomous medium of expression, is often far from difficult, while that of the computer composer, Yannis Xenakis, is often so direct as to appeal more on first than on subsequent hearings.

But if the excessive intellectualisation of *avant-garde* music has occasionally seemed wearisome, it has had the concealed, and salutary, effect of bringing informed popular taste into line with the principal middle-of-the-road composers, who occupy a position which was itself once something of a challenge to lay audiences. Stravinsky's conversion to serialism in the 1950s, for instance, far from realigning him with the *avant-garde*, helped popularise serial music – including that of Webern – in a way which would once upon a time have seemed hopelessly improbable. Similarly, the German dodecaphonist Hans Werner Henze (b. 1926) has fou d himself documented as a latter-day Romantic, though in fact his music is frequently far more demanding and complex than that of a swarm of avant-gardists. In England several leading composers have made profitable use of medieval techniques in rhythm and counterpoint; to a composer like Peter Maxwell Davies (b. 1934), for example, the influence of post-war Stravinsky was crucial in overcoming the modern tendency to Romanticise medievalism.

Meanwhile, such composers as Britten and Shostakovich, who have composed major and highly individual scores in essentially tonal idioms, are all too readily dismissed for failing to take a more extreme stand. Their music is a clear symptom of what many regard as the chronic artistic malady of our time, the increasing distance which divides contemporary music from the layman, a distance which is in fact bridged by a range of styles greater than at any previous time in history. Why this should be thought a malady is not immediately apparent, unless it be that people do not like to feel that there is anything of value in circulation which they themselves cannot comprehend. Art has always contained an element of challenge, and it may be argued that the real malady of our time lies in the widespread reluctance of the ordinary music-lover to extend his senses and intellect beyond the all too accessible territories of the known and familiar.

Certainly there are signs of such an illness in the commercial exploitation of music, almost invariably couched in sub-Romantic idioms whose psychological impact depends entirely on the seriousness with which such styles are treated by the listener. The worst manifestations of this phenomenon, the advertising jingle and the piped music by which restaurants, self-service stores and airlines suborn the public will, are musically beneath contempt, as indeed they should be socially.

Of far greater interest, both artistically and sociologically, are two genres of longer-standing respectability, the incidental film score and commercial pop music – itself largely the creation of the most important of all new media, the gramophone. Film music has been dignified, since the turn of the century, by the contributions of leading serious composers – including such distinguished figures as Saint-Saëns, Milhaud, Prokofiev, Britten, Walton, Copland, Vaughan Williams, Cage and Leonard Bernstein – though these are the high points of what remains a largely murky and featureless landscape.

In the 1960s pop music pulled itself up by its bootstraps to fulfil a true 'popular' role in relation to advanced serious music, many of whose techniques it has explored imaginatively and fruitfully. And yet even here the old malady recurs, for how else can one describe the increasing tendency of serious musicians to discuss pop music as though it were now the most significant musical art of the day? Such an attitude seems more a gesture of despair as to the value of authentic art works than a valid assessment of pop music itself.

STEPHEN WALSH

An early recording session.

The instruments of music in the 20th century

A prominent feature of music during this century has been the increasing interest shown by composers in new tone colours and unusual instrumental timbres. What we may call the conventional instruments of the orchestra, combined by 19th-century composers with the general intention of producing a fundamentally homogeneous texture of sound, have been exploited increasingly for effects of contrast. Instrumental combinations once regarded as harsh and strident have been purposely employed to give piquancy and brilliance to the overall effect. In the general search for new sounds composers have not only redeployed the forces of the Romantic orchestra, but have also investigated completely different areas both old and almost futuristically modern.

Ever since Arnold Dolmetsch began his pioneering work into the revival of instruments of the pre-classical period, research has gone on with an ever-increasing momentum. Thus, it is now possible to hear performances of medieval music on the instruments for which it was written, played by musicians dedicated to authentic techniques and a lively, musical execution. In 1969, for example, the London Promenade concerts included a programme in which a work by Olivier Messiaen could be heard in company with medieval and Renaissance music performed by Musica Reservata, one of Europe's leading ensembles in the field of old music. Like many of his colleagues Messiaen has been actively interested in the procedures of medieval composers, while other 20th-century composers, such as the Swiss Frank Martin, have written works specifically for the harpsichord and other early instruments.

The widening of the range of the orchestral palette has not been simply a matter of the revival of early instruments or the invention of new electronic instruments to be discussed below. There has also been a considerable extension, particularly in the percussion department, by the adaptation of many instruments from popular, folk and 'primitive' musical traditions. The 'battery' of drums used by the jazz percussionist is familiar but instruments such as the tenor drum, the snare drum and the cymbals have been increasingly usual in the concert hall since the last years of the 19th century, while such instruments as the wood block and rattles of various types have added to the scope of the untuned section of the percussion. Among the tuned instruments in this department the most important is the kettledrum. A regular member of the orchestra since the 18th century, its versatility was greatly enhanced in this century with the invention of efficient pedal-operated mechanisms that enabled the player to change the pitch of the drumhead at speed. The glissando is now available to the drummer and in one famous example of its use, Bartók's *Music for Strings, Percussion and Celeste*, the effect is fully vindicated. But in addition to the kettledrums there are a number of fixed note instruments, such as the xylophone, marimba and vibraphone, derived ultimately from African and Indonesian examples, that are now often used by composers of 'serious' music as well as by jazz musicians.

In some cases the mechanisms of the percussion have been possible only because of the improved technology

The fine modernistic case of the municipal organ of the German town of Rohrweiller.

of the last century. No instrument has been subjected to greater technical modifications than the organ, although in some respects these changes might be better described as a return to past styles and as a part of the movement towards the tone colours of the pre-classical age. In the 19th century the qualities of brilliance, contrast and balance that were such an important feature of the Baroque organ used by Bach were abandoned. The sharp tones of the mixture stops and the incisive colour of the reeds were abandoned in favour of more rounded tones, while balance between the various sections of the organ became less important than the capacity to render gradually modulated transitions from loud to soft volume or from one group of tone colours to another. The Romantic organ was in fact designed to emulate as far as possible the qualities admired in the 19th-century orchestra. There was nothing new in the principle. As early as the 17th century organ builders had named the pipes from the wind instruments then common, and some early organs provide valuable clues to the tone qualities expected from these instruments.

With its carefully graduated stops, which made possible the slow build-up of massive crescendos or the most subtle contrast of tone colours, the Romantic organ was an extremely expressive instrument and in the hands of builders such as Cavaillé-Coll of Paris was a magnificent vehicle for the comparatively small number of works, by Liszt, Franck and others, written for the instrument during the Romantic period. However, the tendency to build massive instruments, capable of everything but fit for nothing, gathered strength until, in the early decades of the present century, organs with as many as seven manuals and two hundred ranks of pipes became a matter of pride to their owners.

The general interest in earlier types of instrumental colour was reflected in organ building as early as 1921, when the German firm of Walcker produced the so-called Praetorius organ. Since that time more and more early Baroque and Renaissance instruments have been pressed into service for the recording of early music, while many new organs are now designed with complete Baroque sections.

As interest in early music and its instruments extends and deepens, so the specifications of the new generation of instrument makers become ever more exact; it is now possible to buy excellent modern viols, harpsichords, clavichords, shawms, crumhorns and many other types. Some of the finest makers are working in Germany, both East and West, and the United States, while in England too, lutes and early keyboard instruments are produced.

The pre-classical instrument that has enjoyed the most widespread popularity is undoubtedly the 18th-century recorder. It is used extensively in schools, while at the professional level a new generation of virtuosi, like John Sothcott in England, is revealing the considerable possibilities of the recorder both in its 18th-century and Renaissance styles. The nature and capacities of these early instruments have been described in earlier chapters of this book; here we can only draw attention to the extent and thoroughness of their revival in the modern age. More relevant in a chapter on 20th-century instruments is a study of some of the developments in the application of electronic techniques to music.

Music and electronics

The impact of electronics on music has, on the broadest front, produced what is a revolution in the range of music available to the listener, in his attitude to it and in the structure of the musical establishment in many countries. With the application of the methods of mass production to the long-playing record and the radio, music itself has become an article of mass consumption to which the listener and even the 'music lover' has a passive or even inattentive attitude. In the course of this survey we have seen how, at all stages of man's cultural evolution, music had held a central place. In this sense the modern age is no different from any other. The difference, perhaps, lies in the fact that, without the physical presence of the performer, the music itself is liable to lose its hold on the audience and to fall in their respect. Furthermore, of course, with first-rate performances easily available, the amateur music lover has lost interest in making his own music. That people by and large are not satisfied with this state of affairs is indicated by the popularity of the guitar and other comparatively simple means of music making.

Finally, in this brief review of the electronic revolution in music, we must emphasise the importance of a mass audience on the economics of the world of professional music. Thanks both to the recording fees from the large record companies and, above all, to the enlightened patronage of such bodies as the British Broadcasting Corporation (up to 1970) and the Australian Broadcasting Commission, the musical experience available to large populations has been immensely broadened.

Historically, however, it was in the field of instrument manufacture that the science of electronics first made its appearance in music. Since 1925, with the perfecting of the electronic valve, research into its musical applications has been constantly pursued – in the first place to discover totally new sonorities, in the second to reproduce electrically the tone colours of existing instruments.

The vibraphone derives its highly characteristic tone from the vibrato effect caused by revolving fans set at the top of the tubular resonators and turned by an electric motor.

Electronic instruments

Among the numerous experiments dating from the 1920s, the most brilliant was the *ondes musicales* invented by Maurice Martenot and generally known as Ondes Martenot. But, apart from isolated examples such as

above left
The Ondes Martenot, one of the first and still among the most successful of electronic instruments.

left
Percussion instruments of all kinds have become more and more common in 20th-century orchestral music; a 'battery' of drums and cymbals such as that illustrated here is typical of many jazz bands.

this, many of the instruments invented at this period have fallen into oblivion. Of lasting value, rather, was the contribution that such research made to the clarification of the problems surrounding the production of electronic instruments. Apart from Martenot in France the main work was done by Germans, and the festivals of this 'new music' at Darmstadt and Donaueschingen were rendered the more startling by the frequently astonishing appearance of such instruments as the Mixture Trautonium of Oscar Sala, the oscillator invented by the Russian-born Leon Theremin and the Sphärophon of Jörg Mager, who was primarily interested in the pure rendering of micro-intervals.

In the later 1930s, further advances in technology led to the production of electronic instruments that attempted to reproduce traditional sonorities. From 1936 various models of electronic organs, cheaper than the pipe organ though not as yet an effective replacement for it, competed on the market. Of these the most famous is that produced by the American Hammond Organ Company.

The task of reproducing the exact sounds of traditional instruments proved more difficult than expected, but in the late 1940s the technicians of the American R.C.A. company, grouped around Olson, developed a gigantic machine capable of duplicating, with some accuracy, any required tone colour of the conventional orchestra. But neither it, nor a more advanced device developed by the engineers of Siemens of Germany in 1956, reached any degree of perfection.

Besides these grave drawbacks, a large number of technical experts were needed to run such machines and hopes of an electronic device which would replace the traditional instrument proved illusory. Nevertheless, electronics did effect a fundamental transformation of attitudes among the *avant-garde*; performers, composers and listeners alike entered a new field of experiment.

The base of the revolution lay in a new understanding of acoustics. By electronic means it was possible to produce 'pure' sound, that is sound free from overtones or harmonics, the essential distinguishing features of traditional instruments. From this it gradually became apparent that classic theories of the acoustics of vibrating strings and sounding pipes, when studied in static conditions, relate to a theoretical context as far removed from reality as plane geometry is from nature. The crucial significance of the transitory conditions of reality, as opposed to the stationary conditions of abstract theory, came to be realised, and the classic theories themselves came to be questioned. The frequent divergence between hoped for objectives and actual results, common enough in scientific research in general, provided experimental composers with a new and liberating outlook.

Increasingly, from the 1950s, composers have interested themselves in the business of the editing and mixing studios of the recording companies, and some have made this their special study. In the same period the perfection of the magnetic tape as a means of mass recording has provided them with yet another technique to master, though the first experiments of men like Pierre Schaeffer used earlier transcription methods.

From 1949 Schaeffer became head of a team in an experimental studio provided by O.R.T.F., the French broadcasting corporation. Sound engineers rather than composers were the elite of the enterprise, inventing new apparatus to allow the composer the fullest freedom in recording whatever sound material he wished, whether from the physical world or from the electronic generator. Since those early days most of the major broadcasting bodies in Europe, America and Japan have established experimental studios and at least one, the B.B.C. Radiophonic Workshop, has achieved a 'hit' with the theme music to the science-fiction television series, *Dr Who*.

In Germany in the 1950s, composers such as Herbert Eimert and Karlheinz Stockhausen struck out in a new direction. Whereas the French school under Schaeffer had been fascinated by the richness and diversity offered by the new medium, the Germans concentrated rather on the precise ordering of pre-selected sonorous elements. In Paris the term '*musique concrète*' was coined, thus emphasising that the variegated palette of sound produced by the composer-engineer had its origins in noises produced in the physical world which were then manipulated and transformed in the studio. In Cologne, where the objective was formal organisation and the limiting of the range of tone colour to controllable electrophonically produced noises, the term 'electronic music' was used. This term, taken up by the famous Studio di Phonologia of Milan, subsequently became virtually universal in Europe, while in the United States some experimenters adopted the term 'music for tape'.

In all these types of experimental music, where research and experimentation were ultimately more important than the works that resulted, the method of procedure is basically similar. The work is prepared on the tape and the role of the interpretative artist, where it exists, is relegated to that of a 'push-button' operator, balancing more or less the volumes of sound in the concert hall. Since the mid-1960s the interpreter has made something of a comeback, as often as not in the person of the composer himself, and in works of 'live' electronic music in the forefront of the *avant-garde* the operator of the equipment has, apparently, a real function in the concert hall.

Pierre Schaeffer, one of the leading pioneers of musique concrète *in the studios of French radio in the post-war period.*

Into the future

From investigating and using the possibilities of electronic equipment for the production and assembling of entirely new kinds of sound and their rigorous organisation, composers have moved on to using computers for the process of composition itself. Among the pioneers in America were L. A. Hiller Jr. and L. M. Isaacson, using an Illiac computer at the University of Illinois, while in Europe the Greek-born Yannis Xenakis has been one of the leaders. In this kind of work the creative act of the composer consists in devising a computer programme into which he may build features allowing for random effects; indeed, under the impetus of the kind of experimentation described in this chapter, the element of chance has become of increasing interest to *avant-garde* composers. Thus today, as in the whole history of music, the instruments available to the composer have not only served his intention but also fed back into his work possibilities for further investigation.

We can be sure that experimentation in the production of prepared sounds has not stopped. Equally, there is little doubt that unless some profound and fundamental transformation of the human psyche redirects man's whole outlook on the sensory world, the great music of the past will continue to provide an irreplaceable and sustaining part of his spiritual life. It is an occupational hazard of the experimenter to be derided and an occupational temptation for him to play the charlatan on occasion, but we, as the audience, confused by the blanket application of the word 'music', shut out a world of new experience if we expect from the electronic studio the same kind of procedures as we hear in a familiar symphony.

Unless, through the process of technological evolution, we come to regard the direction of past human cultural effort as ending in a puzzling cul-de-sac (and the possibility of even this has been hinted at by a leading molecular biologist), the works of men such as Beethoven or Mozart will remain firmly entrenched on the heights of musical achievement. The new music made possible by the instruments and procedures described here will not be less, or more, valid – it will be different. It has been said that in a few years' time, our understanding of the reactions of the central nervous system will have advanced so far that it will be possible to produce 'functional' music predetermined according to parameters defined by the laws of sociology and human behaviour. Knowledge of sensory systems will permit the diffusion of this music by direct application of electric stimuli. The musical element will be established by an electronic synthesiser fed with a score in the form of a computer programme. The 'instruments of music' will have become a clinical electrode applied to the forearm.

It is also said that the science-fiction of the present is the reality of the future. Nevertheless, those who enjoy the violin as well as the oscillator face that future with some confidence, convinced that the administrators of its 'sociological laws' will probably be as inept as their ancestors. It may also prove in the final analysis that, however we establish contact with it, the central nervous system of Johann Sebastian Bach was, in fact, up to par.

The interest in the revival of early tone colours has led to the building of a number of organs with complete Baroque registrations as part of their pipe work. This elaborate modern console, with its numerous stops and combinations, allows the player to command a full range of tone colour for music of all periods.

The school of Vienna

During the first twenty years of the 20th century, the three composers treated in this chapter, Schoenberg, Berg and Webern, produced music which was to mark them out as revolutionaries and was to affect the course of Western music in one way or another down to our own day. They are commonly grouped together under some such heading as the twelve-note school but it must be emphasised that, although all three certainly used this technique, it was not fully worked out until towards 1920. Schoenberg was the leader and teacher but, before the twelve-note thesis was completely worked out, his young pupil Anton von Webern wrote a number of compositions characterised by an unparalleled conciseness of form and lucidity of instrumentation that remained virtually unknown until the late 1940s but then deeply influenced the younger generation of composers. Alban Berg, though no less of a musician than his two colleagues, has had less influence on other composers, though a masterpiece such as the opera *Wozzeck* assures his place among the greatest figures of music.

The composers of the modern school of Vienna like those of the classical school, certainly form a well-defined group with shared aims, but their inspiration and achievements were quite different from, and their music as individual as those of their great predecessors, Haydn, Mozart and Beethoven.

Programme for a concert in 1932 of the music of Schoenberg, Berg and Mahler, conducted by Webern.

Schoenberg

With Debussy and Stravinsky, Schoenberg was one of the great musicians responsible for the precipitate evolution which was to change the face of European music at the beginning of the 20th century. His early works, up to about the year 1907, are strongly tinged with Romanticism in the idiom of Wagner, Brahms and Mahler, though he pushes still further their use of chromatic harmonies, while still making use of key signatures. By degrees, however, these disappear from his work, as his music progresses from athematic to radically atonal compositions, Finally, in the year 1912, when Schoenberg was thirty-eight, all pretence of key is abandoned.

Arnold Schoenberg (1874-1951) was born of Jewish parents in Vienna. His father was a prosperous shopkeeper and his mother gave piano lessons. He gave early indications of his musical talent, writing his first compositions when he was seventeen. Although he took some lessons in counterpoint from the Polish-born conductor and composer Alexander von Zemlinsky, his future brother-in-law who was only two years his senior, he was virtually self-taught. His beginnings were difficult and he was obliged to support himself by hack work, orchestrating the light operettas of other composers. In 1901 he was in Berlin as conductor of the Buntes Theater, and while there received the Liszt prize at the instigation of Richard Strauss. But in 1903 he returned to Vienna to teach.

During eight years in Vienna, as a conductor as well as teacher, he became the friend of Mahler and attracted Berg and Webern into his circle of pupils. In 1911 Strauss provided him with the opportunity of returning to Berlin as teacher of composition at the Stern conservatory. In 1912 his *Pierrot Lunaire*, for 'speech-song', piano and flute, finally drew public attention to his work. But his creative activities were interrupted for some ten years, first by his theoretical researches and secondly by his service (1914-17) in the First World War. In 1921 he broke his long silence and published his *Twelve Note System of Composition* which is also illustrated with examples of his own works. In 1925 he was appointed professor of composition at the Academy of Arts in Berlin, in succession to Busoni. Henceforth his influence extended over all Europe.

When the Nazis came to power he left Germany. He took refuge for a while in Spain, then in Paris, where his presence remained unnoticed. He had become a convert to Roman Catholicism, but in 1933 he reverted to his original faith as a mark of solidarity with the Jewish victims of Hitler's persecution. In 1934 he travelled to the United States where he was successively professor at the Malkin Conservatory of Boston and then director of the department of music at the University of California, Los Angeles (1936-44). The end of his life was marked by financial difficulties, and work became more and more arduous for him due to his delicate health and failing eyesight. He died in Los Angeles in 1951.

The twelve-note system and the serial method

The twelve-note system is a method of composition based on a particular use of the twelve notes of the chromatic scale. This system, which reverses all established and traditional 'rules' is not, however, merely fortuitous, nor spontaneously created; on the contrary, it was a carefully considered and formulated principle, a direct issue of past musical forms.

Schoenberg is quite properly regarded as the artistic originator of the system and its founding exponent. Nevertheless, it has now become generally acknowledged that the independent researches in the field by another Viennese composer, Joseph Matthias Hauer (1883-1959), antedate Schoenberg by a few years. But Hauer, who developed his theories by an analogy from Goethe's theory on the nature of light, never extended his work into the practical field, all his music being late Romantic in mood.

The chromatic scale is composed of twelve notes separated by intervals of a semitone and is elusive from the point of view of classical tonality, being quite neutral and implying neither one key nor another. Wagner, and after him Mahler, had progressively enriched their harmonic palettes by making use of notes from the whole of the chromatic scale at will, though still retaining the ideal framework of a given key. Schoenberg was to take this to a logical conclusion, using the chromatic scale in itself as the basic compositional element, without regard to key. The diatonic scale of tones and semitones, and all ideas of tonality that it implied, was deposed from the ruling place that it had long held in Western art music. Furthermore, the twelve notes of the chromatic scale became entirely autonomous and had no function except their own individual sound; they no longer had the superior or subordinate qualities they held in the old system—such as dominant, tonic, leading note—and the old rules of harmony and melody no longer applied. We are in the presence of a dodecaphonic atonality, a statement of fact, which, though novel, is still unformulated and negative. This new state of 'democratic' equality among the notes of the musical scale made Schoenberg's work from about 1907 to about 1912 truly atonal, though it was as yet not subject to theoretical rigour. This was the first phase of the Schoenberg reform.

The second phase was to organise this new atonal system and to bring order out of chaos. The basis of the new structure was called the note row, or *Tonreihe* in German. The 'series' is the kernel of a twelve-note composition, whether it is merely one sheet of piano music or a five-act opera. To form the series, the twelve notes of the semitone scale are arranged by the composer in a determined sequence in which each note appears only once, though at any pitch. This sequence, which may be stated at the opening of the music, determines the interrelations of the notes throughout the piece of music. The row, or fragments of it, can appear in an inverted form, or can be given forwards or backwards with the notes at different pitches.

Arnold Schoenberg.

right
Autograph manuscript of the beginning of the fourth of the Five Pieces for Piano, *Op. 23, by Schoenberg.*

below
Der Rote Blick, *a painting by Schoenberg.*

The aesthetic and style of Schoenberg's works

It is commonly, though mistakenly, claimed that this technique is purely mathematical. Schoenberg insisted all his life that 'in music the heart must guide the head'. He advocated 'expression' at all costs, and indeed he is one of the great German musical Expressionists.

In his very first works, his attitude is made abundantly clear; they have a wealth of emotional expressiveness which surpasses even that of Mahler and Wagner and at times becomes almost unbearably intense. A number of works in a magnificent, sharp, exacerbated post-Wagnerian manner come from Schoenberg's early period. They are: the string sextet *Verklärte Nacht*, Schoenberg's Opus 4 (1899), based on a pre-Expressionist poem by Richard Dehmel; *Pelléas and Mélisande* (contemporary to Debussy's version); and *Die Gurrelieder* (1900, orchestrated in 1911) for soloists, chorus and orchestra and based on a medieval Danish legend. The first string quartet is directly descended from the Romantic tradition – even from the Beethoven tradition – in the subtlety of its scoring and thematic material. The beginnings of the evolution towards atonality are found in the second string quartet; here a soprano voice is introduced in the last two movements (based on poems by Stefan George), where a hint of the twelve-note scale may be noted.

A different but equally significant tendency is apparent in the chamber symphony of 1906. Here we have not only great concentration of expression but also a concentrated exploitation of instrumental possibilities. Instead of a gigantic orchestra of the type so frequently used at the time, Schoenberg uses only fifteen solo instruments. The songs of the *Lieder* cycle, *Hängende Gärten*, to words by Stefan George (1908), are already atonal, although still disorganised, and mark a second stage in Schoenberg's evolution. Its direction is confirmed with his piano pieces Opus 11 and 19, with the monodrama *Erwartung* (1909), about a woman who discovers the dead body of her lover, and the music drama, *Die glückliche Hand* (1908-13). This period in his work has been called 'the phase of unlimited anarchy and liberty'. During this period too the composer developed his use of the half-speaking, half-singing mode of declamation that he called *Sprechgesang* (literally, 'speech-song'). It occurs in both the last named works and was used again in *Pierrot Lunaire*.

The beginning of the third phase of his work was marked by the publication of his theory of composition, and he immediately put this twelve-note theory into practice with his piano pieces, Opus 23; *Serenade*, Opus 24, and the piano suite, Opus 25. We have now passed from the stage of disorganised dodecaphony to serial technique, the height of which is achieved in the wind quintet (1924). These didactic, disciplined works might be called Schoenberg's manifesto.

In the fourth phase of his evolution this rigorous attitude became slightly more flexible and his music was even, to some extent, linked with the classical past. This is noticeable in his third string quartet, but in particular in his orchestral variations, Opus 31, where he returns to the use of a large orchestra and formal classical methods in an expanded form and pays homage to Bach.

In the fifth phase, which corresponds more or less with Schoenberg's American period, his technique becomes even more flexible, to such an extent that it is almost 'tonal' whilst still remaining within a serial framework. This phase is represented by the *Variations for wind orchestra*, *Ode to Napoleon* and *A Survivor of Warsaw* (1947). The last is a cantata with spoken recitation, chorus and orchestra, which evokes the tragedy of the Warsaw Ghetto.

It was during this last period that Schoenberg was becoming increasingly preoccupied with religion, a preoccupation which manifested itself in several different ways. First, in *Moses and Aaron*, which he began in 1930 but whose third act he never completed. This opera, which is a sort of synthesis of all Schoenberg's styles and is hailed by some as his masterpiece, was performed on stage at Zurich in 1957, directed by Hans Rosbaud, in Berlin in 1959 under Hermann Scherchen and at Covent Garden in 1965 under Georg Solti.

But in his very last works, Schoenberg paid even greater homage to the faith of his ancestors – *Prelude to Genesis*, *Psalm CXXX* and the *Moderne Psalmen* (for which he himself wrote the words) for spoken recitation, chorus and orchestra, the publication of which was interrupted by his death.

Schoenberg's work has a double significance – in relation to himself it was one of the most prodigious adventures ever embarked on by any musician. From the purely artistic point of view the results are disputed. There are some who claim that Schoenberg's evolution was marked by a continuous advance; others that, once he had invented his method, he was unable to make use of his discovery, since, instead of creating new forms which would suggest new musical language, he reverted to old forms and never quite escaped from Romanticism.

Berg

Alban Berg's development followed similar lines to that of his master: tonality, atonality, anarchic dodecaphony, serial dodecaphony and finally, the application of serial music within a framework of expanded tonality. Berg was an Expressionist composer who was always attracted to the Romanticism of Schumann and Mahler: he cannot properly be spoken of as a pioneer. He did no more than give expression to an extreme sensibility in a composite musical language, employing basically Schoenberg's technique. Like his master he never entirely freed himself from earlier forms.

The composer was born in 1885 into an upper-middle-class family and, as a student, he was undecided whether to become a poet or a musician. In his first attempts at composition he was encouraged by Schoenberg, with whom he worked from 1904 until 1910. During these years a profound friendship developed between the two men while the younger became a master of his craft. In 1911 he married the singer Helene Nahowski who had a certain influence on his future development. During the war, ill health compelled him to serve in an administrative capacity, and he was able to continue composing. After the war his life continued peacefully; he was entirely bound up in his music, which alternately caused scandal and won him fame. In September 1935, an abscess obliged him to stop work; septicaemia, which a blood transfusion failed to alleviate, ensued; his condition worsened and he died on Christmas Eve.

Aesthetic and style

Berg's compositions can be divided into three periods, the first from 1907 to 1914, the second extending to 1926. In the piano sonata (which is the composer's Opus 1), although the music is in the key of D minor, tonality is already being shaken in its foundations: the composer has entered the new world of atonality, although he was

left
Alban Berg.

below
Poster for the 1963 production of Wozzeck *at the Paris Opera, directed by Jean-Louis Barrault and conducted by Pierre Boulez.*

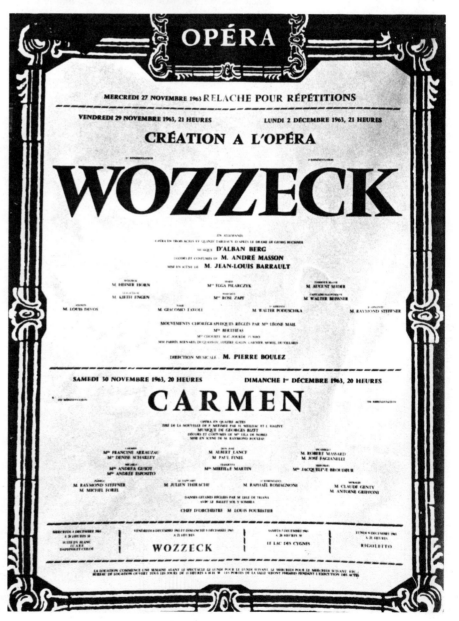

never entirely to break his ties with the Romanticism of Schumann and Mahler. In the quartet Opus 3, there is a complete break with tonality, and the Expressionist character of Berg's music is clearly affirmed.

His first attempt at writing for full orchestra is the *Five Altenbergerlieder*. At its first performance in 1912 the work shocked the public as much by the violence of Peter Altenberger's text as by the powerful, dramatic and Expressionist musical language of the composer; there are also certain parts of the score which show a tendency towards true serialism. In the *Three Orchestral Pieces*, his second work for full orchestra, which are conceived in the grand cyclical style, Berg seems to achieve an original synthesis of Schoenberg's musical 'grammar' with the architecture of Mahler and the subtly coloured harmonies of Debussy.

Berg's second period does not provide any great differences in method, but, thanks to his mastery of his craft, this was the time when he produced his masterpieces. During these years (1917-26) appeared the chamber concerto, the *Lyric Suite* and the opera *Wozzeck*. The chamber concerto for violin, piano and thirteen woodwind is Berg's most radical work in the field of serial music. Three movements, three families of instruments used in three different combinations and the form based on the ternary conception give the work its integral unity. The string quartet, entitled *Lyric Suite*, which was written two years later, is infinitely less rigorous in style. It consists of six movements: the first, third and sixth are serial, the second and fourth are free, and the fifth is a mixture of both styles. These different movements are in fact built on traditional formal lines – sonata, rondo, scherzo and trio, *Lied* and rhapsody. The character of the work consists in the highly charged, emotional mood of each succeeding movement, progressive and regressive, handled with an instrumental invention of unbelievable subtlety which establishes this string quartet as one of the greatest ever written.

Berg's *Wozzeck* is one of the major operatic events of the 20th century. Based on the unfinished drama *Woyzeck*, by the brilliant and intense young genius Georg Büchner (1813-37), it tells the story of a poor wretch of a soldier in the imperial Austrian army, a victim of the sadism of his doctor and captain, who is living with a loose and sensual woman. She deceives him with the drum major and he stabs her and drowns himself.

Behind these events lies a psychological background which Berg's music illuminates in a unique manner. Indeed the atmosphere of Büchner's work is eminently suited to the composer's Expressionist genius. As an operatic experience the work has a direct dramatic appeal which transcends the kind of problems that modernist works are generally expected to present to an audience. Nevertheless, the structure is quite new in the history of opera. The fifteen scenes of the three acts are each treated in one of the classic forms – invention, suite, prelude, fugue or rondo. In the synthesis of various styles of composition, Berg succeeded where Schoenberg himself to some extent failed. The dynamic emotional content of the drama leaves no room for any arid Neo-classicism, nor is *Wozzeck* basically serial; it is in a mixture of genres and contains some portions which are quite straightforwardly tonal. Meanwhile, the orchestral colour is powerfully suggestive and is both richer and more economical than in some earlier works.

Berg uses a half-spoken melodic line, like the *Sprechgesang* of Schoenberg's *Pierrot Lunaire*, but in a subtler form, to maintain the tempo and dramatic rhythm of the libretto. Finally, it is worth noting that Berg even employs the mechanics of the Wagnerian *Leitmotiv*. All

A scene from a production of Berg's opera Wozzeck.

in all, although using what from a theoretical point of view are very disparate styles, *Wozzeck* is one of the great masterpieces in the history of opera.

The third period of Berg's output produced, as its most notable works, the concerto for violin and orchestra and the opera *Lulu*; it should be noted that during this period Berg tends to certain tonalities, and even the series he chooses help to this end. This is particularly noticeable in the violin concerto, inspired by the composer's grief at the death of a young girl whom he knew, and sometimes known as the *Concerto in Memory of an Angel*. The work is charged with an intense emotion. In this respect it is in the direct line of descent from 'Schumannian' Romanticism, but the effect is all the stronger by reason of the music's compulsive Expressionism. Overall the work has a magnificent organic unity, which enables it to introduce the theme and harmonisation of Bach's chorale, *Ich habe genug*, without any sense of awkward incongruity. This synthesis of tonal and serial styles is largely made possible by the fact that the first eight notes of the initial series form a sequence of major and minor chords, while the last four notes progress by whole tones, like the first notes of Bach's chorale.

Lulu, an opera in three acts, was composed between 1928 and 1935, and the third act remained unfinished at the composer's death. It is based on a libretto which the composer himself compiled from two plays by the Expressionist writer Frank Wedekind. The plot concerns a woman of easy virtue and devilish beauty who provokes murder and suicide and ends, in the most ghastly circumstances, as a prostitute assassinated by a casual client (in fact the mass murderer Jack the Ripper). The music is based on a series which is linked to the character of Lulu, from which the composer extracts secondary series for the other characters and the different episodes in the drama. The architectonic structure of the scoring is less strict than in *Wozzeck* and Berg reverts, to some extent, to the forms and vocal techniques of traditional grand opera.

Webern

Anton Webern (1883-1945), who for a long time was unknown in his own country, even to members of the musical *avant-garde*, was the first composer who fully exploited the discoveries of Schoenberg, whose first pupil he was. One could perhaps sum up Webern's contribution to music by saying that, if Schoenberg discovered a new language and syntax, it was Webern who discovered the forms, styles and instrumentation and had the sensibility to create a musical language.

Webern was born in Vienna. After a traditional education he met Schoenberg, with whom he worked for six years (1904-10), and thereby became associated with Alban Berg. To earn a living he took up conducting and worked in various Austrian theatres. His activities were interrupted by the war, the whole of which he spent in uniform. But in 1918 he once again took up his baton and also devoted himself to teaching. He lived an extremely modest life, composing music which was practically never performed and earning a meagre living by correcting music proofs for publishers. Between 1922 and 1934 he was the director of the Vienna Workmen's Symphony Concerts and later he worked for a time for the Austrian broadcasting corporation. On the arrival of the Nazis in Austria, he was, of course, immediately classed as a 'degenerate' artist. He achieved celebrity only once, at the time of the American entry into Austria, when he was killed by a trigger-happy soldier, apparently after failing to understand a challenge given in English.

left
Anton Webern in his last years.

below
Anton Webern, from a drawing by Oskar Kokoschka.

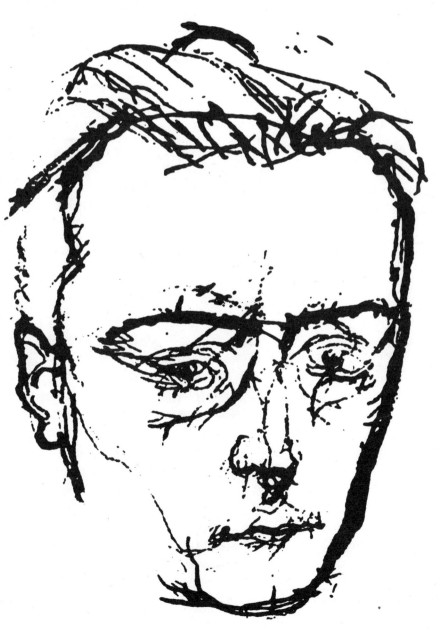

Aesthetic and style

Webern first fell under the influence of Brahms, Mahler and Schoenberg, but such influences were very short lived and he soon found an entirely personal style. The second period, already atonal, begins with the *Lieder*, Opus 3 and 4 (1908-09). The Webern style dates from this moment, although some Expressionist elements still remain. A completely radical outlook appears in the third period in the *Five Pieces for String Quartet* (1909), *Six Pieces* for large orchestra (1910) and the *Four Pieces* for piano and violin (1910). It was at this time that Webern adopted the 'little form', short and concentrated, with a rarefied musical atmosphere, a subtlety of timbre and a transparent quality, which had never been achieved until then. Between 1910 and 1914 the pieces became even shorter, in imitation of the *haiku* verse form of Japan. They contain passages of such extreme delicacy that they are scarcely audible. This is particularly true of the *Six Bagatelles* for string quartet (1913) and the *Five Pieces* for orchestra (1913).

Thereafter, until 1927, Webern wrote exclusively vocal music, and broke with the traditional style of the *Lied* to create a new style in which, to quote Pierre Boulez, 'the voice rules and supervises the arrangement of the ensemble'. Webern, it should be noted, does not use the *Sprechgesang* of Schoenberg but always a sung declamation. But from 1924 onwards he adopted the serial method recently proclaimed by Schoenberg. This, however, did little to change his musical thought, but brought a unifying element into his musical vocabulary.

Between 1927 and 1934 the composer produced a series of 'ascetic' works whose style was of great inspiration to, and was extended by European *avant-garde* composers after 1945. These are the *String Trio* (1927), the symphony (1928), the quartet for violin, clarinet, tenor saxophone and piano (1930) and the *Concerto for Nine Instruments* (1934). The style of this period is characterised by wide intervals, by very colourful instrumental tone and by an extraordinary use of completely

silent passages. It was also the period when Webern established his new 'auditory sensibility' by exploiting the most extreme consequences of '*Klangfarbenmelodie*' ('melody of sound colours'). Propounded but not thoroughly applied by Schoenberg, this was the technique which gave the constituent notes of a polyphonic line to different instruments. In this way a new atmosphere of sound was created, giving music a new dimension and freeing it from the confines of vertical chords. This indeed was one of Webern's great achievements, and he brilliantly applied the technique to a classic masterpiece in his orchestration of Bach's great *Ricercare* from the *Musical Offering*.

The last great period of his evolution took place in the years 1935-45 with such works as the two *Cantatas* and the *Variations* for piano, the *String Quartet* and the *Variations for Orchestra*. These works display unrestrained freedom of style and complete technical mastery. The didacticism expressed in some of his earlier works has disappeared. In his use of voices in the cantatas, Webern deployed a technique that has since been taken up by a later generation of young musicians. The poetic word is now used less for its meaning than for its musical sound and its place in music.

Thus in the course of his career Webern re-established the power of sound in a way somewhat similar to that of Debussy in *The Martyrdom of St Sebastian*, *Jeux*, and the études for piano. This comparison between Webern and Debussy, however strange it may seem at first, has recently been drawn and does help to illuminate some developments in European music. 'In place of families of instruments', it has been said, 'Webern has substituted the less conventional family of timbres'. This pinpoints the way in which Webern created a new auditory sensibility. Finally he promoted those elements – tone colour, attack, nuances and silences – formerly regarded as merely decorative or expressive – to the rank of structural elements, by introducing them into the organic texture of compositions. It is advances such as these that have provided the starting point for the integral serialism of Olivier Messiaen and younger musicians throughout Europe. The art of Webern in fact is practically the only music nurtured in the Viennese school to have had a living posterity.

Page 1 of Webern's autograph manuscript of his Five Pieces for Orchestra, Op. 10.

Stravinsky

By virtue of the number of masterpieces that he has composed; by the range of styles, of each of which he has proved himself a fluent and inspired master; by reason of the position that he has held at the centre of the stage of Western music for the last sixty years; and finally because of the apparently inexhaustible vigour which has made him the leader of many modernisms and receptive to others right up to the eighth decade of his life, Stravinsky is the giant of 20th-century music. The comparison with Picasso in the world of painting seems almost inevitable. And the parallels run not only along the lines of their achievement and their impact on the work of a multitude of lesser men. Both have produced more than their fair share of outrage, both have been, perhaps inevitably, the object of unfavourable reappraisals. However, it is safe to assume that whatever temporary eclipse the reputation of Stravinsky may suffer, he will remain for future generations one of the world's greatest composers.

Yet unlike Schoenberg or Bartók, Stravinsky has pioneered no new system and it might even be questioned whether he had the same revolutionary impact on musical awareness as Claude Debussy. And for the post-war generation of composers in the van of musical development, the work of Anton Webern was the lodestar – indeed with typical versatility Stravinsky himself has learnt from it. His first great departure, which proved a revelation for many other composers, was in the field of rhythm where, more than any other single man, he upset former orthodoxies, disrupting them by the violence and variety of his invention. In the 1920s, moreover, he stood at the head of that return to the inspiration of the past known as Neo-classicism – a movement which may be dated with some precision from the production, in 1920, of his ballet *Pulcinella*, with its self-proclaimed use of 18th-century idioms. Stravinsky's genius has always been of immense versatility, so that he has always been able to achieve a complete, though never facile, mastery of his adopted style. The originality of his genius is apparent in such works as *The Rite of Spring* or *Les Noces*, but an element of inspired pastiche is often to be found in his music. For this kind of reason, and without belittling his achievement, one hesitates to class Stravinsky as one of music's great innovators – the same is after all true of Bach and Mozart. The point was made, with considerable force, though perhaps with less insight, as early as 1914 by the musicologist, Igor Glebov:

'Stravinsky is the last representative of a superior refined civilisation, but a civilisation tired of itself, used up. Its musical world is genuine, but it does not look forward. There is no real future in the music of Stravinsky, it is a very delicate synthesis of discoveries from the past. In spite of all his audacious harmonies, one feels that his real force resides in his own weakness. Thanks to his intuition and prodigious perspicacity, he perceives the spirit and meaning of composers, no matter of what period. He stylises them with diabolical cleverness and offers them up to his contemporaries. He is always sincere because he feels "at home" in no matter what civilisation; because all cultures have left some traces in his brain. When one hears a work by Stravinsky one has the feeling that everything that could be said has been said and that it is impossible to proceed further.'

Biography

The composer's life reflects in a fascinatingly apt way the universality of his music. Born in Russia and inspired in his earliest music by the national idiom, he was to adopt French nationality at a time when Paris was the centre of the world of art, later becoming an American citizen and living in California, the cosmopolitan state of the future.

He was born in June 1882, at Oranienbaum near St Petersburg, into the privileged society of pre-Revolutionary Russia. His father's family, originally of Polish extraction, had been induced into the Russian nobility at the beginning of the 19th century, while his mother too was a member of the great land-owning Russian aristocracy. It was natural for the boy to be brought up strictly in the faith of the Russian Orthodox Church, and this religious upbringing apparently made a real impression on the young man. His comments after a youthful visit to Bayreuth stem from something more

Stravinsky in his early forties.

than a purely aesthetic aversion to the music of Wagner. 'Is not all this brilliant comedy of Bayreuth, with its ridiculous formalities, simply an unconscious aping of a religious rite? . . . It is high time to put an end, once and for all, to this unseemly and sacrilegious conception of art as religion and the theatre as temple.'

From the first, the young Stravinsky was actively involved in the world of music. His father was principal bass singer at the imperial opera, being particularly noted for his interpretation of the part of Boris Godunov; the composer's mother was an excellent pianist. At the age of nine Igor was already revealing a precocious talent for improvisation at the keyboard and at this stage his idols were Glinka and Tchaikovsky. His education followed conventional lines but he was experimenting in composition even then and continued to develop his leanings in this direction while pursuing his university studies as a law student. He completed the course but when he was twenty he had begun to take private lessons in composition from Rimsky-Korsakov, and his commitment to music was made.

Stravinsky came of age in a Russia where the debate between the Easterners and Westerners was still in spate, the first represented in the fervently nationalist group called The Wanderers. These artists were opposed to the recently founded academies and committed to bringing art to the people, while cultivating in their paintings

A scene from Petrushka.

a self-consciously peasant style. Such principles were well in tune with the theories which were engrossing Tolstoy in his old age, and which were so forcefully advocated by the immensely active and influential critic, Vladimir Stassov. Later the whole Soviet ethos of socialist realism in the arts was to find its spiritual ancestors in such manifestations.

It is not surprising, in view of his later development as well as his career up to that time, that Stravinsky should have allied himself to the World of Art movement founded in the early 1890s, with the impresario Diaghilev and the artists Benois and Bakst its most prominent members. Passionately opposed to what they regarded as the provincialism of the Wanderers, and advocating close involvement with developments in the West, the World of Art published their own magazine (1899-1904), edited by Diaghilev. The fruits of their brilliant and intense activity burst on the outside world with the sensational seasons of Diaghilev's *Ballets Russes* which, from 1909 to the outbreak of the First World War, held the Parisian artistic world in thrall.

As a pupil of Rimsky-Korsakov, Stravinsky had already composed the flamboyant *Fireworks* (1909) for orchestra, and a symphony, both influenced by the Romanticism of Brahms and Glazunov, and had begun an opera, *The Nightingale*, which was to be completed in 1914. Possibly he would have turned increasingly to opera had it not been for his association with Diaghilev who, with Stravinsky as with many of the brilliant group of artists that he gathered round him, seems to have revealed the composer to himself by introducing him to the world of the ballet. *The Firebird* was commissioned and performed in Paris, with choreography by Fokine, in 1910; subsequently Stravinsky was to make two arrangements of the music for orchestral suite. In the following season appeared Stravinsky's *Petrushka*, the choreography this time by Benois. In both these ballets the composer's mastery of rhythm is already apparent, while the orchestration is both faultless and audacious. In both, too, Stravinsky has drawn on the world of Russian folklore, and in one sense they may be regarded as the natural extension of the ideals of the school of the Five. In his first great masterpiece, *The Rite of Spring*, that was to follow two years later, the composer also roots his conception in the rituals and ceremonies of peasant Russia; to some extent the music, too, has its origins there, but in all important respects this astonishing work made a revolution.

Living in Switzerland between 1910 and 1914, he became close friends with the conductor Ernest Ansermet, an association which was carried on into the concert hall by Ansermet's enthusiastic advocacy of Stravinsky's music. In 1917, the composer visited Rome, meeting Picasso there for the first time. Stravinsky was now thirty-five and for the last eight years had lived and worked away from his native Russia. In all important respects he had become a citizen of the world of art, and his music can no longer be confined within the limits of any national school. After the Revolution in 1917 he never returned to his native land and, between 1920 and the outbreak of the Second World War, he lived in Paris, adopting French citizenship in 1934.

There he was part of that brilliant society of the arts which gave rise to the 'schools of Paris' in painting and in music, many of whose most talented members were, like Stravinsky, foreigners by nationality if cosmopolitan by achievement. He not only continued to compose but also developed his activities as a conductor and pianist, while his compositions, like those of Ravel and de Falla and many others, contributed to the intense and exciting musical life of the world's artistic capital. In 1936, after a life of fifty-four eventful and creative years, he published his autobiography. In the face of the German invasion of France, Stravinsky, in common with many

others, left Europe and, from 1940, lived in California, also the home during the last eighteen years of his life of that other great figure in the music of our time, Arnold Schoenberg. He died in 1971.

The stage music

The ballet *The Rite of Spring*, with choreography by Nijinsky and decor by N. Roerich, caused a riot in the audience at its first performance in 1913. It took as its subject the primitive rituals of pre-Christian Russia which ended in the sacrifice of a virgin. The theme was in keeping with the contemporary European interest in primitive cultures, and the music, with its abrupt, harsh rhythms and remarkable instrumental colouristic effects, evoked only too well the barbaric and atavistic emotions that lie uncomfortably near the surface of civilised society. The music of *Les Noces* (1923), drawn in part from Russian folk songs, has much of the power of *The Rite*, but, in the years between, Stravinsky had opened out into his Neo-classical style with the ballet *Pulcinella*. His other ballets included *Apollon Musagète* (1928) with choreography by Balanchine; *Jeu de cartes* (1937); *Orpheus* (1948); and the dodecaphonic *Agon* for twelve dancers (1957). He also wrote a number of other works for the stage, among them *Renard* (1922), a burlesque based on Russian folk tales. *The Soldier's Tale* (1918), for speaking voice, dancers and a band of seven instruments, is set to a text of Russian folk stories by the Swiss poet C. F. Ramuz, while the music uses jazz elements.

One of his greatest masterpieces is the opera-oratorio, *Oedipus Rex* (1927). The staging of the work in itself is evidence of Stravinsky's restless search for new ideas in the theatre, and is strangely analogous to Bertolt Brecht's theory of *Verfremdung* (alienation or estrangement). Insofar as the work is based on the classical tragedy of

Sophocles it has nothing of the social objectives of Brechtian drama, but a production of *Oedipus Rex* perfectly fulfils Brecht's demand for the breaking of dramatic illusion as a means of alienating the theatrical experience. The very libretto of *Oedipus* is artificial. While the performers sing a Latin text – translated from the French version of Sophocles prepared by Jean Cocteau, the action is interpreted in the vernacular to the audience by a commentator in evening dress, standing to one side of the stage. Stravinsky took the convention of the chorus and of masked actors from Greek theatrical tradition but, while the classical Greek chorus

above
Stravinsky with Jean Cocteau.

left
A scene from a Sadlers Wells production of Oedipus Rex.

accompanied the singing of its part with dance and mime, the chorus in this work remains stationary throughout the action, while even the main actors are permitted only the most limited movement. The work merits this somewhat lengthy description because it illustrates certain characteristics of the composer's work. First we notice the use of many derivative elements; second the confidence with which they are modified to suit the present purpose; third, a point that is apparent in production, the truly tragic power of this opera of tableaux. It is typical of Stravinsky that a work which so nearly crosses the line between brilliant theatre and gimmickry is fully vindicated on the stage.

In the opera *The Rake's Progress* (1951), ultimately based on the famous series of engravings by Hogarth and to a libretto by W. H. Auden and C. Kallman, the formal device is, in 20th-century terms, equally surprising. However, it is in no way revolutionary, consisting as it does of a return to the conventions of Mozartian opera.

Stravinsky's musical language

below
Scene from the New York City Ballet's production of Orpheus.

bottom
A set for the 1926 production of Firebird *by Goncharova.*

After 1956 Stravinsky committed himself to serialism and the techniques of the twelve-note composers. In this last period, as fertile in great music as any that went before, he followed to its logical conclusion his life-long search in the treasure house of Europe's past for the inspiration of his own magnificent and highly

individual work. It is significant that he came to serialism only when it was already established and, such is the rate of change in the modern world, was already beginning to acquire the aura of a traditional style. He said that he refused to abandon 'well-tempered pitches', the traditional sonorous material of the composer, for the world of sounds and noises being explored by many of his younger colleagues. It may be questioned whether, if he had lived to find electronic music one of the established procedures of the past, Stravinsky would have persisted in rejecting them. Nevertheless, it is perhaps more correct to take the remark at its face value and to regard Stravinsky as the Bach of the music of tonality: a giant at an end of an era.

This refusal 'to abdicate the rule of my ears' can be set against another observation he has made since he turned to serialism. 'I hear certain possibilities and make my choice from them. For me such a choice is every bit as possible in the realm of serial composition as it is in any tonal contrapuntal form. Obviously I hear harmonically and compose in the same manner as before.' And the evidence of his serial works bears him out; as often as not the note-rows that he uses are strongly reminiscent of diatonic procedures. Before his last serial period the harmonic element in Stravinsky's music is characteristically diverse. It may be influenced by that of Russian folk music, of the old church modes or, in his Neoclassical phase, the tonalities of the 18th century (*Pulcinella* is derived from the music of Pergolesi). In other works he makes free use of dissonant episodes at moments of tension, dissonances that depend for their effect on an assumed harmonic background of consonance, or of polytonal techniques. At times he makes use of ancient techniques which are lent new life by their masterly placing in unexpected contexts. However, it was in his rhythms that Stravinsky made perhaps his greatest impact on music. Often apparently wild, always urgent, they are never undisciplined. He achieves the most stunning effects not by bombast or incoherent passion, but by the application to the complex polyrhythms that he so often builds up of the same craftsmanlike technique as is to be found in every other aspect of his music.

Instrumental and choral works

Stravinsky's natural talent for the stage was only one aspect of his genius. During his long career he also wrote much music for instruments and voices. The symphony for wind instruments of 1921, subtitled *In memoriam Claude Debussy*, was to be the first of a number of works commemorating the deaths of famous men, in the worlds of politics and literature as well as music; it was reworked in the 1940s. His interest in the quality of the sound of the wind was followed up in 1924 with a concerto for piano and this section of the orchestra. Stravinsky also composed other works in a symphonic idiom, of which the *Symphony of Psalms* (1930) for orchestra and choir is subtitled 'composed to the glory of God and dedicated to the Boston Symphony Orchestra'. His concerto in E flat, the *Dumbarton Oaks Concerto* (1938) for chamber orchestra, also has American associations, and the symphony in C (1940) and the symphony in three movements (1946) were both composed after he had settled there. Other orchestral works include: a *Capriccio* for piano and orchestra; *Four Studies for Orchestra* (1929), the fourth of which was originally composed for the pianola; a concerto for violin (1931) later reworked as the ballet *Balustrade*; *Circus Polka* for wind band, 'composed for a young elephant' (1942); the *Ebony Concerto* composed for Woody Herman's 'big band' jazz orchestra; the concerto in D for string orchestra, later reworked as the ballet, *The Cage*; and *Movements for piano and orchestra*.

Among the large quantity of chamber works we have space to mention only a few, but it should be remembered that Stravinsky expressed some of his finest conceptions in music for small ensembles, and in his serial period this was to be especially true. His works for the classic combination of the string quartet include *Three Pieces* (1914) and a *Concertino* (1920), reworked for other combinations later. He also wrote for solo instruments, chamber music for wind, as well as much fine music for the piano. Among his choral works we have already referred to the *Symphony of Psalms*, and some of his most important music for this combination was to be written during his last period, which receives treatment of its own in the next section. His music for solo voice and instruments has been the vehicle of intimate and poignant conceptions. *Three Japanese Lyric Poems* for voice and piano (1913) was in tune with the growing interest in Europe in Japanese literature, which was interestingly enough paralleled by Webern. The *Three Songs from William Shakespeare* for mezzo-soprano,

flute, clarinet and viola (1953) and *In Memoriam Dylan Thomas* for tenor, string orchestra and two trombones (1954), are evidence of the growing and genuine attachment for English culture which was a feature of Stravinsky's later years. By the early 1950s the composer was prepared to embark on another adventure, and it may well be that his meeting with Pierre Boulez in 1952 finally decided him on a serious study of serial technique. The first work in the new style was not completed until three years later, but it heralded a decade of creative activity of the first importance and to this we now turn.

Stravinsky's serial music

The first work to be completed in the style was the *Canticum Sacrum*, finished in 1955 but first performed in Venice the following year, being dedicated to the city and its patron saint, St Mark. The work is rich in the

24-5-20-

Stravinsky at the age of thirty-eight, a drawing by Picasso.

characteristically Stravinskian mastery of orchestral colour and, although it signifies a new departure into the world of twelve-note composition, analysis reveals a tonic-dominant structure behind the serial structure. This solemn hymn of praise (in five main sections corresponding to the five great domes of St Mark's Cathedral) has all the qualities of a masterpiece and indicates the stature of Stravinsky's later work in the idiom. But more fascinating, if not more magnificent, is his transcription for choir and orchestra of the great *Canonic Variations* for organ on the chorale *Vom Himmel hoch da komm ich her* by J. S. Bach. This is fascinating not only for the circumstances surrounding Bach's original composition (it constituted his entry piece into a society devoted to mathematics), nor only for the very aptness of the gesture from Stravinsky as he entered a new field, but especially because the young Webern, whose figure loomed so large in the serialist world of the 1950s, had, as early as 1909, made his orchestrated transcription of the Ricercare from Bach's *Musical Offering*.

There followed the ballet *Agon*, begun in 1953 but completed four years later, which reflects Stravinsky's conversion to serial technique as the work progresses. *Threni, that is the lamentations of the Prophet Jeremiah* (1958), for six solo voices, choir and orchestra, represents a completely integrated exercise in serialism. The *Movements for piano and orchestra* of 1960 were regarded by

the composer himself as the central achievement of his later period, and in this work he ventures into serialism proper as distinct from twelve-note composition, extending the principle to the rhythmic as well as the pitch element. Both in its length, a mere twelve minutes, and the use of such medieval techniques as isorhythmy, it is in keeping with the work of Webern. It is also the work in which Stravinsky came nearest to abandoning his often proclaimed allegiance to tonalism, and in which he probes the matter of time in music, so central in the minds of his younger contemporaries.

There is no space here for extended treatment of all Stravinsky's later works, but the inspiration of this astonishing talent continued unabated. This is apparent in such compositions as the two-minute long *Epitaph for the tombstone of Prince Egon Max of Furstenberg* (1959); the lyrical *A Sermon, a Narrative and a Prayer* (1961); the 'choral ballet' *The Flood* (1962); *Elegy for JFK* (1963) for mezzo-soprano or baritone and three clarinets, and *Introitus; T. S. Eliot In Memoriam* (1965), scored for tenor and bass voices, solo viola and double basses, harp, piano, timpani and tam-tam. All these works are outstanding, and yet in *Abraham and Isaac, A Sacred Ballet* (1963), a true masterpiece, Stravinsky revealed himself as one of that rare body of artists capable of great achievements in the extremity of their life.

GEOFFREY HINDLEY

Stravinsky conducting.

French music

After the death of Berlioz, France could not boast a composer of world rank until the young Debussy began to reveal his powers. Nevertheless, his revolutionary achievements had more impact outside France than in his country of birth, where the pupils of such essentially 19th-century masters as Fauré and Franck occupied an important place in the first half of the 20th. The tradition of Debussy was carried on, though in a highly individual manner, by that other great original of French music of the first decades of the century, Maurice Ravel. After him the major figure was to be that of Olivier Messiaen, a generation younger, and then his pupils, notably Pierre Boulez. Besides these major figures France has produced a number of highly talented composers of the second rank such as Milhaud and Poulenc, who, with many of their contemporaries, formed for a brief period one of the numerous groups and schools which sprang up so freely in French arts between the wars. Their programmes and manifestos were not concerned only, or even mainly, with abstract theories as to the nature of music in the modern world. There was also the need to establish a French style free from the colourings of Wagnerianism, which had exerted such a strong influence in the 1880s, and from the extra-musical Impressionism of Debussy's earlier works. Indeed, the official manifesto of the 'Six' rejected not only the German music but even Debussy himself.

Debussy

Born at St Germain en Laye, a suburb of Paris, in 1862, the composer was given the names Achille Claude and only dropped the first of these names, which he had come to regard as absurd, when he was a young man in his twenties. He entered the Conservatoire as a student of the piano at the age of ten, and did not graduate to the school of composition for some time. When he was eighteen he met the wealthy Nadezhda von Meck, Tchaikovsky's patroness, being employed by her as a household musician for some months. When he was twenty-two Debussy won the Prix de Rome, though he left Italy before the statutory three-year period was complete. More important, perhaps, was his visit to Bayreuth in 1888 (the music of Wagner exerted a detectable influence on his youthful works) and the performances of Indonesian gamelan music that he heard at the Paris International Exhibition in 1889. Two years later he met Erik Satie and they become lifelong friends; indeed Satie's admiration for Debussy was so great that it led him to belittle his own achievements as a composer. Debussy's other acquaintances were by no means limited to the world of music and included his close friend, the poet and novelist Pierre Louÿs, the sculptor Rodin and the writers Maeterlinck and Mallarmé, whose works he

set to music. Debussy was for long deeply interested in the relation of music to the other arts and was an admirer not only of the manifestations of the contemporary Art Nouveau, but also of the Japanese prints of Hokusai and the paintings of Turner. His personal life was at first comparatively untroubled; the association with his mistress Gabriel Dupont was amiably concluded when Debussy married his first wife, a provincial girl who had come to Paris to work as a dressmaker. But in 1904 he left her, driving her to attempt suicide, for a rich widow, Emma Bardac, who bore him his beloved daughter Chouchou. In his late thirties the cancer that was to kill him in 1918 made itself apparent, and his life ended in deepening tragedy and bitterness.

Roughly speaking we can distinguish three successive periods in Debussy's musical evolution. The first is that of the prize-winning cantata *L'Enfant prodigue* (1884); the brilliant *Prélude à l'après-midi d'un faune* (1892-94), a musical evocation of the allusive symbolism of Mallarmé's poem; and the *Demoiselle élue* (1888), all of these being dexterous exploitations of incisive harmonies.

Contemporary caricature of Debussy.

The second revolution, marked by the composition of *La mer* (1905), was one in which he emancipated his music and began to explore new musical sensations, a mixture of timbre, chords and prosody, a whole new musical vocabulary evoking impressions then disturbing and unusual. During this period Debussy's music was particularly affected by his interest in painting and literature.

In the third revolution, Debussy was to abandon this attempt to equate nature with music, and to write purely abstract music, such as the *Etudes*, *Sonates* and *Jeux*. Debussy's new harmonic vocabulary soon proved its value; the melodic line by degrees became less and less essential, until finally it disappeared altogether to be replaced by timbre and rhythm that attained a fresh vigour. Few musicians since Beethoven have undergone such a metamorphosis during their lifetime.

Claude Debussy.

Piano works and chamber music

Throughout his life Debussy jotted down projects and sketches which may be compared to the drawings of some of the old masters. From the 'black and white' of the piano, as Debussy himself put it, he extracted the maximum amount of colour. His acquaintance with the works of Liszt and Chopin aroused his powers of invention to a much greater degree than those of his contemporaries, with the exception of Ravel. Debussy perfected the principles of resonance, which is so much richer in the modern pianoforte. His first two piano works, the two *Arabesques* of 1888 and *Suites Bergamasques*, however, only draw some caressing effects from a few bold harmonies, nothing more. The trilogy *Pour le piano* (1896) is a disguised form of the old French suite; but with *Estampes* (1903), *Masques* and *L'Ile joyeuse* (1904), *Images* (1905-07) and *Children's corner* (1908), Debussy explored every sonorous possibility that the piano can produce. His research into timbre and rhythm is definitely established in his two collections of twenty-four *Préludes* (1910-13), which are like a vast palette on which are displayed all the musical moods of the composer. They range from caricature (*Minstrels* and *General Lavinne*) to romances (*La fille aux cheveux de lin*), mysterious evocation (*Canope* and *Danseuse de Delphes*), hallucinatory vision (*Ce qu'a vu le vent d'ouest*) and the rainbow colours of *Feu d'artifice*. This prodigious collection of 'sketches' (a word Debussy was particularly fond of), which contributed so much to a renewal of French piano writing, was to be incorporated in his last great masterpieces. The twelve *Etudes* (1915) show him as a master of all the magic and bravura of which the piano is capable. Each is a concise and vigorous masterpiece in its own right and, if the whole collection represents Debussy at his most subtle in his search for fresh harmonies and colours, he also displays here a new power and grandeur. Dating from the same period is the lovely trilogy, *En blanc et noir*, for two pianos, in which his 'evocative period' has been replaced by one of simple grandeur.

Debussy did not return to writing chamber music until twenty-two years after he had revealed his brilliant talents with the G minor quartet (1893), in which he combines a thematic argument with free fantasy. His three sonatas (1915-17) for cello and piano, for flute, viola and harp and for violin and piano, conceived in the style of the chamber music of Rameau and Couperin, reveal the more dreamy side of his character. This is particularly true of the nostalgic sonata for piano and cello, and the almost painful violin sonata (1917). In the sonata for flute, viola and harp (1915) he momentarily forgets his intimate sorrows, and seeks for 'caressing combinations of timbre' which, as Debussy himself declared, take us back to the happy times of the *Nocturnes*.

Orchestral and vocal works

In the orchestral works, we can find a similar evolution from a sensuous, auditory and visual Impressionism, to a progressive interest in equating music with nature. *Prélude à l'après-midi d'un faune* was the magnificent opening to a series of evocative masterpieces. The three Nocturnes – *Nuages*, *Fêtes* and *Sirènes* – analyse sound, harmony, timbre and rhythm as never before. Already in *La mer* Debussy had dispensed with the naturalistic imitation of wind and waves, but reproduced light and movement and, by the interplay of these two elements, miraculously resolved the problem of structure. *Les images pour orchestre* (1910-12) are still Impressionistic, but his analysis of orchestral colour (already noticeable in *La mer*) and his use of counterpoint are here predominant. Also apparent is his neglect of melodic line in favour of rhythm, a technique which he employed in the dense texture of *Jeux*. This ballet, commissioned by Diaghilev with choreography by Nijinsky, was completed in 1912 and is now widely considered to be Debussy's orchestral masterpiece. It may be said that the music of the ballet *Jeux* is to the orchestra what the *Etudes* are to the piano. The abstract quality of the subject accords with the aesthetic of Debussy's ultimate concept of music – the play of the tennis balls is reflected in the play of notes.

Debussy's numerous projects for opera show just how difficult was the problem confronting an admirer of Wagner, whom he revered as a musician but not as a man of the theatre, since he himself abhorred all traditional operatic conventions.

It was his reading of Maeterlinck's drama, *Pelléas and Mélisande*, in 1892 that decided Debussy to embark on a dramatic work. Maeterlinck's text, with its dream-like quality, its enigmatic characters and settings in a 'never-never land', was admirably suited to his genius, and the resultant opera may be regarded as the central work of Debussy's career. The otherworldliness of the text is admirably adapted to the subtleties of the French language, around which Debussy has woven a mysterious orchestral score. This unique opera occupied Debussy's energies between the ages of thirty-one and forty; it is devoid of any definite action and the characters themselves are unreal, but the work has always fascinated musicians.

The music has a magic power unique in French opera. Debussy retained much of his youthful involvement with Wagner and technically the vocal writing is essentially Wagnerianism in French dress; there is also much of Wagner in the contrapuntal texture and the subtle use of *Leitmotive*.

The elaborate incidental music for the *Martyrdom of St Sebastian*, by the Italian playwright d'Annunzio (1911), has been criticised for its departure from d'Annunzio's original text and conception, and it enjoyed little success at its first performance. Debussy's collaboration with the author was only half-hearted; he was already aware that much of what he admired in the writings of his contemporaries would soon be outdated. D'Annunzio's shattering words and frenzied choreography were too intense for Debussy's introvert character and his concept of Christian martyrdom. Nevertheless, this score contains some of the most remarkable passages ever written by Debussy.

His long list of songs, beginning with his *Ariettes oubliées* (1888) with words by Verlaine, were developments of his youthful cantatas, *L'Enfant prodigue*, which has something of the tenderness of Massenet, and the *Demoiselle élue*. For a time, disturbed by Wagnerian influences as we can see in the *Cinq poèmes de Baudelaire* (1887-89), Debussy eventually found a style of French song which is as subtle as the French language itself, comprising quiet recitatives, but possessed of infinite variety. The *Fêtes galantes* (1892) with words by Verlaine, *Proses lyriques* (1893) with words by the composer and the *Chansons de Bilitis* (1897) with words by Pierre Louÿs mark the apogee of Debussy's sensuous period. Later he turned to earlier poets, who helped to show him a way out from Impressionism and Symbolism. The three *Chansons de France*, *Le Promenoir des deux amants*, the *Ballade de Villon*, the *Trois Poèmes de Mallarmé* (1913) and the *Noël des enfants qui n'ont plus de maison* (1915) belong to Debussy's last period.

Ravel

Maurice Ravel (1875-1937) studied at the Paris Conservatoire under Fauré among others. He was known as a pianist and conductor, and made concert tours, but otherwise he lived a retiring life devoted to composition.

Ravel tapped many sources of inspiration and technique – Mozart, Liszt, Johann Strauss, Saint-Saëns, Chabrier, Borodin, Schoenberg, Stravinsky and, above all, Debussy, yet his style is more personal than that of any of his contemporaries and his synthesising genius was to produce a uniquely personal style in which the

Mary Garden in the role of Mélisande.

use of modal melodies and the intervals of the seventh and the ninth are important. From even the most academic models he produced audacious and novel forms which are pure Ravel. But corresponding with this logical discourse is a curious illogicality which provides a pretext for the introduction of inspired irrational themes into the heart of his music – fairy tales, magic and choreographic incantations – which he strove to depict clearly in the most vivid and easily analysable colours. This incomparable stylist was just as much at home with the form of the old-fashioned classical suite as with the waltz; yet in the Dionysian piano concerto for left hand and the terrifying Romantic *Scarbo* he could express himself in a way which was quintessentially French.

Piano works and chamber music

The *Pavane pour une infante défunte* (1899) and the *Jeux d'eaux* (1901), although influenced by Liszt and Chabrier, already show in which direction Ravel's piano composition was to lead; virtuosity and firmness constitute a solid foundation for his argument and Impres-

sionistic technique. *Miroirs* (1905) shows Ravel more aware of the appeal of Impressionism. After classicism and Impressionism, Ravel turned to Romanticism with *Gaspard de la nuit* (1908) – three fantastic subjects, *Ondine*, *Le Gibet*, *Scarbo*, rendered in terms of black and white like etchings. In *The Mother Goose Suite* of 1908 for two pianos, the simplicity of the score hides a fairy-like quality, a favourite motif of Ravelian escape. A choreographic stylisation dictates the essentials of the last two masterpieces. *Les Valses nobles et sentimentales* (1911) contrast the sensuality of the undulating melodic line and languishing melodies with strict counterpoint. *Le Tombeau de Couperin* (1917) is one of the early works of European Neo-classicism and is in the tradition of French music of the past, which attracted all the masters of the 'new' French school. In Ravel's music virtuosity is linked with the inner life of the composition; in this, Ravel was practising the lesson learnt by Saint-Saëns and was in part inspired by Liszt.

After the youthful but astonishing quartet in F and the *Introduction and allegro* for harp, flute, clarinet and strings, the trio in A minor (1914), the subtle rhythms of which owe something to Saint-Saëns, is a highly finished work. The sonata for violin and cello was deliberately simplified in order to highlight the beauty of the unadorned melodic line. The sonata for piano and violin (1927) stresses even more sharply Ravel's sense of instrumental qualities by the successful exaggeration of the difference between the two instruments.

Orchestral and vocal works

Ravel's first mentor in the art of orchestration was Berlioz. The original separation and distribution of timbres, however, were his principal preoccupations; colour is the servant of the programme, whereas, with Berlioz, colour is part of the whole design. This same attention to discipline makes the *Rhapsodie Espagnole* (1907) much more a 'study' of Spain than an 'impression'. In *La Valse* (1920) and *Boléro* (1928) he uses choreographic themes to evoke a secret magic in the form of the vertiginous rhythm of the waltz. Virtuosity for its own sake tempted Ravel to write the *Tzigane* for violin and orchestra, and in particular the two piano concertos, in G major and for the left hand (1931). The first is a triumph of Ravel's art of pastiche; a musical outburst inspired by Mozart seen through the eyes of Saint-Saëns, intersected by a stylised nocturne whose theme is an act of homage to the *Ballade* of his master, Fauré. In contrast to the luminous and objective score of the G major, the concerto for the left hand (written for the pianist Paul Wittgenstein, who lost his right arm during the First World War) is much more savage and inflammatory, and is almost acrobatic in its virtuosity.

Ravel's fascination with instrumental and orchestral colour led him to arrange some of his own piano compositions, such as *The Mother Goose Suite*, for orchestra, and also those of other composers, most notably Mussorgsky's *Pictures from an Exhibition*.

In *Schéhérazade* (1903), which takes into account the relation between voice and orchestral accompaniment, Ravel achieves a somewhat Debussy-like charm. In *Les Histoires naturelles* he deliberately adapts the music to the trenchant and a-musical prose of Jules Renard to achieve a masterly exercise in prosody; here once again a technical tour de force has produced a masterpiece. In the *Trois Poèmes de Mallarmé* (1913) the verbal alchemy of the poet competes with the music, in combinations made possible by the instrumental ensemble with which the voice is surrounded. Fascinated by the occult, Ravel

left
Decor by E. Steinhof for the 1929 production of Ravel's L'Enfant et les sortilèges *in Vienna.*

below
Ravel on holiday on the Basque coast.

attains a sensuousness uncommon to him in the *Chansons madécasses* (*Songs of Madagascar*, 1926). At the end of his life, he returned to composing songs, writing settings of the ironic poems by Paul Morand, *Don Quichotte à Dulcinée*. What was really to have been music for a film inspired Ravel to compose a separate work which, despite its strictly scientific approach, has become one of his most celebrated groups of songs.

Ravel's works for the theatre are masterpieces of their kind. In *L'Heure espagnole* (1907) he uses the same sort of free declamation as in the *Histoires naturelles*, in order to emphasise the one-act libretto. To use a somewhat scabrous subject and the conventions of the comic opera was yet another new and acrobatically brilliant tour de force on Ravel's part. But his greatest success was the operatic fantasy on a text by Colette, *L'Enfant et les sortilèges* (1920-25), in which Ravel seizes upon the discourse between a child and inanimate objects and nature. The child's reactions (destructive and compassionate) provide the pretext for a series of bizarre and fairy-like episodes, all the more successful for not being human. With this libretto, Ravel found a subject which suited him perfectly and which he made into an 'opera' unique of its kind.

Daphnis and Chloe (1912), commissioned by Diaghilev, is a full-scale ballet with choruses. The somewhat conventional plot led Ravel to make a glorious symphonic version of it in the form of two suites for orchestra. In the ballet itself the contrast between the linking passages and the more successful items, the *Nocturne, Lever du jour* and *Bacchanale*, which the symphonic version has made famous, make the work all the more moving.

Roussel

At the age of twenty-five Albert Roussel (1869-1937) abandoned his career in the navy to take up the study of music. His teachers were to include d'Indy, under whom he worked for four years, but Roussel's music, which has become increasingly well known in England since the 1950s, is highly individualistic and is not to be grouped with any of the schools in France during the inter-war years. He has none of Debussy's literary Im-

right
Albert Roussel.

below
A page from Ravel's manuscript of
L'Heure espagnole.

pressionism and none of Fauré's 'charm', nor the fairy-like qualities dear to Ravel. If Roussel was in fact a late-comer to music, his modesty does not obscure his artistic integrity, and his music reveals an enlightened if lonely figure. Although he borrows sometimes from Impressionism and from d'Indy and Franck, his musical language does not suffer from their faults: it is neither too vague nor too precise. Roussel was wary of systematic atonalism, which he regarded as an agent of unrest. But he did make a freer use of modality than others who turned to this source of inspiration and, above all, he discovered the potentialities of oriental music, his interest being aroused through direct experience gained on his voyages in the navy. By uniting these various influences Roussel enriched the harmony, rhythms and counterpoint of his musical language. But although he was open to the discoveries of his time, he remained disciplined according to classical rules. The influence of d'Indy can be seen in this love of order, and, while he absorbed oriental influences he still remained just as strict a classical conformist as he was modern.

Roussel's style was established by the mid-1910s with *Poème de la forêt*, considered his first symphony (1906), and the ballet *Le festin de l'araignée* (1912). The second symphony (1921) is one of Roussel's most complete and complex works; in it he displays all his versatility and definitely frees himself of all outside influences. His suite in F and the third and fourth symphonies, composed between the mid 1920s and 1930s, mark the apex of Roussel's great orchestral style.

Unlike so much French music of the period, these scores had an immediate and overwhelming success outside France. Roussel's compositions for small orchestral ensembles, e.g. *Concert pour petit orchestre* (1927), are equally remarkable and the *Sinfonietta* (1934) for strings, where the players are divided into groups of soloists, is ideally suited to contrapuntal music inspired by Bach. His chamber works include: *Divertissements* for woodwind, horn and piano and *Joueurs de flûte* (1924) for flute and piano; the *Serenade* for flute, harp, violin, viola and cello and the second trio for flute, cello and viola. But the very best of all Roussel's chamber music are the string quartet (1931-32) and the third trio for strings, which have all the quality of his last symphonies. The scope and variety of French piano music of this period can be seen in Roussel's sharp and precise rhythmic invention, though his vocal compositions are no less original. The songs *Réponse d'une épouse sage* and *Incantation* reveal a more contemplative side of his character, while *Les évocations* for chorus and orchestra was a formative work.

Some of Roussel's best music was inspired by ballet. The *Festin de l'araignée* (1912), which brought him public notice, is a parable of human cruelty in terms of a fairy tale; but it was in particular with *Bacchus and Ariadne* and *Aeneas* that Roussel found an opportunity to dispense with 'pure' abstract music, leaving him free to devote all his Dionysian energies to the creation of tableaux which scintillate with vigour and joy. However, *Padmavâti*, Roussel's great opera-ballet in the style of Rameau and based on an Indian legend, paid the price of an uninspiring libretto.

Dukas, Satie and lesser figures

Paul Dukas (1865-1935), who, as professor of the orchestral class and of composition at the Paris Conservatoire, exercised a great influence as a teacher, has often been misjudged as a composer and his works are seldom performed. The demands made by his piano compositions are not flattering to the virtuosity of executants, nor did the public respond to his operas. *The Sorcerer's Apprentice* and *La Péri* reflect only one aspect of his music. *The Polyeucte overture* (1892) and the C major symphony are the only works still stamped with the influence of Franck. *The Sorcerer's Apprentice* (1897), based on Goethe's poem, is undoubtedly the finest tone poem by a French composer. Goethe's poem gave Dukas an ideal inspiration and vehicle for his talent: he was content to write an orchestral score which positively sparkles with delectable sound but dispenses with all meretricious charms, and, despite the date of its composition, the work is quite free of Wagnerian influence. It is indeed entirely original in style. *La Péri*, the ballet commissioned by Diaghilev in 1912, is an enchanting orchestral piece inspired by Debussy, though more Romantic than Impressionistic in mood, with overtones of oriental harmonies.

His piano sonata in E flat minor, for all its extreme length and technical difficulty, displays Dukas's feeling for structure at its best. On the other hand, the *Variations, interlude and finale* on a theme of Rameau (1901), is one of the greatest French pianistic masterpieces. The magisterial quality of the variations in no way detracts from the splendour of the dazzling finale.

Mention must also be made of the *Plainte au loin du faune*, composed in homage to Debussy, and the *Prélude élégiaque* on a theme derived from the name Haydn. Dukas's piano music is essentially Romantic and draws its inspiration from Beethoven, Brahms and Liszt; it is barely touched by the influence of Debussy.

Satie (1866-1925) was a rebel and a pioneer who thoroughly enjoyed misleading critics and masking his natural candour. He abandoned his studies at the Conservatoire to work as a café pianist and it was thus, in the early 1890s, that he met Debussy. The real Satie is seen at his best in his deliberately economic *Socrates*, where his more audacious passages are doubly disguised under cover of comparatively unambitious short pieces with wilfully fantastic titles to tease the public. A fear of bathos prevented him from writing anything on a grand scale and his originality prevented him from having a large following. But his experiments set an example for innumerable French musicians, and it was this almost legendary 'bohemian' character who was responsible for more than one revolutionary manifesto and the formation of two famous post war groups – the Six and the School of Arcueil.

In his piano works, *Gymnopédies* (1888) and *Piece in the form of a pear*, in which he combines the naïve style of a Douanier Rousseau with revolutionary dissonant harmonies which subscribe to no known rules, one can discern the stirrings of a new harmonic style which inspired Debussy and Ravel, although the more audacious passages are no more than sketched in.

His instrumental contribution is also remarkable for its deliberate economy. *Parade* (1917) a ballet designed by Cocteau with décor by Picasso and choreography by Massine, introduces a spectacular element into his art, with borrowings from jazz and French popular songs. By his forceful reaction against all forms of Impressionism he became the standard-bearer for the new French school of music. *Socrates* (1918), a 'symphonic drama' for voices and orchestra, consists of readings from Plato in recitative.

Maurice Emmanuel (1862-1938), best known for his work as a musicologist, was in fact a fine composer. His perfect knowledge of Greek modes, oriental music and folk songs led him to create a characteristic and expressive musical language. In his *Chansons bourguignonnes* he clothes the folk element in very subtle harmonies, while for his six piano sonatas he uses a modal system influenced by Debussy. However, it is in his orchestral works and dramatic scores that Emmanuel shows himself at his best. *Prométhée enchâiné* (1918), *Salamine* (1928) and *Amphitryon* (1936), are inspired by epic poems and Greek tragedy. Emmanuel's knowledge of Greek metrical modes inspired him to write a very original new form of declamatory recitative, admirably suited to French prosody.

André Caplet (1879-1925), friend of Debussy and Prix de Rome scholar, was more under the influence of Debussy than any other French musician and was especially attracted by Debussy's songs.

Revolution and tradition

Traditional form can be found in manifestations as different as the 'Franckist' heritage, the lyric theatre in the style of Massenet, operettas and organ music, but also in a loyalty to the aesthetic principles of ancient

Erik Satie.

Paul Dukas.

French music, based on Gregorian plainsong and the modes.

The revolution was led by groups and manifestos, which were as numerous in the 1920s as before the war. It was more than just a reaction against Wagner, Franck and Debussy, all of whom were rejected by the proclaimed programme of the so-called group of the Six. Even the 'return to Bach' was under attack from some composers, particularly some members of the group called Young France, while another, that of Arcueil, strove above all for simplicity. It is apparent that all these groups were struggling, among other things, to find a truly French musical idiom after the 19th-century domination by the Germans. Nevertheless, revolutionary inspiration might be of foreign origin.

In 1909 Diaghilev electrified Paris with his *Ballets Russes*, which was to have a European impact. The Swedish ballet also enjoyed its moment of glory. The flood of foreign musicians, a continuing feature of the Parisian scene since the 18th century, continued unabated. The scandal of Stravinsky's *Rite of Spring*, which provoked a riot in the audience on its first performance in 1913, affected a whole stratum of French art represented in music by the Six and Jolivet, just as his later Neo-classical period was to influence another generation. Schoenberg's twelve-note system too, though sometimes mistrusted and sometimes tolerated, began to penetrate France in the 1920s. The cosmopolitan character of Parisian musical life between the wars is emphasised by the fact that the so-called School of Paris, which so influenced French music, consisted of foreign musicians living in Paris. The members of the group were the Czech, Bohuslav Martinů; the Hungarian, Tibor Harsany; the Pole, Alexander Tansmann; the Russian, Alexander Tcherepnin; the Swiss, Conrad Beck and the Rumanian, Marcel Mihalovici.

Honegger, Milhaud, Poulenc and the 'Six'

The official manifesto of *Les Six*, a group, as we shall see, of very disparate personalities, was in fact enunciated by Jean Cocteau, who had no time for German music, with the exception of Bach, but who also rejected the music of Debussy and the Russians. He contended that the new generation of French composers should derive its inspiration from the witty and wordly art of music hall and circus.

The members of the Six were of widely diverse characters and talents: the curious, retiring Durey, the mocking but humble Auric, the mighty Provençal Milhaud and the Swiss Honegger, Poulenc, by turns lighthearted and serious, and the brilliant Germaine Taillefer. Each was in fact soon to break away from the attributes which had been accorded him in Cocteau's *Coq et l'Arlequin*. But there were two points which all had in common: a hostility to French Wagnerianism and Impressionism. They wanted to align their work with painting and literature, and the writers Aragon, Eluard, Claudel, Gide and Apollinaire, as well as Cocteau, were often associated with them. But any actual collaboration between the Six was limited to a single ballet, conceived

Richard Strauss with a number of French composers; Milhaud is behind him and Roussel to his right.

by Jean Cocteau, *Les Mariés de la Tour Eiffel* (1921).

Arthur Honegger (1892-1955), a German Swiss Protestant (born at Le Havre and brought up in France), nicknamed the 'modern Handel', was of strikingly different background from the Mediterranean-Jewish Darius Milhaud. This difference of background points to the lack of any common artistic outlook between the Six.

The work that brought Honegger immediate fame was the oratorio *Le Roi David* (1921), but it was also the work that, from the very start, separated him from the group. Despite his rapid success Honegger suffered the fate of an artist separated from his public and was dogged by disappointment and despair. He prized opera above everything, and regarded *Antigone* as one of his masterpieces, though it was his oratorios that made his reputation – *Le Roi David*, *Judith*, *Les cris du monde*, *La danse des morts* and *Jeanne au bûcher*. In all Honegger's works, despite his harmonic and rhythmic language, we find a marked Romanticism. He was in fact not enough of an innovator for those who considered *avant-garde* music more important than anything else.

Some of Honegger's most effective music is found in his orchestral compositions. The celebrated orchestral tone poem *Pacific 231* (1923), on a crack railway train, is more than mere imitative music; the second symphony, for strings and trumpets (1941), and the third reflect the conflict between the composer and a hostile musical environment. In contrast to the simplicity of the *Pastorale d'été* (1920), *Horace victorieux* (1921) is a violent and uncompromising work which Honegger himself considered 'the most original and successful to have ever come from [his] hands'.

Darius Milhaud was born in Aix-en-Provence in 1892. He studied the violin and was later a pupil at the Paris Conservatoire under Dukas. He spent the First World War in Brazil as attaché at the French embassy under Paul Claudel. His Parisian career was again interrupted in 1940, when he took refuge from the Nazis in the United States and became professor of composition at Mills College, California. On his return to Paris, after the war, he became professor at the Conservatoire.

Milhaud is one of those composers, more common in earlier periods than our own, whose output is huge. His work runs into hundreds of opus numbers – from miniature pieces to vast scores. He attached extreme importance to melodic line, superimposing different keys to produce a polytonal texture characteristic of his style. Of all his works his monumental dramatic compositions are the most remarkable. The three scenes from *Orestes*, adapted from Aeschylus by Claudel, offer a remarkable variety of spoken declamation, a form of speech in measured rhythm. The operas *Christophe Colombe* (1930), *Maximilian* and *Bolivar* are often criticised for being too similar. Nevertheless, *Christophe Colombe* is considered by some to be Milhaud's masterpiece; *Bolivar*, which is a more popular but composite work, does suffer from its closeness to traditional operatic style.

Among his less important works is a successful chamber opera, the *Malheur d'Orphée*, a new version of the myth lit by the hard sun of Provence. Milhaud was very much attached to his meridional background, which explains his brilliant and celebrated orchestral *Suite provençale* and *Service sacré*. The deep impression made on him by Latin America inspired the ballet *Création du monde* (1923) and the *Saudades do Brasil* for piano. Among his vast output, which includes twelve symphonies and eight quartets, it is essential to mention the stunning *Scaramouche* for two pianos.

More than any other of the Six (with the exception of Poulenc), Georges Auric (b. 1899), director of the Paris Opéra since 1962, followed the tenets of Cocteau's manifesto. Equally hostile to Wagnerianism and Impressionism, he cultivated a witty sharp-edged style opposed to

all Romanticism. His deliberate easy grace was admirably suited to the innumerable theatrical and, especially, film scores that he wrote for Cocteau, René Clair and many others. Auric drew on the idiom of the music hall and jazz, and works such as the ballets for Diaghilev, *Les Fâcheux* (1924) and *Les Matelots* (1925), brought him outstanding success. But this overtly witty music was followed by a later period of more seriously intentioned works, such as his partita for two pianos, written in an idiosyncratic 'serial' style.

Francis Poulenc (1899-1963) was born in Paris, and was a remarkable pianist at a very early age. For a long time he had a reputation as a social maverick which he deliberately cultivated and which earned him a fashionable success; for example, in his ballet *Les Biches* (1924), commissioned by Diaghilev, the erotic element refers explicitly to a known person. A tendency to witty pastiche, sometimes harmonious, sometimes not, is evident in a large number of piano pieces, and also in the organ concerto of 1938. But in spite of the immediate charm of these works, the chorale from the *Litanie de la Vierge noire* and *Figures humaines* (1943) and the song cycle *Tel jour, telle nuit* (1937) show a much more profound feeling and are devoid of the many facile mannerisms which earned him popular success. Spicy charms and dissonant harmonies are here replaced by a determined and convincing aesthetic. During his last creative period Poulenc, although sometimes reverting to his youthful flippancy, stressed the serious side of his nature in two operas, *Dialogue des Carmélites* (1957) with libretto by Bernanos, and *La Voix humaine*, based on a play by Cocteau. Even in his Stabat Mater, despite its gravity

Darius Milhaud.

of tone, the element of pastiche is a little over-accentuated. In his last instrumental works, the sonatas for two pianos, for flute and piano, for clarinet and piano and for oboe and piano, the composer deliberately freed his score of all extraneous effects and dispensed with any sort of 'programme music'.

Germaine Taillefer (b. 1892), after brilliant studies at the Paris Conservatoire, met Milhaud and later Satie and became involved with the Six, but later she showed a profound admiration of the French masters of the 18th century. She has written many works for piano and orchestra as well as solo piano pieces, chamber music, a cantata based on Paul Valéry's *Narcisse* and lyric pieces.

Louis Durey (b. 1888), little known save for his association with the Six, was one of the first French composers to be inspired by the theories of Schoenberg in his songs, *L'Offrande lyrique*.

The school of Arcueil and Young France

This school was made up of admirers of the simplicity, naïveté and economy of style of Erik Satie's late works. Its most distinguished member was Henri Sauguet (b. 1901). He had a great admiration for Satie, both as a man and as a musician; moreover, it was not so much the unadorned structural simplicity of *Socrates* that appealed to him as its emotional content. Sauguet's own music displays considerable sensitivity and depth of feeling; it includes the brilliantly successful ballet *Les*

Jean Cocteau.

Forains, his operas *La Chartreuse de Parme* and the *Caprices de Marianne*, his piano concerto, quartets and songs. Sauguet never deliberately seeks a new musical language, but he has experimented with *musique concrète*.

The avowed intention of the Young France group, formed in the 1930s, was to reinstate those deeper and permanent human and spiritual values which the postwar generation had affected to despise and ignore. The group was initiated by Yves Baudrier (b. 1906), more by virtue of his manifesto than his compositions. But the original intention has not survived, as the other members, Daniel-Lesur, André Jolivet and Olivier Messiaen have orientated their music in very different directions.

Daniel-Lesur (b. 1908) is a musician of refined sensibility whose art is distinguished by its lyrical and poetic quality. The problem of musical language interests him less exclusively than it does Jolivet or Messiaen. He very soon adopted a modal form which is dignified and Romantic, noble but not too austere, and is remarkably consistent in quality. He has composed works for the organ and written a mass, but his principal work is the *Song of Songs* (1953) which reflects his interest in medieval and Renaissance polyphony.

André Jolivet (b. 1905) interprets the humanism of the group in a different way. His works as a whole are inspired by the religious feelings which first led him to ritual music. After five years of study with Paul le Flem, who gave him a solid classical foundation, and later with Edgar Varèse, Jolivet first turned his attention to the modes of primitive music. Here he discovered his spiritual vocation, and he has been occupied ever since with the vast new field of sound which this study provided. The rhythms and modes of African, Oriental and Polynesian music inspired his piano suite *Marna* (1935).

But his research into sound effects and the need to escape from tonality incited Jolivet to experiment even further with the modal styles provided by his study of primitive music. He devoted himself to extreme harmonic experimentation, and interested himself in serial music, although not subscribing to it in a systematic way. His combined interest in all musical languages, and his desire for a unifying 'message', give Jolivet's music constant novelty. His compositions include a concerto for the electronic Ondes Martenot (1947), a piano concerto, the first and second symphonies, and a full-scale oratorio, *La Vérité de Jeanne*.

The middle generation

Fauré bequeathed to his pupils a way of musical thinking rather than any definite characteristic language. As a theoretician, Charles Koechlin (1867-1950) exercised a great influence on many musicians and his reputation as a teacher has overshadowed his work as a composer.

The music of Florent Schmitt (1870-1958), a pupil of Dubois, Massenet and Fauré, displays an energetic and independent character, both passionate and spiritual, and he remains an isolated figure in French music of the first half of the 20th century. His very personal style, sometimes on an immense scale, sometimes sarcastic or even Romantic, was altogether too excessive and bewildering for French taste. His output was very large, always interesting and often prophetic. *Soirs* (1890) for piano, was written prior to Debussy's Impressionism, with which he was not familiar; *Psalm XLVII* has a primitive and monumental boldness anticipating Honegger and Stravinsky; while the *Tragédie de Salomé* introduces a sort of intense Romanticism in the 'grand Debussy style' and anticipates at the same time the savagery of the *Rite of Spring*. However, the best of

Schmitt's work was in the manner of the true Romantic that he was. To this period belong *Antony and Cleopatra*, *Salammbô* and the ballets *Le petit elfe ferme l'oeil* and *Oriane*, while his last symphony and his string quartet are among his finest works.

J. Roger-Ducasse (1873-1954) wrote quartets and a 'mimodrama', *Orphée*, inspired by the same themes as Fauré, but his southern temperament asserts itself in *Cantegril*, an *opéra comique*, which is in a different category. His finest work is his *Sarabande* for chorus (1911).

Louis Aubert, a remarkably fine pianist, was at one time world famous as the composer of *Habanera* for orchestra (1918).

Ravel's teaching was more a matter of a subtle relationship between master and pupil than of formal indoctrination. Roland-Manuel (b. 1891), who knew Ravel better than anyone else, thoroughly learnt the lessons of his master and, by taking him as a model, avoided any tendency to Romanticism. Manuel Rosenthal (b. 1904) combined a career as a conductor with composing comic operas and piano works and some deeply sincere sacred compositions.

Tony Aubin has described his master Dukas's teaching as! 'Severity towards any faults in form, or excessive virtuosity or anything that smacks of empty eloquence; he appreciated and defended anything in our works which had a unique flavour – perhaps just one linking passage, or a melodic curve in which he recognised a personal touch'. Like all fine teachers, then, Dukas encouraged his pupils towards individuality of expression, yet all those mentioned here have a predilection for classicism and the purest forms of musical expression.

Georges Dandelot (b. 1895) expresses a natural Romanticism in his operas, oratorio, concert music, songs and chamber music. Henri Barraud (b. 1900) will have nothing to do with any systematic musical programme, and thereby hides the serious and dignified aspect of his music, which is expressed in some remarkable symphonic works. Moreover, his orchestral texture owes its colour to Berlioz. Although Barraud sometimes seems a little too light-hearted, the somewhat remote nobility of his opera *Numance* and the sincerity of the *Mystère des Saints Innocents* show a sensitivity tempered with modesty which is the keynote of all his music.

Straightforward classicism, a taste for delicate poetry, a happy childhood, a rich sense of humour and sudden moments of seriousness, all colour the attractive music of Claude Arrieu (b. 1903). His lyric works (*Cadet Rousselle*), a series of songs, instrumental music, a trio for reed instruments, and much music for radio are all excellent. But by far the best is his cantata *Sept poèmes d'amour en guerre*, with a text by Paul Eluard, which evokes the passion of the French resistance movement in the Second World War. The name of the organist Maurice Duruflé (b. 1903), the teacher of Messiaen, is linked with the *Requiem* (1947) in which he retains Fauré's principles but simplifies them even further by the inclusion of Gregorian plainsong. The same characteristics are to be found in his *Veni Creator* suite for organ.

The music of Tony Aubin (b. 1907) who took up the same position at the Paris Conservatoire as his former master (Fauré) in 1946, is peculiarly lucid and shows great veneration for Dukas, while adhering to the lessons of his master.

The independents

Many French composers and musicians during the first half of the century studied under none of the great figures mentioned so far. Fred Barlow (1881-1951), a pupil of Koechlin, left some truly delightful and sensitive music in his songs, chamber works and *opéra comique*, *Sylvie*.

Lily Boulanger (1893-1918) whose reputation as a composer is steadily rising, won the Grand Prix de

Francis Poulenc.

right
Olivier Messiaen as a young man.

below
A page of Messiaen's autograph manuscript of Chronochromie.

Rome in 1913 with the cantata *Faust et Hélène*, being the first woman composer ever to do so. During her stay in Rome she wrote the *Three Psalms*, the originality and vigour of which compare with similar works by Roussel and Florent Schmitt. Her more famous sister, Nadia, (b. 1887) became one of the most important teachers of the 20th century and has also played a decisive role in the revival of interest in the music of Monteverdi. In 1921 she was appointed to the American Conservatory at Fontainebleau, becoming its director in 1950. Her pupils have included Walter Piston, Aaron Copland and Lennox Berkeley among many others.

Claude Delvincourt (1888-1954) played an important role in music as director of the Paris Conservatoire from 1941. As a composer he made experiments with 'extra-tonal' harmonies with the object of contrasting them with tonality, but he was equally at home with witty compositions like the *Boccaceries* for piano. His more ambitious works, like the dance poem *Offering to Siva* and the mime cantata *Lucifer*, are very closely linked with the traditions of sacred opera.

Jacques Ibert (1890-1962) was director of the Villa Medici (the school of the Prix de Rome) for a number of years. His *Divertissement* for orchestra (1930) possesses all the qualities that make his music so outstanding: his compositions are always concise and elegant with unusual harmonies. His comic vein is particularly evident in his operas, notably *Le Roi d'Yvetot*. The same witty brilliance characterises his flute, saxophone and cello concertos and the *Sinfonia concertante* for oboe, *Escales* for orchestra and his piano pieces, *Histoires*. But in his string quartet and the *Chevalier errant*, a choreographic epic for a large orchestra, Ibert reveals a profounder side of his art.

Georges Migot (b. 1891), a highly cultured and very religious man, uses a severely contrapuntal line; he is inspired by the mystique of numbers and frequently looks back to the old French music of the troubadours. His esoteric preoccupations and lofty spiritual ideals have earned him the nickname 'The Group of One'.

Jean Rivier (b. 1896) succeeded Milhaud as professor of composition at the Paris Conservatoire. His large output, which is both Romantic and tender, is somewhat reminiscent of Honegger, but never quite achieves the latter's genuine intensity of feeling. His best work is in orchestral compositions, notably a *Don Quixote* overture, but he also made a name for himself with his chamber music.

Suzanne Demarquez (b. 1899) is as excellent a musician and technician as she is a critic and musicologist. Her compositions include *Variations, Interlude* and *Tarantella*. Among her literary works are biographies of Purcell, Roussel and Manuel de Falla.

The concert music of Maurice Jaubert (1900-40) has scarcely had time to become known, but the songs he wrote to texts by Giraudoux, and the music he composed for the best films of Marcel Carne and René Clair, are still performed.

Jean Françaix (b. 1912) seems predestined by his very name to carry French music beyond the frontiers of his native country. His somewhat superficial and repetitive work would seem to correspond exactly with what foreigners expect of French music – elegance, brilliance and a variety of styles.

Henri Dutilleux (b. 1916) is one of those rare composers who has found a convincing and personal language without allying himself to any particular composer or any particular new school. Neither does he use ancient or classical forms already exploited. His four major works are his piano sonata (1948), *Le Loup*, a ballet by Anouilh and Neveux (1952), and his first and second symphonies, which display great individuality and a desire to expand the tonal language rather than reject it entirely.

Messiaen

Olivier Messiaen (b. 1908) was a pupil of Jean and Noël Gallon, Caussade, Marcel Dupré and Maurice Emmanuel. He was appointed organist of La Trinité church in Paris in 1931, and in the same year his first big work, *Les Offrandes oubliées*, attracted wide attention. A special chair of musical analysis was created for him at the Paris Conservatoire.

Very early in his career Messiaen felt the need to reconsider the problem of musical language outside the rules of classical tonality. He saw the problem under two aspects – melody and rhythm. His answer was to evolve a new system, born of his studies of nature, which he called 'modes with limited transpositions'. His rhythms consist of a tripartite rhythmic system where the last part picks up the first. In a sense, Messiaen's chief preoccupation is the search for the impossible, but it must not be forgotten that the inspiration behind his systems arises from a wide variety of different elements. His melody is inspired by his intensive study of bird songs of which, with infinite patience, he has collected many examples, while his rhythms are often based on the subtle variations of Indian music. Such rarefied techniques, like others in modern music, may be thought to make his work inaccessible to the lay listener, but Messiaen argues that his music possesses two universal qualities: religious faith and a gift of colour.

A devout Christian, Messiaen has never ceased to refer to religion in carrying out his work, and it was as an organist that he first gave proof of his dedication to the Church in a series of works (1932–51): *L'Apparition de l'église éternelle*, *L'Ascension*, *Le Corps glorieux*, *Messe de la Pentecôte* and the *Livre d'orgue*. In these works Messiaen freed the organ from its role as a symphonic instrument or as an instrument with a purely decorative function, as used by the post-Romantics. Instead he substituted a new musical sound and his main preoccupation is research into colour, which he carried through into his piano works, many of which demand a high degree of virtuosity and were first interpreted by his pupil Yvonne Loriod. These works comprise the *Vision de l'amen*, *Vingt regards sur l'enfant Jésus Christ*, *Catalogue d'oiseaux* (1959) and *Quatre études de rhythme* (1949). The last was immensely influential among younger composers for its application of the principle of continuity of pitch changes in chromatic intervals to the time values and intensity of notes. His powerful faith and astonishingly colourful palette also call on the resources of a large orchestra, as in *Trois petites liturgies de la présence divine* (1944) and the *Turangalíla symphony* (1948), a monumental score which embraces and enlarges on all Messiaen's researches at this period. Among the smaller – but no less important – compositions of the same character are the charming youthful works, *La Fête des Belles Eaux* for sextet of Ondes Martenot; the *Quatuor pour la fin du temps*, composed and first performed in 1941 while Messiaen was in an internment camp, and *Les Oiseaux exotiques* (1956) for piano and instrumental ensemble.

Messiaen's *Technique de mon langage musical* expounds his musical theories in 1944, but since then his research has led him to further explorations. He has also written a treatise on the subject of rhythm.

Messiaen's teaching has had a decisive effect on a number of contemporary composers who have contributed to a renewal of musical language during the 1960s, chief among them being Pierre Boulez.

Messiaen surrounded by his pupils.

Music in Germany and Austria

In the early 20th century Vienna, the home of Haydn, Mozart and Beethoven, once again took the lead in the formation of a new style. The story of the three great figures in this movement, Schoenberg, Berg and Webern, has been told at some length in an earlier chapter, as has also the long post-Romantic 'Indian summer' of Richard Strauss. Here we are concerned with men, some of whom are the continuators of the revolutionary work of the school of Vienna, while others present a direct contrast to it. In the post-war generation, many younger composers have turned to the work of Webern for their inspiration rather than to that of his once better known friends, applying themselves to composition not only for the conventional instruments that were available to him, but also to the new sonorous techniques of concrete music and electronic music. But the German composer who, after the giants of Vienna, for long bulked largest in the music of this century, was Paul Hindemith.

Hindemith

Both in his music and in his theories, Hindemith was explicitly opposed to the rarefied and abstruse music of the twelve-note composers and other extremely *avant-garde* musicians. In his view such experiments, so far in advance of the generally accepted notion of music, produced works whose performance was tantamount to beating the audience into submission. Hindemith was firmly convinced that the composition of music was a craft with direct social usefulness, whether for diversion or for education, and as such must not allow itself to become the ivory-tower preserve of the experts and the cognoscenti. He backed up these convictions by the composition of a large body of what he called functional music (*Gebrauchsmusik*), and of music for amateurs (*Gemeinschaftmusik*). In two early *Lehrstücke*, or plays of instruction, the audience of school children was expected to participate directly; he also composed film, radio and educational music and, for amateurs, sonatas for virtually every commonly used instrument.

Paul Hindemith was born in the German state of Hesse in 1895. After completing his studies at the Conservatory of Frankfurt-am-Main, he was appointed conductor of the orchestra of the opera there (1915-23) and later played viola in the internationally famous Amar String Quartet. In the 1920s he was active in the festivals of contemporary music at Donaueschingen and Baden-Baden; in 1927 he became teacher of composition at the Musikhochschule in Berlin. In the early 1930s he openly opposed Hitler and the reactionary and nationalist doctrines of Goebbels. Stigmatised by the Führer personally as a representative of 'degenerate, effete, anti-German art', Hindemith fled the country. He went into exile, first in Switzerland and then, in 1939, to the United States, where he spent the whole of the war years. He then returned to Europe to take up the post of professor of composition at Zurich University. He died from a heart attack in hospital in Frankfurt in December 1963.

The development of his music

Hindemith first became known as a composer at the beginning of the 1920s. His music was aggressive and volcanic. After some preliminary works, influenced by Brahms, Bruckner and Reger, he broke out on his own. His first opera, *Sancta Suzanna*, caused such a scandal that the police had to be called in. His explosive reputation was to be confirmed with his second string quartet, published in 1921.

In reality there is no very apparent difference of language between the successive Hindemith periods. If the first seemed revolutionary at the time, it was certainly less because of the music itself than because of the aesthetic and philosophic ideas for which it was the vehicle. Once these youthful explosive flashes of genius had revealed themselves, Hindemith's musical development quickly assumed a more level course. The song cycle *Das Marienleben* (1923, revised 1936-48), based on poems by Rilke which were themselves the heralds of a new literary period, is a beautiful work, but it shows traces of the Neo-classical tendencies so common in the music of the time. This return to a more conventional style of composition was confirmed by a return to the manner of Bach, evident in a large series of small instrumental chamber works, in particular in the concertos of 1927. After his early cosmopolitan tendencies, he became more and more traditionally German. The instrumental works of his second period are full of references to the Baroque music of the German courts of the 18th century. Henceforth, Hindemith was only on the fringe of the international movement.

He also reverted to the use of vast orchestras and, beginning with the superb *Konzertmusik* for string orchestra and brass (1930), he was to employ larger and larger combinations of instruments. However, despite this very clear development and change of direction, the youthful Hindemith is still apparent in his opera *Cardillac* (1926), after Hoffmann's *Mademoiselle de Scudéry*. The central theme of the opera is one very close to Hindemith's heart – the problem confronting a creative artist who is a prisoner of a social order which is at odds with his personal genius. This same idea occupies him in his best known opera, *Mathis der Maler*. The music is also used in a symphony, both opera and symphony being written in the years immediately following Hindemith's departure from Nazi Germany. The story is that of the 16th-century German painter, Matthias Grünewald, and his masterpiece the Isenheim altarpiece.

Hindemith's credo rested on clear and strongly held
convictions. First there was the belief in the value of
music as a social activity, summed up in the dictum 'it
is better to make music than to listen to it'. Secondly
came an intense and proud professionalism, which made
Hindemith not only a master of all the intricacies of
traditional harmony and counterpoint, but also an
expert in the performing techniques of the instruments
that he wrote for. Thirdly, in an age when the vanguard
of musical experimentation was leading further and
further away from the notion of tonality, Hindemith
steadfastly opposed the concepts of atonality and twelve-
note composition. In such treatises as *The Craft of
Composition* (1937) and *Traditional Harmony* (1943), and
compositions such as the prelude and fugues for piano,
Ludus Tonalis, the didactic intent is obvious.

His attempt to construct a new ordering of the basic
materials of music which should preserve the concept
of tonality, while neither so thorough-going nor so fruitful as that of Bartók, is nevertheless of considerable
interest. He compared the power of an overall tonal
system to the force of gravity in the physical world, but
melody also played a central part in his own system. In
the new style of melody that he cultivated, the minor
second plays an important part, though not with the
directional quality of the leading note, and the interval
of the fourth is also much used. The result is a melodic
plasticity that is a characteristic feature of Hindemith's
work, while his theory of intervals certainly opened the
way to new harmonic possibilities. In addition to the
works referred to above, mention should also be made of
the ballet, *Noblissima Visione* (1938), on the life of St
Francis of Assisi, with choreography by Massine; the
opera *The Harmony of the World* (1957), on the life of the
German astronomer Kepler, first composed in symphonic form (1951); the orchestral *Metamorphoses on
themes by C. M. von Weber* (1943); and the theme and
variations for piano and strings, *The Four Temperaments* (1940).

Hindemith's own career as a composer shows the full
circle from a violent and iconoclastic youth, through a
period of meditation to a return to the tradition of
Brahms, Bruckner and Reger.

right
*Kurt Weill (left), Hindemith
(centre) and Brecht (far right) at a
chamber music festival at Baden-
Baden in 1929.*

below
*An Italian production (1952) of
Carl Orff's* Carmina Burana.

Hindemith's contemporaries

Among the composers of Hindemith's generation whose work is best known abroad is Carl Orff, who was born in Munich in 1895. Besides his work as a composer, Orff has been an active teacher, holding a position at the Munich Academy of Music and being particularly active in methods of musical education for children, as well as working as a conductor and as an editor of old music. His work in this last field has coloured his own music, most notably the well known scenic cantata, *Carmina Burana*. This was first performed in Frankfurt in 1937, the music being accompanied by mimed action, and consists of settings of songs of wine and women from a 13th-century manuscript found at the Benediktbeuren monastery in Bavaria. The style of this, as of most, of Orff's works, is clear and uncomplicated, using simple but effective melodic and rhythmic elements, building up climaxes by repetition and avoiding contrapuntal procedures. From the age of forty Orff has devoted himself exclusively to music for the theatre, from incidental music to operas such as *Antigone* (1949).

Another composer to have found inspiration in the stage is Boris Blacher (b. 1903). His talent for light and dancing melody is combined with an almost equal gift for contrapuntal structures; and an intense interest in rhythm has led him to a system of variable metre, derived in part from his study of the music of Stravinsky's second period. Although some of his best music is to be found in his operas and, above all, ballets, such as *Hamlet* (1950), he has also composed the brilliant orchestral *Variations on a theme by Paganini* and the opera *The Grand Inquisitor* (1948).

Werner Egk (b. 1901), who studied under Orff for a time, writes in an uncomplicated language which reveals his admiration for the works of Richard Strauss, Stravinsky and, above all, the French school. His music is distinguished by its colourful orchestration. In 1936 he received the Golden Olympic Medal for orchestral music, but he is most admired for such operas as *Die Zaubergeige* (1935), in which he made much use of folk songs, and *The Government Inspector* (1957) after Gogol. Egk has also written a good deal for the radio and a number of ballets and orchestral and choral works, among them *Mein Vaterland* (1937).

But of all the German composers of music for the theatre from this period, the best known and one of the most talented is Kurt Weill (1900–50). His most important work was done before 1935, when he settled in the United States, becoming an American citizen in 1943. Weill was already actively employed in the theatre in his early twenties, though at this time he also took lessons in composition from Busoni in Berlin. His purely instrumental works include two symphonies and a concerto for wind instruments, and he wrote incidental music for the plays of the Expressionist dramatist Georg Kaiser before his famous collaboration with Bertolt Brecht. In 1928 this resulted in the *Dreigroschenoper*.

Ostensibly a modernisation of Gay's *Beggar's Opera* (and produced in its bicentenary year), *The Threepenny Opera* had a far more explicit and self-conscious social programme than its original. The production was clearly imbued with Brecht's views on the theatre as a medium of social evangelism and his theory of *Verfremdung* (alienation), which requires the constant breaking of the theatrical illusion to involve the audience and point to an explicit message in the action. Weill's witty, spiky and sometimes moving music, which borrowed from the music hall and the world of jazz, was the ideal foil for the libretto. *The Threepenny Opera* was followed by the still more bitterly satirical *Rise and Fall of the City of Mahagonny*, in which composer and librettist mercilessly presented the vicious aspects of capitalist society. Weill left Germany in 1933. In New York he soon mastered the requirements of Broadway and wrote a number of successful musicals.

The Austrian composer, Hanns Jelinek (b. 1901), was almost an exact contemporary of Weill and, like him, found the jazz idiom a fruitful source of ideas. Indeed, as a young man he frequently took jobs as a bar pianist to support himself and, although he was able to take some lessons with Berg and Schoenberg, he had no regular training as a composer. He has written an operetta, *Bubi Caligula* (1947), and a certain amount of film music, but with these exceptions most of his work has been in the twelve-note idiom. He held a number of teaching posts as an exponent of the technique, on which he has written a treatise (1952) and a *Twelve-note primer for the piano* (1954). In 1952 he was appointed to the staff of the Viennese Academy of Music. His other works include a *Sinfonia concertante* for string quartet and orchestra, *Prometheus* (a cantata for baritone and orchestra), and *Symphonia Brevis*, commissioned to celebrate the fiftieth anniversary of the founding of the Viennese symphonic society.

Like Jelinek, Karl Amadeus Hartmann (1905–63) took lessons with one of the founders of the twelve-note school, Anton Webern, but his music, though making use of twelve-note techniques and atonality, was never strictly confined to the system. Indeed, after

A still from the film The Threepenny Opera.

Karl Amadeus Hartmann.

1945, Hartmann's essentially Expressionist technique showed leanings towards the early style of Stravinsky, and he developed an interest in rhythmic variations comparable to that of Boris Blacher. In 1934 he wrote an opera based on the 17th-century novel, *Simplicissimus*, by Grimmelshausen. The social commitment and pacifism of Hartmann's opera was directly opposed to the mood of Nazi Germany and the work was not performed until 1949. But Hartmann's finest achievement as a composer lies in his eight symphonies.

After the war he was active in the cause of *avant-garde* music, inaugurating the Musica Viva concerts at Munich. Here many contemporary works have received their first performance at the hands of the world's finest conductors and performers. Closely associated with him in the early years of this venture was his former teacher, the distinguished conductor Hermann Scherchen (1891-1966) who, at the age of twenty, had directed the first performance of Schoenberg's *Pierrot-Lunaire* and who, throughout his life, was an ardent advocate of advanced music, particularly that of the twelve-note school. Scherchen left Germany in the 1930s with the advent of the Nazis as did so many of his colleagues, among whom was the Austrian Ernst Krenek (b. 1900) who settled in America in 1938, where he has held a succession of teaching posts. He has visited Europe on a number of occasions since the war to hold seminars on twelve-note technique. His very large output includes music in a variety of styles, and his reputation was founded by the success of his jazz opera, *Johnny Spielt Auf* (1927), for which he also wrote the libretto. It was followed by a brief period of what Krenek himself has described as 'atavistic Romanticism'. His first exercises in twelve-note composition date from the early 1930s and his subsequent study of the frequently complex procedures of 15th-century Flemish polyphonists, such as Ockeghem, have further enriched his work. His inclination towards the musical *avant-garde* had been prompted in the 1920s by his admiration for the work of Bartók and Hindemith, but his style has been continually receptive to new developments and he has experimented with electronic techniques.

In Germany itself the twelve-note school won a late disciple in Wolfgang Fortner (b. 1907) who, since about 1950, has made use of the technique. He has also worked as a conductor and exercised a certain influence as a teacher, his pupils including Hans Werner Henze. Up to 1945 he had composed in a basically tonal idiom, being influenced as a young man by Reger, Stravinsky and Hindemith. His first twelve-note composition was the third string quartet of 1948. Since then his works, which comprise virtually every type, have included the dramatic choral work *The Sacrifice of Isaac* (1952), scored for numerous instruments including jazz trumpets and trombones, and the opera *Blood Wedding* (1957), based on the play by Garcia Lorca.

Finally in this description of some of Hindemith's near contemporaries we must mention two composers of the German Democratic Republic. Of these the most interesting is Hanns Eisler (1898-1962), the composer of the East German national anthem. After studying with Schoenberg and Webern in Vienna he proved himself an early and apt disciple of their method, producing works using its techniques in the 1920s. This was followed by a period of social commitment and the composition of a number of songs for workers which brought him into contact with Bertold. Brecht. In collaboration they wrote a number of works for the theatre. The Hitler regime drove Eisler, too, from Germany. He went to America where he proved a successful composer of film music, writing a book on the techniques required. In 1948 he returned to Germany to take up the post of professor of composition in the East Berlin Academy of Arts. From that time he wrote a number of compositions which show a return to a late Romantic style, and include a number of workers' choruses. The second of these two East German composers is Rudolf Wagner Regeney (b. 1903). Between the wars he was active in the theatre, composing operas including *The Burghers of Calais* (1939). His music is in a simple pellucid tonal style somewhat influenced by Weill, and, formally, such works as the opera *Johanna Balk* (1941) show a return to the traditional operatic structure of separate numbers. In 1950 he was appointed as professor of composition at the Musikhochschule in East Berlin and since then his works have included the choral works *Cantica Davidi Regis* (1954) and *Genesis* (1957).

The younger generation

Among the most important composers working in Germany now are Henze and Stockhausen, but their *avant-garde* music is balanced by that of composers such as the Austrian Gottfried von Einem, born in Bern in 1918. His work is based on an imaginative use of tonality and draws eclectically on a number of sources including the music of Mahler and Strauss, Stravinsky, Blacher (in his rhythmic interests) and jazz. His works include the operas *Danton's Death* (1947), based on Georg Büchner's play, and *The Trial* (1953), from Kafka's novel.

Hans Werner Henze, born at Gütersloh in 1926, studied at the local music academy in Brunswick, but also took private lessons from Fortner and visited the classes of René Leibowitz in Paris. In his early twenties he was the musical director of the German theatre in Constance and then artistic director of the ballet in Wiesbaden. Since 1953 he has lived on the island of Ischia and in Naples, as a freelance composer. From the first he was hailed as one of the most talented musicians working in Germany; his facility in every type of composition, from tonal to twelve-note and the most advanced techniques, is astonishing and like other younger composers he is prepared to accept dodecaphony as a manner of expression rather than as a strict method. His compositions include a number of

left
A scene from the Hamburg premier of Hans Werner Henze's opera The Prince of Homburg *(1960).*

below
A scene from the first Berlin production of Henze's ballet Jack Pudding *(1957).*

ballets, among them *Jack Pudding* (1949) and *Ondine* (1956); operas such as *The Prince of Homburg* (1960) and the instrumental *Sonata per archi* (1958). But his facility is not simply a matter of stylistic adaptability, from his total mastery of the resources of late Romantic orchestration to deployment of serial methods in all their variety. Henze also has an astonishing rate of production, which before the age of thirty had resulted in an oeuvre of more than fifty works, many of them on the largest scale.

Like Henze, Giselher Klebe (b. 1925), one year his senior, makes use of a variety of styles and techniques though he does not equal his contemporary's speed of composition. Nevertheless, his technical expertise is considerable and his early expressive style was indebted in part to the variable metre of his teacher, Boris Blacher, and in part to his own study of Webern's music. After a musical training interrupted by war service and not completed until he was twenty-six, Klebe worked for a time with the Berlin radio and then went freelance. His compositions include musical metamorphoses on Paul Klee's painting *The Twittering Machine* (1950), a symphony and other orchestral music, chamber music and an opera based on Schiller's play *The Robbers.*

Another of Boris Blacher's pupils is Heimo Erbse (b. 1924), who has worked for much of his professional career in the world of the theatre and cinema. His music lacks richness, and sound is regarded essentially as a means for the expression of intellectual concepts rather than as a sensuous object in its own right. His chamber music is his most intimate work, while for the stage he has composed ballet and the opera *Julietta* for the Salzburg Festival of 1959.

Karlheinz Stockhausen, born near Cologne in 1928, soon made his mark as an experimenter in electronic music and has proved to be a leading theorist among serialist composers. He studied at Cologne with Frank Martin and then, in 1952, at Paris with Messiaen, where he was introduced to the techniques of concrete music. Thereafter he worked in the studio for electronic music of Cologne Radio, and also studied phonetics and communication theory at Bonn University, studies that were of direct importance to his development as a composer. He was one of the first modern composers to reintroduce, as an important factor in performance, the spatial disposition of instrumental forces, which had not been in use since the Baroque period. For Stockhausen the five elements of basic importance are: the spatial one, the duration of the notes, their frequency, their tone colour and their intensity. Much of his theoretical work has been devoted to devising mathematical relationships between these, as precise as those required by the classic twelve-note theory for the ordering of the pitch or frequency of the notes.

However, his work in electronic music led him to introduce the element of indeterminacy into his work. In both electronic and concrete music there was inevitably an element of chance. The author-craftsman often obtained effects that he had not foreseen, and his freedom as a creator then consisted in accepting or rejecting them. As musicians ventured further into this field, known as aleatory music (from the Latin word for dice), they allowed for a certain percentage of unexpected effects, and Stockhausen himself at one point drew up a list of the forms that he used in his works, which ranged from totally determined to a maximum of indetermination.

His professional approach to the problems of the new music has also made Stockhausen insist that composers, now faced with a variety of media, should design specifically for the medium intended. In this way his approach to a commission for the radio would be radically different from that to a composition for the concert hall of the traditional type. In his instrumental compositions he has tended to work on the assumption of considerable liberty for the performer. His *Piano Pieces number XI* (1956), for example, consists of a number of fragments that can be performed in various orders and in different manners. Among his other compositions are *Zeitmasse* or 'tempos' for five wind instruments (1956), *Groups* for three orchestras (1957), *Contacts* for electronic sounds, piano and percussion (1960), and *Moments* for soprano voice, four choirs and an ensemble of thirteen instruments (1962). Stockhausen still retains his position as one of the most important leaders of the new music and some account of later developments in his work is given in the final chapter of this book.

The new Beethoven Room at Bonn.

Hungary in the age of Bartók

Even before the death of Liszt the musical life of Hungary was divided. On the one hand there were the delightful but essentially 'Palm Court' productions of composers whose music was coloured by the Hungarian idiom of a *verbunkos* that had lost its élan. On the other hand was a group of talented musicians who modelled themselves on the great Romantic composers of Germany. This was the situation which led Bartók and Zoltán Kodály to go out into the countryside to find solid foundations for a truly national musical idiom.

Hungary after Liszt

The light Hungarian flavour of their music was a factor in the success of those two delightful operetta composers, Lehár and Kálmán. The name of Franz Lehár (1870-1948), Hungarian by birth but a true Viennese in every other respect, is inevitably associated with the immense reputation of his operetta *The Merry Widow*, performed at Vienna in 1905. Over the next thirty years

there followed many others, such as *The Count of Luxemburg* (1909), *Gipsy Love* (1910), and *The Tsarevitch* (1927), which shows Lehár's interest, later in his career, in a somewhat more intense dramatic content. Apart from the rapid and international acclaim won by his *The Gay Hussars* (1908), the career of Emmerich (originally Imre) Kálmán (1882-1953) was not of equal brilliance.

The violinist and composer Jeno Hubay (1858-1937), whose compositions included the opera *The Violin maker of Cremona* (1894), with a famous violin solo, also wrote orchestral music which, later, in such works as the *Petöfi Symphony*, became consciously Hungarian in intention. Karoly Goldmark (1830-1915), the son of a Jewish cantor, belonged to the earlier generation and, besides the colour that it receives from the Hungarian music of the period and from the music of the synagogue, his work shows such diverse influences as Wagner and Mendelssohn. He wrote six operas, of which *The Queen of Sheba* reveals the composer's considerable orchestral technique, and a number of orchestral works such as the *Sakuntala Overture*, which betrays Goldmark's interest in the discovery of Sanskrit literature which went on

A scene from the operetta The Merry Widow *by Franz Lehár.*

throughout the 19th century.

Such composers as these were worthy representatives of the international European idiom and in his compositions Ernö Dohnányi (1877-1960), more important than any of them, followed the same pattern. His works, mainly in the idiom of Brahmsian Romanticism, include the well known *Variations on a Nursery Theme* for piano and orchestra; a festival overture to celebrate the fiftieth anniversary of the union of the towns of Buda and Pest; a suite *Ruralia Hungarica* and the *American Rhapsody*, written after he had settled in the United States in 1949. But in addition to his compositions, which also included three operas, a ballet and three symphonies, Dohnányi had an important career in Hungary between the wars as a conductor and director in the state broadcasting service. In these capacities he worked hard in the cause of modern music.

Bartók

Béla Bartók (1881-1945) was born the son of a director of an agricultural school in the southern region of the Hungarian plain, and the countryside of his native land was to be an inspiration to him as a composer. He was

Béla Bartók.

trained at the Conservatory in Budapest and his early music shows a natural inclination to the style of Brahms and Dohnányi, and then of Liszt. During these years he wrote the *Kossuth Overture*, first performed under Hans Richter at Manchester in 1904, and a rhapsody for piano and orchestra. Then, in 1905, he undertook with his friend Zoltán Kodály a profound and scientific study of the true folk music of Hungary, Slovakia and Rumania.

The two musicians travelled through the villages with a phonograph, complete with a stock of waxed cylinders, to record not only the music but the performances of peasant musicians. The result of this, the first great exercise in folk musicology in the field, was 16,000 recordings. The outcome of his discoveries decided Bartók to break away from the confines of tonality. He became interested in a form of melody derived from the most ancient pentatonic Magyar airs and with rhythms both firm and complex like those of folk songs, and he also experimented with popular Hungarian instruments, among which percussion plays a major role. However, Bartók was by no means in the general run of 'folklore' composers. It is relatively rare for him to borrow textually from popular folk music, nor does he compose in a 'folk' idiom, as did Liszt, the Russians, Grieg and many others. Rather, he was inspired by his fundamental studies of the creative principles of folk art to write profoundly original music. In 1908 he himself became teacher of the piano at the Academy, Budapest. During the inter-war years Bartók found himself increasingly out of sympathy with the rightist Horthy regime, and this was possibly a factor that led him to resign his teaching post in 1934 to devote himself exclusively to research into folk music. Then, in 1940, disgusted by Hungary's rapprochement with Nazi Germany and the increasingly extreme tendencies of the government, the sixty-year-old composer left his native country for the United States. There he was given an honorary professorship at Columbia University and supported himself as a pianist. When he died of leukaemia in 1945 he was a poor man and his funeral was attended by only a few friends. The tragic circumstances of his death soon became known and there followed a period of intense interest in the man and his music that led to its becoming more widely known than ever before.

The musician

In appearance Bartók was small, slim and ascetic; he gave an impression of energy and constant nervous tension. By character proud, even haughty, he was opposed to any form of compromise and lacked the worldly wisdom of a man such as Stravinsky, or the imperious dogmatism of Schoenberg. Yet his independence, so dearly bought, attracted all the young composers anxious to escape from the Neo-classicism then exemplified by Stravinsky, or, on the other hand, from the stifling atmosphere of dodecaphonic techniques not yet liberated by the post-Webern school. For a long time Bartók was the natural inspiration of all those who rejected serial music, yet nevertheless wished to turn their backs on the past.

Throughout his life Bartók, whose research took him not only through Hungary and the neighbouring territories but also to Bulgaria, Turkey and North Africa, tried to prove scientifically that these traditions had common roots. As a composer he soon realised that to use this new material he would have to invent a new musical language, free from the traditional rules of harmony and from the limitations imposed on rhythms by the use of bars. Liszt had anticipated much of this, but Bartók's final liberation from tradition was stimulated by Debussy, whose work he first heard in 1905. Bartók's resultant synthesis was a minutely elaborated, coherent and original language. The composer never actually codified this language himself, but the analysis of his style by Ernö Lendvai, which provides the basis of this summary, describes it thoroughly.

A new musical language

The major-minor tonal system of the classical period is foreign to folk music and, as a first step towards his new style, Bartók drew on the ancient modes and on the pentatonic scale, which allowed him to emancipate fourths and fifths from their conventional harmonic contexts. But folk music also tends to use not only its own modal system but also its own scales, among them the so-called acoustic octave, with a major third and sixth, a minor seventh and an augmented fourth. This augmented fourth, the interval of the tritone known since the middle ages as the 'devil in music', became the distinguishing mark of Bartók's language and the basis of the system of harmonic axes that he evolved.

This is a coherent use of the twelve notes of the chromatic scale, but is founded on the cycle of fifths and so, unlike twelve-note music, on the natural system of harmonics. Each tonic key under this system possesses two virtually related keys, of which each in its turn possesses two others. The base notes of the two related keys are always a tritone apart, lying a minor third on each side of the tonic. Thus the tritone becomes the basic interval, and two tritones, a minor third apart, form the two axes of the tonic.

Similar pairs of axes are formed starting from the dominant and subdominant, and the tonality of these encompasses the twelve semitones of the chromatic scale. This is why the tritone always occupies a predominant place in Bartók's musical language, and also why he uses without distinction the dominant or subdominant of either the tonic or the related keys. In fact, Bartók's axial system represents a tonal use of the 'chromatic total' of notes, and is the only system which can be set against Schoenberg's serial, non-tonal use of the twelve chromatic notes. Indeed, it has been argued paradoxically that Bartók, not Schoenberg, is the true revolutionary of the early 20th century.

Schoenberg's twelve-note system is, in a sense, the natural and logical consequence of the increasing chromaticism of late 19th-century harmony. This had

above
Ernö Dohnányi at a recording session in New York.

left
Set for a production of Bartók's opera Bluebeard's Castle, *at Budapest in 1959.*

led to the hierarchy imposed on the twelve notes of the chromatic scale by the major-minor tonal system, to the point of breakdown. Schoenberg, it can be argued, simply recognised the true state of affairs and set to work to erect a system of composition on the ruins of the old system. Accepting that the idea of tonality itself was exhausted, he started from the fact of a chromatic scale whose twelve notes have equal weight. Bartók on the other hand undertook the heroic task of building a new tonality on entirely revolutionary acoustic principles.

Certainly, the temptation to join the ranks of the twelve-note school was at times very strong, and occasioned Bartók acute inner conflicts, as the two violin sonatas, the études and improvisations for piano and, to a lesser extent, the third and fourth quartets prove. Bartók had here reached the point of rupture when it was no longer possible to avoid choosing or rejecting 'total' dodecaphony. But he remained faithful to his determination to wed the language of art music, in its most advanced stage, to the deep inspiration of folk. During the period of his decision between the two great alternatives we find shreds of folk themes savagely deformed, but the concept of a tonality is never quite lost.

In his search for a language which was both revolutionary and coherent, rhythm was a powerful help to Bartók. His rhythms were a development from the two

Zoltán Kodály.

opposite poles of Hungarian folk music, such as Liszt had once used: the free melodic recitative, and the dance rhythms based on a binary measure or on irregular groups of 5, 7, 9, 11 beats or more. In certain cases, like the famous 'Bulgarian' rhythms in the *Mikrokosmos* or the fifth quartet, the measure is divided in irregular tempi such as $3+3+2$, or $4+3+2$, etc. Such relatively complex rhythms are the natural counterpart to the advanced tonal structure of his music.

Only in the field of form was Bartók unable to find inspiration in folk melody; in consequence he had recourse to Bach and Beethoven, whose shadow looms over his six quartets. But he also made extensive use of the ratio of the golden section, common enough in painting but rare in music, though some commentators have found traces of its use in the music of Mozart, and the 20th-century composer, Jolivet, makes constant use of it. (A line divided by golden section has two parts, such that the ratio of the smaller to the larger is the same as the ratio of the larger to the whole.) In some of Bartók's major works, the golden section is used to mark a point of climax. A case in point is the first movement of the sonata for two pianos and percussion, in which the number of crotchets, when set against the number of crotchets in the two other movements (together shorter than the first), gives the required ratio. This over-intellectualised procedure was quite in tune with Bartók's almost obsessive concern for detail, and this ratio even determined the choice of melodic intervals in some of his works. His concern for symmetry and architecture manifests itself just as much in his use of an 'arch' structure as in the five-movement *Concerto for orchestra*.

Among Bartók's greatest works are the sonata for two pianos and percussion (1937); the concertos; the six great string quartets; the opera *Bluebeard's Castle* (1911); ballets like *The Wooden Prince* (1914-16) and *The Miraculous Mandarin* (1919); *Music for Strings, Percussion and Celeste* (1936); *Divertissement for strings* (1939) and *Concerto for orchestra* (1943).

Kodály and his contemporaries

Zoltán Kodály (1882-1967) was less ambitious than Bartók, though the latter once said that Kodály's works are the perfect incarnation of the spirit of Hungary and that his music constitutes 'a real profession of faith in the Hungarian soul'. In fact Kodály devoted his services to genuine Hungarian folk music. Nevertheless much of his work is brilliant and picturesque music, curiously allied to the influences of Brahms and Debussy – a music with irresistible rhythms and sumptuous orchestration.

Among his most successful works are the *Meditation on a theme by Claude Debussy*; the choral work *Psalmus Hungaricus* (1923); the *Galánta Dances* and *Marosszek Dances* for orchestra; and the opera *Háry János* (1926). Other compositions include a Te Deum, a Missa Brevis and the magnificent sonata for solo cello.

Kodály, also an erudite musicologist, produced a thesis on the *Strophic structure of Hungarian folk songs*. He was a fervent teacher, in love with his country, and was unsparing in his service of the ideal of a national musical culture. Indeed, in Hungary itself, his influence may well have been even greater than that of Bartók.

Of the contemporaries and successors of Kodály, one of the most important is László Lajtha (1892-1963), a pupil of d'Indy and appointed in 1919 a professor of composition at the Budapest Conservatory. In his music he achieved a successful synthesis of the sources

Plate 48 above
Le Foyer de danse à l'Opéra *by Degas*.

Plate 49 left
The new ceiling of the Paris Opera, designed by Chagall.

Plate 50
*Backdrop designed by Picasso for
Erik Satie's ballet,* Parade.

of Hungarian folk music and the music of Debussy. His works include seven symphonies; religious music; two ballets; a comic opera; and chamber music, including three quartets. Tibor Harsányi (1898–1954), who studied at first under Kodály, was another composer to be inspired by the work of Debussy. He settled in Paris in the 1920s, playing an important part in the school of Paris. Sandor Veress (b. 1907), who since 1949 has lived and worked in Switzerland, was a pupil of both Bartók and Kodály. In the 1930s he was affected by the Neo-classical movement and was one of the first Hungarian composers to be so, but later he turned to a more nationalist style, making much use of Hungarian folk music. Other representatives of the nationalist style are Ferenc Szabo (b. 1902), Endre Szervansky (b. 1911), Gyorgy Ranki (b. 1907) and Pal Jardanyi (b. 1920).

above
A Hungarian csárdás *being performed on the stage of the Royal Opera House, Budapest.*

left
Set for Kodály's one-act opera Soirée de Fileuses Siciliennes *(1932).*

Italian music

Only during the last forty years or so has Italy recovered something of the status in the international musical community that it enjoyed during the 17th and 18th centuries. In a previous chapter we have seen how, during the 19th century, when the German lands were evolving a new international musical language, and a host of new musical traditions were springing up in its orbit, the Italians, rather than research the heritage of their past or investigate the treasuries of national folk-lore, were content to follow the familiar road of their operatic style, which had for so long dominated Europe. Only in the work of Verdi did this tradition prove itself capable of vigorous renewal and true grandeur. In the hands of lesser men it produced much charming and some fine music, while towards the end of the century, affected by the new trend to realism in the arts that was developing abroad, the Italians evolved their own parochial 'realist' style, *verismo*.

To set developments in Italy during this century in their broad historical context we should remember that, from the year 1600, the great tradition of European music had been firmly set in the German countries, France and above all Italy. After superb achievements in the 16th century the Spanish school had fallen away; in England, despite the splendours of Purcell, a once great school had begun a long period of decline, while in the Low Countries the death of Sweelinck in 1621 marked the end of one of the most productive epochs in the music of the Western world. From then on the leadership passed to Italy and France, while in Germany a long line of great composers, much influenced by the two great traditions beyond their frontiers, were intensively developing an art which, during the 19th century, the age of nationalism, emerged as the dominant idiom. During this period the tradition of French music remained alive but, save Berlioz, produced no achievements of note until, towards the end of the century, French composers began to reject the allure of Wagnerianism and forge, in this once proud home of international inspiration, a strictly national language. In Italy, during the same years, the political quest for national identity was still proceeding, and even after its first achievement in the 1860s the idea of nationalism, so long alien to the spirit of Italy as a concept, only slowly began to give birth to a regeneration in the arts. The opera was only reluctantly abandoned in the face of the new ascendancy of the instrumental idiom, which was welcomed in the operas of Wagner and had been since Beethoven's time the frontier of musical advance.

It seemed that Italians had forgotten their own magnificent tradition of instrumental music, stretching from the Gabrielis through Vivaldi to Boccherini, and had even forgotten the classical clarity and elegance of their own school. Many Italians were content to learn from the Romantic composers of Germany and only at the beginning of the 20th century did such important figures as Alfredo Casella begin to revive the language

of the great Italian instrumental composers of the past. By the middle of the century, with such composers as Maderna, Berio and Nono, Italy was once again in the vanguard of musical advance, but the road to this new peak of achievement led through the foothills of nationalism – familiar terrain to many countries with less venerable traditions. Before tracing the main story just outlined we should turn aside to consider the career and music of the last great composer in the long line of Italian expatriates who had for so many generations fertilised the music of Europe.

Busoni

Ferruccio Benvenuto Busoni was born at Empoli near Florence, of mixed Austrian-Italian parentage, in 1866. By the age of eight he had made his first public appearance as a virtuoso pianist and he was in due course to make an international reputation for himself as a performer. At the age of fifteen he had gained the traditional accolade of achievement for an Italian musician by becoming a member of the Accademia Filarmonica at Bologna. Thereafter he toured widely both in Europe and in the United States and held various teaching posts. In 1894 he settled at Berlin where, apart from a number of short periods at other centres, he remained until his death, being appointed, in 1920, to a position as teacher of composition. He died in 1924.

This comparatively late appointment in a field other than the piano squares with the fact that, to his contemporaries, and indeed for some time after his death, Busoni was admired rather as an executant than as a composer. His development from pianist to composer, his virtuosity and his great international reputation provoked comparison with Liszt, and he was in fact noted as an interpreter of Liszt's music. But in his compositions Busoni reveals a truly outstanding talent and one of particular historical interest.

True to his Italian ancestry, he displayed a strong sense of form in his music and can, in most respects, be classed as an anti-Romantic – despite his long sojourn in Germany and his admiration for Liszt. He detested the music of Wagner. As a theorist he was much concerned with the need to evolve new principles of musical language, and his *Sketch of a New Aesthetic of Music* (1907; translation 1911) contains proposals for new scales and even new instruments, but although, as is to be expected of any gifted composer working in the early 20th century, he employs an ambitious system of tonality, he never fully abandoned the principle itself. More interesting is his study of, and sensitivity towards, the music of the classical period, revealed in both the formal clarity of his music and his percipient essays on Mozart. Inevitably, perhaps, post-Romantic elements are apparent in his work but, showing a strange sympathy with the direction that music was to take in his native Italy, Busoni worked towards a style of Neoclassicism. Living in Germany at a time before the revival of Italian composers had gathered strength, Busoni found his inspiration in Mozart and Bach. He wrote piano arrangements of Bach's organ works and in 1910 composed his own *Fantasia contrapuntistica*. Besides a large body of piano music he also wrote operas, *Die Brautwahl* (1912) and *Doktor Faust*, completed by his pupil Jarnach, which contain some of his finest work.

Futurism and other trends

Neither Busoni nor the majority of his Italian compatriots were in the vanguard of musical experimentation in the early years of the century. This was represented by the short-lived movement known as Futurism, launched in 1909 by the poet and dramatist F. T. Mari-

Ferruccio Busoni, a portrait by the Futurist painter Boccioni.

Ancient airs and dances derives from a study of early lute music. He also wrote nine operas and two violin concertos and arranged some of Rossini's diversions for piano as the ballet *La Boutique Fantasque* (1919).

The generation of Casella

The three main composers to be considered here are Gian-Francesco Malipiero, Ildebrando Pizzetti and Casella himself.

Born in Turin in 1883, Alfredo Casella was destined for a career in the tradition of the great cosmopolitan musicians of the past but, as a composer, his ambition was to create a truly national Italian style that could stand with the best that contemporary Europe had to offer.

He studied composition at the Paris Conservatoire under Fauré and also the piano, working for some time as a conductor in Paris. For eight years he taught at the St Cecilia conservatory in Rome, and in 1917 founded the National Society of Music, which was later, under the name Italian Society for Modern Music, to become part of the International Society for Contemporary Music. He worked as Rome correspondent for various foreign newspapers and also toured the United States as a conductor. His early cosmopolitan experiences inevitably coloured his music, and while in some works he explored the possibilities of Italian folk music and in others the dance forms of the Renaissance and Baroque periods, the impact of Russian music and of Stravinsky may also be traced. In his middle thirties he made a close investigation of Schoenbergian atonalism and in such works as the piano sonata of 1916 approached a style of absolute chromaticism. But he found himself unable to follow Schoenberg's logical extension of this and, by the early 1920s, Casella found himself temporarily at a halt.

In terms of historical development this need not surprise us. Italian music was struggling for a new national identity and, following the pattern of nationalist development in music, it was necessary for it to go through a period of rediscovery of its past. In the lesser musical nations this had generally involved intensive research and exploitation of folk music. Casella did indeed experiment in this field but, by the mid 1920s,

netti and represented in music by the work of Luigi Russolo (1885-1947), who was also a painter. Futurism was the self-proclaimed art of the machine age and, in keeping with this aesthetic, Russolo postulated noise as a basic material in composition. He built machines to produce such non-musical noises, composed works like *The Meeting of automobile and aeroplane* and conducted a 'concert' in Milan in 1913 that produced a riot. Russolo's ideas, expressed in his manifesto of 1913, are, to some extent, comparable to the interest of more recent composers in noise as an object of art.

In Italy itself, the various tendencies that we have noticed in the music of Busoni were represented by various composers of his generation, the most important of whom was Alfredo Casella. He was the central figure in the return to Italy's great instrumental heritage, and this essentially Neo-classical inspiration was to provide the natural access point for Italians to the great developments in Europe between the wars; it was to be taken up and developed by such figures as Goffredo Petrassi. But of course some composers, such as Mascagni, whose works have been touched on, Umberto Giordano (1867-1948) and Riccardo Zandonai (1883-1944), were to continue to compose pleasant music in the tradition of *verismo*. Among this company we should also mention Ermanno Wolf-Ferrari (1876-1948), a composer of mixed German-Italian parentage. In such an opera as his *Jewels of the Madonna* he exploits the material of popular rural lore in a manner similar to Mascagni's *Cavalleria Rusticana*, but his individual and straightforward lyrical style is at its best in his many comic operas.

While the trend was to set more and more strongly against German Romanticism, there were some men, of whom Ottorino Respighi (1879-1936) was the chief, who did not follow this development whole-heartedly. A pupil of Max Bruch (1838-1920, a German composer famous for his first violin concerto), Respighi often wrote in an almost Straussian manner, and with such tone poems as *Fountains of Rome* (1916) and *Roman Pines* (1924), he became widely known abroad. From 1925 he taught composition at the St Cecilia conservatory in Rome, but his influence towards his own brand of Romantic Impressionism was slight and in many of his works he showed himself susceptible to the Neo-classicism of his time. His orchestral suite *The Birds* was based on themes by Rameau and Pasquini, and

Casella had evolved a manner of composition which drew heavily on the idioms and forms of the 17th and 18th centuries. He was influenced, apparently, by a journey through Tuscany which showed him the fundamental importance of the brilliant clarity of the light on Italian art. In the *Partita* for piano and orchestra of 1925 the components of this new language are apparent; and the trend is developed by the *Concerto romano*, of the following year, for organ and chamber orchestra.

Anti-Romantic by conviction, Casella developed the classic qualities of lucid tonality and form and did much to restore the contrapuntal element to the Italian tradition, but he seems to have been moving towards a rapprochement with twelve-note technique in his later works. The great *Missa Solemnis* 'pro pace' (1944) shows some slight indications of this. The cycle was to be completed by other, younger men, but Casella's contribution was crucial. He died in 1947.

The other figure in the renovation of Italy's past music is Gian-Francesco Malipiero (1882–1973) whose work as a musicologist and editor was to be almost as important as his contribution as a composer. By the age of twenty his study of Monteverdi's music had fired his imagination, and perhaps his greatest single achievement was an edition of the complete works, published between 1926 and 1942. He also studied the work of other 17th- and 18th-century composers and the results are to be seen in the formal elegance and open lyrical qualities of his music. He has written oratorios and symphonies, but his best work is to be found in his operas, among them *Julius Caesar* (1936), with a libretto by the composer based on Shakespeare's play. In the mid-1950s he approached twelve-note techniques in such compositions as the *Dialogues* for voices and instruments and the *Fantasie concertante*. His nephew, Riccardo Malipiero (b. 1914), representing a younger generation, became a

421

Gian-Francesco Malipiero.

firm convert to dodecaphony in the years after the Second World War, repudiating many of his earlier works.

While the major revival of Italian music has been in the field of instrumental music, Ildebrando Pizzetti (b. 1880) introduced its principles into opera, subordinating the music and the typical Italian talent for lyricism to the requirements of the plot. His first important work as a composer was incidental music for the theatre, and this may have affected his approach to opera and the relative importance of its dramatic and musical elements. His operas include *Deborah and Jael* (1922) and one based on T. S. Eliot's *Murder in the Cathedral* (1958). Finally in this brief account of the Neo-classical generation, we should mention Giorgio Federico Ghedini (1892-1965), who, like Malipiero, made important contributions in the field of musicology. Basically, his style developed from a modal type of tonality towards a stricter use of contrapuntal techniques and the introduction of various aspects of modernism. His interest in the works of the American writer Herman Melville gave rise to an opera, *Billy Budd* (1949), and the *Concerto dell'Albatro* (1945), inspired by *Moby Dick*. In his *Canoni* for violin and cello and in the piano concerto of 1946 he made use of twelve-note methods, but he was by no means fully committed to them.

From Neo-classicism to dodecaphony

For reasons already explained, the evolution of Italian music had been delayed. But the undiminished vigour of the country's tradition was demonstrated by the comparatively rapid growth of a native school of twelve-note composers whose example, as we have indicated, coloured the later work of the generation of Casella. The chief names among the pioneers in this field are those of Dallapiccola and Petrassi.

Born in 1904, Luigi Dallapiccola studied piano and composition at the Florence conservatory where he himself taught the piano from the 1930s. As a young pianist he was closely involved in the performance of contemporary music, and his first hearing of Schoenberg's *Pierrot Lunaire* was an important event for him. Nevertheless, during his twenties his style was based on a

strictly diatonic approach, heavily coloured by modal techniques. With the *Divertimento* (1934) for voice and chamber ensemble and the *Sei cori di Michelangelo il Giovane* (completed in 1936), a change of direction towards intense chromaticism and the abandonment of tonality is observable. This direction is confirmed by three works from the late 1930s which culminate with the *Canti di prigionia* (1938-41) for chorus, piano, harp and percussion. In this, as in the other two works of the group, the tonal element is still apparent. But, by a massive achievement, Dallapiccola synthesises such diverse elements as the Gregorian plainsong of his early inspiration and features of twelve-note composition, to produce in these 'Songs from Prison' one of the most moving musical documents of our century. The same masterly combination of diverse elements is to be heard in the *Tre Laudi* (1937), for voice and chamber orchestra, and the opera (for which they were a study) *Volo di Notte* (1939), based on Saint-Exupéry's account of a night flight over the Andes.

The chromatic element had now become predominant and the transition to complete dodecaphony was indicated. This was confirmed by the three sets of ancient Greek lyrics composed between 1942 and 1949. These years also witnessed the composition of one of his greatest works, the opera *Il prigioniero* (1949), which embodies his passionate love of liberty and hatred of oppression. In its musical language, while making strict application of twelve-note systems, it employs note rows with strong thematic possibilities and develops this thematic material in a way comparable to the *Leitmotiv* of Wagnerian opera. Subsequent works, by and large tending to a more and more strict use of serialism, include the ballet *Sacra rappresentazione*, *Job* (1950) and the magnificent *Canti di Liberazione* (1954) for chorus and orchestra. He died in 1975.

Goffredo Petrassi who, like Dallapiccola, was born in 1904, came later to dodecaphony and between the wars wrote in an essentially Neo-classical diatonic idiom with a strong rhythmic interest, more comparable to such modernists as Casella or Stravinsky than to Schoenberg. Characteristic is the *Partita* (1932) for orchestra that brought him international acclaim, but the next important compositions were a series of three choral works. *Psalm IX* (1936), for chorus and orchestra, is still imbued with a powerful rhythmic drive and boldly dissonant harmonies and, although something of Palestrina is to be found in the choral writing, the contemplative nature of his art is missing. This was followed by a Magnificat and then, in 1941, by the completion of the *Coro di Morti*, which has been described as 'one of the incontestable masterpieces of modern music'.

In this work, which expresses a deep inner inspiration, the chorus is accompanied by an instrumental combination of unusually powerful sonority, consisting as it does of a string section of double basses, brass, percussion and three pianos. Not the least interesting aspect of the work is the fact that the musical procedures are linked with sonority, so that the pianos move in a largely atonal sphere; the voice parts are highly modal in character while the brass uses diatonic harmony, both tonal and polytonal.

Petrassi began to move towards dodecaphony only in the 1950s and then tended to draw on serial technique as his inspiration and artistic requirements dictated: the *Récréation concertante* (1953), one of six concertos for orchestra written between 1934 and 1957, is a good example. His other compositions include operas and ballets; *Nonsense* (1952) for *a cappella* choir, using texts from Edward Lear; a *Serenata* (1958) for a chamber ensemble of woodwind, strings, harpsichord and percussion; and film music.

Other Italian composers have also made use of twelve-note techniques, but in most cases it has been a matter of adapting the system rather than a strict application of it. An early exponent was Riccardo Nielsen (b. 1908), who made ventures into the new field as early as the 1920s and then returned to commit himself to it fully in 1942. Nielsen, despite this application of the most *avant-garde* method, believes firmly that contemporary music should be approachable by the contemporary listener, and in consequence his dodecaphony, although austere and noble, is often more simple than one would at first expect. His work as an arranger and reviser of the music of the 17th and 18th centuries has no doubt influenced his own composition; in 1954 he was appointed director of the Frescobaldi Liceo at Ferrara.

The career of Mario Peragallo (b. 1910) is of special interest. His work before the Second World War was in the theatre and his success as a composer, in the style of a developed *verismo*, was considerable but, after the war, instead of returning to this profitable line of easy success, he worked hard at advancing his technical resources. In this endeavour he drew freely on dodecaphonic procedures, though he was in no way rigorous in his application of them. His violin concerto of 1954 had none of the forbidding aspects usually associated with the twelve-note method and, although his opera *La Cita Campagna* (La Scala, 1954) met with a poor reception, it gradually gained in reputation and was followed by *La Parrucca dell'imperatore*.

Roman Vlad (b. 1919), although born in Bukovina, lived in Italy from the age of twenty, taking Italian citizenship in 1950. His standing in the musical world rests not only on his composition but also on his work as a critic and writer: his books include volumes

left
Goffredo Petrassi.

below
Luigi Dallapiccola.

on Dallapiccola and Stravinsky, and a history of the evolution of twelve-note technique (1958). He was obviously discontented with the concept of tonality from an early age, and even his film music pays scant regard to it. As a twelve-note composer he has extended serial methods to other elements of the musical structure, such as rhythm and tone colour, sometimes using the more advanced permutational procedures of modern serialism. His compositions have included the opera *Storia di una Mamma*, the ballet *La Dama delle Camelie* and the cantata *Le Ciel est vide*.

Luigi Nono.

Avant-garde serial composers in Italy

To the great trinity of Maderna, Berio and Nono, we should also add the name of Camillo Togni (b. 1922). A pupil of Casella, he nevertheless adopted twelve-note methods in his early twenties and has been one of those composers to apply the ideals of serialism to all the main musical elements, showing particular interest in the ordering of rhythm on pre-ordained and closely worked-out lines. In *Ricerca* (1957), for baritone and five instruments, for example, rhythm and intervals were directly connected. Within this rigid system, his liberty of invention as a composer was confined to the organising of the periods of silence, the repetition of notes and their coincidences in vertical groupings. His other works include *Coro di T. S. Eliot* and *Fantasia concertante* for flute and string orchestra.

Far more rigorous in his approach to serialism is Bruno Maderna (b. 1920) who is notable not only as a composer but also as a conductor of contemporary music. His compositional procedures are based on careful mathematical calculations of the potentials of the chosen series for each composition. From this basic material, by the manipulation of dynamics and of the pitch of the various notes of the series, he derives music often of surprising lyricism and directness. His compositions include *Compositions in three tempi*, *Music in two dimensions 1958*, for flute and taped sounds, and a number of compositions for electronic music, such as *Dimensions II* (1960). For, with Luciano Berio, Maderna was the first Italian musician to take up active research into electronic music, working in studios provided by Italian Radio.

In addition to his compositional experiments in electronic techniques, Luciano Berio (b. 1925) has also held teaching posts in the United States and in Europe. He too has written music for mixed media (such as flute and tape), and much of his work has been for the flute, whether unaccompanied or with chamber ensembles. In other compositions he has sought to find musical equivalents for the sounds of speech, using, again, either electronic techniques or the sonorities of traditional instruments. His works in this genre include *Homage to James Joyce*.

The last of these three *avant-garde* muscians to be mentioned here is Luigi Nono (b. 1924). After studies with Malipiero, Hermann Scherchen and Maderna, he went to work for a time at the electronic studio in Darmstadt. In his use of serialism he makes extensive application of the pointillist technique first evolved by Webern. Yet this radically *avant-garde* composer is deeply concerned with artist-to-audience communication and this, together with his native Italian talent for lucidity and elegance, gives his music surprising clarity, despite its often complex procedures. His music has been more often heard in Germany than in his own country, and the performance of his opera *Intolleranza* at Venice in 1961 was met with violent hostility. It was an attack on restrictions of freedom, and together with such works as *Sul Ponte di Hiroshima*, for chorus and orchestra, signifies the composer's strong sense of social commitment. His other works include *Il Canto Sospeso* (1956) for soloists and large orchestra, drawn from the letters of victims of war-time oppression, and *Polyphony-monody-rhythm* for instruments.

These three composers, with their younger contemporaries, have re-established Italy as a major centre of the music of the post-war age. It is probably no coincidence that, after a century of recession during the age of nationalism, Italy has begun to recover its standing in an age of internationalism.

Music in Russia

The period between the maturity of Tchaikovsky and the appearance of Stravinsky and Prokofiev must be regarded as a period of synthesis. The generation of younger composers did their utmost to ensure the survival of Russian music simply as music in its own right. These were no longer passionately addicted self-taught musicians, but serious professional products of the St Petersburg and Moscow Conservatories.

The friendship between Rimsky-Korsakov and Tchaikovsky made a link between the two schools. Yet the schools maintained their own personality. The Muscovites, pupils of Tchaikovsky and Sergey Taneyev, were more occidental in their tastes and inevitably came under the influence of the belated Romanticism of their masters. The St Petersburg school, brought up under the aegis of Rimsky-Korsakov and Lyadov, remained fundamentally nationalist, devotees of the folk idiom and lovers of the fantastic element in music.

The work of Alexander Glazunov (1865-1936) has the vigour and majesty of an oak. He was a pure musician who regarded music as an end in itself. Unlike his teacher Rimsky-Korsakov he never wrote an opera, but started by composing symphonic poems which have only a minimum of narrative content – *Stenka Razin*, *The Forest*, *The Sea*, *Spring* and *The Kremlin*. From the outset, despite his period of study under Rimsky-Korsakov, he eschewed an aggressively nationalist idiom. His early works are in the tradition of European Romanticism and he ended up writing in the most formal classical style. Of his eight completed symphonies, the seventh is a masterpiece. His other works include six string quartets, piano and violin concertos, two piano sonatas, ballets and incidental music. There is no sign of any inward struggle in his scores, which are always serene and beautiful; his music reflects the joy of triumph and not the struggle preceding victory. He was director of the St Petersburg (Leningrad) Conservatory and was the Soviet People's Artist of the Republic. But he left Russia to settle in Paris in 1928 when, after the death of Lenin, the new regime became increasingly repressive.

Serge Rachmaninov (1873-1943) was brought up in the tradition of Tchaikovsky. Rachmaninov, too, was a master of music for its own sake. 'Melodic invention, in the proper meaning of the term', he wrote 'is the real aim of every composer. If he is incapable of inventing melodies that endure, his chances of mastering his material are very slender.'

In Rachmaninov's works there is a refined though by no means insipid lyric quality. He never seeks to surprise. His music is moving and has been criticised for occasional excessive Romanticism, but it is always sincere and sensitive, and his later works are coming to be more and more admired.

His works include three operas; three symphonies; five symphonic poems, including *The Cliff* and *The Island of Death*; four piano concertos; two suites for

above left
Alexander Glazunov.

left
Alexander Nikolayevich Scriabin, an important figure in early Russian modernism.

two pianos; two masses; and seventy-nine songs, for which he could rightly be claimed to be the creator of the Russian *Lied*. Compositions such as the famous prelude in C sharp minor, written before he was twenty, and his renown as a concert pianist in the West after he had left Soviet Russia for good in 1918, made him one of the most popular composers of his age.

Alexander Nikolayevich Scriabin (1872-1915) was a pupil of Taneyev and Arensky at the Moscow Conservatory, and was also a brilliant pianist. When he first started to compose, he was a fervent admirer and follower of Chopin, and wrote eighty-five preludes, twenty-four études, ten sonatas and some nocturnes in a Chopinesque style. Later he elected himself champion of a morbid aesthetic of sorrow and disquiet, which was common to many composers at the beginning of the 20th century, and the interpreter of 'the ecstasy of hyper-aesthetic emotions, of nameless nightmares, of love and suffering', in the words of Savaneyev, one of his great admirers. During a voyage abroad Scriabin discovered Debussy and Richard Strauss and, continuing the lessons learnt from the latter, tried to combine Impressionism with the theories of theosophy in his music. Among works devoted to the exposition of his theories are the symphonic poems *The Divine Poem*, *The Poem of Ecstasy* and *Prometheus* or *The Poem of Fire* (1909-10), and his fifth piano sonata.

In these works he tried to transmute the very essence of music and to translate 'the essence of soul and spirit' into terms of musical notation, with the result that we are led into a strange and captivating musical climate which makes Scriabin a veritable pioneer. The analogies

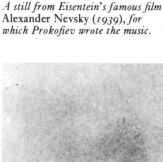

A still from Eisentein's famous film Alexander Nevsky (1939), *for which Prokofiev wrote the music.*

between *The Poem of Ecstasy* and Stravinsky's *Rite of Spring*, written two years later, are too striking to be overlooked and clearly show Scriabin's influence on his younger contemporary. Moreover, Scriabin's melodic idiom and harmonies (he made use of a chord of his own consisting of superimposed fourths which he called the 'mystic chord') and experiments with different timbres, make him one of the most interesting experimental composers of his period. Nevertheless, despite immense talents and great imagination in the development of his new harmonic theories, it is generally held against him that his devotion to his system became so complete as often to hamper his inspiration.

Some minor figures

Anatol Lyadov (1855-1914), a pupil of Rimsky-Korsakov, added a rare delicacy, a penetrating intelligence and an even more delicate sense of orchestration, to the lessons learnt from his master, while his humour and verve sometimes remind one of Mussorgsky. He was very self-critical and only composed a small number of works – though Rimsky-Korsakov regarded each as a precious jewel. They include the symphonic poems based on old Russian legends, *Baba-Yaga* and *Kikimora*, the Impressionist *Enchanted Lake* and the disturbing *Page from the Apocalypse*.

Alexander Arensky (1861-1906) was the spiritual heir of Tchaikovsky and teacher of Scriabin and

Rachmaninov. He was the composer of three operas of uneven quality and a very lovely ballet, *Egyptian Nights*. Nikolay Tcherepnin (1873–1945) was the friend and companion in arms of Glazunov, though musically totally different from him. He was a watercolourist in music, who brought everything he wrote to the highest degree of perfection with an almost 18th-century aristocratic refinement. However, his loveliest and greatest work is *The Passion of Our Lady*, composed in Paris in 1935 and inspired by medieval Orthodox canticles. He wrote a number of ballets, among them *Armida's Pavilion*. His son Alexander Tcherepnin, the pianist (1899–1977), was one of the few emigré Russian composers of the following generation of real merit. His compositions include three piano concertos, eight ballets and chamber music. A more modest but prolific composer is Alexander Gretchaninov (1864–1956). There is perhaps too much candid simplicity and sentiment in his music – even in his opera *Dobrynia Nikititch*, which enjoyed a big success in 1903. His compositions include four symphonies, three quartets, a cello concerto and religious music.

Vladimir Rebikoff (1866–1920) was one of the first Russians to exploit the whole-tone scale seriously and is often considered the father of Russian modernism. However, his profession of faith was purely 'Impressionist'. He wrote nine operas, a mass, symphonic suites and the *Melomimiques*, which, he claimed, 'express . . . moments in the life of man when words are no longer sufficient'. He also wrote a strange work entitled *Music in 1960*.

Sergey Ivanovich Taneyev (1856–1915), a pupil of Tchaikovsky, was opposed to the teaching of 'The Five', and himself exercised a considerable influence as a teacher, holding various professorial posts and becoming director of the Moscow Conservatory. The first symphony of Vassily Kalinnikov (1866–1901) was outstanding but its promise was not fulfilled; Georges Conius (1862–1933) is similarly a composer remembered for one remarkable work, his violin concerto, which is a true masterpiece. Sergey Liapunov (1859–1924) was a friend of Balakirev and a convinced nationalist in his music. He wrote a rhapsody on Ukrainian themes and two fine piano concertos that are unjustly neglected. The most talented of this group of minor figures was Nikolay Karlovich Medtner (1880–1951) of German extraction. For preference he composed for the piano and, largely, it seems, for himself; such works as the delicate *Fairy Tales* (1905–29) for piano have a markedly Schumannesque quality. Medtner was for a time professor at the Moscow Conservatory, but left Russia in 1921. Thereafter he toured France, England and the United States as a concert pianist, and settled in London in 1935.

Thanks to this generation the tradition of classical music in Russia was strong enough to produce and maintain, during their early development, the great talents of Stravinsky and Prokofiev. Both composers left Russia after the Revolution, but whereas Stravinsky was to develop his cosmopolitan characteristics as a man and become one of the very greatest figures in the field of international music, Prokofiev eventually returned to Russia and never sought to win a place in the vanguard of musical development.

Prokofiev

Serge Sergeyevich Prokofiev was born in 1891 in Sontsovka, a little village in the Donetz basin. Precociously gifted, he first studied with his mother and then took private lessons with Reinhold Glière. By the

Serge Sergeyevich Prokofiev.

age of twelve he had composed four operas, one symphony, two sonatas and a collection of piano pieces. His parents entered him at the St Petersburg Conservatory where he studied under Lyadov. He finished his studies in 1909. Four years later he was awarded a prize for piano, playing his first concerto. From 1918 to 1922 he spent a wandering life, visiting the United States, France and England as a concert pianist. In 1922 he settled in Paris, working for a time with Diaghilev's *Ballets Russes*. Afterwards, unable to live abroad, he returned to the U.S.S.R. in 1932 and died in Moscow in 1953.

His music

It is impossible to relate Prokofiev to any particular movement or any particular musical epoch. A pure classicist, he once declared, 'There are still so many beautiful things to be said in C major'; and again, 'I write for nothing simpler or more compact than the sonata form, which contains everything necessary for the development of my ideas'. 'What I want most is simplicity and melody. Of course I have used dissonances, but there have been too many. Dissonance for Bach was the salt in the music. Other composers have added pepper and more and more spices to their dishes until their stomachs have turned and they have become ill and all their music has become nothing but pepper. I think people are tired of it. We need a simpler, more tuneful sort of music, a more direct and tonal appeal, something less complex . . .'

Prokofiev also derives from classicism his integrity as a craftsman. A motif for the music of Eisenstein's film *Ivan the Terrible* came to him as a musical revelation of the heroism of the Russian people; for this reason, he had no hesitation in using it again, to express the same idea, in *War and Peace*. Furthermore, it was certain themes from the opera *The Flaming Angel* that engendered his third symphony, while themes from the ballet *The Prodigal Son* gave birth to the fourth symphony. Prokofiev considered these themes as 'polyvalent', as being at one and the same time motifs suitable for opera, ballet and a symphony. He reused them, just as the 18th-century composers used the same themes in various different works.

Prokofiev's art, fundamentally classic, is, one might say, vigorous, athletic and well balanced. But he is also a great lyric composer, as we can judge from the melodic line of his beautiful themes, as well as from the way in which he was attracted to opera and Romantic or neo-Romantic subjects.

Furthermore, despite his apparent cosmopolitanism and the relatively few works from his hand which are avowedly Slav in inspiration, Prokofiev is essentially a Russian composer. He belongs to the same spiritual generation as Glinka and Tchaikovsky. He expresses the heroism and endurance of the Russian people in *Alexander Nevsky*, *Simeon Kotko* (1930) and *War and Peace* (1941-42); in the ballet *The Stone Flower* (1954) he reveals a fairytale tenderness which has had no equal

since Rimsky-Korsakov. When Diaghilev commissioned him to compose the ironic fairytale *Chout* (*The Buffoon*, 1915-20), he had introduced a lyric quality and sincere emotion, equivalent to those of a real fairytale.

His work is abundant and infinitely varied. The mordant *Sarcasmes* for piano (1919) contrast with the mechanical measures of the ballet *Pas d'acier* (1925). The *cantilenas* of the ballet *Romeo and Juliet* (1940) are followed by the epic majesty of his music for Eisenstein's film *Alexander Nevsky*, on which he later (1938) based a cantata. The biting humour of the opera *The Love of Three Oranges* (first produced in Chicago in 1921), in its turn, contrasts with the deliberately childish simplicity of the musical tale for children, *Peter and the Wolf* (1936), for narrator and orchestra, and the ballet with songs, *Cinderella* (1945).

As a composer of abstract music, Prokofiev wrote

Scene from Prokofiev's opera Love for Three Oranges.

428

seven symphonies, the first of which, the famous *Classical Symphony*, dates from 1918; nine piano sonatas and six sonatas for other instruments; two string quartets; and five piano concertos, including one for the left hand. He also composed suites, cantatas, oratorios and incidental music for the theatre, as well as songs.

Nationalist composers in the Soviet Union

The Revolution of 1917 was heir to the vast tsarist empire of 'all the Russias'. The phrase was no empty one, for, in the course of centuries of conquest, the Russian state, based on Kiev and later Moscow, had spread out to envelop the whole of central Asia, bringing under its sway a large number of peoples of different nationalities, languages and even religions. With the founding of the new state, a number of these nationalities achieved the status of semi-independent Soviet Socialist republics, and their national consciousness, as expressed in language and culture, found some degree of political expression. In some cases, such as that of the Ukraine and Georgia (until 1801 an independent kingdom), the events of 1917 seemed to offer the opportunity of complete national independence. Nevertheless, after five years of fighting, during which time the nationalist movements which had been gathering strength during the 19th century were overwhelmed by the might of the mother state, these countries once again found themselves a part of a greater Russia with the formal proclamation of the Union of Soviet Socialist Republics in 1922. In cultural affairs the central government encouraged a large degree of differentiation, and in music the rich folklore of the various peoples of the Soviet Union has been eagerly exploited by their composers in the search for a national idiom.

In the Ukraine, the most important 19th-century figure was Mykola Lyssenko (1842-1912), who founded a musical institute in Kiev in 1904, and who had by then written a number of operas, drawing on Ukrainian legends and the work of the poet T. Shevtshenko. The spirit of his work was kept alive by the succeeding generation, of whom the most important was B. Liatochinsky (b. 1895). He re-orchestrated two of Lyssenko's operas, as well as writing three operas, four symphonies, a Slav concerto for piano and orchestra and a number of other works. The greatest musician from the Ukraine, Reinhold Glière, despite a certain interest in the folk music of his own people, is more important for his contribution to the central tradition of Soviet music and is dealt with in the next section. In Georgia, the work of Z. P. Paliasvili (1872-1933) is regarded as doing for the music of that country what Glinka did for Russian music as a whole. He was a pupil of Ippolitov-Ivanov, who encouraged his researches into the Georgian folk tradition. The fruits of his work were a number of compositions indebted to the rich polyphony of Georgian folk music; three operas of which the last, *Latrava*, is considered the most important; and a number of followers who constitute a considerable body of musicologists devoted to the music of Georgia. Another composer particularly connected with the tradition of his country of origin is the Azerbaijani, Gadzhibekov, but the best known of these composers is Aram Khatchaturian (1903-1978).

Born in 1903 in Tiflis, Khatchaturian was of Armenian descent and his devotion to the folk music of his ancestral home has led to his being described as the Armenian Glinka. He arrived at music comparatively late in life, and at the age of nineteen had never attended a performance of an opera or symphony concert. He himself once said, 'My horizon was bounded by the

songs and instruments of the people'. He was, indeed, discovered as it were by accident by Gnessin while he was studying at Moscow university; after lessons with Gnessin he also studied under Miaskovsky at the Conservatory. He rose to a high position in the Soviet musical world, being for a time secretary of the Union of Composers. Although criticised for formalism during the Zhdanov period, he later became professor of composition at the Moscow Conservatory. As a composer he never attempts finesse; the exotic beauty of his themes, his astonishing instinctive polyrhythms and the rich texture of his orchestration are direct expressions of his exuberant personality. His music, which is in the tradition of the 19th-century nationalist school, applying its principles to the use of Armenian folk idiom, includes two symphonies, a well known piano concerto, a cello concerto, a symphonic poem with chorus, *Hymn to Stalin* (1937), the ballet *Spartacus* (1956) and the ballet *Gayane* (1942) which includes the famous *Sabre Dance*.

The central tradition

Insofar as folk music was to come to be regarded as one of the prime sources of composition in Soviet musical theory, all composers may be regarded as nationalist. However, those whom we have just described are notable because of their devotion to the traditions of their homelands, and in the section that follows we shall encounter a number of musicians who have drawn freely on the most diverse sources from the rich heritage of folk music of the Soviet Union.

One of the most important figures as a theorist was Boris Asafiev (1884-1949). His writings, which stress the importance of melody in musical communication, emphasise music's capacity for relating to reality, despite its abstract quality. These views were important in

The Soviet Armenian composer Aram Khatchaturian.

right
The young Shostakovich with the theatre producer Meyerhold and the poet Mayakovsky.

below
The Soldiers' Dance from Asafiev's ballet The Fountain of Bakhchisarai (*1934*) *performed by members of the Bolshoi Ballet.*

shaping the official attitude to music. As a composer, Asafiev is best known for his ballet *The Fountain of Bakhchisarai* (1934) which, with other ballets such as *The Flames of Paris* (1931), is still in the regular repertory in Russia.

Asafiev reached maturity before the Revolution and was only one of a number of composers who willingly adopted the principles of the new society which that great event gave birth to. Of an older generation was Mikhail Ippolitov-Ivanov (1859-1935), a pupil of Rimsky-Korsakov and director of the Moscow Conservatory from 1905. As both composer and teacher he devoted himself to folk music, particularly that of Georgia and Armenia, also taking an active interest in the musical life of those countries. He wrote operas, symphonies and orchestral suites, of which *Caucasian Sketches* is the best known, as well as many other works.

Among his many pupils was Reinhold Moritzovich Glière (1873-1956) who, as professor of composition at the Moscow Conservatory, was also to be an important teacher. After the Revolution, Glière became more than academically involved in the folk music movement, devoting himself in particular to that of Azerbaijan. Just as Sergey Vassilenko moved from a study of Japanese and Indian folk music to produce, in his opera *The Snow Storm* (1938), a work that utilised Uzbeki folk idioms in art music, so Glière, in his opera *Shah-Senem* (1925), performed the same function for Azerbaijani music. Among his other works are the ballets *The Red Poppy* (1927), still one of the most popular in the Soviet Union, and *The Bronze Horseman*, based on a story by Pushkin, as well as symphonies, patriotic overtures and much other music.

One of the most influential composers in Russia during this century, and one to whom Prokofiev acknowledged a debt, was Nikolay Yakovlevich Myaskovsky (1881-1950), a pupil of Glière. In terms of sheer output he is among the most important symphonists of the 20th century, producing twenty-seven during his long life. After a youthful interest in the more *avant-garde* work of his contemporaries (he was obviously affected by the music of Scriabin in certain compositions), he developed a style in the tradition of Rimsky-Korsakov and Tchaikovsky which was coloured by his individual use of folk music. From the 1920s his work showed a progressive hardening of harmonic language and the use of a technique of cellular thematic development, reminiscent in some ways of Sibelius. Like many of his contemporaries, Myaskovsky was fully involved in the state direction of the arts and his twelfth symphony, of 1932, was intended as a symphonic expression of the new society and mode of life created by the massive social revolution which the collectivisation of Soviet agriculture brought about.

State directives and the arts

It is important for a Western reader to realise that the stringent requirements demanded of artists by the Soviet authorities at the time of the notorious Seventeenth Party Congress of 1934 were, for musicians at least, not entirely alien to their own tradition or inclination. The great Russian *avant-garde* composer Stravinsky did not hesitate to draw on Russian folk music even after he had left his homeland, and the 19th-century tradition, of which Glinka came to be regarded as the major figure, was founded in the attempt to fuse national folk idioms with the classical tradition of European music. Russia has by no means been alone in developing a national music on these lines, and in many countries, such as for example England, composers for long voluntarily eschewed the more extreme experiments of the *avant-garde*. There is no need to pretend that an environment in which experimentation is officially condemned and proscribed, as was to be the case in Russia, especially during the so-called Zhdanov period from 1948 to about 1953, does not severely hamper the development of original and important work. Nevertheless, in the years that followed the founding of the Union of Soviet Composers, and the official admonitions to composers to make their music accessible to the masses and ideologically acceptable, some fine work was produced. In the years that immediately preceded Russia's declaration of war against Germany, Prokofiev composed his magnificent ballet *Romeo and Juliet* and the touching *Peter and the Wolf*, and Shostakovich produced his fifth symphony. During the war itself, in Russia as in other belligerent countries, artists and composers were expected to contribute to the patriotic business of raising the morale of the civilian population and the armed forces.

Lev Knipper (b. 1898), a pupil of Glière and a keen advocate of oriental folk music, composed the vast *Far Eastern Symphony* in 1933 and this was followed by a symphony called the *Komsomol*. Another important work is his symphonic suite *Vantch* (1932). Another composer of talent who accepted party directives and ideology in his work was Dmitry Kabalevsky (b. 1904), a pupil of Myaskovsky and the composer of a number of symphonies as well as the opera *Under Fire* (1943). During the war, too, both Prokofiev and Shostakovich wrote music in tune with the struggles and aspirations of the Russian people during that period, perhaps the chief work being Shostakovich's seventh, the *Leningrad Symphony* (1941). Later, in the Zhdanov period, when

left
Sergei Pavlovich Diaghilev, founder of the famous Ballets Russes.

below
Shostakovich taking a class at the Leningrad conservatory.

Party strictures on modernism were at their most severe, he was to compose the oratorio *The Song of the Forests*, on the theme of the massive programme of land reclamation and afforestation.

Shostakovich

The career of Dmitri Shostakovich is an instructive commentary on the life of an artist of the highest calibre in a society where culture is officially controlled. Born in St Petersburg in 1906, he revealed his talents as a musician at a very early age, entering the Petrograd Conservatory as a student of the piano at the age of thirteen and winning first prize in the international Chopin competition when he was twenty-one. His first symphony, a work of epic proportions, had already appeared and won him wide acclaim, and it is interesting that even at this early stage his talents as a symphonist should have been apparent. During the 1920s, thanks to the exertions of the Association of Contemporary Music, works by Schoenberg, Berg and Hindemith were to be heard in Soviet concert halls, and this remarkable first symphony of Shostakovich, which shows little evidence of his training in the Russian national school, is clearly affected not only by the late Romanticism of Mahler, but also by Berg and Hindemith.

The composer's commitment to the ideals of Soviet society and his love of Russia have remained central to his outlook, nor does he find the notion of an ideologically directed art absurd, yet at many points during his career he has been the object of attack by official critics for the dissonances and other 'avant-garde' elements in certain of his compositions. The second symphony of 1927, celebrating the tenth anniversary of the Revolution, is a good example. Its theme could hardly be questioned, but the nature of the musical language belongs to a period of Shostakovich's development that was later to be condemned.

Yet, although he has frequently made fruitful use of dissonance and in other compositions has introduced modal elements to his harmony, Shostakovich has never abandoned a basically tonal language for such techniques as polytonalism, atonalism or twelve-note composition. In 1937 he was appointed a professor at the Leningrad Conservatory and occupied an important place in Russian musical life from that time. Many of his compositions were explicitly programmatic, with ideological and contemporary themes. We have already mentioned the *Leningrad Symphony*, on the siege of Leningrad. His epic tenth symphony (1953) is fully in accord with the demands of official requirements, while the eleventh (1957) was on the theme of the 1905 Revolution, and the twelfth (1961) about the great Revolution. Other works include the operas *The Nose* (1930), after Gogol's short story satirising bureaucracy, and *Lady Macbeth of Mzensk* (1934), later renamed *Katerina Ismailova*, which was banned for a time and produced in a revised version in 1963. He also wrote a violin concerto (1955) and a number of piano works, including the important *Twenty-Four Preludes and Fugues* (1951), which were criticised in the Soviet Union for showing traces of his earlier dissonantal techniques. Shostakovich has thus been subject periodically to official reprimands, yet he has not ceased writing fine music and navigating a course between his own original inspiration and the permitted limits.

Shostakovich and his wife at a concert in the great hall of the Moscow conservatory.

Plate 51
*A scene from the Covent Garden
production of Schoenberg's opera*
Moses and Aaron *in 1967.*

American music

The history of music in America and the history of American music are two quite different things. During nearly three centuries the musical life of the New World was almost exclusively in the hands of Europeans or of Americans who performed European music, most of it composed by Europeans, some of it composed by Americans who imitated European models. If American music is understood to be music with a recognisable American character or flavour, then its history begins only in this century. And if it is further to be understood as music of world-wide importance, music that is able to compete artistically with European music, then its emergence is still more recent. Undoubtedly in the 20th century America has developed a new race, which thinks, acts and reacts in special ways. But the further one goes back into the past, the harder it becomes to say what 'American' means in specific terms.

These pages give little attention to such pre-20th-century American composers as represent a more or less unadulterated European tradition, however interesting some of them may be in their local, historical and socio-logical context. And it cannot be stressed too strongly that American musical history is comprehensible only in a broad context of the country's development. During three and a half centuries successive groups of settlers and immigrants have produced an ethnic and cultural complexity that is almost unique among the nations of the world. As a result, only in this century, when it has reached maturity, does American music permit treatment as a fully independent phenomenon.

The beginnings

When in 1492 Christopher Columbus dropped anchor in the port of San Salvador as the first European to set foot in the New World, there was very little music in America. The music of the Indians must have seemed extremely monotonous to the European ears. In general, it moved within a very limited range and consisted of endless repetitions. Singing was accompanied by drums, rattles and the like, playing simple or sometimes fairly complicated rhythms. Indian music consisted of chants which accompanied dancing and which were sung on special occasions (preparation for war, work, weddings, funerals and the like) or were religious in nature.

Just as there were many Indian tribes and nations, each with its own language and customs, so there were also various kinds of music which corresponded to the cultural levels of the tribes. Whereas the Sioux, Iroquois and other northern tribes led a nomadic life, the Hopi of Arizona and the Pueblo Indians of New Mexico had already become more settled and had founded villages. Their music is somewhat less monotonous than that of the nomadic tribes: the melodic range is greater and the

beginnings of stylisation are apparent.

To be sure, one kind of European music did exist at a very early period – that of the liturgical chant of the Catholic Church, which the Spaniards brought with them and cultivated in their missions in California and in other parts of New Spain. Spanish influence, how-ever, proved to be slight, for gradually Spain lost its North American territories, and other countries, above all England, laid the foundations of American culture.

The decisive event for the culture and thus also for the music of America was the arrival of the little ship *May-flower* on the rocky, unfriendly coast of Cape Cod in 1620. The Pilgrim fathers were only a handful, around 100 souls, the refugee separatists who refused to con-form in James I's England, but they had a high-minded religious fervour that left its imprint on the nation they helped to found. They were the first in a stream of religious non-conformists who left England (and later other countries) for the freedom of the New World. After them came the Puritans, some 26,000 of them in twenty years.

The only kind of music officially approved by the Puritans were very simple psalms, while instruments were forbidden as an invention of the devil; thus they had no organs and no bands in their churches. Yet the Puritan tradition of simple church music extends into our own century. The majority of psalm melodies originated in England; many of them are to be found in the Ainsworth Psalter of 1612, but the psalm books of the Huguenots were also a source. The melody was first 'lined out' by the preacher or leader, with the congrega-tion repeating it line by line. Then the whole psalm was sung in unison, or sometimes in parts.

An idea of the awkward texts is given by *The Bay Psalm Book*, the first book to be published in America and a veritable model of wretched poetry. Yet this collection went into 70 editions by 1752. Psalm 137 begins:

> The rivers of Babilon,
>   there when wee did sit downe,
> Yea, even then wee mourned when
>   we remembered Sion.
>
> Our harp wee did hang it amid
>   upon the willow tree
> Because there they that us away
>   led into captivitee.
>
> Required of us a song, and thus
>   askt mirth us waste who laid,
> Sing us among a Sion song,
>   unto us then they said.

The music however had a kind of rude monolithic strength. If ever a music was the expression of its society, this surely is. Since dancing and all forms of theatre were under strict ban in the New England colonies, it is inconceivable that the corresponding forms of secular music were cultivated. In the capital city of Boston no play was produced professionally until 1791. The southern colonies were much more tolerant in all respects – religious, political and cultural. But their role in shaping American thought and *mores* was relatively slight for well over a century after the first English had settled in Jamestown, Virginia, in 1607. Virginia was colonised as a commercial enterprise by fortune-seekers who operated huge plantations with the help of Negro slaves. Throughout the agricultural South there were few cities with an atmosphere conducive to developing the arts, while the growing importance of the Middle Eastern states – particularly of New York and Pennsylvania – did not challenge New England's intellectual supremacy until the 19th century. The folk music which the English brought with them to the New World lived on, and many British folk songs are still sung in such remote regions as Kentucky and Tennessee; but little information has survived to indicate when, how frequently and on what occasions it was sung and played.

The first American composer

It appears that the first native-born American composer was the Philadelphia lawyer Francis Hopkinson. His 'My Days have been so wondrous free' (*c.* 1760), a charming little song in the then current British ballad style, is the first extant piece of American secular music. In dedicating his *Seven Songs for the Harpsichord* (1788) to George Washington, Hopkinson wrote: 'However

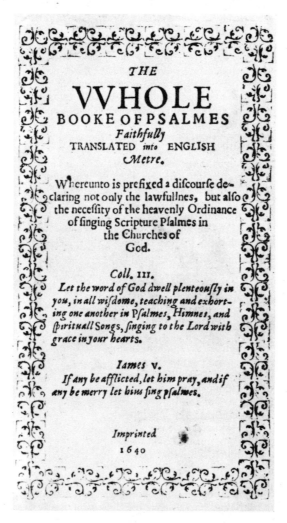

Title page of the Bay Psalm Book.

small the Reputation may be that I shall derive from this Work, I cannot, I believe, be refused the Credit of being the first Native of the United States who has produced a Musical Composition.'

Of greater interest are the works of William Billings (1746-1800), a Boston tanner, whose compositions were a direct outgrowth of the tradition of psalm singing. They might have been a point of departure for an early indigenous American style, but, in fact, they led to no further development and have been rediscovered only recently. Yet his published collections were known and sung very widely – so much so that he gave up his trade to devote himself entirely to music. The popularity of his music was short-lived, however, and he died in poverty.

Billings' musical education was slight, his reliance on inspiration great. As he wrote in *The New England Psalm Singer* (1770): 'Nature must lay the Foundation, Nature must inspire the thought. For my own Part . . . I don't think myself confin'd to any Rules for Composition laid down by any that went before me . . . Art is subservient to genius . . .' In many of his works the spark of genius did indeed burn brightly – in David's touching lamentation for Absalom, the tender melody of the canon *When Jesus Wept* (one of the favourite forms of the period was the round, or 'fuguing tune'), the rousing hymn-tune *Chester* or the grandiose anthem *Be Glad Then America*. Billings was the most gifted of a number of American primitives who composed similar pieces during the second half of the 18th century. It is crude music, in a sense, abounding in parallel fifths and other technical faults that cultivated musicians of the time found barbarous but that have a special appeal to modern ears. But it has a rough-hewn strength and a pioneer freshness, when sung properly, that makes a splendid, often powerful sound.

That there was no substantial art music during the colonial and post-colonial period is not surprising; nowhere could a potential composer or performer obtain an adequate training. From the early 18th century onwards, European musicians came to America, but they gave only sporadic private instruction, principally in singing and piano playing. Conservatories and schools of music were practically non-existent. The only composers who might have produced well trained students were the members of the Moravian Church who, in the 18th century, like the Puritans before them, sought freedom of thought in the New World. One of these Moravians, Johann Friedrich Peter (1746-1813), a German born in Holland, was a gifted composer who left over 80 sacred compositions for chorus and orchestra and six excellent quintets for strings. But the Moravians, among whom were several composers, founded their own small towns and had very little contact with the world around them. As a result their music remained without influence on the future.

The 19th century

That the beginnings of an indigenous American style came to an end around the turn of the century is due largely to the social and cultural change which the 19th century brought with it. In the space of 100 years the immense territory known as the 'West', was explored, exploited and civilised. The wealth of the country grew enormously and though Americans had little time and little energy for the advancement of indigenous arts or for creative activity, cultural life flourished under the aegis of visiting Europeans, whose art and music held the stage. The simple unpolished works of Billings no longer satisfied genteel public taste, but despite the domination by European musicians and models, the basis of a native musical culture was laid.

While the pioneers and settlers led a primitive and often dangerous life in the West, the residents of the East Coast turned their attention to matters of the spirit. In such centres as Boston, Philadelphia, New York and Baltimore, organisations were established which subsequently played an important role in the cultural development of the country. As early as 1815, for instance, the Handel and Haydn Society of Boston, an organisation which still exists today, was founded for the performance of choral music. The New York Philharmonic Orchestra dates from 1842.

The Revolutions of 1848 in Europe sent a flood of German musicians to the New World, among them musicians of outstanding talent, and one can understand the resentment expressed by the Philadelphia-born composer, William Henry Fry (1815-64), who wrote in 1853: 'the Philharmonic Society (of New York) is an incubus on Art, never having asked for or performed a single American composition during the eleven years of its existence'. Yet such pieces as Fry's own overture to *Macbeth* were simply not able to compete with Beethoven, Schumann, Liszt and Mendelssohn. The American public remained indifferent to the aspirations of native composers and accepted the supremacy of German music (and later of Italian opera) without question. So, indeed, did most American composers, who closely followed European models. But, with the establishment of music schools and conservatories, Americans could at last receive their first training at home, although further study abroad was practically obligatory. American art music of the 19th century shows little originality, but it does reveal a progressively more professional technical quality, in itself a prerequisite to the formation of a strong musical tradition.

Such composers as John Knowles Paine (1839-1906) laid solid foundations for future achievement, though, like many others, Paine studied in Germany and wrote essentially German music. Perhaps for that very reason, his success in America was considerable. An eye-witness related that at the Boston premiere of his second symphony *In the Spring*, a leading critic 'stood in his seat,

frantically opening and shutting his umbrella as an expression of uncontrolled enthusiasm'.

Paine's appointment as the first Professor of Music at Harvard University marks the beginnings of university musical activity, today an important factor in American musical life. His pupils included the composers Arthur Foote, Frederick Converse, Daniel Gregory Mason and John Alden Carpenter. In striking contrast to Paine, the academician, stands the exotic figure of Louis Moreau Gottschalk (1829-69), the first American composer to achieve an international reputation. Born in New Orleans, Gottschalk was an American citizen by reason of the Louisiana Purchase, which had attached the for-

above left
Leopold Damrosch (d.1885) and his son Walter, two German musicians who made a successful career in America.

left
Church service in Alabama, U.S.A.

merly French and Spanish territory to the United States. The child prodigy soon became the sensation of Europe, not only for his pianistic virtuosity (Chopin hailed him as the future 'king of pianists'), but also for his compositions. Although many of his piano pieces fall into the category of salon music and others are primarily virtuosic, they represent one of the first attempts to introduce native popular and folk music into art music. Such pieces as *Bamboula* (using Negro tunes), *Ballade Créole*, *La Savane*, *Chanson Nègre* and *Le Bananier* have distinct charm and vitality, however superficially the folk and folk-like material may be treated. In utilising Negro music as early as 1845, Gottschalk indicated a direction which serious composers scorned until Dvořak gave it further impetus fifty years later in his *New World* symphony.

It is not surprising that one of Gottschalk's compositions should be a fantasy on Stephen Foster's *Old Folks at Home*. Foster too drew inspiration from Negro music, which he converted to his own uses, producing his 'darky' songs, for commercial purposes, that have over the years entered into the folk music repertory of America. Foster (1826-64) poses a neat problem for the music historian. Growing up in Pittsburgh, then considered the West, his musical education was slight; he never acquired a technique of composition, and he wrote only songs – some two hundred of them. Yet his best songs have survived all the learned music of his contemporaries: such songs as *Camptown Races*, *My Old Kentucky Home*, *Oh! Susanna* and *Old Black Joe*. His particular genius for melody comes out in his 'darky' songs, inspired in varying degrees by Negro melodies. The texts, most of which he wrote himself, are in unauthentic Negro dialect.

Many of Foster's 'Ethiopian melodies', as they were often called, were written for the then popular minstrel shows. These variety entertainments – in which whites appeared with black faces and in outlandish costumes with a combination of singing, dancing, dialect patter and jokes and instrumental numbers featuring the banjo – had little artistic value, but possessed a vitality which made them popular throughout America and in Great Britain as well. Christy's and Bryant's Minstrels were only two of many troupes which flourished during the heyday of blackface minstrelsy (roughly 1840-70), and which provided the mass of Americans with quantities of vernacular music, some of which (like 'Dixie') have become traditional. However simple and naïve, this music acted at least as a counterpoise to the sentimental ballads and vacuous salon pieces that flooded the market.

Shape-note music and folk hymnody

While 19th-century 'highbrows' listened to European music and the masses were amused by minstrel shows, other Americans found spiritual recreation in singing 'folk hymns'; some of these were adaptations from English and European sources, but many were homegrown and homespun. The number and constant reprinting of such collections as *Songs of Zion* (1821), *Southern Harmony* (1835) and *Sacred Harp* (1844) are a measure of their popularity, which was greatest in rural areas and small communities. A peculiarity of a great part of this musically modest but socially important literature is the form of notation, employing note-heads of varying shapes to indicate the different degrees of the scale. In a few remote parts of the Appalachian Mountains, the tradition of shape-note singing survived well into the 20th century.

These and other folk hymns were sung by thousands at the camp meetings and evangelistic revivals that swept

the country from around 1800 to the time of the Civil War. These meetings, often lasting several days, provided not only social contacts for isolated farmers but also a valid excuse, sanctioned by religion, for the participants to let off steam. The musical result was scarcely edifying. An eye witness wrote: 'As the excitement increases, all order is forgotten, all unison of parts repudiated, each sings his own tune, each dances his own dance, or leaps, shouts, and exults with exceeding great joy'. Many of the 'white spirituals' which constitute a part of American folk hymnody were taken over to varying degrees by the Negroes. Thus a line of development can be traced from such early 18th-century English sources as Dr Isaac Watts' *Hymns and Spiritual Songs*, to American 'white spirituals', to Negro spirituals – and from there to jazz, via the country band of the late 19th century.

The beginning of a tradition

Apart from Gottschalk, the first American composer to achieve international fame was Edward MacDowell (1861-1908). As a clearly gifted student he completed his musical education in Germany and lived for twelve years abroad. Franz Liszt recognised his outstanding talent and arranged for the publication of some of his music in Leipzig. Such pieces as the second piano concerto had considerable success in Germany, and in the United States MacDowell was acclaimed widely. His music is, indeed, of excellent technical quality, but it lacks originality. It is genteel music, and occasionally suffers from sentimentality and bombast. In his *Fireside Tales*, *New England Idylls*, *Indian Suite* and other poetic works, MacDowell does little more than bring a bit of local colour into a thoroughly Germanic style of post-Romantic hue. The same lack of innate vitality characterises the works of other New Englanders of this period: Daniel Gregory Mason (1873-1953), Arthur Foote (1853-1937), George Chadwick (1854-1931) and Horatio Parker (1863-1919) – academic composers, often grouped as 'New England Classicists', who wrote under the strong influence of Brahms.

At the end of the 19th century America was still waiting for its first important composer. The time was

opposite, top
The Fiske Jubilee Singers in the 1870s.

opposite bottom
Music at home in 19th-century America.

below
A 19th-century tutor on shape-note music.

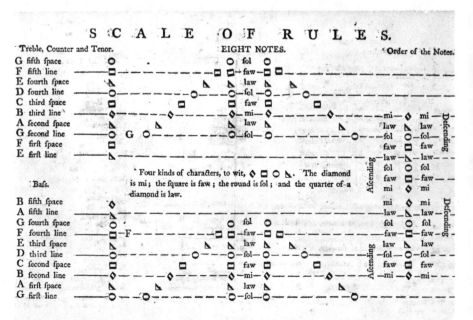

ripe; musical maturity had been long in the making. But another quarter of a century was to elapse before fulfilment, for although the long-awaited American composer was already at work, his existence was universally ignored.

Charles Ives

Charles Ives (1874-1954) is the first truly original and independent American composer – besides being one of the most fascinating figures of modern music. He lived and worked entirely apart from the musical world of his time, yet, by 1916, he had composed works containing bi-tonal, polytonal, atonal, polyrhythmic and aleatory passages – long before his European colleagues, of whom Ives, in any case, had no cognisance.

In Danbury, Connecticut, where Charles Ives was born and brought up, there was little serious music. But young Ives heard music in the everyday sounds that surrounded him: in church bells ringing over the gently rolling hills of New England; the out-of-tune village organ and the equally out-of-tune church choir; the simple hymns with which he grew up; the village brass band which his father conducted; and, later on, sounds and noises of the metropolis, New York.

Although he studied music at Yale University, Ives showed little respect for academicism. Relying on his own imagination he arrived at innovations which, to his teachers and contemporaries, seemed utter madness. He wrote in his *Essays before a Sonata*: 'Beauty in music is too often confused with something that lets the ears lie back in an easy chair'. But when conventional writing served his expressive purpose, he employed it.

Since it was clear that he could not earn a living as a musician without compromising, Ives went into the insurance business and established his own highly successful firm. His few attempts to have his music performed were fruitless; he published some pieces privately and at his own expense. He was 71 before he heard any work of his performed by a full orchestra. Yet nearly all his music had been composed by 1915. During his later life he was an invalid and something of a recluse.

Such titles as *Three Places in New England* and the subtitles he gave to individual movements of other works would seem to place Ives as a regional composer. In other pieces he draws heavily on familiar American songs and dance tunes; elsewhere, and frequently, he alludes to well-known hymns and Civil War songs. The four movements of *Holidays* for orchestra are all-American in scope. Even in his four symphonies and four sonatas for violin and piano, Ives introduces folk and popular material. His second piano sonata, *Concord, Mass., 1840-1860*, one of his most impressive works, contains veiled quotations from many sources, including Beethoven. All these elements are integrated into an idiom that is naturally, never self-consciously, American, and is the expression of a strong musical personality – music characteristically American but never provincial.

The 20th century

To a certain extent, European Romanticism, with its glorification of folk music and its later development towards nationalism in music, was instrumental in hastening American composers' coming of age. Whereas some were content to follow in the footsteps of Wagner and Brahms, others made a conscious and often self-conscious effort to write recognisably American music. Arthur Farwell (1872-1952) wrote: 'The first correction we must bring to our musical vision is to cease to see everything through German spectacles, however wonderful, however sublime those spectacles may be in themselves!' Farwell advocated paying more attention to contemporary French and Russian music, and he was not alone. Gradually the German hegemony was broken and French influence became apparent – that of Debussy, Ravel and, later on, Milhaud and other moderns, from Messiaen to Boulez.

Indigenous American music supplied ready-to-hand material for the creation of 'typically American' sounds. Farwell and several others made a valiant attempt to incorporate Indian melodies, rhythms and idioms into concert music, but with little success. With Negro music, which had already absorbed many European characteristics, the results were somewhat better. But works such as *Negro Rhapsody* for piano and orchestra (1918) by John Powell (1882-1963) remained artificial and unconvincing. Nearly all American folk-music-inspired rhapsodies, fantasies and symphonies give the impression that the native material, whatever its origin, has been applied from without, like a veneer. The nature of folk and vernacular music is such as to make its incorporation into serious music a very difficult, and even doubtful, procedure. Unless the folk or vernacular idiom has been so digested and transformed that it comes out as a normal, integrated ingredient of the composer's musical speech (as in Bartók's works) the music will sound artificial. The composer is by education a sophisticated

Charles Ives, one of the greatest figures of 20th-century American music.

left
The Boston Symphony Orchestra in 1882.

below
P. T. Barnum, the impresario who was a co-founder of Barnum and Bailey's circus, also sponsored the visit of Jenny Lind, the 'Swedish Nightingale', to America. Here he is shown introducing her to Ossian Dodge, a contemporary composer.

musician; the essence of folk material lies in its directness and simplicity. By putting on a peasant costume, the composer does not become a peasant.

For the American composer, lacking a long-established and homogeneous culture, the use of folk material is especially problematical and, in the light of this, an American national school of composition would seem to be a contradiction in terms. If some composers, notably Aaron Copland, have made use of folk material in creating works of artistic value, the credit is due not to the material but to the creative powers brought to bear.

It is generally conceded that jazz is America's most typical musical expression and it would seem to be a logical point of departure for a typically American music. Yet the combination of jazz and serious music has not worked. Many Americans and Europeans have tried to square the stylistic circle involved. Two of the most successful are Copland, in his 'jazz' piano concerto (1927), and Milhaud, in his ballet *La Création du Monde* (1923). But as early as 1926 Milhaud wrote that he saw no future along these lines.

In recent years a new movement, headed by Gunther Schuller, has been under way. To date, this 'Third Stream' has not achieved its aims. But Schuller and his associates are getting closer to an artistically valid solution of their misleadingly simple problem.

Breakthrough

American music reaches maturity in the 1920s. The technical preparation is complete, and composers have lost the inferiority complexes which made them imitate Europe on the one hand and seek a self-conscious Americanism on the other. From now on, they can 'take it or leave it', as they see fit – and 'it' can be anything from the latest European developments to indigenous material, to oriental and other exotic influences, to brand new inventions '*made in U.S.A.*'. To what extent native self-confidence was bolstered by America's part in the First World War is a matter for speculation.

The number of notable composers increases so rapidly from 1920 onwards that a mere list of their names would fill pages. To the non-specialist, the contemporary American picture is, indeed, bewildering, not only because of the enormous quantity of music but also

because of the variety of styles and approaches. The large number of well trained composers results to a certain degree from the American system of education: music is taught in many high schools, and the literally thousands of colleges and universities all have music departments and offer degrees either in music or with music as the major subject. In addition to this the huge geographical dimensions of the United States make it difficult to get a clear view of the enormous amount of creative and other musical acitivity.

The hegemony of German music was definitely broken in the 1920s in favour of a predominantly French orientation, reinforced by the Stravinsky style of his Parisian period. Paris now became the Mecca for budding American composers for some twenty years. The first generation went almost without exception to that remarkable pedagogue Nadia Boulanger, to whom Stravinsky was the one true prophet. From the 'Boulangerie' came Copland, Harris, Piston and Thomson in the 1920s; Berger, Carter, Elwell, Fine and Haieff in the 1930s – to mention only a few. All of them received a first-class technical training and all of them began composing with a strong bias towards Neo-classicism.

Aaron Copland, born in Brooklyn, New York, in 1900, is undoubtedly one of the most gifted composers America has produced to date. His imitators have been numerous and unsuccessful, but his general influence has been great. The 'modernism' of his early works – the piano concerto of 1927, the *Vitebsk* trio for violin, cello and piano (1929), and the piano variations – shocked conservative taste. The *Short Symphony* (1933) and *Statements* for orchestra (1934) are concise, austere pieces, more to be admired than loved. In a conscious effort to reach a broader public, Copland then adopted what he calls 'an imposed simplicity'. *El Salón México* (1936), is attractive and entirely unproblematic; the ballets *Billy the Kid* (1938), *Rodeo* (1942) and *Appalachian Spring* (1944) incorporate folk music of cowboy and religious provenance. The *Lincoln Portrait* (1942) for speaker and orchestra just misses being embarrassingly popular. Copland's only opera, *The Tender Land* (1954), portraying 'plain salt-of-the-earth folk', fails to come off, both musically and dramatically.

In the *Piano Fantasy* (1952–57) Copland returns to a more severe style, employing twelve-note technique in

Aaron Copland (extreme left) speaking to Darius Milhaud.

a fairly rudimentary way and with little success. His major contribution, as creator and influence, ends with the Second World War. And it is very considerable.

Roy Harris, born in Oklahoma in 1898, is a special and puzzling case. His early works led to great expectations; his third symphony (1939) is one of the finest America has produced. It is unmistakably American without benefit of folk material. But the fourth symphony, subtitled *Folk Song Symphony* (1941), piles folk tune on folk tune and adds up to little more than a *pot-pourri*. Nevertheless, today he is perhaps unjustly neglected. His loudly proclaimed determination to achieve rough-hewn Americanism has led all too often to provincialism. Yet his piano trio (1934), his three string quartets and, especially, his piano quintet (1937) contain some splendid music that is typically Harris. Considering his study with Nadia Boulanger, his style is surprisingly untouched by Stravinskian Neo-classicism. Harris' predilection for broad lyricism, polyphonic development and contrapuntal forms (his works abound in fugues), coupled with a spontaneous vitality, produce a unique combination in American music.

Born in Maine in 1894, Walter Piston displayed a continuing enchantment with classicism that has been the undoing of his extremely well written but, in the last analysis, academic music. One admires the fine writing and the economy of means, the clever play of rhythms and the balanced proportions of many of his works – not to mention the dry wit of others. But it is cultivated, unimpassioned, easily-forgotten music – even the best of it, which would include the second, fourth and seventh symphonies and the ballet music, *The Incredible Flutist*.

Virgil Thomson, born in Kansas in 1896, is the prime American exponent of Neo-classicism. His stylistic simplicity is often exasperating, and one feels that this highly sophisticated musician is playing at shepherdess *á la* Marie Antoinette. But Thomson's best music is memorable – especially that which has a text, and specifically when the words are by Gertrude Stein, as they are in *Four Saints in Three Acts* (1934). The sophisticated naïveté of this opera, with its provoking simple harmonies, its unsolicited references to hymn tunes and its intentional vulgarities, reflects Thomson's spiritual affinity with the Paris of the 1920s, especially with the group of the Six and also Erik Satie. When Thomson uses American material 'straight', as in his *Symphony on a Hymn Tune*, the results are less interesting, and his second opera with a Gertrude Stein libretto, *The Mother of Us All*, lags somewhat behind the first. Thomson has remained a Francophile but has not lost a certain native raucousness. The unlikely juxtaposition of Kansas and Paris gives his music a special quality.

In striking contrast to the four Boulanger pupils mentioned above stands Roger Sessions (b. 1896), whose teacher, the Swiss-American Ernest Bloch, influenced him in the direction of German music. Sessions' music is, on the whole, difficult for the listener, not only because of its dissonant harmonic structure but even more because of its often thick, sometimes opaque texture and contrapuntal complexity, notably in the string quartets. He has avoided the pitfalls of Neo-classicism, heart-on-sleeve Americanism and, indeed, any kind of '-ism', following his own lights and accepting his musical ideas 'without theorising as to their source or their other than musical meaning', as he puts it. When his music sounds American, this is because it does not sound like anything else – certainly not like Schoenberg or Berg, to whom Sessions is indebted. In Sessions' relatively small catalogue of works, the second (1947), third (1957) and fourth (1958) symphonies command special respect and are gradually assuming their rightful place in the concert repertoire.

Among the elder statesmen of American music mention should be made of the solitary New England mystic

Carl Ruggles, whose chromatic polyphony bears a certain resemblance to Schoenberg's, although the resulting music does not. The rehabilitation of Ruggles' superbly individualistic works, including the symphonic suite *Men and Mountains* (1924), is long overdue.

Recognition was also long in coming to Wallingford Riegger (1885-1961), a pioneer of serial technique in the United States. From German Romanticism, his style progressed towards greater lucidity, remarkable for its transparent texture and cogent, clearly defined rhythms – the result, perhaps, of Riegger's activity in the field of modern dance. Less aggressive than the earlier works, his *Variations for piano and orchestra* (1954) reflect an individual and thoroughly American concept of serialism of which humour and wit are ingredients.

The second generation

Together with Henry Cowell (1897-1966), an active publicist of new music as well as a fine composer, and the naturalised Frenchman Edgar Varèse, these were the first important composers of the United States.

With the second generation, such a final assessment is still not possible. Twenty years ago, for example, Harold Shapero (b. 1920) would have figured as one of the brightest of coming composers, while Elliott Carter (b. 1908) would have received only passing mention. In the meantime, Shapero has virtually stopped composing, and Carter's development has been enormous.

The second generation has it both easier and harder than the first. On the one hand, modern American music was no longer a cause to bleed and die for. The concerts of Copland and Sessions and those of the League of Composers of the 1920s had won the day. American music was generally accepted as existing, in principle; but it no longer got the publicity and attention that a hot issue does. Notoriety is, in fact, preferable to indifference.

Yet during the 1930s and 1940s it does appear that there are few works by the younger men that can stand up to those of their elders. Neo-classicism provided an easy escape from musical reality for many composers and reduced the hardier ones to silence. On the heels of the Neo-classical came a wave of homespun Americanism which, after the beginning of the war, often took a patriotic turn.

One of the most successful composers of the period is William Schuman (b. 1910), a pupil of Roy Harris whose *American Festival Overture* (1939) brought him nation-wide prominence. His works include a 'baseball opera' called *The Mighty Casey*, the orchestral *William Billings Overture* and *New England Triptych*, the ballets *Undertow*, *Night Journey* and *Judith*, the secular cantata *This is Our Time* and many choral pieces. But Schuman's best writing is to be found in his symphonies and string quartets; it is marked by great rhythmic vitality, tense and often highly dissonant harmonies and complex contrapuntal textures. His Americanisms, superimposed on an essentially cosmopolitan style, have grown thin. If his work survives, it will be on the basis of his exuberant and highly competent abstract works, of which the fifth symphony (for strings) is a good example.

Some of the many outspokenly Americanist works of the 1930s and 1940s have had their day. Although the rise and wide adoption of serial and post-serial techniques tends to make all tonally-based music seem *passé*, however untenable such an attitude may be, it is safe to say that such pieces as *A Walt Whitman Overture* and *Sunday in Brooklyn* by Elie Siegmeister, Ray Green's *Sunday Sing Symphony* and Douglas Moore's *Village Music* have passed the peak of their popularity. In the same category is *The Prairie* (1943), a cantata after Walt Whitman's poem, by the versatile Lukas Foss (b. 1922), who has gone through a number of stylistic transformations and today cultivates a radical post-serial idiom.

A number of composers who began their careers as Neo-classicists have developed since the war in quite different directions. Those who have not (for example Alexei Haieff and Vincent Persichetti) have fallen by the wayside. Like others, Irving Fine (1914-1962) left Piston's classes at Harvard University with a Neo-classical outlook that was strengthened by study with Nadia Boulanger. In his string quartet of 1952, he employed a special, quasi-tonal kind of serialism. The early death of this gifted composer represented a great loss to American music. Elliott Carter (b. 1908) is another Harvard-Boulanger product who has gone far from his Neo-classical beginnings to become one of the most important voices of today. Rejecting serialism as a way of creative life, Carter has developed a personal style in which metrical and time relationships play a basic part. His music is complicated, but the complications are necessary to what he wishes to convey. Carter's is eminently meaningful music, but the meaning is of a

left
Wallingford Riegger.

below
Samuel Barber at the piano.

musical nature; it is expressive without being emotional, the work of a gifted and serious musician who knows his business thoroughly and who pursues it with little regard for passing fashions. Different as his mature works are, they represent an aesthetic entity spanning the cello sonata (1948), string quartet (1951), *Variations for orchestra* (1955), second string quartet (1959), double concerto (1961) and the piano concerto (1965). These works occupy a significant place in 20th-century music – and not only that of America.

Something of the same artistic honesty as informs Carter's music is present in the work of Samuel Barber (b. 1910) who, as a traditionalist, stands at the other end of the stylistic spectrum. Barber's natural form of expression stems from Romanticism, and he has not tried to fight or conceal it. His wide appeal, based on unabashedly subjective expression, has made him perhaps the most frequently performed American composer. In his *Essays for Orchestra*, the *Adagio for Strings* (1932), the virtuosic piano sonata (1949), *Dover Beach* for voice, string quartet (1931) and above all in his songs, Barber is eloquently lyrical. In other works, such as the attractive *Capricorn Concerto* for chamber ensemble, he ventures into a more modern idiom which includes mild polytonality, lively rhythms and extremely expert counterpoint. His two excursions into the field of opera (*Vanessa* and *Anthony and Cleopatra*) have not been notably successful. Barber's particular gifts are not essentially dramatic.

Musical theatre

The first opera to be composed by a native American was Fry's *Leonora* (1845); the first on a native subject was George Bristow's *Rip Van Winkle*. Both followed Italian models of the period, and neither changed the

course of history. In the second half of the 19th century, a few Wagnerian imitations were produced, such as Walter Damrosch's very successful *The Scarlet Letter* (1896) and, with the 20th century, the number of attempts at American music theatre increases: Deems Taylor's *The King's Henchmen* (1927) and *Peter Ibbetson* (1931) had deservedly short runs, as did Howard Hanson's *Merry Mount* (1934). The American composer was, and still is, at a decided disadvantage in this field, for there are few outlets for opera in the United States, although the number has increased in recent years thanks to the founding of university opera workshops and of such companies as the New York City Opera. But American opera has not yet come of age, and probably will not do so until (and if) opera becomes as much part of American culture as concert music has become. There have been some good tries: Douglas Moore's *The Devil and Daniel Webster*, Marc Blitzstein's *The Cradle Will Rock*, Carlisle Floyd's *Susannah*. But none has been able to compete with the best European products, with the possible exception of Gunther Schuller's *The Visitation* (1966).

All the more interesting is it, then, that America has originated the form par excellence of light musical stage work of the 20th century – the musical. Originating in the operetta but stripped of that form's conventional absurdities (and sentimentality!), the musical sets out to entertain and comes close, at times, to being art. It could easily be argued that Richard Rogers' *Oklahoma!* (1934) – one of the first great musicals – shows more originality, and contains more valid music, than the opera *The Consul* by Gian Carlo Menotti (b. 1911). Or that Frank Loesser's *Guys and Dolls* is a better score than Menotti's *Amahl and the Night Visitors*. And there can be little doubt that George Gershwin's *Porgy and Bess* is worth all the serious American operas that had preceded it.

George Gershwin (1898-1937) poses the neat problem as to where commercial music stops and serious music begins. *Porgy and Bess*, Gershwin's most ambitious and

The musical: a scene from a Theatre Guild production of Oklahoma!

best work, was written for, and first produced on, Broadway. It has been called a 'folk opera', but it is in reality a musical that did, indeed, achieve the status of art. It is Gershwin's only work that crosses this border, despite the strong appeal of the piano concerto, the *Rhapsody in Blue*, the piano *Preludes* and *An American in Paris*. Gershwin went from rags to riches as a pop composer; he would have given much of his huge fortune to be a serious one, but he lacked the tools of the composer's trade. His wonderful show tunes sprang from sheer spontaneous genius; in *Porgy and Bess*, the last work of Gershwin's pathetically short life, he leaves a legacy that has yet to be fulfilled. In his opera, Tin Pan Alley and art music meet and are reconciled as never before or since – not even in *West Side Story* (1957) by the brilliant composer and conductor Leonard Bernstein (b. 1918).

The contemporary scene

John Cage (b. 1912) belongs by birth to the second generation, but his influence has been felt only since the Second World War. It has been great and it is continuing. A pupil of Henry Cowell, Cage studied briefly with Arnold Schoenberg in Los Angeles without adopting twelve-note technique. He first attracted attention with his works for 'prepared piano' – i.e. a piano into which various and sundry objects (from bits of wood to weather stripping) have been inserted to produce unusual timbres. It is his employment of chance procedures, however, that has created a following among *avant-garde* composers on both sides of the Atlantic and which, together with a certain amount of pseudo-oriental philosophy, has led to various forms of 'indeterminacy' and, finally, to non-music, consisting entirely of selence, as in his piece *4 minutes and 33 seconds*. Cage's disciples Earle Brown and Morton Feldman have arrived at their

own personal interpetations of Cageism, too complicated for description here and often involving graphic notation which employs signs and symbols rather than notes on staves.

Twelve-note and serial techniques played a relatively small role in American music before 1950 or thereabouts. Since than serialism has been very widely adopted by younger composers, who have produced their versions of post-Webernism, total serialism and, more recently, post-serialism. This last is an overall term covering a multitude of forms and techniques from 'open' (i.e. chance or indeterminate) forms to the musical happening

above left
George Gershwin, aged thirty-eight, working on a portrait of Schoenberg.

left
Leonard Bernstein at the piano.

above
Edgar Varèse, the French-born composer, one of the most important musicians working in America this century.

below
From the ms. of John Cage's concerto for piano and orchestra. Reprinted with permission of the copyright owners: Henmar Press Inc., New York.

and 'action' music, in which the composer gives the performer more or less general directions to play or do 'something' and leaves the rest to him.

Electronic music has also won a wide following. Pioneers in the field are the 'conservatives' Vladimir Ussachevsky (b. 1911) and Otto Luening (b. 1900), both of whom helped to found the electronic studio at Columbia University, where the 'radical' Milton Babbitt (b. 1916) has also worked extensively.

Since serial and other 'advanced' techniques are now taught in a large number of institutions from coast to coast, the problems of distinguishing among young composers is made difficult by reason of their sheer numbers. Gunther Schuller (b. 1925) is certainly a name to be reckoned with. Aside from his experiments in combining jazz and serious music, the 'Third Stream', he has composed concert music (in a serial vein) that for its sheer effectiveness is both remarkable and somewhat suspect. One wonders too whether the effortless assimilation of the trappings of avant-gardism by the gifted Lukas Foss is for better or for worse – whether his later works will stand up to such earlier ones as *A Parable of Death* (1953) and *Time-Cycle* (1960).

Characteristic of a number of the most gifted younger American composers is their heretical attitude towards orthodox and consistent avant-gardism. Charles Wuorinen (b. 1938), Yehudi Wyner (b. 1929) and William Sydeman (b. 1928) adapt serial techniques, or write non-serial music, as they see fit. Billy Jim Layton (b. 1924) has already developed an advanced personal style that has its roots in Ives and Carter. In his highly sensitive Romantically tinged works, Leon Kirchner (b. 1919) has produced some of the most expressive music of the post-war period.

The amount of creative activity in present-day America is enormous, and a great deal of the music gets performed – often in the cloistered atmosphere of the universities. But also the many 'art centres' that have sprung up in recent years give a hearing to new music, and the foundations (Ford, Rockefeller, Guggenheim and others) provide direct and indirect sponsorship.

In the wake of the oft-cited cultural explosion of the 1950s, the American public has been given increasingly greater opportunities to hear music of all periods and varieties – including that of its own composers. New York's Lincoln Center for the Performing Arts and Los Angeles' new centre are visible manifestations of this development, as are the founding of new orchestras and opera companies and the increased number of festivals throughout the country; while such summer schools as Tanglewood in Massachusetts and Interlochen in Michigan are making vital contributions to the training of young musicians.

The evolution of American music has involved the absorption and synthesis of many ethnic and cultural traditions. Much could be written on the contributions made by musical immigrants: from the German conductors Theodor Thomas and Walter Damrosch to the Russian Serge Koussevitzky and the Greek Dimitri Mitropoulos; from the French composers Charles Martin Loeffler and Edgar Varèse to the Germans Weill and Hindemith, the Austrians Schoenberg and Krenek and the Russian Stravinsky – not to mention a host of performers, educators and pedagogues. And, of primary importance, those black 'immigrants' whose ancestors came not of their own volition but under duress and who created the anonymous music of jazz. All these factors have combined to bring American music to the point it has reached today, where American music and musicians, in short, are equal partners with the other musical countries of the world.

EVERETT HELM

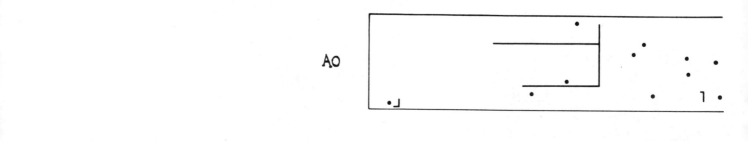

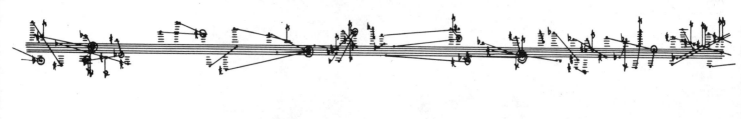

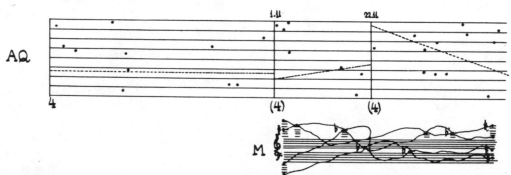

Music in England from 1800

The 19th century is the least distinguished period in English musical history. Yet the renaissance that occurred in the last two decades did not happen purely fortuitously, but was the result of a number of developments during the previous eighty years. Of these, the most significant was the general extension of interest in music and the improvement in education.

The native tradition of choral singing, based firmly on the oratorio since Handel's time and soon to be buttressed by the publication of cheap music, was the principal means by which the new mass culture developed. Although opera has always been a difficult plant to cultivate in England, there has always been a demand for musical drama of a popular kind. The line of descent here can be traced from the late 17th century, from Lawes and Locke through Purcell to the ballad opera, to Balfe and Wallace in the mid-19th century and to the Savoy operas, whose descendants were the musical comedies of the twenties and thirties.

In popular musical education, the pioneers were Joseph Mainzer (1801-51) and John Hullah (1812-84) and, even more successful, John Curwen (1816-80), promoter of the Tonic Sol-Fa method. Many thousands of people who would otherwise have been musically illiterate were enabled by these systems to participate in choral singing and sight-read difficult music to a high degree of accuracy.

The men who first took steps to meet the vastly increased demand for music which resulted from the formation all over the country of singing classes and choral societies were Vincent Novello (1781-1861) and his son Alfred (1810-96). The remarkably versatile Vincent Novello (composer, conductor, pianist, organist, viola player, father of a large and gifted family and host to many artistic figures of the time) produced his first publications in 1811, but it was his son Alfred who expanded the business and in the early 1840s began to produce probably the cheapest music ever published in England.

The proliferation of musical activity, which was not only choral but also (particularly in the north of England) instrumental, through the medium of the brass band, found its outlet first in the choral and later in the competitive festivals. The centring of the choral festivals on the oratorio tradition resulted in a demand for large numbers of works of this type. Of the native products the best known and longest remembered were Crotch's *Palestine* and Sterndale Bennett's *The Woman of Samaria*, but the field was dominated by the foreign composers. Handel remained the foundation of the repertoire, and his pre-eminence was demonstrated by the mammoth Crystal Palace Handel Festivals which began in 1857. But Mendelssohn and Louis Spohr (1784-1851) and a large number of other continental composers were welcomed. They are often remembered for the slight and sentimental works with which they pleased Victorian taste but Spohr himself produced

some fine music, notably his nonet for four strings, double bass, woodwind and horn.

The world of music

The career of Sterndale Bennett (1816-75) exemplified both the achievements and the shortcomings of 19th-century musicians. The promise of the youthful compositions, which caused him to be generously praised by Mendelssohn and Schumann, was never fulfilled. But he did valuable work for English music in teaching and administration, particularly in founding the Bach Society in 1849, which entitles him to be considered one of the main architects of the late renaissance.

The general decline in standards in the established Church in the 18th century and the neglect of the music in parish church and cathedral that ensued reached its nadir in the early 19th century. In the cathedrals a scandalous situation had developed with regard to the pay and working conditions of the organist and choir, the money usually being diverted to other purposes, if not straight into the pockets of the Dean and Chapter. Circumstances improved after the middle of the century, largely as a result of the efforts of two militant reformers. Miss Maria Hackett (1783-1874) adopted the causes of the choirboys and their education, and Samuel Sebastian Wesley (1810-76), in addition to following his father Samuel in promoting the music of

Vincent Novello, the Italian-born composer and conductor, and first of a famous dynasty of English musicians.

445

Bach in England, fought for better music throughout his life against obstructive and apathetic cathedral authorities. His compositions are touched with genius and stand out among those of his worthy but dull contemporaries.

The great increase in concert-giving which had occurred in the 18th century had been mainly organised by 'society' groups, who confined their audiences to subscribers or elected members, though the London 'Gardens' provided excellent concerts for large audiences. The need for concerts at the cheapest price for the greatest number was perceived and met by a Frenchman, Louis Antoine Jullien (1812-60), and a German, August Manns (1825-1907). Jullien imported the 'promenade' idea, which had been adapted by the French from the public garden concerts, and drew large audiences by his mixture of showmanship and solid musical fare. But while Jullien was a populariser Manns was a missionary. The tradition of concert-giving at the Crystal Palace that he began in 1855 not only outlived the Victorian era, but grafted on to a comprehensive repertoire of familiar and unfamiliar classics a large number of works by contemporary composers. The encouragement and sympathetic treatment that Manns gave to English composers were otherwise singularly lacking in their own country.

Muzio Clementi (1751-1832), an Italian who spent most of his working life in England, was outstanding in the development of the piano and its music. Among his pupils were J. B. Cramer (1771-1858) and John Field (1782-1837). Cramer's life and work resembled that of his master. He lived all but the first of his eighty-seven years in England, composed prolifically, had an international reputation as performer and teacher, and founded the business firm that bears his name, first devoted to publishing and later also to pianoforte

manufacture. The Irishman John Field also enjoyed great fame as a performer and teacher, but the music he composed for the pianoforte was in many ways in advance of its time. His influence on Chopin, notably through the conception of the nocturne, is well known, but his compositions are more than mere forerunners. In a great age of English poetry he discovered the poetic capabilities of the pianoforte, and though his output was comparatively small, it contains some lyrical pieces as perfect as any written by his successors.

The Tudor and folk music revival

The renewal of interest in 16th- and 17th-century music and the collection and preservation of English folk song were to be major influences on later composers, though the domination of the English musical scene by foreign-trained academic musicians was initially such that more than fifty years elapsed before a distinctively national character materialised. The English Folk Song Society was founded in 1898, though many collections of English folk songs had been published in the previous fifty years. The man who did most to promote the cause of folk music in England was Cecil Sharp (1859-1924). The fruits of his widespread and innumerable journeys with notebook and pencil were published in several collections containing altogether over 3000 tunes. A year he spent in the southern Appalachian mountains of North America during the First World War produced some 1600 tunes of English origin carried there by the first settlers.

The Musical Antiquarian Society, founded in 1840, produced nineteen volumes on a subscription basis containing madrigals, lute songs, motets, and anthems. Although it survived only seven years it set an example which was widely followed. Later bodies included the Plainsong and Medieval Music Society and the Purcell Society, and individual musicians were also active in rediscovery and editing.

One of the greatest contributors to the movement was E. H. Fellowes (1870-1951) who, early in 1924, finally completed a definitive and practical edition of all surviving English madrigals. His other publications included a series of *English Lutenist Songs* and the complete works of William Byrd.

The work of R. R. Terry (1865-1938) at Westminster Cathedral, where he restored to liturgical use the motets and masses of Palestrina, Byrd and the continental schools, stimulated an interest that resulted in the publication of the ten volumes of *Tudor Church Music*, edited by a committee that included Terry and Fellowes. Instrumental music of the period also had its champions, especially J. A. Fuller-Maitland (1856-1936) for keyboard music and Arnold Dolmetsch (1858-1940) for all old instruments including the viol and recorder families.

Renaissance

Conditions for the would-be professional composer in Victorian England were such that, unless the traditional oratorio or the drawing-room ballad were his chosen medium, he could hope for little in the way of performances and even less in royalties. Nevertheless, four composers showed in their different ways that it was possible to be a professional composer in England and to produce work of high quality without sacrificing individuality or national identity.

Arthur Sullivan (1842-1900) had a conventional

Sir Arthur Sullivan as seen by a contemporary caricaturist.

even more profound effect on the course of English music than his compositions. A consummate and prolific craftsman whose output included nine operas, seven symphonies, twenty-two cantatas, anthems and services for the Anglican church and chamber music, he showed his greatest mastery in the smaller forms. In these, and particularly in his songs, the Irish element that was the essence of his individuality often predominated, and the influence of Brahms and Schumann that was a legacy from his studies in Germany was least in evidence. The setting of the church canticles in B flat that appeared in 1879 had the same radical importance for Anglican church music as Parry's *Prometheus Unbound* had for choral music generally, and his other works for the church, notably the service settings in C and G and the unaccompanied motets, show a similar variety and vitality that are the more remarkable when we consider the egregious dullness of contemporary efforts in this field. Stanford's music has a freshness and creativity that deserve practical recognition and a much wider audience.

Elgar

Though largely self-taught, Edward Elgar (1857-1934) was England's first truly professional composer, holding no official appointment during his life apart from a brief tenure of Birmingham University's chair of music and later the sinecure of Master of the King's Musick. His early life as a working musician, conducting and writing music for the Worcester Asylum band, playing the violin and composing for many different occasions was, together with such private study as he found possible, both the start of his professional life and his apprenticeship. His failure to settle in London early in his career and consequent retirement to Malvern helped to separate him from the influences which had devitalised the

above left
Dr Hubert Parry.

below
Sir Charles Stanford.

musical training as Chapel Royal choirboy, Mendelssohn scholar at the Royal Academy of Music and student at the Leipzig Conservatory, which no doubt explains his life-long conviction that his real business in life was to be a serious composer of oratorios, church music and symphonies. The collaboration with W. S. Gilbert that produced the Savoy operettas was a unique partnership in the world of the theatre. The immediate and lasting popularity of his stage works derives from their perfect expression of the wit, versatility, and irreverent mockery that breathes in the libretto.

Alexander Campbell Mackenzie (1847-1935) began his career as a violinist. His first-hand experience of orchestral and operatic music and his continental training and contacts with international musical figures gave him a cosmopolitanism that combined not unsuccessfully with his Scottish nationalism. In his instrumental music, such as the *Violin Concerto* and the *Scottish Concerto* for piano, there is a freshness that reflects his vigorous personality. Most of his best work as a composer was done before his appointment as principal of the Royal Academy of Music in 1888. Thereafter, composition gave way to teaching and administration: his thirty-six years at the R.A.M. were marked by a massive improvement in the institution's resources and prestige and in the quality of its teaching.

Hubert Parry (1848-1918) and Charles Stanford (1852-1924) mark the beginning of the new epoch. They were associated by age, similarity of education and outlook, and by their shared determination to improve the status of English music and musicians. The performance of Parry's *Prometheus Unbound* at the Gloucester Festival of 1880 was a seminal event. Though the work, a setting of Shelley for soloists, chorus and orchestra, made little subsequent impression, its significance lay in the composer's choice of a text of literary distinction, his bold new approach to choral writing, and his abandonment of the tired musical language, a kind of Handel stereotype diluted with Mendelssohn and Spohr, that had too long been the idiom of the 'festival cantata'. His setting of Milton's *Blest Pair of Sirens* has always held a firm place in the affections of English choral singers, but finer still are the six unaccompanied motets, the *Songs of Farewell*.

In 1894 Parry became Director of the Royal College of Music, where the Irish-born Stanford was professor of composition. Stanford's work as a teacher – his pupils included Vaughan Williams and Holst – had an

work of his contemporaries.

Elgar first emerged as a composer through the medium that had become traditional – the festival cantata. In spite of the vitality and originality that he brought to this overworked form his fame remained only local until his marriage in 1889 to Caroline Alice Roberts. His wife's encouragement and devotion and steadfast belief in his genius were the elements needed to counterbalance his moodiness, which occasionally turned into bitterness, and his lifelong (but unjustified) conviction that his work was neglected and unappreciated. In 1899 the production of the *Enigma Variations* proclaimed to the world that England possessed a composer who could no longer be ignored, and *The Dream of Gerontius*, which received its notorious first performance in Birmingham a year later, was immediately adopted by the Germans and acclaimed as a masterpiece. Two more oratorios followed, *The Apostles* and *The Kingdom*, but the period

succeeding *Gerontius* produced a flood of orchestral works that proved that at least one English composer could work outside the choral tradition. The *Cockaigne* overture, the *Pomp and Circumstance* marches, and the *Introduction and Allegro* for strings enriched the orchestral repertoire, but symphonic composition was delayed by the demands on his time and energy which resulted from his increasing fame and by the necessity to make a regular income. The first symphony eventually appeared in 1908 and ushered in the richest group of Elgar's works; it was followed by the violin concerto, the second symphony, the symphonic study *Falstaff*, and, in 1919, the cello concerto, but after the death of Elgar's wife in 1920 little of significance appeared.

Symptomatic of the greatness in Elgar's music is its renewed appeal at the present time, when performers and listeners are finding elements in it that express aspects of the contemporary mood more exactly than pre-

Sir Edward Elgar.

vious superficial assessments could ever have allowed or expected. Elgar himself said that English music should have 'something broad, noble, chivalrous, healthy, and above all an out-of-door sort of spirit', but underlying all the exuberance and spaciousness are an introspective regret and disquiet that give an added meaning to his favourite *nobilmente*.

Delius

Frederick Delius (1862–1934), the most purely poetic of English composers, was born, prosaically enough, into the wool trade in Bradford. With the very mixed influences that affected him – German and Dutch ancestry, American and German training, Scandinavian associa-

tions and preferences, and French domicile – it is not surprising that his music owes no obvious allegiance to any tradition and founded no school of successors. In spite of his early display of musical talent he had to overcome opposition from his father to the idea of a musical career, but the travels involved in his training for the wool trade took him to countries where he found full scope for his musical proclivities. After even orange-growing in Florida had failed to quench his thirst for music, the intervention of Grieg persuaded his father to allow him to become a composer. He settled in France and married Jelka Rosen, a Norwegian artist, in 1897. In 1899 he moved to the country town of Grez-sur-Loing where he lived, detached from the world, for the rest of his life.

Delius's large output includes concertos and sonatas for violin and cello but, ultra-romantic that he was, his real genius lay in the evocation of atmosphere and in

Frederick Delius.

449

representing his own reactions to nature and solitude. The titles of his finest works, those for chorus and orchestra or orchestra alone, convey some of the essence of his distinctive vision: *Sea Drift, Appalachia; Variations on an Old Negro Song; A Song of the High Hills; Brigg Fair: An English Rhapsody; North Country Sketches*, and on a smaller scale, *In a Summer Garden; On Hearing the First Cuckoo in Spring*, and *Summer Night on the River*. Good exponents of this music have been few because of its elusive and subtle idiom; notable among them were the German conductors who gave the first performances of many of his works including the operas *Koanga, A Village Romeo and Juliet*, and *Fennimore and Gerda*. But it was an English conductor, Sir Thomas Beecham, who was Delius's greatest interpreter and champion.

For the last ten years of his life Delius was afflicted with paralysis and blindness, but with the devoted care of his wife and his amanuensis Eric Fenby he was able to continue composing.

Vaughan Williams and Holst

In the work of Ralph Vaughan Williams (1872-1958) and Gustav Holst (1874-1934), English music found roots in its own country for the first time in two hundred years. Consideration of Vaughan Williams's schooling would give little hint of the creative power that was to be released by his discovery of folk song and Tudor polyphony. An active and vigorous collector of folk song, he went to live among the people in the country, and his early orchestral works *In the Fen Country* and the three *Norfolk Rhapsodies* were the result. In these it was apparent that he had found his own musical language, permeated with the melodic idiom and harmonic implications of folk song. His contact with the public was initially, like Elgar, through works written for competitive and choral festivals: *Towards the Unknown Region* and *A Sea Symphony* are both highly characteristic of the composer and traditional in their debt to Purcell and Parry. The song cycle *On Wenlock Edge* was far removed from these in its intimate dimensions, but the choice of poets, Whitman for the choral works and Housman for the songs, and later such writers as Bunyan and George Herbert, reflects the mysticism, contemplative yet closely in touch with common life, that was his most important characteristic. Even the purely instrumental works, particularly some of the nine symphonies and *Job*, 'a masque for dancing', demonstrate the pattern of his thinking: diatonic or modal music represents the forces of good, and unstable chromatic music those of evil. The fourth, fifth, and sixth symphonies, dated 1935, 1943 and 1948 respectively, the earlier *Fantasia on a Theme by Tallis* for strings (1910) and *Job* (1931) contain the essence of his achievement – reconciliation of symphonic structure with quasi-vocal melodic lines and polyphony. The width of his interests can be seen in his output, which ranges from opera (*Hugh the Drover, The Pilgrim's Progress*) and church music (the Mass in G minor) to music for films (*49th Parallel, Scott of the Antarctic*).

Vaughan Williams and Holst were lifelong friends from their student days. Among other things, they had in common their love of folk song, of 16th- and 17th-century English music and of Whitman's poetry, and a keen and active interest in amateur music making. Holst studied at the Royal College of Music and on leaving became a professional trombonist and opera *répétiteur*. In 1903 he began his career as a teacher, his main posts being at St Paul's Girls' School from 1905 and Morley College from 1907. Both positions were held to the end of his life, and he also taught composition at the Royal College from 1919. Twin influences in his early days were Wagner and the rather less orthodox study of Sanskrit, begun about 1906, which resulted in such works as the operas *Sita* and *Savitri* and the four sets of choral hymns from the *Rig Veda* for chorus and orchestra. His most productive period, which began about 1914, includes the works by which he is best known, the orchestral suite *The Planets, The Hymn of Jesus*, slighter works such as the *St Paul's Suite* for strings, and, towards the end of his life, the work he believed to be his best, the short orchestral piece *Egdon Heath*, based on Hardy's novel *The Return of the Native*.

From the turn of the century song writing flourished in England as it had not done since the death of Purcell. The discovery of folk song was a major stimulus, and while Vaughan Williams, Holst and Delius all made significant contributions, a number of other composers, led by Peter Warlock (1894-1930), left their most enduring work in this medium. Warlock's style was formed mainly by his admiration of Delius combined with a study of Tudor secular music, but his songs cover a wide range, from the bleak nostalgia of *The Curlew* to the swagger of *Captain Stratton's Fancy*. Ivor Gurney (1890-1937) and George Butterworth (1885-1916) were both casualties of the First World War and left a handful of works which contain some masterpieces. Roger Quilter (1877-1953), John Ireland (1879-1962), noted also for his concerto and smaller pieces for the piano, Gerald Finzi (1901-56) and Michael Head (b. 1900) all show a similar sensitivity to English poetry matched with considerable lyrical gifts.

Sir Thomas Beecham at the age of eighty.

The next generation

E. J. Moeran (1894-1950), Arnold Bax (1883-1953) and Edmund Rubbra (b. 1901) represent in their different ways the schools that might have developed if nationalism as a conscious fertilising agent had survived the war and had not been displaced by a reaction against Romanticism. Moeran's style, like Warlock's, was influenced by folk song and the Elizabethans, with harmony from Delius modified by the teaching of John Ireland. Bax was a self-confessed 'brazen Romantic' who had 'no interest in any modernist 'isms or factions'. His predilection for Ireland and the Irish (not due to any known Irish ancestry) extended to publishing verse and stories under an Irish pseudonym, and the Celtic revival is the main influence to be discerned in his music. A prolific composer, both in content and quantity, he wrote seven symphonies and a number of symphonic poems, notably *The Garden of Fand* and *Tintagel*, as well as some fine choral music, songs, and chamber works. Rubbra's music on the other hand shows little of the folk song influence but develops impressively the concept of amalgamating polyphonic lines (based on the principles of Tudor polyphony) with symphonic construction. His seven symphonies form the nucleus of his work, austere in their intellectual demands on the listener and in their eschewing of colour for its own sake. Between the wars, comparatively few English composers wholeheartedly adopted the styles and theories of their foreign contemporaries, though the influx of refugee musicians brought a first-hand opportunity to examine recent Central European trends. Egon Wellesz (1885-1974), composer and musicologist, lived in England after he left Austria in 1938, bringing with him (as a pupil of Schoenberg) direct experience of dodecaphonic principles. Roberto Gerhard (1896-1970) studied with Schoenberg but left Spain for England after the defeat of the Republicans. Though cosmopolitan in outlook, he came to regard himself as an English composer, and he enriched the orchestral repertoire, particularly with his concerto for orchestra, written in 1966. Matyas Seiber (1904-60) was born in Hungary but worked mainly in Germany before emigrating to London in 1935. Here his versatility was displayed in teaching (at Morley College and the Guildhall School of Music), conducting, and composing, his most important work being the cantata *Ulysses*, based on the novel by James Joyce.

The most senior of the native English composers, Arthur Bliss (1891-1975), was an able conductor and administrator and was appointed Master of the Queen's Music in 1953. He started his composing career with works of marked originality that owed a certain debt to the French school and Stravinsky, but the leaning towards experiment gave way to a more traditionally inclined Romanticism in later works such as the *Colour Symphony*, the clarinet quintet and the piano concerto. Three choral works, *Pastoral* (dedicated to Elgar), *Morning Heroes* and *The Beatitudes*, composed for the Coventry Festival of 1962, showed imaginative use of the traditional medium, and a later phase produced ballet music and an opera, *The Olympians*, to a libretto by J. B. Priestley.

William Walton (b. 1902) first received recognition for *Façade*, an 'entertainment' for speaking voice and six instrumental players with poems by Edith Sitwell. More characteristic are the subsequent major works, all of which are firmly entrenched in the repertory; some must be considered classics. The viola concerto and the first symphony are masterly successors to the orchestral tradition of Elgar, and the oratorio *Belshazzar's Feast*,

left
Ralph Vaughan Williams at the age of forty-seven; a drawing by William Rothenstein.

below
Sir Arthur Bliss (right) with Vaughan Williams at a concert in the Royal Festival Hall, London, to celebrate the latter's eightieth birthday.

with its primitive savagery, scintillating colours, and emotion ranging from heart-broken lament to ecstatic rejoicing, is the climax of the emancipation of oratorio from Victorian respectability. Walton's list of works, though not large for a composer of such stature, includes distinguished contributions in many spheres, from film music, particularly for the Shakespearean films *Henry V*, *Hamlet* and *Richard III*, to the operas *Troilus and Cressida* and *The Bear*.

Both Lennox Berkeley (b. 1903) and Alan Rawsthorne (b. 1905) stand a little apart from this group of composers as a result of their non-traditional training and connections. Berkeley lived and studied for some years in Paris and his music displays a typically French elegance, wit, and economy. Rawsthorne first trained for a career as a dentist and only later received his musical training in Manchester. They have both written successful piano concertos and chamber music, but whereas almost all Rawsthorne's work is instrumental, Berkeley later in his career produced a number of vocal works, the most striking being the Stabat Mater, the *Four Poems of St Theresa of Avila*, and the operas *Nelson* and *A Dinner Engagement*. Michael Tippett (b. 1905) has become a dominant figure in contemporary English music as a result of his concern, projected through composing, writing, and teaching, with present-day social and artistic problems. His reputation, like that of most of his contemporaries, is based on comparatively few works. The concerto for double string orchestra and the string quartets are examples of polyphonic method combined with symphonic structure that has proved a germinating principle for many modern English composers. The oratorio *A Child of Our Time* was an impassioned protest against oppression and persecution, and further aspects of Tippett's uncompromising integrity and continual struggle to express his 'inner life' through words and music can be found in the operas *The Midsummer Marriage*, *King Priam* (for which he wrote his own libretti) and the cantata *The Vision of St Augustine* for baritone solo, chorus and orchestra.

Britten

Consideration of the musical scene in England since the Second World War must centre on the figure of Benjamin Britten (1913-1976). Born in East Anglia, he studied composition with Frank Bridge and John Ireland, and after a short stay in America (1939-42) he settled in Aldeburgh, Suffolk, where he established the distinctively individual annual festival. From his first published compositions the brilliance of his technique and talent was incontestable, and international fame came with the *Variations on a Theme of Frank Bridge* for string orchestra, which was given its first performance at the Salzburg Festival of 1937 by the Boyd Neel Orchestra. The works written during the difficult and unsettling 1930s have failed on the whole to sustain a place in the repertory, but the period in America produced the *Sinfonia da Requiem*, *A Ceremony of Carols* and *Les Illuminations*, settings of Rimbaud's poems, and saw the conception of *Peter Grimes* (1945).

While Britten's instrumental works, particularly the popular *Young Person's Guide to the Orchestra* and the later cello symphony, have enhanced his reputation, it is in the setting of words that his real genius lies. His achievement in vocal music is immense. *Peter Grimes* put English opera back on the world opera map and was followed by *The Rape of Lucretia*, *Albert Herring*, *Billy Budd*, *Gloriana*, *The Turn of the Screw* and *A Midsummer Night's Dream*. He has written strikingly original works for children to perform and the impressive set of church

above right
Sir William Walton.

right
Sir Michael Tippett.

parables, *Curlew River*, *The Prodigal Son* and *The Burning Fiery Furnace*. His association with individual artists, particularly the tenor Peter Pears, has called forth many works for solo singers in addition to the concerted works, but perhaps the *War Requiem*, written for the consecration of Coventry Cathedral in 1962, may stand as representative of his genius and of the theme that recurs throughout his work: the indictment of human folly as it shows itself both in the tragedy and wastage of war and in the corruption of human innocence. The profundity of his work epitomises the great distance English music had travelled since 1800.

In 1947 Britten founded the English Opera Group for the performance of chamber opeas. Among these were *The Rape of Lucretia* (1946), *Albert Herring* (1947) and *The Turn of the Screw* (1954). Other important compositions for voice are: the *Serenade for tenor, horn and strings* (1943); Canticle No. 3 *Still falls the Rain*, to a poem by Edith Sitwell; and *Nocturne* (1958) for tenor and orchestra. Finally we must mention the works for cello inspired by his work with the Russian cellist Rostropovich, among them the suite for unaccompanied cello of 1965.

Thanks to the prominence of his Marxist convictions, the music of Alan Bush (b. 1900) has been unduly neglected. The early *Dialectic* for string quartet remains his masterpiece in spite of the large achievements of the operas *Wat Tyler* and *Men of Blackmoor*, but he shares with Britten the ability to make original sounds with very simple means.

Perhaps benefiting from the example of Dame Ethel Smyth (1858-1944), militant feminist and composer of some fine operas (*The Wreckers*, *The Boatswain's Mate*), women composers have made very distinguished contributions to English music. Elisabeth Lutyens (b. 1906) was one of the first English composers to use the twelve-note technique; like Elizabeth Maconchy (b. 1907), her most characteristic work is in chamber music. The music of Phyllis Tate (b. 1911) is striking for its imaginative sonorities; the solo cantata *The Lady of Shalott* is scored for voice, solo violin, two pianos and two percussion, and there are also a saxophone concerto and an opera about Jack the Ripper entitled *The Lodger*. Thea Musgrave, born in Edinburgh in 1928, studied with Nadia Boulanger in Paris. Her earlier works were for chamber ensembles, but the *Sinfonia* and the *Scottish Dance Suite* for orchestra have been much performed, while *The Phoenix and the Turtle* was commissioned for a London Promenade concert.

An important pioneer of twelve-note technique, Humphrey Searle (b. 1915) studied with Webern, but his very individual style shows affinities with Liszt and Schoenberg. It has evolved through four symphonies, two piano concertos and the great choral trilogy – *Gold Coast Customs*, *The Riverrun* and *The Shadow of Cain*. Some of his finest music is in his operas, among them *The Diary of a Madman* and *Hamlet* (1969), with a libretto adapted from Shakespeare by the composer.

Two near contemporaries of Searle, Peter Racine Fricker (b. 1920) and Iain Hamilton (b. 1922) share a

Benjamin Britten at the piano accompanying the Russian cellist Mstislav Rostropovich.

right
A scene from Benjamin Britten's opera Albert Herring.

below
Benjamin Britten conducting.

stylistic debt to Bartók. They have both produced a number of large-scale instrumental works, outstanding among Fricker's being the two symphonies and the viola concerto, and among Hamilton's the violin concerto and the *Symphonic Variations*. The incorporation of some of the newest continental techniques into Hamilton's music since 1958 amounted to something of a change of style, but the *Sonata for Chamber Orchestra* and the *Sinfonia for Two Orchestras* display the same expressiveness and vitality as characterised the earlier works.

Some composers have written mainly for vocal or choral forces: Geoffrey Bush (b. 1920), whose later works include two operas, *If the Cap Fits* and *The Equation*; Anthony Milner (b. 1925), ranging from his impressive Opus 1, *Salutatio Angelica*, to the oratorio *The Water and the Fire* (1961); and John Gardner (b. 1917). John Addison (b. 1920) and Malcolm Arnold (b. 1921) have written a number of instrumental works of a light, uncomplicated nature.

The present generation of English composers reveals a considerable galaxy of talent. Alexander Goehr (b. 1932), with affinities to the style of Schoenberg, has achieved much success as an orchestral composer with such works as *Pastorale* for strings, brass and two wood-wind instruments (1965), but the large-scale choral cantata *Sutter's Gold* has many fine passages. Harrison Birtwistle (b. 1934) is among the growing number of contemporary composers to have studied the methods of medieval and Renaissance masters; his works include *Entr'actes and Sappho Fragments* for female voice and instruments and *Visions of Francesco Petrarcha*, a work of a semi-dramatic character for voices and instruments.

One of the most brilliant younger composers is Richard Rodney Bennett (b. 1936), whose opera *The Mines of Sulphur* (1964) rapidly won a European reputation. Among Bennett's contemporaries are Nicholas Maw (b. 1935), whose fine lyrical style is well displayed in his string quartet; Gordon Crosse (b. 1937), with a distinguished one-act opera based on Yeats's *Purgatory* (1966); and Cornelius Cardew (b. 1936), one of the few English practitioners in the style of John Cage.

In the 20th century English music has at long last recovered something of the splendours of the 16th and 17th centuries. The contemporary generation, notably Peter Maxwell Davies, whose work is discussed in the last chapter of this book, promises equal achievement in the future.

DONALD PAINE

Music in Scandinavia

The four countries of northern Europe only evolved a truly national style in music during the 19th century. They were successively influenced by German Romanticism, then by the modern French school, then by Stravinsky and Hindemith, and finally, and quite recently, by Webern and Boulez. When considering Finnish music, we must of course take account of the proximity of Russia. Nordic folk music is simple, grave and very melodic, with marked rhythms and austere, modal harmonies, and the Scandinavian composers have been profoundly influenced by these traits.

Sweden

Johan Helmich Roman (1694-1758) may be called the father of Swedish music. In the 1720s he became director of the royal music and composed the first Swedish instrumental and vocal works comparable with the mainstream of European music. He himself visited England for a time, where he met Handel, who influenced his compositions.

During the 19th century the country was strongly influenced by German Romanticism and Italian opera, and Franz Berwald (1796-1868), stifled by artistic provincialism, was unable to give expression to his own highly original ideas. Intransigent by character, he drew down on himself the enmity of the mediocre musicians around him and therefore sought, but without success, to make a career abroad – in Berlin, Vienna and Paris, where he met Berlioz. Only Liszt appreciated his worth. To gain a livelihood he had to take numerous jobs which considerably restricted his output, and, apart from a few isolated performances, his work was not heard in the concert hall until the 20th century.

Berwald is a marvellously natural artist: lively and fiery, with something of the audacity and éclat of Berlioz combined with the delicacy of Mendelssohn and the solidity, conciseness and humour of Haydn. His four symphonies – *La Sérieuse* in G minor, *La Capricieuse* in D, *La Singulière* in C (1845) and number four in E flat – are his most representative works. *La Singulière* has only three movements, the scherzo being incorporated in the slow movement. The brilliant orchestration and great virtuosity of these symphonies also characterise his six symphonic poems and his three concertos for violin, bassoon and piano. Berwald also composed two operas, *Estrella da Soria*, with a beautiful tragic overture, and *The Queen of Golconda*, as well as some operettas. His abundant chamber music consists of duos, three trios with piano, three string quartets, two quintets and a septet. These works display a uniformly high level of inspiration and are frequently advanced in construction, using cyclic form and a synthesis of four movements in one in the manner of Liszt.

Franz Berwald, the first important Scandinavian composer.

The 20th century

Hilding Rosenberg (b. 1892) is regarded as the first major figure of Swedish 20th-century music, both by the scope of his work and the fecundity of his teaching. He rapidly turned to Schoenberg and Hindemith and happily reconciles audacity with tradition; in some of his later works he turned to serialism. His linear conception of music is derived from his intensive study of Gregorian plainsong. Among his six symphonies, the third, entitled *The Four Ages of Man*, is inspired by Romain Rolland's *Jean Christophe*, while the colossal fourth, *The Apocalypse of St John*, and the fifth, *Hortulanus*, both of which include soloists and choirs, are a synthesis of symphony and oratorio. Between 1945 and 1948 Rosenberg composed a monumental tetralogy based on Thomas Mann's *Joseph and his Brethren*, a composition half way between an opera and an oratorio.

Gosta Nystroem (b. 1890) was a pupil of Vincent d'Indy and his affinities are more Latin than Nordic. His great *Sinfonia breve* and *Sinfonia espressiva* and particularly the *Sinfonia del mare* possess a striking lyrical, sometimes tragic, quality which calls to mind the works of Honegger. He has also composed some fine songs, concertos and incidental theatre music.

The musicians born at the beginning of the century turned towards the Neo-classicism typical of the inter-war period. Dag Wiren (b. 1905), the eldest and a composer of natural talent, studied for three years in Paris and attained an immense popularity with his *Serenade for Strings* (1937), but he should be judged by his more recent and more mature works. Lars Erik Larsson (b. 1908) is a more sensitive composer, whose work has evolved from his early light Neo-classicist style, via a strong national Romanticism, to a more bold dissonant style influenced by Honegger. Erland von Koch (b. 1910) is very drawn to folk idiom. He also studied in Paris and is the composer of a number of songs and small instrumental compositions as well as four symphonies and the *Oxberg variations*.

Norway

Sheltered by its fjords and mountains and with a mysterious and magical tradition of legend, Norway developed an original folk tradition, particularly in the field of dance. Composers only had to delve into the different sorts of *slaater*, the peasant dances executed to the accompaniment of the *hardangerfell* (the Norwegian fiddle with sympathetic strings). Among these dances are: the *haling* in duple time, the *springar* in triple time and the *gangar* in 6/8 time. However, a national tradition of art music did not begin to develop until the beginning of the 19th century, when the violinist Ole Bull (1810-80) became conductor of the first Norwegian orchestra. With the following generation, Romanticism was firmly entrenched, represented particularly by Rikard Nordraak (1842-66) who, in a tragically short career, composed a few outstandingly lovely songs and provided his country with its national anthem. It was Nordraak who introduced Grieg to Norwegian popular or folk music.

right
Gosta Nystroem, the Swedish composer.

below
Edvard Hagerrup Grieg.

Grieg

Edvard Hagerrup Grieg (1843-1907), the best known of all 19th-century Scandinavian composers, enjoyed incredible success at the turn of the century. He was born in Bergen and received his musical education at Leipzig, but the young Grieg broke away from Mendelssohn's influence (and that of Gade, Mendelssohn's Danish successor) when Nordraak introduced him to folk music. From then onwards, encouraged by Liszt, he made a European career for himself as a virtuoso pianist and conductor. Although the lyricism of his works is related to that of Chopin and Schumann he succeeded in creating a musical language whose harmonies, derived from the modalities of the *slaater*, were to influence the young Debussy. Grieg himself was conscious of his limitations. He was a delightful miniaturist, unable to cope with grand symphonic development, but within these limitations he composed a rich treasure of 'intimate' pieces which contain all the atmosphere of Norwegian native music. Thus, his celebrated piano concerto and various chamber works never seem so convincing as his short pieces directly inspired by folk music. Among these are the two *Norwegian Dances* and the ten collections of *Lyric Pieces* for piano, and the four *Symphonic Dances* and *Lyric Suite* for orchestra. His best known composition, the incidental music for *Peer Gynt* by Ibsen (1876), is famous for the two orchestral suites, but he also wrote incidental music for plays by Bjørnson, while his *Holberg Suite*, a pastiche of 17th- and 18th-century dances composed for the bicentenary of the Norwegian dramatist Ludvig Holbert, is a truly delightful work. Nevertheless, some of Grieg's best work is contained in his songs. Grieg was perhaps only a minor master, but his nostalgic *Solveig's song* from *Peer Gynt* and the remarkable *slaater* for piano, his last work, hold a respected place in European music.

Johan Svendsen (1840-1911), Grieg's contemporary and the conductor of the Copenhagen Royal Court Orchestra, although less original than Grieg, was a more powerful composer. Christian Sinding (1856-1941) was prolific. He is the composer of three symphonies, three concertos, two operas, various orchestral pieces, numerous chamber works and the well-loved *Rustle of Spring*.

A modern movement was late in developing in Norway and Bjarne Brustad (b. 1895) was the first to introduce a modern musical language influenced by Bartók and Hindemith. But one of the most important composers at the beginning of the century was Harald Saeverud (b. 1897). He employed a modal and folk idiom and displays a fine sense of polyphony in his three symphonies, his concertos and his chamber music. His powerful imagination expresses itself in music that is frequently harsh, always vigorous and, as in his piano concerto and *Peer Gynt* suite, often subtle. A major figure in the history of 20th-century Norwegian music is Fartein Valen (1887-1952), an independent and isolated figure who, after study in Berlin, spent his life in the western Norwegian fjords. First inspired by Reger, then by Schoenberg, he was the first Norwegian atonal composer. He succeeded in achieving a synthesis between a quasi-serial linear musical language and a romantic and pantheistic view of nature. Valen's music is lucid, spacious and austere and breathes a sense of profound peace. These qualities are seen to perfection in masterpieces such as his symphonic poems, *Le Cimetière marin* (after Valéry) and *La Isla de las Calmas*, his violin concerto and his four string quartets.

Among the leaders of the younger generation of Norwegian composers are Finn Mortensen (b. 1922), Egil Hovland (b. 1924) and Edvard Fliflet Braein (b. 1924).

Denmark

Denmark owes its rich musical tradition to its relatively close geographic position to Germany and, through it, to the mainstream of European music, although Danish folk music is less original than that of the other Nordic countries. From the 16th century the royal court at Copenhagen became an important musical centre.

Two composers dominate the dawn of the 19th century. Christopher Ernst-Friedrich Weyse (1774-1842), whose cantatas and improvisations made such a deep impression on his contemporaries, is today particularly venerated as the 'father of the Danish *Lied*'. Friedrich Kuhlau (1786-1832) is generally remembered for his piano sonatas and works for flute, but in Denmark he is most highly regarded as the author of the national opera, *Elverhøj* (*The Elfin Mountain*). Weyse and Kuhlau were rather Danish composers in the European style than nationalists; Johann Peter Emilius Harmann (1805-1900), however, aspired to a powerful sombre Nordic style inspired by the myths and history of his native country. A folk ballet, *Et Folkesagn*, written in collaboration with Gade, assured the composer of an immense national popularity.

Niels Wilhelm Gade (1817-90), began with a spontaneity of inspiration which soon won him recognition outside Demark. Among the best of his early works was a piano sonata, while the overture *Ossian* (1841), and the first symphony in C minor (1841) attracted the attention of Mendelssohn, whose assistant at Leipzig Gade was for a time. But Gade's music has paled with time, and of his eight symphonies, seven overtures, suites and choral works little is now regularly performed.

It was only with Carl Nielsen (1865-1931), who wrote the greater part of his work in the 19th century, that Denmark gave the world a truly powerful symphonist. His music, unmistakably Danish in character, has breadth, austerity, vigour and enthusiasm, realism and human understanding. Sometimes Nielsen introduces elements of almost titanesque conflict, as in the fourth and fifth symphonies. His opus of more than one hundred works shows a constant evolution and demonstrates that he is always open to new musical trends. He was the first composer to conclude a symphony in a different key

below
A fragment of manuscript autographed by Grieg.

bottom
Niels Gade, Denmark's first Romantic.

two bold and original sections. Both clearly foreshadow Shostakovich's great dramatic symphonies. Nielsen's sixth symphony, *Sinfonia semplice*, is, despite its title, a work of crisis and problems, of the struggle of a composer faced with an accepted new musical language. Nielsen overcame these problems in the very moving *Commotio* for organ, which is his musical testament. He also wrote three concertos (for violin, flute and clarinet), several symphonic poems, four string quartets, two violin sonatas and a delightful string quintet. Outstanding among his piano works are the astonishing suite (Opus 45) and the pieces (Opus 59), which have a Schoenbergian audacity. His two operas, *Saul and David* and *Mascarade*, were instantly accepted as part of the Danish national repertory.

Knudage Riisåger (b. 1897), pupil of Roussel and Paul le Flem, first opened the way in Denmark to modern musical trends. His music is vivacious and rhythmic, anti-conformist and full of humour. His ballets are eminently successful, among them *Pays de Cocagne*, *X cos d* (for 'trigonometric marionettes'), *Etudes*, in the repertory of the Paris Opéra, and particularly *Qartsiluni* (a very original work based on the magic rites of sorcerers in Greenland). Jørgen Bentzon (1897-1951), although a pupil of Nielsen, was more influenced by Hindemith. His first and most interesting manner is experimental and difficult, and consists of chamber music. In his second symphony, written in 1946-47, known under the title of *Energy – Growth – Construction*, he arrives at a synthesis of innovation and tradition.

Finn Høffding (b. 1899) is best known for his *Fantaisies Symphoniques*, which owe their inspiration to many different sources, and are monothematic in structure. Ebbe Hamerik (1898-1951), the composer of five *Symphonies brièves* constructed on a *cantus firmus*, also wrote two operas, *Maria Grubbe* (1940) and the *Travelling Companion* (1946, after a story by Andersen), which placed him at the head of modern Danish lyric composers.

Hermann D. Koppel (b. 1908), an excellent pianist, was first of all greatly taken with jazz, which, together

from that in which he began. This we find in his first symphony, written in 1892, and he continued to develop this fruitful principle of 'progressive tonality'. His second symphony, *The Four Temperaments* (1902), is a forceful example of his interest in psychology. The third, *Sinfonia espansiva* (1911), is a hymn representing the joy of the sun for the earth, the friend of man. The grand fourth, *The Inextinguishable* (1916), is the triumph of art, represented by a hymn, over barbarity, represented by a dialogue between two timpani, and sums up in its title the composer's credo – 'Music is life, and like life is inextinguishable'.

He reached his highest achievement with his titanesque fifth symphony (written in 1920-22), which is in

above right
Carl Nielsen, the major figure in Danish music.

right
A musical soirée at Fredericksborg in the 1830s. Note that the cello, without a tailpin, is on a raised sounding board.

opposite page
Portrait of Sibelius as a young man.

with his admiration for Bartók and Stravinsky, gave his first works a primarily rhythmic quality. But after 1941 a lyric and melodic expression began to take an ever-growing importance, as in his fine *Psalms of David* (1949) for tenor chorus and orchestra, and his second and third piano concertos.

Svend Erik Tarp (b. 1908) follows the same line as Riisåger–that of a light and lively French style not unlike that of his Swedish contemporaries Wiren and Larsson. His recent works, however, give evidence of a profounder understanding. Vagn Holmboe (b. 1909) is Denmark's most important orchestral writer since Nielsen and one of her leading 20th-century composers. He was also influenced by Bartók (to whose memory he dedicated his first string quartet in 1949) as well as Balkan folk music. He has written ten large symphonies, of which the fifth and the seventh have been especially praised, symphonic works like *Epitaph* (1956) and *Monolith* (1960), and twelve chamber concertos for various instruments.

Finland

Finnish folk music is as rich as it is original. The Finns are Finno-Ugrians and not Germanic by origin like the other Nordic peoples, and these Asiatic origins are revealed in their ancient chants, with their asymmetric periodic structure, and in their often pentatonic songs. The foreign influence was represented chiefly by the Lutheran chorale, introduced into Finland in the 16th century, and by the music of 19th-century Russia, which governed Finland from 1814 to 1917, when she received her independence.

The beginnings of Finnish national artistic awareness may be dated from 1835, when the poet Elias Lonnrot produced the first published version of the *Kalevala*, the great national epic poem, which until this time had, like the Homeric epics in their first form, been handed down by oral tradition. A short while after, Lonnrot published *Kanteletar*, a collection of lyric poems which derived its title from the *kantele*, the plucked instrument with which the bards accompanied their songs. Nevertheless, it was at first a German, Frederick Pacius (1809-91), who dominated musical life, although far from imposing any sort of German musical hegemony; he composed patriotic anthems and the first national Finnish opera, *King Charles's Hunt*, in 1852.

In the second half of the 19th century we find native Finnish composers appearing on the scene. Axel Gabriel Ingelius' overture *Kullervo* (1860) was the first work to be inspired by the *Kalevala*. Martin Wegelius (1846-1906), the founder of the first Finnish musical conservatory, was an eminent teacher and the master of the young Sibelius. Robert Kajanus (1856-1933), an eminent conductor and composer, also found inspiration in the *Kalevala* for his choral symphony *Aino*, his symphonic poem *The Death of Kullervo* and his Finnish rhapsodies.

Sibelius

In view of this attenuated national musical tradition, the case of Jean Sibelius (1865-1957) may be regarded as truly extraordinary. When he was only thirty-two he was granted a state pension to devote himself to composition, and in the Scandinavian countries, Britain and the United States he is generally acclaimed as a major symphonist. In Germany, on the other hand, he tends to be treated with a certain reserve, while in France he is

459

dismissed altogether. But the symphonies and a handful of other works from the 113 which make up his entire *oeuvre* justify his high reputation, though it is interesting to note that after 1929 he wrote nothing.

From the outset Sibelius was an artist in full possession of his own language and style. The only definite influences on him were firstly Borodin, then Grieg and finally Tchaikovsky, though the latter's influence was much less strong than has been claimed. After this first manner, which was palpably Romantic and lasted until about 1905, Sibelius returned to his estate at Jarvenpaa, some thirty kilometres from Helsinki, where he settled down to the serious business of composition and rid himself of the last elements of outside influences. It is only in his harmony, which became increasingly subtle, that we may detect the influence of Debussy. Passages from the sixth symphony or from *Tapiola* truly suggest a northern Debussy in their clarity and perfect conciseness. It is a pure art of classic sobriety, which, despite its intense poetic magic, is in the final analysis much more Latin in feeling than German.

The majestic series of his seven symphonies are his crowning achievement. The first two, the E minor (1899) and the D major (1902), are frankly Romantic, heroic and nationalist. After the second, Sibelius employed a technique of thematic growth which constitutes a complete reversal of the traditional form by developing, little by little, great melodic themes from 'cells' which in themselves seem to be completely unrelated. Sibelius's sober and limpid third symphony in C major, *The Northern Pastoral* (1907), marks the first step towards a greater conciseness of form, consisting as it does of only three movements (the scherzo and finale being fused into one), and demanding only light orchestration. The fourth symphony in A minor is a tense and emotional work rich in polytonal passages and has been described as the quintessence of northern music. In contrast to its asceticism there is the fifth in E flat (1919), with its triumphal peroration. The first movement is in the form of a sonata-cum-scherzo. The sixth symphony in D minor (1923), the most intimate of all, is a fascinating study in half-tones of light, exalting the beauties of northern summers. With the seventh in C major (1924), the composer achieves great concision by successfully creating one single great movement, lasting twenty minutes, which encompasses all the usual movements of a symphony.

The symphonic poems are more freely evocative than descriptive, in the manner of Liszt or Richard Strauss. The cycle of four legends for orchestra (1893-96) was inspired by the exploits of Liminkainen, the hero of the *Kalevala* and the Achilles of Finnish mythology; although early works, they still retain their spell. The second, *The Swan of Tuonela*, composed in 1893, is an example of Nordic Impressionism, while the *Karelia Suite* written in the same year evokes the Finnish province of that name. After the popular *Finlandia* (1899), which expressed the desire of the Finnish people for independence of tsarist Russia, Sibelius turned again to the *Kalevala* for *Pohjola's Daughter* (1906). The series of symphonic poems ends with *Tapiola* (1926), a poem of the Finnish forests.

Sibelius' instrumental music also includes the famous D minor violin concerto (1905) and the outstanding string quartet, the so-called *Voces intimae* (1909), which, foreshadowing his fourth symphony, is in direct descent from the last Beethoven quartets. He also wrote for the theatre, though the works vary very much in quality; they comprise the famous *Valse triste* (1903); music for Maeterlinck's play *Pelléas and Mélisande* and for Shakespeare's *The Tempest* (1925), with its most impressive prelude.

After Sibelius

Among Sibelius' contemporaries and followers Oskar Merikanto (1868-1924) composed the first opera in the Finnish language, *Daughter of the North*, based on the *Kalevala*. Selim Palmgren (1878-1951), known as the 'Chopin of the North', a brilliant pianist, wrote a number of piano works, in particular five concertos in a very delicate harmonic style which might be described as Impressionist, together with an impressive opera, *Daniel Hjort*.

The next generation includes Toivo Kuula (1883-1918) a vehement and passionate composer, influenced by the Impressionist school, who wrote a number of dramatic cantatas and songs and two orchestral suites; Leevi Madetoja (1887-1947), the most outstanding of Sibelius' followers, who was a native of the extreme north of Finland. He conjures up the desolate landscape in his three symphonies, in his sombre symphonic poem *Kullervo*, and in particular in his two operas *Pohjalaisai* and *Juha*. The former of these is regarded as the Finnish national opera par excellence.

The first of a series of modern composers was Vaino Raitio (1891-1945), who developed from a youthful Romanticism to post-Impressionism and displays the most extraordinary gifts as an orchestrator. Undoubtedly his masterpiece is his symphonic poem *The Swans*. Towards the end of his life he wrote five remarkable operas. Yrjö Kilpinen (1892-1959), probably Finland's finest composer after Sibelius, became world-renowned as a master of *Lieder*; he wrote some six hundred with Finnish, Swedish and German texts, and may be compared with Hugo Wolf both in the nature and in the quality of his work. Unno Klami (1900-61) took lessons in Paris, where he wrote his first piano concerto, entitled *Nuit à Montmartre*. In his Finnish-inspired works, *Karelian Rhapsody* (1928) and the great symphonic suite *Kalevalan*, he approaches folk music in a positive manner.

Peasant musician playing the kantele *zither, the ancient bardic instrument of Finland.*

Central European music

In this chapter we shall be concerned with the important composers and musical developments which are to be observed in the Slav states of Central Europe, Poland and Czechoslovakia, since the conclusion of the First World War, when both countries finally received full statehood. In the case of Poland we have already dealt with certain figures, such as the pianist and composer Paderewski, who, although they lived well into the 20th century, may more naturally be regarded as the musical heirs of the late Romantic movement. In Czechoslovakia the career of Leoš Janáček, who was born in 1854, seemed destined to take a similar course and indeed, even in his latest works, the memory of his earlier Romantic period is still to be found. But, in the 1900s, he evolved what amounted to a new style, deriving much of its inspiration from the folk music and speech rhythms of his native Bohemia, and also clearly associated with the developments in contemporary Europe.

These facts of musical development prompt certain generalisations about the pattern of the evolution of the national schools of Central and Northern Europe. In almost every case we find that the first important composer in a new national school achieves recognition as a master of the current international style, or that of the generation immediately prior to his own. Often his music has a characteristic quality derived from the incorporation of certain, usually not fully understood, elements of his national folk music. The next generation of nationalist composers have tended to research their national folk heritage in a far more rigorous manner, and have set out to embody their new and deeper understanding of this heritage in their music. The final stage may, in this very broad general analysis, be said to have been reached when the composers of the third generation, heirs of a fully established tradition of musical excellence and totally familiar with their own particular national idiom, react against this necessarily parochial environment and seek full identity with the most advanced work going on in the international field.

If this general pattern is a fair representation of the facts, then we see that, like Janáček in Bohemia, the great Polish composer Szymanowski may be regarded as the great master in the second stage of the Polish renaissance in music and the pioneer towards the third.

Poland

By and large, Polish composers of the generation before the First World War are representative in different ways of the schools of Romanticism and neo-Romanticism. The influences of Wagner, the Impressionist composers and, above all, Richard Strauss are there, but the national accent is particularly marked in all their works. During the first years of the 20th century, the youthful Bartók

and the revolutionary Stravinsky were already making a name for themselves, composers like Scriabin, Debussy and Ravel were writing in their own definitive way, and Schoenberg had already broken away from tonal principles, but Poland still remained strictly conservative. At the beginning of the century a number of talented young musicians founded a group under the name of 'Young Poland', in revolt against this reactionary atmosphere. This group, which was however comparatively short-lived, comprised Mieczylaw Karłowicz, Grzegorz Fitelberg, Ludomir Różycki and Apollinary Szeluto; their first compositions before the First World War reveal their innovatory tendencies, though they remained primarily interested in symphonic compositions.

Mieczylaw Karłowicz (1876-1909) was the most eminent of this group. His seven symphonic tone poems, which include *Episode at the Masquerade* and *Lithuanian Rhapsody*, are filled with literary and philosophic ideas. He also wrote a symphony, the *Renaissance*, an excellent violin concerto in A major, and songs; all his compositions are in a very personal style, though the combined influences of Strauss and Tchaikovsky are apparent. The works of Karłowicz are some of the most remarkable of all Polish orchestral composers, filled with a dreamy melancholy and imbued with a Slav lyricism.

Grzegorz Fitelberg (1879-1953) began his career as a composer during this same period with the symphonic poems *The Song of the Falcon* and *The Sea*, but soon abandoned composition to become a conductor. This

Leoš Janáček.

gave him the opportunity of propagating the new works of young composers, particularly those of Karol Szymanowski, the most noteworthy of them all. Ludomir Różycki (1883-1953) was particularly intrigued by German neo-Romanticism. Both his symphonic poems and his operas contain Polish motifs influenced by the orchestration of Richard Strauss. All his works are based on Polish dramas, either historical, legendary or literary. Rozycki retained the same musical idiom throughout the period between the two World Wars, and even during the years of the Second World War and beyond. His works include the *Warsaw Pietà* (1942), a tone poem, a piano concerto and chamber music.

Szymanowski

But it is the figure of Karol Szymanowski (1882-1937) that dominates the 'Young Poland' group. The preludes of his Opus 1, written in his late teens, revealed a creative talent which exceeded anything seen in Poland since Chopin; his evolution was to pass through several stages. To begin with, Szymanowski's style showed marked affinities with that of Scriabin; later with that of Strauss and Reger. Then we find a definite influence of Impressionism, which he introduces in a quite unique way in his violin compositions, such as the first violin concerto and *Myths* for violin and piano. Then, for a period, Szymanowski came under the influence of Expressionism, as in the third symphony and the piano compositions, *Masques*. But these were only passing experiments which led to the crystallisation of a definite personal style. After the First World War, he may be said to have joined the new 20th-century current, represented by Bartók and Stravinsky; the inspiration of this new style in his development was derived from folk music.

After the First World War the Polish state was reborn out of a hundred years of occupation and division, and the culture of the three provinces had to be united. This need affected the reforms introduced into musical teaching in the communal schools and into the organisation of the two state conservatories. The number of orchestras and opera houses increased, amateur choral societies developed, musicians began to tour the country, and the treasury provided bursaries for composers in order to help them study abroad.

Szymanowski was at the very centre of the musical life of this period. The renaissance of Polish music and its future depended on him, but he found himself alone, confronted by a group of reactionaries. Karłowicz had died and Fitelberg, except for a short period when he was director of the Warsaw Radio symphony orchestra, was conducting concerts all over the world. During the war years Szymanowski was under the influence of Impressionism and, in certain works, of Expressionism – even atonality. But in the 1920s he returned to the traditions of folk music and researched into the authentic examples of the idiom, not yet the victim of clumsy adaptations, notably the music of the mountaineers of Podhale. This period is represented by works like the Stabat Mater (1929), the mountaineers' ballet *Harnasie* (1926), mazurkas for piano and a *Sinfonia Concertante* (1932) for piano and orchestra.

Szymanowski came up against much opposition in his attempts to reorganise the Warsaw Academy during the course of his two rectorships. However, for the younger generation of composers brought up in the twenties and thirties, he was both master and leader into a closer involvement with the most modern musical movements in Europe.

Yet, although he was their inspiration, this young generation followed quite a different path from that of

below
Karol Szymanowski.

bottom
Witold Lutosławski.

Szymanowski and, as a result of studies made in Paris, Berlin and Vienna, came under the influence of Stravinsky, thus becoming orientated towards Neo-classicism and also serial technique. They introduced the most recent innovations into Poland, although some of them remained abroad; Aleksander Tansman (b. 1897) settled in Paris and became a naturalised Frenchman, while Karol Rathaus (1895-1954), after some years in Berlin, moved to London and then the United States. The Polish public, which was, in any case, unable to understand Szymanowski, was antagonistic to the music of these young composers, and the gap between audiences and composers became even wider.

But, besides the work of the men in the vanguard, others combined traditional elements of Polish music with the lessons of Szymanowski – with some very varied results. Stanislaw Wiechowicz (b. 1893) has concentrated on choral music but has also written a symphonic scherzo; Piotr Perkowski (b. 1902) attempted a synthesis between Neo-classicism and Szymanowski; and others wrote in the Neo-classical idiom, using intensely rhythmic beats, clear orchestration and a return to Baroque forms. Michal Kondracki (b. 1902) has made intensive use of folk music, while Boleslaw Szabelski (b. 1896), the organist, has allowed himelf to be beguiled by the neo-Baroque style of Hindemith. The compositions of Kazimierz Sikorski (b. 1895), a teacher of the first order and author of several works on harmony, counterpoint and instrumentation, are eclectic in character.

Other important composers between the wars were: Jozef Koffler (1896-1943) the first Polish twelve-note composer; Jan Adam Maklakiewicz (1899-1954), whose early post-Impressionist works, including a symphony and *Japanese Songs* for voice and orchestra, were followed by a return to folk music and later neo-Romanticism; Artur Malawski (1904-57), whose Neo-classicism was also touched by the folk idiom; and the talented Roman Palester (b. 1907), for a time associated in Paris with the Six, then influenced by Stravinsky and since 1947 working abroad.

Post-war Poland

Immediately after 1945 the Polish state was in ruins, and cultural life had come to a standstill. In the years that followed, Poland was brought into the orbit of the Soviet bloc and her cultural life seemed likely to be dominated by the theories of socialist realism in the arts which, however strong its social and political justifications may be, is explicitly opposed to that ceaseless experimentation with new forms thought in the West to be the prerequisite of the creative mind. However, the vigour of Polish art, above all in the film and in music, was never effectively sapped, and after the political revolution of 1956 experimentation and advance continued, so that Polish composers have gained world-wide recognition.

Among the composers of the older generation one of the best-known outside Poland is Witold Lutosławski, who was born in Warsaw in 1913. After study at the Warsaw Conservatory he devoted himself to full-time composition, displaying in his earlier works the influence of Stravinsky and of Bartók. The element of folk music was important in many of his post-war works, such as the first symphony (1947), his *Overture for Strings* (1949) and his *Concerto for Orchestra* (1954), in which the folk idiom was deployed in an entirely modern context. In other works, such as the *Muzyka zalobna*, funeral music in homage to Bartók, Lutosławski made use of atonalism in a very personal manner and later works have shown a strong interest in and brilliant talent for instrumental colour. With Lutosławski, one of the finest Polish

left
The Tyl Theatre in Prague.

below
Krzysztof Penderecki.

musicians of his generation is Andrzej Panufnik (b. 1914), probably best-known as a conductor successively of the Cracow and Warsaw philharmonic orchestras and then, in England, of the Birmingham municipal orchestra; he has also composed some fine music.

Among the more important members of the next generation are Tadeusz Baird (b. 1928), whose works include a *Sinfonietta*, two symphonies, a concerto for orchestra, and then a number of serial compositions including *Four Essays for Orchestra* and *Variations on a theme for orchestra* (1962); and Kazimierz Serocki (b. 1922) whose teachers include Nadia Boulanger. Certain of his works show an inclination to folk music, but later compositions, which include a *Sinfonietta* and a trombone concerto, show an advance on their earlier style.

Of the younger generation of Polish composers the best-known abroad is undoubtedly Krzysztof Penderecki, who was born in 1933. He studied with Malawski but his style was also much influenced by Debussy and Szymanowski, and he has since developed an expressive and individual serial technique. His versatility is shown by the mastery he displays in handling the full range of ensembles from full orchestra to *a cappella* choir, while his music also reveals his fascination and concern with the growing complexity and vast range of stimuli in the modern world. Among his works are *Dimensions in Time and Silence*, *Threnody for the victims of Hiroshima* for fifty-two strings (1960) and a *Stabat Mater* for three *a cappella* choirs (1962). His idiom and his interests are essentially those of the international school, while his religious faith as a Catholic is of great importance to his work – one of Penderecki's works best known abroad is his *St Luke Passion*.

Czechoslovakia

Leoš Janáček, who at the age of fifty produced in the opera *Jenůfa* (1904) one of the great works of the 20th century, thereafter developed still further in this new direction. Well before the end of the 19th century, as part of the growing movement of scientific research into Europe's folk heritage, he had begun collecting Moravian folk music. It was this that increasingly came to form the basis of his music. He studied at first hand the rhythms of language, laughter and tears and even bird songs. It was these elements that conditioned a succinct staccato thematic style of extraordinary expressive vigour, combined with a rhythmic and periodic structure, which is as free as his harmonies. At the same time as Debussy, but independent of him, Janáček emancipated dissonance and integrated the whole tone scale, modes and even polytonality into a new musical language. With such an idiom, classical forms were no longer applicable; fascinated by conciseness, Janáček ignored sonata form and thematic development and, instead, juxtaposed short 'cells' and employed melodic and rhythmic repeated figures of extraordinary power, in which one seems to hear echoes of the human voice, although they are purely instrumental. His highly coloured, incisive orchestration, often using extreme registers, and disregarding repeats and 'padding', fully expresses a vigorous mind.

His most important works were vocal and choral,

including operas which are so intimately related to the Czech language that any translation is bound to lose a truly essential aspect of the music.

Janáček is first and foremost a dramatist. His conciseness, sharpness and burning lyricism are marvellously suited to the stage; his choice of subjects reveals a humanist, full of pity for human suffering. The character of the man is fully revealed in the peasant tragedy *Jenůfa*, which has remained his most popular work. Yet the same is true in an even greater degree in *Katya Kabanova* (1921), the moving story of a Russian Madame Bovary of the last century while his last opera, *The House of the Dead* (1930), inspired by Dostoyevsky's description of exile in Siberia, is the work of a visionary and humanist. The almost unbearable violence is only lightened by the faith of the composer, who claimed that 'in every human being there is a divine spark'. But Janáček can also be a violent satirist and writer of comedy; we only have to take *The Journeys of M. Broucek on the moon in the 15th century* (1917), which has an almost surrealist flavour; or the disquieting philosophy of *The Makropoulos affair* (1926), which treats the problem of immortality and the elixir of eternal life. Finally, we have a delightful ray of sunshine with *The Cunning little Vixen* (1923), a fable full of smiling wisdom and a dedicated and deeply moving poem to life and nature.

Janáček's choral music is dominated by the *Glagolithic Mass* (1926), based on the old Slavonic rite; it is exultant and filled with an almost barbaric joy, an act of common faith. But he also wrote dramatic male choruses based on the revolutionary poems of Bezruc, which are the finest choral works in the Czech repertory, and the

part-song cycle *Diary of a Man who disappeared* (1918).

Of his orchestral works, apart from the ever popular *Lasské dances*, there are two major works: the rhapsody *Taras Bulba* (1918), and the brilliant *Sinfonietta* (1926) with twelve trumpets. Of his chamber music, the most important works are the two string quartets of 1923 and 1928, the second of which is entitled *Private letters*. Written in old age, it is nevertheless a hymn to a youthful unfulfilled love and burns with true ardour. The most important of his piano works are the revolutionary-inspired dramatic sonata, *J.X. 1905*, and two lyric cycles that have an almost Fauréan delicacy.

Martinů

Bohuslav Martinů (1890-1959), born in eastern Moravia, ranks as one of the most talented composers of the 20th century. His more than 400 works are not widely known, and indeed still remain to be fully discovered. Martinů, however, is well known in France, where he lived between 1923 and 1940, and where he was regarded as leader of the school of Paris.

At an early date he was attracted by French music and art, and felt stifled by the German-Romantic atmosphere at the Prague Conservatory. He turned instead to Debussy, and later to Dukas and Roussel, who afforded him an effective counterbalance to the influence of Strauss and Mahler; while in folk music he found an antidote to an excess of somewhat 'decadent' refine-

Scene from a production of Janáček's opera Jenůfa *at the Royal Opera House, Covent Garden, in 1957. Sylvia Fisher as the Kostelnická (centre), and Amy Shuard as Jenůfa (right).*

ment. However, he never studied folklore as scientifically as Janáček. In Paris he took lessons with Albert Roussel, and the influence of Stravinsky and the Six contributed a rhythmic force to his music and a feeling for construction, polytonality and vigorous counterpoint. Yet after about 1930 this exile wrote music which was more and more imbued with national elements, and his dominating rhythms gave way gradually to a warm lyricism. From 1941 to 1953, forced to leave France by the German invasion, Martinů lived in the United States. This was his great period of abstract music and is dominated by his six symphonies. After 1953 he divided his last years between Nice, Rome and Basel, where he died.

Martinů himself has defined the sources of his musical language as Czech, and more specifically Moravian folk music, Debussy and French music, the Elizabethan madrigal – the origin of his polyphony and asymmetry and his freer rhythms – and the Italian concerto grosso. This last helps to explain the great originality of his instrumental style and form, for Martinů was unattracted by the dualism of the classical sonata form and thematic development. He preferred the example of the Baroque masters, using very simple thematic 'cells', which, carried along on a rhythmic current, developed into full-blown melodies. The method has obvious affinities with the 'thematic growth' technique of Sibelius. Similarly, in his orchestration, in which the piano plays a major role, Martinů tends, in the manner of the concerto grosso, to oppose small groups of soloists with a mass of instruments: in his own phrase – 'chamber music on a symphonic scale'.

His harmony, always tonal, is nevertheless of extreme richness and originality, pushing harmonic procedures to their limit. His rhythm is distinguished by its subtlety and its free syncopation, which gives it an airy grace. Finally, although at times capable of the greatest tragic vehemence – as in the third and sixth symphonies, the double concerto and the fifth quartet – Martinů is primarily an interpreter of joy who can be both serene and light-hearted.

Of his innumerable works, let us select for preference the six symphonies (1942-53) and the preceding three orchestral works, *Concerto grosso*, *Tre Ricercari*, and *Double Concerto* for two string orchestras, piano and timpani. These instrumental masterpieces were followed by the brilliant colours of *Les Fresques de Piero Della Francesca* (1955) and *Paraboles* (1958). Of his thirty concertos, mention must be made of *Incantation* (1956) for piano and orchestra, and the astonishing concerto for two pianos (1943). Martinů is also a master of chamber music and has written some seventy works from duets to nonets, among which are the second piano quintet, the three *Madrigals for violin and viola* and, above all, the fifth (1938) of his seven string quartets. His abundant piano works are dominated by his *Fantasia and toccata* (1940) and his unique *Sonata* (1954).

Martinů is the author of fifteen operas and twelve ballets. His most important lyric works are *Juliette, ou la Clef des Songes* (1937), a surrealist dream, and *Passion grecque* (1959), based on Nikos Kazantzakis' *Christ crucified*. But other works of interest are *Les Jeux de Marie*, an adaptation of medieval miracle plays, and *Les Tréteaux*, a combination of the *commedia dell'arte* and

Scene from a production of Janáček's The Cunning little Vixen *in Prague.*

right
Alois Hába (left).

below
A caricature drawn by Bohuslav Martinů.

Czech folklore. His most important ballet is the folk epic *Spalicek* (1931). The cantata, *Boutique de fleurs*, is conceived in the same spirit, while his numerous choral works (rich in fine unaccompanied madrigals) culminate with the moving oratorio *Gilgamesh* (1955).

A third Czech composer of considerable interest is Alois Hába (b. 1893), who has been one of the most convinced exponents of microtone music, expounding and practising the techniques of composing in semitones, quarter tones and sixth tones. After studies at Prague and Berlin, Hába was professor of composition at the Prague conservatory from 1923 to 1953 and, in 1945, undertook the direction of the newly founded Smetana opera in Prague. Since the war his style has tended to return to more orthodox methods, and he has made use of folk music in such compositions as the *Wallachian suite* for orchestra of 1952. It is an interesting fact that one of the first stimuli that prompted him towards the study of micro-intervals seems to have been his encounter with the modified scales used by the folk singers of his native country, and he subsequently tried to lend further force to his theory by analogies with the scales presumed to have been used in ancient Greek music. The problems presented by the performance of his music led him to devise new types of instrument – piano, clarinet and trumpet for example. His most ambitious project in the idiom is the quarter-tone opera *The Mother* (1930). His brother Karel Hába (b. 1898), also a composer, is influenced by his brother's theories; he was appointed as a teacher in the theory of musical education at the Prague institute of education in 1951.

Spanish music in the 19th and 20th centuries

The first important composers of the modern Spanish school naturally belong to Romanticism and use a musical language borrowed from the classic post-Beethoven manner; but while they employed the classical four-movement symphony and quartet, their melodies and modulations were much bolder than those of their models. Essentially their starting point was a style like Schubert's, but with a more strongly Italian than Viennese flavour. To this they added an element of 'Spanish' colour, to produce a style which, in the hands of composers such as Arriaga, García, Sor and Aguado, captivated the fashionable if hardly profound musical world of Paris. Juan Crisostimo Arriaga, born in Bilbao in 1806, studied at the Paris Conservatoire under Cherubini and Fétis and died before he was twenty in 1826, when he was assistant tutor in the class of his late master. His opera *Los Esclavos felices* has recently been republished and his three quartets are still played today. A symphony, a cantata and various religious works complete the oeuvre of a talented composer with undeniable gifts of freshness and grace.

The brief though precocious career of Arriaga was overlapped by that of Manuel García, born in Seville in 1775 and dying in Paris in 1832. He started his career in Cadiz in 1798, then proceeded to Madrid with his wife, who, like him, was a singer, thence went to the Opéra in Paris, where he had a brilliant success, and later toured Europe and America with a company recruited from members of his family. For, apart from being a composer of operas, *zarzuelas* and *tonadillas*, Manuel was chiefly famous as a singer and as the teacher of his three children, all of whom were outstanding musicians. Manuel García (1805-1906), who invented the laryngoscope, was also a fine singing teacher, numbering Jenny Lind among his pupils and being professor of singing at the Royal Academy of Music in London from 1848 to 1895; Maria Felicitá was the famous singer (1808-36) who was better known by her married name of Malibran; and Michelle Ferdinand Pauline Vardot (1821-1910) was a fine pianist and singer. The tradition of this talented musical family was continued by the next generation.

The guitar

The guitar, the Spanish instrument par excellence, had an immense vogue at the beginning of the last century and even usurped the place of the harp in the salon. Two great executants and composers, Sors and Aguado, were responsible for restoring the technique and literature of the instrument. The Catalan, Fernando Sors, or Sor (1778-1839), who spent much of his career in Paris, wrote operas and ballets but is best known for his *Guitar Method* (published in French, English and German) and for his compositions for guitar. Dionisio Aguado y

García (1784-1849) was obliged to leave Spain on the fall of the Bonapartist regime and lived in Paris from 1825 to the late 1830s. Apart from his compositions and studies, he published his *Método de guitarra* (Madrid, 1825); finally completed in 1849, it remains a classic. In the second half of the century Francisco Tarrega (1852-1909) was the recognised master. He was the author of many transcriptions for the guitar, which still remain in the concert repertoire. His main disciples were another Catalan, Miguel Llobet (1875-1938), a distinguished composer, and Emilio Pujol (b. 1886), also known as the editor and writer of transcriptions of the works of vihuelists. Among contemporary 20th-century guitarists Regino Sainz de la Maza and Narciso Yepes are in the first rank, but the undisputed king of the instrument is of course Andres Segovia.

Born in 1893, Segovia, by his technical brilliance and deep musicianship, has ensured the guitar's status as a major concert solo instrument. It is largely his example that has inspired such outstanding musicians as Julian Bream in England and John Williams in Australia to continue the tradition. Moreover, Segovia has added to the repertoire of the guitar not only by his own transcriptions and compositions but also by inspiring leading contemporary composers to write for the instrument. These include not only Spaniards such as Turina but also the Frenchmen Ibert and Roussel, the Polish composer Tansman and Latin-Americans such as Villa-Lobos.

Other Spanish virtuosi, such as the violinists Jesus

Title page of a collection of string quartets by Boccherini, the Italian who was the most important composer working in Spain at the end of the 18th century.

Monasterio (1836-1903) and Pablo de Sarrasate (1844-1908) also had international success, but probably the most remarkable of all was Pablo Casals, in his prime the world's greatest cellist. Born at Vendrell in Catalonia in 1876, Casals was proud of his Catalan homeland and adopted Pau, the Catalan as opposed to the Castilian version of his christian name. During an intensely active career he became renowned not only as a virtuoso but also as a conductor, founding the Pau Casals Orchestra in 1919 and, from 1950, the year of the Bach bicentary, holding an annual festival in his home at Prades in the French Pyrenees. Like many of Spain's most talented artists Casals chose to live in exile after the Fascist victory in the civil war. He died in 1973.

Music for the stage

Andres Segovia, whose virtuosity and musicianship led to the revival of the Spanish guitar as a concert instrument.

Opera and *zarzuela*, the Spanish type of *Singspiel* or ballad opera, have been the testing grounds and battlefields for Spanish music. In opera, Spanish composers inevitably succumbed to foreign influences – Rossini and

the Italians in the first half of the 19th century, and French composers in the second half, but more particularly Wagner. The latter even affected Spanish composers, such as Felipe Pedrell, who were addicted to 'National Opera'. It is therefore perhaps not surprising that the *zarzuela* was the chosen field for a renewal of Spanish music. Although more 'popular' than the opera and artistically less ambitious, precisely because of the audience to which it was addressed, the *zarzuela* was obliged to speak in a 'national' language in every sense of the word. It was a native Spanish form using folk tales and Spanish literature for its plots and drawing heavily on folk music, while opera remained based on dramatic themes and the Italian musical idiom.

Nevertheless Spain produced some competent operatic composers in the Italian manner. Ramón Carnicer (1789-1855) was conductor of the orchestra of the Barcelona opera house, then of the Madrid Opera, and professor of the Madrid Conservatory from 1830, when it was founded, until 1854. Like all the composers of that period, he composed symphonies and religious music, in addition to a number of Spanish songs, but his reputation rests on his seven Italian operas. His pupil, Baltasar Saldoni (1807-89) who was also professor at the Madrid Conservatory, composed several operas, but is best known as the author of a four-volume dictionary of Spanish music, a work which despite its faults showed a definite advance on the *History* by the composer Mariano Soriano Fuertes (1817-80). As has been observed, all the best Spanish musicians of the 19th century were historians as well as composers, seeking to recover the treasures of their country's rich musical tradition and to associate themselves with that tradition. Hilarión Eslava (1807-78), musical director of the cathedral of Seville and then of the Chapel Royal, was a composer of operas in the style of Meyerbeer, but also professor of composition at the conservatory. Brought up on a study of the great ecclesiastical music of Spain, Eslava wrote some good church music himself, but he is more important for having published a ten-volume anthology of Spanish church music from the 16th century up to his own time (1869).

Among the most prolific and successful composers of *zarzuelas* was Asenjo Barbieri (1822-94), an accomplished musician and musical historian who composed principally for the lyric theatre. He wrote more than 70 *zarzuelas*, with Spanish texts – of these, *Pan y toros* (1864) is probably his best work and had the distinction of being banned for political reasons. As a historian, one of his greatest claims to fame was his edition of the *Cancionaro de Palacio*, published in 1890, which revealed that there was a rich Spanish school of secular polyphonic music in the 15th and 16th centuries. Today, his magnificent library, together with many of his own annotations, is housed in the Biblioteca Nacional of Madrid. Probably the most popular of all the composers of the *zarzuela* was Ruperto Chapi y Lorente (1851-1909). After beginning his career as an opera composer he went on to write over 150 *zarzuelas*, also producing some fine instrumental music.

But the greatest figure in 19th-century Spain was Felipe Pedrell. Born in Tortosa in 1841 and dying in Barcelona in 1922, he was a composer of some stature, producing music very unlike that of the delightful, light-hearted *zarzuelas*. His chief importance, however, was as a musicologist of unparalleled energy. He edited and published a large quantity of old Spanish music, including the complete works of Victoria, two anthologies of sacred music, two of organ music, a collection of Spanish popular songs (the last two volumes of which are devoted to ancient art music), two musical dictionaries – one technical, the other (which he was unable to complete) biographical and bibliographical. He also published the extensive catalogue of works in the library of the Diputación de Barcelona, as well as writing a vast number of articles and essays.

In addition to all this, Pedrell also found time to compose six national operas – of which *El Pirineus* and *La Celestina*, based on the 16th-century tragedy by Tirso da Molina, are the most often cited – as well as tone poems, vocal music and a quartet. Despite his altogether unique position in Spanish music, Pedrell, as a composer, is today almost entirely neglected, even in Spain itself. Apart from a few arrangements and adaptations, the only music by Pedrell that is at all known is to be found in the rarely played *Hommage* that de Falla composed in his honour.

Regional schools

Complementary to researches into national Spanish music was the revival of regional schools, the most important of which was the Catalan school. The initiator of the Catalan choral movement which is so active today was the poet and composer José Anselmo Clavé (1824-74) who wrote a number of vocal works for the institute which he founded and directed. Enrique Morera (1865-1942) founded the *Catalunya Nova* choral society, but it must not be imagined that the musical movement in Catalonia was limited to choral activities. It also produced pianist/composers of the first rank such as Albéniz and Granados, distinguished guitarists like Llobet and Tarrago, and, of course, the cellists Casals and Cassado. Leading composers were also interested in spreading the teaching and musical practice and, as a result, in Catalonia good music is not confined to a minority, as it is in other regions of Spain. This fact was to prove exceptionally favourable for the production of Catalan composers and a homogeneous song literature with words of real poetic value.

After Catalonia, and to some extent within its zone of influence, comes the school of Valencia, which can boast musicologists of the calibre of Pujol, *zarzuelistas* such as Chapi, and internationally distinguished composers such as Oscar Esplá and Joaquín Rodrigo. The Basque provinces have also produced a galaxy of musicologists and composers. Thanks to centralisation, intellectual life in Madrid was enriched by contributions from the various provinces. Castile, nevertheless, can claim some distinguished personalities of its own, of whom the most important was Frederico Olmeda (1865-1909). Organist and composer, he also published a rich collection of Castilian folk songs and made a study of the *Codex Calixtimis*; his compositions, nearly 350 in all, and many of outstanding value, include four symphonies, sacred music and songs.

Albéniz and Granados

The two most important composers at the end of the 19th and beginning of the 20th century were the Catalans Isaac Albéniz (1860-1909) and Enrique Granados (1867-1916). Pedrell had set himself the difficult task of reviving an interest in Spanish folk music and dance on the one hand and in the works of Victoria, Morales and Cabezón on the other, and was the forerunner of a Spanish national school, but it was left to Granados and Albéniz to establish it on an international footing.

Born in Gerona province, Isaac Albéniz was one of music's more remarkable prodigies. He made his public debut before he was five and by the age of fifteen had

travelled through Spain and the Americas, supporting himself as a pianist. He studied in Paris and later worked in Leipzig and Brussels before becoming a pupil of Vincent d'Indy. His early works, in particular his piano compositions, are influenced by Schumann and Liszt (he knew the latter personally) but are often very obviously the result of the lavish patronage he enjoyed at the hands of the London millionaire, Money-Coutts. Nevertheless Albéniz's real musical contribution began to be manifest with certain picturesque piano pieces and really revealed itself with his opera *Pepita Jiménez*, commissioned by Money-Coutts to his libretto after the novel of the same name by Juan Valera, and with a symphonic piece entitled *Catalonia* (1899).

But Albéniz's crowning achievement was undoubtedly the suite *Iberia* (1906-09), twelve pieces for piano that are evocative of the mood typical of Spanish fiestas. It was thanks to contacts with his French friends, Debussy, Chausson, Fauré and Dukas, that Albéniz perfected his harmonic and pianoforte writing, though his music is sometimes too complex. Nevertheless his finest works, such as *Corpus Christi at Seville* from the *Iberia* suite, have 'the eloquence of a language with national elements yet inalienably the composer's and entirely mod-

A painting of a guitar player by Goya.

right
Isaac Albéniz.

centre right
Enrique Granados.

bottom right
The castanets were a familiar part of Spanish music making from the middle ages.

ern'. Several of his pieces have been arranged for orchestra by Enrique Fernandez Arbos (1863-1939). A violinist and pupil of Vieuxtemps and Gevaert at Brussels and of Joachim in Berlin, Arbos also had a brilliant career as a conductor in Europe and in the United States.

Enrique Granados, a pupil of Pedrell and later of Charles-Wilfrid de Bériot in Paris, was born at Lerida in 1867. He wrote a large quantity of orchestral, theatrical and vocal music and songs such as the *Tonadillas*, which are models of their kind, but it was in his piano music that he expressed himself best. His talents are well revealed in his youthful *Danses Espagnoles* and the *Goyescas*, inspired by the paintings of Goya and used as the material for an opera in 1916. Granados, like Albéniz, was too willing to write drawing-room music, and perhaps he wrote too much altogether for his instrument. Nevertheless, in his best work he displays an extreme sensitivity, combining melancholy with fervour in a typically Spanish manner.

De Falla and Turina

In the first half of the 20th century it is de Falla and Turina who stand in the front rank of Spanish music. Indeed, Manuel de Falla, who was born in Cadiz in 1876 and died in the Argentine in 1946, is perhaps the most important Spanish composer of the century. His production is linked with that of Albéniz; his first important work, a two-act prize-winning opera, *La Vida breve*, appeared a year before the performance of the first volume of *Iberia*, but it is more restrained in feeling. It was followed by the four Spanish pieces for piano (1909) and the *Siete Canciones* (*c.* 1912) and with these he established his name. He reached full maturity with his *Nights in the Gardens of Spain* (1916) and the ballets *El amor brujo* and *The Three Cornered Hat* (1919). Two years after its operatic debut this was reworked for Diaghilev as a ballet with choreography by Massine. His last works, *El retablo de Maese Pedro* (1923), a one-act opera for three voices and small orchestra based on a chapter of *Don Quixote*, and his harpsichord concerto for small orchestra (1928), opened new horizons and are undoubtedly the masterpieces of a Spanish musical style that was by now unquestionably of international stature.

Nearly all de Falla's works achieved polished precision and each responds precisely to the demands of its genre, exploiting to the full the instrumental means employed – both the concerto and the *Retablo* achieve great power and fullness of tone, although the instrumental resources are small in both instances. The ambitious *Atlantida* for chorus, soloists and orchestra was left unfinished, but even those passages completed by the composer lack his characteristic polish. It received a posthumous performance in 1961 in a version completed by de Falla's pupil Ernesto Halffter.

Joaquin Turina, who was born in Seville in 1882 and died in Madrid in 1949, is the exact opposite of de Falla in that he produced a vast amount of work in which the influence of his two Parisian teachers, Moszkowski and d'Indy, is noticeable in a certain unnecessary virtuosity and a too evident preoccupation with form. But in his best works, the symphonic poem *La Procesion del Rocio* (1913), the three *Fantastic Dances* for orchestra and the *Symphonic Rhapsody*, Turina, while remaining essentially Spanish, manages to achieve a richness of texture which is anything but parochial.

One of Spain's most important composers during the 20th century has undoubtedly been Oscar Esplá, who was born in Alicante in 1886. He was at first bent on a career in engineering, but after studying with Saint-

Saëns and Reger he was fully confirmed in his passion for music. He was an important figure in the life of the musical world under the Republican regime, but left Spain for exile in Brussels in 1936 when the Falangist victory became apparent. However, Esplá returned to Spain in 1951 and has played a leading part in her musical life. His music, which includes numerous orchestral works, among them two folk music suites and chamber music and songs, relies less on the outright adoption of the forms of folk music than does that of other Spanish composers but often displays a characteristic colour in Esplá's use of scales and harmonies that derive from his study of the music of his native Alicante. His work and example have been a major source of inspiration to younger Spanish composers.

Deeply conscious of the long break in Spain's musical tradition, he strongly felt the need for establishing a tradition of professional technique and intellectual rigour. Of the composers born about the turn of the century the most important is Roberto Gerhard. Of Swiss descent, he was born in the province of Tarragona in 1896. He began his studies under Granados in Barcelona but then went to Germany where he worked under Schoenberg for five years from 1923 to 1925. This period decisively affected his creative objectives, and his interest in twelve-note and serial technique has been basic to much of his work. After the Spanish Civil War Gerhard left Spain and settled in England, where he won considerable international reputation. While in no way denying the value of compositional techniques such as that of serialism as the scaffolding on which the composer works, Gerhard was convinced that music of all kinds demonstrates its validity and can only be properly approached from the intuitive response in the listener. His works, many of which do use serial techniques, include two ballets, a radio opera *The Duenna* (1947), based on Sheridan, a string quartet (1955) and two symphonies. He died in 1970.

After de Falla

In Spain itself the immense achievements of Manuel de Falla exerted, as is to be expected, a considerable influence. Esplá was not immune, and other composers of note to come under the spell include the Catalans Manuel Blancafort (b. 1897) and Federico Mompou (b. 1893). Of these the latter has produced music of great sensitivity and subtlety and has sometimes been called the miniaturist of modern Spanish music.

A more significant figure is perhaps that of Joaquín Rodrigo, born in the province of Valencia in 1902. Taking his inspiration, like many of his contemporaries, from the tendency in de Falla's later work towards Neo-classicism, which not only put Spanish composers in touch with their own distant past but also gave them objectives common to many European musicians, he soon developed a personal direction of his own. Questioning the validity of 'classicism' for its own sake, he has sought a more objective and less nationalistic musical language. In this respect one of his most important works has been the *Musica para un Codice Salmantino* (1952), in which any compromise between 'picturesque' Spanishisms and pure music is eschewed.

Rodrigo was one of the group of Eight founded in Madrid in 1930 which also numbered among its members the two brothers Rodolfo and Ernesto Halffter (b. respectively in 1900 and 1905). Both began their careers as students of de Falla, whose influence remained strong in the work of Ernesto, long resident in Portugal and the continuator of de Falla's *Atlantida*. Rodolfo, on the other hand, who settled in Mexico, made use of

left
A portrait of Manuel de Falla at the age of forty-five.

below
The Teatro Liceo at Barcelona, in the latter half of the 19th century.

polytonal techniques and in his *Three pieces for String orchestra* (1957) makes use of twelve-note methods.

Maurice Ohana, born in 1914, has claimed that his musical education owed more to Andalusian folk music of the African and Berber tribes, which he heard as a young child in Casablanca, where he was born of Gibraltarian parents, than to the mainstream of the classical European tradition. During the Second World War he served in the British Army but has since lived in Paris where he works as a pianist and composer. An early work which is also among his best known is *Llanto por Ignacio Sanchez Mejias* (1950), based on a poem by Lorca on the death of a famous bull-fighter; his other works include an opera for puppets and a guitar concerto.

The younger generation

Among the composers born about the early thirties there is a tendency to regard the purely Spanish tradition as secondary to their aim of integrating their work into the main development of European music. The influence of the modern Parisian school and above all that of Stravinsky is to be found in their work, and one of the most characteristic figures is Cristobal Halffter, born in Madrid in 1930 and a cousin of Ernesto and Rodolfo. Despite the fact that he belongs to a much younger generation, the late music of de Falla, notably the *Retablo*, was important in his formative years though as his music has matured the influence of Bartók and Stravinsky has made itself felt; he has also investigated the implications of atonalism and twelve-note technique. Halffter was associated with the New Music group of Madrid founded by Ramon Barce (b. 1928), and its members form an important body in Spanish music. Luis de Pablo (b. 1930) is a twelve-note composer who, in addition to his admiration for Webern, has obviously studied and learnt from the music of Messiaen and even Bartók. Alberto Blancafort (b. 1928), son of the distinguished Catalan composer and for a long time a pupil of Milhaud, has tended to reject the more *avant-garde* experiments of his contemporaries and has developed a highly personal harmonic style in which the influence of his teacher and the traditions of his native province have obviously been important. Manuel Moreno

Buendia (b. 1932) is the last of the New Music group to be mentioned here. Aiming to come to grips with the main trends in European music, he has shown interest in the rhythmic procedures of Stravinsky and has made intensive experiments in twelve-note composition.

While the tendency among the younger generations of Spanish composers has been towards the main European current, that tendency may be thought to be more marked in Barcelona, which prides itself as a more cosmopolitan music centre, than in Madrid. Barcelona has been the centre of an active cult of serialism with José Cercos (b. 1925) as one of its main devotees; he has not only produced work rigorously conforming to the twelve-note aesthetic but is also convinced of the value of jazz as a vivid and living musical experience. Other highly respected Catalan composers of the present period are Xavier Berenguel (b. 1931) and Narciso Bonet (b. 1933). Both have tended towards the music of Stravinsky and the modern Parisian school without rejecting out of hand the traditions of Spain itself. Indeed, the conflict between the desire to assimilate the most recent main achievements of other European schools and the desire to cultivate a truly national idiom has produced not only a divide within the world of Spanish music but also dilemmas for the composers themselves.

Portugal

The cultural history of Portugal up to today is closely linked with that of Brazil, a contact which has worked in both directions. Antonio José da Silva, known as 'the Jew' (1705-39), condemned by the Inquisition and author of Portuguese *opéras comiques*, was born in Brazil. The Portuguese composer André Gomes da Silva (1752-1844) settled in São Paulo in 1774. Among his pupils were Manuel José Gomes, the father of Carlos Gomes, the first great 19th-century Brazilian composer. These exchanges were intensified in 1808 with the arrival of the court and the Portuguese royal family, who were fleeing from the Napoleonic invasion. The court returned to Portugal in 1821, but the prince, dom Pedro, who became constitutional emperor in 1822 (he was forced to abdicate in 1831) retained among other musicians the important composer Marcos Portugal.

A production of de Falla's El Retablo de Maese Pedro *at La Scala, Milan.*

Marcos Antonio de Fonseca, known as Marcos Portugal, was born in Lisbon in 1762. After having composed operas for Lisbon and Madrid, he left for Italy to perfect his technique (1792). Here he started a brilliant international career, his operas being performed not only in Italy but also in Germany and Russia. Between 1799 and 1810 he was director of the São Carlos opera at Lisbon, and during these years he wrote some ten operas, including among others a new version of his best-known work, *Demofoonte* (Milan 1794, Lisbon 1807). Under French occupation he composed a work to celebrate Napoleon's birthday, but then left Lisbon for Brazil with the court. He remained in Rio until his death in 1830, his works being regularly performed in the Real Teatro de São João.

A new period in Portuguese music began with the foundation of the Lisbon conservatory (1835). This institution, which owed its creation in part to the tenacious efforts of J. A. Rodriguez da Costa (1798-1870), is associated with a brilliant line of Portuguese piano virtuosi. João Domingos Bontempo (1775-1842), who was feted in London and Paris, was appointed director. Artur Napoleão (1843-1925) visited Rio in 1857 and then settled there ten years later, becoming the master of a number of Brazilian composers. Raphael Coelho Machado, born in the Azores in 1814, lived in Brazil from 1835 and died in Rio in 1887; Alexandre Rey Colaço (1864-1928), a pupil of Matthias in Paris and of Hartel and Spitta in Berlin, published a collection of Portuguese folk dances and songs. The most outstanding of all these virtuosi was José Viana da Motta (1868-1948). He was a pupil of Scharwenka in Berlin, and then

The great Catalan cellist, Pablo Casals.

later, at Weimar, of Liszt (1885) and von Bülow (1887). He was later to publish his memoirs of both. As a teacher he did much to raise standards in the Lisbon Conservatory and as a composer he wrote a symphony, a quartet and many piano pieces inspired by popular music. Da Motta's prestige was such that he was invited to edit the piano works of Liszt for the German publishing house of Breitkopf and Härtel. Alfredo Keil (1850-1907), a composer and painter of German descent, wrote some fine operas, of which *Serrana* (Turin and Lisbon, 1899) may be regarded as the first opera in Portuguese to be imbued with a truly national spirit. Francisco de Gazul (1842-1925), one of the major figures in the formation of the Portuguese national school, wrote some thirty operettas and an opera, *Frei Luiz da Souza* (1891), as well as symphonies, chamber works and church music, including seven masses. João Marcellino Arroyo (1861-1930) composed two operas, four symphonic suites, songs and piano pieces. Augusto Machado (1845-1925) studied first in Lisbon and then in Paris. He was director of the São Carlos theatre and of the conservatory. He also composed operas, as well as an operetta, a cantata (*Camoens*) on the great Portuguese Renaissance poet, and other lesser works.

Among Portugal's leading 20th-century composers are: Luiz de Freitas (b. 1890), a pupil of Humperdinck in Berlin, director of the São Carlos theatre in 1926 and composer of two symphonies, orchestral and chamber music and music for piano and organ; Ruy Coelho (b. 1892), also a pupil of Humperdinck, and creator of modern Portuguese opera with *Ines de Castro* among others; and Claudio Carneygo (b. 1895), a pupil of Widor and Dukas and the composer of symphonic, chamber and choral works.

Frederico Freitas Branco (b. 1905) uses polytonality and was the first to make use of colonial folk music; he has composed an opera, chamber music and music for films. Ivo Cruz was born in Brazil in 1901, but studied

in Lisbon, where in 1923 he founded an important periodical – the *Rinascimento musical*. From 1924 he spent five years in Germany and on his return to Lisbon he founded, in 1930, the *Duarte Lobo* society, for the performances of old polyphonic music. He established the Cintra Festival in 1949. In addition to his orchestral works and chamber music (including a saraband for two guitars) and choral works (on texts by Camoens) he has also made arrangements of old Portuguese music. Fernando Lopez Graça (b. 1906) was influenced by European composers in atonality and microtonality. Apart from his orchestral and chamber works, piano pieces, choral works and songs, he has also written works on theory and musical history.

In Portugal, as in Spain, scholarship has made major contributions in editing much music of the middle ages and the Renaissance.

The music of South America

In music, as in the other arts, the cultural history of the countries of the South American continent is broadly divided into three main periods: the Pre-Columbian, the colonial (or Spanish and Portuguese) centuries and the modern era, in which a characteristic style has begun to establish itself.

At the time of the European conquest in the 16th century Central America and the northern part of South America were dominated by two great empires: the Aztec, in the area largely comprising modern Mexico, and the Inca, centred upon the lands of the modern state of Peru. In both, as in other cultures on the continent, music played an important role in social, political and religious life. The point was noted by the invaders and towards the end of the 16th century Father Jerome de Mendieta in his *Historia ecclesiastica indiana* states that 'one of the main things to be found in this land of Mexico is the prevalence of songs and dances'. In the absence of Aztec or Inca musical notation it is now extremely difficult to make any certain observations on the nature of this ancient music. However, it is known, from eyewitness accounts, that court feasts and ceremonies were accompanied by music provided by highly-trained singing girls and percussion players. A certain amount of information as to the musical instruments employed has also been recovered.

The Aztec empire and its many highly developed subject populations had numerous wind instruments, including fipple flutes, panpipes and various types of trumpet; there was also a wide range of percussion instruments and xylophones. The flute, which reached its most varied and complete development in this part of the world, was also much cultivated in Peru; indeed the melancholy sound of the *quena* flute was so evocative that the Spanish ecclesiastical authorities attempted to prevent its use. Peru, like many other parts of the continent, now has a number of stringed instruments, harps and guitars of various types, all of which date from the colonial period.

While we can be fairly sure of the instruments used, the nature of the music itself is less easy to determine. But it seems that the melodic line was based on the pentatonic scale without being slavishly bound to it. This characteristic is to be found in the music of the aboriginal Mexican Indians of today, some of which, notably that of the Huichol tribes, appears to be very close to the ancient musical tradition. In a similar way we can gain some idea of the music of the Incas from the songs and dances still performed among the populations of the high plateaus of the Andes. These too display a strongly pentatonic structure and studies have revealed the use of five modes, each of which is based on one of the notes of the pentatonic scale in turn.

The generally nomadic and culturally less advanced populations elsewhere in South America did nevertheless betray a delight in and respect for music common to all human societies, and music held a high place in their social and religious ceremonies. However, here, as with so much of the culture of the ancient populations of this region, study and recovery of the lost art have been made more difficult by the disgraceful dealings of the European populations and their successors towards the more primitive peoples of the interior. Accordingly the integration of the autochthonous music of the various regions has proceeded unevenly. In many cases it has remained entirely outside the orbit of the Westernised popular and art traditions and has survived, in an attenuated form, among the isolated and vulnerable groups of the interior. Certain native instruments, such as the *teponaztli* xylophone and the maracas, now familiar in Western dance and jazz bands, were introduced into the larger communities of half-caste or totally non-Indian societies. To a lesser extent, even the characteristically Indian style of recitative chant has infiltrated certain types of popular music, particularly in Brazil. But the strongest survivals of this ancient music are to be found in the Cordillera of the Andes among the descendants of the Inca, while it has also survived, in a pure or in a degenerate state, in parts of Peru, Ecuador and Bolivia. It is a curious fact that, although Mexico is the heir to a vigorous Pre-Columbian culture based on the achievements of the Toltecs and Maya, and although their descendants and those of the conquering Aztecs predominate in the peasant population, the ancient musical tradition is least strong there. Late 19th-century researchers did discover a primitive musical tradition among remote communities in the north-west of the country, but otherwise Mexican popular music is almost completely an extension of the European art.

Mayan wall painting showing musicians playing rattles and a large drum.

475

The centuries of European influence: Mexico

A Spanish manuscript from the 1560s gives not only a list of Aztec instruments and musicians but also information on rhythmic patterns, which show some points of comparison with those used in oriental music. An important centre of this ancient Mexican music was the temple of Macuilxochitl, the god of music, which probably held the same sort of position as the great churches of Europe in musical life. By degrees Roman Catholic music came to be superimposed on this existing tradition, and the popular Christmas carols and hymns to the Virgin still heard today are no doubt the first fruits of this period of conversion to Christianity. Spanish influence also coloured secular music from the 16th century, and later, in such music as that of the *habañera* dance, we find traces of the music of the African slave population introduced into the Central American area by the Europeans. In the 19th century, even the effects of Italian operatic arias were felt in the *cancion*, while the European idiom also shaped the music of village funerals, feasts and weddings.

The first Christian missionaries in Mexico were a group of Franciscans led by Pedro de Gante, who arrived in 1527. The Church was the chief patron of the arts. The first notated missal was printed in Mexico in 1556, and by the last quarter of the 16th century Spanish musicians in Mexico were producing polyphonic church compositions. Spanish colonial rule finally came to an end in Mexico in the 1820s, though Spain's cultural influence was to live for a long time thereafter.

After the winning of political independence Mexico witnessed the rise of a group of composers eager to shape a truly national style. Among them were Aniceto Ortega (d. 1875) whose opera *Guatimotzin* was the first on a Mexican subject; Melesio Morales (1838-1908), who wrote five operas; Filipe Villanueva (1862-93), the composer of a number of popular *danza mexicana* in imitation of the Cuban dance idiom of the period; and Juventino Rosa (1868-94), whose fame as the composer of *Sobre las olas* spread beyond the frontiers of his own land. In the 1870s the Mexican national conservatory was founded, and with it began a new epoch in Mexican music in which a number of the pupils of Morales featured prominently. Among them were Gustavo Campa (1863-1934), a professor at the conservatory and the composer of operas and symphonies, and Ricardo Castro (1866-1907) who, in addition to four operas, wrote a piano concerto.

The northern republics

An important feature of the musical life of Venezuela and the island republics of Haiti, Dominica and Cuba was the western African tradition introduced by the slave populations which were imported by the European plantation owners.

The Spanish *conquistadores* in Dominica at the beginning of the 16th century were fascinated by the *areito*, a round dance of importance in the ceremonies of the local population. But the indigenous music was inevitably supplanted by that of the invaders, and over the centuries this in its turn was highly coloured by Negro elements, while the principal instrument of the area, the *marimbulla*, on the xylophone principle but with metal tongues, is clearly derived from the African *marimba*.

The cathedral of Santo Domingo was completed in the first half of the 16th century and became the focus of musical life until the 19th century, when a number of composers, chief among them Juan Bautista Alfonseca (1810-75), worked for the establishment of a strong tradition in secular music.

The Republic of Haiti, the first Negro republic in the world, has a strong tradition of popular music which has been the object of much musicological research. African musical influence is apparent not only in the instruments but in the music and the dances such as the *moundongue*, a ritual dance, and the *meringo*, analogous to the Mexican *merengo*. In the composer Ludovic Lamothe (b. 1882), who studied at the Paris Conservatory, Haiti produced a musician whose gifts, both as pianist and composer, have led to his being compared to Chopin.

In Cuba, the original population of Tainos and Siboneyes Indians has long since disappeared, and the music of the island is almost exclusively African in origin. Cuban music is inevitably rich in rhythmic variety, and this is provided by a wide range of instruments of which the best-known are probably the bongo drums. The African musical idiom has infected even the popular dances of Spanish origin, such as the rumba and the bolero, while the Roman Catholic religion itself and the music of its smaller shrines betrays the effect of African ideas.

Art music has an almost equally venerable tradition in Venezuela. After its foundation in the 1570s, Caracas

Musicians in a procession in the Cuzco region of Peru. A violin, guitar and flutes provide the music, and behind them the harpists, who will play when the procession reaches its destination, are carrying their instruments.

became the leading city of Spanish Latin America and, from the beginning of the 17th century, the music of its cathedral was administered by a professional organist. In 1671 a musical director was appointed on the European model. The first composer known by name was the Capuchin friar Diego de los Rios (d. 1670); he wrote church music intended for the edification and conversion of the Indian population, and, though the music is now lost, it is known that de los Rios set his music to the local native language. It may perhaps be assumed that he introduced elements of the indigenous musical idiom.

In the last year of the 17th century the first professor of music was appointed at Caracas university, but the 18th century was dominated by the figure of Pedro Palacios y Sojo (1739-99). It is not known whether he himself composed or even whether he was noted as a performer, but his contribution to the musical life of Venezuela fully justified the high regard in which he is still held. It was Sojo who founded the Oratory of St Philip Neri at Caracas and who, following his extensive travels in Europe, introduced to his native country the music of the Viennese school. Furthermore, in 1784, Sojo founded an academy of music at Caracas, appointing as its director Juan Manuel Olivares (1760-97), the most distinguished composer of a talented generation. His many pupils shaped the course of music in Venezuela during the 19th century. The pianist and composer Teresa Carreño (1853-1917) won an international reputation, and mention should also be made of José Angel Montero (d. 1881), whose first opera *Virginia* was produced in 1873, and the talented composer Reynaldo Hahn (1875-1947) who, although he made his career in France, was in fact born in Caracas.

The most important relics of Colombian ethno-musicology are the gold trumpets and other instruments of the Chibchas tribe, but the folk tradition of this country also boasts a wide range of drums, the variety of flutes (transverse, straight and of the panpipe type) so characteristic of South America, and many types of string instruments, mostly the fruit of European contacts. Of the music itself, the national folk dance, the *bambuco*, displays features of the three main traditions in Colombian music – the native Indian, the African and the Spanish. As in other parts of Spanish America, art music flourished from the 16th century, but in Colombia the tradition was not so vigorous as, for example, in Venezuela. When the Spanish *tonadilla* dance and the music of the Italian opera were introduced to the main towns of Cartagena and Bogotá in the late 18th century, these two influences swamped the weak native tradition.

During the 19th century musical life developed. Juan Antonio de Velasco (d. 1859) introduced the music of Beethoven and Rossini; the Englishman Henry Price (1819-63) founded the Bogotá Philharmonia Society, while his son, Jorge W. Price (1853-1953), founded the national academy of music. There were also a number of native Colombian composers of whom the chief was Guillermo Uribe Holguin (b. 1880) who, after training in Paris, returned to refound the academy and refurbish the whole Colombian system of musical education.

The southern states of Spanish America

In Chile, the Araucan and Alacalufe Indians in the south of the country still retain a vigorous tradition. Their melodies tend to use four or five notes of the diatonic scale, while their instruments display the same emphasis on the wind families as we have seen elsewhere in Latin America. In Manuel Robles (1780-1837) Chile produced her first native composer of any stature. There-

after musical life flourished with increasing vigour – Federico Guzman (1837-85) produced the first notated example of the national dance known as the *cueca*, while the German composer Aquinas Reid (d. 1868) produced the first opera set to Spanish words to be heard in Chile.

The folk-music traditions of the vast country of Argentina offer the student a remarkable diversity of types: from the aboriginal music of the deserted zone of la Puna in the north west, whose melodies, using the interval of the tritone, may represent an ancient pre-

below
Devil dancers at a religious festival in Venezuela. The maracas they are holding are obviously derived from the rattles of the early Mayan priest musicians.

bottom
A Mexican peasant violinist; note the way he holds his instrument and its primitive bow.

Inca culture, to the heavily Europeanised gaucho melodies of the central pampas regions. In the western provinces of the Argentine the music shows the influence of Chilean styles; to the north it approaches in style the music of Bolivia and Peru; and in the frontier regions with Paraguay and Uruguay we find similar approximations to a common idiom.

But undoubtedly it is the music of the gauchos or cowboys of the central plains which is to be considered the most characteristic of Argentine popular and folk tradition. The gaucho tradition of poetry is generally regarded as beginning with the patriotic songs and political dialogues of Bartolome Hidalgo (d. 1823), and the tradition was continued by Hilario Ascasubi (1807-75), who wrote political ballads and an epic on an 18th-century gaucho hero. It will be seen that the central feature of this tradition was the poetry of the texts, but these ballads and epics would have been inconceivable without the guitar accompaniment to which they were always performed.

The tradition of art music in the Argentine owed much during the 17th century to the Jesuits who here, as elsewhere in South America, played a vital part in cultural and indeed political life. During the 18th century the influence was continued by a number of European musicians, among them Germans and Italians. The first native Argentinian composer of merit was Juan Pedro Esnaola (1808-78), who studied in Madrid and Paris before returning to his native country, where he wrote a number of religious works, operas and pieces for the piano.

It is not until the later 19th century that we can speak of a school of Argentinian composers. In the year 1890 Alberto Williams (1862-1952), a composer of British and Basque descent, returned to the Argentine after studies at the Paris Conservatory which had included some work under César Franck. His output was vast,

above right
A peasant musician from Ecuador playing the panpipes.

right
Shawm player and a player of the Mexican guitar at a local festival.

perhaps too vast in view of its uneven quality, and included nine symphonies, a multitude of works for piano and choral works, as well as many songs and chamber compositions. The number of compositions explicitly nationalist in tone, of which the orchestral suite *Milongas* is the best, is comparatively small. Nevertheless, Williams provided the point of departure for a group of composers who were to produce a body of Argentinian operas, drawing not only on the cult of *verismo* prevalent in Italian opera but also on native Argentinian tradition.

The music of the 20th century: Brazil

During this century the countries of South America have produced a number of composers of the first rank, of whom the most notable is probably Heitor Villa-Lobos of Brazil. This country, by far the largest of the sub-continent, is heir to the Portuguese cultural tradition as the consequence of the conquests of the 16th century. Like the coastal states to the north, however, it has also been subject to African influences on its musical development. The music of the aboriginal populations is little known, since large parts of the country are still unexplored and many tribes have been exterminated by freebooting profiteers. From what is known of the customs of these apparently peaceable and gentle people, music is of central importance in their religious and social rituals. Here, as in so many parts of aboriginal South America, instruments of the flute family have reached a particular stage of development. The Indians of the Kamaiuras tribe, for example, use great bass flutes of the recorder type which may be of four or five feet in length and as much as six inches in external diameter.

In the coastal areas, the music of Pre-Columbian Brazil has yielded to the music of the African immigrants, which has done much to shape the characteristic music of Brazil and give it its rich rhythmic character and wide range of percussion instruments, including friction drums and the *marimba*. But if such dances as the *catira* reflect the indigenous music, while the *modinha* or the *toadas* are imbued with nostalgia of the Portuguese *saudade* (solitude in the spiritual sense of that word), the great mass of Brazilian popular music is indebted to Negro influence or to a variety of cultural sources. In the first category we may place the liturgical or dramatic forms such as the *macumba* or the *congada*, while to the second belong the *choro* and the *samba*.

In Brazil, as in the Argentine, the first European representatives of music were the Jesuits. By the 18th century the district controlled by the Jesuit mission stations, so bitterly attacked by Voltaire in his novel *Candide*, was, whatever other faults it may have had, a veritable conservatory for music. At this period too, the district of the modern province of Minas Gerais enjoyed an intense musical life. Local composers produced many competent works, while European developments as represented in the compositions of such men as Haydn or Boccherini were copied and performed within a few years of their European publication.

The most important composer of this period, José Nuñes Garcia (1767-1830), was of Negro extraction and displayed a precocious talent, his earliest composition, an antiphon, dating from his sixteenth year. In 1798 he was appointed director of music of the viceroy's establishment in Rio.

As a result of the temporary exile of the Portuguese court in the 1810s, Brazil benefited from the talent of the gifted Portuguese musician Marcos Portugal, who settled there and with whom Nuñes Garcia had to contend for the favours of court patronage. It was a pupil of Nuñes Garcia, Francisco Manuel da Silva (1796-1865), who reflected changing tastes in 19th-century Brazil. His compositions include not only religious music in the tradition of his master but also an opera and music for chamber ensembles. Da Silva also composed the Brazilian national anthem.

After Da Silva, Brazilian composers turned decisively to opera, and the way was prepared for Antonio Carlos Gomes (1836-96), undoubtedly the greatest Brazilian composer of the 19th century and the first South American composer to win world recognition. Thanks to the success of his opera *Joana de Flandre* (1863) which, despite its name, already had a definable Brazilian style, Gomes received a bursary to study abroad. After six years in Italy he received the accolade of a production at La Scala, Milan, with his opera *Il Guarany*. Thereafter his career both in Europe and Brazil continued successfully until his final achievements, *Lo Schiavo* at Rio and *Condor* (1891) at La Scala.

After Gomes, Brazil produced a number of talented composers. Leopoldo Miguiz (1850-1902), who studied in Portugal and Brussels, was the founder of the national institute of music, which succeeded the conservatory. He composed an opera, a number of symphonic poems and pieces for piano. Henrique Oswald (1852-1931) succeeded at the institute in 1903 and was also a composer of merit. Alberto Nepomuceno (1864-1920) was a composer of immense gifts who studied in Berlin, Rome and Paris. His oeuvre, which comprises orchestral and chamber music, reveals a talent of rich sensibility.

Villa-Lobos

But undoubtedly the most important figure in Brazilian musical life of the first half of the 20th century was Heitor Villa-Lobos (1887-1959). Initially self-taught, he toured Europe in the 1920s, meeting many leading

The recording of folk music has been an important aspect of 20th-century music; nowhere has this been more thoroughly conducted than in South America.

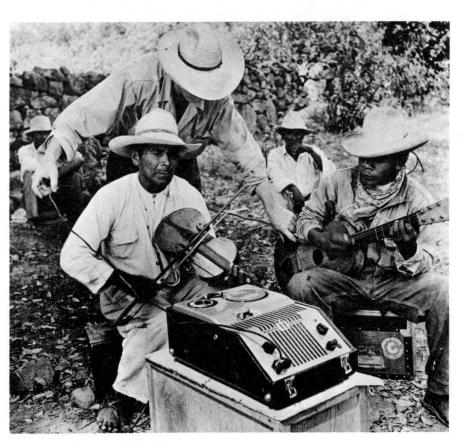

composers. In 1930 he was appointed director of the national music academy and two years later given charge of the country's musical education. In 1942 Villa-Lobos founded the Conservatorio Nacional de Canto Orfeônico, with the aim of providing qualified music teachers for Brazilian schools. As a pedagogue and administrator and as folklorist and musicologist he did much to improve Brazilian music. In the early 1910s he undertook a long tour of Brazil in search of its folk-musical heritage, and in his own compositions he introduced it into the mainstream of Brazilian music.

Villa-Lobos has been criticised for an indiscriminate facility of composition, and his output is certainly immense. However, there can be no doubt that at his best Villa-Lobos, the most famous of 20th-century Latin American composers, is also one of the best. His music, despite the strong colouring it derives from Brazilian folk elements and its stylistic affinities to European Impressionism, is essentially Romantic in mood though eclectic in inspiration. His compositions include four operas, a number of ballets including *Emperor Jones* (1955) and thirteen programmatic symphonies. But perhaps his best music is to be found in the *Noneto* for mixed choir of 1923, the first and second of the nine *Bachianas Brasileiras*, for eight cellos and for cellos and soprano voice respectively and in his 'Choros', a new type of composition of which he wrote fourteen examples.

The choro is essentially a popular composition, consisting of variations on the basic combination of a wind instrument accompanied by strings. The orchestration

above
Manuel Ponce.

below
Villa-Lobos of Brazil, one of South America's leading 20th-century composers.

can be extremely varied, ranging from a single guitar to a double orchestra. It was the composer's declared intention to provide in his Choros a synthesis of Brazilian popular and folk music, using their rhythms, melodies and even, on some occasions, their instruments. Among the best of the Choros are No. 7 for strings and woodwind and No. 10 for chorus and orchestra.

Thanks to the work of Villa-Lobos and his contemporaries, music occupied a far higher place in the life of Brazil during the second half of the 20th century than at any other time in the country's history. And this general activity was reinforced by a number of fine composers such as Luciano Gallet (1893-1931), also a keen student of folk and popular music. These interests are reflected in such compositions as *Cancoes populares* and *Suite sobre temas negro-brasileiros* for orchestra (1929). He was a friend of Villa-Lobos and, like him, of Darius Milhaud. Francisco Mignone (b. 1897) was trained in Milan but also sought his musical identity in the popular tradition of his native land. The *congada* dance of his opera *O contratador de diamantes*, for example, is inspired by a popular song recorded in the 1830s. Oscar Lorenzo Férnández (1897-1948), who founded another large music school in Rio, the Conservatorio Brasileiro, derived much of the material for his compositions from folklore. Examples are the second quartet and the *batuque* dance from his opera *Malasarte*, perhaps his best-known piece.

For Brazilian composers of the next generation the most important influence was that of the German-born Hans Joachim Koellreutter (b. 1915), resident in Brazil from 1937. He gathered round him a group of composers known collectively as Musica Viva, among whom Cesar Guerra Peixe (b. 1914) and Claudio Santoro (b. 1919) were the first Brazilian twelve-note composers. Other members of the group are Eunice Catunda (b. 1915) and Edino Krieger (b. 1928). An essential complement to their work has been that of a flourishing and talented body of musicologists, among the chief of whom has been Oneyda Alvarenga (b. 1911) with his publication *Musica popular brasilena* (1947).

The 20th century in Chile and Argentina

A most important figure in Chilean music in the first half of the 20th century was that of Humberto Allende (b. 1885). Both as a composer and more significantly as a teacher of composition at the Santiago conservatory from 1928 to 1946 he did much to further the advance of music in Chile. Allende also made folk-song collections, and his own works include the symphonic poem *La voz de las calles*.

But the impetus for the advance of which we have spoken came from one man, the greatest figure in Chilean music, Domingo Santa Cruz Wilson (b. 1899). Trained in Madrid, he returned to Chile in 1918 and in that year founded the Sociedad Bach, which he directed until its dissolution in the 1930s. He was behind the creation of the faculty of fine arts at the university of Chile in 1929, which became the centre of a completely restructured system of musical education throughout the country. Santa Cruz was also a powerful composer in a nationalist Romantic idiom, his compositions including the *Cantata de los rios de Chile*. After Allende and Santa Cruz, Juan Orrego Salas (b. 1919) is probably Chile's best all-round musician of the older generation, though better known internationally is the brilliant and powerful pianist Claudio Arrau (b. 1903). The upsurge in Chile's musical life has been so dramatic during this century that her composers are already joining the *avant-garde* movement and there has been a sizeable school of twelve-note composers.

Unlike Chile, her large neighbour Argentina has had a flourishing musical life since the earliest years of the century. We have already seen the important part played in this development by Alberto Williams. Buenos Aires now has two other large conservatories in addition to the one that he founded, it supports several symphony and chamber orchestras and boasts the internationally famed opera house of the Colon theatre.

The most prominent Argentinian musicians in the generation succeeding Williams are the conductor Juan José Castro (b. 1895), also the composer of some fine music, and the composer Juan Carlos Paz (b. 1899). Paz has exerted a wide and deep influence on the musical life of his country as teacher and critic. As director of the Concerts of New Music since 1937, he has introduced virtually every major contemporary work to the Argentine. In his own music, which has inspired a generation of young composers, he has progressed from Impressionism to twelve-note techniques by a natural development through chromaticism, polytonality and atonality. A school of young twelve-note composers sprang up around the figure of Paz, while more traditional music was continued by followers of Williams, such as Albert Ginastera (b. 1916), until recently professor of music at the La Plata university. Ginastera is the first Argentine-trained composer of real stature, and his music owes much not only to Williams but also to the popular music of the Argentine itself. He has considerable facility as a composer for the orchestra and is able to blend modern with traditional effects.

Mexico

Following the musical activity of the 19th century, Mexico was well placed to advance in the 20th. The three great figures of the first half of the century are Manuel Ponce, Julián Carrillo and Carlos Chávez and they will occupy most of our attention in this section.

Manuel Maria Ponce (1882-1948) was of great importance in the musical life of Mexico not only as a composer but also as a teacher and, like many other Latin American musicians, he devoted part of his working life to the study of folk music. After initial training in Mexico he went to Bologna and then Berlin, where he studied the piano, becoming teacher of that instrument and of musical history at the national conservatory on his return to Mexico in 1906. Later he was to live for a period in New York until in 1923 he went to Paris to work under Dukas for some eight years. His music, in a typically nationalist idiom, includes symphonic compositions, three concertos, among them one for the guitar dedicated to Segovia, chamber music and the very popular song Estrellita. His country recognised the value of his work by renaming the chief concert hall in Mexico City after him.

Julián Carrillo (b. 1875) was the pupil of Melesio Morales at the Mexican national conservatory before going to study in Leipzig for a period. He also made an intensive study of the violin and this no doubt helped to direct his interest in microtones. In some of his works he writes for an octave divided equally into sixteen intervals; in others he uses quarter tones, and in others still smaller intervals. Nevertheless his music is not merely experimental but is truly expressive, whether he uses the standard instruments of the orchestra or prepared instruments (flutes, clarinets, harps etc.) modified to yield the micro-intervals sometimes needed.

The dominating figure in 20th-century Mexican music is Carlos Chávez (1899–1978) who, indeed, is one of the major composers produced by the Americas.

He studied with Ponce at the national conservatory, though he started by teaching himself the basics of composition. Like many of his Latin American colleagues he made early visits to Europe and to North America; this has naturally coloured much of his music, a good example being the abrupt rhythms of his ballet H.P. (i.e. 'horsepower'), written in 1926-27, showing affinities with the music of the Italian Futurist composers. In the diverse sources of his inspiration Chávez epitomises the freedom with which the artist, maturing in the eclectic culture of Latin America, can draw on the various traditions offered by his own country and Europe. Some of his music consciously embodies Mexican elements and at times attempts to reconstruct the sonorities of Pre-Columbian music in much the same way as Mexican painters have looked to their ancient traditions for inspiration. Indeed, the work of Chávez shows many traits found in the post-Revolutionary period of Mexican culture. The ballet H.P. concerned itself with the problems of a revolutionary proletariat, and he founded a series of workers' concerts for which he wrote a Sinfonia proletaria for choir and chamber orchestra (1934) and a republican overture in the following year. In an explicitly Mexican idiom we have such works as the Sinfonia India and Xochipilli Macuilxochitl, which uses native Mexican instruments and is dedicated to the ancient god of music. But although his music is predominantly nationalist in inspiration, compositions such as the chamber works Espiral, Exagonos, Poligonos, influenced by the work of Edgar Varèse, show his keen interest in European developments. The founder-conductor of the Mexican symphony orchestra and director of the national conservatory from 1928 to 1952, Chávez also expounded

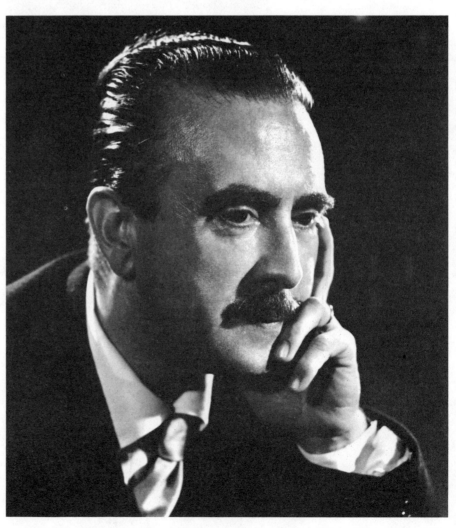

The brilliant and world famous Chilean pianist, Claudio Arrau.

his musical credo in *Towards a New Music* (1937) and *La Musica Mexicana* (1949). As yet no other Mexican composer has contested the ascendancy of Chávez.

Silvestre Revueltas (1899-1940) studied for a time in the United States and later produced music which admirably expresses his verve and good humour, while some of his later works veer towards polytonality. Of a somewhat younger generation we should mention the composers of the short-lived 'Group of Four': Daniel Ayala (b. 1908), Blas Galindo (b. 1911), a pupil of Chávez; Salvador Contreras (b. 1912), a pupil of both Chávez and Revueltas, and José Pablo Moncayo (b. 1912), also a pupil of Chávez.

With this account of Mexican music we come to the end of the main musical traditions in Latin America, but we must mention the flourishing and vigorous tradition of music in Cuba. The leading figures have been the Spaniard José Ardévol (b. 1911), who in 1930 founded the group known as the *Renovacion musical* and four years later a chamber orchestra to perform their music; Alejandro García Caturla (1906-40), trained in Paris; and Amadeo Roldán (1900-39), who made intensive use of popular instruments performed in a diversity of manners and playing music of great rhythmic interest. Among Cuban composers of a younger generation are Esther Rodríguez (b. 1920) and Julián Orbón (b. 1926).

All in all it may be said that the music of the countries of South America exhibits the same development from 'classical' through folk to a national idiom as is found, in broad outline, in other new national traditions.

Music in Switzerland

Insofar as Switzerland is a federal state with three main linguistic groups, German, French and Italian, it may be questioned whether it can have a true national music. Yet Switzerland possesses a stimulating folk music tradition and a long national tradition of communal choral singing. The Reformed Church, which is slightly the more preponderant, has helped to nourish this activity. German Switzerland and French-speaking Switzerland have developed a sufficiently original musical life for it to be necessary to study each independently. Switzerland, like Belgium, is a country which is subjected to both Latin and Germanic cultures. Arthur Honegger of Zurich and Conrad Beck of Basel, both from German Switzerland, nevertheless, spontaneously turned to Paris, while Frank Martin of Geneva was attracted by Vienna and lives in Holland.

The founder of the German Swiss choral tradition was the Zurich-born Hans Georg Nageli (1773-1836). The great *Festspiele*, or choral festivals, were the most important musical events in the 19th century. Friedrich Hegar (1841-1927), the friend of Brahms, gave an extraordinary impulse to the musical life of Zurich as a conductor of orchestras and choirs, and by the foundation of a school of music which later became a conservatory. He also composed numerous choral and some orchestral works. Hans Huber of Basel (1852-1921), who followed in his footsteps, was a much more prolific composer. He first came under the influence of Brahms and later of Richard Strauss, but despite this he remained essentially Swiss. His nationalist feelings are expressed in the titles of his eight symphonies, such as *William Tell*. His works also include symphonic poems, choral music and many chamber works. Hermann Suter (1870-1926), his pupil, was also inspired by nationalist and Romantic inclinations. His work culminated in his masterpiece, the noble oratorio based on the *Laudi* of St Francis of Assisi (1924).

Paradoxically, German musicians contributed powerfully to the awakening of an original form of expression in the Suisse Romande (i.e. French Switzerland). A major event in popular music in the Suisse Romande has been the famous Wine Growers' Festival (*Fête des Vignerons*), held at Vevey about every twenty-five years. Hugo de Senger (1835-92), a Bavarian by origin, but a citizen of Geneva by adoption and very much attracted by France, was the great architect of the Suisse Romande musical revival and wrote, among other things, the music for the Wine Growers' Festival of 1889. He was succeeded in Geneva by the eminent organist Otto Barblan (1860-1943), also educated in Germany, and Joseph Lauber (1864-1952), another German, the pupil of Hegar and also, in Paris, of Massenet. His prolific output, of great freshness and imbued with echoes of folk music, is particularly brilliantly orchestrated. Jacques-Dalcroze and Gustave Doret, two of his French-speaking contemporaries, have acquired popularity thanks to their many songs for chorus, inspired by folk tunes of French Switzerland.

Emile Jacques-Dalcroze (1865-1950) was born in Vienna where he was a pupil of Bruckner. Nevertheless, he was entirely Latin in temperament, and was the creator of a genuine neo-folk popular music in the Suisse Romande. He is also the author of several symphonic works and music for the stage. Outside Switzerland he achieved fame as the author of a definite and carefully worked-out system of musical training through physical movement, to which he gave the name eurhythmics. Gustave Doret (1866-1943), a pupil of Massenet and Saint-Saëns, a violinist and excellent conductor, was associated with the rustic theatre of Jorat, which later became famous for its production of Honegger's *King David*, and for which Doret composed numerous operas and other stage works strongly inspired by the countryside. He, too, wrote for the Wine Growers' Festivals of 1905 and 1927 and composed a quasi-folk

Emile Jacques-Dalcroze.

right
Ernest Bloch.

below
The interior of the Grand Theatre, Geneva.

music drama, produced by the Opéra Comique of Paris in 1906. He is also remembered for his songs, of which he wrote a very large number.

One of the more important figures in German Swiss music was Othmar Schoeck (1886-1957), a pupil of Reger. His work became well known outside Switzerland, especially in Germany. His popularity there is probably because Schoeck's main work consists of *Lieder*, sometimes arranged in large cycles with orchestral accompaniment. The finest of these cycles, and possibly Schoeck's masterpiece, is the harsh, dramatic *Lebendig begraben* (*Buried alive*, 1926), based on poems by Gottfried Keller. These cycles are in a rich post-Romantic idiom which also permeates his six operas; the most perfect of these is *Penthesilea* (1925), based on the tragedy by the German dramatist Kleist. Schoeck also wrote a number of choral works while his instrumental works, which are less numerous, include three concertos, two quartets, and several sonatas. Another leading figure in the musical life of German Switzerland was Volkmar Andreae (1879-1962). Most important as a conductor, he also composed orchestral and chamber works which reveal the influence of Strauss and Reger. Fritz Brun (1878-1962), from Lucerne, is the author of two great symphonies faithful to the tradition of Brahms.

Bloch

Ernest Bloch (1880-1959), one of the greatest composers produced by Switzerland, belongs like his younger contemporary Honegger to the international world of music. He was born in Geneva but studied in Brussels (with Ysaye), Frankfurt, Munich and Paris. He left for the United States in 1916 and spent most of the rest of his life there, except between the years 1930 and 1938, which he spent between Italian Switzerland and Haute-Savoie. He had many American composers among his pupils, and the United States claim Bloch as an American just as often as the Swiss claim him as their own. Yet in a sense neither claim is fully justified, since Bloch's Judaism was such an important element in his work that he may be regarded as the true creator of a Jewish national tradition in art music.

He was a Romantic independant whose music, although admittedly not always free from over-emphasis, prolixity and heaviness, is a synthesis of Germanic and Latin schools. Franck and Strauss were his original models, but his music soon became more complex and, in his last works, his tonality was so greatly expanded as to include twelve-note serial technique. Deeply inspired by the musical tradition of his people and the music of the synagogue, his work has at times an oriental sumptuousness which he raises to the highest pitch. But Bloch could also write marvellously simple passages, evocative of the gentle pastoral uplands of his beloved Swiss mountains.

His output, consisting of more than seventy works, can be divided into five great periods. At the early age of twenty-two he established his name as a composer with his symphony in C sharp minor, which the French critic, Romain Rolland, greeted with enthusiasm. This early Romantic phase culminated with Bloch's one and only opera, the powerful *Macbeth* (1910), which was staged in Paris by the Opéra Comique. The next period belongs to his early thirties and is marked by his pride of race. From this sprang the *Trois poèmes juifs* for orchestra; *Trois Psaumes*, for voices and orchestra; the vehement second symphony known as 'The Israel', and the rhapsody for cello and orchestra, *Schelomo* (1916), one of Bloch's most famous works. Bloch's evolution as man and artist was completed in his first string quartet in B minor (1916), written in America. The following chapter of his life (1916-29) is represented by the American period, during which he was not only very active as a teacher but also composed a great deal, though mainly minor works. From these years only the viola suite, the first quintet with piano, and the two violin sonatas are worthy of mention. During the years 1930-38, when he retired to his Alpine retreat, he began to write masterpieces once more: *Avodath Hakodesh* (*Holy Service for Sabbath morning*), which forms the keystone of all Bloch's music; *Voix dans le désert*, a symphonic poem for cello and orchestra, the supreme expression of what we may call Bloch's prophetic style; and, finally, the violin concerto of 1937-38, one of the most successful works of this genre.

Bloch's final period from 1944 till his death in 1959 was more productive than any other. During these years he wrote the *Concerto Symphonique* for piano and orchestra, three new symphonies and a quantity of chamber music. The second quartet, with its great *passacaglia* and fugue, the third quartet, the most concentrated of all, and the fourth, more intimate and peaceful, are all outstanding. In his *Two Last Poems* for flute and orchestra (1958), his swan song, this great tormented composer at last found peace.

Bloch's contemporaries in the Suisse Romande were Henri Gagnebin (b. 1886), a pupil of Vincent d'Indy, and Blanche Selva (1884-1946). For more than thirty years Gagnebin was director of the Geneva Conservatory. His prolific compositions follow the traditions of the Schola Cantorum, while some of his great religious works express his Calvinist beliefs. In addition, we should mention the Genevan, Jean Duperier, author of the opera *Le Malade Imaginaire*, after Molière; Alexandre Mottu and Fernande Peyrot from Lausanne; the fine and delicate Jean Binet (1893-1960), and Aloïs Fornerod. One of Switzerland's important contributions to world music was the distinguished conductor Ernest Ansermet (1883-1969), who founded the famous Suisse Romande Orchestra in 1918. During his fifty years as a conductor he played a major role in introducing new music to the concert halls of the world.

German Switzerland

Willy Burkhardt (1900-55), abrupt and austere by nature, profoundly religious and a powerful and complex contrapuntist, symbolises perfectly the severe and serious side of German music. His fragile health and comparatively early death did not prevent him from writing a hundred works, dominated by two fine oratorios, *The Vision of Isaiah* and *The Year*, and by his opera *The Black Spider* (1948). His choral and religious works are particularly abundant. His instrumental works, no less numerous, include three symphonies, numerous concertos, chamber music and piano pieces.

Conrad Beck (b. 1901), although typically Germanic in temperament, has turned to France for inspiration. He lived in Paris during his twenties and early thirties, studying under Nadia Boulanger and receiving advice from Arthur Honneger, whom he considered, with Ravel, as his mentor. He has put his hand to every sort of music except opera. His language, essentially linear and contrapuntal, is robust and sober and is within the orbit of Hindemith, although lightened by Beck's admiration for French music. The two peaks of his musical achievement are two great oratorios; the first, composed in 1936, is to words by Angelus Silesius, a 17th-century German mystic; the second (1952), *Der Tod zu Basel*, subtitled *A Great Miserere*, was inspired by late medieval representations of the Dance of Death. He has also written some fine cantatas to words by Rilke. Beck's orchestral works comprise a number of symphonies and concertos. The first five symphonies, written prior to 1931, are particularly concise in a Neoclassical linear style. The sixth (1950), Romantic in inspiration, is sombre and tormented, but opposed to it we have the freshness of the seventh (1959), dedicated to the memory of Aeneas Silvius, the Renaissance humanist (and pope as Pius II) and founder of the University of Basel. Among Beck's other orchestral works, particular mention should be made of his sym-

The ballet Arbres de Mai *at the* Fête des Vignerons *in Vevey.*

phonic poem, *Innominata* (1931). This was inspired by the very difficult ascent of Mont Blanc on the Italian side, which Beck, a passionately addicted mountaineer, was the first to make. His vast output of chamber music includes four quartets, two string trios, and a number of sonatas and sonatinas for various instruments.

Walther Geiser (b. 1897), who also lived in Basel, was a pupil of Busoni, whose Neo-classical ideals he has perpetuated in four orchestral fantasias and a symphony. Albert Moeschinger (b. 1897), also from Basel, was brought up in Germany, but perhaps he owes the asperity and vigour of his musical style to the setting of the Valaise Alps where he has lived in retirement since 1943. His works include five symphonies and a number of concertos. Robert Oboussier (1900–57) divided his studies and career between France and Germany. His musical output was comparatively small but very polished, and comprises *Antigone*, for contralto and orchestra (1939), the opera *Amphitryon*, after Molière

and Kleist (1949), one symphony, two concertos, and *Musique de Deuil* (Mourning Music) for orchestra.

Vladimir Vogel (b. 1896) although Russian by origin, has lived in Switzerland for over thirty years and is a naturalised Swiss. A pupil of Busoni, he has nevertheless a passionately inquiring mind which led him, in the 1950s, to adopt serial techniques. His broad humanism and bold libertarian spirit find expression in his master work, the colossal oratorio *Thyl Claes*, based on the *Légende d'Uylenspiegel* by Charles de Coster, which was composed between the years 1937 and 1945, and which which requires two evenings to perform.

right
Conrad Beck.

below
Frank Martin.

Frank Martin

Undoubtedly the greatest Swiss composer is Frank Martin (1890–1974). This Calvinist from Geneva and pupil of Lauber lived in Amsterdam from 1946. More so than any of his compatriots, he bestrides both the Latin and Germanic worlds. First influenced by Franck and Fauré and later by Ravel, he passed through a period of serialism and the Expressionism of Berg and Schoenberg to arrive finally at a purely personal style. Few other composers in the history of music have shown such an example of late development. Martin's world-wide reputation dates from the late 1930s. His works since that period constitute more than half his relatively small oeuvre. His works prior to 1938 are the results of a long and often painful search towards self-knowledge. In particular among these should be noted *Rhythms*, three symphonic movements; the violin and piano sonata; the piano concerto; the twelve-note string trio; and the symphony, in which the instrumentation shows Martin's predilection for jazz.

In 1938, Martin began to compose the secular cantata *Le Vin Herbé*, for twelve voices, seven instruments and piano, based on Joseph Bédier's version of the Tristan story. At this time he had suffered a tragic personal bereavement and he was obviously deeply inspired by the subject itself. Certainly it was a critical point in his career; for the first time Martin emerges as a composer with a truly individual and indeed masterly style. In effect *Le Vin Herbé*, which he only completed in 1941, is the real key to his work. It reveals a serious, meditative and even tortured character. A synthesis of Impressionist harmonies, obviously indebted to Ravel and Viennese atonal chromaticism, produced a harmonic language which is extraordinarily subtle and expressive. Martin excels in nuances of orchestral colour, and his musical palette is perfectly suited to giving life to impalpable concepts and fantasy. But he is equally capable of expressing a tragic vehemence, and of showing an epic quality necessary to the construction of immense choral and religious works.

Everything he produced since *Le Vin Herbé* is of great excellence. His work includes the five *Ballades Concertantes* (1938–50); *Le Cornette* (1942–43), a great song cycle based on poems by Rainer Maria Rilke; and the six profoundly moving monologues of *Everyman* (1944) with Hofmannsthal's famous text. His admirable *Passacaille* for organ (1944), transcribed for strings and later for full orchestra, was succeeded by the oratorio *In Terra Pax*, written to celebrate the end of the war. This same year (1944) saw the birth of a masterpiece which did more than anything else to secure Martin's reputation. This was the *Petite Symphonie Concertante* for piano, harpsichord, harp and two string ensembles, commissioned by the conductor Paul Sacher. After this, Martin continued his search for a more refined new instrumental colour in the concerto for seven wind instruments, percussion and strings (1949), and in the concertos for violin (1951) and harpsichord (1952).

During this period he was also working on his great oratorio *Golgotha*, completed in 1948, perhaps the only modern Passion to take its place besides those of J. S. Bach. He then composed eight piano *Preludes* (1948), one of the finest cycles since Debussy and Fauré. Between 1952 and 1955 he wrote his first opera, *The Tempest*. The libretto is based on Schlegel's German translation of Shakespeare's play, and Martin's score contains the fine and well-known settings of the *Five Songs of Ariel*. Two *Etudes* for strings and two overtures

lead us to *The Mystery of the Nativity* (1959), a grandiose conception which forms a pendant to *Golgotha*, and has a remarkable and almost medieval mystic fervour. After so many grave and intimate works, Martin gave free rein to his humour with his comic opera *Monsieur de Pourceagnac* (1962), which faithfully follows Molière's text. *Les Quatre Eléments*, an orchestral suite, was written in 1964.

In the figure of Frank Martin, Switzerland gave the world one of the finest composers on the international scene.

Ernest Ansermet.

Music in Belgium and the Netherlands

The modern Belgian school comprises both Flemish music, influenced by German culture, and Walloon music, essentially Latin in character.

César Franck was of Belgian origin but quite apart from the fact that he was a naturalised Frenchman, every aspect of his career makes him unquestionably a member of the French school. Yet there was no lack of brilliance in the musical life of Belgium in the 19th century; the Théâtre Royal de la Monnaie in Brussels dates from 1700, and by 1900 it had assumed international importance. However, until the 1870s, Belgium was richer in scholars and musical executants than in creative artists. François Joseph Fétis (1784-1871) and Auguste Gevaert (1828-1908), both important as scholars and pedagogues, were the only composers of any note.

The great Belgian school of violinists was established in the 19th century by Charles de Bériot (1802-70), a pupil of Viotti. Henri Vieuxtemps (1820-81), an infant prodigy who started on world tours at the age of thirteen, was Bériot's greatest disciple. A better composer than his master, he deserves to be remembered for the fourth and fifth of his seven concertos. His pupil, Eugène Ysaÿe (1858-1931), who also studied with the Polish violinist Wieniawski, was certainly the greatest violinist of his period. His romantic temperament naturally attracted him to the school of César Franck, of whom he was the

interpreter and enthusiastic advocate, and he used his influence to introduce a number of French symphonic and vocal works to Brussels. He played most of Franck's masterpieces either as a soloist or as leader of the string quartet which he founded in 1892. His own compositions, which include six concertos, six violin sonatas, a symphonic poem for strings and a Walloon opera *Pier li Houyeu*, display a tormented, complex and tense chromatic style.

Guillaume Lekeu (1870-94) was the last of Franck's disciples. Although he died at twenty-four, his work shows an extraordinary depth of feeling, a profound and sad nostalgia as well as a wayward, exalted and fanciful temperament. His chromaticisms anticipate the early works of Schoenberg, but his music could also be joyous and fresh, as in the *Fantaisie sur deux thèmes angevins*—his most complete score. His symphonic study *Ophélie* is a marvellously poetic work, while the heart-breaking *Adagio for strings*, the violin sonata and the unfinished piano quartet are all outstanding.

Joseph Jongen (1873-1953), the leading figure in Belgian music in the first half of the 20th century, has been called the spiritual successor of César Franck. His *Symphonie concertante* with organ (1926) is of tremendous intensity and is his major work, but he also composed many other orchestral works, an immense amount

The Belgian composer François Auguste Gevaert.

of chamber music, songs and sacred pieces including a mass for choirs, brass and organ.

Lesser composers of a traditional stamp were Victor Vreuls (1876-1944), a pupil of Vincent d'Indy, who was attracted to the stage, and his co-disciple Albert Dupuis among whose vast output were eleven operas.

The birth of the Flemish school

During this time, Flanders tried to evolve a music which was expressive of the national temperament, and a strong movement arose for the development of a truly homogeneous Flemish culture with no division between an intellectual élite and the community at large. It fell to Peter Benoit (1834-1901) to found a national Flemish school of music. Benoit devoted all his life to the service of his people and established a musical academy at Antwerp where, for the first time, instruction was given in Flemish. In 1889, his academy was raised to the official status of a 'royal conservatory'. Benoit was a conscientious nationalist who believed that music should be the faithful expression of a people. Although he is much respected in Flanders his music now seems old-fashioned and is perhaps of little more than local interest. His use of unison and huge orchestral effects and his rather grandiloquent Romanticism are all deliberately popular in style. Among his immediate successors was Jan Blockx (1851-1912), whose lyricism and musical language is more subtle. Blockx's best music was written for the stage and, among his operas, *Princesse d'auberge* and *La Fiancée de la mer* are still regularly performed. Edgar Tinel (1854-1912), a pupil of Gevaert, devoted himself to sacred music, developing a Roman Catholic equivalent of the oratorio so popular in 19th-century Protestant Germany; his finest works were *Franciscus*, a music drama *Godelieve* and the dramatic legend *Katharina*.

The Brussels-born Paul Gilson (1865-1942) was a composer, theoretician and eminent teacher who had a very considerable influence. He himself was much impressed by the concerts given in about 1884 by the Russian composers of the 'Five', and to them he owes his sparkling orchestral colour. His healthy, vigorous and richly textured work comprises the symphonic sketches *La Mer*, a dramatic cantata *Francesco da Rimini*, *Variations symphoniques* and the opera *Prinses Zonneschijn* and *Gens de mer*.

Auguste de Boeck (1865-1937) became known in 1893 with his *Rhapsodie Dahomienne*, a highly coloured symphonic work; his G minor symphony dates from the same year and reveals Russian influences. His sensuous, generous and tender nature is reflected in his songs, piano pieces and delightful children's choruses and particularly in his operas, which include one on the story of Reynard the Fox. Another important Flemish musician of this generation was Lodewijk (Louis) Mortelmans (1868-1952), born in Antwerp, and a pupil of Benoit and Blockx. He was a fervent and introspective artist, an *intimiste*, whom Gilson rightly described as the 'prince of the Flemish *Lied*'.

Flor Alpaerts (1876-1954) from Antwerp, a pupil of Blockx, was inspired by Gilson's florid orchestration, and even more by Richard Strauss. Thoroughly Flemish both by temperament and in the choice of his subjects, he composed a number of symphonic works, among which the most remarkable are the tone poem *Pallieter*, based on a work by the Flemish novelist Felix Timmermans, and, in particular, the *James Ensor Suite*, inspired by the fantasy world of the Belgian painter.

The music of Tinel's pupil Arthur Meulemans (b. 1884) reveals a richly imaginative composer in a post-

Impressionist manner owed to Ravel and heightened by an orchestral technique of the highest order. Primarily a symphonist, Meulemans wrote fifteen symphonies between 1931 and 1959, of which three include choirs. In addition he has produced some fifty orchestral works of different sorts and forty concertos, and has composed some thirty chamber works, while his songs and choral compositions run into hundreds.

The Walloons

Jean Absil (b. 1893), a native of Hainaut, was a pupil of Paul Gilson and assumed the mantle of his master as the leader of young talent. A subtle but bold harmonist, Absil employs an original, lively and concise atonal

style, with brilliant instrumental decoration, entirely Latin in feeling. Until 1945, his music was constructed on grand classic lines, culminating with his second and third symphonies (1936 and 1943), the symphonic variations and his concertos for violin, for viola and, in particular, for piano (1937). His chamber music comprises four string quartets, a remarkable quartet for piano, two string trios and quintets. After 1945, Absil showed a marked preference for freer forms deriving from rhapsodies and variations. A predilection for folk music became more evident; he is often inspired by Bulgarian and Rumanian themes, whose rhythms fascinate him. His major works are the great cantata *Benedictions* (1940); *Le Zodiaque* (1949), a symphonic cantata in the form of variations; several works for the theatre including an opera, and the vast *Peter Breughel the Elder* (1950) for radio.

In the 1920s some pupils of Gilson, both Flemish and Walloon, formed the *Synthétiste* group, following the Parisian example of the 'Six'. The oldest member, Francis de Bourguignon (1890-1961), of French descent, lived an adventurous life in his youth as an itinerant pianist, and it was not until 1925 that he settled in Brussels and devoted himself to composing music in a clear, lively and subtle style, which owes something to Ravel. Gaston Brenta (b. 1902) has a preference for sharper harmonies, but his inspiration also blossoms into wide melodic phrasing and generous lyricism. Two of his most important dramatic works, *Aucassin and Nicolette* (1934) and *Héraklès* (1955), after Euripides, were specially written for broadcasting, but he has also written an opera, a ballet *Candide*, after Voltaire, a symphony and a piano concerto.

André Souris (b. 1899), an exceptionally intelligent and witty musician, has fought unremittingly in the cause of *avant-garde* music. His very limited production is dictated by clear-sightedness and pitiless self criticism. Some of his compositions are the works of a true surrealist, and sometimes he makes use of music of the past or Walloon folk music.

The tragic life of Albert Huybrechts (1899-1938), dominated by misery and ill health, is revealed in his anguished music. Its sincerity and intensity is reminiscent of Lekeu; but it is chromatic and polytonal and extremely complex. René Bernier (b. 1905), the youngest of the *Synthétistes*, is undoubtedly the most French of

above
Marcel Poot, one of the best-known Flemish composers of this century.

right
Flor Peeters, the distinguished Flemish organist.

all Belgian composers. Fauré and Ravel are the inspiration for this melodious, delicate composer who belongs to the tradition of modal music.

Leaving the *Synthétistes*, we come to Raymond Chevreuil (b. 1901), the Belgian composer closest to Absil. Full of verve, prolific at the risk of uneven quality, Chevreuil remains an independent, using tonal, atonal and polytonal techniques. His freedom of expression is indicative of a self-taught composer, and it assures him of a constantly youthful outlook and great variety. He has written six symphonies, the second of which is choral. The tragic and violent mood of the large-scale third symphony (1951) is in contrast with the freshness of the *Symphonie printanière* (1954). We must also mention the vigorous *Concerto pour orchestre* and some ten concertos.

August Baeyens (b. 1890) was the first to make a radical break with the Romanticism of his predecessors, and this is obvious in his eight symphonies (1923-61), as well as in recent concertos, five quartets and two operas.

Marcel Poot (b. 1901), director of the Brussels conservatory and formerly a *Synthétiste*, is the Flemish composer best known abroad. He is very much a compatriot of Breughel, with the same sort of truculence and straightforward vitality as the great painter. His *Ouverture Joyeuse* (1934) and *Allegro symphonique* (1935) have been universally acclaimed. However, he has written more important works of greater depth: three symphonies, a string quartet (1952), an octet (1948), an oratorio, *Icarus* (1945) and an opera, *Moretus* (1943). Belonging to the same generation are Flor Peeters (b. 1903), the eminent organist, director of the Antwerp conservatory and composer of innumerable liturgical works, chorales, and important organ works; and Daniel Sternefeld (b. 1905), a pupil of Gilson and an indefatigable advocate of contemporary music. The last of this generation is Louis de Meester (b. 1904), who spent his youth in Morocco and completed his musical education with Absil. A bold and vivacious composer, he is also capable of a cutting irony and a high degree of concentration. The middle generation was represented by the Expressionist Jef van Durme (1907-65), a pupil of Alban Berg and Scherchen and the first of the Belgian twelve-note composers.

Holland

After Sweelinck the Netherlands produced practically no composers for three hundred years. But the 20th century has seen the birth of a flourishing school who, in reacting against the strong German influence of the 19th century, accepted the hegemony of French music; indeed, perhaps nowhere else in the world has Debussy had such a wide and enthusiastic audience. Bernard Zweers (1854-1924), although he received his musical education at Leipzig, was the first Dutch composer to make a bid for an independent nationalist style, at least in the choice of his subjects, and his third symphony, *To my Country* (1890), marks a milestone in this direction.

Alphons Diepenbrock (1862-1921) was the first great Dutch composer since Sweelinck, who lived exactly three hundred years previously (1562-1621). Diepenbrock, a devout Christian, expressed his faith in large-scale works where Wagnerian harmonies are curiously mixed with a very free melodic line based on Gregorian plain-song. After his discovery of Debussy, which came as a revelation, the Wagnerian influence gradually disappeared, to be replaced by a refined Impressionism. The German 'poets of the night' – Novalis, Hölderlin and Nietzsche – inspired many *Lieder* with orchestral accompaniment, although Diepenbrock preferred the more intimate type of song with piano accompaniment

for his settings of Baudelaire, Verlaine and Laforgue. The most important scores in his last manner were written for the stage and are very obviously influenced by Debussy in style: *Marsyas*, *Les Oiseaux*, after Aristophanes, *Faust* and *Elektra*, after Sophocles.

Johann Wagenaar (1862-1941) was of quite a different temperament, a realist, a *bon vivant*, humorous but at the same time an eminent pedagogue. His best works for the orchestra are his overtures *Cyrano de Bergerac* and *The Taming of the Shrew*, the symphonic poem *Saul and David*, inspired by a painting by Rembrandt, and the *Sinfonietta*.

To the same generation belongs the Germanist Peter van Anrooy (1879-1954), composer of a brilliant rhapsody for orchestra, *Piet Hein*, inspired by popular folklore, and Willem Landré (1874-1948), the descendant of an old Huguenot family and a devotee of Debussy. The work of this elegaic composer culminated in the lovely Requiem written in memory of his wife.

After 1914 four important musicians took the decisive step of putting Dutch music in touch with European developments. Henri Zagwijn (1878-1954), the biographer of Debussy, was a partisan of atonal techniques, polytonality and polyrhythms, which he expressed in an esoteric manner. Sem Dresden (1881-1957) was a much more prolific composer, turning constantly towards France from his very first chamber works right up to his posthumously performed opera *François Villon*. He wrote a great deal of chamber music and some beautiful unaccompanied choruses, but at the end of his life he

Alphons Diepenbrock, the first major composer fom the Netherlands since the death of Sweelinck.

enlarged his scope with a series of concertos and some fine works for chorus and orchestra.

Daniel Fuyneman (1886-1963) was an indefatigable promoter and advocate of all *avant-garde* music. In 1918, his *Hiéroglyphes* for three flutes, celeste, harp, piano, two mandolins, two guitars and special bells (replaced today by the vibraphone) anticipated the world of sound of the young musicians of today. In *Appel* and in his sonata for chorus and chamber orchestra (1931), he extended the voice parts by including them in his bold research into sound colour. During the following period, he employed a constructive linear style, which he gradually expanded. His work terminated with the series entitled *Reflexion I–IV* for various combinations

Hendrik Andriessen, Dutch Catholic composer of religious music.

of instruments in strictly serial style (1959-62).

In comparison with these advanced musicians, the eminent musicologist Bernard van den Sigtenhorst-Meyer (1888-1953), a specialist on Sweelinck, appears a very traditional composer.

Pijper

The genius of Willem Pijper (1894-1947) dominates all modern Dutch music. Like many of his contemporaries he fell much under the influence of Mahler, notably in his first symphony, *Pan* (1917). It was not long before Debussy's influence superimposed itself and Pijper created a harmonious synthesis of these two, so dissimilar, masters. But at the same time he evolved a revolutionary polytonal and polyrhythmic language founded on the use of brief melodic and rhythmic 'cells', from which springs the organic growth of the work. He reached his most audacious period between about 1923 and 1933, after which his polytonality became gentler and his teaching work restricted his output. His later music has brevity and stylistic perfection to commend it. Pijper was a strict Calvinist, but he shows an exceptionally elegant sensuousness in his music, expressed in exotic rhythms (particularly the tango) and glittering harmonies.

He wrote three symphonies of which the third (1926), dedicated to Pierre Monteux who performed it all over the world, remains the masterpiece of modern Dutch music. Six movements, lasting in all only fifteen minutes, are played without a break by a small orchestra of ten players (with piano and mandolin); the violent changes are worthy of Stravinsky's *Rite of Spring* yet are extremely subtle. A similar style is followed with great brilliance in the one-movement piano concerto (1927) and in the *Six épigrammes symphoniques* (1928), written with a conciseness reminiscent of Webern. His last period gave birth to the concerto for violin and cello and the *Six Adagios for orchestra*.

Pijper also wrote the operas *Halewijn*, preceded by a choral version, and *Merlijn*, which remained unfinished, as well as stage music. His chamber music comprises twenty compositions, from duets to septets; particularly notable are his five string quartets of which the last was left unfinished.

Hendrik Andriessen (b. 1892) is a Roman Catholic and a prolific composer of sacred music (numerous masses and a Te Deum), in which he seeks for truly medieval simplicity. He is a traditionalist; his art springs from the organ music of César Franck, whom he followed with four chorales, a sonata and various other pieces. But he is by no means cut off from new forms, nor from secular music: his bold piano sonata and his opera *Philomèle* are evidence of this, and in his last works he often uses serial structures.

Four names stand out from musicians born at the beginning of this century. Guillaume Landré (b. 1905), son of Willem Landré, studied composition with Pijper. At an early date he was fascinated by Debussy and Ravel. However, he found his own road in 1936 with his suite for piano and strings. While remaining faithful to Pijper's thematic 'cells' (to which, in the 1950s, he was to add the twelve-note scale), he enlarged his melodic range in a very moving manner with elegaic and even funerary undertones. In addition to his four symphonies he wrote the *Sinfonia sacra in memoriam patris* (1948). He has written some very original orchestral scores based on the principle of thematic metamorphoses: *Kaleidoscope* (1956), *Permutazioni Sinfoniche* (1957) and *Anagrammes* (1960). His chamber music includes four string quartets.

Badings and his contemporaries

Henk Badings, born in 1907 in Indonesia, studied composition with Pijper. With the latter, he is the Dutch composer best known internationally. None of his colleagues have achieved such fecundity, and in this he reminds one of Milhaud. By temperament Neo-classical and indebted to Brahms, Reger and Hindemith, Badings contributes his own individual style by his vigour and freshness of expression and by the really powerful architectural structure of his music. His great symphonies, moreover, possess strikingly original and memorable themes. From the middle 1950s he was Holland's pioneer in the field of electronic music. Of his twelve concertos, the concerto for two violins (1954) is one of the masterpieces of contemporary Dutch music. Badings has written seven piano sonatas and numerous chamber works; his vocal music includes songs and choral works some on religious themes. He has also written operas – *Rembrandt, Martin Korda* (1960) – music for various plays, and an 'electronic' ballet, *Cain and Abel* (1956).

The major work by Bertus van Lier (b. 1906), a pupil of Pijper and Hermann Scherchen, is the *Cantique de Cantique*, for soloists, chorus and small orchestra. But he has also written a ballet, *Katharsis* (1945), three symphonies, concertos, and choral and chamber music.

It is only recently that Kees van Baaren (b. 1906) has been recognised as one of the most important Dutch composers. This pupil of Pijper, who during a visit to Berlin made the acquaintance of Schoenberg and Berg, was the first Dutch composer to become actively interested in serial music. His septet of 1952 is the first important Dutch work to be written entirely in this style. Since then, each new composition has been a milestone in his career: *Sinfonia, Variations for orchestra*, and two string quartets (*Sovraposizioni II*, 1963).

Escher, Henkemans, Flothuis and Van Delden are the most remarkable composers of the next generation. Although the first two were students of Pijper, the others are self taught.

Rudolf Escher (b. 1912) made his name in 1946 with his *Music for a Soul in Mourning* for orchestra, which has a noble and generous lyric quality, both elegaic and dream-like. Although belonging to the thematic 'cellular' school of Pijper, he has developed an ample poly-melodic style. However, he shows a distinct affinity with the art of Ravel, to whom he has paid magnificent homage with his suite *Tombeau de Ravel* for flute, oboe, string trio and harpsichord. He has also written two symphonies, in the second of which he embarks for the first time on serial technique.

Hans Henkemans (b. 1913) is famous as a pianist and as an excellent interpreter of Mozart and Debussy. His best known composition is his *Passacaglia and Gigue* for piano and orchestra (1942), but he has also composed a series of concertos, sonatas and a remarkable *Partita* for orchestra (1960).

For Marius Flothuis (b. 1914) Mozart is the prime inspiration. A lyric and *intimiste* composer, he is particularly attracted by the use of quite small groups of instrumentalists. He is one of the most delicate and unassuming of the Dutch composers. He has written some excellent concertos as well as several works for the harp and a quantity of chamber music. His production is dominated by two more profound works: the string quartet and his *Symphonic music* for large orchestra.

Guillaume Landré, Dutch composer of outstanding orchestral music.

Music in the Balkan countries

It is only in the 20th century that the peoples of this troubled and long-subjugated area of Europe have achieved statehood. In the middle ages Montenegro and Serbia, two of the constituent republics of modern Yugoslavia, had both been powerful and independent states, while Greece had been one of the central provinces of the Byzantine empire. But, during the 15th century, the Turkish advance had obliterated the ancient Christian empire and its client states in the Balkans, and for four hundred years they had been subject to the rule of an alien race and an alien religion. The traces of this period are still very much apparent in both the art and the music of the region, and we have seen, in the chapter on European folk music, the way in which elements of Turkish and Arab music are still to be found in modern Balkan folk music. For if this long age of cultural subjection handicapped the development of strong native traditions of art music in the area, its folk music is probably the richest and least corrupted in Europe. In this chapter we shall be mainly concerned with the musical traditions of Greece, Rumania and Yugoslavia, all of whom, and especially the first two, have produced composers of considerable stature. But first we should notice that Bulgaria, although not so advanced musically as these countries, has rich potentialities.

The liturgical music of the Bulgarian Church is one of the richest of the Orthodox community, and the variety and originality of Bulgarian folk music greatly impressed Bartók when he visited this country during his years as an ethnomusicologist. In common with other folk music traditions of the area, that of Bulgaria betrays marked oriental and Turkish influence in its melodic structure. But here this influence has also made itself felt on the rhythms of the music, and as a consequence there are a number of unequal rhythms in Bulgarian folk music. Thus, what in the West might be considered, should it ever occur, as a measure of seven beats in the bar (until recently a very unusual measure), is treated by the Bulgarian folk musician as one bar of three beats and two bars of two beats, and would not be found at all out

A Ukrainian orchestra of bandouras.

of the ordinary. Indeed measures of five, seven, nine or eleven beats are quite common.

But the most significant composers from the Balkans up to the mid-1960s have been the Greeks, Skalkottas and Xenakis, and our account of Greek music occupies the final section of this chapter. First we shall consider developments in Yugoslavia.

Yugoslavia

Yugoslavia was constituted as a country only at the end of the First World War, by the union of three peoples, admittedly closely related ethnically but with very different histories. The Catholic Slovenes and Croatians were in touch with European music as members of the Austrian empire. The Serbs, on the contrary, who were only freed from the Turkish yoke at the beginning of the 19th century, belonged to the Orthodox Church and looked eastwards. Like all Balkan countries, however, the three states of Yugoslavia all possess an extraordinarily rich, brilliant and colourful folk music, charged with bold and complex rhythms. The whirling *kolo* is the national dance. This folk music has been the source of inspiration for Yugoslav composers, though the younger ones have broken away more and more to join the ranks of the international *avant-garde*.

Slovenia, situated in the northwest corner of the country, and at that time part of the kingdom of Bohemia, gave the world one of the great 16th-century composers in the person of Jacobus Gallus (Jacob Handl). Davorin Jenko (1835-1914) is considered as the founder of Slovene national music; Risto Savin (1859-1948) created a national tradition of opera; Gojmir Krek (1875-1942) introduced new international trends into the country at the beginning of the century; while Marij Kogoj (1895-1956) followed in the path of the early Schoenberg. Slavko Osterc (1895-1941), a disciple of Schoenberg and the Czech Alois Hába, threw himself boldly into the total use of chromaticism, atonality and athematic music, and the symphonies of Lucijan-Maria Skerjanc (b. 1900) reveal the influence of his teacher d'Indy and the French Impressionist composers.

The Croatian school has its capital at Zagreb, which was already a musical centre during the 18th century. Indeed Zagreb has become established as the cultural capital of Yugoslavia itself. It possesses a flourishing conservatory, an orchestra famous for its conductors and a first-class ballet and opera company. Its Biennale, founded in 1961, is one of the most important international festivals of contemporary music.

In the Romantic period, Vatroslav Lisniski (1819-54) was the founder-father of Croatian opera. He was followed by the prolific Ivan Zajc (1832-1914), a composer of more than 1,200 works, and by Franjo Kuhac (1830-1911), the ethnologist and expert on folk music. 20th-century Croatian composers display a common enough division between the national 'folklorists' – Josip Slavenski (1896-1955), a pupil of Kodály, Jakov Gotovac (b. 1895), a conductor who has also composed operas, incidental theatre music, symphonic poems and an orchestral *Kolo*, Kresimir Baranovic (b. 1894), a well-known conductor and composer of ballets and operas— and the cosmopolitan 'modernists'. These include Blagoje Bersa (1873-1934), Boris Papandopoulo (b. 1906), the author of a remarkable *Sinfonietta* for strings, and Albe Vidakovic (b. 1914), the Rumanian-educated composer of polyphonic church music and organist. The most important of this group is the Neo-classicist Stevan Sulek (b. 1914). Since 1945 he has written four symphonies, three concertos and other works, and is the teacher of many young composers. Among the best of

A folk dance in Yugoslavia.

these is Milko Kelemen (b. 1924), who is considered one of the leading lights of present-day *avant-garde* European music.

Kelemen was influenced by Bartók in his youthful period, and was also a pupil of Messiaen in Paris and later of Fortner in Germany. His development as a composer has led him away from the folk idiom towards a post-serial style of the most advanced kind. A man of dynamic personality, professor at the Zagreb Conservatory and founder of the Biennale mentioned above (which has familiarised the Yugoslav public with modern international music), he has established himself as the leading musical figure of his country. He is also an important composer.

During the 19th century, Serbia was again an independent kingdom. The formation of the Belgrade symphony orchestra in 1899, of the opera and the Academy of Music after 1918, and finally of the Institute of Musicology (1945), were important dates in the musical history of modern Serbia. The first composers devoted their talents chiefly to liturgical works and to arrangements of folk songs and operas of a popular character. Among their successors, whose Impressionism and Expressionism was influenced by Mussorgsky and Richard Strauss, particular mention must be made of Peter Konjovic (b. 1883), a prolific composer of all genres and author of four operas, and Stevan Hristic (b. 1885), who owes his fame in particular to his nationalist ballet *The Legend of Ochrida*. Young Serbian composers working today include Vlastimir Pericic (b. 1927) and D. Radjic (b. 1929).

Rumania

A Latin people, the Rumanians have always been in close contact with their neighbours, the Slavs. They adopted Orthodox Christianity through the agency of Byzantium, and for many centuries were under Turkish rule.

If, in addition, we take into account the presence in Transylvania of important Magyar and German minorities, and the large gipsy population throughout the country, we obtain a picture of a medley of races probably unique in Europe.

One result is that Rumania can boast one of the richest, largest and most varied traditions of folk music in all Europe. Turko-Arab influence is evident in the long drawn out melismas of the *doinas*, songs in a free 6/8 time which express love or mourning. The violin bands, the *lautari*, sometimes achieve an astonishing ingenuity in improvisation – indeed they staggered Liszt. But the true Rumanian national instrument is the *nai*, or panpipe, whose performers reach a degree of virtuosity that is hardly credible.

Complete independence for Rumania was obtained only in 1860. Thereafter a national school of music began to develop, first in the field of religious music, with the work of such composers as George Muzicescu (1847-1903). Secular music was still largely imported from Austria and Italy. Philharmonic societies had already been established at Bucharest (1834) and Jassy (1835), and by 1870 conservatories had been opened in these two centres.

The first Rumanian composers with a Western training were Adolf Flechtenmacher (1823-98), who composed *Baba Hirca* (the national anthem) as well as the first Rumanian operetta, based on folk themes; and Edward Caudella (1841-1923), of Italian extraction, a virtuoso violinist and pupil of Vieuxtemps, who wrote the popular opera *Olteanca* (which was a definite advance on Flechtenmacher's) and the grand opera *Petru Raresch*. George Stefanescu founded a permanent opera company which sang in Rumanian, and as a composer produced an operetta and the first Rumanian symphony.

Demetri Kiriac (1866-1928), a pupil of d'Indy and a professor at the Schola Cantorum in Paris, made arrangements of folk tunes and composed a large amount of religious music, while the study of folk music received great impetus in 1928 with the foundation of the Phonographic Archives, based on the researches of Béla

A Rumanian panpiper.

Bartók. In Transylvania, previously part of Hungary, the archives initiated by the Rumanian government and under the original direction of Professor G. Breazul, now include many thousands of classified recordings of folk music. Rumania also gave the world one of the greatest ethnologists and experts on folk music in Constantin Brăiloiu (1893-1960).

In the meanwhile, the genius of George Enesco (1881-1955) was developing, and he was soon to become for his country what Bartók was for Hungary. A great humanist and complete artist, a conductor, violinist, pianist and eminent interpreter of Bach, he showed such precocious and brilliant gifts as a youth that he was sent to the conservatory at Vienna, where he made the acquaintance of Brahms. Very soon, however, Enesco left for Paris where he joined the classes of Gédalge and Gabriel Fauré. Already his mastery as a composer was evident and his *Poème roumaine*, written when he was sixteen, received a public performance. Henceforth, Enesco was to spend the greater part of his life in Paris, where he died. Among his pupils were the violinist Yehudi Menuhin and the Rumanian pianist Dinu Lipatti.

The multiplicity of Enesco's artistic activities limited his production to thirty-three works. True to the first sources of his inspiration, Brahms and Reger, he remained a classicist in style, while the mood of his music is tinged with Romanticism. Nevertheless, what might be called a sublimated Rumanian folk music colours all his work. Its language is completely original and profoundly poetic and sometimes produces extremely audacious harmonies.

The keystone of his work is the noble opera, *Oedipe*, produced at the Paris Opera in 1936, and the fruit of fifteen years' work (1917-32). The tragic horror of the third act and the grandiose serenity of the fourth are worthy of Sophocles' tragedy, while the echoes of Rumanian folk song convey an impression of earthy and brotherly warmth under a clear sky. Enesco also wrote three symphonies, three orchestral suites, an *Ouverture concertante*, a *Symphonie de chambre* for twelve solo instruments (his last work), and two popular early

works, *Rhapsodies roumaines*. His chamber music includes three sonatas for violin and piano, of which the third 'in popular Rumanian style', is undoubtedly the finest one.

Stan Golestan (1875-1956) was the pupil of d'Indy, Roussel and Dukas. A Parisian by adoption, he introduced the folk music of his native country into the academic architecture of his concertos, quartets and symphonies. His compositions include *Rhapsodie roumaine*, a 'Rumanian' concerto for violin, and a 'Moldavian' concerto for cello.

Among the chief composers active in Rumania in the inter-war years were the intensely nationalistic Michel Audrico (b. 1894) and Alfred Alessandrescu (b. 1893), a student of d'Indy at the Schola Cantorum in Paris and composer of the symphonic poem *Acteon*, which reflects

left
Portrait of George Enesco.

below
A scene from George Enesco's opera Oedipe *on the stage of the Opera and Ballet Theatre, Bucharest.*

Dinu Lipatti.

the influence of Dukas and Debussy.

Marcel Mihalovici (b. 1898) settled in Paris as a young man and later took French nationality. This fact however has not prevented this eminent member of the international school of Paris from remaining firmly attached to his native country. His compositions, well over a hundred in number, reflect the degree to which he has assimilated the lessons of his master d'Indy as well as those of Brahms and Reger. Mihalovici is the composer of solidly constructed and deeply considered music, in which elements of folk music happily correct a tendency to a too cerebral conciseness, though his chromaticism often leads to atonality. He has written several operas, including *Krapp, ou la Dernière Bande* (1962), based on Samuel Beckett's play *Krapp's Last Tape*, and several very original symphonies.

Filip Lazar (1894-1937) was also affiliated to the school of Paris. His compositions are in a contemporary European idiom but are imbued with the spirit of his native folk music. His work is vigorous and concise and possesses a noble simplicity.

Among the Rumanian composers working in Rumania itself, the dominant personality has been that of Paul Constantinesco (b. 1900), who has written choral works, symphonies, a liturgy, a ballet and the opera *Night of Torment*. The country has also produced some great interpretative artists with world-wide reputations, such as the conductors George Georgescu (b. 1889), Sergiu Celibidache (b. 1912) and Constantin Silvestri, and, above all, the pianist Dinu Lipatti (1917-50) who was also a fine composer and a pupil of Dukas and Nadia Boulanger.

Greece

During the four centuries of Turkish occupation, Greek musical life was confined to the Byzantine liturgy and folk music. The latter, which is very rich and interesting, consists of a synthesis of elements inherited from antiquity and others borrowed from the Orient and from the Turkish conquerors themselves. Its very unusual modal colour and rhythmic structure demand a wide range of instruments, which are as diverse as they are colourful, and, although its structure is basically monodic, there are also examples of a sort of primitive instrumental polyphony.

The foundation of the Athens Conservatory in 1871 marks the beginning of a musical florescence, but the first native Greek composers, members of the so-called Ionian school – like Nicolas Mantzaros (1795-1872), the author of the Greek national anthem, Paul Carrere (1829-96) and Spiros Samaras (1861-1917) – were in fact no more than imitators of the Italians. It was only after the First World War that a true Greek musical life began to develop in Athens. Among the many native composers who reached maturity during this period, two names are outstanding as the real founders of a national school. These are Manolis Kalomiris (1883-1962), who received his musical education in Vienna, and Petro Petridis (b. 1892), who studied with Roussel in Paris. Both have written many works in all fields, including music for the theatre, and the five symphonies by Petridis testify to a remarkable mastery of construction.

Skalkottas

It was the succeeding generation however which produced one of the greatest of all Greek composers – Nikos Skalkottas (1904-49). Nothing could be more extraordinary than his career. Precociously gifted, he was able to study in Germany thanks to a wealthy patron, and lived there from 1921 to 1933. First as a violinist and then as a composer, he studied with Jarnach and Kurt Weill, but mostly with Schoenberg, with whom he stayed for four years (1927-31). In 1933, when his name was already becoming well known in *avant-garde* circles, financial difficulties obliged him to return to Athens. From that time onwards until his premature death sixteen years later, he completely disappeared from active musical life and earned a living as a simple orchestral player. Henceforth he was to know nothing further of contemporary musical developments, since the repertoire of his orchestra was strictly traditional. Yet after his death some 150 compositions were found among his papers. They were of all types, and were of a quality that staggered even his most intimate friends. Most of these compositions were on a large scale and together they represent one of the most important musical achievements of our time. They are still being published.

With the exception of his charming arrangements of folk music, including the *Thirty-six Greek Dances* (1936), all Skalkottas' music is atonal. Between 1927 and 1938 he wrote in strict serial form, but thereafter more freely.

Skalkottas seems to have composed in successive waves, separated by periods of inactivity. His work has the same warmth and lyricism (and is often as sombre) as that of Alban Berg; sometimes it is as subtle and delicate as Webern; sometimes as rhythmical as Stravinsky or Bartók. But above all it has a truly Mediterranean clarity and lucidity, particularly in the twelve great symphonic works. These include a monumental symphony in one movement – originally planned as the overture to *The Return of Ulysses*, an opera which was in fact never written – and the giant second symphonic suite in six movements lasting an hour and a half (1943-49). Skalkottas left fourteen concertos – for violin, for cello, for violin and viola, for two violins and three for piano; a *Sinfonietta*; several chamber works and a mythological drama; ballets, *Death and the Maiden* (1938) and *La Mer* (1948); choral works, cantatas, songs, some fifty chamber works, numerous piano pieces and a treatise on orchestration. A society was founded in Athens to ensure that the works of this great recluse should become widely known.

Charilaos Perpessas (b. 1904), who has lived in the United States since 1948, is, like Skalkottas, a serial composer and a disciple of Schoenberg, whereas the prolific Jean Papaloannou (b. 1910), the author of four symphonies, symphonic poems, concertos, chamber music and songs, remains faithful to the tonal language and exploits the riches of Greek folk music explored by Kalomiris and Petridis. The young generation has produced several talented composers such as Yorgos Sicilianos (b. 1922); Manos Hadjidakis (b. 1925), an excellent composer of folk music for the bouzouki, who has attained fame as the author of the music for the film *Never on Sunday;* and Jani Christou (b. 1926), whose grand religious works and two symphonies reveal a profound and original talent. Of them all however, Mikis Theodorakis (b. 1925) is probably the best known outside Greece. A brilliant orchestrator, symphonist and vivid dramatic writer, he composed a song which became the rallying call of opposition to the military regime.

Greece, which has also given the world one of the best conductors of the 20th century in Dimitri Mitropoulos (1896-1960), an ardent advocate of contemporary music, shares a brilliant part in the international *avant-garde* movement thanks to the career of Yannis Xenakis and the work of Arghyris Koureadis (b. 1924), the author of five ballets, a *Sinfonietta*, several *concertante* works, chamber music, songs and piano pieces.

Yannis Xenakis

Born in 1922 Xenakis studied with Honegger, Milhaud and Messiaen in Paris, and at the same time studied architecture; for a long time he was assistant to Le Corbusier. His technical and mathematical training led him to master quickly the techniques of serial and electronic music, *musique concrète* and, finally, the so-called 'stochastic' technique of which he himself is a practitioner and whose use he advocates. This technique, which has limitless possibilities, is largely speculative and dependent on the element of chance.

He has said, 'If you wish to play with chance, learn the rules of the game, the scientific rule'. And similarly, in the mid-1950s, Xenakis also reacted against the trend in serialism: 'Linear polyphony is destroying itself with its present complexity. What we hear is in reality nothing but an accumulation of notes at varied registers. The enormous complexity prevents the listener from following the interweaving of lines, and has, as a macroscopic effect, an unreasoned and fortuitous dispersion of sounds throughout the whole range of the sonorous spectrum. There is, consequently, a contradiction between the linear polyphonic system and the heard result'.

It is a paradoxical fact that much of Xenakis' work, although it may be guided by a certain number of mathematical data, still appears to the ordinary listener as music – admittedly not a conventional music, but still one that is relatively clear to perceive and very striking. *Metastasis* (1955), *Pithoprakta* (1956), *Achorripsis* (1957) and the subsequent works are all the rather unexpected results of a creative effort which seems to incarnate itself quite naturally within a preliminary mathematical network.

Such a method has at times been misunderstood. It is not a question of composing with numbers but, after the elements of the language have been chosen, of establishing the criteria of qualitative and quantitative distribution which will permit the vastest and surest use of the chosen elements. To establish these criteria by statistical laws can be considered as valid a method as that which consisted in defining a sonorous scale and harmonic rules for the distribution of voices.

left
The Greek composer Nikos Skalkottas.

below
The Greek composer Mikis Theodorakis (right) talking to his lawyer in January 1968.

Music in Australia

During the 1930s and 1940s, Australian literature witnessed a move by some writers to draw on the language and thought-world of the Aborigines. Similar tendencies, though with a less doctrinaire intention, had occurred in Australian music more than a century earlier, though with what ineffective results we shall see in a later section. However, since the pioneering work of Sir Baldwin Spencer, who made a number of recordings of music from north and central Australia in the first decade of this century, and of E. H. Davies of Adelaide, from 1926, the work of a number of musicologists and anthropologists, chief among them A. P. Elkin, T. G. H. Strethlow, C. P. Mountford, Alice Moyle, Professor Trevor Jones and Dr Catherine Ellis, has done much to advance the study and preservation of this music.

Music of the Australian Aborigines

Although there are numerous points of difference between the various tribes, the music of the Aborigine has common cultural roots. Music is of central importance in Aboriginal religious and social life. It is affected by the totemism which colours all aspects of the society; members of a given clan, or moiety as it is called, tend to use only those songs whose subject is traditionally regarded as being related to their totem. As in all non-literate societies, poetry and song form a vital function in the transmission of the legends and traditions of the tribe, as well as in its dealings with the gods and spirits. In the first case the performance of the songs is entrusted to professionals who enjoy considerable prestige, but in the religious field the 'owner' of a sacred song, whose task, one of the most honourable of all, is to memorise a holy chant, may be chosen more for his tribal seniority than his musical ability. Since it is believed that only by the exact rendering of the age-old chant can contact be established with the supernatural, mistakes can be punished with severe penalties, sometimes even death. With such a responsibility on his shoulders, it is not surprising that the song owner sometimes delegates the actual performance of the chant to someone with special musical skill. In addition to this type of song, some of which may be accessible only to tribesmen who have achieved a certain hierarchical status, there are songs for entertainment which are more or less formally composed, and may take as their subject matter the gossip of the camp fire or the doings of the white man.

As to the actual nature of the music, a full account cannot yet be given. Nevertheless, researchers have found evidence of the use of various types of scales, including the pentatonic and a six-note scale (omitting

Aboriginal boys experimenting with a dijeridu.

the seventh degree of the diatonic scale); the use of a tonic note and of intervals smaller than the semitone. Among the intervals most commonly used is that of the minor third, and some sacred songs are confined entirely within this interval. Other songs have a far wider compass and may begin at a very loud volume, at the top of this compass from which a descending melodic line sung with ever decreasing volume continues to the end of the verse. Harmony, as such, is not used, but chance effects of two-part chords at the third, the fourth or the fifth have been heard, and in some cases the musicians themselves, delighted by these accidents, have attempted to prolong them.

Melodically Aboriginal music depends on the human voice, but its vigorous and often complicated rhythms are provided by a small group of instruments of which the famous dijeridu, clapper sticks and parts of the human body itself are the main members. Occasionally various types of rattle are also found. The dijeridu, consisting of an open wooden tube three or four feet in length, is sounded by blowing across one of the ends. Essentially, two notes are available, the fundamental and a harmonic usually about a tenth above it, though sometimes the player may produce a two-note chord by singing a note while playing another. Melodically then, the instrument is extremely limited, but as a rhythm instrument, in the hands of a skilled performer, it is capable of the most complex effects. The lower note is used to maintain a basic rhythm while the higher note is used for setting up counter-rhythms to it.

Even from this brief survey it is obvious that Aboriginal music is capable of both subtlety and complexity, and in the pattern of tribal life it is crucial. For all such reasons it is lamentable that, thanks to the eager work of earlier missionary workers, who in the place of this musical culture could only offer the most flaccid examples of European hymnody, and to the general decline of Aboriginal life, many tribal traditions have already been lost and the age-old music of Australia is doomed to extinction.

Traditional music

A body of songs rapidly sprang up out of the society bred by the penal settlements, out of the conditions of pioneering as the century advanced, and in the boom towns which grew from the gold rush of the 1850s. Many

Aboriginal corroboree dancers acting out the events of a kangaroo hunt.

such songs have easily identifiable antecedents in Irish, English or Scottish folk music, while others are related to songs spawned in the pioneering regions of the United States. In some cases they are by known authors, and for this type the term 'bush ballad' is sometimes used. Much research has been done in the whole field of popular music by such scholars as Rev. Dr Percy Jones, John Manifold and the American John Greenway.

The Australian version of a song found elsewhere has usually lost much of the melodic variety of its original; perhaps because of the use of the guitar and piano to provide harmonic accompaniments, and the tendency of unskilled performers to flatten out a melodic line to avoid awkward harmonies. Nevertheless, some of the early convict songs, such as *Jim Jones* and *Moreton Bay*, have words and music which are often powerful and

haunting, and the era offers a remarkable testimony to man's delight in, and need of, music. An eye-witness of a convict ship in 1827 observed how the prisoners did 'turn the jingling of their chains into music whereto they dance and sing'. As the 19th century advanced, Australia acquired its own style of lawlessness in the bush rangers who, by the time of Ned Kelly, could make claims as leaders of a populist revolt. They too contributed songs, often Irish in origin, of which the best known were *Bold Jack Donahue* and *The Wild Colonial Boy*.

These later examples, such as the Ben Hall songs and the Kelly ballads themselves, are less interesting musically. In the songs of the stockmen, shearers and other members of the pioneering community, the English tradition predominates and we find such examples as *The Banks of Condamine* (related to *Sweet Polly Oliver*)

Dame Nellie Melba of Melbourne, the first of a great succession of Australian operatic singers.

and the splendid *Queensland Drover*.

In this music as well as that of the gold rush towns served by professional entertainers, who incidentally also brought the tradition of the English music hall to new environments, we find parallels with American frontier society. At first this music was accompanied by concertina or accordion, which often simply doubled the melody line, though later, as we have seen, piano and guitar were used for harmonic backing. The confused ancestry of the most famous of all Australian popular songs offers an interesting example of the mixture of traditions and manners which lay behind them. The exact provenance of *Waltzing Matilda* is still disputed, yet it seems probable that it arose in the 1890s as an arranged version of the Scottish song *Craigielea* with the words provided, according to tradition, by A. B. 'Banjo' Paterson, the finest of the bush balladists.

The colonial period

The first European music to be heard in Australia was that of the military band, and the first compositions produced there were probably the 'Set of Quadrilles for Australia . . .', advertised in 1825 in the *Sydney Gazette* by Bandmaster Reichenberg. The almost desperate attempts of the exiles in Botany Bay to build a familiar life are most piquantly illustrated by the immense importation of pianos and the touching devotion with which the rough and hardy pioneers transported their drawing-room status symbol to the desolate, unwelcoming lands of the outback. The music, too, was for the drawing-room, and Sir Henry Bishop's *Home Sweet Home* spawned a numerous progeny of still more mediocre imitations. The worthy Bishop had another tie with Australia when his wife eloped with the fascinating French harpist, Nicholas Bochsa, who had fled to London to avoid bankruptcy in Paris and ended his days with his mistress in Sydney.

A somewhat more valuable contribution to Australian music was made by Isaac Nathan (1792-1864), who settled there in 1841 after fleeing his London creditors.

He vaunted his friendship with Lord Byron, who had provided the words for his *Hebrew Melodies*, but the opening passage of his elegaic ode *Leichardt's Grave* shows much talent. Nathan was also among the first to attempt a transcription of Aboriginal music, yet his settings, if not so complete a travesty as those which were to follow, inevitably distorted the music to fit European taste. Other English musicians who played a part in the beginnings of Australian music were William Vincent Wallace and John Phillip Deane.

Despite their meagre talents, Wallace, Deane and Nathan were the progenitors of the tradition of art music in Australia, but the strength of that tradition, moderately reinforced by the arrival of a number of English organists later in the century, lay in the numerous amateur choral societies modelled on the English movement. The repertory came to include, besides Handel's *Messiah*, Haydn's *Creation* and Mendelssohn's *Elijah*, works by Spohr and others; the first performance of Bach's *St Matthew Passion* was in 1875.

In the late 19th century some young Australians, among them Alfred Hill (1870-1960), went to Leipzig to study. Hill, if only for the size of his output, may be regarded as the first important Australian composer; yet his works, which include twelve symphonies and seven operas, appear to show little originality or power.

Percy Grainger and the 20th century

It was the tragedy of Grainger, which he himself felt keenly, to become irredeemably associated in the public mind with such delightful but secondary pleasantries as his suites *Handel in the Strand* and *Country Gardens*. It was also a misfortune that his imaginative pioneering was frequently so far in advance of his time as to be dubbed eccentric. He dismayed his professor, while a student in Germany, by proposing to use some prize money for the study of Chinese music in China. This youthful intention presaged the remarkable experiments in tone colour that he was to make in later life.

Born in Melbourne in 1882, he left Australia for

The magnificent opera house at Sydney, if controversial, is one of those buildings where man's imagination has matched the natural setting.

Percy Grainger, the first major Australian composer and still one of the most interesting figures in Australian music.

Germany when only thirteen, thereafter travelling in England and northern Europe collecting folk songs; he became an American citizen in 1914. Yet throughout his life he claimed his roots in Australia, and most of his most important work was done before the age of thirty. One of his early works, *Marching Song of Democracy*, though completed only in 1916 and dedicated to Walt Whitman, was a manifesto for the arts in America and 'Australia and the other younger democracies'. His *Tribute to Foster*, also completed in America and comprising variations on Stephen Foster's *Camptown Races*, is interesting for the extraordinary instrumentation of the lullaby section. Here Grainger used musical glasses and the bars of a marimba sounded by a cello bow to sustain chords, against a horn and a celeste. Later in the piece he directs some of the performers to produce discordant notes at random within a range of two and a half octaves.

The orchestra for *The Warriors, Music for an Imaginary Ballet*, one of his finest works, includes three pianos and a large body of tuned percussion instruments, and his interest in unusual sonorities extended to the prophetic view that Western composers would come to learn much from African and Asian music. He was convinced that Australians in particular would come to draw on Asian sources of inspiration, a prediction which is now being fulfilled. He put his beliefs into practice during a lecture tour of Australia and New Zealand in 1933-35, in which he introduced his audiences to music from various non-Western countries and also to medieval European music. At this time he was also experimenting with the idea of what he called 'free music', in which 'reigns complete freedom from scales, complete rhythmic freedom and complete freedom from what I call "harmonic morality" . . . ' Grainger was an experimentalist to the end, and developed a composing machine for the production of his free music. This, like so much of his work, was consigned to the Grainger Museum in Melbourne after his death in 1961.

Grainger is undoubtedly the most important composer from Australia in the first half of the 20th century, and his true stature is becoming recognised more and more. His older contemporary, Henry Tate (1873-1926), is a far more provincial figure but is of particular interest both because of his early appreciation of the work of Bartók, and because of his study of Australian bird

song and his awareness of the urgency for scientific study of Aboriginal music. His attempt at a specifically Australian music is best represented by *Dawn: An Australian Rhapsody for Full Orchestra* (1922).

Arthur Benjamin (1893-1960), another composer of real if minor talent, settled early in England, teaching at the Royal College of Music from 1926, where Benjamin Britten was among his pupils. His work included two one-act operas, *The Devil Take Her* and *Prima Donna*, and the full opera *A Tale of Two Cities* (1957), orchestral, piano and ballet music and much for the film. Of more interest from an Australian point of view is the work of John Antill (b. 1904), and notably his ballet *Corroboree* (1946). This work, inspired by the Aboriginal tribal assembly of the same name, was first performed under the English musician, Sir Eugene Goossens (1893-1962), who as conductor and director of the Sydney Conservatorium played an important part in Australian music of the late 1940s and 1950s. *Corroboree*, obviously indebted to Stravinsky's *Rite of Spring*, is nevertheless both original and one of the first Australian works in a truly 20th-century idiom. Antill's later ballet scores include *Black Opal* (1961), also on an Aboriginal theme, and of his other works, *Symphony for a City* should also be mentioned.

Among other Australian composers of this generation are Miriam Hyde (b. 1913) whose work, even if largely in a Brahmsian Romantic idiom, reveals high technical competence; Margaret Sutherland (b. 1897), unusual among Australian composers for her affinities with French music, and a creative artist of vigour and distinction revealing an authentic individual talent in such works as *Discussion for String Quartet* and *Concerto for Strings*; Roy Agnew (1893-1944), whose piano music is coloured by the style of Bax and Delius; and Clive Douglas (b. 1903), whose strength lies in colourful programmatic music such as his *Olympic Overture* (1956) for the Melbourne Games, and *Sturt 1829*, commemorating one of Australia's most renowned explorers. Douglas is also committed to the value of Aboriginal music as a source of inspiration.

Raymond Hanson (b. 1913), whose chief influence stems from his work as a teacher at the New South Wales Conservatorium, has revealed a real, if little known talent for composition in his trumpet concerto (1948). Dorian Le Gallienne (1915-63), of Melbourne, demonstrated considerable skill in the lesser idioms of the first half of the century, and among his best works are the *Sinfonietta* of 1956; the symphony in E (1951), indebted to the fourth symphony of Vaughan Williams, but nevertheless a considerable achievement; and, above all, the duo for violin and viola.

The contemporary world

Two of Australia's leading composers of the generation of the 1920s are Felix Werder (b. 1922) and Eric Gross (b. 1926). Gross, although born in Vienna, was trained in England and his music, such as the *Four Psalms* for *a cappella* choir, influenced by Walton, often betrays his debt. Werder, born in Berlin, left Germany with his family in 1934, coming to Australia in 1941. His practical approach to composition owes something to Hindemith, but the influence of Jewish liturgical music is more important, and he has learnt from the work of Schoenberg and Bartók, who powerfully influence his fourth quartet. Other important works are the elegy for strings *Actomos* (1952), *Fantasias* for string trio (1955) and the excellent orchestral *Monostrophe* (1962).

Two gifted Australians, Banks and Williamson, have spent most of their working careers in England. Don

Banks (b. 1923), who studied under Matyas Seiber, Milton Babbitt and Luigi Dallapiccola, still retains a strong sense of identity with his Australian background. He has written in twelve-note technique and it colours other works such as the trio for horn, violin and piano written for the Edinburgh Festival of 1962. This work, like the outstanding horn concerto of 1966 (a masterpiece of international stature), was written for another distinguished Australian musician – the horn virtuoso Barry Tuckwell.

Malcolm Williamson (b. 1931) studied at the New South Wales Conservatorium, and in England under Elizabeth Lutyens and Erwin Stein, both of whom directed his interest to twelve-note techniques. But Williamson, who for a time worked as a night club pianist, is also interested in popular music. In addition, he made an intensive study of the work of Messiaen and of medieval techniques, writing a number of extended works for organ indebted to these studies, among them *The Vision of Christ-Phoenix* for the dedication of Coventry Cathedral. Other works include the magnificent *Elevamini Symphony* (1956), the *Symphony for Voices* (1962), and the fine third piano concerto of 1964.

The important composers' conference at Hobart in 1963 proclaimed the maturity of a new generation of composers, such as Peter Sculthorpe (b. 1929) of Tasmania, Larry Sitsky (b. 1934), Nigel Butterly (b. 1935) and Richard Meale (b. 1932). Of these, Sculthorpe, whose teachers include Egon Wellesz and Edmund Rubbra, rapidly won a wide reputation. His music also owes debts to Bartók, early Webern and Balinese gamelan music, and includes *Irkanda I* (1958) for unaccompanied viola, and a series of works under the title *Sun Music*, of which the second experiments with the integration of the performers with the audience. These and other works, notably the sonata for viola and percussion, reveal the considerable potential of this composer. His near contemporary Meale, whose flute sonata of 1963 won international acclaim, reflects the rare influence of French music, notably Boulez, in Australia and assures the future of the new music there.

In this context the last name to be mentioned is that of George Dreyfus (b. 1928), whose *From Within*

Looking Out (1962) for soprano, flute, celeste, vibraphone and viola (based on the words of an Indo-Chinese street song), and the two-act opera *Garni Sands* are works of considerable distinction.

Music in Australia, still most strongly represented abroad by a succession of outstanding opera singers, chief among them Dame Nellie Melba and Joan Sutherland, is emerging in the 1970s as a vigorous and independent school.

above left
Peter Sculthorpe, one of the leaders of Australia's younger generation of composers. He is playing an Indonesian gong chime, and on the table is a Chinese sheng.

left
The Chinese-born conductor Helen Quash (b.1941) rehearsing the Melbourne Symphony Orchestra with the Australian pianist Roger Woodward.

Music in Canada

For the first two centuries of its history, Canada was a French colony. In 1763, however, the treaty of Paris formally transferred it to Great Britain, an event celebrated in grand style by the English master of the Chapel Royal to George II with *A Thanksgiving Anthem, for the taking of Montreal and making us Master of all Canada*. However, the first composer in Canada, and indeed on the North American continent, was Jean Biancourt, called the Baron de Poutrinourt, who worked in the colony for a few years at the beginning of the 17th century. The predominance of French culture was an assured fact in Canada for many generations to come and the music of the court of Louis XIV was eagerly listened to. But the earliest missionaries were seriously intent on approaching the Indian population and at the baptism of grand chief Memberton we learn that the assembled company sang a version of the Te Deum.

Throughout the 17th century the Church continued to play a dominant part in the musical life of the province of New France. In 1664 the bishop, Monseigneur de Laval, was able to write in an address to Rome: 'The great feasts of the church are attended by the music of choirs and instruments while the organ of the church blends its sounds with those of the singers.' Indeed, thanks to the importance attached to music by the Catholic Church during the period of the Counter Reformation, Canada could boast organs and instruments of all the main families more than a generation ahead of Boston, one of the centres of music in the British colonies to the south. There is of course evidence of secular music-making during the first century of Canada, but the place of the Church was central and the first known Canadian composition is a piece for the liturgy of the third Sunday after Pentecost in 1685. In the 18th century, however, Quebec and Montreal became the centres of a comparatively sophisticated society which naturally called for music as a diversion and to accompany its dancing.

In the years immediately following the British conquest of the province, Canadian cultural life was seriously disrupted. But if one tradition was cut short, another was introduced which, if not so rich in its creative potential (18th-century England was, after all, hardly the most fertile field in the history of music), did bring an important new element into the musical life of Canada. It is in fact very probable that the beginnings of an orchestral tradition in Canada as a whole should be dated from the vogue for military bands and their music which was exported from the London of Vauxhall and Ranelagh to Halifax, Toronto and even Quebec. The conductors and musicians who directed these concerts came not only from Britain but also from Germany and other continental countries. The circumstances of British rule and the taste of the British officer corps for band music – and for the theatre – led to the first opera performance, Grétry's tactful *Richard the Lionheart*, in 1798.

During the 19th century, Canada's music continued to be largely indebted to foreign visitors. Among them were the German Theodor Molt (1796-1856) who, as professor and organist at Quebec, had an important influence, and Antoine Dessane (1826-73), who introduced the music of César Franck to the population of French Canada. The preference of the British settlers was for German music; in 1860, for example, a full-scale performance of Weber's *Der Freischütz* was given in Toronto. Of the native musicians of the period, Calixa Lavalle (1842-91) enjoyed a considerable reputation in the United States as well as in his own country; Guillaume Couture (1851-1915), who studied in Paris, was an important teacher in the Montreal musical world and also produced some good music himself; while Alexis Constant (1858-1918), largely self-taught as a composer, was a stubborn opponent of modernism. An important figure in the musical life of the country during the present century has been Sir Ernest Campbell Macmillan (1893-1973), the principal of the Toronto conservatory, dean of the faculty at Toronto university and conductor of the Toronto symphony orchestra.

Although it is not easy to talk of a specifically 'Canadian' style of music in the 20th century, Canadian composers have been able to draw on the most diverse folklore sources – including not only French, English or Scottish, but also American Indian and even Eskimo. Nevertheless the roots of their art lie in the established traditions of European art music. Two important centres of music during this century have been Toronto and Montreal.

The school of Toronto

As professor of composition and orchestration in the faculty of music at the university of Toronto, John Weinzweig has been of immense importance as a teacher and has shaped many of Canada's younger composers. Born in Toronto of Polish parents in 1913, he himself studied at Toronto university under Sir Ernest Macmillan and Healey Willan (b. 1880), the English-born organist and composer of symphonic and church music. As a student, Weinzweig was fully initiated into the idiom of the late Romantics, but as his style matured and developed he became one of the first Canadian composers to break away from traditional tonality, exploring first atonalism and then serial techniques. Indeed his significance as a teacher consists largely in the central part he played in introducing the techniques of the school of Vienna to the composers of Toronto and western Canada.

In his symphonic poem *The Edge of the World* (1946) Weinzweig drew on the melodies and rhythms of Eskimo dances and songs; the *Divertissement for*

bassoon and string orchestra (1959) shows a happy combination of swing rhythms and twelve-note technique; while in *Red Ear of Corn* (1949) he had drawn on the folk music of the Indians and of French Canada. But these interesting and successful examples of eclecticism are less significant in his development than the string quintet *Interlude in the life of an artist* (1943). In this the ternary form receives its unifying force from the use of a melody of twelve notes dominated by the interval of a fourth.

One of Weinzweig's most important compositions is the violin concerto, in which he reveals a positively Neoclassical sense of structure, while the instrumentation of his *Vin de paix*, 'Two dramatic songs for soprano and orchestra' (1957), is among the most remarkable

right
Harry Somers, a Toronto-trained composer.

below
Claude Champagne seated at the piano with other Montreal composers, among them Papineau-Couture (extreme right).

achieved by any Canadian composer. The work is dedicated to the United Nations and reveals the composer's preoccupation with the problems that confront man in the contemporary world. In the third string quartet (1963), which marks a new stage in Weinzweig's musical development, his deployment of serial techniques reaches its most rigorous form, although there are traces of the influence of German Expressionism and the pointillist technique of Webern.

Harry Somers (b. 1925) began his training at Toronto under Weinzweig, went to San Francisco to study with the pianist Robert Schmitz, then to Paris where he worked under Milhaud. His free atonalism, joined with the occasional use of tonal elements, as in the suite for harp and chamber ensemble (1949), proclaimed him true to the school of Toronto. But his subtle and authentic talent led him to research into new sonorities, and this is reflected in the *Fantasy for Orchestra* of 1959. Three years later he produced two works which indicated another change of direction in his musical development. These were *Abstract*, commissioned by Canadian radio, and *Five concepts for orchestra*. In the first the composer sought to integrate electronic sounds with traditional instruments, in this case strings, harp and percussion. *Concepts* consists of four movements that are veritable studies in orchestral technique and also comprise serial treatments of pitch, intensity and rhythm, the fifth movement being concerned with dynamics. For a time, Somers worked at the studio for electronic music at Toronto University directed by Myron Schaeffer; his studies there are reflected in *Stereophony* (1963). Here the composer's interest in sonorities and tempi are expressed, not through the medium of electronic equipment, but by the use of traditional musical instruments disposed about the auditorium to introduce the spatial element to the purely sonorous effect. In addition to those already mentioned, his works include the opera *The Madman* (1953), a passacaglia and fugue for orchestra and a symphony.

Another Canadian composer who studied under Weinzweig is Harry Freedman (b. 1922). His work also shows the trait of atonalism coloured by serial technique. He came to Canada as a child and began his musical studies at Winnipeg, transferring later to Toronto. His training included serious study of the technique of the reed instruments; he was taught by Ernst Krenek as well as Weinzweig, and he attended the course given by Copland and Messiaen at Tanglewood, Massachusetts. Freedman has combined his work as a composer with that of a professional musician, playing the cor anglais with the Toronto symphony orchestra. Jazz has formed an important source of his inspiration as a composer. In *Tableaux* (1952) he has evoked the immensity and solitude of the Arctic wastes and, using a rigorously atonal and contrapuntal technique, he has rivalled the skill of the poet and painter in presenting the true aspect of that desert of ice. This poetic and visual imagination is again present in *Images* (1958) on Canadian themes. Works which show his interest in dodecaphony and serialism include *Nocturne* (1949), five pieces for string orchestra (1949) and a symphony (1961). In this brief account of the composers of the Toronto school, mention should be made of John Beckwith (b. 1927), a student of Nadia Boulanger and later a professor at the University of Toronto. His inspiration, which is essentially literary, finds its fullest expression in vocal music. Among the best of his works are the cantata *Jonah* (1963) and *Five Lyrics of the T'ang Dynasty*.

Barbara Pentland (b. 1912), whose considerable output includes four symphonies, three concertos, chamber music and an opera, studied in Paris and New York. She taught for a time at the Toronto Conservatory and was appointed to a post at the faculty of music in the University of British Columbia.

The school of Montreal

The doyen of French Canadian composers, Claude Champagne, was born at Montreal in 1891. He submitted his first work, the comparatively late symphonic poem *Hercule et Omphale* (1918), to Rachmaninov, who was at the time on tour in Canada. Champagne's first love was the Russian school of Borodin and Rimsky-Korsakov and he only began to be interested in French music when he was about thirty. He took lessons with Gédalge in counterpoint and, learning from the music of such masters as Debussy and Ravel, ventured outside the field of strict tonality, producing in the *Suite Canadienne* (1928) a work which demonstrated his allegiance to the French school but also betrayed his fascination with Canadian folk music. On returning to Canada he wrote *Danse villageoise*, again obviously inspired by the folk idiom and showing clear indications of his French and Irish ancestry. His later works include *Images du Canada Français* (1943) for choir and orchestra, a piano concerto (1950), the string quartet of 1951, which is one of his deepest works, and *Altitude* (1959). This vast fresco-like composition for choirs and orchestra, inspired by mountain scenery, is divided into three sections entitled 'The Primitive Age', 'Meditation' and 'The Modern Age'.

Jean Papineau-Couture (b. 1916) studied composition under Champagne and with Nadia Boulanger. She had a decisive influence on his development as a composer, directing him towards an essentially international idiom in which Neo-classicism is combined with a rhythmic interest derived from Stravinsky. His penchant for traditional forms such as the sonata and the concerto has not prevented him from exploring to the full the extreme territories of harmony and rhythm pioneered by the vanguard of 20th-century composers. In the *Concerto Grosso* of 1943 he uses tonality; in the second movement of the suite for flute, polytonal methods; and, in his ballet *Papotages*, atonalism. However, he held aloof from dodecaphony until the 1950s when, with his suite for violin solo, he made use of it – though very much on his own terms and with strong tonal reservations. From 1956 he went through a period of 'constructivism', exploring a private and poetic universe to which such a work as *Cinq pièces concertantes* bears witness.

Another member of the younger generation of Montreal composers is François Morel (b. 1926). In his work *Antiphonie* (1953) he revealed an essentially Impressionistic technique which nevertheless achieved a close-knit synthesis of medieval and modern elements. In 1956, with the symphony for brass, his music took a new direction in which the modal character of his earlier work is associated with certain elements derived from jazz. He completed his first venture into atonalism with *Space Ritual* (1959). *Boreal* (1959), in which he superimposed influences derived from Boulez and Edgar Varèse, represents his first major work in serial technique. Other works include *Mythe de la Roche Percée* (1960), a serial work for two bands of wind instruments, and the second string quartet (1963).

The passionate temperament of Clermont Pépin (b. 1926) imbues all his works, despite their essentially Romantic lyrical quality, with great intensity. A rhythmic tension, almost obsessional in quality yet combined with a vigorous polyphonic sense, drives through such works as the symphonic poems *Guernica* (1952), based on Picasso's famous painting, and the *Rite du soleil noir* (1955). The quartet that he entitled *Hyperbole* (1961) shows elements of a serialist approach to counterpoint

and signifies a new stage of development, while in the later work, *Monade*, for fourteen string instruments, we can see the composer orientating himself towards the procedures of electronic music.

One of the most interesting composers of the younger generation of the school of Montreal is Roger Matton (b. 1929), among whose works the concerto for two pianos and orchestra is particularly fine. In the 1960s a number of other composers have also come to the fore, such as Serge Garant, composer of *Ennéade* (1964), and Gilles Tremblay, whose *Cantique de Durée* appeared in 1963. A studio for electronic music has also been established at McGill university for the use of the composers of the *avant-garde*.

In conclusion, we can observe that the younger generation of composers in Canada, as elsewhere in the Western world, is now fully committed to the development of music in a completely international idiom and that while the school of Toronto, unimpeded by any sentimental attachment to the French school, was introduced to the techniques of serial composition somewhat in advance of the musicians of Montreal, both these centres of Canadian music are now proceeding along similar lines.

below
Roger Matton, of the Montreal school.

bottom
Montreal composers grouped around the conductor Wilfred Pelletier.

The World of Jazz

In discussing jazz music, there is one overriding difficulty, which is that nobody has ever defined it to anybody else's satisfaction. But although jazz, like Hegel's beach, is neither land nor sea, it is a very definite musical entity, and is perhaps the most intriguing phenomenon with which the 20th-century musicologist has had to come to terms. The two words most frequently applied to it are 'syncopation' and 'improvisation', each of which represents only a half-truth. All jazz is syncopated music, but not all syncopated music is jazz. Even more perversely, jazz is by very definition an improvised music, and yet some of its most brilliant and subtle performances have been achieved at least partly by the stratagems of pre-arrangement.

If there is a factor common to all jazz performances, it is that the musician is creating his own melodic variations on a given melodic theme, these variations being based on the underlying harmonies of the original material, the whole being conceived against a background of rhythmic syncopation. The student of jazz history can do no better than to concentrate on the harmonic aspect of the music, for only then do the shifting styles of jazz begin to reveal any logical pattern.

The story of jazz is in fact a story of harmonic exploration. Its greatest figures have been those adventurers who extended the harmonic territory available to the jazz musician, although it is wise to remember that so far as the history of harmonic advance in music is concerned, jazz has, until very recently, remained strictly within its own confines, so that what is defined in jazz as 'modern' is only modern in the jazz sense. Perhaps the most convincing demonstration of this vital fact is found in the chord of the minor seventh, one of the characteristic effects of the modern movement which transformed the face of jazz in the 1940s. Although the minor-seventh chord was virtually new to jazz, it was by no means an unfamiliar sound to the world of music at large. As early as 1859, the Russian novelist Turgenev describes one of his characters 'pausing entranced over minor sevenths', and in 1907, Maurice Ravel's *Introduction and Allegro* opens with a comprehensive exposition of the use of the chord precisely as it was later to be deployed by the jazz musicians of the 1940s.

Jazz, then, has not only lived a curious existence isolated from the main body of music, but has lived that existence for no more than sixty or seventy years, which explains the feverish haste with which it has

Willy 'Bunk' Johnson and his band about 1905; note that the leader is holding a violin and that the bassist is using a bow.

evolved from era to era. In those seventy years, it has moved from the crudest primitivism to the most hypersophisticated Neo-classicism; so baffling has the overlapping of styles and generations become that it is possible for a founding father of the music to share the same concert stage with the most ferocious exponent of the *avant-garde* of the 1960s. And it is only if the rapid progression from style to style is observed in harmonic terms that the history of jazz falls at once into a logical, indeed inevitable pattern.

New Orleans

The beginnings of the music are obscured by an impenetrable fog, although it seems quite certain that the emancipation of the Negro after the American Civil War made it inevitable that in time this oppressed minority, dumped in an alien environment, would seek its own forms of artistic self-expression. To the Negro of Louisiana at the turn of the century, music was an integral part of his life and experience, and yet the conventional paths to musical accomplishment were closed to him. Not only was it impossible for him to attend a conservatory, or even more humble music lessons, but very often even the conventional musical instruments were beyond his grasp. For this reason much early jazz was vocal, and it was only very gradually that its influence began to stretch out from the church choirs where the seeds of its later stylistic devices were sown.

New Orleans at that time is usually described by the cliché, 'melting pot of the nations' and, like all clichés, that particular one is accurate enough. Old French, New American, Creole, Negro and Indian, all races and cultures mingled, until gradually a new musical language arose from the chaos. People there not only thought in terms of making their own music, but also associated it with the mundane episodes of daily life. There was music at weddings, funerals, christenings,

confirmations, picnics and birthdays, and because a great deal of this music-making took place out of doors, the loudness of a musician's tone became as important as the subtlety of his ideas or the proficiency of his technical execution. For this reason, bands were always led by trumpeters, and the rivalry between them was intense. The figure who stands on the border between legend and fact is the trumpeter Buddy Bolden, who, around 1900, was the undisputed trumpet champion of the city and, although no recordings of his work survive, it is evident from eye-witness accounts that, with Bolden, the convention of collective improvisation known as New Orleans Style had already evolved.

The classic New Orleans style was based on the interplay of three front-line instruments, trumpet (or cornet), trombone and clarinet; the trumpet embellished the melody, the clarinet contributing filigree effects above, and the trombone a bass foundation below. There was little or no solo playing as the modern student knows it. Integration of ensemble was everything, and it was even felt in some quarters, and still is among diehards, that solo extravagance stained the purity of a New Orleans performance. Perhaps more to the point is the fact that in Bolden's day individual techniques were so primitive that to avoid long solos was an act of personal prudence rather than of aesthetic morality.

It was evident that this classic style, which concentrated exclusively on ensemble textures, was doomed the moment a virtuoso appeared with the technique and imagination required to produce long bravura passages. This virtuoso arrived in the person of Louis Daniel Armstrong, born in New Orleans in 1900, and a protégé of Joe 'King' Oliver, Bolden's successor as the trumpet champion of the bayou. As a teenager Armstrong played second trumpet in Oliver's band, but by his early twenties it was obvious that a whole new concept of jazz technique was evolving. In the face of Armstrong's gathering virtuosity, the New Orleans ensemble style, too restrictive to contain the prolific music of an unquestioned genius, was soon to split at the seams.

But apart from the titanic proportions of Armstrong's

King Oliver and his band.

gift, there was another factor which helped to kill off New Orleans as the centre of the new music. In 1917 its notorious Red Light district, Storyville, whose bars and brothels gave employment to hundreds of young jazz musicians, was closed by order of the U.S. secretary of the navy, alarmed by the regularity with which his sailors became involved in incidents of violence and dissipation. As we shall see, this was by no means the first time that a social or economic event was to turn the course of jazz history.

With the closing down of New Orleans' Storyville, the first watershed had arrived. Virtually expelled from his own city, the New Orleans jazz musician had now either to turn inward and restrict his music to the proportions of a local dialect, or seek new audiences. Inevitably the music spread, and it did so through two agencies, the northward migration of many of the best players and the riverboats plying their way up the Mississippi from New Orleans to Memphis, St Louis and points north. All the riverboats employed bands, and their importance as an evangelising agency can hardly be exaggerated. For many young white men, the sound of a riverboat band, as the great cumbersome vessels drifted into some small-town levee, was their first experience of the new music. The white cornettist Leon 'Bix' Beiderbecke, destined to make so profound an impact on the jazz art, was only one of thousands of teenagers galvanised by this experience.

The greatest of the New Orleans masters, King Oliver, soon became one of the leading attractions of Chicago night life, and it was not long before he sent to New Orleans for young Armstrong to join him. From this point on, the future of jazz as an international music was assured, although nobody suspected it at the time. New York had seen a feeble white imitation of the real thing as early as 1917 with the début of the Original Dixieland Jazz Band, the first group in history to make a commercial jazz recording, but it was not till the supreme art of men like Armstrong began to gather support that jazz really began to move away from its origins.

Louis Armstrong in 1948.

Chicago

By 1927 the central base of the music had moved to Chicago. Not surprisingly the jazz style which takes its name from that city was a musical reflection of conditions in Chicago at the time. A brash, coarse and excitable city enjoying its dubious distinction as the capital of Al Capone's bootleg empire, Chigago teemed with gin mills and speakeasies where illegal liquor was consumed to an accompaniment of loud, aggressive music. Chicago style was really no more than a modification of the old New Orleans methods, a compromise between the ensemble convention of the pioneers and the great age of solo virtuosity soon to come. The Chicago groups, composed of fiery, extrovert players who thrived in the brassy, violent environment of the town, usually began and ended each tune with the ensemble effect, but filled in the middle with a string of solos, thus following the precepts laid down by Armstrong in a monumental series of recordings with groups he called The Hot Five and The Hot Seven (1927-28). In these remarkable performances Armstrong established once and for all the hegemony of the individual virtuoso over the group, but unfortunately not all who followed his example were able to shoulder the immense responsibilities which solo freedom endows. Most of the Chicago stars were white players whose talents varied from excellent to mediocre, but none remotely approached the heroic stature of Armstrong's music.

The three most interesting products of this school were the clarinettist Benny Goodman, destined to alter the whole social context of the music, Jack Teagarden, a Texas trombonist of sublime melodiousness, and Bix Beiderbecke, perhaps the most intriguing and romantic figure in jazz history. Beiderbecke symbolises the middleclass white American with a musical aptitude, whose whole course of existence was changed through exposure to the new Negro art. Beiderbecke had a harmonic sense which occurs perhaps once or twice in every generation, and had it not been for the fortuitous confluence of this aptitude and the sound of the new music, he would no doubt have been one of thousands of musicians who enjoyed a reasonably successful professional life without ever thinking about jazz at all.

Beiderbecke enjoyed a brief and riotous career, beginning in 1923 with a band of college boys called The Wolverines, and ending in bathos with the pseudo-

Plate 55
Ben Webster on baritone saxophone.

Plate 56 above
Modern jazz organist

Plate 57 right
Modern jazz drummer

symphonic puerilities of the Paul Whiteman Orchestra. At his peak, around 1927, Beiderbecke, through the agency of an exquisite bell-like tone, produced sequences of subtle phrases which made up in introspective intensity what they lacked of the fire and passion of an Armstrong. Bix was also a self-taught pianist and casual composer, and his piano recordings of his own work remain a testimony both to his own gifts and to the twin influences of jazz and the concert hall, which he never resolved. He died in 1931 at the age of twenty-eight.

Recordings of the period give an impression of white and black musicians operating in hermetically sealed compartments, but although a tacit colour bar operated both on the bandstand and in the recording studio, there was much mingling after hours, a truism illustrated by the mutual admiration of Armstrong and Beiderbecke. Towards the end of the decade Armstrong made history with *Knockin' a Jug*, the first jazz record to be created by white and black musicians working together, Jack Teagarden being among the players involved.

The pianists and the Blues

While the soloists were pursuing their quest for the subtler solo based on more sophisticated harmonies, a parallel development was taking place which was to have enormous influence in the years that followed. The

Bix Beiderbecke.

pianist Fletcher Henderson, one of the few pioneer jazzmen to have the advantage of an academic musical education, had been experimenting with the larger type of jazz orchestra since 1923. His method was to hire outstanding soloists, cushioning their playing with simply conceived, written ensemble figures which might enhance the individual's effectiveness. A few earlier men, especially the New Orleans pianist-composer Ferdinand 'Jelly Roll' Morton, had been working along similar lines with smaller groups, but with Henderson the convention of sections of instruments within the frame of the large orchestra was born. Today, naturally, much of Henderson's scoring sounds crude, but his recordings retain their interest through the superlative work of his soloists, among them Louis Armstrong and the first of the tenor saxophone virtuosi, Coleman Hawkins.

However, in retrospect, by far the most important single event of the later 1920s was the arrival in New York from Washington, D.C. of the pianist-bandleader-composer Edward Kennedy 'Duke' Ellington. In his early New York days Ellington aligned himself with the flourishing school of two-handed pianists headed by James P. Johnson and Willie 'the Lion' Smith. The playing of this school was characterised by the towering rhythmic strength of the left hand and the ten-note harmonies of the right. Johnson and Smith were undisputed masters, but ironically the flower of their school was produced by their two pupils, Ellington and Thomas 'Fats' Waller, both of whom amended Johnson's 'stride' style to their own ends. Within a few years of arriving in New York, Ellington was destined to far outstrip orchestral experimenters like Henderson, but for the moment he contented himself with a mere quintet which grew by the end of the decade to exactly twice the size.

Although there is no question that Johnson was one of the most influential as well as one of the most gifted of all the early jazz figures, his style was soon to be superseded by a new piano approach which laid down the pre-cepts followed by jazz pianists to this day. The man responsible for this revolution was the Chicago pianist Earl Hines, who, through his work with Armstrong, conceived the possibility of the pianist producing right-hand figures consisting of single notes instead of Johnson's two-fisted clusters. Because the lines which Hines produced could be transposed on to any of the instruments able to play only one note at a time, the new style became known as 'Trumpet-style piano', and within a short time it was the Hines approach rather than Johnson's which spread across the face of jazz.

The late 1920s also saw the maturing of perhaps the greatest of all the authentic jazz singers, Bessie Smith, who specialised in countless variations of the traditional twelve-bar blues, singing lyrics whose earthiness and realism stand in stark contrast to the sentimentality of Tin Pan Alley which superseded the Smith repertoire in the 1930s. Bessie Smith interpreted the folk poetry of the blues with incomparable power and pathos. Her successors in the vocal field would find themselves deprived of that poetry and faced instead with the mawkishness of the conventional commercial love song.

Big band

Throughout the burgeoning period of the late 1920s and early 1930s, jazz was tied economically to the prohibition laws which had caused the mushrooming of thousands of illegal drinking rooms, most of them employing a band, or at least a pianist and a jazz-tinged cabaret. And just as the closing of Storyville had brought about a radical amendment in the location of the jazz centre, so did the repeal of Prohibition become a prime factor in the next great development in jazz history. It is interesting to note that so far jazz had been more or less the music of illegality, the background effect of the brothel and the speakeasy. Now, in the mid-1930s, it

Jelly Roll Morton, at the piano, and his Red Hot Peppers.

was to take the first of its giant steps towards respectability, enjoying in the process its first taste of genuine mass popularity, and also a remarkably brilliant Golden Age of individual virtuosity, when the art of constructing a solo evolved with amazing rapidity.

The area which jazz now invaded was the ballroom of the Roosevelt era. The phenomenon was born of the touring Big Band, groups of twelve or fourteen musicians, meticulously drilled to meet the demands of strict-tempo dancers and ballroom managers who required the balanced programming of different types of dances. Although the jazz world hardly realised it, the age of innocence was over. The carefree days of the small group with its hit-or-miss approach were passing and, because the technical demands of playing in an orchestral setting were so severe, the jazz musician found himself equipped, for the first time in the music's history, to sell himself in more commercial markets. And most significant of all, the orchestrator now came into his own.

In retrospect the era of the big bands is the most hysterical and least comprehensible of any in jazz history. Orchestras became as keenly supported as

above left
Bessie Smith.

left
James P. Johnson at the piano.

right
Benny Goodman.

below
Coleman Hawkins.

football teams, and their individual stars as admired as boxing champions. Audiences were numbered in thousands, Hollywood beckoned to the more successful bandleaders, magazines conducted annual popularity polls evoking response from people all over America. Police had sometimes to be called out to control adoring crowds, and the profits soared into five figures, then six, then seven. Jazz now enjoyed the questionable prestige of its first millionaires.

What had happened was that the general public became aware of the surface excitement of jazz. A new generation of college students was delighted to find that the music it danced to was also an emergent art. Benny Goodman, the Chicago clarinettist who led the march into the ballrooms, later wrote that he and his musicians were totally unprepared for anything like the hysterical response they received. Goodman played for dancing and saw that instead of shuffling round the floor to his music, hundreds of the customers were crowding the bandstand instead, watching with rowdy fascination the feats of his drummer Gene Krupa, or his trumpet soloist Harry James, or his own dazzling pyrotechnics. Others soon followed Goodman, among them Tommy and Jimmy Dorsey, a rival clarinet virtuoso to Goodman called Artie Shaw, Woody Herman, James himself, and literally hundreds of others. Eventually the big band boom was to peter out, musically if not commercially, in the decadence of the Glenn Miller Orchestra, which cultivated felicity of dancing rhythms at the expense of the jazz content, but for a long time it was the mastodons of the Swing Age who produced music artistically ingenious as well as commercially viable.

But it must be remembered that now that jazz was a saleable commodity, non-musical considerations were bound to impinge. Although it was Benny Goodman who was referred to as the King of Swing, neither he nor his business rivals were representative of the best in the big band art. Because of the curious tendency to include pigmentation of skin as one of the relevant factors in assessing artistic merit, the truly outstanding bands of the 1930s were placed out of court in the dash for popularity. The orchestras of men like Count Basie, Jimmy Lunceford and Chick Webb, although musically superior to those of Goodman and company, were not eligible for appearances everywhere in America, and so remained far behind in public acclaim. It was the Basie

left
Count Basie.

below
Lester Young.

band which included one of the greatest of all solo masters, the saxophonist Lester Young, whose work as virtuoso in this age of the great soloist was to have far-reaching consequences among the young men of the generation which followed him.

Young's name is bracketed with that of Coleman Hawkins as the man who gave his instrument complete coherence. Hawkins, rescuing the saxophone from the status of a vaudeville joke, had endowed the tenor with the full, rich sound of the romantic. He favoured a hot, sensuous tone and a passionate stream of arpeggios, grouped together in a way which hinted at an instinctive mastery of form. Young provided an alternative approach, in which the tone was distilled to a metallic honk, in which selection of notes superseded a proliferation of notes, and in which silence was used for the first time as a telling weapon in the soloist's armoury.

Ellington

But a greater figure than even Young or Hawkins, and leader of an orchestra far greater than Basie's or Goodman's, was Duke Ellington. By the late 1930s, Ellington's mastery of orchestral textures had flowered to the point where his work was no longer in the same category as anyone else's in jazz. Unlike all other jazz orchestral writers, Ellington wrote not for grouped instruments, but for the individuals who played those instruments, so that the number of different effects he could achieve with a simple C major chord was limited only by the number of permutations he could command in a band of fifteen men. Ellington represents the greatest paradox of all for those people who believe that all authentic jazz must be improvised. A truer definition, seen in the light of Ellington's prolific achievements, would seem to be that all authentic jazz need not be improvised, but must at any rate create the illusion of improvisation.

Ellington's development as orchestrator and composer has been of profound significance, because it alone refutes the otherwise justifiable claim that jazz music, although it can express deep emotions, is strictly limited in the breadth of its sensibilities. Through the agency

right
Billie Holiday.

below
Jack Teagarden.

of orchestral mastery, interpreted by outstanding soloists, Ellington contrived vastly to extend the area in which jazz can operate with any validity, producing after the 1940s a whole range of extended works running concurrent with his more conventional exercises. These extended works, ranging from a series of Shakespearean vignettes (*Such Sweet Thunder*, 1957) to paraphrases of Grieg and Tchaikovsky (1959-60) have passed the acid test of remaining faithful to the original programmatic intent without sacrificing the animation and vitality of jazz. He died in 1974.

Ellington apart, the musicians of the pre-war years, whether working inside the framework of the big bands or devoting their time to small-group work, were busily involved in the task of assimilating all the harmonic possibilities of the diatonic system. That is to say, whatever they played, there was implicit in every performance a home key, a key centre, so that the harmonic conception of each essay in improvisation was strictly conventional in the 18th-century sense. There was to come a time when the limitations of the diatonic approach appeared repressive, but this was only because throughout the 1930s the great soloists plumbed so thoroughly all the diatonic possibilities. It is doubtful whether jazz had ever known before, or ever will again, such a proliferation of brilliant individual talents, ranging through every instrument from trumpet to string bass, and even incorporating one or two new ones, like the vibraphone and the electric guitar.

The first generation of virtuosi

While Young and Hawkins between them extended the possibilities of the tenor saxophone and unwittingly created a tradition which has endured to this day, Ellington's Johnny Hodges was perfecting an elegiac, rhapsodic style on the alto saxophone whose reverse was the dandified elegance of his rival Benny Carter. Although Louis Armstrong had by now succumbed to the fleshpots of Hollywood, and his influence as a developing musician was on the wane, his effectiveness as a player remained enormous. The younger school was represented by the pyrotechnics of Roy Eldridge, the muted ferocity of Cootie Williams, the swaggering romanticism of Bunny Berigan and the quiet felicities of Buck Clayton. Jack Teagarden remained the classical trombonist, and while Thomas 'Fats' Waller became the sunset master of the now all but discredited stride school, disciples of Earl Hines' trumpet-style piano like Teddy Wilson were attaining a degree of technical proficiency which would have astonished the founding fathers of jazz. Belonging to no category and transcending them all was the solo pianist Art Tatum, a blind virtuoso whose technical command was so staggering that he was able to decorate his work with rococo flourishes so complex that even today the debate goes on as to his qualifications as a purely jazz artist. With the big bands came the day of the drummer-showman, symbolised by the frenetic Gene Krupa; while Ellington's string bassist Jimmy Blanton provided the first

proof that the string bass could be a solo instrument as well as a harmonic pulse in the rhythm section.

Perhaps the two greatest figures of this era were the singer who came at the beginning of it and the electric guitarist who symbolises its close. Billie Holiday, daughter of an itinerant guitarist who had once played in the Fletcher Henderson Orchestra, may be said in one sense to have transcended even the achievements of Bessie Smith. Where Bessie Smith had utilised the genuine poetry of an ancient folk tradition, Billie Holiday had only the depressing pap of the commercial songwriting business at her hand. It is one of the miracles of jazz that, restricted in this way, she should have produced so many recorded masterpieces. It has been said that while Bessie Smith interpreted the poetry of the blues, Billie Holiday had to create her own, and

Duke Ellington, one of the great figures of American music.

on the evidence of her recorded small-group work, and particularly her exquisite duets with Lester Young, it is doubtful whether her equal will ever be heard.

If she represented the flower of the old diatonic thinking, then the guitarist Charlie Christian stands for its imminent dissolution. Christian was an unknown Mid-West musician who burst suddenly into the ranks of the Benny Goodman band, eclipsing not only all the other musicians in the group, but also every guitarist in jazz. Using an instrument amplified by electric power, Christian overnight transformed the guitar from a rhythm to a front-line instrument as powerful and as exciting as any trumpet or saxophone. But by the time of his advent, in 1939, the diatonic era was already drawing to a close. Men like Hawkins, Young and Carter had extended that system to its limits, and the new wave of players, which included Christian (he died in 1942 in his early twenties), having digested all that the old masters could offer, once again began to chafe at the restrictions of a convention whose widest possibilities had already been explored.

The birth of 'modernism'

The introduction of conscription in the United States in 1942 dealt the big band boom its death blow, and this accident, combined with the effect of revolutionary thinkers like Christian, was to change the face of jazz so dramatically that within a few years diehards would be denying that the new music was jazz at all. Christian is a vitally significant figure in the emergence of the new modernism, not because he played a very dominant part, but because he is the sole figure who could be said to link the diatonic and modern ages of jazz, the one instrumentalist of great stature to bestride the two eras. His partners in the experimentalism of the 1940s, Bebop as it was then called, were all strange young men with un-

above right
Dizzy Gillespie.

right
Charlie 'Bird' Parker with Thelonious Monk on piano and Charlie Mingus on bass.

opposite page
Miles Davis.

familiar names, whose acceptance was to be a protracted and harrowing affair for all concerned.

Assessment of the new modernism of the 1940s is always made difficult by the fact that its outstanding figure, the alto saxophonist Charlie Parker, was the greatest improvising genius since Louis Armstrong and would unquestionably have excelled himself no matter which era he had been born into. A staggering technician with a tone of wild beauty, Parker's great achievement was to resolve the deep complexities of his harmonic thought into melodic patterns of the most ravishing beauty. Where his early partner in the modern revolution, the trumpeter Dizzy Gillespie, was a shrewd and calculating musician with a professional grasp of harmony, Parker was much more the instinctive jazzman able to improvise on any theme, from the most sophisticated ballads to the basic blues formula. Several of his blues recordings, *Now's The Time*, *Billie's Bounce*, *Parker's Mood*, *Chi Chi* and dozens of others, rank among the finest versions in the entire jazz repertoire.

The Parker-Gillespie generation, by grasping the nettle of chromatic harmony, at one blow increased the size of the jazz musician's harmonic vocabulary tenfold. The dream of Bix Beiderbecke, that one day the jazzman would have at his disposal the complete harmonic palette used by the formal composer, had come true. But at a terrible price. Even the most indifferent layman can listen to a performance by anyone from Armstrong to Christian and recognise in it the same language with which he has been made familiar since birth, by lullabies, by nursery rhymes, by national anthems, and the rest of the daily diet of music to which Western man is exposed. But the new musicians, almost as interested in the thought processes of Debussy and Bartók as in those of any of their jazz predecessors, divorced the music once and for all from the mass ear. From here on jazz was to be a musician's music, its harmonic conventions so convoluted that it became increasingly difficult for the untrained ear to distinguish the justified neologism from the unjustified solecism.

What was most surprising of all about the new chromatic jazz was the incredible speed with which its implications were grasped by the younger musicians. Instead of a long period of digestion, by the mid-1950s musicians were once again showing impatience at the restrictions of the new harmony. Only this time the dilemma was a far more baffling one. The old diatonic player had at least chromaticism to look forward to. What was the chromatic thinker to do, now that disenchantment had set in once again? The modern movement in jazz gradually evolved into a campaign to free the soloist once and for all from the tyranny of discord and resolution, to win what one or two of its younger theorists called 'freedom', by which they appear to have meant anarchy.

New frontiers

The break away from the conventions of harmonic structure was not sudden but slow and steady. One of the key figures in the early days of this movement was the trumpeter Miles Davis, an exquisite soloist whose introspective melancholia introduced a new mood into the jazz context. In a highly significant album, *Kind of Blue*, Davis probed the possibilities of improvising on a modal instead of a harmonic base, with the soloist guided not by chords but by scales. But even this revolutionary step did not endow the soloist with his hypothetical freedom. The great break was made around the end of the 1950s by the saxophonist Ornette Coleman, who explained that a musician must be free to

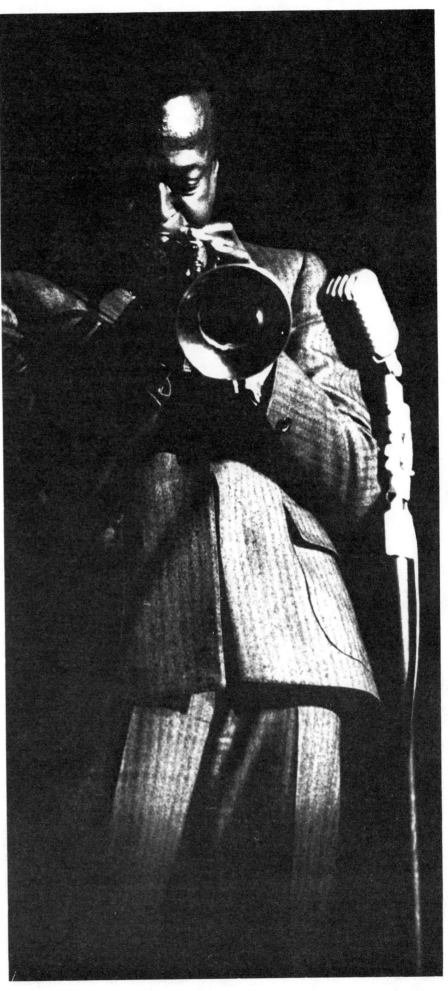

right
Ornette Coleman.

below
Sidney Bechet.

create any sound at any given time, and then produced quartet recordings to prove his intense seriousness about his theory.

The great paradox which has outfaced the attempts by Coleman and the avant-gardists who followed him to create coherent jazz that was yet utterly free (Coleman's music has been referred to as 'free form') is that although jazz is the one musical art which glorifies the individual performer, it is by its very nature a communal enterprise, so that the moment any two jazzmen come together, they either have to agree on some prearranged pattern, or drift into chaos. Coleman's dialectics would be more to the point if he and his followers were each satisfied to play alone in a room.

Another attempt to find a way out of the impasse has been the quite different movement to integrate the vitality and stylistic devices of jazz with the formal conventions of concert music. This has taken several forms, from the austere Europeanisation of jazz by the pianist John Lewis and the Modern Jazz Quartet, to the use of flamboyant Afro-Cuban rhythms and textures by Dizzy Gillespie, the experiments in arcane time signatures by Dave Brubeck, and the 'third stream' movement involving the brass player Gunther Schuller and the trombonist Bill Russo. So far the wedding has been barren. Lewis, in attempting to refine the coarsenesses of the jazz muse, has thrown out the baby with the bath water; Gillespie's rhythmic eccentricities are really the old modernism hiding behind a battery of percussive exotica; while Brubeck's thumping platitudes, when seen in the light of the grace of Tatum or Hines, are reduced to very minor proportions.

Third stream experiments have shown so far that after all the soloist, happy or not with the old-fashioned business of resolving his discords, sounds more effective inside the frame of a jazz unit than in the ranks of a classical orchestra. To what extent the instrumental mannerisms of jazz will eventually influence the classical composer remains to be seen, but there is no question that the modern orchestral writer will ignore the innovations of jazz at his own peril. From the jazz standpoint there are parallel dangers. Evidence so far suggests that, in his attempts to merge with the main stream of Western orchestral music, the jazzman is exposing himself to the possibility of losing the one property of his art which justifies its existence, its vigour. The jazz soloist is, after all, an impromptu composer, and the degree to which he can subordinate this talent to the notes on the printed sheet is problematical.

The 1960s and beyond

In the meantime the influence of jazz continues to grow. In the 1960s there is no film score entirely free of its presence. Indeed, a few jazz figures, among them Ellington, Miles Davis and John Lewis, have already composed full film scores of their own with a considerable degree of success. Television commercials, popular music, operetta, musical comedy, all now bear the stamp of the jazz influence, and it is extremely doubtful whether in fifty years time any composer of music in the world will be considered to know his craft without at least an elementary grasp of the processes of making jazz.

However, the most serious question currently faced by the jazz world concerns its very existence. Jazz is based on the principles of improvisation on a given harmonic base. Already the jazz musician, frustrated by the limitations of harmony, is rejecting this convention and in the process destroying the frame which has lent

left
John Lewis of the Modern Jazz Quartet.

below
Gary Burton.

coherence to his art in the past. It may well be that jazz music is, after all, a finite art, that all practical possibilities have now been exhausted, that the intrepid explorer, having crossed a whole continent of harmonic thought, has finally reached the sea. But if no new styles seem imminent, the jazz follower of the 1960s can at least console himself with two thoughts; first, that jazz has always proved in the past to be an utterly unpredictable form, and second, that masters of all styles coexist today in an atmosphere of healthy exchange. As to the unpredictability of jazz developments, the history of the music contains too much proof to be denied. Who could have predicted that a contemporary of Louis Armstrong, the soprano saxophonist Sidney Bechet, would emigrate in old age to Paris and there enjoy a new career of such staggering brilliance that those who never saw him in the flesh could not credit the fact that he was a septuagenarian? Who could have predicted that jazz, an essentially Black American art form, would find in the music of a Basque gipsy called Django Reinhardt some of its finest moments, or that Reinhardt would reverse the order of things and cause American guitarists to copy him?

Above all, who could have known that jazz, the art of the improvisor, would achieve its apotheosis in the work of Duke Ellington, a musician who for fifty years has been committing jazz to manuscript without impaling its vitality on the end of his pen-nib? Posterity may well come to acknowledge that Ellington, who started out as a primitive stride pianist, ranks among the great orchestral innovators of 20th-century music, and that his jazz label is irrelevant.

Jazz is now an eclectic affair. Stan Getz, a stylistic descendant of Lester Young, co-exists with Sonny Rollins, a saxophonist whose work shows jazz extended as far as it can go without abandoning entirely the harmonic frame. The pianist Oscar Peterson has developed the findings of Earl Hines to the very highest point of sophistication, while Parker's old contemporary Thelonious Monk, with his fetish for jagged dissonance, has contrived to preserve much of the primitive fire of the early pianists. That it is still possible for the young player to achieve originality of style without

either pillaging the works of the past or throwing formal discipline out of the window is proved by the young vibraphonist Gary Burton, perhaps the strongest candidate for greatness among the new generation. What is quite certain is that whether the future of jazz lies in the wedding with formal music, or in its reckless pursuit of free form, there can be no turning back. One of the essential acts of the harmonic explorer is that he burns all his bridges. The jazz musician today is a hyper-sophisticated animal, versed in every harmonic subtlety. Whether he has left himself any fresh fields to conquer remains to be seen.

BENNY GREEN

The last five years — new directions

There has certainly been no lack of new, often startling developments in music during the past five years. Indeed we are now living through the most diversified and exciting period in its entire history, and for this we must count ourselves fortunate. The most outstanding general characteristic of recent new music is the fact that it has broken away from the line of development (which seemed so inescapable only a few years ago) established by Schoenberg and Webern and continued in the early works of Boulez and Stockhausen. These composers laid great emphasis on the autonomous development of their musical language. The works themselves were primarily concerned with the resolution of their own internally created dialectics – between form and content, audible and non-audible and so on. Music now is generally less self-regarding than this; it has become more outward-looking and more conscious of itself as a social force, and it requires participation and involvement from performers and listeners alike for its com-

pletion. To many people, of course, this has also meant that it has become less like music, but it has brought increased relevance and urgency to the art.

Boulez

We may begin by considering the rather alarming case of Pierre Boulez (b. 1925). During the past few years Boulez has developed into one of the finest conductors in the world; he regularly conducts most of the major symphony orchestras in Europe and America; he has been appointed chief conductor of both the New York Philharmonic and the B.B.C. Symphony Orchestra. On the other hand, since 1965 he has completed only two works, *Eclat* for chamber ensemble (1965, duration eight minutes) and *Domaines* for solo clarinet (1968,

Boulez conducting.

duration twenty minutes). This shows an astonishing falling-off of creative activity when compared with the spate of brilliant works which he wrote at the beginning of his compositional career. (The first and second piano sonatas, flute sonatina, *Livre pour quatuor* and *Le Soleil des Eaux* were all written between 1946 and 1948).

What has gone wrong? The music which he most frequently performs or conducts provides several clues. The basis of his repertoire is the work of Stravinsky, Debussy, Schoenberg, Berg and Webern. His own published statements show that he still feels very close to these composers and especially cherishes the ideal of the complete integration of form and content found in Webern: 'I am very attached to the formal structure of a work, but not only to that . . . I think that the formal structure exists only to express particular feelings; you see, I like a precious stone, a diamond, for instance, to serve a practical purpose, not just to be a valuable ornament. And a knife is sharp in order to kill: the 'form' of a knife is not confined to the knife alone but depends on the uses to which it is put; it's the same with the formal structure of a piece of music'.

His view of a composer's task today is one of extreme emotional and intellectual purity and it leads him to condemn what he sees as gross and unsubtle developments in composition. These include indeterminate music which is *genuinely* indeterminate (as opposed to the strictly limited and controlled freedoms of choice to be found in his own third piano sonata). He quotes, with obvious approval, the critic Jacques Scherer on Mallarmé's *Le Livre*: 'The only thing that can be considered is directed freedom'. He also appears to reject

Pierre Boulez.

the new developments in live electronics: 'Contact microphones and so on are a facile solution. They're just a practical solution, not a theoretical one'.

It is this insistence on theoretical solutions which sets him, as he says himself, *au contre-courant* to many of the important new developments in composition. Any form of compromise would be anathema to a composer of his integrity and so he has wisely decided to channel his creative energies into the *re*creative activity of conducting. His close study of the classic scores of the first half of the 20th century is having a reciprocal effect on his compositions, and may eventually help him to extricate himself from his present dilemma.

Barraqué and Carter

Naturally, Boulez is not the only composer to have continued to develop within the context of a previously established style. In his book *Since Debussy*, André Hodeir claimed that a young French composer, Jean Barraqué, had taken over where Boulez had left off (just before *Le Marteau sans Maitre* of 1954, according to Hodeir) and precipitated a storm of controversy by comparing him very favourably with Beethoven. In terms of quality this judgment must remain a personal one, but as regards compositional techniques it contains more than a grain of truth. During the past five years, Barraqué has composed several more instalments of his major life's work, *La Mort de Virgile*, inspired by the novel of Hermann Broch. This vast series of vocal, choral and instrumental works will eventually have an estimated duration of twenty-five hours. The latest sections are *Chant après chant* for soprano, piano and six percussionists and *Le Temps Restitué* for soprano, chorus and orchestra, a fine and compelling work that shows very clearly the Beethovenian features of his style. Barraqué uses a highly developed serial system which results in music of a density and complexity far more reminiscent of Schoenberg than of Webern (and hence the viable parallel with late Beethoven). Although the sound of his music is always finely calculated, its surface aspects remain subservient to the uncompromisingly thematic nature of his musical argument and this results in a texture which is at the same time resilient and tough.

The music of Elliot Carter (b. 1908), probably the most distinguished American composer of his generation, might appear, on the surface, to have little connection with that of Barraqué. For instance, he employs no strict serial system at all but an entirely personal technique based on the characteristic use of different intervals. But his concentration on a continuously developing thematic argument articulated in dramatic terms seems remarkably similar in spirit to that of Barraqué. He works very slowly on his complex scores and the piano concerto (1964-65) is the only new work that has appeared since his double concerto for harpsichord, piano and two chamber orchestras of 1961.

Writing about his recent works, Carter says: 'I regard my scores as scenarios, auditory scenarios, for performers to act out with their instruments, dramatising the players as individuals and as participants in the ensemble'. With the idea of warring instrumental factions as the basis of his style, the concerto was obviously a natural form of expression for Carter, and in fact his piano concerto is a masterly recreation, in contemporary terms, of the ideal of the Romantic concerto. Carter extends the principle further by having a concertino of seven solo instruments grouped round the piano, which act as intermediaries between the soloist and the orchestra.

above right
Elliot Carter.

right
Jean Barraqué.

The rhythmic difficulties and the resulting problems of ensemble posed by this work are extreme – not only for the soloist, but for each individual player. Carter's piano concerto in fact typifies many of the problems inherent in the music under discussion in this section. It is founded on a premise of total thematicism which means (or, from the evidence of the works themselves, seems to mean) that the only way to progress is by increasing complexity of the substance of the music. This is a problem which beset many composers in the 1950s; by now most of them have succeeded in reversing this trend, with the results which will be discussed later. Another crucial question must be – how successful is the relationship between the complexity of the individual parts and that of the total result? In many works, the labour of writing and executing such complicated scores hardly seems worth the effort.

Xenakis, Ligeti and Penderecki

It does seem that, aurally speaking, there is an optimum level of complexity obtaining for any given work, beyond which the functional identity of each discrete element becomes absorbed into a more general and textural foreground. Many composers have recognised this fact, and have exploited it – Stockhausen's *Gruppen* for instance, is composed on the knife-edge of discrete and textural sound and the balance is continually shifting from one to the other. On the other hand, a large number of composers are using textural blocks as the basis of their compositions, viewing these as a natural outcome of total serialism. These composers include Xenakis (b. 1922), Ligeti (b. 1923), Penderecki (b. 1933), Lutosławski (b. 1913) and many other Polish composers. Their approach is fraught with difficulties; textural blocks are very difficult to handle with any degree of formal subtlety.

It must be noted that Xenakis's very individual approach sets him apart from the other composers in the above list. Formerly an assistant to Le Corbusier (1947-59), he sees his impressive agglomerations of pizzicati and glissandi (in works like *Pithoprakta*, 1955-56, and *Syrmos*, 1959) as being aural transliterations of architectural phenomena (curves, planes etc.). In another composition – *Terretektorh* (1965-6) – he developed his interest in musical space even further. The eighty-eight musicians (who in addition to their usual instruments also play one woodblock, one whip, one maraca and one siren-whistle each) are seated among the audience. 'Terretektorh is a sonotron: an accelerator of sonorous particles, a disintegrator of sonorous masses, a synthesiser. It places the sound and the music around the man, near to him. It tears down the psychological and auditive curtain which separates the listener from the musicians placed far away on a

Yannis Xenakis.

527

pedestal stage itself placed often in a box. The player in the orchestra rediscovers his responsibility as an artist, an individual'.

Ligeti has also considerably extended his range in recent years. From his earliest works (*Atmospheres* and *Apparitions* for example) he has always created the most subtle sound-pictures of any textural composer. Recently he has written a remarkable series of 'pianissimo-pieces': *Etude No 1–Harmonies* for organ (1967), *Lux aeterna* (1966) for 16-part choir and *Lontano* for orchestra, in which shifts of pitch and colour occur almost imperceptibly. He has also developed away from the one-dimensional, harmonic structure of these works to a sound-world of increased diversity and drama in his two miniature 'operas without words' *Aventures* and *Nouvelles Aventures*, and two chamber works, the ten

pieces for wind quintet and a string quartet.

Penderecki, on the other hand, in an attempt to broaden the range of his musical language, notably in the *St Luke Passion*, has only succeeded in rather unsuccessfully grafting onto it other styles (pseudo-plainchant for the recitatives, a primitive twelve-note technique for the arias), and has finally composed a work which satisfies neither formally nor stylistically.

In fact, the medium of the large orchestral and choral work seems to have borne little fruit during the past few years. This is in marked contrast to many of the earlier successes of new music, which were achieved in these traditional, and therefore more acceptable media (e.g. Nono, *Il Canto Sospeso*; Boulez, *Le Soleil des Eaux*; Stockhausen, *Gruppen*; Berio, *Allelujah II*). The many factors that have contributed to this change may

Karlheinz Stockhausen.

Plate 58
*Scene from a performance in 1964
of* La Création du Monde, *a ballet
with music by Milhaud and choreography by Kenneth MacMillan.*

Plate 59
*The organ of the Royal Festival
Hall, London.*

Plate 60
*An opera recording in progress. At
the EMI studios in London the
cast of* Don Giovanni *are placed on
a raised platform with their movements carefully planned to enhance
the atmosphere of a performance.*

be enumerated as follows: the economic difficulties of mounting performances of large-scale works; the antagonism of orchestral players towards new music (due in the main, to the poor quality of advanced music education); the short-sightedness of orchestral managements in programming important new works; and the tremendous development of electronic music, especially of live electronics, which have enabled composers to achieve greater volume and diversity of sound than any orchestra could ever achieve, with only a few performers. There is also a new generation of performers, who are dedicated not merely to re-interpreting the past but to actively creating the present – a selective list would include David Tudor (piano), Siegfried Palm (cello), Heinz Hollinger (oboe), Christoph Caskel (percussion), Alan Hacker (clarinet), Alfons and Aloys Kontarsky (piano duo), Karl-Erik Welin (organ), Severino Gazelloni (flute) and Vinko Globokar (trombone). Finally there is the activity of composers themselves as performers, organisers and promoters of their own groups, such as Luciano Berio's Juilliard Ensemble of New York, Stockhausen's Performing Group of Cologne, the Pierrot Players of Peter Maxwell Davies and Harrison Birtwistle in London, Cornelius Cardew's AMM of London, the Sonic Arts Group of New York, and Larry Austin's New Music Ensemble in Davis, California.

Stockhausen (I)

The developments just outlined can be followed particularly clearly in the work of the most important and influential composer of the post-war world, Karlheinz Stockhausen (b. 1928). 1964 saw the completion of *Moments*, his (then) largest work, with a total duration of 75 minutes. In spite of its great length and the astonishing diversity of its sound-world it is scored only for a soprano solo, medium-sized chorus and 13 instrumentalists for its realisation. It can be viewed in retrospect as the culmination of his previous music and is cast in 'Moment' form, as are *Carré* (1959–60) and *Contacts* (1959–60). But for the first time the Moments are mobile and their relative positions can be changed from performance to performance. All the musical elements (pitch, rhythm, instrumental combinations etc.) form part of a large-scale serial design, although the way in which these parameters are serialised is related more and more to the way in which we hear music and far less to the purely abstract criteria of his earlier works. This fact obviously has a bearing on the use of instrumental and vocal characteristics as form-building elements.

But as well as marking a far-reaching extension of many of his earlier compositional techniques, *Moments* also initiated many new facets of Stockhausen's genius, and these have formed the basis of his work since then. Perhaps due to the humanising effect of voices, the all-embracing emotionalism characteristic of Stockhausen's large-scale works (but previously kept on a tight rein) comes bursting unforgettably to the surface of the music in the intense lyricism of the soprano part and the choral outbursts of almost Messiaenic fervour.

Stockhausen's choice of texts for *Moments* is also very revealing. There are several different kinds of text. The first includes typical audience reactions (clapping, shouts of *bis*, *encore* etc.) and extracts from letters he received during the composition of the work. These express his increasing acceptance of the artistic validity of every aspect of our everyday life, an idea paralleled in his alternative description of Moment form as NOW-form (*Jetztform*). The second quotes the names of his wife, children and friends, representing the private,

personal aspect of his work. The third has extracts from the Song of Songs and two lines of William Blake ('He who kisses the joy as it flies Lives in eternity's sun rise'). In an interview, he has explained the reasons for this choice of texts: 'First of all I used text which is extremely spiritual, which goes very obviously beyond the logic-information in the text, and also beyond its descriptive quality. It must always have something which is super-rational (I purposely don't say irrational). Secondly it must be as common as possible. When I take these two qualities together, then the texts are all sources which have been translated into all languages. . . . The same thing is true of the texts I quote; they are very short works by world-famous poets. But already less true, much less true. These are the two things, that what I take is quickly recovered in the memory of as many people as possible, and that it is highly spiritual'. This notion of gathering up the threads of past and present experience in a grand historical synthesis is even more clearly expressed in his subsequent works and marks a major breakthrough in the history of 20th-century music.

Now that the initial shock of Schoenberg's atonal and serial revolutions has receded we can see that he actually rejected very little of what his predecessors (Bach, Mozart, Beethoven and Brahms, on his own admission) had evolved, except – at least in the serial works – the guiding principle of tonality. Webern abandoned much more, especially in his evolution of rhythmic structure and his increasingly structural use of timbre. With the first important post-war music the structuralisation and fragmentation of all parameters became pervasive. In *Moments* and Stockhausen's succeeding works, we witness a gradual reintegration and recombination of these fragments – a totally new stage in the history of music is not merely (as in previous works by Cage) made

An experimental sound studio of the French radio and television corporation.

possible, but is actually composed.

Following the completion of *Moments*, Stockhausen wrote, in quick succession, three works in which he used, for the first time, electronic processing of live sound in real time. In *Mikrophonie I* (1964), a large tam-tam is 'excited' from both sides by two players with dozens of different objects (made of paper, glass, wood, metal, plastic etc.). Two other players pick up the sounds produced with directional microphones. This sonorous 'raw material' is then processed by two more players who each have a filter (which alters the timbre of the sound) and a potentiometer (which controls its volumes). The parts of all the players are precisely notated in the score. The transformed and live sounds are heard, simultaneously over four loud speakers.

In *Mixtur* (1964), a different procedure is used. The sounds from five orchestral groups are picked up by microphones and modulated by sine-wave frequencies in a ring-modulator. A ring-modulator is a single piece of electronic equipment which both adds and subtracts the frequencies of any two sounds fed into it. Because even a single note played on any musical instrument contains a very large number of frequencies the ring-modulation of orchestral groups produces incredibly rich and infinitely variable sound mixtures (hence the title of the work). *Mikrophonie II* uses the same process, the two sound sources being a choir of 12 voices and a Hammond organ (which functions as a sophisticated tone-generator).

Live electronics

The foregoing gives a brief idea of some of the techniques of live electronic music. Its possibilities are endless, governed only by the amount and sophistication of the equipment available. Never since the middle ages has music been so closely bound up with scientific thought.

As increasingly complex and adaptable pieces of electronic apparatus are developed, new compositions will be able to make use of them. Already in his *Music for solo performer* (1965), Alvin Lucier (b. 1931) has employed three small Grass Instrument silver electrodes to pick up alpha-waves from the brain of the performer. They are then relayed through a number of loud-speakers and used to activate percussion instruments placed in front of them. In his *North American Time Capsule 1967*, the performers are asked 'to prepare material using any sound at all that would describe to beings far from our environment, either in space or in time, the physical, spiritual, social, scientific or any other situation in which we currently find ourselves'. These sounds are processed by a vocoder, an electronic device developed by Sylvania Electronic Systems to encode speech sounds into digital information lists for transmission over narrow band-widths via telephone lines or radio channels. Many scores – those of the two works by Alvin Lucier just mentioned, *Mesa* for cybersonic bandoneon by Gordon Mumma, and *Max-feed* by Max Neuhaus – consist only of circuit diagrams showing how the relevant electronic equipment is to be set up. Some of Cage's recent works (e.g. *Variations VI* for a plurality of sound systems) consist only of instructions for connecting randomly derived numbers of sound sources, amplifiers and loudspeakers.

Live electronic music is the best possible confirmation of Marshall McLuhan's contention that we have emerged from the visual, mechanical and linear-print culture of Renaissance man into a new, aural, tribal and electronic age.

The parallel is drawn by Robert Ashley, a member of the ONCE group, an ensemble of musicians, dancers, artists and designers based on Ann Arbor, Michigan. 'We have made pieces by working together. Just practice. You get together with an idea. You describe the idea, and everybody talks about it, and then we try to work it out. When a piece gets to a certain point you know that it is in at least good enough form to show to an

Peter Maxwell Davies.

audience. By the time of a public performance all the things that have gone into it are so complex that I can't notate them any longer'.

A new musical tradition is thus being created and transmitted aurally. In this respect it resembles folk song, the music of Indian, Japanese and Chinese cultures and all forms of primitive tribal music. Some groups play without any form of written score whatsoever (notably AMM Music), all decisions being made by spontaneous mutual interaction during the performance. In Stockhausen's most recent scores only a musical *process* is notated, and not a final aural result. The performances of these works given by his own group, both on concert tours and on records, are thus invaluable in enabling us to form a complete picture of the works, only half of which is contained in the score.

Stockhausen (II)

This is an appropriate moment to return to Stockhausen and the historical synthesis mentioned earlier. The process begins, in fact, with the last work described in that section, *Mikrophonie II*. From time to time, in this work, tape-recorded extracts from previous pieces by Stockhausen are heard on a distantly placed loudspeaker. His next work, *Prozession* (1967), written for an ensemble made up from the players who gave the original performances of *Mikrophonie I*, goes much further than this. The score consists of a symbolically expressed process for developing musical material. The precise material which is fed into this process is recalled from memory by the players themselves from previous (designated) works by Stockhausen. *Prozession* obviously demands players who are very familiar with Stockhausen's own works, and future performers will have to 'learn' this work not only from the score, but also from listening to performances given of it by Stockhausen's own ensemble – a striking example of the new aural culture in evolution.

In 1966 Stockhausen spent six months in Japan. His experiences there have had a profound effect on all his subsequent music. He describes the first impact of the country on him as follows: 'The first eight or nine days in Tokyo I was unable to sleep. I was happy about it, because thousands of sound-visions, ideas, movements passed through me while I lay awake. One vision came back more and more openly: it was what I like – a vision of sounds, new technical processes, formal relations, pictures of notation, human relationships etc. etc.' The first fruit of this new aesthetic orientation was his work for four-channel tape, *Telemusik* (1966), and it was soon followed by *Hymnen* (1966-67), described as electronic and concrete music for tape and four instrumentalists (those of *Prozession*). Both these works are based on already existing music – recordings of folk music in *Telemusik* and of over fifty different national anthems in *Hymnen*. Distorted, filtered, modulated, altered in pitch (but always retaining their identity) and mixed with purely electronically produced sound, these '*objets trouvés*' from the past form both the musical and poetic substance of these works. Asked why he chose to use national anthems in *Hymnen*, Stockhausen replied simply, 'In order to know what I have done with them'. Interviewer: 'You don't want any associations which are extra-musical?' Stockhausen: 'Well, that happens also. But then I don't mind what they are like.' This statement, although obviously true in itself, underestimates (probably deliberately) the overwhelming emotional impact of this huge work, which lasts 115 minutes.

Peter Maxwell Davies

Many composers have used quotations from already existing works and references to earlier styles in their recent works. Most of these differ from Stockhausen in their intent, which is primarily parodistic. Some such works are *Sinfonia* by Berio, *Blues and Screamer* by David Reck, the opera *Votre Faust* by Henri Pousseur

An electronic concert.

The American composer John Cage, whose work has greatly influenced many young avant-garde composers.

and many recent works of Maxwell Davies (b. 1934).

Throughout his career this composer has made extensive use of pre-existing material. His *Alma Redemptoris Mater* for woodwind sextet (1957) is based on a motet by Dunstable; *St Michael* (1957) on the plainsong of the requiem mass; the string quartet (1961), *Leopardi Fragments* (1961) and *Sinfonia* (1962) on movements from Monteverdi's Vespers. In all these earlier works, however, the sources never appear in their original form, but are always transmuted through complex serial and contrapuntal techniques into a musical structure which, although exhibiting the same kind of intellectual and emotional toughness of much late medieval music, nevertheless sounds totally different. After a period of transition a startling new departure occurs in *Antechrist* (1967). This piece begins with an instrumental version of the original motet on which it is based (*Deo confitemini*), scored in a raucous fashion reminiscent of a Baroque organ. The dislocated rhythms and shrill instrumentation are immediately continued and heightened in the rest of the piece. The process of derivation which, in his earlier works, was a pre-compositional technique (as he said, 'the plainsong was first reduced to a sequence of notes and intervals and then subjected to the process of proportional organisation'), now becomes a living part of the musical fabric. In *L'Homme Armé* of 1968, the stylistic net is thrown even wider. The composer's starting point was the completion of an anonymous 15th-century mass. To this he added 'glosses' in widely diverging styles in a manner suggested by the 'Sirens' chapter of James Joyce's novel *Ulysses*. The deliberate grotesquerie of this work, and the expressionistic intensity of *Revelation and Fall* (1965), a setting of a prose-poem by Georg Trakl, emphasise the irony, reminiscent of Mahler, which lies behind his use of this material. These pieces are never merely amusing; the distortion of the originals is so extreme that we feel almost a personal affront that they should be treated in this way. The aesthetic behind these works can be related back as far as *St Michael*, of which he has said, 'I was much torn by the fundamental question of good and evil at that time and, in fact, I still am. Writing that work was an attempt to come to terms with that problem'.

John Cage

In spite of his assertion that he is 'less and less interested in music', Cage has recently completed his most elaborate work, entitled *HPSCHD*. The fruit of two years work with Lejaren Hiller in the computer studios at Illinois university, it uses seven harpsichords, 52 tape machines, 59 amplifiers and speakers together with 40 movie films and 6,400 slides connected with the theme of manned space flight. At its first performance on May 16, 1969, it lasted five hours and was given before an audience of 8,000 people. Apart from this unprecedented work the most significant product of Cage's recent activities has been the appearance of his second book of collected writings, *A Year From Monday*. Compared with his earlier book *Silence*, this new volume records a very significant change of attitude. Instead of the withdrawn contemplation and search for a 'will-less' music, he now sees the composer in a more dynamic role and believes that he must now bring his private thought processes out into the world 'where our central nervous system effectively now is.' The sphere of his influence has also been steadily widening. In one way or another he has affected many – indeed most – of the composers mentioned in this chapter. His debt to oriental philosophy has been reciprocated by the influence that he has had on Eastern, particularly Japanese, composers.

Throughout this discussion of 'new directions' it has been thought more valuable to write in some detail – however superficial – about the work of the best and most significant composers working today, rather than overwhelm the reader in an attempt to mention every composer who is writing music of interest. Even the work of these few composers should indicate that never has the field of musical composition been so rich, nor the possibilities for its future so wide.

ROGER SMALLEY

Glossaries

Glossary of
Technical Terms

This glossary contains three main types of entry: descriptions of all the important musical forms; brief definitions of the main technical terms relating to music; and one line definitions of the more important foreign words commonly used to indicate modes of performance. Instruments are described in a separate section.

absolute pitch. Anyone able to identify by name a note heard, or able to sing any note asked for by name, is said to have a sense of absolute pitch.

abstract music. Used of music which is considered not to describe or relate to any extra-musical concept such as phenomena of nature or a human activity. It is used as the opposite of programme music, but the boundaries between the two types are blurred.

a cappella (Italian, 'as in church'). The term is used to describe unaccompanied vocal music although, of course, the use of instrumental accompaniment has been known in church music since the middle ages.

accidental. A sign, such as a sharp or flat, which modifies the pitch of a note but which is not in the key signature. An accidental is placed immediately in front of the note it applies to and is effective only within the bar in which it occurs. The natural sign is used to cancel a sharp or flat marking.

acoustics. The term is used in two senses. Firstly, to mean the science of sound; secondly, of the properties of a concert hall or other building as they affect the sounds produced in it.

acoustic bass. An effect sometimes used on small organs to achieve a range of low notes without full-length pipes by using the principle of the resultant note.

adagio (Italian, 'at ease'). Indication that the music is to be performed at a slow, relaxed pace. A movement or piece of music with this marking.

ad lib (Latin *ad libitum*, 'at will'). A piece of music so marked may be performed, as to its tempo, at the performer's discretion. A part so marked may be omitted if desired. The term may also indicate that a cadenza may be included at the place marked.

Agnus Dei. A section of the mass.

Alberti bass. A type of broken chord accompaniment in the left hand of a keyboard composition, particularly common in 18th-century music, and named after the composer D. Alberti (d. 1740).

aleatory (from the Latin *alea*, 'dice'). A type of contemporary music in which the composer intentionally allows chance events to play a part in either the composition or performance of the music, e.g. the admission of extraneous sounds.

allegretto. The Italian diminutive of *allegro*; music so marked is to be performed in a slightly less lively manner.

allegro (Italian, 'lively'). The term indicates a fairly fast tempo.

allemande (French, 'German'). One of the dances, often the opening one, in the classical dance suite which evolved in the 17th century. The allemande, also called in English, alman, almand, or almain, was in an easy 4/4 time. It had two sections.

alto (Italian, 'high'). The term is used of the high male voice, also known as counter-tenor, and sometimes of the female voice normally called contralto. In vocal music the second highest part is always called alto, whether sung by men or women; instruments of approximately this range are also given the name and there is an alto clef for parts lying in the range. In France the viola is called an *alto* (i.e. alto violin).

Ambrosian chant. Early type of plainsong supposedly developed by St Ambrose, bishop of Milan in the 4th century.

andante (Italian, 'walking'). Indicating a steady, flowing tempo.

andantino. Indicating a somewhat faster tempo than the above.

answer: see **fugue**

anthem. A short choral composition for religious services, particularly in the English Church. The words are not usually part of the liturgy. Anthems may be either accompanied or unaccompanied. A 'full' anthem is for chorus throughout; one with passages for soloists is a 'verse' anthem. During the Restoration, the verse anthem, with brilliant instrumental passages, was a major form.

antiphon (Greek, 'sound across'). A short passage, usually from the psalms, sung or intoned before and after the psalms in the liturgy of the Catholic Church. They are often sung as responses between groups of singers or between a single voice and the choir, hence the adjective antiphonal for any music performed thus.

aria (Italian, 'air'). A song for solo voice in an opera or oratorio. Unlike an arioso it has a clear formal structure which, in the case of a da capo aria, frequent in 18th-century opera, requires the repetition of the first section after a central contrasting passage.

arioso. An operatic passage for solo voice, melodic but with no clearly defined form.

arpeggio (from the Italian for 'harp'). A broken chord in which the notes are played in succession with an effect, whether on the piano or other instrument, reminiscent of the harpist sweeping the strings.

ars antiqua. The style of developed organum evolved and perfected by the school of Paris in the late 12th and 13th centuries.

ars nova. The musical style of the 14th century, above all in France, marked by extreme theoretical complexity and often aridity.

atonal: see **tonality**

augmentation. The lengthening of the notes of a musical theme or motif, usually by multiples of two or four applied to all the notes. Diminution is the reduction in length of the notes by a similar process. For augmented interval see **interval**.

Ave Maria (Latin, 'Hail Mary'). A Latin prayer which has been the subject of many settings. Notable are those by Schubert and by Gounod in his adaptation of the first prelude of Book I of Bach's *Well Tempered Clavier*.

ayre. English strophic song, usually with lute accompaniment, of the late 16th and early 17th centuries.

B. In German notation, the name for the note in English designated B flat. B natural (English notation) is H in German.

bagatelle. Short, lightweight piano piece.

ballad. Narrative verse type of simple stanzaic form and rhyming scheme; such ballads have frequently been set to music. The term also applied in 19th-century England to a type of sentimental strophic song.

ballade. A form in medieval French poetry. Typically it consists of three eight-line stanzas, the last line of each being a repeated refrain, and an *envoi* which also has the refrain. It and its cognate musical form were immensely popular during the 14th and 15th centuries. The term and the form were revived in the 19th century both in poetry and in music, the most famous *ballades* being those of Chopin.

ballad opera. English dramatic form with spoken dialogue alternating with songs. The origins of the form go back to the jig of the 16th century, but it reached its classic expression with John Gay's *Beggars' Opera* of 1728.

bar. A metrical unit marked by the vertical 'bar' lines in the score.

barcarolle. A boatman's song or a piece in that type of swaying rhythm; Chopin wrote a famous one for the piano.

baritone. Man's voice, intermediate between bass and tenor.

bass. The lowest part in a musical score or the lowest male voice. The term is also used of low pitched musical instruments, those of the lowest pitch being termed 'double-' or 'contra-bass'.

bel canto (Italian, 'beautiful song'). Loosely used to cover any particular style of singing, now past, especially admired by the user. It is also used with particular reference to the style cultivated in the 18th and early 19th centuries in Italian opera. This demanded precise intonation, clarity of tone and enunciation and a virtuoso mastery of the most florid passages.

Benedictus. A section of the ordinary of the Roman Catholic mass.

berceuse (French, 'cradle song'). The term is used of an instrumental piece, usually for piano, with a rocking accompaniment. A famous example is the *Berceuse* by Chopin.

bergamasca. Italian dance of a full-blooded, boisterous nature from the town of Bergamo; in England it applied to a specific tune which was a very popular basis for lute compositions. Since the 17th century the term has come to mean 'picturesque' in a vigorous sort of way.

binary form. A simple musical form in two sections which develop a simple harmonic pattern; the first modulates from the home key to a related one, the second returns to the home key. This simple formula, established as a recognised form in the early 18th century, contained the seeds of sonata form.

bitonality: see **tonality**

blues. A vocal and instrumental style which provided one of the major streams from which jazz flowed. The blues scale is distinct from the other scales of Western music in that the third and seventh degrees can be modified by flattening to a greater or lesser extent.

bolero. Spanish dance in triple time originally accompanied by singing and castanets. It dates from the 17th century but brilliant boleros were written for the piano by Chopin and for orchestra by Ravel.

boogie-woogie. Style of piano playing springing from the blues. The typical elements are the form of the twelve-bar blues, which modulates from tonic to dominant to sub-dominant back to tonic, and the ostinato figures of the left hand.

bourdon. A low pitched diapason stop on the organ.

bourrée. French dance in duple time which became one of the movements in the classical dance suite.

bowing. This is an important element in the techniques of all bowed stringed instruments and is an extensive field. There are many types of bowing, and the composer usually gives thorough instructions to ensure that the performer gives the music the required phrasing.

brass. Collective term for a family of musical instruments.

breve. Rarely used time value, double the semibreve in length.

cabaletta. The final short, fast section of a type of aria in 19th-century Italian opera.

caccia (Italian, 'hunt'). A late medieval musical form which evolved in Italy and continued to be used during the 16th century. The *caccia* was programmatic, using voices and instruments to describe episodes in the hunt (hence the name) or similar scenes of outdoor life.

cadence. A chord progression at the end of a phrase or a piece of music which gives the hearer the sense of finality. Usually the final chord of such a progression falls on a strong beat, but

when on a weak beat the cadence is described as 'feminine'. There are various types of cadence: the 'perfect', a progression from dominant to tonic; the 'imperfect', ending on the dominant; the 'plagal', sub-dominant to tonic; the 'interrupted' cadence moves from the dominant to some chord other than the tonic.

cadenza (Italian, 'cadence'). A passage in a concerto in which the solo instrument performs without the orchestra. The cadenza usually occurs just before a cadence in the music and developed from the practice of embellishing this with elaborate ornamentations. Hence, of course, the name and hence, also, the fact that the cadenza, usually little more than a display of virtuosity, was originally left to the improvisatory skill of the performer. From the time of Mozart, however, composers began to write out the cadenzas for their concertos. However, even as it became an increasingly integral part of the concerto, the cadenza retained its brilliant and florid character.

cancrizans (from Latin *cancer*, 'crab'). A type of canon in which the second voice consists of the notes of the first given in reverse order.

canon. A style of contrapuntal composition in which the first voice or part is followed at fixed time intervals by other parts which imitate it note for note, or as exactly as the harmony of the resulting polyphonic structure will allow. Canons may be in two or more parts, four-part canon being common, and may be extremely complex. The imitating voices may take the first by augmentation, diminution, or inversion; two two-part canons may proceed simultaneously to give 'double canon' and in 'crab' canon (cancrizans) the notes of the first part appear in retrograde order. A canon is usually so arranged that the parts end together, but in 'perpetual' canon, well known in the form of the 'round', each voice on completing its brief theme begins again and the music ends when the last voice to enter has completed its last repetition of the theme. Canons may also be written with harmonic accompaniments which have no share in the main contrapuntal development of the canonic parts.

cantabile. In a flowing style; from the Italian 'singing'.

cantata. A musical form for voices and instruments. The text may be secular or religious and the form originated in the Italian chamber cantata of the late 16th century for solo voice with lute or keyboard accompaniment. During the 17th century the church cantata developed and reached its highest peak in Germany, above all in the work of J. S. Bach. Solo cantatas continued to be written, but the form was usually choral. However, it always consisted of a number of arias and instrumental or choral sections; the German church cantata, usually composed for specific days in the liturgical year, commonly opened with a chorus and closed with a chorale. The instrumental resources soon grew beyond the simple accompaniment of the earliest cantatas. The formal concept has been employed in this century by Stravinsky and Britten.

canticles. Sacred songs, other than psalms, which form part of the church liturgy and draw their texts from the Bible.

cantilena. A term adopted from Italian to describe a flowing, song-like melodic line or performance, whether by voice or instruments.

cantillation. The unaccompanied chanting or

'intonation' of a sacred text, employed especially in Jewish worship. The rhythm follows that of the words and the melody line is very restricted, long passages of text being intoned on a single note, though some styles of cantillation are more ornate.

cantor (Latin, 'singer'). This term is commonly used as the equivalent of *chazan*, the title of the official who leads the music of the synagogue and is responsible for the cantillation of the liturgy. The director of music in a German Evangelical church is also called the Cantor.

cantus firmus (Latin, 'fixed song'). From the earliest days of polyphony, composition proceeded by building a contrapuntal structure of independent parts on the firm foundation of a slow moving theme taken from the plainsong of the liturgy, or from a secular song. At first called the 'tenor' and as such increasingly modified and distorted, the *cantus firmus* gained renewed importance in the cyclic mass of the 15th century. *Cantus firmus* composition continued after the high age of polyphony, if largely as a pedagogical exercise.

canzone (Italian, 'song'). The most important application of this term is to the Italian 17th-century form of instrumental composition, also called, in English, 'canzona', which often opened with a fugal introduction. In the 16th century, Italian composers had applied the term *canzoni* to their instrumental arrangements of French *chansons*. Earlier still, the *canzone* was a verse form whose text might be set as a *frottola*. In opera, the term may be used to describe any song without the formal pretensions of an aria.

canzonet (abbreviation from the Italian *canzonetta*, 'little song'). A type of part song, similar to the madrigal, highly popular with English composers of the early 17th century.

capriccio (Italian, 'caprice'). In the 17th century, a light composition using fugal techniques; later, a piece in free form, or short variations on a theme by another composer.

carol. A lyric form originating in the middle ages, consisting of verses with refrain; performed in religious and secular processions and composed for notable occasions. The term is now almost exclusively reserved for the carols of Christmas.

cassation. A musical form of the 18th century with similarities to the divertimento. It was for instruments, was in a number of short movements and often opened with a march.

castrato. A eunuch singer, one of a group who enjoyed immense vogue during the 17th and, even more, the 18th century. The boy was castrated before puberty to preserve the soprano, or more rarely alto, pitch of the voice. The greatest *castrati* achieved remarkable heights of virtuosity, and the quality of their voices, in range and purity like boys', in power and control like men's, gained them immense wealth and prestige.

catch. A part song for unaccompanied voices, very popular in England in the 17th and 18th centuries. Related to the round and the glee, the catch became something of a cult until the Catch Club (founded in the 1760s) could claim the prince regent as one of its members. The texts were often written so that the slowest imagination or the simplest mispronunciation produced secondary, usually obscene, meanings.

cavatina. A type of short operatic song or an instrumental piece in a similar style, such as the legendary cavatina for violin and piano by J. J. Raff.

chaconne. Originally a dance in slow triple time composed on a ground bass. From the 17th century onwards it was used, like the passacaglia, by composers as a musical form. The chaconne in D minor for violin by Bach, and the 'chacony' in G minor for strings by Purcell, are among their noblest works.

chamber music. The name given by convention to music for a small group of instrumentalists, each part being played by one performer only. The classic form is that of the string quartet, though there are many other combinations. Most common of these are the string quintet, the string trio and the piano trio for piano, violin and cello. There is a considerable repertory of music for wind instruments alone, but by far the most usual chamber music ensembles are those in which stringed instruments predominate. The piano trio has already been mentioned but there are also many fine examples of flute or oboe in conjunction with violin, viola or cello as well as famous works by Brahms and Mozart for clarinet and string quartet.

change ringing. The art of ringing a 'peal' of bells (commonly eight in number) through a series of permutations. The number of possible permutations of eight bells is 40,320, and out of these certain sequences are established in the change-ringing repertory. This style of bell-ringing, quite distinct from carillon music, in which melodies are played, is most fully developed in England.

changing note: see **nota cambiata**

choir. 1) The body of singers who lead the music in church. While most usually designating singers, the term is also sometimes used, particularly in the context of Renaissance music, of groups of instrumentalists. 2) The word is also used of a section of the organ.

chopsticks. The name of a simple melody 'chopped' out with the sides of the hands on the black notes of the piano while another player, the more advanced member of this primitive duo, provides a vamp bass. A number of 19th-century composers, among them Liszt, contributed to a set of variations on it published in 1880.

chorale. The English name for the hymn tunes of the German Reformed Church, many of which were derived from the earlier plainsong melodies – the German word *Choral* referring, strictly, to the plainsong. Luther and his contemporaries set words to these melodies and also composed some of them – later composers made new harmonisations of them and used them in their Passions and cantatas.

chorale prelude. A style of German organ composition in which the melody of a chorale was used as the basis of the music. The form probably grew out of the practice of the organist of embellishing the chorale tune as he played it over, preliminary to the singing of the hymn by the congregation. The art of such improvisation was much cultivated during the 17th century, J. S. Bach being the greatest and the last representative, but many chorale preludes were published by Bach and his predecessors and the form enjoyed something of a revival in the 20th century, in the work of Karg Elert. Either the whole tune is used as a *cantus firmus* or for a series of variations, or only a part of it is used.

chord. A group of notes sounded together.

Systems of harmony are concerned with rules governing the use of chords that are considered pleasing or acceptable, but the word itself is quite neutral in its application. The term 'chording' is used in three ways, to describe: the intonation of a group of performers; the composer's spacing of the notes of a chord; and, particularly in the United States, to describe the improvisation of harmonies to a melody.

chorus. 1) a body of singers. 2) A section of a dramatic, religious or other work sung by such a body – the Hallelujah Chorus of Handel's *Messiah* being the most famous example. 3) The refrain in, for example, a folk song, which is sung by a number of voices between the verses sung by a solo voice. 4) A solo improvisatory passage in classical jazz.

chromatic. This musical term is derived from the Greek word for colour. In music written according to the rules of diatonic harmony, notes not in the scale of the key of the music can be used, but they are felt to have a specially charged, 'colourful' quality. They are called chromatic notes and the harmonies that they introduce, chromatic harmonies. As composers in the 19th century came to make increasingly intense use of this kind of 'chromaticism', the validity of the key system was weakened.

clarino. In the Baroque period, a high lying trumpet part.

clausula. In 13th-century polyphony, a musical fragment based on a section of plainsong for a single word or clause. Such a section could be taken from the plainsong melody to which it originally belonged and the two parts, plainsong fragment and the vocalised part above it, inserted into another polyphony. When composers began to add words to the vocalised part a new form, the motet, came to be born.

clef (French, 'key'). This term describes the symbol which, placed at the beginning of a line of music, fixes the pitches of the lines of the staff. Thus the treble clef, in the form of an elaborately decorative 'G', fixes the second line up as the G above middle C; the bass clef, derived ultimately from the florid Gothic 'F', fixes the second line down as the F below middle C; while the third clef, the movable 'C' clef, fixes the central line of the staff as middle C for music lying in the alto register, and the second line from the top as middle C for music lying in the tenor register. The objective of the various clefs is to ensure as far as possible that the music of any given part lies on the five lines of the staff, but the use of the C clef is now very limited.

close. A synonym for cadence, a 'full' close being a perfect cadence, a 'half' close, imperfect.

cluster. The American composers Henry Cowell and Charles Ives, at the beginning of the 20th century, were probably the first to use the 'tone-cluster' (English usage, 'note-cluster') in their piano music. It is simply a massed chord produced by depressing a cluster of keys with the forearm.

coda. From the Italian word for 'tail', a coda is a concluding section to a piece of music or part of it. In fully developed sonata form as evolved by Beethoven, the coda is an integral and important section of the music. CODETTA, the diminutive of the word, applies to any brief concluding passage to a section of a movement; or, in fugue, to the episode between the second and third subjects.

coloratura. An elaborate and highly orna-

mented, usually high-lying, part for soprano voice. The term is also applied to those singers who specialise in the mastery of the demanding technique required for such parts.

compass. The compass of a voice or instrument is the range of pitch that it can command from its lowest note to its highest. In the case of the trombone, the lowest 'pedal' notes of the compass are separated by the interval of a fourth from the others, so that the instrument does not have a fully chromatic compass.

concertante. A piece of music or style in the nature of a concerto, with a small group of players contrasting with the main body.

concertato. Italian term for a new style of instrumental music introduced in the late 16th and early 17th century in which contrast – between various bodies of performers, between instrumental timbres and dynamics of volume – was of the essence.

concerto. A work for solo instrument, or instruments, and orchestra. It usually has three movements, of which the first is in sonata form. The term originated in the 17th century and was loosely applied to many kinds of instrumental and vocal music; by the end of the 18th century the classical concerto had emerged. Of central importance is the idea of contrast, and Bartók's use of this explains the title of his *Concerto for orchestra*.

concerto grosso. A type of composition much in vogue in the late 17th century and the first half of the 18th, in which the main body of the orchestra, the *grosso* or *ripieno*, is in dialogue with a small group of instruments, the *concertino*.

concord. A combination of notes in a chord that seems pleasing and restful to the ear.

concrete music. 'Music' made with pre-recorded sounds. It originated with the experiments of Pierre Schaeffer in the French radio and television corporation in the late 1940s. The raw material is recordings of sounds of all kinds from music to traffic noises; the artist-technician manipulates and distorts these sounds at will to yield a new tape 'composition'.

conductor. The director of a musical performance for any sizeable body of performers. During the 17th and 18th centuries the body of musicians was led from the harpsichord, often by the composer himself, playing the continuo bass; in other cases the performance would be kept together by someone giving the *tactus*, i.e. literally beating out time. In the 19th century the use of a baton became increasingly general and the authority of the conductor in all matters of interpretation became increasingly great.

conductus. Originally a monodic processional chant. In the 13th century it developed as a polyphonic form less complex than the motet and with a composed *cantus firmus*.

conservatory. English equivalent of the Italian *conservatorio* and the French *conservatoire*. The first schools of music seem to have originated in the Italian orphanages of the 17th century where music was an important subject; from these origins the name derives. The famous Paris Conservatoire was founded in 1784.

console. The keyboard and pedal-board of an organ.

consort. In 17th-century English music, a group of instruments playing together; a 'whole consort' consisted of instruments of the same family, a 'broken consort' of instruments of various families.

continuo. For much music written between 1600 and 1730 the basis was provided by a *basso continuo*. This was a bass line on which the harmonies of the music were to be built up, often extemporarily, by the keyboard player. Sometimes the line of notes was reinforced with figures over the notes to specify the required harmonies and the result was called a 'figured bass'. The keyboard player, who was often also both composer and conductor, was usually supported by a bass stringed instrument. The English for *basso continuo* is 'thorough bass' but the term usually used is the abbreviation of the Italian that heads this article.

contralto. Low-pitched woman's voice.

contra-tenor. A part in 15th-century music with a semi-harmonic function.

contredanse. French derivative word from English country dance.

counterpoint. The aspect of musical composition in which the horizontal movement of the parts rather than the vertical structures of the chords is of primary consideration. The polyphonic music of the 16th century and much 19th- and 20th-century music is truly contrapuntal but the great age of such composition is generally placed between about 1650 and 1750 and its characteristic mode of expression is canon and fugue. In 'invertible' counterpoint, two or more parts can exchange positions without producing a non-musical effect.

counter-tenor. High male voice of roughly the same range as the female contralto.

country dance. During the 17th century English village dances, already popular at court, enjoyed a vogue both at home and abroad. John Playford's *English Dancing Master* (1650) was a compilation of many of them.

coupler: see **organ**

Credo (Latin, 'creed'). Part of the ordinary of the Roman Catholic mass.

crescendo. Italian word meaning 'growing', used as a musical direction to indicate that the music is to get gradually louder.

cross relation. American term for false relation.

crotchet. The American term 'quarter note' derives from the fact that the crotchet is a time value one quarter the length of the semibreve.

csárdás. A Hungarian national dance with slow and quick sections; it has occasionally been used in classical ballet, an example being the *csárdás* in *Coppelia*.

cyclic form. Composition in which the same theme recurs in more than one movement as a main principle of formal unity. The earliest example was that of the cyclic tenor mass, but the technique is most usually associated with César Franck.

da capo. A direction from the Italian 'from the beginning'. It is usually abbreviated D.C. which, at the end of a piece, indicates that the first section is to be repeated as a conclusion. The *da capo* aria of the form A–B–A was one of the conventions of 18th-century Italian opera.

descant. A decorative line, often improvised, added above a harmonised melody. The descant recorder is pitched higher than the treble of the family. Also see **discant.**

development: see **sonata form**

devil in music: see **interval**

diabolus in musica: see **interval**

diapason. The characteristic tone of the organ.

diaphony. A type of two-part organum.

diatonic. A type of scale and the harmony resulting from using it.

differential note: see **resultant note**

dies irae (Latin 'day of wrath'). A 13th-century metrical sequence in the Roman Catholic requiem mass. It has been quoted to great effect by later composers.

diminished: see **interval**

diminuendo. Direction to performers for a gradual lessening in volume.

diminution: see **augmentation**

discant. In medieval music English discant was a type of three-part polyphony with the *cantus firmus* in the lowest part, the upper two parts moving so as to produce intervals of a third and a sixth above it. Also see **organum.**

discord. A chord which, in a harmonic context, seems to be in tension and to need resolution.

disjunct: see **motion**

divertimento. A musical form primarily of the classical period. It was for instruments and was in a number of short movements somewhat like the suite.

divertissement. Similar to the above though the music may be based on popular tunes.

divisions. A 17th-century term for embellishments to a melodic line consisting of florid runs that 'divided' the time values of the original melody. Composers often wrote sets of divisions on a ground bass.

dodecaphony (from Greek *dodeka*, 'twelve'): see **twelve-note music**

dominant. The fifth degree of the scale. The key of the dominant is of prime importance in diatonic harmony.

Dona nobis pacem (Latin, 'Grant us peace'). The concluding section of the Roman Catholic mass.

Dorian mode: see **mode**

dotted note. The dot is used in notation in two ways: above the note, to indicate staccato, or after the note to give a 'dotted note'. The dot in this case lengthens the time value of the note it follows by half.

double. 1) Of low-pitched instruments, e.g. double bass. 2) for two instruments, e.g. a 'double' concerto. 3) As in 'double octaves', i.e. octaves played by both hands simultaneously on the piano. 4) When a line is reinforced by another, thus – 'the violins are doubled by the oboes'. 5) A 'double-handed' performer is one skilled in two instruments which, if they are of the same family, he may play in the course of one piece. The third flautist may 'double' on piccolo.

double bar. A bar-line followed closely by a thick bar-line is the notational sign that marks the end of the piece, or of a section of it.

down-beat. The first beat of the bar: see **up-beat.**

drone. A note or chord held in the bass throughout the performance of a song or dance. Most common in folk music in which such instruments as the bagpipes and hurdy-gurdy are fitted with drone pipes and strings. In European folk music the drone is part of the music; in Indian music it has rather the function of providing a barely audible reference note for the main performers to correct their intonation as needed.

dumka (Ukrainian, 'lament'). A folk-music type used by Dvořák in some of his compositions.

dynamics. The variations of volume from loud to soft.

écossaise. An 18th-century French dance supposedly with Scottish characteristics. Beethoven and other 19th-century composers wrote examples in triple time; the original *écossaise* was in duple time.

eighth note. American term for quaver.

electronic music. Whereas concrete music uses recordings of sounds made by physical objects, including musical instruments, electronic music uses noises produced in the laboratory by electronic oscillators. Since its development in Germany in the 1950s it has been taken up in many parts of the world.

enharmonic. In ancient Greek music a specific scale. In harmonic music the term is used to describe the minute differences in pitch between, for example, c sharp and d flat. On the piano and other fixed-note instruments these two pitches are regarded as equivalent and are served by a single note. Enharmonic modulation exploits the nearness in pitch for moving from a sharp to a flat key.

ensalada. Spanish name for quodlibet.

ensemble. From the French word for 'together', this term is used when discussing the degree of effective teamwork among a body of performers. The word may also be used as a collective noun for the group of performers themselves or, in opera, for a set piece for a group of soloists.

entr'acte. A French term for music that may be played between the acts of a play or opera.

episode. Passage in a fugue between expositions of the subject.

equale. Composition for four trombones, usually funeral music. Beethoven wrote three fine *equali*.

estampie or **estampida.** A medieval instrumental form with the pattern a, a, b, b, which may have developed from the sequence.

exposition. 1) The statement of the subjects in sonata form. 2) Passage in a fugue containing the subject.

Expressionism. A term taken from painting to describe the music of certain early 20th-century composers, among them Schoenberg, whose work, by virtue of its extreme contrasts in pitch, instrumentation and rhythm, is often concerned with the explicit presentation of an interior emotional state. The term is sometimes contrasted with the music of such composers as Debussy, which is seen as parallel to Impressionism in painting.

faburden. A 16th-century English type of composition in which a tenor was derived from a plainsong melody according to certain rules and then used as the *cantus firmus*, the plainsong being discarded.

false relation. The English term for the effect produced in harmonic writing when a given note is followed, in another part, by its sharpened or flattened unison or octave, or when they are sounded simultaneously. d flat in the treble followed by d in the bass would be an example.

falsetto. A register available to the adult voice (usually male) above the normal pitch of utterance. Most male altos and counter-tenors are falsettists and, exceptionally, a soprano voice can be produced.

fandango. Vigorous Spanish and Latin American dance in triple time.

fanfare. A flourish of trumpets.

fantasia. The Italian equivalent of fantasy, sometimes used in English instead of the native word.

fantasy. 1) Polyphonic instrumental composition, especially for viols, much cultivated by English 16th- and 17th-century composers. 2) A piece in free form by 19th-century Romantic composers. 3) A pot-pourri of melodies from some larger work such as an opera.

farandole. Provençal folk dance accompanied by pipe and tabor.

fauxbourdon. A 15th-century manner of composition probably derived by Dufay from an attempt to emulate English discant. The top part carries the *cantus firmus*, the bottom two parts moving at the intervals of a fifth and an octave below it.

fifteenth: see **mutation stop**

fifth. A musical interval. The cycle of fifths, used in tuning keyboard instruments and in some harmonic procedures, is the progression of perfect fifths which eventually leads back to the starting note. In academic counterpoint and harmony consecutive fifths, that is two parts moving by parallel motion at the distance of a fifth, are forbidden, as are consecutive octaves.

figured bass: see **continuo**

final: see **mode**

fioritura (from the Italian for 'flower'). Florid improvised ornamentation employed by singers, especially in the 18th century.

flamenco (possibly from Spanish word for 'Flemish'). Spanish type of strongly rhythmic guitar playing derived from the traditional folk song type known as *cante hondo* and its related form of *cante flamenco*.

flat. The notational symbol placed before a note (accidentals) or in the key signature to indicate that it is to be lowered a semitone in pitch. Conventions of notation sometimes lead to the use of two flats or a 'double' flat before the same note, indicating that it is to be lowered a full tone.

Folia, La. Name of Portuguese dance immensely popular with composers during the 17th century.

forte, fortissimo. The Italian for 'loud' and 'very loud'; the abbreviations *f* and *ff* are used in scores.

fourth. An interval.

frottola. A 15th-century Italian verse form, a forerunner of the madrigal and more popular in style. Like the madrigal it had its own accompanying musical form.

fugue. The foremost type of contrapuntal composition. It is not, properly speaking, a form since about the only essential requirements are two or more parts and a fragment of thematic material called the 'subject' which forms the centre of interest in the composition. However, in a 'typical' fugue in four parts or 'voices' the pattern is roughly as follows. In the first 'exposition' each voice enters in turn with the subject and, as it relinquishes it, takes up the 'counter-subject' which normally accompanies the subject in all its later appearances. After the initial exposition there may follow a passage, called an 'episode', in which the subject is absent. In the course of a fugue there may be a number of episodes and expositions but there is no established and obligatory form. The subject can be modified by giving it inverted intervals (i.e. the intervals of the original are reversed – upward leaps become downward

steps), by augmentation or by diminution. Sometimes harmonic considerations require the actual intervals and notes of the subject to be changed slightly, and when this happens in the opening exposition we have what is called a 'tonal' rather than a 'real' answer; a requirement of strict fugal writing is that the initial and third entries of a four-part fugue should be in the tonic key and the second and fourth in the dominant. 'Stretto' occurs when one voice enters with the subject before another has completed the statement of it; depending on the composer's skill this entry can occur at various points in the subject. A fugue may have two or more subjects and can be written in 'mirror' fashion so that the parts may change places and the effect still be pleasing and musical.

fundamental. The base note in a harmonic series.

Futurism. In music, as in the other arts, the movement was primarily Italian and was inspired by the poet Marinetti. An early Futurist manifesto proclaimed a racing car more beautiful than the *Winged Victory of Samothrace*. In music the idea was a 'renovation' of the art through the use of noise. The Futurists even built special instruments, but in the 1950s their ideas find an echo in the techniques of concrete music.

galante. The *style galante* is the French term most commonly used for the style of composition, elegant, harmonically uncomplicated and avoiding contrapuntal techniques, which evolved in Germany, Vienna and France during the Rococo period of the mid-18th century.

galliard. A vigorous 16th-century court dance in triple time. It was commonly danced after the pavan.

gamba: see **viol family**

gamelan. A type of orchestra, consisting predominantly of fixed key instruments of the xylophone type, from the islands of Bali and Java in Indonesia.

gamut. In the early systems of vocal training (hexachord) the lowest note was the G of the bass stave; i.e. gamma was ut. From this the term came to be applied to the scale above this note and now the word 'gamut' has the general connotation of range.

gavotte. French dance enjoying a fashionable vogue in the 17th century. It became one of the more regular components of the dance suite of the 18th century.

Gebrauchsmusik. The German for 'utility music', a term coined by the composer Hindemith. He believed that composers should accept the obligation of providing music for functional use.

gigue (French 'jig'). Dance that was often the final movement of the 18th-century suite.

glee. (Probably from the Old English *gleo*, 'a musical entertainment'). In medieval England the gleeman was a strolling minstrel. In the 18th-century the term glee came to be applied to simple vigorous part-songs, usually for male voices, and many glee clubs were founded. In the U.S. glee clubs perform many types of short unaccompanied vocal works.

glissando. The word – an Italianised formation from the French *glisser*, 'to slide' – applies to the effect deliberately achieved by dragging the fingers across the keys of the piano or the

strings of the harp. The effect is also well known on the trombone.

Gloria. A section of the Roman Catholic mass.

grace note. An imprecise equivalent for certain types of ornament.

gradual. A section of the Proper of the Roman Catholic mass.

Gregorian chant: see **plainsong**

ground bass. A bass line consisting of a single, simple figure, repeated throughout a movement and implying a harmonic superstructure that colours the movement of the parts above it. The device, often rich in harmonic ambiguities, was much used in the late 17th century.

Guidonian hand. A mnemonic, devised by the 11th-century Italian monk, Guido d'Arezzo, to assist singers learning to read music. See also **hexachord**.

gymel. In medieval music a style of singing, probably of folk origin, in which two voices (the word comes from the Latin for 'twin') sing at intervals of the sixth and the third.

H. In German musical notation the name for B natural in English notation.

half-note. In American terminology, the minim, the semibreve being a 'whole-note'.

harmonic. A note derived on the violin or the harp by lightly placing the finger at a specific point on an already vibrating string to make one of the natural harmonics set up by the vibrations to ring clear. These 'natural harmonics' are members of the harmonic series.

harmonic series. When a string or column of air, or any other resonator, vibrates, it produces one loudly heard note, the 'fundamental', and a number of others above it, the 'harmonics', which may be faintly heard or only subconsciously perceived. These harmonics are related by simple mathematical ratios to give a series of decreasing intervals. From the fundamental, or first harmonic, to the second is an octave, from the second to the third the interval is a fifth, the next interval up is a fourth and so on up the series so that from about the seventh harmonic the series gives a number of notes approximating to a diatonic scale. The series is of special importance on two counts. First, the tone colour of the musical instruments is largely affected by which of the upper harmonics (also called 'upper partials') predominate in their individual sound 'spectrum'. Second, the notes of the brass instruments are all harmonics and the player selects the ones in the series by variations in wind pressure and lip.

harmony. In music of the Western tradition, the combination of sounds in a way deemed musically significant according to a system based on the concept of tonality and the major and minor keys. These systems were only explicitly established in the early 17th century and for the next two hundred years the structure of harmony rested on the chord of the triad – three notes separated by two intervals of a third (for example C-E-G in the key of C major). Further chords were derived by superimposing other thirds and all chords could be regarded in three aspects: the root position – i.e., C-E-G; the 'first inversion', E-G-C; the 'second inversion', G-C-E. The notes first available to the composer are those of the diatonic scale of the key in which he is writing, but of course other notes more or less remote from this key are used and are called chromatic notes. Chords may also be derived from these and furthermore the music can, according to certain rules, move, or 'modulate', into other keys. As such movement became increasingly free, and as more and more chromatic effects were introduced, the nature of harmony necessarily changed, so that in the 20th century new systems were investigated. Some were based on different scales; some used different principles for chord building – such as the interval of the fourth; others abandoned tonality (see also **twelve-note music**) or made use of several keys simultaneously.

head motif. Melodic fragment repeated at the beginning or head of phrases; a device used in the early 15th century to give unity to the music of the mass.

head voice. The upper part of a singer's range, usually with a lighter, less vibrant quality than the chest voice.

heroic tenor (From German *Heldentenor*). A singer specialising in the heavy and demanding operatic roles by composers such as Wagner.

hexachord. A group of six (Greek, *hex*) notes embracing a semitone interval, thus G, A, B, C, D, E, with the semitone between B and C. The system was devised by the 11th-century Italian monk, Guido d'Arezzo, to aid singers learning to sight-read. The six notes each received a name – ut, re, mi, fa, sol, la, with the semitone between mi and fa. Guido took the lowest G on the bass stave as base note for his system so that the first hexachord ran from G to E, the second from C to A, the third from F to D, and the 'grid' was repeated over two octaves. In this way the singer had a familiar structure to which to refer the music in front of him.

hill-billy music. White folk music of the Appalachian Mountains region of America.

histrion. Type of folk bardic singer still found in Balkan folk music.

hocket. In medieval music the effect achieved by the rapid passing of a short rhythmic motif from one part to another, with rests in the voices that do not have it for the moment.

homophony. Music in which the parts tend to move in step with one another – that is in block chords like a hymn tune. The term is also sometimes used, by extension, of music where there is slight movement in the parts but where the top, melodic line is clearly predominant.

hornpipe. Lively 17th-century English dance. Now associated with sailors but deriving its name from the folk instrument of the same name which originally accompanied it.

hymn. A song of praise for congregational singing, with a metrical verse form. The earliest hymns of the Church date from the 4th and 5th centuries.

idée fixe (French, 'fixed idea'). Device of composition used by Berlioz anticipating and similar to Wagner's *Leitmotiv*.

imitation. For long a staple element in compositional techniques. It occurs when a melodic phrase is repeated by different voices either more or less modified; it was particularly developed by late 15th-century composers.

Impressionism. Term used in painting of artists of the late 19th century who aimed to present on canvas the impression, usually in the most strictly visual sense, made on them by

the object of their painting. Debussy was much attracted by their work and his music, as well as that of Ravel, has something of the same quality.

impromptu. Despite its name a type of composition, but one intended to give the impression of improvisation. Schubert wrote well-known examples.

improvisation. Once a central part of the musician's art and remaining of importance down to the 19th century. It has always been basic in folk music, where the performer draws on a huge vocabulary of rhythms and melodic conventions, learned during a long apprenticeship, to create his own original musical 'sentences'. Such conventions and the use of improvisation were also known in the art music of the past and are still the basis of the art music of India. Improvisation also remains an important element in the art of the jazz musician.

incidental music. Music written for stage plays.

In nomine. A type of viol composition cultivated by English composers of the 16th and 17th centuries. It is in fact a polyphonic fantasy and is based on a *cantus firmus* drawn from the In nomine section of a mass by John Taverner, who started the vogue by transcribing this section of his mass for keyboard.

instrumentation. A term used when appraising a composer's skill in writing for individual instruments, the familiarity he shows with their techniques and the fullness to which he exploits their peculiar qualities.

interlude. A short dramatic entertainment sometimes given between the acts of a larger work or in the intervals of a feast or celebration. Late medieval interludes were important contributors to secular drama, and the music that accompanied them was important in the development of ballet and instrumental music.

intermezzo. Like the above a term now of indeterminate application. Formerly it referred to a piece of music played between the acts of an opera or sometimes to a short comic opera performed in the intervals of a grand opera; in such intermezzi were the origins of *opera buffa*. During the Renaissance, *intermedii* or interludes were an important part of court entertainment.

interval. The difference of pitch between two notes is described as the interval between them and this is conventionally measured by the steps of the major diatonic scale. The 'interval' between the first and fifth degrees of the scale is a 'fifth' and so on. With the fourth and the octave, the fifth is classed as one of the 'perfect' intervals – so called both for theoretical reasons and because they sound 'stable' in a way that the other intervals do not. These are classed as major and minor, the latter being a semitone smaller than the former. A compound interval is one larger than an octave. One interval, the 'tritone', has occupied a unique place in musical history. Composed of three whole tones (the distance between F and B) it was considered peculiarly ugly, was avoided at all costs and was named *diabolus in musica*, the 'devil in music'. The smallest interval conventionally used is the semitone, but some composers have experimented with quarter-tones and other 'micro'-intervals.

intonation. 1) The quality of pitching notes accurately in performance, i.e. singing or playing them 'in tune'. 2) In plainsong the

'intonation' is the opening phrase sung over by the precentor to give the singers the pitch of the chant.

invention. Two-part composition for the keyboard by J. S. Bach, who himself gave this name to fifteen such works written for his son Wilhelm Friedemann Bach.

inversion. 1) In counterpoint the 'mirror' image of a melodic line in which the intervals are reversed, the upward leaps becoming downward and vice versa. 2) The notes of a chord in other than their root position: see **harmony**.

isorhythm. The term, from the Greek meaning 'equal' rhythms, is applied to compositions of the 14th and 15th century in which the *cantus firmus* tenor is divided into rhythmically identical sections, without respect to its melodic character. The techniques of such isorhythmic motets have been used by certain *avant-garde* 20th-century composers.

Janissary music. The name given in the 18th century to music employing the percussion instruments, such as the bass drum, large cymbals and triangle, used by the Janissary regiments of the Turkish army. These were introduced in military bands and were used in such works as Haydn's 'Military' symphony.

jig. The name of an English country dance and also of a stage entertainment given by travelling players. They toured Germany in the early 17th century and may have contributed to the formation of the *Singspiel*.

jongleurs. Medieval travelling musicians and entertainers.

jota. Spanish folk dance in triple time. A well-known example occurs in de Falla's ballet, *The Three Cornered Hat*.

K. The initial of L.A.F. Ritter von Köchel, whose chronological and thematic catalogue of the works of Mozart was published in 1862. The 'K' numbers now conventionally quoted when referring to the composer's works derive from this catalogue.

Kapellmeister. German term (literally, 'master of the chapel') for the director of music at a court or similar establishment. *Kapelle* has a more general meaning than its literal English equivalent, referring to the full body of musicians on the establishment.

key. The notes and intervals of the diatonic scale are found at various pitches depending on which note the scale begins on. This note may be called the 'keynote', and music which uses primarily the notes of the scale based on it is said to be in the key of that note. For example, a passage in the key of C major will tend to use the notes of the scale of C major. Certain of these notes are of course shared by other keys, and those with many notes in common are said to be related; keys with very few notes in common are 'remote' from one another. In classical harmony a single key tends to dominate the music or a movement and the work is said to be 'in' that key, even though during its course the music may modulate to others either related to or remote from this 'home' key. The key of the music is indicated at the beginning of the staff by the KEY SIGNATURE i.e. the sharps or flats relevant to that key.

Klangfarbenmelodie. This German word, literally translated 'sound-colour-melody', was coined by Webern to describe his use of instrumental timbres as a primary element in his compositions.

Kyrie eleison. Greek for 'Lord have mercy upon us': the first section of the Roman Catholic mass.

Lamentations of Jeremiah. A book of the Bible from which are drawn the lessons for the Matins of the last three days of Holy Week in the Roman Catholic liturgy. These are also known as the services of *Tenebrae*, and the lessons have been the subject of many fine polyphonic settings by 16th-century composers as well as of the *Leçons de Tenèbre* by the great François Couperin.

Ländler. Southern German folk dance in waltz time. The great composers of the Viennese classical school used it occasionally.

largamente. Italian, 'broadly'.

larghetto. Diminutive of the Italian word *largo* and indicating a speed rather less slow.

largo. Italian for 'broad', indicating a stately, measured performance. The famous 'Handel's largo' comes from one of the arias in his opera *Serse*.

laudi spirituali. Congregational devotional songs of the Counter Reformation in 16th-century Italy, but their antecedents stretch back to the music of medieval religious fraternities.

lay. Medieval verse form with a corresponding musical form.

leader. The senior member of the first violins in an orchestra is the 'leader' of the orchestra in that he may take rehearsals and is an important factor in the orchestra's morale. The U.S. term is 'concert master', a direct translation of the German *Konzertmeister*.

leading note. The seventh degree of the major scale.

ledger lines. The short extra lines added above or below the staff in notation for notes that rise too high or go below it.

legato. (In Italian, literally, 'bound together'). A direction for smooth performance without detached notes.

Leitmotiv. Melodic element used by Wagner in his operas to represent musically the character of dramatis personae or events in the plot.

libretto (Italian, 'little book'). The text of an opera. The term derives from the fact that, bound in the form of a little book, these were sold to the audience.

Lied (plural, *Lieder*). Most simply, the German word for 'song'. But from the 15th century on the German *Lied*, like the French *chanson*, had sufficient rhythmic and other characteristics to be regarded as a distinct genre of composition. In the 19th century the Romantic *Lied*, set to words by contemporary poets and distinguished by the integral part played by the accompaniment, influenced song composition throughout Europe.

ligature. A line placed over a number of notes to indicate that they are to be phrased together.

long. Time value in medieval notation.

madrigal. A secular polyphonic composition for unaccompanied voices reaching its most fully developed form in Italy during the 16th century. The earliest madrigals, of the late 14th and 15th centuries, were light expressive part-songs, but by the 16th century the finest poets were writing examples, and composers set increasingly complex and powerful music to them with a new attention to expressing the sentiments and atmosphere of the words. At its height the Italian madrigal was a vehicle of the most passionate expression. A late-flowering madrigal school in England wrote much fine music but the texts were generally of lesser quality and the music was suitable for performance by amateurs rather than being the highly professional art usually demanded by the Italians.

maestoso. Italian, 'majestic'.

maestro di cappella. Italian term for 'director of music'. The German *Kapellmeister* is an exact equivalent.

Magnificat. The song of Mary (Luke I, 46-55), 'My soul doth magnify the Lord . . .' Plainsong and many polyphonic settings exist.

major: see **scale** and **interval**

marcato. Italian direction requiring *marked* emphasis of a part of the music.

marcia, alla marcia. Italian, 'in the manner of march music'.

masque. English 16th- and 17th-century dramatic entertainment in which poetry, costumes, scenery and music (which included singing and dances) were more important elements than the plot. It was analogous to the French court ballet.

mass. The central service of worship in the Roman Catholic Church. Much of the service remains the same throughout the liturgical year; this is called the 'Ordinary' and has been the vehicle of some of the finest compositions in the history of music. The sections which change, according to the feast day or the occasion, are called the 'proper' and are, for the most part, sung in plainsong versions. The five main divisions of the Ordinary are: the Kyrie, the Gloria, the Credo, the Sanctus and Benedictus, and the Agnus Dei, concluding with Dona nobis pacem. The first extended form in the history of music was the 'cyclic tenor' mass, developed during the 15th century, in which composers gave unity to the various 'movements' by employing the same *cantus firmus* in each. In the 'parody' mass the composer used material either from other works by himself or from works by other composers. The mass received its name from the concluding words of the service – *ita missa est*, 'it is concluded'. The term *missa brevis* refers either to a short setting of the whole service or to a setting of the Kyrie and Gloria only, usual earlier in the Lutheran liturgy. A *missa solemnis* is a full setting of particularly magnificent proportions. Some masses of the polyphonic period were described as *missa sine nomine*; such masses had 'no name' since they were not based on any previous named *cantus firmus*, such as a popular song or a section of plainsong.

mastersingers (German, *Meistersinger*). Guild musicians in the German towns of the late 15th to 17th centuries. Like all guilds the mastersingers were subject to hierarchical organisation and their art was governed by elaborate rules, lampooned in Wagner's opera *The Mastersingers of Nuremberg*. This townsman's art seems to have grown out of that of the aristocratic *Minnesänger*.

mazurka. Polish folk dance in triple time. It was used by various Russian composers but was introduced to the repertoire of concert music by Chopin, who wrote more than fifty examples for piano.

mediant. The third degree of the scale.

Meistersinger: see **mastersingers**

melisma. A long musical phrase of many notes set to a single vowel. Melismata (the plural) were a common feature of plainsong and early polyphonic music but the term may also be used of similar features in later music.

melodrama. Stage production of words and music, created in the second half of the 18th century. In melodrama there is singing, but the characteristic combination is of the spoken word against a background of music. It is thus distinct both from the opera and the ballad opera etc.

ménestrel: see **minstrel**

mezzo (Italian, 'half'). The dynamic marking *mezzo-forte*, abbreviated as *mf*, means of average loudness. The mezzo-soprano voice has a range intermediate between soprano and contralto.

microtone: see **interval**

minim. English term for the note with half the time value of a semibreve and twice that of the crotchet. The American term is 'half-note'.

Minnesänger. German poets of the late 12th to early 14th centuries. Their theme, in the tradition of the Provençal troubadours, was that of courtly love ('*Minne*') and the service of their lady. As with the troubadours a musical tradition sprang up and this was continued to some extent by the mastersingers.

minor: see **scale** and **interval**

minstrel (Old French, *ménestrel*). In the middle ages a musician usually attached permanently to some lay musical establishment, though the term was later applied to travelling entertainers.

minuet. European court dance of the late 17th and 18th centuries. It is in a steady triple time and in ternary form, and became one of the regular movements in the dance suite. Two minuets, of which the second is conventionally called the trio, together constituted the third movement of the classical symphony.

miserere. The opening word of the fiftieth psalm (numbered 51 in the Vulgate). This psalm, which concludes the service of Matins and Lauds during the last three days of Holy Week (*Tenebrae*), has been the subject of many musical settings. The most famous was that by Gregorio Allegri (b. 1652), for long the jealously guarded property of the Sistine Chapel.

missa: see **mass**

Mixolydian mode. One of the authentic modes.

mode. The system of scales that governed European music from the early middle ages to the 16th century was based on the modes. Each mode started on a different note and while each had five intervals of a tone and two of a semitone, the semitones fell differently in each mode. The effect can be appreciated if a scale is played from each of the white notes on the piano using only the white notes. Each mode has its own *finalis*, the note on which a melody in that mode ends, and its own *tenor* or 'dominant' (usually a fifth above the *finalis*), the note around which a melody in the mode tends to revolve. These considerations and the different placing of the semitones gives each mode a characteristic flavour or mood. The modal system was codified during the middle ages to produce four 'authentic' modes and four 'plagal' modes, the plagal modes having the same *finalis* as their equivalent authentic modes but extending a fourth lower. Modal systems, basically evolved for the organisation of melody, are found in other traditions, such as the Indian (see **rāg**), where harmony is absent.

modulation. In harmony the movement from one key, through intervening ones, to another.

moderato (Italian, 'moderate'). By itself it indicates a moderate pace, but it is also used adjectivally, e.g. *allegro moderato*, to modify the force of another direction.

molto. Italian, 'much' or 'very'.

monody. The style of declamation by a solo voice with harmonically restricted instrumental accompaniment evolved at the turn of the 16th and 17th centuries in Florence, as an attempt to return to what was considered the manner of declamation in the ancient Greek theatre.

monophony, monophonic. Music for one voice alone or with the most limited of accompaniments.

monothematic. Literally, 'single theme'. Commonly used of a more or less extended work in which only one main theme is developed.

mordent. Old type of musical ornament.

morris dance. Vigorous English folk dance, possibly of Moorish origins (hence, perhaps, the name). Sticks and bells feature in some of the dances, whose performers once had a reputation for bawdy riot.

motet. 1) In medieval music a composition in three parts, each often moving at a different speed, the bottom moving the slowest, and each set to different words. The lowest part, a plainsong tenor, would be set to Latin while the *motetus* and *triplum* above it might have texts related in meaning but in French. The motet, religious in origin, soon became a secular form. Also see **isorhythm.** 2) Any religious choral composition using words not part of the liturgy. 3) Also sometimes used of serious secular choral works.

motion. Term describing the movement of parts. 1) A single part is said to have 'conjunct' motion when the intervals between its notes do not exceed a tone, 'disjunct' motion when they do. 2) Two parts moving away from one another or towards one another have 'contrary' motion. 3) If one part holds a note and the other moves away from it or towards it, there is 'oblique' motion. 4) When parts move in the same direction they have 'similar' motion. 5) Parts moving in the same direction, and maintaining the same interval between them, have 'parallel' motion.

moto (Italian, 'movement'). A piece marked *con moto* is to be played with a strong sense of rhythmic movement. The term *moto perpetuo* (literally, perpetual motion) is sometimes given to rapidly moving display pieces.

musica ficta. Modifications to the pitch of notes, not indicated by accidentals but required by convention to avoid discordant clashes. *Musica ficta* was common during the 15th and 16th centuries, as the modal system was gradually displaced by the harmonic.

musica reservata. A term encountered in the late 16th and early 17th centuries. The meaning is not now clearly known but it may have referred to music considered too complex for any but connoisseurs.

musique concrète. The original French term for concrete music, which was developed first in France.

Natural. An accidental sign used in notation to cancel any sharp or flat governing a given note.

Neo-classical. The musical style of the 1920s and 1930s, associated particularly with the name of Stravinsky and the music of the Italian composers. The style, foreshadowed by Prokofiev's *Classical symphony* of 1918, was a conscious return to the idioms and forms of the 18th century, which were used and re-presented in contemporary guise.

neume. Musical unit in plainsong and, by extension, the symbol for that unit and later for individual notes: also see **notation.**

new music, the. Phrase used of revolutionary changes in the language of music since the *ars nova* of the 14th century and the new art of the English in the 15th century. But the phrase itself had special significance in the early 17th century in Italy, when the avowed advocates of the new music included Monteverdi, and Caccini published his *Nuove musiche* (1601) containing examples of monody, and also in 19th-century Germany, when the advocates of the 'new music' were Wagner and Liszt, opposed by Schumann and Brahms.

ninth. A compound interval of an octave plus a tone.

nocturne. A piece of music felt to be programmatic of the night. The term as applied to atmospheric piano pieces was coined by the English composer John Field and adopted by Chopin.

nonet. A composition for chamber ensemble of nine instruments.

nota cambiata. A melodic convention involving three or four notes in which the characteristic feature is a leap of a third away from a note not part of the main harmony.

notation. Any system of recording music with written symbols. In 'stave' notation each note of the music has a symbol set on a five line stave that: 1) specifies the pitch of the note by its position on the staff; 2) defines the pitch more precisely, if need be, by the use of accidentals that indicate sharpening or flattening by a semitone; 3) indicates the duration of the note, by its shape (also see **dotted**). Directions as to the mode of performance can also be made by words or their abbreviations written in the score or by markings (tie, slur).

note. In English terminology: 1) a musical sound of specific pitch and duration; 2) its symbol in stave notation; 3) the actual key of a keyboard instrument which, when struck, produces the note. In American terminology the word 'tone' is used for the first of these meanings. For 'note row' (American 'tone row') see **twelve-note music**

obbligato (Italian, 'obligatory'). A direction in a musical score that first carried its full literal meaning to indicate a part that could not be omitted. Later it was applied to a specially elaborate or decorative part accompanying the main melodic line.

oblique motion: see motion

octave. A musical interval defined by the ratio 2:1. A note an octave above another is produced by a resonator vibrating at twice the frequency; to the ear the effect is of the same note at a higher pitch. A 'diminished' octave is a semitone less, an 'augmented', a semitone larger than a 'perfect' octave.

octet. A chamber work for eight instruments.

oeuvre. French word for 'work', used in English to refer to the total output of works by a composer.

offertorium (Latin for 'offertory'). The section of the Roman Catholic mass during which the priest prepares and offers up the unconsecrated elements. The name is also given to the antiphons and the other music which accompanies this act.

opera. Among the many types of dramatic work with music, such as ballad opera, *Singspiel* or *zarzuela*, opera is distinguished in having all the words of the text set to music. It originated about the year 1600 in an attempt to reconstruct the theatre of ancient Greece and from the 1650s to the late 1700s it found in Italy a classic form known as *opera seria*. In this the chorus became increasingly less important, elaborate stage scenery and spectacle were essential and the music dominated the action. Broadly speaking, the music was divided between arias and narrative recitative passages. Gluck strove to restore dramatic cohesion to opera; Verdi gave the classic Italian opera new vitality and emotional power; and Wagner brought features of symphonic music to the opera to produce what he called 'music drama'. The term opera may also be applied loosely to works in some of the categories listed below.

opéra-ballet. A characteristically French form of the 17th century in which dances gradually became an important part of the action.

opera buffa. An Italian form in which the spoken word was also used. It was usually on a comedy theme and originated as an interlude between the acts of an *opera seria*. The finale for several soloists was first introduced into the *opera buffa*. The French term *opéra bouffe* describes a similar type, though it may have an explicitly satirical intent.

opéra comique. This French term first applied to comic opera with spoken dialogue, but in the 19th century it came to be used of any opera, comic or serious, with spoken dialogue. After it had been officially recognised in the early 18th century it was granted a special theatre and the Opéra Comique is now one of the leading Parisian theatres.

operetta. A light opera, whether full-length or not, often using spoken dialogue.

opus. This Latin word meaning 'work' is often used instead of its English equivalent when speaking either 1) of specific compositions, or 2) of a composer's whole output. In the first case composers often give their works 'opus numbers'–Op. 1, Op. 25, etc.–and these may be used when referring to a piece of music to identify it exactly. In some cases an opus number may cover several short pieces or a group of works of a similar type; these are then further defined as, for example, 'Op. 46, No 3' etc.

oratorio. A work of a dramatic nature for voices and usually instruments, but not acted. In its first use it applied to religious works, with texts often based on the Bible, which arose in the early 17th century as a kind of church opera (a 'religious opera' as such was acted, and differed from its secular counterpart only in the subject matter). During the 18th century the chorus remained important in oratorio as opposed to opera and some composers, above all Handel in England, made use of this dramatic but unstaged musical form as an alternative to opera, producing oratorios with secular subjects.

orchestra. A large body of instrumentalists. The constitution of an orchestra has varied during its evolution over about three centuries and also depends on its function. A full symphony orchestra of the Romantic period was made up as follows: a large string section consisting of violins divided into first and second sections, violas, cellos and double basses. Harps are sometimes called on but are not considered part of the 'string section' of the orchestra. A woodwind section consisting of two flutes, with perhaps a bass flute and piccolo; two or three oboes and a cor anglais; two or three clarinets and a bass clarinet; two bassoons and perhaps a double bassoon. A brass section consisting of four horns, three trumpets and, exceptionally, a bass trumpet, two tenor and one bass trombone, and one tuba. A percussion section consisting of from two to five timpani, a bass drum, side drums of various kinds, cymbals and perhaps a triangle. Many other types of percussion are also available and in the orchestra such keyboard instruments as the celeste, glockenspiel and also the piano (when not the solo instrument) are classed in this section. The orchestra of Haydn and Mozart had the same classifications as the above but had a smaller body of string players, two flutes, two oboes, two bassoons, clarinets on occasion, two horns and sometimes trumpets and two timpani. Composers have of course written for an infinite variety of instruments but a 'symphony orchestra' in terms of resources and cost refers to the large body described above. Some works have been written for string orchestra alone – that is the string section as described above.

orchestration. The art of combining and exploiting the forces of the orchestra without the specific connotation, as to exact understanding of the techniques of the various instruments, implied by instrumentation.

organum. The earliest form of polyphonic composition, in which a *cantus firmus* was accompanied by other parts at fixed intervals. The term is also applied to somewhat more elaborate compositions of the 12th century.

ornamentation. Since the beginning of the 19th century composers have tended to write out in full every note that they want played. But in earlier periods conventions of performance allowed and indeed required the singer or instrumentalist to embellish the written line with notes and runs not necessarily given in the score. This may be regarded as the fossilised remnant of the tradition of improvisation within accepted conventions, once so strong a part of European music. The composers' revolt against the growing extravagance of performers began in the early 18th century, Handel's imprecations on the matter being well known, while Bach took the more practical step of writing out his parts far more fully than many of his contemporaries. During the 18th century composers evolved a shorthand of symbols to indicate the kind of ornament required at a given point; of these, that for the 'trill' or 'shake' *tr.* is one of the few to remain in regular use. Vibrato, once considered an ornament, seems now to be an obligatory part of a musician's technique which he applies, indiscriminately, to music of all periods, whether by Purcell or Brahms.

ostinato (Italian, 'obstinate, persistent'). A melodic or rhythmic figure repeated throughout a piece of music or a long section of it. Such a figure usually occurs in the bass, hence *basso ostinato*. Obvious examples are the ground bass of the 17th century and the bass line of 20th-century boogie-woogie jazz piano playing.

overtone. An upper harmonic in the harmonic series.

overture. 1) A piece of music preceding an opera or play. 2) A concert piece for orchestra in one movement, preceding nothing in particular, unless it be the concert programme itself.

part. Any piece of music for an ensemble of players is made up of a number of 'parts' or lines of music, each of which may be given to one or more players. Polyphonic or contrapuntal music may be described as in 'four parts' (also see **voice**). When music is published a full score is printed, containing all the parts, for the use of the conductor, and separate copies of the individual parts for the players. Much early music survives only in PART BOOKS. These may be either for each individual performer (as described), or printed with the individual parts laid out round the opened page so as to be easily read by singers or players seated round a table.

partial: see **harmonic series**

partita. An Italian term equivalent to suite; the most famous examples are Bach's partitas for unaccompanied violin.

part-song. Strictly speaking any song-type of composition for more than one voice, but the term is not used of earlier forms such as the madrigal. It refers particularly to vocal compositions, sometimes with piano accompaniment, in which the melodic interest tends to lie with the highest part.

passacaglia. Like the chaconne, a dance and musical form properly composed on a ground bass, but the most famous examples of both types, by Bach, either use the 'ground' in higher parts or retain only its harmonic structure.

passamezzo. Italian dance of the 16th and 17th centuries. It was in a stately measure, like the pavan, but was composed on a ground bass; of the grounds used, the *passamezzo antico* and the *passamezzo moderno* were the most popular.

passepied. French dance fashionable at the court of Louis XIV; it had affinities with the minuet.

passing-note. A note which carries the melodic line, in conjunct motion, between two notes which are concordant in the harmonic context, even though it is, itself, discordant.

Passion. A musical form which grew out of the Gospel account of the sufferings and death (the 'Passion') of Jesus as it is given in the liturgy for Holy Week. From the simple antiphonal setting of the account, with various singers taking the various parts of the dramatis personae of the story, there developed an increasingly elaborate style of setting, with solo voices, chorus and instruments, that reached its apogee in the works of J. S. Bach. In German settings of the Passion, chorales sung by the congregation were a constituent element.

pastorale or **pastoral.** A stage performance, often with music, on a pastoral or other theme drawn from classical literature. It first arose in Renaissance Italy but was taken up in France, where it was found to be an ideal vehicle for the French love of ballet.

pastourelle. A medieval lyric verse form and also a musical entertainment based on it.

pause. An indication to the performer to hold the note, or rest, marked, longer than its strict time value requires. In a 'general pause' in an orchestral work all the performers are held silent for a period indicated by the composer and interpreted by the conductor.

pavan (French, '*pavane*'; original Italian, '*paduana*'). A stately court dance of the Renaissance, in common time. It was often paired with the sprightly galliard.

pedal. 1) A mechanism found on various musical instruments. 2) In harmony, a note held, usually in the bass, over many bars while the other parts move above it. The term 'pedal point' is also used.

penillion. A style of improvised performance by singer and harpist deriving from the traditional art of the ancient Welsh bards.

pentatonic: see **scale**

perpetuum mobile. The Latin equivalent of the Italian, *moto perpetuo*.

pesante. Italian, 'heavily'.

phrase. Used in music of a section of a melodic line in much the same way as it is used in language of a part of a sentence. Phrasing, i.e. the art of articulating and shaping the various elements of the musical parts, is an important part of musical performance.

pianissimo. Italian, 'very softly', abbreviated as a musical direction to *pp*.

piano. Italian, 'softly' or 'quietly', abbreviated to *p*.

pitch. The 'highness' or 'lowness' of a musical note according to the frequency of the vibrations producing it. During the past, standards of pitch have varied from place to place and from time to time and indeed the general standard of pitch seems to have risen over the centuries. Since 1939 the pitch of the A above middle C has been defined at a frequency of 440 vibrations per second; this is now generally accepted in concert performances, but brass bands in Britain use a somewhat higher standard.

pizzicato (Italian, 'pinched'). Direction for performance, abbreviated to *pizz.*, indicating, for bowed string instruments, that the strings are to be plucked.

plainsong. The ancient monodic chant of the Christian Church. The earlier type of Ambrosian chant was gradually displaced, from the 7th century, by Gregorian chant, named after Pope Gregory I. Also see **mode**.

pointillism. Term taken over from painting to describe a technique of using sounds as isolated points or dots rather than parts of a phrase or melody. Webern used sound in this way and he has been followed by some *avant-garde* composers of the post-war generation.

polonaise. A stately court dance in triple time. Originally a Polish folk dance, it was adopted by high society during the Renaissance; composers outside Poland have used a formalised version of it since the time of Bach, but it is best known in the more vigorous manner found in Chopin's polonaises for piano.

polymodality. Term applied to the works of some 20th-century composers who have adapted the principles of the ancient modes to the practices of modern harmonic music, using the scales of several modes at once.

542

polyphony. This term, from the Greek, 'many voices', is used in a limited sense to apply to the music of the Renaissance period in which the horizontal, 'melodic' interest of the separate parts tends to predominate over the harmonic combinations that result from their movement.

polytonality. The use, in some 20th-century music, of several keys simultaneously – bitonality is the use of two keys. See **harmony**.

portamento (Italian, 'carrying'). The effect achieved by a singer or player on a bowed instrument when he moves from one note to another at some distance from it by sliding onto it and touching on the notes in between.

post-Romantic. The idiom of composers such as Mahler who continued the essential Romantic expression in music after its high period in the mid-19th century.

presto. Italian, 'fast', with its superlative '*prestissimo*'. As directions to performance, the terms are used without abbreviations.

primadonna (Italian, 'first lady'). The leading woman singer in an operatic cast or company.

prelude. Most simply, a piece of music that leads up to another. In the case of Bach's famous preludes and fugues for keyboard the two pieces are of equal weight and the result is nearly a two-movement work. The word was used by Chopin to title short independent piano pieces.

programme music. Used of music which is avowedly aimed at expounding an extra-musical experience or concept. In its earliest forms, the 14th-century *caccia* for example, programme music simply reproduced the sounds of familiar activities such as the hunt, or painted sound pictures of physical events or scenes. In the 19th century music became much involved with literary and philosophical concepts, and composers aimed to portray such concepts in their work or their own emotional or psychological states.

quadruplet. Four notes of equal duration to be played in the time of three where the time signature would indicate three notes.

quartered note. The American term for crotchet.

quarter tone. A micro-interval, half the value of a semitone.

quartet. 1) An instrumental or vocal composition in four parts, or a group of players who perform such music. 2) Commonly used with the specific meaning of a chamber work written for two violins, viola and cello. It is usually in four movements and the classical string quartet, perfected by Haydn, has its first movement in sonata form.

quaver. A note with a duration half as long as a crochet; the American term is 'eighth note'.

quint. An organ stop.

quintet. A chamber work for five players, also used of the group of players themselves. A string quintet is composed of a standard string quartet with an additional viola or cello. A piano quintet is usually a string quartet with piano added. But there are exceptions, such as Schubert's 'Trout' quintet, scored for piano, violin, viola, cello and double bass.

quintuplet. Five notes of equal duration to be played in a time interval which, from the time signature, would normally be occupied by four or some other number of notes.

quodlibet (Latin, 'what you please'). A piece of music in which a number of popular tunes are combined; the Spanish term *ensalada* (literally, 'salad') has the same meaning. The *quodlibet* may be either composed (an example concludes Bach's *Goldberg Variations*), or extemporised – a favourite pastime in Bach's own family.

rallentando. Italian, 'slowing down'; abbreviated as a direction to performers, in the score, as *rall.*

rag. The Hindu word, often spelt raga in transliteration, for a mode. There are very many *rāgs* employing some or all of the notes of the diatonic scale and modifications of them. In the theory of Indian music the *rāg* has an elaborate philosophical and poetic symbolism which is also open to interpretation in painting.

rag, ragtime. Ragtime is an early type of classical jazz, often for the piano, a rag being a piece of music in this idiom.

rank. A set of organ pipes.

real answer: see **fugue**

realise. In music of the pre-classical period conventions of performance were sufficiently widely understood and established for a composer to omit elements in the music which would now be considered necessary. The classic example is that of the continuo bass, which would appear in the score simply as a single line, sometimes with figures above indicating harmonies, and from which the performer would reconstruct or 'realise' the omitted parts. In modern performances of such music the player often makes use of 'realisations' provided by a musicologist or editor. Providing a good realisation has always been a matter of considerable musicianship.

recapitulation. A passage in a composition that restates, usually in clearly recognisable form, a section or material from an earlier passage. The term has specific significance in the sonata form.

recitative. A style of sung declamation used in opera. It may be either accompanied or unaccompanied save for punctuating chords from the harpsichord; in the latter form it is called *recitativo secco* (literally, 'dry recitative'). It evolved as a more expressive and dramatic form of the early 17th-century monody and came to be used for narrative and dialogue passages between the arias and choruses of the opera.

register. A part of the compass of an instrument or voice; usually the different registers also have characteristic tone qualities. The term is also used of the tone qualities of groups of organ pipes.

relative major, minor. A major and minor key that are said to be relative to one another share the same key signature. The scale of C major, without sharps or flats, opens with a major third (see **intervals**): C–D–E; if a scale using the same notes is started on A, the result is a minor third: A–B–C.

répétiteur. The coach and conductor of an opera cast at rehearsals.

reprise. A direct repetition of an earlier section in a piece of music or, in musical comedy, the repeat of a song.

requiem. The Roman Catholic mass for the dead. There have been many fine settings from Palestrina to Verdi; Brahms's 'German Requiem' (*Ein Deutsches Requiem*) draws its text from Luther's translation of the Bible.

resolution. When a discord is brought to rest on a concord by movement of some of its notes, it is said to be resolved.

resultant note. An acoustical effect produced when two notes are sounded loudly together. A third note may then be heard either above them, which is the result of the sum of their frequencies and is called the 'summational note'; or below, produced by the difference of their frequencies and called the 'differential note'.

retrograde motion. The playing of the notes of a theme in reverse order; an intellectual musical device used by certain *ars nova* composers of the 14th century, by contrapuntalists such as Bach and by contemporary serial composers.

rhythm. One of the basic elements of music. Rhythm concerns the organisation of sounds in time; a framework pattern or metre is established with unit bars of so many beats, while the rhythmic accents give rise to longer units or phrases which play about this basic structure producing new, more or less complex patterns. The term 'polyrhythm' is sometimes used to describe music in which different parts move in different rhythms whose conflicts and tensions give the music dynamic strength.

ricercare (Italian, 'search'). During the Renaissance period an instrumental composition similar to the fugue; thereafter, into the 18th century, it was sometimes used of a specially elaborate fugue.

ripieno (Italian, 'full'). In the concerto grosso the musicians were in two groups, the full orchestra or *ripieno*, and the *concertino*, the smaller group of solo instruments. A *ripieno* part may also be one added to fill out the musical structure.

ritornello (Italian, 'return'). In 17th and 18th century music a passage for the full body of performers in a piece for solo instrument, when the soloist is silent. Such passages, not necessarily using the same material, recur at various points during the work.

ritardando. The Italian for 'slowing down', used as a direction to performers and abbreviated in the score to *rit.*

Rococo. A term usually applied to a period of architecture and the visual arts which began in France in the early 18th century and continued, particularly in southern Germany, into the 1770s. It was first a reaction to the heavy style and formality of decoration of the age of Louis XIV and its characteristic productions were light and elegant interior decors and the painting of men like Boucher and Fragonard. In music the term may be applied to the *style galante* of Vienna and the French contemporaries of Rameau, and in general it denotes a lighter, less involved manner than the contrapuntal splendours of the Baroque period in northern Europe.

romanesca bass. One of the ground basses of the late medieval and Renaissance periods, used in dance music.

Romanticism. The movement that dominated the arts during the greater part of the 19th century and was closely bound up in the aspirations of contemporary nationalism. The main themes were an interest in nature as an object of artistic inspiration in its own right; study of Europe's medieval past and of folk literature, art and music; an emphasis on art as a vehicle of emotional self-expression; and the preponderating influence of literature on the other arts. In music the forms of the classical age of Haydn and Mozart were extended and joined by others less precisely articulated, the orchestra became larger, harmony tended towards greater chromaticism and programme music invaded the concert hall. Overtures, symphonies and piano works were written depicting natural phenomena or expressing ideals and moods. The movement culminated in the operas of Wagner, based on myths and rich in new effects of harmony and instrumentation. Composers such as Mahler, Bruckner or Strauss are classed as late or post-Romantics, both because of the huge orchestral resources they employed and because their harmonic procedures are the natural continuation of Wagner's.

rondeau. Medieval French verse form of three stanzas and having two rhymes. It was intended for singing and many settings were composed.

rondo. A form in which an initial theme is repeated between a number of episodes in the pattern ABACADA. The sonata rondo sometimes used by Beethoven makes use of the harmonic structure of the sonata form in the context of the rondo.

rota. The Latin name of a type of medieval round song.

round. A part-song with one or more simple melodies which are sung in perpetual canon.

rubato, tempo (Italian, 'robbed time'). As a direction to performance, usually of keyboard music, '*rubato*' indicates that the player should, at his discretion, fractionally accelerate or retard the tempo of the music for expressive effect. Sometimes *rubato* is applied in one hand while the music of the other is maintained at a steady tempo.

rumba. Latin American dance from Cuba with eight beats to the bar divided: 3, 3, 2.

running set. Appalachian Mountain folk dance, possibly of English origin.

S. The initial letter of the name of Wolfgang Schmieder, a 20th-century musicologist whose index of the works of J. S. Bach displaced earlier catalogues. The 'S.' or 'Schmieder' number is now regularly used in identifying a work by Bach.

Sanctus. A section of the Roman Catholic mass.

saraband, French *sarabande*. Stately court dance of Spanish origins in a slow triple time. It was a regular movement in the 18th-century suite.

scale. A progression of notes that comprises all those available to the composer or musician according to the tradition within which he is working. There are an infinite variety of scales – four note, five note, six note, eight note etc. The five-note pentatonic scale, which can be heard by sounding the black notes of the piano, is frequently found in folk music; the blues scale used in some jazz music has slightly flattened third and sixth degrees; but for centuries the diatonic scale has been the basis of European art music. The major scale, with seven notes between the octave, has five intervals of a tone and two of a semitone; there are three variants of the minor scale but all have a minor third interval between the first and the third degrees where the major scale has a major interval. Each of the notes or 'degrees' of the scale is named.

The keynote or tonic gives its name to the key which the scale defines; then come the supertonic, the mediant, the subdominant, the dominant – after the tonic the most important note in the scale – the submediant and, finally, the leading note. This last, being at the interval of only a semitone from the tonic, gives an irresistible feeling of moving onto it. In all there are twelve notes spaced at semitone intervals between the octaves and these all taken together are collectively known as the chromatic scale; this scale removed from the harmonic context is the twelve note scale. The whole tone scale sometimes used by Debussy is, as its name suggests, without any semitone intervals.

scherzo (Italian, 'joke'). A movement in vigorous triple time which from Beethoven onwards tended to displace the minuet in the symphony, though the trio was retained. The origin of the name has little bearing on the nature of the symphonic scherzo or on the independent pieces for piano of the same name composed by Chopin.

scordatura. The tuning of a stringed instrument in an unconventional manner, either to extend its range downwards or to produce open string effects on different notes from those usually available, or to facilitate fingering in certain keys.

score. The written or printed book containing all the parts of a piece of music laid out one above the other (by convention the strings are at the bottom and the high woodwind at the top). A full score has all the parts individually written out; a condensed version or 'short' score may also be made. In a 'vocal' score the voice parts are given in full but the orchestral accompaniment is printed in a short score version arranged for piano. A piece originally written for keyboard may be laid out in 'open' score to facilitate an analysis. The word is also used as a verb in such a phrase as 'scored' (i.e. written) for strings, percussion and celeste.

Scotch snap. A short note on the accented beat followed by a longer one.

second: see **interval**

semibreve. A note with a duration equivalent to four crotchets. It is the longest note conventionally used in modern notation and in United States terminology is called the 'whole' note, this being a direct translation of the German *Ganzenote*. Its name is explained by the fact that note values have got progressively shorter since the middle ages when the 'breve' was the short time value as opposed to the '*longus*'. The semibreve, or half breve, was shorter still.

semiquaver. A note with half the duration of the quaver or one-sixteenth that of the breve described above; in American terminology called the 'sixteenth note'.

semitone: see **interval**

septet. A chamber work for seven instrumentalists, or the group of players themselves.

sequence. A monodic hymn-like composition, so called because it followed the gradual in the mass. Numerous sequences were written during the high middle ages.

serenade. 1) In its general sense a song by a lover at the window of his mistress. 2) An 18th-century form of the suite, analogous to the divertimento or the cassation.

serial music. Technique of composition evolved by the followers of Schoenberg and Webern

which applies the idea of a strictly arranged series, as used for pitch in a twelve-note composition, to the other elements of music. Thus, as well as pitch, duration, dynamics, timbre and even the players' methods of attack are subjected to systematised arrangement.

sextet. Chamber work for six instruments, or the group of players themselves.

sextuplet. Six notes of equal duration to be played over the period where the time signature would imply four or some other number of notes.

sforzando (Italian, 'forced'). Musical direction abbreviated as *sf.*, indicating that the note so marked is to be played with special emphasis.

shake. Alternative name for the trill ornament.

shanty. Sailor's work song, the word being derived, it is thought, from the French *chantez*, 'sing!'

sharp. In notation an accidental sign indicating that the note to which it refers is to be raised in pitch by a semitone. In performance, a note that is wrongly played or sung somewhat higher than its correct pitch is said to be 'sharp'.

siciliano. Dance of the 17th and 18th centuries in moderate tempo and in the minor key. It was sometimes one of the movements in the suite.

sinfonia. This term, with its English equivalent 'symphony', was used in the Renaissance to designate various types of instrumental composition and in the late 17th and early 18th centuries was used of instrumental passages in an opera. The *sinfonie* (plural) of Alessandro Scarlatti anticipated some of the features of the later symphony. A *sinfonia concertante* was, in the classical period, the term used for a concerto with more than one solo instrument.

sinfonietta. A short work in symphonic form. In United States terminology also the name for a small-sized orchestra.

Singspiel. German musical stage entertainment which developed from the middle of the 18th century and reached its highest peak in the works of Mozart. The extensive use of spoken dialogue distinguishes it from Italian opera.

sixteenth note. American term for the semiquaver, which has a time value one-sixteenth that of the semibreve or 'whole note'.

sixth. A musical interval.

slur. In notation a curved line over a group of notes indicating that they are to be played as a smooth unbroken phrase. The tie, also a curved line, has another significance.

sol-fa: see **tonic sol-fa**

solfège (derived from the Italian, *solfeggio*). A system of musical training for the ear, for sight-reading and for other basic elements of music, occupying an important position in the curriculum of all French musical academies.

solmisation. A mnemonic system used to aid sight-reading by naming the notes of the scale with syllables: see also **hexachord** and **tonic sol-fa**.

solo. A part for unaccompanied instrument or for an instrument or voice with the dominant role in a work.

sonata (from the Italian, 'to sound'). At the beginning of the 17th century the word was used to mean simply a piece for instruments as opposed to one for voices. Later in the century the sonata emerged as a formalised structure for two or more instruments with continuo in a number of movements. There was a somewhat vague distinction between the *sonata da camera*, or chamber sonata, and the *sonata da chiesa*, the church sonata, somewhat graver in mood, perhaps using the organ rather than the harpsichord as the main continuo instrument and not having dance movements. The trio sonata for two solo instruments only and continuo was the most favoured form for small ensembles at the end of the 17th century. The classical sonata, which developed during the 18th century to its peak in the period of Haydn and Mozart, was for solo keyboard instrument, or keyboard and one other instrument. It was in three or four movements, the first of which was in sonata form.

sonata form. Also called first-movement sonata form. This form was used during the classical period not only in sonatas but also in the quartet and the symphony, usually in the first movement and occasionally in others. There are two main elements: the thematic and the harmonic. Evolving from the binary form of the early 18th century, a movement in sonata form usually had two, generally contrasting, themes; the music moved from the tonic key to the dominant, or some other key, and back to the tonic. The pattern was for the two themes to be stated in an 'exposition' section which moved towards the dominant key; there then followed a 'development' section in which the themes and new material were explored, and this was followed by the 'recapitulation', basically a repeat of the opening section and ending in the tonic key. As the form developed, a concluding coda was added, to be greatly extended by Beethoven.

sonatina. The Italian diminutive of the word 'sonata' and denoting a piece of the same form but of slighter dimensions.

sopranino. Diminutive of the word soprano and used of instruments to describe the highest member of a family.

soprano (Italian, literally 'upper'). 1) The high female voice. 2) The high, often highest, member of a family of instruments. 3) The soprano clef, now obsolete, was the movable C clef that fixed the lowest line of the stave as middle C (in the treble clef middle C is on a ledger line below the stave).

sordino (plural, *sordini*). The Italian word for 'mute', used as a direction to performance (sometimes abbreviated to *sord.*) to indicate the use of mutes, *con sordini*, and their removal, *senza sordini*. If found in piano music (a famous example is the first movement of Beethoven's 'Moonlight' sonata) these directions refer to the dampers. The French term for the first meaning is *sourdine*.

speech-song. Literal English translation of Schoenberg's German coinage *Sprechgesang*.

spiccato (Italian, 'picked out'). Abbreviated to *spicc.*, a direction to bowed instrument performers to play a rapid passage in a light detached manner by bouncing the bow on the strings.

spiritual. A religious part-song with its origins in the Black American folk tradition and heavily influenced by European harmony.

Sprechgesang (German, 'speech-song'). A style of half-spoken, half-sung declamation asked for by Schoenberg in such works as *Gurrelieder*.

Stabat Mater. A hymn by the 13th-century friar, Jacopone da Todi, on Mary the mother of Jesus standing before the cross. It was set as a sequence in the middle ages and later by many composers, notably Pergolesi.

staccato (Italian, 'detached'). A direction to performers, symbolised by a dot over the notes concerned, to play these in a sharply detached way.

stave or **staff**. The basic five-line 'grid' in musical notation on which the notes are written. Their position on the stave determines their relative pitch and the point of reference is provided by the clef.

stretto: see **fugue**

strophic song. One in which each stanza of the poetry is set to the same music.

subdominant. A degree of the scale.

subject. A usually non-melodic but pregnant figure that provides the basic musical idea in a fugue.

submediant. A degree of the scale.

suite. 1) In the 17th and 18th centuries an instrumental composition in several movements in different stylised dance forms. A typical sequence was: allemand, courante, saraband, gigue. 2) In later periods a light work lacking strict formal structure.

summational note: see **resultant note**

superius. The term for the upper part in medieval polyphony.

supertonic. A degree of the scale.

suspension. A note held over from one chord so as to make a temporary dissonance with the next chord before it is satisfactorily resolved by moving to a note that is part of the new harmony.

symphonic poem. A one-movement form for orchestra developed by Liszt. The work is symphonic because of its dimensions and poetic because it has a non-musical programme (see **programme music**).

symphony. The major musical form throughout the 19th century, brought to perfection in the late 18th by Haydn and Mozart and thereafter extended to ever larger proportions until the symphonies, vast both in length and orchestral resources, of Mahler. The classical symphony was in four movements, the first of which was in sonata form and in a vigorous tempo. In Haydn's symphonies and some of Beethoven's the first movement was preceded by a slow introduction; the second movement was usually slow; the third was a minuet and trio; and the last movement, like the first, was fast. Even in the 19th century this was to prove the most general form, but after Beethoven the expressive and emotional content of the work changed its nature. The elegant minuet was replaced by the vigorous scherzo; new instruments, beginning with the trombones, became regular members of the symphony orchestra; choral passages were introduced to certain movements; and the number of movements was sometimes as many as five or six or as few as one. The term symphony has been used by 20th-century composers both for true symphonies as here described and, in a more general sense, for large scale instrumental works. For an early usage see **sinfonia**. In the United States the word symphony is also used alone to mean symphony orchestra.

syncopation. A rhythmic effect produced when the accent is placed on a normally unaccented beat in the bar.

tablature. A system of musical notation in which the notes are represented not by abstract symbols on a stave but rather by code letters or symbols which direct the player where to place his fingers so as to obtain the notes. The system is still used for the guitar and lute but, in the Renaissance, tablatures were also used for keyboard instruments and notably, in German countries, the organ.

tacet. This word, from the Latin verb 'to be silent', is used as a direction in performance to indicate that an instrument is to remain silent for a large section of the work, usually a whole movement.

tāl. In Indian music a rhythmic pattern which may extend over as many as sixteen bars and provides the rhythmic framework of the performance. It is made up of a number of metrical units around which the performers build elaborate counter-rhythms; but at the beginning of each new section, called the *sam*, they must all be together. The word is also transliterated as tala.

tango. Latin American dance introduced into European ballroom music during the First World War.

Tantum ergo. A Latin hymn from the 13th century by St Thomas Aquinas.

tarantella. An Italian dance in quick tempo. It is supposed either to be caused by the bite of the tarantula spider or to be the cure for it.

Te deum laudamus (English 'We praise thee O God!'). A Latin hymn dating from the 5th century.

temperament. The practice of so tuning the notes of the chromatic scale that the slight differences that exist in acoustical terms between for example C sharp and D flat are modified or 'tempered' so that one note on the keyboard can serve for both. During the 17th century numerous experiments in temperament were made, since perfect tuning required the use of a separate string and key for each of the sharps and flats or, alternatively, the tuning of the instrument for a single key only. The keys nearest to it could also be used, but as music became more harmonically complex composers demanded greater freedom of movement. By the system of 'equal temperament', widely adopted from the beginning of the 18th century and publicised by works such as Bach's volume of preludes and fugues, which he called the *Well Tempered Clavier*, all semitone intervals were treated as equal, i.e. C to C sharp was the same as D to D flat. By accepting this slight inaccuracy of intonation throughout the scale, all the keys could be played with equal ease on a single standard keyboard instrument and modulation from one to another presented no problems.

tempo (Italian, 'time'). Now an English term used to mean the pace of a piece of music, hence 'fast' tempo etc.

Tenebrae (Latin, 'darkness'). Name sometimes used for the services of Matins and Lauds on the Thursday, Friday and Saturday of Holy Week in the Roman Catholic liturgical calendar. Hence the term is also used of the music composed for these services, notably settings of the Lamentations.

tenor (from the Latin, 'to hold'). In the age of polyphony the tenor was the part that held the *cantus firmus* while the other parts moved above it. As music developed towards the beginnings of a harmonic system during the 15th century, other parts, without melodic interest but with semi-harmonic functions, came to be set against the old tenor both above and below it. These were known as the '*contra-tenor altus*', later called simply altus (i.e. alto), and the '*contra-tenor bassus*', later the 'bass'. The term tenor itself also came to denote simply a part or high male voice. Instruments of about the same range are said to have the same tenor.

ternary form. A movement in three sections of the pattern A-B-A, the last section being a very close imitation of the first. The first section may sometimes be repeated immediately after its original statement and before the beginning of the second; the second is in a key related to the first and third.

tessitura (Italian, 'texture'). The Italian word is used in English, with a meaning quite distinct from texture, to describe the predominant range of a voice or a part. Thus a generally high-lying part is said to have a high tessitura.

tetrachord. Group of four consecutive notes in the diatonic scale, a unit sometimes used in musical theory but of greatest importance in ancient Greek music.

theme. A musical figure, usually melodic, providing the initial material of which a movement is built up. It is not usually used of fugue, where the term subject is more common, but symphonic themes, like the subject of some fugues, are often less melodies in their own right than pregnant musical ideas which await development. In the musical 'form' of a 'theme and variations' the theme is a self-contained melody, and each of the following movements presents it complete, though in a much embellished manner.

third: see **interval**

thirty-second note. American term for demisemiquaver, a note value half that of the semiquaver and a thirty-second part of a semibreve.

thorough bass: see **continuo**

threnody. A song for the dead, used as the title of some pieces of a mournful nature. The Greek word *threni*, from which it is ultimately derived, is also so used.

tie. A curved line used in notation to link two notes of the same pitch which are to be played as one continuous note. The tie is needed when the bar line falls across the note that is to be held. Thus, if the composer wants a time value of a minim across the bar line he writes two crotchets either side of the line, linking them with a tie. Although the symbol is the same for both, the tie is quite distinct in its use from the slur.

tierce de Picardie (French, 'Picardy third'). A chord with a major third used at the final cadence of a piece in the minor key, especially common in music of the 17th and 18th centuries. The major third, being one of the natural harmonics in the harmonic series, was liable to be heard in any case in a long held chord on the keynote or fundamental, reverberating in a resonant building like a church, and this may explain why composers avoided the minor third in the final chord.

timbre. A French word, commonly used in English to describe the tone colour of an individual instrument. The term tone colour is often confined to mean the effect of the combined timbres of a number of instruments.

time. A term referring to the metrical unit of a piece of music. A piece in 'triple' time has three main beats in the bar: e.g. 3/4 time is three crotchets to the bar, 9/8 is nine quavers divided into three groups of three. 'Duple' time indicates two main beats in the bar, but note that a piece marked 6/8 is regarded as having two groups of three quavers (eighth notes) to the bar and is thus in duple time. 'Compound' time occurs when two times are combined; thus, if one part is in 3/4 and another is in 6/8 each has six quavers to the bar but one divides them 2:2:2, triple time, and the other divides them 3:3, duple time. The term 'common' time is used of a measure of four beats in the bar; for this the time signature, which indicates at the beginning of the music the time being used, is 3/4. The actual speed of the beats, rather than their number, is indicated by a tempo marking.

toccata. At first, in the early 17th century, a term which, like sonata, *sinfonia* etc. might be used of any instrumental composition, though sometimes with the specific meaning of a fanfare of trumpets. By the middle of the century, however, it had become limited to a keyboard piece in free form, usually of considerable brilliance.

tonality. A general abstract term relating to the use of keys in music, though it can also be used as a synonym for key itself. The harmonic system recognises tonality as a basic principle of organisation using a number of keys, one of which is predominant and provides the overall tonality of the music. 'Progressive' tonality, first used by Carl Nielsen, describes music which starts in one key and ends in another; usually the composer returned to the original or 'home' key at the conclusion of a movement. Other 20th-century developments have been 'polytonality', the use of many keys at once, and 'atonality', the abandonment of key as a system of organisation.

tone. 1) A musical interval. 2) Used when discussing the quality of sound reproduction in a voice or instrument. For the American usage see **note**.

tone colour: see **timbre**

tonic. 1) The first degree of the scale. 2) Also called the 'keynote', since both the scale and the key derived from it take their name from the tonic. 3) The main key of a piece of music in which it starts and ends, and thus sometimes called the 'home' key.

tonic sol-fa. A simplified system of notation devised in the 1840s by John Curwen (d. 1880) to assist musically untrained singers in reading music. The degrees of the major scale are named – doh, re, mi, fa, soh, la, te, and then the keynote repeated an octave higher, doh. But these names are relative, doh being the tonic of the main key of the piece whether it be C major, E flat minor or any other key. Thus the singer is freed from the symbols of stave notation and can sing at sight the simple run 'doh, re, mi', once he knows the key note, whether it denotes C-D-E, A flat – B flat – C, or is at some other pitch. Other symbols are used to denote time durations etc.

transcribe. To arrange a piece of music composed for one instrument or combination of instruments for performance by another. Thus, piano transcriptions have been made of Bach's organ music and of 19th-century orchestral works. A musicologist is said to have transcribed a piece of medieval music when he has written it out in modern notation after having interpreted the original notation.

transition. A linking passage of music or a sudden shift of key without modulation.

transpose. To perform a piece of music in a higher or lower key than its original one, or to rewrite music in another key. A piece is usually transposed to suit the range of a voice or instrument other than the one originally intended.

transposing instrument. A specialised use of the word 'transpose' described in the Glossary of Instruments.

treble. 1) A high boy's voice. 2) High pitched members of various instrumental families, notably the treble recorder. 3) By convention the treble clef is also used for tenor parts, a figure eight attached to the bottom of the clef indicating that the notes are to be sung an octave lower than they appear.

tremolo. 1) A 'trembling' effect achieved on bowed instruments by a rapid reiteration of a note by means of a quick succession of backward and forward movements of the bow. 2) On any instruments the rapid alternation between one note and another.

tremulant. An organ stop.

triad. The basic chord of classical harmony consisting of three notes spaced by two intervals of a third.

trill. Musical ornament consisting of the rapid alternation between the note and the note above it; also called 'shake'.

trio. 1) A chamber music composition for three performers, or the group of performers themselves. 2) In a symphony, a second minuet, which may have derived its name because it was first composed for only three instruments, for the sake of contrast, though the derivation is unsure. 3) A trio sonata was an early chamber music form, but Bach wrote trio sonatas for organ with three distinct parts usually played one on each of two manuals, the other on the pedals.

triplet. A group of three notes required to be played in the duration allowed by the time signature for two of the same denomination.

tritone. The interval of three whole tones, for example from F to B, called the 'devil in music' during the middle ages because it was both difficult to sing and was considered ugly.

trope. 1) In early medieval music an interpolation, whether of words or music, into a standard piece of plainsong. Such tropes came to be used in various contexts and books called 'tropers' were compiled containing a selection of them for easy access. 2) A term coined in the 20th century by twelve-note theorists to name the combinations of the series selected for use in composition.

troppo. Italian for 'too much', used in such phrases as *allegro ma non troppo* – literally, 'fast but not too much'.

troubadour. Poet-composer and singer of 11th- and 12th-century Provence. The music of the troubadours, set to poems on the themes of courtly love, was the first great flowering of European secular music. Their work was taken up by the *trouvères* of northern France and by the *Minnesänger* of Germany.

tune. Used as a verb to describe the act of bringing the mechanism of any instrument – the strings of the violin or piano, the head of a kettledrum – to the correct pitch. A tuning fork is quite simply a two-pronged fork manufactured with great precision so that when struck it vibrates at an exact frequency, acting as an aid to a musician in finding an accurate pitch.

turn. A musical ornament; a flourish of four

notes beginning on the note above the one to be decorated and then falling to the note below it.

tutti. The Italian word for 'all', used generally to refer to those passages in a concerto or other work in which the main body of instrumentalists are playing.

twelve-note composition. 20th-century technique of composition effectively evolved by Schoenberg. Accepting that traditional harmony and the system of tonality were exhausted, Schoenberg postulated a system in which all twelve notes of the chromatic scale were treated as equal and were not subject to the kind of 'hierarchy' of relationships set up by the tonic-dominant system of tonality. Robbed of the idea of key and the harmonic devices of organisation, the composer sets up his own terms of reference. Basic is the 'note row' (American, 'tone row'), the twelve notes of the old chromatic scale arranged in a sequence determined for the piece by the composer. This row may be subjected to various types of distortion, such as inversion or retrograde motion, but the sequence it has established governs the relations of the notes throughout the piece, at whatever pitch they appear. When this kind of formalisation is applied to the elements of rhythm, timbre etc., the term serial music is used.

unison. Term used of two or more voices or instruments performing the same note at the same pitch. Less strictly, voices are said to be singing 'in unison' if all are singing the same part even when the men's and women's voices are in fact an octave apart. A canon 'at the unison' is one where the subsequent parts enter on the same note as the first one.

up-beat. The unaccented beat preceding the first accented beat of a bar, so called because it is indicated by a conductor with an upward gesture of the baton. The term 'down-beat' refers to the accented beat and for a similar reason.

'utility music'. Literal English translation of the term *Gebrauchsmusik*, coined by the German composer Hindemith.

valve. A mechanism on brass instruments.

vamp. Used in music as a verb. To provide a simple, improvised chordal accompaniment on the piano.

variation. The term 'theme and variations' is more or less self-explanatory. But the variation can range from the simplest embellishment to the melodic line, to a passage which retains only the harmonic structure of the original, or to a passage which takes up some musical idea perceived in the theme and develops it at greater or less length.

verismo. A type of 'realism' in Italian opera at the turn of the 19th and 20th centuries, in which the plot was on a contemporary, often violent, theme.

verse: see anthem

vibrato. An effect, once an ornament but now a standard part of tone production, whereby a singer or instrumentalist imparts a throbbing quality to a note by oscillating between it and a pitch slightly below. With singers the louder the note, the more pronounced, usually, the vibrato – and the oscillation can become so wide that the hearer may be left in doubt as to just which note is being aimed for. If the technique is applied, as it often is, to a fairly rapid passage, the result is quite unnerving and totally unmusical (except, apparently, in the opera house).

villanella. A type of part-song popular in Italy during the 15th and 16th centuries. It was much less elaborate and intense than the madrigal, but many composers wrote examples.

virelay. A medieval French song, with equivalents in other parts of Europe, having an involved rhyming structure.

virtuoso. A musical performer of outstanding technical skill.

vivace. The Italian for 'lively', used as a direction to performance; *vivo* has the same meaning.

vocalise. To sing without words. A vocalisation is a passage where the music continues over a greatly extended single syllable.

voice. Apart from its general connotation, the word has two specific meanings. 1) A part in a fugue. 2) As a verb, meaning the fine adjustment of organ pipes to obtain accurate intonation and the required shade of timbre. Hence the term 'voicing'.

voice-leading (from the German, *Stimmeführung*). The American term for part-writing, that is the composer's success and skill in laying out the various parts of his composition to achieve his effects.

volta. An Italian dance of the Renaissance period. One of the steps was a jump, hence the name. In English it was sometimes called 'lavolta'.

voluntary. A piece of organ music usually played as a prelude to the church service and once improvised, as it still is sometimes.

vox humana. An organ stop.

waits. Town musicians in England during the middle ages and flourishing into the 17th century.

waltz. A dance in a lilting triple time that swept the ballrooms of Europe during the early 19th century, though it probably had its origins in the *Ländler*, an Austrian folk dance.

whole-note. The American term for the semibreve, which is equivalent to four crotchets.

yodel. Also spelt jodel. A type of singing, associated with the mountains of Switzerland and the Tyrol, in which the singer alternates between his natural and falsetto voice.

zapateado. Spanish show dance of great vigour in which the performer stamps out rhythms with his feet.

zarzuela. Spanish type of ballad opera with singing and spoken dialogue; often the mood is satirical.

Glossary of Musical Instruments

accordion. A portable instrument in which free reeds are vibrated by wind from a large expandable bellows slung across the player's body; it was invented in Germany in the 1820s. The flow of wind to the reeds is controlled by melody keys, operated by the player's right hand, and chord buttons (which each affect three reeds), operated by the left hand, which also works the bellows.

action. Term used to describe the mechanism, primarily of keyboard instruments, by which the performer operates the strings or pipes of the piano or organ. The traditional 'tracker' action of the organ, in which the key operates a series of articulated rods, is still considered the best musically since it gives the player direct mechanical contact with the pipe itself.

aeolian harp. A stringed instrument 'played' by the wind. It consists of a frame about five feet high, strung with strings of varying thicknesses that vibrate as a chord in the breeze. The name derives from Aeolus, god of the winds, but although the principle was known in ancient times the instrument enjoyed a particular vogue in the early Romantic period.

alphorn. Instrument of conical bore and usually about ten feet long. It is played with a cup mouthpiece and has been used in the Alps, primarily for signalling, since the middle ages.

American organ. A free reed organ like the harmonium, except that the reeds are vibrated by a suction bellows.

anvil. A percussion instrument consisting of a metal bar hit by a metal striker and having no definite pitch.

archlute. Generic term for all instruments of the lute family with strings on an additional neck. Examples are the theorbo and the chitarrone.

arpeggione. An instrument invented in Vienna during the 1820s. Of the size and pitch of a cello, it has the smooth waist, flat back and frets of a guitar. Schubert wrote a sonata for it, now played on the cello.

aulos. Ancient Greek instrument consisting of two divergent pipes with finger-holes and blown with a double reed.

bagpipe. Folk instrument of ancient origins, probably in the Middle East. The 'bag' is an animal bladder which is held under the player's arm and acts as a reservoir of air; the piper blows into it through a mouth pipe and keeps up the wind pressure with his arm. From the bag lead off the 'chanter', a melody pipe with finger holes, and one, two or three drone pipes, a medieval addition. All the pipes are activated by a reed while the mouth pipe is fitted with a non-return valve. There are numerous types of bagpipe; in some the chanter and the drones are played by different performers, in others, such as the Irish Union pipes and the French musette, the wind is supplied by a bellows. In all, however, the flow of air and hence of sound is unbroken, giving rise to a characteristic type of ornamentation as an essential aid to clear articulation of the melody.

balalaika. Russian stringed instrument of the guitar type. It is triangular in shape, has three strings and four moveable frets and is played with a plectrum. There are six sizes, and balalaika bands are common.

bandora: see **pandora**

bandurria. Spanish plucked stringed instrument of medieval provenance. The modern type has six pairs of strings and a round flat body similar to a cittern; it is usually about two feet long.

banjo. A plucked instrument, from the first associated with the Negro slaves of America and probably brought by them from Africa. In its first form it was a tambourine with strings stretched across it and a long neck. Now the banjo has a fretted finger board, retains its parchment table, but is backed by a wooden resonator. It is played either with a plectrum (four-stringed type) or with the fingers, in which case a fifth, drone string is added.

baritone. A type of brass band instrument, very similar to the euphonium.

baryton. Bass stringed instrument, evolved in the late 17th century but obsolete by the early 19th century. Similar in tone quality and range to the bass viol, it had between 16 and 40 wire sympathetic strings running under the neck, which not only vibrated sympathetically but also were plucked. Haydn wrote 175 works for this very difficult instrument for his patron, Prince Nicolas Esterhazy.

basset horn. A tenor instrument of the clarinet family, much used by Mozart and still occasionally heard in performances of his works for it.

bassoon. Bass double reed instrument of conical bore. It derived, in the 17th century, from the curtal and was soon used in the orchestra as the bass equivalent of the oboe, although for about a century it simply doubled the bass line. The 'double' or 'contra'-bassoon has a range an octave lower. The Russian bassoon was an entirely different instrument.

battery. Generic term for the untuned percussion instruments of the orchestra.

bell. An instrument, some type or another of which has been known since the most remote times. Whereas the gong vibrates at its centre, the bell vibrates primarily near the rim at what is called the sound bow. Bells, which may vary in size from a few ounces to several tons, can be rung either by a clapper inside the bell which strikes the sound bow as the bell is swung, or by hammers, striking inside or outside the stationary bell. They are cast of an alloy of about 78% copper to 22% bronze, and their casting and tuning call for considerable skill. The tone of the bell is made up of a number of partials, but the exact acoustics are not agreed among theorists. However, the tone is conventionally divided into the 'strike' note, the 'hum' note, and the major overtones. Bells, grouped in carillons, are used as melodic instruments, but they are also rung, especially in England, in changes. In medieval times the bell chime, a group of bells sounded with a hammer, was a common instrument; its place in the modern orchestra is taken by the tubular bells.

biwa. A type of Japanese flat-backed lute.

bladder pipe. Common enough in medieval Europe and still surviving as a folk instrument in the remoter parts of the continent. It is essentially a simple double-reed instrument. The reed is in an elastic animal bladder, which acts as a temporary wind reservoir, between the mouthpiece and the pipe itself.

bombard. This word and its variants and corruptions, such as *pommer*, were the general terms in continental Europe, from the 15th to the 17th century, for the bass and tenor members of the shawm family of reed instruments.

bombarde. A type of bass reed stop on the organ.

bombardon. Alternative term for the bass tuba in a brass band.

bonang. A chime of bossed gongs used in the Indonesian gamelan orchestra.

bongo drums. A pair of small drums of Afro-Cuban origin. They are fixed together side by side, are of the same height but different diameters and are played with the hands.

bore. The internal diameter of a tube; hence loosely used to mean the bore at every point along the tube. An instrument with a 'cylindrical' bore has the same diameter throughout the greater part of its length; an instrument with 'conical' bore gradually widens from mouthpiece to bell.

bourdon. 1) A low-pitched stopped organ stop. 2) The bass strings of plucked instruments, particularly the off-board strings of the archlutes. 3) The drone pipes of the bagpipes, in earlier usage.

bow. 1) A primitive type of musical instrument consisting simply of a hunting bow of which the string is vibrated in some way while the stick is flexed so as to alter the tension in the string and hence the pitch of the note. 2) An implement used for vibrating the strings of many types of stringed instruments. During a long history the bow has had many shapes. The modern violin bow consists of a slightly curved stick with a ribbon of horsehair running down the convex side between the tip and an adjustable 'nut' which can vary the tension of the hair; the bow is held in the right hand of the player. The standard modern shape is thought to date from the design of François Tourte (1747-1835). The bows of the cello and double bass are both shorter and heavier; the bows used for the viols have the horsehair on the concave side, as once the violin bow did. See also the technical term **bowing**

brass band: see **military band**

brass instruments. The generic term for all instruments, of which the most familiar are the horn, the trumpet, the trombone and the tubas, which are made of metal and are blown with some kind of cup-shaped or cone-shaped mouthpiece. The quality of the tone is importantly affected by the shape of the mouthpiece – i.e. whether deep or shallow, cup or cone – and the nature of the bore – i.e. whether cylindrical like the trumpet or conical like the horn. The tone is also affected by the type of metal used to make the instrument, by the largeness or smallness of the bore, and by the degree to which the terminal section of the tube, called the 'bell', flares out. An open tube of a certain length gives the notes of the harmonic series related to the fundamental note of an air column of that length. In the 19th century valve mechanisms were developed that allowed the player to alter the length of his instrument instantaneously and thus select any note from a variety of harmonic series. Previously, the pitch of the 'natural', i.e. unvalved, horns and trumpets could only be changed by fixing different lengths of tube, called 'crooks', between the mouthpiece and the instrument. This of course meant that the player could perform in a higher or lower key but still only had the notes of the harmonic series available.

bridge. The part of any instrument using strings that transfers their vibrations to the sounding board or sound box. On the bowed instruments the strings pass over the bridge, holding it in place against the belly of the instrument by their pressure. In plucked instruments, such as the guitar, the bridge is anchored to the belly, and the strings stretch from it to the peg box. On keyboard instruments, the strings are anchored by wrest pins and pass over two bridges that define their vibrating length.

buccina. Ancient Roman type of horn, made either of animal horn or of metal.

bugle. A wide bore, conical brass instrument without valves. It is high pitched and played with a cup mouthpiece. Much modified, and with valves added, it became the basic instrument of the saxhorn family. See also **keyed bugle**

buisine. A medieval long straight trumpet, made of several sections jointed together with ornamental bosses.

bull-roarer. This instrument of prehistoric origins is also called 'thunder stick'. It consists of a shaped piece of wood attached to a string which is whirled round the head; in primitive societies it is a cult object of great potency, its sound being reckoned to be the voices of ancestors or spirits.

carillon. A set of tuned bells with a compass of between one and a half and two octaves. The bells are hung stationary and are sounded by hammers operated from a keyboard.

castanets. A pair of shell-like clappers made of wood, held in one hand and manipulated by the fingers. They have been used to accompany dances in the Mediterranean region since the earliest times.

caval. Turkish end-blown flute of cylindrical bore; it is also found in Balkan folk music.

celeste. A keyboard instrument invented in the 1880s in which tuned metal bars are struck by hammers similar to those of the piano.

cembalo. Italian word, cognate with the Hungarian *cimbalom*, a type of dulcimer, and used as the shortened form of '*clavicembalo*' or keyed dulcimer. Hence it came to mean any keyboard instrument but specially the harpsichord.

chalumeau. Formerly a single-reed folk instrument which was modified and improved in the first half of the 18th century to produce the clarinet. The term is now used of the lowest register of the clarinet.

chanter: see **bagpipe**

ch'in. Ancient Chinese type of zither. Of the seven strings one is a melody string, the others providing the accompaniment. The strings are of equal length but of different thicknesses and are stretched over a long, narrow, slightly convex board.

chitarrone. An archlute whose overall length was sometimes as much as six feet to accommodate the long off-board strings. See also **theorbo**

cimbalom. Hungarian gipsy instrument of the dulcimer family; it was 'improved' and standardised during the 19th century and in this form has been used in the orchestra.

citole. The forerunner of the cittern.

cittern. Plucked stringed instrument popular from the early 16th to the mid 19th century. It had a flat back, fretted finger board and a variable number of wire strings and was played with the fingers, not with a plectrum.

clappers. An old percussion instrument consisting of two hinged arms with wooden shells or little metal cymbals at their extremities; when the hinged arms, usually attached to a handle, are shaken, the cymbals clash together.

clarinet. A woodwind instrument of cylindrical bore with a single reed, developed in the early 18th century. It did not become a regular member of the orchestra until Mozart recognised its potentialities; like the other woodwind it was improved during the 19th century by the addition of a more elaborate key mechanism. The clarinet is a transposing instrument; the B flat model has a range of about three octaves from the D below middle C. The bass clarinet is an octave lower than this in pitch and the basset horn, now rarely heard, is the tenor of the family.

clarino. A high trumpet part.

clavecin. The French word for 'harpsichord'; hence *claveciniste*, a performer on the *clavecin*.

clavicembalo: see **cembalo**

clavichord. A keyboard instrument in use from the 15th to the 18th centuries and now revived. It is in the shape of a horizontal rectangular box with or without legs (some were small enough to be carried easily); the keyboard was in one of the long sides and the strings ran the length of the case. The string was struck by a small metal tangent fixed in the end of the key; since there was no escapement it remained in contact with the string so long as the key was depressed, the string's vibrating length stretching between the tangent and the bridge. In early models one string might be used for two or three notes, which could of course not be sounded simultaneously; this type was called a 'fretted' clavichord. Unlike the harpsichord it was capable of varied dynamics depending on the power with which the key was struck.

Clavier or **Klavier.** The German word for keyboard and hence stringed keyboard instruments.

concertina. Free reed instrument with hexagonal bellows and finger studs controlling notes and chords; patented by Charles Wheatstone in 1829.

console: see **organ**

cor anglais. An alto oboe.

cornet. Soprano brass instrument with valves. It is similar in range to the trumpet but has a wider, conical bore, is played with a deeper cup mouthpiece and is less brilliant in tone. Lower pitched instruments of the same family are the althorn and the tenor horn.

cornett. Soprano wind instrument used in music of the 16th and 17th centuries. It is made of wood bound in leather, has finger holes and is played with a cup mouthpiece, which in the 'mute' cornett was carved out of the tube itself and was not detachable.

coupler. Part of organ mechanism enabling the player to link the mechanism and stops of one keyboard to those of another.

crook: see **brass instruments**

crumhorn. Double reed instrument, made in various sizes, and used from the 15th to 17th centuries. The reed is blown through a reed cap and thus does not vibrate in the player's mouth.

crwth. Ancient Welsh bowed lyre with melody and drone strings.

curtal. Renaissance double-reed instrument similar in range to the bassoon, but, unlike it, the conical tube of the curtal was hollowed out of a single piece of wood and was not jointed.

cymbal. An untuned percussion instrument consisting of a metal dish and usually played in pairs, the two cymbals being clashed together. The orchestral cymbal, adopted from Turkey, is a concave dish with a boss through which is threaded a leather thong. The cymbals may be struck by full clashes ('let ring') or short clashes, muted against the player's body ('sec'). A single cymbal may be freely suspended and struck with drum sticks. The 'Chinese' cymbal is less convex than the standard model and the edges turn up; the tone quality is similar to the tam-tam's. The choke cymbals are mounted on a column, the upper fixed and the lower worked by a pedal to clash against it. The so-called 'ancient' cymbals are tuned and have a diameter of about four inches.

dawul. Two-headed Turkish drum, one head being struck with a stick, the other with a switch.

diapason. The foundation tone of the organ.

double bass. The lowest stringed instrument used in the orchestra. The shape and size have never been standardised, but it is usually between five and six feet high and has the same shape as the other members of the violin family. The instrument commonly has four strings but three- and five-stringed basses are also known.

drum. Percussion instrument found in innumerable varieties the world over and since the earliest times. In Western music the commonest types are the kettledrum and those listed here; various other types, such as the dawul and the bongo, have separate entries. The bass drum as used in the orchestra is between four and five feet in diameter and sometimes has two 'heads' or skins, but often only one. The bass drum in jazz or dance music is much smaller and always double-headed; sometimes it is struck with a pedal-operated drumstick. The side drum is about fifteen inches in diameter and only some six inches deep. The upper or 'batter' head is somewhat thicker than the lower or 'snare' head; as with the bass drum the heads can be given greater or lesser tension by means of screws round the rim, while across the lower head are often stretched springs of wound silk, gut or wire which give the instrument a bright sound; there is usually a mechanism that allows these 'snares' to be released from contact with the head. Side drums of various types are used in military and jazz bands and in the latter case may be played with a wire brush. The tenor drum, much deeper than the side drum but of the same diameter and having a more sombre tone, is now more commonly met with in the military band.

dulcimer. A stringed instrument of zither type but with moveable bridges and played with light, hand-held hammers, not plucked.

dulzian. An alternative, German name for the curtal.

echo. Department of a large organ.

electric. Instruments such as the electric guitar are simply modifications of the original instrument, designed to be electrically amplified.

electronic instruments. Various invented instruments, such as the *Ondes Martenot*, using electronic oscillations as a means of sound generation.

embouchure. French term for the mouthpiece of a wind instrument, used in English of the player's lip technique and also of the blow hole of a flute.

end-blown flute. A type of flute in which the player blows across the open end of the instrument, directing the air stream at the opposite rim.

English horn: see **cor anglais**

enharmonic harpsichord. Instrument constructed during the Renaissance which permitted the playing of a number of microtone intervals in an attempt, in the first instance, to demonstrate and return to the acoustical principles of ancient Greek music.

escapement. Mechanism in a piano action that allows the hammer to fall back from the string even while the key is still depressed. The double escapement enables the rapid repetition of a note.

euphonium. Brass instrument of wide conical

bore with a range of about three and a half octaves from the B flat below the bass stave.

Fagot or **Fagott.** German term from the Italian *fagotto* for instruments of the curtal and bassoon type.

f-hole. The holes on either side of the bridge in the belly of the instruments of the violin family, so-called because shaped like an *f*.

fiddel. In fact the German equivalent of the fiddle. The term is used in this book to describe the medieval bowed instrument distinguished by a flat peg disc with pegs inserted above or below. Neither size nor shape were standardised, but usually the fiddel was flat-backed and lacked the well defined waist of the violin.

fiddle. Colloquial term for the violin; bass fiddle is sometimes used of the double bass.

fife. Small, soprano-pitched transverse flute; introduced as a military instrument with the drum by the Swiss in the 15th century.

fipple flute. A type in which the vibrations are set up by a lip cut in the wall of the flute below the mouthpiece. The air is directed through a narrow duct formed between the wall of the flute and a plug or block, called the 'fipple'. The recorder is a familiar example.

flageolet. Type of fipple flute with narrow, contracting bore and two thumb holes at the back, invented in the late 16th century. It subsequently developed in the direction of the recorder.

flugelhorn. Brass instrument with wide conical bore and cup mouthpiece; the same pitch as the cornet but with a somewhat mellower tone.

flute. Wind instrument in which the vibrations are initiated by some part of the wall of the instrument itself (see fipple flute and end-blown flute). There is an endless variety of flutes from all times and places, but the term is now used specifically of the orchestral woodwind instrument also called the transverse flute. About two feet in length, this is held projecting beyond the player's right shoulder and is played by blowing across a small aperture a few inches from the stopped end of the pipe. Since the 17th century the flute has been made in a number of sections, and in the 19th century it was greatly modified and improved by T. Böhm. The flute's range is about three octaves above middle C; the alto or bass flute is about a fourth lower.

foot. The length of organ pipes determines their pitch and is also used to describe it. Thus 'eight foot tone' means playing at written pitch, the C two octaves below middle C being obtained from a pipe eight feet long and the notes above from pipes proportionately shorter. Four foot tone means an octave above written pitch.

fortepiano. Term now used of 18th-century pianos.

fret. On stringed instruments, such as the guitar, lute and viol, the bars or pieces of gut placed across the fingerboard beneath the strings, against which the player stops the strings.

gamba. Abbreviation for viola da gamba, a term now conventionally limited to the bass viol. Also an organ stop with this tone quality.

gamelan. Indonesian orchestra consisting of percussion instruments of the fixed note type such as xylophones etc.

gedackt. German word for 'stopped', used in

English of certain types of organ pipes.

gemshorn (German, 'goat's horn'). An early type of fipple flute made apparently from the horn of a mountain goat. Now used of an organ stop.

gender. Type of marimba used in the Indonesian gamelan orchestra.

glass harmonica. An instrument consisting of a number of differently sized glasses, threaded on a horizontal axle and rotated through a partially filled trough of water by a treadle mechanism. This instrument, whose strange ethereal sound is produced by the player's fingers rubbing on the moistened rims of the glasses, had a particular vogue in the late 18th century.

glockenspiel. Tuned percussion instrument consisting of a series of tuned metal plates struck with hard hammers, either hand-held or operated by a keyboard.

gong. Percussion instrument, probably, like its name, of Javanese or at least south-east Asian origin. It is a bronze disc with edges turned up and often with a boss in the centre; the rim is dead and the instrument sounds from the vibrations at the centre when struck.

great. Department of the organ.

guitar. Plucked stringed instrument related to the earlier cittern and vihuela. The modern Spanish guitar is flat backed, has six strings, a flat peg box with rear mounted pegs, a fretted fingerboard and a pronounced 'figure of eight' shape. The earlier guitar had only five strings and a less marked waist. The electric guitar common in pop music is a heavily modified adaptation of the principle of the guitar to electrical amplification.

gusle. Yugoslav folk instrument consisting of a single bowed string stretched over a sound box and neck.

guzli. Russian folk psaltery with medieval antecedents.

Hammond organ. Patent American electronic keyboard instrument, simulating the effects of the pipe organ.

Hammerklavier. A German word for piano, used by Beethoven in titling his sonata in B flat, Opus 106, and certain others.

harmonica. Mouth blown instrument employing free reeds.

harmonium. Keyboard instrument, invented by Alexandre-François Debain of Paris in 1840, employing free reeds vibrated by air blown through from a bellows. It has been used by some composers, among them Dvořák and Webern. See also **American organ**

harp. One of the most ancient of stringed instruments, consisting basically of a frame carrying strings of different lengths, and hence different pitches, which are plucked. The frame is essentially of two members, the 'body', which acts as a resonator, and the neck, and between these the strings are tensioned. Many harps also have a 'pillar', joining neck and body to make a rigid triangular frame; the Irish or Celtic harp has a curving pillar, the modern 'double-action' orchestral harp has a straight pillar rising from a 'pedestal'. From the 17th century on, attempts were made to provide a string for each note of the chromatic scale without making the instrument too cumbersome, but in the modern harp, with a range of some eight octaves, this has proved difficult.

The instrument has therefore remained diatonic, i.e. with seven, not twelve strings to the octave. But a mechanism, operated by pedals in the pedestal and levers rising through the pillar, has been evolved since the early 19th century enabling each string to be raised either a semitone or a tone, thus permitting the performance of the diatonic scale in all keys.

harpsichord. A stringed keyboard instrument of major importance from the 16th to the 18th centuries. The range is only slightly less than that of the modern piano but the action is quite different. Operation of the keys causes the strings to be plucked rather than struck and it is virtually impossible to achieve gradations of volume by the degree of pressure on the key. Fixed vertically at the end of the key is a 'jack'. This carries at its top a damper that rests on the string and, just below this, a pivoted tongue of wood rotating in a slit cut in the jack and carrying a quill. When the key is depressed the jack rises, the quill plucking the string to produce the note as it moves upwards; the movement of the jack upwards is arrested by a strip of wood called a jack rail. When the key is released the jack falls back, a spring-operated escapement preventing the quill from plucking the string on its descent, and the damper falls back on to the string, stopping its vibrations. In most instruments of the 16th and 17th centuries there was only one keyboard and each note had only a single string, or course of strings, tuned to the unison. In later models duplicate sets of jacks and strings were provided for each note and the player, by moving a hand stop, could select the jacks and strings to be used and thus vary the tone quality of the instrument; in the 18th century, double-manual harpsichords were common and some models were built with pedal boards. The instrument has been revived in the 20th century, but both the size of the orchestra against which it is required to play and the loss of the secret of making the sound board in particular, have led some makers to use electrical methods of sound amplification and even swell mechanisms.

hautbois. French word meaning literally 'high wood', from which is derived the English 'oboe'.

hazozrah. Ancient Hebrew straight trumpet.

Heckelphone. Instrument invented by the German firm of Heckel; played with a double reed like the oboe but having a wider bore and being of baritone pitch.

helicon. A bass tuba wound in a ring so as to be more easily carried by a marching bandsman.

hoboy. A 17th-century English equivalent of the French *hautbois*.

horn. Of the innumerable instruments derived from the horns of various animals (see, for example, **oliphant**), the term is now generally reserved for the orchestral brass instrument, of conical bore, with a range of about three octaves from the B below the bass stave. It is played with a conical mouthpiece and has a widely flaring bell; from the early 19th century it has been fitted with valves. During the 18th century hornists developed a technique of hand-stopping the bell so as to modify the pitch of the instrument at will and thus produce notes not naturally occurring in the harmonic series of an open tube. It was also possible to raise or lower the pitch of the whole instrument, and thus enable it to play in a variety of keys, by

introducing additional lengths of tubing, called 'crooks', between the mouthpiece and the instrument proper. There are important differences between the French and German horn; the former, narrower in bore and with a different valve system, is brighter in tone but more difficult to play than the latter.

hornpipe. An early folk instrument, consisting of a reed pipe fitted with a bell of cowhorn.

hurdy-gurdy. A stringed instrument popular in the middle ages and continuing in folk music since then. It has a large pear-shaped body which runs straight into the peg box. The strings are stopped not by the fingers but by wooden sliders moving in slots in a casing either side of them. The instrument is sometimes bowed, but far more usually the strings are vibrated by a wooden wheel turned by a handle projecting from the bottom of the body; in addition to the melody strings there are two drone strings.

hydraulis or **hydraulos** (from the Greek for 'water' and 'pipe'). The organ known to classical antiquity. It seems that its only essential difference from the modern organ was the use of water pressure to maintain a steady air pressure to the pipes.

jack: see **harpsichord**

jew's harp or **trump.** The derivation is unclear: the instrument is not a harp and has no definable connection with the Jews – possibly it comes from the Dutch, *Jeugd tromp*, 'child's trumpet'. Possibly of Asiatic origin, it is in the shape of an open stirrup with a metal tongue attached to the centre of its long side. This part is placed in the mouth of the performer and the projecting metal tongue plucked; by varying the shape of the mouth cavity selected natural harmonics of the instrument can be emphasised and a melody produced.

jingling johnny, also called '*pavillon chinois*' and 'Turkish crescent'. Military band instrument (particularly in Germany), introduced to Europe from Turkey in the 19th century, consisting of a 'Christmas-tree' structure hung with little bells that jingle when shaken.

kaval: see **caval**

kantele. The Finnish 'national instrument'; a type of psaltery.

kettledrum (for the plural, the Italian word '*timpani*' is often used). A tuned percussion instrument, coming to Europe from the Arab world and the descendant of the medieval naker. The instrument has a 'head', which may be made either of animal skin or plastic, of between two and three feet in diameter. This is stretched across the open top of a copper shell or 'kettle' and is held in place by a circlet of metal. Tuning is effected either by keys that screw down on to the metal circlet, depressing it and thus stretching the head, or by a pedal-operated mechanism that allows almost immediate tuning of the head. This latter type, perfected in the 20th century, is called a 'pedal' or 'machine' drum. In the classical orchestra the kettledrums were usually in pairs, tuned to the tonic and dominant of the music; from the 1830s three or more were commonly used, sometimes needing two performers. The tone quality of the kettledrum varies according to the type of stick used and as to whether the head is struck near the rim or between it and the

centre.

keyed bugle. A brass instrument of bugle type to which keys were fitted instead of valves as in the cornet etc.

kit. A high-pitched, pocket-sized violin (hence the French name, '*pochette*') commonly used by dancing masters in the 18th century.

koto. Japanese stringed instrument of zither type derived from the Chinese *ch'in*. It has thirteen strings and a range of two octaves, and is played with plectra attached to the fingers of the right hand.

lira da braccio. Bowed stringed instrument of the 15th and 16th centuries. It had a wide fingerboard with five strings and two additional, unstopped strings off the fingerboard, a flat peg disc and a not very pronounced waist. The bass version was called a *lirone*.

lituus. Ancient Roman trumpet with conical bore.

lur. Celtic bronze trumpet with conical bore, terminating in a flat decorated disc. It was apparently most common in Denmark, and the examples found date from 1100 to 500 BC.

lute. Plucked stringed instrument of Arabic origins (the name comes from the Arabic *al'ud*). It was one of the most important instruments in European music during the 16th and 17th centuries; but in various primitive forms it is known from about 2000 BC. It has a deep body in the shape of a half pear, a short neck carrying the fretted fingerboard and a long peg box turned back at right angles to the neck. There are five pairs, or courses, of strings, each pair tuned to the octave or unison. The instrument is still common in Arab countries where it is unfretted and played with a plectrum; in Europe it has been plucked with the fingers since the early 15th century and was capable of elaborate polyphonic music in the hands of a virtuoso.

lyra viol. Term which primarily denoted a style of playing the bass viol – holding it across the knees like a lute and plucking the strings. Sometimes, however, smaller instruments were made specially for this style.

lyre. An ancient type of plucked stringed instrument. It consists of a sound box or resonator on which is mounted a yoke of two vertical arms joined by a cross-piece. The strings are stretched between this cross-piece and some form of bridge on the belly of the resonator. The classic lyre of ancient Greece was of this type. In the middle ages various types of bowed lyre evolved of which the Welsh *crwth* was one to which a fingerboard had been added.

machine drum: see **kettledrum**

mandoline. Plucked stringed instrument originating, in its present form, in early 18th-century Italy. It is about two feet long, has a fretted fingerboard, four pairs of wire strings tuned like those on the violin and a deeply arched back. It is played with a plectrum.

mandora. A type of small lute.

manual. Alternative name for the keyboard of a harpsichord or organ – both being instruments which commonly have more than one.

maraca. A type of rattle consisting of a dried gourd containing a number of hard dried seeds. It originated with the South American Indians, but has been used in Western music.

marimba. A xylophone with resonators beneath the keys, adopted by the West from Africa and modified for orchestral and band use.

marine trumpet: see **tromba marina**

metronome. A clockwork-operated pendulum mechanism which enables composers and performers to establish and to reproduce the required tempo of a piece. The pendulum can be set to beat out a variety of speeds and by setting the metronome marking at the beginning of the piece the composer can indicate the number of metrical units per minute that should be maintained. The device was patented in the early 19th century by the inventor J. N. Maelzel.

military band. A band consisting of brass, woodwind and percussion. The 'brass' band does not have woodwind and rarely percussion.

mirliton. A membrane used on a musical instrument to produce a 'buzzing' effect; the child's kazoo and the comb-and-paper are familiar uses of the mirliton.

mixture stop. On the organ a stop with a number of pipes to each note, so tuned as to sound selected harmonics in the series above that note and thus reinforce its brilliancy.

monochord. As its name suggests, an instrument consisting of a single string stretched between two nuts fixed to a rectangular sound box and usually passing over a moveable bridge. This primitive device was used in ancient Greece to demonstrate acoustic ratios, but in the middle ages it was used as an instrument in its own right and gave rise, by the addition of more strings, to various types of psaltery.

mouth music. Style of wordless vocal performance found in Scottish folk music.

mouth organ: see **harmonica**

musette. This French word for bagpipe is now generally reserved for a soft-toned 'society' instrument, blown by bellows and often delicately and richly decorated. It enjoyed a great vogue in the 18th century.

mutation stop. On the organ a stop that brings into action pipes pitched at one of the harmonics above the note played; it is always used in conjunction with a foundation stop. Thus, when the player draws the 'twelfth' mutation stop he adds the note an interval of a twelfth above to the one already sounding.

mute. Device applied to wind and stringed instruments to lessen the volume of their tone or to modify it in some way. Mutes for brass instruments are on some variant of the stopper principle; for stringed instruments they consist of some type of clip, applied to the bridge to damp its vibrations.

naker. Small type of kettledrum used by the armies of medieval Islam and brought to Europe by soldiers in the later Crusades. The Arabic word is *naqqara*.

nut. The ridge of the upper end of the neck of stringed instruments over which the strings pass into the peg box. In English usage the moving part at the lower end of the bow, called in American usage the 'frog'.

oboe. Woodwind instrument, played with a double reed, having a conical bore and a range of about three octaves above the B flat below middle C. It was a refined and more expressive modification of the shawm, being for example made in three jointed sections, of more accurate bore, and was invented by the musicians of the *Écurie* of the court of Louis XIV. The soft-tone *oboe d'amore*, in vogue during the 18th century, was pitched a minor third below the oboe proper. The cor anglais (the term's derivation is unknown) is a double-reed instrument of tenor range but with a much richer and heavier tone than the oboe. It was originally curved and bound in leather; later angled, jointed versions were made. The modern instrument is straight but is distinguished from the oboe by the curved 'crook' carrying the reed and by its globular bell. The term *oboe da caccia*, used by Bach, may possibly have referred to the curved cor anglais, or simply to an oboe with a flaring bell.

ocarina. A small globular flute, usually of clay.

octobass. A vast stringed instrument invented in the mid-19th century. It was pitched an octave below the double bass, stood some twelve feet high and had a lever-operated mechanism to stop the strings.

oliphant. Medieval ceremonial horn made from elephant tusk and often most elaborately carved and decorated.

Ondes Martenot. Instrument devised in the 1920s by the French inventor Maurice Martenot, in which the generation of the tone is achieved by means of the interference effect produced between a fixed and a variable radio-frequency oscillator.

ophicleide. Keyed brass instrument invented by a Paris maker in about 1817. Identical in principle to the keyed bugle, i.e. using keyed holes like the woodwind, the ophicleide had a tube of wide conical bore and was played with a cup mouthpiece. The bass member of the family was adopted in the orchestra and the military band; its career in the latter was longer than in the former, since from the mid-19th century it was displaced by the tubas.

organ. A vast battery of single-pitched pipes, blown with air from a mechanical bellows and controlled from a keyboard by either mechanical or electropneumatic action. The largest medieval organs could be heard, it was said, at over a mile's distance, though the delicate portative and positive organs were also used in this period. The modern instrument, whose development may be traced from the 15th century, is in effect three or more organs, each of which is allotted a keyboard in the organ 'console', the term for the keyboards and controls from which the player operates the instrument. The 'great' organ has, in the main, full-sounding diapason pipes. The 'swell', so called because it is enclosed within louvred doors which can be gradually opened so as to 'swell' the volume of sound, has mainly reed stops, often of very brilliant tone, and mixture and mutation stops. The 'choir' organ has predominantly small soft-toned pipes. Large organs have additional departments, such as the 'echo' and 'solo' organ. There is an almost infinite variety of types of organ pipe, but the two main divisions are between the flute pipe, sounding on the principle of the fipple flute, and the reed pipe, using a beating reed. Within these broad categories differences of tone quality are gained by using varying materials, wood and various types of metal, varying the shape of the pipe and modifying it in other ways. The length of the pipe determines its pitch; hence organ pipes and their tone may be described in terms of feet – eight foot tone being the basic pitch of the instrument, four foot being an octave higher and so on. Most organs have sixteen-foot pipes; thirty-two foot is less common and sixty-four rare. All these deep pipes are played from the pedal board. In small organs, the effect of sixteen-foot tone can be achieved with an eight-foot pipe plugged or 'stopped' at its upper end; this has the acoustic effect of lowering the pitch of a flue pipe by an octave. Such 'stopped' pipes also have a different quality of tone as well as a lower pitch.

The flow of air to the pipes from the wind chest is controlled by a 'pallet' across the bottom of the pipe; this is opened by depressing the keys. In tracker action, pressure on the key activates a number of articulated rods, called trackers and stickers, which connect the key to the pallet; in electro-pneumatic action, movement of the key activates an electric current which, in its turn, operates a pneumatic mechanism that opens the pallet. By a system of 'sliders', operated by 'tabs' or 'stops' at the console, the player can select the 'rank' of pipes that he wishes to use.

organistrum. Medieval name for the hurdy-gurdy.

orpharion. A small pandora, tuned like a lute.

pandora. A wire-stringed instrument invented in the 1560s. Flat-backed and fretted, it was in effect a bass cittern, but had a characteristically scalloped shape.

pandoura. A long-necked lute with small body, dating from classical times and persisting, in numerous variants, in Persia and other countries.

panharmonicon. Mechanical organ invented in the early 19th century by J. N. Maelzel, inventor also of the metronome; Beethoven wrote his *Battle Symphony* for it.

panpipes. An instrument consisting of a number of stopped, end-blown pipes (one to each note) bound together in a row.

pavillon chinois: see **jingling johnny**

percussion instruments. That vast family of instruments which sound when struck. It is divided into tuned, e.g. the kettledrum, xylophone etc., and untuned, a far bigger class.

piano. A stringed instrument in which the strings are vibrated by felt-covered hammers operated from a keyboard. The essential quality of the piano that distinguished it from the outset from the harpsichord is its ability to produce varying gradations of volume according to the force with which the key is struck. A feature of the action is the escapement, perfected only after much experimentation from the invention of the piano in the early 18th century. This allows the hammer to fall back from the string while the key is still held down. When the key is released a damper falls back on to the string thus deadening the sound. During the 19th century the piano was the main keyboard instrument, and the development of its mechanism, so important to the music written for it, is described in the chapter on 19th-century musical instruments. In the 'grand' piano the strings run horizontally; in the 'upright', a more compact instrument, they run vertically. The piano has more than one string to each note except, in some models, on the very lowest notes; the 'sustaining' pedal allows the player to hold the dampers off the strings at will, while the 'soft' pedal reduces the 'travel' of the hammers, thus causing them to strike less violently, or shifts the hammers so that they strike fewer of the strings available for each note. In the early-19th-century 'square' piano the strings were placed at right angles to the direction of the keys and the instrument was in the shape of a horizontal rectangular box.

pianola. A mechanical piano, also called 'player' piano. The hammers are operated by air jets passing through holes in a moving paper roll, the perforations being printed to reproduce a performance by some renowned pianist.

piccolo. A small flute pitched an octave higher than the concert flute.

p'i-p'a. Chinese short-necked lute.

pipe and tabor. Combination of a three-holed pipe and small drum played by one performer. Used in many types of dance music during the middle ages, but now confined to folk music and chiefly found in the south of France.

pirouette. A small disc or cylindrical cover on old reed instruments, both to protect the reed and to provide a platform for the player's lips.

player piano: see **pianola**

plectrum. A device used for plucking the strings of some instruments of the lute and guitar type. It is made of wood, metal or, now, plastic and is either held by the fingers or attached to them.

pluriarch. A primitive instrument, consisting in effect of a number of musical bows fixed to a sound box resonator.

pochette. Small violin, pitched an octave higher than the standard model, used as an orchestral instrument by Monteverdi in the early 17th century, but more usual later as the dancing master's kit.

pommer. German term for bass shawm.

portative organ. Small high-pitched medieval organ with a single row of pipes and a range of not more than three octaves. It was slung from the player's body with a strap or rested on his knee and was blown by a gravity bellows operated by the left hand while the right played on the keyboard.

positive organ (from Latin *positus*, 'placed'). A small but not portable organ (see above) of the middle ages and the Renaissance. It had a range of five or six octaves, was lower in pitch than the portative and was played with both hands by one performer whose assistant worked the bellows.

principal. 1) In the early 18th century a type of trumpet part. 2) An organ diapason stop sounding an octave higher than written pitch.

psaltery. A medieval type of zither plucked by the fingers of both hands or by two plectra (see **plectrum**).

qanun. Arab psaltery still played in Islamic countries including parts of Pakistan and Indonesia.

quint. Organ mutation stop sounding, originally, a fifth higher than written though the name is used for other mutations. On some organs, a quint at the fifth is used with the bass note to exploit the acoustic principle of the resultant note and thus provide, without the expense of large thirty-two foot pipes, the effect of thirty-two foot tone. This is also termed an acoustic bass.

rabab. Arab stringed instrument of the spike fiddle type.

rackett. Medieval and Renaissance bass double-reed instrument of cylindrical bore. A short solid cylinder of wood or ivory was bored through its length with a number of cylindrical channels which were then connected in such a way as to form a single long narrow tube 'folded up' in the material.

rank. Set of organ pipes operated by one stop.

Rauschpfeife. Medieval and Renaissance double-reed instrument with a reed cap, like the crumhorn, and wide conical bore.

rebec. Medieval and Renaissance bowed stringed instrument, probably derived from the Arab *rabab*, but no longer a spike fiddle.

recorder. Woodwind instrument of the fipple flute type important in the music of the Renaissance and Baroque periods, the Renaissance instrument tending to have a wider bore and a more incisive tone than that of the 18th century, which has provided the model for the modern revival. The members of the recorder family are the bass, about four feet long and played through a side pipe, the tenor, the treble, the descant and the sopranino, the lower three members occasionally having one or two keys. The complete range of the family is about four octaves from the F below middle C.

reed instruments. The innumerable wind instruments in which the air column is activated by a reed are divided broadly between the double-reed class, in which two reeds together forming a narrow tube (as with the oboe) constitute the vibrating mechanism, and the single-reed class. In the latter case the reed, which may be cut out of the wall of the instrument itself, as with some bagpipe reeds, is either 'beating' or 'free'. A beating reed, e.g. that of the clarinet, vibrates against the edges of the aperture over which it is fixed; the reeds in reed pipes of the organ are of this kind. A free reed is also fixed at one end but is free to vibrate backwards and forwards at the other; in instruments using this type each note is served by a separate reed which determines itself the pitch of the note. See **reed organ** and also **sheng**

reed organ. A group of instruments, derived in the early 19th century from the Chinese *sheng*, in which the sound is produced by free reeds, one to each note. Examples are the harmonium and the mouth organ or harmonica.

regal. An 'organ' of the late middle ages and Renaissance in which reeds, vibrated by air from a small gravity bellows, provided the notes. The reeds were either entirely without pipe resonators or with only very small ones. Gradually true organs came to have 'regal' stops. The 'Bible' regal was one that folded up like a book for ease of transport.

resin or **rosin.** A dried gum preparation used on the bows of stringed instruments to increase their grip on the strings.

rote. A type of medieval plucked stringed instrument.

Russian bassoon. Type of serpent.

sackbut. Old name for the trombone, which, in fact, formerly had a narrower bore and less flaring bell than the modern instrument.

samisen. Long-necked Japanese lute having a square body with wooden walls and skin belly and back. It is played with a large axe-shaped plectrum and has a number of tunings designed to allow for the maximum use of open strings.

sanayi. Double-reed instrument of northern India, equivalent of the old European shawm or Turkish zurna.

sansa. African instrument consisting of a number of metal tongues attached to a small wooden soundbox. It is held in the two hands, the thumbs plucking the metal tongues.

sarangi. Northern Indian bowed instrument with large clumsy body carved out of a single piece of wood and wide fingerboard. There are three or four speaking strings and a number of sympathetic strings.

sārod. Northern Indian stringed instrument with very deep body, either plucked or played with a bow.

saron. Metal tuned percussion instrument of xylophone type, used in the Indonesian gamelan orchestra.

sarrusophone. Double-reed instrument made of brass. Invented in the mid-19th century for military band use, though the bass sarrusophone has occasionally been substituted for the double bassoon in the orchestra.

saxhorn. Wind instrument of the bugle type, but fitted with valves and invented by Adolphe Sax in the 1840s. Strictly he did not invent anything, but merely standardised the number of existing valved bugles into a homogeneous family, over the whole pitch range from sopranino to double bass.

saxophone. Keyed brass instrument with single beating reed (like the clarinet) and wide conical bore, invented by Adolphe Sax in the 1840s. Designed originally for the military band, the saxophone became one of the prime instruments of jazz.

serpent. Obsolete brass instrument apparently invented in the late 16th century. It consisted of an S-shaped wooden tube of wide bore, about seven feet long and bound with leather. It was regarded as the natural bass of the cornett, was played with a cup mouthpiece and had six finger holes. Later, keys were added.

shawm. Double-reed instrument with conical bore used in European art music up to the middle of the 17th century, when it came to be replaced by the newly evolved oboe. It had a heavier, coarser tone then the oboe, and the bass members of the family, called pommers or bombards, were also louder than the curtal. It is still used as a folk instrument, particularly in Spain.

sheng. Chinese mouth organ of ancient origins, using the free reed principle. It consists of a gourd-like wind chest from which project upwards a number of bamboo pipes, each of which has a hole bored near the base. At the bottom of the pipes is a free metal reed which speaks only when the hole in the pipe is closed by the player's fingers. It is used not as a melody instrument, but rather to produce long chords, the reeds speaking with both exhalation and inhalation.

sho. The Japanese equivalent of the *sheng* and derived from it.

shofar. Ancient Hebrew cult instrument, still used in worship. It consists of a ram's horn and produces only two notes.

short octave. An arrangement in the lowest octave of old keyboard instruments, particularly the organ, which consisted of omitting certain notes not generally used at this register so as to bring the remaining notes more easily under the player's fingers and to spare the expense of unnecessary pipes.

sistrum. Ancient type of rattle consisting of a U-shaped piece of metal on a handle with two metal cross bars that rattled when the instrument was shaken.

sitār. Long-necked Indian lute, the body made from a large gourd. It has melody and sympathetic strings and the melody strings are stopped against arched hoops of metal rising over the neck; these allow the player to stretch the string by pulling it down the hoops, and the consequent distortions of the pitch through various degrees of a tone are a feature of *sitar* music.

slit drum. African type of drum, consisting of a hollowed-out tree trunk, so made that the lips of the slit yield different notes when struck.

soundpost: see **violin**

spike fiddle. Primitive type of stringed instrument in which the long tubular neck runs the length of the instrument, piercing the body to emerge at the bottom as a foot.

spinet. Small instrument of the harpsichord type. It differs from the harpsichord in its flat triangular shape, the keyboard forming one of the long sides rather than the short side as with the harpsichord, and by virtue of the fact that the strings are strung diagonally from left to right of the player rather than running away from him in the line of the keys. The action, however, is identical with that of the harpsichord.

stop. On the organ both the actual lever or tab that controls a rank of pipes and, by extension, the rank of pipes itself. Thus an organ with many reed 'stops' is one with a number of reed as opposed to flue pipes.

swell and **swell box:** see **organ**

sympathetic strings. Strings which, although not bowed or plucked, vibrate 'in sympathy' with the other strings and so reinforce their tone. Occasionally strings that are bowed or plucked can also act at other times as sympathetic strings (see **baryton**).

tabor. Type of drum: see **pipe and tabor**
tabor pipe: see **pipe and tabor**
tambourine. Untuned percussion instrument. A frame drum with only one head and with metal discs set in pairs in slits in the frame so as to jingle when the head is struck by the palm of the hand.

tambura or **tampura.** Long-necked lute used as drone instrument in the classical music of India.

tam-tam. Gong of uncertain pitch.

theorbo. Archlute devised in the late 16th century in which the off-board strings, controlled by a second peg box, are shorter than those on the chitarrone.

timpani: see **kettledrum**

tof. Ancient type of Middle Eastern frame drum.

tonguing. The use of the tongue in the technique of wind instruments, so as to produce elegant phrasing or rapid execution.

tracker: see **action**

transposing instrument. One for which the music is written at a different pitch from that at which it is sounded. As a result of their historical development it was frequently easier for the players of instruments built in several different keys to finger them all alike. The composer was thus obliged to score his music to accommodate this singularity.

tremulant. Organ stop which, when drawn, produces marked variations of pitch in the note being sounded; the effect is achieved by producing pulsations in the wind supply to the pipes.

triangle. Percussion instrument consisting, as its name implies, of a triangle of metal struck by a metal striker.

tromba marina (Italian, 'marine trumpet'). A single-stringed instrument, about five feet long. It had a moveable bridge and was bowed above the bridge, depending, in fact, upon harmonics for the production of its sound.

trombone. A brass instrument of cylindrical bore, played with a cup mouthpiece. It seems to have been invented in the 15th century in essentially the same form as it is now used. The distinguishing feature of the trombone is a simple slide mechanism; this enables the player to lengthen the tube of the instrument at will and thus to obtain a variety of harmonic series and consequently a variety of notes and a full chromatic scale. The most common trombone is now the tenor, with a full chromatic range from E natural below the bass clef.

trumpet. Brass instrument of cylindrical bore played with a cup mouthpiece. From the Renaissance down to the early 19th century, when it received a valve mechanism, it sounded only the notes of the harmonic series. Because of this limitation specialised types of players arose who devoted themselves to the high, virtually chromatic so-called 'clarino' register, or else to the lower range, called the *principale* or principal. The old trumpet, pitched in F, was the one for which Bach wrote his trumpet parts. The modern trumpet is shorter in length and has a valve mechanism to make it chromatic.

tuba. Loose generic term for bass brass instruments of wide conical bore and vertically-pointing bell, played with a cup mouthpiece.

tuning fork. Two-pronged metal fork, precision-made to yield an exact pitch when vibrated.

'ugab. Ancient Hebrew, generic name for wind instruments other than the horns.

ukelele. Small plucked stringed instrument of guitar type.

Union pipes: see **bagpipes**

valve. Mechanism adapted to the natural horns and trumpets in the early 19th century so as to give them a fully chromatic range. This it does by enabling the player to divert the passage of air through additional lengths of tubing and in effect to extend or shorten the length of the instrument at will. There are two main types of valve on the horn – the rotary and the piston, the first being preferred by German makers, the second by French. The trumpet is always fitted with piston valves.

vihuela. Originally the Spanish word for any type of stringed instrument. In the Renaissance it became limited to a plucked instrument similar to the guitar of that time but having six instead of four courses of strings.

vīnā. The classical Indian stringed instrument. Unlike the *sitar* it usually has two gourd resonators.

viol. The stringed instrument that held pride of place from the late 15th century to the mid 17th, when it was displaced by the violin. The viol differs from the violin in having a flat, rather than arched back, a fretted fingerboard, sloping shoulders, where the body joins the neck, and C- or flame-shaped, as opposed to *f* shaped, sound holes. The frets and other details of construction give it a 'reedier' and less brilliant tone than the violin. There are four main members of the family: treble, alto, tenor, bass. All have six strings and all are played resting either on or between the legs. The term *viola da gamba*, meaning 'leg viol', was used to distinguish instruments of this family from the *viola da braccia*, or 'arm viol', that is the violin family.

viola bastarda. A viol slightly smaller than the normal bass and with special tunings to allow for the more easy execution of chords. In England it was called the lyra viol.

viola d'amore. In the 18th century, an unfretted stringed instrument played under the chin like the violin but shaped like a viol. Its most characteristic feature was its sympathetic strings.

viola pomposa. In the 18th century, a large-sized viola with five strings.

violin. Family of bowed stringed instruments that emerged in the early 16th century and by the late 17th century had almost completely displaced the viol. From the outset they had a brighter tone than the viols. They were without frets, had an arched rather than flat back, high shoulders, *f*-shaped sound holes and, like the viols, a soundpost that amplified the vibrations of the bridge within the body. The violins tended to be strung under higher tension than the viols and this contributed greatly to the brilliancy of the tone and power. The violin itself has remained virtually unchanged since the beginning of the 16th century, apart from small though important details. The tenor member of the family is called the 'viola', and the bass the 'violoncell', now in English 'cello'. The lowest of the orchestral strings, the double bass, is related to the violin family.

violone. The largest member of the viol family; it is played resting on the floor as is the double bass.

virginal. A keyboard instrument of the 16th and 17th centuries, particularly common in England, where the name was the generic term for all keyboard instruments. The virginal used the same plucking action as the harpsichord, but it was oblong rather than wing-shaped and the keyboard was in the long side. The derivation of the name is not clear.

Wagner tuba. The English name for a type of bass brass instrument conceived by the composer for use in his opera cycle, *The Ring*. It is, in effect, a horn with a slightly wider bore than normal.

woodwind. This classification of instruments embraces the vast families of the flutes and the reed instruments. In the symphony orchestra the woodwind consists of the flutes, oboes, clarinets and bassoons, even though both flutes and clarinets are now sometimes made of metal.

xylophone. A type of instrument consisting of tuned wooden blocks set on a frame in front of the player and struck with hard wooden sticks.

Xylophones are among the numerous fixed-note percussion instrument of south-east Asia and may have originated there.

zampogna. Type of Italian bagpipe with double chanter.

zither. In general terminology any type of stringed instrument consisting merely of strings and a string bearer and with or without some form of resonator. In particular the word is used of a folk instrument of the Austrian and Bavarian Alps consisting of a rectangular board over which are strung a number of strings (usually four melody strings and between twenty and thirty accompaniment strings). The melody strings are stopped against frets on the finger board while they are plucked with a plectrum.

zurna. Shawm of Turkey and the Middle East.

Supplementary Reading List

Abraham, Gerald. *A Hundred Years of Music*. London, 1964.

Adler, G. *Handbuch der Musikgeschichte*. 2 vols. 1930.

Anderton, H. Orsmond. *Early English Music*. London, 1920.

Apel, Willi. *Harvard Dictionary of Music*. London, 1944.

Bagar, Robert and Louis Biancolli. *The Concert Companion*. London, 1947.

Baines, Anthony. *Woodwind Instruments and Their History*. London, 1957.

Baines, Anthony. *European and American Musical Instruments*. London, 1966.

Baines, Anthony, (ed.). *Musical Instruments through the Ages*. London, 1966.

Barrett, William A. *English Church Composers*. London, 1894.

Bekker, P. *The Story of the Orchestra*. New York, 1936.

Bekker, P. *Beethoven*. London, 1925.

Bessaraboff, Nicholas. *Ancient European Musical Instruments*. Boston, 1941.

Blom, Eric (ed.). *Grove's Dictionary of Music and Musicians* (10 vols.). London, 1954–61.

Blom, Eric. *Some Great Composers*. London, 1961.

Blom, Eric. (ed.). *Everyman's Dictionary of Music*. London, 1962.

Boyd, Morrison. *Elizabethan Music and Musical Criticism*. Philadelphia, 1940.

Bragard, R. and F. J. de Hen. *Musical Instruments in Art and History*. London, 1968.

Bridges, Robert. 'English Chanting', *Musical Antiquary*, II (1911), 125–141.

Buchner, A. *Mechanical Musical Instruments*. London, n.d.

Bukofzer, Manfred F. *Music in the Baroque Era from Monteverdi to Bach*. New York, 1947.

Burney, Charles. *A General History of Music*. ed. by Frank Mercer. London, n.d.

Clément, F., and Larousse, P. *Dictionnaire des Opéras*. Paris, 1905.

Cobbett, W. W. *Cyclopedic Survey of Chamber Music*, (1929–30). London, 1963.

Colles, H. C. *The Growth of Music*, (1923). Oxford, 1956.

Combarien, Jules. *Histoire de la Musique.*

Paris, 1913–19.

Dart, R. Thurston. *Interpretation of Music*. London, 1967.

Davey, Henry. *History of English Music*. 2nd edition, London, 1921.

David, H. T. and A. Mendel (eds.). *The Bach Reader*. London, 1967.

Dent, Edward J. *Foundations of English Opera*. Cambridge, 1928.

Dolmetsch, Arnold. *The Interpretation of the Music of the XVIIth and XVIIIth Centuries Revealed by Contemporary Evidence*. London, 1946 (new edn.).

Donington, Robert. *The Instruments of Music*. London, 1970.

Donington, Robert. *The Interpretation of Early Music*. London, 1963.

Dorf, Richard A. *Electronic Musical Instruments*. New York, 1959.

Einstein, Alfred. *Gluck*. London, 1936.

Einstein, Alfred. *Schubert*. London, 1951.

Einstein, Alfred. *Mozart*. London, 1971.

Einstein, Alfred. *A Short History of Music*. London, 1953.

Fellowes, E. H. *William Byrd*. London, 1948.

Flower, Norman. *Handel*. London, 1923.

Foss, Herbert J. (ed.). *The Heritage of Music*. Oxford, 1928–1934.

Galpin, Francis W. *Old English Instruments of Music. Their History and Character*. London, 1965.

Geiringer, K. *The Bach Family*. London, 1954.

Geiringer, K. *Brahms, His Life and Work*. New York, 1936.

Glyn, M. H. *About Elizabethan Virginal Music and its Composers*. 2nd edn. London, 1934.

Grassineau, James. *A Musical Dictionary*. London, 1740.

Grout, Donald J. *A History of Western Music*. London, 1962.

Grout, Donald J. *A Short History of the Opera*. Columbia, 1966.

Hadden, J. Cuthbert. *Haydn*. London, 1902.

Harding, Rosamond E. M. *The Pianoforte*. Cambridge, 1933.

Harrison, Frank. *Music in Medieval Britain*. London, 1958.

Hayes, Gerald. *Musical Instruments and*

their *Music 1500–1750*. London, 1928–1930.

Hitchcock, H. Wiley. *Music in the United States: A Historical Introduction*. New Jersey, 1969.

Holst, Imogen. *An A.B.C. of Music*. London, 1963.

Hughes, A. (ed.). *Early Medieval Music up to 1300*. London, 1954.

Hunt, Reginald. *A First Harmony Book*. London, 1962.

Hunt, Reginald. *A Second Harmony Book*. London, 1966.

Hyatt King, A. *Chamber Music*. New York, 1948.

James, Philip. *Early keyboard instruments, Proceedings of the Musical Association, 57th session (1931)*, 23–39.

Lang, Paul Henry. *Music in Western Civilization*. London, 1942.

Macmillan. *Encyclopedia of Music*. London, 1938.

Marcuse, Sybil. *Musical Instruments: A Comprehensive Dictionary*. London, 1966.

Mees, Arthur. *Choirs and Choral Music*. New York, 1901; reprint 1969.

Mellers, Wilfred. *Music and Society*. London, 1950.

Meyer, Ernest H. *English Chamber Music*. London, 1946.

Nettl, Bruno. *Folk and Traditional Music of the Western Continents*. New Jersey, 1965.

New Oxford History of Music. Vol. 1, 'Ancient and Oriental Music'. London, 1957.

O'Brien, Grace. *The Golden Age of German Music*. London, 1953.

O'Brien, Grace. *The Golden Age of Italian Music*. London, 1949.

Palisca, Claude V. *Baroque Music*. New Jersey, 1968.

Parry, Sir C. *Evolution in the Art of Music*. London, 1896.

Parry, Sir C. *The Heritage of Music*. London, 1927.

Pulver, Jeffrey. *A Dictionary of Old English Music and Musical Instruments*. London, 1923.

Pulver, Jeffrey. *A Biographical Dictionary of Old English Music*. London, 1927.

Reese, Gustave. *Music in the Middle Ages.*

New York, 1940.

Reese, Gustave. *Music in the Renaissance*. New York, 1959.

Robbins Landon, H. C. *Beethoven*. London, 1970.

Robertson, A. and D. Stevens. *Cassell's A History of Music* (2 vols.). London, 1960–2.

Sachs, Curt. *World History of the Dance*. New York, 1963.

Sachs, Curt. *The History of Musical Instruments*. New York, 1940.

Salzman, Eric. *Twentieth-Century Music: An Introduction*. New Jersey, 1967.

Scholes, Percy A. *Oxford Companion to Music*. London, 1968.

Schwarz, Boris. *Music & Musical Life in Soviet Russia, 1917–1970*. New York, 1971; London, 1972.

Seay, Albert. *Music in the Medieval World*. New Jersey, 1965.

Shirlaw, M. *The Theory of Harmony*. London and New York, 1917, reprint 1969.

Slonimsky, N. *Music Since 1900*, 4th ed., New York, 1971.

Stevenson, Ronald. *Western Music*. London, 1971.

Stracten, E. van der. *The History of the Violin*. London, 1933.

Stuckenschmidt, H. H. *Twentieth-Century Composers: Germany and Central Europe*. London, 1970.

Terry, Charles Sanford. *Bach*. London, 1933.

Thayer, A. *The Life of Ludwig van Beethoven*. New York, 1921.

Thomson, Virgil. *Twentieth-Century Composers: American Music since 1910*. London, 1971.

Tovey, D. *Essay in Musical Analysis*. London, 1964.

Turner, W. J. *Music: A Short History*. London, 1949.

Walker, Ernest. *A History of Music in England*. London, 1952.

Westrup, J. A. *An Introduction to Musical History*. London, 1967.

Winternitz, E. *Musical Instruments of the Western World*. London, 1967.

Winternitz, E. *Musical Instruments and their Symbolism in Western Art*. London, 1967.

Index

Index

The numbers in heavy type indicate main references; those in italics refer to illustrations.

Abdelazar, Purcell's music for 196
Abduction from the Seraglio (Mozart) 243
Abegg Variations (Schumann) 278
Abel, Carl Friedrich 162, 219
Abelard, Peter 74, 75
Aborigines, Australian *see* Australia
Abraham and Isaac (Stravinsky) 392
Abranyi, Kornel 318
Absil, Jean 489-490; *489*
Abstract (Somers) 508
Abu-Hassan (Weber) 270
Académie de poésie et de musique 111
Academy of Ancient Music 214
Academy of Arts, Berlin 380
a capella style 48, 174, 212, 228, 306; *and see* glossary of technical terms
Accademia Filarmonica, Bologna, 204, 418
Achorripsis (Xenakis) 499
Acteon (Alessandrescu) 497-498
Actomos (Werder) 504
Adagio for Strings (Barber) 442
Adam, Adolphe 292, 340
Adam of Ileborgh 114
Addison, John 454
Adelaide (Beethoven) 268
Admeto (Handel) 216
Adson, John 164
adufe 45
Aeneas (Roussel) 398
Africa, African music 21-24
Agazzari, Agostina 167
Agincourt carol 143
Agnew, Roy 504
Agon (Stravinsky) 389, 392
Agricola, Alexander 105
Agricola, J. F. 231
Agricola, Martin 91
Agrippina (Handel) 215
Aguado y García, Dionisio 467
Aichinger, Georg 179
Aichinger, Gregor 120
Aïda (Verdi) 357; *356*
Aino (Kajanus) 459
air 185, 186, 190
air de cour 185, 187
air en rondeau 186
Akathistos, the 60
aksak rhythms 45, 46
alba 74
Albania, folk music 45
Albéniz, Isaac 469-470; *470*
Albert, E. 255
Albert, Heinrich 184
Albert Herring (Britten) 452, 453; *454*
Alberti bass 206; *and see* glossary of technical terms
Albinoni, Tommaso 206
Albrecht V, duke of Bavaria 118
Albrechtsberger, J. G. 236, 263
Alceste (Gluck) 234
Alcuin of York 50
aleatorism 373 412; *and see* glossary of

technical terms (aleatory)
Alessandrescu, Alfred 497-498
Alexander IV, Pope 135
Alexander Nevsky, music for (Prokofiev) 428
Alexander's Feast (Handel) 217
Al-Farabi 39
Al-Faradj al-Isfahani, Abu 39;
Book of Songs 39
Alfonseca, Juan Bautista 476
Alfonso II, duke of Ferrara 92, 119
Alfonso V, the Magnanimous 136
Alfonso the Wise of Castile 74, 135;
Cantigas 135; *135*
Alfred (Arne) 218
Alkan, Charles 292
Al-kindi 39
Allgemeine Musikalische Zeitung 252
Allegro symphonique (Poot) 491
Allende, Humberto 480
Alma Redemptoris Mater (Davies) 532
Alma Redemptoris Mater (Leonel) 142
Almenraeder, Karl 256
Alpaerts, Flor 489
Alpensymphonie (R. Strauss) 363
Altenberger, Peter 384
Altitude (Champagne) 509
Alvarenga, Oneyda 480
Alzira (Verdi) 356
Amadigi (Handel) 215
Amahl and the Night Visitors (Menotti) 442
Amalaire 63
Amants Magnifiques, les (Lully) 222
Amati family 96
Ambros 252
America (North), early church music 433-434; 18th C 434; beginnings of art music in the 19th C 434-437; Negro melodies in popular music 437; Ives 438; 20th C 438-444
America (South) pre-colonial 475; Andes peoples 475; Spanish colonial music in Mexico 476; beginnings of national style (Mexico) 476; Dominica 476; Haiti 476; Cuba 476; Venezuela 476-477; Colombia 477; Chile 477; Argentina 480-481; 20th-C Mexico 481
American Festival Overture (W. Schuman) 441
American in Paris, An (Gershwin) 443
American Rhapsody (Dohnányi) 414
Amfiparnasso (Vecchi) 129
Amir Khusru 34
Ammerbach, Nicholas 115
AMM, London 529, 531
*Amon, Blasius 120
Amor brujo, el (de Falla) 470
Amphitryon (Emmanuel) 399
Amphitryon (Oboussier) 486
Amusing masquerades and buffooneries for carnival 128-129
Anagrammes (G. Landré) 492
Anchieta, Juan de 136
Ancient airs and dances (Respighi) 420
An die Geliebte (Beethoven) 268
André Johann 271
Andreae, Volkmar 484

Andriessen, Hendrik 492; *492*
Andromeda (Ferrari and Manelli) 169
Animuccia, Giovanni 130, 138
Annette et Lubin (Gossec) 281
Anne of Austria 188, 190
Anne of England 215
Anouilh, Jean 404
Ansermet, Ernest 388, 485; *487*
Antar (Rimsky-Korsakov) 346
Antechrist (Davies) 532
anthems 145; Byrd 148; Gibbons 149; in the Baroque 156; in 17th-C France 188; in 17th-C England 192, 194; Purcell 196; Handel 215, 216; Croft 218; Boyce 218; *and see* glossary of technical terms
Antica Musica ridotta alla moderna prattica 127
Antigone (Honegger) 401
Antigone (Oboussier) 486
Antigone (Orff) 408
Antill, John 504
Antiphonary, 1891 edition 64
Antiphonie (Morel) 509
Antoni, Giovanni Battista 204
Antoni, Pietro degli 204
Antony and Cleopatra (Schmitt) 403
Anweisung die Flöte traversiere zu Spielen (Quantz) 231
Apocalypse of St John, The (Rosenberg) 455
Apostles, the (Elgar) 448
Appalachia (Delius) 450
Appalachian Spring (Copland) 440
Apparitions (Ligeti) 528
Appel (Fuyneman) 492
Apollon Musagète (Stravinsky) 389
Apotheosis of Corelli, The (F. Couperin) 224
Apotheosis of Lully, The (F. Couperin) 224
Arab countries, music of 37-40 *and see* Islam
Arabesques (Debussy) 394
Araja, Francesco 337
Arbeau, Thoinot 78, 95
Arbos, Enrique Fernandez 470
Arcadelt, Jacques 89, 122, 126, 130
Arceuil, School of 399, 402
Ardevol, José 482
Arensky, Alexander 426-427
Ariadne auf Naxos (Benda) 231
Ariadne on Naxos (Strauss) 363
Arianna (Monteverdi) 173
arieto 476
arietta 223, 225
Ariettes oubliées (Debussy) 395
arioso 169, 170, 175, 226, 225; *and see* glossary of technical terms
Armida's Pavilion (Tcherepnin) 427
Armide (Gluck) 234
Armstrong, Louis Daniel 511-512, 513, 521, 522; *512*
Arne, Thomas Augustine 218
Arnold, Malcolm 454
Aroldo (Verdi) 356
Arrau, Claudio 480; *481*
Arriaga, Juan Crisostimo 467
Arrieu, Claude 403

Arroyo, João Marcellino 474
ars antiqua 52-53, 124; absence of in Italy 122; in England 141; *and see* glossary of technical terms
ars nova 53; France 70-72, 88; Italian influence on Franco-Flemish school 97; in Italy 122, 123-125; influence of on Polish music (early 15th C) 304; *and see* glossary of technical terms
Art of Fugue, The (Bach) 201; *201*
Art of Playing on the Violin, The (Geminiani) 212
Art of the Future (Wagner) 324
Artusi, Giovanni 173; *133*
Asafiev, Boris 429
Ascasubi, Hilario 478
A Sermon, a Narrative and a Prayer (Stravinsky) 392
Ashley, Robert 530
Asia, South-East 19, 21, 24 *and see* Indonesia
Association of Contemporary Music 432
Aston, Hugh 144
Athens Conservatory, the 498
Atlandida (de Falla) 470
Atmospheres (Ligeti) 528
Attaingnant, Pierre 108, 109, 112
Attila (Verdi) 356
Auber, Daniel François 248, 291-292, 340
Aubert, Louis 403
Aubin, Tony 403
Aucassin and Nicolette (Brenta) 490
Auden, W. H. 390
Audrico, Michel 497
Augustus II of Poland 306
Augustus III of Poland 337
Augustus II of Saxony 154
Auric, Georges 400, 401
Aus Italien (R. Strauss) 363
Austin, Larry 529
Australia, music of, Aborigines 17, 21, 500-501; traditional 501-503; colonial period 503; Grainger 503-504; 20th C 504-505
Austrian music *see* Germany and Austria
Aventures (Ligeti) 528
Avicenna 39
Avodath Hakodesh (Bloch) 485
Ayala, Daniel 482
ayres, in Elizabethan England 147, 150; in 17th-C England 194

Baba Hirca 496
Baba-Yaga (Lyadov) 426
Babbitt, Milton 444, 505
Babcock, Alpheus 260
Bacchanale (Ravel) 397
Bacchus and Ariadne (Roussel) 398
Bach, Carl Philip Emmanuel 197, 201, 230, **231**, 232, 237, 260; *231*
Bach, Johann Ambrosius 197
Bach, Johann Christian 179, 197, 211, 218-219, 231, 235, 242; *232*
Bach, Johann Sebastian 102, 154, 157, 158, 165, 176, 178, 180, 184, 195,

202, 228, 233, 235, 252, 263,
chapter pp. 197-201;
transcriptions of Vivaldi's concertos
205; performances of by
Singakademie (18th C) 232; *200*
Bach, Wilhelm Friedemann 197, 218,
232
Bachianas Brasileiras (Villa-Lobos) 480
Badings, Henk 493
Baermann 255
Baeyens, August 491
Baffo, Giovanni Antonio 95
Bagatelles (Beethoven) 273
bagpipes 20, 55-56, 57; Mediterranean
countries 45; Scotland 47-48;
Brittany 47-48 *and see biniou bras;*
Ireland 47-48; in medieval European
dance 77; in 15th-c Europe 90;
in Henry VIII's collection 92; in
17th c 162, 164; in the Ecurie 221;
*47, 72, 95, 124, 177; and see glossary
of musical instruments*
Baïf, Jean Antoine de 111, 119, 187
Baird, Tadeusz 463
Bakfark, Valentin 315
Bakst, Léon 388; *between pp. 384 and
385, 396*
Balakirev, Mily 309, 339, 341, 342;
341
Bali 30, 31, 32
ballade 72, 73, structure of 74; in
dance 77; Dufay 100; increasing
complexity and decline in popularity
100; Binchois 101; Busnois 103;
and see glossary of technical terms
Ballade Créole (Gottschalk) 437
Ballade de Villon (Debussy) 395
Ballade for piano and orchestra (Fauré)
302
Ballades (Brahms) 326
Ballades (Chopin) 309
Ballades Concertantes (Martin) 486
ballad opera 217; *and see* glossary of
technical terms
Ballard, Robert (publisher) 108, 112,
118
Ballard, Robert (lutenist) 161, 191
ballate 123, 124; increasing popularity
of 125; Landini 124; Ciconia 125
ballet, *ballets de cour* (17th-c France)
161, 186-187, 222; in 17th-c
English masques 194; of Lully 222;
opéra-ballet see separate entry;
Moniuszko 310; Tchaikovsky 350;
Stravinsky 371, 388, 389; Debussy
395; Ravel 397; Hindemith 407;
Bartók 416; Arensky 427; N.
Tcherepnin 427; Prokofiev 428;
Riisäger 458; Martinů 465; De
Falla 470; Chávez 481; 'electronic'
(Badings) 493
Ballet comique de la Reyne 159, 160, 186
ballet de cour see ballet
Ballet de la nuit 187
Ballet de Madame 161
ballets dramatiques 185
ballet mascarade 186
ballet mélodramatique 186
Ballets Russes 388, 400, 427
Ballo delle Ingrate (Monteverdi) 173
Ballo in Maschera (Verdi) 356
Balustrade (Stravinsky) 390
Bamberg manuscript 68
Bamboula (Gottschalk) 437
bambuco 477
Bananier, le (Gottschalk) 437
Banister, John 194
Banks, Don 504-505
Banks of Condamine, the 502
Baoule 23
Baranovic, Kresimir 495
Barbaja, Domenico 354
Barber, Samuel 442; *441*
Barberini theatre, Rome 169, 175
Barbiere di Siviglia (Pergolesi) 210
Barblan, Otto 483
Barce, Ramon 472

Barcewicz, Stanislaw 311
Bardac, Emma 393
Barley, William 150
Barlow, Fred 403
Barraqué, Jean 526; *526*
Barraud, Henri 403
Bartered Bride, The (Smetana) 331;
331
Bartók, Béla 46, 48, 371, 407, **414-416**;
414
Basie, Count 516, 517; *517*
basse danse 77, 78, 89
basset horn 256; *and see* glossary of
musical instruments
bass-horn 256
basso continuo 88, 89; in 16th-c Italy
132; in the Baroque 158, 160, 161,
162, 163, 167, 174, 176, 180, 184,
187, 188, 191, 193
bassoon, in 17th c 160, 161, 164, 165;
in work of Scarlatti 107; in the
Ecurie 221; addition of keys in the
early 19th c 255; improvements to
256; Heckel bassoon 256;
contrabassoon (Heckel) 256; *256,
and see* glossary of musical
instruments
bassoon serpent see Russian bassoon
Battle of the Huns, The (Liszt) 320
Baudrier, Yves 402
Bauyn manuscript 162
Bax, Arnold 451
Bay Psalm Book, The 433; *434*
Bayreuth opera house 322; *324*
Bear, The (Walton) 452
Beatitudes, The (Bliss) 451
Beatrice and Benedict (Berlioz) 290
Beaujoyeux 186
Beaumarchais 244
Bechet, Sidney 523; *522*
Bechstein 260
Beck, Conrad 400, 483, 485-486; *486*
Beckwith, John 508
Beecham, Sir Thomas 450; *450*
Beethoven, Ludwig van 48, 155, 203,
213, 217, 236, 237, 250; development
of symphony and sonata forms 237,
250, 251, 265; symphonies 237, 248,
265-267; chamber music 237, 267;
works for piano 260-261; opera,
choral works etc **chapter pp.
263-269**; *romances* 286;
symphonies performed in 19th-c
Paris 291; *264, 266, 267, between
pp. 272 and 273*
Beggar's Opera (Gay) 216, 217; *217*
Be Glad Then America (Billings) 434
Beheim, Michel 77
Beiderbecke, Leon 'Bix' 512-513, 521;
513
bel canto 354; *and see* glossary of
technical terms
Belgiojoso, Baldassarino di *see*
Beaujoyeux
Belgium and Netherlands, music of,
19th-c Belgium 488-489; Flemish
school (late 19th-20th c) 489; the
Walloons 490-491; Holland (20th c)
491-493; Pijper 492; Badings and
contemporaries 493
bell 90; *61, 69, 73; and see* glossary of
musical instruments
Belle Hélène, La (Offenbach) 294
Bellini, Vicenzo 287, 291, 307, 354;
354
Belshazzar's Feast (Walton) 451-452
Bembo, Pietro 126
Benda, Georg 231, 237, 244
Benda, Jiří 333
Benedicam Dominum (Buxtehude) 160
Benedictions (Absil) 490
Benjamin, Arthur 504
Bennett, Richard Rodney 454
Bennett, Sterndale 445
Benois, Alexander 388
Benoit, Peter 489
Benserade, Isaac de 187
Bentivoglio, Guido 176
Bentzon, Jørgen 458
Benvenuto Cellini (Berlioz) 289, 290,
319
Berceo, Gonzalado 134

Berenguel, Xavier 472
Berenice (Handel) 216
Berezovsky, Maxim 339
Berg, Alban 371, 372, 380, **383-385**,
432; *383*
Berger, Ludwig 276
bergerette 77
Berigan, Bunny 519
Berio, Luciano 373, 418, 424, 529
Berkeley, Lennox 404, 452
Berlin, Irving 372
Berlioz, Hector 64, 248, 250, 251, 252,
284, 287, **288-290**, 300, 307, 319,
352, 354, 362; *252, 288, 289*
Bermudo, Juan 139
Bernasconi, A. 229
Bernhard, Christoph 180
Bernier, René 490-491
Bernini, Gianlorenzo 169, 174; *177*
Bernstein, Leonard 374, 443; *443*
Bersa, Blagoje 495
Bertali, Antonio 180
Bertolotti of Venice 95
Berwald, Franz 455; *455*
Besard, Jean-Baptiste 163, 191
Bèze, Theodore 107, 111
Bharata 33
Bhatkande, V. N. 33
Biancourt, Jean 506
Biber, Heinrich 184, 330
Biches, Les (Poulenc) 401
Bihary, Janos 317
Billie's Bounce (Parker) 521
Billings, William 434
Billy Budd (Britten) 452
Billy Budd (Ghedini) 422
Billy the Kid (Copland) 440
Binchois 100-101, 113; *98*
Binet, Claude 187
Binet, Jean 485
biniou bras 47
Birds, The (Respighi) 420
Birtwistle, Harrison 454, 529
Bishop, Henry 503
biwa 28; *and see* glossary of musical
instruments
Bizet, Georges 256, 292, 294, 297-298;
297
Blacher, Boris 408, 410, 411
Black Domino, The (Auber) 292
Black Opal (Antill) 504
Black Spider, The (Burkhardt) 485
Blainville, Charles Henri de 281
Blancafort, Alberto 472
Blancafort, Manuel 471
Blanchet et Rollet 261
Blanton, Jimmie 519
Blest Pair of Sirens (Parry) 447
Blitheman, William 150
Blitzstein, Marc 442
Bloch, Ernest 440, 484-485; *484*
Blockx, Jan 489; *489*
Blodeck, Vilem 333
Blood Wedding (Fortner) 410
Blow, John 194, 195, 196, 214; *195*
Bluebeard's Castle (Bartók) 416; *415*
blues *see* jazz *and* glossary of technical
terms
Blues and Screamer (Reck) 531
Bluhmel, Friedrich 253, 257
Boccaccio 50, 57, 85
Boccherini, Luigi 203, 213, 282, 351
Bochsa, Nicholas-Charles 262, 503
Boëly, Alexandre 292
Boesset, Antoine 185, 186, 187, 188
Boesset, Jean-Baptiste 188
Boethius 60
Bogotá Philharmonia Society 477
Bogurodzica 303
Bohème, La (Puccini) 358
Bohemia, music of, 121, 233, 330-331;
Smetana 331-332; Dvořák and
contemporaries 332-333; Janáček
333
Böhm, Georg 165, 197
Böhm, Theobald 253, 254
Boïeldieu, Adrien 284, 286, 287, 292
Boito, Arigo 357, 358
Bolden, Buddy 511
Bold Jack Donahue 502
Boléro (Ravel) 396

Boleslas, King of Poland 303
Bolivar (Milhaud) 401
bombard 57, 77; *and see* glossary of
musical instruments
bonang 30, 32 *and see* glossary of
musical instruments
Boniface VIII, Pope 70
Bonifaci 337
Bononcini, Antonio 228
Bononcini, Giovanni Battista 204, 214,
215, 228
Bontempi, G. A. 183
Bontempo, João Domingos 473
Booke of Common Praier noted
(Merbecke) 145
*Book of Esther, drawn from the Bible,
The* 336
Book of Psalms, the 58
Book of Songs, The (Al-Faradj
al-Isfahani) 39
Bordes, Charles 63, 300; *301*
Bordoni, Faustina 233
Boréal (Morel) 509
Boris Godunov (Mussorgsky) 340, 343,
346; *345*
Borodin, Alexander 339, 340, 341,
342, **343-344**, 346, 460; *342*
Bororos 23, 24
Bortniansky, Dmitri 338-339
Bosch, Laux 92
Bossinensis, Franciscus 91
Bouffes Parisiennes 294
Boulanger, Lily 403-404
Boulanger, Nadia 404, 440, 441, 485
Boulez, Pierre 298, 373, 386, 391, 393,
405, **524-525**; *524, 525*
bourdon 93
Bourgeois, Loys 111
Bourgeois Gentilhomme, music for
(Lully) 222
Boutique de fleurs (Martinů) 465
Boutique Fantasque, La (Respighi) 420
Boutique Fantasque, La (Rossini) 353
Bouzignac, Guillaume 160, 188
bouzouki 45, 499
bow fiddle 77
Boyce, William 214, 218; *218*
Boyd Neel Orchestra 452
Brahms, Johannes 248, 250, 252, 278,
325, 370; piano works 326-327;
chamber music 327-328; symphonic
music 328; *Lied* 328-329; choral
works 329; *327*
Brăiloiu, Constantin 497
Branco, Frederico Freitas 474
Brandenburg concertos (Bach) 157,
199, 200
Brandenburgers in Bohemia, The
(Smetana) 331
Brandowski, Aleksander 311
Brautwahl, Die (Busoni) 419
Breazul, G. 497
Brecht, Bertold 217, 372, 389, 409, 410
Brenta, Gaston 490
Bridge, Frank 452
Brief Introduction to the Skill of Music
(Playford) 193
Briegel, Carl 179
Brigg Fair (Delius) 450
Bristow, George 442
British Broadcasting Corporation 376;
Radiophonic Workshop 378
Brittany, folk music 47
Britten, Benjamin 48, 374, **452-453**;
453, 454
Britton, Thomas 194; *195*
Broadwood, John 259, 260, 261
'broken consort', in 15th c 90; in
16th c 92; growth of (16th c) 93;
art of (16th-c England) 94-95, 147;
in 17th c 162, 163, 164
Bronze Horseman, The (Glière) 430
Brown, Earle 443
Browne, John 143
Brubeck, Dave 522
Bruch, Max 420
Bruckner, Anton **329**, 333, 370; *329*
Brudieu, Joan 138
Bruhns, Nicolas 184
bruitismo 372
Brumel, Antoine 108

Brun, Fritz 484
Brustad, Bjarne 457
Bryant's Minstrels 437
Bubi Caligula (Jelinek) 409
Büchner, Georg 384, 410
Buendia, Manuel Moreno 472
Buffet, Auguste 255
Bugaku 28
bugle, keyed 257 *and see* glossary of musical instruments
buka 38
Bulgaria 46, 494
Bull, John 144, 145, 150; *150*
Bull, Ole 456
'bull-roarer' 24; *and see* glossary of musical instruments
Bunraku theatre 28
Buntes Theater, the 380
Buona figliuola, La (Piccini) 210
Burghers of Calais, The (Regeney) 410
Burgkmair, Hans 92
Burgtheater, Vienna 234
Burkhardt, Willy 485
Burney, Dr. Charles 205, 214, 330
Burning Fiery Furnace, The (Britten) 453
Burton, Gary 523; *523*
Bush, Alan 453
Bush, Geoffrey 454
'bush ballad' (Australia) 502-503
Bushmen 23, 24
Busnois 102-103, 105; *113*
Busoni, Ferruccio Benvenuto 358, 371, **418-419**; *419*
Butterly, Nigel 505
Butterworth, George 450
Buxheim, Charterhouse of 90; Organ Book 114
Buxtehude, Dietrich 160, 179, 183, 197
buylini 334, 347
Byrd, William 94, 144, 145, 146, **148**, 150, 192; *148*
Byron 249, 250, 279

cabaletta 354
Cabezón, Antonio de 139, 163; *139*
Cabezón, Hernando de 139
caccia, in 14th c 123-124; Piero 124; Jacopo da Bologna 125; Gherardello 125; Ciconia 125; *and see* glossary of technical terms
Caccini, Francesco 305
Caccini, Giulio 94, 129, 133, 168, 169, 172, 174
Cadet Rousselle (Arrieu) 403
Caesar and Cleopatra (Graun) 231
Carfarelli 208, 209
Cage, John 373, 443, 520, **532**; *532*
Cage, The (Stravinsky) 391
Cain and Abel (Badings) 493
Ça ira 285
Caldara, Antonio 209, 211, 228-229, 237
Calixtus III, Pope 135
Calvisius, Sethus 178
Calzabigi, R. da 234
Cambert 187, 194, 222
Cambiale di Matrimonio, La (Rossini) 352
Cambini, Giovanni Giuseppe 212, 213, 351
Cambodia 32 *and see* Indonesia
Cambrensis, Geraldus 140
Cambridge song-book 74
camerata 89
camerata fiorentina 133, 168
Campa, Gustavo 476
Campion, Thomas 147
Campra, André 223, 225
Camptown Races (Foster) 437; variations on (Grainger) 504
Camus, Sébastien 186
Canada, music of, 506-509; Toronto school 506-508; Montreal school 509
Cancionero de la Colombina 136
Cancionero de Palacio 136, 137, 468
Cancionero del Real Alcázar de Segovia 136
Cancionero of Upsala 138
Canciones y villanescas (F. Guerrero) 137
Cancoes populares (Gallet) 480

Candide (Brenta) 490
Cannabich, Christian 229, 230
Canonic Variations for organ (Stravinsky) 392
cantabile (piano) 308
cantata 156; origins and early history 174-175; popularity of in 17th-c Italy 175; church cantata in 17th-c Germany 178, 179, 181, 183, 184; secular in 17th-c Germany 179, 183; Bach 197, 199, 201; evolution of in 18th-c Italy 212; dramatic 225 *and see grand motet*; Haydn 241; Beethoven 267-268; Moniuszko 310; Brahms 329; Schoenberg 382-383; Webern 386; Vlad 424; Elgar 448; Tippett 452; Beck 485; Absil 490; *and see* glossary of technical terms
Cantata de los rios de Chile (Santa Cruz Wilson) 480
Cantatas (Webern) 386
Cantegril (Roger-Ducasse) 403
Cantica Davidi Regis (Regeney) 410
Canticle no 3 (Britten) 453
canticles 60; *and see* glossary of technical terms
Canticum Sacrum (Stravinsky) 391-392
Canti di Liberazione (Dallapiccola) 422
Canti di prigonia (Dallapiccola) 422
Cantigas de Santa Maria 76, 135
cantillation 20, 25, 38, 58, 59, 60, 63 *and see* glossary of technical terms
Cantiones Sacrae (Byrd) 148
cantipanchi 125
Cantique de Durée (Tremblay) 509
Cantique de Cantique (van Lier) 493
Canto Sospeso, il (Nono) 424
cantus firmus, folk music themes in 48; in *ars antiqua* period 53; as device for unification of mass 88; in 15th-c England 97-98; in Franco-Flemish music 99-107; development of by Ockeghem 101-102; Brumel 108; 16th-c Germany 117; 17th-c Germany 181; *and see* glossary of technical terms
cantus spiritualis 123
canzona da sonar 89, 94, 95, 132-133, 176
canzone 126; of A. Gabrieli 132; of G. Gabrieli 132-133; development of as independent musical form 133; in the Baroque 157, 163, 176; of Bach 199; in 17th-c Poland 306; *and see* glossary of technical terms
canzonet, Reformation Germany 117; Elizabethan England 150; *and see* glossary of technical terms
Canzonets for two voices (Morley) 146
Canzone villanesche (Willaert) 129
Canzone villanesche alla napolitana 129
Caplet, André 396
Capriccio (R. Strauss) 363
Capriccio for piano and orchestra (Stravinsky) 390
Capriccio stravagante (Farini) 177
Caprices (Brahms) 327
Caprices de Marianne (Sauguet) 402
Capricieuse, La (Berwald) 455
Capricorn Concerto (Barber) 442
Captain Stratton's Fancy (Warlock) 450
Cardew, Cornelius 454, 529
Cardillac (Hindemith) 406
carillon 55; *and see* glossary of musical instruments
Carissimi Giacomo 156, 175, 179; *175*
Carmagnole, La 285
Carmen (Bizet) 297-298, 357
Carmen saeculare (Philidor) 282
Carmina Burana (Orff) 74, 408; *408*
Carneygo, Claudio 474
Carnicer, Ramón 468
Carnival (Schumann) 279
carol 143; *and see* glossary of technical terms
carole 89
Carpenter, John Alden 435
Carré (Stockhausen) 529
Carreño, Teresa 477
Carrère, Paul 498

Carrillo, Julián 372, 481
Carteccia, Francesco 133
Carter, Benny 518
Carter, Elliott 440, 441-442, 526-527; *526*
Carver, Robert 144
Casali, Giovanni Battista 211
Casals, Pablo 468, 469; *473*
Casella, Alfredo 358, 420-421
Caskel, Christoph 529
Cassado G. 469
Castor and Pollux (Sarti) 338
castrati 170, 171, 208; *and see* glossary of technical terms
Castro, Juan José 481
Castro, Ricardo 476
Catalogue d'oiseaux (Messiaen) 405
Catalonia (Albéniz) 469
Catalunya Nova choral society 469
catch, in Elizabethan England 147; replaces madrigal in popularity (17th c) 193; in 18th-c England 218; *and see* glossary of technical terms
Cathedral Music (Boyce) 214, 218
Catherine the Great of Russia 338
catira 479
Cattaneo, Claudia 172
Catunda, Eunice 480
Caturla, Alejandro García 482
Caucasian Sketches (Ippolitov-Ivanov) 430
Caudella, Edward 496
Cavaillé-Coll 376
Cavalieri, Emilio de' 94, 133, 168, 169, 175
Cavalleria Rusticana (Mascagni) 358, 420
Cavalli, Pietro Francesco 166, 170, 187
Cavendish, Michael 150
Cazzati, Morizio 204
Celestina, La (Pedrell) 469
Celibidache, Sergiu 498
Cellini, Giovanni 95
cello 162, 163; increasing importance as solo instrument 203, 204; in church sonatas of Corelli 205; concertos (18th-c Italy) 207; importance of Boccherini 213; as solo instrument in concerto of classical era 237; *162, 165, 216; and see* glossary of musical instruments (violoncello)
Celtic harp 47
Cercos, José 472
Ceremony of Carols, A (Britten) 452
Certon, Pierre 110, 111
Cesti, Mercantonio 160, 170; *171*
Chabrier, Emmanuel 294, 298; *298*
Chadwick, George 437
chalemie 56
Chamber, the (France) 220, 221, 222, 225
chamber music, in Elizabethan England 148; in the Baroque 157, 176; in 17th-c Germany 183; Purcell 195; development of in 18th-c Naples 207-208; Boccherini 213; *Stil galant* in 18th-c Germany 228; growing distinction between chamber and symphonic music (Mannheim school) 229; popularity of in late 18th-c Vienna 236-237; Mozart 237, 242; Haydn 237; development of in classical era 238; Beethoven 267; Schubert 273; Mendelssohn 277-278; Schumann 280; Lalo 295; Saint-Saëns 297; Franck 299; Fauré 302; Brahms 327-328; Smetana 332; Dvořák 332; Stravinsky 391; Debussy 394; Ravel 396; Roussel 398; Martinů 465; Pijper 492; Badings 493; *and see* glossary of technical terms
Chambonnières, Jacques Champion de 182, 190
Champagne, Claude 509
Champion, Jacques 190
Champmesle, Marie 222
Chandos Anthems (Handel) 216
chanson 76, 89; Binchois 101; Busnois 103; J. des Prez 105; Brumel 108;

golden age of French 108-111; 'Parisian' 108-110; Janequin 109; de Sermisy 110; influence of madrigal on 110-111, 126; Goudimel 111; de Monte 118; Lassus 118, 119; transpositions for lute (16th c) 121; Arcadelt 127; in 13th-c Spain 135; in 15th-c Spain 136; in 16th-c Spain 139; in Portugal (15th and 16th c) 139; in 14th-c Poland 304; in 16th-c Poland 304, 305
chansonettes 111
Chanson Nègre (Gottschalk) 437
Chansons bourgignonnes (Emmanuel) 399
Chansons de Bilitis (Debussy) 395
Chansons de France (Debussy) 395
chansons de geste 50, 55, 73
Chansons madécasses (Ravel) 397
Chant du départ 285
Chant après chant (Barraqué) 526
Chapel Royal (France) 220, 221, 223, 225
Chapel Royal (Poland) 304
Chapi y Lorente, Ruperto 468, 469
Charlemagne, Emperor 50, 65, 134
Charles I of England 153, 192, 194
Charles II of England 191, 193, 194, 195
Charles IV of Bohemia 121
Charles V, Holy Roman Emperor 72, 86, 106; 118, 137, 139
Charles VI, Holy Roman Emperor 228, 229
Charles IX of France 111, 119
Charles the Bold 102; *103*
Charles the Great (Manfredini) 337
Charles Theodore, Elector Palatine 155, 229
Charles the Rash 98
Charpentier, Marc Antoine 175, 222-223, 226
Chartreuse de Parme, La (Sauguet) 402
Chatter of laundry women, The (Striggio) 128
Chaturdandi Prakāshika 33
Chausson, Ernest 300
Chávez, Carlos 481-482; *482*
Cherokee, The (Storace) 217
Cherubini, Luigi 213, 276, 285, 287, 351; *212*
Chester (Billings) 434
Chevalier errant (Ibert) 404
Chevreuil, Raymond 491
Chi Chi (Parker) 521
chifonie see hurdy-gurdy
Child, William 192
Child of Our Time, A (Tippett) 452
Children's Corner (Debussy) 394
ch'in zither 19, 27, 28, 29, 40; *26; and see* glossary of musical instruments
China and Chinese music 18, 19, 25, 26-27, 30
chitarrone 94, 160, 163, 177; *169, 202; and see* glossary of musical instruments
Chopin, Frédéric 48, 247, 248, 261, 278, 291, 292; **307-309**, 319; *between pp. 320 and 321, 306, 307, 310*
chorale 89, 178; as feature of church cantata 178, 179, 183; sections in Passion 179; as *cantus firmus* (17th-c Germany) 181; variations for organ (Scheidt) 181; of Reger 363; *and see* glossary of technical terms
Chorale Improvisations (Karg-Elert) 364
chorale prelude 157, 178, 180 *and see* glossary of technical terms
Chorale Preludes and Postludes (Karg-Elert) 364
Chorales (Franck) 299
Choral Fantasy (Beethoven) 251
Choral symphony (Beethoven) 265
choro 479, 480
choron 56
Choron, Alexandre 292
Choron, E. A. 63
Chout (Prokofiev) 428
Christian, Charlie 520, 521
Christian IV of Denmark 150, 153

Christina of Sweden 176, 209
Christmas Oratorio (Bach) 201
Christofori 203
Christ on the Mount of Olives (Beethoven) 267
Christophe Colombe (Milhaud) 401
Christou, Jani 499
Christy's Minstrels 437
Chrodegand of Metz 62
Chromatic Fantasia and Fugue (Bach) 201
Chronicles of my Life (Rimsky-Korsakov) 346
church music, in medieval Europe 52; in *ars antiqua* period 53; decline in 14th-c Europe 53; origins of Christian plainsong 58; Hebrew 59; Byzantine 59-60; Early Christian 60; unification of liturgy (W. Europe) 61-62; increasing complexity of plainsong 63; School of Paris 66; mass as musical form (14th c) 72; *cantus firmus* mass 88; regains predominance in 15th c 97-98, 99; 15th-c Franco-Flemish composers 101-107; revival of popularity in France during Reformation 111-112; in Germany during Reformation 115-119; Lassus 119; Palestrina 129, 130-131; 16th-c Italy 129-132; Hispanic liturgy 134; 15th-c Spain 136-138; medieval England 140; 15th-c England 142-144; Byrd 144, 148; Tallis 145; effect of Reformation 144; banned in England under Protectorate 154; infiltration of dramatic elements in the Baroque 156; instruments in (17th c) 160-161; in 17th-c Italy 174-175; Monteverdi 174; in 17th-c Germany 178, 179, 180, 183, 184; in 17th-c France 187-189; of Rome school (18th c) 211; evolution of styles (18th-c Italy) 212; 18th-c England 216-217, 218; Handel 216-217; late 17th-c France 222; Charpentier 222; Haydn 239, 240-241; Beethoven 267-268; Schubert 275-276; Berlioz 290; Rossini 291; revival of interest in polyphonic (19th-c France) 292; 17th-c Poland 306; Dvořák 333; chant of Russian Orthodox Church 336; American Puritan 433-434; Stanford 447; Andriessen 492
Ciconia, Johannes 97, 100, 125
Cigogne, Jean *see* Ciconia
Cimarosa, Domenico 210, 281, 338
Cimetière marin (Valen) 457
Cinderella (Prokofiev) 428
Cinq pièces concertantes (Papineau-Couture) 509
Cinq poèmes de Baudelaire (Debussy) 395
Cintra Festival 474
Circus Polka (Stravinsky) 390
Cisneros, *see* Ximenes de Cisneros
Cita Campagna, La (Peragallo) 423
cittern 57; in 15th-c Europe 90; compositions for in 16th-c Europe 91, 92; in ensembles (16th c) 94; music for by Thomas Morley 95; tablatures for (16th c) 96; published music for (16th c) 112; in 17th c 160; *and see* glossary of musical instruments
clarinet 45, 226; in Mozart symphonies 243; Weber's works for solo clarinet 255; improvements to in 19th c 255; 'Albert system' 255; 'Böhm clarinet' 255; alto clarinet 256; bass clarinet 256; Besson pedal clarinet 256; in jazz 511; *254; and see* glossary of musical instruments
Classic, the (Mussorgsky) 343
Classical Symphony (Prokofiev) 371, 429
Claudel, Paul 401
clausula 67, 68 *see also* motet *and* glossary of technical terms
'clavechimbolon' *see* harpsichord
clavichord 57; in 15th-c Europe 90; in

16th-c Europe 91; in Henry VIII's collections 92; makers of (16th c) 95; in 17th c 173; Bach's work for 201; contribution to invention of piano 258; in 20th c 376; *69, 160, 186; and see* glossary of musical instruments
'clavecin à maillets' 259
clavicembalum 57
Clavierbüchlein (J. S. Bach) 232
Clavé, José Anselmo 469
Clayton, Buck 519
Clemens non Papa *see* Cl´ment, Jacques
Clement VII, Pope 50
Clément, Jacques 107
Clementi, Muzio 203, 212, 219, 261, 351, 446; *212*
Clemenza di Tito, La (Mozart) 244
Cliff, The (Rachmaninov) 425
cobza 47
Cockaigne overture (Elgar) 448
Cocteau, Jean 389, 399, 400; *389, 402*
Códax, Martín 135
Coelho, Ruy 474
Colaço, Alexandre Rey 473
Colbran, Isabella 353
Coleman, Ornette 521-522; *522*
Collection of Lessons for the Harpsichord, A (Boyce) 218
Collegium musicum 183, 232
Colour Symphony (Bliss) 451
Combattimento di Tancredi e Clorinda (Monteverdi) 174
Comédie Française 222
Comédie Italienne 281
Comes, J. B. 160
Compère, Loyset 107
Commedia dell' Arte 128, 129, 363
Commotio (Nielsen) 458
Communiones (Zieleński) 304, 305, 306
complaint 71, 74
Composition Method (Albrechtsberger) 236
Composition in three tempi (Maderna) 424
computers, use of in composition 379
Comte Ory, Le (Rossini) 291, 353
Comus (Milton) 192
concertato style 167, 174, 179, 180, 188, 191, 196, 306; *and see* glossary of technical terms
Concertino (Stravinsky) 391
concerto 157, 176; Bach 199, 200; solo 203, 204, 205; orchestral (17th-c Italy) 205; Vivaldi 205; in 18th-c Italy 206, 207; Handel 217; F Couperin 224; for solo instruments in classical era 237; Haydn 237; Mozart 237, 242; Beethoven 237, 267; Mendelssohn 277; Brahms 326, 328; Dvořák 332; Tchaikovsky 350; Berg 385; Stravinsky 390; Bartók 416; Glazunov 425; Rachmaninov 425; 'jazz' piano concerto (Copland) 439; Elgar 448; Nielsen 458; Martinů 465; Martin 486-487; Pijper 492; Skalkottas 498; Weinzweig 508; Carter 526-527; *and see* glossary of technical terms
Concerto dell' Albatro (Ghedini) 422
Concerto for Nine Instruments (Webern) 386
Concerto for orchestra (Bartók) 416
concerto grosso 157, 165, 176, 203, 204; Corelli 205; Geminiani 212; Handel 217; *and see* glossary of technical terms
Concerto grosso (Martinů) 465
Concerto grosso (Papineau-Couture) 509
Concerto in Memory of an Angel (Berg) 385
Concerto romano (Casella) 421
Concerto Symphonique (Bloch) 485
Concerto without Orchestra (Schumann) 279
Concert pour petit orchèstre (Roussel) 398
concerts spirituels 223, 224, 225, 232, 262, 281, 282
Concord, Mass., 1840-1860 (Ives) 438
Condor (Gomes) 479

conductus, monodic 69; polyphonic 69, 72, 123; in medieval England 140; *and see* glossary of technical terms
Confucius 27
congada 479
Congo, music of 19
Congregation of the Oratory 130
Conius, Georges 427
Conservatorio di Loretto, Naples 209
Conservatorio Nacional de Canto Orfeônico 480
consorts, in 15th c 90; in 16th c 92; in 16th-c England 147 *and see* 'broken consort'; emergence of instrumental in 17th c 176; *and see* glossary of technical terms
Constant, Alexis 506
Constantine, Emperor 49
Constantinescu, Paul 498
consueta 135
Consul, The (Menotti) 442
Contacts (Stockhausen) 412, 529
contrabassoon *see* bassoon
Contreras, Salvador 482
Converse, Frederick 435
Cooke, Deryck 362
Cooke, Henry 194, 195
Cooper, John *see* Coperario
Copenhagen Royal Court Orchestra 457
Coperario 162
Copland, Aaron 374, 404, 439, 440; *440*
Coq et l' Arlequin (Cocteau) 400
cor anglais 256; *255; and see* glossary of musical instruments
Corelli, Arcangelo 157, 163, 176, 177, 199, 202-203, **204-205**, 212; *205*
Cornago, Johannes 136
Cornale, Ludovico 177
cornemuse see bagpipes
cornet 257; in jazz (Beiderbecke) 512, 513; *and see* glossary of musical instruments
cornett 55; in medieval European dance 77; in 15th-c Europe 90; in ensembles (16th c) 92; in Henry VIII's collection 92; as sustaining instrument 93; in consorts 93; use and importance of in 16th c 93-94; music for (G. Gabrieli) 95; in 16th-c Germany 120; in 17th c 160, 161, 163, 173; *74; 164; and see* glossary of musical instruments
Cornette, le (Martin) 486
Cornyshe, William 147
Coro di Morti (Petrassi) 422
Coro di T. S. Eliot (Togni) 424
Corps glorieux (Messiaen) 405
Corregidor, The (Wolf) 359
Corroboree (Antill) 504
Corsair, The (Berlioz) 289
Corsair, The (Verdi) 356
Corsi, Jacopo 133, 168
Corvinus, Matthias 313; *313*
Così fan tutte (Mozart) 244
Cosimo III, duke of Tuscany 160
Costeley, William 111, 189
Cother, Hans 115
Council of Laodicea 60
Council of Trent 63, 86, 120, 129, 130
Council of Venice 60
countertenor 71, 160 *and see* glossary of technical terms
Countess, The (Moniuszko) 310
Count of Luxembourg, The (Lehár) 413
Country Gardens (Grainger) 504
Couperin, François (the Great) 220, 223, **224**, 226, 248, 281
Couperin, Louis 161, 182, 189, 190; *224*
Course of Composition (d'Indy) 301
Courtois 256
Cousineau, Georges 262
Couture, Guillaume 506
Covent Garden Opera House 383
Coventry Festival of Music 451
Cowell, Henry 441, 443
Cracovienne (Chopin) 308
Cradle will rock, The (Blitzstein) 442
Craft of Composition, The (Hindemith) 407

Cramer, J. B. 213, 446
Creation (Haydn) 238, 241, 503; *240*
Création du monde, La (Milhaud) 439; *between pp. 528 and 529*
Crequillon, Thomas 107
Cries of London (Gibbons) 48, 149
Cris du monde, Les (Honegger) 401
Cristofori, Bartolommeo 258, 259
Croce, Giovanni 128
Croft, William 218
Cromwell, Oliver 153, 192
Crosse, Gordon 454
Cruelty of the Spaniards in Peru, The 194
crumhorn, in Henry VIII's collection 92; in 17th c 157, 164; in Lully's orchestra 162; in 20th c 375; *and see* glossary of musical instruments
Cruz, Ivo 474
Crystal Palace Handel Festivals 445
csárdás 317; *417; and see* glossary of technical terms
Cui, César 339, 341, 342, 348; *343*
Cunning little Vixen, The (Janáček) 464; *465*
Cupid and Death 193
Curlew, The (Warlock) 450
Curlew River (Britten) 453
curtal 164, 165, 174; *161; and see* glossary of musical instruments
Curwen, John 445
Cutting, Francis 150
cyclic tenor 88
cymbalon 47
cymbals 56; Hebrew 59; in 15th-c Europe 90; increasing use in concert music (late 19th and 20th c) 375; *95; and see* glossary of musical instruments
Cyrano de Bergerac (Wagenaar) 491
Czechoslovakia, music of (20th c) 463-466; for earlier periods *see* Bohemia
Czech polkas and dances (Smetana) 332
Czerny, Carl 236, 318; *289*

Da Bologna, Jacopo 124-125
da capo aria 209, 225, 234; *and see* glossary of technical terms
Da Cascia, Giovanni 124, 125
Da Costa, J. A. Rodrigues 473
Dafne (Peri) 133
Dafne (Rinuccini) 168
D'Agoult, Countess Marie 319; *319*
D'Alayrac 285; *285*
Dalibor (Smetana) 331
Dall'Abaco, Evaristo Felice 230
Dallapiccola, Luigi 422, 424, 505; *423*
Dall'Aquila, Serafino 126
Dama delle Camelie, La (Vlad) 424
Dame Blanche, La (Boïeldieu) 292
Damnation of Faust, The (Berlioz) 289, 317
Da Motta, José Viana 473-474
Damrosch, Walter 442, 444; *435*
dance and dance music, in medieval Europe 77; Church attitude to 77; round 77; instrumental music in 89, 94; ecclesiastical in Catalonia 135; dance suite in Baroque age 157; 17th-c court ballets 161, 186-187; influence of dance music on *concertato* style 191; popularity of in 17th-c England 194; role of in *opéra-lirique* 224; in 17th-c Poland 306; Hungary 316, 317; *and see* ballet
danceries 95
dance 'suites' (17th c) 95, 176, 183, 184, 190, 191; form of in chamber sonata 202; in late 17th-c France 225; in lyric drama and *opéra ballet* 225
Dandelot, Georges 403
Daniel Hjort (Palmgren) 460
Daniel-Lesur 402
D'Annunzio, Gabriele 395
Danse des morts, La (Honegger) 401
danse macabre 78
Danse Macabre (Saint-Saëns) 297
Danses Espagnoles (Granados) 470

Danse villageoise (Champagne) 509
Dante 51, 85
Dante Symphony (Liszt) 319
Danton's Death (von Einem) 410
Danyel, John 147
danza mexicana 476
Daphnis and Chloe (Ravel) 345, 397
Da Ponte, Lorenzo 244
D'Arezzo, Guido 62, 63
Dargomizsky, Alexander 339, 340, 347
D'Arras, Jean Bodel 81
Da Salo, Gaspar 96
Da Silva, André Gomes 472
Da Silva, Antonio José 472
Da Silva, Francisco Manuel 479
Daughter of the North (Merikanto) 460
Daughter of the Regiment, The (Donizetti) 354
David, Félicien 292
David, Ferdinand 277
Davidsbündler March against the Philistines (Schumann) 279
Davidsbündler-Tänze (Schumann) 279
Davies, E. H. 500
Davies, Peter Maxwell 374, 454, 529, **531-532**; *530*
Davis, Miles 521; *521*
Davy, Richard 143
Dawn: An Australian Rhapsody for Full Orchestra (Tate) 504
De Adamo, Salimbeno 123
Deane, John Philip 503
Death and the Maiden (Schubert) 273
Death and the Maiden (Skalkottas) 498
Death and Transfiguration (R. Strauss) 363
Death of Jesus, The (Graun) 231
Death of Kullervo, The (Kajanus) 459
De' Bardi, Giovanni 133
De Beaujoyeux, Balthazar 94
De Bériot, Charles 488
De Bertrand, Antoine 111
De Binches, Gilles *see* Binchois
De Boeck, Auguste 489
Deborah (Handel) 216
Deborah and Jael (Pizzetti) 422
De Bourguignon, Francis 490
De Bournonville, Jean 188
De Bus, Gervais 70
De Busnes, Antoine *see* Busnois
Debussy, Claude 32, 248, 255, 290, 292, 300, 301, 370, 371, 386, 414; piano works and chamber music 394; orchestral works 394-395; ballet and opera 395; *393, 394*
De Chancy, F. 191
De Châtillon, Gautier 74, 76
Declaración (J. Bermudo) 139
De Coster, Charles 486
De Courville, Thibault 111
De Dalza 91
Deering, Richard 149, 192
def 45
De Falla, Manuel 48, 388, 469, 470; *471, 474*
De Florentia, Johannes *see* Da Cascia, Giovanni
De Fonseca, Marcos Antonio *see* Portugal, Marcos
De Freitas, Luiz 474
De Gallienne, Dorian 504
De Gante, Pedro 476
De Gazul, Francisco 474
De Goes, Damião 139
Dehmel Richard 382
De la Fresnaye, Vauquelin 111
De la Halle, Adam 48, 72, 77, 82
Delalande, Louis 220
Delalande, Michel Richard 223, 225, 226; *222*
De la Maza, Regino Sainz 467
De Lantins, Hugo 100
De la Pouplinière, Le Riche 262
De la Rue, Pierre 106-107, 115
De Lenclos, Ninon 190, 191
De Lescurel, Johannot 70
Delius, Frederick 449-450, 451; *449*
Déliverance de Renaud (Guédron) 186
Del Fontego, Silvestro Ganassi 93
Della Casa, Giovanni 127
Della Scala family 124

De Lorme, Marion 190
De los Rios, Diego 477
Delvincourt, Claude 404
De Mandricourt, Pierre 107
Demarquez, Suzanne 404
De' Medici, Catherine 94, 186, 226
De' Medici, Ferdinand 94
De' Medici, Francesco 133
De' Medici, Lorenzo 98, 105, 115, 125-126; *125*
De' Medici, Marie 191
De Meester, Louis 491
Demetrio e Polibia (Rossini) 352
Demofoonte (Marcos Portugal) 473
Demoiselle élue (Debussy) 393, 395
De Monte, Philip 107, 115, **117-118**, 127; *117*
De Musica (Aurelian) 60
De Musica (Fulda) 114
De Musica (St Augustine) 60
De musica mensurabili (Garland) 140
De musica practica (de Pareja) 136
Denmark *see* Scandinavia, music of
De Nesle, Blondel 76
De Nyert, Pierre 186, 187
De organographia see Syntagma musicum
De Orto, Marbriano 106
De Pablo, Luis 472
De Pestain, Chaillou 70
De Rippe, Albert 112
De Rore, Cypriano 107, 127, 128, 131; *127*
De Sarrasate, Pablo 468
Desert, The (David) 292
Desportes, Philippe 189
De Sermisy, Claudin 110
Desmarets, Henri 225
Des Prez, Josquin 85, 89, **103-105**, 107, 108; *103*
Dessane, Antoine 506
D'Este, Hercule, Duke 106
D'Este, Ippolito 137
D'Este, Isabella 92, 126; *126*
Destouches 225, 300
De Troyes, Chrétien 76
De Ventadour, Bernard 75, 76; *75*
Devienne, François 286
Devil and Daniel Webster, The (Moore) 442
Devil and Kate, The (Dvořák) 333
Devil's Wall, The (Smetana) 332
Devil Take Her, The (Benjamin) 504
De Vitry, Philippe 70, 71, 72, 124, 125
Devotia Moderna 98
De Wert, Jacques 107, 127, 128, 129, 171
De Zwolle, Arnaut 57, 90
Diaghilev, Serge 371, 388, 395, 397, 399, 400, 401, 428; *431*
Dialectic (Bush) 453
Dialogo della Natività del Nostro Signor (Animuccia) 130
Dialogue des Carmélites (Poulenc) 401
Dialogues (Malipiero) 421
diaphony 52-53, 66 *and see* glossary of technical terms
Diary of a Madman (Searle) 453
Diary of a Man who disappeared (Janáček) 464
Dias Melgaço, Diego 139
Dibdin, Charles 217
Dichterliebe (Schumann) 279
didjeridu 501; *500*
Dido and Aeneas (Purcell) 194, 195, 252; *194*
Didone (Cavalli) 170
Diepenbrock, Alphons 491; *491*
Dietrich, Sixtus 116
Di Lasso, Orlando *see* Lassus
Dimanche breton (Ropartz) 300
Dimensions II (Maderna) 424
Dimensions in Time and Silence (Penderecki) 463
D'Indy, Vincent 48, 63, 300-302
Dinner Engagement, A (Berkeley) 452
Dioclesian (Purcell) 195
Dittersdorf, Ditters von 235, 236; *236*
Divertimento (Dallapiccola) 422
Divertissement à la Hongroise (Schubert) 273

Divertissement for bassoon and string orchestra (Weinzweig) 506-508
Divertissement for strings (Bartók) 416
Divertissements (Roussel) 398
Divine Poem, The (Scriabin) 426
Division violist (Simpson) 193
Dixieland Jazz Band, the Original 512
Dizi, François-Joseph 262
Dmitri (Dvořák) 333
Dobrynia Nikititch (Gretchaninov) 427
Dobrzyński, Ignacy Feliks 309
dodecaphony *see* serial method
Dohnányi Ernö 414
doinas 496
Doktor Faust (Busoni) 419
Dolmetsch, Arnold 375, 446
Domaines (Boulez) 524-525
Donato 125
Don Carlos (Verdi) 291, 356, 357
Don Giovanni (Mozart) 244, 352
Donizetti, Gaetano 287, 291, 354; *354*
Don Juan (R. Strauss) 363
Don Pasquale (Donizetti) 354
Don Quichotte à Dulcinée (Ravel) 397
Don Quixote (R. Strauss) 363
Don Quixote overture (Rivier) 404
Doret, Gustave 483
Dorfbarbier, Der (Schenk) 235
Dorico, Valerio 126
Dorsey, Jimmy 516
Dorsey, Tommy 516
D'Ortigue, Joseph 292
Dostoyevsky, Fyodor 341, 464
Double Concerto (Martinů) 465
Double Dealer, The, Purcell's music for 196
Douglas, Clive 504
Dover Beach (Barber) 442
Dowland, John 94, 145, 147, 149, 150
drama, ecclesiastical origins in medieval Europe 79; evolution as secular form 79 *and see* miracle play; Greek (revival of) 89; musical in 15th-c Italy 133; music for in Portugal (15th-16th c) 139; influence on church music in Baroque age 156
Dream of Gerontius, The (Elgar) 448
Dresden, Sem 491-492
Dreyfus, George 505
drone 20, 45, 46, 56; *and see* glossary of technical terms
Drouet 254
drum, Africa 21, 22-23; Indonesia 32; Japan 28; India 34, 36; Arab 38, 40; Mediterranean countries 47; Hebrew *see* tof; in medieval European dance 77; in 16th-c dance 95; in 17th-c Europe 161; use in jazz 375; tenor drum 375; snare drum 375; varieties in Colombia 477; *28, 45, 54; and see* glossary of musical instruments
Drum mass (Haydn) 241
'Drum Roll' symphony (Haydn) 240
Dr Who, music for 378
Dryden, John 195-196
Duarte Lobo society 474
Dubinushka (Rimsky-Korsakov) 346
Dubois, Théodore 402
Du Caurroy, Eustache 187, 188, 189
Ducis, Benedictus 116
Duenna, The (Gerhard) 471
Dufay, Guillaume 88, 97, 99, **98-101**, 113, 114; *98*
duff 38, 40
Due Foscari, I (Verdi) 356
Dukas, Paul 301, 398-399, 403; *399*
dulcimer, 90; *90; and see* glossary of musical instruments
dulzian 56; *and see* glossary of musical instruments
Dumbarton Oaks Concerto (Stravinsky) 390
Du Mont, Henry 188, 225
Dunstable, John 88, 97, 98, 114, **142-143**, 214
Duparc, Henri 294, 295, 300
Duperier, Jean 485
Dupuis, Albert 489
Dupont, Gabriel 393

Durante, Francesco 176, 205, 209, 211
Durey, Louis 400, 402
Duruflé, Maurice 403
Dussek, Johann Ladislaus 269, 287, 333
Dutilleux, Henri 404
Duza, Esteban 139
Dvořák, Antonin 332-333; *332, 333*

Easte, Thomas 148
Eberlin, J. E. 235
Ebner, Wolfgang 182
Ebony Concerto (Stravinsky) 390
Eccard, Johannes 116, 120
echiquier d'Angleterre 57
Eclat (Boulez) 524
Ecurie, the 220, 221
Edge of the World, The (Weinzweig) 506
Edict of Nantes 87, 185
Edward VI of England 144
Egdon Heath (Holst) 450
Egisto (Cavalli) 187
Egk, Werner 408-409
Egmont (Goethe, Beethoven) 268
Egyptian Nights (Arensky) 427
Ehren Pforte (Mattheson) 232
Eight Scenes from Faust (Berlioz) 284, 288
Eimert, Herbert 378
Ein Heldenleben (R. Strauss) 363
Einstein, Alfred 275
Ein Versuch über die wahre Art das Clavier zu Spielen (C.P.E. Bach) 231
Eisenstein, Sergei 427
Eisler, Hanns 410
Eldridge, Roy 518
Eleanor of Aquitaine 50, 75
electronic music 373, 376, **378**, 379, 529, 530; Jolivet 402; Stockhausen 412, 530; Maderna 424; in America 444; Badings 493; Xenakis 499; in Canada 509; 531; *and see* glossary of technical terms
Elegischer Gesang (Beethoven) 268
Elegy for J F K (Stravinsky) 392
Elektra (Diepenbrock) 491
Elektra (R. Strauss) 363
Elevamini Symphony (Williamson) 505
Elfin Mountain, The (Kuhlau) 457
Elgar, Edward 447-449; *448*
Elijah (Mendelssohn) 276, 503
Elixir of Love, The (Donizetti) 354
Elizabeth I of England 144, 193
Elizabeth, Queen of England (Rossini) 352
Elkin, A. P. 500
Ellington, Edward Kennedy 'Duke' 514, 517-518, 522; *519*
Ellis, Catherine 500
Elsner, Joseph 307
Eluard, Paul 403
Emmanuel, Maurice 399
Emperor concerto (Beethoven) 267
Emperor Jones (Villa-Lobos) 480
En blanc et noir (Debussy) 394
Enchanted Lake (Lyadov) 426
Encina, Juan del 137
Energy-Growth-Construction (Bentzon) 458
Enesco, George 497; *497*
Enfance du Christ (Berlioz) 290
Enfantines (Mussorgsky) 343
England, music of 88, 97; diaphony and polyphony in middle ages 140; of *ars nova* period 140-141; *ars antiqua* in 141; predominance of church music in 15th c 142; influence on Burgundian school 142-143; becomes universal style 143; instrumental music and secular song of 15th and 16th c 144, 145, 150; church music (16th c) 145, 148; in Elizabethan age 145-146; madrigal in Elizabethan age 146-147; instrumental music in Elizabethan age 150; in the 17th c 192-196; masque and early opera 193-194, 195; in the 18th c 214-219; ballad opera 217; 19th c 445-447; revival of Tudor and folk music (19th c) 446; Elgar 447-448;

Delius 448-450; Vaughan-Williams and Holst 449-450; discovery of folk song as stimulus to English song-writing 450; 20th C 451-454; Britten 452-453
English Dancing Master (Playford) 193
'English descant' 141
English Lutenist Songs 446
English Folk Song Society 446
English Rhapsody, An (Delius) 450
Enigma Variations (Elgar) 448
Ennéade (Garant) 509
ensaladas 136, 138
Entr'actes and Sappho Fragments (Birtwistle) 454
epic song 73, 75, 125, 336
Episode at the masquerade (Karłowicz) 461
Epitaph (Holmboe) 459
Epitaph (Rimsky-Korsakov) 346
Epitaph for the Tombstone of Prince Egon Max of Furstenberg (Stravinsky) 392
Erard, Pierre 260, 261
Erard Sébastian 259, 260, 262
Erasmus 105, 115
Erbach, Christoph 179
Erbse, Heimo 411
Ercole Amanti (Cavalli) 170, 187
Erigena, Johannes Scotus 140
Erkel, Ferenc 317
Erlkönig (Schubert) 274
Ernani (Verdi) 356, 357
Eroica symphony (Beethoven) 248, 251, 265; *265*
Erwartung (Schoenberg) 370, 382
Erwin et Elmire (Goethe and André) 235
Escales (Ibert) 404
Escher, Rudolf 493
Esclavos felices, Los (Arriaga) 467
Escobedo, Bartolomé de 138
Escribano, Juan 138
Eslava, Hilarión 468
Esmeralda (Dargomizsky) 340
Esnaolo, Juan Pedro 478
España (Chabrier) 298
Espinel, Vicente 139
Espiral (Chávez) 481
Esplá, Oscar 469, 470-471
esrāj 34
Essays before a Sonata (Ives) 438
Essays for Orchestra (Barber) 442
Estampes (Debussy) 394
Esteban of Seville, Fernando 136
Esterhazy family 155; 238, 262, 269, 318; *238*
Esterhazy, Pal 316; *316*
Esther (Handel) 216
estive see bagpipes
Estella da Soria (Berwald) 455
Estrellita (Ponce) 481
Et Folkesagn (Harman) 457
Eton choir book 142, 143; *143*
Etudes (Debussy) 394
Etudes (Gershwin) 442
Etudes (Riisåger) 458
Etudes d'exécution transcendante (Liszt) 219
Etudes for piano (Debussy) 386
Etudes pour piano (Liszt) 319
Etudes symphoniques (Schumann) 279
Eugene Onegin (Tchaikovsky) 350
Euridice (Peri) 133
Euryanthe (Weber) 270
eurhythmics 483
Evenings in the Orchestra (Berlioz) 290
Everyman (Martin) 486
Exagonos (Chávez) 481

Façade (Walton) 451
Fâcheux, Les (Auric) 401
Fairy Queen, The (Purcell) 196
Fairy Tales (Medtner) 427
Fall of Arkun, The (Fibich) 333
Falstaff (Elgar) 448
Falstaff (Verdi) 355
Fantaisie (Chopin) 308
Fantaisie sur deux thèmes angevins (Lekeu) 488
Fantaisies Symphoniques (Hoffding) 458

Fantasia and Fugue in G minor (Bach) 200
Fantasia and toccata (Martinů) 465
Fantasia concertante (Togni) 424
Fantasia contrapuntistica (Busoni) 419
Fantasia on a Theme by Tallis (Vaughan Williams) 449
fantasias, in 16-c Spain 138; in 17th-c Germany (harpsichord) 181; for keyboard in 17th-c France 189; see also viol fantasies *and* glossary of technical terms
Fantasias (Werder) 504
Fantasie concertante (Malipiero) 421
Fantasien (Brahms) 327
Fantasiestücke (Schumann) 279
Fantastic Dances (Turina) 470
Fantastic Symphony (Berlioz) 250, 320
Fantasy for Orchestra (Somers) 508
Fantasy for piano and orchestra (Fauré) 302
Fantasy on popular French themes (D'Indy) 301
Far Eastern Symphony (Knipper) 431
'Farewell' symphony (Haydn) 239-240
Farinelli 171, 208, 209; *208*
Farnaby, Giles 150
Faroe Islands, folk music 47
Farrant, Richard 145
Farwell, Arthur 438
Fasch, Carl Friedrich 232
Fauré, Gabriel 290, 292, 295, 301, **302**, 393, 402; *302*
Faust (Diepenbrock) 491
Faust (Gounod) 294
Faust (Schumann) 319
Faust et Hélène (Boulanger) 404
Faust Symphony (Liszt) 319
fauxbourdon 141, 304; *and see* glossary of technical terms
Fayrfax, Robert 143-144
Febi Armonici 170
Feldman, Morton 443
Feen, Die (Wagner) 322
Fellowes, E. H. 446
Fenby, Eric 450
Fennimore and Gerda (Delius) 450
Feodor, Tsar 336
Fer, Philibert Jambe de 93
Ferdinand I, Emperor 114, 133
Ferdinand II, Emperor 153
Ferdinand of Tyrol, Archduke 92
Ferdinand the Catholic 136
Fernand Cortez (Spontini) 287
Fernandez de Castilleja, Pedro 137
Fernández, Oscar Lorenzo 480
Ferrabosco, Alfonso II 150
Ferrabosco, Domenico 127
Ferrante of Aragon 86, 136
Ferrari, Benedetto 169
Ferri, Baldassare 171
Fervaal, l'étranger (D'Indy) 300
Festa, Costanzo 126-127, 129
Festin de l'araignée (Roussel) 398
Festival Overture (Schumann) 280
Festspiele (Switzerland) 483
Fête des Belles Eaux (Messiaen) 405
Fêtes galantes (Debussy) 395
Fétis, François Joseph 252, 294, 488
Fezandat 112
Fiancée de la mer, La (Blockx) 489
Fibich, Zdeněk 333
Fidelio (Beethoven) 268-269; *between pp. 288 and 289*
fiddel 55, 56, 90; *44, 56, 67, 68, 72, 76, 77, 91; and see* glossary of musical instruments
Field, John 213, 308, 446
Fields and Forests of Bohemia, The (Smetana) 332
Fiesta de Elche 135
fiestas 135
fife 164; *and see* glossary of musical instruments
Figures humaines (Poulenc) 401
Finck, Heinrich 114, 304
Fine, Irving 440, 441
Finel, Edgar 489
Finland see Scandinavia, music of
Finlandia (Sibelius) 460
Finta Pazza, La (Sacrati) 187

Finzi, Gerald 450
Fiori Musicali (Frescobaldi) 176
Firebird, The (Stravinsky) 388; *390*
Fireside Tales (MacDowell) 437
Fireworks (Stravinsky) 388
Fischer, J. F. C. 201
Fitelberg, Grzegorz 461-462
Fitzwilliam Virginal Book 150
'Five', the 339, 341-342, 343, 347, 427
Five Altenbergerlieder (Berg) 384
Five concepts for orchestra (Somers) 508
Five Lyrics of the T'ang Dynasty (Beckwith) 508
Five Pieces for orchestra (Webern) 386; *386*
Five Pieces for String Quartet (Webern) 386
Five Songs of Ariel (Martin) 487
flageolets 57, 77, 95; *and see* glossary of musical instruments
Flaming Angel, The (Prokofiev) 427
Flaminio, Il (Pergolesi) 210
Flames of Paris, The (Asafico) 430
Flecha, Mateo the Elder 138
Flecha, Mateo the Younger 138
Flechtenmacher, Adolf 496
Flood, The (Stravinsky) 392
Flothuis, Marius 493
Floyd, Carlisle 442
flugelhorn 257, 258; *and see* glossary of musical instruments
flute 56; Africa 22; Indonesia 31 *and see suling;* India 34, 36; Arab countries 38, 40; Mediterranean countries 45; Balkan countries 47; Hebrew see '*ugab*; transverse 55; in 15th-c Europe 90; in 16th-c Europe 91; in ensembles (16th c) 92, 93, 94; in Henry VIII's collection 92; treatises on 93; as sustaining instrument 93; makers of (16th c) 96; published music for (16th c) 112; in 17th c 161, 162, 164, 165; in work of Scarlatti 207; in the Chamber (France) 221; in Mozart concerto 237; seven-keyed flute 254; improved by T. Böhm (cylindrical Böhm flute) 254; bass and alto flutes (revived by Böhm) 256; work of Berio 424; *quena* flute (Peru) 475; varieties in Colombia 477; *18, 22, 25, 28, 78, 255; and see* glossary of musical instruments
Flying Dutchman, The (Wagner) 319, 322, 324
Fokine 388
Folk Song Symphony (Harris) 440
Foltz, Hans 77
Fontana, Giovanni Battista 177
Foote, Arthur 435, 437
Forains, Les (Sauguet) 402
Ford, Thomas 147
Forest, The (Glazunov) 425
Forgotten One, The (Mussorgsky) 343
Formé, Nicolas 166, 188
Fortner, Wolfgang 410
Forza del Destino (Verdi) 356
Foss, Lukas 441, 444
Foster, Stephen 437
Fountain of Bukhchisarai, The (Asafiev) 430; *430*
Fountains of Rome (Respighi) 420
Fountains of the Villa d'Este (Liszt) 320, 321
Four Ages of Man, The (Rosenberg) 455
Four minutes and thirty-three seconds (Cage) 443
Four Pieces (Webern) 388
Four Poems of St Theresa of Avila (Berkeley) 452
Four Psalms (Gross) 504
Four sacred pieces (Verdi) 357
Four Saints in Three Acts (Thomson) 440
Four Serious Songs (Brahms) 329
Four Studies for Orchestra (Stravinsky) 390
Four Temperaments, The (Hindemith) 407

Four Temperaments, The (Nielsen) 458
Fra Diavolo (Auber) 291-292
Françaix, Jean 404
France, music of, medieval 66-67, 70-72, 74-76, 81-82 *and see* Franco-Flemish school; in 16th c 108-112; dominance of secular music in 16th c 108; golden age of *chanson* 108-111; revival of religious music after Reformation 111; in 17th c 185-191; institutions in the reign of Louis XIV 220-221; increasing popularity of opera 222; religious music under Louis XIV 222-223; in the reign of Louis XV 224-226; conflict with Italian styles 226; *opéra-comique* (18th c) 281; during the Revolution 285, 286; *théâtre-lyrique* 287; Berlioz 288-290; contribution of foreign composers (19th c) 290-291; revival of interest in polyphonic church music 292; renaissance in 19th c 294-295; Debussy 393-395; Ravel 395-397; Roussel 397-398; Dukas, Satie and contemporaries 398-399; the 'Six' 400-402; School of Arcueil 402; Young France group 402; the Independents 403-404; Messiaen 405
Francesca da Rimini (Gilson) 489
Francesca da Rimini (Tchaikovsky) 350
Francis I of France 86, 92, 108, 137, 221; *109*
Franciscello 162
Franciscus (Tinel) 489
Francisque, Antoine 191
Franck, Cesar 284, **298-300**, 301, 393, 488; *299*
Franco-Flemish school 93, 97-107, 122; contribution of *ars nova* to 88, 89, 97; influence of Italian and English music 97; end of predominance 108
François Villon (Dresden) 491
Francs-Juges, Les (Berlioz) 289
Franz Josef, Emperor 248
Frauenliebe und Leben (Schumann) 279
Frauenlob 76, 330; *76*
Frau ohne Schatten, Die (Strauss) 363
Frederick I of Prussia 230
Frederick II (the Great) of Prussia 154, 198, 230, 231, 232, 233; *230*
Frederick, elector palatine 153, 305
Frederick Augustus I (the Strong) of Saxony 233, 305
Frederick William I of Prussia 154, 230
Freedman, Harry 508
Freischütz, Der (Weber) 270, *271*
French horn 166, 243, 247; *257*
Frescobaldi, Girolamo 127, 176, 182, 199, 205, 230; *176*
Fresques de Piero Della Francesca, Les (Martinů) 465
fretel 55
Frey, Hans 95
Fricker, Peter Racine 453-454
Froberger, Johann Jacob 176, 181, 182, 183
From the Cradle to the Grave (Liszt) 320
From the New World symphony (Dvořák) 332
From Within Looking Out (Dreyfus) 505
frottola 89, 105, 108, 126, 129; *and see* glossary of technical terms
Fry, William Henry 435, 442
Frye, Walter 114, 143
Fuenllano, Miguel de 139
Fuertes, Mariano Soriano 468
Fugger family 92
fugue 157, 178, 184; Bach 199, 200, 201; in sonatas of Corelli 205; Handel 217; Reger 363; *and see* glossary of technical terms
Fulbert of Chartres 74
Fuller-Maitland, J. A. 446
Fundamentum organisandi (Paumann) 114
Futurism 419-420
Fux, Johann Joseph 229

Fuyneman, Daniel 492

Gabrieli, Andrea 95, 120, 128, 131, 132
Gabrieli, Giovanni 95, 107, 128, 129, 131, 132-133, 157, 172, 180
Gade, Niels Wilhelm 457-458; *457*
Gadzhibekov, Useir 429
gafta 40
Gagaku 25, 28
Gagnebin, Henri 485
Galanta Dances (Kodály) 416
Galindo, Blas 482
Gallet, Luciano 480
Gallus, Jacobus *see* Handl
Galuppi, Baldassare 206, 210, 211, 229, 338
gamelan 30-32, 393; *and see* glossary of musical instruments
Garant, Serge 509
García, José Nuñes 479
García, Manuel 467
García, Maria Felicità 467
Garden of Fand, The (Bax) 451
Gardner, John 454
Garland, John 140
Garni Sands (Dreyfus) 505
Gaspard de la Nuit (Ravel) 396
Gastoldi, G. G. 146, 172
gaucho tradition 478
Gaultier, Denys 190, 191
Gaultier, Ennemond 191
Gay, John 217
Gayane (Khatchaturian) 429
Gay Hussars, The (Kálmán) 413
Gazelloni, Severino 529
Gédalge, André 497, 509
Geiser, Walther 486
Gelasian sacramentary 61
Geminiani, Francesco 205, 212, 219
gender 32
General History of Music, The (Hawkins) 214
Genesis (Regeney) 410
Gens de mer (Gilson) 489
Gentleman's Catch Club 214
George, Stefan 359, 382
George I of England 215
Georgescu, George 498
Gerhard, Roberto 451, 471
Gerle, Georg 95
Gerle, Hans 92, 120
'German' mass (Schubert) 276
German Requiem (Brahms) 329
Germany and Austria: early music of 113-121; *Minnesänger see separate entry;* elements of Franco-Flemish style 114, 117; emergence of national style 114; organ music (15th and 16th c) 114-115; Protestant congregational song 116; church music (16th c) 116-119; secular music (16th c) 115, 119; Italian influence on 120; instrumental music (16th c) 120; in 17th c 178-184; church music 178, 180, 183; organ music 180-183; secular music 183-184; Bach 197-201; in the 18th c 227-244; French and Italian influence on music of south Germany 228, 230; Italian influence on music in Vienna 229; Mannheim school 229-230; Munich 230; Berlin 230-232; Hamburg 232; the court of Saxony-Poland 233; opera 233-235; age of classicism 236-244; Beethoven 263-269; Weber 269-270; *Lied* in 18th c 271-272; Romantic composers (Schubert, Mendelssohn, Schumann) 273-280; Wagner 322-325; Brahms 325-329; Bruckner 329; late Romantic composers (Wolf, Mahler, Strauss, Reger etc.) 359-364; early 20th c (Schoenberg, Berg, Webern) 380-386; Hindemith and contemporaries 406-410; later 20th-c composers 410-412
Gershwin, George 372, 442-443; *443*
Gesellschaft der Musikfreunde 237
Gesualdo (Don) Carlo 128, 172, 176
Getz, Stan 523
Gevaert, Auguste 488; *488*

Gewandhaus Concerts, Leipzig 251
Gewandhaus Orchestra, Leipzig 276
Geystliche Gesangk Buchleyn 116
Ghedini, Giorgio Federico 422
Gherardello 125
Ghiselin, Johannes 106
Giacoso, G. 358
Giardini, Felice di 212
Giasone, Il (Cavalli) 170
Gibbons, Christopher 193
Gibbons, Orlando 48, 94, 145, 146, 149, 192; *149*
Gilbert, W. S. 447
Gilgamesh (Martinů) 466
Gillespie, Dizzy 521, 522; *520*
Gilson, Paul 489
Ginastera, Albert 481
Gioconda, La (Ponchielli) 357
Giordani, Domenico Antonio 205
Giovanna d'Arco (Verdi) 356
Gipsy Love (Lehár) 413
Girl of the Golden West, The (Puccini) 358
Giselle (Adam) 292
Giustini, Ludovico 258
Giustiniani, Leonardo 125
Glagolitic Mass (Janáček) 464
Glazunov, Alexander 348, 425, 427; *425*
Glenn Miller Orchestra 516
Glière, Reinhold 427, 429, 430
Glinka, Mikhail Ivanovich 310, 339-340, 342, 347; *338*
Globokar, Vinko 529
Glogauer songbook 113
Gloriana (Britten) 452
Glorious Moment, The (Beethoven) 267
Gluck, Christoph Willibald 202, 209, 210, 233-234, 236, 271, 352; *234*
Glückliche Hand, Die (Schoenberg) 382
Gobert, Thomas 189
Godeau, Antoine 189
Godelière (Tinel) 489
Godunov, Boris 336
Goehr, Alexander 454
Goethe, Johann Wolfgang 235, 268, 271, 274, 279, 319, 359; *235*
Gogol, Nikolai 432
Goldberg Variations (J. S. Bach) 201
Gold Coast Customs (Searle) 453
Golden Cockerel, The (Rimsky-Korsakov) 340, 345, 346; *347*
Goldmark, Karoly 413
Goldoni, Carlo 210
Golestan, Stan 497
Golgotha (Martin) 487
goliards, songs of 74, 75; influence on *trouvère* songs 76
Gombert, Nicolas 107, 121, 174
Gomes, Antonio Carlos 472, 479
Gomes, Manuel José 472
Gomolka, Mikolaj 304
Gonzaga, Fernando 118
Goodman, Benny 512, 516; *516*
Goossens, Eugene 504
Gorczcki, Grzegorz Gerwazy 306
Gossec, François-Joseph 224, 281, 287; *283*
Gotovac, Jakov 495
Gottschalk, Louis Moreau 435-436
Goudimel, Claude 111, 314
Gounod, Charles 284, 292, 294-295, 300, *295*
goût mixte 228
Government Inspector, The (Egk) 409
Goyescas (Granados) 470
Grabu, Louis 194
Graça, Fernando Lopez 474
Graduale, Medicean edition 63; 1883 edition 64
Gradus ad Parnassum (Clementi) 213, 261
Gradus ad Parnassum (Fux) 229
Graew, Valentin 121
Grainger, Percy 503-504; *504*
Granados, Enrique 469, 470
Grand Ballet de Nemours 161
Grande Duchesse de Gérolstein, La (Offenbach) 294
Grande Messe des Morts (Berlioz) 290
Grandi, Alessandro 174

Grand Inquisitor, The (Blacher) 408
Grand Mass in C minor (Mozart) 243
grand motet 223, 225
Gran mass (Liszt) 319, 320
Graun, Carl Heinrich 231
Graupner, Johann Cristoph 197
'grazing songs' (Scandinavia) 47
Great Russian Easter, The (Rimsky-Korsakov) 346
'Great' symphony (Schubert) 275
Greban, Arnoul 82
Greece, music of 45, 498-499
Green, Ray 441
Greene, Maurice 218
Greenway, John 502
Gregorian chant 52, 63, 64, 66, 68, 313 *and see* plainsong
Gregory, Johann Gottfried 336
Gregory the Great, Pope *see* St Gregory
Gretchaninov, Alexander 427
Gretchen am Spinnrade (Goethe, setting by Schubert) 273, 274
Grétry, André Erneste Modeste 286, 506; *286*
Grieg, Edvard Hagerrup 449, **456-457**, 460; *456*
Grillparzer, Franz 268
griots 19, 24
griotte 24
Griselda, La (A. Scarlatti) 209
Gross, Eric 504
grosses bombardes 56
Grossin, Estienne 90
Grossman, Ludwik 310
ground bow (Uganda) 21
'Group of Four' 482
Groups (Stockhausen) 412
Guarany, Il (A. C. Gomes) 479
Guatimotzin (Ortega) 476
Guédron, Pierre 185, 186, 187
Guernica (Pépin) 509
Guerre des Bouffons 226, 281
Guerrero, Francisco 137
Guerrero, Pedro 137
Guignol (Mussorgsky) 343
Guillet, C. 189
Guilmant, A. 63
guitar, in 16th-c Europe 91, 92; in Henry VIII's collection 92; tablatures for (16th c) 96; replaces *vihuela* in 16th c Spain 139; in 17th c 162, 163, 191; in the Chamber (France) 221; as accompanying instrument in *romances* 281; in 19th- and 20th-c Spain 467-468; electric 518, (Christian) 519, 520; *190, 478; and see* glossary of musical instruments
Guitar method (Sor) 467
Guittara Española (Espinel) 139
gunbri 40
Günther von Schwarzburg (Holzbauer) 235
Gurney, Ivor 450
Gurrelieder, Die (Schoenberg) 382
Gussakovsky 341, 342
Gustavus Adolfus of Sweden 153, 175
Guys and Dolls (Loesser) 442
guzli 47, 304, 334, 335; *335; and see* glossary of musical instruments
Guzman, Federico 477
gymel 140
Gymnopédies (Satie) 399

Hába, Alois 372, 466, 495; *466*
Hába, Karel 466
habañera 476
Habanera (Aubert) 403
Habeneck, F. A. 251, 287
Hacker, Alan 529
Hackett, Maria 445
Hadjidakis, Manos 499
Haffner symphony (Mozart) 242
Hagen, Georg 77
Hahn, Reynaldo 477
Haieff, Alexei 440, 441
Hakon Jarl (Smetana) 332
Halary 257
Halévy, J. L. F. 287, 292; *292*
Halévy, Ludovic 294, 340
Halewijn (Pijper) 492

Halffter, Cristobal 472
Halffter, Ernesto 470, 471
Halffter, Rodolfo 471-472
haling 456
Halka (Moniuszko) 310
Halliday 257
Hamerik, Ebbe 458
Hamilton, Iain 453-454
Hamlet (Blacher) 408
Hamlet (Liszt) 320
Hamlet (Searle) 453
Hammerklavier see piano *and* glossary of musical instruments
Hampel, Anton Joseph 166
Handel, Georg 214-215
Handel, George Frederick 48, 157, 183, 195, 197, 214, 218, 219, 241; as virtuoso performer 214-215; opera 215, 216; instrumental work 215; religious music 215, 216; secular choral works 217; *215, 217, between pp. 224 and 225*
Handel and Haydn Society of Boston 435
Handel in the Strand (Grainger) 503
Handel Variations (Brahms) 326
Handl, Jacob 121, 330, 331, 495
Hängende Gärten (Schoenberg) 382
Hanslick, Eduard 252
Hanson, Howard 442
Hanson, Raymond 504
hardangerfele 47, 456
Hardy, Thomas 450
Harmann, Johann Peter Emilius 457
Harmonia Caelestis (P. Esterhazy) 316
Harmonicum instrumentorum libri IV (Praetorius) 159
Harmony mass (Haydn) 241
Harmony of the World, The (Hindemith 407
Harnasie (Szymanowski) 462
Harold In Italy (Berlioz) 289
harp 54, 56, 57; Africa 21; Hebrew 59; in epic song 73; in 15th c Europe 90; in collections (16th c) 92; in ensembles (16th c) 93, 94; in 17th c 160, 161, 163, 173; in Mozart concerto 237; pedal harp (18th c) and music for 262; double-action harp and improvements to (18th and 19th c) 262; popularity in the reign of Louis XVI 281; *21, 261, 262; and see* glossary of musical instruments
Harpist, The (Mussorgsky) 343
harpsichord 57; in 16th-c Europe 91; in collections (16th c) 92; as *continuo* instrument (16th c) 94; 16th-c makers of 95; in 17th c 159, 160, 161, 163, 176, 190; Bach's work for 201; in sonatas (17th-c Italy) 205; sonatas (18th-c Italy) 207; work of Handel 215, 217; work of F. Couperin 224; contribution to invention of piano 258; decline in popularity 280; in 20th c 375; *166, 187, between pp. 208 and 209; and see* glossary of musical instruments
Harris, Roy 440, 441
Harsányi, Tibor 400, 417
Hartmann, Karl Amadeus 409-410; *410*
Hartmann, Victor 341
Háry János (Kodály) 416
Hasse, Johann Adolf 209, 229, 230, 233; *233*
Hassler, Hans Leo 116
Hauer, Joseph Matthias 381
Haunted Castle, The (Moniuszko) 310
Hauptmann, Gerhart 359
hautbois baryton 256
hautboy 77, 164; *and see* glossary of musical instruments
Hawkins, Coleman 514, 517; *516*
Hawkins, Isaac 261
Hawkins, Sir John 214
Haydn, Joseph 48, 155, 202, 217, 219, 229, 236, 237, 240, 243, 250, 263, 308; development of symphony form 237; chamber music 237-238; symphonies 237, 239-240; religious music 238, 240-241; trumpet concerto 253; works for piano 260;

Lied 271-272; *between pp. 216 and 217*, 239
Haydn, Michael 269
hazozra 58, 59; *and see* glossary of musical instruments
Head, Michael 450
Hebrew Melodies (Nathan) 503
Hebrew music 58-59
Hebrides overture (Mendelssohn) 277
Heckel family 256
Hedy (Fibich) 333
Hegar, Friedrich 483
Heine, Heinrich 278, 279; *276*
Heinrich of Saxony 113
Heller, Stephen 292
Henderson, Fletcher 514
Henestrosa, Venegas de 139
Henkemans, Hans 493
Henry II of France 50
Henry III of France 50, 111, 186
Henry IV of France 87, 142, 154, 161, 185, 186, 187
Henry V of England 142
Henry VII of England 143
Henry VIII of England 85, 92, 143-144
Henze, Hans Werner 374, 410-411
Héraklès (Brenta) 490
Hercule et Omphale (Champagne) 509
Heredia, Sebastian Aguilera de 138
Herman, Woody 390, 516
Hérold, Ferdinand 284, 287, 292
Hibernian Catch Club 214
hichiriki 28
Hidalgo, Bartolomé 478
Hiéroglyphes (Fuyneman) 492
Hill, Alfred 503
Hiller, J. A. 235
Hiller, L. A. Jr. 379
Hiller, Lejaren 532
Hindemith, Paul 371-372, **406-407**, 432; *407*
Hines, Earl 514, 519, 522
Hippodamie (Fibich) 333
Hippolyte et Aricie (Rameau) 225, 226
Histoires naturelles, Les (Ravel) 396, 397
History of Music (Burney) 214
History of Sir Francis Drake 194
histrion *see* epic song *and* glossary of technical terms
Hitler, Adolf 368, 380, 406
Hochbrucker, Christian 262
Hochbrucker, Simon 262
hocket 72
Hodeir, André 526
Hodges, Johnny 518
Høffding, Finn 458
Hoffmann, Ernst Theodor Amadeus 269
Hoffmann, Leopold 236, 238
Hofhaimer, Paul 114, 115, 121
Hofmannsthal, Hugo von 363, 486
Holberg Suite (Grieg) 456-457
Holbert, Ludvig 457
Holborne, Anthony 164
Holguin, Guillermo Uribe 477
Holiday, Billie 519-520; *518*
Holidays (Ives) 438
Holland, music of *see* Belgium and Netherlands
Hollinger, Heinz 529
Holmboe, Vagn 459
Holst, Gustav 447, 450
Holzbauer, Ignaz 229, 230, 235
Homage to James Joyce (Berio) 424
Home Sweet Home (Bishop) 503
Hommage (De Falla) 469
Honegger, Arthur 400, 401, 483
Hopkinson, Francis 434
horns, in 17th C 162, 164, 166, 171 *and see* French horns: in work of Scarlatti 107; improvements to in 19th C 257, 258; *and see* glossary of musical instruments
Hortulanus (Rosenberg) 455
Hot Five, The 512
Hothby, John 143
Hot Seven, The 512
Hotteterre, Jean 164, 165; *223*
House of the Dead, The (Janáček) 464
Housman, A. E. 450
Hovland, Egil 457

H.P. (ballet, Chávez) 481
HPSCHD (Cage) 532
Hristic, Stevan 496
Hubay, Jeno 413
Huber, Hans 483
huda song 37
Hugh of Orléans (Primat) 74, 75
Hugh the Drover (Vaughan Williams) 450
Hugo, Victor 250, 319, 357
Hullah, John 445
Humfrey, Pelham 194, 195
Hummel, Johann Nepomuk 236, **269**, 308
Hundred Years War 88, 98, 142
Hungaria (Liszt) 320
Hungarian Rhapsodies (Liszt) 48, 319
Hungaro, Francesco 95
Hungary, music of, medieval to 15th C 313-314; 16th and 17th C 315-316; 18th C 316-317; 19th C 317-318; Liszt 318-321; early 20th C 413-414; Bartók 414-415; Kodály and contemporaries 416-417
Hunyadi Laszlo (Erkel) 317
hurdy-gurdy 20, 56, 57; in Balkan countries 47; in medieval European dance 77; *57, 160, 181*; *and see* glossary of musical instruments
Hus, Jan 86, 121
Hussite hymns 121, 330-331
Huybrechts, Albert 490
Hyde, Miriam 504
hymn, in Early Christian Church 60; in Byzantine Church 60; Lutheran 166 *and see* chorale; Hussite 330-331; in medieval Russia 336; 'folk hymns' in 19th-C America 437; *and see* glossary of technical terms
Hymnen (Stockhausen) 531
Hymn of Jesus, The (Holst) 450
Hymn of St Wenceslas 330
Hymns and Spiritual Songs (Watts) 437
Hymn to Liberty, The 285
Hymn to Stalin (Khatchaturian) 429
Hymnus: the Heirs of the White Mountain (Dvořák) 332
Hyperbole (Pépin) 509

Iberia (Albéniz) 469
Ibert, Jacques 404
Ibn Misjah 38
Ibrahim ibn al-Mahdi 38
Icarus (Poot) 491
Idomeneo (Mozart) 244
If the Cap Fits (Bush) 454
Illica, L. 358
Illuminations, Les (Britten) 452
Images (Debussy) 394
Images (Freedman) 508
Images du Canada Français (Champagne) 509
Images pour orchestre, Les (Debussy) 395
Impromptus on an Air by Clara Wieck (Schumann) 279
In a Summer Garden (Delius) 450
Incantation (Martinů) 465
Incantation (Roussel) 398
Incredible Flutist, The (Piston) 440
Indes galantes (Rameau) 225
India, music of 28, 30, 33-36
Indian Queen (Purcell) 196
Indian Suite (MacDowell) 437
Indonesia, music of 30-31
Iñes de Castro (Coelho) 474
Inextinguishable, The (Nielsen) 458
Ingegneri, Marc Antonio 128, 171
Ingelius, Axel Gabriel 459
In memoriam Claude Debussy (Stravinsky) 390
In memoriam Dylan Thomas (Stravinsky) 391
Innominata (Beck) 486
In nomine 144, 145, 149; *and see* glossary of technical terms
Institute of Musicology, Serbia 496
Institutioni Harmoniche (Zarlino) 132
Interlude (Demarquez) 404
Interlude in the life of an artist (Weinzweig) 508
intermedi 128, 133
Intermezzi (Brahms) 327

Intermezzi (Schumann) 279
Intermezzo (R. Strauss) 363
International Society for Contemporary Music 420
In Terra Pax (Martin) 486
In the Fen Country (Vaughan Williams) 450
In the Spring (Paine) 435
In the steppes of Central Asia (Borodin) 344
Intolleranza (Nono) 424
Intonazioni d'organo (G. Gabrieli) 132
Introduction and Allegro (Elgar) 448
Introduction and Allegro (Ravel) 396
Introitus (Stravinsky) 392
Iphigenia in Tauris (Galuppi) 338
Iphigénie en Aulide (Gluck) 234
Iphigénie en Tauride (Gluck) 234
Ippolitov-Ivanov, Mikhail 430
Ireland, folk music 47
Ireland, John 450, 451, 452
Irkanda I (Sculthorpe) 505
Isaacson, L. M. 379
Isaak, Heinrich 89, 105, **115**, 121
Ishaq al-Mausili 38-39
Isidore of Seville 60
Isla de las Calmas, La (Valen) 457
Islamey (Balakirev) 342
Islam, music of 17, 21, 24, 30, 37-40, 50
Island of Death, The (Rachmaninov) 425
Israel in Egypt (Handel) 217
'Israel' symphony (Bloch) 484
Italian concerto (J. S. Bach) 201
Italian Girl in Algiers, The (Rossini) 352
Italian madrigals Englished 149
Italian Serenade (Wolf) 359
Italian Society for Modern Music 420
Italian symphony (Mendelssohn) 277
Italy, music of 122-133; influence of Franco-Flemish school 122, 125; 14th-C religious song 123; 14th-C secular music 123-125; secular of 15th C 125-129; religious of 16th C 129-132; instrumental of 16th C 132-133; in 17th C 159-177; opera 156; (17th C) 159, 167-174; oratorio 156; (17th C) 175-176; instrumental (17th C) 157-158, 162, 163, 177; church music (17th C) 160-161, 174; instrumental in late 17th and 18th C 202-208; opera in 18th C 208-211; church music in 18th C 211-212; migration of Italian composers in 18th C 212; 19th C 351-352; Rossini and contemporaries 352-355; Verdi 355-357; Puccini 357-358; Busoni 418-419; Futurism 419-420; Casella and contemporaries 420-422; dodecaphony 422-424; serial composers 424
Ivan Sussanin (Glinka) 339, 340
Ivan the Terrible (Prokofiev) 427
Ives, Charles 373, **438**; *438*

Jacchini, Giuseppe Maria 204
Jack Pudding (Henze) 411; *411*
Jacobin, The (Dvořák) 333
Jacques-Dalcroze, Emile 483; *483*
Jagd, Die (Hiller) 235
James, Harry 516
James I of England 145, 147, 149, 153, 192
James II of England 153
James Ensor Suite (Alpaerts) 489
Janáček, Leoš 333, 371, 461, **463-464**; *461*
Janequin, Clément 47, 108, **109**, 121
jank 38
Jannaconi, Giuseppe 211
Janotha, Natalia 311
Janson brothers 163
Japan, music of 19, 25, 28-29
Jardanyi, Pal 417
Jarecki, Henryk 310
Jarnach, Philipp 419
Jarzebski, Adam 306
Jaubert, Maurice 404
Jausions 64
Java 28, 30, 32; *and see* Indonesia

jazz 372, 373; elements of in Stravinsky's music 389; elements of in Weill's music 409; jazz opera (Krenek) 410; attempts at combination with serious music 439; 'jazz' piano concerto (Copland) 439; **chapter pp. 510-523**
Jeanne au bûcher (Honegger) 401
Jean-Paul 278
Jelinek, Hanns 409
Jenkins, John 192
Jenko, Davorin 495
Jennens, Charles 217
Jenůfa (Janáček) 333, 463, 464
Jerome of Bologna 95
Jerusalem (Verdi) 356
Jeu d'Adam 81
Jeu de Robin et Marion 48, 82; *82*
Jeu de Saint Nicolas (d'Arras) 81
Jeux (Debussy) 386, 394, 395
Jeux de Marie, Les (Martinů) 465
Jeux d'enfants (Bizet) 297
Jewels of the Madonna (Wolf-Ferrari) 420
Jew's harp 90; *91*; *and see* glossary of musical instruments
Jim Jones 502
Joachim, Joszef 318, 326
Joana de Flandre (Gomes) 479
Job (Vaughan Williams) 450
Johanna Balk (Regeney) 410
Johanneum, Hamburg 232
John XXII, Pope 67, 72
John George of Saxony 153
Johnny Spielt Auf (Krenek) 410
John of Lublin 304
Johnson, James P. 514; *515*
Johnson, Robert 144, 150
Jolivet, André 400, 402, 416
Jommelli, Niccolò 207, 209, 210, 229; *207*
Jonah (Beckwith) 508
Jones, C. M. 23
Jones, Inigo 192, 193; *192*
Jones, Percy 502
Jones, Robert 147
Jones, Trevor 500
Jongen, Joseph 488
jongleurs 51, 53, 55, 56, 57, 73, 75; *73*; *and see* glossary of technical terms
Jonson, Ben 193; *150*
Jorat, theatre of 483
Joseph I, Emperor 228
Jota Aragonese (Glinka) 340
Joueurs de flûte (Roussel) 398
Journal des Débats 252, 290
Journeys of M. Broucek on the moon in the 15th century (Janáček) 464
Judas Maccabaeus (Handel) 216, 217
Judenkönig, Hans 120
Judith (Honegger) 401
Judith (Serov) 340
Juive, La (Halévy) 292
Julian the Apostate, Emperor 49
Julietta (Erbse) 411
Juliette, ou la Clef des Songes (Martinů) 465
Julius III, Pope 130
Julius Caesar (Malipiero) 421
Julius Caesar (Schumann) 280
Juilliard Ensemble of New York 529
Jullien, Louis Antoine 293
Jupiter symphony (Mozart) 242, 243
Justinian I, Emperor 49
J.X. 1905 (Janáček) 464

Kabalevsky, Dmitry 431
Kabuki theatre 28
Kafka, Franz 359, 410
kagura dance (Japan) 28
Kaiser, Georg 409
Kajanus, Robert 459
Kajoni, Janos 314, 315
Kaleidoscope (G. Landré) 492
Kalevala, the 459, 460
Kalevalan suite (Klami) 460
Kalinnikov, Vassily 427
Kalkbrenner, Friedrich 292
Kallman, C. 390

Kálmán, Emmerich 413
Kalomiris, Manolis 498
Kamarinskaya (Glinka) 340
kan ha diskan 47
kantele zither 47; *47, 460; and see*
    glossary of musical instruments
Kapsberger, H. 163
Karelian Rhapsody (Klami) 460
Karelia Suite (Sibelius) 460
Karg-Elert, Sigrid 364
Karłowicz, Mieczyław 461
Kassel Manuscript 161
Kastchey (Rimsky-Korsakov) 346
Katerina Ismailova (Shostakovich) 340,
    347, 432
Katharsis (Van Lier) 493
Katherina (Tinel) 489
Katski, Antoine 310
Katski, Apollinaire 310, 311
Katya Kabanova (Janáček) 464
kaval 47; *and see* glossary of musical
    instruments
Keil, Alfredo 474
Keleman, Milko 496
kendang drum 32
Kerala, boat song 36
Kerle, Christoph von 174, 179
Kerle, Jacobus 107, 120, 129
Ketner, Fritz 77
kettle drums 40, 55; in Lully's
    orchestra 162; in 17th c 164, 166;
    in the Ecurie 221; improvement to
    and increasing use of 375; *54; and
    see* glossary of musical instruments
keyboard instruments and music, in
    16th c 89, 91; technique of
    variations (16th c) 89, 150; in
    ensembles (16th c) 94; works
    (Sweelinck) 107; accompaniment in
    16th-c madrigal 128; in 16th-c
    Italy 132; in 16th-c England 144,
    145, 146, 150; Byrd's work for 149,
    150; dance suite adapted for 157;
    as continuo (17th c) 167; in early
    opera 174; Frescobaldi's work for
    176; in 17th-c Germany 181-182,
    183; in 17th-c France 189-190;
    Purcell's work for 195; concertos of
    Bach 20; styles in late 17th-c Italy
    202; invention of piano and effect on
    style 203; compositions in 18th-c
    England 218; F. Couperin's work
    for 224; blend of Italian and French
    styles in work of Muffat 228; work
    of C. P. E. Bach 231; work of W. F.
    Bach 232; work of Mozart 237 *and
    see* piano; work of Haydn 237 *and
    see* piano; popularity in 17th-c
    Hungary 315; production of in 20th
    C 376; *319; see also* individual
    instruments
Khatchaturian, Aram 429; *429*
Khovansky Affair, The (Mussorgsky)
    342, 347
Kikimora (Lyadov) 426
Kilpinen, Yrjö 460
Kinderszenen (Schumann) 279
Kind of Blue (Davis) 521
King, Robert 195
King Arthur (Chausson) 300
King Arthur (Purcell) 195
King Charles's Hunt (Pacius) 459
King David (Honegger) 483
Kingdom, The (Elgar) 448
King Lear (Berlioz) 289
King Priam (Tippett) 452
King's Henchmen, The (Taylor) 442
kinnor 59
Kircher, Athanase 159
Kirchner, Leon 444
Kiriac, Demetri 496-497
kirtān 36
Kiss, The (Smetana) 332
Kitezh (Rimsky-Korsakov) 344, 347
Klami, Unno 460
Klangfarbenmelodie 386
Klavierstücke (Brahms) 326
Klebe, Giselher 411
Kleber, Leonhard 115
Klopstock, F. G. 231, 274, 361
Klose, H. 255
Knipper, Lev 431

Knockin' a Jug (Armstrong) 513
Koango (Delius) 450
Kodály, Zoltán 413, 414, **416**; *416*
Koechlin, Charles 402
Koellreutter, Hans Joachim 480
Koffler, Jozef 462
Kogoj, Marij 495
Kohaut 163
Kolberg, Oskar 310
koliada 335
kolo 495
Komsomol (Knipper) 431
Kondracki, Michal 462
Konjovic, Peter 496
Kontarsky, Alfons 529
Kontarsky, Aloys 529
Konzertmusik (Hindemith) 406
Koppel, Hermann D. 458-459
Koran, the 38, 40
Körner, Theodor 270
Kossuth Overture (Bartók) 414
koto 28, 29; *25, 28, between pp. 32 and
    33; and see* glossary of musical
    instruments
Koureadis, Arghyris 499
Koussevitzky, Serge 444
Kovařovic, Karel 333
Kozeluch, Anton 330
krakovia 306
Krapp, ou la Dernière Bande
    (Mihalovici) 498
Kreisleriana (Schumann) 279
Krek, Gojmir 495
Krenek, Ernst 372, 410, 508
Kreutzer, Rodolphe 287
Krieger, Adam 175, 184, 204
Krieger, Edino 480
Krieger, Johann Philipp 214
Krumpholz J. B. 262
Krupa, Gene 516, 519
Kuhac, Franjo 495
Kuhlau, Friedrich 457
Kuhnau, Johann 197
Kullervo (Ingelius) 459
kuruc 316, 317
Kuula, Toivo 460

Lac, Le (Niedermeyer) 292
Lachrymae (Dowland) 150
Ladislas IV of Poland 306
*Lady Macbeth of Mzensk see Katerina
    Ismailova*
Lady of Shalott, The (Tate) 453
lai see lay
Lajtha, László 416-417
L'Allegro, il Penseroso ed il Moderato
    (Handel) 217
Lalo, Edouard 294, 295-296; *295*
Lamartine, A. M. L. 292, 319
Lambert, Michel 186
Lamentations of Jeremiah (Tallis) 145
Lamothe, Ludovic 476
Landé, Jean-Baptiste 337
Landi, Stefano 169, 175
Landini, Francesco 97, 114, 124, *125*
Landré, Guillaume 492; *493*
langue d'oc dialect, in troubadour
    songs 74
Lanier, Nicholas 193
La Pouplinière 224
L'Apparition de l'église éternelle
    (Messiaen) 405
L'Arlésienne (Bizet) 297
Larsson, Lars Erik 456
L'Ascension (Messiaen) 405
Lasské dances (Janáček) 464
Lassus, Roland de 78, 85, 88, 89, 94,
    107, 115, **118-120**, 121, 127, 129;
    118, 119
Laube, Heinrich 322
Lauber, Joseph 483
laudi spirituali 76, 99, 122-123, 125,
    129-130, 175; *and see* glossary of
    technical terms
lautari 496
Lavalle, Calixa 506
Lawes, Henry 192, 193
Lawes, William 192, 193
lay (*lai*) 70, 71, 74, 75, 76; *and see*
    glossary of technical terms

Layton, Billy Jim 444
Lazar, Filip 498
League of Composers (U.S.A.) 441
Lebendig begraben (Schoeck) 484
Leblanc 256
Le Blanc, Hubert 162
Lechner, Leonhard 120
Leclair, Jean-Marie 165, 220; *226*
Le Flem, Paul 402, 458
Le Franc, Martin 136, 142
Légende de St Christophe, La (d'Indy)
    301
Legend of Ochrida, The (Hristic) 496
Legrenzi, Giovanni 175, 202, 203, 206
Lehár, Franz 413; *413*
Lehrstücke (Hindemith) 406
Leibowitz, René 410
Leich see lay
Leichardt's Grave (Nathan) 503
Leitmotiv 324, 333, 350, 357, 384, 395,
    422; *and see* glossary of technical
    terms
Le Jeune, Claude 111-112, 189; *111*
Lekeu, Guillaume 300, 488
Lendvai, Ernö 415
L'Enfant et les Sortilèges (Ravel) 397;
    397
L'Enfant prodigue (Debussy) 393, 395
Lenin 425
Leningrad Symphony (Shostakovich)
    431, 432
Leo III, Pope 50
Leo X, Pope 137
Leo, Leonardo 207, 209, 210, 211
Leoncavallo, Ruggiere 358
Leonel see Power, Leonel
Léonin 66
Leonine sacramentary 61
Leonora (Fry) 442
Leonora No. 3 (Beethoven) 269
Leopardi Fragments (Davies) 532
Leopold I, Emperor of Austria 170,
    228
Le Roy, Adrien 108, 112, 118, 185
Leroy, Alfred 321
Letters (Berlioz) 290
Levites, the 19-20
Lewis, John 522; *523*
L'Hermite, Tristan 186
L'Heure espagnole (Ravel) 397; *398*
L'Homme Armé (Davies) 532
L'Horizon chimérique (Fauré) 302
Liapunov, Sergey 427
Liatochinsky, B. 429
Libussa (Smetana) 331
*Liberazione di Ruggero dell' Isola di
    Alcina, La* (F. Caccini) 305
Libro di Cifra nueva 139
*Libro del musica de vihuela de mano
    intitulado El Maestro* (Milán) 138
Lichnowsky, Prince 263
Lied, in 16th c 89; of *Minnesänger* 113;
    Hofmaier 114; Senfl 117; Lassus
    119; in 17th-c Germany 183, 184;
    in 18th-c Germany 232; Beethoven
    268; in 18th c 271-272; Reichardt
    271; Haydn 271-272; Mozart 272;
    Schubert 273, 274-275; Schumann
    279-280; Schubert *Lied* introduced
    to French public 287, 291; Brahms
    328-329; Wolf 359; Mahler 360;
    Schoenberg 382; Webern 386;
    Russian (Rachmaninov) 426;
    Danish 457; Finnish (Kilponen) 460;
    Schoek 484; Diepenbrock 491; *and
    see* glossary of technical terms
Liederkreis I (Schumann) 279
Liederkreis II (Schumann) 279
Life and Love of a Woman (Chamisso,
    settings by Schumann) 280
Life for the Tzar, A (Glinka) 344, 346
Ligeti, 528
Lincoln Center for the Performing
    Arts 444
Lincoln Portrait (Copland) 440
L'incoronazione di Poppea
    (Monteverdi) 174; *173*
L'innocenza giustificata (Gluck) 234
Linz symphony (Mozart) 242
Lipatti, Dinu 497, 498; *498*
L'isle joyeuse (Debussy) 394
Lisniski, Vatroslav 495

Liszt, Franz 249, 250, 251, 261, 287,
    289, 291, 292, 297, 307, **317-321**,
    324, 333, 370, 456; *289, 318, 321*
Litanie de la Vierge noire (Poulenc) 401
Lithuanian Rhapsody (Karłowicz) 461
Little Russian symphony
    (Tchaikovsky) 350
Little Symphony for Wind Instruments
    (Gounod) 294
liturgical drama 52, 76, 79, 80, 135, 303
liuti soprani 163
Livre d'orgue (Messiaen) 405
Livre pour quatuor (Boulez) 525
Llanto por Ignacio Sanchez Mejias
    (Ohana) 472
Llivre Vermell 135
Llobet, Miguel 467
Lobo, Duardo 139
Locatelli, Pietro Antonio 205, 212, 338
Lochamer songbook 113
Locke, Matthew 193, 194
Locqueville 90
Lodger, The (Tate) 453
Lodygensky, N. N. 341, 342
Loesser, Frank 442
L'Offrande lyrique (Durey) 402
Lo Frato'n amorato (Pergolesi) 210
Logroscino, Niccolò 210
Lohengrin (Wagner) 270, 319, 322, 324,
    325; *323*
Lombardi alla prima crociata, I (Verdi)
    356
Lonnrot, Elias 459
Lontano (Ligeti) 528
Lorca, Garcia 410
Lorée 256
Loriod, Yvonne 405
Lotti, Antonio 206, 211, 215, 233
Louis XIII of France 154, 160, 185,
    187, 191, 221, 222, 225
Louis XIV of France 153, 154, 161,
    163, 164, 170, 187, 220, 221, 222,
    226; *220, 221*
Louis XV of France 220, 223, 224
Louis Philippe of France 248
Loup, Le (Dutilleux) 404
Louÿs, Pierre 393, 395
Love of Three Oranges, The (Prokofiev)
    428; *428*
Löwe, Johann Carl 271
Löwe, J. J. 197
Lower Rhine musical festival,
    Düsseldorf 276
Low Mass (Fauré) 302
Lucas, *magnus organista* of Tarragona
    135
Lucia di Lammermoor (Donizetti) 354;
    353
Lucier, Alvin 530
Lucifer (Delvincourt) 404
Ludus Tonalis (Hindemith) 407
Ludwig of Bavaria 248, 322
Luening, Otto 444
Luisa Miller (Verdi) 356, 357
Lully, Jean-Baptiste 154, 161-162, 164,
    165, 170, 194, 220, **222**, 224, 226;
    222
Lulu (Berg) 385
Lunceford, Jimmy 516
Luscinius, Othmar 91, 115
lute 39, 56, 57; Spain 39 *and see 'ud*
    and *gunbri*; Arab 39, 40;
    Mediterranean countries 45; in
    15th-c Europe 90; tablatures
    (15th c) 90; technique (15th c)
    90-91; compositions for in 16th-c
    Europe 91, 92; in Henry VIII's
    collection 92; treatises on (16th c)
    92; in ensembles (16th c) 93, 94;
    music for by T. Morley 95;
    tablatures for (16th c) 96, 315;
    published music for (16th c) 112; in
    16th-c Germany 120; tablature for
    (16th-c Germany) 120, 121; in
    Elizabethan England 145, 150;
    compositions of Dowland 150; use of
    in 17th c 160, 161, 163; music for in
    17th and 18th c 163; in 17th-c
    France 185, 186, 190-191; in the
    Chamber (France) 221; music for in
    16th-c Poland 304, 305; music for
    in 16th-c Hungary 315; in 20th c

376; *35, 39, 40, 44, 63, 67, 71, 77, 94, 168, 174, 188, 208; and see* glossary of musical instruments
Luther, Martin 85, 86, 115, 116, 117; *116*
Lutosławski, Witold 373, 462; *462*
Lutyens, Elizabeth 453, 505
luwitra 40
Lux aeterna (Ligeti) 528
Luzzaschi, Luzzasco 128, 176
Lyadov, Anatol 309, 341, 425, 426, 427
Lyon, Gustave 262
lyra da braccio 94; makers of (16th C) 95; in 17th C 159, 160; *94; and see* glossary of musical instruments
lyra viol 162; *and see* glossary of musical instruments
lyre 54, 73; Hebrew *see kinner; and see* glossary of musical instruments
Lyre and Sword (settings by Weber) 270, 271
lyric drama 224-225; *and see opéra-lyrique*
Lyric Pieces (Grieg) 456
lyric songs 74, 75, 76, 77
Lyric Suite (Berg) 384
Lyric Suite (Grieg) 456
Lyrische Stücke (Brahms) 327
Lyssenko, Mykola 429

Macbeth (Bloch) 484
Macbeth (Verdi) 356
MacDowell, Edward 437
Mace, Thomas 195
Machado, Augusto 474
Machado, Raphael Coelho 473
Machaut, Guillaume de 57, 71-72, 73, 88, 97, 98, 99, 100, 330
Macht der Liebe und des Weins, Die (Weber) 270
Mackenzie, Alexander Campbell 447
Macmillan, Ernest Campbell 506
Maconchy, Elizabeth 453
Macuilxochitl 476
macumba 479
Madame Butterfly (Puccini) 358; *358*
Maderna, Bruno 418, 424
Madetoja, Leevi 460
Madman, The (Somers) 508
Madrid Conservatory 468
Madrid Opera 468
madrigal 89, 109; instruments in 93; influence of on French *chanson* 110-111; De Monte 117-118, 127; Lassus 118, 119; transpositions for lute (16th C) 121; Handl 121; of *ars nova* period 123-124; first performance of polyphonic 124; Da Cascia 124; Da Bologna 125; Ciconia 125; golden age in 16th-C Italy 126-129; Arcadelt 127; Willaert 127; De Rore 127; Lassus 127; Palestrina 127, 130; Marenzio 128; Gesualdo 128; Monteverdi 128; solo voice madrigals 128; 'dramatic' madrigal 128-129; in Elizabethan England 146-147; Morley 146; Weelkes 147; Wilbye 147; Frescobaldi 176; in 17th-C England 193; *and see* glossary of technical terms
Madrigali de diversi autori 126
Madrigals for violin and viola (Martinů) 465
Madrigal Society 214
Maeterlinck, Maurice 393, 395, 460
Magalhaes, Felipe de 139
Mager, Jörg 378
Magic Flute, The (Mozart) 235, 243, 244, 338; *243*
Mahillon 256, 258
Mahler, Gustav 248, 250, 359, 360-362, 370, 380, 381
Mainzer, Joseph 445
Maklakiewicz, Jan Adam 462
Makropoulos affair, The (Janáček) 464
Malade Imaginaire, Le (Dupérier) 485
Malawski, Artur 462
Maler, Laux 92, 95
Malherbe 185, 186
Malheur d'Orphée (Milhaud) 401

Malipiero, Gian-Francesco 358, 420, 421; *422*
Malipiero, Riccardo 421-422
Malkin Conservatory of Boston 380
Malarmé, Stéphane 393
Malvezzi, Cristofano 94, 133
mandolin 163; *and see* glossary of musical instruments
mandora, in ensembles (16th C) 94; makers of (16th C) 96; published music for (16th C) 112; in 17th C 163; *and see* glossary of musical instruments
Manelli, Francesco 169
Manelli, Madalena 169
Manfordi 213
Manfred (Schumann) 319
Manfredini Vincenzo 337
Manfred symphony (Tchaikovsky) 350
Manifold, John 502
Manns, August 446
Manon Lescaut (Puccini) 358
Manru (Paderewski) 312
Mantzaros, Nicolas 498
maqam 37
maqama 37
Marais, Martin 162, 165; *225*
Marais, Roland 162
Marazzoli, Marco 169
Marcabru 75
Marcello, Alessandro 206
Marcello, Benedetto 206, 211, 215; *206*
Marcellus II, Pope 130
Marche joyeuse, La (Chabrier) 298
Marchettus of Padua 124, 125
Marching Song of Democracy (Grainger) 504
Marenzio, Luca 128, 133, 172
Maria Grubbe (Hamerik) 458
Maria Theresa of Austria 228, 236
Mariazell mass (Haydn) 240
Marienleben, Das (Hindemith) 406
Mariés de la Tour Eiffel, Les (the 'Six') 401
marimba 375, 479
marimbulla 479
Marinetti, F. T. 419-420
Marini, Biagio 177
Marius, Jean 258
Marlowe, Christopher 145
Marna (Jolivet) 402
Marosszek Dances (Kodály) 416
Marot, Clément 107, 108, 111, 119
Marriage, The (Mussorgsky) 343
Marriage of Figaro, The (Mozart) 217, 244, 338
Marseillaise 285
Marsyas (Diepenbrock) 491
Martenot, Maurice 376, 378
Martin, Frank 375, 411, 486-487; *486*
Martini, Giambattista 211, 230, 287, 338; *211*
Martinů, Bohuslav 400, 464-465
Martyrdom of St Sebastian (Debussy) 386, 395; *396*
Marx, Karl 294
Mary II of England 196
Mascagni, Pietro 358, 420
Mascarade (Nielsen) 458
Masnadieri, I (Verdi) 356
masque 144, 192, 193, 194; *150, 192; and see* glossary of technical terms
Masques (Debussy) 394
Masques (Szymanowski) 462
Mason, Daniel Gregory 435, 437
mass, the 52, 66, 72; *cantus firmus* 88; Ordinary of 88; cyclic 98, 99, 101, 142; unification of 99; Lutheran 116; De Monte 118; Lassus 119; 'parody' mass 121; Handl 121; Hispanic 134; Catalonian 134; in 16th-C England 144; abolition of in England 144; 'cyclic' in 15th-C England 142; in Elizabethan England 148; Byrd 148; evolution in 18th-C Italy 212; Charpentier 222; Haydn 239, 240; Mozart 242, 243; Beethoven 268; Schubert 275-276; Berlioz 290; Rossini 291; cyclic in 16th-C Poland 304; Dvořák 333; *and see* glossary of technical terms
Massenet, Jules 256; *301*

Mass in B minor (J. S. Bach) 199, 201
Massine, Leonide 399, 407
Mastersingers, The (Wagner) 322, 334
Masurgia universalis (Kircher) 159
Matelots, Les (Auric) 401
Mathieu of Vendôme 74
Mathis der Maler (Hindemith) 406
Matrimonio Segreto, Il (Cimarosa) 210
Mattheson, Johann 232
Matton, Roger 509
Mauduit, Jacques 111, 187
Maurice the Learned, Landgrave of Hesse-Kassel 180
Mavra (Stravinsky) 340
Maw, Nicholas 454
Maxfeed (Neuhaus) 530
Maximilian (Milhaud) 401
Maximilian I, Emperor 85, 115; *114*
Maximilian II, Emperor 117
Max-Joseph III, elector of Bavaria 230
Mayr, Giovanni Simone 352
Mazeppa (Liszt) 319, 320
mazurka 304, 306; *and see* glossary of technical terms
Mazurkas (Chopin) 309
Mazzaferrata, Giovanni Battista 204
Mazzochi, Domenico 169
Mazzochi, Virgilio 169
McLuhan, Marshall 530
Meale, Richard 505
Medea (Charpentier) 222
Médecin malgré lui, Le (Gounod) 294
Meditation on a theme by Claude Debussy (Kodály) 416
Mediterranean diptych (d'Indy) 301
Medtner, Nikolay Karlovich 427
Meeresstille, Die (Beethoven) 268
Meeting of automobile and aeroplane, The (Russolo) 420
Méhul, Etienne Nicolas 286, 287; *287*
Meilhac, Henri 294
Meisterlieder 77
Meistersinger 76-77; *120; and see* glossary of technical terms
Melii, Pietro Paulo 163
melodiaria 316
melodrama, in 18th-C Germany 231, 244; of Weber 270; of Moniuszko 310; *and see* glossary of technical terms
Melomimiques (Rebikoff) 427
Melville, Herman 454
Men and Mountains (Ruggles) 441
Mendelssohn, Felix 232, 251, 257, 261, **276-278**, 445, 456 457; symphonic music 277; chamber music and piano works 277; *277*
Mendes, Manoel 139
Men of Blackmoor (A. Bush) 453
Menotti, Gian Carlo 442
Menuhin, Yehudi 497
Mer, La (Debussy) 394-395
Mer, La (Skalkottas) 498
Mebecke, John 145
Mercadante, Giuseppe 384
Merikanto, Oskar 460
meringo 476
Merry Mount (Hanson) 442
Merry Widow, The (Lehár) 413; *413*
Mersenne, Marin 159, 163, 164, 187, 189, 262; *161, 186, 191*
Merulo, Claudio 132; *132*
Mesa (Mumma) 530
Messager, André 292
Messe de la Pentecôte (Messiaen) 405
Messe des Morts (Gossec) 282
Messiaen, Olivier 298, 372-373, 374, 386, 393, 402, 405, 411; *404, 405*
Messiah, The (Handel) 48, 216, 217, 503
Metamorphoses (R. Strauss) 363
Metamorphoses on themes by C. M. von Weber (Hindemith) 407
Metastasio, Pietro 209, 233
Metastasis (Xenakis) 499
Methodius 121
Método de guitarra (Aguado y Garcia) 467
Metternich 248
Metropolitan Opera House, New York 360

Metru, N. 162
Meulemans, Arthur 489
Meyerbeer, Giacomo 230, 248, 250, 287, **291**; *292*
Mexico *see* America, South
Michalowski, Aleksander 311
Michelangelo 126, 127
Mickiewicz, Adam 307, 309
microtonalism 372
Midsummer Marriage, The (Tippett) 452
Midsummer Night's Dream, A (Britten) 452
Midsummer Night's Dream (Mendelssohn) 257, 276, 277
Mielezewski, Martin 305
Mierzwinski, Władysław 311
Mighty Casey, The (W. Schuman) 441
Mignon (Thomas) 292
Mignone, Francisco 480
Migot, Georges 404
Miguiz, Leopoldo 479
Mihalovich, Ödön 318
Mihalovici, Marcel 400, 498
Mikrokosmos (Bartók) 416
Mikrophonie I (Stockhausen) 530, 531
Mikrophonie II (Stockhausen) 530, 531
Milán, Luis 138; *139*
Milhaud, Darius 48, 372, 374, 393, 400, **401**, 402, 480; *400, 401, 440*
'Military' symphony (Haydn) 240
milking songs (Hebrides) 47
Miller, Glenn 516
Miller, Sorcerer, Liar and Matchmaker (Sokolovsky) 338
Milner, Anthony 454
Milton, John 192, 241
Mines of Sulphur, The (Bennett) 454
Minheimer, Adam 310
Minnesänger 50, 74; origins of melodies 76, 113; *and see* glossary of technical terms
Miracle de Théophile 81
miracle play 80, 81-82, 334
Miraculous Mandarin, The (Bartók) 416
Mirecki, Franciszek 310
Miroirs (Ravel) 396
Missa Brevis (Kodály) 416
Missa mappa mundi (Cornago) 136
Missa Papae Marcelli (Palestrina) 130
Missa sine nomine (Palestrina) 48
Missa Solemnis (Casella) 421
Missa Solemnis (Beethoven) 208
Missa Super Maria zart (Obrecht) 105
Mitridate (A. Scarlatti) 209
Mitropoulos, Dimitri 444, 499
Mixtur (Stockhausen) 530
Mixture Trautonium 378
mizaf 38
Mocquereau 64
Moderne Psalmen (Schoenberg) 383
Modern Jazz Quartet 521
Modes de valeur et d'intensités (Messiaen) 373
modinha 479
Moeran, E. J. 451
Moeschinger, Albert 486
Moldau (Smetana) 332
Molière 165, 222
Molt, Theodor 506
Moments (Stockhausen) 412, 529
Mompou, Federico 471
Monade (Pépin) 509
Monasterio, Jesus 467-468
Moncayo, José Pablo 482
Moniuszko, Stanislaw 310, 342; *311*
Monk, Thelonious 523
monody 89, 167, 168, 172, 173, 174, 175, 185, 187; *and see* glossary of technical terms
Monolith (Holmboe) 459
Monostrophe (Werder) 504
Monsieur de Pourceaugnac (Martin) 487
Montéclair, Michel de 225
Montero, José Angel 477
Monteux, Pierre 392
Monteverdi, Claudio 93, 94, 128, 159, 160, 163, 168, 169, 170, **171-174**, 252, 300; *128, between pp. 192 and 193*
Montpellier manuscript 68
Moore, Douglas 441, 442

Morales, Cristobal de 137; *137*
Morales, Melesio 476, 481
Moravian duets (Dvořák) 332
Morel, François 509
Morera, Enrique 469
Moreton Bay 502
Moretus (Poot) 491
Morlaye, Guillaume 112
Morley, Thomas 94, 145, *146*, 147
Morning Heroes (Bliss) 451
Mort de Sardanapale, La (Berlioz) 288
Mort de Virgile, La (Barraqué) 526
Mortelmans, Lodewijk (Louis) 489
Mortensen, Finn 457
Morton, Ferdinand 'Jelly Roll' 514; *514*
Morton, Robert 98, 114, 143
Moscheles, Ignaz 333
Moses and Aaron (Schoenberg) 383; between *pp. 448 and 449*
Mosonyi, Mihály 317·
motet, origins of 66, 67; as secular form 68, 69, 70; isorhythmic in *ars nova* period 71, 72; transcriptions of for instruments 91; performance of in 16th-c Europe 94; revival as liturgical form (15th c) 97, 100-107; 16th-c Germany 118, 119; in Bohemia (16th c) 121; in Italy (14th c) 125; (16th c) 130, 131, 132; in Spain (16th c) 137; in medieval England 140; in 15th- and 16th-c England 143, 144; in the Baroque 156, 174, 180, 188, 189; evolution of in 18th-c Italy 212; in late 17th-c France 223; in late 18th-c France 282; in 16th-c Poland 304
motetus see motet, origins of
Mother, The (Hába) 466
Mother Goose Suite, The (Ravel) 396
Mother of us All, The (Thomson) 440
Mottu, Alexandre 485
Moulinié, Etienne 162, 186, 188
moundongue 476
Mountford, C. P. 500
Movements for piano and orchestra (Stravinsky) 391, 392
Moyle, Alice 500
Mozart, Leopold 165, 237, 241
Mozart, Maria Anna 241-245
Mozart, Wolfgang Amadeus 165, 166, 196, 202, 209, 211, 219, 226, 230, 235, 241, **241-244**, 250, 308; development of symphony form 237; chamber music 237; symphonies 237, 242-243; sonatas 243; church music 243; opera 243-244; works for piano 260; *Lied* 272; *romance* 286; between *pp. 272 and 273, 237, 242*
Mozart and Salieri (Rimsky-Korsakov) 340
mridangam 34
Mudarra, Alonso 139
Muette de Portici, La (Auber) 291
Muffat, Georg 176, 204, 205, 228, 237
Muffat, Gottlieb 229
Müller, Ivan 255
Müller, Matthias 261
Mulliner Book 150
Mumma, Gordon 530
Mundy, William 145
Muses, The (Lully) 222
Muset, Colin 75
Musgrave, Thea 453
Musica Enchiriadis 66
Musica getutscht (Virdung) 91
Musica instrumentalis deudsch (Agricola) 91
Musical Antiquarian Society (England) 446
musical bow (Africa) 21
Musical Offering (J. S. Bach) 198; 201; *Ricecare* of orchestrated by Webern 386, 392
Musical panacea, The (de Monte) 129
Musica Mexicana, La (Chávez) 482
musica naturalis 75
Musica para un Codice Salmantino (Rodrigo) 471
Musica popular brasiliana (Alvarenga) 480
Musica Nova (Willaert) 127

Musica Reservata 375
Musica Teutsch 120-121
Musica Transalpina (Yonge) 146
Musica Viva concerts, Munich 410
Music for an Imaginary Ballet (Grainger) 504
Music for a Soul in Mourning (Escher) 493
Music for solo performer (Lucier) 530
Music for Strings, Percussion and Celeste (Bartók) 375, 416
'music for tape' see electronic music
Music for the Royal Fireworks (Handel) 217
Music in 1960 (Rebikoff) 427
Music in the Renaissance (Reese) 146
Music in two dimensions (Maderna) 424
Musick's Monument (Mace) 195
'Music of Versailles' 220, 224
Music's Recreation on the Lyra viol (Playford) 193
Musikhochschule, Berlin 406
musique concrète 373, 378, 499; *and see* electronic music *and* glossary of technical terms
Musique de Deuil (Oboussier) 486
Mussorgsky, Modest Petrovich 48, 339, 340, 341, 342-343, 346, 347, 371; between *pp. 384 and 385*
Musurgia (Luscinius) 91
Muzicescu, George 496
Myaskovsky, Nikolay Yakovlevich 430
My Country (Smetana) 332
My Lady Nevell's Booke 149, 150
My Old Kentucky Home (Foster) 437
Mystère des Saints Innocents (Barraud) 403
Mystery of the Nativity, The (Martin) 487
mystery plays 81-82, 135, 334
Mysliweczek, Josef 330
Mythe de la Roche Percée (Morel) 509
Myths (Szymanowski) 462

Nabucco (Verdi) 355
Nadermann, François-Joseph 262
nāgasvaram 34
Nageli, Hans Georg 483
Nahowski, Hélène 383
Namouna (Lalo) 295
Napoleão, Artur 473
Napoleon III 248
Napoleon Buonaparte 247, 248
Nārada 33
Nardini, Pietro 207, 213
Nasco, Giovanni 127
Nathan, Isaac 503
Nations, The (F. Couperin) 224
Nātya-Shāstra, the 33
nauba 40
Navarro, Juan 137
Nedbal, Oskar 333
Neefe, C. G. 263
Negro music see America, American music
Negro Rhapsody (Powell) 438
Nekrassov, N. A. 341
Nelson (Berkeley) 452
Nelson mass (Haydn) 241
Nepomuceno, Alberto 479
Neue Zeitschrift für Musik (Schumann) 252, 326
Neuhaus, Max 530
Neumeister, Erdman 179, 199
neumes 62, 65, 74; *and see* notation, origins of
Neuschel, Hans 120
Neusiedler, Hans 121
Neusiedler, Melchior 121
Neusiedler family 315
New England Idylls (MacDowell) 437
New England Psalm Singer, The (Billings) 434
New Music Ensemble, California 529
New Music group of Madrid 472
New Orleans style see jazz
Newton, Sir Isaac 155
New York City Opera 442
New York Philharmonic Orchestra 435

Ney, Napoléon Joseph 292
Nicholas of Radom 304
Nicholson 254
Nidecki, Tomasz 309
Niedermeyer, Louis 292; School of 292
Nielsen, Carl 457; *458*
Nielsen, Riccardo 423
Nigeria see Africa, music of
Nightingale, The (Stravinsky) 388
Night of Torment (Constantinescu) 498
Nights in the Gardens of Spain (De Falla) 470
Nijinsky 389, 395
Nikisch, Artur 360
Nine Preludes (Fauré) 302
Nobilissima Visione (Hindemith) 406
Noces, Les (Stravinsky) 371, 387, 389
Nocturne (Britten) 453
Nocturne (Freedman) 508
Nocturnes (Debussy) 394
Noël des enfants qui n'ont plus de maison (Debussy) 395
Noh theatre 25, 28
Noise of Darkness, the 18
Noneto (Villa-Lobos) 480
Nono, Luigi 418, 424; *423*
Nonsense (Petrassi) 422
Nordraak, Rikard 456
Norfolk Rhapsodies (Vaughan Williams) 450
Norma (Bellini) 354; *355*
North American Time Capsule 1967 (Lucier) 530
North Country Sketches (Delius) 450
Northern Pastoral symphony (Sibelius) 460
North Pacific Indians 18
Norway see Scandinavia, music of
Norwegian Dance (Grieg) 456
Nose, The (Shostakovich) 432
Noskowski, Zygmunt 311, 312; *312*
No song, no supper (Storace) 217
Nostalgia of the Spring (Mozart) 272
notation, musical, Chinese 27; origins and early systems (Europe) 52, 62-63; Hebrew 59; Byzantine 59; invention of new n. in 14th c 70; n. of troubadour and *trouvère* songs 75; *and see* glossary of technical terms
note row 381
Notre-Dame mass (Machaut) 72, 97
Notre Dame, Paris, School of 66
nouba 20
Nourrit, Adolphe 287, 291
Nouvelles Aventures (Ligeti) 528
Novello, Alfred 445
Novello, Vincent 445; *445*
Nowakowski, Josef 309
Now's the Time (Parker) 521
Nozzi di Teti e di Pelso (Cavalli) 166
Nuage gris (Liszt) 321
Nuits d' Eté, Les (Berlioz) 290
Numance (Barraud) 403
Nunnenbeck 77
Nuove musiche, Le (Caccini) 172
nuqayrat 40
Nystroem, Gosta 455; *456*

Oberon (Vranicky) 235
Oberon (Weber) 270
Oberte (Verdi) 355
oboe, in 17th c 161, 162, 164, 165, 166; concertos for (18th-c Italy) 106; oboe d'amore 165, 256; in work of Scarlatti 207; in the Ecurie 221; in the Chamber (France) 221; thirteen-keyed oboe (Sellner) 255; Viennese oboe (Zuleger) 255; improvements by Triebert family 255; Böhm system 255; *and see* glossary of musical instruments
O bone Jesu (Carver) 144
Oboussier, Robert 486
Obrecht, Jacob 103, 105
Occasional Oratorio (Handel) 216
Ockeghem, Johannes 99, **100-102**, 103, 113; *101*
O contratador de diamantes (Mignone) 480
Octavian Fugger II 116
Ode on the Death of Mr Henry Purcell (Blow) 196

Ode to Joy (Schiller) 265, 267
Ode to Napoleon (Schoenberg) 382
Odes and Lieder by Klopstock for Singing to the Clavier (Gluck) 271
Odington, Walter 141
Oedipe (Enesco) 497
Oedipus Rex (Stravinsky) 371, 389; *389*
Offenbach, Jacques 292, 294; *294*
Offering to Siva (Delvincourt) 404
Offertoria (Zieleński) 304, 306
Offrandes Oubliées, Les (Messiaen) 405·
Oginsky 308
Ohana, Maurice 472
Oh! Susanna (Foster) 437
Oiseaux, Les (Diepenbrock) 491
Oiseaux exotiques, Les (Messiaen) 405
Oklahoma (Rogers) 442
Old Black Joe (Foster) 437
Old Hall Manuscript, the 97, 141, 142
oliphant 55
Olivares, Juan Manuel 477
Oliver, Joe 'King' 511, 512; *511*
Olmeda, Frederico 469
Olympians, The (Bliss) 451
Olympic Overture (Douglas) 504
ONCE group 530
Ondes Martenot 376, 402, 405; *377;* *and see* glossary of musical instruments (electronic instruments)
ondes musicales see Ondes Martenot
Ondine (Henze) 411
Ondine (Hoffmann) 269
Ondine (Ravel) 396
On Hearing the First Cuckoo in Spring (Delius) 450
On the Accession of the Emperor Leopold II (Beethoven) 268
On the Death of the Emperor Joseph II (Beethoven) 267-268
On Wenlock Edge (Vaughan Williams) 450
opera 89, 133, 156; first performance in England 154; religious in 17th-c Rome 156, 169 *and see* oratorio; 17th-c Italian 168-174; in Rome (17th c) 169; Italian in Paris (17th c) 169; Venetian (17th c) 170; founding of Hamburg opera 183; in 17th-c Germany 183; in 17th-c England 193-194, 195; in 18th-c Italy 208-211; *opera seria* 208, 209, 234-243; *opera buffa* 209, 210, 225, 244, 287; effect on *opéra-comique* 210, 211; increasing importance of orchestra 209; attitude to in 18th-c England 214, 216; of Handel 215, 216; ballad opera in 18th-c England 217; popularity of in late 17th-c France 222; *opéra-comique* 223, 225, 234, 235, 281, 287, 332; *opéra-lyrique* 224-225; reform of in 18th-c Germany (Gluck) 233-234; role of *Singspiel* in formation of national German style 235; Mozart 243-244; Berlioz 290; Monteverdi 172-174; Beethoven 268-269; Weber 270; Romantic Opera 270; in 19th-c France 291-292, 294; Gounod 294; Bizet 297-298; Italian opera in 17th-c Poland 305; in 19th-c Poland 310; Wagner 322-325; Italian opera in Russia (18th c) 337-338; Glinka and contemporaries 340-341; Mussorgsky 343; Borodin 344; Rimsky-Korsakov 346; Russian 346-348; Rossini 352-354; 19th-c Italy 354; Verdi and successors 355-358; Strauss 363; Berg 384; Stravinsky 389-390; Debussy 395; Hindemith 406, 407; jazz opera (Krenek) 410; Bartók 416; Malipiero 421; Pizzetti 422; Dallapiccola 422; Peragallo 423; Vlad 423; Gretchaninov 427; Thomson 440; in America 442; Tippett 452; Britten 452-453; Searle 453; Bennett 454; Nielsen 458; Janáček 463-464; in 19th-c Spain 468-469; Bloch 484; Martin 487; *and see* glossary of technical terms

Opera and Drama (Wagner) 270, 324, 325
opéra-ballet 223, 225, 281; *and see* glossary of technical terms
opera buffa see opera
Opéra d'Issy (Cambert) 187
'Opera of the Nobility' 216
opera seria see opera
operetta, of Offenbach 294; Moniuszko 310; Lehár 413; Kálmán 413; *and see* glossary of technical terms
Ophélie (Leken) 488
ophicleide 257; *and see* glossary of musical instruments
Opus musicum (Handl) 121
oratorio, origins of 156; in 17th-C Italy 175-176; in 17th-C Germany 180; in 18th-C Italy 209, 211; evolution of in 18th-C Italy 212; Handel 216-217; Charpentier 223; Haydn 239, 241; popularity of in 18th-C England 251; Beethoven 267; Franck 299; Dvořák 333; Honegger 401; Elgar 448; Walton 451-452; Tippett 452; Martinů 466; Burkhardt 485; Vogel 486; Martin 486-487; *216; and see* glossary of technical terms
Orbón, Julián 482
Orchesographie, the 77
Orestes (Milhaud) 401
Orff, Carl 408
Orfeo (Monteverdi) 159-160, 163, 168, 173
Orfeo (Politian) 133
Orfeo (Rossi) 169, 187
Orfeo ed Euridice (Gluck) 156, 234; *234*
organ and organ music 54, 56, 57; tablatures in 15th-C Europe 90, 114, 115; in 16th-C Europe 91; in Henry VIII's collection 92; chamber (16th C) 93; in ensembles (16th C) 94; works (Sweelinck) 107; published music for (16th C) 112; in 15th- and 16th-C Germany 113, 114-115; in 16th-C Italy 132; in 16th-C Spain 137-138; 15th-C England 142; in Baroque Germany 157; in 17th C 159, 160, 161, 163, 164, 176; in 17th-C Germany 179, 180-183; Buxtehude 183; in 17th-C France 189-190; Bach 197, 199, 200, 201; separation from style of harpsichord works (late 17th-C Italy) 202; sonatas for (late 17th-C Italy) 204; Handel 216, 217; F. Couperin 224; Franck 299; in 16th-C Poland 304; Reger 363-364; improvements and alterations (19th and 20th C) 375; Praetorius 375; Royal Festival Hall 375; electronic 378; Messiaen 405; Ligeti 528; *between pp. 112 and 113, 192 and 193, 208 and 209, 189, 197, 198, 375, 379, between pp. 528 and 529; and see* glossary of musical instruments
organetti, makers of 96
organistrum see hurdy-gurdy
organum 52-53, 55, 63, 65-66, 67, 140; *and see* glossary of technical terms
Oriane (Schmitt) 403
Original Dixieland Jazz Band, The 512
Orlande *see* Lassus
O rosa bella (Dunstable) 143
Orphée (Roger-Ducasse) 403
Orpheus (Liszt) 320
Orpheus (Stravinsky) 389; *390*
Orpheus in the Underworld (Offenbach) 294
Ortega, Aniceto 476
Ortiz, Diego 93, 138, 139
oscillator 378, 379
Osiander, Lukas 178
Ospizio della Pietà 206
Ossian (Gade) 457
Osterc, Slavko 495
Ostrovsky, A. N. 340
Oswald, Henrique 479
Otello (Verdi) 355, 356
Otger 66
Ouverture concertante (Enesco) 497
Ouverture Joyeuse (Poot) 491

O Woful Orpheus (Byrd) 149
Oxberg Variations (von Koch) 456

Pachelbel, Johann 183
Pacific 231 (Honegger) 401
Pacini, Giovanni 354
Pacius, Frederick 459
Paderewski, Ignacy Jan 311, 312; *311*
Padmavâti (Roussel) 398
Paganini, Niccolò 389, 354-355
Page from the Apocalypse (Lyadov) 426
Pagliacci, I (Leoncavallo) 358
Paine, John Knowles 435
Paisiello, Giovanni 208, 210, 287, 338, 351; *210*
Paix, Jacob 115
Palacios y Sojo, Pedro 477
Palester, Roman 462
Paléographie musicale 64
Palestrina, Giovanni Pierluigi 48, 63, 88, 102, 107, 120, 127, **129-131**, 174; *130*
Palestrina (Pfitzner) 364
Paliasvili, Z. P. 429
Pallavicino, Benedetto 172
Pallavicino, Carlo 170
Pallieter (Alpaerts) 489
Palm, Siegfried 429
Palmgren, Selim 460
Pan (Pijper) 492
pandora 95, 96; *162; and see* glossary of musical instruments
pandoura 54
Pankiewicz, Eugeniuz 310
panpipes 55, 164, 475; Rumania *see* nai; *95, 478; and see* glossary of musical instruments
Panufnik, Andrzej 463
Pan y toros (Barbieri) 468
Papalounnou, Jean 499
Papandopoulo, Boris 495
Pape, Henri 261, 262
Papillons (Schumann) 278, 279
Papineau-Couture, Jean 509
Papotages (Papineau-Couture) 509
Parable of Death (Foss) 444
Paraboles (Martinů) 465
Parade (Satie) 399
Paradise Lost (Milton) 241
Pareja, Ramos de 136
Paria (Moniuszko) 310
Paris-Alvars, Elias 262
Paris Opera House 248, 291; *246*
Paris, School of 400
Parker, Charlie 521; *520*
Parker, Horatio 437
Parker's Mood (Parker) 521
Parry, Hubert 447; *447*
Parrucca dell' imperatore, La (Peragallo) 423
Parsifal (Wagner) 322, 324, 325, 360
Partita for orchestra (Petrassi) 422
Partita for piano and orchestra (Casella) 421
Pas d'acier (Prokofiev) 428
Pasquini, Bernardo 175, 176, 204
Passacaglia and Gigue (Henkemans) 493
Passacaille (Martin) 486
Passion, in 17th-C Germany 156, 179; of Bach 198, 201; in 18th-C Italy 212; *and see* glossary of technical terms
Passion grecque (Martinů) 465
Passion of Our Lady, The (Tcherepnin) 427
Pastoral (Bliss) 451
Pastorale (Goehr) 454
Pastorale d'été (Honegger) 401
pastorals (Brittany) 47
Pastoral symphony (Beethoven) 265, 320
Pastor Fido (Handel) 215
pastourelle 77, 82; *and see* glossary of technical terms
Paterson, A. B. 'Banjo' 503
Pathétique symphony (Tchaikovsky) 350
Pau Casals Orchestra 468
Paul III, Pope 137
Paul IV, Pope 130

Paul Whiteman Orchestra 513
Paumann, Conrad 114
Pavane pour une infante défunte (Ravel) 396
Pays, Le (Ropartz) 300
Pays de Cocagne (Riisåger) 458
Paz, Juan Carlos 481
Peace of Westphalia 153, 178, 227
Pears, Peter 453
Pedrell, Felipe 468-469
Peer Gynt (Grieg) 456
Peer Gynt suite (Saeverud) 457
Peerson, Martin 192
Peeters, Flor 491; *491*
Peixe, Cesar Guerra 480
Pekiel, Bartlomej 306
Pelléas and Mélisande (Debussy) 395
Pelléas and Mélisande (Schoenberg) 382
Pellegrina, La 133, 160
pelog 30, 31
Penderecki, Krzysztof 463, 528; *463*
Pénélope (Fauré) 302
penillion 47
Penthesilea (Schoeck) 484
Penthesilea (Wolf) 359
Pentland, Barbara 508
Pépin, Clermont 509
Pepin the Short 50
Pepusch, John 217, 218
Peragallo, Mario 423
Performing Group of Cologne 529
Pergolesi, Giovanni Battista 207, 210, 226, 371; *210*
Peri, Jacopo 94, 133, 168, 169
Péri, La (Dukas) 399
Pericic, Vlastimir 496
Perkowski, Piotr 462
Permutazione Sinfoniche (G. Landré) 492
Pérotin 66, 69, 70, 75
Perpessas, Charilaos 499
Perrin, Pierre 194, 222
Persichetti, Vincent 441
pes 141
Pesaro, Domenico de 95
Peter, Johann Friedrich 434
Peter and the Wolf (Prokofiev) 428, 431
Peter Breughel the Elder (Absil) 490
Peter Grimes (Britten) 452
Peter Ibbetson (Taylor) 442
Peterson, Oscar 522
Peter the Great of Russia 155, 337; *336*
Petit elfe ferme l'oeil, Le (Schmitt) 403
Petite Suite (Borodin) 344
Petite Symphonie Concertante (Martin) 486
Petöfi Symphony (Hubay) 413
Petrarch 50, 85, 125, 126
Petrassi, Goffredo 420, 422; *423*
Petridis, Petro 498
Petrini, Francesco 262
Petrucci 108
Petrushka (Rimsky-Korsakov) 345
Petrushka (Stravinsky) 388; *388*
Peyrot, Fernande 485
Pfitzner, Hans 364
Phantoms (Moniuszko) 310
Philharmonic Concerts (Hungary) 317
Philharmonic Society, London 255
Philidor, André Danican 164, 165; *226*
Philip II of Spain 86, 107, 137, 139
Philip the Handsome 105, 106
Philippe, 'Chancellor of Paris' 75
Philips, Peter 146, 150
Philomèle (Andriessen) 492
Phoenix and the Turtle, The (Musgrave) 453
'pianino' 261
piano 198; invention of 203, 258; importance of Clementi 212-213; sonatas of Clementi 213; increasing popularity in 18th-C England 219; favoured as solo instrument in concerto (classical era) 237; work of Mozart 237-238; work of Haydn 237; history of and types in 18th and 19th C 258-261; work of Beethoven 267; 'singing manner' (Dussek) 269; method of Hummel 269; work of Schubert 273; importance as accompaniment in

Schubert *Lied* 274-275; work of Mendelssohn 277-278; work of Schumann 278-279, 280; work of Saint-Saëns 297; work of Chabrier 298; work of Franck 299; work of Fauré 302; work of Chopin 308; work of Paderewski 312; work of Liszt 319, 321; work of Brahms 326-327, 328; importance in Wolf's *Lied* 360; work of Debussy 394; work of Ravel 396; work of Roussel 398; work of Dukas 399; work of Satie 399; work of Messiaen 405; work of Busoni 418-419; work of Rachmaninov 425-426; work of Scriabin 426; work of Gottschalk 437; 'prepared piano' 443; work of Martinů 465; work of Martin 487; as jazz instrument 513-514, 519; 'trumpet-style piano' (Hines) 514, 519; Art Tatum 519; work of Carter 526-527; *258, 259, 260, 264; and see* glossary of musical instruments
Piano concerto (Sauguet) 402
Piano Fantasy (Copland) 440
Piano Pieces number XI (Stockhausen) 412
Picasso, Pablo 387, 388, 399; *between pp. 416 and 417*
Piccini, Niccolò 209-210, 233
Pictures from an Exhibition (Mussorgsky) 341, 343; arranged for orchestra by Ravel 396
Piece in the form of a pear (Satie) 399
Pièces pittoresques, Les (Chabrier) 298
Pièces pour orgue (Franck) 299
pien ch'ing 27
Pierli Houyen (Ysaye) 488
Pierluigi, Giovanni *see* Palestrina
Piero 124
Pierre de Blois 74
Pierrot Lunaire (Schoenberg) 370, 380, 382, 410, 422
Pierrot Players 529
Piet Hein (van Anrooy) 491
Pijper, Willem 492
Pilgrim's Progress, The (Vaughan Williams) 450
Pilkington, Francis 147
p'i-p'a 27, 28; *and see* glossary of musical instruments
pipe 95
Pirineus, El (Pedrell) 469
Pisador, Diego 139
Pisari, Pasquale 211
Piston, Walter 404, 440
Pithoprakta (Xenakis) 499, 527
Pitoni, Giuseppe 211, 212
piyyutim 59
Pizzetti, Ildebrando 420, 422
plainsong 52-53, 54-55, 57, 59, 62, 63-64, 65, 66, 67, 68, 69; origins of 58, 59; themes in *trouvère* and troubadour compositions 73, 75; pre-Norman England 140; Gregorian in Hungarian Church 313; of Russian Orthodox Church (medieval) 336, 339; *and see* Gregorian chant
Plainsong and Medieval Music Society (England) 446
Plainte au loin du faune (Dukas) 399
planctus *see* complaint
Planctus (Abelard) 74
Planer, Minna 322
Planets, The (Holst) 450
Platée (Rameau) 225
Playford, John 193; *193*
Pléiade poets 111, 119
Pleyel 260, 261, 262
Podbielski, Jean 306
Poema del Mio Cid 134
Poème, Le (Chausson) 300
Poème de la forêt (Roussel) 398
Poème roumaine (Enesco) 497
Poem of Ecstasy, The (Scriabin) 246
Poem of Fire, The (Scriabin) 426
poesia per musica 126
Pohjalaisai (Madetoja) 460
Pohjola's Daughter (Sibelius) 460
Poland, Polish music 233; 13th and 14th C 303-304; 15th C 304; 16th C

304; in the Baroque 305-306; Romanticism 307; Chopin 307-309; in the 19th c 309; opera (19th c) 310; late 19th and early 20th c 309-312; 20th c 461-463

Poligonos (Chávez) 481

Polish Blood (Nedbal) 333

polonaise 306; *and see* glossary of technical terms

Polovtsian dances (Borodin) 346

polycounterpoint 373

Polyeucte overture, The (Dukas) 399

'polymelody' 65

polyphony, vocal in African music 23; in Japanese music 28; in folk music of Mediterranean countries 45; in folk music of Central and Eastern Europe 46; early European origins and practice 52-53, 64, 65, 66; of School of Paris 66; secular in 14th c 67 68, 69; in *ars nova* period 70, 71; new euphonious style of (15th c) 88; movement away from in 16th c 89; style of in French *chanson* 109; beginnings of in German song 114; opposition to in 16th-c Bohemia 121; in 13th-c Italian church music 122; in Italian *ars nova* 125-126; in 16th-c Italian madrigal 126; in 16th-c Italian church music 132; in medieval Spain 135; religious and secular in 16th-c Spain 137; in 16th-c Portugal 139; in medieval England 140-141; in 15th-c England 142-143; in Elizabethan England 148, 149; increasing complexity in the Baroque 158; decline of in 17th c 158, 167; in Monteverdi's early church music 172, 174; polyphonic music for violin (17th-c Germany) 183; in 17th-c France 187; in 17th-c English church music 192; influence on Bach's style 199; in 18th-c Italian church music 211; revival of interest in polyphonic church music (19th-c France) 292; in 13th- and 14th-c Poland 303-304; flowering of in 16th-c Poland 304-305; vocal in Hungary (17th c) 314; Vaughan Williams' use of 450; Rubbra's use of 451; Tippett's use of 452; *and see* glossary of technical terms

Polyphony-monody-rhythm (Nono) 424

polyrhythm 373

polytonality 363

Pomo d'Oro, Il (Cesti) 160, 170-171; *171*

Pomone 187

Pomp and Circumstance marches (Elgar) 448

Pompadour, Mme de 223

Ponce, Manuel Maria 481; *481*

Ponchielli, Amilcare 375

Poot, Marcel 491; *490*

Porgy and Bess (Gershwin) 442-443; *between pp. 448 and 449*

Porpora, Nicola 208, 209-210; *209*

Porsile, Giuseppe 228

Porter, Walter 192

Portugal, Marcos 472-473, 479

Portugal, music of 139; 18th c 472-473; 19th c 473; 20th c 474

Posch, Laux 95

Postillon de Longjumeau (Adam) 292

post-serialism 443, 444

Pothier, Joseph 64

Poulenc, Francis 393, 400, 401-402; *403*

Pour le piano (Debussy) 394

Pousseur, Henri 531

Powell, John 438

Power, Leonel 88, 97, 142

Power of Evil, The (Serov) 340

Praetorius, Michael 159, 178, 191; *159, 178*

Praetorius, Jacob 183

Praetorius organ *see* organ

Prague symphony (Mozart) 242

Prairie, The (Foss) 441

Pré-aux-Clercs, Le (Hérold) 292

Prélude à l'après-midi d'un faune (Debussy) 393, 394

prelude and fugue, in 17th-c Germany 178, 181; of Bach 199, 201

Prelude, chorale and fugue (Franck) 300

Prélude élégiaque (Dukas) 399

Préludes (Debussy) 394

Preludes (Fauré) 302

Preludes (Liszt) 319, 320

Preludes (Martin) 487

Prelude to Genesis (Schoenberg) 383

Preziosa (Weber) 270

Price, Henry 477

Price, Jorge W. 477

Prigioniero, Il (Dallapiccola) 422

Prima Donna (Benjamin) 504

prima prattica 172, 174

'Primat' *see* Hugh of Orléans

Prince Igor (Borodin) 340, 344, 346, 347; *344*

Prince of Homburg, The (Henze) 411; *411*

Princesse d'auberge (Blockx) 489

Princesse d'Elide (Lully) 162, 166

Prinses Zonneschijn (Gilson) 489

Printemps (Le Jeune) 111

Prix de Rome 393, 399, 404

Procesion del Rocio, La (Turina) 470

Procurans odium 76

Prodigal Son, The (Animuccia) 130

Prodigal Son, The (Britten) 453

Prodigal Son, The (Prokofiev) 427

Prokofiev, Serge Sergeyevich 340, 347, 348, 367, 371, 372, 374, 427-428, 431; *427*

Promenoir des deux amants, Le (Debussy) 395

Prométhée enchaîné (Emmanuel) 399

Prometheus (Fauré) 302

Prometheus (Jelinek) 409

Prometheus (Liszt) 320

Prometheus (Scriabin) *see Poem of Fire, The*

Prometheus Unbound (Parry) 447

Prophète, Le (Meyerbeer) 291

Proses lyriques (Debussy) 395

Provençal dialect in troubadour songs 74

Provençal lyric 50

Provence 50, 51

Provenzale, Francesco 209

Prozession (Stockhausen) 531

Psalm IX (Petrassi) 422

Psalm CXXX (Schoenberg) 383

Psalm XLVII (Schmitt) 402

psalms, Hebrew 59; Christian 60; settings by Goudimel 111; in 'measured verse' (Le Jeune) 111; polyphonic in Reformation France 111-112; in Reformation Germany 117; in 16th-c Italy 131; in 17th-c Italy 177; in 17th-c France 187, 189; evolution of in 18th-c Italy 212; in 16th-c Poland 304; Puritan (U.S.A.) 433

Psalms and Sonnets (Byrd) 147

Psalms of David (Koppel) 459

Psalmus Hungaricus (Kodály) 416

psaltery 56, 57, 90, 94; *56, 67, 69;* and *see* glossary of musical instruments

Psyche (Lully) 222

Psyche and Eros (Franck) 299

Puccini, Giacomo 357; *358*

Pujol, Emilio 467, 468

Pulcinella (Stravinsky) 371, 387, 389, 390

Purcell, Henry 94, 142, 154, 162, 194, **195-196**, 214, 251; *between pp. 208 and 209*

Purcell Society (England) 446

Puritani, I (Bellini) 291, 354

Puschmann, Adam 77

Pushkin, Alexander 340; *338*

Pygmies 23, 24

Pythagoras 33

qanun 40

Qartsiluni (Riisager) 458

Quam pulchra es (Dunstable) 143

Quantz, Johann Joachim 165, 230-231; *231*

Quatre Eléments, Les (Martin) 487

Quatre études de rhythmes (Messiaen) 372, 405

Queen of Sheba, The (Goldmark) 413

Queen of Spades (Tchaikovsky) 350; *350*

Queen of the Golconda, The (Berwald) 455

Queensland Drover 503

quena flute (Peru) *see* flute

Quilter, Roger 450

Quinault, Philippe 222

qussaba 38

rabab 30; Indonesia 30, 32; Spain 39; Arab 40

Rabindra Sangit 36

Rachmaninov, Serge 348, 425-426, 427

Racine 222

Radicati, F. A. 351

Radjic, D. 496

rāg 17, 27, 34, 35-36; *bilāval* 34, 35; *bhairavi* 35; *megh* 35; *dipak* 35; *and see* glossary of technical terms

Rāga-Vibodha, the 33

rāginis 36

Raimondi, Ignazio 351

Raitio, Vaino 460

rackett 164; *161, 164;* and *see* glossary of musical instruments

Rake's Progress, The (Stravinsky) 390

Rakoczy march 317; Berlioz setting of 317, 354

Rameau, Jean-Philippe 220, 223, 224, **225-226,** 300; *between pp. 224 and 225*

Ramuz, C. F. 389

Ranki, Gyorgy 417

Rape of Lucretia, The (Britten) 452, 453

Rappresentazione dell'anima e di corpo (Cavalieri) 133, 169, 175

Rathaus Karol 462

rattles 375

Raugel, Félix 241

Raupach 337

Ravel, Maurice 48, 255, 290, 292, 297, 301, 343, 371, 372, 388, 393, 395; piano works and chamber music 396; orchestral music 396; vocal music 397; ballet 397, 403; *397*

Ravenscroft, Thomas 147

Rawsthorne, Alan 452

R.C.A. company 378

rebec 56, 57, 90, 92, 96; *61, 74;* and *see* glossary of musical instruments

Rebello, Soares 139

Rebikoff, Vladimir 427

recitative, origins of 89; development of in late 16th-c Italy 133, 156, 167, 168; in 17th-c Italy 169, 170, 172 173, 175; in 17th-c Germany 179; in 17th-c French court ballet 186; in 17th-c England 193, in 18th-c *opera seria* 108-109; developed by Lully 222, 224; reform of (Gluck) 234; in Russian opera 347; *and see* glossary of technical terms

recitativo arioso 360

recitativo secco 234, 244, 363

Reck, David 531

Reconciliation of the Styles, The (F. Couperin) 224

recorder 57; in 15th-c Europe 90; in 16th-c Europe 91; treatises on 93; as sustaining instrument 93; in consorts 93; in 16th-c England 95; in 17th-c 157, 160, 162, 164, 165; in the Chamber (France) 221; revival of in 20th c 376; *71, 164;* and *see* glossary of musical instruments

Récréation concertante (Petrassi) 422

Red Ear of Corn (Weinzweig) 508

Redford, John 144, 150

Red Poppy, The (Glière) 430

Reese, Gustave 146

Reflexion I-IV (Fuyneman) 492

Reformation symphony (Mendelssohn) 277

regal organ, in 17th c 160, 161, 173; *and see* glossary of musical instruments

Regeney, Rudolf Wagner 410

Reger, Max 363-364

Reicha, Antonin 284, 294

Reichardt, J. F. 231-232, 271

Reid, Aquinas 477

Reinhardt, Django 523

Reinken, Jan Adam 183, 197

Reményi, E. 326

Renaissance symphony (Karłowicz) 461

Renard, Jules 396

Renard (Stravinsky) 389

Renovacion musical group 482

Réponse d'une épouse sage (Roussel) 398

Requiem (Fauré) 302

Requiem (Liszt) 320

Requiem (Verdi) 357

Requiem Mass (Berlioz) 288

Residenz theatre, Munich 230

Respighi, Ottorino 420; *420*

'Resurrection' symphony (Mahler) 361

Reszko family 311

Retablo de Maese Pedro, El (De Falla) 470; *472*

Return of Ulysses, The (overture, Skalkottas) 498

Reutter, Johann Georg 229

Revelation and Fall (Davies) 532

Revolutionary Study (Chopin) 247, 309

Revueltas, Silvestre 482; *482*

Rhapsodie Dahomienne (Gilson) 489

Rhapsodie Espagnole (Ravel) 396

Rhapsodies (Brahms) 327

Rhapsodies roumaines (Enesco) 497

Rhapsody in Blue (Gershwin) 442

Rhaw, Georg 116, 178

Rhenish symphony (Schumann) 280

Rhinegold, The (Wagner) 324

Rhythms (Martin) 486

Riabinin 336

ribbon flute (Indonesia) *see* suling

ricercare 94; of Palestrina 130; of A. Gabrieli 132; of G. Gabrieli 132; of Titelouze 189; *and see* glossary of technical terms

Ricerca (Togni) 424

Richard, Etienne 189

Richard III (Smetana) 332

Richard the Lionheart (Grétry) 506

Richelieu, cardinal 154, 190

Richter, Franz Xaver 229, 281, 333; *229*

Rieger, Wallingford 441; *441*

Rienzi (Wagner) 322

Ries, Ferdinand 269

Rigoletto (Verdi) 356, 357

Riisäger, Knudage 458

Rilke, Rainer Maria 359, 406, 486

Rimsky-Korsakov, Nikolai Andreyevich 48, 339, 340, 341, 344-346, 347, 371, 388, 425; *344*

Rinaldo (Brahms) 329

Rinaldo (Handel) 215

Rinascimento musical 474

Ring of the Nibelung, The (Wagner) 322, 324

Rinuccini, Ottavio 133, 168, 173

Rip Van Winkle (Bristow) 442

Riquier, Guiraut 75

Rise and Fall of the City of Mahagonny (Weill and Brecht) 409

rispetti 125

Rite du soleil noir (Pépin) 509

Rite of Spring, The (Stravinsky) 335, 367, 387, 388, 389, 400, 426

Ritorno d'Ulisse in patria, Il (Monteverdi) 174

Ritter, Alexander

Riverrun, The (Searle) 453

Rivier, Jean 404

Roberday, François 189

Robert le Diable (Meyerbeer) 291

Robert of Anjou 124

Roberts, Caroline Alice 448

Robinson, Thomas 150

Robledo, Melchor 138

Robles, Manuel 477

Rob Roy (Berlioz) 289

Rochlitz, J. F. 252

Rodeo (Copland) 440

Rodin, Auguste 393

Rodrigo, Joaquín 469, 471
Rodrigo (Handel) 215
Rodriguez, Esther 482
Roerich, N. 389
Roger-Ducasse, J. J. A. 403
Rogers, Richard 442
Rogneda (Serov) 340
Rohaczewski, Andrej 306
Roi David, Le (Honegger) 401
Roi d' Ys, Le (Lalo) 295
Roi d' Yvetot, Le (Ibert) 404
Roland-Manuel 403
Roldán, Amadeo 482
Rolland, Romain 484
Rollins, Sonny 523
Roman, Johan Helmich 455
Roman Carnival (Berlioz) 289
romances 136, 139, 281, 286-287
Romances (Brahms) 327
Roman de Fauvel, the 70
Roman de Guillaume de Dole 77
Roman Pines (Respighi) 420
Romanzen aus Magelone (Brahms) 329
Romberg, A. 213
Romeo and Juliet (Berlioz) 289
Romeo and Juliet (Prokofiev) 428, 431
Romeo and Juliet (Tchaikovsky) 350
rommelpot 43
rondeau 69, 70, 72, 73; structure of 74; in liturgical drama 76; in dance 77, 89; by Dufay 100; by Binchois 101; by Busnois 103
rondet de carole see dance, round
rondo-sonata form 265
Ronsard, P. de 111, 119
Ropartz, Joseph Guy 300
Rosa, Juventino 476
Rosaura, La (A. Scarlatti) 209
Rosbaud, Hans 383
Rose, John 96
Roseingrave, Thomas 218
Rosen, Jelka 449
Rosenberg, Hilding 455
Rosenkavalier, Der (Strauss) 363; *364*
Rosenmuller, Johann 184
Rosenthal, Manuel 403
Rosseter, Philip 147
Rossi, Luigi 169, 174, 187
Rossi, Michelangelo 176, 204
Rossi, Salomon 177
Rossini, Gioacchino Antonio 210, 284, 287, 291, **352-354**; *351*
Rostropovich, Mstislav, 453; *453*
rote 54, 56
Rousseau, Jean-Jacques 226, 231, 235
Roussel, Albert 301, 371, **397-398**, 458, 464; *398*, *400*
Royal Academy of Dancing (France) 220
Royal Academy of Music (England) 447
Royal Academy of Music (France) 220, 221, 225
Royal Choral Society (France) 292
Royal College of Music (England) 450
Royal Society of Musicians (England) 218
Różycki, Jacek 306
Różycki, Ludomir 461, 462
Rubbra, Edmund 451, 505
Rubezahl (Weber) 370
Rubinstein, Anton 310, 341, 348, 349; *340*
Rubinstein, Nicolas 341
Ruckers, Andries 95
Ruckers, Hans 95; *148*
Ruckers, Johannes 95
Rudolf II, Emperor 118, 120, 331
rudra-vina 19
Ruffo, Vicenzo 127, 128
Ruggles, Carl 440-441
'Rule, Britannia!' (Arne) 218
Rules for the realisation of a basso continuo (Giordani) 205
Rumania, music of 496-498
Rupsch, Conrad 116
Russia, music of 334-335; folk song 335-336; sacred song 336; epic song 336; beginnings of art music 336-337; Italian musicians in Russia

337-338; 18th C 339-341; 19th C 341-346; opera 346-348; Tchaikovsky 348-350; early 20th C 425-432; Prokofiev 427-429
Russia (Balakirev) 342
Russian bassoon 256
Russlan and Ludmilla (Glinka) 339, 340, 344
Russo, Bill 522
Russolo, Luigi 420
Rust, Friedrich Wilhelm 243
Rustle of Spring (Sinding) 457
Rutebeuf 81
Rutkowski, Antoni 310
Ruysbroeck, Jan Van 98

Sabbatini, Luigi Antonio 211
Sabinus (Gossec) 281
Sabre Dance (Khatchaturian) 429
Sacchini, Antonio 208
Sacher, Paul 486
Sachs, Curt 54
Sachs, Hans 77
sackbut 57; in 15th-C Europe 90; in ensembles (16th C) 92, 93; as continuo instrument (16th C) 94; music for by G. Gabrieli 95; in 16th-C Germany 120; in 17th C 159, 160, 161, 164, 173, 174; *166*; and see glossary of musical instruments
Sacrae Symphoniae (G. Gabrieli) 132, 133
Sacra rappresentazione, Job (Dallapiccola) 422
Sacrati, Francesco 187
Sacred Ballet, A (Stravinsky) 392
Sacred Harp 437
Sacrifice of Isaac, The (Fortner) 410
Sadko (Rimsky-Korsakov) 346, 347
saetas 45
Saeverud, Harald 457
Safi al-Din 39
sagas (Norse) 73
Saibara songs (Japan) 28
Saint-Amand, Hucbald de 66
St Ambrose 60; *60*
St Augustine 60, 140
St Cecilia Ode (Blow) 196
St Cecilia Ode (Handel) 217
St Elizabeth (Liszt) 320
St Francis of Assisi, hymns of 123
St Gelasius 61
St Gregory I, Pope 49, 52, 61; *61*
St Ignatius Loyola 153
St Isidore 134
St John Passion (Bach) 198, 201
St John's Night on the Bare Mountain (Mussorgsky) 343
St Luke Passion (Penderecki) 463
St Martial of Limoges, Abbey of 66
St Matthew Passion (Bach) 199, 201, 232; edited and conducted by Mendelssohn 276; first performed in Australia 503
St Matthew Passion (Sebastiani) 179
St Michael (Davies) 532
St Paul (Mendelssohn) 276
St Paul's Suite (Holst) 450
St Philip Neri 129-130, 137, 156, 175
Saint-Requier, Micon de 74
Saint-Saëns, Camille 292, 294, **296-297**, 320, 374; *296*
Sakuntala Overture (Goldmark) 413
Sala, Oscar 378
Salamine (Emmanuel) 399
Salas, Juan Orego 480
Saldoni, Baltasar 468
Salieri, A. 263, 318
Salome (R. Strauss) 363
Salon Mexico, El (Copland) 440
Salutatio Angelica (Milner) 454
Samaras, Spiros 498
Samaveda, the 33
samba 479
samisen 28; *29*; and see glossary of musical instruments
Sammartini, Giuseppe 212, 233
Samson (Corelli) 204
Samson and Delilah (Saint-Saëns) 296; *296*
San Cassiano theatre, Venice 169, 170

Sances, Felice 169
Sancta Susanna (Hindemith) 406
Sand, Georges 308; *307, 308*
Sandrin, Pierre 119
Sangita Makarandah, the 33
Sangita-Ratnakāra, the 33, 36
sansa 22; and see glossary of musical instruments
Sanskrit drama, Indonesian adaptation 30
Santero, Claudio 480
santur 40
sarangi 34
Sarabande for chorus (Roger-Ducasse) 403
sārangi 34
Sarcasmes (Prokofiev) 428
Sarka (Fibich) 333
sārod 34; and see glossary of musical instruments
saron 30, 32
Sarti, G. 338
Sarum rite, role of in English church music 140
Satie, Erik 301, 371, 372, 393, **399**, 402; *399*
Saudades do Brasil (Milhaud) 401
Sauguet, Henri 402
Saul (Handel) 217
Saul and David (Nielsen) 458
Saul and David (Wagenaar) 491
Savanarola, G. 126
Savane, La (Gottschalk) 437
Savin, Risto 495
Savitri (Holst) 450
Sax, Adolphe 256, 258
Sax, C. 255
saxhorns 258
saxophone 256; jazz (Young) 517, 518 (Hawkins) 517, 518 (Hodges) 518 (Carter) 518; *256*; and see glossary of musical instruments
Sayn-Wittgenstein, Princess Caroline 319
Scandinavia, music of, Sweden (18th-20th C) 455-456; Norway (19th-20th C) 456-457; Denmark (19th-20th C) 457-459; Finland (19th-20th C) 459-460; Sibelius 459-460
Scaramouche (Milhaud) 401
Scarbo (Ravel) 396
Scarlatti, Alessandro 165, 175, 205, 207, 209;
Scarlatti, Domenico 157, 203, 205, 207, 209, 218, 237, 251; *207*
Scarlet Letter, The (Damrosch) 442
Scenes from town and village (Mussorgsky) 343
Schaeffer, Myron 508
Schaeffer, Pierre 373, 378; *378*
Schaeffner, André 54
Schaubankes, Fredericus 113
Schedelscher songbook 113
Schéhérézade (Ravel) 396
Scheherezade (Rimsky-Korsakov) 346; between pp. *384 and 385*
Scheidemann, Heinrich 183
Scheidt, Samuel 180, 181, 183; *181*
Schein, Johann Hermann 178, 180, 181, 184
Schelomo (Bloch) 484
Schenk, Johann 235
Scherchen, Hermann 383, 410
Scherbatchov 341
scherzo 204, 250, 273; of Chopin 309; of Brahms 325; and see glossary of technical terms
Scherzo capriccioso (Dvořák) 332
Schikaneder, E. J. *237*
Schiller, F. von 265, 271, 274, 319, 357
Schlick, Arnolt 114-115, 120
Schmid, Bernhard 115
Schmitt, Florent 402-403
Schmitz, Robert 508
Schobert, Johann 231
Schoeck, Othmar 484
Schoenberg, Arnold 300, 360, 361, 370, 372, **380-383**, 385, 386, 400, 410, 415, 416, 422, 432, 524; *381, 382*
Schola Cantorum, The 63, 300
Schöne Müllerin, Die (Schubert) 275
School of Arcueil 399, 402
School of Paris 400

Schop, Johann 184
Schroter, Gottlieb 259
Schubart, C. F. D. 271
Schubert, Franz 207, 250, 269, 271, 328; piano works and chamber music 273; *Lied* 274-275, 287; symphonies 275; religious music 275-276; *274*
Schulkomödie 235
Schuller, Gunther 439, 442, 444, 522
Schulz, Johann 271
Schuman, William 441
Schumann, Clara 326; *278*
Schumann, Robert 252, 278, 309, 328; works for piano 261, 278-279; *Lied* 279-280; chamber music 280; symphonies 280; music criticism 290; *278, 280*
Schütz, Heinrich 94, 132, 160, 165, 178, 179, **180**, 181, 183, 184, 197, 227, 233, 252; *180*
Schwanengesang (Schubert) 275
Schwarzwald trio (Brahms) 328
Schweigsame Frau, Die (Strauss) 263
Schweizer Familie, Die (Weigl) 235
Scotland, folk music 47
Scott, Sir Walter 249, 250
Scottish Concerto (Mackenzie) 447
Scottish Dance Suite (Musgrave) 453
Scottish symphony (Mendelssohn) 277
Scott of the Antarctic, film music (Vaughan William) 450
Scriabin, Alexander Nikolayevich 309, 348, 370, **426**; *425*
Sculthorpe, Peter 505; *505*
Sea, The (Fitelberg) 461
Sea, The (Glazunov) 425
Sea Drift (Delius) 450
Searle, Humphrey 453
Seasons, The (Haydn) 236, 238, 241
Sea Symphony, A (Vaughan Williams) 450
Seaven passionate Pavans (Dowland) 149
Sebastiani, Johann 179
seconda prattica 172, 174
Secret, The (Smetana) 332
Secret of the Muses (Vallet) 163
Sedulius Scottus 74
Segovia, Andres 467; *468*
Sehnsucht 243
Seiber, Matyas **451**, 505
Sei cori di Michelangelo il Giovane (Dallapiccola) 422
sequence, the 52, 63, 66, 67, 70
Sella, Giorgio 96
Sella, Matteo 96
Sellner 255
Selva, Blanche 485
Sembrick-Kochanska, Marcelina 311
Senfl, Ludwig 115, 116, 117, 121; *117*
Serenade (Roussel) 398
Serenade, Opus 24 (Schoenberg) 382
Serenade for Strings (Wiren) 456
Seranade for tenor, horn and strings (Britten) 453
Serenade for the Prince of Stigliano (Scarlatti) 207
Serenade (Petrassi) 422
Serenata, La (Cesti) 160
serial method and compositions 373-374, 381, 400, 415; Boulez 373; Stockhausen 373, 529; Schoenberg 380; Berg 386; Webern 386; Stravinsky 390, 391-392; Jelinek 409; Hartmann 409; Krenek 410; Dallapiccola 422; Petrassi 422; Nielsen 424; Togni 424; Maderna 424; Berio 424; Nono 424; in America 443-444; Schuller 444; Foss 444; Searle 453; in Poland 463; in Chile 480; in Argentina 481; Bloch 484; in Belgium 491; Skalkottas 498; Xenakis 499; Banks 504; Morel 509; in Canada 509; and see glossary of technical terms
Sérieuse, La (Berwald) 455
Sermisy, Claudin, de 93
Serocki, Kazimierz 463
Serov, Alexander 340
serpent 256; and see glossary of musical instruments

serpent Forveille 256
Serrana (Keil) 474
Serse (Handel) 216
Serva Padrona, La (Cimarosa) 281
Serva Padrona, La (Pergolesi) 210, 226
Service sacré (Milhaud) 401
Sessions, Roger 440, 441
setar 40
Seven Last Words from the Cross (Haydn) 241
Seven Songs for the Harpsichord (Hopkinson) 434
Sforza, Galeazzo Maria 105
Shadow of Cain, The (Searle) 453
Shadwell, Thomas 193
shahnāi 34
Shah-Senem (Glière) 430
shape-note music 437; 437
Shapero, Harold 441
Shārangadeva 33
Sharp, Cecil 446
Shaw, Artie 516
shawm 20, 55, 56, 57; China 27; Arab 40, and see surnay; Mediterranean countries 45; Hebrew 59; in 15th-c Europe 96; in ensembles (16th c) 92; in collections 92; in 17th c 157, 160, 161, 164, 165; in 20th c 378; 45, 48, 55, 73, 90, 123, 161, 162, 478; and see glossary of musical instruments
sheng 19, 27, 28; 27, between pp. 32 and 33; and see glossary of musical instruments
Shepherd, John 145
Shepherd King, The (Galuppi) 338
Shevtshenko, T. 429
Shield, William 217
sho 28; and see glossary of musical instruments
shofar 58, 59; 58; and see glossary of musical instruments
Short Solemn Mass (Rossini) 291
Short Symphony (Copland) 440
Shostakovich, Dmitri 340, 347, 348, 367, 374, 431, 432, 458; 430, 431, 432
Sibelius, Jean 459-460; 459
Siciliano, Antonio 96
Sicilianos, Yorgos 499
Sicilian Vespers (Verdi) 291, 356
Siege of Corinth (Rossini) 353
Siege of Rhodes, The 193, 194
Siegmeister, Elie 441
Siete Canciones (De Falla) 470
Sigismund I of Poland 304
Sikorski, Kazimierz 462
Silbermann, Gottlieb 259
Silence (Cage) 532
Silvana (Weber) 270
Silvestre de Mesa, Grigorio 139
Silvestri, Constantin 498
Simeon Kotko (Prokofiev) 428
Simon Boccanegra (Verdi) 356
Simpson, Thomas 193
Sinding, Christian 457
sinfonia 157, 177, 203, 207; and see glossary of technical terms
Sinfonia (Davies) 532
Sinfonia (Musgrave) 453
Sinfonia (Van Baaren) 493
Sinfonia breve (Nystroem) 455
Sinfonia concertante (Ibert) 404
Sinfonia Concertante (Szymanowski) 462
Sinfonia concertante for piano (Jelinek) 409
sinfonia da chiesa 176
Sinfonia da Requiem (Britten) 452
Sinfonia del mare (Nystroem) 455
Sinfonia Domestica (R. Strauss) 363
Sinfonia espansiva (Nielsen) 458
Sinfonia espressiva (Nystroem) 455
Sinfonia for Two Orchestras (Hamilton) 454
Sinfonia India (Chávez) 481
Sinfonia proletaria (Chávez) 481
Sinfonia sacra in memoriam patris (G. Landré) 492
Sinfonia semplice (Nielsen) 458
Sinfonia di concerto grosso (A. Scarlatti) 207

Sinfonietta (Janáček) 464
Sinfonietta (Roussel) 398
Singakademie, Vienna 232, 276, 325
Singers of St Gervais, the 63
Singspiel 211, 229, 232; origins of and role of in German operatic style 235, 243; style of in Magic Flute 244; songs by Beethoven for 268; of Weber 270; spirit of in Viennese Lied 271; of Schubert 273; and see glossary of technical terms
Singulière, La (Berwald) 455
sirventes 303
Sita (Holst) 450
sitar 20, 34; 34; and see glossary of musical instruments
Sitsky, Larry 505
Sitwell, Edith 451, 453
'Six', the 300, 371, 372, 393, 399, 400-402, 464
Six Adagios for orchestra (Pijper) 492
Six Bagatelles (Webern) 386
Six canonic studies (Schumann) 261
Six épigrammes symphoniques (Pijper) 492
Six Pieces for large orchestra (Webern) 386
Six sketches (Schumann) 261
Skalkottas, Nikos 495, 498; 499
Skerjanc, Lucijan-Maria 495
Sketch of a New Esthetic of Music (Busoni) 418
slaater 456; Grieg 457
Slavenski, Josip 495
Slavonic Dances (Dvořák) 332
Sleeping Beauty (Tchaikovsky) 350
slendro 30, 31
Smetana, Bedřich 249, 331; 330
Smith, Bessie 514, 519; 515
Smith, Willie 'the Lion' 514
Smithson, Harriet 288, 289
Smyth, Ethel 453
Snow Maiden, The (Rimsky-Korsakov) 346
Snow Storm, The (Vassilenko) 430
Sociedad Bach (Chile) 480
Société des concerts du Conservatoire 287
Society for Concerts of Religious and Classical Vocal Music (France) 292
Society of Jesus 153
Socrates (Satie) 399
Soirs (Schmitt) 402
Sokolovsky 338
Soldier's Tale, The (Stravinsky) 389
Soleil, Le (Boulez) 525
Solér, Antonio 207
Solesmes, monastery 63, 64
Solti, Georg 383
Solveig's song (Grieg) 457
Somanātha 33
Somers, Harry 508; 508
Somis, Giovanni Battista 205
sonata 157, 163, 164, 167, 176, 177; church sonata (sonata da chiesa) 167, 177, 202, 204, 205; chamber sonata (sonata da camera) 167, 177, 202, 205, 228; solo sonata 177, 200, 203, 204, 207; trio sonata 177, 194, 195, 196, 202, 204, 205; of Purcell 195, 196; of Bach 200-201; with basso continuo 202; bithematic 202; stabilisation of number of movements 203; of Clementi 203; of Corelli 204, 205; of Veracini 204; of Vivaldi 206; in 18th-c Italy 206; of A. Scarlatti 207; of D. Scarlatti 207; of Clementi 213; of Cherubini 213; of Boccherini 213; of Handel 217; of Boyce 218; replaces suite in popularity (18th-c Germany) 228; of Mannheim school 229; first movement sonata form 237; development of in classical era 237; of J. C. Bach 237; of Mozart 237-238, 243; of Haydn 237-238; of Beethoven 238, 267; of Schubert 273; of Franck 299; of Chopin 309; of Brahms 326; of Reger 363; of Bartók 416; of Kodály 416; of Glazunov 425; of Scriabin 426; of Martin 486; of Badings 493; and see glossary of technical terms

Sonata (Martinů) 465
sonata da camera see sonata
sonata da chiesa see sonata
Sonata for Chamber Orchestra (Hamilton) 454
Sonata per archi (Henze) 411
Sonata pian e forte (G. Gabrieli) 132
Sonates (Debussy) 394
Song of Deborah, the 58
Song of Miriam, the 58
Song of Roland 73
Song of Songs (Daniel-Lesur) 402
Song of the Earth, The (Mahler) 360, 362
Song of the Falcon (Fitelberg) 461
Song of the Forests, The (Shostakovitch) 432
Song of the High Hills, A (Delius) 450
'Song of the Night' symphony (Mahler) 361-362
Songs and dances of death (Mussorgsky) 343
'Songs from Prison' (Dallapiccola) 422
Songs of Farewell (Parry) 447
Songs of Sundrie Natures (Byrd) 148
Songs of Zion 437
Songs without Words (Mendelssohn) 277
Sonic Arts Group, New York 529
Sonnambula, La (Bellini) 354
Sonnets of the Crimea (Moniuszko) 310
Sonnleithner, J. von 269
Sor, Fernando 218, 467
Sorcerer's Apprentice (Dukas) 399
Soto de Langa, Francisco 138
Souris, André 490
Southern Harmony 437
sou youe 25
Space Ritual (Morel) 509
Spain, music of; Moorish see Islam; medieval 134-135; sources of 135; polyphony in medieval S. 135; influence of France and Italy in 15th c 135-136; in 16th c 137 Andalusian school 137; Castilian school 138; Aragon school 138; instrumental music in 16th c 138-139; 19th and 20th c 467-469; 471-472; revival of regional schools 469; De Falla and Turina 470-471; later 20th c 472
Spalicek (Martinů) 465
Spanisches Liederbuch (Wolf) 359
Spanish Capriccio (Rimsky-Korsakov) 346
Spartacus (Khatchaturian) 429
Spem in alium (Tallis) 145
Spencer, Baldwin 500
Sphärophon 378
Spinacino 91
spinet 57; in 15th-c Europe 90; in collections (16th c) 92; in ensembles (16th c) 93; in consorts 93; makers of (16th c) 95; and see glossary of musical instruments
Spohr, Ludwig 251, 445
Sponsus, the 76, 80, 81
Spontini, Gasparo 234, 251, 287, 351-352
Sprechgesang 360, 382, 384
Spring (Glazunov) 425
springar 456
Spring day in the mountains (d'Indy) 300, 301
Squarcialupi, Antonio 98, 115
Stabat Mater (Berkeley) 452
Stabat Mater (Rossini) 291, 353
Stamitz, Johann 213, 224, 229, 230, 238
Stanford, Charles 447; 447
Stanley, John 218
Starzer, Joseph 236, 238
Stassov, Vladimir 341, 342, 388
Statements for orchestra (Copland) 440
Stefanescu, George 496
Steffan, J. A. 271
Steffani, Agostino 170, 211, 215, 230
Stegreifkomödie 235
Stein, Andreas 259
Stein, Erwin 505
Stein, Gertrude 440

Steinway 260, 261
Steinweg 260
Stenka Razin (Glazunov) 425
Steppes, The (Noskowski) 312
Stereophony (Somers) 508
Sternefeld, Daniel 491
Stil galant 227, 228, 231
Still falls the rain (Britten) 453
Stockhausen, Karlheinz 373, 378, 411-412, 523, 529-531; 528
Stodart 261
Stölzel, Heinrich 253, 257
Stone Flower, The (Prokofiev) 428
Stone Guest (Dargomizsky) 340
Storace, Nancy 217
Storace, Stephen 217
Storia di una Mamma (Vlad) 424
Strabo, Walafrid 74
Stradella, Alessandro 170, 174, 175-176, 205
strambotto 126
Strauss, Franz 362
Strauss, Johann 248; 327
Strauss, Richard 300, 362-363, 370 380; between pp. 384 and 385, 400
Stravinsky, Igor 201, 300, 335, 348, 367, 371-372, 373, 374, chapter pp. 387-392, 424, 430; 387, 389, 391, 392
Stretblow, T. G. H. 500
Striggio, Alessandro 128, 133, 173
String Trio (Webern) 386
Strophic Structure of Hungarian folk songs (Kodály) 416
Strozzi, Pietro 133
Studies on a Theme of Paganini, I and II (Schumann) 278
Studio di Phonologia, Milan 378
Sturm und Drang 213
style brillant 308
style galant 227, 228, 231, 236, 308
style galant alla polacca 235
Such Sweet Thunder (Ellington) 518
Suisse Romande Orchestra 485
Suite Canadienne (Champagne) 509
Suite Provençale (Milhaud) 401
Suites Bergamasques (Debussy) 394
Sulek, Stevan 495
suling flute 31, 32
Sullivan, Arthur 446-447; 446
Sul Ponte di Hiroshima (Nono) 424
Sumer is icumen in 140-141
Summer Night in Madrid (Glinka) 340
Summer Night on the River (Delius) 450
Sunda Isles 19
Sunday in Brooklyn (Siegmeister) 441
Sunday Sing Symphony (Green) 441
Sun Music (Sculthorpe) 505
surnay 38
'Surprise' symphony (Haydn) 239
Survivor of Warsaw, A (Schoenberg) 382
Susannah (Floyd) 442
Susato, Tielman 108
Susato of Antwerp 110
Suter, Hermann 483
Sutherland, Joan 505
Sutherland, Margaret 504
Sutter's Gold (Goehr) 454
Svendsen, Johan 457
Swan Lake (Tchaikovsky) 350; 358
Swan of Tuonela, The (Sibelius) 460
Swans, The (Raitio) 460
Sweden, see Scandinavia, music of
Sweelinck, Jan Pieterszoon 107, 115, 107, 150, 176, 183; 107
Swiss Alps 17
Switzerland, music of, German choral tradition 483; French Swiss musical revival 483; German Swiss (19th and 20th c) 484, 485; Bloch 484-485; Martin 486
Sydeman, William 444
Sydney Conservatorium 504
Sylvania Electronic Systems 530
Symphonia Brevis (Jelinek) 409
Symphonic Dances (Grieg) 456
Symphonic music (Flothuis) 493
symphonic poem, Liszt 250-251, 319, 320; Smetana 332; Rimsky-Korsakov 346; Tchaikovsky 350;

Strauss 363; Glazunov 425; Rachmaninov 425; Scriabin 426; Berwald 455; Nielsen 458; Sibelius 460; Beck 486; *and see* glossary of technical terms
Symphonic Rhapsody (Turina) 470
Symphonic Variations (Dvořák) 332
Symphonic Variations (Franck) 299
Symphonic Variations (Hamilton) 454
symphonie concertante form 281
Symphonie concertante (Jongen) 488
Symphonie de chambre (Enesco) 497
Symphonie Espagnol (Lalo) 295, 296
Symphonie Fantastique (Berlioz) 288, 289
Symphonie Funèbre et Triomphale (Berlioz) 289
Symphonie printanière (Chevreuil) 491
Symphonies pour les soupers du roi 225
symphony 157; origins of 202, 203, 207; of Stradella 205; Vivaldi 206; introduction of minuet into 206; in 18th-c Italy 208; Clementi 213; Cherubini 213; Boyce 218; Mannheim school 229; development in classical era 237, 243; Haydn 237, 239, 240; Mozart 237, 242-243; Beethoven 237, 265; development of (Beethoven) 250; development in the 19th c 250; Schubert 275; Mendelssohn 277-278; Schumann 280; in late 18th-c France 281; Berlioz 289; Brahms 326, 328; Bruckner 329; Dvořák 332; Tchaikovsky 350; Mahler 360, 361-362; Stravinsky 390; Glazunov 425; Rachmaninov 425; Shostakovich 432; Elgar 448; Vaughan Williams 450; Rubbra 451; Berwald 455; Rosenberg 455; Nielsen 458; Sibelius 460; Beck 485; Martin 486; Pijper 492; Enesco 497; *and see* glossary of technical terms
Symphony for a City (Antill) 504
Symphony for Voices (Williamson) 505
Symphony in Three Movements (Stravinsky) 371
Symphony of Psalms (Stravinsky) 390, 391
Symphony on a French montagnard's song (d'Indy) 300, 301
Symphony on a Hymn Tune (Thomson) 440
Syntagma musicum (Praetorius) 159
Synthétiste group 490, 491
Syrmos (Xenakis) 527
Szabelski, Boleslaw 461
Szabo, Ferenc 417
Szarzynski, Stanislas Sylvestre 306
Szeluto, Apollinary 461
Szervansky, Endre 417
Szymanowski, Karol 309, 461, 462; *462*

tabor 55, 56, 57, 95; *78, 90; and see* glossary of musical instruments
Tableaux (Freedman) 508
tablā bāyan 34
tafsil 46
Tagelied see alba
Tagore, Rabindranath 36
tagwid 40
tāl, the 35, 36; *haptāl* 36; *sultāl* 36; *vishnutāl* 36; *and see* glossary of technical terms
Tale of Two Cities, A (Benjamin) 504
Tales of Hoffmann (Offenbach) 269, 294
Taillefer, Germaine 400, 402
Tallis, Thomas 144-145, 148, 149, 150; *145*
tambourine 56, 77; *20, 38; and see* glossary of technical terms
Tamil peoples 17
Taming of the Shrew, The (Wagenaar) 491
Tancredi (Rossini) 352
Taneyev, Sergey 425, 427
Tannhäuser (Wagner) 319, 322, 324; *325*
tānpurā (tamburā) 34, 35
Tan Sen 35
Tansmann, Alexander 400, 462

tapan 45
Tapiola (Sibelius) 460
tar 40
taragota 316
Tarantella (Demarquez) 404
Taras Bulba (Janáček) 464
Tarp, Svend Erik 458
Tarrega, Francisco 467
Tartini, Giuseppe 202, 205, 206-207
Tate, Henry 504
Tate, Phyllis 453
Tatum, Art 519, 522
Taucher, Der (Schiller, setting by Schubert) 275
Taverner, John 144
Taylor, Deems 442
Tchaikovsky, Piotr Ilyitch 340, 347, **348-350**, 425, 460; *349*
Tcherepnin, Alexander 400, 427
Tcherepnin, Nikolay 427
Teagarden, Jack 512, 513, 519; *518*
Technique de mon langage musical (Messiaen) 405
Te Deum, in late 17th-c France 225; of Haydn 240; of Berlioz 390; Dvořák 333; Kodály 416
Te Deum (Berlioz) 290
Te Deum (Kodály) 416
Telemann, Georg Philip 183, 198, 215, 225, 231, **232**; *233*
Telemusik (Stockhausen) 531
Tel jour, telle nuit (Poulenc) 401
Tempest, The (Martin) 487
Tempest, The (Purcell) 195
Temps Restitué, Le (Barraqué) 526
Tender Land, The (Copland) 440
Terpsichore Musarum (Praetorius) 191
Terretektorh (Xenakis) 527
Terry, R. R. 446
Thailand 32; *and see* Indonesia
Thalberg, Sigismond 292
Thamar (Balakirev) 342
thāt 35
théâtre-lyrique 287
Théâtre Royal de la Monnaie, Brussels 488
Theile, Johann 184
Theodorakis, Mikis 499; *499*
Theodosius I, Emperor 49
theorbo, in 16th-c Europe 94; in 17th c 160, 161, 162, 163; in the Chamber (France) 221; *and see* glossary of musical instruments
theorbo-cittern 163
Theremin, Leon 378
'The Thousand' symphony (Mahler) 362
Thibaut of Champagne 75
'Third Stream' 439, 444
Thirty-six Greek Dances (Skalkottas) 498
Thirty Variations on an Original Aria (Goldberg Variations, Bach) 201
Thirty Years War 153, 178, 180, 229 233
This is Our Time (Schuman) 441
Thomas, Ambroise 292
Thomas, Theodor 444
Thomas à Kempis 86
Thompson, James 236, 241
Thomson, Virgil 440
Three Choirs Festival 214, 218, 251
Three Cornered Hat, The (De Falla) 470
Three Japanese Lyric Poems (Stravinsky) 391
Three Orchestral Pieces (Berg) 384
Threepenny Opera, The (Weill and Brecht) 217, 409; *409*
Three Pieces (Stravinsky) 391
Three pieces for String Orchestra (R. Halffter) 472
Three Places in New England (Ives) 438
Three Psalms (Boulanger) 404
Three Songs from William Shakespeare (Stravinsky) 391
Threni, that is the lamentations of the Prophet Jeremiah (Stravinsky) 392
Threnody for the victims of Hiroshima (Penderecki) 463
Thus spake Zarathustra (R. Strauss) 363
Thyl Claes (Vogel) 486

ti 27
Tieffenbrucker, Magnus 92, 95
tientos 139
Till Eulenspiegel (R. Strauss) 363
Time-Cycle (Foss) 444
Tinctoris, Johannes 90, 91, 136, 142
Tinódi, Sebestyen 314
Tintagel (Bax) 451
Tippett, Michael 452; *452*
'Titan' symphony (Mahler) 361
Titelouze, Jean 189
Titus, Emperor 59
toccata, 94; in 16th-c Italy 132; in 16th-c England 145; in 17th-c Germany 181; of Bach 199, 200; for harpsichord (Leo) 207
Toccata and Fugue in D minor (Bach) 200
Tod zu Basel, Der (Beck) 485
tof 59
Togni, Camillo 424
Togo, music of 18
Tolstoy, Leo 341
Tombeau de Couperin, Le (Ravel) 371, 396
Tombeau de Ravel (Escher) 493
Tomkins, Thomas 146, 192
To my Country (Zweers) 491
tonadillas 467, 477
Tonic Sol-Fa method 445; *and see* glossary of technical terms
Tonkünstler Sozietät 236
Tonreihe see note-row
Torelli, Giuseppe 157, 187, 204; *204*
Tosca (Puccini) 358
'Toulouse' mass 72
'Tournai' mass 72
Towards a New Music (Chávez) 482
Towards the Unknown Region (Vaughan Williams) 450
Traditional Harmony (Hindemith) 407
Traetta, Tommaso 209
Tragédie de Salomé (Schmitt) 402
tragédie lyrique 281
'Tragic' symphony (Mahler) 361
Traité de l'harmonie (Rameau) 225
Traité des instruments (Mersenne) 159
Traité des instruments de musique (Trichet) 159
Traité d'instrumentation et d'orchestration modernes (Berlioz) 345
Trakl, Georg 359
Transuntinis, Vitus de 95
Tratado, de glosas . . . en la musica de violones (Ortiz) 139-
Travelling Companion (Hamerick) 458
Traviata, La (Verdi) 356, 357
Treatise on Instruments (Praetorius) see *Syntagma musicum*
Treatise on Orchestration (Berlioz) 290, 345
Treaty of Versailles 368
Tre Laudi (Dallapiccola) 422
Tremblay, Gilles 509
Trepak of Death (Mussorgsky) 343
Tre Ricercari (Martinů) 465
Tréteaux, Les (Martinů) 465
Tretis of the Gam (Leonel) 142
Trial, The (von Einem) 410
triangles 90; *and see* glossary of musical instruments
Tribute to Foster (Grainger) 504
Trichet, Pierre 159
Triébert family 256
Trinity Mass 62
Tristan and Isolde (Wagner) 322, 324, 360, 370
Triumph of Bacchus (Dargomizsky) 340
Troilus and Cressida (Walton) 452
Trois petites liturgies de la présence divine (Messiaen) 405
Trois Poèmes de Mallarmé (Debussy) 395
Trois Poèmes de Mallarmé (Ravel) 396
Trois poèmes juifs (Bloch) 484
Trois Psaumes (Bloch) 484
Trojans, The (Berlioz) 290
tromba marina 90; *91; and see* glossary of musical instruments
trombone 57; invention of 94; in 17th

c 164; introduced into symphonic writing (Beethoven) 250; modification in 19th c 256; valve trombone 258; in New Orleans style jazz 511; *257; and see* glossary of musical instruments
troparion 60, 63
trope, the 63, 67, 134
troubadours, in southern France 50, 53, 69; in northern France *see* *trouvères*; in Catalonia 74; in northern Italy 74; notated songs of 75; influence on *Minnesänger* 76; role in dance 77; *and see* glossary of technical terms
Trout quintet (Schubert) 273
trouvères 71, 72; compositions 73, 74; in northern France 74; notated songs 75; melodies in folk song 76; influence on goliard songs and *Minnesänger* 76; elements of in *chanson* 76; in dance 77
Trovatore, Il (Verdi) 356
trumpet 55, 56; in Africa 21; in Hebrew music *see hazozra*; in medieval European dance 77; in 15th-c Europe 90; in 17th c 159, 160, 161, 162, 164, 166, 171, 173; in work of Scarlatti 207; in the Ecurie 221; Viennese keyed trumpet 253, 256; Haydn concerto for 253; types and uses in 19th c 256, 257-258; modern trumpet 258; in New Orleans style jazz 511; *78, 90, 95, 121, 123, 180, 191; and see* glossary of musical instruments
Tsarevitch, The (Lehár) 413
T. S. Eliot in Memoriam (Stravinsky) 392
tuba 258; *and see* glossary of musical instruments
Tuckwell, Barry 505
Tudor, David 529
Tudor Church Music 446
Tulou 254
tunbur 38, 40
Tunder, Franz 183
Turandot (Puccini) 358
Turangalla symphony (Messiaen) 405
Turgenev, Ivan 341
Turina, Joaquin 470
Turn of the Screw, The (Britten) 452, 453
Turovsky, Cyril 335
twelve-note method *see* serial method
Twelve-note primer for the piano (Jelinek) 409
Twelve Note System of Composition (Schoenberg) 380
Twenty-Four Preludes (Chopin) 308
Twenty-Four Preludes and Fugues (Shostakovich) 432
Twilight of the Gods, The (Wagner) 324
Two last Poems (Bloch) 485
Two Widows, The (Smetana) 332
Tye, Christopher 144-145
Tyrol 17
Tzar Sattan (Rimsky-Korsakov) 346
Tzigane for violin and orchestra (Ravel) 396

'ud 39, 40
'ugab 58; *and see* glossary of musical instruments
Uganda *see* Africa, music of
Ulibishev, A. D. 342
Ulysses (Seiber) 451
Umayyad caliphate 38
Umlauf, Ignaz 235
Umlauf, Michael 235
Under Fire (Kabalevsky) 431
'Unfinished' symphony (Schubert) 274
Ungaro, Francesco 92
Un Giorno di Regno (Verdi) 355
Urban VIII, Pope 169; *169*
Ussachevsky, Vladimir 444

Vaet, Jacob 107
Valderrabano, Enriquez de 139
Valen, Fartein 457
Valentini 179
Valéry, Paul 402, 457

Valkyrie, The (Wagner) 324
Vallet, Nicolas de 163
Vallotti, Antonio 211, 230
Valse, La (Ravel) 396
Valses nobles et sentimentales, Les (Ravel) 396
Valses romantiques (Chabrier) 298
Valse triste (Sibelius) 460
Van Anrooy, Peter 491
Van Baaren, Kees 493
Van Delden 493
Van den Sigtenhorst-Meyer, Bernard 492
Van Durme, Jef 491
Van Ghizeghem, Hayne 105
Vanhal, J. B. 236
Van Lier, Bertus 493
Van Swieten, Gottfried 237
Vantch (Knipper) 431
Van Weerbecke, Gaspar 105-106
Vardot, Michelle Ferdinand Pauline 467
Varèse, Edgar 372, 402, 441; *444*
Variations (Demarquez) 404
Variations VI (Cage) 530
Variations and Fugue on a Joyous Theme by Johann Adam Hiller (Reger) 363
Variations and Fugue on a Theme from 'The Magic Flute' (Reger) 363
Variations for Orchestra (Carter) 442
Variations for orchestra (van Baaren) 493
Variations for Orchestra (Webern) 386
Variations for piano (Webern) 386
Variations for piano and orchestra (Riegger) 441
Variations for Wind Orchestra (Schoenberg) 382
Variations, interlude and finale (Dukas) 399
Variations on an Old Negro Song (Delius) 450
Variations on a Nursery Theme (Dohnányi) 414
Variations on a Theme by Paganini (Blacher) 408
Variations on a Theme of Beethoven (Saint-Saëns) 297
Variations on a Theme of Frank Bridge (Britten) 452
Variations on the St Anthony Chorale (Brahms) 328
Variations sérieuses (Mendelssohn) 277-278
Vasari 126
Vasquez, Juan 137
Vassilenko, Sergey 430
Vaughan Williams, Ralph 48, 256, 374, 447, 449-450; *451*
Vecchi, Orazio 129
Veilchen, Das (Goethe, setting by Mozart) 272
Veillot, Jean 188
Velasco, Juan Antonio de 477
Venanrius, Fortunatus 59, 60
Venus and Adonis (Blow) 194
Veracini, Antonio 204
Veracini, Francesco Maria 204, 233
Verbonnet *see* Ghiselin, Johannes
Verbum nobile (Moniuszko) 310
verbunkos style 316-317
Verdelot, Philippe 126-127, 131, 132
Veress, Sandor 417
Verdi, Giuseppe 250, 251, 291, 333, 352, 354, 355-357; *between pp. 352 and 353, 357*
Verfremdung 389, 409
verismo 357, 358, 418, 420
Vérité de Jeanne, La (Jolivet) 402
Verklärte Nacht (Schoenberg) 382
Verlaine, Paul 395
Verrotto, Michele 128
Verstovsky, A. N. 339
Vespers of 1610 (Monteverdi) 174
Vestale, La (Spontini) 234, 287, 351
Viadana, Lodovico 167, 172
Viaggio a Reims, Il (Rossini) 353

vibraphone 375, 518; *376*
Vicente, Gil 139
Vicentino, Nicolas 92, 95, 127
Victor Emmanuel of Sardinia 248
Victoria, Luiz de 138; *138*
Victory of the Cross, The (Beethoven) 267
Vida breve, La (De Falla) 470
Vidakovic, Albe 495
Vidal, Pierre 313
Vienna Workmen's Symphony Concerts 385
Vie Parisienne, La (Offenbach) 294
Vieuxtemps, Henri 488
vihuela and compositions for 91, 92, 137, 138, 139, 160, 163; *134; and see* glossary of musical instruments
Village Music (Moore) 441
Village Romeo and Juliet, A (Delius) 450
Villa-Lobos, Heitor 479-480; *480*
villancicos 136, 138, 139
Villancicos de diversos autores see Cancionero of Upsala
villanelle 129, 304
villanescha 89, 129
Villanueva, Filipe 476.
vinā 33-34, 40; *33; and see* glossary of musical instruments
Vinci, Leonardo 209, 210
Vin de paix (Weinzweig) 508
Vingt-quatre violons du Roy 159, 161, 221, 226
Vingt regards sur l'enfant Jesus Christ (Messiaen) 405
Vin Herbé, Le (Martin) 486
viol 57; in 16th-c England 89, 94, 144; in 15th-c Europe 90; in ensembles (16th c) 92, 93; in Henry VIII's collection 92; treatises on (16th c) 93; as 'continuo' instrument (16th c) 94; in Elizabethan England 146 *and see* viol consort *and* viol fantasy; use of in 17th c 159, 160, 161, 163, 164, 173, 174; music of in 17th c 162-163; bass viol as solo instrument 162, replaced by cello 163; in 17th-c France 191; in 17th c England 192, 193, 195; in the Chamber (France) 221; in 20th c 375; *96, 150, 188, 225; and see* glossary of musical instruments
viola bastarda 94, 159; *and see* glossary of musical instruments
viola da braccio 90, 93, 121, 159
viola da gamba 121
viola pomposa 163; *and see* glossary of musical instruments
viol consorts 148, 149; *188*
viol fantasy 146; by Gibbons 149; in 17th-c England 162; by Purcell 162, 195; by Lawes 192
violin and music for 89, 90; in 1th c 92, 94, 95; displaces viol as basic string instrument 157; introduction into serious music 159; in 17th c 161-162, 163, 164, 174, 176, 177; as instrument in sonata (17th c) 177, 203, 204, 205; in 17th-c Germany 183-184; in 17th-c France 191; in 17th-c English church music 194; concertos of Bach 201; specific instrumental style (late 17th-c Italy) 202; solo instrument in concerto (17th-c Italy) 204; developments in technique (Corelli) 105; solos for (Marcello) 206; importance of (Tartini 206-207; concertos in 18th-c Italy 207; technique in 18th-c England 212; sonatas of Handel 217; in the Ecurie 221; influence of Italian technique on 18th-c French 226; solo instrument in concerto (classical era) 237; sonatas of Schubert 273; work of Mendelssohn 277; work of Franck 299; in Hungarian *kuruc* music 316; concertos of Brahms 328; *162, 174, 190; and see* glossary of musical instruments
violoncello piccolo 163
Violon maker of Cremona (Hubay) 413
violone 160, 161, 173; *and see* glossary

of musical instruments
violons à la française 160, 173
Viotti, G. B. 202, 213, 351
Virdung 91
virelay 71; structure of 74; influence on *Minnesänger* 76; in dance 77
Virgil 137
virginal 92, 145, 150; *between pp. 128 and 129, 148; and see* glossary of musical instruments
Visconti, Luchino 125
Visigothic rite 61
Vision de l'amen (Messiaen) 405
Vision of Christ- Phoenix, The (Williamson) 505
Vision of Isaiah, The (Burkhardt) 485
Vision of St Augustine, The (Tippett) 452
Visions of Francesco Petrarcha (Birtwistle) 454
Visitation, The (Schuller) 442
Vitali, G. B. 202, 204
Vitali, Tommaso Antonio 204
Vitebsk trio (Copland) 440
Vitore, Loreto 171
Vivaldi, Antonio 157, 163, 165, 199, 202, 203, 205, **206**; *206*
Viviane (Chausson) 300
Vlad, Roman 423-424
Vladimir of Kiev 335
Vogel, Vladimir 486
Vogler, Abbé 211, 230, 269, 291
Voix dans le désert (Bloch) 485
Voix humaine, La (Poulenc) 401
Vollkommene Kapellmeister (Mattheson) 232
Volo di Notte (Dallapiccola) 422
Von Bruck, Arnolt 116, 117
Von Bülow, Hans 251, 320, 322, 362
Von Einem, Gottfried 410
Von Fulda, Adam 114
Von Hausen, Friedrich 76
Von Horheim 76
Von Kerll, Johann Kaspar 182, 183, 215, 230
Von Koch, Erland 456
Von Meck, Nadezhda 349, 393
Von Meissen, Heinrich *see* Frauenlob
Von Morungen 76
Von Watt, Benedict 77
Von Zemlinsky, Alexander 380
Votre Faust (Pousseur) 531
vox organalis 66, 67, 68, 71
Voz de las calles, La (Humberto) 480
Vreuls, Victor 489

Wagenaar, Johann 491
Wagenseil, Georg Cristoph 229, 236
Wagenseil, Johann Christoph 77
Wagner, Cosima 322, 359
Wagner, Richard 77, 244, 248, 249, 250, 251, 252, 270, 289, 291, **322-325**, 333, 357, 361, 370, 371, 381; *between pp. 320 and 321, 323, 325*
Walcker, firm of 375
Waldmädchen, Das (Weber) 270
Wales, folk music 47
Wallace, William Vincent 503
Wallachian suite (Hába) 466
Wallenstein 153
Wallenstein (d'Indy) 301
Wallenstein's Camp (Smetana) 332
Waller, Thomas 'Fats' 514, 519
Walter, Bruno 362
Walther, J. J. 184
Walther, Johann 116, 120
Walton, William 374, 451-452; *452*
Walt Whitman Overture, A (Siegmeister) 441
Waltzing Matilda 503
Wanderer (Schubert) 273, 275
wann 38
War and Peace (Prokofiev) 427
Ward, John 147
Warlock, Peter 450, 451
War Requiem (Britten) 453
Warriors, The (Grainger) 504
Warsaw Pietà (Różycki) 462
Wars of Religion 87
Water and the Fire, The (Milner) 454
Water Music (Handel) 217

Watts, Dr Isaac 437
Wat Tyler (Bush) 453
Washington, George 434
Waverley (Berlioz) 289
Wayang Kulit theatre 28, 30, 31
Webb, Chick 516
Weber, Constance 242
Weber, Carl Maria von 230, 249, 251, 255, 263, **269-270**, 286, 320; *270, 272*
Weber, G. 256
Webern, Anton von 370, 372, 373, 380, **385-386**, 387, 392, 409, 524; *385*
Weckmann, Matthias 183
Wedekind, Frank 359, 385
Weelkes, Thomas 145, 146, 192; *147*
Wegelius, Martin 459
Weigl, Joseph 235
Weill, Kurt 217, 372, 409; *408*
Weinzweig, John 506-508; *507*
Weiss, Leopold 163
Weisse, C. F. 235
Welin, Karl-Erik 529
Well-song, the 58
Well Tempered Clavier (Bach) 201, 263
Wenceslas III of Bohemia 330
Werder, Felix 504
Werfel, Franz 359
Werrecoren, Hermann 118
Wesendonck, Mathilde 322
Wesley, Samuel Sebastian 445-446
West Side Story (Bernstein) 442
Weyse, Christopher Ernst-Friedrich 457
When Jesus Wept (Billings) 434
White, Robert 145
Whitman, Walt 441, 450
Wicenty of Kielce 303
Wichram, Jorg 77
Wiechowicz, Stanislaw 462
Wieck, Clara 278
Wieck, Friedrich 278
Wieland, L. M. 270
Wieniawski, Henryk 310, 311, 488; *311*
Wierzbillowkz, Aleksander 311
Wilbye, John 145, 147, 192
Wild Colonial Boy, The 502
Willaert, Adriano 85, 89, 107, 108, 122, 126, 127, 131, 313; *127*
Willan, Healey 506
William I of Prussia 248
William IV, Kaiser 359
William V, duke of Bavaria 118
William IX, duke of Aquitaine 75
William and Mary 153
William Billings Overture (Schuman) 441
Williams, Alberto 478-479, 480
Williams, Cootie 518
Williamson, Malcolm 504-505
William Tell (Huber) 483
William Tell (Rossini) 291, 353, 354; *352*
Wilson, Domingo Santa Cruz 480
Wilson, Teddy 519
Winckelmann, J. J. 236
Wine Growers' Festival (Switzerland) 483
Winterreise (Schubert) 275
Wiren, Dag 456
Without Sunshine (Mussorgsky) 343
Wittgenstein, Paul 396
Wolf, Hugo 252, 359-360; *360*
Wolf-Ferrari, Ermanno 420
Wolkenstein, Oswald von 313
Wolmuth, Janos 315
Wolverines, the 512
Woman of Samaria, The (Bennett) 445
Wonne der Wehmut (Beethoven) 268
Wooden Prince, The (Bartók) 416
World of Art movement 388
Wornum, Robert 261
Wozzeck (Berg) 372, 380, 384-385; *383, 384*
Wuorinen, Charles 444
Wyclif, John 86
Wyner, Yehudi 444

Xenakis, Yannis 373, 379, 495, **499**, **527-528**; *527*
Ximenes de Cisneros, Cardinal 134; *135*

Xochipilli Macuilxochitl (Chávez) 481
xylophone, Africa 21; Indonesia 30, 32; use in 20th C 375; *and see* glossary of musical instruments

ya yue 25
Year, The (Burkhardt) 485
Year from Monday, A (Cage) 532
Years of Pilgrimage (Liszt) 321
Yepes, Narciso 467
Yonge, Nicholas 146
Yoruba 22
Young, Lester 517, 520, 522; *517*
Young France group 400, 402
Young Germany movement 322

Young Person's Guide to the Orchestra (Britten) 452
'Young Poland' group 461; *309*
Ysaÿe, Eugène 488
Yugoslavia, music of 45, 495

Zachow, F. W. 214
Zagwijn, Henri 491
Zajc, Ivan 495
Zampa (Hérold) 292
Zandonai, Riccardo 420
Zarebski, Julius 310
Zaremba, N. I. 341
Zarlino, Gioseffo 131, 132
zarzuelas 467, 468

Zaubergeige, Die (Egk) 409
Zeitmasse for five wind instruments (Stockhausen) 412
Zeleński, Władysław 311
Zelter, Carl Friedrich 232, 271, 276, 291
Zieleński, Mikołaj 304-305
zil 40
Zipoli, Domenico 208
Ziryab 39
zither 20, 54; Africa 21; Indonesia 30; Arab 40 *and see qanum;* Balkan countries 47 *and see cobza* and *guzla;* Finland 47 *and see kantele;* published music for (16th-C France)

112; *65; and see* glossary of musical instruments
zither-harp (Africa) 21
znoudi 40
Zodiaque, Le (Absil) 490
zo kugaku 25
Zoroastre (Rameau) 281
Zumpe, Johannes 259
Zumsteeg, J. R. 271
zurna 40, 45; *and see* glossary of musical instruments
Zweers, Bernard 491
Zweig, Stefan 363
zymbalom 316

The black and white photographs were supplied by: A. C. L. Brussels: 163, 164r, 166t, 189t; A. G.: 100t; A.P.N.: 429; Agence Intercontinentale: 237; Agraci: 162t; Alinari: 51, 64, 174; Anderson: 76b, 122, 131b; F. Arborio Mella: 126, 129t, 129b, 132, 133t, 168t, 205, 272t, 419, 421, 422, 423b; Archives Photographiques: 56l, 109b, 310, 332; Erich Auerbach: 392, 453, 468, 473, 486b, 487, 524, 530, 531; Australian News & Information Bureau: 500, 501, 502, 503, 505t, 505b; Bärenreiter: 180t; Bassano Ltd.: 447b; Belgian National Tourist Office: 102; Bildarchiv Foto Marburg: 66, 98r, 99, 100b; Bischoff-Magnum: 47b; Bonaglia: 260b; E. Boudot-Lamotte: 158, 275t, 285b, 319b; G. Bourdelon: 31; British Council: 454t; Brogi: 55b; Bruckmann: 91; Ilse Buhs: 407t; Bulloz: 55t, 90, 103r, 262r, 295b, 308, 318t; Bundesbildstelle, Bonn: 412; Camera Press: 389t, 402, 450, 452b, 454b, 481b; Cameraphoto, Venice: 424; Canadian Broadcasting Corporation: 509t; Jean-Loup Charmet: 416; Consoli: 354b; Courtauld Institute, London: 150l; Crea, Rome: 178; 215b; Culver Pictures, New York: 435t; Czechoslovak Legation, Paris: 295; P. Delbo: 390b; Delius, Paris: 212t; Henri Denis: 489b; Zoë Dominic: 194; Duong Tran Orang: 25; Editura Enciclopedicǎ Românǎ, Bucharest: 348t, 496, 497b, 498; Henry Ely: 110b; English Bach Festival Trust: 499t; W. L. Entwistle, Canterbury: 149t; Evers: 133b; Heinz Eysell: 324; Ferrania: 423t; Festspielleitung, Bayreuth: 324, 325t; Finnish Embassy, Paris: 286; John Freeman, London: 146t, 193, 218; Gisèle Freund: 475, 478t; Gabinetto Fotografico Nazionale, Rome: 177b; Giraudon: 53, 95t, 97, 98l, 81, 109t, 110t, 112, 191, 245r, 272, 274t, 275b, 282, 293b, 383t, 391; Godin: 511, 514, 518, 520b; Karnine: 528; Keystone: 403, 499b, 504, 512, 522b; W. Knopff: 490t; Larousse: 26, 45, 48, 54, 57, 61tr, 62b, 63, 65, 67t, 68, 69, 70, 71t, 71b, 72, 73l, 73r, 74, 76t, 77b, 78b, 82, 93t, 93b, 94t, 94b, 96t, 104, 107, 111, 116b, 117t, 118, 119, 123t, 123b, 124, 127t, 127b, 147, 159, 160t,

160b, 165, 168b, 169r, 175, 179, 180b, 181l, 182, 185, 187, 188b, 189b, 190, 195t, 199, 202, 203, 204, 206b, 207t, 208t, 211b, 213, 216t, 216b, 221, 222l, 222r, 223, 224, 225, 226t, 226c, 226b, 227, 229, 231t, 232, 233l, 234t, 236, 238t, 241t, 241b, 242t, 244, 254l, 255t, 255b, 256t, 256b, 257t, 257b, 258, 259b, 260t, 264b, 270, 271, 274b, 276t, 276b, 279, 283t, 283b, 284, 285t, 286, 287, 298, 299, 300, 301l, 319t, 323tl, 327t, 328, 329, 332, 334, 335b, 339, 341, 345, 346, 349t, 351, 360t, 361, 376, 377t, 377b, 385t, 396b, 436t, 467, 469, 470b, 471t, 481t, 488, 508b, 527; Mander & Mitchenson Theatre Collection: 80, 171t, 331, 352; Mansell-Alinari: 125, 152, 169l, 210r, 212b; Mansell-Alinari-Anderson: 131t; Mansell Collection: 60l, 60r, 61tl, 67b, 87, 103l, 106, 114, 116tl, 120/1, 130, 141, 142, 145, 148t, 150r, 176, 192l, 195b, 196, 197, 198l, 198r, 208b, 210l, 211t, 217t, 230, 235, 238b, 239b, 240t, 240b, 265, 277t, 277b, 297t, 304, 311b, 313, 336, 446, 447t, 451t, 456b, 459; Marn, Frankfurt: 484t; Luis Marques: 477b; MAS, Barcelona: 95b, 104b, 135tl, 135tr, 136, 137, 138, 139t, 139b, 471b; Mary Evans Picture Library: 166r, 117b, 192r, 209, 233r, 307t, 354t; Melody Maker: 513, 515t, 517b, 518b, 522t; F. Meyer: 280; Gilbert A. Milne: 508t; Mission Ogooué-Congo: 22c; Morath-Magnum: 46t; National Film Archive, London: 297b, 409, 426; Neprajzi: 47t; Sidney W. Newberry: 147b; Novello & Co.: 445; Novosti Press Agency, London: 300, 337, 338t, 339b, 342, 344b, 349b, 425b, 430t, 430b, 431b, 432; O.R.T.F.: 261, 262l, 378, 529; Jose de Prado Herranz: 135b; Pic: 20b, 27; E. Piccagliani, Milan: 173t, 408b, 472; Pictorial Press: 401; Polish Cultural Institute: 249, 305, 311tr, 462b, 463b; Popperfoto: 417t, 451t, 452t; Public Archives of Canada: 507t; R.C.A.: 374; Radio Times Hulton Picture Library: 431t, 448, 449; Benedict Rast: 162b; Raugel: 215t; David Redfern: 516t, 517t, 520t, 521, 523b; Réunion des Musées Nationaux, Versailles: 220; Ringier: 486t; Houston Rogers: 234b, 243, 291, 353, 355, 358t, 389b, 413, 464; Roger-Viollet: 38t, 259t, 263, 266b, 267, 278, 289, 290, 292t, 292b, 293t, 294, 302, 319c, 321, 325b, 330, 340, 343, 357, 358b, 362, 387, 393, 394, 398t, 399t, 399b, 404t, 425t, 427, 470c, 474; Rouget: 21, 22b, 23t; Sylvia Salmi, Connecticut: 381; A. Seeberger: 348b; A. Serres: 61b, 62t; Sammlung Schmidt: 113; Sirot: 295t, 323tr, 327b; Society for Cultural Relations with the U.S.S.R.: 353t; Studio Jac-Guy: 509b; Dr. J. Svoboda-Art Centrum: 463t, 465, 466t; Swedish Radio: 456t; Swiss Foto, Lima: 476; Tresseniers: 489t; Unations: 18; Unesco: 19bl, 32t, 34, 40; Ullstein Bilderdienst, Berlin: 184, 408t;

United States Information Service: 439t, 440, 441b, 510, 515b, 519, 523t; Fr. Van der Werf: 492; Marcel Viaud Studio: 181r; Viennot: 35t, 35b; K. P. Wachsmann: 24; Watzeck: 375; John Webb: 42; Willinger: 397t; X: 29, 56r, 92, 96l, 104t, 164l, 264t, 306, 307b, 309, 312, 316b, 320, 379, 415b, 417b, 455, 457t, 457b, 458t, 458b, 470t, 477t, 482t, 482b, 490b, 491, 493, 507b; Yugoslav National Tourist Office: 495; Zaiks: 303; Gramafone Zavody: 466b.

The colour illustrations have been reproduced by kind permission of the following collections, galleries, and museums: Abbey Aldrich Rockefeller Folk Art Collection: 54; The Beethoven-Haus, Bonn: 37 (Sg. H. C. Bodmer); Dr. Attilio Bigo, Turin: 21, 22; Cathedral of St Bavo, Ghent: 2; E.M.I. Ltd., London: 60; Ferdinandeum, Innsbruck: 19; The Viscount FitzHarris: 28; Galleria Nazionale d'Arte Moderna, Rome: 43; Gesellschaft der Musikfreunde, Vienna: 32; Historisches Museum der Stadt, Vienna: 39; G. K. Kanoria: 4; Kunsthistorisches Museum, Vienna: 16; Louvre: 41, 30, 48; Memlingmuseum, Bruges: 11; Musée des Arts Décoratifs, Paris: 46; Musée Instrumental du Conservatoire, Paris: 23, 40, 13, 35; Musée National d'Art Moderne, Paris: 50; Musée de Rennes: 12; Museo d'Arte Antica, Milan: 8; Museo della Scala, Milan: 36; Metropolitan Museum of Art, New York: 29; Faculty of Music, Oxford: 20; Nationalgalerie, Berlin: 47; National Gallery, London: 9, 14, 15, 27; Nationalhistoriske Museum, Frederiksborg, Copenhagen: 20; National Portrait Gallery, London: 25; Richard-Wagner Museum, Bayreuth: 42; Rosenborg Castle, Copenhagen: 17; Theatermuseum, Munich: 38; Tretyakov Gallery, Moscow: 45; The Wallace Collection, London: 33; Lord Willoughby de Broke: 34. Plate 49 © Rights Reserved A.D.A.G.P., Paris; Plates 46, 47, 50 © Rights Reserved S.P.A.D.E.M., Paris.

The transparencies were supplied by the following: F. Arborio Mella, Milan: 19, 30, 42; J. Blauel, Munich: 38; Chomon-Perino, Turin: 21, 22; Condominas: 6; Dominguez Ramos, Madrid: 17; R. B. Fleming & Co., London: 34; John Freeman, London: 33; Giraudon, Paris: 2, 12, 24, 36, 41, 46; Hawkley Studios, London: 28; Michael Holford, London: 15, 27; Japanese Embassy, Paris: 5; Keystone, London: 53; Larousse Archives, Paris: 1, 7, 26, 56, 57; Godfrey MacDominic, London: 60; Meyer: 39; Novosti, London: 45, 52; Photo Brusselle, Bruges: 11; Erio Piccagliani, Milan: 44; Rapho, Paris: 49; David Redfern, London: 55; Houston Rogers,

London: 58; Sachsse, Bonn: 37; Scala, Florence: 10, 43; Skira: 4; Studio Yan, Toulouse: 50; The Sunday Times-Donald McCullin: 5; Reg Wilson, London: 51; Woodmansterne, Watford: 59.

The illustration at the base of page 146 is reproduced by Gracious Permission of Her Majesty the Queen. The other black and white illustrations are reproduced by kind permission of the following collections, galleries and museums: Lord Aldenham: 190; Badische Landesbibliothek, Karlsruhe: 79br (Cod. Aug. L.X, f.93°); Bayerisches Nationalmuseum, Munich: 164l; The Beethoven-Haus, Bonn: 266r, 269; Biblioteca de Bologna: 104t; Biblioteca Central de Barcelona: 138, 139b; Biblioteca Civica Gambalunga, Rimini: 54; Biblioteca del Monasterio de San Lorenzo el Real: 135b; Biblioteca Nacional, Madrid: 137, 467; Biblioteca Nazionale Marciana, Venice: 123b, 124, 129t; Biblioteca Piccolomini, Siena: 64; Bibliothèque Espagnole, Paris: 471t; Bibliothèque Inguimbertine, Carpentras: 280; Bibliothèque Municipale, Grenoble: 419; Bibliothèque du Musée des Arts Décoratifs, Paris: 56l, 78t, 78b, 182; Bibliothèque Nationale, Paris: 68, 73l, 73r, 75, 77b, 82, 93b, 98l, 101, 123t, 290, 319t; Bibliothèque Nationale du Conservatoire National de Musique, Paris: 160t, 169r, 238t, 276t, 328, 332; Bibliothèque de l'Opéra, Paris: 271, 339; Bibliothèque de Valence: 95b; Bodleian Library, Oxford: 434; Bodmer, Zurich: 266t; British Museum, London: 142, 144, 145, 146t, 148t, 149b, 193, 216b, 218, 219; Canterbury Cathedral: 149t; Castello Sforzesco, Milan: 123t, 421; Cathedral of Salamanca: 57; Cathédrale de Puy: 103r, Château de Gaun, Denmark: 179; Château de Versailles: 220, 262r; Chichester Cathedral: 147t; Chiostri Monumentali di Santa Maria Novella, Florence: 72; Conservatorio Martini, Bologna: 232; Dayton C. Miller, Cleveland: 255t; Deutsche Staatsbibliothek, Berlin: 201; Devonshire Collection, Chatsworth: 150l; Enel: 96l, 165; Eton College: 143; Faber & Faber Ltd.: 333t, 333b (from *Antonin Dvořák, Musician & Craftsman* by John Chapman); Faculty of Music, Oxford: 150r; Free Press U.S.A.: 382; Galleria dell' Accademia, Venice: 122; Galleria Corsini, Rome: 174; Galleria Nazionale d'Arte Antica, Rome: 208t; Galleria Nazionale d'Arte Moderna, Rome: 419; Händelhaus, Halle: 215t; Hauptamt für Hochbauwesen, Nuremberg: 113; Hermitage Museum, Leningrad: 345; Historisches Museum der Stadt Wien: 94b; Imperial Collection, Vienna: 222l; Instituto d'Arco, Mantua: 172b; Kenner, Vienna: 267; Kunsthistorisches Mu-